מחזור לב שלם
MAḤZOR LEV SHALEM

מחזור לב שלם

MAHZOR LEV SHALEM

לימים הנוראים

FOR ROSH HASHANAH

AND YOM KIPPUR

THE RABBINICAL ASSEMBLY

The Rabbinical Assembly
3080 Broadway
New York, NY 10027
www.rabbinicalassembly.org

Permissions and copyrights for quoted materials may be found on page 467.

Library of Congress Cataloging-in-Publication Data
Mahzor (Conservative, Rabbinical Assembly). High Holidays. English & Hebrew.
 880-01 [Mahzor Lev shalem la-Yamim ha-Nora'im] = Mahzor Lev shalem for
Rosh Hashanah and Yom Kippur.
    p. cm.
 Text of mahzor in Hebrew with English translation; commentary in English.
 "Mahzor Lev shalem editorial committee, Rabbi Edward Feld, chair."
 ISBN 978-0-916219-46-8 (alk. paper)
 1. High Holidays—Liturgy—Texts. 2. Mahzorim—Texts. 3. Conservative
Judaism—Liturgy—Texts. 4. Mahzor (Conservative, Rabbinical Assembly).
High Holidays. I. Feld, Edward, 1943– II. Rabbinical Assembly of America.
III. Title.

 BM675.H5Z647213 2010
 296.4'531047—dc22

              2009075051

Designed, composed, and produced by
Scott-Martin Kosofsky at The Philidor Company,
Lexington, Massachusetts. www.philidor.com

The principal Hebrew type, Milon, was designed and made
by Scott-Martin Kosofsky and Rabbi Scott Israel Seldowitz;
it was inspired by the work of Henri Friedlaender. The other
types are Arno and Cronos, by Robert Slimbach; Chapparal,
by Carol Twombly; David, after Ismar David; Adobe Hebrew,
by John Hudson; and Magma (titling), by Sumner Stone.

Printed and bound in the United States of America
by Courier Corporation and Acme Bookbinding.

Fifth Printing
18 17 16 15 14 13 12 11 10 9 8 7 6 5a

The publication of

Mahzor Lev Shalem

has been made possible

through the devotion

and generosity of

IRMA AND PAUL MILSTEIN

in honor of their children

ROSLYN AND JEROME MEYER

ABBY AND HOWARD MILSTEIN

BARBARA AND DAVID ZALAZNICK

ROBIN AND EDWARD MILSTEIN

תוכן העניינים   TABLE OF CONTENTS

A detailed list of subsections
may be found on the opening pages
of the major sections listed here.

תוכן העניינים   TABLE OF CONTENTS

MAḤZOR LEV SHALEM EDITORIAL COMMITTEE

Rabbi Edward Feld, *Senior Editor and Chair*

Rabbi Leonard Gordon

Rabbi Stuart Kelman

Rabbi Alan Lettofsky

Cantor Joseph Levine

Cantor Ken Richmond

Rabbi Robert Scheinberg

Rabbi Laurence Sebert

Rabbi Jan Robyn Uhrbach

Rabbi Jan Caryl Kaufman, *ex-officio*

INTRODUCTION

T HE PRAYERBOOK represents the theology of the Jewish people throughout the generations. Not only is it an expression of popular religious feeling, but it is also a textbook of, and gateway into, the world of Jewish thought and imagination of the past two thousand years.

The prayerbook is a work of collective genius. On the one hand, learned and artful poets turned biblical verses and commentary into prayer; they even made legal texts into liturgical poems. On the other hand, the basic liturgy is simple and direct, reflecting its origin in common communal experience. On several occasions, the will of the people overrode the decision of rabbis in determining the text and customary practice of prayer.

Our hope is that this High Holy Day maḥzor will allow each congregant to engage the world of Jewish prayer in a vital way. In Jewish tradition, study and prayer have always been intimately linked. With this in mind, this maḥzor consists of four main elements linking study and prayer—the liturgical Hebrew text, translation, commentary, and meditational readings—each carefully prepared with attention to the contemporary worshipper.

The Hebrew Text

All Jewish prayerbooks are anthologies of liturgical materials produced by generations of Jews living in many lands. Traditional maḥzorim include biblical texts and prayers so old and so embedded in the liturgy that dating can only be approximated, sometimes only within hundreds of years. Moreover, because Jews in every land have adapted the liturgy for their own use, a variety of liturgical strands have come down to us. The standard liturgy has come to include poems written throughout the Middle Ages enhancing earlier prayers and expressing the religious sensibilities of their times. This maḥzor follows the form customarily used by Ashkenazic Jewry—the Jews descended from Central and Eastern Europeans. Our manuscript sources show that while many *piyyutim*, liturgical poems, have been added or removed over time, the foundational texts have remained fairly consistent for the last several centuries, and we have tried to remain faithful to that longstanding tradition. To these basic texts we have added some prayers used only by Sephardic Jewry—Jews descended from those living in the Iberian peninsula and Arab lands—and by Italian Jewry. We have also added contemporary prayers, since the prayerbook must give voice to the needs of our own generation, as it did for those in the past.

The Translation

Several principles have guided this translation:

1. We believe the translation ought to reflect the Hebrew original as closely as possible, allowing the English reader to experience the text without a filter, and allowing the congregant who has some basic familiarity with Hebrew to find familiar words. When the Hebrew text is jarring, which it sometimes is, the English translation ought not to smooth over the difficulty.

2. The Hebrew prose frequently borders on the poetic, and the translation ought to convey some sense of that in its cadence, in its form, and in its use of language.

3. The translation ought to be prayerful; it ought to put the English reader in the mood of prayer.

4. Because each language has a distinct grammar, we have sometimes changed the word order, syntax, and sentence structure to create an appropriate English translation.

5. A contemporary American translation needs to be gender-neutral as far as possible, while conveying the intent and meaning of the original. Sometimes this has necessitated changing the third person in the original to the second person, in this translation.

6. We have consulted previous translations, especially the most recent version of the maḥzor for the Conservative movement (1972), which was edited and translated by Rabbi Jules Harlow, as well as the re-edited Shabbat and Festival prayerbook, *Siddur Sim Shalom* (1998). We owe these sources a debt of gratitude— they were always our starting point, though the reader will readily recognize this as a new and original translation. For the Morning Blessings and P'sukei D'zimra (Verses of Song), we have for the most part used the translations found in *Siddur Sim Shalom*. And for the Torah and Haftarah readings, we have adapted David E. S. Stein's *The Contemporary Torah: A Gender-Sensitive Adaptation of the JPS Translation* and the Jewish Publication Society's *TaNaKh: The Holy Scriptures*, respectively.

7. The formula with which a *b'rakhah* begins, *Barukh atah Adonai*, is often translated as "blessed are You" or "praised are You." We decided, however, not to translate these standard opening words, for we felt that neither "blessed" nor "praised" is an adequate translation of *barukh*, and that it was important to convey that these words in Jewish liturgy function primarily as the formal introduction of a *b'rakhah*. A few other basic Jewish vocabulary words such as *mitzvah* lose all their deep overtones when translated, so most often they have simply been transliterated when they appear in English.

Running Commentary

We believe that a modern commentary ought to accompany the ancient texts to inform the reader of their history, to explain unusual vocabulary, to comment on difficult ideas and key concepts, and to explain why a particular prayer appears in a certain context and is recited at a particular moment in the service. The commentary generally appears in the right margin. The commentary on Birkhot Ha-shaḥar and P'sukei D'zimra is adapted from *Or Hadash*, by Rabbi Reuven Hammer.

Readings and Meditations

In the left margin, we have included *kavvanot*, meditational readings to help congregants focus at central moments, as well as readings that may be recited aloud. We have also provided some alternative renderings that offer a different approach to the theological ideas raised by the text. Some of these *kavvanot* and readings are drawn from classical sources, while others are new prayers and meditations related to the traditional context in which they are placed, that we hope will resonate with contemporary Jews. These readings do not represent a particular point of view or consistent theological perspective. Rather, we have been conscious that a High Holy Day congregation is a diverse community and that what speaks to some will not resonate with others. We hope that among the different voices you will find something that inspires your prayer.

Special Vowels and Symbols

We have noted where it is traditional to bow with the sign ſ. Readings are marked by roman type (prayer leader) alternating with *italic* (congregation). Readings that may be recited by the congregation as supplements to the standard liturgy are marked with a ſ. The moment when the leader begins reciting aloud is marked by an open triangle pointer ◁.

The Hebrew text font, made especially for this maḥzor by Scott-Martin Kosofsky, the book's designer, includes the *pataḥ g'nuvah*, printed prior to a final guttural letter (עַ– חַ– הַ–), indicating that the vowel should be pronounced *before* the final consonant (for example, רוּחַ as *ru·aḥ*, not *ruḥa*). A special symbol is used for the *kamatz katan* (אָ), the enlarged *kamatz* that denotes a vowel sound between *ah* and *oh*.

The Transliteration

We have transliterated those parts of the service that are most often sung or chanted out loud, in order to encourage participation by all congregants. (These passages are generally indicated in the Hebrew by a bold typeface.) The following guidelines have been followed:

CONSONANTS: The transliteration distinguishes between gutturals ח (*ḥ*) and כ (*kh*). ה is always represented by *h* (even when silent). Neither א or ע is generally represented in the transliteration.

VOWELS: *a* represents בַ בָ בֶ and is pronounced as in "father."

e represents בֶ בּ and is pronounced as in "red."

ei represents בֶ בֵי and is pronounced as in "eight."

i represents בִי בִ and is pronounced as in "antique."

o represents בָ בֹ בָ בֳ בוֹ and is pronounced as in "crow."

u represents בֻ בוּ and is pronounced as in "tuba."

ai represents בַי and is pronounced as in "aisle."

APOSTROPHE: Vocal *sh'va* is represented by an apostrophe (e.g., *b'rakhah*, בְּרָכָה).

HYPHEN: Hyphens are used to indicate prefixes (e.g., *ha-b'rakhah*, הַבְּרָכָה).

RAISED DOT: Raised dots are used to indicate *patah g'nuvah* (e.g., *elo·ah*, אֱלוֹהַּ), as well as to break up a vowel cluster in the middle of a word (e.g., *yisra·el*, יִשְׂרָאֵל).

Our transliteration strives to facilitate accurate pronunciation of the Hebrew words, and so exceptions to these guidelines have been made, from time to time, in favor of a more user-friendly rendering; note also that the names of the prayers and services follow a more familiar transliteration style.

Acknowledgments

Throughout our work on *Mahzor Lev Shalem* we realized that this mahzor was not the product of our committee's work, but rather represents a window into the legacy of generations of Jews for whom the High Holy Day liturgy was a heightened experience. Our hope is that our efforts continue in this tradition and serve as inspiration for our own generation. Each meeting of the mahzor committee began with the prayer recorded in the Mishnah that our work would not contain errors, mislead our readers, or be an impediment to true prayer. Now that we have completed our task, we hope that this mahzor will be a source of inspiration to all who pray from it.

Words cannot convey the gratitude we who served on the editorial committee felt as we met each month and grappled with this text. We learned much from our work and much more from each other. The fellowship that matured through these years will not be forgotten by us. Over the course of many years, members of the *Mahzor Lev Shalem* committee volunteered their time and energy for this new effort, and each member of the committee had a significant role in the production of *Mahzor Lev Shalem*. Rabbi Stuart Kelman wrote the commentaries for the evening and morning Sh'ma and Its Blessings. He also contributed to the titling of all the sections of the mahzor and, along with Rabbi Leonard Gordon, wrote the commentary for the Torah and Haftarah readings. Rabbi Gordon wrote the commentary for Kol Nidrei, prepared the section of home rituals, worked with me in editing the Eilleh Ezk'rah for Yom Kippur Musaf, and contributed creative material used throughout the mahzor. Rabbi Alan Lettofsky worked on Rosh Hashanah Musaf as well as Ne·ilah and devotedly corrected each page of the entire manuscript. The committee utilized his linguistic skills throughout. Cantor Joseph Levine read the entire manuscript, with particular attention to the indications for congregational singing and leader's chant, and helped in our preparation of Ne·ilah; he also wrote the chants for several of the new prayers included in the maḥzor. Cantor Kenneth Richmond also served as a consultant regarding the needs of musical leaders and he contributed several musical pieces. Rabbi Larry Sebert, along with Cantor Richmond, worked on the Torah service and Yizkor and made many helpful suggestions incorporated throughout the maḥzor. Rabbi Jan Uhrbach was responsible for a major share of Rosh Hashanah Musaf and added her literary sensibility to several other sections. Rabbi Robert Scheinberg was a source of expert advice on liturgical matters, as well as the author of the commentary on the Shaḥarit and Arvit Amidah for Rosh Hashanah and Yom Kippur. Rabbi Jan Kaufman served as the Rabbinical Assembly liaison for the committee. She coordinated our meetings, shared her insights and expertise, and reviewed and commented on the entire manuscript at every stage of development.

Several people served shorter terms on the committee: Francine Klagsbrun, who contributed an important early editorial voice and served as a representative layperson; Rabbi Nina Beth Cardin, whose liturgical sensibility was helpful in the development of our thinking and who composed several new prayers for Kol Nidrei; Rabbi Amy Eilberg, who developed the innovative Prayers of Brokenness and Wholeness; and Rabbi Lawrence Troster, who provided thoughtful insights.

Maḥzor Lev Shalem owes a tremendous debt to the editors of other Rabbinical Assembly prayerbooks, most especially to Rabbi Jules Harlow, editor and translator of the original *Siddur Sim Shalom*, published in 1985, and the *Rabbinical Assembly Maḥzor*, published in 1972. Many of the innovations that Rabbi Harlow pioneered in the daily, Shabbat and Festival, and High Holy Day liturgy have been incorporated in this maḥzor. One example is his addition—based on the 10th-century siddur of R. Saadia Gaon—of the word *ba-olam* to the final blessing of the Amidah, thus broadening the prayer for peace into a universal statement. We also used selections from the new edition of *Siddur Sim Shalom for Sabbath and Festivals* (1998), edited by Rabbi Leonard Cahan, and *Siddur Sim Shalom for Weekdays* (2002), edited by Rabbi Avram Reisner, as well as the forthcoming volume of *Siddur Sim Shalom—Home Rituals*, also edited by Rabbi Leonard Cahan.

Members of the Committee on Jewish Law and Standards of the Rabbinical Assembly reviewed the manuscript and made some important suggestions. Special thanks to its chair, Rabbi Elliot Dorff, and the chair of the Subcommittee on Liturgical Publications, Rabbi Robert Fine, for their cooperation and help.

Many volunteer readers contributed valuable editorial suggestions at different stages of development. Thanks are due to the many rabbis, cantors, scholars, and congregants who contributed feedback over the years. While it is not possible to name everyone who commented, we appreciate the extensive suggestions we received. Special thanks to the following readers: Rabbis Martin Cohen, Michelle Fisher, David Freidenreich, Lilly Kaufman, Allan Kensky, Vernon Kurtz, Kenneth Leitner, Chai Levy, David Lincoln, Daniel Nevins, Perry Rank, Joel Rembaum, Michelle Robinson, Peretz Rodman, Daniel Shevitz, Michael Singer, Robert Slosberg, Max Ticktin and Jeffrey Wohlberg; as well as to Joy Ladin, Catherine Madsen, and Merle Feld. Special thanks to Michael Bohnen who commented on almost every page, corrected both Hebrew and English grammar, cross-checked the translation, and suggested felicitous phrasing. He engaged in this labor of love in memory of his father, Rabbi Eli Bohnen, who had been a member of the editorial committee of the first and pioneering Rabbinical Assembly maḥzor. Professor Avraham Holtz was always at the ready to respond to our liturgical and grammatical questions. He reviewed the preliminary Kol Nidrei booklet and made extensive corrections. Professors Menahem Schmelzer and Raymond Scheindlin were consulted at various stages of our work.

Sections of the maḥzor were piloted by six congregations and the participation of the rabbis, cantors, and members of the congregations in offering helpful feedback was greatly appreciated. Our thanks to Temple Israel Center (White Plains, New York); Har Zion Temple (Penn Valley, Pennsylvania); Congregation Beth Yeshurun (Houston, Texas); Beth Jacob Congregation (Mendota Heights, Minnesota); Congregation Netivot Shalom (Berkeley, California); and Congregation B'nai Israel (Northampton, Massachusetts).

The secretaries to the maḥzor committee, Evan Schreiber and Jonah Rank, ensured that we had the necessary source material available to us. Jonah Rank also contributed his knowledge of synagogue practice, compiled the glossaries that appear in this volume, and prepared the materials needed for permissions. Melissa Flamson handled the permissions requests with care and professionalism.

We owe a tremendous debt to the editorial and proofreading team, whose extensive knowledge, high standards, and painstaking devotion to detail is exemplary. Elisheva Urbas served as literary editor; her careful reading and extensive suggestions clarified and improved the volume. Michelle Kwitkin-Close served as primary copyeditor at each stage of production; she lived with this book for many years and her thoughtful editing is reflected on every page. At the final stages, Rabbi David E. S. Stein, chief proofreader, provided oversight and coordination for an extensive and complex proofreading process and we are grateful for his diligence and care. Thanks also to proofreaders Cynthia Goldstein, Emily Law, Eric Schramm, and Rabbi Reena Spicehandler.

Maḥzor Lev Shalem was expertly designed by Scott-Martin Kosofsky. His understanding and commitment to this project is apparent in the design, composition, and aesthetic of every page; it was a labor of love for him and he became a true partner in the process of publishing this volume. Adrianne Onderdunk Dudden, the maḥzor's earlier designer, set the stage for our first preliminary edition. Her death was mourned by all of us who worked with her.

The staff of the Rabbinical Assembly helped at every stage of production. Rabbi Joel Meyers was the executive vice president of the Rabbinical Assembly during the years of this project's development. He ensured that the resources were available to bring this project to fruition, and he was the one who suggested *Lev Shalem* as the title of the mahzor. Rabbi Julie Schonfeld, the current executive vice president of the Rabbinical Assembly, brought this mahzor to its completion. Amy Gottlieb, publications director of the Rabbinical Assembly, coordinated and supervised editing, proofreading, and production.

Rabbi Wayne Franklin, chair of the publications committee, encouraged our work and helped smooth our way. Thank you to the former chairs of that committee, Rabbis Ira Stone, Ronald Isaacs, Martin Cohen, and especially Gordon Freeman, who originally invited me to take on this project. I would also like to acknowledge the current president of the Rabbinical Assembly, Rabbi Jeffrey Wohlberg, as well as his predecessors, Rabbis Alvin Berkun, Perry Rank, Reuven Hammer, Vernon Kurtz, and Seymour Essrog ל"ז.

A special debt of gratitude is owed to Irma and Paul Milstein, whose generous gift has enabled the publication of *Mahzor Lev Shalem*. May they and their family be blessed through the prayers of the community of Israel.

—RABBI EDWARD FELD
January 2010 / Tevet 5770

I T HAS BEEN A RARE PLEASURE and privilege to work together under the expert leadership of Rabbi Edward Feld, a creative and masterful editor, scholar, team-builder, and mensch. Over the years of this mahzor's development, Rabbi Feld delegated responsibilities, built consensus, nurtured our relationships, managed processes, and informed our decisions with his wide knowledge and fine sensibility. He focused our collective attention on the sacred work of producing a mahzor that would best facilitate meaningful prayer experiences in our diverse communities. The words in this mahzor come from a wide range of sources, but every page is imprinted by a single and singular intellect and *n'shamah*. We are all very grateful.

—*Members of the Editorial Committee*

עֲרָבִית לְרֹאשׁ הַשָּׁנָה · EVENING SERVICE OF ROSH HASHANAH

שָׁלוֹם שָׁלוֹם לָרָחוֹק וְלַקָּרוֹב אָמַר יהוה.

שַׁדַּי, אֲשֶׁר יַקְשִׁיב לַדַּל וְיַעְתַּר,
עַד אָן תְּהֵא רָחוֹק מֶנִּי וְתִסָּתֵר?
לֵיל וָיוֹם אֶעְטוֹף, אֶקְרָא בְּלֵב נָכוֹן,
אוֹדֶה לְךָ תָמִיד, כִּי חַסְדְּךָ יֶתֶר.
מַלְכִּי, לְךָ אוֹחִיל לִבִּי בְּךָ יִבְטַח,
חוֹלֵם חֲלוֹם סָתוּם יִבְטַח עֲלֵי פוֹתֵר.
הִנֵּה שְׁאֵלָתִי: לַקְשִׁיב תְּחִנָּתִי,
אוֹתָהּ אֲבַקֵּשׁ, לֹא פָחוֹת וְלֹא יוֹתֵר.

ROSH HASHANAH. The celebration of the New Year involves a mixture of emotions. On the one hand there is a sense of gratitude at having lived to this time. Last year, we may have prayed that we be given another year, and thankfully we are here to see this day. Many of us come to synagogue and joyously greet old friends and members of the community, both those we know well and those we have not seen for some time. Some of us celebrate that we are once again with family. Traditionally, one wears new clothes on the holy day and we look forward to a festive meal.

On the other hand, the beginning of a new year raises anxiety: What will my fate be this year? Will I live out the year? Will I be healthy? Will I spend my time wisely, or will it be filled in a way that does not truly bring happiness? In turn these questions inspire even deeper self-reflection: What do I want out of life? What makes me proud? What makes me ashamed? What are my most fundamental commitments? Rightfully, this day is called the "Day of Judgment," for in asking ourselves where we have been and where we are going, what have we done, and in what ways we need to strike out on different and new paths, our lives this past year are judged and our future is determined. To stand before God means that we must face ultimate questions.

The Rabbis formulated the variety of emotions of this day by having God say to us, "Half this day is for you and half for Me" (Babylonian Talmud, Pesaḥim 68b). It is a day of extraordinary seriousness as we face our Creator and reveal our deepest selves. It is a day of joy as we revel in the community surrounding us and celebrate the gift of life with them.

WELCOME שָׁלוֹם. Isaiah 57:19.

MIGHTY GOD שַׁדַּי. This poem by Solomon Ibn Gabirol (Spain, 11th century), written as a liturgical introduction (or r'shut), is recited in many different traditions, though at differing holy day times.

PREPARATORY PRAYERS

❡ This Rosh Hashanah, each of us enters this sanctuary with a different need.

Some hearts are full of
  gratitude and joy:
they are overflowing with
  the happiness of love and
  the joy of life;
they are eager to confront
  the day, to make the world
  more fair;
they have recovered from
  illness or have escaped
  misfortune.
And we rejoice with them.

Some hearts ache with
  sorrow:
disappointments weigh
  heavily upon them, and
  they have tasted despair;
families have been broken;
loved ones lie in bed in pain;
death has taken those whom
  they cherished.
May our presence and
  sympathy bring them
  comfort.

Some hearts are embittered:
they have sought answers
  in vain;
they have had their ideals
  mocked and betrayed;
life has lost its meaning and
  value.
May the knowledge that we
  too are searching
restore their hope that there
  is something to find.

Some spirits hunger:
they long for friendship;
they crave understanding;
they yearn for warmth.
May we in our common
  need gain strength from
  one another, sharing
  our joys, lightening each
  other's burdens, and praying for the welfare of our
  community.
  —CHAIM STERN (*adapted*)

Words of Welcome

Shalom: shalom to those who are far off, shalom to those who are near, says ADONAI.

Mighty God who listens to the poor and hears their prayer:
how long will You be distant and hidden from me?
Night and day I turn, calling out with a true heart,
always thanking You, for Your kindness, so great.
My sovereign, my hope is in You; my heart trusts in You,
as a dreamer of dreams depends on an interpreter.
This I ask: hear my prayer.
This I seek—not more, not less.
  —SOLOMON IBN GABIROL

TO SEEK RENEWAL

On this night, O God, we have come into Your house
to pray in Your sanctuary.

But if the heavens are merely Your throne,
if the earth is but Your footstool,

If the heaven of heavens cannot contain You,
how much less this house, built by mere human hands.

Yet although Your dwelling place is every place,
and although You can be sought and found in any place,

It is to this place that we come most confidently—
to seek renewal in Your purifying presence.
  —HERSHEL J. MATT
  (*Mahzor Hadash*)

A Meditational Psalm for the New Year

Bless ADONAI, O my soul,
all my being, God's holy name.
Bless ADONAI, O my soul,
and do not forget all God's bounties.

God forgives all your sins,
heals all your diseases.
God redeems your life from destruction,
surrounds you with steadfast love and mercy.

ADONAI acts justly,
ruling in favor of the oppressed.
God has not dealt with us according to our sins,
nor punished us according to our iniquities.

For as the heavens are high above the earth,
so is God's steadfast love great toward those who
stand in awe of God.
As a father has compassion for his children,
so does ADONAI have compassion for those who
stand in awe of God.

For God knows how we are formed;
God is mindful that we are dust.
The days of humans are like grass;
they bloom like a flower of the field.
But a wind passes by and they are no more,
and where they were planted is no longer known.

But ADONAI's steadfast love toward those who
fear God is for all eternity, lasting through the
generations, for those who keep God's covenant
and remember to observe God's precepts.

Bless ADONAI, all you messengers of God,
people of strength, doing God's will,
obeying God's word.

Bless ADONAI, all God's creatures,
through the length and breadth of God's realm.
Bless ADONAI, O my soul.   Psalm 103 (selected verses)

לְדָוִד. בָּרְכִי נַפְשִׁי אֶת־יהוה,
וְכָל־קְרָבַי אֶת־שֵׁם קָדְשׁוֹ.
בָּרְכִי נַפְשִׁי אֶת־יהוה,
וְאַל־תִּשְׁכְּחִי כָּל־גְּמוּלָיו.
הַסֹּלֵחַ לְכָל־עֲוֺנֵכִי,
הָרֹפֵא לְכָל־תַּחֲלֻאָיְכִי.
הַגּוֹאֵל מִשַּׁחַת חַיָּיְכִי,
הַמְעַטְּרֵכִי חֶסֶד וְרַחֲמִים.
עֹשֵׂה צְדָקוֹת יהוה,
וּמִשְׁפָּטִים לְכָל־עֲשׁוּקִים.
לֹא כַחֲטָאֵינוּ עָשָׂה לָנוּ,
וְלֹא כַעֲוֺנֹתֵינוּ גָּמַל עָלֵינוּ.
כִּי כִגְבֹהַּ שָׁמַיִם עַל־הָאָרֶץ,
גָּבַר חַסְדּוֹ עַל־יְרֵאָיו.
כְּרַחֵם אָב עַל־בָּנִים,
רִחַם יהוה עַל־יְרֵאָיו.
כִּי הוּא יָדַע יִצְרֵנוּ,
זָכוּר כִּי־עָפָר אֲנָחְנוּ.
אֱנוֹשׁ כֶּחָצִיר יָמָיו,
כְּצִיץ הַשָּׂדֶה כֵּן יָצִיץ.
כִּי רוּחַ עָבְרָה־בּוֹ וְאֵינֶנּוּ,
וְלֹא־יַכִּירֶנּוּ עוֹד מְקוֹמוֹ.
וְחֶסֶד יהוה מֵעוֹלָם וְעַד־עוֹלָם
עַל־יְרֵאָיו, וְצִדְקָתוֹ לִבְנֵי בָנִים.
לְשֹׁמְרֵי בְרִיתוֹ
וּלְזֹכְרֵי פִקֻּדָיו לַעֲשׂוֹתָם.
בָּרְכוּ יהוה מַלְאָכָיו,
גִּבֹּרֵי כֹחַ עֹשֵׂי דְבָרוֹ,
לִשְׁמֹעַ בְּקוֹל דְּבָרוֹ.
בָּרְכוּ יהוה כָּל־מַעֲשָׂיו
בְּכָל־מְקֹמוֹת מֶמְשַׁלְתּוֹ,
בָּרְכִי נַפְשִׁי אֶת־יהוה.

תהלים קג

The Powerful Prayer

Once on the eve of the New Year, when they were in synagogue, Rabbi Naḥum of Chernobyl was reciting the afternoon prayer with great fervor, but his grandson-in-law who stood near him felt a sinking spirit. Everyone seemed to be praying with great concentration, but it took all the strength he could muster just to be able to figure out a single word and to grasp its meaning. Afterward he approached Rabbi Naḥum, concerned that his prayer was unacceptable, for he had been unable to make his way through the service. Rabbi Naḥum said to him: "My son, how your prayer took Heaven by storm today! It lifted up all those prayers that could not come through the gates."

—A ḤASIDIC TALE

NOW IS THE TIME FOR TURNING

To everything there is a season,
and there is an appointed time for every purpose
  under heaven.
  Now is the time for turning.
The seasons change
as does the balance of day and night.
  The birds are beginning to turn
  and are heading once more toward the south.
The animals are beginning to turn
to storing their food for the winter.
  For the earth, for birds and animals,
  turning comes naturally,
  but for us, turning does not come so easily.
It takes an act of will
for us to make a turn.
  It means breaking with old habits.
  It means admitting that we have been wrong;
  and this is never easy.
It means losing face;
it means starting all over again;
and this is always painful.
  It means saying: "I am sorry."
  It means admitting that we have the ability to change;
  and this is always embarrassing.
These things are terribly hard to do.
But unless we turn, we will be trapped forever
in yesterday's ways.
  Dear God, help us to turn—
from callousness to sensitivity,
from hostility to love,
  from pettiness to purpose,
  from envy to contentment,
from carelessness to discipline,
from fear to faith.
  Turn us around, O God, and bring us back toward You.
  Revive our lives, as at the beginning.
And turn us toward each other, God,
for in isolation there is no life.

—JACK RIEMER
(*Mahzor Hadash*)

מִזְמוֹר שִׁיר לְיוֹם הַשַּׁבָּת.

טוֹב לְהֹדוֹת לַיהוה, וּלְזַמֵּר לְשִׁמְךָ עֶלְיוֹן.

לְהַגִּיד בַּבֹּקֶר חַסְדֶּךָ, וֶאֱמוּנָתְךָ בַּלֵּילוֹת.

עֲלֵי־עָשׂוֹר וַעֲלֵי־נָבֶל, עֲלֵי הִגָּיוֹן בְּכִנּוֹר.

כִּי שִׂמַּחְתַּנִי יהוה בְּפָעֳלֶךָ, בְּמַעֲשֵׂי יָדֶיךָ אֲרַנֵּן.

מַה־גָּדְלוּ מַעֲשֶׂיךָ יהוה, מְאֹד עָמְקוּ מַחְשְׁבֹתֶיךָ.

אִישׁ־בַּעַר לֹא יֵדָע וּכְסִיל לֹא־יָבִין אֶת־זֹאת.

בִּפְרֹחַ רְשָׁעִים כְּמוֹ עֵשֶׂב וַיָּצִיצוּ כָּל־פֹּעֲלֵי אָוֶן,
לְהִשָּׁמְדָם עֲדֵי־עַד.

וְאַתָּה מָרוֹם לְעֹלָם יהוה.

כִּי הִנֵּה אֹיְבֶיךָ יהוה, כִּי הִנֵּה אֹיְבֶיךָ יֹאבֵדוּ,
יִתְפָּרְדוּ כָּל־פֹּעֲלֵי אָוֶן.

וַתָּרֶם כִּרְאֵים קַרְנִי, בַּלֹּתִי בְּשֶׁמֶן רַעֲנָן.

וַתַּבֵּט עֵינִי בְּשׁוּרָי, בַּקָּמִים עָלַי מְרֵעִים, תִּשְׁמַעְנָה אָזְנָי.

◁ צַדִּיק כַּתָּמָר יִפְרָח, כְּאֶרֶז בַּלְּבָנוֹן יִשְׂגֶּה.

שְׁתוּלִים בְּבֵית יהוה, בְּחַצְרוֹת אֱלֹהֵינוּ יַפְרִיחוּ.

עוֹד יְנוּבוּן בְּשֵׂיבָה, דְּשֵׁנִים וְרַעֲנַנִּים יִהְיוּ.

לְהַגִּיד כִּי־יָשָׁר יהוה, צוּרִי וְלֹא עַוְלָתָה בּוֹ. תהלים צב

יהוה מָלָךְ גֵּאוּת לָבֵשׁ, לָבֵשׁ יהוה עֹז הִתְאַזָּר,
אַף־תִּכּוֹן תֵּבֵל בַּל־תִּמּוֹט.

נָכוֹן כִּסְאֲךָ מֵאָז, מֵעוֹלָם אָתָּה.

נָשְׂאוּ נְהָרוֹת יהוה, נָשְׂאוּ נְהָרוֹת קוֹלָם,
יִשְׂאוּ נְהָרוֹת דָּכְיָם.

◁ מִקֹּלוֹת מַיִם רַבִּים, אַדִּירִים מִשְׁבְּרֵי יָם,
אַדִּיר בַּמָּרוֹם יהוה.

עֵדֹתֶיךָ נֶאֶמְנוּ מְאֹד לְבֵיתְךָ נָאֲוָה קֹדֶשׁ, יהוה,
לְאֹרֶךְ יָמִים. תהלים צג

*Many congregations recite Mourner's Kaddish
(page 26) following the Shabbat psalms.*

SHABBAT. When any holy day falls on Friday night, the evening service begins with an abridged Kabbalat Shabbat, and only traces of the Shabbat liturgy are included.

PSALM 92. This psalm includes themes appropriate to Shabbat. Contemplating creation, the poet begins with an expression of wonder and ends with hope: a vision of future peace and wholeness is captured in the image of being firmly planted in God's house. Shabbat is both a remembrance of creation and a foretaste of redemption.

PALM TREE . . . CEDAR כַּתָּמָר . . . כְּאֶרֶז. Palm trees grow in the Jericho Valley, one of the lowest places on earth; cedars grow on the mountaintops of Lebanon, the highest in the Middle East. Palm trees grow straight up, losing their leaves each year; cedars grow wide and are evergreens. Palms yield dates, one of the most nutritious fruits; cedars bear no fruit, though their wood is precious. Both will be planted in God's house, for all difference is united in the God who is one.

PSALM 93. This psalm describes God's enthronement as Sovereign. It may have become associated with Shabbat because it is only with rest, peace, and the sense of completion on Shabbat that God can be seen as truly enthroned.

The Angelic Song of Shabbat: Psalm 92

This psalm inspired a legend that as the sixth day ended and the sun set, Adam began to be afraid that permanent darkness would be his fate. Angels descended from heaven and began to sing this psalm. Reassured that new days would come, he was filled with joy and joined in the song.

—AVOT OF RABBI NATAN

❧ *Psalm 93: An Interpretive Translation*

Entwined in worlds,
enwrapped in glory,
    You are.
*So has it been,
and so it is—*
    eternally You are.
Waves pounding out their
song reach up to God
from their depths,
    for the song of the sea,
    beaten to the sound of
    the breakers, tells of the
    God within.
These are proof enough
for the faithful—that You
are the lord of time.

—EDWARD FELD
and ARTHUR GOULD

ON SHABBAT, WE RECITE THESE PSALMS:

PSALM 92: A SONG FOR SHABBAT

It is good to thank You, ADONAI,
to sing Your praise, exalted God,
    to speak of Your love each morning,
    and of Your faithfulness at night,
    to the music of the lute and the melody of the harp.
Your creation, ADONAI, gives me joy; I sing of Your handiwork.
    How vast Your works, ADONAI,
    how intricate Your designs.
The thoughtless cannot comprehend,
the foolish cannot fathom this:
    the wicked flourish like grass, those who commit evil blossom,
    only to be destroyed in the end.
But You, ADONAI, are supreme forever.
    Surely, Your enemies, ADONAI, surely, Your enemies shall perish;
    those who commit evil shall crumble.
And You will raise my head high, like the horn of the ox,
anointing me with fragrant oil.
    Were enemies to gather against me, my gaze would remain
    steady, for my ears would hear:
The righteous shall flourish like the palm tree; they shall endure
like a cedar in Lebanon, transplanted in the house of ADONAI,
thriving in our God's courtyard.
    In old age, they are yet fruitful, always fresh and fragrant,
    proclaiming that ADONAI is flawless, my stronghold, never unjust.
Tzaddik ka-tamar yifraḥ, k'erez ba-l'vanon yisgeh. Sh'tulim b'veit
Adonai, b'ḥatzrot eloheinu yafriḥu. Od y'nuvun b'seivah, d'sheinim
v'ra·anannim yihyu, l'haggid ki yashar Adonai, tzuri v'lo avlatah bo.

PSALM 93

ADONAI is sovereign, robed in splendor, girded in strength.
Surely the earth stands firm; it will not be shaken.
Your kingdom stands from earliest time, You are eternal.
The rivers rise to You, ADONAI, the rivers raise their voices,
the rivers raise up their waves,
from the roaring of the deep, and the mighty breakers of
    the sea: "ADONAI is supreme."
Your teaching, ADONAI, never fails.
Holiness befits Your house, ADONAI, until the end of time.

Many congregations recite Mourner's Kaddish
(page 26) following the Shabbat psalms.

We rise. Leader:

בָּרְכוּ אֶת־יְהוה הַמְבֹרָךְ.

Congregation, then the leader repeats:

↑ בָּרוּךְ יהוה הַמְבֹרָךְ לְעוֹלָם וָעֶד.

We are seated.

בָּרוּךְ אַתָּה יהוה אֱלֹהֵינוּ מֶלֶךְ הָעוֹלָם,
אֲשֶׁר בִּדְבָרוֹ מַעֲרִיב עֲרָבִים,
בְּחָכְמָה פּוֹתֵחַ שְׁעָרִים,
וּבִתְבוּנָה מְשַׁנֶּה עִתִּים,
וּמַחֲלִיף אֶת־הַזְּמַנִּים,
וּמְסַדֵּר אֶת־הַכּוֹכָבִים בְּמִשְׁמְרוֹתֵיהֶם בָּרָקִיעַ כִּרְצוֹנוֹ.
בּוֹרֵא יוֹם וָלָיְלָה,
גּוֹלֵל אוֹר מִפְּנֵי חֹשֶׁךְ, וְחֹשֶׁךְ מִפְּנֵי אוֹר.
◁ וּמַעֲבִיר יוֹם וּמֵבִיא לָיְלָה,
וּמַבְדִּיל בֵּין יוֹם וּבֵין לָיְלָה,
יהוה צְבָאוֹת שְׁמוֹ.
אֵל חַי וְקַיָּם, תָּמִיד יִמְלוֹךְ עָלֵינוּ לְעוֹלָם וָעֶד.
בָּרוּךְ אַתָּה יהוה, הַמַּעֲרִיב עֲרָבִים.

THE SH'MA AND ITS BLESSINGS קְרִיאַת שְׁמַע וּבְרְכוֹתֶיהָ. The evening service (Arvit) always includes two climactic moments: the Sh'ma and the Amidah. The Sh'ma, the affirmation of faith in the One God, has often been called Judaism's only creed. B'rakhot surround the Sh'ma and serve to interpret the themes enunciated in the biblical verses that make up the Sh'ma itself. Two b'rakhot precede the Sh'ma: the first reflects on God's presence in the cycle of the day and the cycle of seasons, while the second acknowledges God's love, represented by the gift of Torah, God's instruction as to how we should live. Two b'rakhot also follow the Sh'ma: the first acknowledges the Exodus from Egypt, which has set us on the path of freedom and responsibility; the last speaks to our concrete concerns for safety in the darkness of night.

WHOSE WISDOM OPENS THE GATES OF DAWN בְּחָכְמָה פּוֹתֵחַ שְׁעָרִים. Some of our liturgical texts reflect biblical and rabbinic metaphorical understandings of the operation of the heavenly bodies—for instance, this depiction of the sun marching from and toward gates in the sky in the east and west. These images should be taken as representations of subjective experiences, rather than as astronomical observations; they can evoke for us the sense of awe people have had throughout time as they contemplated the wonders of the universe.

CREATES בּוֹרֵא. The word בּוֹרֵא, "creates," is used as a verb in the Bible only when the subject is God, for ultimately creation of the world is a mystery.

ADONAI TZ'VA·OT יהוה צְבָאוֹת. In the ancient world, the sun, the moon, and the stars were all seen as divine powers. Biblical monotheism deposed these ancient gods and they were then depicted as handmaidens of God, God's army. Thus this phrase, which has sometimes been translated as "Lord of hosts," alludes to God's mastery of all the forces of the universe.

THE SH'MA AND ITS BLESSINGS

Beginning to Pray

Where do I begin?
Where do I find God?
How do I begin to pray?
There is a *tzelem Elohim*, an image of God, implanted in me. The image of God is found in myself, in whom God breathes *nishmat hayyim*—the divine breath of life. In each of us is a *n'shamah*, a soul whose origin is God. In prayer, I enter into the deepest parts of my self, discover who I am, and touch God's presence.

— HAROLD SCHULWEIS
(adapted)

¶ *God and Nature: An Interpretive Translation*

Beloved are You,
  eternal God,
by whose design the
  evening falls,
by whose command
  dimensions open up
and eons pass away and
  stars spin in their orbits.
You set the rhythms of
  day and night;
the alternation of light
  and darkness
sings Your creating word.
In rising sun and in
  spreading dusk,
Creator of all, You are
  made manifest.
Eternal, everlasting God,
may we always be aware
  of Your dominion.
Beloved are You,
  Adonai, for this hour
  of nightfall.

— ANDRÉ UNGAR

Bar'khu: The Call to Worship Together

We rise as we are called by the leader's words of invitation to prayer. The leader bows when saying the word "bar'khu" (praise) and stands straight when reciting the name of God. Similarly, the congregation bows at the word "barukh" (praise) and straightens to full height at the recitation of God's name.

Leader:

Praise ADONAI, to whom all prayer is directed.

Congregation, then the leader repeats:

ſ Praise ADONAI, to whom all prayer is directed
forever and ever.

Barukh Adonai ha-m'vorakh l'olam va·ed.

We are seated.

First B'rakhah before the Sh'ma: The Evening Light

Barukh atah ADONAI, our God, ruler of time and space,
whose word brings the evening dusk,
whose wisdom opens the gates of dawn,
whose understanding changes the day's division,
whose will sets the succession of seasons and arranges the
    stars in their places in the sky,
who creates day and night,
who rolls light before darkness and darkness from light,
who makes day pass into night,
who distinguishes day from night;
Adonai Tz'va·ot is Your name.
Living and ever-present God,
may Your rule be with us, forever and ever.
Barukh atah ADONAI, who brings each evening's dusk.

אַהֲבַת עוֹלָם בֵּית יִשְׂרָאֵל עַמְּךָ אָהָבְתָּ, תּוֹרָה וּמִצְוֹת, חֻקִּים וּמִשְׁפָּטִים אוֹתָנוּ לִמַּדְתָּ. עַל כֵּן יהוה אֱלֹהֵינוּ, בְּשָׁכְבֵּנוּ וּבְקוּמֵנוּ נָשִׂיחַ בְּחֻקֶּיךָ, וְנִשְׂמַח בְּדִבְרֵי תוֹרָתֶךָ וּבְמִצְוֹתֶיךָ לְעוֹלָם וָעֶד. כִּי הֵם חַיֵּינוּ וְאֹרֶךְ יָמֵינוּ, וּבָהֶם נֶהְגֶּה יוֹמָם וָלַיְלָה, ◁ וְאַהֲבָתְךָ אַל תָּסִיר מִמֶּנּוּ לְעוֹלָמִים. בָּרוּךְ אַתָּה יהוה, אוֹהֵב עַמּוֹ יִשְׂרָאֵל.

קְרִיאַת שְׁמַע

Some people may wish to pause here for a moment. Some may close their eyes; others place a hand over their eyes. The intention is to concentrate on the one-ness of God. These words are added in the absence of a minyan: אֵל מֶלֶךְ נֶאֱמָן

שְׁמַע יִשְׂרָאֵל יהוה אֱלֹהֵינוּ יהוה אֶחָד:
בָּרוּךְ שֵׁם כְּבוֹד מַלְכוּתוֹ לְעוֹלָם וָעֶד.

וְאָהַבְתָּ אֵת יהוה אֱלֹהֶיךָ בְּכָל־לְבָבְךָ וּבְכָל־נַפְשְׁךָ וּבְכָל־מְאֹדֶךָ: וְהָיוּ הַדְּבָרִים הָאֵלֶּה אֲשֶׁר אָנֹכִי מְצַוְּךָ הַיּוֹם עַל־לְבָבֶךָ: וְשִׁנַּנְתָּם לְבָנֶיךָ וְדִבַּרְתָּ בָּם בְּשִׁבְתְּךָ בְּבֵיתֶךָ וּבְלֶכְתְּךָ בַדֶּרֶךְ וּבְשָׁכְבְּךָ וּבְקוּמֶךָ: וּקְשַׁרְתָּם לְאוֹת עַל־יָדֶךָ וְהָיוּ לְטֹטָפֹת בֵּין עֵינֶיךָ: וּכְתַבְתָּם עַל־מְזֻזוֹת בֵּיתֶךָ וּבִשְׁעָרֶיךָ:   דברים ו ד-ט

TORAH AND GOD'S LOVE אַהֲבַת עוֹלָם. The Sh'ma is our affirmation of God as well as a statement of our obligation to God. In the *b'rakhot* before the Sh'ma, we affirm God's gifts to us—first as the creator of the universe, and second by giving us instruction as to how to live: the Torah. Similarly, since the Sh'ma commands that we love God "with all our hearts," this *b'rakhah* emphasizes God's antecedent love of human beings and the people Israel. Jewish tradition teaches that God's love for us and our own love of each human being ("Love your neighbor as yourself," Leviticus 19:18) live in our hearts side by side.

THE SH'MA. The Sh'ma is recited twice daily: morning and evening. It is a קְרִיאָה (*k'ri·ah*), a reading or declaration. The three paragraphs from the Torah that comprise the Sh'ma were selected because they express basic aspects of Jewish belief. According to the Rabbis, the first of the three paragraphs proclaims allegiance to the sovereignty of heaven, עַל מַלְכוּת שָׁמַיִם (*ol malkhut shamayim*); the second proclaims allegiance to the commandments, עַל מִצְוֹת (*ol mitzvot*); and the third reminds us of the Exodus, יְצִיאַת מִצְרַיִם (*y'tziat mitzrayim*), our primary sacred story.

HEAR שְׁמַע. To hear is to emphasize the nonmaterial over the physical, to internalize the sense of God.

ALONE אֶחָד. The word *eḥad* literally means "one." As an affirmation about God, it can be understood in multiple ways. The present rendering emphasizes the monotheistic claims of Jewish faith. Others translate *eḥad* as "unique," emphasizing God's otherness. Mystic commentators interpret "oneness" as a unity of heaven and earth, saying that we are ultimately all connected to the One.

PRAISED BE THE NAME בָּרוּךְ שֵׁם. According to the Mishnah, when God's name was pronounced by the High Priest on Yom Kippur, the people would respond, "Praised be the name . . ." (Yoma 3:8). Since this is a response but not part of the biblical text, it is normally not recited out loud, in order not to interrupt the flow of biblical verses—though the memory of how it was recited in the Temple remains with us in a whisper.

Faith is not something that we acquire once and for all. Faith is an insight that must be acquired at every single moment. . . . Those who honestly search, those who yearn and fail, we did not presume to judge. Let them pray to be able to pray, and if they do not succeed, if they have no tears to shed, let them yearn for tears, let them try to discover their heart and let them take strength from the certainty that this too is a high form of prayer.

—ABRAHAM JOSHUA HESCHEL

¶ *Sh'ma:*
Declaration of Faith

Loving life
and its mysterious source
with all our heart
and all our spirit,
all our senses and strength,
we take upon ourselves
and into ourselves
these promises:
to care for the earth
and those who live upon it,
to pursue justice and peace,
to love kindness and
  compassion.
We will teach this to our
  children
throughout the passage of
  the day—
as we dwell in our homes
and as we go on our
  journeys,
from the time we rise
until we fall asleep.
And may our actions
be faithful to our words
that our children's children
may live to know:
Truth and kindness
have embraced,
peace and justice have
  kissed
and are one.

—MARCIA FALK

Second B'rakhah before the Sh'ma: Torah and God's Love

You have loved Your people, the House of Israel, with infinite love; You taught us Torah and mitzvot, statutes and laws. Therefore, Adonai our God, as we lie down or rise up, we shall think of Your laws and speak of them, rejoicing in Your words of Torah and Your mitzvot forever and ever. For they are our life and the fullness of our days, and on them we will meditate day and night. May You never withdraw Your love from us. *Barukh atah* Adonai, who loves the people Israel.

Ahavat olam beit yisra·el am'kha ahavta. Torah u-mitzvot, ḥukkim u-mishpatim otanu limmadta. Al kein Adonai eloheinu, b'shokhveinu u-v'kumeinu nasi·aḥ b'ḥukkekha, v'nismaḥ b'divrei toratekha u-v'mitzvotekha l'olam va·ed. Ki heim ḥayyeinu v'orekh yameinu, u-va-hem nehgeh yomam va-lailah.

Recitation of the Sh'ma

Some people may wish to pause here for a moment. Some may close their eyes; others place a hand over their eyes. The intention is to concentrate on the oneness of God. These words are added in the absence of a minyan: God is a faithful sovereign.

Hear, O Israel, Adonai is our God, Adonai alone.
Sh'ma yisra·el Adonai eloheinu Adonai eḥad.

Praised be the name of the One whose glorious sovereignty is forever and ever.

You shall love Adonai your God with all your heart, with all your soul, and with all that is yours. These words that I command you this day shall be taken to heart. Teach them again and again to your children, and speak of them when you sit in your home, when you walk on your way, when you lie down, and when you rise up. Bind them as a sign upon your hand and as a symbol above your eyes. Inscribe them upon the doorposts of your home and on your gates. Deuteronomy 6:4–9

V'ahavta eit Adonai elohekha b'khol l'vav'kha u-v'khol nafsh'kha u-v'khol m'odekha. V'hayu ha-d'varim ha-eilleh asher anokhi m'tzav'kha ha-yom al l'vavekha. V'shinnantam l'vanekha v'dibbarta bam, b'shivt'kha b'veitekha u-v'lekht'kha va-derekh u-v'shokhb'kha u-v'kumekha. U-k'shartam l'ot al yadekha v'hayu l'totafot bein einekha. U-kh'tavtam al m'zuzot beitekha u-vi-sh'arekha.

וְהָיָה אִם־שָׁמֹעַ תִּשְׁמְעוּ אֶל־מִצְוֹתַי אֲשֶׁר אָנֹכִי מְצַוֶּה
אֶתְכֶם הַיּוֹם לְאַהֲבָה אֶת־יהוה אֱלֹהֵיכֶם וּלְעָבְדוֹ בְּכָל־
לְבַבְכֶם וּבְכָל־נַפְשְׁכֶם: וְנָתַתִּי מְטַר־אַרְצְכֶם בְּעִתּוֹ
יוֹרֶה וּמַלְקוֹשׁ וְאָסַפְתָּ דְגָנֶךָ וְתִירֹשְׁךָ וְיִצְהָרֶךָ: וְנָתַתִּי
עֵשֶׂב בְּשָׂדְךָ לִבְהֶמְתֶּךָ וְאָכַלְתָּ וְשָׂבָעְתָּ: הִשָּׁמְרוּ לָכֶם
פֶּן יִפְתֶּה לְבַבְכֶם וְסַרְתֶּם וַעֲבַדְתֶּם אֱלֹהִים אֲחֵרִים
וְהִשְׁתַּחֲוִיתֶם לָהֶם: וְחָרָה אַף־יהוה בָּכֶם וְעָצַר אֶת־
הַשָּׁמַיִם וְלֹא־יִהְיֶה מָטָר וְהָאֲדָמָה לֹא תִתֵּן אֶת־יְבוּלָהּ
וַאֲבַדְתֶּם מְהֵרָה מֵעַל הָאָרֶץ הַטֹּבָה אֲשֶׁר יהוה נֹתֵן
לָכֶם: וְשַׂמְתֶּם אֶת־דְּבָרַי אֵלֶּה עַל־לְבַבְכֶם וְעַל־נַפְשְׁכֶם
וּקְשַׁרְתֶּם אֹתָם לְאוֹת עַל־יֶדְכֶם וְהָיוּ לְטוֹטָפֹת בֵּין
עֵינֵיכֶם: וְלִמַּדְתֶּם אֹתָם אֶת־בְּנֵיכֶם לְדַבֵּר בָּם בְּשִׁבְתְּךָ
בְּבֵיתֶךָ וּבְלֶכְתְּךָ בַדֶּרֶךְ וּבְשָׁכְבְּךָ וּבְקוּמֶךָ: וּכְתַבְתָּם עַל־
מְזוּזוֹת בֵּיתֶךָ וּבִשְׁעָרֶיךָ: לְמַעַן יִרְבּוּ יְמֵיכֶם וִימֵי בְּנֵיכֶם
עַל הָאֲדָמָה אֲשֶׁר נִשְׁבַּע יהוה לַאֲבֹתֵיכֶם לָתֵת לָהֶם
כִּימֵי הַשָּׁמַיִם עַל־הָאָרֶץ:

דברים יא יג-כא

וַיֹּאמֶר יהוה אֶל־מֹשֶׁה לֵּאמֹר: דַּבֵּר אֶל־בְּנֵי יִשְׂרָאֵל
וְאָמַרְתָּ אֲלֵהֶם וְעָשׂוּ לָהֶם צִיצִת עַל־כַּנְפֵי בִגְדֵיהֶם
לְדֹרֹתָם וְנָתְנוּ עַל־צִיצִת הַכָּנָף פְּתִיל תְּכֵלֶת: וְהָיָה לָכֶם
לְצִיצִת וּרְאִיתֶם אֹתוֹ וּזְכַרְתֶּם אֶת־כָּל־מִצְוֹת יהוה
וַעֲשִׂיתֶם אֹתָם וְלֹא־תָתוּרוּ אַחֲרֵי לְבַבְכֶם וְאַחֲרֵי עֵינֵיכֶם
אֲשֶׁר־אַתֶּם זֹנִים אַחֲרֵיהֶם: לְמַעַן תִּזְכְּרוּ וַעֲשִׂיתֶם
אֶת־כָּל־מִצְוֹתָי וִהְיִיתֶם קְדֹשִׁים לֵאלֹהֵיכֶם: אֲנִי יהוה
אֱלֹהֵיכֶם אֲשֶׁר הוֹצֵאתִי אֶתְכֶם מֵאֶרֶץ מִצְרַיִם לִהְיוֹת
לָכֶם לֵאלֹהִים אֲנִי ◁ יהוה אֱלֹהֵיכֶם:

במדבר טו לז-מא

אֱמֶת

וֶאֱמוּנָה כָּל־
זֹאת, וְקַיָּם עָלֵינוּ, כִּי הוּא יהוה אֱלֹהֵינוּ וְאֵין זוּלָתוֹ,
וַאֲנַחְנוּ יִשְׂרָאֵל עַמּוֹ. הַפּוֹדֵנוּ מִיַּד מְלָכִים, מַלְכֵּנוּ
הַגּוֹאֲלֵנוּ מִכַּף כָּל־הֶעָרִיצִים. הָאֵל הַנִּפְרָע לָנוּ
מִצָּרֵינוּ, וְהַמְשַׁלֵּם גְּמוּל לְכָל־אֹיְבֵי נַפְשֵׁנוּ,

IF YOU WILL HEAR וְהָיָה אִם־שָׁמֹעַ. This passage, like many in the Torah, reflects the tradition's insistence that moral coherence underlies the world. The text's plain meaning describes a very literal form of the idea of divine reward and punishment, one with which every generation of Jews since biblical times has struggled theologically. Some Reform and Reconstructionist liturgists have gone so far as to remove this paragraph from their recitation of the Sh'ma. Traditional Jewish prayer, however, has retained it, reflecting a deep belief that in a way we may not grasp, the consequences of our moral and immoral behavior resound in the world.

ADONAI SAID TO MOSES וַיֹּאמֶר יהוה אֶל־מֹשֶׁה. The Rabbis emphasized the last words of this paragraph as the prime reason for its inclusion in the Sh'ma: the remembrance of the Exodus from Egypt. In Jewish theology, the historical Exodus anticipates the redemption in the future: true freedom. The means of achieving redemption, we are taught, is remembering our responsibility to live lives that are holy.

TRULY—THIS IS OUR FAITHFUL AFFIRMATION אֱמֶת וֶאֱמוּנָה. So closely was the Sh'ma linked with this next b'rakhah, the blessing of redemption, that the Rabbis insisted that the first word—truly—be recited along with the very last words of the Sh'ma, so we always read the *(continued)*

¶ *Faithfulness:*
An Interpretive
Translation

If you faithfully obey My laws today, and love Me, I shall give you your livelihood in good time and in full measure. You shall work and reap the results of your labor, satisfied with what you have achieved. Be careful, however. Let not your heart be seduced, lured after false goals, seeking alien ideals, lest God's image depart from you and you sink into dissoluteness and lose your joyous God-given heritage.

—ANDRÉ UNGAR

If you will hear and obey the mitzvot that I command you this day, to love and serve ADONAI your God with all your heart and all your soul, then I will grant the rain for your land in season, rain in autumn and rain in spring. You shall gather in your grain and wine and oil—I will also provide grass in your fields for cattle—and you shall eat and be satisfied. Take care lest your heart be tempted, and you stray to serve other gods and bow to them. Then ADONAI's anger will flare up against you, and God will close up the sky so that there will be no rain and the earth will not yield its produce. You will quickly disappear from the good land that ADONAI is giving you.

Therefore, impress these words of mine upon your heart and upon your soul. Bind them as a sign upon your hand and as a symbol above your eyes; teach them to your children, speaking of them when you sit in your home, when you walk on your way, when you lie down and when you rise up; inscribe them upon the doorposts of your home and on your gates.

Then the length of your days and the days of your children, on the land that ADONAI swore to give to your ancestors, will be as the days of the heavens over the earth.

Deuteronomy 11:13–21

ADONAI said to Moses: Speak to the people Israel, and instruct them that in every generation they shall put *tzitzit* on the corners of their garments, placing a thread of blue on the *tzitzit*, the fringe of each corner. That shall be your *tzitzit* and you shall look at it, and remember all the mitzvot of ADONAI, and fulfill them, and not be seduced by your heart and eyes as they lead you astray. Then you will remember and fulfill all My mitzvot, and be holy before your God. I am ADONAI your God, who brought you out of the land of Egypt to be your God. I am ADONAI your God—

Numbers 15:37–41

Truly—

This is our faithful affirmation, binding on us: that ADONAI is our God and there is none other, and we, Israel, are God's people. God redeems us from earthly rulers, our sovereign delivers us from the hand of all tyrants, *God brings judgment upon our oppressors, retribution upon all our mortal enemies,*

הָעֹשֶׂה גְדוֹלוֹת עַד אֵין חֵקֶר, וְנִפְלָאוֹת עַד אֵין מִסְפָּר.
הַשָּׂם נַפְשֵׁנוּ בַּחַיִּים, וְלֹא נָתַן לַמּוֹט רַגְלֵנוּ,
הַמַּדְרִיכֵנוּ עַל בָּמוֹת אוֹיְבֵינוּ, וַיָּרֶם קַרְנֵנוּ עַל כָּל־
שׂוֹנְאֵינוּ. הָעֹשֶׂה לָּנוּ נִסִּים וּנְקָמָה בְּפַרְעֹה, אוֹתוֹת
וּמוֹפְתִים בְּאַדְמַת בְּנֵי חָם. הַמַּכֶּה בְעֶבְרָתוֹ כָּל־בְּכוֹרֵי
מִצְרָיִם, וַיּוֹצֵא אֶת־עַמּוֹ יִשְׂרָאֵל מִתּוֹכָם לְחֵרוּת עוֹלָם.
הַמַּעֲבִיר בָּנָיו בֵּין גִּזְרֵי יַם סוּף, אֶת־רוֹדְפֵיהֶם וְאֶת־
שׂוֹנְאֵיהֶם בִּתְהוֹמוֹת טִבַּע, וְרָאוּ בָנָיו גְּבוּרָתוֹ, שִׁבְּחוּ
וְהוֹדוּ לִשְׁמוֹ.
◁ וּמַלְכוּתוֹ בְּרָצוֹן קִבְּלוּ עֲלֵיהֶם, מֹשֶׁה וּמִרְיָם וּבְנֵי
יִשְׂרָאֵל לְךָ עָנוּ שִׁירָה בְּשִׂמְחָה רַבָּה, וְאָמְרוּ כֻלָּם:

מִי־כָמֹכָה בָּאֵלִם יהוה, מִי כָּמֹכָה נֶאְדָּר בַּקֹּדֶשׁ,
נוֹרָא תְהִלֹּת, עֹשֵׂה פֶלֶא.

מַלְכוּתְךָ רָאוּ בָנֶיךָ, בּוֹקֵעַ יָם לִפְנֵי מֹשֶׁה, זֶה אֵלִי עָנוּ
וְאָמְרוּ:

יהוה יִמְלֹךְ לְעוֹלָם וָעֶד.

וְנֶאֱמַר: כִּי־פָדָה יהוה אֶת־יַעֲקֹב, וּגְאָלוֹ מִיַּד חָזָק מִמֶּנּוּ.
בָּרוּךְ אַתָּה יהוה, גָּאַל יִשְׂרָאֵל.

(continued from previous page)
יהוה אֱלֹהֵיכֶם אֱמֶת (Adonai eloheikhem emet). Thus we affirm that God is true, or truth itself. The world as it is presented to us is a world in which truth is hidden: its full revelation constitutes redemption. When we recite the Sh'ma and affirm God's oneness, we may have a token of that redemption.

GOD SMOTE הַמַּכֶּה. The reality is that the cost of achieving freedom may be violence. America, for instance, won its independence through revolution. In the Italian liturgical tradition, this sentence is omitted on Shabbat, since it is not considered to be in keeping with the peaceful mood of the day.

MIRIAM מִרְיָם. After the deliverance at the Sea, we are told that Moses led the men in song and Miriam led the women in response, joyously singing מִי כָמֹכָה "Who is like You . . ."

WHO IS LIKE YOU מִי כָמֹכָה. Exodus 15:11.

ADONAI WILL REIGN יהוה יִמְלֹךְ. Exodus 15:18.

ADONAI HAS RESCUED כִּי פָדָה יהוה. Jeremiah 31:11.

REDEEMED גָּאַל. The verb is in the past tense, unlike all the other b'rakhot of the Sh'ma, which are in the present tense. It is as if a community that truly is able to recite the Sh'ma together must already have been redeemed.
(adapted from Franz Rosenzweig)

¶ *A Prayer for Redemption*

True redemption will arrive when enemies understand the humanity common to us all, when the praises sung by Israel can be sung by all peoples, forever rescued from their fears and hates, their cowardice and cruelty.

As our ancestors sang Your praise all alone by the Sea of Reeds, so we sing Your praise here, in the hope that soon, in our days, we may be joined by people of good will everywhere and sing . . . —RICHARD LEVY *(adapted)*

God performs wonders beyond understanding, marvels beyond all reckoning.

> *God places us among the living,*
> *not allowing our steps to falter,*
> *and leads us past the false altars of our enemies.*

God exalted us above all those who hated us, avenged us with miracles before Pharaoh, offered signs and wonders in the land of Egypt.

> *God smote, in anger, all of Egypt's firstborn,*
> *brought Israel from its midst to lasting freedom,*
> *led them through the divided water of the Sea of Reeds.*

As their pursuing enemies drowned in the depths, God's children beheld the power of the Divine;

> *they praised and acknowledged God's name,*
> *willingly accepting God's rule.*

Then Moses, Miriam, and the people Israel joyfully sang this song to You:

> *"Who is like You, ADONAI, among the mighty! Who is like You, adorned in holiness, revered in praise, working wonders!"*
> *Mi khamokha ba-eilim Adonai, mi kamokha ne·dar ba-kodesh, nora t'hillot, oseih fele.*

Your children recognized Your sovereignty, as You split the sea before Moses. "This is my God," they responded, and they said:

> *"ADONAI will reign forever and ever."*
> *Adonai yimlokh l'olam va·ed.*

And so it is written: "ADONAI has rescued Jacob and redeemed him from the hand of those more powerful than he."
Barukh atah ADONAI, who redeemed the people Israel.

הַשְׁכִּיבֵנוּ יהוה אֱלֹהֵינוּ לְשָׁלוֹם,
וְהַעֲמִידֵנוּ מַלְכֵּנוּ לְחַיִּים,
וּפְרוֹשׂ עָלֵינוּ סֻכַּת שְׁלוֹמֶךָ,
וְתַקְּנֵנוּ בְּעֵצָה טוֹבָה מִלְּפָנֶיךָ,
וְהוֹשִׁיעֵנוּ לְמַעַן שְׁמֶךָ,
וְהָגֵן בַּעֲדֵנוּ,
וְהָסֵר מֵעָלֵינוּ אוֹיֵב, דֶּבֶר, וְחֶרֶב, וְרָעָב וְיָגוֹן,
וְהָסֵר שָׂטָן מִלְּפָנֵינוּ וּמֵאַחֲרֵינוּ,
וּבְצֵל כְּנָפֶיךָ תַּסְתִּירֵנוּ.
כִּי אֵל שׁוֹמְרֵנוּ וּמַצִּילֵנוּ אָתָּה,
כִּי אֵל מֶלֶךְ חַנּוּן וְרַחוּם אָתָּה,
וּשְׁמֹר צֵאתֵנוּ וּבוֹאֵנוּ, לְחַיִּים וּלְשָׁלוֹם, מֵעַתָּה וְעַד עוֹלָם.
◁ וּפְרוֹשׂ עָלֵינוּ סֻכַּת שְׁלוֹמֶךָ.
בָּרוּךְ אַתָּה יהוה, הַפּוֹרֵשׂ סֻכַּת שָׁלוֹם עָלֵינוּ וְעַל כָּל־
עַמּוֹ יִשְׂרָאֵל וְעַל יְרוּשָׁלָיִם.

We rise.

ON SHABBAT WE RECITE:

וְשָׁמְרוּ בְנֵי יִשְׂרָאֵל אֶת־הַשַּׁבָּת, לַעֲשׂוֹת אֶת־הַשַּׁבָּת
לְדֹרֹתָם בְּרִית עוֹלָם. בֵּינִי וּבֵין בְּנֵי יִשְׂרָאֵל אוֹת הִיא
לְעוֹלָם, כִּי־שֵׁשֶׁת יָמִים עָשָׂה יהוה אֶת־הַשָּׁמַיִם וְאֶת־
הָאָרֶץ, וּבַיּוֹם הַשְּׁבִיעִי שָׁבַת וַיִּנָּפַשׁ.

ALLOW US . . . TO SLEEP
הַשְׁכִּיבֵנוּ. Nighttime may provoke fear: Who will protect us as we sleep? Will we wake up? We beseech God to protect us from those threatening forces that we can see, as well as from those we cannot observe. Ten verbs are enunciated in this prayer, creating a powerful drama of motion and movement, an expression of the will to live.

EVIL FORCES שָׂטָן. "Satan," in the Bible, is a term generally used to refer either to evil impulses or to a celestial adversary, but never to a fallen angel.

CANOPY OF PEACE סֻכַּת שְׁלוֹם. This phrase is not found in the Bible but may allude either to Amos 9:11, where the prophet sees the rebuilding of the fallen *sukkah* of David as an image of redemption, or to Psalm 27:5, where the poet prays to be hidden in God's *sukkah*, protected from enemies, while gazing peacefully at God's countenance.

JERUSALEM יְרוּשָׁלָיִם. In Jewish thought, the peace of Jerusalem symbolizes universal peace.

THE PEOPLE ISRAEL SHALL OBSERVE וְשָׁמְרוּ בְנֵי־יִשְׂרָאֵל. Exodus 31:16–17.

AND RESTED וַיִּנָּפַשׁ. Or: "was refreshed." The basic root meaning of this verb is "to breathe" and it is related to the noun נֶפֶשׁ (*nefesh*), "life" or "soul" (i.e., that which breathes). When one rests, one infuses oneself with a new breath of life. The peculiarity of the phrasing of this verse gave birth to the idea of the נְשָׁמָה יְתֵרָה (*n'shamah y'teirah*), the "additional soul" granted us on Shabbat. (*Reuven Hammer*)

Peace

Peace comes to us in the recognition that even in our weakest and most fragile moments, redemption can be achieved. The central image in this prayer is the "*sukkah* of peace." The *sukkah* is a fragile structure, temporary and open to the elements. Peace is pictured not as a temple, solidly built, gilded, perhaps ornate, but rather as created out of the most fragmentary of materials, leaving us vulnerable, at risk.

Shabbat

We are obsessed with work. During the week we rest so we can go back to work. We play so that we can go back to work. We love so that we can go back to work. One ulterior motive after another. Worrying over the past, living in the future. But one day each week there is a day devoted to being present, the seventh day. On that day, we do not have to go anywhere or do anything. Everything is done and we are already here.

—LAWRENCE KUSHNER

Second B'rakhah after the Sh'ma: Peace in the Night

Allow us, ADONAI our God, to sleep peacefully and to awaken again to life, our sovereign.

> *Spread over us Your canopy of peace,*
> *restore us with Your good counsel,*
> *and save us for the sake of Your name.*

Shield us: Remove from us enemies and pestilence, sword, starvation, and sorrow, and remove the evil forces that surround us.

> *Shelter us in the shadow of Your wings,*
> *for You, God, watch over and deliver us,*
> *and You are the Sovereign, merciful and compassionate.*

Ensure our going and coming for life and peace, now and forever.

> *May You spread over us Your canopy of peace.*

Barukh atah ADONAI, who spreads the canopy of peace over us, and over all the people Israel, and over Jerusalem.

Biblical Sanctification of the Day

We rise.

ON SHABBAT WE RECITE:

The people Israel shall observe the Shabbat, to maintain it as an everlasting covenant throughout all generations. It is a sign between Me and the people Israel for all time, that in six days ADONAI made the heavens and the earth, and on the seventh day, ceased from work and rested.

V'sham'ru v'nei yisra·el et ha-shabbat,
la·asot et ha-shabbat l'dorotam b'rit olam.
Beini u-vein b'nei yisra·el ot hi l'olam,
ki sheishet yamim asah Adonai et ha-shamayim v'et ha-aretz,
u-va-yom ha-sh'vi·i shavat va-yinnafash.

תִּקְעוּ בַחֹֽדֶשׁ שׁוֹפָר, בַּכֶּֽסֶה לְיוֹם חַגֵּֽנוּ.
כִּי חֹק לְיִשְׂרָאֵל הוּא, מִשְׁפָּט לֵאלֹהֵי יַעֲקֹב.

חֲצִי קַדִּישׁ

יִתְגַּדַּל וְיִתְקַדַּשׁ שְׁמֵהּ רַבָּא, בְּעָלְמָא דִּי בְרָא, כִּרְעוּתֵהּ,
וְיַמְלִיךְ מַלְכוּתֵהּ בְּחַיֵּיכוֹן וּבְיוֹמֵיכוֹן וּבְחַיֵּי דְכָל־בֵּית
יִשְׂרָאֵל, בַּעֲגָלָא וּבִזְמַן קָרִיב, וְאִמְרוּ אָמֵן.

יְהֵא שְׁמֵהּ רַבָּא מְבָרַךְ לְעָלַם וּלְעָלְמֵי עָלְמַיָּא.

יִתְבָּרַךְ וְיִשְׁתַּבַּח וְיִתְפָּאַר וְיִתְרוֹמַם וְיִתְנַשֵּׂא וְיִתְהַדָּר
וְיִתְעַלֶּה וְיִתְהַלָּל שְׁמֵהּ דְּקֻדְשָׁא, בְּרִיךְ הוּא, לְעֵֽלָּא לְעֵֽלָּא
מִכָּל־בִּרְכָתָא וְשִׁירָתָא תֻּשְׁבְּחָתָא וְנֶחֱמָתָא דַּאֲמִירָן
בְּעָלְמָא, וְאִמְרוּ אָמֵן.

SOUND THE SHOFAR תִּקְעוּ בְחֹֽדֶשׁ שׁוֹפָר. Psalm 81:4–5. On each holy day and every Shabbat, a biblical passage relating to the special character of the day is inserted before the Amidah of the evening service. The Rabbis understood this verse from Psalms as referring to Rosh Hashanah because it mentions the shofar's being sounded on the new moon. They may also have had in mind the dual meaning of the word מִשְׁפָּט, here translated as "ordinance." It can also mean "judgment," and Rosh Hashanah is the day on which the world is judged.

KADDISH קַדִּישׁ. This Kaddish marks the break between the recitation of the Sh'ma and Its Blessings, the public declaration of our faith, and the more private, introspective part of our liturgy, the Amidah.

MAY GOD'S GREAT NAME יְהֵא שְׁמֵהּ רַבָּא. The seven words of this response are an almost exact Aramaic translation of the Hebrew refrain commonly used in the ancient Temple in Jerusalem, בָּרוּךְ שֵׁם כְּבוֹד מַלְכוּתוֹ לְעוֹלָם וָעֶד "Praised be the name of the One whose glorious sovereignty is forever and ever." This is familiar to us today as the response following the first verse of the Sh'ma.

TRULY FAR BEYOND לְעֵֽלָּא לְעֵֽלָּא. Distinctively during the High Holy Day period, Ashkenazic versions of the Kaddish emphasize God's sovereignty by repeating the word l'eilla, "beyond." Evidently that was already an alternate version of this prayer, given that some Jewish communities, including those of Rome and Yemen, repeat the word l'eilla all year long. Ashkenazim preserved both versions—reciting one year round, the other from Rosh Hashanah through Yom Kippur.

*May God's
Great Name
Be Acknowledged*

Whenever the people
Israel enter the syna-
gogue and house of study
and proclaim: יְהֵא שְׁמֵהּ
רַבָּא מְבָרַךְ לְעָלַם וּלְעָלְמֵי
עָלְמַיָּא, "May God's great
name be acknowledged
forever and ever," the
Holy One nods and says:
"Happy is the sovereign
in whose house such
praise is spoken!"

—BABYLONIAN TALMUD,
BERAKHOT

Sound the shofar on our feast day, on the new moon, when
it is hidden. For it is Israel's law, a decree of the God of Jacob.
*Tik·u va-ḥodesh shofar, ba-keseh l'yom ḥaggeinu.
Ki ḥok l'yisra·el hu, mishpat leilohei ya·akov.*

Ḥatzi Kaddish

May God's great name be exalted and hallowed throughout the
created world, as is God's wish. May God's sovereignty soon be
established, in your lifetime and in your days, and in the days of
all the House of Israel. And respond with: *Amen.*

May God's great name be acknowledged forever and ever!
Y'hei sh'meih rabba m'varakh l'alam u-l'almei almayya.

May the name of the Holy One be acknowledged and celebrated, lauded and worshipped, exalted and honored, extolled
and acclaimed—though God, who is blessed, *b'rikh hu*, is truly
far beyond all acknowledgment and praise, or any expressions
of gratitude or consolation ever spoken in the world. And
respond with: *Amen.*

We recite this Silent Amidah at the evening and morning services of Rosh Hashanah.

Before the Amidah begins, it is customary to take three steps backward, as if we are leaving our familiar surroundings, and then three steps forward, as we approach God's presence.

When reciting the words בָּרוּךְ אַתָּה on this page, we customarily bend the knees and bow, standing up straight by the time we reach the word יהוה. We repeat these motions at the end of the first b'rakhah when we come to the words בָּרוּךְ אַתָּה יהוה. The sign ⅂ indicates the places to bow.

אֲדֹנָי שְׂפָתַי תִּפְתָּח, וּפִי יַגִּיד תְּהִלָּתֶךָ.

AMIDAH. The Amidah, literally "the prayer said while standing," is the moment of personal meditation and is also known as the "Silent Prayer." It always contains three introductory b'rakhot. The first recalls our ancestors and their relation to God; the second describes God's continuing presence in the world; the third emphasizes God's uniqueness and the path to God: holiness. Similarly, every Amidah ends with three b'rakhot. The first looks toward the restoration of God's presence to Zion; the next thanks God for all the gifts we experience in life; and the final one asks for peace. On holidays, the middle b'rakhah concerns itself with themes of the day.

BENDING THE KNEES AND BOWING. The Babylonian Talmud encourages us to pay attention to the movement of each of our vertebrae as we bow, enabling us to focus on the miracle of our bodies' construction. We stand up straight when we reach God's name, for we speak to God face to face (Berakhot 28b). The Talmud confined bowing to the beginning and end of this first b'rakhah and to the beginning and end of the next-to-last b'rakhah, which thanks God for the gift of life (Berakhot 34b).

Version with Patriarchs and Matriarchs:

⅂ בָּרוּךְ אַתָּה יהוה,
אֱלֹהֵינוּ וֵאלֹהֵי אֲבוֹתֵינוּ
[וְאִמּוֹתֵינוּ], אֱלֹהֵי אַבְרָהָם,
אֱלֹהֵי יִצְחָק, וֵאלֹהֵי יַעֲקֹב,
אֱלֹהֵי שָׂרָה, אֱלֹהֵי רִבְקָה,
אֱלֹהֵי רָחֵל, וֵאלֹהֵי לֵאָה,
הָאֵל הַגָּדוֹל הַגִּבּוֹר וְהַנּוֹרָא,
אֵל עֶלְיוֹן, גּוֹמֵל חֲסָדִים
טוֹבִים, וְקוֹנֵה הַכֹּל, וְזוֹכֵר
חַסְדֵי אָבוֹת [וְאִמָּהוֹת],
וּמֵבִיא גוֹאֵל לִבְנֵי בְנֵיהֶם
לְמַעַן שְׁמוֹ בְּאַהֲבָה.

Version with Patriarchs:

⅂ בָּרוּךְ אַתָּה יהוה,
אֱלֹהֵינוּ וֵאלֹהֵי אֲבוֹתֵינוּ,
אֱלֹהֵי אַבְרָהָם, אֱלֹהֵי
יִצְחָק, וֵאלֹהֵי יַעֲקֹב, הָאֵל
הַגָּדוֹל הַגִּבּוֹר וְהַנּוֹרָא,
אֵל עֶלְיוֹן, גּוֹמֵל חֲסָדִים
טוֹבִים, וְקוֹנֵה הַכֹּל, וְזוֹכֵר
חַסְדֵי אָבוֹת, וּמֵבִיא גוֹאֵל
לִבְנֵי בְנֵיהֶם לְמַעַן שְׁמוֹ
בְּאַהֲבָה.

ADONAI, OPEN MY LIPS אֲדֹנָי שְׂפָתַי תִּפְתָּח. Psalm 51:17, where prayer is exalted over sacrifice.

GOD OF ABRAHAM אֱלֹהֵי אַבְרָהָם. Why don't we say *eloheinu melekh ha-olam*, "ruler of time and space," as part of the opening b'rakhah as we do with every opening b'rakhah, but immediately proceed to "God of Abraham"? Because Abraham was the first to discover that God is the ruler of the entire universe, by mentioning him we also acknowledge God's sovereignty.

GOD OF SARAH אֱלֹהֵי שָׂרָה. Many congregations add the names of the four matriarchs at the beginning of this b'rakhah because of their significance as founders of our people and as part of our effort to reclaim women's voices and to honor women's experiences.

GREAT, MIGHTY, AWE-INSPIRING הַגָּדוֹל הַגִּבּוֹר וְהַנּוֹרָא. This phrase is a quotation from Deuteronomy 10:17–18, where God's might is characterized by the befriending of the stranger, the widow, and the orphan.

REDEEMER גּוֹאֵל. Judaism's messianic impulse reminds us that the world, as broken as it sometimes appears, is ultimately perfectible; God's teachings, carried out by us, will help the world achieve such perfection. Some liberal prayerbooks use the word גְּאֻלָּה (g'ullah), "redemption," in place of "redeemer," to de-emphasize the role of any single individual in facilitating the world's healing.

THE SILENT AMIDAH

Meditation on Prayer

In the Bible, God speaks to us, and we listen. At the moment of prayer, we speak to God and God listens.

—ISAAC ARAMA

God of Abraham, God of Isaac, and God of Jacob

Why is the word "God" repeated each time? We might more easily have said it once. The repeated use of the word "God" highlights that each patriarch—and matriarch—knew God personally and sought a distinct relationship with God.

—A ḤASIDIC TEACHING

We recite this Silent Amidah at the evening and morning services of Rosh Hashanah.

Before the Amidah begins, it is customary to take three steps backward, as if we are leaving our familiar surroundings, and then three steps forward, as we approach God's presence.

When reciting the words "barukh atah" on this page, we customarily bend the knees and bow, standing up straight by the time we reach the word "Adonai." We repeat these motions at the end of the first b'rakhah when we come to the words "barukh atah Adonai." The sign ſ indicates the places to bow.

ADONAI, open my lips that my mouth may speak Your praise.

First B'rakhah: Our Ancestors

Version with Patriarchs:

ſ Barukh atah ADONAI,
our God and God of our
  ancestors,
God of Abraham, God of
  Isaac, and God of Jacob,
great, mighty, awe-inspiring,
  transcendent God,
who acts with lovingkindness
  and creates all things,
who remembers the loving
  deeds of our ancestors,
and who will send a redeemer
  to their children's children
  with love
  for the sake of divine honor.

Version with Patriarchs and Matriarchs:

ſ Barukh atah ADONAI,
our God and God of our
  ancestors,
God of Abraham, God of
  Isaac, and God of Jacob,
God of Sarah, God of
  Rebecca, God of Rachel,
  and God of Leah,
great, mighty, awe-inspiring,
  transcendent God,
who acts with lovingkindness
  and creates all things,
who remembers the loving
  deeds of our ancestors,
and who will send a redeemer
  to their children's children
  with love
  for the sake of divine honor.

זָכְרֵנוּ לְחַיִּים, מֶלֶךְ חָפֵץ בַּחַיִּים,
וְכָתְבֵנוּ בְּסֵפֶר הַחַיִּים, לְמַעַנְךָ אֱלֹהִים חַיִּים.

Version with Patriarchs and Matriarchs: *Version with Patriarchs:*

מֶלֶךְ עוֹזֵר וּפוֹקֵד
וּמוֹשִׁיעַ וּמָגֵן.
בָּרוּךְ אַתָּה יהוה, מָגֵן
אַבְרָהָם וּפוֹקֵד שָׂרָה.

מֶלֶךְ עוֹזֵר וּמוֹשִׁיעַ וּמָגֵן.
בָּרוּךְ אַתָּה יהוה, מָגֵן
אַבְרָהָם.

אַתָּה גִבּוֹר לְעוֹלָם אֲדֹנָי, מְחַיֵּה מֵתִים אַתָּה,
רַב לְהוֹשִׁיעַ.

מְכַלְכֵּל חַיִּים בְּחֶסֶד, מְחַיֵּה מֵתִים בְּרַחֲמִים רַבִּים,
סוֹמֵךְ נוֹפְלִים, וְרוֹפֵא חוֹלִים, וּמַתִּיר אֲסוּרִים, וּמְקַיֵּם
אֱמוּנָתוֹ לִישֵׁנֵי עָפָר. מִי כָמוֹךָ בַּעַל גְּבוּרוֹת וּמִי דּוֹמֶה
לָּךְ, מֶלֶךְ מֵמִית וּמְחַיֶּה וּמַצְמִיחַ יְשׁוּעָה.

מִי כָמוֹךָ אַב הָרַחֲמִים, זוֹכֵר יְצוּרָיו לְחַיִּים בְּרַחֲמִים.

וְנֶאֱמָן אַתָּה לְהַחֲיוֹת מֵתִים. בָּרוּךְ אַתָּה יהוה,
מְחַיֵּה הַמֵּתִים.

אַתָּה קָדוֹשׁ וְשִׁמְךָ קָדוֹשׁ, וּקְדוֹשִׁים בְּכָל־יוֹם
יְהַלְלוּךָ, סֶּלָה.

REMEMBER US זָכְרֵנוּ. This brief prayer is the first of four that are added on the ten days of the High Holy Day season. Each of the four phrases of this short addition ends with the word חַיִּים (ḥayyim), "life."

SHIELD OF ABRAHAM מָגֵן אַבְרָהָם. After Genesis 15:1.

GUARDIAN OF SARAH פוֹקֵד שָׂרָה. Or: "the One who remembered Sarah" (after Genesis 21:1). We, who stand here today, are the fruit of God's promise to Abraham and Sarah.

SUPPORT THE FALLING סוֹמֵךְ נוֹפְלִים. After Psalm 145:14.

HEAL THE SICK רוֹפֵא חוֹלִים. After Exodus 15:26, following God's self-description there as "the One who heals."

LOOSEN THE CHAINS OF THE BOUND מַתִּיר אֲסוּרִים. Psalm 146:7.

BRINGS DEATH AND LIFE מֵמִית וּמְחַיֶּה. 1 Samuel 2:6.

WHO IS LIKE YOU, SOURCE OF COMPASSION מִי כָמוֹךָ אַב הָרַחֲמִים. Jewish mystical tradition highlights the theological tension between God's qualities of power and strict judgment, גְּבוּרָה (g'vurah), and God's qualities of mercy and lovingkindness, חֶסֶד (ḥesed). Throughout the year, this b'rakhah reminds us that God is unsurpassed in power. At this season of judgment, we add this line to remind us—and God—that God is also unsurpassed in mercy.

GIVES LIFE TO THE DEAD מְחַיֵּה הַמֵּתִים. Over the millennia, many Jewish perspectives on the afterlife have been proposed. Many sages (including Saadiah Gaon, 10th century, and Maimonides, 12th century) caution against speculation about the specific implications of the doctrine of bodily resurrection of the dead. They understand it to be an articulation of God's supreme power: God cares even for the dead.

HOLY קָדוֹשׁ. We become holy when we imitate God's qualities: "As God is called 'merciful' so should you be merciful . . . as God is called 'righteous' and 'loving,' so should you be righteous and loving" (Babylonian Talmud, Sotah 14a).

Each morning You restore consciousness to my sleep-filled body, and I awake.

Each spring You restore vitality to trees, plants, and animals that have hibernated through the winter, and they grow once more.

Each day I remember those who have died; they live on beyond the grave.

Each moment I contemplate the rebirth of our people; I recall that You put the breath of life into dry bones.

Praised are You, Adonai, for planting immortality in my soul, in my people, and in our world.

—ROBERT SCHEINBERG

Remember us for life,
Sovereign who delights in life,
and inscribe us in the Book of Life,
for Your sake, God of life.

Version with Patriarchs:	*Version with Patriarchs and Matriarchs:*
You are the sovereign who helps and saves and shields.	You are the sovereign who helps and guards, saves and shields.
ſ *Barukh atah* ADONAI, Shield of Abraham.	ſ *Barukh atah* ADONAI, Shield of Abraham and Guardian of Sarah.

Second B'rakhah: God's Saving Care

You are mighty forever, ADONAI—
You give life to the dead;
great is Your saving power.

You sustain the living through love,
    and with great mercy give life to the dead.
You support the falling,
    heal the sick,
    loosen the chains of the bound,
    and keep faith with those who sleep in the dust.
Who is like You, Almighty,
    and who can be compared to You?—
    Sovereign, who brings death and life,
    and causes salvation to flourish.

Who is like You, source of compassion,
    who remembers with compassion Your creatures for life?

You are faithful in bringing life to the dead.
Barukh atah ADONAI, who gives life to the dead.

Third B'rakhah: God's Holiness

Holy are You and holy is Your name;
    holy ones praise You each day.

וּבְכֵן תֵּן פַּחְדְּךָ יהוה אֱלֹהֵינוּ עַל כָּל־מַעֲשֶׂיךָ
וְאֵימָתְךָ עַל כָּל־מַה־שֶּׁבָּרֱאתָ,
וְיִירָאֽוּךָ כָּל־הַמַּעֲשִׂים
וְיִשְׁתַּחֲווּ לְפָנֶֽיךָ כָּל־הַבְּרוּאִים,
וְיֵעָשׂוּ כֻלָּם אֲגֻדָּה אַחַת לַעֲשׂוֹת רְצוֹנְךָ בְּלֵבָב שָׁלֵם,
כְּמוֹ שֶׁיָּדַֽעְנוּ יהוה אֱלֹהֵֽינוּ שֶׁהַשִּׁלְטוֹן לְפָנֶֽיךָ,
עֹז בְּיָדְךָ וּגְבוּרָה בִּימִינֶֽךָ,
וְשִׁמְךָ נוֹרָא עַל כָּל־מַה־שֶּׁבָּרֱאתָ.

וּבְכֵן תֵּן כָּבוֹד יהוה לְעַמֶּֽךָ,
תְּהִלָּה לִירֵאֶֽיךָ וְתִקְוָה לְדוֹרְשֶֽׁיךָ,
וּפִתְחוֹן פֶּה לַמְיַחֲלִים לָךְ,
שִׂמְחָה לְאַרְצֶֽךָ וְשָׂשׂוֹן לְעִירֶֽךָ
וּצְמִיחַת קֶֽרֶן לְדָוִד עַבְדֶּֽךָ,
וַעֲרִיכַת נֵר לְבֶן־יִשַׁי מְשִׁיחֶֽךָ, בִּמְהֵרָה בְיָמֵֽינוּ.

וּבְכֵן צַדִּיקִים יִרְאוּ וְיִשְׂמָֽחוּ
וִישָׁרִים יַעֲלֹֽזוּ,
וַחֲסִידִים בְּרִנָּה יָגִֽילוּ,
וְעוֹלָֽתָה תִּקְפָּץ־פִּֽיהָ
וְכָל־הָרִשְׁעָה כֻּלָּהּ כְּעָשָׁן תִּכְלֶה,
כִּי תַעֲבִיר מֶמְשֶֽׁלֶת זָדוֹן מִן הָאָֽרֶץ.

וְתִמְלֹךְ אַתָּה יהוה לְבַדֶּֽךָ עַל כָּל־מַעֲשֶֽׂיךָ,
בְּהַר צִיּוֹן מִשְׁכַּן כְּבוֹדֶֽךָ
וּבִירוּשָׁלַֽיִם עִיר קָדְשֶֽׁךָ,
כַּכָּתוּב בְּדִבְרֵי קָדְשֶֽׁךָ:
יִמְלֹךְ יהוה לְעוֹלָם, אֱלֹהַֽיִךְ צִיּוֹן לְדֹר וָדֹר, הַלְלוּ־יָהּ.

קָדוֹשׁ אַתָּה וְנוֹרָא שְׁמֶֽךָ, וְאֵין אֱלֽוֹהַּ מִבַּלְעָדֶֽיךָ,
כַּכָּתוּב: וַיִּגְבַּהּ יהוה צְבָאוֹת בַּמִּשְׁפָּט, וְהָאֵל הַקָּדוֹשׁ
נִקְדַּשׁ בִּצְדָקָה. בָּרוּךְ אַתָּה יהוה, הַמֶּֽלֶךְ הַקָּדוֹשׁ.

U-V'KHEIN וּבְכֵן. These three paragraphs, which are introduced by the same word, וּבְכֵן (u-v'khein), are ascribed by many scholars to the 2nd or 3rd century, and may constitute the earliest poetic additions to the High Holy Day Amidah.

Stages of redemption are described in this series of prayers. The first paragraph implores God to cause the entire world to live with reverence for God. The next paragraph discusses not the universal, but the particular: the return of the people Israel to its land and specifically to Jerusalem, and the kingship of David. The third paragraph describes the rejoicing that will come to the righteous "when You remove the tyranny of arrogance from the earth" and God will rule alone over the entire world from Zion and Jerusalem.
(adapted from Reuven Hammer)

AWE . . . FEAR . . . פַּחְדְּךָ . . . וְאֵימָתְךָ. These emotions are meant to describe obedience to God's will and inspire us to bring sanctity to the world.

THE LIGHT OF DAVID קֶרֶן לְדָוִד. See Psalm 132:17.

YOU ALONE . . . WILL RULE וְתִמְלֹךְ אַתָּה לְבַדֶּךָ. God's sovereignty is always envisioned as the rule of justice, and therefore a time of peace. It is the ultimate conclusion of history.

ADONAI WILL REIGN FOREVER יִמְלֹךְ יהוה לְעוֹלָם. Psalm 146:10.

ADONAI TZ'VA·OT WILL BE EXALTED וַיִּגְבַּה יהוה צְבָאוֹת. Isaiah 5:16. In concluding the b'rakhah, this verse highlights its themes as expanded on the High Holy Days: We await the day when earthly powers become subservient to the divine ideals of justice and righteousness.

THE HOLY SOVEREIGN הַמֶּלֶךְ הַקָּדוֹשׁ. The rest of the year, this b'rakhah concludes with the words הָאֵל הַקָּדוֹשׁ "the Holy God." God's sovereignty is a central theme of the High Holy Days.

May All Be Bound Together

The purpose of creation is not division, nor separation. The purpose of the human race is not a struggle to the death between classes, between nations. Humanity is meant to become a single body. . . . Our purpose is the great upbuilding of unity and peace. And when all nations are bound together in one association living in justice and righteousness, they atone for each other. —MARTIN BUBER

All Wickedness Will Disappear

There were once some lawless men who caused Rabbi Meir a great deal of trouble. Rabbi Meir accordingly prayed that they should die. His wife, Beruriah, said to him: "How can you think that such a prayer is permitted? . . . When sin ceases there shall be no more wicked people. Therefore pray for them that they turn from their ways, and there will be no more wicked people." Then he prayed on their behalf.

—BABYLONIAN TALMUD, BERAKHOT

U-v'khein—ADONAI our God,
instill Your awe in all You have made,
and fear of You in all You have created,
so that all You have fashioned revere You,
all You have created bow in recognition,
and all be bound together, carrying out Your will wholeheartedly.
For we know that true sovereignty is Yours,
power and strength are in Your hands,
and Your name is to be revered beyond any of Your creations.

U-v'khein—Bestow honor to Your people, ADONAI,
praise to those who revere You,
hope to those who seek You,
recognition to those who await You,
joy to Your land, and gladness to Your city.
May the light of David, Your servant, dawn,
and the lamp of the son of Jesse, Your anointed,
be kindled speedily in our day.

U-v'khein—The righteous, beholding this, will rejoice,
the upright will be glad,
the pious will celebrate with song,
evil will be silenced,
and all wickedness will disappear like smoke,
when You remove the tyranny of arrogance from the earth.

You alone, ADONAI, will rule all Your creation,
from Mount Zion, the dwelling-place of Your glory,
and from Jerusalem, Your holy city.
As it is written in the Book of Psalms:
"ADONAI will reign forever;
Your God, O Zion, from generation to generation. Halleluyah!

You are holy, and Your name is revered, for there is no God
but You. As Your prophet Isaiah wrote: "*Adonai Tz'va·ot* will
be exalted through justice, the holy God sanctified through
righteousness."
Barukh atah ADONAI, the Holy Sovereign.

אַתָּה בְחַרְתָּנוּ מִכָּל־הָעַמִּים,
אָהַבְתָּ אוֹתָנוּ וְרָצִיתָ בָּנוּ,
וְרוֹמַמְתָּנוּ מִכָּל־הַלְּשׁוֹנוֹת,
וְקִדַּשְׁתָּנוּ בְּמִצְוֹתֶיךָ,
וְקֵרַבְתָּנוּ מַלְכֵּנוּ לַעֲבוֹדָתֶךָ,
וְשִׁמְךָ הַגָּדוֹל וְהַקָּדוֹשׁ עָלֵינוּ קָרָאתָ.

AT THE CONCLUSION OF SHABBAT:

וַתּוֹדִיעֵנוּ יהוה אֱלֹהֵינוּ אֶת־מִשְׁפְּטֵי צִדְקֶךָ וַתְּלַמְּדֵנוּ
לַעֲשׂוֹת חֻקֵּי רְצוֹנֶךָ. וַתִּתֶּן־לָנוּ יהוה אֱלֹהֵינוּ, מִשְׁפָּטִים
יְשָׁרִים וְתוֹרוֹת אֱמֶת חֻקִּים וּמִצְוֹת טוֹבִים, וַתַּנְחִילֵנוּ זְמַנֵּי
שָׂשׂוֹן וּמוֹעֲדֵי קֹדֶשׁ וְחַגֵּי נְדָבָה. וַתּוֹרִישֵׁנוּ קְדֻשַּׁת שַׁבָּת
וּכְבוֹד מוֹעֵד וַחֲגִיגַת הָרֶגֶל. וַתַּבְדֵּל יהוה אֱלֹהֵינוּ בֵּין קֹדֶשׁ
לְחֹל, בֵּין אוֹר לְחֹשֶׁךְ, בֵּין יִשְׂרָאֵל לָעַמִּים, בֵּין יוֹם הַשְּׁבִיעִי
לְשֵׁשֶׁת יְמֵי הַמַּעֲשֶׂה, בֵּין קְדֻשַּׁת שַׁבָּת לִקְדֻשַּׁת יוֹם טוֹב
הִבְדַּלְתָּ, וְאֶת־יוֹם הַשְּׁבִיעִי מִשֵּׁשֶׁת יְמֵי הַמַּעֲשֶׂה קִדַּשְׁתָּ.
הִבְדַּלְתָּ וְקִדַּשְׁתָּ אֶת־עַמְּךָ יִשְׂרָאֵל בִּקְדֻשָּׁתֶךָ.

All services continue:

וַתִּתֶּן־לָנוּ, יהוה אֱלֹהֵינוּ, בְּאַהֲבָה אֶת־יוֹם [הַשַּׁבָּת הַזֶּה
וְאֶת־יוֹם] הַזִּכָּרוֹן הַזֶּה, יוֹם [זִכְרוֹן] תְּרוּעָה [בְּאַהֲבָה]
מִקְרָא קֹדֶשׁ, זֵכֶר לִיצִיאַת מִצְרָיִם.

אֱלֹהֵינוּ וֵאלֹהֵי אֲבוֹתֵינוּ [וְאִמּוֹתֵינוּ], יַעֲלֶה וְיָבֹא, וְיַגִּיעַ
וְיֵרָאֶה, וְיֵרָצֶה וְיִשָּׁמַע, וְיִפָּקֵד וְיִזָּכֵר זִכְרוֹנֵנוּ וּפִקְדוֹנֵנוּ,
וְזִכְרוֹן אֲבוֹתֵינוּ [וְאִמּוֹתֵינוּ], וְזִכְרוֹן מָשִׁיחַ בֶּן־דָּוִד
עַבְדֶּךָ, וְזִכְרוֹן יְרוּשָׁלַיִם עִיר קָדְשֶׁךָ, וְזִכְרוֹן כָּל־עַמְּךָ בֵּית
יִשְׂרָאֵל לְפָנֶיךָ לִפְלֵיטָה לְטוֹבָה, לְחֵן וּלְחֶסֶד וּלְרַחֲמִים,
לְחַיִּים וּלְשָׁלוֹם, בְּיוֹם הַזִּכָּרוֹן הַזֶּה. זָכְרֵנוּ יהוה אֱלֹהֵינוּ
בּוֹ לְטוֹבָה, וּפָקְדֵנוּ בוֹ לִבְרָכָה, וְהוֹשִׁיעֵנוּ בוֹ לְחַיִּים,
וּבִדְבַר יְשׁוּעָה וְרַחֲמִים חוּס וְחָנֵּנוּ, וְרַחֵם עָלֵינוּ
וְהוֹשִׁיעֵנוּ, כִּי אֵלֶיךָ עֵינֵינוּ, כִּי אֵל מֶלֶךְ חַנּוּן
וְרַחוּם אָתָּה.

Fourth B'rakhah: The Holiness of Rosh Hashanah

You have chosen us among all peoples, loving us, wanting us. You have distinguished us among all nations, making us holy through Your commandments, drawing us close to Your service, and calling us by Your great and holy name.

AT THE CONCLUSION OF SHABBAT:

You, ADONAI our God, have instructed us with Your laws of righteousness, and You have taught us to observe the precepts that accord with Your will. ADONAI our God, You gave us true teachings, just laws, and goodly precepts and mitzvot. You bestowed upon us times for joy, days of holiness, and festivals celebrated with generous gifts. You have endowed us with the holiness of Shabbat, glorious festival times, and pilgrimage feasts. ADONAI our God, You have distinguished between the holy and the weekday, light and darkness, Israel and the peoples of the world, between the seventh day and the six days of creation. You have differentiated the holiness of Shabbat from the holiness of the festival, by granting the seventh day a sanctity above all other days, enabling Your people Israel to share in Your holiness.

All services continue:

With love, You have bestowed on us, ADONAI our God, [this Shabbat and] this Day of Remembrance, a day for [recalling] the shofar sound [with love], a day for holy assembly and for recalling the Exodus from Egypt.

Our God and God of our ancestors, may the thought of us rise up and reach You. Attend to us and accept us; hear us and respond to us. Keep us in mind, and keep in mind the thought of our ancestors, as well as the Messiah, the descendant of David; Jerusalem, Your holy city; and all Your people, the House of Israel. On this Day of Remembrance respond to us with deliverance, goodness, compassion, love, life, and peace. Remember us for good; respond to us with blessing; redeem us with life. Show us compassion and care with words of salvation and kindness; have mercy on us and redeem us. Our eyes are turned to You, for You are a compassionate and loving sovereign.

אֱלֹהֵֽינוּ וֵאלֹהֵי אֲבוֹתֵֽינוּ [וְאִמּוֹתֵֽינוּ],

מְלֹךְ עַל כָּל־הָעוֹלָם כֻּלּוֹ בִּכְבוֹדֶֽךָ,

וְהִנָּשֵׂא עַל כָּל־הָאָֽרֶץ בִּיקָרֶֽךָ,

וְהוֹפַע בַּהֲדַר גְּאוֹן עֻזֶּֽךָ

עַל כָּל־יוֹשְׁבֵי תֵבֵל אַרְצֶֽךָ.

וְיֵדַע כָּל־פָּעוּל כִּי אַתָּה פְעַלְתּוֹ

וְיָבִין כָּל־יְצוּר כִּי אַתָּה יְצַרְתּוֹ,

וְיֹאמַר כֹּל אֲשֶׁר נְשָׁמָה בְאַפּוֹ:

יהוה אֱלֹהֵי יִשְׂרָאֵל מֶֽלֶךְ, וּמַלְכוּתוֹ בַּכֹּל מָשָֽׁלָה.

אֱלֹהֵֽינוּ וֵאלֹהֵי אֲבוֹתֵֽינוּ [וְאִמּוֹתֵֽינוּ], [רְצֵה בִמְנוּחָתֵֽנוּ]

קַדְּשֵֽׁנוּ בְּמִצְוֹתֶֽיךָ, וְתֵן חֶלְקֵֽנוּ בְּתוֹרָתֶֽךָ, שַׂבְּעֵֽנוּ מִטּוּבֶֽךָ

וְשַׂמְּחֵֽנוּ בִּישׁוּעָתֶֽךָ [וְהַנְחִילֵֽנוּ, יהוה אֱלֹהֵֽינוּ, בְּאַהֲבָה

וּבְרָצוֹן שַׁבַּת קָדְשֶֽׁךָ, וְיָנֽוּחוּ בָהּ יִשְׂרָאֵל מְקַדְּשֵׁי שְׁמֶֽךָ]

וְטַהֵר לִבֵּֽנוּ לְעָבְדְּךָ בֶּאֱמֶת, כִּי אַתָּה אֱלֹהִים אֱמֶת,

וּדְבָרְךָ אֱמֶת וְקַיָּם לָעַד. בָּרוּךְ אַתָּה יהוה, מֶֽלֶךְ עַל כָּל־

הָאָֽרֶץ, מְקַדֵּשׁ [הַשַּׁבָּת וְ] יִשְׂרָאֵל וְיוֹם הַזִּכָּרוֹן.

רְצֵה, יהוה אֱלֹהֵֽינוּ, בְּעַמְּךָ יִשְׂרָאֵל וּבִתְפִלָּתָם, וְהָשֵׁב

אֶת־הָעֲבוֹדָה לִדְבִיר בֵּיתֶֽךָ, [וְאִשֵּׁי יִשְׂרָאֵל]

וּתְפִלָּתָם בְּאַהֲבָה תְקַבֵּל בְּרָצוֹן, וּתְהִי לְרָצוֹן תָּמִיד

עֲבוֹדַת יִשְׂרָאֵל עַמֶּֽךָ.

וְתֶחֱזֶֽינָה עֵינֵֽינוּ בְּשׁוּבְךָ לְצִיּוֹן בְּרַחֲמִים.

בָּרוּךְ אַתָּה יהוה, הַמַּחֲזִיר שְׁכִינָתוֹ לְצִיּוֹן.

מוֹדִים אֲנַֽחְנוּ לָךְ, שָׁאַתָּה הוּא יהוה אֱלֹהֵֽינוּ

וֵאלֹהֵי אֲבוֹתֵֽינוּ [וְאִמּוֹתֵֽינוּ] לְעוֹלָם וָעֶד,

צוּר חַיֵּֽינוּ מָגֵן יִשְׁעֵֽנוּ אַתָּה הוּא.

לְדוֹר וָדוֹר נֽוֹדֶה לְּךָ וּנְסַפֵּר תְּהִלָּתֶֽךָ עַל חַיֵּֽינוּ הַמְּסוּרִים

בְּיָדֶֽךָ, וְעַל נִשְׁמוֹתֵֽינוּ הַפְּקוּדוֹת לָךְ, וְעַל נִסֶּֽיךָ שֶׁבְּכָל־יוֹם

עִמָּֽנוּ, וְעַל נִפְלְאוֹתֶֽיךָ וְטוֹבוֹתֶֽיךָ שֶׁבְּכָל־עֵת,

עֶֽרֶב וָבֹֽקֶר וְצָהֳרָֽיִם.

הַטּוֹב, כִּי לֹא כָלוּ רַחֲמֶֽיךָ, וְהַמְרַחֵם, כִּי לֹא תַֽמּוּ חֲסָדֶֽיךָ,

מֵעוֹלָם קִוִּֽינוּ לָךְ.

RESTORE WORSHIP TO YOUR SANCTUARY וְהָשֵׁב אֶת־הָעֲבוֹדָה לִדְבִיר בֵּיתֶֽךָ. According to the Babylonian Talmud, "Ever since the day when the Temple was destroyed, there has been an iron barrier separating Israel from God" (Berakhot 32b). The destructions of the Temple in Jerusalem, first by the Babylonians in 586 B.C.E. and then by the Romans in 70 C.E., were cataclysmic events in early Jewish history. The prayer for restoration of the Temple service expresses longing to recover the sense of immediate connection with God that is believed to have characterized the Temple service.

FIERY OFFERINGS וְאִשֵּׁי יִשְׂרָאֵל. The phrase "fiery offerings" originally referred to the sacrifices in the Temple, but later medieval and Ḥasidic commentators understood it as a description of the intensity of religious fervor required of true prayer. It is as if to say, "May our prayers have the same meaning and effect as burnt offerings once did for our ancestors."

YOUR DIVINE PRESENCE שְׁכִינָתוֹ. The Hebrew word shekhinah has been used for centuries to refer to God's immanence, the presence of God that is felt in the world. The word shekhinah is grammatically feminine. Accordingly, Jewish mystical tradition has tended to personify as female the Divine Presence, who is known as the Shekhinah.

You know what is for my good. If I recite my wants, it is not to remind You of them, but so that I may better understand how great is my dependence on You. If, then, I ask You for the things that may not be for my well-being, it is because I am ignorant; Your choice is better than mine and I submit myself to Your unalterable decree and Your supreme direction.

—BAHYA IBN PAKUDA

Fiery Offerings

The fire that was on the altar entered into the hearts of the priests and worshippers so that their song was full of passion, and the power of prayer filled their beings.   —THE ZOHAR

Your Miracles That Accompany Us Each Day

The 20th-century Ḥasidic master, the Netivot Shalom, remarks that each day we are confronted with new tasks of repair of the world, but each day God renews creation and so there is new energy that we may call on for the new day.

Our God and God of our ancestors: May You be exalted over the entire universe in Your glory, may You be raised up over all the earth in Your splendor, and may You manifest Yourself to all the inhabitants of the world in the majestic beauty of Your strength. Then all creatures will know that You created them; all living things will understand that You gave them life; and everything that breathes will proclaim: ADONAI, the God of Israel, is sovereign, ruling over all.

Our God and God of our ancestors, [embrace our rest,] make us holy through Your mitzvot and let the Torah be our portion. Fill our lives with Your goodness and gladden us with Your triumph. [ADONAI our God, grant that we inherit Your holy Shabbat, lovingly and willingly, so that the people Israel, who sanctify Your name, may find rest on this day.] Purify our hearts to serve You truly, for You are the God of truth, and Your word is true, eternal, and unchanging. *Barukh atah ADONAI*, ruler of all the earth, who makes [Shabbat,] Israel and the Day of Remembrance holy.

Fifth B'rakhah: The Restoration of Zion

ADONAI our God, embrace Your people Israel and their prayer. Restore worship to Your sanctuary. May the [fiery offerings and] prayers of the people Israel be lovingly accepted by You, and may our service always be pleasing.

Let our eyes behold Your merciful return to Zion. *Barukh atah ADONAI*, who restores Your Divine Presence to Zion.

Sixth B'rakhah: Gratitude for Life and Its Blessings

ʄ We thank You,
You who are our God and the God of our ancestors through all time, protector of our lives, shield of our salvation.
From one generation to the next we thank You and sing Your praises—for our lives that are in Your hands, for our souls that are under Your care, for Your miracles that accompany us each day, and for Your wonders and Your gifts that are with us each moment—evening, morning, and noon.
You are the One who is good, whose mercy is never-ending; the One who is compassionate, whose love is unceasing. We have always placed our hope in You.

וְעַל כֻּלָּם יִתְבָּרַךְ וְיִתְרוֹמַם שִׁמְךָ מַלְכֵּנוּ תָּמִיד לְעוֹלָם וָעֶד.

וּכְתוֹב לְחַיִּים טוֹבִים כָּל־בְּנֵי בְרִיתֶךָ.

וְכֹל הַחַיִּים יוֹדוּךָ סֶּלָה,
וִיהַלְלוּ אֶת־שִׁמְךָ בֶּאֱמֶת,
הָאֵל יְשׁוּעָתֵנוּ וְעֶזְרָתֵנוּ סֶלָה.
בָּרוּךְ אַתָּה יהוה, הַטּוֹב שִׁמְךָ וּלְךָ נָאֶה לְהוֹדוֹת.

When the Silent Amidah is recited in the morning, the following is said:

שִׂים שָׁלוֹם בָּעוֹלָם, טוֹבָה וּבְרָכָה, חֵן וָחֶסֶד וְרַחֲמִים עָלֵינוּ וְעַל כָּל־יִשְׂרָאֵל עַמֶּךָ. בָּרְכֵנוּ אָבִינוּ כֻּלָּנוּ כְּאֶחָד בְּאוֹר פָּנֶיךָ, כִּי בְאוֹר פָּנֶיךָ נָתַתָּ לָּנוּ, יהוה אֱלֹהֵינוּ, תּוֹרַת חַיִּים וְאַהֲבַת חֶסֶד, וּצְדָקָה וּבְרָכָה וְרַחֲמִים וְחַיִּים, וְשָׁלוֹם. וְטוֹב בְּעֵינֶיךָ לְבָרֵךְ אֶת־עַמְּךָ יִשְׂרָאֵל, בְּכָל־עֵת וּבְכָל־שָׁעָה בִּשְׁלוֹמֶךָ.

When the Silent Amidah is recited in the evening, the following is said:

שָׁלוֹם רָב עַל יִשְׂרָאֵל עַמְּךָ וְעַל כָּל־יוֹשְׁבֵי תֵבֵל תָּשִׂים לְעוֹלָם, כִּי אַתָּה הוּא מֶלֶךְ אָדוֹן לְכָל־הַשָּׁלוֹם. וְטוֹב בְּעֵינֶיךָ לְבָרֵךְ אֶת־עַמְּךָ יִשְׂרָאֵל בְּכָל־עֵת וּבְכָל־שָׁעָה בִּשְׁלוֹמֶךָ.

All services continue:

בְּסֵפֶר חַיִּים, בְּרָכָה וְשָׁלוֹם וּפַרְנָסָה טוֹבָה, נִזָּכֵר וְנִכָּתֵב לְפָנֶיךָ, אֲנַחְנוּ וְכָל־עַמְּךָ בֵּית יִשְׂרָאֵל, לְחַיִּים טוֹבִים וּלְשָׁלוֹם.

בָּרוּךְ אַתָּה יהוה, עוֹשֶׂה הַשָּׁלוֹם.

MAY YOUR NAME BE PRAISED AND EXALTED יִתְבָּרַךְ וְיִתְרוֹמַם שִׁמְךָ. In the language of the Bible and the prayerbook, "God's name is exalted" when we acknowledge God, recognize God's goodness in creation, and act to enable God's justice and compassion to be visible in the world.

AND INSCRIBE וּכְתוֹב. This is the third of the four special insertions in the Amidah for the Ten Days of Repentance. There is a progression of thought: at first we prayed for God's mercy that we may live another year; now we pray that the life we are granted be good.

IN THE BOOK OF LIFE בְּסֵפֶר חַיִּים. This is the last of the four special insertions in the Amidah, added for the Ten Days of Repentance. In this final addition, the theme of a "good life" is expanded to include peace and prosperity.

WHO BRINGS PEACE עוֹשֶׂה הַשָּׁלוֹם. In the words of the Midrash, "Great is peace, for all the prayers conclude with pleas for peace" (Sifrei Numbers 42). In addition to the Amidah, the Grace after Meals, Priestly Blessing, Kaddish Shalem, Mourner's Kaddish, and evening Sh'ma and Its Blessings all conclude with prayers for peace.

The Blessing of Shalom

When the blessing of *shalom* is lacking, however much we have of other blessings—wealth or power, fame or family, even health—these all appear as nothing. But when *shalom* is present, however little else we have somehow seems sufficient.

Shalom means "peace," of course, but it means so much more as well:
wholeness, fullness, and
  completion;
integrity and perfection;
healing, health, and
  harmony;
utter tranquility;
loving and being loved;
consummation;
forgiveness and reconciliation;
totality of well-being.

And even all of these together do not spell out sufficiently the meaning of *shalom*. But though we cannot accurately translate or adequately define *shalom*, we can experience it.

—HERSHEL J. MATT

For all these blessings may Your name be praised and exalted, our sovereign, always and forever.

And inscribe all the people of Your covenant for a good life.

May all that lives thank You always, and praise Your name faithfully forever, God of our deliverance and help.
ʩ *Barukh atah ADONAI*, whose name is goodness and to whom praise is fitting.

Seventh B'rakhah: Prayer for Peace

In the evening, we say:

Grant abundant and lasting peace to Your people Israel and all who dwell on earth, for You are the sovereign master of all the ways of peace. May it please You to bless Your people Israel at all times with Your gift of peace.

In the morning, we say:

Grant peace to the world: goodness and blessing, grace, love, and compassion to us and all the people Israel. Bless us, our creator, united as one in the light of Your counte-nance; by that light, ADONAI our God, You gave us a guide to life: the love of kindness, righteousness, blessing, compassion, life, and peace. May it please You to bless Your people Israel at every season and at all times with Your gift of peace.

All services continue:

May we and the entire House of Israel be called to mind and inscribed for life, blessing, sustenance, and peace in the Book of Life.

Barukh atah ADONAI, who brings peace.

On the first day the following may be added:

אֱלֹהַי, נְצוֹר לְשׁוֹנִי מֵרָע, וּשְׂפָתַי מִדַּבֵּר מִרְמָה, וְלִמְקַלְלַי נַפְשִׁי תִדֹּם, וְנַפְשִׁי כֶּעָפָר לַכֹּל תִּהְיֶה. פְּתַח לִבִּי בְּתוֹרָתֶךָ, וּבְמִצְוֹתֶיךָ תִּרְדּוֹף נַפְשִׁי. וְכָל־הַחוֹשְׁבִים עָלַי רָעָה, מְהֵרָה הָפֵר עֲצָתָם וְקַלְקֵל מַחֲשַׁבְתָּם. עֲשֵׂה לְמַעַן שְׁמֶךָ, עֲשֵׂה לְמַעַן יְמִינֶךָ, עֲשֵׂה לְמַעַן קְדֻשָּׁתֶךָ, עֲשֵׂה לְמַעַן תּוֹרָתֶךָ. לְמַעַן יֵחָלְצוּן יְדִידֶיךָ, הוֹשִׁיעָה יְמִינְךָ וַעֲנֵנִי. יִהְיוּ לְרָצוֹן אִמְרֵי פִי וְהֶגְיוֹן לִבִּי לְפָנֶיךָ, יהוה צוּרִי וְגוֹאֲלִי. עֹשֶׂה שָׁלוֹם בִּמְרוֹמָיו, הוּא יַעֲשֶׂה שָׁלוֹם עָלֵינוּ, וְעַל כָּל־יִשְׂרָאֵל [וְעַל כָּל־יוֹשְׁבֵי תֵבֵל] וְאִמְרוּ: אָמֵן.

On the second day the following may be added:

יְהִי רָצוֹן מִלְּפָנֶיךָ יהוה אֱלֹהַי וֵאלֹהֵי אֲבוֹתַי [וְאִמּוֹתַי], יוֹצֵר בְּרֵאשִׁית, כְּשֵׁם שֶׁהִמְצֵאתָ אֶת עוֹלָמְךָ בְּיוֹם זֶה וְנִתְיַחַדְתָּ בְּעוֹלָמֶךָ וְתָלִיתָ בּוֹ עֶלְיוֹנִים וְתַחְתּוֹנִים בְּמַאֲמָרֶיךָ, כֵּן בְּרַחֲמֶיךָ הָרַבִּים תְּיַחֵד לְבָבִי וּלְבַב כָּל־עַמְּךָ בֵּית יִשְׂרָאֵל לְאַהֲבָה וּלְיִרְאָה אֶת־שְׁמֶךָ. וְהָאֵר עֵינֵינוּ בִּמְאוֹר תּוֹרָתֶךָ, כִּי עִמְּךָ מְקוֹר חַיִּים, בְּאוֹרְךָ נִרְאֶה אוֹר. וְזַכֵּנוּ לִרְאוֹת בָּאוֹר הַצָּפוּן לַצַּדִּיקִים לֶעָתִיד לָבוֹא. יִהְיוּ לְרָצוֹן אִמְרֵי־פִי וְהֶגְיוֹן לִבִּי לְפָנֶיךָ, יהוה צוּרִי וְגֹאֲלִי.

On Rosh Hashanah morning, continue on page 81.

MY GOD אֱלֹהַי. The Babylonian Talmud says that every Amidah must be accompanied by a personal prayer (Berakhot 17a). The prayer that is printed here for the first day is one of the Talmud's exemplars; it is attributed to Mar son of Ravina (5th century). The prayer for the second day appears in the Prague prayerbook *Sha'arei Tziyon* (1662); its English rendering is by Jules Harlow. Both prayers are distinguished by their use of the first-person singular ("I," "me," "my"), whereas almost all other prayers are in the first-person plural ("we," "us," "our").

MAY THE WORDS יִהְיוּ לְרָצוֹן Psalm 19:15.

FOR IN YOUR LIGHT DO WE SEE LIGHT בְּאוֹרְךָ נִרְאֶה אוֹר. Psalm 36:10.

Personal Prayers Concluding the Amidah

On the first day the following may be added:

My God, keep my tongue from evil, my lips from lies. Help me ignore those who would slander me. Let me be humble before all. Open my heart to Your Torah, that I may pursue Your mitzvot. Frustrate the designs of those who plot evil against me; make nothing of their schemes. Act for the sake of Your name, Your power, Your holiness, and Your Torah. Answer my prayer for the deliverance of Your people. May the words of my mouth and the meditations of my heart be acceptable to You, ADONAI, my rock and my redeemer. May the One who brings peace to the universe bring peace to us and to all the people Israel [and to all who dwell on earth]. Amen.

On the second day the following may be added:

Creator of beginnings, as You created Your world on this day, uniting fragments into a universe, so may it be Your will to help unite my fragmented heart and the heart of all Your people Israel to love and revere You. Illumine our lives with the light of Your Torah, for in Your light do we see light. Grant us this year a hint of the light of redemption, healing, and peace. May the words of my mouth and the meditations of my heart be acceptable to You, ADONAI, my rock and my redeemer.

On Rosh Hashanah morning, continue on page 81.

וַיְכֻלּוּ הַשָּׁמַיִם וְהָאָרֶץ וְכָל־צְבָאָם.
וַיְכַל אֱלֹהִים בַּיּוֹם הַשְּׁבִיעִי מְלַאכְתּוֹ אֲשֶׁר עָשָׂה,
וַיִּשְׁבֹּת בַּיּוֹם הַשְּׁבִיעִי, מִכָּל־מְלַאכְתּוֹ אֲשֶׁר עָשָׂה.
וַיְבָרֶךְ אֱלֹהִים אֶת־יוֹם הַשְּׁבִיעִי וַיְקַדֵּשׁ אֹתוֹ,
כִּי בוֹ שָׁבַת מִכָּל־מְלַאכְתּוֹ, אֲשֶׁר בָּרָא אֱלֹהִים לַעֲשׂוֹת.

Version with Patriarchs and Matriarchs:	Version with Patriarchs:
◁ בָּרוּךְ אַתָּה יהוה, אֱלֹהֵינוּ וֵאלֹהֵי אֲבוֹתֵינוּ [וְאִמּוֹתֵינוּ], אֱלֹהֵי אַבְרָהָם, אֱלֹהֵי יִצְחָק, וֵאלֹהֵי יַעֲקֹב, אֱלֹהֵי שָׂרָה, אֱלֹהֵי רִבְקָה, אֱלֹהֵי רָחֵל, וֵאלֹהֵי לֵאָה, הָאֵל הַגָּדוֹל הַגִּבּוֹר וְהַנּוֹרָא, אֵל עֶלְיוֹן, קוֹנֵה שָׁמַיִם וָאָרֶץ.	◁ בָּרוּךְ אַתָּה יהוה, אֱלֹהֵינוּ וֵאלֹהֵי אֲבוֹתֵינוּ, אֱלֹהֵי אַבְרָהָם, אֱלֹהֵי יִצְחָק, וֵאלֹהֵי יַעֲקֹב, הָאֵל הַגָּדוֹל הַגִּבּוֹר וְהַנּוֹרָא, אֵל עֶלְיוֹן, קוֹנֵה שָׁמַיִם וָאָרֶץ.

מָגֵן אָבוֹת בִּדְבָרוֹ, מְחַיֵּה מֵתִים בְּמַאֲמָרוֹ, הַמֶּלֶךְ הַקָּדוֹשׁ
שֶׁאֵין כָּמוֹהוּ, הַמֵּנִיחַ לְעַמּוֹ בְּיוֹם שַׁבַּת קָדְשׁוֹ, כִּי בָם רָצָה
לְהָנִיחַ לָהֶם. לְפָנָיו נַעֲבוֹד בְּיִרְאָה וָפַחַד, וְנוֹדֶה לִשְׁמוֹ בְּכָל־
יוֹם תָּמִיד. מְעוֹן הַבְּרָכוֹת, אֵל הַהוֹדָאוֹת, אֲדוֹן הַשָּׁלוֹם,
מְקַדֵּשׁ הַשַּׁבָּת וּמְבָרֵךְ שְׁבִיעִי, וּמֵנִיחַ בִּקְדֻשָּׁה לְעַם
מְדֻשְּׁנֵי־עֹנֶג, זֵכֶר לְמַעֲשֵׂה בְרֵאשִׁית.

◁ אֱלֹהֵינוּ וֵאלֹהֵי אֲבוֹתֵינוּ [וְאִמּוֹתֵינוּ], רְצֵה בִמְנוּחָתֵנוּ.
קַדְּשֵׁנוּ בְּמִצְוֹתֶיךָ, וְתֵן חֶלְקֵנוּ בְּתוֹרָתֶךָ,
שַׂבְּעֵנוּ מִטּוּבֶךָ, וְשַׂמְּחֵנוּ בִּישׁוּעָתֶךָ,
וְטַהֵר לִבֵּנוּ לְעָבְדְּךָ בֶּאֱמֶת,
וְהַנְחִילֵנוּ יהוה אֱלֹהֵינוּ בְּאַהֲבָה וּבְרָצוֹן שַׁבַּת קָדְשֶׁךָ,
וְיָנוּחוּ בָהּ יִשְׂרָאֵל מְקַדְּשֵׁי שְׁמֶךָ.
בָּרוּךְ אַתָּה יהוה, מְקַדֵּשׁ הַשַּׁבָּת.

שבת

THE HEAVENS AND THE EARTH וַיְכֻלּוּ הַשָּׁמַיִם וְהָאָרֶץ. Genesis 2:1–3.

PROTECTION TO OUR ANCESTORS מָגֵן אָבוֹת. Literally, "shield of our ancestors." The evening service contains no repetition of the Amidah. This paragraph, which includes the themes of each of the seven b'rakhot of the Shabbat Amidah, is added on Shabbat eve. As elsewhere in the High Holy Day liturgy, the word מֶלֶךְ (melekh), "sovereign," is substituted for the word אֵל (El), "God" (which is recited in the year-round version of this prayer), to emphasize the metaphor of God's sovereignty on this day.

The heavens and the earth, and all they contain, were completed. On the seventh day God finished the work, ceasing from all work on the seventh day. Then God blessed the seventh day, making it holy, because on it, God had ceased from all the work of creation.

Va-y'khullu ha-shamayim v'ha-aretz v'khol tz'va·am. Va-y'khal Elohim ba-yom ha-sh'vi·i m'lakhto asher asah, va-yishbot ba-yom ha-sh'vi·i mi-kol m'lakhto asher asah. Va-y'varekh Elohim et yom ha-sh'vi·i va-y'kaddeish oto, ki vo shavat mi-kol m'lakhto, asher bara Elohim la·asot.

Version with Patriarchs:
Barukh atah ADONAI, our God and God of our ancestors, God of Abraham, God of Isaac, and God of Jacob, great, mighty, awe-inspiring, transcendent God, Creator of heaven and earth.

Version with Patriarchs and Matriarchs:
Barukh atah ADONAI, our God and God of our ancestors, God of Abraham, God of Isaac, and God of Jacob, God of Sarah, God of Rebecca, God of Rachel, and God of Leah, great, mighty, awe-inspiring, transcendent God, Creator of heaven and earth.

God, who promised protection to our ancestors and assures life to the dead, the incomparable holy sovereign, desired to give rest to the people Israel and so provided them with the holy Shabbat. We worship in awe and reverence in God's presence and offer thanks, each day, always, to God. The source of blessings, the master of peace, God, whom we praise, sanctifies Shabbat, blesses the seventh day, and provides sacred rest to a people overflowing with joy, as a symbol of the work of creation.

Magein avot bi-d'varo, m'ḥayyeih meitim b'ma·amaro, ha-melekh ha-kadosh she-ein kamohu, ha-meini·aḥ l'ammo b'yom shabbat kodsho, ki vam ratzah l'hani·aḥ la-hem. L'fanav na·avod b'yir·ah va-faḥad, v'nodeh li-sh'mo b'khol yom tamid. M'on ha-b'rakhot, El ha-hoda·ot, adon ha-shalom, m'kaddeish ha-shabbat u-m'vareikh sh'vi·i, u-meini·aḥ bi-k'dushah l'am m'dush'nei oneg, zeikher l'ma·aseih v'reishit.

Our God and God of our ancestors,
embrace our rest.
Make us holy through Your mitzvot
and let the Torah be our portion.
Fill our lives with Your goodness
and gladden us with Your triumph.
Purify our hearts to serve You faithfully.
ADONAI our God, grant that we inherit Your holy Shabbat, lovingly and willingly, so that the people Israel, who sanctify Your name, may find rest on this day.
Barukh atah ADONAI, who makes Shabbat holy.

קַדִּישׁ שָׁלֵם

יִתְגַּדַּל וְיִתְקַדַּשׁ שְׁמֵהּ רַבָּא, בְּעָלְמָא דִּי בְרָא, כִרְעוּתֵהּ, וְיַמְלִיךְ מַלְכוּתֵהּ בְּחַיֵּיכוֹן וּבְיוֹמֵיכוֹן וּבְחַיֵּי דְכָל־בֵּית יִשְׂרָאֵל, בַּעֲגָלָא וּבִזְמַן קָרִיב, וְאִמְרוּ אָמֵן.

יְהֵא שְׁמֵהּ רַבָּא מְבָרַךְ לְעָלַם וּלְעָלְמֵי עָלְמַיָּא.

יִתְבָּרַךְ וְיִשְׁתַּבַּח וְיִתְפָּאַר וְיִתְרוֹמַם וְיִתְנַשֵּׂא וְיִתְהַדָּר וְיִתְעַלֶּה וְיִתְהַלָּל שְׁמֵהּ דְּקֻדְשָׁא, בְּרִיךְ הוּא, לְעֵלָּא לְעֵלָּא מִכָּל־בִּרְכָתָא וְשִׁירָתָא תֻּשְׁבְּחָתָא וְנֶחֱמָתָא דַּאֲמִירָן בְּעָלְמָא, וְאִמְרוּ אָמֵן.

תִּתְקַבֵּל צְלוֹתְהוֹן וּבָעוּתְהוֹן דְּכָל־יִשְׂרָאֵל קֳדָם אֲבוּהוֹן דִּי בִשְׁמַיָּא, וְאִמְרוּ אָמֵן.

יְהֵא שְׁלָמָא רַבָּא מִן שְׁמַיָּא וְחַיִּים עָלֵינוּ וְעַל כָּל־יִשְׂרָאֵל, וְאִמְרוּ אָמֵן.

עֹשֶׂה שָׁלוֹם בִּמְרוֹמָיו הוּא יַעֲשֶׂה שָׁלוֹם עָלֵינוּ וְעַל כָּל־יִשְׂרָאֵל [וְעַל כָּל־יוֹשְׁבֵי תֵבֵל], וְאִמְרוּ אָמֵן.

KADDISH SHALEM קַדִּישׁ שָׁלֵם is recited at the end of every worship service that features an Amidah. Its distinguishing sentence is the line תִּתְקַבֵּל צְלוֹתְהוֹן, "May the prayers . . . of all Israel be accepted."

PEACE . . . HARMONY שְׁלָמָא שָׁלוֹם. Originally marking the end of the service, this prayer ends with thoughts of peace.

AND TO ALL WHO DWELL ON EARTH וְעַל כָּל־יוֹשְׁבֵי תֵבֵל. Our maḥzor follows the liturgical practice begun in some earlier Conservative movement prayerbooks by adding these words after mentioning Israel. (See, for example, the Shalom Rav prayer just recited at the end of the Amidah, page 16, above.)

At many moments in the liturgy, prayers focus on "Israel" or "the people Israel." The 20th-century philosopher Emmanuel Levinas pointed out that the designation "Israel" focuses our attention outward into the broader world of humanity and all those to whom we owe an ethical obligation of caring. In our prayers, we may move among various understandings of "Israel": Israel as Jewish community, Israel as national home, and Israel as symbolic of all those who uphold an ethical universe.

Kaddish Shalem

May God's great name be exalted and hallowed throughout the created world, as is God's wish. May God's sovereignty soon be established, in your lifetime and in your days, and in the days of all the House of Israel. And respond with: *Amen.*

May God's great name be acknowledged forever and ever!
Y'hei sh'meih rabba l'alam u-l'almei almayya.

May the name of the Holy One be acknowledged and celebrated, lauded and worshipped, exalted and honored, extolled and acclaimed— though God, who is blessed, *b'rikh hu*, is truly far beyond all acknowledgment and praise, or any expressions of gratitude or consolation ever spoken in the world. And respond with: *Amen.*

May the prayers and pleas of all Israel be accepted by their creator in heaven. And respond with: *Amen.*

May abundant peace from heaven, and life, come to us and to all Israel. And respond with: *Amen.*

May the One who brings harmony on high, bring harmony to us and to all Israel [and to all who dwell on earth]. And respond with: *Amen.*

Oseh shalom bi-m'romav hu ya·aseh shalom aleinu v'al kol yisra·el [v'al kol yosh'vei teiveil], v'imru amen.

בְּרֵאשִׁית בָּרָא אֱלֹהִים אֵת הַשָּׁמַיִם וְאֵת הָאָרֶץ: וְהָאָרֶץ
הָיְתָה תֹהוּ וָבֹהוּ וְחֹשֶׁךְ עַל־פְּנֵי תְהוֹם וְרוּחַ אֱלֹהִים
מְרַחֶפֶת עַל־פְּנֵי הַמָּיִם: וַיֹּאמֶר אֱלֹהִים יְהִי אוֹר וַיְהִי־
אוֹר: וַיַּרְא אֱלֹהִים אֶת־הָאוֹר כִּי־טוֹב וַיַּבְדֵּל אֱלֹהִים בֵּין
הָאוֹר וּבֵין הַחֹשֶׁךְ: וַיִּקְרָא אֱלֹהִים | לָאוֹר יוֹם וְלַחֹשֶׁךְ
קָרָא לָיְלָה וַיְהִי־עֶרֶב וַיְהִי־בֹקֶר יוֹם אֶחָד: בראשית א א-ה

מִי נָטָה גַלְגַּל נְגֹהִים,　　מִי יָסַד שְׁמֵי גְבוֹהִים,
מִי יְמַלֵּל גְּבוּרוֹת אֱלֹהִים?　　מִי אֵל גָּדוֹל כֵּאלֹהִים,
לְךָ דוּמִיָּה תְהִלָּה אֱלֹהִים!

יוֹם מְתִיחַת שְׁחָקָיו?　　מִי אָמַר וַתְּהִי אִמְרָתוֹ
יוֹם נְטִיַּת אֲרָקָיו?　　מִי בָט וַיִּכּוֹן מִבְּטָאוֹ
יוֹם שׂוּמוֹ חֻקָּיו?　　מִי גָדַר גְּדֵרוֹת מַצְלוּלִים
יוֹם הֲכִינוֹ עֲמָקָיו?　　מִי דִּבֵּק רִגְבֵי אָרֶץ
מִי שָׂם מְמַדֶּיהָ כִּי תֵדַע אוֹ מִי נָטָה עָלֶיהָ קָּו?
לְךָ דוּמִיָּה תְהִלָּה אֱלֹהִים!

הַרְבֵּה נִימִין בְּגָדְלוֹ?　　מִי קָבַע בְּרֹאשׁ אֱנוֹשׁ
מִי רָשַׁם לְכָל נִימָה וְנִימָה בִּפְנֵי עַצְמָהּ
מִלְּהַכְחִישׁ נְהוֹלוֹ?
כְּתֹאַר אָדָם הָרִאשׁוֹן וְכָלֻלוֹ?　　מִי שִׁפֵּר תְּאַר כָּל יְצוּר
בְּצוּרָתוֹ וַאֲמִירָתוֹ וְקוֹלוֹ?　　מִי תִכֵּן לְהַשְׁווֹת לָז לְלָז
מִי יַגִּיד עַל פָּנָיו דַּרְכּוֹ, וְהוּא עָשָׂה – מִי יְשַׁלֶּם לוֹ?
לְךָ דוּמִיָּה תְהִלָּה אֱלֹהִים!

INTRODUCTION TO KIDDUSH HA-SHANAH. Whereas some *piyyutim* (liturgical poems) were composed specifically for the evening of Rosh Hashanah, they did not become a standard part of the liturgy. This maḥzor introduces a series of readings—biblical readings, medieval *piyyutim*, and modern readings—to dedicate the new year. Opinions in the Babylonian Talmud consider the first day of the month of Tishrei (Rosh Hashanah) as the first day of creation (Rosh Hashanah 10b–11a). Yet the Midrash records an opinion that the world was created on the 25th day of the preceding month, Elul (Pesikta D'rav Kahana, Piska 23:1). That is, the sixth day of creation—the day on which God created human beings—fell on the first day of Tishrei. Thus according to this opinion, Rosh Hashanah celebrates the creation of humankind. As we dedicate the new year, we keep both opinions in mind, and in this ceremonial moment we celebrate both views with the appropriate verses from Genesis and also with poetic reflections.

WHO ESTABLISHED מִי יָסַד. The poem excerpted here was written by Joseph Ibn Abitur (10th–11th centuries, Spain) to be recited as a *piyyut* on the new year. It takes its inspiration from God's speech at the end of the Book of Job (chapter 38), where God questions Job as to whether the latter truly understands what powers are at work in the universe. The images that Abitur uses are taken both from Job and from talmudic midrashim.

EVEN SILENCE לְךָ דֻמִיָּה. Psalm 65:2.

WHO EXACTLY MEASURED מִי שָׂם מְמַדֶּיהָ. Job 38:5.

WHO CAN DESCRIBE מִי יַגִּיד עַל פָּנָיו. Job 21:31.

WHO CAN BATTLE מִי הִקְשָׁה. Job 9:4.

THE DEDICATION OF THE NEW YEAR

B'REISHIT

Each year we sit expectantly,
waiting to hear how it all began.
We strain and stretch ourselves,
not to imagine darkness, chaos—
darkness and chaos are states
with which we are well acquainted.
No, we begin

by trying to conjure first light,
form and order and sense emerging
from *tohu va-vohu*. And how can it be
that on Day One there was light,
night and day, but sun and moon
not till Day Four? OK, we think,
put aside that question
for the moment

as we struggle to see how it was,
for light has limitless possibilities
to consider—shimmering white heat
of the Negev, June sunset over
the Pacific, the way it sparkles
on early morning maple leaves
in Maine woods when everything
seems new and promising.

And yes, before sun and moon,
the Yangtze, the Nile, Mississippi,
Danube, North Sea, Finger Lakes,
Victoria Falls, Ein Gedi.
And fig trees, fuchsia, redwood,
rhubarb, palm, eucalyptus, birch,
blueberries, mango, mustard seed,
dogwood, dill, the mighty oak,
oregano, arugula, climbing roses,
cinnamon and cyclamen.

A fifth day brings us dolphin and
wren, duck and swan, seagull and
whale, crocodile, crab, bat, octopus,
butterfly, sockeye salmon and shark,
trout, snapping turtle, blue jay,
hawk and dove, ladybug, lobster,
falling sparrow, heron and herring
and hummingbird,
whooping cranes, and bees.
Now our hearts are pounding wildly,
our eyes fill with tears
at the glory of this world—

(continued)

The Creation of the World

FROM THE TORAH: THE FIRST DAY OF CREATION

When God began to create heaven and earth, the earth was unformed and void, darkness was over the surface of the deep, and the spirit of God swept over the water. God said, "Let there be light," and there was light. God saw that the light was good, and God separated the light from the darkness. God called the light Day and the darkness Night. And there was evening and there was morning, one day. Genesis 1:1–5

CREATION: A MEDIEVAL PIYYUT

Who established the highest heights?
Who propelled the sphere's rays?
Who is as great as the Divine?
Who can describe the Most Sublime?
          Even silence is Your praise!

Who spoke and with word day came to be?
Who glanced, and in that gaze created land?
Who propelled the waves and set limits to the seas?
Who raised up mountains and formed the valleys?
Who exactly measured the distance the world
     spanned?
          Even silence is Your praise!

Who placed hair on human heads and caused it
     to grow?
Who made each worm slither, and move only
     that way?
Who formed each person, each in Adam's mold?
Who created species, members alike, numbers
     untold?
Who can describe God's ways; and what God
     has given, who can repay?
          Even silence is Your praise!

וַיִּבְרָא אֱלֹהִים | אֶת־הָאָדָם בְּצַלְמוֹ בְּצֶלֶם אֱלֹהִים בָּרָא
אֹתוֹ זָכָר וּנְקֵבָה בָּרָא אֹתָם: וַיְבָרֶךְ אֹתָם אֱלֹהִים וַיֹּאמֶר
לָהֶם אֱלֹהִים פְּרוּ וּרְבוּ וּמִלְאוּ אֶת־הָאָרֶץ וְכִבְשֻׁהָ וּרְדוּ
בִּדְגַת הַיָּם וּבְעוֹף הַשָּׁמַיִם וּבְכָל־חַיָּה הָרֹמֶשֶׂת עַל־
הָאָרֶץ: . . . וַיַּרְא אֱלֹהִים אֶת־כָּל־אֲשֶׁר עָשָׂה וְהִנֵּה־טוֹב
מְאֹד וַיְהִי־עֶרֶב וַיְהִי־בֹקֶר יוֹם הַשִּׁשִּׁי: בראשית א כז-כח, לא

One or more of the following selections may be included.

א

קָרְבִּי, לִבִּי, נַפְשִׁי –
יוֹצְאִים אֶל נִיחוֹחַ הַחֲבַצֶּלֶת.
נְשִׁימַת הָאֹשֶׁר
מְשׂוֹשׂ הַחוֹלוֹת,
הִנֵּה הִיא עוֹלָה אֵלַי מִן הַטַּחַב
מִן הָרִיק
מֵאֵין אֹפֶק,
פּוֹרַחַת בִּכְנָפֶיהָ הַלְּבָנוֹת,
שׁוּב הָעוֹלָם מַמָּשׁוּת מְלֻטֶּשֶׁת
מַזָּל עֶלְיוֹן
בַּעַל קְדֻשָּׁה וַדַּאי.

MY BEING, MY HEART
קָרְבִּי, לִבִּי. A poem by the
modern Israeli poet Zelda
Schneerson Mishkovsky
(1914–1984), known simply
as "Zelda."

(continued from previous page)
all in a jumble then, frantically
getting ready for Shabbos,
come antelope and alley cat,
Irish setter, polar bear, black bear,
beaver, tiger, squirrel, chipmunk
and camel, lioness and spring lamb,
zebra, elephant, rattlesnake,
hippopotamus, giraffe,
monkey, mountain goat—
and just as it's time to reach into
the box at the back of the cupboard
to pull out two candles and find
the matches for *licht bentschen*—

miraculously comes the human
who can strike the match
and sanctify all the work
that God has done, eons ago
and every moment since,
battling *tohu va-vohu*,
the chaos that threatens
to once again engulf it all.
Shaken and humbled, we
reach for the match
and the blessing,
full of gratitude
for this holy world.

— MERLE FELD

The Creation of Humanity

FROM THE TORAH: THE SIXTH DAY OF CREATION

And God made human beings in God's image—
thus were they created: God created them male and
female. And God blessed them and said to them, "Be
fruitful and multiply, fill the earth and conquer it;
rule over the fish of the sea, the birds of the heavens,
and all living things that crawl on earth." . . . And God
saw all that had been done and thought it very good.
And there was evening and there was morning, the
sixth day.   Genesis 1:27–28, 31

One or more of the following selections may be included.

א

THE ROSE OF SHARON

My being, my heart, my soul
set out toward the fragrance of the rose.
The smell of happiness,
the joy of the sand dunes,
rises toward me through the damp,
through the emptiness
of endless space,
flies on its white wings,
and the world again becomes a discernible reality,
a heavenly charm,
an instrument of holiness, surely.

ב

בְּצַלְמְךָ בִּדְמוּתְךָ בָּרֵאתָ אוֹתָנוּ
וְחַיָּב אַתָּה לִהְיוֹת נוֹכֵחַ לָנוּ.

עָלֵינוּ לְהִשְׁתַּחֲווֹת אֵלֶיךָ
לְבַקֵּשׁ אֶת־סְלִיחָתֶךָ
וּלְחַיֵּב אוֹתְךָ עַל כָּל־הָאִי־צֶדֶק וְהַמְכֹעָר בָּעוֹלָם.

עָלֵינוּ לָשׁוּב אֵלֶיךָ
וּלְבַקֵּשׁ דִּין וְחֶשְׁבּוֹן עַל כָּל־שֶׁלֹּא מוּבָן
שֶׁאָז נוּכַל לִפְנוֹת אֵלֶיךָ בְּכַוָּנָה
לְהוֹדוֹת לְךָ עַל הָעִתִּים וְעַל הַכּוֹכָבִים,
עַל הַיּוֹם וְעַל הַלַּיְלָה.

לִפְנֵי פִּלְאֵי הָעוֹלָם אָנוּ מוּשְׁפָּלִים
אֲסִירֵי תּוֹדָה עַל חַנּוּן הַדַּעַת
עַל כָּל־חֲלוֹמוֹתֵינוּ וְתִקְווֹתֵינוּ
עַל אַשְׁלָיוֹתֵינוּ שֶׁאֵין לָהֶן סוֹף
וְעַל הַנְּשָׁמוֹת הַיָּפוֹת שֶׁחַיּוֹת חַיֵּי עוֹלָם.

אֵל הַכּוֹפְרִים
וֵאלֹהֵי הַמַּאֲמִינִים
אֱלוֹהַּ בְּכָל־דְּמֻיּוֹת וְשֶׁאֵין לוֹ דְּמוּת
שֶׁהָיָה הֹוֶה וְיִהְיֶה
אַתָּה הוּא אֱלֹהֵינוּ לְעוֹלָם וָעֶד.

ג

כֹּל הַנְּשָׁמָה תְּהַלֵּל יָהּ, הַלְלוּ־יָהּ.

ד

תִּכְלֶה שָׁנָה וְקִלְלוֹתֶיהָ.
תָּחֵל שָׁנָה וּבִרְכוֹתֶיהָ.

IN YOUR IMAGE בְּצַלְמְךָ בִּדְמוּתְךָ. This poem, composed in French by Myriam Kubovy and published in 1956, draws upon recognizable phrases of the liturgy. It asserts that the "image of God" in human beings includes not only the ability to appreciate the wonder of creation and the Creator's wisdom, but also the ability to struggle with God. The English translation of this excerpt is by Amy Gottlieb; the Hebrew translation, by Alan Lettofsky.

TIKHLEH תִּכְלֶה. This refrain is taken from a popular Rosh Hashanah Arvit *piyyut* in the Sephardic liturgy.

ב

IN YOUR IMAGE

In Your Image You fashioned us;
You owe us Your Presence.

We need to bow to You, ask Your forgiveness,
hold You responsible for the unfair, the ugly.

We need to return to You,
hold You accountable for what defies comprehension,
that we may turn to You more fervently, with gratitude for
the seasons and the stars and the day and the night.

We are humbled by the wonder of the world,
grateful for the gift of thought,
grateful for our dreams, our hopes,
grateful for our never-ending illusions,
grateful for these beautiful souls that transcend death.

God of the faithless,
God of the faithful,
God in all forms and formless,
who was and who is and who will be:
You are the Eternal One.

ג

Let every breath of life praise ADONAI. Halleluyah!
Kol ha-n'shamah t'hallel yah, hal'luyah.

ד

May this year's troubles end, and a year of blessing begin.
Tikhleh shanah v'kil'loteha,
taḥeil shanah u-virkhoteha.

יְהִי רָצוֹן מִלְּפָנֶיךָ יהוה אֱלֹהֵינוּ וֵאלֹהֵי אֲבוֹתֵינוּ
[וְאִמּוֹתֵינוּ], שֶׁתְּחַדֵּשׁ עָלֵינוּ אֶת־הַשָּׁנָה הַזֹּאת, שְׁנַת
חֲמֵשֶׁת אֲלָפִים _____ וּתְהִי זוֹ שָׁנָה שֶׁל שִׂגְשׂוּג
שָׁקוּל לָנוּ לְמִשְׁפְּחוֹתֵינוּ וְלִקְהִלּוֹתֵינוּ. יְהִי רָצוֹן שֶׁנָּשׁוּב
בַּשָּׁנָה הַבָּאָה לַמָּקוֹם הַזֶּה בִּבְרִיאוּת וּבְרִגְשֵׁי הוֹדָאָה
לְשָׁנָה שֶׁל שָׁלוֹם, שָׁנָה בָּהּ נִמְצָא דְרָכִים לְהֵיטִיב אֶת־
חַיֵּינוּ בְּלִמּוּד תּוֹרָה וְקִיּוּם מִצְוֹת,
שָׁנָה בָּהּ נִהְיֶה פְּתוּחִים לְנוֹכְחוּת הַשְּׁכִינָה,
שָׁנָה בָּהּ נְחַזֵּק אֶת־יַחֲסֵינוּ הָאִישִׁיִּים לַאֲחֵרִים וְשִׁתּוּף
פְּעוּלָתֵנוּ בְּתִקּוּן עוֹלָם. כֵּן יְהִי רָצוֹן.

MAY IT BE YOUR WILL יְהִי
רָצוֹן. This meditation is
adapted from the writings
of the 20th-century rabbi
and liturgist, Chaim Stern.

תַּעַזְרֵנוּ יהוה אֱלֹהֵינוּ, בְּרַחֲמֶיךָ הָרַבִּים שֶׁנִּזְכֶּה לְקַבֵּל
אֶת־רֹאשׁ הַשָּׁנָה, מַתָּנָה טוֹבָה שֶׁנָּתַתָּ־לָנוּ, בְּאַהֲבָה
וּבְשִׂמְחָה רַבָּה. וּבִזְכוּת קְדֻשַּׁת רֹאשׁ הַשָּׁנָה נִזְכֶּה
לֶאֱמוּנָה שְׁלֵמָה בֶּאֱמֶת. וְתַעַזְרֵנוּ וְתוֹשִׁיעֵנוּ שֶׁיִּתְקַבְּצוּ
יַחַד כָּל־נִיצוֹצוֹת הָאֱמוּנָה הַקְּדוֹשָׁה שֶׁבְּתוֹכֵנוּ, עַל יְדֵי
הַקִּבּוּץ הַקָּדוֹשׁ שֶׁל עַמְּךָ יִשְׂרָאֵל הַמִּתְקַבְּצִים בְּכָל־
הַקְּהִלּוֹת יַחַד בְּכָל־מְקוֹמוֹת מוֹשְׁבוֹתֵיהֶם בִּימֵי רֹאשׁ
הַשָּׁנָה הַקְּדוֹשִׁים לְבָרֵךְ אֶת־שֵׁם קָדְשֶׁךָ.

IN YOUR GREAT KINDNESS
תַּעַזְרֵנוּ. A prayer adapted
from Rabbi Nathan Stern-
harz (1780–1845), the chief
student of the Ḥasidic
master Naḥman of Bratzlav
and the compiler of the
main body of the Bratzlav
corpus. Naḥman's teachings
stress a life of faith and
joyfulness.

May it be Your will, Adonai our God and God of our ancestors, that the year _____ be one of balanced and mindful growth for us as individuals, for our families, and our communities. May we return next year in good health and in appreciation of a year of greater peace, a year in which we deepened our lives through learning and the performance of mitzvot, a year in which we were conscious of the Divine Presence, a year in which we strengthened our shared commitment to *tikkun olam*, the betterment of the world.

MEDITATION

In Your great kindness, aid us, Adonai our God, to embrace this Rosh Hashanah with love and overwhelming joy, as a gift from You. Through the celebration of this sacred Rosh Hashanah may we attain a full and true faith. Help us to gather together the sparks of holiness within ourselves, as we join with all the people Israel congregating from their individual homes and joining together on these holy days of Rosh Hashanah to bless Your sacred name.

קִדּוּשׁ

We rise.

בָּרוּךְ אַתָּה יהוה אֱלֹהֵֽינוּ מֶֽלֶךְ הָעוֹלָם,
בּוֹרֵא פְּרִי הַגָּֽפֶן.

בָּרוּךְ אַתָּה יהוה אֱלֹהֵֽינוּ מֶֽלֶךְ הָעוֹלָם, אֲשֶׁר בָּחַר בָּֽנוּ
מִכָּל־עָם וְרוֹמְמָֽנוּ מִכָּל־לָשׁוֹן, וְקִדְּשָֽׁנוּ בְּמִצְוֹתָיו. וַתִּתֶּן־
לָֽנוּ יהוה אֱלֹהֵֽינוּ בְּאַהֲבָה אֶת־יוֹם [הַשַּׁבָּת הַזֶּה וְאֶת־
יוֹם] הַזִּכָּרוֹן הַזֶּה, יוֹם [זִכְרוֹן] תְּרוּעָה [בְּאַהֲבָה] מִקְרָא
קֹֽדֶשׁ, זֵֽכֶר לִיצִיאַת מִצְרָֽיִם. כִּי בָֽנוּ בָחַֽרְתָּ וְאוֹתָֽנוּ קִדַּֽשְׁתָּ
מִכָּל־הָעַמִּים, וּדְבָרְךָ אֱמֶת וְקַיָּם לָעַד. בָּרוּךְ אַתָּה יהוה,
מֶֽלֶךְ עַל כָּל־הָאָֽרֶץ מְקַדֵּשׁ [הַשַּׁבָּת וְ] יִשְׂרָאֵל וְיוֹם
הַזִּכָּרוֹן.

On Saturday night, we add the following two b'rakhot. While reciting the first, we view our upraised fingers in the light of the holy day candles.

בָּרוּךְ אַתָּה יהוה אֱלֹהֵֽינוּ מֶֽלֶךְ הָעוֹלָם,
בּוֹרֵא מְאוֹרֵי הָאֵשׁ.

בָּרוּךְ אַתָּה יהוה אֱלֹהֵֽינוּ מֶֽלֶךְ הָעוֹלָם, הַמַּבְדִּיל בֵּין
קֹֽדֶשׁ לְחוֹל, בֵּין אוֹר לְחֹֽשֶׁךְ, בֵּין יִשְׂרָאֵל לָעַמִּים, בֵּין
יוֹם הַשְּׁבִיעִי לְשֵֽׁשֶׁת יְמֵי הַמַּעֲשֶׂה, בֵּין קְדֻשַּׁת שַׁבָּת
לִקְדֻשַּׁת יוֹם טוֹב הִבְדַּֽלְתָּ, וְאֶת־יוֹם הַשְּׁבִיעִי מִשֵּֽׁשֶׁת
יְמֵי הַמַּעֲשֶׂה קִדַּֽשְׁתָּ, הִבְדַּֽלְתָּ וְקִדַּֽשְׁתָּ אֶת־עַמְּךָ
יִשְׂרָאֵל בִּקְדֻשָּׁתֶֽךָ. בָּרוּךְ אַתָּה יהוה, הַמַּבְדִּיל בֵּין
קֹֽדֶשׁ לְקֹֽדֶשׁ.

On all nights, we conclude:

בָּרוּךְ אַתָּה יהוה אֱלֹהֵֽינוּ מֶֽלֶךְ הָעוֹלָם,
שֶׁהֶחֱיָֽנוּ וְקִיְּמָֽנוּ וְהִגִּיעָֽנוּ לַזְּמַן הַזֶּה.

KIDDUSH. Every Shabbat and festival is sanctified by a *b'rakhah* recited over wine and a second *b'rakhah* centered on the holiness of the day. When a festival begins or continues after Shabbat, a *b'rakhah* is recited over a lit candle as well as a *b'rakhah* formally marking the end of Shabbat. Unlike Shabbat, the use of fire is permitted on the festival, save that rather than kindling a new flame, the fire is passed from one already kindled.

LOVINGLY . . . WITH LOVE בְּאַהֲבָה . . . בְּאַהֲבָה. The holy day is seen as a gift from God—a special moment in the relationship between God and Israel, a time when the love between God and Israel is self-evident. Each weekly Shabbat is also a moment of personal quiet and rest as well as communal prayer and study, on which it is possible to experience the spiritual in one's life; thus the Kiddush also uses the word "love" in connection with Shabbat.

Kiddush

We rise.

Barukh atah ADONAI, our God, ruler of time and space,
who creates the fruit of the vine.
Barukh atah Adonai eloheinu melekh ha-olam, borei p'ri ha-gafen.

Barukh atah ADONAI, our God, ruler of time and space, who has chosen and distinguished us by sanctifying our lives with the commandments. With love, You have bestowed on us, ADONAI our God, [this Shabbat and] this Day of Remembrance, a day for [recalling] the shofar sound [with love], a day for holy assembly and for recalling the Exodus from Egypt. For You have chosen us, sanctifying us among all people, and Your faithful word endures forever. *Barukh atah ADONAI*, ruler of all the earth, who makes [Shabbat,] the people Israel and the Day of Remembrance holy.
Barukh atah Adonai eloheinu melekh ha-olam, asher baḥar banu mi-kol am v'rom'manu mi-kol lashon, v'kid'shanu b'mitzvotav. Va-titten lanu Adonai eloheinu b'ahavah et yom [ha-shabbat ha-zeh v'et yom] ha-zikkaron ha-zeh, yom [zikhron] t'ru·ah [b'ahavah] mikra kodesh, zeikher litzi·at mitzrayim. Ki vanu vaḥarta v'otanu kiddashta mi-kol ha-ammim, u-d'var'kha emet v'kayyam la·ad. Barukh atah Adonai, melekh al kol ha-aretz m'kaddesh [ha-shabbat v'] yisra·el v'yom ha-zikkaron.

On Saturday night, we add the following two b'rakhot. While reciting the first, we view our upraised fingers in the light of the holy day candles.

Barukh atah ADONAI, our God, ruler of time and space,
who creates the lights of fire.
Barukh atah Adonai eloheinu melekh ha-olam, borei m'orei ha-eish.

Barukh atah ADONAI, our God, ruler of time and space, who distinguishes the sacred from the everyday, light from darkness, Israel from the nations, and Shabbat from all other days. As You distinguished between Shabbat and the festivals, imbuing the seventh day with a sanctity above all other days, so have You distinguished and endowed Your people Israel with Your holiness. *Barukh atah ADONAI*, who distinguishes one holy day from another.

On all nights, we conclude:
Barukh atah ADONAI, our God, ruler of time and space,
for granting us life, for sustaining us, and for bringing us to this moment.
*Barukh atah Adonai eloheinu melekh ha-olam,
she-heḥeyanu v'kiy'manu v'higi·anu la-z'man ha-zeh.*

עָלֵינוּ לְשַׁבֵּחַ לַאֲדוֹן הַכֹּל,
לָתֵת גְּדֻלָּה לְיוֹצֵר בְּרֵאשִׁית,
שֶׁלֹּא עָשָׂנוּ כְּגוֹיֵי הָאֲרָצוֹת,
וְלֹא שָׂמָנוּ כְּמִשְׁפְּחוֹת הָאֲדָמָה,
שֶׁלֹּא שָׂם חֶלְקֵנוּ כָּהֶם,
וְגֹרָלֵנוּ כְּכָל־הֲמוֹנָם.

וַאֲנַחְנוּ כּוֹרְעִים וּמִשְׁתַּחֲוִים וּמוֹדִים,
לִפְנֵי מֶלֶךְ מַלְכֵי הַמְּלָכִים, הַקָּדוֹשׁ בָּרוּךְ הוּא.
שֶׁהוּא נוֹטֶה שָׁמַיִם וְיֹסֵד אָרֶץ, וּמוֹשַׁב יְקָרוֹ בַּשָּׁמַיִם
מִמַּעַל, וּשְׁכִינַת עֻזּוֹ בְּגָבְהֵי מְרוֹמִים, הוּא אֱלֹהֵינוּ אֵין
עוֹד. אֱמֶת מַלְכֵּנוּ אֶפֶס זוּלָתוֹ, כַּכָּתוּב בְּתוֹרָתוֹ:
וְיָדַעְתָּ הַיּוֹם וַהֲשֵׁבֹתָ אֶל־לְבָבֶךָ, כִּי יהוה הוּא הָאֱלֹהִים
בַּשָּׁמַיִם מִמַּעַל, וְעַל הָאָרֶץ מִתָּחַת, אֵין עוֹד.

עַל כֵּן נְקַוֶּה לְךָ יהוה אֱלֹהֵינוּ, לִרְאוֹת מְהֵרָה בְּתִפְאֶרֶת
עֻזֶּךָ, לְהַעֲבִיר גִּלּוּלִים מִן הָאָרֶץ וְהָאֱלִילִים כָּרוֹת יִכָּרֵתוּן,
לְתַקֵּן עוֹלָם בְּמַלְכוּת שַׁדַּי, וְכָל־בְּנֵי בָשָׂר יִקְרְאוּ בִשְׁמֶךָ,
לְהַפְנוֹת אֵלֶיךָ כָּל־רִשְׁעֵי אָרֶץ. יַכִּירוּ וְיֵדְעוּ כָּל־יוֹשְׁבֵי תֵבֵל,
כִּי לְךָ תִּכְרַע כָּל־בֶּרֶךְ, תִּשָּׁבַע כָּל־לָשׁוֹן. לְפָנֶיךָ יהוה
אֱלֹהֵינוּ יִכְרְעוּ וְיִפֹּלוּ, וְלִכְבוֹד שִׁמְךָ יְקָר יִתֵּנוּ. וִיקַבְּלוּ
כֻלָּם אֶת־עֹל מַלְכוּתֶךָ, וְתִמְלֹךְ עֲלֵיהֶם מְהֵרָה לְעוֹלָם וָעֶד.
כִּי הַמַּלְכוּת שֶׁלְּךָ הִיא, וּלְעוֹלְמֵי עַד תִּמְלֹךְ בְּכָבוֹד.
כַּכָּתוּב בְּתוֹרָתֶךָ: יהוה יִמְלֹךְ לְעֹלָם וָעֶד.
וְנֶאֱמַר: וְהָיָה יהוה לְמֶלֶךְ עַל כָּל־הָאָרֶץ,
בַּיּוֹם הַהוּא יִהְיֶה יהוה אֶחָד, וּשְׁמוֹ אֶחָד.

ALEINU עָלֵינוּ. This prayer was originally composed for, and recited during, the Malkhuyot/מַלְכֻיּוֹת ("Sovereignty") section of the Rosh Hashanah Musaf service. Since the late Middle Ages, it has acquired a special pride of place in Ashkenazic liturgy and is recited as part of the conclusion of every service. It is customary to physically bow when we recite the line וַאֲנַחְנוּ כּוֹרְעִים (*va-anaḥnu kor'im*), "And so we bow."

KNOW THIS DAY וְיָדַעְתָּ הַיּוֹם. Deuteronomy 4:39, Moses' speech enunciating the meaning of God's revelation at Sinai.

ESTABLISHING IN THE WORLD THE SOVEREIGNTY OF THE ALMIGHTY לְתַקֵּן עוֹלָם בְּמַלְכוּת שַׁדַּי. Beginning in the 19th century, this phrase came to be seen as similar to Isaiah's call to be "a light unto the nations," and it was reinterpreted as a call to universal justice. In this vein, the phrase לְתַקֵּן עוֹלָם (*l'takken olam*) was understood to mean "to repair the world," to be partners with God in achieving a time of peace and righteousness. Even earlier, Maimonides (12th century) had argued that the single most important characteristic of God's sovereignty would be an end to one people dominating another.

ADONAI WILL REIGN FOREVER AND EVER יהוה יִמְלֹךְ לְעֹלָם וָעֶד. From the Song at the Sea, Exodus 15:18.

ON THAT DAY ADONAI SHALL BE ONE בַּיּוֹם הַהוּא יִהְיֶה יהוה אֶחָד. Zechariah 14:9. In reciting the Sh'ma, we declare that God is one. Through our prayer we hope to make the world at one with God.

CONCLUDING PRAYERS

Aleinu

It is for us to praise the ruler of all, to acclaim the Creator, who has not made us merely a nation, nor formed us as all earthly families, nor given us an ordinary destiny.

ℓ And so we bow, acknowledging the supreme sovereign, the Holy One, who is praised—the One who spreads out the heavens and establishes the earth, whose glorious abode is in the highest heaven, whose powerful presence is in the loftiest heights. This is our God, none else; ours is the true sovereign, there is no other. As it is written in the Torah: "Know this day and take it to heart, that ADONAI is God in heaven above and on earth below; there is no other."

Aleinu l'shabbei·aḥ la-adon ha-kol, la-teit g'dullah l'yotzeir b'reishit,
she-lo asanu k'goyei ha-aratzot, v'lo samanu k'mishp'ḥot ha-adamah,
she-lo sam ḥelkeinu ka-hem, v'goraleinu k'khol hamonam.
ℓ Va-anaḥnu kor'im u-mishtaḥavim u-modim,
lifnei melekh malkhei ha-m'lakhim, ha-kadosh barukh hu.
She-hu noteh shamayim v'yoseid aretz, u-moshav y'karo ba-shamayim mi-ma·al,
u-sh'khinat uzzo b'govhei m'romim, hu eloheinu ein od. Emet malkeinu efes zulato,
ka-katuv b'torato: v'yadata ha-yom va-hasheivota el l'vavekha, ki Adonai hu ha-Elohim
ba-shamayim mi-ma·al, v'al ha-aretz mi-taḥat, ein od.

And so, ADONAI our God, we await You, that soon we may behold Your strength revealed in full glory, sweeping away the abominations of the earth, obliterating idols, establishing in the world the sovereignty of the Almighty. All flesh will call out Your name—even the wicked will turn toward You. Then all who live on earth will recognize and understand that to You alone all knees must bend and allegiance be sworn. All will bow down and prostrate themselves before You, ADONAI our God, honor Your glorious name, and accept the obligation of Your sovereignty. May You soon rule over them forever and ever, for true dominion is Yours; You will rule in glory until the end of time.

As is written in Your Torah: "ADONAI will reign forever and ever." And as the prophet said: "ADONAI shall be acknowledged sovereign of all the earth. On that day ADONAI shall be one, and the name of God, one."

V'ne·emar: v'hayah Adonai l'melekh al kol ha-aretz,
ba-yom ha-hu yihyeh Adonai eḥad, u-sh'mo eḥad.

Some congregations recite Mourner's Kaddish after Aleinu; some, after the recitation of Psalm 27 (next page).

קַדִּישׁ יָתוֹם

Mourners and those observing Yahrzeit:

יִתְגַּדַּל וְיִתְקַדַּשׁ שְׁמֵהּ רַבָּא,
בְּעָלְמָא דִּי בְרָא, כִּרְעוּתֵהּ,
וְיַמְלִיךְ מַלְכוּתֵהּ בְּחַיֵּיכוֹן וּבְיוֹמֵיכוֹן
וּבְחַיֵּי דְכָל־בֵּית יִשְׂרָאֵל,
בַּעֲגָלָא וּבִזְמַן קָרִיב,
וְאִמְרוּ אָמֵן.

Congregation and mourners:

יְהֵא שְׁמֵהּ רַבָּא מְבָרַךְ לְעָלַם וּלְעָלְמֵי עָלְמַיָּא.

Mourners:

יִתְבָּרַךְ וְיִשְׁתַּבַּח
וְיִתְפָּאַר וְיִתְרוֹמַם
וְיִתְנַשֵּׂא וְיִתְהַדָּר
וְיִתְעַלֶּה וְיִתְהַלָּל
שְׁמֵהּ דְּקֻדְשָׁא, **בְּרִיךְ הוּא,**
לְעֵלָּא לְעֵלָּא מִכָּל־בִּרְכָתָא וְשִׁירָתָא
תֻּשְׁבְּחָתָא וְנֶחֱמָתָא
דַּאֲמִירָן בְּעָלְמָא,
וְאִמְרוּ אָמֵן.

יְהֵא שְׁלָמָא רַבָּא מִן שְׁמַיָּא וְחַיִּים
עָלֵינוּ וְעַל כָּל־יִשְׂרָאֵל,
וְאִמְרוּ אָמֵן.

עֹשֶׂה שָׁלוֹם בִּמְרוֹמָיו
הוּא יַעֲשֶׂה שָׁלוֹם
עָלֵינוּ וְעַל כָּל־יִשְׂרָאֵל
[וְעַל כָּל־יוֹשְׁבֵי תֵבֵל],
וְאִמְרוּ אָמֵן.

KADDISH קַדִּישׁ. The custom of mourners reciting Kaddish began sometime after the 11th century. Though its origin is obscure, it has become an essential element of Jewish prayer. It is not a private prayer; rather, it is recited in community with a minyan present. In that context the mourner affirms that tragedy has not separated him or her from God or the Jewish people, and, in turn, the communal response then constitutes a way of acknowledging the mourner.

Grant that the memories of those who have gone before us be a source of strength for me and for everyone of the House of Israel. May the souls of our departed find peace in Your sheltering care, and may we all be blessed with peace, tranquility, and the fullness of life.

The Blessing of Memory

It is hard to sing of oneness when our world is not complete, when those who once brought wholeness to our life have gone, and nothing but memory can fill the emptiness their passing leaves behind.

But memory can tell us only what we were, in company with those we loved; it cannot help us find what each of us, alone, must now become. Yet no one is really alone; those who live no more echo still within our thoughts and words, and what they did is part of what we have become.

We do best homage to our dead when we live our lives most fully, even in the shadow of our loss. For each of our lives is worth the life of the whole world; in each one is the breath of the Divine. In affirming God we affirm the worth of each one whose life, now ended, brought us closer to the source of life, in whose unity no one is alone and every life finds purpose. —CHAIM STERN

Some congregations recite Mourner's Kaddish after Aleinu; some, after the recitation of Psalm 27 (next page).

Mourner's Kaddish

May God's great name be exalted and hallowed throughout the created world, as is God's wish. May God's sovereignty soon be established, in your lifetime and in your days, and in the days of all the House of Israel. And respond with: *Amen.*

May God's great name be acknowledged forever and ever!

May the name of the Holy One be acknowledged and celebrated, lauded and worshipped, exalted and honored, extolled and acclaimed—though God, who is blessed, *b'rikh hu*, is truly far beyond all acknowledgment and praise, or any expressions of gratitude or consolation ever spoken in the world. And respond with: *Amen.*

May abundant peace from heaven, and life, come to us and to all Israel. And respond with: *Amen.*

May the One who brings harmony on high, bring harmony to us and to all Israel [and to all who dwell on earth]. And respond with: *Amen.*

Mourners and those observing Yahrzeit:
Yitgaddal v'yitkaddash sh'meih rabba, b'alma di v'ra, ki-r'uteih,
v'yamlikh malkhuteih b'ḥayyeikhon u-v'yomeikhon
u-v'ḥayyei d'khol beit yisra·el,
ba-agala u-viz'man kariv,
v'imru amen.

Congregation and mourners:
Y'hei sh'meih rabba m'varakh l'alam u-l'almei almayya.

Mourners:
Yitbarakh v'yishtabbaḥ v'yitpa·ar v'yitromam v'yitnassei v'yit·haddar
v'yit·alleh v'yit·hallal sh'meih d'kudsha, b'rikh hu,
l'eilla l'eilla mi-kol birkhata v'shirata tushb'ḥata v'neḥamata
da-amiran b'alma, v'imru amen.

Y'hei sh'lama rabba min sh'mayya v'ḥayyim aleinu v'al kol yisra·el,
v'imru amen.

Oseh shalom bi-m'romav hu ya·aseh shalom aleinu
v'al kol yisra·el [v'al kol yosh'vei teiveil],
v'imru amen.

לְדָוִד.

יהוה אוֹרִי וְיִשְׁעִי מִמִּי אִירָא,

יהוה מָעוֹז־חַיַּי מִמִּי אֶפְחָד.

בִּקְרֹב עָלַי מְרֵעִים לֶאֱכֹל אֶת־בְּשָׂרִי,

צָרַי וְאֹיְבַי לִי הֵמָּה כָשְׁלוּ וְנָפָלוּ.

אִם־תַּחֲנֶה עָלַי מַחֲנֶה לֹא־יִירָא לִבִּי,

אִם־תָּקוּם עָלַי מִלְחָמָה בְּזֹאת אֲנִי בוֹטֵחַ.

אַחַת שָׁאַלְתִּי מֵאֵת־יהוה, אוֹתָהּ אֲבַקֵּשׁ,

שִׁבְתִּי בְּבֵית־יהוה, כָּל־יְמֵי חַיַּי

לַחֲזוֹת בְּנֹעַם־יהוה וּלְבַקֵּר בְּהֵיכָלוֹ.

כִּי יִצְפְּנֵנִי בְּסֻכֹּה בְּיוֹם רָעָה,

יַסְתִּרֵנִי בְּסֵתֶר אָהֳלוֹ, בְּצוּר יְרוֹמְמֵנִי.

וְעַתָּה יָרוּם רֹאשִׁי עַל אֹיְבַי סְבִיבוֹתַי

וְאֶזְבְּחָה בְאָהֳלוֹ זִבְחֵי תְרוּעָה,

אָשִׁירָה וַאֲזַמְּרָה לַיהוה.

שְׁמַע־יהוה קוֹלִי אֶקְרָא, וְחָנֵּנִי וַעֲנֵנִי.

לְךָ אָמַר לִבִּי בַּקְּשׁוּ פָנָי, אֶת־פָּנֶיךָ יהוה אֲבַקֵּשׁ.

אַל־תַּסְתֵּר פָּנֶיךָ מִמֶּנִּי,

אַל תַּט־בְּאַף עַבְדֶּךָ, עֶזְרָתִי הָיִיתָ,

אַל־תִּטְּשֵׁנִי וְאַל־תַּעַזְבֵנִי אֱלֹהֵי יִשְׁעִי.

כִּי־אָבִי וְאִמִּי עֲזָבוּנִי, וַיהוה יַאַסְפֵנִי.

הוֹרֵנִי יהוה דַּרְכֶּךָ, וּנְחֵנִי בְּאֹרַח מִישׁוֹר, לְמַעַן שׁוֹרְרָי.

אַל־תִּתְּנֵנִי בְּנֶפֶשׁ צָרָי,

כִּי קָמוּ־בִי עֵדֵי־שֶׁקֶר וִיפֵחַ חָמָס.

◁ לוּלֵא הֶאֱמַנְתִּי, לִרְאוֹת בְּטוּב־יהוה בְּאֶרֶץ חַיִּים.

קַוֵּה אֶל־יהוה, חֲזַק וְיַאֲמֵץ לִבֶּךָ וְקַוֵּה אֶל־יהוה. תהלים כז

Some congregations recite Mourner's Kaddish after the recitation of this psalm; see previous page.

PSALM 27 is recited on each of the ten days from Rosh Hashanah to Yom Kippur. It has also become customary to recite it during the entire month before Rosh Hashanah, in preparation for the High Holy Days. In mystical Jewish tradition, the days of judgment are extended through the seventh day of Sukkot, known as Hoshana Rabbah, and so the psalm is recited until then.

Psalm 27 expresses two opposite feelings, each of which may be felt on this day. From the very beginning, the psalmist expresses absolute faith in God, culminating in the striking sentence: "Though my father and mother abandon me, Adonai will gather me in. . . ." But at the same time, the psalmist experiences God's absence—the speaker longs to "see God," yet receives no response to this longing. The poem's last line leaves us with a thin, consoling thread of hope, making us realize, perhaps, how much our lives depend on faith.

DO NOT HIDE YOUR FACE FROM ME אַל־תַּסְתֵּר פָּנֶיךָ מִמֶּנִּי. "Face" suggests "presence"; the concrete metaphor serving the poet more than the abstract sense behind it. The speaker desperately seeks God's face (a privilege denied Moses). The practical manifestation of God's turning away would be the abandonment of the person to the enemies gathered about. (*Robert Alter*)

IF I COULD ONLY TRUST לוּלֵא הֶאֱמַנְתִּי. This is the only verse in the psalm that has no parallel. It is as if the speaker's voice simply trails off and then hears an inner voice calling: קַוֵּה אֶל־יהוה, "place your hope in Adonai." Or, perhaps someone else, in turn, urges the despairing supplicant to continue trusting that God will respond and asks that the person not lose faith.

To Hold On to Life

The Ḥasidic master Simḥah Bunam once remarked: "On New Year's Day the world begins anew; and before it begins anew, just as before dying, all the powers of the body clutch hard at life, so too a person at the turn of the year ought to clutch at life with all of that person's might."

—MARTIN BUBER

Psalm 27

Psalm 27 seems anything but a single, unified psalm. The first verses bespeak self-assurance, while later, the poem asks God to have pity and not to abandon the worshipper. It is both a psalm of confidence as well as a psalm of desperation. No wonder, then, that scholars have claimed that Psalm 27 is essentially composed of two psalms. Yet, there are others who are able to see the unity in the psalm and its use ritually during these Days of Awe. Psalm 27 offers an unanswered challenge, not a solution; a question to be dealt with, not a response. It does so by describing two contradictory situations, which share certain terminology, a framework, and a call for "one" understanding. It describes two well-known extremes of life: total assurance or belief and a deep, almost incurable, despondency. Out of these the reader is to create one life of faith.

—BENJAMIN SEGAL
(adapted)

A Psalm for the Season of Repentance—Psalm 27

A PSALM OF DAVID.

ADONAI is my light and my help. Whom shall I fear?
ADONAI is the stronghold of my life. Whom shall I dread?
When evil people assail me to devour my flesh
it is they, my enemies and those who besiege me,
who stumble and fall.
Should an armed camp be arrayed against me,
my heart would show no fear;
should they war against me, of this I would be sure.

One thing I ask of ADONAI—this I seek:
to dwell in the House of God all the days of my life,
to behold God's beauty and visit in God's sanctuary.

Aḥat sha·alti mei·eit Adonai, otah avakkeish
shivti b'veit Adonai, kol y'mei ḥayyai
la-ḥazot b'no·am Adonai u-l'vakkeir b'heikhalo.

Were God to hide me in God's *sukkah* on the calamitous day,
were God to enfold me in the secret recesses of God's tent,
I would be raised up in a protecting fort.
Now, I raise my head above the enemies that surround me,
and come with offerings, amidst trumpet blasts, to God's tent,
chanting and singing praise to ADONAI.
ADONAI, hear my voice as I cry out;
be gracious to me, and answer me.
It is You of whom my heart said, "Seek my face!"
It is Your presence that I seek, ADONAI.
Do not hide Your face from me; do not act angrily toward me.
You have always been my help; do not forsake me;
do not abandon me, my God, my deliverer.
Though my father and mother abandon me,
ADONAI will gather me in.
Show me Your way, ADONAI, and lead me on a straight path
despite those arrayed against me.
Do not hand me over to the grasp of those who besiege me;
for false witnesses and those who seek ill have risen against me.

If only I could trust that I would see God's goodness
in the land of the living . . .
Place your hope in ADONAI.
Be strong, take courage, and place your hope in ADONAI.

Some congregations recite Mourner's Kaddish after the recitation of this psalm; see previous page.

YIGDAL יִגְדַּל. This song was written by Daniel ben Yehudah of Rome in the 14th century. It is a poetic summary of Maimonides' thirteen articles of faith.

Although it has become a popular hymn, recited both before the morning blessings and at the conclusion of many services, there have always been objections to its use since many have argued that Judaism cannot be reduced to thirteen articles of faith. Some have altered the last lines, objecting to the affirmation that the dead will one day be resurrected.

In at least one of the cities of Hungary, the Ḥevra Kaddisha (Burial Society) would proceed from house to house on the 7th day of Adar, the legendary anniversary of the birth and death of Moses, and would sing Yigdal, repeating the last stanza declaiming the resurrection of the dead.

(Macy Nulman)

יִגְדַּל אֱלֹהִים חַי וְיִשְׁתַּבַּח,
נִמְצָא וְאֵין עֵת אֶל מְצִיאוּתוֹ.
אֶחָד וְאֵין יָחִיד כְּיִחוּדוֹ,
נֶעְלָם, וְגַם אֵין סוֹף לְאַחְדּוּתוֹ.

אֵין לוֹ דְּמוּת הַגּוּף וְאֵינוֹ גוּף,
לֹא נַעֲרוֹךְ אֵלָיו קְדֻשָּׁתוֹ.
קַדְמוֹן לְכָל־דָּבָר אֲשֶׁר נִבְרָא,
רִאשׁוֹן וְאֵין רֵאשִׁית לְרֵאשִׁיתוֹ.

הִנּוֹ אֲדוֹן עוֹלָם וְכָל־נוֹצָר
יוֹרֶה גְדֻלָּתוֹ וּמַלְכוּתוֹ.
שֶׁפַע נְבוּאָתוֹ נְתָנוֹ
אֶל אַנְשֵׁי סְגֻלָּתוֹ וְתִפְאַרְתּוֹ.

לֹא קָם בְּיִשְׂרָאֵל כְּמֹשֶׁה עוֹד
נָבִיא וּמַבִּיט אֶת־תְּמוּנָתוֹ.
תּוֹרַת אֱמֶת נָתַן לְעַמּוֹ אֵל,
עַל יַד נְבִיאוֹ נֶאֱמַן בֵּיתוֹ.

לֹא יַחֲלִיף הָאֵל וְלֹא יָמִיר דָּתוֹ
לְעוֹלָמִים לְזוּלָתוֹ.
צוֹפֶה וְיוֹדֵעַ סְתָרֵינוּ,
מַבִּיט לְסוֹף דָּבָר בְּקַדְמָתוֹ.

גּוֹמֵל לְאִישׁ חֶסֶד כְּמִפְעָלוֹ,
נוֹתֵן לְרָשָׁע רָע כְּרִשְׁעָתוֹ.
יִשְׁלַח לְקֵץ יָמִין מְשִׁיחֵנוּ,
לִפְדּוֹת מְחַכֵּי קֵץ יְשׁוּעָתוֹ.

מֵתִים יְחַיֶּה אֵל בְּרוֹב חַסְדּוֹ,
בָּרוּךְ עֲדֵי עַד שֵׁם תְּהִלָּתוֹ.

בִּרְכַּת פְּרֵידָה
לְשָׁנָה טוֹבָה תִּכָּתֵבוּ וְתֵחָתֵמוּ.

Maimonides' Thirteen Articles of Faith

God is Creator.

God is one, unique, eternal.

God is incomparable, with neither body nor form.

God precedes all and is beyond all.

Only God is to be worshipped.

The words of the prophets are true.

Moses was the spiritual ancestor of all the prophets.

The Torah was given to Moses.

The Torah is immutable.

God, as Creator, knows our deeds and thoughts.

Reward and punishment issue from God.

The Messiah will come.

God, in God's own time, will give life to the dead.

YIGDAL

Revere the living God, sing praises to God's name,
  both immanent and timeless, through eternity.

God's oneness is unique, no other can compare;
  unlimited and boundless is God's majesty.

No image can be seen, no form or body known;
  no mortal mind can fathom God's totality.

Before creation's start, the world as yet unformed,
  the living God endured in endless mystery.

The ruler of the world, whose creatures all declare
  the glory and the greatness of God's sovereignty.

God chose devoted servants, wise and faithful seers,
  and showered on each one the gift of prophecy.

In Israel none arose like Moses—touched by God—
  whose visions probed the limits of humanity.

The Torah, in its truth, God granted to us all,
  which loyal servant Moses taught us faithfully.

Our God will neither change nor modify God's law,
  its place remains established for eternity.

God penetrates our minds, the promptings of our hearts,
  anticipating actions that are yet to be.

God grants reward to those who lead a noble life,
  while punishing transgressors sinning wantonly.

Our Messiah, God will send, to greet the end of days,
  redeeming all who long for God to make them free.

In love our God restores the life to all our souls—
  may God be ever praised until eternity.

Yigdal Elohim ḥai v'yishtabbaḥ nimtza v'ein et el m'tzi·uto.
* Eḥad v'ein yaḥid k'yiḥudo ne·lam, v'gam ein sof l'aḥduto.*
Ein lo d'mut ha-guf v'eino guf lo na·arokh eilav k'dushato.
* Kadmon l'khol davar asher nivra rishon v'ein reishit l'reishito.*
Hinno adon olam, v'khol notzar yoreh g'dullato u-malkhuto.
* Shefa n'vu·ato n'tano el anshei s'gullato v'tifarto.*
Lo kam b'yisra·el k'mosheh od navi u-mabbit et t'munato.
* Torat emet natan l'ammo El al yad n'vi·o ne·eman beito.*
Lo yaḥalif ha-El v'lo yamir dato l'olamim l'zulato.
* Tzofeh v'yodei·a s'tareinu mabbit l'sof davar b'kadmato.*
Gomel l'ish ḥesed k'mif·alo notein l'rasha ra k'rish·ato.
* Yishlaḥ l'keitz yamin m'shiḥeinu lifdot m'ḥakkei keitz y'shu·ato.*
Meitim y'ḥayyeh El b'rov ḥasdo barukh adei ad shem t'hillato.

Traditional High Holy Day Greeting

May you be inscribed and sealed for a good year.

L'shanah tovah tikkateivu v'teiḥateimu.

ROSH HASHANAH ראש השנה
AT HOME בבית

Candlelighting

On the first night, we light candles eighteen minutes before sunset, as on Shabbat. On the second night, we light candles from an existing flame after nightfall. It is traditional to light a minimum of two candles, although some light more, corresponding to the number of people in one's family.

After lighting the candles, we customarily cover our eyes while reciting the following two b'rakhot, which we recite on both nights:

בָּרוּךְ אַתָּה יהוה אֱלֹהֵינוּ מֶלֶךְ הָעוֹלָם, אֲשֶׁר קִדְּשָׁנוּ
בְּמִצְוֹתָיו וְצִוָּנוּ לְהַדְלִיק נֵר שֶׁל [שַׁבָּת וְשֶׁל] יוֹם טוֹב.

Barukh atah ADONAI, our God, ruler of time and space, who has made us holy through mitzvot and instructed us to light the [Shabbat and] festival candles.

Barukh atah Adonai, eloheinu melekh ha-olam, asher kid'shanu b'mitzvotav v'tzivvanu l'hadlik neir shel [shabbat v'shel] yom tov.

בָּרוּךְ אַתָּה יהוה אֱלֹהֵינוּ מֶלֶךְ הָעוֹלָם, שֶׁהֶחֱיָנוּ וְקִיְּמָנוּ
וְהִגִּיעָנוּ לַזְּמַן הַזֶּה.

Barukh atah ADONAI, our God, ruler of time and space, for granting us life, for sustaining us, and for bringing us to this moment.

Barukh atah Adonai, eloheinu melekh ha-olam, she-heheyanu v'kiy'manu v'higgi·anu la-z'man ha-zeh.

ROSH HASHANAH EVE. Beginning on the new moon of Tishrei, Rosh Hashanah lasts for two days in both the Land of Israel and the Diaspora. In ancient times there was doubt about the exact starting date of the new month. Today, when we follow a precise calendar rather than astronomical observations to determine the date of Rosh Hashanah, we nevertheless preserve the tradition of celebrating two days. To justify the recitation of the prayer Sheheheyanu (the blessing over new events and things) on the eve of the second night, it is customary to wear new clothing and eat new fruits at the evening meal.

I LIGHT THE CANDLES. *T'hinnot* (תְּחִנּוֹת) are prayers, mostly from the European Yiddish tradition, written by or for women as introductions to rituals and statutory prayers. *T'hinnot* (*tkhines* in Yiddish) often have a deeply personal character and may serve as a model for our own personal prayers. The *t'hinnah* printed here is a contemporary prayer.

LA ORASION DE LA MUJER. A contemporary Judeo-Spanish prayer by Flory Jagoda, modeled after traditional women's prayers for candlelighting.

BLESSING THE FAMILY. After lighting the candles, it is customary to bless the family with blessings based on biblical verses that express our hopes for peace and protection during the year ahead. For sons, we fulfill Jacob's blessing to his grandsons Manasseh and Ephraim, in which he told them, "By you shall the people Israel invoke blessings, saying: 'May God make you like Ephraim and Manasseh'" (Genesis 48:20). For daughters, Jews have long recited a parallel blessing naming the four matriarchs. We follow that with a recitation of the Priestly Blessing (Numbers 6:24–26).

Candlelighting

One or more of these three meditations may accompany the candlelighting.

א

With these lights we welcome (Shabbat and) Rosh Hashanah. In the glow of contrasting colors we discern the light and dark of our lives. We recall the disappointments and joys we have shared, and the hopes and intentions we now nurture for the year ahead.

—MITCHELL SILVER (adapted)

ב

T'ḥinnah for Today
I light the candles, close my eyes, shield my face with my hands and retreat into solitude to find my way to You.

Please, a new year, fresh, a clean slate, a true beginning. A year of health and strength, work which brings sustenance and meaning, permission to rest and savor, abundant love, laughter, joy.
The same and more for my beloved family, my cherished friends. Cessation of the horrors, the throbbing of war, violence, cruelty. Peace for us, the human family, and for our home, Your world.

I chant the ancient words, uncover my face, open my eyes. I am ready for a new year.

—MALKA ALIZA BAT LEIBA

Blessing the Children

For a son:

יְשִׂימְךָ אֱלֹהִים כְּאֶפְרַיִם וְכִמְנַשֶּׁה.

May God make you like Ephraim and Manasseh.
Y'sim'kha elohim k'efrayim v'khi-m'nasheh.

For a daughter:

יְשִׂימֵךְ אֱלֹהִים כְּשָׂרָה רִבְקָה רָחֵל וְלֵאָה.

May God make you like Sarah, Rebecca, Rachel, and Leah.
Y'simeikh elohim k'sarah, rivkah, raḥeil, v'lei·ah.

Recited for all:

יְבָרֶכְךָ יהוה וְיִשְׁמְרֶךָ.
יָאֵר יהוה פָּנָיו אֵלֶיךָ וִיחֻנֶּךָּ.
יִשָּׂא יהוה פָּנָיו אֵלֶיךָ וְיָשֵׂם לְךָ שָׁלוֹם.

May ADONAI bless and protect you.
May ADONAI's countenance shine upon you
and grant you kindness.
May ADONAI's countenance be lifted toward you
and grant you peace.
Y'varekh'kha Adonai v'yishm'rekha.
Ya·eir Adonai panav eilekha vi-ḥunnekka.
Yissa Adonai panav eilekha v'yaseim l'kha shalom.

ג

La Orasion de la Mujer / The Woman's Prayer
Kun estas kandelas arrogamos al Dio, el Dio de muestros padres Avram, Isak i Yakov, ke muz de vida saludoza a todus miz keriduz i al mundo intero. Kun estas kandelas arrogamos al Dio, el Dio de muestros madres Sara, Rifka, Lea i Rachel, ke muz de vida saludoza a todus miz keriduz i al mundo intero.

With these candles we pray to God, the God of our fathers Abraham, Isaac, and Jacob, to grant us good life and health to all our dear ones and the whole world. With these candles we pray to God, the God of our mothers Sarah, Rebecca, Leah, and Rachel, to grant us good life and health to all our dear ones and the whole world. —FLORY JAGODA

Kiddush

ON SHABBAT, BEGIN HERE:

וַיְהִי־עֶרֶב וַיְהִי־בֹקֶר יוֹם הַשִּׁשִּׁי. וַיְכֻלּוּ הַשָּׁמַיִם וְהָאָרֶץ וְכָל־צְבָאָם. וַיְכַל אֱלֹהִים בַּיּוֹם הַשְּׁבִיעִי מְלַאכְתּוֹ אֲשֶׁר עָשָׂה, וַיִּשְׁבֹּת בַּיּוֹם הַשְּׁבִיעִי, מִכָּל־מְלַאכְתּוֹ אֲשֶׁר עָשָׂה. וַיְבָרֶךְ אֱלֹהִים אֶת־יוֹם הַשְּׁבִיעִי וַיְקַדֵּשׁ אֹתוֹ, כִּי בוֹ שָׁבַת מִכָּל־מְלַאכְתּוֹ, אֲשֶׁר בָּרָא אֱלֹהִים לַעֲשׂוֹת.

There was evening and there was morning, the sixth day. The heavens and the earth, and all they contain, were completed. On the seventh day God finished the work, ceasing from all work on the seventh day. Then God blessed the seventh day, making it holy, because on it, God had ceased from all the work of creation.

On other days, begin here:

סַבְרִי מָרָנָן וַחֲבֵרַי:

בָּרוּךְ אַתָּה יהוה אֱלֹהֵינוּ מֶלֶךְ הָעוֹלָם, בּוֹרֵא פְּרִי הַגָּפֶן.

With the assent of teachers and friends:

Savri maranan va-ḥaveirai:

Barukh atah ADONAI, our God, ruler of time and space, who creates the fruit of the vine.

Barukh atah Adonai, eloheinu melekh ha-olam, borei p'ri ha-gafen.

בָּרוּךְ אַתָּה יהוה אֱלֹהֵינוּ מֶלֶךְ הָעוֹלָם, אֲשֶׁר בָּחַר־בָּנוּ מִכָּל־עָם, וְרוֹמְמָנוּ מִכָּל־לָשׁוֹן, וְקִדְּשָׁנוּ בְּמִצְוֹתָיו. וַתִּתֶּן־ לָנוּ יהוה אֱלֹהֵינוּ בְּאַהֲבָה אֶת־יוֹם [הַשַּׁבָּת הַזֶּה וְאֶת־ יוֹם] הַזִּכָּרוֹן הַזֶּה, יוֹם [זִכְרוֹן] תְּרוּעָה [בְּאַהֲבָה] מִקְרָא קֹדֶשׁ, זֵכֶר לִיצִיאַת מִצְרָיִם, כִּי בָנוּ בָחַרְתָּ וְאוֹתָנוּ קִדַּשְׁתָּ מִכָּל־הָעַמִּים, וּדְבָרְךָ אֱמֶת וְקַיָּם לָעַד. בָּרוּךְ אַתָּה יהוה, מֶלֶךְ עַל כָּל־הָאָרֶץ מְקַדֵּשׁ [הַשַּׁבָּת וְ] יִשְׂרָאֵל וְיוֹם הַזִּכָּרוֹן.

Barukh atah ADONAI, our God, ruler of time and space, who has chosen and distinguished us by sanctifying our lives with the commandments. With love, You have bestowed on us, ADONAI our God, [this Shabbat and] this Day of Remembrance, a day for [recalling] the shofar sound [with love], a day

KIDDUSH קִדּוּשׁ. The day is sanctified, and the spirit of the holy day is formally welcomed into our homes, through the recitation of the blessing over a cup of wine. This blessing is introduced on Shabbat by verses that recognize Shabbat as the culminating moment in creation (Genesis 2:1–3). The blessings that follow introduce the themes of Israel's chosenness, Rosh Hashanah as a day of memory, and the story of the Exodus from Egypt. On Saturday night, Havdalah, defining the transition from Shabbat to weekday Holy Day, is recited. The latter differs from the Havdalah service recited at the conclusion of Shabbat, for the day after Shabbat on Rosh Hashanah is not a day of work, but a holy day.

Compassionate God, grant us the understanding and the will to love mercy, to live justly, and to walk humbly before You. May our hearts be open with generosity and our hands ready with kindness. May our faith in the attainment of harmony and peace for all humanity remain unshaken.

ב

May the words of our mouths and the meditations of our hearts find expression in our lives day by day, helping us to fulfill our potential to live up to the divine image in which we are created. May all our aspirations for good be fulfilled. Amen.

—BERNARD RASKAS
(adapted)

for holy assembly and for recalling the Exodus from Egypt. For You have chosen us, sanctifying us among all people, and Your faithful word endures forever. *Barukh atah ADONAI*, ruler of all the earth, who makes [Shabbat,] the people Israel and the Day of Remembrance holy.

(*For transliteration, see page 24.*)

On Saturday night, we add the following two b'rakhot. While reciting the first, we view our upraised fingers in the light of the holy day candles.

בָּרוּךְ אַתָּה יהוה אֱלֹהֵינוּ מֶלֶךְ הָעוֹלָם,
בּוֹרֵא מְאוֹרֵי הָאֵשׁ.

בָּרוּךְ אַתָּה יהוה אֱלֹהֵינוּ מֶלֶךְ הָעוֹלָם, הַמַּבְדִּיל בֵּין קֹדֶשׁ
לְחוֹל, בֵּין אוֹר לְחְשֶׁךְ, בֵּין יִשְׂרָאֵל לָעַמִּים, בֵּין יוֹם הַשְּׁבִיעִי
לְשֵׁשֶׁת יְמֵי הַמַּעֲשֶׂה. בֵּין קְדֻשַּׁת שַׁבָּת לִקְדֻשַּׁת יוֹם טוֹב
הִבְדַּלְתָּ, וְאֶת־יוֹם הַשְּׁבִיעִי מִשֵּׁשֶׁת יְמֵי הַמַּעֲשֶׂה קִדַּשְׁתָּ,
הִבְדַּלְתָּ וְקִדַּשְׁתָּ אֶת־עַמְּךָ יִשְׂרָאֵל בִּקְדֻשָּׁתֶךָ. בָּרוּךְ אַתָּה
יהוה, הַמַּבְדִּיל בֵּין קֹדֶשׁ לְקֹדֶשׁ.

Barukh atah ADONAI, our God, ruler of time and space, who creates the lights of fire.

Barukh atah ADONAI, our God, ruler of time and space, who distinguishes the sacred from the everyday, light from darkness, Israel from the nations, and Shabbat from all other days. As You have distinguished between Shabbat and the festivals, imbuing the seventh day with a sanctity above all other days, so have You distinguished and endowed Your people Israel with Your holiness. *Barukh atah ADONAI*, who distinguishes one holy day from another.

On all nights, we conclude:

בָּרוּךְ אַתָּה יהוה אֱלֹהֵינוּ מֶלֶךְ הָעוֹלָם,
שֶׁהֶחֱיָנוּ וְקִיְּמָנוּ וְהִגִּיעָנוּ לַזְּמַן הַזֶּה.

Barukh atah ADONAI, our God, ruler of time and space, for granting us life, for sustaining us, and for bringing us to this moment.

Barukh atah Adonai, eloheinu melekh ha-olam,
she-heḥeyanu v'kiy'manu v'higgi·anu la-z'man ha-zeh.

Hand Washing

It is customary to pour water two or three times over each hand.
After this ritual washing of the hands, we each recite the following b'rakhah:

בָּרוּךְ אַתָּה יהוה אֱלֹהֵינוּ מֶלֶךְ הָעוֹלָם,
אֲשֶׁר קִדְּשָׁנוּ בְּמִצְוֹתָיו וְצִוָּנוּ עַל נְטִילַת יָדָיִם.

Barukh atah ADONAI, our God, ruler of time and space, who
has made us holy through mitzvot by instructing us to wash
our hands.

Barukh atah Adonai, eloheinu melekh ha-olam,
asher kid'shanu b'mitzvotav v'tzivvanu al n'tilat yadayim.

Ha-motzi: The B'rakhah before the Meal

בָּרוּךְ אַתָּה יהוה אֱלֹהֵינוּ מֶלֶךְ הָעוֹלָם,
הַמּוֹצִיא לֶחֶם מִן הָאָרֶץ.

Barukh atah ADONAI, our God, ruler of time and space, who
brings forth bread from the earth.

Barukh atah Adonai, eloheinu melekh ha-olam,
ha-motzi leḥem min ha-aretz.

Prayer for a Sweet Year

We recite the following over an apple dipped in honey:

בָּרוּךְ אַתָּה יהוה אֱלֹהֵינוּ מֶלֶךְ הָעוֹלָם, בּוֹרֵא פְּרִי הָעֵץ.

Barukh atah ADONAI, our God, ruler of time and space,
who creates the fruit of the tree.

Barukh atah Adonai, eloheinu melekh ha-olam, borei p'ri ha-eitz.

יְהִי רָצוֹן מִלְּפָנֶיךָ יהוה אֱלֹהֵינוּ וֵאלֹהֵי אֲבוֹתֵינוּ
[וְאִמּוֹתֵינוּ] שֶׁתְּחַדֵּשׁ עָלֵינוּ שָׁנָה טוֹבָה וּמְתוּקָה.

May it be Your will, ADONAI our God, and God of our
ancestors, to renew for us a new, sweet, and good year.

Y'hi ratzon mi-l'fanekha Adonai eloheinu veilohei avoteinu
[v'immoteinu] she-t'ḥaddeish aleinu shanah tovah u-m'tukah.

HAND WASHING. After the
destruction of the Temple
in 70 C.E., the home table
took on some of the rules
governing the ritual altar.
Washing hands before a
meal reflects the Temple
ritual that required purity
for all those involved in
the handling of sacrificial
offerings.

THE MEAL. The *ḥallot* used
on the evenings of Rosh
Hashanah (as well as at the
midday meals) are custom-
arily round, to represent the
cyclical nature of the year.
The blessing over bread
constitutes the blessing of
all that is consumed during
the meal. It is also customary to dip the *ḥallah* in
honey. The meal concludes
with בִּרְכַּת הַמָּזוֹן, the Grace
after Meals.

AN APPLE DIPPED IN HONEY.
It is customary to eat an
apple dipped in honey,
representing the promise of
a sweet new year. Customs
differ as to whether the
apple is eaten before the
meal or during the meal.
Similarly, customs differ
as to whether a formal
b'rakhah is said when the
apple is eaten during the
meal. On the second night
of Rosh Hashanah it is
traditional to taste a new
fruit (one not yet tasted
that year) and to keep it in
mind during Kiddush when
reciting the Sheheḥeyanu
blessing for special occasions. This new fruit is often
a pomegranate, which is said to have 613 seeds, equal to the
number of mitzvot in the Torah.

KIDDUSH קִדּוּשׁ. Kiddush is recited before the midday meal.
The paragraphs added for Shabbat (Exodus 31:16–17 and
Exodus 20:11) are recited before the meal on each Shabbat.
The final passages are from Leviticus 23:44 and Psalm 81:4–5.

Kiddush for the Midday Meal

Before the midday meal on Shabbat, we recite the following paragraph; some add the second paragraph as well:

וְשָׁמְרוּ בְנֵי יִשְׂרָאֵל אֶת־הַשַּׁבָּת, לַעֲשׂוֹת אֶת־הַשַּׁבָּת לְדֹרֹתָם
בְּרִית עוֹלָם. בֵּינִי וּבֵין בְּנֵי יִשְׂרָאֵל אוֹת הִיא לְעוֹלָם, כִּי שֵׁשֶׁת
יָמִים עָשָׂה יהוה אֶת־הַשָּׁמַיִם וְאֶת־הָאָרֶץ, וּבַיּוֹם הַשְּׁבִיעִי
שָׁבַת וַיִּנָּפַשׁ.

The people Israel shall observe the Shabbat to maintain it as an everlasting covenant throughout all generations. It is a sign between Me and the people Israel for all time that in six days Adonai made the heavens and the earth and on the seventh day ceased from work and rested.

V'sham'ru v'nei yisra·el et ha-shabbat, la-asot et ha-shabbat l'dorotam, b'rit olam. Beini u-vein b'nei yisra·el hi l'olam, ki sheishet yamim asah Adonai et ha-shamayim v'et ha-aretz, u-va-yom ha-sh'vi·i shavat va-yinnafash.

עַל כֵּן בֵּרַךְ יהוה אֶת יוֹם הַשַּׁבָּת וַיְקַדְּשֵׁהוּ.

Therefore Adonai blessed Shabbat and made it holy.
Al kein beirakh Adonai et yom ha-shabbat va-y'kad'sheihu.

On all days:

וַיְדַבֵּר מֹשֶׁה אֶת מוֹעֲדֵי יהוה אֶל בְּנֵי יִשְׂרָאֵל.

Moses declared to the Israelites the sacred occasions of God.
Ya-y'dabbeir moshe et mo·adei Adonai el b'nei yisra·el.

תִּקְעוּ בַחֹדֶשׁ שׁוֹפָר בַּכֶּסֶה לְיוֹם חַגֵּנוּ.
כִּי חֹק לְיִשְׂרָאֵל הוּא מִשְׁפָּט לֵאלֹהֵי יַעֲקֹב.

Sound the *shofar* on our feast day, on the new moon, when it is hidden.
For it is Israel's law, a decree of the God of Jacob.
Tik'u va-ḥodesh shofar ba-keseh l'yom ḥaggenu.
Ki ḥok l'yisra·el hu mishpat leilohei ya·akov.

סַבְרִי מָרָנָן וַחַבֵּרַי:
בָּרוּךְ אַתָּה יהוה אֱלֹהֵינוּ מֶלֶךְ הָעוֹלָם, בּוֹרֵא פְּרִי הַגָּפֶן.

With the assent of teachers and friends:
Savri maranan va-ḥaveirai:
Barukh atah Adonai, our God, ruler of time and space,
who creates the fruit of the vine.
Barukh atah Adonai, eloheinu melekh ha-olam, borei p'ri ha-gafen.

שחרית לראש השנה וליום כיפור
MORNING SERVICE OF ROSH HASHANAH AND YOM KIPPUR

ברכות השחר

MORNING SERVICE

שַׁחֲרִית. The core sections of the morning service are the Sh'ma and the Amidah. Over the centuries, two preliminary sections have been added. First, P'sukei D'zimra, featuring selections from the Book of Psalms (page 47), was added as preparation for reciting the main service itself. Later, בִּרְכוֹת הַשַּׁחַר (Birkhot Ha-shahar), b'rakhot and other readings that had originally been recited individually upon arising, were moved from their private setting in the home to public recitation in the synagogue service. In the 13th and 14th centuries, biblical verses, prayers, and poems were added to the liturgy to mark the opening and closing of the service.

Birkhot Ha-shahar has become a generic name for

Upon entering the synagogue:

מַה־טֹּבוּ אֹהָלֶיךָ יַעֲקֹב, מִשְׁכְּנֹתֶיךָ יִשְׂרָאֵל.
וַאֲנִי בְּרֹב חַסְדְּךָ אָבוֹא בֵיתֶךָ,
אֶשְׁתַּחֲוֶה אֶל־הֵיכַל־קָדְשְׁךָ בְּיִרְאָתֶךָ.
יהוה אָהַבְתִּי מְעוֹן בֵּיתֶךָ, וּמְקוֹם מִשְׁכַּן כְּבוֹדֶךָ.
וַאֲנִי אֶשְׁתַּחֲוֶה וְאֶכְרָעָה, אֶבְרְכָה לִפְנֵי־יהוה עֹשִׂי.
וַאֲנִי תְפִלָּתִי־לְךָ, יהוה, עֵת רָצוֹן.
אֱלֹהִים בְּרָב־חַסְדֶּךָ, עֲנֵנִי בֶּאֱמֶת יִשְׁעֶךָ.

עֲטִיפַת טַלִּית

While reciting the meditation and the b'rakhah, it is customary to hold the tallit. After saying the b'rakhah we first wrap the tallit around our head and body, symbolically enclosing ourselves in a sacred garment, and then drape it around our shoulders.

בָּרְכִי נַפְשִׁי אֶת־יהוה. יהוה אֱלֹהַי גָּדַלְתָּ מְאֹד, הוֹד וְהָדָר לָבָשְׁתָּ. עֹטֶה־אוֹר כַּשַּׂלְמָה, נוֹטֶה שָׁמַיִם כַּיְרִיעָה.

**בָּרוּךְ אַתָּה יהוה אֱלֹהֵינוּ מֶלֶךְ הָעוֹלָם,
אֲשֶׁר קִדְּשָׁנוּ בְּמִצְוֹתָיו וְצִוָּנוּ לְהִתְעַטֵּף בַּצִּיצִית.**

כְּשֵׁם שֶׁגּוּפִי מִתְעַטֵּף בְּטַלִּית, כָּךְ תִּתְעַטֵּף נִשְׁמָתִי בְּאוֹר שְׁכִינָתֶךָ.

all those b'rakhot that were considered appropriate to recite upon arising. The Mishnah records that "the pious men of old would pause for an hour before praying in order to direct their hearts toward God" (Berakhot 5:1). Individuals also had their own ways of approaching prayer. Some would recite the Book of Psalms; others created their own meditations.

HOW LOVELY מַה טֹּבוּ (Numbers 24:5). These words were uttered by the gentile prophet Balaam, who had been hired to curse Israel; they have the distinction of being the only prayer in the classical siddur attributed to a non-Jew. Balaam's blessing of Israel's dwelling place, together with the verses from Psalms that follow, were seen as appropriate for entering a synagogue, as many rabbinic readings of this verse understood the dwellings of Jacob (literally, "tents of Jacob") and the "sanctuaries of Israel" to be houses of study and of worship.

YOUR HOUSE בֵיתֶךָ (Psalm 5:8). The verse refers to the Temple. The prophet Ezekiel, comforting the exiles in Babylonia, assures them that God is with them in the small sanctuaries of foreign lands. The Sages understood Ezekiel as referring to the synagogue, which they called a מִקְדָּשׁ מְעַט "minor sanctuary." Thus, words originally describing the Temple were also deemed appropriate when applied to the synagogue.

I LOVE YOUR HOUSE אָהַבְתִּי (Psalm 26:8). Here too the original reference was to the Temple, and it was later applied to the synagogue.

FOR MY PRAYER וַאֲנִי תְפִלָּתִי (Psalm 69:14). Perhaps the most primal prayer. May our words be heard and responded to.

PUTTING ON THE TALLIT. The fringes of the *tallit*, the *tzitzit*, as explained in Numbers 15:39–40, serve to remind us of the Torah's mitzvot, and the ideal of holiness to which we are summoned. (*T'fillin* would normally be donned next, but they are not worn on Shabbat and festivals.)

LET ALL MY BEING PRAISE בָּרְכִי נַפְשִׁי. Psalm 104:1–2.

MORNING BLESSINGS

Morning Prayer

The Bible mentions that Abraham rose early in the morning to greet God. The Rabbis envisioned Abraham's act as the model of morning prayer. We follow in Abraham's path.

The Effect of Prayer

Prayer is a way of sensitizing ourselves to the wonder of life, of expressing gratitude, and of praising and acknowledging the reality of God. One need not believe that God will interfere with the ongoing process of nature to feel that prayer is worthwhile. We may have different understandings of what God is. No definition we have is sufficient or answers all doubts and questions. To be aware that God exists—that there is more in the universe than physical matter, that a moral order is inherent in creation, that humans are responsible for their conduct and can help to bring about the perfection, or at least the improvement, of the world and of life—that is sufficient reason for prayer.

—REUVEN HAMMER

Upon entering the synagogue:

How lovely are your dwellings, people of Jacob;
your sanctuaries, people of Israel!
As for me, God,
Your great love inspires me to enter Your house,
to worship in Your holy sanctuary, filled with awe for You.
ADONAI, I love Your house, the place where Your glory dwells.
Before my maker I humbly bow in worship.
May this be an auspicious time, ADONAI, for my prayer.
God, in Your abundant mercy,
answer me with Your faithful deliverance.

Mah-tovu ohalekha ya·akov, mishk'notekha yisra·el.
Va-ani b'rov ḥasd'kha avo veitekha,
eshtaḥaveh el heikhal kodsh'kha b'yir·atekha.
Adonai ahavti m'on beitekha, u-m'kom mishkan k'vodekha.
Va-ani eshtaḥaveh v'ekhra·ah, evr'khah lifnei Adonai osi.
Va-ani t'fillati l'kha, Adonai, eit ratzon.
Elohim b'rov ḥasdekha, aneini be-emet yish·ekha.

Putting on the Tallit

While reciting the meditation and the b'rakhah, it is customary to hold the tallit. After saying the b'rakhah we first wrap the tallit around our head and body, symbolically enclosing ourselves in a sacred garment, and then drape it around our shoulders.

Let all my being praise ADONAI.
ADONAI, my God, You are great indeed:
clothed in splendor and majesty,
wrapped in light as in a garment,
unfolding the heavens like a curtain.

Barukh atah ADONAI, our God, ruler of time and space, who has made us holy through mitzvot and instructed us to wrap ourselves in *tzitzit*.

Barukh atah Adonai eloheinu melekh ha-olam,
asher kid'shanu b'mitzvotav v'tzivvanu l'hit·atteif ba-tzitzit.

Just as I wrap my body in a *tallit*, so may my soul wrap itself in the light of Your Presence.

מַה־יָּקָר חַסְדְּךָ, אֱלֹהִים, וּבְנֵי אָדָם בְּצֵל כְּנָפֶיךָ יֶחֱסָיוּן.
יִרְוְיֻן מִדֶּשֶׁן בֵּיתֶךָ, וְנַחַל עֲדָנֶיךָ תַשְׁקֵם.
כִּי עִמְּךָ מְקוֹר חַיִּים, בְּאוֹרְךָ נִרְאֶה־אוֹר.
מְשֹׁךְ חַסְדְּךָ לְיֹדְעֶיךָ, וְצִדְקָתְךָ לְיִשְׁרֵי־לֵב.

בָּרוּךְ אַתָּה יהוה אֱלֹהֵינוּ מֶלֶךְ הָעוֹלָם, אֲשֶׁר יָצַר אֶת־
הָאָדָם בְּחָכְמָה וּבָרָא בוֹ נְקָבִים נְקָבִים חֲלוּלִים חֲלוּלִים.
גָּלוּי וְיָדוּעַ לִפְנֵי כִסֵּא כְבוֹדֶךָ שֶׁאִם יִפָּתֵחַ אֶחָד מֵהֶם אוֹ
יִסָּתֵם אֶחָד מֵהֶם אִי אֶפְשָׁר לְהִתְקַיֵּם וְלַעֲמֹד לְפָנֶיךָ.
בָּרוּךְ אַתָּה יהוה, רוֹפֵא כָל־בָּשָׂר וּמַפְלִיא לַעֲשׂוֹת.

אֱלֹהַי, נְשָׁמָה שֶׁנָּתַתָּ בִּי טְהוֹרָה הִיא. אַתָּה בְרָאתָהּ,
אַתָּה יְצַרְתָּהּ, אַתָּה נְפַחְתָּהּ בִּי, וְאַתָּה מְשַׁמְּרָהּ בְּקִרְבִּי,
וְאַתָּה עָתִיד לִטְּלָהּ מִמֶּנִּי, וּלְהַחֲזִירָהּ בִּי לֶעָתִיד לָבוֹא.
כָּל־זְמַן שֶׁהַנְּשָׁמָה בְקִרְבִּי, מוֹדֶה/מוֹדָה אֲנִי לְפָנֶיךָ,
יהוה אֱלֹהַי וֵאלֹהֵי אֲבוֹתַי [וְאִמּוֹתַי] רִבּוֹן כָּל־הַמַּעֲשִׂים
אֲדוֹן כָּל־הַנְּשָׁמוֹת. בָּרוּךְ אַתָּה יהוה, הַמַּחֲזִיר נְשָׁמוֹת
לִפְגָרִים מֵתִים.

הֲרֵינִי מְקַבֵּל/מְקַבֶּלֶת עָלַי מִצְוַת הַבּוֹרֵא: וְאָהַבְתָּ לְרֵעֲךָ
כָּמוֹךָ.

בִּרְכוֹת הַתּוֹרָה

בָּרוּךְ אַתָּה יהוה אֱלֹהֵינוּ מֶלֶךְ הָעוֹלָם,
אֲשֶׁר קִדְּשָׁנוּ בְּמִצְוֹתָיו וְצִוָּנוּ לַעֲסוֹק בְּדִבְרֵי תוֹרָה.
וְהַעֲרֶב־נָא יהוה אֱלֹהֵינוּ אֶת־דִּבְרֵי תוֹרָתְךָ בְּפִינוּ וּבְפִי
עַמְּךָ בֵּית יִשְׂרָאֵל, וְנִהְיֶה אֲנַחְנוּ וְצֶאֱצָאֵינוּ וְצֶאֱצָאֵי עַמְּךָ
בֵּית יִשְׂרָאֵל כֻּלָּנוּ יוֹדְעֵי שְׁמֶךָ וְלוֹמְדֵי תוֹרָתֶךָ לִשְׁמָהּ.
בָּרוּךְ אַתָּה יהוה, הַמְלַמֵּד תּוֹרָה לְעַמּוֹ יִשְׂרָאֵל.

HOW PRECIOUS מַה־יָּקָר.
Psalm 38:8–11. These verses
speak of God's protection.
With their recitation, being
enwrapped in the *tallit*
becomes an embodiment
of the metaphor of being
enfolded in God's wings.
The *tallit* thus becomes
symbolic of the Shekhinah,
God's presence.

**WHO FASHIONS THE HU-
MAN BODY WITH WISDOM**
אֲשֶׁר יָצַר אֶת־הָאָדָם בְּחָכְמָה.
This prayer (Babylonian
Talmud, Berakhot 60b) is a
b'rakhah to be recited after
taking care of bodily functions. Even these private
acts become a moment of
marvelling at the miracle
of creation.

**WHO RESTORES THE SOUL
TO THE LIFELESS BODY**
הַמַּחֲזִיר נְשָׁמוֹת לִפְגָרִים
מֵתִים. According to the
Rabbis, sleep is a taste of
death; thus, when we arise
in the morning we recog-
nize the gift of a new day.

LOVE YOUR NEIGHBOR
וְאָהַבְתָּ לְרֵעֲךָ. Leviticus
19:18. Rabbi Isaac Luria
(Safed mystic, 1534–1572)
began each day with this
reminder of the command
to love, believing that
through its fulfillment
redemption would be
achieved.

OUR CHILDREN וְצֶאֱצָאֵינוּ.
Torah is an ongoing pro-
cess of teaching and learning, from one generation to
the next.

How precious is Your constant love, God! Mortals take shelter under Your wings. They feast on the abundance of Your house; You give them drink from Your stream of delights. With You is the fountain of life; in Your light we are bathed in light. Maintain Your constant love for those who know You, and Your righteousness for those who are upright.

THE BODY
Barukh atah ADONAI, our God, ruler of time and space, who fashions the human body with wisdom, creating openings, arteries, glands, and organs, marvelous in structure, intricate in design. It is known and revealed to You that should but one of them fail to function, it would be impossible to exist. *Barukh atah* ADONAI, healer of all flesh, sustaining our bodies in wondrous ways.

THE SOUL
The soul that You, my God, have given me is pure. You created it, You formed it, You breathed it into me; You keep body and soul together. One day You will take my soul from me, to restore it to me in life eternal. So long as this soul is within me I acknowledge You, ADONAI my God, my ancestors' God, master of all creation, sovereign of all souls. *Barukh atah* ADONAI, who restores the soul to the lifeless body.

THE WORLD
I hereby accept the obligation of fulfilling my Creator's mitzvah as written in the Torah: Love your neighbor as yourself.

B'rakhot for the Study of Torah
Barukh atah ADONAI, our God, ruler of time and space, who instills in us the holiness of mitzvot by commanding us to study words of Torah. May the words of Torah, ADONAI our God, be sweet in our mouths and in the mouths of all Your people so that we, our children, and all the children of the House of Israel may come to love You and study Your Torah for its own sake. *Barukh atah* ADONAI, who teaches Torah to Your people Israel.

בָּרוּךְ אַתָּה יהוה אֱלֹהֵינוּ מֶלֶךְ הָעוֹלָם, אֲשֶׁר בָּחַר בָּנוּ מִכָּל־הָעַמִּים וְנָתַן לָנוּ אֶת־תּוֹרָתוֹ. בָּרוּךְ אַתָּה יהוה, נוֹתֵן הַתּוֹרָה.

Passages from the Torah:

יְבָרֶכְךָ יהוה וְיִשְׁמְרֶךָ.

יָאֵר יהוה פָּנָיו אֵלֶיךָ וִיחֻנֶּךָּ.

יִשָּׂא יהוה פָּנָיו אֵלֶיךָ וְיָשֵׂם לְךָ שָׁלוֹם. במדבר ו כד-כו

קְדֹשִׁים תִּהְיוּ כִּי קָדוֹשׁ אֲנִי יהוה אֱלֹהֵיכֶם. לֹא־תְקַלֵּל חֵרֵשׁ, וְלִפְנֵי עִוֵּר לֹא תִתֵּן מִכְשֹׁל. לֹא־תַעֲשׂוּ עָוֶל בַּמִּשְׁפָּט, לֹא־תִשָּׂא פְנֵי־דָל וְלֹא תֶהְדַּר פְּנֵי גָדוֹל, בְּצֶדֶק תִּשְׁפֹּט עֲמִיתֶךָ. לֹא תַעֲמֹד עַל־דַּם רֵעֶךָ. לֹא־תִשְׂנָא אֶת־אָחִיךָ בִּלְבָבֶךָ. וְאָהַבְתָּ לְרֵעֲךָ כָּמוֹךָ, אֲנִי יהוה. ויקרא יט ב, יד-יח

A passage from the Mishnah:

אֵלּוּ דְבָרִים שֶׁאֵין לָהֶם שִׁעוּר: הַפֵּאָה וְהַבִּכּוּרִים וְהָרֵאָיוֹן וּגְמִילוּת חֲסָדִים וְתַלְמוּד תּוֹרָה. משנה פאה א א

A passage from the Gemara:

אֵלּוּ דְבָרִים שֶׁאָדָם אוֹכֵל פֵּרוֹתֵיהֶם בָּעוֹלָם הַזֶּה וְהַקֶּרֶן קַיֶּמֶת לוֹ לָעוֹלָם הַבָּא, וְאֵלּוּ הֵן: כִּבּוּד אָב וָאֵם, וּגְמִילוּת חֲסָדִים, וְהַשְׁכָּמַת בֵּית הַמִּדְרָשׁ שַׁחֲרִית וְעַרְבִית, וְהַכְנָסַת אוֹרְחִים, וּבִקּוּר חוֹלִים, וְהַכְנָסַת כַּלָּה, וּלְוָיַת הַמֵּת, וְעִיּוּן תְּפִלָּה, וַהֲבָאַת שָׁלוֹם בֵּין אָדָם לַחֲבֵרוֹ וּבֵין אִישׁ לְאִשְׁתּוֹ, וְתַלְמוּד תּוֹרָה כְּנֶגֶד כֻּלָּם. תלמוד בבלי, קדושין לט ב

MAY ADONAI BLESS YOU יְבָרֶכְךָ יהוה. The Priestly Blessing (Numbers 6:24–26) and the following passages are recited in order to fulfill the command to study Torah, immediately after reciting the *b'rakhah* for the study of Torah. No longer having Temple priests to bless us each morning, we read this passage as an act of study. Thus study becomes prayer, and prayer, blessing.

BEFORE THE BLIND וְלִפְנֵי עִוֵּר. The Sages took this to mean that we must not deceive anyone who is unaware—blind—regarding what is happening.

THESE ARE THE DEEDS אֵלּוּ דְבָרִים. The list from tractate Kiddushin was expanded through the Middle Ages and several versions of it exist.

AND THE STUDY OF TORAH IS THE MOST BASIC OF THEM ALL וְתַלְמוּד תּוֹרָה כְּנֶגֶד כֻּלָּם. Studying Torah provides the basis for all of these actions. In a discussion of the relative importance of Torah and deeds, the Rabbis came to the conclusion that Torah is more important because it leads to proper actions (Babylonian Talmud, Kiddushin 39b).

Torah

The word "Torah" means "teaching." It came to refer to the Five Books of Moses—the central teaching of Judaism—and its primary association is with the scroll of the Five Books that is placed in the ark at the front of the synagogue. In traditional Jewish thought "Torah" has a wider meaning, including the teaching of the later Rabbis down to the present day. Thus the Talmud speaks of both the Written Torah and the Oral Torah, the former referring to the Five Books, the latter to the interpretive teachings that grew in association with it. In one formulation the Rabbis said that all interpretations of Torah emanate from Sinai. In the blessing just before the Sh'ma that we recite later in the service, Torah is referred to as "the laws of life." Thus in this wider sense all teaching about the life of holiness, all understandings of God, all insight into life, all truths that we can know, are aspects of Torah.

Barukh atah ADONAI, our God, ruler of time and space, who has chosen us from among all peoples, giving us the Torah. *Barukh atah* ADONAI, who gives the Torah.

Passages from the Torah:

May ADONAI bless and protect you.
May ADONAI's countenance shine upon you
    and grant you kindness.
May ADONAI's countenance be lifted toward you
    and grant you peace. Numbers 6:24–26

You shall be holy for I, ADONAI your God, am holy. You shall not insult the deaf, nor put a stumbling block before the blind. You shall not render an unjust decision: do not be partial to the poor nor show deference to the rich. Judge your neighbor fairly. Do not stand idly by the blood of your neighbor. You shall not hate your brother in your heart. Love your neighbor as yourself; I am ADONAI. Leviticus 19:2, 14–18

A passage from the Mishnah:

These are the deeds for which there is no prescribed measure: leaving crops at the corner of a field for the poor, offering first fruits as a gift to the Temple, bringing special offerings to the Temple on the three Festivals, doing deeds of lovingkindness, and studying Torah. Mishnah Peah 1:1

A passage from the Gemara:

These are the deeds that yield immediate fruit and continue to yield fruit in time to come: honoring parents; doing deeds of lovingkindness; attending the house of study punctually, morning and evening; providing hospitality; visiting the sick; helping the needy bride; attending the dead; probing the meaning of prayer; making peace between one person and another, and between husband and wife. And the study of Torah is the most basic of them all. Babylonian Talmud, Kiddushin 39b

בָּרוּךְ אַתָּה יהוה אֱלֹהֵינוּ מֶלֶךְ הָעוֹלָם,

אֲשֶׁר נָתַן לַשֶּׂכְוִי בִינָה לְהַבְחִין בֵּין יוֹם וּבֵין לָיְלָה.

בָּרוּךְ אַתָּה יהוה אֱלֹהֵינוּ מֶלֶךְ הָעוֹלָם, שֶׁעָשַׂנִי בְּצַלְמוֹ.

בָּרוּךְ אַתָּה יהוה אֱלֹהֵינוּ מֶלֶךְ הָעוֹלָם, שֶׁעָשַׂנִי יִשְׂרָאֵל.

בָּרוּךְ אַתָּה יהוה אֱלֹהֵינוּ מֶלֶךְ הָעוֹלָם,

שֶׁעָשַׂנִי בֶּן/בַּת־חוֹרִין.

בָּרוּךְ אַתָּה יהוה אֱלֹהֵינוּ מֶלֶךְ הָעוֹלָם, פּוֹקֵחַ עִוְרִים.

בָּרוּךְ אַתָּה יהוה אֱלֹהֵינוּ מֶלֶךְ הָעוֹלָם, מַלְבִּישׁ עֲרֻמִּים.

בָּרוּךְ אַתָּה יהוה אֱלֹהֵינוּ מֶלֶךְ הָעוֹלָם, מַתִּיר אֲסוּרִים.

בָּרוּךְ אַתָּה יהוה אֱלֹהֵינוּ מֶלֶךְ הָעוֹלָם, זוֹקֵף כְּפוּפִים.

בָּרוּךְ אַתָּה יהוה אֱלֹהֵינוּ מֶלֶךְ הָעוֹלָם,

רוֹקַע הָאָרֶץ עַל הַמָּיִם.

בָּרוּךְ אַתָּה יהוה אֱלֹהֵינוּ מֶלֶךְ הָעוֹלָם,

שֶׁעָשָׂה לִי כָּל־צָרְכִּי.

בָּרוּךְ אַתָּה יהוה אֱלֹהֵינוּ מֶלֶךְ הָעוֹלָם,

הַמֵּכִין מִצְעֲדֵי־גָבֶר.

בָּרוּךְ אַתָּה יהוה אֱלֹהֵינוּ מֶלֶךְ הָעוֹלָם,

אוֹזֵר יִשְׂרָאֵל בִּגְבוּרָה.

בָּרוּךְ אַתָּה יהוה אֱלֹהֵינוּ מֶלֶךְ הָעוֹלָם,

עוֹטֵר יִשְׂרָאֵל בְּתִפְאָרָה.

בָּרוּךְ אַתָּה יהוה אֱלֹהֵינוּ מֶלֶךְ הָעוֹלָם, הַנּוֹתֵן לַיָּעֵף כֹּחַ.

BLESSINGS UPON ARISING בְּרְכוֹת הַשַּׁחַר. The *b'rakhot* in this collection were originally recited upon arising in the morning, as one went through the daily acts of awaking and rising. Each passage extols God as we begin the day: on arising from sleep, on noticing the daylight, on dressing, on taking one's first steps, and so on. Maimonides stated: "These *b'rakhot* are without a prescribed order; each is to be recited only on the appropriate occasion, and not as part of the synagogue service." Other authorities, however, beginning with the siddur of Rabbi Amram Gaon in the 9th century, recommended the public recitation of these *b'rakhot*. This has been the standard Ashkenazic practice to this day. Some other communities recite these *b'rakhot* only privately.

WHO GIVES SIGHT TO THE BLIND פּוֹקֵחַ עִוְרִים. Said when opening the eyes. Many of these blessings are taken from the psalmist's descriptions of God's actions: "… sets prisoners free … restores sight to the blind … makes those who are bent stand straight …" (Psalm 146:7–8).

WHO CLOTHES THE NAKED מַלְבִּישׁ עֲרֻמִּים. Said when dressing. God's clothing of Adam and Eve (Genesis 3:21) was an act of kindness. Isaiah mentions clothing the naked as one of the moral actions that God expects of us, along with feeding the hungry and providing for the homeless (Isaiah 58:7).

WHO RELEASES THE BOUND מַתִּיר אֲסוּרִים. Releasing the fetters of wickedness and letting the oppressed go free are also mentioned by Isaiah (58:6).

WHO STRAIGHTENS THOSE WHO ARE BENT DOWN זוֹקֵף כְּפוּפִים. Literally, "making those who are bowed down stand upright." This phrase, as found in Psalm 146:8, is the biblical warrant for standing straight after bowing when God's name is pronounced in the Amidah.

WHO STRETCHES OUT THE DRY EARTH OVER THE WATERS רוֹקַע הָאָרֶץ עַל הַמָּיִם. Literally, "spreading the earth over the waters" (Psalm 136:6).

A Morning Prayer

Master of the Universe, grant me the ability to be alone;

may it be my custom to go outdoors each day among the trees and grass, among all growing things

and there may I be alone, and enter into prayer, to talk with the One to whom I belong.

May I express there everything in my heart, and may all the foliage of the field (all grasses, trees, and plants) awake at my coming,

to send the powers of their life into the words of my prayer so that my prayer and my speech are made whole

through the life and spirit of all growing things, which are made as one by their transcendent Source.

—NAHMAN OF BRATZLAV

Blessings Upon Arising

Barukh atah ADONAI, our God, ruler of time and space,

who enables us to distinguish day from night,

who made me in the divine image,

who made me a Jew,

who made me free,

who gives sight to the blind,

who clothes the naked,

who releases the bound,

who straightens those who are bent down,

who stretches out the dry earth over the waters,

who has provided for all my needs,

who steadies our steps,

who strengthens the people Israel with courage,

who crowns the people Israel with glory,

who gives strength to the weary.

בָּרוּךְ אַתָּה יהוה אֱלֹהֵינוּ מֶלֶךְ הָעוֹלָם, הַמַּעֲבִיר שֵׁנָה
מֵעֵינָי וּתְנוּמָה מֵעַפְעַפָּי. וִיהִי רָצוֹן מִלְּפָנֶיךָ יהוה
אֱלֹהֵינוּ וֵאלֹהֵי אֲבוֹתֵינוּ [וְאִמּוֹתֵינוּ], שֶׁתַּרְגִּילֵנוּ בְּתוֹרָתֶךָ
וְדַבְּקֵנוּ בְּמִצְוֹתֶיךָ, וְאַל תְּבִיאֵנוּ לֹא לִידֵי חֵטְא, וְלֹא
לִידֵי עֲבֵרָה וְעָוֹן, וְלֹא לִידֵי נִסָּיוֹן, וְלֹא לִידֵי בִזָּיוֹן, וְאַל
תַּשְׁלֶט־בָּנוּ יֵצֶר הָרָע, וְהַרְחִיקֵנוּ מֵאָדָם רָע וּמֵחָבֵר רָע.
וְדַבְּקֵנוּ בְּיֵצֶר הַטּוֹב וּבְמַעֲשִׂים טוֹבִים, וְכוֹף אֶת־יִצְרֵנוּ
לְהִשְׁתַּעְבֶּד־לָךְ. ◁ וּתְנֵנוּ הַיּוֹם וּבְכָל־יוֹם לְחֵן וּלְחֶסֶד
וּלְרַחֲמִים בְּעֵינֶיךָ וּבְעֵינֵי כָל־רוֹאֵינוּ, וְתִגְמְלֵנוּ חֲסָדִים
טוֹבִים. בָּרוּךְ אַתָּה יהוה, גּוֹמֵל חֲסָדִים טוֹבִים לְעַמּוֹ
יִשְׂרָאֵל.

יְהִי רָצוֹן מִלְּפָנֶיךָ, יהוה אֱלֹהַי וֵאלֹהֵי אֲבוֹתַי [וְאִמּוֹתַי],
שֶׁתַּצִּילֵנִי הַיּוֹם וּבְכָל־יוֹם מֵעַזֵּי פָנִים וּמֵעַזּוּת פָּנִים,
מֵאָדָם רָע וּמֵחָבֵר רָע, וּמִשָּׁכֵן רָע וּמִפֶּגַע רָע וּמִשָּׂטָן
הַמַּשְׁחִית, מִדִּין קָשֶׁה וּמִבַּעַל דִּין קָשֶׁה, בֵּין שֶׁהוּא בֶן־
בְּרִית, וּבֵין שֶׁאֵינוֹ בֶן־בְּרִית.

לְעוֹלָם יְהֵא אָדָם יְרֵא שָׁמַיִם בַּסֵּתֶר וּבַגָּלוּי,
וּמוֹדֶה עַל הָאֱמֶת וְדוֹבֵר אֱמֶת בִּלְבָבוֹ, וְיַשְׁכֵּם וְיֹאמַר:

רִבּוֹן כָּל־הָעוֹלָמִים, לֹא עַל צִדְקוֹתֵינוּ, אֲנַחְנוּ מַפִּילִים
תַּחֲנוּנֵינוּ לְפָנֶיךָ, כִּי עַל רַחֲמֶיךָ הָרַבִּים. מָה אֲנַחְנוּ, מֶה
חַיֵּינוּ, מֶה חַסְדֵּנוּ, מַה־צִּדְקֵנוּ, מַה־יְשׁוּעֵנוּ, מַה־כֹּחֵנוּ,
מַה־גְּבוּרָתֵנוּ. מַה־נֹּאמַר לְפָנֶיךָ, יהוה אֱלֹהֵינוּ וֵאלֹהֵי
אֲבוֹתֵינוּ [וְאִמּוֹתֵינוּ], הֲלֹא כָּל־הַגִּבּוֹרִים כְּאַיִן לְפָנֶיךָ,
וְאַנְשֵׁי הַשֵּׁם כְּלֹא הָיוּ, וַחֲכָמִים כִּבְלִי מַדָּע, וּנְבוֹנִים כִּבְלִי
הַשְׂכֵּל, כִּי כָל־מַעֲשֵׂינוּ תֹהוּ, וִימֵי חַיֵּינוּ הֶבֶל לְפָנֶיךָ.
וּמוֹתַר הָאָדָם מִן הַבְּהֵמָה אָיִן, כִּי הַכֹּל הָבֶל.

אֲבָל אֲנַחְנוּ עַמְּךָ בְּנֵי בְרִיתֶךָ, בְּנֵי אַבְרָהָם אֹהַבְךָ
שֶׁנִּשְׁבַּעְתָּ לּוֹ בְּהַר הַמּוֹרִיָּה, זֶרַע יִצְחָק יְחִידוֹ, שֶׁנֶּעֱקַד
עַל גַּבֵּי הַמִּזְבֵּחַ, עֲדַת יַעֲקֹב בִּנְךָ בְּכוֹרֶךָ שֶׁמֵּאַהֲבָתְךָ
שֶׁאָהַבְתָּ אוֹתוֹ וּמִשִּׂמְחָתְךָ שֶׁשָּׂמַחְתָּ בּוֹ קָרָאתָ אֶת־
שְׁמוֹ יִשְׂרָאֵל וִישֻׁרוּן.

MAY IT BE YOUR WILL יְהִי רָצוֹן. This prayer was recited by Rabbi Yehudah Ha-Nasi, the editor of the Mishnah, as a private meditation when completing the Amidah (Babylonian Talmud, Berakhot 16b).

AND FROM ARROGANCE IN MYSELF וּמֵעַזּוּת פָּנִים. We should not ourselves exhibit that behavior which we do not want to suffer from others.

WE SHOULD ALWAYS REVERE GOD לְעוֹלָם יְהֵא אָדָם יְרֵא שָׁמַיִם. This brief meditation, advising us that our inward stance should accord with our outward acts, precedes another personal prayer. This passage from the 10th-century text Tanna D'vei Eliyahu 19 incorporates various earlier rabbinic sources.

NOT UPON OUR MERIT לֹא עַל צִדְקוֹתֵינוּ. Parts of this prayer were originally written for the Yom Kippur service (Babylonian Talmud, Yoma 87b) and will be recited in Ne·ilah. The Talmud recommends it as constituting the essence of confession.

WHOM YOU NAMED ISRAEL קָרָאתָ אֶת־שְׁמוֹ יִשְׂרָאֵל. Jacob was the first person in the Bible to have God's name intertwined with his own.

AND JESHURUN וִישֻׁרוּן. Another name for the people Israel (Deuteronomy 32:15, Isaiah 44:2).

You should act in prayer as if you were a farmer: first you plow, then you seed, afterward you water, and finally things begin to grow. In prayer, first you have to dig deeply to open your heart, then you place the words of prayer in your heart, then you allow your heart to cry. That's how salvation grows.

—THE ḤASIDIC MASTER ABRAHAM OF SLONIM

Barukh atah ADONAI, our God, ruler of time and space, who removes sleep from my eyes and slumber from my eyelids. May we feel at home with Your Torah and cling to Your mitzvot. Keep us from error, from sin and transgression. Bring us not to trial or to disgrace; let our evil impulse not control us. Keep us far from wicked people and corrupt companions. Strengthen our impulse to do good deeds; and subdue our will, that we may serve You. May we find grace, love, and compassion in Your sight and in the sight of all who look upon us, this day and every day. Grant us a full measure of lovingkindness. *Barukh atah* ADONAI, who bestows lovingkindness upon the people Israel.

Morning Meditations

May it be Your will, ADONAI my God and God of my ancestors, to protect me, this day and every day, from insolence in others and from arrogance in myself. Save me from vicious people, from evil neighbors, and from corrupt companions. Preserve me from misfortune and from powers of destruction. Save me from harsh judgments; spare me from ruthless opponents, whether they are members of the covenant or not.

We should always revere God, in private as in public. We should acknowledge the truth in our hearts, and practice it in thought as in deed. On arising one should declare:

Master of all worlds! Not upon our merit do we rely in our supplication, but upon Your limitless love. What are we? What is our life? What is our piety? What is our righteousness? What is our attainment, our power, our might? What can we say, ADONAI our God and God of our ancestors? Compared to You, all the powerful are nothing; the famous, insignificant; the wise lack wisdom, and the clever lack reason. In Your sight, all that we do is meaningless, the days of our lives empty. Human preeminence over beasts is an illusion, for all is futile.

But we are Your people, partners to Your covenant, descendants of Your beloved Abraham to whom You made a pledge on Mount Moriah. We are the heirs of Isaac, his son bound upon the altar. We are Your firstborn people, the congregation of Isaac's son Jacob, whom You named Israel and Jeshurun because of Your love for him and Your delight in him.

לְפִיכָךְ אֲנַחְנוּ חַיָּבִים לְהוֹדוֹת לְךָ וּלְשַׁבֵּחֲךָ וּלְפָאֶרְךָ וּלְבָרֵךְ וּלְקַדֵּשׁ וְלָתֵת שֶׁבַח וְהוֹדָיָה לִשְׁמֶךָ.

◁ אַשְׁרֵינוּ, מַה־טּוֹב חֶלְקֵנוּ וּמַה־נָּעִים גּוֹרָלֵנוּ וּמַה־יָּפָה יְרֻשָּׁתֵנוּ. אַשְׁרֵינוּ שֶׁאֲנַחְנוּ מַשְׁכִּימִים וּמַעֲרִיבִים עֶרֶב וָבֹקֶר, וְאוֹמְרִים פַּעֲמַיִם בְּכָל־יוֹם:

שְׁמַע יִשְׂרָאֵל יהוה אֱלֹהֵינוּ יהוה אֶחָד.

On Yom Kippur the following is recited aloud;
on Rosh Hashanah it is recited quietly:

בָּרוּךְ שֵׁם כְּבוֹד מַלְכוּתוֹ לְעוֹלָם וָעֶד.

אַתָּה הוּא עַד שֶׁלֹּא נִבְרָא הָעוֹלָם,
אַתָּה הוּא מִשֶּׁנִּבְרָא הָעוֹלָם,
אַתָּה הוּא בָּעוֹלָם הַזֶּה,
וְאַתָּה הוּא לָעוֹלָם הַבָּא.
◁ קַדֵּשׁ אֶת־שִׁמְךָ עַל מַקְדִּישֵׁי שְׁמֶךָ,
וְקַדֵּשׁ אֶת־שִׁמְךָ בְּעוֹלָמֶךָ.
וּבִישׁוּעָתְךָ תָּרִים וְתַגְבִּיהַּ קַרְנֵנוּ.
בָּרוּךְ אַתָּה יהוה, מְקַדֵּשׁ אֶת־שִׁמְךָ בָּרַבִּים.

אַתָּה הוּא יהוה אֱלֹהֵינוּ בַּשָּׁמַיִם וּבָאָרֶץ, וּבִשְׁמֵי הַשָּׁמַיִם הָעֶלְיוֹנִים. אֱמֶת, אַתָּה הוּא רִאשׁוֹן וְאַתָּה הוּא אַחֲרוֹן וּמִבַּלְעָדֶיךָ אֵין אֱלֹהִים. קַבֵּץ קוֹיֶךָ מֵאַרְבַּע כַּנְפוֹת הָאָרֶץ. יַכִּירוּ וְיֵדְעוּ כָּל־בָּאֵי עוֹלָם כִּי אַתָּה הוּא הָאֱלֹהִים לְבַדְּךָ לְכֹל מַמְלְכוֹת הָאָרֶץ. אַתָּה עָשִׂיתָ אֶת־הַשָּׁמַיִם וְאֶת־הָאָרֶץ, אֶת־הַיָּם וְאֶת־כָּל־אֲשֶׁר בָּם, וּמִי בְּכָל־מַעֲשֵׂה יָדֶיךָ בָּעֶלְיוֹנִים אוֹ בַתַּחְתּוֹנִים שֶׁיֹּאמַר לְךָ מַה תַּעֲשֶׂה. אָבִינוּ שֶׁבַּשָּׁמַיִם, עֲשֵׂה עִמָּנוּ חֶסֶד בַּעֲבוּר שִׁמְךָ הַגָּדוֹל שֶׁנִּקְרָא עָלֵינוּ, וְקַיֶּם־לָנוּ, יהוה אֱלֹהֵינוּ, מַה שֶּׁכָּתוּב: בָּעֵת הַהִיא אָבִיא אֶתְכֶם, וּבָעֵת קַבְּצִי אֶתְכֶם, כִּי אֶתֵּן אֶתְכֶם לְשֵׁם וְלִתְהִלָּה בְּכֹל עַמֵּי הָאָרֶץ, בְּשׁוּבִי אֶת־שְׁבוּתֵיכֶם לְעֵינֵיכֶם, אָמַר יהוה.

HEAR, O ISRAEL שְׁמַע יִשְׂרָאֵל. Perhaps this line was inserted here so that we would fulfill our obligation of reciting the Sh'ma early enough in the day, as it is written: "when you lie down and when you rise up" (Deuteronomy 6:7). In an earlier age, this was recited at home.

YOU ARE אַתָּה הוּא. This emphatic phrase, literally "You are the One who . . . ," appears four times in this paragraph and three more in the next paragraph—a total of seven times. Given that the number seven has mystical significance, this sevenfold refrain may have served originally as a meditational exercise.

BEFORE CREATION עַד שֶׁלֹּא נִבְרָא הָעוֹלָם. Two pairs of periods are mentioned: before and after creation; this world and the next. Collectively, the enumeration emphasizes that God is beyond time.

TRULY YOU ARE FIRST, אֱמֶת, אַתָּה הוּא רִאשׁוֹן. The words come from Isaiah 44:6, where God proclaims God's own eternity.

A TIME WILL COME בָּעֵת הַהִיא. Zephaniah 3:20.

Therefore it is our duty to thank You and praise You, to glorify and sanctify Your name. How good is our portion, how pleasant our lot, how beautiful our heritage! How blessed are we that twice each day, morning and evening, we are privileged to declare:

Hear, O Israel, ADONAI is our God, ADONAI alone.
Sh'ma yisra·el Adonai eloheinu Adonai eḥad.

On Yom Kippur the following is recited aloud;
on Rosh Hashanah it is recited quietly:
Praised be the name of the One whose glorious sovereignty
is forever and ever.
Barukh shem k'vod malkhuto l'olam va·ed.

You are eternal, before creation and since creation,
in this world and in the world to come.
Manifest Your holiness through those who hallow You,
raising us to dignity and strength.
Barukh atah ADONAI, who manifests Your holiness to all.

You are ADONAI our God on earth and in all the spheres of heaven. Truly You are first and You are last; there is no God but You. From the four corners of the earth, gather those who hope in You under Your protecting presence. All who dwell on earth will acknowledge You alone as God over all the kingdoms of the world. You made the heavens, earth, and sea, and all that they contain. Who among all of Your creatures, in the heavens or on earth, can question You? Our guardian in heaven, be merciful to us for we bear Your great name. Fulfill the prophetic promise: "'A time will come when I will gather you in, a time when I will bring you home. Renown and praise shall be yours among all the peoples of the earth. This you yourself will see as I bring your captives back home,' says ADONAI."

Devotional Rabbinic Texts

On Rosh Hashanah:

לְפִיכָךְ נִבְרָא אָדָם יְחִידִי, לְלַמֶּדְךָ שֶׁכָּל־הַמְאַבֵּד נֶפֶשׁ
אַחַת מַעֲלֶה עָלָיו הַכָּתוּב כְּאִלּוּ אִבֵּד עוֹלָם מָלֵא, וְכָל־
הַמְקַיֵּם נֶפֶשׁ אַחַת מַעֲלֶה עָלָיו הַכָּתוּב כְּאִלּוּ קִיֵּם עוֹלָם
מָלֵא. וּמִפְּנֵי שְׁלוֹם הַבְּרִיּוֹת, שֶׁלֹּא יֹאמַר אָדָם לַחֲבֵרוֹ:
אַבָּא גָדוֹל מֵאָבִיךָ. וְשֶׁלֹּא יְהוּ הַמִּינִין אוֹמְרִים: הַרְבֵּה
רְשֻׁיּוֹת בַּשָּׁמָיִם. וּלְהַגִּיד גְּדֻלָּתוֹ שֶׁלְּהַקָּדוֹשׁ בָּרוּךְ הוּא.
שֶׁאָדָם טוֹבֵעַ כַּמָּה מַטְבְּעוֹת בְּחוֹתָם אֶחָד וְכֻלָּן דּוֹמִין
זֶה לָזֶה, וּמֶלֶךְ מַלְכֵי הַמְּלָכִים הַקָּדוֹשׁ בָּרוּךְ הוּא טָבַע
כָּל־הָאָדָם בְּחוֹתָמוֹ שֶׁלְאָדָם הָרִאשׁוֹן וְאֵין אֶחָד מֵהֶן
דּוֹמֶה לַחֲבֵרוֹ. לְפִיכָךְ כָּל־אֶחָד וְאֶחָד חַיָּב לוֹמַר: בִּשְׁבִילִי
נִבְרָא הָעוֹלָם. משנה סנהדרין ד ה

On Yom Kippur:

הָאוֹמֵר: אֶחֱטָא וְאָשׁוּב אֶחֱטָא וְאָשׁוּב, אֵין מַסְפִּיקִין
בְּיָדוֹ לַעֲשׂוֹת תְּשׁוּבָה. אֶחֱטָא וְיוֹם הַכִּפּוּרִים מְכַפֵּר, אֵין
יוֹם הַכִּפּוּרִים מְכַפֵּר. עֲבֵרוֹת שֶׁבֵּין אָדָם לַמָּקוֹם,
יוֹם הַכִּפּוּרִים מְכַפֵּר. עֲבֵרוֹת שֶׁבֵּין אָדָם לַחֲבֵרוֹ, אֵין
יוֹם הַכִּפּוּרִים מְכַפֵּר עַד שֶׁיְרַצֶּה אֶת־חֲבֵרוֹ. אֶת־זוֹ דָּרַשׁ
רַבִּי אֶלְעָזָר בֶּן־עֲזַרְיָה: מִכֹּל חַטֹּאתֵיכֶם לִפְנֵי יְהוָה
תִּטְהָרוּ (ויקרא טז ל). עֲבֵרוֹת שֶׁבֵּין אָדָם לַמָּקוֹם, יוֹם
הַכִּפּוּרִים מְכַפֵּר. עֲבֵרוֹת שֶׁבֵּין אָדָם לַחֲבֵרוֹ, אֵין יוֹם
הַכִּפּוּרִים מְכַפֵּר עַד שֶׁיְרַצֶּה אֶת־חֲבֵרוֹ. משנה יומא ח ט

Conclude with one of the following meditations:

◁ יְהִי רָצוֹן מִלְּפָנֶיךָ יְהוָה אֱלֹהֵינוּ וֵאלֹהֵי אֲבוֹתֵינוּ
[וְאִמּוֹתֵינוּ], שֶׁתִּתֵּן חֶלְקֵנוּ בְּתוֹרָתֶךָ, וְנִהְיֶה מִתַּלְמִידָיו
שֶׁל אַהֲרֹן הַכֹּהֵן, אוֹהֵב שָׁלוֹם וְרוֹדֵף שָׁלוֹם, אוֹהֵב אֶת־
הַבְּרִיּוֹת וּמְקָרְבָן לַתּוֹרָה.

◁ יְהִי רָצוֹן מִלְּפָנֶיךָ יְהוָה אֱלֹהֵינוּ וֵאלֹהֵי אֲבוֹתֵינוּ
[וְאִמּוֹתֵינוּ], שֶׁיִּבָּנֶה בֵּית הַמִּקְדָּשׁ בִּמְהֵרָה בְיָמֵינוּ וְתֵן
חֶלְקֵנוּ בְּתוֹרָתֶךָ. וְשָׁם נַעֲבָדְךָ בְּיִרְאָה כִּימֵי עוֹלָם
וּכְשָׁנִים קַדְמֹנִיּוֹת.

Devotional Rabbinic Texts

On Rosh Hashanah:

The Bible relates that God created Adam, a single human being, as the ancestor of all humanity. This teaches us that to destroy a single life is to destroy a whole world, even as to save a single life is to save a whole world. That all people have a common ancestor should make for peace, since no one can say to anyone else: "My ancestor was greater than your ancestor." That humanity began with a single human being is an answer to heretics who could claim the existence of more than one Creator. That humanity began with a single human being proclaims forever the greatness of the Holy One. For humans stamp many coins with one die and they all look alike, but the Holy One stamped every human being with the die of Adam, yet no person is like any other. Therefore, every human being must declare, "It is for my sake that the world was created." Mishnah Sanhedrin 4:5

On Yom Kippur:

Whoever says, "I shall sin and repent, and sin again and repent," will have no opportunity to repent. Whoever says, "I shall sin and gain atonement through Yom Kippur," will gain no atonement through Yom Kippur. Yom Kippur brings atonement only for transgressions between people and God. Atonement for transgressions between one person and another can be gained only when the wrong has been righted and the offended person has been reconciled. "For on this day, atonement shall be made for you to purify you from all your transgressions. In the presence of ADONAI you shall be pure" [Leviticus 16:30]. Rabbi Elazar ben Azariah has expounded this verse in the following way: Yom Kippur brings atonement for transgressions between people and God [i.e., "before ADONAI"], but Yom Kippur can bring atonement for transgressions between one person and another only if the person offended has first been reconciled. Mishnah Yoma 8:9

Conclude with one of the following meditations:

May it be Your will, ADONAI our God and God of our ancestors, to grant our portion in Your Torah. May we be disciples of Aaron the *kohen*, loving peace and pursuing peace, loving our fellow creatures and drawing them near to the Torah.

May it be Your will, ADONAI our God and God of our ancestors, that the Temple be restored in our day, and grant us a portion among those devoted to Your Torah. May we be privileged to worship You there, in splendor and in awe, as in ancient days.

קַדִּישׁ דְּרַבָּנָן

יִתְגַּדַּל וְיִתְקַדַּשׁ שְׁמֵהּ רַבָּא, בְּעָלְמָא דִּי בְרָא, כִּרְעוּתֵהּ,
וְיַמְלִיךְ מַלְכוּתֵהּ בְּחַיֵּיכוֹן וּבְיוֹמֵיכוֹן וּבְחַיֵּי דְכָל־בֵּית
יִשְׂרָאֵל, בַּעֲגָלָא וּבִזְמַן קָרִיב, וְאִמְרוּ אָמֵן.

יְהֵא שְׁמֵהּ רַבָּא מְבָרַךְ לְעָלַם וּלְעָלְמֵי עָלְמַיָּא.

יִתְבָּרַךְ וְיִשְׁתַּבַּח וְיִתְפָּאַר וְיִתְרוֹמַם וְיִתְנַשֵּׂא וְיִתְהַדָּר
וְיִתְעַלֶּה וְיִתְהַלָּל שְׁמֵהּ דְּקֻדְשָׁא, **בְּרִיךְ הוּא,** לְעֵלָּא לְעֵלָּא
מִכָּל־בִּרְכָתָא וְשִׁירָתָא תֻּשְׁבְּחָתָא וְנֶחֱמָתָא דַּאֲמִירָן
בְּעָלְמָא, וְאִמְרוּ אָמֵן.

עַל יִשְׂרָאֵל וְעַל רַבָּנָן וְעַל תַּלְמִידֵיהוֹן, וְעַל כָּל־תַּלְמִידֵי
תַלְמִידֵיהוֹן, וְעַל כָּל־מָאן דְּעָסְקִין בְּאוֹרַיְתָא, דִּי בְאַתְרָא
הָדֵין וְדִי בְכָל־אֲתַר וַאֲתַר, יְהֵא לְהוֹן וּלְכוֹן שְׁלָמָא רַבָּא,
חִנָּא וְחִסְדָּא וְרַחֲמִין, וְחַיִּין אֲרִיכִין, וּמְזוֹנָא רְוִיחָא,
וּפֻרְקָנָא מִן קֳדָם אֲבוּהוֹן דִּי בִשְׁמַיָּא, וְאִמְרוּ אָמֵן.

יְהֵא שְׁלָמָא רַבָּא מִן שְׁמַיָּא וְחַיִּים טוֹבִים עָלֵינוּ וְעַל
כָּל־יִשְׂרָאֵל, וְאִמְרוּ אָמֵן.

עֹשֶׂה שָׁלוֹם בִּמְרוֹמָיו, הוּא בְּרַחֲמָיו יַעֲשֶׂה שָׁלוֹם עָלֵינוּ
וְעַל כָּל־יִשְׂרָאֵל [וְעַל כָּל־יוֹשְׁבֵי תֵבֵל], וְאִמְרוּ
אָמֵן.

KADDISH D'RABBANAN.
The Kaddish is an ancient prayer written in Aramaic, a sister-language of Hebrew and a spoken language of the Jewish people during the period of the Second Temple and for many centuries thereafter. (For more on the Kaddish, see p. 26.) The Kaddish D'rabbanan, recited after the study of rabbinic texts, contains a special prayer for the well-being of teachers, their disciples, and all who study Torah.

MOVEMENT AT THE END OF KADDISH. Before reciting the last line of the Kaddish, it is customary to take three steps backward. Bow to the left at the word *oseh*, to the right at *hu*, and to the center at *aleinu*. These actions, taken from court etiquette, heighten our awareness of standing in the presence of God.

Kaddish D'rabbanan

May God's great name be exalted and hallowed throughout the created world, as is God's wish. May God's sovereignty soon be established, in your lifetime and in your days, and in the days of all the House of Israel. And respond with: *Amen.*

May God's great name be acknowledged forever and ever!

May the name of the Holy One be acknowledged and celebrated, lauded and worshipped, exalted and honored, extolled and acclaimed—though God, who is blessed, *b'rikh hu,* is truly far beyond all acknowledgment and praise, or any expressions of gratitude or consolation ever spoken in the world. And respond with: *Amen.*

Grant lasting peace, God, to our people and their leaders, to our teachers and their disciples, and to all who engage in the study of Torah in this land and in all other lands. Let there be grace and kindness, compassion and love, for them and for us all. Grant us fullness of life and sustenance. Save us from all danger and distress. And respond with: *Amen.*

May abundant peace from heaven, and a good life, come to us and to all Israel. And respond with: *Amen.*

May the One who brings harmony on high, mercifully bring harmony to us and to all Israel [and to all who dwell on earth]. And respond with: *Amen.*

Yitgaddal v'yitkaddash sh'meih rabba, b'alma di v'ra, ki-r'uteih,
v'yamlikh malkhuteih b'ḥayyeikhon u-v'yomeikhon u-v'ḥayyei d'khol beit yisra·el
ba-agala u-viz'man kariv, v'imru amen.

Y'hei sh'meih rabba m'varakh l'alam u-l'almei almayya.

Yitbarakh v'yishtabbaḥ v'yitpa·ar v'yitromam v'yitnassei v'yit·haddar v'yit·alleh
v'yit·hallal sh'meih d'kudsha, b'rikh hu, l'eilla l'eilla mi-kol birkhata v'shirata
tushb'ḥata v'neḥamata da-amiran b'alma, v'imru amen.

Al yisra·el v'al rabbanan v'al talmideihon, v'al kol talmidei talmideihon,
v'al kol man d'as'kin b'oraita, di v'atra hadein v'di v'khol atar va-atar,
y'hei l'hon u-l'khon sh'lama rabba, ḥinna v'ḥisda v'raḥamin, v'ḥayyin arikhin
u-m'zona r'viḥa, u-furkana min kodam avuhon di vi-sh'mayya, v'imru amen.

Y'hei sh'lama rabba min sh'mayya
v'ḥayyim tovim aleinu v'al kol yisra·el, v'imru amen.

Oseh shalom bi-m'romav, hu b'raḥamav ya·aseh shalom
aleinu v'al kol yisra·el [v'al kol yosh'vei teiveil], v'imru amen.

הַיּוֹם רֹאשׁ הַשָּׁנָה, שֶׁבּוֹ אוֹמְרִים:

לַמְנַצֵּחַ עַל־הַגִּתִּית מִזְמוֹר לְדָוִד.

יהוה אֲדֹנֵינוּ מָה־אַדִּיר שִׁמְךָ בְּכָל־הָאָרֶץ
אֲשֶׁר תְּנָה הוֹדְךָ עַל־הַשָּׁמָיִם.
מִפִּי עוֹלְלִים וְיֹנְקִים יִסַּדְתָּ עֹז לְמַעַן צוֹרְרֶיךָ
לְהַשְׁבִּית אוֹיֵב וּמִתְנַקֵּם.
כִּי־אֶרְאֶה שָׁמֶיךָ, מַעֲשֵׂה אֶצְבְּעֹתֶיךָ
יָרֵחַ וְכוֹכָבִים אֲשֶׁר כּוֹנָנְתָּה.
מָה־אֱנוֹשׁ כִּי־תִזְכְּרֶנּוּ
וּבֶן־אָדָם כִּי תִפְקְדֶנּוּ.
וַתְּחַסְּרֵהוּ מְּעַט מֵאֱלֹהִים
וְכָבוֹד וְהָדָר תְּעַטְּרֵהוּ.
תַּמְשִׁילֵהוּ בְּמַעֲשֵׂי יָדֶיךָ
כֹּל שַׁתָּה תַחַת־רַגְלָיו.
צֹנֶה וַאֲלָפִים כֻּלָּם
וְגַם בַּהֲמוֹת שָׂדָי.
◁ צִפּוֹר שָׁמַיִם וּדְגֵי הַיָּם
עֹבֵר אָרְחוֹת יַמִּים.
יהוה אֲדֹנֵינוּ מָה־אַדִּיר שִׁמְךָ בְּכָל־הָאָרֶץ.   תהלים ח

PSALM 8. The post-talmudic tractate Soferim (8th century) reports a tradition of reciting psalms specific to each holy day, rather than reciting the usual psalm of the day. Abudarham (14th century) recommended this psalm as one of those to be recited upon entering the sanctuary on Rosh Hashanah.

THE SOUNDS OF INFANTS מִפִּי עוֹלְלִים וְיֹנְקִים. The psalmist demonstrates God's power through what most consider weakness! A baby is fully vulnerable, yet it is depicted here as ultimately triumphant. That reversal is also true of all humans: we are weak and finite, yet, in the words of the psalmist, "little less than divine."

SILENCING ENEMIES AND THE VENGEFUL לְהַשְׁבִּית אוֹיֵב וּמִתְנַקֵּם. The psalmist uses the verb that has the same root as the noun Shabbat (שַׁבָּת). Surprisingly, the victory over enemies is described in pacific language, as a sabbatical peace. That victory is achieved through the least obvious of warriors—a child—in the least violent manner.

Human Responsibility

Before God gave the Torah to Moses the angels protested, "We are pure and Your Torah is pure, how can you give that which is pure to the impure?" And so they said, "What are mortals that You should be mindful of them?" God replied by saying that the Torah cannot be fulfilled in heaven: "I have given mortals dominion over all that I have fashioned. It is only on earth that the Torah can be fulfilled."

—THE MIDRASH
ON PSALMS

Psalm of the Day: Rosh Hashanah

PSALM 8

FOR THE LEADER, ON THE GITTITH. A PSALM OF DAVID.
ADONAI, our master,
what majesty is Yours throughout the world!
The heavens display Your splendor.

The sounds of infants attest to Your power;
nurslings are an answer to Your foes,
silencing enemies and the vengeful.

When I look at Your heavens, Your handiwork;
the moon and the stars, which You have shaped—

What are mortals, that You should be mindful of them,

mere mortals, that You should take account of them,
that You have made them little less than divine?

You have given them mastery over that which You fashioned,
placing all creation at their feet,

all sheep and oxen, all the wild beasts,
birds of the air and fish of the sea,
all that inhabit the ocean deep.

ADONAI, our master,
what majesty is Yours throughout the world!

הַיּוֹם יוֹם הַכִּפּוּרִים, שֶׁבּוֹ אוֹמְרִים:

לַמְנַצֵּחַ מִזְמוֹר לְדָוִד. בְּבוֹא־אֵלָיו נָתָן הַנָּבִיא כַּאֲשֶׁר־בָּא אֶל־בַּת־שָׁבַע.

חָנֵּנִי אֱלֹהִים כְּחַסְדֶּךָ, כְּרֹב רַחֲמֶיךָ מְחֵה פְשָׁעָי.

הֶרֶב כַּבְּסֵנִי מֵעֲוֹנִי, וּמֵחַטָּאתִי טַהֲרֵנִי.

כִּי־פְשָׁעַי אֲנִי אֵדָע, וְחַטָּאתִי נֶגְדִּי תָמִיד.

לְךָ לְבַדְּךָ חָטָאתִי, וְהָרַע בְּעֵינֶיךָ עָשִׂיתִי

לְמַעַן תִּצְדַּק בְּדָבְרֶךָ תִּזְכֶּה בְשָׁפְטֶךָ.

הֵן־בְּעָווֹן חוֹלָלְתִּי, וּבְחֵטְא יֶחֱמַתְנִי אִמִּי.

הֵן־אֱמֶת חָפַצְתָּ בַטֻּחוֹת, וּבְסָתֻם חָכְמָה תוֹדִיעֵנִי.

תְּחַטְּאֵנִי בְאֵזוֹב וְאֶטְהָר, תְּכַבְּסֵנִי וּמִשֶּׁלֶג אַלְבִּין.

תַּשְׁמִיעֵנִי שָׂשׂוֹן וְשִׂמְחָה, תָּגֵלְנָה עֲצָמוֹת דִּכִּיתָ.

הַסְתֵּר פָּנֶיךָ מֵחֲטָאָי, וְכָל־עֲוֹנֹתַי מְחֵה.

לֵב טָהוֹר בְּרָא־לִי אֱלֹהִים, וְרוּחַ נָכוֹן חַדֵּשׁ בְּקִרְבִּי.

אַל־תַּשְׁלִיכֵנִי מִלְּפָנֶיךָ, וְרוּחַ קָדְשְׁךָ אַל־תִּקַּח מִמֶּנִּי.

הָשִׁיבָה לִּי שְׂשׂוֹן יִשְׁעֶךָ, וְרוּחַ נְדִיבָה תִסְמְכֵנִי.

אֲלַמְּדָה פֹשְׁעִים דְּרָכֶיךָ, וְחַטָּאִים אֵלֶיךָ יָשׁוּבוּ.

הַצִּילֵנִי מִדָּמִים אֱלֹהִים אֱלֹהֵי תְּשׁוּעָתִי

תְּרַנֵּן לְשׁוֹנִי צִדְקָתֶךָ.

אֲדֹנָי שְׂפָתַי תִּפְתָּח וּפִי יַגִּיד תְּהִלָּתֶךָ.

כִּי לֹא־תַחְפֹּץ זֶבַח וְאֶתֵּנָה עוֹלָה לֹא תִרְצֶה.

◁ זִבְחֵי אֱלֹהִים רוּחַ נִשְׁבָּרָה,

לֵב־נִשְׁבָּר וְנִדְכֶּה אֱלֹהִים לֹא תִבְזֶה. תהלים נא א-יט

PSALM 51. Ascribing this song to David, the psalmist conveys David's regret for his sin regarding Bathsheba. He tells of his "broken heart," and indeed the Rabbis point to our broken hearts as the aim of fasting on this day.

HIDE YOUR FACE הַסְתֵּר פָּנֶיךָ. Hiding the face is usually an image of God's turning away from the human; it is seen as such when prayer goes unanswered. Here the poet invokes the image for opposite effect. The psalmist pleads, "hide Your face from my sins," confident that if God were to do so, the distance that has been created in relation to the Divine would be immediately bridged.

FASHION A PURE HEART לֵב טָהוֹר בְּרָא־לִי. It is as if the poet now asks for a new creation: a human being who is no longer attracted to sin. The implicit argument is that God created us as imperfect human beings; therefore, God should understand how we have come to stray. After all, our needs and desires are the result of God's will. Similarly, Ezekiel at one point asks Israel to change its heart from the ways of sin and acquire a new heart (18:31), but he also says that the return from exile will be accompanied by God instilling in the people a new heart and a new spirit (11:31).

ADONAI, OPEN MY LIPS אֲדֹנָי שְׂפָתַי תִּפְתָּח. This verse became the opening line for every Amidah.

YOU DO NOT WANT . . . SACRIFICES כִּי לֹא־תַחְפֹּץ זֶבַח. Ritual acts are acceptable only when they are accompanied by internal transformation.

Psalm of the Day: Yom Kippur—Psalm 51

The words of this psalm are to be considered in light of the verse "Death and life are in the power of the tongue" (Proverbs 18:21). People's tongues can bring them to dwell in the world to come. What brought David into the world to come? The tongue in his mouth, which said, "I have sinned," as it is said, "David said to Nathan, 'I have sinned against Adonai'" (2 Samuel 12:13). David was in darkness and the Holy One kindled light for him, as David said, "It is You who kindle my lamp" (Psalm 18:29).

—THE MIDRASH
ON PSALMS

FOR THE LEADER: A PSALM OF DAVID. WHEN NATHAN THE PROPHET CAME TO DAVID AFTER HE HAD GONE TO BATHSHEBA.

Have mercy upon me, God, as befits Your faithfulness;
in keeping with Your abundant compassion,
blot out my transgressions.
Wash me thoroughly of my iniquity, and purify me of my sin;
for I recognize my transgressions,
and am ever conscious of my sin.
Against You alone have I sinned,
and done what is evil in Your sight;
so You are just in Your sentence, and right in Your judgment.
Indeed, I was born with iniquity;
with sin my mother conceived me.

You desire truth about that which is hidden;
teach me wisdom about secret things.
Purge me with hyssop till I am pure;
wash me till I am whiter than snow.
Let me hear tidings of joy and gladness;
let the bones You have crushed exult.
Hide Your face from my sins; blot out all my iniquities.

Fashion a pure heart for me, God;
create in me a steadfast spirit.
Do not cast me out of Your presence,
or take Your holy spirit away from me.
Let me again rejoice in Your help;
let a vigorous spirit sustain me.
I will teach transgressors Your ways,
that sinners may return to You.
Save me from bloodguilt, God—God, my deliverer—
that my tongue may sing of Your righteousness.

ADONAI, open my lips that my mouth may speak Your praise.
You do not want me to bring sacrifices;
You do not desire burnt offerings.
True sacrifice to God is a contrite spirit;
God, You will not despise a contrite and crushed heart.

Psalm 51:1–19

לְדָוִד.

יהוה אוֹרִי וְיִשְׁעִי, מִמִּי אִירָא,
יהוה מָעוֹז־חַיַּי, מִמִּי אֶפְחָד.
בִּקְרֹב עָלַי מְרֵעִים לֶאֱכֹל אֶת־בְּשָׂרִי,
צָרַי וְאֹיְבַי לִי הֵמָּה כָשְׁלוּ וְנָפָלוּ.
אִם־תַּחֲנֶה עָלַי מַחֲנֶה לֹא־יִירָא לִבִּי,
אִם־תָּקוּם עָלַי מִלְחָמָה בְּזֹאת אֲנִי בוֹטֵחַ.
אַחַת שָׁאַלְתִּי מֵאֵת־יהוה, אוֹתָהּ אֲבַקֵּשׁ:
שִׁבְתִּי בְּבֵית־יהוה כָּל־יְמֵי חַיַּי,
לַחֲזוֹת בְּנֹעַם־יהוה וּלְבַקֵּר בְּהֵיכָלוֹ.
כִּי יִצְפְּנֵנִי בְּסֻכֹּה בְּיוֹם רָעָה,
יַסְתִּרֵנִי בְּסֵתֶר אָהֳלוֹ, בְּצוּר יְרוֹמְמֵנִי.
וְעַתָּה יָרוּם רֹאשִׁי עַל־אֹיְבַי סְבִיבוֹתַי,
וְאֶזְבְּחָה בְאָהֳלוֹ זִבְחֵי תְרוּעָה, אָשִׁירָה וַאֲזַמְּרָה לַיהוה.
שְׁמַע־יהוה קוֹלִי אֶקְרָא, וְחָנֵּנִי וַעֲנֵנִי.
לְךָ אָמַר לִבִּי בַּקְּשׁוּ פָנָי, אֶת־פָּנֶיךָ יהוה אֲבַקֵּשׁ.
אַל־תַּסְתֵּר פָּנֶיךָ מִמֶּנִּי,
אַל תַּט־בְּאַף עַבְדֶּךָ, עֶזְרָתִי הָיִיתָ,
אַל־תִּטְּשֵׁנִי וְאַל־תַּעַזְבֵנִי, אֱלֹהֵי יִשְׁעִי.
כִּי־אָבִי וְאִמִּי עֲזָבוּנִי, וַיהוה יַאַסְפֵנִי.
הוֹרֵנִי יהוה דַּרְכֶּךָ, וּנְחֵנִי בְּאֹרַח מִישׁוֹר, לְמַעַן שׁוֹרְרָי.
אַל־תִּתְּנֵנִי בְּנֶפֶשׁ צָרָי, כִּי קָמוּ־בִי עֵדֵי־שֶׁקֶר וִיפֵחַ חָמָס.
◁ לוּלֵא הֶאֱמַנְתִּי לִרְאוֹת בְּטוּב־יהוה בְּאֶרֶץ חַיִּים.
קַוֵּה אֶל־יהוה, חֲזַק וְיַאֲמֵץ לִבֶּךָ וְקַוֵּה אֶל־יהוה. תהלים כז

*Some congregations recite Mourner's Kaddish after the recitation of this psalm;
see page 46.*

PSALM 27. This very personal, intimate psalm progresses from a triumphalist faith to a meditation on the fragility of life and hope. In many communities, it came to be recited twice each day, morning and evening, in the month before the High Holy Days, throughout the Days of Repentance, and up to the last day of Sukkot. Perhaps it was seen as appropriate for this season because of its focus on the wish for God's presence in our lives.

TO HIDE ME IN GOD'S SUKKAH יִצְפְּנֵנִי בְּסֻכֹּה. Note the progress from "House" to "sukkah" to "tent." The movement in the psalm is to greater fragility.

ADONAI, HEAR MY VOICE שְׁמַע יהוה קוֹלִי. This phrase achieves special prominence in the central Yom Kippur prayer Sh'ma Koleinu (שְׁמַע קוֹלֵנוּ), "Hear our voice," which precedes each recitation of the confessional.

DO NOT HIDE YOUR FACE FROM ME אַל תַּסְתֵּר פָּנֶיךָ מִמֶּנִּי. Four times the psalmist uses the word אַל (al), "do not": do not hide, do not act angrily, do not forsake, do not abandon. It appears again later: "do not hand me over." The psalmist reveals here that beneath the facade of confidence, great fear and feelings of abandonment are lurking.

IF ONLY I COULD TRUST לוּלֵא הֶאֱמַנְתִּי. Or: "Did I not believe." Understood that way, the sentence is left unfinished, as if to say, "I would not be able to continue, were it not that I believe that I will experience God's graciousness while I am yet alive." And yet the poet knows that reality and faith do not coincide.

PLACE YOUR HOPE IN ADONAI קַוֵּה אֶל־יהוה. The entire psalm has been recited in the first person, but here we have a second-person command. Either this is meant as an address to oneself, or else another voice is heard speaking: "You have voiced your faith and your doubts; have courage and your hopes will be fulfilled." Rashi (1040–1105), following the Midrash, says that the repetition of the injunction to hope, emphasizing the need for hope, indicates that even if one's prayer does not have a visible response, one should not lose faith.

A Psalm for the Season of Repentance — Psalm 27

A PSALM OF DAVID.

ADONAI is my light and my help. Whom shall I fear?
ADONAI is the stronghold of my life. Whom shall I dread?
When evil people assail me to devour my flesh,
    it is they, my enemies and those who besiege me,
    who stumble and fall.
Should an armed camp be arrayed against me,
    my heart would show no fear;
    should they war against me, of this I would be sure.

One thing I ask of ADONAI—this I seek:
    to dwell in the House of God all the days of my life,
    to behold God's beauty and visit in God's sanctuary.
Were God to hide me in God's *sukkah* on the calamitous day,
    were God to enfold me in the secret recesses of God's tent,
    I would be raised up in a protecting fort.
Now, I raise my head above the enemies that surround me,
    and come with offerings, amidst trumpet blasts, to God's tent,
    chanting and singing praise to ADONAI.
ADONAI, hear my voice as I cry out;
    be gracious to me, and answer me.
It is You of whom my heart said, "Seek my face!"
It is Your presence that I seek, ADONAI.
Do not hide Your face from me; do not act angrily toward me.
You have always been my help; do not forsake me;
    do not abandon me, my God, my deliverer.
Though my father and mother abandon me,
    ADONAI will gather me in.
Show me Your way, ADONAI, and lead me on a straight path
    despite those arrayed against me.
Do not hand me over to the grasp of those who besiege me;
    for false witnesses and those who seek ill have risen against me.

If only I could trust that I would see God's goodness
    in the land of the living . . .
Place your hope in ADONAI.
Be strong, take courage, and place your hope in ADONAI.

Some congregations recite Mourner's Kaddish after the recitation of this psalm; see page 46.

Love Me

Oh my Father, love me,
love me, dear Father,
and I will in goodness
be shattered and
  dispersed
like dust, like a spindrift
my goodness will settle
over everything and
  everyone,
everything and
  everyone.

Love me, sweet Father.

     —MALKA HEIFETZ
         TUSSMAN
    (trans. Marcia Falk)

PSALM 30. This psalm was undoubtedly selected to introduce the section of psalms because the experience of awakening in the morning is seen as escaping from the clutches of death. Turning mourning to joy becomes a metaphor for the way one should celebrate the gift of a new day.

מִזְמוֹר שִׁיר־חֲנֻכַּת הַבַּיִת לְדָוִד.

אֲרוֹמִמְךָ יהוה כִּי דִלִּיתָנִי, וְלֹא־שִׂמַּחְתָּ אֹיְבַי לִי.

יהוה אֱלֹהָי, שִׁוַּעְתִּי אֵלֶיךָ וַתִּרְפָּאֵנִי.

יהוה הֶעֱלִיתָ מִן־שְׁאוֹל נַפְשִׁי, חִיִּיתַנִי מִיָּרְדִי־בוֹר.

זַמְּרוּ לַיהוה חֲסִידָיו, וְהוֹדוּ לְזֵכֶר קָדְשׁוֹ.

כִּי רֶגַע בְּאַפּוֹ חַיִּים בִּרְצוֹנוֹ, בָּעֶרֶב יָלִין בֶּכִי וְלַבֹּקֶר רִנָּה.

וַאֲנִי אָמַרְתִּי בְשַׁלְוִי, בַּל־אֶמּוֹט לְעוֹלָם.

יהוה בִּרְצוֹנְךָ הֶעֱמַדְתָּה לְהַרְרִי עֹז,

הִסְתַּרְתָּ פָנֶיךָ, הָיִיתִי נִבְהָל.

אֵלֶיךָ יהוה אֶקְרָא, וְאֶל־אֲדֹנָי אֶתְחַנָּן.

מַה־בֶּצַע בְּדָמִי בְּרִדְתִּי אֶל שָׁחַת,

הֲיוֹדְךָ עָפָר, הֲיַגִּיד אֲמִתֶּךָ.

שְׁמַע־יהוה וְחָנֵּנִי, יהוה הֱיֵה־עֹזֵר לִי.

◁ הָפַכְתָּ מִסְפְּדִי לְמָחוֹל לִי,

פִּתַּחְתָּ שַׂקִּי וַתְּאַזְּרֵנִי שִׂמְחָה.

לְמַעַן יְזַמֶּרְךָ כָבוֹד וְלֹא יִדֹּם, יהוה אֱלֹהַי לְעוֹלָם אוֹדֶךָּ.

תהלים ל

YOU HEALED ME וַתִּרְפָּאֵנִי. Although the poet seems to have recovered from illness and has been healed, he then mentions external enemies, a common poetic movement in psalms where internal states are externalized.

YOU SAVED ME FROM THE PIT OF DEATH הֶעֱלִיתָ מִן־שְׁאוֹל נַפְשִׁי, חִיִּיתַנִי מִיָּרְדִי־בוֹר. Literally, "You brought me up from Sheol / revived me from my descent into the Pit." In the Bible, Sheol was the realm of the dead. Archaeological evidence supports the view that there was a popular belief in ancient Israel that some shadow of the person descended to the netherworld. Holes for feeding the dead have been found in ancient Israelite burial sites.

Psalms

The biblical psalms are essentially a record of the human quest for God. Hence, the variety of forms in which the ancient psalmists expressed themselves, reflective of the diverse and changing moods that possessed them as they do all human beings. In short, the psalms constitute a revealing portrayal of the human condition.

—NAHUM M. SARNA

To Sing

The emotions of our inner life are so strong, so tied to the essence of life, that they constantly desire to give rise to poetry and song. We need to be able to find words to express our emotions; when we can name them, the inner vitality that is touched by these words gives rise to melody that is the origin of song.

—ABRAHAM ISAAC KOOK
(*adapted*)

INTRODUCTION TO P'SUKEI D'ZIMRA: PSALM 30

A PSALM OF DAVID.
A SONG FOR THE DEDICATION OF THE HOUSE.

I extol You, ADONAI. You raised me up.
You did not permit foes to rejoice over me.

> *ADONAI, I cried out and You healed me.*
> *You saved me from the pit of death.*

Sing to ADONAI, you faithful!
Acclaim God's holiness!

> *God's anger lasts a moment;*
> *divine love is lifelong.*
> *Tears may linger for a night;*
> *joy comes with the dawn.*

While at ease I once thought: Nothing can shake my security.
Favor me and I am a mountain of strength.
Hide Your face, ADONAI, and I am terrified.

> *To You, ADONAI, would I call;*
> *before the Eternal would I plead.*

What profit is there if I am silenced?
What benefit if I go to my grave?
Will the dust praise You? Will it proclaim Your faithfulness?

> *Hear me, ADONAI!*
> *Be gracious, be my help!*

You transformed my mourning into dancing,
my sackcloth into robes of joy,
that I might sing Your praise unceasingly,
that I might thank You, ADONAI my God, forever.

קַדִּישׁ יָתוֹם

Mourners and those observing Yahrzeit:

יִתְגַּדַּל וְיִתְקַדַּשׁ שְׁמֵהּ רַבָּא, בְּעָלְמָא דִּי בְרָא, כִּרְעוּתֵהּ,
וְיַמְלִיךְ מַלְכוּתֵהּ בְּחַיֵּיכוֹן וּבְיוֹמֵיכוֹן וּבְחַיֵּי דְכָל־בֵּית
יִשְׂרָאֵל, בַּעֲגָלָא וּבִזְמַן קָרִיב, וְאִמְרוּ אָמֵן.

Congregation and mourners:

יְהֵא שְׁמֵהּ רַבָּא מְבָרַךְ לְעָלַם וּלְעָלְמֵי עָלְמַיָּא.

Mourners:

יִתְבָּרַךְ וְיִשְׁתַּבַּח וְיִתְפָּאַר וְיִתְרוֹמַם וְיִתְנַשֵּׂא וְיִתְהַדָּר
וְיִתְעַלֶּה וְיִתְהַלָּל שְׁמֵהּ דְּקֻדְשָׁא, בְּרִיךְ הוּא,
לְעֵלָּא לְעֵלָּא מִכָּל־בִּרְכָתָא וְשִׁירָתָא תֻּשְׁבְּחָתָא
וְנֶחָמָתָא דַּאֲמִירָן בְּעָלְמָא, וְאִמְרוּ אָמֵן.

יְהֵא שְׁלָמָא רַבָּא מִן שְׁמַיָּא וְחַיִּים עָלֵינוּ
וְעַל כָּל־יִשְׂרָאֵל, וְאִמְרוּ אָמֵן.

עֹשֶׂה שָׁלוֹם בִּמְרוֹמָיו הוּא יַעֲשֶׂה שָׁלוֹם עָלֵינוּ
וְעַל כָּל־יִשְׂרָאֵל [וְעַל כָּל־יוֹשְׁבֵי תֵבֵל], וְאִמְרוּ אָמֵן.

KADDISH קַדִּישׁ. The central moment of the Kaddish is the communal response expressing praise of God. The Kaddish, then, is not a private prayer, but is recited in community with a minyan present. Its form is a dialogue between the leader and the community. The mourner affirms that tragedy has not separated him or her from God or the Jewish people; the communal response, in turn, constitutes a way of acknowledging the mourner as a member of the congregation.

Mourner's Kaddish

Mourners and those observing Yahrzeit:

May God's great name be exalted and hallowed throughout the
created world, as is God's wish. May God's sovereignty soon be
established, in your lifetime and in your days, and in the days of
all the House of Israel. And respond with: *Amen.*

Congregation and mourners:

May God's great name be acknowledged forever and ever!

Mourners:

May the name of the Holy One be acknowledged and celebrated, lauded and worshipped, exalted and honored, extolled
and acclaimed—though God, who is blessed, *b'rikh hu*, is truly
far beyond all acknowledgment and praise, or any expressions
of gratitude or consolation ever spoken in the world. And
respond with: *Amen.*

May abundant peace from heaven, and life, come to us and to
all Israel. And respond with: *Amen.*

May the One who brings harmony on high, bring harmony to
us and to all Israel [and to all who dwell on earth].
And respond with: *Amen.*

Mourners and those observing Yahrzeit:
Yitgaddal v'yitkaddash sh'meih rabba, b'alma di v'ra, ki-r'uteih,
v'yamlikh malkhuteih b'ḥayyeikhon u-v'yomeikhon
u-v'ḥayyei d'khol beit yisra·el,
ba-agala u-viz'man kariv,
v'imru amen.

Congregation and mourners:
Y'hei sh'meih rabba m'varakh l'alam u-l'almei almayya.

Mourners:
Yitbarakh v'yishtabbaḥ v'yitpa·ar v'yitromam v'yitnassei v'yit·haddar
v'yit·alleh v'yit·hallal sh'meih d'kudsha, b'rikh hu,
l'eilla l'eilla mi-kol birkhata v'shirata tushb'ḥata v'neḥamata
da-amiran b'alma, v'imru amen.

Y'hei sh'lama rabba min sh'mayya v'ḥayyim aleinu v'al kol yisra·el,
v'imru amen.

Oseh shalom bi-m'romav hu ya·aseh shalom aleinu
v'al kol yisra·el [v'al kol yosh'vei teiveil],
v'imru amen.

פְּסוּקֵי דְזִמְרָא

בָּרוּךְ שֶׁאָמַר וְהָיָה הָעוֹלָם,   בָּרוּךְ הוּא.

בָּרוּךְ עֹשֶׂה בְרֵאשִׁית,   בָּרוּךְ שְׁמוֹ.

בָּרוּךְ אוֹמֵר וְעֹשֶׂה,   בָּרוּךְ הוּא.

בָּרוּךְ גּוֹזֵר וּמְקַיֵּם,   בָּרוּךְ שְׁמוֹ.

בָּרוּךְ מְרַחֵם עַל הָאָרֶץ,   בָּרוּךְ הוּא.

בָּרוּךְ מְרַחֵם עַל הַבְּרִיּוֹת,   בָּרוּךְ שְׁמוֹ.

בָּרוּךְ מְשַׁלֵּם שָׂכָר טוֹב לִירֵאָיו,   בָּרוּךְ הוּא.

בָּרוּךְ חַי לָעַד וְקַיָּם לָנֶצַח,   בָּרוּךְ שְׁמוֹ.

בָּרוּךְ פּוֹדֶה וּמַצִּיל,   בָּרוּךְ הוּא וּבָרוּךְ שְׁמוֹ.

בָּרוּךְ אַתָּה יהוה אֱלֹהֵינוּ מֶלֶךְ הָעוֹלָם, הָאֵל הָאָב הָרַחֲמָן הַמְהֻלָּל בְּפִי עַמּוֹ, מְשֻׁבָּח וּמְפֹאָר בִּלְשׁוֹן חֲסִידָיו וַעֲבָדָיו. וּבְשִׁירֵי דָוִד עַבְדֶּךָ נְהַלֶּלְךָ יהוה אֱלֹהֵינוּ, בִּשְׁבָחוֹת וּבִזְמִרוֹת, נְגַדֶּלְךָ וּנְשַׁבֵּחֲךָ וּנְפָאֶרְךָ וְנַזְכִּיר שִׁמְךָ וְנַמְלִיכְךָ מַלְכֵּנוּ אֱלֹהֵינוּ, ◁ יָחִיד חֵי הָעוֹלָמִים. מֶלֶךְ מְשֻׁבָּח וּמְפֹאָר עֲדֵי עַד שְׁמוֹ הַגָּדוֹל. בָּרוּךְ אַתָּה יהוה, מֶלֶךְ מְהֻלָּל בַּתִּשְׁבָּחוֹת.

VERSES OF SONG פְּסוּקֵי דְזִמְרָא. By the year 225 C.E., when the Mishnah was edited, the morning liturgy consisted of two major sections: the Sh'ma and Its Blessings, and the Amidah. It was common, however, for individuals to recite psalms and other sections of the Bible as preparation for worship. The Geonim, the heads of the post-talmudic academies of Babylonia, formalized this devotion sometime in the second half of the first millennium. Psalms of praise were specifically chosen for this section; hence its title, "Verses of Song." The core of the psalmic selection began with Psalm 145 (Ashrei), which was chosen because it was thought to express the essential concepts of praise of God. The following five psalms, the last ones in the Book of Psalms, were included so that each day the Book of Psalms is symbolically completed. Over the centuries other psalms and appropriate biblical selections have been added to P'sukei D'zimra, to help us to prepare for the actual service. These passages recall major events in Jewish history and climax with the Song at the Sea, the great hymn of salvation recorded in Exodus 15.

PRAISED IS GOD WHOSE WORD בָּרוּךְ שֶׁאָמַר. The repetition of the word בָּרוּךְ (barukh), "blessed," turns this prayer into a poetic imitation of the Bar'khu, which is the formal beginning of the prayer service. The first lines of this poem are found in Midrash Tanna D'vei Eliyahu Zuta 4:9 (10th century). Arising in the morning, the poet sees God, the Creator, in all things.

CREATED THE WORLD וְהָיָה הָעוֹלָם. God is often referred to by the Sages as "the One who spoke and the world came into being." This is based on the creation story in Genesis 1, in which the entire Creation is accomplished by God's spoken fiat. In Pirkei Avot 5:1 we read: "The world was created through ten utterances."

BARUKH HU בָּרוּךְ הוּא. Literally, "blessed is God." In the following line we read: בָּרוּךְ שְׁמוֹ (barukh sh'mo), "Praised (Blessed) is God's name." Taken together, these words form the phrase בָּרוּךְ הוּא וּבָרוּךְ שְׁמוֹ, "blessed is God and blessed is God's name," which is commonly used as a response to hearing the name of God. Different communities recite this poem with a variety of responses.

MAGNIFIED WITH SONGS OF PRAISE מְהֻלָּל בַּתִּשְׁבָּחוֹת. The biblical selections that follow this passage are preceded by a b'rakhah: מֶלֶךְ מְהֻלָּל בַּתִּשְׁבָּחוֹת, "Sovereign magnified with songs of praise." They are concluded (p. 69) with another b'rakhah, הַבּוֹחֵר בְּשִׁירֵי זִמְרָה, מֶלֶךְ אֵל חֵי הָעוֹלָמִים, "who delights in the chorus of song, the sovereign God, giving life to all worlds." Nothing in between these two b'rakhot was written by the Sages or liturgical poets; all the selections are biblical.

VERSES OF SONG

Creator

In praising the Creator, we begin to be in touch with our own selves. We marvel at our being and feel the vitality of our inner lives. Normal speech arises out of images we have of the self; prayerful speech arises out of our sense of mystery, out of our lack of ability to grasp the full extent of the universe and ourselves. What prayer induces is this sense of awe. That is why it is such a special language.

—ABRAHAM ISAAC KOOK
(adapted)

It is customary to stand for the opening and closing b'rakhot of P'sukei D'zimra.

Introductory B'rakhah

Praised is God whose word created
   the world.   *Barukh hu.*

Glorified is the Author of creation.   *Barukh sh'mo.*

   Laud the One whose word is performance.   *Barukh hu.*

Revered is God whose decree is fulfillment.   *Barukh sh'mo.*

   Acclaim the One whose mercy envelops
   the world.   *Barukh hu.*

Adored is God whose kindness embraces
all creatures.   *Barukh sh'mo.*

   Honor the One who rewards those who
   are reverent.   *Barukh hu.*

Blessed is God who lives forever, endures
eternally.   *Barukh sh'mo.*

   Celebrate the One who redeems and rescues. *Barukh hu.*

Praised is God and praised is God's name.   *Barukh hu*
                                            u-varukh sh'mo.

Barukh atah ADONAI, our God, ruler of time and space, compassionate creator extolled by Your people, glorified by Your faithful servants. We laud You with the psalms of Your servant David. We extol You in song; we celebrate Your fame in melody. We proclaim You sovereign, singular, eternal God. *Barukh atah* ADONAI, Sovereign extolled with songs of praise.

Some congregations select from among the psalms and biblical texts that follow.

הוֹדוּ לַיהוה, קִרְאוּ בִשְׁמוֹ, הוֹדִיעוּ בָעַמִּים עֲלִילֹתָיו.
שִׁירוּ לוֹ זַמְּרוּ־לוֹ, שִׂיחוּ בְּכָל־נִפְלְאֹתָיו. הִתְהַלְלוּ בְּשֵׁם
קָדְשׁוֹ, יִשְׂמַח לֵב מְבַקְשֵׁי יהוה. דִּרְשׁוּ יהוה וְעֻזּוֹ, בַּקְּשׁוּ
פָנָיו תָּמִיד. זִכְרוּ נִפְלְאֹתָיו אֲשֶׁר עָשָׂה, מֹפְתָיו וּמִשְׁפְּטֵי־
פִיהוּ. זֶרַע יִשְׂרָאֵל עַבְדּוֹ, בְּנֵי יַעֲקֹב בְּחִירָיו. הוּא יהוה
אֱלֹהֵינוּ, בְּכָל־הָאָרֶץ מִשְׁפָּטָיו. זִכְרוּ לְעוֹלָם בְּרִיתוֹ, דָּבָר
צִוָּה לְאֶלֶף דּוֹר, אֲשֶׁר כָּרַת אֶת־אַבְרָהָם, וּשְׁבוּעָתוֹ
לְיִצְחָק, וַיַּעֲמִידֶהָ לְיַעֲקֹב לְחֹק, לְיִשְׂרָאֵל בְּרִית עוֹלָם,
לֵאמֹר: לְךָ אֶתֵּן אֶרֶץ־כְּנָעַן, חֶבֶל נַחֲלַתְכֶם. בִּהְיוֹתְכֶם
מְתֵי מִסְפָּר, כִּמְעַט וְגָרִים בָּהּ. וַיִּתְהַלְּכוּ מִגּוֹי אֶל גּוֹי,
וּמִמַּמְלָכָה אֶל עַם־אַחֵר. לֹא־הִנִּיחַ לְאִישׁ לְעָשְׁקָם,
וַיּוֹכַח עֲלֵיהֶם מְלָכִים: אַל־תִּגְּעוּ בִּמְשִׁיחָי, וּבִנְבִיאַי אַל
תָּרֵעוּ. שִׁירוּ לַיהוה כָּל־הָאָרֶץ, בַּשְּׂרוּ מִיּוֹם אֶל יוֹם
יְשׁוּעָתוֹ. סַפְּרוּ בַגּוֹיִם אֶת־כְּבוֹדוֹ, בְּכָל־הָעַמִּים נִפְלְאֹתָיו.
▷ כִּי גָדוֹל יהוה וּמְהֻלָּל מְאֹד, וְנוֹרָא הוּא עַל־כָּל־אֱלֹהִים.
כִּי כָּל־אֱלֹהֵי הָעַמִּים אֱלִילִים, וַיהוה שָׁמַיִם עָשָׂה.

הוֹד וְהָדָר לְפָנָיו, עֹז וְחֶדְוָה בִּמְקֹמוֹ. הָבוּ לַיהוה
מִשְׁפְּחוֹת עַמִּים, הָבוּ לַיהוה כָּבוֹד וָעֹז. הָבוּ לַיהוה כְּבוֹד
שְׁמוֹ, שְׂאוּ מִנְחָה וּבֹאוּ לְפָנָיו, הִשְׁתַּחֲווּ לַיהוה בְּהַדְרַת־
קֹדֶשׁ. חִילוּ מִלְּפָנָיו כָּל־הָאָרֶץ, אַף תִּכּוֹן תֵּבֵל בַּל־תִּמּוֹט.
יִשְׂמְחוּ הַשָּׁמַיִם וְתָגֵל הָאָרֶץ וְיֹאמְרוּ בַגּוֹיִם יהוה מָלָךְ.

1 CHRONICLES 16:8–36. The first biblical text of P'sukei D'zimra is taken from 1 Chronicles. It represents an early addition to the verses from Psalms that originally exclusively constituted this section. The chronicler describes David bringing the Ark to Jerusalem, accompanied by the singing of psalms. David's song recorded here is drawn from a variety of verses from the Book of Psalms. According to a midrashic text, during the Second Temple period this passage was sung by the Levites when the daily offering, the *tamid*, was sacrificed (Seder Olam 14). It is probably for this reason that these verses entered the liturgy. The synagogue is thought of as a reflection of the Temple, and so David's bringing the Ark to Jerusalem is symbolic of our synagogue ark. David sang these verses even though the Temple was built only after his death. Conversely, we recite them today—long after the destruction of the Temple.

This passage is also included in the Sephardic rite, but there it is placed before Barukh She-amar instead of after it. The Sephardic rite preserves the original form of P'sukei D'zimra, in which Barukh She-amar is followed specifically by chapters of Psalms.

ACCLAIM הוֹדוּ. More specifically, "give thanks" or "acknowledge," from the same root as תּוֹדָה (*todah*), "thanks." The word thus has the secondary meaning of praise, here translated as "acclaim."

TREASURED CHILDREN OF JACOB בְּנֵי יַעֲקֹב בְּחִירָיו. The adjective *bahir* literally means "chosen." Here we render it as "treasured" in light of the Books of Deuteronomy and Isaiah, which assert this motivation for God's having selected the people Israel.

A THOUSAND GENERATIONS לְאֶלֶף דּוֹר. An unlimited time; forever.

LET THE HEAVENS REJOICE יִשְׂמְחוּ הַשָּׁמַיִם. In the order in which they were created, each of the elements of the world is called upon to offer praise. First, the heavens and the earth; then, the sea and the fields; and finally, the trees.

DAVID'S PRAYER: THE DEDICATION OF THE ARK

Acclaim ADONAI; invoke God's name! Make God's deeds known among all people. Praise God in song and in psalm, recalling all of God's wonders. Exult in God's hallowed name; let God's seekers rejoice in their heart. Seek ADONAI and gather strength; seek God's presence always. Descendants of Israel, God's servant, treasured children of Jacob: Remember the wonders God has wrought, God's marvels and justice. This is ADONAI our God, whose justice fills the earth. Remember God's covenant always, God's word to a thousand generations—God's covenant with Abraham, God's oath to Isaac, God's unchanging compact with Jacob; the everlasting promise to Israel: "I will give you the land of Canaan as your inheritance, your possession." You were very few in number, little more than strangers in the land, wandering from nation to nation, from kingdom to kingdom. God would let no one oppress you, admonishing kings for your sake: "Touch not My anointed ones; harm not My prophets." Sing to ADONAI, all the earth; proclaim God's triumph day by day. Declare God's glory among the nations, God's marvels among all peoples. Great is ADONAI, and worthy of praise, to be revered beyond all gods. For all the pagan gods are mere idols, but ADONAI created the heavens.

Grandeur and glory attend God; strength and joy abide in God's dwelling. Acclaim ADONAI, you families of nations! Acclaim God's glory and might. Come into God's presence with an offering; worship ADONAI in the splendor of holiness. Let all on earth tremble before God, who fashioned and steadied the world. Let the heavens rejoice; let the earth be glad. Declare to the world: ADONAI is sovereign.

יִרְעַם הַיָּם וּמְלֹאוֹ, יַעֲלֹץ הַשָּׂדֶה וְכָל־אֲשֶׁר־בּוֹ. אָז יְרַנְּנוּ עֲצֵי הַיָּעַר, מִלִּפְנֵי יהוה כִּי־בָא לִשְׁפּוֹט אֶת־הָאָרֶץ. הוֹדוּ לַיהוה כִּי טוֹב, כִּי לְעוֹלָם חַסְדּוֹ. וְאִמְרוּ הוֹשִׁיעֵנוּ אֱלֹהֵי יִשְׁעֵנוּ וְקַבְּצֵנוּ וְהַצִּילֵנוּ מִן־הַגּוֹיִם, לְהֹדוֹת לְשֵׁם קָדְשֶׁךָ לְהִשְׁתַּבֵּחַ בִּתְהִלָּתֶךָ: בָּרוּךְ יהוה אֱלֹהֵי יִשְׂרָאֵל מִן־הָעוֹלָם וְעַד הָעֹלָם, וַיֹּאמְרוּ כָל־הָעָם אָמֵן וְהַלֵּל לַיהוה. דברי הימים א טז ח-לו

◁ רוֹמְמוּ יהוה אֱלֹהֵינוּ וְהִשְׁתַּחֲווּ לַהֲדֹם רַגְלָיו, קָדוֹשׁ הוּא. רוֹמְמוּ יהוה אֱלֹהֵינוּ וְהִשְׁתַּחֲווּ לְהַר קָדְשׁוֹ, כִּי קָדוֹשׁ יהוה אֱלֹהֵינוּ.

וְהוּא רַחוּם יְכַפֵּר עָוֹן וְלֹא־יַשְׁחִית, וְהִרְבָּה לְהָשִׁיב אַפּוֹ וְלֹא־יָעִיר כָּל־חֲמָתוֹ. אַתָּה יהוה לֹא־תִכְלָא רַחֲמֶיךָ מִמֶּנִּי, חַסְדְּךָ וַאֲמִתְּךָ תָּמִיד יִצְּרוּנִי. זְכֹר־רַחֲמֶיךָ יהוה וַחֲסָדֶיךָ, כִּי מֵעוֹלָם הֵמָּה. תְּנוּ עֹז לֵאלֹהִים, עַל־יִשְׂרָאֵל גַּאֲוָתוֹ, וְעֻזּוֹ בַּשְּׁחָקִים. נוֹרָא אֱלֹהִים מִמִּקְדָּשֶׁיךָ, אֵל יִשְׂרָאֵל הוּא נֹתֵן עֹז וְתַעֲצֻמוֹת לָעָם, בָּרוּךְ אֱלֹהִים. אֵל־נְקָמוֹת יהוה, אֵל נְקָמוֹת הוֹפִיעַ. הִנָּשֵׂא שֹׁפֵט הָאָרֶץ, הָשֵׁב גְּמוּל עַל־גֵּאִים.

PRAISED BE ADONAI בָּרוּךְ יהוה. After completing all of these words of praise, David proclaims the blessedness of God, to which the people respond "Amen." This is a precedent of our own recitation of the formula for blessing, *barukh atah Adonai*, to which the congregation responds, "Amen."

EXTOL ADONAI OUR GOD רוֹמְמוּ יהוה אֱלֹהֵינוּ (Psalm 99:5). The first of a series of verses from various psalms that have been collected and placed together, creating a new composition. Different traditions have included different verses in this passage.

TOWARD GOD'S HOLY MOUNTAIN לְהַר קָדְשׁוֹ. Namely, Mount Zion, upon which the Temple was built. We pray facing Jerusalem, directing our prayers symbolically to the Holy of Holies that existed on the Temple Mount.

GOD, BEING MERCIFUL וְהוּא רַחוּם. Psalm 78:38. This is one of the most frequently quoted verses in the liturgy, perhaps because it is the clearest possible statement about God's mercy. Mercy, not punishment, is fundamental to God's nature. The entire verse has thirteen words, reminding us of the "Thirteen Attributes" of God's mercy disclosed in Exodus 34:6–7. The psalm's verse likewise hints at confession of sins and emphasizes God's patience and forgiveness. In some early medieval traditions, the worshipper began each morning with a confession of sins.

ADONAI אַתָּה יהוה. Psalm 40:12.

REMEMBER YOUR COMPASSION זְכֹר רַחֲמֶיךָ. Psalm 25:6. This verse is the third in a row that emphasizes God's merciful, loving nature.

ACCLAIM THE POWER תְּנוּ עֹז. Psalm 68:35–36.

GOD OF RETRIBUTION—ADONAI אֵל נְקָמוֹת יהוה. Psalm 94:1–2. In this verse, God's retribution is invoked against the wicked who, with no thought of morality, oppress the poor, the widow, and the stranger.

Let the sea roar, and all that is in it; let the fields exult, and all they contain. Let field and forest sing for joy, for ADONAI comes to rule the earth. It is good to acclaim ADONAI, whose love endures forever. Cry out: "Save us, God of our salvation; gather us and deliver us from oppression, that we may acknowledge Your holiness, that we may take pride in Your praise!" "Praised be ADONAI, God of Israel, from age to age." And all the people said "Amen" and "Praise ADONAI!" I Chronicles 16:8–36

AN ANTHOLOGY OF VERSES FROM PSALMS
Extol ADONAI our God;
worship God,
who is holy.
> *Extol ADONAI our God;*
> *and bow toward God's holy mountain.*
> *ADONAI our God is holy.*

God, being merciful, grants atonement for sin and does not destroy.
Time and again God restrains wrath, refusing to let rage be all-consuming.
> *ADONAI, do not withhold Your compassion from me;*
> *may Your unfailing love always guard me.*

ADONAI, remember Your compassion and lovingkindness—
for they are eternal.
> *Acclaim the power of God, whose pride is in the people Israel,*
> *whose majesty is in the heavens.*

God, You are awe-inspiring in Your holy place;
the God of Israel gives courage and strength to this people.
Praised be God.
> *God of retribution—ADONAI, God of retribution, appear!*
> *Judge of the earth, bring the arrogant to judgment.*

לַיהוה הַיְשׁוּעָה, עַל־עַמְּךָ בִרְכָתֶךָ סֶּלָה.

◁ יהוה צְבָאוֹת עִמָּנוּ, מִשְׂגָּב־לָנוּ אֱלֹהֵי יַעֲקֹב סֶלָה.

יהוה צְבָאוֹת, אַשְׁרֵי אָדָם בֹּטֵחַ בָּךְ.

יהוה הוֹשִׁיעָה, הַמֶּלֶךְ יַעֲנֵנוּ בְיוֹם־קָרְאֵנוּ.

הוֹשִׁיעָה אֶת־עַמֶּךָ וּבָרֵךְ אֶת־נַחֲלָתֶךָ,
וּרְעֵם וְנַשְּׂאֵם עַד־הָעוֹלָם.

נַפְשֵׁנוּ חִכְּתָה לַיהוה, עֶזְרֵנוּ וּמָגִנֵּנוּ הוּא.

כִּי־בוֹ יִשְׂמַח לִבֵּנוּ, כִּי בְשֵׁם קָדְשׁוֹ בָטָחְנוּ.

יְהִי־חַסְדְּךָ יהוה עָלֵינוּ כַּאֲשֶׁר יִחַלְנוּ לָךְ.

הַרְאֵנוּ יהוה חַסְדֶּךָ, וְיֶשְׁעֲךָ תִּתֶּן־לָנוּ.

קוּמָה עֶזְרָתָה לָנוּ וּפְדֵנוּ לְמַעַן חַסְדֶּךָ.

אָנֹכִי יהוה אֱלֹהֶיךָ הַמַּעַלְךָ מֵאֶרֶץ מִצְרָיִם,
הַרְחֶב־פִּיךָ וַאֲמַלְאֵהוּ.

אַשְׁרֵי הָעָם שֶׁכָּכָה לּוֹ,
אַשְׁרֵי הָעָם שֶׁיהוה אֱלֹהָיו.

◁ וַאֲנִי בְּחַסְדְּךָ בָטַחְתִּי, יָגֵל לִבִּי בִּישׁוּעָתֶךָ,
אָשִׁירָה לַיהוה כִּי גָמַל עָלָי.

TRIUMPH IS YOURS, ADONAI לַיהוה הַיְשׁוּעָה. Psalm 3:9. Although these next four verses are taken from various psalms, each with its own subject, they are connected by similar words and phrases so that they create a new, coherent composition. The same verses are found in Havdalah, recited at the conclusion of Shabbat. They represent a creedal statement of faith.

ADONAI TZ'VA·OT, BE WITH US יהוה צְבָאוֹת עִמָּנוּ. Psalm 46:8.

ADONAI TZ'VA·OT, BLESSED ARE THOSE יהוה צְבָאוֹת, אַשְׁרֵי אָדָם. Or: "happy the person." Psalm 84:13.

ADONAI, HELP US יהוה הוֹשִׁיעָה. Or: ". . . save us." Psalm 20:10.

HELP YOUR PEOPLE הוֹשִׁיעָה אֶת־עַמֶּךָ. Psalm 28:9. What began as a personal plea in the previous paragraph now becomes a plea for national salvation.

WE WAIT HOPEFULLY FOR ADONAI נַפְשֵׁנוּ חִכְּתָה לַיהוה. Psalm 33:20–22.

SHOW US YOUR LOVE הַרְאֵנוּ יהוה חַסְדֶּךָ. Psalm 85:8. The key word חֶסֶד (hesed), "love," is mentioned three times in this and the following verses. The biblical meaning of the word hesed is love that is manifested in action.

ARISE AND COME TO OUR HELP קוּמָה עֶזְרָתָה לָנוּ. Psalm 44:27.

I AM ADONAI YOUR GOD אָנֹכִי יהוה אֱלֹהֶיךָ. Psalm 81:11. One of the remarkable literary aspects of Psalms is that it records God's speech in the first person: It is as if we hear God's voice answering our prayers. The phrases uttered here are reminiscent of the first words of the Decalogue.

EXPRESS YOUR NEED AND I WILL FULFILL IT הַרְחֶב־פִּיךָ וַאֲמַלְאֵהוּ. Literally, "open your mouth wide and I will fill it." The reference is to the manna that nourished Israel in the desert, but this phrase also takes on a spiritual meaning in this context, as if to say that God will provide us with the strength to pray and the words appropriate for prayer.

BLESSED THE PEOPLE אַשְׁרֵי הָעָם. Psalm 144:15.

I HAVE TRUSTED IN YOUR LOVE וַאֲנִי בְּחַסְדְּךָ בָטַחְתִּי. Psalm 13:6. The conclusion of this string of psalmic verses that talk of God's sovereignty is an expression of faith in God's kindness and compassion.

Triumph is Yours, ADONAI; may Your blessing be upon Your people.
Adonai Tz'va·ot, be with us. God of Jacob, be our protection.
Adonai Tz'va·ot, blessed are those who trust in You.
ADONAI, help us. Answer us, Sovereign, when we call.

Help Your people, bless Your heritage; nurture and sustain them forever.
We wait hopefully for ADONAI; God is our help and our shield.
In God our hearts rejoice, for in God's holy name do we trust.
May Your lovingkindness be extended to us, ADONAI,
    for we have placed our hope in You.
Show us Your love; grant us Your saving power.
Arise and come to our help; redeem us because of Your love.
"I am ADONAI your God who brought you out of the land of Egypt.
Express your need and I will fulfill it."
Blessed the people who are so privileged,
    blessed the people whose God is ADONAI.
I have trusted in Your love; may I rejoice in Your saving power.
I shall sing to ADONAI, for God has been bountiful to me.

לַמְנַצֵּחַ מִזְמוֹר לְדָוִד.

הַשָּׁמַיִם מְסַפְּרִים כְּבוֹד־אֵל, וּמַעֲשֵׂה יָדָיו מַגִּיד הָרָקִיעַ.
יוֹם לְיוֹם יַבִּיעַ אֹמֶר, וְלַיְלָה לְּלַיְלָה יְחַוֶּה־דָּעַת.
אֵין־אֹמֶר וְאֵין דְּבָרִים, בְּלִי נִשְׁמָע קוֹלָם.
בְּכָל־הָאָרֶץ יָצָא קַוָּם וּבִקְצֵה תֵבֵל מִלֵּיהֶם,
לַשֶּׁמֶשׁ שָׂם־אֹהֶל בָּהֶם.
וְהוּא כְּחָתָן יֹצֵא מֵחֻפָּתוֹ, יָשִׂישׂ כְּגִבּוֹר לָרוּץ אֹרַח.
מִקְצֵה הַשָּׁמַיִם מוֹצָאוֹ, וּתְקוּפָתוֹ עַל־קְצוֹתָם,
וְאֵין נִסְתָּר מֵחַמָּתוֹ.
תּוֹרַת יהוה תְּמִימָה, מְשִׁיבַת נָפֶשׁ.
עֵדוּת יהוה נֶאֱמָנָה, מַחְכִּימַת פֶּתִי.
פִּקּוּדֵי יהוה יְשָׁרִים, מְשַׂמְּחֵי־לֵב.
מִצְוַת יהוה בָּרָה, מְאִירַת עֵינָיִם.
יִרְאַת יהוה טְהוֹרָה, עוֹמֶדֶת לָעַד.
מִשְׁפְּטֵי־יהוה אֱמֶת, צָדְקוּ יַחְדָּו.
הַנֶּחֱמָדִים מִזָּהָב וּמִפַּז רָב, וּמְתוּקִים מִדְּבַשׁ וְנֹפֶת צוּפִים.
גַּם־עַבְדְּךָ נִזְהָר בָּהֶם, בְּשָׁמְרָם עֵקֶב רָב.
שְׁגִיאוֹת מִי־יָבִין, מִנִּסְתָּרוֹת נַקֵּנִי.
גַּם מִזֵּדִים חֲשֹׂךְ עַבְדֶּךָ, אַל־יִמְשְׁלוּ־בִי.
אָז אֵיתָם וְנִקֵּיתִי מִפֶּשַׁע רָב.
◁ יִהְיוּ לְרָצוֹן אִמְרֵי־פִי וְהֶגְיוֹן לִבִּי לְפָנֶיךָ,
יהוה צוּרִי וְגֹאֲלִי. תהלים יט

PSALM 19. This psalm is composed of three parts. The first celebrates the magnificence of creation, especially the light of the sun. The second is a hymn to Torah, God's teachings. The third is a personal plea by the psalmist for God's understanding of human shortcomings.

THE HEAVENS DECLARE הַשָּׁמַיִם מְסַפְּרִים. Poetically, the inanimate universe is pictured as alive, singing the praises of God and all that God has created.

THE SKY הָרָקִיעַ. Biblical cosmology envisions the sky (also called the firmament) as the vault of the heavens, from which the heavenly bodies are suspended.

SOUNDLESS THE SPEECH אֵין אֹמֶר. A paradox. Though nature does not verbally communicate, it nevertheless does relate the story of creation.

THE TORAH OF ADONAI תּוֹרַת יהוה. Torah means "teaching." Sometimes the word refers to the Five Books of Moses and at other times to any and all divine instruction.

THE DECREES OF ADONAI עֵדוּת יהוה. The Hebrew word is the same as the word used in the Bible to refer to the tablets on which the Ten Commandments (לֻחֹת הָעֵדוּת, luḥot ha-eidut) were written.

OPENING THE EYES מְאִירַת עֵינָיִם. Literally, "enlightening the eyes." This image of "light" connects back to the physical light described in the first section of the psalm.

REVERENCE OF ADONAI יִרְאַת יהוה. In the ancient Near East, to revere a sovereign was to be completely loyal.

MORE PRECIOUS THAN GOLD הַנֶּחֱמָדִים מִזָּהָב. The poet has used six phrases to describe God's teaching and this seventh phrase is climactic, describing the fullness and wonder of the totality. The number seven recalls Genesis, where the seventh day is the culmination of creation. The identification of Torah with creation is a recurrent theme in later rabbinic literature.

MAY THE WORDS יִהְיוּ לְרָצוֹן. This verse is often quoted as an ending to prayers—for instance, in the final meditation of the Amidah.

Psalm 19—
A Personal Prayer

... Help me to be aware
of my selfishness,
  but without undue
  shame or self-judgment.
Let me know that You are
always present,
  in every atom of my life.
Let me keep surrendering
my self
  until I am utterly
  transparent.
Let my words be rooted
in honesty
  and my thoughts be lost
  in Your light,
Unnamable God, my
  essence,
my origin, my lifeblood,
  my home.
          —STEPHEN MITCHELL

PSALM 19

FOR THE LEADER, A SONG OF DAVID.
The heavens declare the glory of God;
the sky proclaims God's handiwork.

Day after day the word goes forth;
night after night the story is told.
Soundless the speech, voiceless the talk,
yet the tale is echoed throughout the world.

The sun, from its tent in the heavens,
emerges like a bridegroom from his chamber—
as exhilarated as a champion, eager to run his course.

From the rim of the east it rises,
to sweep in majesty upward, westward,
warming all on earth as it passes.

The Torah of ADONAI is perfect, reviving the spirit.
The decrees of ADONAI are sure, enlightening the simple.
The precepts of ADONAI are just, gladdening the heart.
The mitzvah of ADONAI is clear, opening the eyes.

Reverence of ADONAI is pure, enduring forever.
The laws of ADONAI are true, altogether just.
They are more precious than gold, even the purest gold,
and sweeter than honey, the drippings of the honeycomb.

Your servant strives to keep them;
to observe them brings great reward.
Yet who can discern one's own errors?

Cleanse me of secret faults.
Restrain Your servant from willful sins;
may they not control me.
Then shall I be clear of wrongs,
innocent of grave transgression.

May the words of my mouth
and the meditations of my heart
be acceptable to You, ADONAI,
my Rock and my Redeemer.

אֲבָרֲכָה אֶת־יהוה בְּכָל־עֵת, תָּמִיד תְּהִלָּתוֹ בְּפִי.

בַּיהוה תִּתְהַלֵּל נַפְשִׁי, יִשְׁמְעוּ עֲנָוִים וְיִשְׂמָחוּ.

גַּדְּלוּ לַיהוה אִתִּי, וּנְרוֹמְמָה שְׁמוֹ יַחְדָּו.

דָּרַשְׁתִּי אֶת־יהוה וְעָנָנִי, וּמִכָּל־מְגוּרוֹתַי הִצִּילָנִי.

הִבִּיטוּ אֵלָיו וְנָהָרוּ, וּפְנֵיהֶם אַל־יֶחְפָּרוּ.

זֶה עָנִי קָרָא וַיהוה שָׁמֵעַ, וּמִכָּל־צָרוֹתָיו הוֹשִׁיעוֹ.

חֹנֶה מַלְאַךְ־יהוה סָבִיב לִירֵאָיו וַיְחַלְּצֵם.

טַעֲמוּ וּרְאוּ כִּי־טוֹב יהוה, אַשְׁרֵי הַגֶּבֶר יֶחֱסֶה־בּוֹ.

יְראוּ אֶת־יהוה קְדֹשָׁיו, כִּי־אֵין מַחְסוֹר לִירֵאָיו.

כְּפִירִים רָשׁוּ וְרָעֵבוּ, וְדֹרְשֵׁי יהוה לֹא־יַחְסְרוּ כָל־טוֹב.

לְכוּ־בָנִים שִׁמְעוּ־לִי, יִרְאַת יהוה אֲלַמֶּדְכֶם.

מִי הָאִישׁ הֶחָפֵץ חַיִּים, אֹהֵב יָמִים לִרְאוֹת טוֹב.

נְצֹר לְשׁוֹנְךָ מֵרָע, וּשְׂפָתֶיךָ מִדַּבֵּר מִרְמָה.

סוּר מֵרָע וַעֲשֵׂה־טוֹב, בַּקֵּשׁ שָׁלוֹם וְרָדְפֵהוּ.

עֵינֵי יהוה אֶל־צַדִּיקִים, וְאָזְנָיו אֶל־שַׁוְעָתָם.

פְּנֵי יהוה בְּעֹשֵׂי רָע, לְהַכְרִית מֵאֶרֶץ זִכְרָם.

צָעֲקוּ וַיהוה שָׁמֵעַ, וּמִכָּל־צָרוֹתָם הִצִּילָם.

קָרוֹב יהוה לְנִשְׁבְּרֵי־לֵב, וְאֶת־דַּכְּאֵי־רוּחַ יוֹשִׁיעַ.

רַבּוֹת רָעוֹת צַדִּיק, וּמִכֻּלָּם יַצִּילֶנּוּ יהוה.

שֹׁמֵר כָּל־עַצְמוֹתָיו, אַחַת מֵהֵנָּה לֹא נִשְׁבָּרָה.

תְּמוֹתֵת רָשָׁע רָעָה, וְשֹׂנְאֵי צַדִּיק יֶאְשָׁמוּ.

◁ פֹּדֶה יהוה נֶפֶשׁ עֲבָדָיו,

וְלֹא יֶאְשְׁמוּ כָּל־הַחֹסִים בּוֹ. תהלים לד

PSALM 34. This is an alphabetical psalm. One letter, *vav*, is elided with the contiguous *zayin*. The poem expresses the pilgrim's yearning for God and stresses God's constancy.

AND WAS FORCED TO FLEE וַיְגָרֲשֵׁהוּ. David fled from Saul to the city of Gath, where the Philistines ruled. Realizing that he might be arrested and killed, David acted insane. The governor, seeing David, declared: "Do I lack madmen that you have brought this fellow to rave for me?" (1 Samuel 21:16). Thus David escaped.

PROCLAIM GOD'S GREATNESS WITH ME גַּדְּלוּ לַיהוה אִתִּי. This verse is recited in the synagogue service just before the Torah is paraded around the room.

ANGEL OF ADONAI מַלְאַךְ יהוה. The Bible frequently speaks of God's angels—messengers—aiding people. These biblical angels have no personality and seem to come and go as needed for specific tasks. As messengers for God, they often cannot be differentiated from God. See for instance Exodus 3:2–4, where one moment an angel appears to Moses in the burning bush, but in the next instant it is God who speaks. Likewise, in the story of the sacrifice of Isaac, God directly addresses Abraham in the first half of the chapter but then an angel appears in the second half (Genesis 22).

THE HOLY ONES קְדֹשָׁיו. The term is applied to the entire congregation of Israel, which is bidden to be God's holy nation (Exodus 19:6).

KEEP YOUR TONGUE FROM EVIL נְצֹר לְשׁוֹנְךָ מֵרָע. The first requirement for being God-fearing is being careful in one's speech. Note the importance of speech in biblical thinking: God spoke and the world came into being.

SEEK PEACE AND PURSUE IT בַּקֵּשׁ שָׁלוֹם וְרָדְפֵהוּ. This theme is reflected in Hillel's saying: "Be of the disciples of Aaron: loving peace and pursuing peace, loving humanity and bringing them close to the Torah" (Avot 1:12). The Bible asks us to "pursue" only two things: peace and justice (see Deuteronomy 16:20).

I Will Praise Adonai at All Times

It is truly a blessing to be able to praise God in each moment, but most of us see God only in extraordinary events. Would that we could see each moment as a new creation, a special time, a manifestation of the holy.

—ABRAHAM ISAAC KOOK
(*adapted*)

Taste and See How Good Adonai Is

That God can be "tasted" implies that God can be beheld intuitively, confronted and related to. The human can share in God....

The human does not only think of God or comply with God's will, but feels the touch of God's hand, the warmth that God's eyes radiate, so to speak.

—JOSEPH BER
SOLOVEITCHIK
(*adapted*)

PSALM 34

A PSALM OF DAVID, WHO FEIGNED MADNESS
BEFORE ABIMELEKH AND WAS FORCED TO FLEE.

I will praise ADONAI at all times, God's glory always on my lips. In ADONAI will I exult; let the humble hear and be glad. Proclaim God's greatness with me; let us exalt God together. I sought ADONAI, who answered me, freeing me from all my fears. Look to God and be radiant, never to be downcast. This poor wretch cried out; ADONAI heard and delivered him from all his troubles. The angel of ADONAI dwells round about those who revere ADONAI, protecting them. Taste and see how good ADONAI is; blessed is the one who takes refuge in God. Let the holy ones revere ADONAI; those who revere God lack for nothing. Even lion cubs may starve and moan, but those who seek ADONAI will not lack any good.

Come, children, listen to me; I will teach you to revere ADONAI.
Which of you desires life,
loves long years discovering goodness?
Keep your tongue from evil, your lips from speaking lies.
Shun evil and do good; seek peace and pursue it.
Mi ha-ish he-ḥafeitz ḥayyim,
ohev yamim lir·ot tov.
N'tzor l'shon'kha mei-ra
u-s'fatekha mi-dabbeir mirmah.
Sur mei-ra va-aseih tov,
bakkeish shalom v'rodfeihu.

The eyes of ADONAI are on the righteous; God's ears are open to their cry. The face of ADONAI is set against evil-doers, to erase all memory of them from the earth. When the righteous cry out, ADONAI listens and sets them free from all their troubles. ADONAI is close to the brokenhearted and helps those who are crushed in spirit. Many are the troubles of the righteous, but with ADONAI's help, they are overcome. God protects every limb; not one is broken. Misfortune slays the wicked, and those who hate the righteous are doomed. ADONAI redeems the life of those who serve God; none who take refuge in God will be forsaken.

אֲדֹנָי, מָעוֹן אַתָּה הָיִיתָ לָּנוּ בְּדֹר וָדֹר. בְּטֶרֶם הָרִים יֻלָּדוּ
וַתְּחוֹלֵל אֶרֶץ וְתֵבֵל, וּמֵעוֹלָם עַד־עוֹלָם אַתָּה אֵל.

תָּשֵׁב אֱנוֹשׁ עַד־דַּכָּא, וַתֹּאמֶר שׁוּבוּ בְנֵי־אָדָם. כִּי אֶלֶף
שָׁנִים בְּעֵינֶיךָ כְּיוֹם אֶתְמוֹל כִּי יַעֲבֹר, וְאַשְׁמוּרָה בַלָּיְלָה.
זְרַמְתָּם שֵׁנָה יִהְיוּ, בַּבֹּקֶר כֶּחָצִיר יַחֲלֹף. בַּבֹּקֶר יָצִיץ
וְחָלָף, לָעֶרֶב יְמוֹלֵל וְיָבֵשׁ. כִּי־כָלִינוּ בְאַפֶּךָ, וּבַחֲמָתְךָ
נִבְהָלְנוּ.

שַׁתָּ עֲוֹנֹתֵינוּ לְנֶגְדֶּךָ, עֲלֻמֵנוּ לִמְאוֹר פָּנֶיךָ. כִּי כָל־יָמֵינוּ
פָּנוּ בְעֶבְרָתֶךָ, כִּלִּינוּ שָׁנֵינוּ כְמוֹ־הֶגֶה. יְמֵי־שְׁנוֹתֵינוּ בָהֶם
שִׁבְעִים שָׁנָה, וְאִם בִּגְבוּרֹת שְׁמוֹנִים שָׁנָה וְרָהְבָּם עָמָל
וָאָוֶן, כִּי־גָז חִישׁ וַנָּעֻפָה. מִי־יוֹדֵעַ עֹז אַפֶּךָ וּכְיִרְאָתְךָ
עֶבְרָתֶךָ.

לִמְנוֹת יָמֵינוּ כֵּן הוֹדַע, וְנָבִא לְבַב חָכְמָה. שׁוּבָה יהוה,
עַד־מָתָי, וְהִנָּחֵם עַל־עֲבָדֶיךָ. שַׂבְּעֵנוּ בַבֹּקֶר חַסְדֶּךָ,
וּנְרַנְּנָה וְנִשְׂמְחָה בְּכָל־יָמֵינוּ. שַׂמְּחֵנוּ כִּימוֹת עִנִּיתָנוּ,
שְׁנוֹת רָאִינוּ רָעָה. יֵרָאֶה אֶל־עֲבָדֶיךָ פָעֳלֶךָ, וַהֲדָרְךָ עַל־
בְּנֵיהֶם.

◁ וִיהִי נֹעַם אֲדֹנָי אֱלֹהֵינוּ עָלֵינוּ, וּמַעֲשֵׂה יָדֵינוּ כּוֹנְנָה
עָלֵינוּ, וּמַעֲשֵׂה יָדֵינוּ כּוֹנְנֵהוּ. תהלים צ

PSALM 90. This is the only psalm attributed to Moses. Perhaps it reflects the despair Moses expressed at the end of his life, when he felt that all was for naught. The poet calls upon God to "return" to earth (שׁוּבָה יהוה)—that is, for God, who is infinite, to understand the human situation, which is finite.

MAN OF GOD אִישׁ־הָאֱלֹהִים. This title is given to Moses in Deuteronomy 33:1: "This is the blessing with which Moses, the man of God, bade the Israelites farewell before he died." Some prophets are also called "men of God" in the Bible, as is King David.

RETURN שׁוּבוּ. As God said to Adam, "You will return to the ground, for from it you were taken. For dust you are, and to dust you shall return" (Genesis 3:19). The word אָדָם (adam), meaning "human being," resembles אֲדָמָה (adamah), "earth."

AS A PASSING DAY כְּיוֹם אֶתְמוֹל. Our own time on earth of seventy (or even eighty) years is paltry compared with the universe's time.

TO USE ALL OF OUR DAYS לִמְנוֹת יָמֵינוּ. Literally, "to count our days," meaning: "Make each of our days count."

RELENT, ADONAI שׁוּבָה יהוה. On the High Holy Days we are especially conscious of the plea in the penultimate stanza of this psalm, which asks God to move from anger and strict judgment to mercy and forgiveness. Then our work and labor will bear fruit and not be in vain.

ESTABLISH THE WORK OF OUR HANDS וּמַעֲשֵׂה יָדֵינוּ כּוֹנְנָה עָלֵינוּ. The final plea of the psalmist is that we might be partners of God in creation—that our work, like God's, may last.

Psalm 90—
A Poetic Rendering

…Teach us how short
our time is;
  let us know it in the
  depths of our souls.
Show us that all things
are transient,
  as insubstantial as
  dreams,
and that after heaven and
earth
  have vanished, there is
  only You.
Fill us in the morning
with Your wisdom;
  shine through us all our
  lives.
Let our hearts soon grow
transparent
  in the radiance of Your
  love.
Show us how precious
each day is;
  teach us to be fully here.
And let the work of our
hands
  prosper, for our little
  while.
        —STEPHEN MITCHELL

PSALM 90

A PRAYER OF MOSES, MAN OF GOD.

ADONAI, You have been our refuge through all generations.
Before the mountains emerged, before the earth was formed,
from age to age, You are God.

> *But humans You crumble into dust,*
> *and You say: "Return, O mortals."*
> *For a thousand years in Your sight*
> *are as a passing day, as an hour of night.*

You engulf all human beings in sleep;
they flourish for a day, like grass.
In the morning it sprouts afresh;
by nightfall it fades and withers.

> *By Your anger we are consumed;*
> *by Your wrath we are overcome.*
> *You set out our transgressions before You,*
> *our secret sins before Your presence.*

Your wrath darkens our days;
our lives are over like a sigh.

> *Threescore and ten our years may number,*
> *fourscore years if granted the vigor.*
> *Laden with trouble and travail,*
> *life quickly passes and flies away.*

Who can know the power of Your wrath?
Who can measure the reverence due You?
Teach us to use all of our days,
that we may attain a heart of wisdom.

> *Relent, ADONAI! How long must we suffer?*
> *Have compassion upon Your servants.*
> *Grant us Your love in the morning,*
> *that we may sing in gladness all our days.*

Match days of sorrow with days of joy
equal to the years we have suffered.
Then Your servants will see Your power;
their children will know Your glory.

> *May ADONAI our God show us compassion,*
> *and establish the work of our hands.*
> *May the work of our hands be firmly established.*

יֵשֵׁב בְּסֵתֶר עֶלְיוֹן, בְּצֵל שַׁדַּי יִתְלוֹנָן.
אֹמַר לַיהוה מַחְסִי וּמְצוּדָתִי, אֱלֹהַי אֶבְטַח־בּוֹ.
כִּי הוּא יַצִּילְךָ מִפַּח יָקוּשׁ, מִדֶּבֶר הַוּוֹת.
בְּאֶבְרָתוֹ יָסֶךְ לָךְ וְתַחַת־כְּנָפָיו תֶּחְסֶה,
צִנָּה וְסֹחֵרָה אֲמִתּוֹ.
לֹא־תִירָא מִפַּחַד לָיְלָה, מֵחֵץ יָעוּף יוֹמָם.
מִדֶּבֶר בָּאֹפֶל יַהֲלֹךְ, מִקֶּטֶב יָשׁוּד צָהֳרָיִם.
יִפֹּל מִצִּדְּךָ אֶלֶף וּרְבָבָה מִימִינֶךָ, אֵלֶיךָ לֹא יִגָּשׁ.
רַק בְּעֵינֶיךָ תַבִּיט, וְשִׁלֻּמַת רְשָׁעִים תִּרְאֶה.
כִּי־אַתָּה יהוה מַחְסִי, עֶלְיוֹן שַׂמְתָּ מְעוֹנֶךָ.
לֹא־תְאֻנֶּה אֵלֶיךָ רָעָה וְנֶגַע לֹא־יִקְרַב בְּאָהֳלֶךָ.
כִּי מַלְאָכָיו יְצַוֶּה־לָּךְ לִשְׁמָרְךָ בְּכָל־דְּרָכֶיךָ.
עַל־כַּפַּיִם יִשָּׂאוּנְךָ, פֶּן־תִּגֹּף בָּאֶבֶן רַגְלֶךָ.
עַל־שַׁחַל וָפֶתֶן תִּדְרֹךְ, תִּרְמֹס כְּפִיר וְתַנִּין.
כִּי בִי חָשַׁק וַאֲפַלְּטֵהוּ, אֲשַׂגְּבֵהוּ כִּי־יָדַע שְׁמִי.
◁ יִקְרָאֵנִי וְאֶעֱנֵהוּ, עִמּוֹ־אָנֹכִי בְצָרָה,
אֲחַלְּצֵהוּ וַאֲכַבְּדֵהוּ.
אֹרֶךְ יָמִים אַשְׂבִּיעֵהוּ, וְאַרְאֵהוּ בִּישׁוּעָתִי.
אֹרֶךְ יָמִים אַשְׂבִּיעֵהוּ, וְאַרְאֵהוּ בִּישׁוּעָתִי. תהלים צא

PSALM 91. This psalm promises God's protection. The worshipper affirms his or her faithfulness and a responding voice offers reassurance of God's protection. Finally, at the end of the psalm, ultimate reassurance is affirmed as God's own voice is heard, promising the supplicant fullness of days.

THE ALMIGHTY שַׁדַּי. Shaddai is a name for God that appears many times throughout the Bible. Already by rabbinic times, its original meaning had been lost and the Rabbis offered a poetic explanation of its etymology as she-dai, "the One who declared that the works of creation were sufficiently complete (dai)."

GOD'S WINGS וְתַחַת־כְּנָפָיו. The image of God as a bird that shelters its young is an ancient metaphor that first appears in the Bible when God speaks to Israel at the foot of Mount Sinai, saying: "You have seen . . . how I bore you on eagles' wings and brought you to Me" (Exodus 19:4).

SINCE YOU ARE DEVOTED TO ME כִּי בִי חָשַׁק. The last three verses of the psalm introduce the voice of God, as if God (rather than any human) is giving assurance of help for the person who dwells "in the shelter of the Most High."

I WILL BE WITH YOU IN TIME OF TROUBLE עִמּוֹ אָנֹכִי בְצָרָה. The Rabbis gave a radical interpretation to this verse, saying that whenever an individual suffers, God suffers with that person (Mekhilta Pisḥa 14).

I WILL SATISFY YOU WITH FULLNESS OF DAYS אֹרֶךְ יָמִים אַשְׂבִּיעֵהוּ, וְאַרְאֵהוּ בִּישׁוּעָתִי. God's ultimate gift is the gift of time.

I Know Not Your Ways

I know not your ways.
A sunset is for me
a Godset.
Where are you going,
God?
Take me along,
if in the along,
it is light,
God,

I am afraid of the dark.

—MALKA HEIFETZ
TUSSMAN
(trans. Marcia Falk)

PSALM 91

Dwelling in the shelter of the Most High,
abiding in the shadow of the Almighty,
I call ADONAI my refuge and fortress,
my God in whom I trust.

> *God will save you from the hidden snare,*
> *from deadly pestilence;*
> *God's wings will cover you*
> *and in God's shelter you will find refuge.*

Fear not terror by night nor the arrow that flies by day,
the pestilence that stalks in darkness
nor the plague that rages at noon.

> *A thousand may fall by your side,*
> *ten thousand close at hand, but it will never touch you;*
> *God's faithfulness will shield you.*

You need only look with your eyes
to see the recompense of the wicked.

> *You have made ADONAI your refuge,*
> *the Most High your haven.*
> *No evil shall befall you;*
> *no plague shall approach your dwelling.*

God will instruct angels to guard you in all your paths,
to carry you in their hands lest you stumble on a stone.

> *You will step on cubs and cobras,*
> *tread safely on lions and serpents.*

"Since you are devoted to Me I will deliver you;
I will protect you because you care for Me.

> *"When you call to Me I will answer;*
> *I will be with you in time of trouble.*
> *I will rescue you and honor you.*

"I will satisfy you with fullness of days,
and show you My salvation."

> *"I will satisfy you with fullness of days,*
> *and show you My salvation."*

הַלְלוּ יָהּ. הַלְלוּ אֶת־שֵׁם יהוה, הַלְלוּ עַבְדֵי יהוה. שֶׁעֹמְדִים בְּבֵית יהוה, בְּחַצְרוֹת בֵּית אֱלֹהֵינוּ. הַלְלוּ־יָהּ כִּי־טוֹב יהוה, זַמְּרוּ לִשְׁמוֹ כִּי נָעִים. כִּי־יַעֲקֹב בָּחַר לוֹ יָהּ, יִשְׂרָאֵל לִסְגֻלָּתוֹ. כִּי אֲנִי יָדַעְתִּי כִּי־גָדוֹל יהוה, וַאֲדֹנֵינוּ מִכָּל־אֱלֹהִים. כֹּל אֲשֶׁר־חָפֵץ יהוה עָשָׂה, בַּשָּׁמַיִם וּבָאָרֶץ בַּיַּמִּים וְכָל־תְּהֹמוֹת. מַעֲלֶה נְשִׂאִים מִקְצֵה הָאָרֶץ, בְּרָקִים לַמָּטָר עָשָׂה, מוֹצֵא־רוּחַ מֵאוֹצְרוֹתָיו. שֶׁהִכָּה בְּכוֹרֵי מִצְרָיִם, מֵאָדָם עַד־בְּהֵמָה. שָׁלַח אוֹתֹת וּמֹפְתִים בְּתוֹכֵכִי מִצְרָיִם, בְּפַרְעֹה וּבְכָל־עֲבָדָיו. שֶׁהִכָּה גּוֹיִם רַבִּים, וְהָרַג מְלָכִים עֲצוּמִים. לְסִיחוֹן מֶלֶךְ הָאֱמֹרִי וּלְעוֹג מֶלֶךְ הַבָּשָׁן, וּלְכֹל מַמְלְכוֹת כְּנָעַן. וְנָתַן אַרְצָם נַחֲלָה, נַחֲלָה לְיִשְׂרָאֵל עַמּוֹ. יהוה שִׁמְךָ לְעוֹלָם, יהוה זִכְרְךָ לְדֹר־וָדֹר. כִּי־יָדִין יהוה עַמּוֹ, וְעַל־עֲבָדָיו יִתְנֶחָם. עֲצַבֵּי הַגּוֹיִם כֶּסֶף וְזָהָב, מַעֲשֵׂה יְדֵי אָדָם. פֶּה־לָהֶם וְלֹא יְדַבֵּרוּ, עֵינַיִם לָהֶם וְלֹא יִרְאוּ. אָזְנַיִם לָהֶם וְלֹא יַאֲזִינוּ, אַף אֵין־יֶשׁ־רוּחַ בְּפִיהֶם. כְּמוֹהֶם יִהְיוּ עֹשֵׂיהֶם, כֹּל אֲשֶׁר־בֹּטֵחַ בָּהֶם. ◁ בֵּית יִשְׂרָאֵל בָּרְכוּ אֶת־יהוה, בֵּית אַהֲרֹן בָּרְכוּ אֶת־יהוה. בֵּית הַלֵּוִי בָּרְכוּ אֶת־יהוה, יִרְאֵי יהוה בָּרְכוּ אֶת־יהוה. בָּרוּךְ יהוה מִצִּיּוֹן, שֹׁכֵן יְרוּשָׁלָיִם. הַלְלוּ־יָהּ. תהלים קלה

PSALM 135. This psalm is one of many "Halleluyah" psalms praising God for wondrous interventions in the history of the people Israel. It begins and ends with a call to the people standing in the Temple to praise and bless God. At the end, all who assembled in the Temple precincts—priests, Israelites, non-Israelites—are asked to join in.

HALLELUYAH הַלְלוּ יָהּ. A compound word in Hebrew: "Praise Yah." "Yah" is a shortened form of the name of God.

SERVANTS OF ADONAI עַבְדֵי יהוה. The phrase refers to Israel, of whom it is written: "My servants, whom I freed from the land of Egypt" (Leviticus 25:42). It is also a play on words, since those gathered are participating in the Temple service, called עֲבוֹדָה (avodah), from the same root as עֶבֶד (eved), "servant." The Rabbis called prayer עֲבוֹדָה שֶׁבַּלֵּב (avodah she-ba-lev), "the service of the heart."

IN THE COURTS OF THE HOUSE OF OUR GOD בְּחַצְרוֹת בֵּית אֱלֹהֵינוּ. The Temple consisted largely of open courts in which the people stood; sacrifices were offered on an upper platform.

SMOTE THE FIRSTBORN OF EGYPT שֶׁהִכָּה בְּכוֹרֵי מִצְרָיִם. This begins the recounting of God's deeds in the history of Israel. Smiting of the firstborn is singled out because it was the ultimate plague that broke the will of the Egyptians. (Ibn Ezra)

SIHON, KING OF THE AMORITES לְסִיחוֹן מֶלֶךְ הָאֱמֹרִי. Numbers 21:21–35. Israel offered to make peace with Sihon, king of the Amorites, and Og, king of Bashan, asking only permission to cross their land on the way to Canaan. These kings chose instead to fight, and they were defeated by the Israelites.

GAVE THEIR LAND וְנָתַן אַרְצָם. The lands of Sihon and Og, which were on the eastern side of the Jordan River and not part of Canaan, were occupied by the tribes of Reuben, Gad, and half of the tribe of Manasseh.

ADONAI, YOUR GLORY ENDURES FOREVER יהוה שִׁמְךָ לְעוֹלָם. Or: "Your name endures forever." "Name" and "fame" often are coupled, to connote "an enduring reputation." Both the workings of nature and the events of our history are ways that God's presence is made known in the world.

YOU WHO REVERE ADONAI יִרְאֵי יהוה. In biblical literature this is a technical term referring specifically to the non-Israelites who attended the Temple worship service.

WHO DWELLS IN JERUSALEM שֹׁכֵן יְרוּשָׁלָיִם. Even though the entire world is not sufficient to contain the Almighty, God is described as dwelling amidst God's people. A similar thought is expressed in Solomon's prayer at the dedication of the Temple (1 Kings 8).

Idols

What is an idol? A thing, a force, a person, a group, an institution or an ideal, regarded as supreme. God alone is supreme. . . .

Even the laws of the Torah are not absolutes. Nothing is deified: neither power nor wisdom, neither heroes nor institutions. To ascribe divine qualities to all of these, to anything, sublime and lofty as it may be, is to distort both the idea it represents and the concept of the Divine which we bestow upon it . . .

Nothing exists for its own sake, nothing is valid by its own right. What seems to be a purpose is but a station on the road. All is set in the dimension of the holy. All is endowed with bearing on God.

To be a Jew is to renounce allegiance to false gods; to be sensitive to God's infinite stake in every finite situation; to bear witness to God's presence in the hours of God's concealment; to remember that the world is unredeemed. . . . We are chosen to remain free of infatuation with worldly triumphs, to retain independence of hysteria and deceptive glories; never to surrender to splendor, even at the price of remaining strangers to fashion. . . .

It is impossible to grasp spirit in itself. Spirit is a *direction*, the turning of all beings to God.

—ABRAHAM JOSHUA
HESCHEL

PSALM 135

Halleluyah! Praise the name of ADONAI.
Give praise, servants of ADONAI
who stand in the House of ADONAI,
in the courts of the House of our God.
Halleluyah! For ADONAI is good.
Sing to God, who is gracious.

God chose Jacob, the people Israel as a special treasure.
I know that ADONAI is great,
greater than everything worshipped as divine.
Whatever ADONAI has willed
has come to be in the heavens and on earth,
in the sea and all the depths.
God gathers clouds from the ends of the earth,
makes lightning for the rain,
and releases the wind from its vaults.

God smote the firstborn of Egypt, human and beast alike,
and sent signs and portents in Egypt
against Pharaoh and all of his subjects.
God smote many nations and slew mighty kings:
Sihon, king of the Amorites;
Og, king of Bashan; and all the princes of Canaan.
God gave their land as a heritage to the people Israel.
ADONAI, Your glory endures forever;
Your fame, ADONAI, for all generations.
ADONAI will vindicate the people;
God will have compassion for God's servants.

The idols of the nations are silver and gold,
made by human hands.
They have mouths that cannot speak;
they have eyes that cannot see.
They have ears that cannot hear,
nor have they breath in their mouths.
Their makers shall become like them,
so shall all who trust in them.

House of Israel, praise ADONAI;
House of Aaron, praise ADONAI.
House of Levi, praise ADONAI;
you who revere ADONAI, praise ADONAI.
Praised from Zion be ADONAI who dwells in Jerusalem.
Halleluyah!

הוֹדוּ לַיהוה כִּי־טוֹב   כִּי לְעוֹלָם חַסְדּוֹ.
הוֹדוּ לֵאלֹהֵי הָאֱלֹהִים   כִּי לְעוֹלָם חַסְדּוֹ.
הוֹדוּ לַאֲדֹנֵי הָאֲדֹנִים   כִּי לְעוֹלָם חַסְדּוֹ.

לְעֹשֵׂה נִפְלָאוֹת גְּדֹלוֹת לְבַדּוֹ   כִּי לְעוֹלָם חַסְדּוֹ.
לְעֹשֵׂה הַשָּׁמַיִם בִּתְבוּנָה   כִּי לְעוֹלָם חַסְדּוֹ.
לְרֹקַע הָאָרֶץ עַל־הַמָּיִם   כִּי לְעוֹלָם חַסְדּוֹ.

לְעֹשֵׂה אוֹרִים גְּדֹלִים   כִּי לְעוֹלָם חַסְדּוֹ.
אֶת־הַשֶּׁמֶשׁ לְמֶמְשֶׁלֶת בַּיּוֹם   כִּי לְעוֹלָם חַסְדּוֹ.
אֶת־הַיָּרֵחַ וְכוֹכָבִים לְמֶמְשְׁלוֹת בַּלָּיְלָה   כִּי לְעוֹלָם חַסְדּוֹ.

לְמַכֵּה מִצְרַיִם בִּבְכוֹרֵיהֶם   כִּי לְעוֹלָם חַסְדּוֹ.
וַיּוֹצֵא יִשְׂרָאֵל מִתּוֹכָם   כִּי לְעוֹלָם חַסְדּוֹ.
בְּיָד חֲזָקָה וּבִזְרוֹעַ נְטוּיָה   כִּי לְעוֹלָם חַסְדּוֹ.

לְגֹזֵר יַם־סוּף לִגְזָרִים   כִּי לְעוֹלָם חַסְדּוֹ.
וְהֶעֱבִיר יִשְׂרָאֵל בְּתוֹכוֹ   כִּי לְעוֹלָם חַסְדּוֹ.
וְנִעֵר פַּרְעֹה וְחֵילוֹ בְיַם־סוּף   כִּי לְעוֹלָם חַסְדּוֹ.

לְמוֹלִיךְ עַמּוֹ בַּמִּדְבָּר   כִּי לְעוֹלָם חַסְדּוֹ.
לְמַכֵּה מְלָכִים גְּדֹלִים   כִּי לְעוֹלָם חַסְדּוֹ.
וַיַּהֲרֹג מְלָכִים אַדִּירִים   כִּי לְעוֹלָם חַסְדּוֹ.

לְסִיחוֹן מֶלֶךְ הָאֱמֹרִי   כִּי לְעוֹלָם חַסְדּוֹ.
וּלְעוֹג מֶלֶךְ הַבָּשָׁן   כִּי לְעוֹלָם חַסְדּוֹ.

וְנָתַן אַרְצָם לְנַחֲלָה   כִּי לְעוֹלָם חַסְדּוֹ.
נַחֲלָה לְיִשְׂרָאֵל עַבְדּוֹ   כִּי לְעוֹלָם חַסְדּוֹ.

◁ שֶׁבְּשִׁפְלֵנוּ זָכַר לָנוּ   כִּי לְעוֹלָם חַסְדּוֹ.
וַיִּפְרְקֵנוּ מִצָּרֵינוּ   כִּי לְעוֹלָם חַסְדּוֹ.

נֹתֵן לֶחֶם לְכָל־בָּשָׂר   כִּי לְעוֹלָם חַסְדּוֹ.
הוֹדוּ לְאֵל הַשָּׁמָיִם   כִּי לְעוֹלָם חַסְדּוֹ.

תהלים קלו

PSALM 136. According to some rabbis, Psalms 135 and 136 originally formed one unit and were known as הַלֵּל הַגָּדוֹל (hallel ha-gadol), "the great Hallel" (Jerusalem Talmud, Pesaḥim 5:7; Babylonian Talmud, Pesaḥim 118a). Each verse of Psalm 136 contains the liturgical response found in thanksgiving psalms: כִּי לְעוֹלָם חַסְדּוֹ (ki l'olam ḥasdo), "God's love endures forever." When the Levites used to recite such psalms in the Temple, this refrain was the people's response. Here the refrain occurs twenty-six times, which is the numerical equivalent of God's name, יהוה (yod-hei-vav-hei). (Abudarham)

GOD, WHO IS ALMIGHTY לֵאלֹהֵי הָאֱלֹהִים. This and other phrases that follow are reminiscent of the language of Deuteronomy.

GOD GIVES FOOD TO ALL FLESH נֹתֵן לֶחֶם לְכָל־בָּשָׂר. Turning from Israel's history to a more general topic, God is praised for sustaining all life. Thus the psalm comes full circle: it begins and ends by praising God as the creator of all.

Exodus

In an early rabbinic commentary on Exodus, the famous sage Judah Ha-Nasi is quoted as saying: "Through the strength of God Israel went out of Egypt, as it is said: 'By strength of hand, the Lord brought us out of Egypt.'" But, the commentary continues, there is "another interpretation": "With an alertness of their own Israel went out of Egypt, as it is said: 'And thus shall ye eat [the paschal lamb]: with your loins girded, your shoes on your feet, and your staff in your hand.'". . . Many men and women, believing in God's mighty hand, have nevertheless girded their loins, challenged the pharaohs of their own time, marched into the wilderness—and understood what they were doing by reading Exodus.

—MICHAEL WALZER
(adapted)

PSALM 136

Praise ADONAI, for God is good;
praise God, who is almighty;
praise the supreme sovereign: *ki l'olam ḥasdo*;
        God's love endures forever.

Praise God, who works great wonders alone,
making the heavens with wisdom,
suspending earth over waters: *ki l'olam ḥasdo*;
        God's love endures forever.

God made the great lights,
the sun to rule by day,
the moon and stars to rule by night: *ki l'olam ḥasdo*;
        God's love endures forever.

God smote the Egyptian firstborn,
and brought Israel out of their midst
with strong hand and outstretched arm: *ki l'olam ḥasdo*;
        God's love endures forever.

God split the Sea of Reeds,
and brought Israel through,
while sweeping Pharaoh and his
  troops into the sea: *ki l'olam ḥasdo*;
        God's love endures forever.

God led the people in the wilderness,
smiting great kings—slaying the mighty Sihon,
king of the Amorites, and Og, king of Bashan: *ki l'olam ḥasdo*;
        God's love endures forever.

God gave their land
as a heritage to God's servant Israel,
remembering us when we were low,
and rescuing us from our oppressors: *ki l'olam ḥasdo*;
        God's love endures forever.

God gives food to all flesh,
Praise the Sovereign of heaven;   *ki l'olam ḥasdo*;
        God's love endures forever.

רַנְּנוּ צַדִּיקִים בַּיהוה, לַיְשָׁרִים נָאוָה תְהִלָּה. הוֹדוּ לַיהוה בְּכִנּוֹר, בְּנֵבֶל עָשׂוֹר זַמְּרוּ־לוֹ. שִׁירוּ־לוֹ שִׁיר חָדָשׁ, הֵיטִיבוּ נַגֵּן בִּתְרוּעָה. כִּי־יָשָׁר דְּבַר־יהוה, וְכָל־מַעֲשֵׂהוּ בֶּאֱמוּנָה. אֹהֵב צְדָקָה וּמִשְׁפָּט, חֶסֶד יהוה מָלְאָה הָאָרֶץ.

בִּדְבַר יהוה שָׁמַיִם נַעֲשׂוּ, וּבְרוּחַ פִּיו כָּל־צְבָאָם. כֹּנֵס כַּנֵּד מֵי הַיָּם, נֹתֵן בְּאוֹצָרוֹת תְּהוֹמוֹת. יִירְאוּ מֵיהוה כָּל־הָאָרֶץ, מִמֶּנּוּ יָגוּרוּ כָּל־יֹשְׁבֵי תֵבֵל. כִּי הוּא אָמַר וַיֶּהִי, הוּא צִוָּה וַיַּעֲמֹד. יהוה הֵפִיר עֲצַת־גּוֹיִם, הֵנִיא מַחְשְׁבוֹת עַמִּים. עֲצַת יהוה לְעוֹלָם תַּעֲמֹד, מַחְשְׁבוֹת לִבּוֹ לְדֹר וָדֹר.

אַשְׁרֵי הַגּוֹי אֲשֶׁר־יהוה אֱלֹהָיו, הָעָם בָּחַר לְנַחֲלָה לוֹ. מִשָּׁמַיִם הִבִּיט יהוה, רָאָה אֶת־כָּל־בְּנֵי הָאָדָם. מִמְּכוֹן־שִׁבְתּוֹ הִשְׁגִּיחַ, אֶל כָּל־יֹשְׁבֵי הָאָרֶץ. הַיֹּצֵר יַחַד לִבָּם, הַמֵּבִין אֶל־כָּל־מַעֲשֵׂיהֶם.

אֵין הַמֶּלֶךְ נוֹשָׁע בְּרָב־חָיִל, גִּבּוֹר לֹא־יִנָּצֵל בְּרָב־כֹּחַ. שֶׁקֶר הַסּוּס לִתְשׁוּעָה, וּבְרֹב חֵילוֹ לֹא יְמַלֵּט. הִנֵּה עֵין יהוה אֶל־יְרֵאָיו, לַמְיַחֲלִים לְחַסְדּוֹ. לְהַצִּיל מִמָּוֶת נַפְשָׁם, וּלְחַיּוֹתָם בָּרָעָב.

נַפְשֵׁנוּ חִכְּתָה לַיהוה, עֶזְרֵנוּ וּמָגִנֵּנוּ הוּא. ◁ כִּי־בוֹ יִשְׂמַח לִבֵּנוּ, כִּי בְשֵׁם קָדְשׁוֹ בָטָחְנוּ. יְהִי־חַסְדְּךָ יהוה עָלֵינוּ כַּאֲשֶׁר יִחַלְנוּ לָךְ. תהלים לג

PSALM 33. This psalm begins as a call to worship God, after which it sets forth a credo announcing God's justice and compassion. At the conclusion, the assembled worshippers express their trust in God and pray for God's protecting care. There is a recurrent use of the number seven: seven teachings about God, seven words indicating praise at the beginning of the psalm, and seven expressions in the last three verses ending in the suffix נו- (-nu), "we" or "us" or "our." Each verse of the psalm forms a perfect parallelism, as if it too calls for a reader and congregational response, like the previous psalm.

SING TO ADONAI, YOU RIGHTEOUS רַנְּנוּ צַדִּיקִים בַּיהוה. The leader calls upon the assembled multitude in the Temple to joyfully sing to God. They are called "righteous" and "upright" since they are devoted to God and have come to worship.

WITH THE TEN-STRINGED LUTE בְּנֵבֶל עָשׂוֹר. Some think that the instrument mentioned here, נֵבֶל (neivel), is a wind instrument and the "ten" refers to holes. Furthermore, it is not clear if the psalm mentions two or three instruments. Ibn Ezra thinks the עָשׂוֹר (asor), "ten," is a separate instrument.

LOVES RIGHTEOUSNESS AND JUSTICE אֹהֵב צְדָקָה וּמִשְׁפָּט. Divine attributes that we are called upon to imitate.

ALL THEY CONTAIN כָּל־צְבָאָם. Literally, "all their host." The verse paraphrases Genesis 2:1, which sums up all creation thus: "The heavens and the earth were finished, and all their host." The phrase probably includes the sun, moon, and stars, as well as trees, fish, birds, and animals.

GATHERS . . . AS A MOUND כֹּנֵס כַּנֵּד. Another reference to the story of creation, where the waters are gathered together so that dry land appears (Genesis 1:9).

HORSES ARE A DELUSION OF SECURITY שֶׁקֶר הַסּוּס לִתְשׁוּעָה. Chariots were a critical element in Egyptian military formations. Psalms frequently contrast faith in God to belief in military might.

LONGINGLY WE HOPE IN ADONAI נַפְשֵׁנוּ חִכְּתָה לַיהוה. At the end of the psalm, the assembled group speaks and identifies itself as those worthy of God's concern.

שחרית לראש השנה וליום כיפור · פסוקי דזמרא **57**

Sing

The Baal Shem Tov taught that the way to praise God is first to begin with words and then, as our souls rise, to give expression to the words with song; the music moves us to sing without words, and finally, our whole body wants to praise God and we dance.

PSALM 33

Sing to ADONAI, you righteous;
it is fitting for the upright to praise God.
Praise ADONAI on the harp;
sing to God songs with the ten-stringed lute.
Sing to God a new song; play sweetly and shout for joy,
for the word of ADONAI holds true; all God's deeds endure.
God loves righteousness and justice;
the earth is filled with divine love.

By the word of ADONAI were the heavens made;
at God's command, all they contain.
God gathers the waters of the sea as a mound,
and stores the deep in vaults.

Let all the earth revere ADONAI, and all who inhabit the world stand in awe.
For God spoke, and it came to be; God commanded, and it stood firm.

ADONAI annuls the plans of nations and thwarts the designs of peoples.
ADONAI's plans stand firm forever; God's designs shall endure throughout the ages.
Blessed is the nation for whom ADONAI is God, the people chosen as God's heritage.

ADONAI looks out from heaven and beholds all mortals.
From God's dwelling place God surveys all the inhabitants of the earth;
the One who fashioned the hearts of all, discerns all their deeds.

A king is not rescued by an army, nor is a warrior saved by sheer strength.
Horses are a delusion of security; their great power provides no escape.

ADONAI watches over those who revere the Divine,
over those who hope for God's lovingkindness,
to save them from death, and sustain their lives during famine.

Longingly we hope in ADONAI; God is our help and our shield.
In God our hearts rejoice; in God's holy name have we put our trust.
May we enjoy Your lovingkindness, ADONAI, as we have placed our hope in You.

טוֹב לְהֹדוֹת לַיהוה, וּלְזַמֵּר לְשִׁמְךָ עֶלְיוֹן.
לְהַגִּיד בַּבֹּקֶר חַסְדֶּךָ, וֶאֱמוּנָתְךָ בַּלֵּילוֹת.
עֲלֵי־עָשׂוֹר וַעֲלֵי־נָבֶל, עֲלֵי הִגָּיוֹן בְּכִנּוֹר.
כִּי שִׂמַּחְתַּנִי יהוה בְּפָעֳלֶךָ, בְּמַעֲשֵׂי יָדֶיךָ אֲרַנֵּן.
מַה־גָּדְלוּ מַעֲשֶׂיךָ יהוה, מְאֹד עָמְקוּ מַחְשְׁבֹתֶיךָ.
אִישׁ־בַּעַר לֹא יֵדָע, וּכְסִיל לֹא־יָבִין אֶת־זֹאת.
בִּפְרֹחַ רְשָׁעִים כְּמוֹ עֵשֶׂב, וַיָּצִיצוּ כָּל־פֹּעֲלֵי אָוֶן,
לְהִשָּׁמְדָם עֲדֵי־עַד.
וְאַתָּה מָרוֹם לְעֹלָם יהוה.
כִּי הִנֵּה אֹיְבֶיךָ יהוה,
כִּי־הִנֵּה אֹיְבֶיךָ יֹאבֵדוּ,
יִתְפָּרְדוּ כָּל־פֹּעֲלֵי אָוֶן.
וַתָּרֶם כִּרְאֵים קַרְנִי, בַּלֹּתִי בְּשֶׁמֶן רַעֲנָן.
וַתַּבֵּט עֵינִי בְּשׁוּרָי,
בַּקָּמִים עָלַי מְרֵעִים תִּשְׁמַעְנָה אָזְנָי.

צַדִּיק כַּתָּמָר יִפְרָח,
כְּאֶרֶז בַּלְּבָנוֹן יִשְׂגֶּה.
שְׁתוּלִים בְּבֵית יהוה,
בְּחַצְרוֹת אֱלֹהֵינוּ יַפְרִיחוּ.
◁ עוֹד יְנוּבוּן בְּשֵׂיבָה, דְּשֵׁנִים וְרַעֲנַנִּים יִהְיוּ.
לְהַגִּיד כִּי־יָשָׁר יהוה, צוּרִי וְלֹא־עַוְלָתָה בּוֹ.   תהלים צב

PSALM 92. Perhaps this psalm received the title "A Song for Shabbat" because of its reference to creation and its expression of hope for the time to come. Shabbat celebrates the culmination of creation and also foreshadows the tranquility of the end of days. The days of the Jewish week are enumerated as a progression toward Shabbat and so this psalm has been included in holy day prayers even when they fall on weekdays.

THE THOUGHTLESS CANNOT COMPREHEND אִישׁ־בַּעַר לֹא יֵדָע. The psalm raises the perennial problem of the suffering of the just and the prosperity of the wicked. Only the foolish and thoughtless, says the psalmist, will assume that this is a permanent situation.

YOUR ENEMIES SHALL PERISH אֹיְבֶיךָ יֹאבֵדוּ. In pagan mythology, the gods have divine enemies whom they must battle. The Bible came to view the primal struggle not as one between competing divinities, but rather as one between God and human evil.

LIKE THE HORN OF THE OX וַתָּרֶם כִּרְאֵים קַרְנִי. The identity of the animal referred to here is pure conjecture. Early English translations call it a "unicorn" because the Hebrew refers to a single horn.

TRANSPLANTED IN THE HOUSE OF ADONAI שְׁתוּלִים בְּבֵית יהוה. According to rabbinic tradition, there were two stones in front of the ancient Temple, one short and one tall. In the psalm, the tall palm and the broad cedar of Lebanon are seen as a living representation of that image. The righteous become the living monuments who, planted at the entrance to God's house, now greet all worshippers.

Psalm 92—An Interpretive Translation

It is good to sing praise to You, Lord,
  and to thank You for all Your blessings,
to proclaim Your love in the morning
  and Your faithfulness every night,
with the music of the human voice
  or the melody of my silence.
For You let me delight in Your world, Lord;
  You make my heart sing with joy.
How great is Your goodness, Lord;
  how unfathomable Your justice!
It can't be seen by our eyes
  and can't be grasped by our thinking;
but every secret is told,
  every crime is punished,
every good deed is rewarded,
  every wrong is redressed.
Though chaos rules on the surface,
  in the depths all becomes law.

And the wise flourish like palm trees;
  they grow like the cedars of Lebanon.
They are planted in the dark soil of God,
  and their leaves keep turning to [God's] light.
Even in old age they bear fruit;
  they are green and supple and strong:
living proof that the Lord is just and [the Lord's] way is perfect.

—STEPHEN MITCHELL

PSALM 92

A SONG FOR SHABBAT.

It is good to thank You, ADONAI,
to sing Your praise, exalted God,
  to affirm Your love each morning,
  and Your faithfulness in the night,
  to the music of the lute
  and the melody of the harp.
Your creation, ADONAI, gives me joy,
I sing of Your handiwork.
  How vast Your works, ADONAI,
  Your designs are wonderfully intricate.
The thoughtless cannot comprehend,
the foolish cannot fathom this:
  the wicked flourish like grass,
  and those who commit evil blossom,
  only to be destroyed in the end.
  But You, ADONAI, are supreme forever.
Surely, Your enemies, ADONAI,
surely, Your enemies shall perish;
those who commit evil shall crumble.
  And You will raise my head high, like the horn of the ox,
  anointing me with fragrant oil.
My eyes will look directly at the ranks of my foes,
and as enemies gather against me, my ears will hear:
  The righteous shall flourish like the palm tree;
  they shall endure like a cedar in Lebanon,
  transplanted in the house of ADONAI,
  thriving in our God's courtyard.
In old age, they are yet fruitful,
always fresh and fragrant,
proclaiming that ADONAI is flawless,
my stronghold, never unjust.

Tzaddik ka-tamar yifraḥ, k'erez ba-l'vanon yisgeh.
Sh'tulim b'veit Adonai, b'ḥatzrot eloheinu yafriḥu.
Od y'nuvun b'seivah, d'sheinim v'ra·anannim yihyu,
l'haggid ki yashar Adonai, tzuri v'lo avlatah bo.

יְהוֹה מָלָךְ גֵּאוּת לָבֵשׁ,
לָבֵשׁ יְהוֹה עֹז הִתְאַזָּר,
אַף־תִּכּוֹן תֵּבֵל בַּל־תִּמּוֹט.
נָכוֹן כִּסְאֲךָ מֵאָז מֵעוֹלָם אָתָּה.
נָשְׂאוּ נְהָרוֹת יְהוֹה,
נָשְׂאוּ נְהָרוֹת קוֹלָם,
יִשְׂאוּ נְהָרוֹת דָּכְיָם.
מִקֹּלוֹת מַיִם רַבִּים אַדִּירִים מִשְׁבְּרֵי־יָם,
אַדִּיר בַּמָּרוֹם יְהוֹה.
◁ עֵדֹתֶיךָ נֶאֶמְנוּ מְאֹד,
לְבֵיתְךָ נָאֲוָה־קֹּדֶשׁ יְהוֹה, לְאֹרֶךְ יָמִים. תהלים צג

יְהִי כְבוֹד יְהוֹה לְעוֹלָם, יִשְׂמַח יְהוֹה בְּמַעֲשָׂיו. יְהִי שֵׁם
יְהוֹה מְבֹרָךְ מֵעַתָּה וְעַד־עוֹלָם. מִמִּזְרַח־שֶׁמֶשׁ עַד־
מְבוֹאוֹ, מְהֻלָּל שֵׁם יְהוֹה. רָם עַל־כָּל־גּוֹיִם יְהוֹה, עַל
הַשָּׁמַיִם כְּבוֹדוֹ. יְהוֹה שִׁמְךָ לְעוֹלָם, יְהוֹה זִכְרְךָ לְדֹר־וָדֹר.
יְהוֹה בַּשָּׁמַיִם הֵכִין כִּסְאוֹ, וּמַלְכוּתוֹ בַּכֹּל מָשָׁלָה. יִשְׂמְחוּ
הַשָּׁמַיִם וְתָגֵל הָאָרֶץ, וְיֹאמְרוּ בַגּוֹיִם יְהוֹה מָלָךְ. יְהוֹה
מֶלֶךְ, יְהוֹה מָלָךְ, יְהוֹה יִמְלֹךְ לְעֹלָם וָעֶד. יְהוֹה מֶלֶךְ
עוֹלָם וָעֶד, אָבְדוּ גוֹיִם מֵאַרְצוֹ. יְהוֹה הֵפִיר עֲצַת־גּוֹיִם,
הֵנִיא מַחְשְׁבוֹת עַמִּים. רַבּוֹת מַחֲשָׁבוֹת בְּלֶב־אִישׁ, וַעֲצַת
יְהוֹה הִיא תָקוּם. עֲצַת יְהוֹה לְעוֹלָם תַּעֲמֹד, מַחְשְׁבוֹת
לִבּוֹ לְדֹר וָדֹר. כִּי הוּא אָמַר וַיֶּהִי, הוּא־צִוָּה וַיַּעֲמֹד. כִּי־
בָחַר יְהוֹה בְּצִיּוֹן, אִוָּהּ לְמוֹשָׁב לוֹ. כִּי־יַעֲקֹב בָּחַר לוֹ יָהּ,
יִשְׂרָאֵל לִסְגֻלָּתוֹ. כִּי לֹא־יִטֹּשׁ יְהוֹה עַמּוֹ, וְנַחֲלָתוֹ לֹא יַעֲזֹב.
◁ וְהוּא רַחוּם יְכַפֵּר עָוֹן וְלֹא יַשְׁחִית, וְהִרְבָּה לְהָשִׁיב
אַפּוֹ וְלֹא־יָעִיר כָּל־חֲמָתוֹ. יְהוֹה הוֹשִׁיעָה, הַמֶּלֶךְ יַעֲנֵנוּ
בְיוֹם־קָרְאֵנוּ.

PSALM 93. Some modern commentators see this psalm as a "coronation psalm," proclaiming God's sovereignty over the entire cosmos. It is thought that such psalms may have been written for the celebration of the biblical new year.

THE RIVERS RAISE UP THEIR WAVES יִשְׂאוּ נְהָרוֹת דָּכְיָם. Whereas in other ancient cultures there were divine forces that ruled the sea and threatened other divinities, here the waters reach up to praise God.

ADONAI'S GLORY ENDURES FOREVER יְהִי כְבוֹד יְהוֹה לְעוֹלָם. According to the Rabbis, this verse was recited by "the Angel of the Universe" (i.e., the chief angel) at the creation, marveling at the way in which all things obeyed God's will (Babylonian Talmud, Ḥullin 60a). This prayer is made up of a collection of biblical verses, mostly from the Book of Psalms: Psalm 104:31; Psalm 113:2–4; Psalm 135:13; Psalm 103:19; 1 Chronicles 16:31; Psalm 10:16; Psalm 93:1; Exodus 15:18; Psalm 10:16; Psalm 33:10; Proverbs 19:21; Psalm 33:11; Psalm 33:9; Psalm 132:13; Psalm 135:4; Psalm 94:14; Psalm 78:38; and Psalm 20:10. The themes include: God's rule over the entire universe, both heaven and earth;

the destruction of the evildoers; God's covenantal relationship with Israel; and a plea for compassion for the people Israel, though they may sin. A seemingly natural poetic flow from one verse to the next is created by the presence of similar words in each one.

GOD, BEING MERCIFUL, GRANTS ATONEMENT FOR SIN וְהוּא רַחוּם יְכַפֵּר עָוֹן. These last two verses are found in other prayers that—like this one—date from the first millennium c.e. and comprise a sequence of biblical verses. (For example, see Kedushah D'sidra, p. 180, and Taḥanun, the weekday penitential prayers following the Amidah.) These same verses precede the Bar'khu, the call to worship, in the weekday evening service. The theme of God's mercy is thus constantly evoked.

*Psalm 93—An
Interpretive Translation*

God acts within every
moment
   and creates the world
   with each breath.
[God] speaks from the
center of the universe,
   in the silence beyond all
   thought.
Mightier than the crash of
a thunderstorm,
   mightier than the roar
   of the sea,
is God's voice silently
speaking
   in the depths of the
   listening heart.

   —STEPHEN MITCHELL

PSALM 93

ADONAI is sovereign, robed in splendor,
girded in strength.
   So the earth is established,
   on sure foundation.
Your kingdom stands from earliest time;
You are eternal.
   The rivers rise to You, ADONAI,
   the rivers raise their voices,
   the rivers raise up their waves.
From the roaring of the deep,
and the mighty breakers of the sea:
"ADONAI is supreme."
   Your teaching, ADONAI, never fails;
   holiness befits Your house, ADONAI,
   in the fullness of days.

GOD'S JUST RULE AND GOD'S MERCY:
AN ANTHOLOGY OF BIBLICAL VERSES

ADONAI's glory endures forever; may God rejoice with God's
creation. May ADONAI be praised now and forever. Praised be
God from the rising to the setting of the sun. ADONAI is exalted
beyond all nations; God's glory extends beyond the heavens.
Your glory, ADONAI, endures forever; Your fame throughout
all generations. ADONAI established a throne in heaven; God's
sovereignty encompasses all. The heavens rejoice and the earth
is glad; the nations declare: "ADONAI is sovereign." ADONAI
reigns, ADONAI has reigned, ADONAI shall reign throughout
all time. ADONAI shall reign forever and ever; many peoples
shall vanish from God's land. ADONAI thwarts the designs of
such nations, foiling the plans of such peoples. Many plans rise
in human hearts, but ADONAI's designs are fulfilled. For when
God spoke it came to be; God issued a command and the world
took form. ADONAI has chosen Zion, desiring it for God's
dwelling place. God has chosen Jacob for God's own, the people
Israel as God's treasure. ADONAI will not abandon this people,
nor forsake those who inherit ADONAI's favor. God, being merciful, grants atonement for sin and does not destroy. Time and
again God restrains wrath, refusing to let rage be all-consuming.
Save us, ADONAI. Answer us, Sovereign, when we call.

אַשְׁרֵי יוֹשְׁבֵי בֵיתֶךָ, עוֹד יְהַלְלוּךָ סֶּלָה.
אַשְׁרֵי הָעָם שֶׁכָּכָה לּוֹ, אַשְׁרֵי הָעָם שֶׁיהוה אֱלֹהָיו.

תְּהִלָּה לְדָוִד.

אֲרוֹמִמְךָ אֱלוֹהַי הַמֶּלֶךְ, וַאֲבָרְכָה שִׁמְךָ לְעוֹלָם וָעֶד.
בְּכָל־יוֹם אֲבָרְכֶךָּ, וַאֲהַלְלָה שִׁמְךָ לְעוֹלָם וָעֶד.
גָּדוֹל יהוה וּמְהֻלָּל מְאֹד, וְלִגְדֻלָּתוֹ אֵין חֵקֶר.
דּוֹר לְדוֹר יְשַׁבַּח מַעֲשֶׂיךָ, וּגְבוּרֹתֶיךָ יַגִּידוּ.
הֲדַר כְּבוֹד הוֹדֶךָ, וְדִבְרֵי נִפְלְאֹתֶיךָ אָשִׂיחָה.
וֶעֱזוּז נוֹרְאוֹתֶיךָ יֹאמֵרוּ, וּגְדֻלָּתְךָ אֲסַפְּרֶנָּה.
זֵכֶר רַב־טוּבְךָ יַבִּיעוּ, וְצִדְקָתְךָ יְרַנֵּנוּ.
חַנּוּן וְרַחוּם יהוה, אֶרֶךְ אַפַּיִם וּגְדָל־חָסֶד.
טוֹב־יהוה לַכֹּל, וְרַחֲמָיו עַל־כָּל־מַעֲשָׂיו.
יוֹדוּךָ יהוה כָּל־מַעֲשֶׂיךָ, וַחֲסִידֶיךָ יְבָרְכוּכָה.
כְּבוֹד מַלְכוּתְךָ יֹאמֵרוּ, וּגְבוּרָתְךָ יְדַבֵּרוּ.
לְהוֹדִיעַ לִבְנֵי הָאָדָם גְּבוּרֹתָיו, וּכְבוֹד הֲדַר מַלְכוּתוֹ.
מַלְכוּתְךָ מַלְכוּת כָּל־עוֹלָמִים, וּמֶמְשַׁלְתְּךָ בְּכָל־דּוֹר וָדֹר.
סוֹמֵךְ יהוה לְכָל־הַנֹּפְלִים, וְזוֹקֵף לְכָל־הַכְּפוּפִים.
עֵינֵי־כֹל אֵלֶיךָ יְשַׂבֵּרוּ, וְאַתָּה נוֹתֵן לָהֶם אֶת־אָכְלָם בְּעִתּוֹ.

PSALM 145. This psalm, which was treasured by the Rabbis, is recited thrice daily. It was in liturgical use during the Second Temple period, as attested by the Dead Sea Scrolls, where it appears with a congregational response attached to each verse: "Blessed is Adonai and blessed is God's name."

Psalm 145 begins and ends with personal verses of praise. In the middle verses, the author affirms God's sovereignty, and then immediately connects that affirmation to God's love and compassion.

For synagogue use, Psalm 115:18 was appended to the end, referring to those who are praying in the synagogue. Two additional verses (Psalms 84:5 and 144:15), both of which begin with the word אַשְׁרֵי (ashrei, "joyous"), were added to the opening, apparently in imitation of the Book of Psalms itself, which begins with that word. Originally, P'sukei D'zimra, the preparatory morning psalms, began here and consisted simply of Ashrei followed by the last five psalms in the Book of Psalms.

Ashrei is an alphabetical acrostic and thus easy to remember, which may help to explain its popularity in Jewish liturgy. Many readers relate to individual verses more than to the literary flow of the whole poem.

MY GOD, MY SOVEREIGN אֱלוֹהַי הַמֶּלֶךְ. The psalmist addresses God directly, not in the third person, establishing a feeling of closeness. On the other hand, the psalmist speaks to God as הַמֶּלֶךְ (ha-melekh), "my sovereign." This tension is one that classical Jewish thinkers constantly seek to maintain.

ADONAI IS MERCIFUL AND COMPASSIONATE חַנּוּן וְרַחוּם יהוה. Confirmed by the proclamation of God's attributes to Moses: "A God compassionate and merciful" (Exodus 34:6). This psalm paints a picture of a loving God, who cares for all creatures.

ADONAI SUPPORTS ALL WHO FALTER סוֹמֵךְ יהוה לְכָל־הַנֹּפְלִים. This verse marks a turning point in the psalm. Until now, the poet has praised God's greatness and splendor; now, the focus shifts to God's concern for those in need. Here, God's sovereignty is primarily manifest in love and care.

Day In, Day Out

Day in, day out
I swallow
the beauty of the world
this hungering beauty

My God
open windows within me
to let the world enter
calmly and peacefully
that more of the world
enter

the world that I love
cry over
and love again and again
—MIRIAM BARUCH HALFI

ASHREI

Joyous are they who dwell in Your house;
they shall praise You forever.
> *Joyous the people who are so favored;*
> *joyous the people whose God is ADONAI.*

PSALM 145
A PSALM OF DAVID.

I exalt You, my God, my sovereign;
I praise Your name, always.
> *Every day I praise You, glorifying Your name, always.*

Great is ADONAI, greatly to be praised,
though God's greatness is unfathomable.
> *One generation praises Your works to another,*
> *telling of Your mighty deeds.*

I would speak of Your majestic glory
and of Your wondrous acts.
> *People speak of Your awe-inspiring deeds;*
> *I, too, shall recount Your greatness.*

They recount Your great goodness,
and sing of Your righteousness.
> *ADONAI is merciful and compassionate,*
> *patient, and abounding in love.*

ADONAI is good to all,
and God's mercy embraces all of creation.
> *All of creation acknowledges You,*
> *and the faithful bless You.*

They speak of the glory of Your sovereignty;
and tell of Your might,
> *proclaiming to humanity Your mighty deeds,*
> *and the glory of Your majestic sovereignty.*

Your sovereignty is eternal,
Your dominion endures through each generation.
> *ADONAI supports all who falter,*
> *and lifts up all who are bent down.*

The eyes of all look hopefully to You,
and You provide them nourishment in due time.

פוֹתֵחַ אֶת־יָדֶךָ, וּמַשְׂבִּיעַ לְכָל־חַי רָצוֹן.
צַדִּיק יהוה בְּכָל־דְּרָכָיו, וְחָסִיד בְּכָל־מַעֲשָׂיו.
קָרוֹב יהוה לְכָל־קֹרְאָיו, לְכֹל אֲשֶׁר יִקְרָאֻהוּ בֶאֱמֶת.
רְצוֹן־יְרֵאָיו יַעֲשֶׂה, וְאֶת־שַׁוְעָתָם יִשְׁמַע וְיוֹשִׁיעֵם.
שׁוֹמֵר יהוה אֶת־כָּל־אֹהֲבָיו, וְאֵת כָּל־הָרְשָׁעִים יַשְׁמִיד.
◁ תְּהִלַּת יהוה יְדַבֶּר־פִּי,
וִיבָרֵךְ כָּל־בָּשָׂר שֵׁם קָדְשׁוֹ לְעוֹלָם וָעֶד. תהלים קמה

וַאֲנַחְנוּ נְבָרֵךְ יָהּ, מֵעַתָּה וְעַד־עוֹלָם. הַלְלוּ־יָהּ.

הַלְלוּ־יָהּ.
הַלְלִי נַפְשִׁי אֶת־יהוה.
אֲהַלְלָה יהוה בְּחַיָּי, אֲזַמְּרָה לֵאלֹהַי בְּעוֹדִי.
אַל־תִּבְטְחוּ בִנְדִיבִים, בְּבֶן־אָדָם שֶׁאֵין לוֹ תְשׁוּעָה.
תֵּצֵא רוּחוֹ יָשֻׁב לְאַדְמָתוֹ,
בַּיּוֹם הַהוּא אָבְדוּ עֶשְׁתֹּנֹתָיו.
אַשְׁרֵי שֶׁאֵל יַעֲקֹב בְּעֶזְרוֹ, שִׂבְרוֹ עַל־יהוה אֱלֹהָיו.
עֹשֶׂה שָׁמַיִם וָאָרֶץ, אֶת־הַיָּם וְאֶת־כָּל־אֲשֶׁר־בָּם,
הַשֹּׁמֵר אֱמֶת לְעוֹלָם.
עֹשֶׂה מִשְׁפָּט לָעֲשׁוּקִים, נֹתֵן לֶחֶם לָרְעֵבִים,
יהוה מַתִּיר אֲסוּרִים,
יהוה פֹּקֵחַ עִוְרִים,
יהוה זֹקֵף כְּפוּפִים,
יהוה אֹהֵב צַדִּיקִים.
יהוה שֹׁמֵר אֶת־גֵּרִים,
◁ יָתוֹם וְאַלְמָנָה יְעוֹדֵד, וְדֶרֶךְ רְשָׁעִים יְעַוֵּת.
יִמְלֹךְ יהוה לְעוֹלָם, אֱלֹהַיִךְ צִיּוֹן לְדֹר וָדֹר.
הַלְלוּ־יָהּ. תהלים קמו

ALL THAT IS MORTAL
כָּל־בָּשָׂר. Unlike many other psalms that concentrate on Israel, this psalm is universal. There are no references to the Temple, to Israel, or to historical events. God is depicted as the sovereign of the world who cares for all creatures.

PSALM 146. The final five psalms of the Book of Psalms, recited here in sequence, each begin and end with the compound word "Halleluyah." The first of these, Psalm 146, speaks of God's greatness and loving care in remarkably simple yet eloquent language.

THEY RETURN TO DUST
יָשֻׁב לְאַדְמָתוֹ. The imagery is from Genesis, where Adam is told that he "will return to the earth, for from it you were taken: for dust you are, and to dust you shall return" (Genesis 3:19).

ADONAI FREES THE BOUND
יהוה מַתִּיר אֲסוּרִים. "Adonai," the personal name of God, is repeated five times, expressing God's personal interest in the proper treatment of the needy. The qualities attributed to God in this psalm formed the basis of several of the morning b'rakhot (p. 37).

ADONAI PROTECTS THE STRANGER, SUPPORTS THE ORPHAN AND WIDOW
יהוה שֹׁמֵר אֶת־גֵּרִים, יָתוֹם וְאַלְמָנָה יְעוֹדֵד. In biblical society, these were the three groups least able to defend themselves.

You open Your hand,
satisfying all the living with contentment.
ADONAI is righteous in all that is done,
faithful to all creation.
ADONAI is near to all who call,
to all who sincerely call.
God fulfills the desire of those who are faithful,
listening to their cries, rescuing them.
ADONAI watches over all those who love the Holy One,
but will destroy all the wicked.
My mouth shall utter praise of ADONAI.
May all that is mortal praise God's name forever and ever.

We shall praise ADONAI now and always. Halleluyah!

Justice

A prominent biblical motif is that God is the master of creation and that therefore justice rules. Were there warring divinities of equal power, then the world could become the site of competing heavenly forces, but God's single rule allows justice to be the ultimate principle by which the world exists. The biblical standard of justice is always defined by the treatment of the poor, the weak, the powerless, the infirm, the unprotected. God's care is especially directed toward the most vulnerable, and societies are judged by how they are treated. The lack of justice is the undoing of God's creation.

PSALM 146

Halleluyah! Let my soul praise ADONAI.
I will praise ADONAI all my life,
and sing to my God with all my being.
Put no trust in the powerful, in mortals who cannot save.
Their breath departs, they return to dust,
and that is the end of their grand designs.

Blessed are those whose help is Jacob's God,
whose hope is ADONAI our God,
maker of the heavens and the earth,
the seas and all they contain,
who keeps faith forever,

who brings justice to the oppressed
and provides food for the hungry.
ADONAI frees the bound, ADONAI gives sight to the blind,
ADONAI raises those bowed down, and loves the just.

ADONAI protects the stranger, supports the orphan and widow,
but frustrates the designs of the wicked.
ADONAI will reign forever;
your God, O Zion, from generation to generation.
Halleluyah!

הַלְלוּ יָהּ. כִּי־טוֹב זַמְּרָה אֱלֹהֵינוּ, כִּי־נָעִים נָאוָה תְהִלָּה.
בּוֹנֵה יְרוּשָׁלַיִם יְהוָה, נִדְחֵי יִשְׂרָאֵל יְכַנֵּס. הָרֹפֵא לִשְׁבוּרֵי
לֵב וּמְחַבֵּשׁ לְעַצְּבוֹתָם. מוֹנֶה מִסְפָּר לַכּוֹכָבִים, לְכֻלָּם
שֵׁמוֹת יִקְרָא. גָּדוֹל אֲדוֹנֵינוּ וְרַב־כֹּחַ, לִתְבוּנָתוֹ אֵין
מִסְפָּר. מְעוֹדֵד עֲנָוִים יְהוָה, מַשְׁפִּיל רְשָׁעִים עֲדֵי־אָרֶץ.
עֱנוּ לַיהוָה בְּתוֹדָה, זַמְּרוּ לֵאלֹהֵינוּ בְכִנּוֹר. הַמְכַסֶּה שָׁמַיִם
בְּעָבִים, הַמֵּכִין לָאָרֶץ מָטָר, הַמַּצְמִיחַ הָרִים חָצִיר. נוֹתֵן
לִבְהֵמָה לַחְמָהּ, לִבְנֵי עֹרֵב אֲשֶׁר יִקְרָאוּ. לֹא בִגְבוּרַת
הַסּוּס יֶחְפָּץ, לֹא בְשׁוֹקֵי הָאִישׁ יִרְצֶה. רוֹצֶה יְהוָה אֶת־
יְרֵאָיו, אֶת־הַמְיַחֲלִים לְחַסְדּוֹ. שַׁבְּחִי יְרוּשָׁלַיִם אֶת־יְהוָה,
הַלְלִי אֱלֹהַיִךְ צִיּוֹן. כִּי־חִזַּק בְּרִיחֵי שְׁעָרָיִךְ, בֵּרַךְ בָּנַיִךְ
בְּקִרְבֵּךְ. הַשָּׂם גְּבוּלֵךְ שָׁלוֹם, חֵלֶב חִטִּים יַשְׂבִּיעֵךְ. הַשֹּׁלֵחַ
אִמְרָתוֹ אָרֶץ, עַד־מְהֵרָה יָרוּץ דְּבָרוֹ. הַנֹּתֵן שֶׁלֶג כַּצָּמֶר,
כְּפוֹר כָּאֵפֶר יְפַזֵּר. מַשְׁלִיךְ קַרְחוֹ כְפִתִּים, לִפְנֵי קָרָתוֹ מִי
יַעֲמֹד. יִשְׁלַח דְּבָרוֹ וְיַמְסֵם, יַשֵּׁב רוּחוֹ יִזְּלוּ־מָיִם.
‹ מַגִּיד דְּבָרָו לְיַעֲקֹב, חֻקָּיו וּמִשְׁפָּטָיו לְיִשְׂרָאֵל. לֹא עָשָׂה
כֵן לְכָל־גּוֹי, וּמִשְׁפָּטִים בַּל־יְדָעוּם. הַלְלוּ־יָהּ.   תהלים קמז

הַלְלוּ יָהּ. הַלְלוּ אֶת־יְהוָה מִן הַשָּׁמַיִם, הַלְלוּהוּ בַּמְּרוֹמִים.
הַלְלוּהוּ כָל־מַלְאָכָיו, הַלְלוּהוּ כָּל־צְבָאָיו. הַלְלוּהוּ שֶׁמֶשׁ
וְיָרֵחַ, הַלְלוּהוּ כָּל־כּוֹכְבֵי אוֹר. הַלְלוּהוּ שְׁמֵי הַשָּׁמָיִם,
וְהַמַּיִם אֲשֶׁר מֵעַל הַשָּׁמָיִם. יְהַלְלוּ אֶת־שֵׁם יְהוָה, כִּי
הוּא צִוָּה וְנִבְרָאוּ. וַיַּעֲמִידֵם לָעַד לְעוֹלָם, חָק־נָתַן וְלֹא
יַעֲבוֹר. הַלְלוּ אֶת־יְהוָה מִן־הָאָרֶץ, תַּנִּינִים וְכָל־תְּהֹמוֹת.
אֵשׁ וּבָרָד שֶׁלֶג וְקִיטוֹר, רוּחַ סְעָרָה עֹשָׂה דְבָרוֹ. הֶהָרִים
וְכָל־גְּבָעוֹת, עֵץ פְּרִי וְכָל־אֲרָזִים. הַחַיָּה וְכָל־בְּהֵמָה,
רֶמֶשׂ וְצִפּוֹר כָּנָף. מַלְכֵי־אֶרֶץ וְכָל־לְאֻמִּים, שָׂרִים וְכָל־
שֹׁפְטֵי אָרֶץ. בַּחוּרִים וְגַם־בְּתוּלוֹת, זְקֵנִים עִם־נְעָרִים.
יְהַלְלוּ אֶת־שֵׁם יְהוָה, כִּי־נִשְׂגָּב שְׁמוֹ לְבַדּוֹ, ‹ הוֹדוֹ עַל־
אֶרֶץ וְשָׁמָיִם. וַיָּרֶם קֶרֶן לְעַמּוֹ תְּהִלָּה לְכָל־חֲסִידָיו, לִבְנֵי
יִשְׂרָאֵל עַם קְרֹבוֹ, הַלְלוּ־יָהּ.   תהלים קמח

PSALM 147. This psalm focuses on Jerusalem, but the psalmist also stresses God's hand in nature. With great skill, the poet has created a paean to both peace and prosperity.

HEALS THE BROKEN-HEARTED הָרֹפֵא לִשְׁבוּרֵי לֵב. This line is especially evocative on the High Holy Days, when we approach God with broken hearts.

GOD'S WORD IS REVEALED TO JACOB מַגִּיד דְּבָרָו לְיַעֲקֹב. The same Hebrew phrase דְּבָרוֹ (d'varo), "God's word," appeared in the previous line referring to the ice, which God melts with speech. The speech of God is "heard" both in nature and in the teachings of Torah.

PSALM 148. As we approach the conclusion of the Book of Psalms and of the morning recitation of songs of praise, the emotional intensity increases. The key word הַלְלוּ־יָהּ (halleluyah), "praise Yah," or some form of the root הַלֵּל (hallel), "praise," appears twelve times in this psalm. Using short, rhythmic, staccato phrases, the psalmist calls upon all creatures and all parts of the universe to join in praise of the Creator. The psalm is divided into two parts. The heavens and all that they contain are called upon to praise God in the first part; the earth and all its creatures, in the second.

The Broken-Hearted

There is nothing as
whole as a broken heart.

—attributed to
MENAḤEM MENDEL
OF KOTZK

The Sun Lit a
Wet Branch

The sun lit a wet branch
and gold leaves captured
    my eyes.
The gold leaves that
    coursed
night and day
through my heart's blood
changed their
    configuration.

When they reached
    the soul
in its solitude,
they became distant signs
of light,
clues from heaven,
ancient wonders.

—ZELDA
(trans. Marcia Falk)

PSALM 147

Halleluyah! It is good to sing psalms to our God. How pleasant
it is to chant praise! ADONAI rebuilds Jerusalem, gathers Israel's
dispersed, heals the broken-hearted, binds up their wounds,
and numbers the stars, giving each one a name. Great is our
ruler, vast God's power; beyond measure is God's wisdom.
ADONAI heartens the humble, but casts evildoers to the
ground. Lift your voice in thanks to ADONAI. Sound the harp
in praise of our God. God covers the sky with clouds, provides
rain for the earth, and makes grass grow upon the hills. God
gives the beasts their food, and the ravens that for which they
call—caring not for the power of horses, nor delighting in
vaunted human strength. God delights in those who revere
God, those who look expectantly to God's love. Jerusalem,
praise ADONAI. Zion, sing to your God, who has fortified your
gates and blessed your children within, bringing peace to your
borders, satisfying you with choice wheat. God's commands
go forth to the earth; swiftly the Divine word descends. God
sends down snow, white as wool, and scatters frost thick as
ashes. God pelts the earth with a storm of ice. Who can with-
stand these wintry blasts? At God's command the ice melts;
the wind is stilled, and the waters flow. God's word is revealed
to Jacob, statutes and decrees to the people Israel. God has not
done this for other nations, nor has God taught them these
decrees. Halleluyah!

PSALM 148

Halleluyah! Praise ADONAI from the heavens. Praise God,
angels on high. Praise God, sun and moon, all shining stars.
Praise God, highest heavens. Let them praise the glory of
ADONAI at whose command they were created, at whose decree they endure forever, and by whose laws nature abides.
Praise ADONAI, all who share the earth: all fierce sea creatures,
even the ocean depths, fire and hail, snow and smoke, storms—
which obey God's command; all mountains and hills, all fruit
trees and cedars, all beasts, wild and tame, creeping creatures,
winged birds; earthly rulers, all the nations, officers and mortal
judges, men and women, young and old. Let all praise the glory
of ADONAI! God alone is to be exalted, whose glory is beyond
heaven and earth. God has exalted the fame of God's people as
a name of praise for all who are faithful. God has exalted the
people Israel, the people drawn close. Halleluyah!

הַלְלוּ יָהּ. שִׁירוּ לַיהוה שִׁיר חָדָשׁ, תְּהִלָּתוֹ בִּקְהַל
חֲסִידִים. יִשְׂמַח יִשְׂרָאֵל בְּעֹשָׂיו, בְּנֵי־צִיּוֹן יָגִילוּ
בְמַלְכָּם. יְהַלְלוּ שְׁמוֹ בְמָחוֹל, בְּתֹף וְכִנּוֹר יְזַמְּרוּ־לוֹ.
כִּי־רוֹצֶה יהוה בְּעַמּוֹ, יְפָאֵר עֲנָוִים בִּישׁוּעָה. יַעְלְזוּ
חֲסִידִים בְּכָבוֹד, יְרַנְּנוּ עַל־מִשְׁכְּבוֹתָם. רוֹמְמוֹת אֵל
בִּגְרוֹנָם, וְחֶרֶב פִּיפִיּוֹת בְּיָדָם. לַעֲשׂוֹת נְקָמָה בַּגּוֹיִם,
תּוֹכֵחוֹת בַּלְאֻמִּים. ◁ לֶאְסֹר מַלְכֵיהֶם בְּזִקִּים
וְנִכְבְּדֵיהֶם בְּכַבְלֵי בַרְזֶל. לַעֲשׂוֹת בָּהֶם מִשְׁפָּט כָּתוּב,
הָדָר הוּא לְכָל־חֲסִידָיו. הַלְלוּ־יָהּ.   תהלים קמט

הַלְלוּ יָהּ,
הַלְלוּ אֵל בְּקָדְשׁוֹ, הַלְלוּהוּ בִּרְקִיעַ עֻזּוֹ.
הַלְלוּהוּ בִגְבוּרֹתָיו, הַלְלוּהוּ כְּרֹב גֻּדְלוֹ.
הַלְלוּהוּ בְּתֵקַע שׁוֹפָר, הַלְלוּהוּ בְּנֵבֶל וְכִנּוֹר.
הַלְלוּהוּ בְתֹף וּמָחוֹל, הַלְלוּהוּ בְּמִנִּים וְעֻגָב.
הַלְלוּהוּ בְצִלְצְלֵי־שָׁמַע, הַלְלוּהוּ בְּצִלְצְלֵי תְרוּעָה.
◁ כֹּל הַנְּשָׁמָה תְּהַלֵּל יָהּ, הַלְלוּ־יָהּ.
כֹּל הַנְּשָׁמָה תְּהַלֵּל יָהּ, הַלְלוּ־יָהּ.   תהלים קנ

בָּרוּךְ יהוה לְעוֹלָם, אָמֵן וְאָמֵן. בָּרוּךְ יהוה מִצִּיּוֹן, שֹׁכֵן
יְרוּשָׁלָיִם, הַלְלוּ־יָהּ. בָּרוּךְ יהוה אֱלֹהִים אֱלֹהֵי יִשְׂרָאֵל,
עֹשֵׂה נִפְלָאוֹת לְבַדּוֹ. ◁ וּבָרוּךְ שֵׁם כְּבוֹדוֹ לְעוֹלָם,
וְיִמָּלֵא כְבוֹדוֹ אֶת־כָּל הָאָרֶץ, אָמֵן וְאָמֵן.

Some congregations proceed with נִשְׁמַת, *page 67.*

PSALM 149. This Psalm may have been written in exile, where it would not have been out of place for the wish to overcome enemies and oppressors to be expressed in especially urgent language.

LET THEM DANCE בְמָחוֹל. A characteristic of "Halleluyah" psalms is the accompaniment of instrumental music and dance, further heightening the emotional experience.

A DOUBLE-EDGED SWORD IN THEIR HANDS וְחֶרֶב פִּיפִיּוֹת בְּיָדָם. The image of vengeance invoked in this psalm might be explained by its last line, where the poet evokes the promised judgment. Israel's oppression at the hands of its enemies is a product of the injustice that must be fought.

PSALM 150. This psalm brings the Book of Psalms to an exultant close. The Book of Psalms begins with the praise of the single righteous individual, "Blessed is the One who declared that the works of creation were sufficiently complete (*dai*)," and concludes with every living being praising God. Although this psalm is recited every day, its reference to the blowing of the shofar gives it special meaning on the High Holy Days. Its ten repetitions of the word *hall'luhu* became the basis for the compilation of ten biblical verses that punctuate each of the three special sections of the Musaf service on Rosh Hashanah, and those special sections culminate in another recitation of Psalm 150.

WITH THE SHOFAR CALL בְּתֵקַע שׁוֹפָר. The psalmist refers to the clarion call of the shofar, the *t'ki·ah*, which we hear so dramatically on Rosh Hashanah and at the end of Yom Kippur.

PRAISED BE ADONAI FOREVER בָּרוּךְ יהוה לְעוֹלָם. Psalms 89:53, 135:21, and 72:18–19. Two of these verses conclude with a doubled "Amen," which in the Book of Psalms punctuates the end of three of its five major divisions. All four verses begin with the word בָּרוּךְ (*barukh*), "blessed." Thus, just as we began P'sukei D'zimra with a multiple repetition of "blessed" in Barukh She-amar (page 47), so here, too, we repeat that word over and over. The oldest versions of P'sukei D'zimra ended here and so it is appropriate to conclude with the repetition of the word "Amen."

Isaac says: Reciting the
Sh'ma while in bed is
like wielding a double-
edged sword. For it is
said: "Let praise of God
be on their lips, and a
double-edged sword in
their hands." How does it
indicate this? Mar Zutra,
(some say, R. Ashi) says:
[The lesson is] from the
preceding verse. For it is
written: "Let the saints
exult in glory, let them
sing for joy upon their
beds."
—BABYLONIAN TALMUD,
BERAKHOT

PSALM 149

Halleluyah! Sing a new song to ADONAI. Where the faithful
gather, let God be praised. Let the people Israel rejoice in their
maker; let the people of Zion delight in their sovereign. Let
them dance in praise of God, celebrate with drum and harp.
The people of ADONAI are cherished, the humble are crowned
with triumph. Let God's faithful sing exultantly and rejoice
both night and day. Let praise of God be on their lips, and a
double-edged sword in their hands to execute judgment on the
godless, to bring punishment upon the nations; to bind their
kings in chains and put their princes in irons—carrying out the
judgment decreed against them. This is glory for all of God's
faithful. Halleluyah!

Psalm 150—
A Rendering

Praise God in the depths
of the universe;
  praise [God] in the
  human heart.
Praise God's power and
beauty,
  God's all-feeling,
  fathomless love.
Praise [God] with drums
and trumpets,
  with string quartets and
  guitars.
Praise [God] in market
and workplace,
  with computer, with
  hammer and nails.
Praise [God] in bedroom
and kitchen;
  praise [God] with pots
  and pans.
Praise [God] in the
temple of the present;
  let every breath be
  God's praise.
  —STEPHEN MITCHELL

PSALM 150

Halleluyah! Praise God in the sanctuary,
praise God in the powerful heavens.
  Praise God for the mighty deeds,
  praise God for infinite greatness.
Praise God with the shofar call,
praise God with harp and lyre.
  Praise God with drum and dance,
  praise God with flute and strings.
Praise God with crashing cymbals,
praise God with resounding cymbals.
  Let every breath of life praise ADONAI. Halleluyah!

Hal'luyah.
Hal'lu El b'kodsho, hal'luhu bi-r'ki·a uzzo.
Hal'luhu vi-g'vurotav, hal'luhu k'rov gudlo.
Hal'luhu b'teika shofar, hal'luhu b'neivel v'khinnor.
Hal'luhu b'tof u-maḥol, hal'luhu b'minnim v'ugav.
Hal'luhu v'tziltz'lei shama, hal'luhu b'tziltz'lei t'ru·ah.
Kol ha-n'shamah t'hallel yah, hal'luyah.
Kol ha-n'shamah t'hallel yah, hal'luyah.

Conclusion of the Selection of Psalms

Praised be ADONAI forever. Amen! Amen! Praised from Zion
be ADONAI who abides in Jerusalem. Halleluyah! Praised be
ADONAI, God of the people Israel, who alone works wonders.
Praised be God's glory throughout all time. May God's presence fill the whole world. Amen! Amen!

Some congregations proceed with Nishmat, page 67.

It is customary to stand through the middle of page 66.

וַיְבָרֶךְ דָּוִיד אֶת־יהוה לְעֵינֵי כָּל־הַקָּהָל וַיֹּאמֶר דָּוִיד:
בָּרוּךְ אַתָּה יהוה אֱלֹהֵי יִשְׂרָאֵל אָבִינוּ, מֵעוֹלָם וְעַד־
עוֹלָם. לְךָ יהוה הַגְּדֻלָּה וְהַגְּבוּרָה וְהַתִּפְאֶרֶת וְהַנֵּצַח
וְהַהוֹד, כִּי־כֹל בַּשָּׁמַיִם וּבָאָרֶץ, לְךָ יהוה הַמַּמְלָכָה
וְהַמִּתְנַשֵּׂא לְכֹל לְרֹאשׁ. וְהָעֹשֶׁר וְהַכָּבוֹד מִלְּפָנֶיךָ, וְאַתָּה
מוֹשֵׁל בַּכֹּל, וּבְיָדְךָ כֹּחַ וּגְבוּרָה, וּבְיָדְךָ לְגַדֵּל וּלְחַזֵּק
לַכֹּל. וְעַתָּה אֱלֹהֵינוּ מוֹדִים אֲנַחְנוּ לָךְ, וּמְהַלְלִים לְשֵׁם
תִּפְאַרְתֶּךָ. דברי הימים א כט, י‑יג

אַתָּה־הוּא יהוה לְבַדֶּךָ, אַתָּה עָשִׂיתָ אֶת־הַשָּׁמַיִם, שְׁמֵי
הַשָּׁמַיִם וְכָל־צְבָאָם, הָאָרֶץ וְכָל־אֲשֶׁר עָלֶיהָ, הַיַּמִּים
וְכָל־אֲשֶׁר בָּהֶם, וְאַתָּה מְחַיֶּה אֶת־כֻּלָּם, וּצְבָא הַשָּׁמַיִם
לְךָ מִשְׁתַּחֲוִים. ◁ אַתָּה־הוּא יהוה הָאֱלֹהִים אֲשֶׁר בָּחַרְתָּ
בְּאַבְרָם, וְהוֹצֵאתוֹ מֵאוּר כַּשְׂדִּים, וְשַׂמְתָּ שְּׁמוֹ אַבְרָהָם,
וּמָצָאתָ אֶת־לְבָבוֹ נֶאֱמָן לְפָנֶיךָ,

וְכָרוֹת עִמּוֹ הַבְּרִית לָתֵת אֶת־אֶרֶץ הַכְּנַעֲנִי הַחִתִּי
הָאֱמֹרִי וְהַפְּרִזִּי וְהַיְבוּסִי וְהַגִּרְגָּשִׁי לָתֵת לְזַרְעוֹ, וַתָּקֶם
אֶת־דְּבָרֶיךָ כִּי צַדִּיק אָתָּה. וַתֵּרֶא אֶת־עֳנִי אֲבֹתֵינוּ
בְּמִצְרָיִם, וְאֶת־זַעֲקָתָם שָׁמַעְתָּ עַל־יַם־סוּף. וַתִּתֵּן אֹתֹת
וּמֹפְתִים בְּפַרְעֹה, וּבְכָל־עֲבָדָיו וּבְכָל־עַם אַרְצוֹ, כִּי יָדַעְתָּ
כִּי הֵזִידוּ עֲלֵיהֶם, וַתַּעַשׂ־לְךָ שֵׁם כְּהַיּוֹם הַזֶּה.
◁ וְהַיָּם בָּקַעְתָּ לִפְנֵיהֶם וַיַּעַבְרוּ בְתוֹךְ־הַיָּם בַּיַּבָּשָׁה, וְאֶת־
רֹדְפֵיהֶם הִשְׁלַכְתָּ בִמְצוֹלֹת, כְּמוֹ־אֶבֶן בְּמַיִם עַזִּים.
נחמיה ט ו‑יא

DAVID'S FINAL PRAYER.
Originally, P'sukei D'zimra (Verses of Song) consisted only of selections from the Book of Psalms; later, a series of biblical prayers, beginning here and culminating with the Song at the Sea, was added. These prayerful additions take us from Abram's leaving his home and setting out for an unknown destination, to the Exodus from Egypt, and to the promised entrance into the Land. Praise of God, the covenant with Israel, and the promise of redemption are consecutive themes here.

DAVID PRAISED וַיְבָרֶךְ דָּוִיד. This passage from the Book of 1 Chronicles forms part of David's last speech as he hands his kingdom over to his son Solomon. Having just read selections from the Psalms of David, we begin the closing section of Verses of Song with David's own concluding words.

PRAISED ARE YOU בָּרוּךְ אַתָּה יהוה. This is one of only two times that these words, which became the formula for all Jewish b'rakhot, are found in the Bible.

WE THANK YOU מוֹדִים אֲנַחְנוּ לָךְ. These became the first words of the second to last b'rakhah of the Amidah, in which we thank God for the gifts of life.

YOU ALONE, ADONAI אַתָּה־הוּא יהוה לְבַדֶּךָ. This prayer was offered in the Second Temple when the people rededicated themselves under the guidance of Ezra and Nehemiah. Perhaps it was placed here to instill a feeling of rededication as we recite our morning prayers. Central to Ezra's act of rededication was the reading of the entire Torah, and we face the ark and rise as we recite this prayer.

OUT OF UR OF THE CHALDEES מֵאוּר כַּשְׂדִּים. Although God's call to Abram came in Ḥaran (Genesis 12:4), the journey had begun farther east, in Ur, when Abram's father Terah set out for Canaan but got only as far as Ḥaran (Genesis 11:31).

DAVID'S FINAL PRAYER
It is customary to stand through the middle of page 66.

David praised ADONAI in the presence of all the assembled, saying:
Praised are You, God of our ancestor Israel, from the eternal past to
the eternal future. Yours is the greatness and power, glory, splendor
and majesty, ADONAI—for everything in the heavens and on earth
is Yours. Sovereignty is Yours: You are exalted as ruler of all. You
are the source of wealth and honor; dominion over all the earth is
Yours. Might and courage come from You, greatness and strength
are Your gifts. We thank You now, our God, and we extol Your
glory.   I Chronicles 29:10–13

THE COVENANT

You alone, ADONAI, created the heavens, the high heavens and all
their array, the land and all that is on it, the seas and all they contain. You sustain them all; the hosts of the heavens revere You. You
are ADONAI, the God who chose Abram and brought him out of
Ur of the Chaldees, naming him Abraham, finding in him a faithful
servant:

You made a covenant with him, to give the land of the Canaanites,
the Hittites, the Amorites, the Perizzites, the Jebusites, and the
Girgashites to his descendants; and You kept Your promise, for You
are just. You saw the suffering of our ancestors in Egypt, You heard
their cry at the Sea of Reeds. With signs and wonders You confronted Pharaoh, all of his servants, and all the people of his land,
because You knew of their shameless treatment of our ancestors;
and You gained for Yourself a name that lives on to this day. You
divided the sea for our ancestors, and they passed through it as on
dry land. But their pursuers You cast into the depths, like a stone
into turbulent waters.   Nehemiah 9:6–11

וַיּוֹשַׁע יהוה בַּיּוֹם הַהוּא אֶת־יִשְׂרָאֵל מִיַּד מִצְרַיִם וַיַּרְא
יִשְׂרָאֵל אֶת־מִצְרַיִם מֵת עַל־שְׂפַת הַיָּם: וַיַּרְא יִשְׂרָאֵל אֶת־
הַיָּד הַגְּדֹלָה אֲשֶׁר עָשָׂה יהוה בְּמִצְרָיִם
◁ וַיִּירְאוּ הָעָם אֶת־יהוה וַיַּאֲמִינוּ בַּיהוה וּבְמֹשֶׁה עַבְדּוֹ:

שמות יד ל-לא

אָז יָשִׁיר־מֹשֶׁה וּבְנֵי יִשְׂרָאֵל אֶת־הַשִּׁירָה הַזֹּאת לַיהוה וַיֹּאמְרוּ
לֵאמֹר אָשִׁירָה לַיהוה כִּי־גָאֹה גָּאָה סוּס
וְרֹכְבוֹ רָמָה בַיָּם: עָזִּי וְזִמְרָת יָהּ וַיְהִי־לִי
לִישׁוּעָה זֶה אֵלִי וְאַנְוֵהוּ אֱלֹהֵי
אָבִי וַאֲרֹמְמֶנְהוּ: יהוה אִישׁ מִלְחָמָה יהוה
שְׁמוֹ: מַרְכְּבֹת פַּרְעֹה וְחֵילוֹ יָרָה בַיָּם וּמִבְחַר
שָׁלִשָׁיו טֻבְּעוּ בְיַם־סוּף. תְּהֹמֹת יְכַסְיֻמוּ יָרְדוּ בִמְצוֹלֹת כְּמוֹ־
אָבֶן: יְמִינְךָ יהוה נֶאְדָּרִי בַּכֹּחַ יְמִינְךָ
יהוה תִּרְעַץ אוֹיֵב: וּבְרֹב גְּאוֹנְךָ תַּהֲרֹס
קָמֶיךָ תְּשַׁלַּח חֲרֹנְךָ יֹאכְלֵמוֹ כַּקַּשׁ: וּבְרוּחַ
אַפֶּיךָ נֶעֶרְמוּ מַיִם נִצְּבוּ כְמוֹ־נֵד
נֹזְלִים קָפְאוּ תְהֹמֹת בְּלֶב־יָם: אָמַר
אוֹיֵב אֶרְדֹּף אַשִּׂיג אֲחַלֵּק שָׁלָל תִּמְלָאֵמוֹ
נַפְשִׁי אָרִיק חַרְבִּי תּוֹרִישֵׁמוֹ יָדִי: נָשַׁפְתָּ
בְרוּחֲךָ כִּסָּמוֹ יָם צָלְלוּ כַּעוֹפֶרֶת בְּמַיִם
אַדִּירִים: מִי־כָמֹכָה בָּאֵלִם יהוה מִי
כָּמֹכָה נֶאְדָּר בַּקֹּדֶשׁ נוֹרָא תְהִלֹּת עֹשֵׂה
פֶלֶא: נָטִיתָ יְמִינְךָ תִּבְלָעֵמוֹ אָרֶץ: נָחִיתָ
בְחַסְדְּךָ עַם־זוּ גָּאָלְתָּ נֵהַלְתָּ בְעָזְּךָ אֶל־נְוֵה

THE SONG AT THE SEA שִׁירַת הַיָּם. This song of triumph and praise to God is one of the great biblical poems. It emphasizes Israel's faith in God and God's redemptive role, leading to the climactic proclamation: "Adonai will reign forever and ever!" (Exodus 15:18). The recitation of the Song at the Sea is a later addition to P'sukei D'zimra and is not found in first-millennium orders of prayer. The experience of the long exile may have created the need for the memory of triumph. The Midrash associated this Song with the final redemption.

THEN MOSES . . . SANG אָז יָשִׁיר־מֹשֶׁה. The Hebrew יָשִׁיר (yashir) can be understood as either a present or future tense. This led the Sages to say that this song would be sung in the future by the Messiah, thus linking the past and the future redemptions (Mekhilta, Shirata 1).

THIS IS MY GOD זֶה אֵלִי. The Midrash expounds on the demonstrative pronoun "this" and says that it indicates that the Israelites pointed to God and visually identified the Holy One. "Even a maidservant at the Sea saw God more clearly than the greatest of the prophets!" (Mekhilta Shirata 3). The experience at the Sea was an unequalled moment of faith.

ADONAI IS A WARRIOR; GOD'S NAME IS ADONAI יהוה אִישׁ מִלְחָמָה יהוה שְׁמוֹ. The entire poem emphasizes God's role as warrior, triumphing over Israel's enemies. On the phrase "God's name is Adonai," the Rabbis remarked that God appears in many different guises: here as a warrior, elsewhere as a sage. No matter how varied God's manifestations, "God's name is Adonai"—the One God is always the same (Mekhilta, Shirata 4). Though we each may perceive God differently and our experience of God may vary with our life experience, one reality exists behind all.

Thus ADONAI saved the people Israel from the Egyptians on that day; Israel saw the Egyptians lying dead on the shore of the sea. When the people Israel witnessed the great power that ADONAI wielded against the Egyptians, the people feared ADONAI and kept faith with ADONAI, trusting Moses, ADONAI's servant.   Exodus 14:30–31

THE SONG AT THE SEA

Then Moses and the people Israel sang this song to ADONAI:

I will sing to ADONAI, mighty in majestic triumph!
Horse and driver God has hurled into the sea.
ADONAI is my strength and my might; God is my deliverance.
This is my God, to whom I give glory—
my ancestor's God, whom I exalt.

ADONAI is a warrior; God's name is ADONAI.
Pharaoh's chariots and army God has cast into the sea;
Pharaoh's choicest captains have drowned in the Sea of Reeds.
The depths covered them; they sank in the deep like a stone.

Your right hand, ADONAI, singular in strength—
Your right hand, ADONAI, shatters the enemy.
With Your majestic might You crush Your foes;
You let loose Your fury, to consume them like straw.
In the rush of Your rage the waters were raised;
the sea stood motionless, the great deep congealed.

The enemy said: "I will pursue and plunder!
I will devour them, I will draw my sword.
With my bare hands will I dispatch them."
You loosed the wind—the sea covered them.
Like lead they sank in the swelling waters.

Who is like You, ADONAI, among all that is worshipped?
Who is like You, majestic in holiness,
awe-inspiring in splendor, working wonders?

You stretched out Your hand—the earth swallowed them.
In Your love You lead the people You redeemed;
with Your strength You guide them to Your holy habitation.

חַיִל ׀ שָׁמְעוּ עַמִּים יִרְגָּזוּן ׀ קׇדְשֶׁךָ׃

אָז נִבְהֲלוּ אַלּוּפֵי ׀ אָחַז יֹשְׁבֵי פְּלָשֶׁת׃

אֱדוֹם ׀ אֵילֵי מוֹאָב יֹאחֲזֵמוֹ רָעַד נָמֹגוּ

כֹּל יֹשְׁבֵי כְנָעַן׃ ׀ תִּפֹּל עֲלֵיהֶם אֵימָתָה

וָפַחַד ׀ בִּגְדֹל זְרוֹעֲךָ יִדְּמוּ כָּאָבֶן עַד־

יַעֲבֹר עַמְּךָ יְהֹוָה ׀ עַד־יַעֲבֹר עַם־זוּ

קָנִיתָ׃ ׀ תְּבִאֵמוֹ וְתִטָּעֵמוֹ בְּהַר נַחֲלָתְךָ מָכוֹן

לְשִׁבְתְּךָ פָּעַלְתָּ יְהֹוָה ׀ מִקְּדָשׁ אֲדֹנָי כּוֹנְנוּ

יָדֶיךָ׃ ׀ יְהֹוָה יִמְלֹךְ לְעֹלָם וָעֶד׃

שמות טו א-יח

⊲ כִּי לַיהֹוָה הַמְּלוּכָה וּמֹשֵׁל בַּגּוֹיִם. וְעָלוּ מוֹשִׁעִים בְּהַר
צִיּוֹן לִשְׁפֹּט אֶת־הַר עֵשָׂו, וְהָיְתָה לַיהֹוָה הַמְּלוּכָה. וְהָיָה
יְהֹוָה לְמֶלֶךְ עַל כׇּל־הָאָרֶץ, בַּיּוֹם הַהוּא יִהְיֶה יְהֹוָה אֶחָד
וּשְׁמוֹ אֶחָד.

שַׁחַר אֲבַקֶּשְׁךָ צוּרִי וּמִשְׂגַּבִּי
אֶעֱרֹךְ לְפָנֶיךָ שַׁחְרִי וְגַם עַרְבִּי.
לִפְנֵי גְדֻלָּתְךָ אֶעֱמֹד וְאֶבָּהֵל
כִּי עֵינְךָ תִרְאֶה כׇּל־מַחְשְׁבוֹת לִבִּי.
מַה־זֶּה אֲשֶׁר יוּכַל הַלֵּב וְהַלָּשׁוֹן לַעֲשׂוֹת
וּמַה־כֹּחַ רוּחִי בְּתוֹךְ קִרְבִּי.
⊲ הִנֵּה לְךָ תִּיטַב זִמְרַת אֱנוֹשׁ
עַל כֵּן אוֹדְךָ בְּעוֹד נִשְׁמַת אֱלוֹהַּ בִּי.

FOR SOVEREIGNTY BELONGS TO ADONAI כִּי לַיהוה הַמְּלוּכָה. Psalm 22:29. The biblical selections of P'sukei D'zimra, the Verses of Song, conclude by framing the powerful climax of the Song at the Sea with verses from Psalms and the Prophets that emphasize God's sovereignty and the universal recognition of God that will mark the end of days.

DELIVERERS SHALL RISE וְעָלוּ מוֹשִׁעִים. Obadiah 1:21. Obadiah predicted that though Israel and Judah were bent low in his time, redemption would come soon. Thus the victory described in the Song at the Sea is connected to the hope in redemption and turned into a vision of ever-renewed salvation of the people Israel.

AND THE NAME OF GOD ONE וּשְׁמוֹ אֶחָד. Zechariah 14:9. That is, at the end of days not only will God be universally revealed, but also people's understanding of God will align completely with who God truly is. Whenever we conclude a worship service by reciting the Aleinu, we quote this verse again and express its millennial hope.

AT DAWN I SEEK YOU שַׁחַר אֲבַקֶּשְׁךָ. This poem was written by the great medieval poet Solomon Ibn Gabirol (Spain, 11th century) to be recited by the prayer leader when rising to the *bimah* to begin public prayer. Its last line, which talks of the soul/*n'shamah*, is a bridge to the traditional Nishmat prayer, which begins on the next page and which, on Shabbat and holy days, precedes the Bar'khu, the call to worship. The poet evokes the spirit of God within each human being as the source of prayer. The translation is adapted from Jules Harlow.

Miracles

The concept of miracle
... can be defined at
its starting point as an
abiding astonishment.
The philosopher and
the religious person
both wonder at the phe-
nomenon, but the one
neutralizes his wonder in
ideal knowledge, while
the other abides in that
wonder; no knowledge,
no cognition, can weaken
his astonishment. Any
causal explanation only
deepens the wonder for
him. To live with the miracle means to recognize
this power on every given
occasion as the effecting
one.

—MARTIN BUBER

Nations take note and tremble;
panic grips the dwellers of Philistia.
Edom's chieftains are chilled with terror,
trembling seizes the mighty of Moab,
all the citizens of Canaan are confused,
dread and dismay descend upon them.
Your overwhelming power makes them still as stone,
while Your people, ADONAI—the people
whom You have redeemed—pass peacefully over.
Lead them to Your lofty mountain;
let them lodge there in Your abode,
the sanctuary You have established.
ADONAI shall reign forever and ever.
 ADONAI shall reign forever and ever. Exodus 15:1–18

For sovereignty belongs to ADONAI, who rules the nations.
Deliverers shall rise on Mount Zion to judge the mountain of
Esau, and ADONAI shall be supreme. ADONAI shall be sovereign over all the earth. On that day ADONAI shall be one and
the name of God one.

INTRODUCTION TO NISHMAT

At dawn I seek You, Refuge, Rock sublime;
my morning prayers I offer, and those at evening time.
I tremble in Your awe-inspiring presence, contrite,
for my deepest secrets lie stripped before Your sight.

My tongue, what can it say? My heart, what can it do?
What is my strength, what is my spirit too?
But should music be sweet to You in mortal key,
Your praises will I sing so long as God's soul is in me.

נִשְׁמַת כָּל־חַי תְּבָרֵךְ אֶת־שִׁמְךָ, יהוה אֱלֹהֵינוּ.
וְרוּחַ כָּל־בָּשָׂר תְּפָאֵר וּתְרוֹמֵם זִכְרְךָ, מַלְכֵּנוּ, תָּמִיד.
מִן הָעוֹלָם וְעַד הָעוֹלָם אַתָּה אֵל,
וּמִבַּלְעָדֶיךָ אֵין לָנוּ מֶלֶךְ גּוֹאֵל וּמוֹשִׁיעַ,
פּוֹדֶה וּמַצִּיל, וּמְפַרְנֵס וּמְרַחֵם בְּכָל־עֵת צָרָה וְצוּקָה.
אֵין לָנוּ מֶלֶךְ אֶלָּא אָתָּה.
אֱלֹהֵי הָרִאשׁוֹנִים וְהָאַחֲרוֹנִים,
אֱלוֹהַּ כָּל־בְּרִיּוֹת,   אֲדוֹן כָּל־תּוֹלָדוֹת,
הַמְהֻלָּל בְּרֹב הַתִּשְׁבָּחוֹת,
הַמְנַהֵג עוֹלָמוֹ בְּחֶסֶד,   וּבְרִיּוֹתָיו בְּרַחֲמִים.
וַיהוה לֹא יָנוּם וְלֹא יִישָׁן,
הַמְּעוֹרֵר יְשֵׁנִים,   וְהַמֵּקִיץ נִרְדָּמִים,
וְהַמֵּשִׂיחַ אִלְּמִים,   וְהַמַּתִּיר אֲסוּרִים,
וְהַסּוֹמֵךְ נוֹפְלִים,   וְהַזּוֹקֵף כְּפוּפִים.
לְךָ לְבַדְּךָ אֲנַחְנוּ מוֹדִים.

אִלּוּ פִינוּ מָלֵא שִׁירָה כַּיָּם,
וּלְשׁוֹנֵנוּ רִנָּה כַּהֲמוֹן גַּלָּיו,
וְשִׂפְתוֹתֵינוּ שֶׁבַח כְּמֶרְחֲבֵי רָקִיעַ,
וְעֵינֵינוּ מְאִירוֹת כַּשֶּׁמֶשׁ וְכַיָּרֵחַ,
וְיָדֵינוּ פְרוּשׂוֹת כְּנִשְׁרֵי שָׁמָיִם,
וְרַגְלֵינוּ קַלּוֹת כָּאַיָּלוֹת,
אֵין אֲנַחְנוּ מַסְפִּיקִים לְהוֹדוֹת לְךָ, יהוה אֱלֹהֵינוּ וֵאלֹהֵי
אֲבוֹתֵינוּ [וְאִמּוֹתֵינוּ], וּלְבָרֵךְ אֶת־שִׁמְךָ עַל אַחַת
מֵאֶלֶף אַלְפֵי אֲלָפִים וְרִבֵּי רְבָבוֹת פְּעָמִים הַטּוֹבוֹת
שֶׁעָשִׂיתָ עִם אֲבוֹתֵינוּ [וְאִמּוֹתֵינוּ] וְעִמָּנוּ.

NISHMAT. Nishmat is a fitting conclusion to the psalms and biblical verses we have just recited, as well as an introduction to the b'rakhot we are about to recite. The last psalm we recited, Psalm 150, ends with the line, "Let every breath of life praise Adonai," a thought which is then taken up directly in the opening line of this prayer, "the soul (n'shamah, literally "breath") of all that lives praises Your name." The biblical word for "breath" came to refer to the soul in later Hebrew.

The prayer repeatedly moves from prose statement to rhythmic poetic lines, as if the worshipper cannot stop from breaking into song. Though the speaker emphasizes the limitation of words in describing or praising God, the poet suggests that the actions of our bodies, especially our breathing, can constitute a praise of God. Indeed, in this prayer our entire body is said to praise God.

Nishmat may be artfully woven from several different poems and prayers. For instance, it is likely that the second paragraph was written for a different context since Rabbi Yoḥanan (Land of Israel, 3rd century) recommends reciting it on the occasion of seeing the rain arrive in its season (Babylonian Talmud, Berakhot 59b). Similarly, the Talmud describes a prayer entitled "Nishmat" as concluding the section of praise at the Passover seder (Babylonian Talmud, Pesaḥim 118a).

GOD OF ALL AGES אֱלֹהֵי הָרִאשׁוֹנִים וְהָאַחֲרוֹנִים. All of humanity is included in this prayer, which touches on the prime elements of every human being: the experience of our bodies and souls.

NISHMAT: THE SOUL OF ALL THAT LIVES

The soul of all that lives praises Your name, ADONAI our God;
the spirit of all flesh exalts You, our sovereign, always.
From the very beginning to the very end of time, You are God.
Beside You, we have no sovereign who redeems and liberates us,
rescues and saves us, shows us kindness and sustains us in every
moment of anguish and distress. We have no sovereign but You:
God of all ages, God of all creatures,
master of all generations,
extolled in endless praise,
who guides the world with love
and its creatures with compassion.
ADONAI neither slumbers nor sleeps,
but wakes those who sleep,
rouses those who slumber,
gives voice to those who cannot speak,
frees those who are fettered,
supports those who fall,
straightens those who are bent over.
You alone we thank.

Were our mouths to fill with song as the sea,
our tongues sing endlessly like waves,
our lips offer praise like the limitless sky,
our eyes shine like the sun and the moon,
our arms spread heavenward like eagles' wings,
and our feet run as fast as deer,
we would still be unable to fully express our gratitude to You,
ADONAI our God and God of our ancestors,
or to praise Your name for even one of the myriad moments
of kindness with which You have blessed our ancestors and us.

מִמִּצְרַיִם גְּאַלְתָּנוּ, יהוה אֱלֹהֵינוּ,
וּמִבֵּית עֲבָדִים פְּדִיתָנוּ.
בְּרָעָב זַנְתָּנוּ,   וּבְשָׂבָע כִּלְכַּלְתָּנוּ,
מֵחֶרֶב הִצַּלְתָּנוּ,   וּמִדֶּבֶר מִלַּטְתָּנוּ,
וּמֵחֳלָיִם רָעִים וְנֶאֱמָנִים דִּלִּיתָנוּ.
עַד הֵנָּה עֲזָרוּנוּ רַחֲמֶיךָ,
וְלֹא עֲזָבוּנוּ חֲסָדֶיךָ,
וְאַל תִּטְּשֵׁנוּ, יהוה אֱלֹהֵינוּ, לָנֶצַח.

עַל כֵּן אֵבָרִים שֶׁפִּלַּגְתָּ בָּנוּ,
וְרוּחַ וּנְשָׁמָה שֶׁנָּפַחְתָּ בְּאַפֵּינוּ,
וְלָשׁוֹן אֲשֶׁר שַׂמְתָּ בְּפִינוּ,
הֵן הֵם יוֹדוּ וִיבָרְכוּ וִישַׁבְּחוּ וִיפָאֲרוּ וִירוֹמְמוּ
וְיַעֲרִיצוּ וְיַקְדִּישׁוּ וְיַמְלִיכוּ אֶת־שִׁמְךָ מַלְכֵּנוּ.
כִּי כָל־פֶּה לְךָ יוֹדֶה,   וְכָל־לָשׁוֹן לְךָ תִשָּׁבַע,
וְכָל־בֶּרֶךְ לְךָ תִכְרַע,   וְכָל־קוֹמָה לְפָנֶיךָ תִשְׁתַּחֲוֶה,
וְכָל־לְבָבוֹת יִירָאוּךָ,   וְכָל־קֶרֶב וּכְלָיוֹת יְזַמְּרוּ לִשְׁמֶךָ,
כַּדָּבָר שֶׁכָּתוּב:
כָּל־עַצְמוֹתַי תֹּאמַרְנָה, יהוה מִי כָמוֹךָ,
מַצִּיל עָנִי מֵחָזָק מִמֶּנּוּ, וְעָנִי וְאֶבְיוֹן מִגֹּזְלוֹ.
מִי יִדְמֶה־לָּךְ,   וּמִי יִשְׁוֶה־לָּךְ,   וּמִי יַעֲרָךְ־לָךְ,
הָאֵל הַגָּדוֹל הַגִּבּוֹר וְהַנּוֹרָא, אֵל עֶלְיוֹן, קֹנֵה שָׁמַיִם וָאָרֶץ.
נְהַלֶּלְךָ, וּנְשַׁבֵּחֲךָ, וּנְפָאֶרְךָ, וּנְבָרֵךְ אֶת־שֵׁם קָדְשֶׁךָ,
כָּאָמוּר: לְדָוִד, בָּרְכִי נַפְשִׁי אֶת־יהוה
וְכָל־קְרָבַי אֶת־שֵׁם קָדְשׁוֹ.

FROM EGYPT YOU REDEEMED US מִמִּצְרַיִם גְּאַלְתָּנוּ. Note the connection to the preceding prayer, the Song at the Sea, p. 65.

EVERY TONGUE ... EVERY KNEE וְכָל־לָשׁוֹן ... וְכָל־בֶּרֶךְ. Based on Isaiah 45:23.

EVERY BONE IN MY BODY CRIES OUT כָּל־עַצְמוֹתַי תֹּאמַרְנָה. Psalm 35:10. This verse has been cited as the basis in Jewish tradition for bodily movement during prayer.

GREAT, MIGHTY ... TO WHOM HEAVEN AND EARTH BELONG ... הָאֵל הַגָּדוֹל קֹנֵה שָׁמַיִם וָאָרֶץ. This is the wording of the first blessing of the Amidah, as it was re-cited in the Palestinian rite in the first millennium.

LET MY SOUL BLESS בָּרְכִי נַפְשִׁי. Psalm 103:1.

From Egypt You redeemed us, ADONAI our God,
and from the house of bondage You liberated us.
In famine You nourished us,
in prosperity You sustained us,
from the sword You saved us,
from pestilence You spared us,
and from illness, bitter and long, You raised us up.
Your compassion has maintained us to this day,
Your love has not left us;
do not abandon us, ADONAI our God, ever.

And so the organs You formed within us,
the spirit and soul You breathed into our nostrils,
the tongue You placed in our mouths—
they will all thank and bless, praise and exalt, sanctify
    and crown Your name, our sovereign.
Let every mouth thank You,
every tongue pledge loyalty,
every knee bend to You,
every body bow before You,
every heart be loyal to You,
and every fiber of our being chant Your name,
fulfilling the song of the psalmist:
"Every bone in my body cries out,
ADONAI, who is like You:
saving the afflicted from the powerful,
the afflicted and impoverished from those who prey on them?"
Who resembles You?
Who is equal to You?
Who compares to You?—
great, mighty, awe-inspiring, transcendent God,
to whom heaven and earth belong.
We will praise, acclaim, and bless Your holy name,
    fulfilling David's words:
"Let my soul bless ADONAI,
and every fiber of my being praise God's holy name."

הָאֵל בְּתַעֲצֻמוֹת עֻזֶּךָ, ◄

הַגָּדוֹל בִּכְבוֹד שְׁמֶךָ,

הַגִּבּוֹר לָנֶצַח,

וְהַנּוֹרָא בְּנוֹרְאוֹתֶיךָ,

הַמֶּלֶךְ

יוֹשֵׁב עַל כִּסֵּא רָם וְנִשָּׂא.

שׁוֹכֵן עַד, מָרוֹם וְקָדוֹשׁ שְׁמוֹ.

וְכָתוּב: רַנְּנוּ צַדִּיקִים בַּיהוה, לַיְשָׁרִים נָאוָה תְהִלָּה.

בְּפִי יְשָׁרִים תִּתְרוֹמָם

וּבְדִבְרֵי צַדִּיקִים תִּתְבָּרַךְ

וּבִלְשׁוֹן חֲסִידִים תִּתְקַדָּשׁ

וּבְקֶרֶב קְדוֹשִׁים תִּתְהַלָּל.

וּבְמַקְהֲלוֹת רִבְבוֹת עַמְּךָ בֵּית יִשְׂרָאֵל בְּרִנָּה יִתְפָּאַר שִׁמְךָ מַלְכֵּנוּ בְּכָל־דּוֹר וָדוֹר. שֶׁכֵּן חוֹבַת כָּל־הַיְצוּרִים לְפָנֶיךָ, יהוה אֱלֹהֵינוּ וֵאלֹהֵי אֲבוֹתֵינוּ [וְאִמּוֹתֵינוּ], לְהוֹדוֹת לְהַלֵּל לְשַׁבֵּחַ לְפָאֵר לְרוֹמֵם לְהַדֵּר לְבָרֵךְ ◄ לְעַלֵּה וּלְקַלֵּס עַל כָּל־דִּבְרֵי שִׁירוֹת וְתִשְׁבָּחוֹת דָּוִד בֶּן־יִשַׁי עַבְדְּךָ מְשִׁיחֶךָ.

יִשְׁתַּבַּח שִׁמְךָ לָעַד, מַלְכֵּנוּ הָאֵל הַמֶּלֶךְ הַגָּדוֹל וְהַקָּדוֹשׁ בַּשָּׁמַיִם וּבָאָרֶץ. כִּי לְךָ נָאֶה, יהוה אֱלֹהֵינוּ וֵאלֹהֵי אֲבוֹתֵינוּ [וְאִמּוֹתֵינוּ], שִׁיר וּשְׁבָחָה, הַלֵּל וְזִמְרָה, עֹז וּמֶמְשָׁלָה, נֶצַח, גְּדֻלָּה וּגְבוּרָה, תְּהִלָּה וְתִפְאֶרֶת, קְדֻשָּׁה וּמַלְכוּת. ◄ בְּרָכוֹת וְהוֹדָאוֹת מֵעַתָּה וְעַד עוֹלָם. בָּרוּךְ אַתָּה יהוה, אֵל מֶלֶךְ גָּדוֹל בַּתִּשְׁבָּחוֹת, אֵל הַהוֹדָאוֹת, אֲדוֹן הַנִּפְלָאוֹת, הַבּוֹחֵר בְּשִׁירֵי זִמְרָה, מֶלֶךְ אֵל חַי הָעוֹלָמִים.

GOD הָאֵל. An anonymous early medieval poet created a short poem elaborating each of the adjectives associated with God recited in the first paragraph of the Amidah: הָאֵל הַגָּדוֹל הַגִּבּוֹר וְהַנּוֹרָא, "Great, mighty, awe-inspiring, God," and added one more description declaring God's sovereignty: הַמֶּלֶךְ.

SOVEREIGN הַמֶּלֶךְ. On Shabbat the formal morning service begins with the leader chanting, שׁוֹכֵן עַד "dwelling forever," but on the High Holy Days, the leader begins one line earlier with the word "Sovereign," הַמֶּלֶךְ, with the special High Holy Day melody, since God's rule and judgment are essential images of the High Holy Day liturgy. In many communities the leader chants the opening words from the back of the synagogue and then proceeds to the front lectern.

SING רַנְּנוּ. Psalm 33:1.

IN THE SPEECH OF THE UPRIGHT, YOU ARE EXALTED בְּפִי יְשָׁרִים תִּתְרוֹמָם. The vision of God seated in heaven pans out to the chorus of the faithful singing on earth. Note that the second and third words of each line are acrostics spelling out the names Isaac and Rebecca in Hebrew. In Sephardic tradition, the words always appear in this order; in Ashkenazic tradition, the word order normally spells only Isaac, but for the High Holy Days, the order is rearranged to spell Rebecca as well, perhaps because on the first day of Rosh Hashanah we read of Isaac's birth, and on the second day of Rebecca's.

MAY YOUR NAME BE PRAISED יִשְׁתַּבַּח. This b'rakhah marks the completion of P'sukei D'zimra (Verses of Song), which began with the opening b'rakhah בָּרוּךְ שֶׁאָמַר "Praised be the One," p. 47. The two b'rakhot are considered complementary and one is not recited without the other.

The Stillness

The Ḥasidic master Ze'ev Wolf of Zhitomir remarked that two Hebrew words in the concluding *b'rakhah*, commonly pronounced as *shirei zimrah*, "chorus of song," can be vocalized differently and read as שְׁיָּרֵי זִמְרָה, *shayyarei zimrah*, "what is left over from [our] song." God delights equally in the stillness that remains after the words have been recited and the melodies have come to an end. What remains is the love and gratitude in the human heart. That is what God desires most of all.

The Life of the Soul

God does not need our praise. Rather we need to praise God to keep ourselves aware of our blessings and of the presence of God in the world. To become indifferent to the world is to bring about the death of the soul.
—REUVEN HAMMER

GOD, in the fullness of Your power,

GREAT, in accord with your glorious name,

MIGHTY, in all of time,

AWESOME, in your awe-inspiring deeds,

SOVEREIGN,
enthroned on high,
dwelling forever, exalted and holy is Your name—
as the Psalmist has written:
"Sing, O you righteous, to ADONAI;
for the upright, to praise God is lovely."

In the speech of the upright You are exalted,
in the words of the righteous You are blessed,
in the language of the devoted You are sanctified,
and in the midst of the holy congregation You are praised.

So the choruses of the thousands of Your people, the House of Israel, joyously glorify Your name in every generation. For it is the duty of all Your creations, ADONAI our God and God of our ancestors, to acclaim, laud, and glorify You—extolling, exalting, and adding our own praise to the songs of David son of Jesse, Your anointed servant.

May Your name be praised, always and everywhere, our sovereign, God, great and holy. For it is fitting, ADONAI our God and God of our ancestors, to sing songs of praise to You; to ascribe strength and sovereignty, holiness and eternity, to You; to praise and exalt You; to thank and bless You, now and forever.
Barukh atah ADONAI, Sovereign God, to whom we offer thanks and ascribe wonders, who delights in the chorus of song—the sovereign God, giving life to all worlds.

Some congregations add the following psalm. Some repeat each verse after the leader recites it.

שִׁיר הַמַּעֲלוֹת, מִמַּעֲמַקִּים קְרָאתִיךָ יהוה.
אֲדֹנָי, שִׁמְעָה בְקוֹלִי,
תִּהְיֶינָה אָזְנֶיךָ קַשֻּׁבוֹת לְקוֹל תַּחֲנוּנָי.

אִם־עֲוֹנוֹת תִּשְׁמָר־יָהּ, אֲדֹנָי מִי יַעֲמֹד.
כִּי־עִמְּךָ הַסְּלִיחָה, לְמַעַן תִּוָּרֵא.

קִוִּיתִי יהוה, קִוְּתָה נַפְשִׁי, וְלִדְבָרוֹ הוֹחָלְתִּי.

נַפְשִׁי לַאדֹנָי מִשֹּׁמְרִים לַבֹּקֶר, שֹׁמְרִים לַבֹּקֶר.

יַחֵל יִשְׂרָאֵל אֶל־יהוה, כִּי־עִם־יהוה הַחֶסֶד,
וְהַרְבֵּה עִמּוֹ פְדוּת.
וְהוּא יִפְדֶּה אֶת־יִשְׂרָאֵל מִכֹּל עֲוֹנֹתָיו.

תהלים קל

OUT OF THE DEPTHS
מִמַּעֲמַקִּים. Some congregations add Psalm 130 because it contains some of the central themes of the day: our confession of sin and our search for forgiveness. It begins with the striking phrase "Out of the depths . . ." and ends with the assurance that God will redeem us. In the liturgy of the Land of Israel in the first millennium, this psalm preceded the evening call to worship on the Day of Atonement; over time it became more generally associated with the High Holy Days.
(*adapted from Herman Kieval*)

חֲצִי קַדִּישׁ

יִתְגַּדַּל וְיִתְקַדַּשׁ שְׁמֵהּ רַבָּא. בְּעָלְמָא דִּי בְרָא, כִּרְעוּתֵהּ,
וְיַמְלִיךְ מַלְכוּתֵהּ בְּחַיֵּיכוֹן וּבְיוֹמֵיכוֹן וּבְחַיֵּי דְכָל־בֵּית
יִשְׂרָאֵל, בַּעֲגָלָא וּבִזְמַן קָרִיב, וְאִמְרוּ אָמֵן.

יְהֵא שְׁמֵהּ רַבָּא מְבָרַךְ לְעָלַם וּלְעָלְמֵי עָלְמַיָּא.

יִתְבָּרַךְ וְיִשְׁתַּבַּח וְיִתְפָּאַר וְיִתְרוֹמַם וְיִתְנַשֵּׂא וְיִתְהַדָּר
וְיִתְעַלֶּה וְיִתְהַלָּל שְׁמֵהּ דְּקֻדְשָׁא, **בְּרִיךְ הוּא**, לְעֵלָּא לְעֵלָּא
מִכָּל־בִּרְכָתָא וְשִׁירָתָא תֻּשְׁבְּחָתָא וְנֶחֱמָתָא דַּאֲמִירָן
בְּעָלְמָא, וְאִמְרוּ אָמֵן.

ḤATZI KADDISH. In Jewish liturgical usage, the Ḥatzi (or "partial") Kaddish, calling us to praise the name of God, marks the end of a section of the service.

PSALM 130

Some congregations add the following psalm. Some repeat each verse after the leader recites it.

A SONG OF ASCENTS.

Out of the depths I call to You, ADONAI.
    ADONAI, hear my cry, heed my plea.
If you keep account of sins, ADONAI, who can survive?
    Forgiveness is Yours alone, therefore we revere You.
I wait for ADONAI. O how I wait, yearning for God's response!
    I wait for ADONAI more eagerly than the morning watch
    awaits the dawn.
    Israel, put your hope in ADONAI, for love flows from
    ADONAI, and surely, also, redemption.
God will redeem Israel from all its transgressions.

Shir ha-ma·alot mi-ma·amakkim k'ratikha Adonai.
Adonai shim·ah v'koli tihyenah oznekha kashuvot l'kol taḥanunai.

Im avonot tishmor yah Adonai mi ya·amod.
Ki im'kha ha-s'liḥah l'ma·an tivvarei.

Kivviti Adonai kiv'tah nafshi v'li-d'varo hoḥalti.

Nafshi ladonai mi-shom'rim la-boker, shom'rim la-boker.

Yaḥel yisra·el el Adonai ki im Adonai ha-ḥesed v'harbeih immo f'dut.
V'hu yifdeh et yisra·el mi-kol avonotav.

Ḥatzi Kaddish

May God's great name be exalted and hallowed throughout the created world, as is God's wish. May God's sovereignty soon be established, in your lifetime and in your days, and in the days of all the House of Israel. And respond with: *Amen.*

May God's great name be acknowledged forever and ever!
Y'hei sh'meih rabba m'varakh l'alam u-l'almei almayya.

May the name of the Holy One be acknowledged and celebrated, lauded and worshipped, exalted and honored, extolled and acclaimed—though God, who is blessed, *b'rikh hu*, is truly far beyond all acknowledgment and praise, or any expressions of gratitude or consolation ever spoken in the world. And respond with: *Amen.*

We rise. Leader:

בָּרְכוּ אֶת־יהוה הַמְבֹרָךְ.

Congregation, then the leader repeats:

בָּרוּךְ יהוה הַמְבֹרָךְ לְעוֹלָם וָעֶד.

On Rosh Hashanah:

בָּרוּךְ אַתָּה יהוה אֱלֹהֵינוּ מֶלֶךְ הָעוֹלָם, יוֹצֵר אוֹר
וּבוֹרֵא חֹשֶׁךְ עֹשֶׂה שָׁלוֹם וּבוֹרֵא אֶת־הַכֹּל.

On Yom Kippur:

בָּרוּךְ אַתָּה יהוה אֱלֹהֵינוּ מֶלֶךְ הָעוֹלָם, הַפּוֹתֵחַ לָנוּ
שַׁעֲרֵי רַחֲמִים וּמֵאִיר עֵינֵי הַמְחַכִּים לִסְלִיחָתוֹ, יוֹצֵר
אוֹר וּבוֹרֵא חֹשֶׁךְ, עֹשֶׂה שָׁלוֹם וּבוֹרֵא אֶת־הַכֹּל.

Both services continue:

אוֹר עוֹלָם בְּאוֹצַר חַיִּים, אוֹרוֹת מֵאֹפֶל אָמַר וַיֶּהִי.

We are seated.

ON SHABBAT, TURN TO PAGE 73.

INTRODUCTION TO THE RECITATION OF THE SH'MA. Shaḥarit, the morning service, always includes two central moments, the first of which is the recitation of the Sh'ma. *B'rakhot* surrounding the Sh'ma serve to interpret the themes of the biblical verses that make up the Sh'ma itself. Two *b'rakhot* precede the Sh'ma. The first reflects on the morning light and the wonder of creation. The second acknowledges God's love of the people Israel as manifested through the gift of the teachings of Torah. A single *b'rakhah* follows the Sh'ma and speaks of redemption, a theme introduced in the third paragraph of the Sh'ma.

BAR'KHU: THE CALL TO WORSHIP TOGETHER בָּרְכוּ. The congregation is called together as a minyan by the leader and, by responding, acknowledges its being assembled for prayer.

TO WHOM ALL PRAYER IS DIRECTED הַמְבֹרָךְ. The Jerusalem Talmud explains the word *ha-m'vorakh* to mean "whom all of us praise" (Berakhot 11c).

FORMING LIGHT יוֹצֵר אוֹר. This opening *b'rakhah* before the Sh'ma acknowledges that we experience God, first of all, through witnessing the miracle of creation. Praying in the morning, we are asked to pay attention to the wonder of the dawn of sunlight and of a new day. Many psalms speak of heavenly bodies, stars and planets, praising God; later liturgists attached this idea to prophetic visions of angels singing the praise of God each morning. The break of dawn is then imagined as a chorus of song in which we join, and the flow and changes of time are felt as miracles we experience.

FORMING LIGHT AND CREATING DARKNESS יוֹצֵר אוֹר וּבוֹרֵא חֹשֶׁךְ. This prayer is adapted from a verse in Isaiah (45:7), which reads: עֹשֶׂה שָׁלוֹם וּבוֹרֵא רָע, "makes peace and creates evil." The prophet insists that both good and evil come from the one God. But the prayer focuses on all for which we can be thankful, beginning with the light that makes life possible.

WHO OPENS THE GATES OF MERCY הַפּוֹתֵחַ לָנוּ. While Rosh Hashanah is the Day of Judgment, Yom Kippur is seen as a day of mercy. In this verse, recited only on Yom Kippur, God is pictured as opening the gates of mercy, along with opening the gates of light.

THE ETERNAL LIGHT אוֹר עוֹלָם. This line is a fragment of an ancient *piyyut* written by one of the earliest liturgical poets, Yose ben Yose; the rest of the poem is now lost to us. The traditional melody with which it is usually sung is based on phrases of Kol Nidrei. The fragment reflects the rabbinic legend that the original light of creation is preserved in God's treasury for the use of the righteous in the world to come, and that the light we experience is but a substitute for the supernal light that awaits us (Babylonian Talmud, Ḥagigah 12a).

THE SH'MA AND ITS BLESSINGS

The Call
to Worship Together

Prayer provides a moment when we may search our selves and discover our innermost being. Even the most meditative of world religions emphasize the need for prayer to take place in the midst of a congregation. Paradoxically, when we are with others, silently accompanied by them, we become less fearful of entering into ourselves, as the knowledge of our common quest gives us strength.

It is as if we can find the courage to fully plumb the depths of our own selves only when we know that our private meditations are echoed in the hearts of those who surround us. Our common humanity is the foundation of prayer.

Prayer

Prayer is the microcosm of the soul. It is the whole soul in one moment; the quintessence of all our acts; the climax of all our thoughts.

—ABRAHAM JOSHUA
HESCHEL

Bar'khu: The Call to Worship Together

We rise as we are called by the leader's words of invitation to prayer. The leader bows when saying the word "bar'khu" (praise) and stands straight when reciting the name of God. Similarly, the congregation bows at the word "barukh" (praise) and straightens to full height at the recitation of God's name.

Leader:

Praise ADONAI, to whom all prayer is directed.

Congregation, then the leader repeats:

ʄ Praise ADONAI, to whom all prayer is directed forever and ever.

Barukh Adonai ha-m'vorakh l'olam va·ed.

First B'rakhah before the Sh'ma: The Creation of Light

On Rosh Hashanah:

Barukh atah ADONAI, our God, ruler of time and space, forming light and creating darkness, bringing harmony while creating all.

On Yom Kippur:

Barukh atah ADONAI, our God, ruler of time and space, who opens the gates of mercy, giving light to those who await Your forgiveness, forming light and creating darkness, bringing harmony while creating all.

Both services continue:

The eternal light is found in the treasury of life.
God said, "Let there be light from the darkness," and so it was.

We are seated.

ON SHABBAT, TURN TO PAGE 73.

On weekdays, we recite:

הַמֵּאִיר לָאָרֶץ וְלַדָּרִים עָלֶיהָ בְּרַחֲמִים,
וּבְטוּבוֹ מְחַדֵּשׁ בְּכָל־יוֹם תָּמִיד מַעֲשֵׂה בְרֵאשִׁית.
מָה־רַבּוּ מַעֲשֶׂיךָ יהוה,
כֻּלָּם בְּחָכְמָה עָשִׂיתָ, מָלְאָה הָאָרֶץ קִנְיָנֶךָ.
הַמֶּלֶךְ הַמְרוֹמָם לְבַדּוֹ מֵאָז,
הַמְשֻׁבָּח וְהַמְפֹאָר וְהַמִּתְנַשֵּׂא מִימוֹת עוֹלָם,
אֱלֹהֵי עוֹלָם, בְּרַחֲמֶיךָ הָרַבִּים רַחֵם עָלֵינוּ,
אֲדוֹן עֻזֵּנוּ, צוּר מִשְׂגַּבֵּנוּ, מָגֵן יִשְׁעֵנוּ, מִשְׂגָּב בַּעֲדֵנוּ.

אֵל בָּרוּךְ, גְּדוֹל דֵּעָה,
הֵכִין וּפָעַל זָהֳרֵי חַמָּה.
טוֹב יָצַר כָּבוֹד לִשְׁמוֹ.
מְאוֹרוֹת נָתַן סְבִיבוֹת עֻזּוֹ.
פִּנּוֹת צְבָאָיו קְדוֹשִׁים,
רוֹמְמֵי שַׁדַּי, תָּמִיד מְסַפְּרִים
כְּבוֹד אֵל וּקְדֻשָּׁתוֹ.
◁ תִּתְבָּרַךְ יהוה אֱלֹהֵינוּ עַל שֶׁבַח מַעֲשֵׂה יָדֶיךָ,
וְעַל מְאוֹרֵי אוֹר שֶׁעָשִׂיתָ יְפָאֲרוּךָ סֶּלָה.

Continue on page 75.

HOW VARIED ARE YOUR WORKS מָה־רַבּוּ מַעֲשֶׂיךָ. Psalm 104:24.

ALMIGHTY, BLESSED אֵל בָּרוּךְ. This early anonymous acrostic poem has four beats to the line and a rhyming pattern of *aa, bb, cc*, with a concluding *b*. Joel Hoffman, a contemporary scholar, writes, "The meaning of the individual words here was never the point. They were chosen for their meter and their initial letter." In this conception, the Hebrew alphabet itself was an instrument of creation. Our translation here is impelled by this idea and is alphabetical, capturing the meaning of the text in a non-literal manner.

SELAH [Not translated] סֶלָה. The biblical meaning of this word, which occurs frequently in Psalms, is unknown. The ancient rabbis thought that it meant "forever."

THE MYSTICAL BLESSING OF LIGHT. This first *b'rakhah* before the Sh'ma became a favorite locus for Jewish mystics who flourished in the first millennium of the common era and whose meditations have entered the liturgy here. The subject of creation and the theme of light became a springboard for ecstatic flights that pictured the soul ascending through seven angelic spheres. They imagined that as the heavens opened up, humans might join in that chorus singing, "Holy, holy holy is *Adonai Tz'va·ot*," and so they incorporated references to angels and heavenly spheres in prayers that greeted the break of dawn. While for the Rabbis of the 2nd century the Sh'ma was recited chiefly as an affirmation of Jewish faith, for the later Jewish mystics the Sh'ma became a focal point of meditational exercises. A talmudic story tells that, when the time for the recitation of the Sh'ma had arrived, Rabbi Yehudah would cover his eyes, because he was engaged in other activities (Babylonian Talmud, Berakhot 13b). In its context, the story suggests that he concentrated on the Sh'ma only briefly; yet this text later became a central source for understanding the Sh'ma as a moment of deep inward turning and intense concentration. In keeping with this latter understanding, covering one's eyes became the norm for the recitation of the first sentence of the Sh'ma.

Renewing Creation

Somewhere out there right now a new star is being born. A clump of matter has attracted gas and dust, grown larger, drawn matter to itself more efficiently, until finally the temperature and pressure within are high enough that hydrogen atoms are jammed together and thermonuclear reactions begin. The star turns on and the surrounding darkness is dispelled: matter turns into light. About once a month, somewhere in our galaxy, out of a pitch-black cloud of gas and dust, a new solar system forms. And the observable universe may contain 100 billion galaxies; so perhaps 100 solar systems are forming every second.

—DANIEL MATT

The Sense of Wonder

As civilization advances, the sense of wonder almost necessarily declines. Such decline is an alarming symptom of our state of mind. Mankind will not perish for want of information; but only for want of appreciation. The beginning of our happiness lies in the understanding that life without wonder is not worth living. What we lack is not a will to believe but a will to wonder.

—ABRAHAM JOSHUA HESCHEL

From the Zohar

Rabbi Yitzḥak said: "The light created by God in the act of creation flared from one end of the universe to the other and was hidden away, reserved for the righteous in the world to come, as it is written, "Light is sown for the righteous" (Psalm 97:11).... But until the world to come arrives, it is stored and hidden away."

Rabbi Yehudah responded: "If the light were completely hidden, the world would not exist for even a moment! Rather, it is hidden and sown like a seed that gives birth to other seeds and fruit. Thereby the world is sustained.... Everywhere that Torah is studied at night, one thread-thin ray appears from that hidden light and flows down upon those absorbed in it. Since the first day, the light has never been fully revealed, but it is vital to the world, renewing each day the act of creation."

On weekdays, we recite:

With kindness, You illumine the earth and all who dwell on it;
in Your goodness, You renew creation day after day.
How varied are Your works, ADONAI,
all fashioned with wisdom;
the world in its entirety is Your dominion.
You alone ruled on high from the very beginning,
praised, glorified, and exalted since earliest time.
God of the universe,
with Your great kindness, have compassion on us.
Master of our strength,
protecting fortress,
redeeming shield,
be our stronghold.

Almighty, blessed, creator of all who dwell on earth,
the firmament and goodly heavens are illuminated with
Your justice, kindness, and light; they make Your name
an object of praise; quietly, resolutely, soulfully all tell in
unified voice of Your wise, excellent, and zealous care.
You are to be praised, ADONAI our God, for the wondrous
work of Your hands, and for the radiant lights that You
fashioned, always reflecting Your glory.

Continue on page 75.

הַכֹּל   יוֹדוּךָ
וְהַכֹּל   יְשַׁבְּחוּךָ,
וְהַכֹּל   יֹאמְרוּ אֵין קָדוֹשׁ כַּיהוה.
הַכֹּל   יְרוֹמְמוּךָ סֶּלָה,
יוֹצֵר   הַכֹּל.
הָאֵל הַפּוֹתֵחַ בְּכָל־יוֹם דַּלְתוֹת שַׁעֲרֵי מִזְרָח
וּבוֹקֵעַ חַלּוֹנֵי רָקִיעַ,
מוֹצִיא חַמָּה מִמְּקוֹמָהּ   וּלְבָנָה מִמְּכוֹן שִׁבְתָּהּ,
וּמֵאִיר לָעוֹלָם כֻּלּוֹ   וּלְיוֹשְׁבָיו שֶׁבָּרָא בְּמִדַּת רַחֲמִים.
הַמֵּאִיר לָאָרֶץ וְלַדָּרִים עָלֶיהָ בְּרַחֲמִים
וּבְטוּבוֹ מְחַדֵּשׁ בְּכָל־יוֹם תָּמִיד מַעֲשֵׂה בְרֵאשִׁית.
הַמֶּלֶךְ הַמְרוֹמָם לְבַדּוֹ מֵאָז,
הַמְשֻׁבָּח וְהַמְפֹאָר וְהַמִּתְנַשֵּׂא מִימוֹת עוֹלָם.
אֱלֹהֵי עוֹלָם בְּרַחֲמֶיךָ הָרַבִּים רַחֵם עָלֵינוּ,
אֲדוֹן עֻזֵּנוּ   צוּר מִשְׂגַּבֵּנוּ.
מָגֵן יִשְׁעֵנוּ   מִשְׂגָּב בַּעֲדֵנוּ.

◁ אֵין כְּעֶרְכְּךָ   וְאֵין זוּלָתֶךָ,
אֶפֶס בִּלְתֶּךָ   וּמִי דוֹמֶה לָּךְ.
אֵין כְּעֶרְכְּךָ   יהוה אֱלֹהֵינוּ בָּעוֹלָם הַזֶּה
וְאֵין זוּלָתְךָ   מַלְכֵּנוּ לְחַיֵּי הָעוֹלָם הַבָּא.
אֶפֶס בִּלְתֶּךָ   גּוֹאֲלֵנוּ לִימוֹת הַמָּשִׁיחַ
וְאֵין דּוֹמֶה לָּךְ   מוֹשִׁיעֵנוּ לִתְחִיַּת הַמֵּתִים.

אֵל אָדוֹן עַל כָּל־הַמַּעֲשִׂים,
בָּרוּךְ וּמְבֹרָךְ בְּפִי כָּל־נְשָׁמָה.
גָּדְלוֹ וְטוּבוֹ מָלֵא עוֹלָם,
דַּעַת וּתְבוּנָה סוֹבְבִים אוֹתוֹ.

הַמִּתְגָּאֶה עַל חַיּוֹת הַקֹּדֶשׁ,
וְנֶהְדָּר בְּכָבוֹד עַל הַמֶּרְכָּבָה.
זְכוּת וּמִישׁוֹר לִפְנֵי כִסְאוֹ,
חֶסֶד וְרַחֲמִים לִפְנֵי כְבוֹדוֹ.

ALL הַכֹּל. The word "all," הַכֹּל, occurs five times in quick succession and refers to the totality of humanity, all earthly creatures and forces, as well as the heavenly bodies and the most distant galaxies. It echoes the last word of the opening b'rakhah (p. 71) and anticipates the affirmation of the One God, who is God of all, whom we are about to praise in the Sh'ma.

NOTHING IS AS HOLY AS GOD אֵין קָדוֹשׁ כַּיהוה. Quoted from Hannah's prayer, 1 Samuel 2:2.

NONE EXISTS BESIDES YOU אֵין זוּלָתֶךָ. A pointed polemic against any belief in divine or satanic powers existing outside of God's authority.

THE WORLD TO COME הָעוֹלָם הַבָּא. While conventionally "the world to come" refers to the afterlife or to the messianic era, some Jewish thinkers believe that the Hebrew term refers to the experience of the heavens opening up, that is, the immediate experience of God's presence.

GOD, MASTER אֵל אָדוֹן. This piyyut, commonly attributed to mystics of the first millennium, is based on the visions of Ezekiel that describe a variety of heavenly hosts. Its use of an alphabetical acrostic suggests that God's word is the primary constitutive element of all creation.

ON SHABBAT, WE CONTINUE HERE:

All thank You, all praise You, and all declare:
"Nothing is as holy as God."
All will praise You forever, Creator of all,
for You, ADONAI, raise the gates of the east, each day,
breaking through the openings of the sky,
bringing forth the sun from its place
and the moon from where it sits,
illuminating the entire world and all its inhabitants,
whom You created with mercy.

With kindness You illumine the earth and all who dwell on it;
in Your goodness, day after day You renew creation.
You alone ruled on high from the very beginning, praised and
glorified, exalted since earliest time. God of the universe,
in Your great mercy, have compassion on us.
Master of our strength,   protecting fortress,
redeeming shield,   be our stronghold.

None is like You,
none exists besides You,
the world would be nothing without You,
and none can be compared to You:
none is like You, ADONAI our God, in this world,
none but You will be our sovereign in the world to come,
no one but You, our redeemer, will be acknowledged in the
    messianic age,
and none can compare to You, our savior, giving life to the dead.

God, master of all existence,
praised by all that breathes,
the world is filled with Your greatness and glory,
knowledge and understanding surround You.

Exalted above holy beings,
resplendent in glory,
love and mercy precede You,
integrity and merit stand before Your throne.

El adon al kol ha-ma·asim, barukh u-m'vorakh b'fi kol n'shamah.
Godlo v'tuvo malei olam, da·at u-t'vunah sov'vim oto.
Ha-mitga·eh al ḥayyot ha-kodesh, v'nehdar b'khavod al ha-merkavah.
Z'khut u-mishor lifnei khis·o, ḥesed v'raḥamim lifnei kh'vodo.

טוֹבִים מְאוֹרוֹת שֶׁבָּרָא אֱלֹהֵינוּ,
יְצָרָם בְּדַעַת בְּבִינָה וּבְהַשְׂכֵּל.
כֹּחַ וּגְבוּרָה נָתַן בָּהֶם,
לִהְיוֹת מוֹשְׁלִים בְּקֶרֶב תֵּבֵל.

מְלֵאִים זִיו וּמְפִיקִים נֹגַהּ,
נָאֶה זִיוָם בְּכָל־הָעוֹלָם.
שְׂמֵחִים בְּצֵאתָם וְשָׂשִׂים בְּבוֹאָם,
עֹשִׂים בְּאֵימָה רְצוֹן קוֹנָם.

פְּאֵר וְכָבוֹד נוֹתְנִים לִשְׁמוֹ,
צָהֳלָה וְרִנָּה לְזֵכֶר מַלְכוּתוֹ.
קָרָא לַשֶּׁמֶשׁ וַיִּזְרַח אוֹר,
רָאָה וְהִתְקִין צוּרַת הַלְּבָנָה.

שֶׁבַח נוֹתְנִים לוֹ כָּל צְבָא מָרוֹם,
תִּפְאֶרֶת וּגְדֻלָּה, שְׂרָפִים וְאוֹפַנִּים וְחַיּוֹת הַקֹּדֶשׁ.

לָאֵל אֲשֶׁר שָׁבַת מִכָּל־הַמַּעֲשִׂים, בַּיּוֹם הַשְּׁבִיעִי הִתְעַלָּה
וְיָשַׁב עַל כִּסֵּא כְבוֹדוֹ. תִּפְאֶרֶת עָטָה לְיוֹם הַמְּנוּחָה, עֹנֶג
קָרָא לְיוֹם הַשַּׁבָּת. זֶה שֶׁבַח שֶׁל יוֹם הַשְּׁבִיעִי, שֶׁבּוֹ שָׁבַת
אֵל מִכָּל־מְלַאכְתּוֹ. וְיוֹם הַשְּׁבִיעִי מְשַׁבֵּחַ וְאוֹמֵר: מִזְמוֹר
שִׁיר לְיוֹם הַשַּׁבָּת, טוֹב לְהוֹדוֹת לַיהוה. לְפִיכָךְ יְפָאֲרוּ
וִיבָרְכוּ לָאֵל כָּל־יְצוּרָיו. שֶׁבַח יְקָר וּגְדֻלָּה יִתְּנוּ לָאֵל מֶלֶךְ
יוֹצֵר כֹּל, הַמַּנְחִיל מְנוּחָה לְעַמּוֹ יִשְׂרָאֵל בִּקְדֻשָּׁתוֹ בְּיוֹם
שַׁבַּת קֹדֶשׁ. שִׁמְךָ יהוה אֱלֹהֵינוּ יִתְקַדַּשׁ, וְזִכְרְךָ, מַלְכֵּנוּ,
יִתְפָּאַר בַּשָּׁמַיִם מִמַּעַל וְעַל הָאָרֶץ מִתָּחַת. ◁ תִּתְבָּרַךְ
מוֹשִׁיעֵנוּ, עַל שֶׁבַח מַעֲשֵׂה יָדֶיךָ, וְעַל מְאוֹרֵי אוֹר
שֶׁעָשִׂיתָ, יְפָאֲרוּךָ סֶּלָה.

HAPPY שְׂמֵחִים. Frequently, as is the case here, the letter שׂ (*sin*) is substituted for the similarly sounded ס (*samekh*) in Hebrew alphabetical poetry. Most, if not all, worshippers in ancient times did not have prayerbooks, and so the substitution of letters would have been less noticeable.

GOD, WHO CEASED WORK לָאֵל אֲשֶׁר שָׁבַת. The liturgist forms this prayer out of a series of suggestive biblical verses and rabbinic comments. Already in the Bible, the seventh day is spoken of as affecting God's inner life: God was renewed (*va-yinnafash*) (Exodus 31:17) on the seventh day. The Rabbis pictured God as achieving full sovereignty only on Shabbat. Similarly, the Rabbis depict Shabbat itself praising God and chanting Psalm 92, "A Song of Shabbat." In the formulation of the Zohar, the classic work of Jewish mysticism, the seventh day is identified with the Shekhinah, that aspect of the Divine most accessible to human beings and simultaneously the most spiritual side of our humanity.

Shabbat

God was unable to sit on the "throne of praise" until the work of creation was complete, for until that point, there was no one in the world to praise God. Even after the angels and natural world were created, they needed to work to acclimate themselves to the new world and make it habitable, so they lacked the motivation and opportunity to praise God. It was only with the arrival of the first Shabbat that the angels and creatures truly praised God. This is why God "ascended the throne of praise" on the seventh day.

—THE ZOHAR

Good are the lights that our God has created,
fashioning them with intelligence, understanding, and insight;
endowed with strength and power,
they maintain dominion over earthly realms.

Full of radiance, they gleam brilliantly,
radiating splendor throughout the world.
Happy as they go forth, joyous upon return,
they accomplish, with awe, the will of their creator.

They give glory and honor to the name of God,
declaring with songs of joy God's sovereignty.
God called forth the sun, and light shone,
then saw fit to fix the cycles of the moon.

And so the array of heaven,
s'rafim, ofanim, and holy beings,
all the heavenly hosts,
give praise, glory, and honor to God.

Tovim m'orot she-bara eloheinu, y'tzaram b'da·at b'vinah u-v'haskel.
Ko·aḥ u-g'vurah natan ba-hem, lihyot mosh'lim b'kerev teiveil.

M'lei·im ziv u-m'fikim nogah, na·eh zivam b'khol ha·olam.
S'meiḥim b'tzeitam v'sasim b'vo·am, osim b'eimah r'tzon konam.

P'er v'khavod not'nim lishmo, tzoholah v'rinnah l'zeikher malkhuto.
Kara la-shemesh va-yizraḥ or, ra·ah v'hitkin tzurat ha-l'vanah.

Shevaḥ not'nim lo kol tz'va marom,
Tif·eret u-g'dullah, s'rafim v'ofanim v'ḥayyot ha-kodesh.

All extol God, who ceased work on the seventh day and ascended the throne of praise, robed in majesty for the day of rest, calling Shabbat a delight. Such is the distinction of the seventh day, that God rested from all work, and so the seventh day itself praises God and says, "A song of Shabbat: it is good to thank ADONAI." Let all creatures likewise celebrate and bless God, offering praise, honor, and glory to God—the ruler, creator of all, who, in holiness, grants peaceful rest to the people Israel on the holy Shabbat. May Your name, ADONAI our God, be hallowed and may the thought of You, our sovereign, be celebrated in the heavens above and on earth below, though the praise due You, our redeemer, is beyond any offered by Your handiwork or the lights You have made—may they continue always to sing Your glory.

All services continue here:

תִּתְבָּרַךְ **צוּרֵנוּ** מַלְכֵּנוּ וְגֹאֲלֵנוּ בּוֹרֵא קְדוֹשִׁים, יִשְׁתַּבַּח
שִׁמְךָ לָעַד מַלְכֵּנוּ, יוֹצֵר מְשָׁרְתִים, וַאֲשֶׁר מְשָׁרְתָיו
כֻּלָּם עוֹמְדִים בְּרוּם עוֹלָם וּמַשְׁמִיעִים בְּיִרְאָה יַחַד
בְּקוֹל, דִּבְרֵי אֱלֹהִים חַיִּים וּמֶלֶךְ עוֹלָם.
◁ כֻּלָּם אֲהוּבִים, כֻּלָּם בְּרוּרִים, כֻּלָּם גִּבּוֹרִים,
וְכֻלָּם עֹשִׂים בְּאֵימָה וּבְיִרְאָה רְצוֹן קוֹנָם.
וְכֻלָּם פּוֹתְחִים אֶת־פִּיהֶם בִּקְדֻשָּׁה וּבְטׇהֳרָה,
בְּשִׁירָה וּבְזִמְרָה, וּמְבָרְכִים וּמְשַׁבְּחִים,
וּמְפָאֲרִים וּמַעֲרִיצִים, וּמַקְדִּישִׁים וּמַמְלִיכִים:
אֶת־שֵׁם הָאֵל, הַמֶּלֶךְ הַגָּדוֹל, הַגִּבּוֹר וְהַנּוֹרָא קָדוֹשׁ
הוּא. ◁ וְכֻלָּם מְקַבְּלִים עֲלֵיהֶם עֹל מַלְכוּת שָׁמַיִם זֶה
מִזֶּה, וְנוֹתְנִים רְשׁוּת זֶה לָזֶה, לְהַקְדִּישׁ לְיוֹצְרָם בְּנַחַת
רוּחַ, בְּשָׂפָה בְרוּרָה וּבִנְעִימָה קְדוֹשָׁה, כֻּלָּם כְּאֶחָד עוֹנִים
וְאוֹמְרִים בְּיִרְאָה:

קָדוֹשׁ, קָדוֹשׁ, קָדוֹשׁ יהוה צְבָאוֹת, מְלֹא כׇל־הָאָרֶץ כְּבוֹדוֹ.

◁ וְהָאוֹפַנִּים וְחַיּוֹת הַקֹּדֶשׁ בְּרַעַשׁ גָּדוֹל מִתְנַשְּׂאִים
לְעֻמַּת שְׂרָפִים, לְעֻמָּתָם מְשַׁבְּחִים וְאוֹמְרִים:

בָּרוּךְ כְּבוֹד־יהוה מִמְּקוֹמוֹ.

לְאֵל בָּרוּךְ, נְעִימוֹת יִתֵּנוּ. לַמֶּלֶךְ אֵל חַי וְקַיָּם,
זְמִירוֹת יֹאמֵרוּ, וְתִשְׁבָּחוֹת יַשְׁמִיעוּ. כִּי הוּא לְבַדּוֹ
פּוֹעֵל גְּבוּרוֹת,   עֹשֶׂה חֲדָשׁוֹת,
בַּעַל מִלְחָמוֹת,   זוֹרֵעַ צְדָקוֹת,
מַצְמִיחַ יְשׁוּעוֹת, בּוֹרֵא רְפוּאוֹת,
נוֹרָא תְהִלּוֹת,   אֲדוֹן הַנִּפְלָאוֹת,
◁ הַמְחַדֵּשׁ בְּטוּבוֹ בְּכׇל־יוֹם תָּמִיד מַעֲשֵׂה בְרֵאשִׁית.
כָּאָמוּר: לְעֹשֵׂה אוֹרִים גְּדֹלִים, כִּי לְעוֹלָם חַסְדּוֹ.
אוֹר חָדָשׁ עַל צִיּוֹן תָּאִיר וְנִזְכֶּה כֻלָּנוּ מְהֵרָה לְאוֹרוֹ.
בָּרוּךְ אַתָּה יהוה, יוֹצֵר הַמְּאוֹרוֹת.

KEDUSHAH D'YOTZEIR
קְדֻשָּׁה דְּיוֹצֵר. This version of the Kedushah, recited in the first *b'rakhah* before the Sh'ma, blesses God for the creation of the morning light. Every Kedushah is based on the visions of Isaiah and Ezekiel. Each prophet described an angelic chorus. Isaiah (6:3) saw them singing, "Kadosh, kadosh, kadosh, Holy, holy, holy. . . ."; Ezekiel (3:12) heard them reciting, "Barukh k'vod Adonai, Praised is God's glory. . . ." The angelic chorus can be understood as all the forces of nature personified. All of creation constitutes a praise of God; every created being, animate and inanimate, sings to God.

ALL OF THEM כֻּלָּם. This passage builds on the repetition of the root כל, translated here as "all" and "each." The Holy One is worshipped with one voice, for all of creation represents God's glory.

EACH TURNS TO THE OTHER וְכֻלָּם מְקַבְּלִים. Angels acknowledge each other and recognize a mutual responsibility. This is an ideal of what community should be.

OFANIM . . . S'RAFIM אוֹפַנִּים . . . שְׂרָפִים. Angelic songs figure prominently in ancient mystical texts. Descriptions of different groups of angels singing hymns to God surely mirrored the seekers' own varieties of mystical experience.

THE CREATOR OF THE GREAT LIGHTS לְעֹשֵׂה אוֹרִים גְּדֹלִים. Psalm 136:7.

ZION צִיּוֹן. The liturgist takes the motif of the light of creation and of the dawn found in this *b'rakhah*, and ties it to an image of the Temple of Mount Zion as a source of ultimate illumination.

The real difference between humans and angels is not the fact that we have bodies, because the essential comparison is between the human soul and the angel. Our souls are complex and include a whole world of different existential elements of all kinds, while the angel is a being of single essence and therefore in a sense one-dimensional. Because of our many-sidedness, we have the capacity to contain contradictions, and that spark that marks us as human gives us the ability to distinguish between moral and immoral alternatives. This makes it possible for us to rise to greater heights, and by the same token, creates the possibility for failure and backsliding, neither of which is true for the angel. Essentially, the angel is static, unchanging, whether temporary or eternal, fixed within the limits of quality given at its very creation, charged with a single task. . . . The person who performs a mitzvah, who prays, directs the mind toward the Divine, creates a moment of single-minded purpose and creates an angel, which is a sort of reaching out on our part to higher worlds.

—ADIN STEINSALTZ
(adapted)

All services continue here:

KEDUSHAH D'YOTZEIR: *The Angelic Praise of God*
You are to be praised, our stronghold, our sovereign, our redeemer, creator of celestial beings; Your name is to be acclaimed forever. Our sovereign, You create servants who stand at the edges of the universe, full of awe, proclaiming with one voice the words of the living God and sovereign of the universe.

All of them are beloved, all of them pure, all of them strong, and all of them, reverently and filled with awe, carry out the will of the One who has dominion over them. With holiness and purity, in chant and song, all of them raise their voices to bless, praise, and celebrate, extol, hallow, and acknowledge the majesty of the name of God, the great, mighty, awe-inspiring sovereign, the Holy One.

Each turns to the other as they proclaim their loyalty to God, and each gives permission to joyfully hallow their creator, and so with clear speech, and sacred melody, together as one, filled with awe, they call out and say:

Holy, holy, holy is *Adonai Tz'va·ot*, the whole world is filled with God's glory.
Kadosh, kadosh, kadosh Adonai Tz'va·ot, m'lo khol ha-aretz k'vodo.

The *ofanim* and other holy beings rise up, and, opposite the *s'rafim*, loudly proclaim their praise:
Praised is ADONAI's glory wherever God dwells.
Barukh k'vod Adonai mi-m'komo.

They offer up sweet melodies to God whom they bless. They chant songs to the Sovereign, the living and enduring God, voicing praise. For God alone achieves mighty deeds, creates anew, masters war, sows righteousness, nourishes deliverance, effects healing, is revered in praise, and authors wonders. In God's goodness, the work of creation is renewed each day, as the psalmist declared: "Thank the creator of the great lights, for God's love is everlasting."
Cause a new light to shine on Zion
and may we all soon be worthy of its illumination.
Barukh atah ADONAI, Creator of lights.
Or ḥadash al tziyyon ta·ir v'nizkeh khullanu m'heirah l'oro.

אַהֲבָה רַבָּה אֲהַבְתָּנוּ, יהוה אֱלֹהֵינוּ,
חֶמְלָה גְדוֹלָה וִיתֵרָה חָמַלְתָּ עָלֵינוּ.
אָבִינוּ מַלְכֵּנוּ, בַּעֲבוּר אֲבוֹתֵינוּ [וְאִמּוֹתֵינוּ] שֶׁבָּטְחוּ בְךָ
וַתְּלַמְּדֵם חֻקֵּי חַיִּים, כֵּן תְּחָנֵּנוּ וּתְלַמְּדֵנוּ.
אָבִינוּ, הָאָב הָרַחֲמָן, הַמְרַחֵם, רַחֵם עָלֵינוּ וְתֵן בְּלִבֵּנוּ
לְהָבִין וּלְהַשְׂכִּיל, לִשְׁמֹעַ, לִלְמֹד וּלְלַמֵּד, לִשְׁמֹר וְלַעֲשׂוֹת
וּלְקַיֵּם אֶת־כָּל־דִּבְרֵי תַלְמוּד תּוֹרָתֶךָ בְּאַהֲבָה.
וְהָאֵר עֵינֵינוּ בְּתוֹרָתֶךָ,
וְדַבֵּק לִבֵּנוּ בְּמִצְוֹתֶיךָ,
וְיַחֵד לְבָבֵנוּ לְאַהֲבָה וּלְיִרְאָה אֶת־שְׁמֶךָ,
וְלֹא נֵבוֹשׁ לְעוֹלָם וָעֶד.
כִּי בְשֵׁם קָדְשְׁךָ הַגָּדוֹל וְהַנּוֹרָא בָּטָחְנוּ,
נָגִילָה וְנִשְׂמְחָה בִּישׁוּעָתֶךָ.

Some gather their tzitzit before reciting this line:

◁ וַהֲבִיאֵנוּ לְשָׁלוֹם מֵאַרְבַּע כַּנְפוֹת הָאָרֶץ,
וְתוֹלִיכֵנוּ קוֹמְמִיּוּת לְאַרְצֵנוּ,
כִּי אֵל פּוֹעֵל יְשׁוּעוֹת אָתָּה,
וּבָנוּ בָחַרְתָּ מִכָּל־עַם וְלָשׁוֹן,
וְקֵרַבְתָּנוּ לְשִׁמְךָ הַגָּדוֹל סֶלָה בֶּאֱמֶת,
לְהוֹדוֹת לְךָ וּלְיַחֶדְךָ בְּאַהֲבָה.
בָּרוּךְ אַתָּה יהוה, הַבּוֹחֵר בְּעַמּוֹ יִשְׂרָאֵל בְּאַהֲבָה.

YOU HAVE LOVED US DEEPLY אַהֲבָה רַבָּה. The root אהב, "love," appears six times on this page. The contemporary commentator Reuven Hammer points out that three of them speak of our love of God, and three of God's love for us. While reciting this b'rakhah, the worshipper can anticipate the seventh occurrence, which is found in the first paragraph of the Sh'ma: "You shall love Adonai your God."

AVINU MALKEINU אָבִינוּ מַלְכֵּנוּ. Literally, "our father, our king." The pairing of these two words emphasizes that God is at once both intimate and distant. The word av, "father," suggests the image of God as "source" or "progenitor," and therefore may also be translated as "creator."

TO UNDERSTAND AND DISCERN; TO HEAR, STUDY, AND TEACH; TO OBSERVE, FULFILL, AND PERFORM לְהָבִין וּלְהַשְׂכִּיל לִשְׁמֹעַ לִלְמֹד וּלְלַמֵּד לִשְׁמֹר וְלַעֲשׂוֹת וּלְקַיֵּם This word order implies that study is intimately linked with action—indeed, that study should lead to action.

TORAH תּוֹרָה. The word "Torah" encompasses many different meanings. In its most limited usage, it refers to the Five Books of Moses. But in a larger sense it refers to all of Scripture, and even to all of later Jewish teaching. Thus the Rabbis of the Talmud spoke of the Written Torah and the Oral Torah, the latter referring to the teachings of the Midrash, Mishnah, and Talmud—and even to "whatever new teaching a student of wisdom might impart until the end of time." In this paragraph of the liturgy, "Torah" is given the widest meaning: the laws of life—all those teachings that instruct us in a full and ethical life.

GATHERING THE TZITZIT. In the later Middle Ages, the phrase "bring us safely from the four corners of the earth" evoked the four corners of the *tallit*. As they recited these words, some Jews used to gather together the four *tzitzit* from their *tallit*, symbolizing Israel's unity and ingathering (which God has promised in the Bible to initiate if Jews lead lives of holiness and mitzvot). They would hold their *tzitzit* through the third paragraph of the Sh'ma, where the word *tzitzit* is mentioned three times. As they recited each instance, they would kiss their *tzitzit*. Many Jews today observe this custom, indicating that they have lovingly undertaken to observe these words of Torah.

¶ God's Love

You were God
and we were Israel,
God alone
and lonely people,
long ago.

You loved us with God's love
and You taught us
how to respond to You.

Through mitzvot,
recollections,
celebrations,
Torah.

They are the light of
   our eyes,
the uniqueness of our being.

In the joy of them
You have drawn us close
   to You.
In the truth of them
we have discovered You,
   the only One.

We are together still.

You respond to every people
in Your chosen way;
with Your love You have
chosen to respond to us.

With our love,
we offer You our praise.

—RICHARD LEVY

Unify Our Hearts

There was once a pious
Jew who prayed that he be
saved from *pizzur ha-nefesh*
(literally, "scattering of the
soul"), becoming unfocused,
fragmented, not being
centered, being "all over the
place." Such is the inescapable outcome of trying to
own too many things in too
many places all at the same
time. Since God's oneness is
the root of all being, then to
join oneself with God is to unify oneself. . . . Consider that the source of our alienation from God's
commandments and even from God lies in our
personal disintegration, our fragmentation. Our
brokenness is overcome by saying *eḥad*, "One." By
reflecting on God's unity, we begin to recover our
own.   —ZE'EV WOLF OF ZHITOMIR
            (trans. Lawrence Kushner and Nehemia Polen)

Second B'rakhah before the Sh'ma: God's Great Love

You have loved us deeply, ADONAI our God, and shown us
boundless compassion.

Avinu Malkeinu, for the sake of our ancestors who trusted
in You and whom You taught the laws of life, be gracious to
us as well, and instruct us.

Compassionate Creator, care for us: Allow our hearts
to understand and discern; to hear, study, and teach; to
observe, fulfill, and perform with love all the teachings of
Your Torah. Enlighten our eyes with Your Torah; attach our
hearts to Your mitzvot; unify our hearts to love and revere
Your name so that we never lose hope. As we trust in Your
great, holy, awe-inspiring name, we will delight and rejoice
in Your deliverance.

Some gather their tzitzit before reciting this line:

Bring us safely from the four corners of the earth, and lead
us in dignity to our land, for You are the God who effects
deliverance. You have chosen us from all other peoples and
tongues, always drawing us nearer to Your name, that we
may truly acknowledge You and lovingly proclaim Your
oneness. *Barukh atah* ADONAI, who lovingly cares for the
people Israel.

Ahavah rabbah ahavtanu Adonai eloheinu,
ḥemlah g'dolah vi-teirah ḥamalta aleinu.
Avinu malkeinu, ba·avur avoteinu [v'immoteinu] she-bat'ḥu v'kha
va-t'lam'deim ḥukkei ḥayyim, kein t'ḥonneinu u-t'lam'deinu.
Avinu ha-av ha-raḥaman, ha-m'raḥeim, raḥeim aleinu v'tein
b'libbeinu l'havin u-l'haskil lishmo·a lilmod u-l'lammed lishmor
v'la·asot u-l'kayyem et kol divrei talmud toratekha b'ahavah.
V'ha·eir eineinu b'toratekha
v'dabbeik libbeinu b'mitzvotekha
v'yaheid l'vaveinu l'ahavah u-l'yir·ah et sh'mekha
v'lo neivosh l'olam va·ed.

קְרִיאַת שְׁמַע

If there is no minyan, add these words: אֵל מֶלֶךְ נֶאֱמָן

שְׁמַע יִשְׂרָאֵל יהוה אֱלֹהֵינוּ יהוה אֶחָד:

On Yom Kippur the following is recited aloud;
on Rosh Hashanah it is recited quietly:

בָּרוּךְ שֵׁם כְּבוֹד מַלְכוּתוֹ לְעוֹלָם וָעֶד.

וְאָהַבְתָּ אֵת יהוה אֱלֹהֶיךָ בְּכָל־לְבָבְךָ וּבְכָל־נַפְשְׁךָ וּבְכָל־
מְאֹדֶךָ: וְהָיוּ הַדְּבָרִים הָאֵלֶּה אֲשֶׁר אָנֹכִי מְצַוְּךָ הַיּוֹם
עַל־לְבָבֶךָ: וְשִׁנַּנְתָּם לְבָנֶיךָ וְדִבַּרְתָּ בָּם בְּשִׁבְתְּךָ בְּבֵיתֶךָ
וּבְלֶכְתְּךָ בַדֶּרֶךְ וּבְשָׁכְבְּךָ וּבְקוּמֶךָ: וּקְשַׁרְתָּם לְאוֹת עַל־
יָדֶךָ וְהָיוּ לְטֹטָפֹת בֵּין עֵינֶיךָ: וּכְתַבְתָּם עַל־מְזֻזוֹת בֵּיתֶךָ
וּבִשְׁעָרֶיךָ: דברים ו ד-ט

וְהָיָה אִם־שָׁמֹעַ תִּשְׁמְעוּ אֶל־מִצְוֹתַי אֲשֶׁר אָנֹכִי מְצַוֶּה
אֶתְכֶם הַיּוֹם לְאַהֲבָה אֶת־יהוה אֱלֹהֵיכֶם וּלְעָבְדוֹ בְּכָל־
לְבַבְכֶם וּבְכָל־נַפְשְׁכֶם: וְנָתַתִּי מְטַר־אַרְצְכֶם בְּעִתּוֹ
יוֹרֶה וּמַלְקוֹשׁ וְאָסַפְתָּ דְגָנֶךָ וְתִירֹשְׁךָ וְיִצְהָרֶךָ: וְנָתַתִּי
עֵשֶׂב בְּשָׂדְךָ לִבְהֶמְתֶּךָ וְאָכַלְתָּ וְשָׂבָעְתָּ: הִשָּׁמְרוּ לָכֶם
פֶּן־יִפְתֶּה לְבַבְכֶם וְסַרְתֶּם וַעֲבַדְתֶּם אֱלֹהִים אֲחֵרִים
וְהִשְׁתַּחֲוִיתֶם לָהֶם: וְחָרָה אַף־יהוה בָּכֶם וְעָצַר אֶת־
הַשָּׁמַיִם וְלֹא־יִהְיֶה מָטָר וְהָאֲדָמָה לֹא תִתֵּן אֶת־יְבוּלָהּ
וַאֲבַדְתֶּם מְהֵרָה מֵעַל הָאָרֶץ הַטֹּבָה אֲשֶׁר יהוה נֹתֵן
לָכֶם: וְשַׂמְתֶּם אֶת־דְּבָרַי אֵלֶּה עַל־לְבַבְכֶם וְעַל־נַפְשְׁכֶם
וּקְשַׁרְתֶּם אֹתָם לְאוֹת עַל־יֶדְכֶם וְהָיוּ לְטוֹטָפֹת בֵּין
עֵינֵיכֶם: וְלִמַּדְתֶּם אֹתָם אֶת־בְּנֵיכֶם לְדַבֵּר בָּם בְּשִׁבְתְּךָ
בְּבֵיתֶךָ וּבְלֶכְתְּךָ בַדֶּרֶךְ וּבְשָׁכְבְּךָ וּבְקוּמֶךָ: וּכְתַבְתָּם עַל־
מְזוּזוֹת בֵּיתֶךָ וּבִשְׁעָרֶיךָ: לְמַעַן יִרְבּוּ יְמֵיכֶם וִימֵי בְּנֵיכֶם

SH'MA YISRAEL. Rabbinic literature refers to the Sh'ma as originally a *k'ri·ah,* a reading of a passage of the Torah. Later it became a meditation as well—a way of focusing on the "oneness" of God, so much so that for some it became a heightened moment to experience a mystical union with God.

NO MINYAN. When there is no minyan, and therefore no official prayer leader, we add the three words אֵל מֶלֶךְ נֶאֱמָן, "God is a faithful sovereign," the initial letters of which form an acrostic of the word "amen."

PRAISED IS THE NAME בָּרוּךְ שֵׁם. This phrase is not part of the biblical text but was the customary response of the people to the recitation of the Sh'ma by the priests in the Temple. During the year, it is recited softly, in order not to imply that it has the same holiness as the words of the Torah itself. But on Yom Kippur, when the people Israel pray in purity, they may recite their response out loud.

INSCRIBE THEM UPON THE DOORPOSTS וּכְתַבְתָּם עַל־מְזֻזוֹת. The observant Jew lives a life surrounded by the Sh'ma, reciting it in the morning upon arising and at night before going to sleep, walking past its

---

inscription on the *mezuzah* when entering one's home, and even adorning oneself with the words on weekday mornings upon one's head and near one's heart when putting on תְּפִלִּין (*t'fillin*), phylacteries.

IF YOU WILL HEAR וְהָיָה אִם־שָׁמֹעַ. This paragraph suggests a direct relationship between the righteousness of our acts and our fate. If we are good, God will be good to us, and vice versa. That theology was questioned by biblical writers, most sharply in the Book of Job. Nevertheless, it does speak to a deep human need to see a world as containing a moral balance between good and evil. What is expressed here in concrete terms may be understood more broadly: moral and immoral actions have consequences, both seen and unseen.

Monotheism

Monotheism is the capacity to glimpse the One in and through the changing forms of the many, to see the whole in and through infinite images. "Hear, O Israel": despite the fractured, scattered, and conflicted nature of our experience, there is a unity that embraces and contains our diversity and that connects all things to each other.

—JUDITH PLASKOW

Witnessing

Why are the last letter of the first word of the Sh'ma, the ע, and the last letter of the last word, ד, enlarged, when they are written in the Torah? Together they form the word עֵד, "witness," as Isaiah says about Israel, "You are my witnesses" (43:10). By reciting the Sh'ma, we become witnesses to God's existence.

The Blessing of the Priests before the Sh'ma

The priests in the Temple would say the following *b'rakhah* before the Sh'ma: May the One who dwells in this House always grant you love, harmony, peace, and friendship.

—JERUSALEM TALMUD, BERAKHOT

Love of God

Once the Baal Shem Tov became so depressed that he thought, "I have no share in the world to come." And then he said to himself, "If I love God, what need have I of paradise?" —A HASIDIC TALE

Recitation of the Sh'ma

If there is no minyan, add these words: God is a faithful sovereign.

Hear, O Israel, ADONAI is our God, ADONAI alone.

Sh'ma yisra·el Adonai eloheinu Adonai eḥad.

On Yom Kippur the following is recited aloud; on Rosh Hashanah it is recited quietly:

Praised be the name of the One whose glorious sovereignty is forever and ever.

Barukh shem k'vod malkhuto l'olam va·ed.

You shall love ADONAI your God with all your heart, with all your soul, and with all that is yours. These words that I command you this day shall be taken to heart. Teach them again and again to your children, and speak of them when you sit in your home, when you walk on your way, when you lie down, and when you rise up. Bind them as a sign upon your hand and as a symbol above your eyes. Inscribe them upon the doorposts of your home and on your gates.   Deuteronomy 6:4–9

V'ahavta eit Adonai elohekha b'khol l'vav'kha u-v'khol nafsh'kha u-v'khol m'odekha. V'hayu ha-d'varim ha-eilleh asher anokhi m'tzav'kha ha-yom al l'vavekha. V'shinnantam l'vanekha v'dibbarta bam, b'shivt'kha b'veitekha u-v'lekht'kha va-derekh u-v'shokhb'kha u-v'kumekha. U-k'shartam l'ot al yadekha v'hayu l'totafot bein einekha. U-kh'tavtam al m'zuzot beitekha u-vi-sh'arekha.

If you will hear and obey the mitzvot that I command you this day, to love and serve ADONAI your God with all your heart and all your soul, then I will grant the rain for your land in season, rain in autumn and rain in spring. You shall gather in your grain and wine and oil—I will also provide grass in your fields for cattle—and you shall eat and be satisfied. Take care lest your heart be tempted, and you stray to serve other gods and bow to them. Then ADONAI's anger will flare up against you, and God will close up the sky so that there will be no rain and the earth will not yield its produce. You will quickly disappear from the good land that ADONAI is giving you.

Therefore, impress these words of mine upon your heart and upon your soul. Bind them as a sign upon your hand and as a symbol above your eyes. Teach them to your children, speaking of them when you sit in your home, when you walk on your way, when you lie down and when you rise up. Inscribe them upon the doorposts of your home and on your gates.

עַל הָאֲדָמָה אֲשֶׁר נִשְׁבַּע יְהֹוָה לַאֲבֹתֵיכֶם לָתֵת לָהֶם
כִּימֵי הַשָּׁמַיִם עַל־הָאָרֶץ: דברים יא יג-כא

וַיֹּאמֶר יְהֹוָה אֶל־מֹשֶׁה לֵּאמֹר: דַּבֵּר אֶל־בְּנֵי יִשְׂרָאֵל
וְאָמַרְתָּ אֲלֵהֶם וְעָשׂוּ לָהֶם צִיצִת עַל־כַּנְפֵי בִגְדֵיהֶם
לְדֹרֹתָם וְנָתְנוּ עַל־צִיצִת הַכָּנָף פְּתִיל תְּכֵלֶת: וְהָיָה לָכֶם
לְצִיצִת וּרְאִיתֶם אֹתוֹ וּזְכַרְתֶּם אֶת־כָּל־מִצְוֹת יְהֹוָה
וַעֲשִׂיתֶם אֹתָם וְלֹא תָתוּרוּ אַחֲרֵי לְבַבְכֶם וְאַחֲרֵי עֵינֵיכֶם
אֲשֶׁר־אַתֶּם זֹנִים אַחֲרֵיהֶם: לְמַעַן תִּזְכְּרוּ וַעֲשִׂיתֶם
אֶת־כָּל־מִצְוֹתָי וִהְיִיתֶם קְדֹשִׁים לֵאלֹהֵיכֶם: אֲנִי יְהֹוָה
אֱלֹהֵיכֶם אֲשֶׁר הוֹצֵאתִי אֶתְכֶם מֵאֶרֶץ מִצְרַיִם לִהְיוֹת
לָכֶם לֵאלֹהִים אֲנִי ◁ יְהֹוָה אֱלֹהֵיכֶם:
במדבר טו לז-מא

אֱמֶת

וְיַצִּיב וְנָכוֹן

וְקַיָּם וְיָשָׁר וְנֶאֱמָן וְאָהוּב וְחָבִיב וְנֶחְמָד וְנָעִים וְנוֹרָא
וְאַדִּיר וּמְתֻקָּן וּמְקֻבָּל וְטוֹב וְיָפֶה הַדָּבָר הַזֶּה עָלֵינוּ
לְעוֹלָם וָעֶד.

אֱמֶת אֱלֹהֵי עוֹלָם מַלְכֵּנוּ, צוּר יַעֲקֹב מָגֵן יִשְׁעֵנוּ.
◁ לְדֹר וָדֹר הוּא קַיָּם וּשְׁמוֹ קַיָּם, וְכִסְאוֹ נָכוֹן וּמַלְכוּתוֹ
וֶאֱמוּנָתוֹ לָעַד קַיָּמֶת. וּדְבָרָיו חָיִים וְקַיָּמִים, נֶאֱמָנִים
וְנֶחֱמָדִים, לָעַד וּלְעוֹלְמֵי עוֹלָמִים, עַל אֲבוֹתֵינוּ
[וְאִמּוֹתֵינוּ] וְעָלֵינוּ, עַל בָּנֵינוּ וְעַל דּוֹרוֹתֵינוּ, וְעַל
כָּל־דּוֹרוֹת זֶרַע יִשְׂרָאֵל עֲבָדֶיךָ. עַל הָרִאשׁוֹנִים וְעַל
הָאַחֲרוֹנִים דָּבָר טוֹב וְקַיָּם לְעוֹלָם וָעֶד,
אֱמֶת וֶאֱמוּנָה חֹק וְלֹא יַעֲבֹר.
◁ אֱמֶת שָׁאַתָּה הוּא יְהֹוָה אֱלֹהֵינוּ וֵאלֹהֵי אֲבוֹתֵינוּ
[וְאִמּוֹתֵינוּ], מַלְכֵּנוּ, מֶלֶךְ אֲבוֹתֵינוּ [וְאִמּוֹתֵינוּ], גֹּאֲלֵנוּ
גֹּאֵל אֲבוֹתֵינוּ [וְאִמּוֹתֵינוּ], יוֹצְרֵנוּ, צוּר יְשׁוּעָתֵנוּ, פּוֹדֵנוּ
וּמַצִּילֵנוּ מֵעוֹלָם שְׁמֶךָ, אֵין אֱלֹהִים זוּלָתֶךָ.

TZITZIT צִיצַת. The biblical scholar Israel Knohl, expanding a medieval Jewish comment, suggests that the word tzitzit may derive from tzitz, a garment worn by the High Priest and tied in back with a פְּתִיל תְּכֵלֶת, a "thread of blue." On it were the words קֹדֶשׁ לַיהֹוָה, "holy before Adonai." Wearing the tzitzit (literally, the "little tzitz"), we are asked to serve God in a holy way, much as the High Priest did; thus the paragraph commands us to be "holy before your God." The act of wearing tzitzit turns us all, metaphorically, into high priests.

BROUGHT YOU OUT OF THE LAND OF EGYPT הוֹצֵאתִי אֶתְכֶם מֵאֶרֶץ מִצְרַיִם. The Exodus serves as the paradigmatic, ongoing model for the search for freedom, and when we recall the Exodus, we continue to hope that our own true freedom will be achieved.

TRULY אֱמֶת. This word may be read as the acknowledgment of all that has gone before. That is: all that we have recited is true. Thus, the next paragraph makes explicit some of the affirmations implied in the Sh'ma and spells out a Jewish creed, with each assertion preceded by the word אֱמֶת. Additionally, the word אֱמֶת may be attached to the last two words of the Sh'ma and be read as a description of God: the essence of God is truth—absolute truth may be elusive to us, but God is the ultimate knower of truth. This reading is based

(continued)

The overarching theme of the second paragraph of the Sh'ma is that history is not chaotic. Actions do have consequences. Individuals may not find a direct relation between behavior and just or unjust outcomes, but the course of history frequently illustrates that moral corruption leads to the downfall of even the greatest powers.

The text of the second paragraph of the Sh'ma speaks of group responsibility; interestingly, it emphasizes our relationship to the earth.

In our time, the fate of our planet is not only an issue of individual concern or responsibility, but also has become a global matter. How we collectively respond to this problem will affect every life on the planet.

Redemption

The end of the Exodus story, entering the promised land, was present at the beginning as a hope and an aspiration. . . . God said, "I will bring you into a land flowing with milk and honey," and also said, "You shall be to Me a kingdom of priests and a holy nation." The land is the opposite of Egyptian bondage: free farming instead of slave labor. . . . The kingdom is the opposite of Egyptian corruption: holiness instead of idolatry. Both these promises require human cooperation.

—MICHAEL WALZER
(*adapted*)

Then the length of your days and the days of your children, on the land that ADONAI swore to give to your ancestors, will be as the days of the heavens over the earth.   Deuteronomy 11:13–21

ADONAI said to Moses: Speak to the people Israel, and instruct them that in every generation they shall put *tzitzit* on the corners of their garments, placing a thread of blue on the *tzitzit*, the fringe of each corner. That shall be your *tzitzit* and you shall look at it, and remember all the mitzvot of ADONAI, and fulfill them, and not be seduced by your heart and eyes as they lead you astray. Then you will remember and fulfill all My mitzvot, and be holy before your God. I am ADONAI your God, who brought you out of the land of Egypt to be your God, I am ADONAI your God—

Numbers 15:37–41

Truly—
this teaching is

constant, well-founded and enduring,

righteous and trustworthy,

beloved and cherished,

desirable and pleasing,

awe-inspiring and majestic,

well-ordered and established,

good and beautiful,

and so incumbent on us forever.

Truly, the God of the universe, our sovereign, is the protector of Jacob and the shield of our deliverance. In each generation God is present, God's name endures, God's throne is established, and God's sovereignty and faithfulness abide forever; God's teaching is living and enduring, truthful and beloved throughout all time. As our ancestors accepted it as incumbent on them, we accept it as incumbent on us, our children, and all the future seed of the House of Israel who serve You. Whether in ancient time, or in future time, it is a good, enduring teaching, a constant truth, a never-changing principle.

Truly, You are ADONAI our God and the God of our ancestors, our sovereign and our ancestors' sovereign, our redeemer and our ancestors' redeemer. You are our creator, and the rock of our deliverance, our redeemer and help. So You are known throughout time, for there is no God but You.

עֶזְרַת אֲבוֹתֵינוּ [וְאִמּוֹתֵינוּ] אַתָּה הוּא מֵעוֹלָם,
מָגֵן וּמוֹשִׁיעַ לִבְנֵיהֶם אַחֲרֵיהֶם בְּכָל־דּוֹר־וָדוֹר.
בְּרוּם עוֹלָם מוֹשָׁבֶךָ,
וּמִשְׁפָּטֶיךָ וְצִדְקָתְךָ עַד אַפְסֵי־אָרֶץ.
אַשְׁרֵי אִישׁ שֶׁיִּשְׁמַע לְמִצְוֹתֶיךָ,
וְתוֹרָתְךָ וּדְבָרְךָ יָשִׂים עַל לִבּוֹ.
אֱמֶת אַתָּה הוּא אָדוֹן לְעַמֶּךָ, וּמֶלֶךְ גִּבּוֹר לָרִיב רִיבָם.
אֱמֶת אַתָּה הוּא רִאשׁוֹן, וְאַתָּה הוּא אַחֲרוֹן,
וּמִבַּלְעָדֶיךָ אֵין לָנוּ מֶלֶךְ גּוֹאֵל וּמוֹשִׁיעַ.

מִמִּצְרַיִם גְּאַלְתָּנוּ יהוה אֱלֹהֵינוּ
וּמִבֵּית עֲבָדִים פְּדִיתָנוּ.
כָּל־בְּכוֹרֵיהֶם הָרָגְתָּ   וּבְכוֹרְךָ גָּאָלְתָּ
וְיַם סוּף בָּקַעְתָּ   וְזֵדִים טִבַּעְתָּ
וִידִידִים הֶעֱבַרְתָּ
וַיְכַסּוּ מַיִם צָרֵיהֶם, אֶחָד מֵהֶם לֹא נוֹתָר.
עַל זֹאת שִׁבְּחוּ אֲהוּבִים, וְרוֹמְמוּ אֵל,
וְנָתְנוּ יְדִידִים זְמִירוֹת שִׁירוֹת וְתִשְׁבָּחוֹת,
בְּרָכוֹת וְהוֹדָאוֹת לַמֶּלֶךְ אֵל חַי וְקַיָּם.
רָם וְנִשָּׂא,   גָּדוֹל וְנוֹרָא,
מַשְׁפִּיל גֵּאִים   וּמַגְבִּיהַּ שְׁפָלִים
מוֹצִיא אֲסִירִים   וּפוֹדֶה עֲנָוִים
וְעוֹזֵר דַּלִּים
וְעוֹנֶה לְעַמּוֹ בְּעֵת שַׁוְּעָם אֵלָיו.

(continued from the previous page)
on the words of Jeremiah,
"Adonai is true, is indeed
the living God, and the
sovereign of time and the
world" (10:10). The tradition read the word "truly,"
אֱמֶת, as referring both
backward and forward. It
is the first word of the next
paragraph but is recited as
if it were the last word of
the preceding paragraph.
This maḥzor's placement of
the word between the two
paragraphs highlights that
tradition. It should also be
noted that this traditional
placement emphasizes one
of the biblical meanings
of the word אֱמֶת (emet):
steadfast, or faithful. In this
reading, what is affirmed
is that God will always be
present for us.

HELP OF OUR ANCESTORS
עֶזְרַת אֲבוֹתֵינוּ [וְאִמּוֹתֵינוּ].
Two contrasting theologi-
cal concepts are at work
in this poem and in the
previous prayer. The first
emphasizes the value of
personal observance of
Torah and mitzvot; the
second emphasizes com-
munal redemption and the
need for God to destroy
oppression. The first is
non-violent, speaking of
personal practice and
virtue, through performing acts of
love and care; the second insists that
God must war against evil, rooting it
out. These two views echo a talmudic
argument as to whether the future
redemption will come through war or
non-violence.

Renewing the Miracle of Redemption

God miraculously redeemed our ancestors at the Sea of Reeds in days of old, and God has renewed the miracle of redemption each day since.

From that first moment at the shores of the Sea until this present moment, we, the Children of Israel, chant the same song of gratitude and wonderment: "Who is like You, God, who performs miracles on our behalf, that we may be redeemed?"

Not by mere accident have we survived attempts throughout the ages to destroy us. Not by any laws of history can our survival in the face of all the perils that beset us be explained. Only by our continuous faith in You can our survival be accounted for. And so we sing, "Who is like You, Adonai, doing wonders, working miracles without number?"

—HERSHEL J. MATT
(adapted)

Redemption

You cannot find redemption until you see the flaws in your own soul, and try to efface them. Nor can a people be redeemed until it sees the flaws in its soul and tries to efface them. But whether it be an individual or a people, whoever shuts out the realization of their flaws is shutting out redemption. We can be redeemed only to the extent to which we confront and come to understand our own selves. . . . The world is in need of redemption, but the redemption must not be expected to happen as an act of sheer grace. Our task is to make the world worthy of redemption. Our faith and our works are preparation for ultimate redemption.

—MARTIN BUBER (adapted)

You were always the help of our ancestors,
a shield and deliverer for their descendants in every generation.
You abide at the pinnacle of the universe—
Your judgment and Your righteousness extend to the ends
 of the earth.
Blessed are the ones who hear Your commands,
and place Your teaching and words on their hearts.
Truly, You are the ruler of Your people,
 a mighty sovereign, who takes up their cause.
Truly, You were at the beginning and You will be at the end—
 aside from You we have no ruler who can redeem and deliver.

ADONAI our God, You redeemed us from Egypt,
and freed us from the house of bondage.
Their firstborn You slayed,
Your firstborn You redeemed,
You split the sea,
You drowned the wicked,
You rescued Your cherished ones.
The waters engulfed their oppressors,
not one of them survived.
Then Your beloved sang in praise, acclaiming God for all
 these things.
Your cherished ones offered songs of thanks, hymns of praise,
 psalms of adoration to the sovereign ever-living God,
 who is transcendent, powerful, and awe-inspiring,
overthrowing the proud,
raising up the lowly,
freeing the imprisoned,
redeeming the poor,
helping the weak,
and answering God's people when they cry out.

תְּהִלּוֹת לְאֵל עֶלְיוֹן בָּרוּךְ הוּא וּמְבֹרָךְ. מֹשֶׁה וּמִרְיָם ◁
וּבְנֵי יִשְׂרָאֵל לְךָ עָנוּ שִׁירָה בְּשִׂמְחָה רַבָּה, וְאָמְרוּ כֻלָּם:

מִי־כָמֹכָה בָּאֵלִם יהוה, מִי כָּמֹכָה נֶאְדָּר בַּקֹּדֶשׁ,
נוֹרָא תְהִלֹּת, עֹשֵׂה פֶלֶא.

שִׁירָה חֲדָשָׁה שִׁבְּחוּ גְאוּלִים לְשִׁמְךָ עַל שְׂפַת הַיָּם, ◁
יַחַד כֻּלָּם הוֹדוּ וְהִמְלִיכוּ וְאָמְרוּ:

יהוה יִמְלֹךְ לְעוֹלָם וָעֶד.

צוּר יִשְׂרָאֵל,
קוּמָה בְּעֶזְרַת יִשְׂרָאֵל,
וּפְדֵה כִנְאֻמֶךָ יְהוּדָה וְיִשְׂרָאֵל.
גֹּאֲלֵנוּ, יהוה צְבָאוֹת שְׁמוֹ, קְדוֹשׁ יִשְׂרָאֵל.
בָּרוּךְ אַתָּה יהוה, גָּאַל יִשְׂרָאֵל.

The Silent Amidah for Rosh Hashanah may be found on page 11.
The Silent Amidah for Yom Kippur may be found on page 213.

A NEW SONG שִׁירָה חֲדָשָׁה.
According to the liturgical scholar Yosef Heinemann, just as mystics of the first millennium added the song of the angels—the Kedushah, "holy, holy, holy…"—to the *b'rakhot* before the Sh'ma, they also added this central quotation from Israel's Song at the Sea (Exodus 15:11) following the Sh'ma, thus surrounding the recitation of the Sh'ma with song. Through the recitation of the Sh'ma, our song and the angels' song become a chorus of melody and harmony, a signal of redemption.

ADONAI WILL REIGN יהוה יִמְלֹךְ. Exodus 15:18.

STRONGHOLD OF THE PEOPLE ISRAEL צוּר יִשְׂרָאֵל. We have translated the Hebrew word *tzur* as "stronghold," rather than its more literal meaning, "rock." In ancient times, a fortress was built on a high rocky hill, thus the stronghold was atop the *tzur*, and the two were identified by the same word. With this usage in mind, the Psalmist speaks of God as our fortress or stronghold. Maimonides, relating to the more literal translation, asks: Why is God called צוּר, "rock"? He suggests that a possible meaning is that God is to be compared to a quarry, and we are all hewn from God's rock (*Guide to the Perplexed*, part 1, chapter 16).

ISRAEL יִשְׂרָאֵל. The name "Israel" is mentioned five times just before the conclusion of the *b'rakhah*, emphasizing the plea for Israel's redemption.

OUR REDEEMER גֹּאֲלֵנוּ. Isaiah 47:4.

LIBERATED THE PEOPLE ISRAEL גָּאַל יִשְׂרָאֵל. This *b'rakhah*, in contrast to most, concludes with a verb in the past tense. We can properly bless God for the redemptive acts that have already occurred—not those we still hope and pray for (Babylonian Talmud, Pesaḥim 117b).

SH'MA AND THE AMIDAH. The Babylonian Talmud links this last *b'rakhah* of the Sh'ma, mentioning God's redeeming the people Israel from Egypt, to the personal prayers that now follow in the Amidah, and recommends that there be no verbal interruption at this point (Berakhot 9b). It is as if to say that the possibility of prayer flows out of our experience of God's love as exhibited in freeing us from Egyptian slavery.

The Ḥasidic master Jacob Joseph of Polnoye taught that we each have within us a pharaoh—the hard one, the cruel one, the one who is closed to empathy and faith. When we are able to find and uproot the pharaoh who strangles us from within, that is the beginning of our liberation, our truly becoming whom we need to be.

What the Exodus Taught

So pharaonic oppression, deliverance, Sinai, Canaan are still with us, powerful memories shaping our perceptions of the political world. The "door of hope" is still open; things are not what they might be —even when what they might be isn't totally different from what they are. . . . We still believe, or many of us do, what the Exodus first taught, or what it has commonly been taken to teach, about the meaning and possibility of politics and about its proper form: first, that wherever you live, it is probably Egypt; second, that there is a better place, a world more attractive, a promised land; and third, that "the way to the land is through the wilderness." There is no way to get from here to there except by joining together and marching.

—MICHAEL WALZER

Our homage is to God on high who is ever praised. Moses, Miriam, and the people Israel joyfully sang this song to You:

"Who is like You, ADONAI, among the mighty!
Who is like You, adorned in holiness,
revered in praise, working wonders!"
Mi khamokha ba-eilim Adonai, mi kamokha ne·dar ba-kodesh, nora t'hillot, oseih fele.

At the edge of the sea, the redeemed sang a new song of praise to Your name. Together, as one, they thanked You and acclaimed Your sovereignty, saying:

"ADONAI will reign forever and ever."
Adonai yimlokh l'olam va·ed.

Stronghold of the people Israel,
arise and help the people Israel!
In fulfillment of Your promise,
    redeem Judah and the people Israel.
Our redeemer is called *Adonai Tz'va·ot,*
    the Holy One of the people Israel.
Tzur yisra·el, kumah b'ezrat yisra·el,
u-f'deih khi-n'umekha
y'hudah v'yisra·el.
Go·aleinu Adonai Tz'va·ot sh'mo, k'dosh yisra·el.
Barukh atah ADONAI, who liberated the people Israel.

The Silent Amidah for Rosh Hashanah may be found on page 11.
The Silent Amidah for Yom Kippur may be found on page 213.

We rise as the ark is opened.

כִּי שֵׁם יהוה אֶקְרָא, הָבוּ גֹדֶל לֵאלֹהֵינוּ.
אֲדֹנָי שְׂפָתַי תִּפְתָּח, וּפִי יַגִּיד תְּהִלָּתֶךָ.

Version with Patriarchs and Matriarchs:	*Version with Patriarchs:*

THE READER'S REPETITION OF THE AMIDAH. In the ancient and medieval synagogue, the silent Amidah was repeated aloud by the service leader since individual prayerbooks were virtually unknown through the first millennium. Even as manuscript copies became more available in the latter half of the Middle Ages, they were largely the possession of the wealthy, and most ordinary people still did not have access to one. The reader's repetition was especially important and became an occasion for poetic embellishments of the standard prayer. The Rosh Hashanah additions emphasize the themes of God's sovereignty and the judgment that is effected on this day. Interestingly, Maimonides (Egypt, 12th century) favored abolishing the silent Amidah and retaining only a reader's repetition, since he felt that the recitation of both was prompting too much chatter and disturbance during the repetition.

בָּרוּךְ אַתָּה יהוה,
אֱלֹהֵינוּ וֵאלֹהֵי אֲבוֹתֵינוּ
[וְאִמּוֹתֵינוּ], אֱלֹהֵי אַבְרָהָם,
אֱלֹהֵי יִצְחָק, וֵאלֹהֵי יַעֲקֹב,
אֱלֹהֵי שָׂרָה, אֱלֹהֵי רִבְקָה,
אֱלֹהֵי רָחֵל, וֵאלֹהֵי לֵאָה,
הָאֵל הַגָּדוֹל הַגִּבּוֹר וְהַנּוֹרָא,
אֵל עֶלְיוֹן, גּוֹמֵל חֲסָדִים
טוֹבִים, וְקוֹנֵה הַכֹּל, וְזוֹכֵר
חַסְדֵי אָבוֹת [וְאִמָּהוֹת],
וּמֵבִיא גוֹאֵל לִבְנֵי בְנֵיהֶם
לְמַעַן שְׁמוֹ בְּאַהֲבָה.

בָּרוּךְ אַתָּה יהוה,
אֱלֹהֵינוּ וֵאלֹהֵי אֲבוֹתֵינוּ,
אֱלֹהֵי אַבְרָהָם, אֱלֹהֵי
יִצְחָק, וֵאלֹהֵי יַעֲקֹב, הָאֵל
הַגָּדוֹל הַגִּבּוֹר וְהַנּוֹרָא,
אֵל עֶלְיוֹן, גּוֹמֵל חֲסָדִים
טוֹבִים, וְקוֹנֵה הַכֹּל, וְזוֹכֵר
חַסְדֵי אָבוֹת, וּמֵבִיא גוֹאֵל
לִבְנֵי בְנֵיהֶם לְמַעַן שְׁמוֹ
בְּאַהֲבָה.

מִסּוֹד חֲכָמִים וּנְבוֹנִים,
וּמִלֶּמֶד דַּעַת מְבִינִים,
אֶפְתְּחָה פִי בִּתְפִלָּה וּבְתַחֲנוּנִים,
לְחַלּוֹת וּלְחַנֵּן פְּנֵי מֶלֶךְ מַלְכֵי הַמְּלָכִים
וַאֲדוֹנֵי הָאֲדוֹנִים.

The ark is closed.

GOD OF ABRAHAM . . . GOD OF SARAH אֱלֹהֵי אַבְרָהָם . . . אֱלֹהֵי שָׂרָה. The tradition of reciting the names of each of the patriarchs originates with God's own speech: at the burning bush, God begins addressing Moses by saying, "I am the God of Abraham, the God of Isaac, and the God of Jacob." Some congregations add the names of the four matriarchs at the beginning of this b'rakhah, because of their significance as founders of our people, and as part of our effort to reclaim and honor women as role models of faith.

INSPIRED BY THE INSIGHT מִסּוֹד חֲכָמִים. These lines serve to introduce *piyyutim*, poetic additions to the Amidah, that address the holy day's themes. The reference to "sages" and "those who acquired wisdom" is a relic of the era when adding *piyyutim* was a matter of controversy, which prompted this appeal to the authority of those sages who permitted them. This introduction proclaimed that the Amidah's *piyyutim* are faithful to tradition, in that they are saturated with biblical and midrashic quotations. Its words continue to have meaning as the leader's personal plea for inspiration to guide the congregation appropriately—a poignant reminder of the leader's responsibility as one who represents the congregation before God.

REPETITION OF THE AMIDAH

Prayer

Prayer takes the mind
out of the narrowness of
self-interest, and enables
us to see the world in the
mirror of the holy.

—ABRAHAM JOSHUA
HESCHEL

We rise as the ark is opened.

As I proclaim God's name, ADONAI, exalt our God.
ADONAI, open my lips that my mouth may speak Your praise.

First B'rakhah: Our Ancestors

God of Our Ancestors

As Jews on a religious
quest, we recognize
that we are, first of all,
inheritors. Our spiritual
vocabulary, our values,
the lives that we lead are
pathways built on mark-
ers laid down by those
who came before us.
Beginning on the roads
that they surveyed, we
are each able to proceed
on our own religious
journey. Surely, if we
grow at all religiously,
we will end up in a dif-
ferent place than they;
but as we look back, we
will always be reminded
that it was possible for
us to begin on our way
because of the journey
they undertook.

Version with Patriarchs:
Barukh atah ADONAI,
our God and God of our
   ancestors,
God of Abraham, God of
   Isaac, and God of Jacob,
great, mighty, awe-inspiring,
   transcendent God,
who acts with lovingkindness
   and creates all things,
who remembers the loving
   deeds of our ancestors,
and who will send a redeemer
   to their children's children
   with love
   for the sake of divine honor.

Version with Patriarchs and Matriarchs:
Barukh atah ADONAI,
our God and God of our
   ancestors,
God of Abraham, God of
   Isaac, and God of Jacob,
God of Sarah, God of
   Rebecca, God of Rachel,
   and God of Leah,
great, mighty, awe-inspiring,
   transcendent God,
who acts with lovingkindness
   and creates all things,
who remembers the loving
   deeds of our ancestors,
and who will send a redeemer
   to their children's children
   with love
   for the sake of divine honor.

Inspired by the insight of sages
   and the teachings of those who acquired wisdom,
I open my lips in prayer and supplication
   to entreat the sovereign of all sovereigns,
   the supreme ruler.

The ark is closed.

זָכְרֵנוּ לְחַיִּים,
מֶלֶךְ חָפֵץ בַּחַיִּים,
וְכָתְבֵנוּ בְּסֵפֶר הַחַיִּים,
לְמַעַנְךָ אֱלֹהִים חַיִּים.

<table>
<tr><td>Version with Patriarchs and Matriarchs:</td><td>Version with Patriarchs:</td></tr>
</table>

Version with Patriarchs and Matriarchs: ⟵ *Version with Patriarchs:*

מֶלֶךְ עוֹזֵר וּפוֹקֵד
וּמוֹשִׁיעַ וּמָגֵן.
בָּרוּךְ אַתָּה יהוה, מָגֵן
אַבְרָהָם וּפוֹקֵד שָׂרָה.

מֶלֶךְ עוֹזֵר וּמוֹשִׁיעַ וּמָגֵן.
בָּרוּךְ אַתָּה יהוה, מָגֵן
אַבְרָהָם.

אַתָּה גִּבּוֹר לְעוֹלָם אֲדֹנָי, מְחַיֵּה מֵתִים אַתָּה,
רַב לְהוֹשִׁיעַ.

מְכַלְכֵּל חַיִּים בְּחֶסֶד,
מְחַיֵּה מֵתִים בְּרַחֲמִים רַבִּים,
סוֹמֵךְ נוֹפְלִים, וְרוֹפֵא חוֹלִים,
וּמַתִּיר אֲסוּרִים,
וּמְקַיֵּם אֱמוּנָתוֹ לִישֵׁנֵי עָפָר.
מִי כָמוֹךָ בַּעַל גְּבוּרוֹת,
וּמִי דּוֹמֶה לָּךְ,
מֶלֶךְ מֵמִית וּמְחַיֶּה וּמַצְמִיחַ יְשׁוּעָה.

REMEMBER US זָכְרֵנוּ. On the Days of Awe, we pray for the gift of life and consider how to live fully and responsibly. This brief prayer is the first of four additions to the Amidah on the ten days of the High Holy Day season. Each of its four phrases ends with the word חַיִּים (ḥayyim), "life."

SHIELD OF ABRAHAM מָגֵן אַבְרָהָם. Based on Genesis 15:1, where God appears to Abraham and says, "Do not fear, Abram, for I will shield you. . . ."

GUARDIAN OF SARAH וּפוֹקֵד שָׂרָה. The phrase is based on Genesis 21:1, the Torah reading for the first day of Rosh Hashanah, describing Sarah's pregnancy with Isaac as an expression of God's care and protection. The Jewish people who stand here today are the fulfillment of the promise of God to Abraham and Sarah.

YOU SUPPORT THE FALLING סוֹמֵךְ נוֹפְלִים. For centuries, human rulers have defined "power" as the ability to exert control over others, often through the threat of physical injury. Power was—and in many places around the world, continues to be—measured by the ability to overcome a strong enemy, or to enfeeble and imprison others. In this b'rakhah, the definition of power is the opposite: God's power is manifest through ḥesed, love and kindness, especially to those who are most vulnerable: the fallen, the sick, and the bound.

Remember us for life,
Sovereign who delights in life,
and inscribe us in the Book of Life,
for Your sake, God of life.

*Zokhreinu l'ḥayyim, melekh ḥafeitz ba-ḥayyim,
v'khotveinu b'seifer ha-ḥayyim, l'ma·ankha Elohim ḥayyim.*

Version with Patriarchs:	*Version with Patriarchs and Matriarchs:*
You are the Sovereign who helps and saves and shields.	You are the Sovereign who helps and guards, saves and shields.
Barukh atah ADONAI, Shield of Abraham.	*Barukh atah ADONAI,* Shield of Abraham and Guardian of Sarah.

This World and the Next
One way to think of life and death as mentioned in this *b'rakhah* is to contemplate our own continuous spiritual death and rebirth. Simḥah Bunam, a Ḥasidic master, taught: A person is always passing through two doors: out of this world and into the next, and out and in again.

Second B'rakhah: God's Saving Care

You are mighty forever, ADONAI—
You give life to the dead;
great is Your saving power.

You sustain the living through love,
　and with great mercy give life to the dead.
You support the falling,
　heal the sick,
　loosen the chains of the bound,
　and keep faith with those who sleep in the dust.
Who is like You, Almighty,
　and who can be compared to You?—
　Sovereign, who brings death and life,
　and causes salvation to flourish.

*M'khalkeil ḥayyim b'ḥesed, m'ḥayyeih meitim b'raḥamim rabbim,
someikh nof'lim, v'rofei ḥolim, u-mattir asurim, u-m'kayyeim emunato
li-sheinei afar. Mi khamokha ba·al g'vurot u-mi domeh lakh, melekh
meimit u-m'ḥayyeih u-matzmi·aḥ y'shu·aḥ.*

מִי כָמוֹךָ אַב הָרַחֲמִים, זוֹכֵר יְצוּרָיו לְחַיִּים בְּרַחֲמִים.

וְנֶאֱמָן אַתָּה לְהַחֲיוֹת מֵתִים. בָּרוּךְ אַתָּה יהוה, מְחַיֵּה הַמֵּתִים.

יִמְלֹךְ יהוה לְעוֹלָם אֱלֹהַיִךְ צִיּוֹן לְדֹר וָדֹר, הַלְלוּ־יָהּ. וְאַתָּה קָדוֹשׁ, יוֹשֵׁב תְּהִלּוֹת יִשְׂרָאֵל.

אֵל נָא:

Many congregations recite this piyyut responsively:

א

אַתָּה הוּא אֱלֹהֵינוּ

גִּבּוֹר וְנַעֲרָץ	בַּשָּׁמַיִם וּבָאָרֶץ
הוּא שָׂח וַיֶּהִי	דָּגוּל מֵרְבָבָה
זִכְרוֹ לָנֶצַח	וְצִוָּה וְנִבְרָאוּ
טָהוֹר עֵינַיִם	חַי עוֹלָמִים
כִּתְרוֹ יְשׁוּעָה	יוֹשֵׁב סֵתֶר
מַעֲטֵהוּ קִנְאָה	לְבוּשׁוֹ צְדָקָה
סִתְרוֹ יֹשֶׁר	נֶאְפַּד נְקָמָה
פְּעֻלָּתוֹ אֱמֶת	עֲצָתוֹ אֱמוּנָה
קָרוֹב לְקוֹרְאָיו בֶּאֱמֶת	צַדִּיק וְיָשָׁר
שׁוֹכֵן שְׁחָקִים	רָם וּמִתְנַשֵּׂא
תּוֹלֶה אֶרֶץ עַל בְּלִימָה	
חַי וְקַיָּם נוֹרָא וּמָרוֹם וְקָדוֹשׁ.	

SOURCE OF COMPASSION אַב הָרַחֲמִים. The word אַב (*av*) literally means "father." In the liturgy, it is—as here—almost always modified by the adjective רַחֲמִים (*raḥamim*), "compassionate." Thus the metaphor of God as father depicts a figure who is caring and kind. In rabbinic usage, the word *av* can also mean "creator, root, or foundation." Hence our translation of the expression as "source of compassion."

ADONAI WILL REIGN יִמְלֹךְ יהוה. Psalm 146:10. After stating God's care for the poor, the psalmist concludes with this verse, describing God's eternal majesty.

AND YOU, O HOLY ONE, ARE ENTHRONED THROUGH THE PRAISES OF ISRAEL וְאַתָּה קָדוֹשׁ, יוֹשֵׁב תְּהִלּוֹת יִשְׂרָאֵל. Psalm 22:4. One midrash provocatively implies that God's dominion in the world is dependent on human activity: "'You are My witnesses,' says Adonai, 'and I am God' (Isaiah 43:12)—when you are My witnesses, I am God, but when you are not My witnesses, it is as if I am not God" (Sifrei Deuteronomy 346).

GOD, PLEASE HEAR US אֵל נָא (literally: "God, may it please You!"). These two words, *El na*, have served as an introduction to heartfelt prayer since biblical times, beginning with Moses' prayer for his sister, Miriam, when she was ill (Numbers 12:13), אֵל נָא רְפָא נָא לָהּ (*El na r'fa na lah*), "God, please heal her." Here, they serve as an introduction to the series of *piyyutim* that leads up to the Kedushah.

YOU ARE ADONAI OUR GOD אַתָּה הוּא אֱלֹהֵינוּ. This alphabetical *piyyut* is attributed to Elazar Kallir, the most well-known of the early masters of liturgical poetry, believed to have lived in the Land of Israel in the 5th or 6th century.

CROWNED WITH SALVATION כִּתְרוֹ יְשׁוּעָה. This line and the next three lines, all using the metaphor of God's clothing, are based on Isaiah 59:17.

SUSPEND THE EARTH IN SPACE תּוֹלֶה אֶרֶץ עַל בְּלִימָה. From Job 26:7. This verse states the traditional belief that in the absence of God's sustaining care, the earth would tumble into the abyss. Our understanding of how the world operates may not be that of the Book of Job but we can share with Job a wonder at the complexity of forces at work in the universe.

Images of God

Ultimately, we have no recourse but to think of God in metaphors. The only real question is how we choose the images we use. In that process we would reject images that are ineffective because they do not touch us; those which distort or falsify our experience; and those which undermine the community's cohesiveness. . . . We must seek images that have immediacy of meaning . . . those that evoke the emotions and actions that powerful images should; those that are true to our experience, even if they cannot be totally so; and those that enjoy the community's validation in thought and action.   —ELLIOT DORFF

The Crown of Glory

You are alive,
though not established
   in time,
and not of a time that's
   known.

You are alive,
though not in spirit
   and soul:
for you're soul to
   spirit's soul.

You are alive,
but not like breath in
   a human—
whose end is the moth
   and the worm.

You are alive,
and those who reach Your
   secret discover
delight in the world,
and eat and live forever.
                —IBN GABIROL
          (trans. Peter Cole)

Who is like You, source of compassion,
who remembers with compassion Your creatures for life?
Mi khamokha av ha-raḥamim, zokheir y'tzurav l'ḥayyim b'raḥamim.

You are faithful in bringing life to the dead. *Barukh atah* ADONAI, who gives life to the dead.

Third B'rakhah: God's Holiness

ADONAI will reign forever; your God, O Zion, from generation to generation. Halleluyah! And You, O Holy One, are enthroned through the praises of the people Israel.

THREE PIYYUTIM INTRODUCE THE KEDUSHAH

God, please hear us.

א

Many congregations recite this piyyut responsively:

You are our God   *in heaven and on earth—*
powerful and revered,   *celebrated by multitudes.*
You spoke, and the world
   came to be,   *commanded, and it was created.*
Your name endures forever;   *You are eternal.*
Perceiving perfectly   *You dwell in secret.*
Crowned with salvation,   *You are attired in righteousness,*
wrapped in zeal,   *and armed with retribution.*
Urging uprightness,   *You counsel faithfulness.*
Your actions are truthful,   *righteous and just.*
You are close to those who
   call honestly.
You dwell in the heavens   *Though elevated and exalted,*
You live and endure,   *and suspend the earth in space.*
                               revered, exalted, and holy.

El na.
Atah hu eloheinu
Ba-shamayim u-va-aretz   gibbor v'na·aratz.
Dagul mei-r'vavah   hu saḥ va-yehi.
V'tzivvah v'nivra·u   zikhro la-netzaḥ.
Ḥai olamim   t'hor einayim.
Yosheiv seiter   kitro y'shu·ah.
L'vusho tz'dakah   ma·ateihu kin·ah.
Nepad n'kamah   sitro yosher.
Atzato emunah   p'ullato emet.
Tzaddik v'yashar   karov l'kor'av be-emet.
Ram u-mitnassei   shokhein sh'ḥakim.
Toleh eretz al b'limah.   Ḥai v'kayyam nora v'kadosh.

ב

וּבְכֵן נַמְלִיכְךָ יהוה מֶלֶךְ

יהוה מֶלֶךְ, יהוה מָלָךְ, יהוה יִמְלֹךְ לְעוֹלָם וָעֶד.

כָּל־שִׂנְאַנֵּי שַׁחַק בְּאִמֶּר מַאֲדִירִים   **יהוה מֶלֶךְ.**

כָּל־שׁוֹכְנֵי שֶׁקֶט בִּבְרָכָה מְבָרְכִים   **יהוה מָלָךְ.**

אֵלּוּ וָאֵלּוּ בְּגֹבַהּ מַגְדִּילִים   **יהוה יִמְלֹךְ.**

יהוה מֶלֶךְ, יהוה מָלָךְ, יהוה יִמְלֹךְ לְעוֹלָם וָעֶד.

כָּל־מַלְאֲכֵי מַעֲלָה בְּדֵעָה מַדְגִּילִים   **יהוה מֶלֶךְ.**

כָּל־מוֹשְׁלֵי מַטָּה בְּהַלֵּל מְהַלְלִים   **יהוה מָלָךְ.**

אֵלּוּ וָאֵלּוּ בְּוַדַּאי מוֹדִים   **יהוה יִמְלֹךְ.**

יהוה מֶלֶךְ, יהוה מָלָךְ, יהוה יִמְלֹךְ לְעוֹלָם וָעֶד.

כָּל־עָרִיצֵי עֶלְיוֹנִים בְּזֶמֶר מְזַמְּרִים   **יהוה מֶלֶךְ.**

כָּל־עוֹבְרֵי עוֹלָמִים בְּחַיִל מְחַסְּנִים   **יהוה מָלָךְ.**

אֵלּוּ וָאֵלּוּ בְּטַעַם מְטַכְּסִים   **יהוה יִמְלֹךְ.**

יהוה מֶלֶךְ, יהוה מָלָךְ, יהוה יִמְלֹךְ לְעוֹלָם וָעֶד.

כָּל־קְדוֹשֵׁי קָדוֹשׁ בִּקְדֻשָּׁה מַקְדִּישִׁים   **יהוה מֶלֶךְ.**

כָּל־קְבוּצֵי קָהָל בְּקֹשֶׁט מְקַשְּׁטִים   **יהוה מָלָךְ.**

אֵלּוּ וָאֵלּוּ בְּנֹעַם מַנְעִימִים   **יהוה יִמְלֹךְ.**

יהוה מֶלֶךְ, יהוה מָלָךְ, יהוה יִמְלֹךְ לְעוֹלָם וָעֶד.

כָּל־חַשְׁמַלֵּי זְקִים לַבְּקָרִים מִתְחַדְּשִׁים   **יהוה מֶלֶךְ.**

כָּל־תַּרְשִׁישֵׁי גֹבַהּ בִּדְמָמָה מְלַחֲשִׁים   **יהוה מָלָךְ.**

אֵלּוּ וָאֵלּוּ בְּשִׁלּוּשׁ מְשַׁלְּשִׁים   **יהוה יִמְלֹךְ.**

יהוה מֶלֶךְ, יהוה מָלָךְ, יהוה יִמְלֹךְ לְעוֹלָם וָעֶד.

ADONAI REIGNS יהוה מֶלֶךְ. In each stanza of this *piyyut* (five of which are presented here, out of the twelve stanzas in the entire poem), the first line describes how the angels and celestial beings proclaim God's praise. The second line refers to the praise of God that originates from mortals on earth, and the third line emphasizes that heaven and earth together extol God. The final stanza, however, is ambiguous, and its second line, *kol tarshishei govah*, is understood by some translators and commentators as a reference to the heavenly sphere but by others as a reference to the earthly sphere. (*Tarshish* is the name of one of the precious stones in the High Priest's breastplate [Exodus 28:20, 39:13].) The distinction between heavenly and earthly creatures seems to fade away by the end of the poem, as both groups come together to praise God. The final phrase, *b'shillush m'shal'shim*, "recite the threefold sanctification," is a reference to Isaiah 6:3, the verse at the centerpiece of the Kedushah: "Holy, holy, holy is *Adonai Tz'va·ot*," which is pointedly described as recited by both angels and humans. This joint praise by divine and earthly beings is the hallmark of the Kedushah, the core of which is the human articulation of verses of praise that, according to the prophets Isaiah and Ezekiel, were overheard from God's ministering angels (Isaiah 6:3; Ezekiel 3:12). This poem, by Simon ben Isaac ben Abun of Mayence (11th century), was modeled after a similar poem by Elazar Kallir (5th–6th century). The poem combines three biblical references to the Divine: "Adonai reigns" (Psalm 96:1), "Adonai has reigned" (1 Chronicles 16:31), and "Adonai will reign forever and ever" (Exodus 15:18).

ALL THOSE WHO DWELL ON EARTH כָּל־שׁוֹכְנֵי שֶׁקֶט. Literally, "All those who dwell in quietness," a poetic reference to earth found in the Book of Job (37:17).

THE THREEFOLD SANCTIFICATION בְּשִׁלּוּשׁ מְשַׁלְּשִׁים. The daily recitation of the Kedushah is seen as the unification of heaven and earth. This *piyyut* was originally composed as introduction to the Kedushah, as were all the *piyyutim* in this section.

ב

And so, let us declare ADONAI our sovereign!

ADONAI reigns! ADONAI has reigned!
Adonai melekh! Adonai malakh!

ADONAI will reign forever and ever!
Adonai yimlokh l'olam va·ed!

All those who dwell on high announce God's glory:

ADONAI reigns!
Adonai melekh!

All those who dwell on earth offer blessings:

ADONAI has reigned!
Adonai malakh!

Those above and those below raise up their voices, exalting God:

ADONAI will reign!
Adonai yimlokh!

ADONAI reigns! ADONAI has reigned!
ADONAI will reign forever and ever!
Adonai melekh! Adonai malakh! Adonai yimlokh l'olam va·ed!

All the angels on high skillfully acclaim:

ADONAI reigns!

All earthly rulers offer words of praise:

ADONAI has reigned!

Those above and those below acknowledge with certainty:

ADONAI will reign!

ADONAI reigns! ADONAI has reigned!
ADONAI will reign forever and ever!

All powerful forces on high sing:

ADONAI reigns!

All mortals vigorously declare:

ADONAI has reigned!

Those above and those below harmoniously recite:

ADONAI will reign!

ADONAI reigns! ADONAI has reigned!
ADONAI will reign forever and ever!

All holy beings sanctify God with holiness:

ADONAI reigns!

All the communities of worshippers truthfully declaim:

ADONAI has reigned!

Those above and those below peacefully proclaim:

ADONAI will reign!

ADONAI reigns! ADONAI has reigned!
ADONAI will reign forever and ever!

All the fiery sparks are renewed each morning, saying:

ADONAI reigns!

All those treasured from on high whisper quietly:

ADONAI has reigned!

Those above and those below join in reciting
the threefold sanctification:

ADONAI will reign!

ADONAI reigns! ADONAI has reigned!
ADONAI will reign forever and ever!

We recite each line and the leader repeats it.

וּבְכֵן לְךָ הַכֹּל יַכְתִּירוּ
לְאֵל עוֹרֵךְ דִּין

לְגוֹלֶה עֲמֻקוֹת בַּדִּין.	בְּיוֹם דִּין,	לְבוֹחֵן לְבָבוֹת
לְהוֹגֶה דֵעוֹת בַּדִּין.	בְּיוֹם דִּין,	לְדוֹבֵר מֵישָׁרִים
לְזוֹכֵר בְּרִיתוֹ בַּדִּין.	לְוָתִיק וְעוֹשֶׂה חֶסֶד בְּיוֹם דִּין,	
לְטַהֵר חוֹסָיו בַּדִּין.	בְּיוֹם דִּין,	לְחוֹמֵל מַעֲשָׂיו
לְכוֹבֵשׁ כַּעֲסוֹ בַּדִּין.	בְּיוֹם דִּין,	לְיוֹדֵעַ מַחֲשָׁבוֹת
לְמוֹחֵל עֲווֹנוֹת בַּדִּין.	בְּיוֹם דִּין,	לְלוֹבֵשׁ צְדָקוֹת
לְסוֹלֵחַ לַעֲמוּסָיו בַּדִּין.	בְּיוֹם דִּין,	לְנוֹרָא תְהִלּוֹת
לְפוֹעֵל רַחֲמָיו בַּדִּין.	בְּיוֹם דִּין,	לְעוֹנֶה לְקוֹרְאָיו
לְקוֹנֶה עֲבָדָיו בַּדִּין.	בְּיוֹם דִּין,	לְצוֹפֶה נִסְתָּרוֹת
לְשׁוֹמֵר אוֹהֲבָיו בַּדִּין.	בְּיוֹם דִּין,	לְרַחֵם עַמּוֹ
	בְּיוֹם דִּין.	לְתוֹמֵךְ תְּמִימָיו

ARBITER OF JUSTICE עוֹרֵךְ דִּין. This short *piyyut* by Elazar Kallir (the Land of Israel, 5th–6th century) contains the first enunciation in the liturgy of the major High Holy Day theme of God as the judge of the world.

VOICE OF RIGHTEOUSNESS לְדוֹבֵר מֵישָׁרִים Isaiah 33:15, where the phrase refers to a righteous person (and not God). In the mind of the poet, righteous behavior is godly behavior.

WHO IS WISE AND ACTS LOVINGLY ON THE DAY OF JUDGMENT לְוָתִיק וְעוֹשֶׂה חֶסֶד בְּיוֹם דִּין. The Hebrew word *din*, translated here as "judgment" or "justice" depending on the context, is one of the most heavily weighted words in the Jewish tradition. It usually connotes God's quality of strict judgment and the insistence on holding us to high standards of behavior. Indeed, this *piyyut* begins with an imposing, even intimidating tone, but soon the theme of God's compassion enters. God's judgment is then depicted as tempered with love and therefore redemptive.

WHO REMEMBERS THE COVENANT WHILE DISPENSING JUSTICE לְזוֹכֵר בְּרִיתוֹ בַּדִּין. In the Book of Exodus, when God is enraged at the people Israel after the golden calf episode and declares an intention to destroy them, Moses reminds God of the covenant that God had established with Abraham, Isaac, and Jacob—and God relents (Exodus 32:13). Thus, reminding God of the covenant supports the argument that the people Israel must be judged for life in the coming year.

EXONERATES US לְסוֹלֵחַ לַעֲמוּסָיו. Literally, "forgives the carried ones." This is a reference to Isaiah 46:3, which uses a maternal image to describe God's relationship with Israel ("carried since the womb").

HOLDS CLOSE THOSE WHO SERVE GOD WITH JUSTICE לְקוֹנֶה עֲבָדָיו בַּדִּין. More literally, "who acquires servants via justice." When we act justly, we serve the Divine.

God's Justice

Upon setting out to create the world, God thought: If I create the world through My attribute of mercy, then sinners will be plentiful; if I create the world through My attribute of justice, then how will the world endure? I will create the world with a mixture of both attributes and hope that it will be able to endure.

—MIDRASH
GENESIS RABBAH

Human Justice

The words in Scripture "justice, justice shall you pursue" (Deuteronomy 16:20) were interpreted in the following way by the Ḥasidic master Jacob Isaac, the Seer of Lublin: When you believe that you are wholly just and need not strive further, then justice cannot be ascribed to you. You must constantly pursue justice and never stand still; and in your own eyes, you must always be like a newborn child who has not yet achieved anything at all—that is truly the pursuit of justice.

We recite each line and the leader repeats it.

And so, let all crown You, Sovereign,
the ultimate arbiter of justice,

who probes all hearts on the Day of Judgment,
and reveals what is hidden, with justice;
 who is the voice of truth on the Day of Judgment,
 and pronounces rules of justice;
who is wise and acts lovingly on the Day of Judgment,
and remembers the covenant, while dispensing justice;
 who has compassion for all creation on the Day of Judgment,
 and purifies the faithful with justice;
who knows our thoughts on the Day of Judgment,
and overcomes anger with justice;
 who is clothed in righteousness on the Day of Judgment,
 and whose forgiveness of wrongdoing is a hallmark of justice;
who is revered in praises on the Day of Judgment,
and exonerates us as an exercise of justice;
 who responds to those who cry out on the Day of Judgment,
 and demonstrates mercy in justice;
who discerns all mysteries on the Day of Judgment,
and holds close those who serve God with justice;
 who has compassion for the people Israel on the
  Day of Judgment,
 and guards those who love God, with justice;
and who upholds those who trust wholeheartedly in the Divine,
on the Day of Judgment.

L'vokhein l'vavot b'yom din	*l'goleh amukkot ba-din.*
L'doveir meisharim b'yom din	*l'hogeh dei·ot ba-din.*
L'vatik v'oseh ḥesed b'yom din	*l'zokheir b'rito ba-din.*
L'ḥomeil ma·asav b'yom din	*l'taheir ḥosav ba-din.*
L'yodei·a maḥashavot b'yom din	*l'khoveish ka·aso ba-din.*
L'loveish tz'dakot b'yom din	*l'moheil avonot ba-din.*
L'nora t'hillot b'yom din	*l'solei·aḥ la-amusav ba-din.*
L'oneh l'kor'av b'yom din	*l'fo·eil raḥamav ba-din.*
L'tzofeh nistarot b'yom din	*l'koneh avadav ba-din.*
L'raḥeim ammo b'yom din	*l'shomeir ohavav ba-din.*
L'tomeikh t'mimav b'yom din.	

קְדֻשָּׁה

וּבְכֵן וּלְךָ תַעֲלֶה קְדֻשָּׁה, כִּי אַתָּה אֱלֹהֵינוּ מֶלֶךְ.

נְקַדֵּשׁ אֶת־שִׁמְךָ בָּעוֹלָם, כְּשֵׁם שֶׁמַּקְדִּישִׁים אוֹתוֹ בִּשְׁמֵי
מָרוֹם, כַּכָּתוּב עַל יַד נְבִיאֶךָ, וְקָרָא זֶה אֶל זֶה וְאָמַר:
**קָדוֹשׁ, קָדוֹשׁ, קָדוֹשׁ יהוה צְבָאוֹת,
מְלֹא כָל־הָאָרֶץ כְּבוֹדוֹ.**

אָז בְּקוֹל רַעַשׁ גָּדוֹל אַדִּיר וְחָזָק מַשְׁמִיעִים קוֹל,
מִתְנַשְּׂאִים לְעֻמַּת שְׂרָפִים, לְעֻמָּתָם בָּרוּךְ יֹאמֵרוּ:
בָּרוּךְ כְּבוֹד־יהוה מִמְּקוֹמוֹ.

מִמְּקוֹמְךָ מַלְכֵּנוּ תוֹפִיעַ, וְתִמְלֹךְ עָלֵינוּ, כִּי מְחַכִּים אֲנַחְנוּ
לָךְ. מָתַי תִּמְלֹךְ בְּצִיּוֹן, בְּקָרוֹב בְּיָמֵינוּ, לְעוֹלָם וָעֶד
תִּשְׁכּוֹן. תִּתְגַּדַּל וְתִתְקַדַּשׁ בְּתוֹךְ יְרוּשָׁלַיִם עִירְךָ, לְדוֹר
וָדוֹר וּלְנֵצַח נְצָחִים. וְעֵינֵינוּ תִרְאֶינָה מַלְכוּתֶךָ, כַּדָּבָר
הָאָמוּר בְּשִׁירֵי עֻזֶּךָ, עַל יְדֵי דָוִד מְשִׁיחַ צִדְקֶךָ:
יִמְלֹךְ יהוה לְעוֹלָם, אֱלֹהַיִךְ צִיּוֹן לְדֹר וָדֹר, הַלְלוּ־יָהּ.

לְדוֹר וָדוֹר נַגִּיד גָּדְלֶךָ, וּלְנֵצַח נְצָחִים קְדֻשָּׁתְךָ נַקְדִּישׁ.
וְשִׁבְחֲךָ אֱלֹהֵינוּ מִפִּינוּ לֹא יָמוּשׁ לְעוֹלָם וָעֶד, כִּי אֵל מֶלֶךְ
גָּדוֹל וְקָדוֹשׁ אָתָּה.

We are seated.

KEDUSHAH קְדֻשָּׁה. In this ancient prayer, composed by Jewish mystics, we pattern our praise after the angelic glorification of God. The Kedushah of the Amidah occurs in many different versions, but always contains three biblical quotations: "Holy, holy, holy" (Isaiah 6:3), "Praised is Adonai's glory wherever God dwells" (Ezekiel 3:12), and "Adonai will reign forever" (Psalm 146:10). The prayers surrounding these verses vary. On weekdays, they are brief; on Shabbat and holy days, they are more elaborate. Antiphonal proclamations of God's holiness are recited only in the presence of a minyan.
(adapted from Reuven Hammer)

HOLY קָדוֹשׁ. The words uttered by the angels that Isaiah (6:3) recorded when he had an overwhelming experience of being in the very presence of God surrounded by angelic hosts. Holiness is God's essential quality, a quality of which humans can partake when dedicated to God and when acting in imitation of God's mercy and love.

THE WHOLE WORLD IS FILLED WITH GOD'S GLORY! מְלֹא כָל־הָאָרֶץ כְּבוֹדוֹ. There are two contrasting themes in the Kedushah: God is to be found everywhere, and God is hidden from us. The paradox of the religious life is that at times we feel a divine presence close at hand and at other times God's absence is terribly palpable.

"PRAISED IS ADONAI'S GLORY WHEREVER GOD DWELLS" בָּרוּךְ כְּבוֹד־יהוה מִמְּקוֹמוֹ. Ezekiel heard this cry as he was carried away by the wind transporting him to preach to the exiles in Babylonia (3:12).

WILL REIGN FOREVER יִמְלֹךְ. Every Kedushah of the Amidah ends with this verse proclaiming God's sovereignty (Psalm 146:10).

The Kedushah

Now, may our sanctification rise up to You,
for You, our God, are sovereign.

Let us hallow Your name in this world as it is hallowed in the
high heavens, as Isaiah wrote of his vision,
Each cried out to the other:
"Holy, holy, holy is *Adonai Tz'va·ot*, the whole world is filled
with God's glory!"
Kadosh, kadosh, kadosh Adonai Tz'va·ot, m'lo khol ha-aretz k'vodo.

Then in thunderous voice, rising above the chorus of *s'rafim*,
other heavenly beings cry out words of blessing:

"Praised is Adonai's glory wherever God dwells."
Barukh k'vod Adonai mi-m'komo.

Our sovereign, manifest Yourself from wherever You dwell, and
rule over us, for we await You. When shall You rule in Zion?
Let it be soon, in our day, and throughout all time. May You
be exalted and sanctified in Jerusalem, Your city, from generation to generation, forever and ever. May our eyes behold Your
dominion, as described in the songs of praise offered to You by
David, anointed to proclaim Your just rule:

Adonai will reign forever;
your God, O Zion, from generation to generation. Halleluyah!
Yimlokh Adonai l'olam, elohayikh tziyyon l'dor va-dor, hal'luyah.

From one generation to another we will declare Your greatness,
and forever sanctify You with words of holiness. Your praise
will never leave our lips, for You are God and Sovereign, great
and holy.

We are seated.

וּבְכֵן תֵּן פַּחְדְּךָ יהוה אֱלֹהֵינוּ עַל כָּל־מַעֲשֶׂיךָ
וְאֵימָתְךָ עַל כָּל־מַה־שֶׁבָּרָאתָ,
וְיִירָאוּךָ כָּל־הַמַּעֲשִׂים
וְיִשְׁתַּחֲווּ לְפָנֶיךָ כָּל־הַבְּרוּאִים,
וְיֵעָשׂוּ כֻלָּם אֲגֻדָּה אֶחָת
לַעֲשׂוֹת רְצוֹנְךָ בְּלֵבָב שָׁלֵם,
כְּמוֹ שֶׁיָּדַעְנוּ יהוה אֱלֹהֵינוּ שֶׁהַשִּׁלְטוֹן לְפָנֶיךָ,
עֹז בְּיָדְךָ וּגְבוּרָה בִּימִינֶךָ,
וְשִׁמְךָ נוֹרָא עַל כָּל־מַה־שֶׁבָּרָאתָ.

וּבְכֵן תֵּן כָּבוֹד יהוה לְעַמֶּךָ
תְּהִלָּה לִירֵאֶיךָ וְתִקְוָה לְדוֹרְשֶׁיךָ,
וּפִתְחוֹן פֶּה לַמְיַחֲלִים לָךְ,
שִׂמְחָה לְאַרְצֶךָ וְשָׂשׂוֹן לְעִירֶךָ
וּצְמִיחַת קֶרֶן לְדָוִד עַבְדֶּךָ
וַעֲרִיכַת נֵר לְבֶן־יִשַׁי מְשִׁיחֶךָ,
בִּמְהֵרָה בְיָמֵינוּ.

וּבְכֵן צַדִּיקִים יִרְאוּ וְיִשְׂמָחוּ
וִישָׁרִים יַעֲלֹזוּ,
וַחֲסִידִים בְּרִנָּה יָגִילוּ,
וְעוֹלָתָה תִּקְפָּץ־פִּיהָ
וְכָל־הָרִשְׁעָה כֻּלָּהּ כְּעָשָׁן תִּכְלֶה,
כִּי תַעֲבִיר מֶמְשֶׁלֶת זָדוֹן מִן הָאָרֶץ.

וְתִמְלֹךְ אַתָּה יהוה לְבַדֶּךָ עַל כָּל־מַעֲשֶׂיךָ
בְּהַר צִיּוֹן מִשְׁכַּן כְּבוֹדֶךָ
וּבִירוּשָׁלַיִם עִיר קָדְשֶׁךָ,
כַּכָּתוּב בְּדִבְרֵי קָדְשֶׁךָ:
יִמְלֹךְ יהוה לְעוֹלָם, אֱלֹהַיִךְ צִיּוֹן לְדֹר וָדֹר, הַלְלוּ־יָהּ.

U-V'KHEIN וּבְכֵן. These three paragraphs, which are introduced by the same word, וּבְכֵן (u-v'khein), are ascribed by many scholars to the 3rd century, and may constitute the earliest poetic additions to the Amidah.

Stages of redemption are described in this series of prayers. The first paragraph implores God to cause the entire world to live with reverence for God. The next paragraph discusses not the universal, but the particular: the return of Israel to its land (and specifically to Jerusalem) and the kingship of David. The third paragraph describes the rejoicing that will come to the righteous "when You remove the tyranny of arrogance from the earth" and God will rule alone over the entire world from Zion and Jerusalem. *(adapted from Reuven Hammer)*

ADONAI WILL REIGN יִמְלֹךְ יהוה, *yimlokh Adonai.* Psalm 146:10.

U-v'khein—ADONAI our God,
instill Your awe in all You have made,
and fear of You in all You have created,
so that all You have fashioned revere You,
all You have created bow in recognition,
and all be bound together, carrying out Your will
     wholeheartedly.
For we know that true sovereignty is Yours,
power and strength are in Your hands,
and Your name is to be revered beyond any of Your creations.

U-v'khein—Bestow honor to Your people, ADONAI,
praise to those who revere You,
hope to those who seek You,
recognition to those who await You,
joy to Your land, and gladness to Your city.
Simḥah l'artzekha v'sason l'irekha
May the light of David, Your servant, dawn,
and the lamp of the son of Jesse, Your anointed,
be kindled speedily in our day.

U-v'khein—The righteous, beholding this, will rejoice,
the upright will be glad,
the pious will celebrate with song,
evil will be silenced,
and all wickedness will disappear like smoke,
when You remove the tyranny of arrogance from the earth.

You alone, ADONAI, will rule all Your creation,
from Mount Zion, the dwelling-place of Your glory,
and from Jerusalem, Your holy city.
As it is written in the Book of Psalms:
"ADONAI will reign forever;
your God, O Zion, from generation to generation.
Halleluyah!"
Yimlokh Adonai l'olam, elohayikh tziyyon l'dor va-dor, hal'luyah.

קָדוֹשׁ אַתָּה וְנוֹרָא שְׁמֶךָ
וְאֵין אֱלוֹהַּ מִבַּלְעָדֶיךָ,
כַּכָּתוּב: וַיִּגְבַּהּ יהוה צְבָאוֹת בַּמִּשְׁפָּט, וְהָאֵל הַקָּדוֹשׁ
נִקְדַּשׁ בִּצְדָקָה. בָּרוּךְ אַתָּה יהוה, הַמֶּלֶךְ הַקָּדוֹשׁ.

אַתָּה בְחַרְתָּנוּ מִכָּל־הָעַמִּים,
אָהַבְתָּ אוֹתָנוּ וְרָצִיתָ בָּנוּ,
וְרוֹמַמְתָּנוּ מִכָּל־הַלְּשׁוֹנוֹת,
וְקִדַּשְׁתָּנוּ בְּמִצְוֹתֶיךָ,
וְקֵרַבְתָּנוּ מַלְכֵּנוּ לַעֲבוֹדָתֶךָ,
וְשִׁמְךָ הַגָּדוֹל וְהַקָּדוֹשׁ עָלֵינוּ קָרָאתָ.

וַתִּתֶּן־לָנוּ, יהוה אֱלֹהֵינוּ בְּאַהֲבָה אֶת־יוֹם [הַשַּׁבָּת הַזֶּה
וְאֶת־יוֹם] הַזִּכָּרוֹן הַזֶּה, יוֹם [זִכְרוֹן] תְּרוּעָה [בְּאַהֲבָה]
מִקְרָא קֹדֶשׁ, זֵכֶר לִיצִיאַת מִצְרָיִם.

אֱלֹהֵינוּ וֵאלֹהֵי אֲבוֹתֵינוּ [וְאִמּוֹתֵינוּ], יַעֲלֶה וְיָבֹא, וְיַגִּיעַ
וְיֵרָאֶה, וְיֵרָצֶה וְיִשָּׁמַע, וְיִפָּקֵד וְיִזָּכֵר זִכְרוֹנֵנוּ וּפִקְדוֹנֵנוּ,
וְזִכְרוֹן אֲבוֹתֵינוּ [וְאִמּוֹתֵינוּ], וְזִכְרוֹן מָשִׁיחַ בֶּן־דָּוִד
עַבְדֶּךָ, וְזִכְרוֹן יְרוּשָׁלַיִם עִיר קָדְשֶׁךָ, וְזִכְרוֹן כָּל־עַמְּךָ בֵּית
יִשְׂרָאֵל לְפָנֶיךָ לִפְלֵיטָה לְטוֹבָה, לְחֵן וּלְחֶסֶד וּלְרַחֲמִים,
לְחַיִּים וּלְשָׁלוֹם, בְּיוֹם הַזִּכָּרוֹן הַזֶּה.
זָכְרֵנוּ יהוה אֱלֹהֵינוּ בּוֹ לְטוֹבָה,   אָמֵן.
וּפָקְדֵנוּ בוֹ לִבְרָכָה,   אָמֵן.
וְהוֹשִׁיעֵנוּ בוֹ לְחַיִּים,   אָמֵן.
וּבִדְבַר יְשׁוּעָה וְרַחֲמִים חוּס וְחָנֵּנוּ, וְרַחֵם
עָלֵינוּ וְהוֹשִׁיעֵנוּ, כִּי אֵלֶיךָ עֵינֵינוּ, כִּי אֵל מֶלֶךְ
חַנּוּן וְרַחוּם אָתָּה.

ADONAI TZ'VA·OT WILL BE EXALTED וַיִּגְבַּהּ יהוה צְבָאוֹת, Isaiah 5:16. Isaiah depicts the terror of God's judgment, but in this liturgical context God's strict justice is seen as an element of awe-inspiring holiness.

HOLY SOVEREIGN הַמֶּלֶךְ הַקָּדוֹשׁ. This is one of several changes made to the text of the Amidah during the High Holy Day season. Throughout the year, the Kedushah concludes with the b'rakhah "Praised are You, Adonai, the holy God." On Rosh Hashanah, Yom Kippur, and the days between them, we substitute the word melekh, literally "King," for the word El, "God." Symbolically, Rosh Hashanah is the day of God's coronation—God became sovereign as the world came into being.

MAY THE THOUGHT OF US RISE UP AND REACH YOU יַעֲלֶה וְיָבֹא. This paragraph is added to the Amidah on Rosh Ḥodesh (the new moon), the pilgrimage festivals, Rosh Hashanah and Yom Kippur, with the name of the appropriate festival inserted in the prayer at the appropriate point. The modern liturgical scholar Yosef Heinemann believed that this paragraph was composed especially for Rosh Hashanah, as it repeatedly addresses the theme of remembrance that is central to Rosh Hashanah, known also as the Day of Remembrance (yom ha-zikkaron).

You are holy, and Your name is revered,
for there is no God but You.
As Your prophet Isaiah wrote: "*Adonai Tz'va·ot* will be exalted
through justice, the holy God sanctified through righteousness."
Barukh atah ADONAI, the Holy Sovereign.

Fourth B'rakhah: The Holiness of Rosh Hashanah

You have chosen us among all peoples,
loving us, wanting us.
You have distinguished us among all nations,
making us holy through Your commandments,
drawing us close to Your service,
and calling us by Your great and holy name.

With love, You have bestowed on us, ADONAI our God, [this
Shabbat and] this Day of Remembrance, a day for [recalling]
the shofar sound [with love], a day for holy assembly and for
recalling the Exodus from Egypt.

Our God and God of our ancestors,
may the thought of us rise up and reach You.
Attend to us and accept us;
hear us and respond to us.
Keep us in mind,
and keep in mind the thought of our ancestors,
as well as the Messiah, the descendant of David;
Jerusalem, Your holy city;
and all Your people, the House of Israel.
On this Day of Remembrance respond to us
with deliverance, goodness, compassion, love, life, and peace.

Remember us for good;   *Amen.*

respond to us with blessing;   *Amen.*

redeem us with life.   *Amen.*

Show us compassion and care with words of salvation and kindness; have mercy on us and redeem us. Our eyes are turned to
You, for You are a compassionate and loving sovereign.

You Have Chosen Us
A difficult task was as-
signed this people in its
history. It is so easy to
listen to the voices of
idols, and it is so hard to
receive the word of the
One God into oneself.
It is so easy to remain a
slave, and it is so difficult
to become a free person.
But this people can only
exist in the full seriousness of its task. It can
only exist in this freedom
which reaches beyond
all other freedoms. Its
history began when it
heard the word, rising
out of the mystery, and
emerging into clarity: "I
am the One-Who-Is thy
God, who brought you
out of the land of Egypt,
out of the House of
Bondage...." This people
traveled through the his-
tory of humanity, century
after century, millennium
after millennium. Its very
history became divine
guidance for it.
　　　　—LEO BAECK

אֱלֹהֵינוּ וֵאלֹהֵי אֲבוֹתֵינוּ [וְאִמּוֹתֵינוּ],
מְלֹךְ עַל כָּל־הָעוֹלָם כֻּלּוֹ בִּכְבוֹדֶךָ,
וְהִנָּשֵׂא עַל כָּל־הָאָרֶץ בִּיקָרֶךָ,
וְהוֹפַע בַּהֲדַר גְּאוֹן עֻזֶּךָ
עַל כָּל־יוֹשְׁבֵי תֵבֵל אַרְצֶךָ.
וְיֵדַע כָּל־פָּעוּל כִּי אַתָּה פְעַלְתּוֹ
וְיָבִין כָּל־יְצוּר כִּי אַתָּה יְצַרְתּוֹ,
וְיֹאמַר כֹּל אֲשֶׁר נְשָׁמָה בְּאַפּוֹ:
יהוה אֱלֹהֵי יִשְׂרָאֵל מֶלֶךְ, וּמַלְכוּתוֹ בַּכֹּל מָשָׁלָה.

אֱלֹהֵינוּ וֵאלֹהֵי אֲבוֹתֵינוּ [וְאִמּוֹתֵינוּ], [רְצֵה בִמְנוּחָתֵנוּ]
קַדְּשֵׁנוּ בְּמִצְוֹתֶיךָ וְתֵן חֶלְקֵנוּ בְּתוֹרָתֶךָ, שַׂבְּעֵנוּ מִטּוּבֶךָ
וְשַׂמְּחֵנוּ בִּישׁוּעָתֶךָ [וְהַנְחִילֵנוּ, יהוה אֱלֹהֵינוּ, בְּאַהֲבָה
וּבְרָצוֹן שַׁבַּת קָדְשֶׁךָ, וְיָנוּחוּ בָהּ יִשְׂרָאֵל מְקַדְּשֵׁי שְׁמֶךָ]
וְטַהֵר לִבֵּנוּ לְעָבְדְּךָ בֶּאֱמֶת, כִּי אַתָּה אֱלֹהִים אֱמֶת,
וּדְבָרְךָ אֱמֶת וְקַיָּם לָעַד. בָּרוּךְ אַתָּה יהוה, מֶלֶךְ עַל כָּל־
הָאָרֶץ, מְקַדֵּשׁ [הַשַּׁבָּת וְ] יִשְׂרָאֵל וְיוֹם הַזִּכָּרוֹן.

רְצֵה יהוה אֱלֹהֵינוּ, בְּעַמְּךָ יִשְׂרָאֵל וּבִתְפִלָּתָם, וְהָשֵׁב
אֶת־הָעֲבוֹדָה לִדְבִיר בֵּיתֶךָ, [וְאִשֵּׁי יִשְׂרָאֵל]
וּתְפִלָּתָם בְּאַהֲבָה תְקַבֵּל בְּרָצוֹן, וּתְהִי לְרָצוֹן תָּמִיד
עֲבוֹדַת יִשְׂרָאֵל עַמֶּךָ.

וְתֶחֱזֶינָה עֵינֵינוּ בְּשׁוּבְךָ לְצִיּוֹן בְּרַחֲמִים.
בָּרוּךְ אַתָּה יהוה, הַמַּחֲזִיר שְׁכִינָתוֹ לְצִיּוֹן.

RESTORE WORSHIP TO YOUR SANCTUARY וְהָשֵׁב אֶת־הָעֲבוֹדָה לִדְבִיר בֵּיתֶךָ. According to the Babylonian Talmud, "Ever since the day when the Temple was destroyed, there has been an iron barrier separating Israel from God" (Berakhot 32b). Each destruction of the Temple in Jerusalem (first by the Babylonians in 586 B.C.E., then by the Romans in 70 C.E.) was a cataclysmic event in early Jewish history. In praying for the restoration of the Temple, we express our wish both for the sense of immediate connection with God that is believed to have characterized the Temple service, and for the common sense of purpose and religious community that was experienced there.

FIERY OFFERINGS וְאִשֵּׁי יִשְׂרָאֵל. The phrase "fiery offerings" originally referred to the sacrifices in the Temple, but later medieval and Ḥasidic commentators understood it as a description of the intensity of religious fervor required of true prayer. It is as if to say, "May our prayers have the same meaning and effect as burnt offerings once did for our ancestors."

YOUR DIVINE PRESENCE שְׁכִינָתוֹ. The Hebrew word *shekhinah* has been used for centuries to refer to God's immanence, the presence of God that is felt in the world. The word *shekhinah* is grammatically feminine. Accordingly, the Jewish mystical tradition generally describes the Divine Presence—known as the Shekhinah—in feminine imagery.

Our God and God of our ancestors:
May You be exalted over the entire universe in Your glory,
may You be raised up over all the earth in Your splendor,
and may You manifest Yourself to all the inhabitants of the world
in the majestic beauty of Your strength.
Then all creatures will know that You created them;
all living things will understand that You gave them life;
and everything that breathes will proclaim:
ADONAI, the God of Israel, is sovereign, ruling over all.

May the Torah Be Our Portion
Each one of us is given a share of this world. The people Israel ask that Torah be our share.

The Holiness of the New Year
Every year, there descends and radiates a new and renewed light that has never yet shone. For the light of every year withdraws to its source in the Infinite One, who is beyond time. . . . But through the shofar's sounding and by means of the prayers we utter, a new and superior light is elicited . . . that has never yet shone since the beginning of the world. Its manifestation, however, depends on the actions of those below, and on their merits and penitence during the Ten Days of Repentance.
—SHNEUR ZALMAN OF LIADI

Our God and God of our ancestors, [embrace our rest,] make us holy through Your mitzvot and let the Torah be our portion. Fill our lives with Your goodness and gladden us with Your triumph. [ADONAI our God, grant that we inherit Your holy Shabbat, lovingly and willingly, so that the people Israel, who sanctify Your name, may find rest on this day.] Purify our hearts to serve You truly,
V'taheir libbeinu l'ovd'kha be-emet.

for You are the God of truth, and Your word is true, eternal, and unchanging. *Barukh atah ADONAI*, ruler of all the earth, who makes [Shabbat,] the people Israel and the Day of Remembrance holy.
[*Leader: Barukh atah Adonai,*] Congregation: *melekh al kol ha-aretz, m'kaddeish [ha-shabbat v'] yisra·el* [*Leader: v'yom ha-zikkaron*].

Fifth B'rakhah: The Restoration of Zion

ADONAI our God, embrace Your people Israel and their prayer. Restore worship to Your sanctuary. May the [fiery offerings and] prayers of the people Israel be lovingly accepted by You, and may our service always be pleasing.

Let our eyes behold Your merciful return to Zion. *Barukh atah ADONAI*, who restores Your Divine Presence to Zion.

While reciting the first words, by custom we remain seated while bowing our head.

Leader recites: *Congregation recites:*

מוֹדִים אֲנַחְנוּ לָךְ   ┐ מוֹדִים אֲנַחְנוּ לָךְ

שָׁאַתָּה הוּא יהוה אֱלֹהֵינוּ   שָׁאַתָּה הוּא יהוה אֱלֹהֵינוּ

וֵאלֹהֵי אֲבוֹתֵינוּ [וְאִמּוֹתֵינוּ]   וֵאלֹהֵי אֲבוֹתֵינוּ [וְאִמּוֹתֵינוּ],

לְעוֹלָם וָעֶד, צוּר חַיֵּינוּ,   אֱלֹהֵי כָל־בָּשָׂר, יוֹצְרֵנוּ,

מָגֵן יִשְׁעֵנוּ אַתָּה הוּא.   יוֹצֵר בְּרֵאשִׁית. בְּרָכוֹת

לְדוֹר וָדוֹר נוֹדֶה לְךָ   וְהוֹדָאוֹת לְשִׁמְךָ הַגָּדוֹל

וּנְסַפֵּר תְּהִלָּתֶךָ, עַל חַיֵּינוּ   וְהַקָּדוֹשׁ, עַל שֶׁהֶחֱיִיתָנוּ

הַמְּסוּרִים בְּיָדֶךָ וְעַל   וְקִיַּמְתָּנוּ. כֵּן תְּחַיֵּינוּ

נִשְׁמוֹתֵינוּ הַפְּקוּדוֹת לָךְ,   וּתְקַיְּמֵנוּ, וְתֶאֱסוֹף

וְעַל נִסֶּיךָ שֶׁבְּכָל־יוֹם   גָּלֻיּוֹתֵינוּ לְחַצְרוֹת קָדְשֶׁךָ,

עִמָּנוּ וְעַל נִפְלְאוֹתֶיךָ   לִשְׁמוֹר חֻקֶּיךָ וְלַעֲשׂוֹת

וְטוֹבוֹתֶיךָ שֶׁבְּכָל־עֵת, עֶרֶב   רְצוֹנֶךָ, וּלְעָבְדְּךָ בְּלֵבָב שָׁלֵם,

וָבֹקֶר וְצָהֳרָיִם. ◁ הַטּוֹב, כִּי   עַל שֶׁאֲנַחְנוּ מוֹדִים לָךְ.

לֹא כָלוּ רַחֲמֶיךָ, וְהַמְרַחֵם,   בָּרוּךְ אֵל הַהוֹדָאוֹת.

כִּי לֹא תַמּוּ חֲסָדֶיךָ, מֵעוֹלָם

קִוִּינוּ לָךְ.

וְעַל כֻּלָּם יִתְבָּרַךְ וְיִתְרוֹמַם שִׁמְךָ מַלְכֵּנוּ תָּמִיד
לְעוֹלָם וָעֶד.

וּכְתוֹב לְחַיִּים טוֹבִים כָּל־בְּנֵי בְרִיתֶךָ.

וְכֹל הַחַיִּים יוֹדוּךָ סֶּלָה,
וִיהַלְלוּ אֶת־שִׁמְךָ בֶּאֱמֶת,
הָאֵל יְשׁוּעָתֵנוּ וְעֶזְרָתֵנוּ סֶלָה.
בָּרוּךְ אַתָּה יהוה, הַטּוֹב שִׁמְךָ וּלְךָ נָאֶה לְהוֹדוֹת.

THE CONGREGATIONAL RESPONSE. A second version of Modim, the *b'rakhah* of thanksgiving, was created by the Rabbis of the talmudic period to be recited by the congregation while the leader chants the official prayer (Babylonian Talmud, Sotah 40a). In this way, both the leader and the congregation personally fulfill the imperative of acknowledging God. The central idea expressed in this second version is *modim anaḥnu lakh… al she-anaḥnu modim lakh*, "we thank You for the ability to thank You." Gratitude is seen as a special gift of our humanity. The expression of thankfulness connects us to the world with a sense of humility and a joyful spirit of openness.

FOR ALL THESE וְעַל כֻּלָּם. In the language of the Bible and the prayerbook, "God's name is exalted" when we acknowledge God, recognize God's goodness in creation, and act to enable God's justice and compassion to be visible in the world.

AND INSCRIBE וּכְתוֹב. This is the third of the four special insertions in the Amidah for the Ten Days of Repentance. With the first two insertions, we prayed for God's mercy that we may live another year; now we pray that the life we are granted be good.

Sixth B'rakhah: Gratitude for Life and Its Blessings

*While reciting the first words, by custom we remain seated
while bowing our head.*

Leader recites:

We thank You, You who are
our God and the God of our
ancestors through all time,
protector of our lives, shield
of our salvation. From one
generation to the next we
thank You and sing Your
praises—
for our lives that are in Your
hands,
for our souls that are under
Your care,
for Your miracles that accompany us each day,
and for Your wonders and
Your gifts that are with us
each moment—
evening, morning, and noon.
You are the One who is good,
whose mercy is never-ending;
the One who is compassionate, whose love is unceasing.
We have always placed our
hope in You.

Congregation recites:

ℸ We thank You for the ability to acknowledge You. You
are our God and the God of
our ancestors, the God of
all flesh, our creator, and the
creator of all. We offer praise
and blessing to Your holy and
great name, for granting us
life and for sustaining us. May
You continue to grant us life
and sustenance. Gather our
dispersed to Your holy courtyards, that we may fulfill Your
mitzvot and serve You wholeheartedly, carrying out Your
will. May God, the source of
gratitude, be praised.

For all these blessings may Your name be praised and exalted,
our sovereign, always and forever.

And inscribe all the people of Your covenant for a good life.
U-kh'tov l'ḥayyim tovim kol b'nei v'ritekha.

May all that lives thank You always, and praise Your name
faithfully forever, God of our deliverance and help.
Barukh atah ADONAI, whose name is goodness
and to whom praise is fitting.

אֱלֹהֵינוּ וֵאלֹהֵי אֲבוֹתֵינוּ [וְאִמּוֹתֵינוּ], בָּרְכֵנוּ בַּבְּרָכָה הַמְשֻׁלֶּשֶׁת בַּתּוֹרָה הַכְּתוּבָה עַל יְדֵי מֹשֶׁה עַבְדֶּךָ, הָאֲמוּרָה מִפִּי אַהֲרֹן וּבָנָיו, כֹּהֲנִים, עַם קְדוֹשֶׁךָ, כָּאָמוּר:

כֵּן יְהִי רָצוֹן.   יְבָרֶכְךָ יהוה וְיִשְׁמְרֶךָ.

כֵּן יְהִי רָצוֹן.   יָאֵר יהוה פָּנָיו אֵלֶיךָ וִיחֻנֶּךָּ.

כֵּן יְהִי רָצוֹן.   יִשָּׂא יהוה פָּנָיו אֵלֶיךָ וְיָשֵׂם לְךָ שָׁלוֹם.

שִׂים שָׁלוֹם בָּעוֹלָם, טוֹבָה וּבְרָכָה, חֵן וָחֶסֶד וְרַחֲמִים עָלֵינוּ וְעַל כָּל־יִשְׂרָאֵל עַמֶּךָ. בָּרְכֵנוּ אָבִינוּ כֻּלָּנוּ כְּאֶחָד בְּאוֹר פָּנֶיךָ, כִּי בְאוֹר פָּנֶיךָ נָתַתָּ לָּנוּ, יהוה אֱלֹהֵינוּ, תּוֹרַת חַיִּים וְאַהֲבַת חֶסֶד, וּצְדָקָה וּבְרָכָה וְרַחֲמִים וְחַיִּים, וְשָׁלוֹם. וְטוֹב בְּעֵינֶיךָ לְבָרֵךְ אֶת־עַמְּךָ יִשְׂרָאֵל, בְּכָל־עֵת וּבְכָל־שָׁעָה בִּשְׁלוֹמֶךָ.

בְּסֵפֶר חַיִּים, בְּרָכָה וְשָׁלוֹם וּפַרְנָסָה טוֹבָה, נִזָּכֵר וְנִכָּתֵב לְפָנֶיךָ, אֲנַחְנוּ וְכָל־עַמְּךָ בֵּית יִשְׂרָאֵל, לְחַיִּים טוֹבִים וּלְשָׁלוֹם.

בָּרוּךְ אַתָּה יהוה, עוֹשֵׂה הַשָּׁלוֹם.

ON SHABBAT, WE CONTINUE WITH KADDISH SHALEM ON PAGE 94.

MAY ADONAI BLESS YOU יְבָרֶכְךָ יהוה. Numbers 6:24–26. This biblical blessing, known as Birkat Kohanim (the Priestly Blessing), is prescribed in the Torah to be recited by Aaron and his descendants, the *kohanim* (priests). In most synagogues in Jerusalem, this blessing is recited every day. The *kohanim*, who come to the front of the synagogue after preparing themselves ritually, extend their hands toward the congregation in a traditional gesture, thus serving as a conduit of blessing. In many synagogues in the Diaspora, the *kohanim* re-enact this ancient blessing only during the Musaf service on High Holy Days and festivals, while in other congregations the blessing is recited by the service leader. The text of the Priestly Blessing has been found on silver amulets in Jerusalem that date from the 7th century B.C.E., the only known inscription of a biblical text predating the Babylonian exile.

GRANT PEACE שִׂים שָׁלוֹם. The wording of this paragraph, which is known by its first two words as Sim Shalom, is related directly to the conclusion of the Priestly Blessing, both in its mention of the blessings of peace and in its reference to the light of God's countenance. Thus, the Sim Shalom b'rakhah is traditionally recited at all services at which the Priestly Blessing occurs. An alternative version of this blessing, Shalom Rav, is recited most afternoons and in the evening.

TO THE WORLD בָּעוֹלָם. Following the text of the 10th century prayerbook of Saadiah Gaon, Conservative movement prayerbooks insert the word *ba-olam*, "to the world," to emphasize that Jewish prayers for peace are universalistic and encompass the entire world.

IN THE BOOK OF LIFE בְּסֵפֶר חַיִּים. This is the fourth of the special insertions in the Amidah of the High Holy Days. This final addition expands the theme of goodness enunciated in the previous addition. In the end, we pray not only for life but also for blessing, peace, and prosperity.

Great is peace, for the
only vessel that can con-
tain blessings is peace.

Great is peace, for all the
prayers conclude with
pleas for peace.

Great is peace, for we
must seek it even in time
of war.

Great is peace, for it is the
reward of the righteous.

Great is peace, for it is
bestowed upon those
who love the Torah.

Great is peace, for it is
bestowed upon the
humble.

Great is peace, for it is
bestowed upon those
who act justly.

Great is peace, for it is
equal to all of the work
of creation.

Great is peace, for even
those who dwell on high
need peace, as it is said,
עֹשֶׂה שָׁלוֹם בִּמְרוֹמָיו "God
imposes peace in God's
heights" (Job 25:2). If
in a place where there
is no hatred and envy,
enmity or malice, peace
is needed, how much
more so in a place where
all these qualities are
lacking!

Great is peace, for the
name of the Holy One
is Peace.

—MIDRASH
SIFREI NUMBERS
(trans. Reuven Hammer, adapted)

Seventh B'rakhah: Prayer for Peace

Our God and God of our ancestors,
bless us with the threefold blessing of the Torah
written by Moses Your servant,
recited by Aaron and his descendants, the *kohanim*,
the consecrated priests of Your people:

May ADONAI bless and protect you.

> *So may it be God's will.* Kein y'hi ratzon.

May ADONAI's countenance shine upon you
and grant you kindness.

> *So may it be God's will.* Kein y'hi ratzon.

May ADONAI's countenance be lifted toward you
and grant you peace.

> *So may it be God's will.* Kein y'hi ratzon.

Grant peace to the world: goodness and blessing, grace, love,
and compassion to us and all the people Israel. Bless us, our
creator, united as one in the light of Your countenance; by that
light, ADONAI our God, You gave us a guide to life: the love of
kindness, righteousness, blessing, compassion, life, and peace.
May it please You to bless Your people Israel at every season
and at all times with Your gift of peace.

May we and the entire House of Israel be called to mind and
inscribed for life, blessing, sustenance, and peace in the Book
of Life.

*B'seifer ḥayyim b'rakhah v'shalom u-farnasah tovah,
nizzakheir v'nikkateiv l'fanekha, anaḥnu v'khol am'kha beit yisra·el,
l'ḥayyim tovim u-l'shalom.*

Barukh atah ADONAI, who brings peace.

ON SHABBAT, WE CONTINUE WITH KADDISH SHALEM ON PAGE 94.

We rise as the ark is opened. An alternate version begins on the next page.
Avinu Malkeinu is not recited on Shabbat.

אָבִֽינוּ מַלְכֵּֽנוּ! חָטָֽאנוּ לְפָנֶֽיךָ.

אָבִֽינוּ מַלְכֵּֽנוּ! אֵין לָֽנוּ מֶֽלֶךְ אֶלָּא אָֽתָּה.

אָבִֽינוּ מַלְכֵּֽנוּ! עֲשֵׂה עִמָּֽנוּ לְמַֽעַן שְׁמֶֽךָ.

אָבִֽינוּ מַלְכֵּֽנוּ! חַדֵּשׁ עָלֵֽינוּ שָׁנָה טוֹבָה.

אָבִֽינוּ מַלְכֵּֽנוּ! בַּטֵּל מֵעָלֵֽינוּ כָּל־גְּזֵרוֹת קָשׁוֹת.

אָבִֽינוּ מַלְכֵּֽנוּ! בַּטֵּל מַחְשְׁבוֹת שׂוֹנְאֵֽינוּ.

אָבִֽינוּ מַלְכֵּֽנוּ! הָפֵר עֲצַת אוֹיְבֵֽינוּ.

אָבִֽינוּ מַלְכֵּֽנוּ! כַּלֵּה כָּל־צַר וּמַשְׂטִין מֵעָלֵֽינוּ.

אָבִֽינוּ מַלְכֵּֽנוּ! כַּלֵּה דֶֽבֶר וְחֶֽרֶב וְרָעָב וּשְׁבִי וּמַשְׁחִית וְעָוֹן
וּשְׁמַד מִבְּנֵי בְרִיתֶֽךָ.

אָבִֽינוּ מַלְכֵּֽנוּ! סְלַח וּמְחַל לְכָל־עֲוֹנוֹתֵֽינוּ.

אָבִֽינוּ מַלְכֵּֽנוּ! מְחֵה וְהַעֲבֵר פְּשָׁעֵֽינוּ וְחַטֹּאתֵֽינוּ מִנֶּֽגֶד עֵינֶֽיךָ.

After the leader has recited each of these lines, we repeat it:

◁ אָבִֽינוּ מַלְכֵּֽנוּ! הַחֲזִירֵֽנוּ בִּתְשׁוּבָה שְׁלֵמָה לְפָנֶֽיךָ.

אָבִֽינוּ מַלְכֵּֽנוּ! שְׁלַח רְפוּאָה שְׁלֵמָה לְחוֹלֵי עַמֶּֽךָ.

אָבִֽינוּ מַלְכֵּֽנוּ! זָכְרֵֽנוּ בְּזִכָּרוֹן טוֹב לְפָנֶֽיךָ.

אָבִֽינוּ מַלְכֵּֽנוּ! כָּתְבֵֽנוּ בְּסֵֽפֶר חַיִּים טוֹבִים.

אָבִֽינוּ מַלְכֵּֽנוּ! כָּתְבֵֽנוּ בְּסֵֽפֶר גְּאֻלָּה וִישׁוּעָה.

אָבִֽינוּ מַלְכֵּֽנוּ! כָּתְבֵֽנוּ בְּסֵֽפֶר פַּרְנָסָה וְכַלְכָּלָה.

אָבִֽינוּ מַלְכֵּֽנוּ! כָּתְבֵֽנוּ בְּסֵֽפֶר זְכִיּוֹת.

אָבִֽינוּ מַלְכֵּֽנוּ! כָּתְבֵֽנוּ בְּסֵֽפֶר סְלִיחָה וּמְחִילָה.

אָבִֽינוּ מַלְכֵּֽנוּ! הַצְמַח לָֽנוּ יְשׁוּעָה בְּקָרוֹב.

אָבִֽינוּ מַלְכֵּֽנוּ! הָרֵם קֶֽרֶן יִשְׂרָאֵל עַמֶּֽךָ.

אָבִֽינוּ מַלְכֵּֽנוּ! הָרֵם קֶֽרֶן מְשִׁיחֶֽךָ.

אָבִֽינוּ מַלְכֵּֽנוּ! שְׁמַע קוֹלֵֽנוּ, חוּס וְרַחֵם עָלֵֽינוּ.

אָבִֽינוּ מַלְכֵּֽנוּ! קַבֵּל בְּרַחֲמִים וּבְרָצוֹן אֶת־תְּפִלָּתֵֽנוּ.

אָבִֽינוּ מַלְכֵּֽנוּ! נָא אַל תְּשִׁיבֵֽנוּ רֵיקָם מִלְּפָנֶֽיךָ.

אָבִֽינוּ מַלְכֵּֽנוּ! זְכוֹר כִּי עָפָר אֲנָֽחְנוּ.

אָבִֽינוּ מַלְכֵּֽנוּ! חֲמוֹל עָלֵֽינוּ וְעַל עוֹלָלֵֽינוּ וְטַפֵּֽנוּ.

AVINU MALKEINU אָבִֽינוּ מַלְכֵּֽנוּ. The Babylonian Talmud reports that Rabbi Akiva prayed with the words *avinu malkeinu* and his prayers were accepted (Taanit 25b). Originally, this was a prayer for material blessing. In time, verses were added asking for deliverance from natural and human devastation. References to martyrdom, as well as meditations on the new year, were also added.

Avinu malkeinu literally means "our father, our king." The image of God as "father" represents related-ness and closeness. (In the ancient world the term "father" is associated with the one who gives life, and so many modern prayer-books reflect this nuance by translating the word as "creator" or "source.") The figure of God as king, or sovereign, conveys authority, particularly that of judge, and so connotes greater distance. Jewish theology has always recognized this paradoxical sense of God, speaking both of God's being close at hand, and also as distant and inscrutable—similarly of God's kindness and caring as well as God's punishing hand for sinful behavior.

Avinu Malkeinu

We rise as the ark is opened. An alternate version begins on the next page.
Avinu Malkeinu is not recited on Shabbat.

Avinu Malkeinu, we have sinned in Your presence.

Avinu Malkeinu, we have no sovereign but You.

Avinu Malkeinu, act toward us kindly in accord with Your name.

Avinu Malkeinu, make this a good new year for us.

Avinu Malkeinu, annul every harsh decree against us.

Avinu Malkeinu, nullify the designs of our foes.

Avinu Malkeinu, frustrate the plots of our enemies.

Avinu Malkeinu, rid us of every oppressor and adversary.

Avinu Malkeinu, rid Your covenanted people of disease, war, hunger, captivity, and destruction.

Avinu Malkeinu, forgive and pardon all our sins.

Avinu Malkeinu, do not look toward our sins and transgressions; blot them out.

Avinu Malkeinu, return us to Your presence, fully penitent.

Avinu Malkeinu, send complete healing to the sick among Your people.

Avinu Malkeinu, remember us favorably.

Avinu Malkeinu, inscribe us for good in the Book of Life.

Avinu Malkeinu, inscribe us in the Book of Redemption.

Avinu Malkeinu, inscribe us in the Book of Sustenance.

Avinu Malkeinu, inscribe us in the Book of Merit.

Avinu Malkeinu, inscribe us in the Book of Forgiveness.

Avinu malkeinu, haḥazireinu bi-t'shuvah sh'leimah l'fanekha.
Avinu malkeinu, sh'laḥ r'fu·ah sh'leimah l'ḥolei ammekha.
Avinu malkeinu, zokhreinu b'zikkaron tov l'fanekha.
Avinu malkeinu, kotveinu b'seifer ḥayyim tovim.
Avinu malkeinu, kotveinu b'seifer g'ullah vi-shu·ah.
Avinu malkeinu, kotveinu b'seifer parnasah v'khalkalah.
Avinu malkeinu, kotveinu b'seifer z'khuyyot.
Avinu malkeinu, kotveinu b'seifer s'liḥah u-m'ḥilah.

Avinu Malkeinu, cause our salvation to flourish soon.

Avinu Malkeinu, cause Your people Israel to be exalted.

Avinu Malkeinu, raise up Your anointed with strength.

Avinu Malkeinu, hear our voice, be kind, sympathize with us.

Avinu Malkeinu, accept our prayer, willingly and lovingly.

Avinu Malkeinu, do not turn us away empty-handed.

Avinu Malkeinu, remember that we are but dust.

Avinu Malkeinu, have compassion for us, our infants, and our children.

אָבִינוּ מַלְכֵּנוּ! עֲשֵׂה לְמַעַן הֲרוּגִים עַל שֵׁם קׇדְשֶׁךָ.

אָבִינוּ מַלְכֵּנוּ! עֲשֵׂה לְמַעַן טְבוּחִים עַל יִחוּדֶךָ.

אָבִינוּ מַלְכֵּנוּ! עֲשֵׂה לְמַעַן בָּאֵי בָאֵשׁ וּבַמַּיִם עַל קִדּוּשׁ שְׁמֶךָ.

אָבִינוּ מַלְכֵּנוּ! עֲשֵׂה לְמַעַנְךָ אִם לֹא לְמַעֲנֵנוּ.

אָבִינוּ מַלְכֵּנוּ! חׇנֵּנוּ וַעֲנֵנוּ, כִּי אֵין בָּנוּ מַעֲשִׂים, עֲשֵׂה עִמָּנוּ צְדָקָה וָחֶסֶד וְהוֹשִׁיעֵנוּ.

אָבִינוּ מַלְכֵּנוּ! חָטָאנוּ לְפָנֶיךָ.

בּוֹרְאֵנוּ מְבָרְכֵנוּ, אֵין לָנוּ מֶלֶךְ אֶלָּא אָתָּה.

גּוֹאֲלֵנוּ מִשַּׁמְּרֵנוּ, עֲשֵׂה עִמָּנוּ לְמַעַן שְׁמֶךָ.

דּוֹרְשֵׁנוּ מְפַרְנְסֵנוּ, חַדֵּשׁ עָלֵינוּ שָׁנָה טוֹבָה.

הוֹדֵינוּ מוֹשִׁיעֵנוּ, בַּטֵּל מֵעָלֵינוּ כׇּל־גְּזֵרוֹת קָשׁוֹת.

וָתִיקֵנוּ מְפַלְּטֵנוּ, בַּטֵּל מַחְשְׁבוֹת שׂוֹנְאֵינוּ.

זָנֵנוּ מְנוּסֵנוּ, כַּלֵּה דֶּבֶר וְחֶרֶב וְרָעָב וּשְׁבִי וּמַשְׁחִית וְעָוֺן וּשְׁמַד מִבְּנֵי בְרִיתֶךָ.

חוֹסֵנוּ מְחַיֵּינוּ, הָפֵר עֲצַת אוֹיְבֵינוּ.

טְהוֹרֵנוּ מְרַחֲמֵנוּ, סְלַח וּמְחַל לְכׇל־עֲוֺנוֹתֵינוּ.

יוֹצְרֵנוּ מְלַמְּדֵנוּ, הַחֲזִירֵנוּ בִּתְשׁוּבָה שְׁלֵמָה לְפָנֶיךָ.

כּוֹנֵנוּ מְכַלְכְּלֵנוּ, שְׁלַח רְפוּאָה שְׁלֵמָה לְחוֹלֵי עַמֶּךָ.

לְבוּבֵנוּ מְגַדְּלֵנוּ, זׇכְרֵנוּ בְּזִכָּרוֹן טוֹב לְפָנֶיךָ.

אָבִינוּ מַלְכֵּנוּ, כׇּתְבֵנוּ בְּסֵפֶר חַיִּים טוֹבִים.

אָבִינוּ מַלְכֵּנוּ, כׇּתְבֵנוּ בְּסֵפֶר גְּאֻלָּה וִישׁוּעָה.

אָבִינוּ מַלְכֵּנוּ, כׇּתְבֵנוּ בְּסֵפֶר פַּרְנָסָה וְכַלְכָּלָה.

אָבִינוּ מַלְכֵּנוּ, כׇּתְבֵנוּ בְּסֵפֶר זְכֻיּוֹת.

אָבִינוּ מַלְכֵּנוּ, כׇּתְבֵנוּ בְּסֵפֶר סְלִיחָה וּמְחִילָה.

אָבִינוּ מַלְכֵּנוּ **AVINU MALKEINU** אָבִינוּ מַלְכֵּנוּ. The images of God as "our father" (*avinu*) and "our sovereign" (*malkeinu*) are central to much of the High Holy Day liturgy. Yet these images may not have the same resonance for us as they once did for our ancestors. At the same time, the tradition is filled with many different metaphors for God. Therefore we offer this alternative version, featuring a variety of imagery. Its synonyms and metaphors for God are mostly taken from usages in other parts of the liturgy. Its alphabetical listing conveys the idea that we grasp the ineffable God through an infinite number of images.

Avinu Malkeinu, do this for the sake of those who were martyred for Your holy name.

Avinu Malkeinu, do this for the sake of those who were slaughtered for their exclusive devotion to You.

Avinu Malkeinu, do this for the sake of those who went through fire and water to sanctify Your holy name.

Avinu Malkeinu, do this for Your sake if not for ours.

Avinu Malkeinu, have mercy on us, answer us, for our deeds are insufficient; deal with us charitably and lovingly, and redeem us.

*Avinu malkeinu, ḥonneinu va-aneinu, ki ein banu ma·asim,
aseih immanu tz'dakah va-ḥesed v'hoshi·einu.*

AVINU MALKEINU: ALTERNATE VERSION

Avinu Malkeinu, we have sinned in Your presence.

Our creator, who blesses us, we have no sovereign but You.

Our redeemer, who guards us, act kindly, in keeping with Your name.

You who seek us out and sustain us, make this new year a good one for us.

You who are our glory, our savior, annul every harsh decree against us.

Ancient One, our rescuer, nullify the designs of our foes.

Provider, our refuge, rid Your covenanted people of disease, war, hunger, captivity, and destruction.

You who are our strength, who gives us life, rid us of every oppressor and adversary.

You who purify us and have mercy on us, forgive and pardon all our sins.

You who form us and instruct us, return us to Your presence, fully penitent.

You who establish us and provide for us, send complete healing to the sick among Your people.

You, our beloved, who raised us, remember us favorably.

Avinu Malkeinu, inscribe us for good in the Book of Life.

Avinu Malkeinu, inscribe us in the Book of Redemption.

Avinu Malkeinu, inscribe us in the Book of Sustenance.

Avinu Malkeinu, inscribe us in the Book of Merit.

Avinu Malkeinu, inscribe us in the Book of Forgiveness.

*Avinu malkeinu, kotveinu b'seifer ḥayyim tovim.
Avinu malkeinu, kotveinu b'seifer g'ullah vi-shu·ah.
Avinu malkeinu, kotveinu b'seifer parnasah v'khalkalah.
Avinu malkeinu, kotveinu b'seifer z'khuyyot.
Avinu malkeinu, kotveinu b'seifer s'liḥah u-m'ḥilah.*

נוֹטְרֵנוּ מְפַלְּטֵנוּ, הַצְמַח לָנוּ יְשׁוּעָה בְּקָרוֹב.
סוֹמְכֵנוּ מַצִּילֵנוּ, הָרֵם קֶרֶן יִשְׂרָאֵל עַמֶּךָ.
עֶזְרֵנוּ מַקְשִׁיבֵנוּ שְׁמַע קוֹלֵנוּ, חוּס וְרַחֵם עָלֵינוּ.
פּוֹדֵנוּ מְשַׁמְּרֵנוּ, קַבֵּל בְּרַחֲמִים וּבְרָצוֹן אֶת־תְּפִלָּתֵנוּ.
צוּרֵנוּ מְנוּסֵנוּ, נָא אַל תְּשִׁיבֵנוּ רֵיקָם מִלְּפָנֶיךָ.
קְדוֹשֵׁנוּ מַצְדִּיקֵנוּ, זְכוֹר כִּי עָפָר אֲנָחְנוּ.
רַחֲמֵנוּ מְחַיֵּינוּ, חֲמוֹל עָלֵינוּ וְעַל עוֹלָלֵינוּ וְטַפֵּנוּ.
שׁוֹמְרֵנוּ מוֹשִׁיעֵנוּ, עֲשֵׂה לְמַעַן הֲרוּגִים עַל שֵׁם קָדְשֶׁךָ.
תּוֹמְכֵנוּ מִסְעָדֵנוּ, עֲשֵׂה לְמַעַנְךָ אִם לֹא לְמַעֲנֵנוּ.
אָבִינוּ מַלְכֵּנוּ, חָנֵּנוּ וַעֲנֵנוּ, כִּי אֵין בָּנוּ מַעֲשִׂים,
עֲשֵׂה עִמָּנוּ צְדָקָה וָחֶסֶד וְהוֹשִׁיעֵנוּ.

The ark is closed.

קַדִּישׁ שָׁלֵם

יִתְגַּדַּל וְיִתְקַדַּשׁ שְׁמֵהּ רַבָּא, בְּעָלְמָא דִּי בְרָא, כִּרְעוּתֵהּ,
וְיַמְלִיךְ מַלְכוּתֵהּ בְּחַיֵּיכוֹן וּבְיוֹמֵיכוֹן וּבְחַיֵּי דְכָל־בֵּית
יִשְׂרָאֵל, בַּעֲגָלָא וּבִזְמַן קָרִיב, וְאִמְרוּ אָמֵן.

יְהֵא שְׁמֵהּ רַבָּא מְבָרַךְ לְעָלַם וּלְעָלְמֵי עָלְמַיָּא.

יִתְבָּרַךְ וְיִשְׁתַּבַּח וְיִתְפָּאַר וְיִתְרוֹמַם וְיִתְנַשֵּׂא וְיִתְהַדָּר
וְיִתְעַלֶּה וְיִתְהַלָּל שְׁמֵהּ דְּקֻדְשָׁא, בְּרִיךְ הוּא, לְעֵלָּא לְעֵלָּא
מִכָּל־בִּרְכָתָא וְשִׁירָתָא תֻּשְׁבְּחָתָא וְנֶחֱמָתָא דַּאֲמִירָן
בְּעָלְמָא, וְאִמְרוּ אָמֵן.

תִּתְקַבֵּל צְלוֹתְהוֹן וּבָעוּתְהוֹן דְּכָל־יִשְׂרָאֵל קֳדָם אֲבוּהוֹן
דִּי בִשְׁמַיָּא, וְאִמְרוּ אָמֵן.

יְהֵא שְׁלָמָא רַבָּא מִן שְׁמַיָּא וְחַיִּים עָלֵינוּ וְעַל כָּל־
יִשְׂרָאֵל, וְאִמְרוּ אָמֵן.

עֹשֶׂה שָׁלוֹם בִּמְרוֹמָיו הוּא יַעֲשֶׂה שָׁלוֹם עָלֵינוּ וְעַל כָּל־
יִשְׂרָאֵל [וְעַל כָּל־יוֹשְׁבֵי תֵבֵל], וְאִמְרוּ אָמֵן.

KADDISH SHALEM. Every service that features an Amidah is brought to a close with Kaddish Shalem, the complete Kaddish, so called because in addition to the words of the Kaddish recited at other times in the service, it adds a line asking God to accept our prayers: "May the prayers and pleas of all Israel be accepted by their creator in heaven." Here, the placement of Kaddish Shalem marks the end of the morning Shaḥarit prayers. The liturgy now moves on to the Torah service. In a formal sense, though introduced and followed by b'rakhot and prayers, the reading of the Torah and the Haftarah constitutes study, not prayer. For the ancient Rabbis, prayer was quintessentially defined by the Amidah, which we have now completed.

Our protector and savior, cause our salvation to flourish soon.

Our support and rescuer, cause Your people Israel to be exalted.

Our helper, who listens to us, hear our voice, be kind, sympathize with us.

Our redeemer, who watches over us, accept our prayer, willingly and lovingly.

Our fortress, who is our refuge, do not send us away empty-handed.

Holy One, who justifies us, remember that we are but dust.

Merciful One, who gives us life, have compassion for us, our infants, and our children.

Guardian, who grants us victory, do this for the sake of those who were martyred for Your holy name.

Benefactor, who provides for our welfare, do this for Your sake if not for ours.

Avinu Malkeinu, have mercy on us, answer us, for our deeds are insufficient; deal with us charitably and lovingly, and redeem us.

*Avinu malkeinu, ḥonneinu va·aneinu ki ein banu ma·asim,
aseih immanu tz'dakah va-ḥesed v'hoshi·einu.*

The ark is closed.

Kaddish Shalem

May God's great name be exalted and hallowed throughout the created world, as is God's wish. May God's sovereignty soon be established, in your lifetime and in your days, and in the days of all the House of Israel. And respond with: *Amen.*

May God's great name be acknowledged forever and ever!

Y'hei sh'meih rabba m'varakh l'alam u-l'almei almayya.

May the name of the Holy One be acknowledged and celebrated, lauded and worshipped, exalted and honored, extolled and acclaimed—though God, who is blessed, *b'rikh hu*, is truly far beyond all acknowledgment and praise, or any expressions of gratitude or consolation ever spoken in the world. And respond with: *Amen.*

May the prayers and pleas of all Israel be accepted by their creator in heaven. And respond with: *Amen.*

May abundant peace from heaven, and life, come to us and to all Israel. And respond with: *Amen.*

May the One who brings harmony on high, bring harmony to us and to all Israel [and to all who dwell on earth]. And respond with: *Amen.*

Oseh shalom bi-m'romav hu ya·aseh shalom aleinu v'al kol yisra·el [v'al kol yosh'vei teiveil], v'imru amen.

סדר קריאת התורה ותקיעת שופר לראש השנה

THE TORAH SERVICE AND SHOFAR BLOWING ON ROSH HASHANAH

אֵין־כָּמְוֹךָ בָאֱלֹהִים, אֲדֹנָי, וְאֵין כְּמַעֲשֶׂיךָ.
מַלְכוּתְךָ מַלְכוּת כָּל־עוֹלָמִים, וּמֶמְשַׁלְתְּךָ בְּכָל־דּוֹר וָדֹר.
יהוה מֶלֶךְ, יהוה מָלָךְ, יהוה יִמְלֹךְ לְעֹלָם וָעֶד.
יהוה עֹז לְעַמּוֹ יִתֵּן, יהוה יְבָרֵךְ אֶת־עַמּוֹ בַשָּׁלוֹם.

אַב הָרַחֲמִים, הֵיטִיבָה בִרְצוֹנְךָ אֶת־צִיּוֹן, תִּבְנֶה חוֹמוֹת
יְרוּשָׁלָיִם. כִּי בְךָ לְבַד בָּטֶחְנוּ, מֶלֶךְ אֵל רָם וְנִשָּׂא, אֲדוֹן
עוֹלָמִים.

We rise as the ark is opened.

וַיְהִי בִּנְסֹעַ הָאָרֹן וַיֹּאמֶר מֹשֶׁה:
קוּמָה יהוה וְיָפֻצוּ אֹיְבֶיךָ, וְיָנֻסוּ מְשַׂנְאֶיךָ מִפָּנֶיךָ.
כִּי מִצִּיּוֹן תֵּצֵא תוֹרָה, וּדְבַר־יהוה מִירוּשָׁלָיִם.
בָּרוּךְ שֶׁנָּתַן תּוֹרָה לְעַמּוֹ יִשְׂרָאֵל בִּקְדֻשָּׁתוֹ.

THE TORAH SERVICE סֵדֶר קְרִיאַת הַתּוֹרָה. It is a widespread view in Jewish thought that since the Temple's destruction, our most direct connection to the divine will is through Torah. Thus, the opening of the ark, the Torah's procession through the congregation, and the reading aloud from the scroll are all symbolic moments when the presence and will of the Divine may be most closely felt. It is as if with the opening of the ark, the doorway to heaven itself is opened. Over time, taking out the Torah has come to be seen as a royal procession. The Torah is adorned with a crown, and its cover's hem kissed as it passes through the congregation. Additionally, the Torah is dressed with accoutrements of the High Priest, including a breastplate and bells (originally used to signal his presence). In short, our way of treating the Torah scroll combines the three "crowns" about which our Rabbis spoke: the crown of sovereignty, the crown of priesthood, and the crown of Torah.

NONE COMPARES TO YOU אֵין כָּמְוֹךָ. As etiquette in Europe's royal courts became more elaborate (14th century), the Ashkenazic rite incorporated verses emphasizing God's sovereignty, as if to say that God alone—and no earthly ruler—is the true sovereign.

ADONAI IS SOVEREIGN יהוה מֶלֶךְ. This sentence is a compilation of biblical phrases referring to God's sovereignty. Stitched together, they form a creed: God has ruled the world since before creation and will continue to rule eternally. The other verses in this passage are from Psalms 86:8, 145:13, and 29:11.

COMPASSIONATE CREATOR אַב הָרַחֲמִים. Literally, "merciful father." This address, followed by a verse that calls for Jerusalem's reconstruction (Psalm 51:20), is all that remains from prayers for forgiveness that were recited during the Torah service in an earlier era.

AS THE ARK WAS CARRIED FORWARD וַיְהִי בִּנְסֹעַ. Numbers 10:35. This verse is from a description of how the people moved from one encampment to another. It depicts the Ark as the seat of divine protection, leading the march and warding off the fledgling nation's enemies. Reciting this verse evokes a period of special closeness between God and Israel, both at Sinai and in their journey through the desert.

TORAH SHALL GO FORTH FROM ZION כִּי מִצִּיּוֹן. Isaiah 2:3. As the ark is opened, we express our belief that Torah contains ideals appropriate to all humanity. Isaiah envisioned all the nations of the world coming to Mount Zion and worshipping one God.

TAKING OUT THE TORAH

*Meditations on the
Meaning of Torah*

א

Open my eyes, that
through the study of
Your Torah I may see
wondrous things.
——PSALM 119:18

ב

What Torah means to us
depends on what God
means to us.
——JACOB PETUCHOWSKI

ג

The custom of our ances-
tors has the status of
Torah.
——TOSAFOT TO
BABYLONIAN TALMUD,
MENAHOT

ד

The people Israel, the
Torah, and the Holy One
are all one. ——THE ZOHAR

None compares to You, ADONAI,
and nothing is like Your works.
Your sovereignty is everlasting;
Your rule endures through all generations.
ADONAI is sovereign, ADONAI has always been sovereign,
ADONAI will be sovereign forever and ever.
ADONAI, give strength to Your people;
ADONAI, bless Your people with peace.

Malkhut'kha malkhut kol-olamim, u-memshalt'kha b'khol dor va-dor.
Adonai melekh, Adonai malakh, Adonai yimlokh l'olam va-ed.
Adonai oz l'ammo yittein, Adonai y'vareikh et-ammo va-shalom.

Compassionate Creator, may it please You that Zion flourish;
build the walls of Jerusalem. For in You alone do we put our
trust, transcendent Sovereign—Master of all time.

Av ha-rahamim, hetivah virtzon'kha et tziyyon,
tivneh homot y'rushalayim.
Ki v'kha l'vad batahnu, melekh El ram v'nissa, adon olamim.

We rise as the ark is opened.

As the Ark was carried forward, Moses would say:
ADONAI! Scatter Your foes,
so that Your enemies flee Your Presence.

Kumah Adonai v'yafutzu oy'vekha,
v'yanusu m'san·ekha mi-panekha.

Torah shall go forth from Zion,
and the word of ADONAI from Jerusalem.
Praised is the One who gave Torah to the people Israel
in holiness.

Ki mi-tziyyon teitzei torah, u-d'var Adonai mirushalayim.
Barukh she-natan Torah l'ammo yisra·el bi-k'dushato.

ON SHABBAT, *CONTINUE AT THE BOTTOM OF THIS PAGE.*

We recite three times:

יהוה יהוה, אֵל רַחוּם וְחַנּוּן, אֶרֶךְ אַפַּיִם וְרַב חֶסֶד וֶאֱמֶת,
נֹצֵר חֶסֶד לָאֲלָפִים, נֹשֵׂא עָוֹן וָפֶשַׁע וְחַטָּאָה, וְנַקֵּה.

אָבִינוּ מַלְכֵּנוּ, אֲדוֹן הַשָּׁלוֹם, עָזְרֵנוּ וְהוֹשִׁיעֵנוּ שֶׁנִּזְכֶּה תָּמִיד
לֶאֱחֹז בְּמִדַּת הַשָּׁלוֹם. וְיִהְיֶה שָׁלוֹם בֵּין כָּל־אָדָם לַחֲבֵרוֹ וּבֵין
אִישׁ לְאִשְׁתּוֹ, וְלֹא תִהְיֶה שׁוּם מַחֲלֹקֶת בֵּין כָּל־בְּנֵי מִשְׁפַּחְתִּי.
אַתָּה עוֹשֶׂה שָׁלוֹם בִּמְרוֹמֶיךָ, כֵּן תַּמְשִׁיךְ שָׁלוֹם עָלֵינוּ וְעַל
כָּל־הָעוֹלָם כֻּלּוֹ, נִתְקָרֵב אֵלֶיךָ וּלְתוֹרָתְךָ בֶּאֱמֶת וְנַעֲשֶׂה כֻלָּנוּ
אֲגֻדָּה אַחַת לַעֲשׂוֹת רְצוֹנְךָ בְּלֵבָב שָׁלֵם. אֲדוֹן הַשָּׁלוֹם, בָּרְכֵנוּ
בַשָּׁלוֹם. אָמֵן.

יִהְיוּ לְרָצוֹן אִמְרֵי־פִי וְהֶגְיוֹן לִבִּי לְפָנֶיךָ יהוה צוּרִי וְגוֹאֲלִי.

Some recite the following three times:

וַאֲנִי תְפִלָּתִי־לְךָ, יהוה, עֵת רָצוֹן.
אֱלֹהִים בְּרָב־חַסְדֶּךָ, עֲנֵנִי בֶּאֱמֶת יִשְׁעֶךָ.

ON SHABBAT, *THE FOLLOWING MEDITATION IS RECITED:*

בְּרִיךְ שְׁמֵהּ דְּמָרֵא עָלְמָא, בְּרִיךְ כִּתְרָךְ וְאַתְרָךְ. יְהֵא
רְעוּתָךְ עִם עַמָּךְ יִשְׂרָאֵל לְעָלַם, וּפֻרְקַן יְמִינָךְ אַחֲזֵי לְעַמָּךְ
בְּבֵית מִקְדְּשָׁךְ, וּלְאַמְטוּיֵי לָנָא מִטּוּב נְהוֹרָךְ וּלְקַבֵּל צְלוֹתָנָא
בְּרַחֲמִין. יְהֵא רַעֲוָא קֳדָמָךְ דְּתוֹרִיךְ לָן חַיִּין בְּטִיבוּתָא, וְלֶהֱוֵי
אֲנָא פְּקִידָא בְּגוֹ צַדִּיקַיָּא, לְמִרְחַם עָלַי, וּלְמִנְטַר יָתִי וְיָת כָּל־
דִּי לִי וְדִי לְעַמָּךְ יִשְׂרָאֵל. אַנְתְּ הוּא זָן לְכֹלָּא, וּמְפַרְנֵס לְכֹלָּא.
אַנְתְּ הוּא שַׁלִּיט עַל כֹּלָּא. אַנְתְּ הוּא דְּשַׁלִּיט עַל מַלְכַיָּא,
וּמַלְכוּתָא דִּי לָךְ הִיא. אֲנָא עַבְדָּא דְקֻדְשָׁא בְּרִיךְ הוּא
דְּסָגֵדְנָא קַמֵּהּ וּמִקַּמָּא דִּיקַר אוֹרַיְתֵהּ בְּכָל־עִדָּן וְעִדָּן.

BEFORE THE OPEN ARK. The sight of the Torah in the opened ark evokes a sense of reverence, inspiring reflection and meditation. Over time, various personal prayers have been added to the Torah service. Rabbi Isaac Luria (1534–1572, Egypt and the Land of Israel) suggested that the Thirteen Attributes be recited before the open ark, as a communal plea for forgiveness.

AVINU MALKEINU אָבִינוּ מַלְכֵּנוּ. Adapted by Jules Harlow from a meditation written by Rabbi Nathan Sternharz (1780–1845), the chief recorder of the teachings of the Ḥasidic master Naḥman of Bratzlav.

MAY THIS BE . . . FOR MY PRAYER וַאֲנִי תְפִלָּתִי־לְךָ. Psalm 69:14. This poetic phrase can be literally translated as: "And I, I am a prayer to You..." Our lives may be seen as prayers offered to God.

PRAISED BE YOUR NAME בְּרִיךְ שְׁמֵהּ. From the Zohar (part 2, 206a), the central text of Jewish mysticism, composed in Aramaic. A translation of the Zohar's introduction to this meditation appears in the leftmost column.

As soon as the Torah scroll is placed on [the reading desk] the whole congregation below should assume an attitude of awe and fear, of trembling and quaking, as though they were at that moment standing at Mount Sinai to receive the Torah, and should pay attention and listen carefully; for it is not permitted then to open one's mouth, even for discussing the Torah, still less other subjects. All must be in awe and fear, as though they were speechless, as it is written: "And when he opened it, all the people stood up," and also, "And the ears of all the people were attentive to the Torah scroll" (Nehemiah 8:5 and 8:3). Rabbi Shimon said: "When the Torah scroll is taken out to be read before the congregation, the heavenly gates of mercy are opened and the attribute of love is stirred up, and each one should then recite the following prayer: "Ruler of the universe, praised be Your name and Your sovereignty. . . ."

—THE ZOHAR

ON SHABBAT, CONTINUE AT THE BOTTOM OF THIS PAGE.
We recite three times:

Adonai, Adonai, God merciful and compassionate, patient, abounding in love and faithfulness, assuring love for thousands of generations, forgiving iniquity, transgression, and sin, and granting pardon.

Adonai, Adonai, El raḥum v'ḥannun, erekh appayim v'rav ḥesed ve-emet.
Notzeir ḥesed la-alafim, nosei avon va-fesha v'ḥatta·ah v'nakkeih.

PRIVATE MEDITATION

Avinu Malkeinu, Master of peace, help us and strengthen us so that we always strive for peace. May there be harmony among all people, their companions, and friends. May there be no discord among the members of my family. You who establish peace above, extend peace upon us and the whole world. May we draw close to You and Your Torah in truth and may we all be bound together, carrying out Your will wholeheartedly. Master of peace, bless us with peace. Amen.

May the words of my mouth and the meditations of my heart be acceptable to You, Adonai, my rock and my redeemer.

Some recite the following three times:

May this be an auspicious time, Adonai, for my prayer. God, in Your abundant mercy, answer me with Your faithful deliverance.

Va-ani t'fillati l'kha, Adonai, eit ratzon.
Elohim b'rov ḥasdekha, aneini be-emet yish·ekha.

ON SHABBAT, THE FOLLOWING MEDITATION IS RECITED:

Ruler of the universe, praised be Your name and Your sovereignty. May Your favor abide with Your people Israel forever, and may Your liberating power be revealed to them in Your sanctuary. Extend to us the goodness of Your light and with compassion accept our prayers. May it be Your will to grant us long life and well-being; may I be counted among the righteous, and in Your compassion protect me, my family, and all the people Israel. You are the One who nourishes and sustains all life. You rule over all—even kings—for true sovereignty is Yours. I am a servant of the Holy One, whom I revere and whose precious Torah I revere in every time and place. Not on

לָא עַל אֱנָשׁ רָחֵצְנָא, וְלָא עַל בַּר אֱלָהִין סָמְכְנָא, אֶלָּא בֶּאֱלָהָא דִשְׁמַיָּא, דְּהוּא אֱלָהָא קְשׁוֹט, וְאוֹרַיְתֵהּ קְשׁוֹט, וּנְבִיאוֹהִי קְשׁוֹט, וּמַסְגֵּא לְמֶעְבַּד טַבְוָן וּקְשׁוֹט.

◁ בֵּהּ אֲנָא רָחֵץ, וְלִשְׁמֵהּ קַדִּישָׁא יַקִּירָא אֲנָא אֵמַר תֻּשְׁבְּחָן. יְהֵא רַעֲוָא קֳדָמָךְ דְּתִפְתַּח לִבִּי בְּאוֹרַיְתָא, וְתַשְׁלִים מִשְׁאֵלִין דְּלִבִּי וְלִבָּא דְכָל־עַמָּךְ יִשְׂרָאֵל, לְטָב וּלְחַיִּין וְלִשְׁלָם. אָמֵן.

Two scrolls of the Torah are taken from the ark.

We repeat each of these lines after the leader has recited it:

שְׁמַע יִשְׂרָאֵל יהוה אֱלֹהֵינוּ יהוה אֶחָד.

אֶחָד אֱלֹהֵינוּ גָּדוֹל אֲדוֹנֵנוּ קָדוֹשׁ וְנוֹרָא שְׁמוֹ.

Leader:

ᒥ גַּדְּלוּ לַיהוה אִתִּי, וּנְרוֹמְמָה שְׁמוֹ יַחְדָּו.

The Torah is carried in a circuit around the congregation.

לְךָ יהוה הַגְּדֻלָּה וְהַגְּבוּרָה וְהַתִּפְאֶרֶת וְהַנֵּצַח וְהַהוֹד, כִּי־כֹל בַּשָּׁמַיִם וּבָאָרֶץ,
לְךָ יהוה הַמַּמְלָכָה וְהַמִּתְנַשֵּׂא לְכֹל לְרֹאשׁ.
רוֹמְמוּ יהוה אֱלֹהֵינוּ וְהִשְׁתַּחֲווּ לַהֲדֹם רַגְלָיו, קָדוֹשׁ הוּא.
רוֹמְמוּ יהוה אֱלֹהֵינוּ, וְהִשְׁתַּחֲווּ לְהַר קָדְשׁוֹ, כִּי קָדוֹשׁ יהוה אֱלֹהֵינוּ.

HEAR, O ISRAEL שְׁמַע יִשְׂרָאֵל. Taking out the Torah becomes a moment of affirming Israel's most fundamental creed, as if we are standing before our sovereign, God, and affirming our loyalty.

AWE-INSPIRING וְנוֹרָא. This word is added on the High Holy Days.

ACCLAIM גַּדְּלוּ *gad'lu*. Psalm 34:4.

YOURS, ADONAI לְךָ יהוה (*l'kha Adonai*). 1 Chronicles 29:11. According to the Chronicler, these verses were part of David's last speech to the people Israel.

EXALT ADONAI רוֹמְמוּ יהוה (*rom'mu Adonai*). Two verses with the same opening words, taken from Psalm 99:5, 9, chosen as appropriate to the Torah's procession.

A Personal Meditation

Avinu Malkeinu, bless
my family with peace.
Teach me to appreciate
the treasures of my life
and help us always to
find contentment in one
another. Save us from
dissension and jealousy;
shield us from pettiness
and rivalry. May selfish
pride not divide us; may
pride in one another
unite us. Help us to
renew our love for one
another continually. In
the light of Your Torah
grant us, the people
Israel, and all humanity,
Your handiwork, health
and fulfillment, harmony,
peace, and joy in the new
year. Amen.

—NAVAH HARLOW

mortals nor on angels do I rely, but rather on the God of heaven, the God of truth, whose Torah is truth and whose prophets are true and who abounds in deeds of goodness and truth.

I put my trust in God and I utter praise to God's holy, precious name. May it be Your will that You open my heart to Your Torah, and that You fulfill the desires of my heart and the hearts of all Your people Israel, for goodness, for life, and for peace. Amen.

Beih ana raḥeitz,
v'li-shmeih kaddisha yakkira ana eimar tushb'ḥan.
Y'heih ra·ava kodamakh d'tiftaḥ libbi b'oraita,
v'tashlim mishalin d'libbi v'libba d'khol ammakh yisra·el,
l'tav u-l'ḥayyin v'lish'lam. Amen.

Two scrolls of the Torah are taken from the ark.

We repeat each of these lines after the leader has recited it:

Hear, O Israel, ADONAI is our God, ADONAI alone.

Sh'ma yisra·el, Adonai eloheinu, Adonai eḥad.

Our God is one; great is our sovereign; holy and awe-inspiring is God's name.

Eḥad eloheinu, gadol adoneinu, kadosh v'nora sh'mo.

Leader:

ʄ Acclaim ADONAI with me; let us exalt God's name together.

The Torah is carried in a circuit around the congregation.

Yours, ADONAI, is the greatness, the power, the splendor, the triumph, and the majesty—for all in heaven and on earth is Yours.

Yours is the sovereignty, above all else.

Exalt ADONAI our God, and bow down at God's throne, for our God is holy.

Exalt ADONAI our God, bow toward God's holy mountain, for ADONAI our God is holy.

L'kha Adonai ha-g'dullah v'ha-g'vurah
v'ha-tiferet v'ha-neitzaḥ v'ha-hod,
ki khol ba-shamayim u-va-aretz.
L'kha Adonai ha-mamlakhah v'ha-mitnassei l'khol l'rosh.
Rom'mu Adonai eloheinu v'hishtaḥavu la-hadom raglav,
kadosh hu.
Rom'mu Adonai eloheinu v'hishtaḥavu l'har kodsho,
ki kadosh Adonai eloheinu.

אַב הָרַחֲמִים הוּא יְרַחֵם עַם עֲמוּסִים, וְיִזְכֹּר בְּרִית
אֵיתָנִים, וְיַצִּיל נַפְשׁוֹתֵינוּ מִן הַשָּׁעוֹת הָרָעוֹת, וְיִגְעַר
בְּיֵצֶר הָרָע מִן הַנְּשׂוּאִים, וְיָחֹן אוֹתָנוּ לִפְלֵיטַת עוֹלָמִים,
וִימַלֵּא מִשְׁאֲלוֹתֵינוּ בְּמִדָּה טוֹבָה יְשׁוּעָה וְרַחֲמִים.

Torah Reader (or Gabbai):

וְיַעֲזֹר וְיָגֵן וְיוֹשִׁיעַ לְכֹל הַחוֹסִים בּוֹ, וְנֹאמַר אָמֵן.
הַכֹּל הָבוּ גֹדֶל לֵאלֹהֵינוּ, וּתְנוּ כָבוֹד לַתּוֹרָה.

(כֹּהֵן, קְרַב: יַעֲמֹד _____ בֶּן _____ הַכֹּהֵן.)
(בַּת כֹּהֵן, קִרְבִי: תַּעֲמֹד _____ בַּת _____ הַכֹּהֵן.)
(יַעֲמֹד _____ בֶּן _____ רִאשׁוֹן.)
(תַּעֲמֹד _____ בַּת _____ רִאשׁוֹנָה.)
בָּרוּךְ שֶׁנָּתַן תּוֹרָה לְעַמּוֹ יִשְׂרָאֵל בִּקְדֻשָּׁתוֹ.

Congregation and Torah Reader:

וְאַתֶּם הַדְּבֵקִים בַּיהוה אֱלֹהֵיכֶם, חַיִּים כֻּלְּכֶם הַיּוֹם.

בִּרְכוֹת הַתּוֹרָה

The person who is honored with an aliyah recites the following
before the Torah is read:

בָּרְכוּ אֶת־יהוה הַמְבֹרָךְ.

The congregation responds:

בָּרוּךְ יהוה הַמְבֹרָךְ לְעוֹלָם וָעֶד.

The person repeats the above response, then continues:

בָּרוּךְ אַתָּה יהוה אֱלֹהֵינוּ מֶלֶךְ הָעוֹלָם,
אֲשֶׁר בָּחַר בָּנוּ מִכָּל־הָעַמִּים וְנָתַן לָנוּ אֶת־תּוֹרָתוֹ.
בָּרוּךְ אַתָּה יהוה, נוֹתֵן הַתּוֹרָה.

The person who is honored recites the following after the Torah is read:

בָּרוּךְ אַתָּה יהוה אֱלֹהֵינוּ מֶלֶךְ הָעוֹלָם,
אֲשֶׁר נָתַן לָנוּ תּוֹרַת אֱמֶת, וְחַיֵּי עוֹלָם נָטַע בְּתוֹכֵנוּ.
בָּרוּךְ אַתָּה יהוה, נוֹתֵן הַתּוֹרָה.

ALIYOT. During the talmudic era, each person called to the Torah would chant the assigned passage directly from the scroll. The first person would recite the opening *b'rakhah*, while the last recited the closing one. Over time, the practice evolved. Today, each person called to the Torah recites both *b'rakhot*, and the Torah is chanted by a designated reader.

The Rabbis instituted a practice of calling a *kohen* for the first aliyah and a *levi* for the second, in order to mitigate arguments about who deserved the opening honors. Some modern congregations retain this traditional practice; others call their congregants to *aliyot* without regard to priestly status.

Each person called to the Torah uses either the corner of the *tallit* or the Torah binder to touch the scroll at the starting place (indicated by the reader) and then kisses the *tallit* or binder, reciting the *b'rakhah* while holding the handles of the Torah. When the reading is completed, that person repeats the kissing gesture at the ending place, rolls the Torah closed, and, holding the handles of the Torah, recites the final *b'rakhah*.

WHO HAS CHOSEN US בָּחַר בָּנוּ. At the moment of approaching the Torah, one may feel especially chosen and may also experience the moment as being directly commanded.

GIVING US THE TORAH . . . WHO GIVES THE TORAH נוֹתֵן . . . וְנָתַן לָנוּ אֶת־תּוֹרָתוֹ הַתּוֹרָה. In Hebrew, the *b'rakhah* uses both the present and the past tense. God not only gave us the Torah in the past, but also we receive it anew whenever we devote ourselves to studying it.

When I read Torah, I
am a link in a very long
chain that shapes my
identity; it is a ritual of
personal and communal
self-definition, as well
as a reenactment of the
first public reading of the
Torah by Ezra and the
scribes rededicating the
Temple. I enunciate the
words, and add my own
meaning to the centuries
of interpretation that
preceded me; thus they
serve both as a key to my
own inner life and as a
form of historical identification.

—RAYMOND SCHEINDLIN

May the One who is the source of compassion, who has always
sustained us, have mercy on us, and remember the covenant
with our ancestors. May God save us in difficult times, restrain
the impulse to evil within us, and grace our lives with enduring deliverance. May our pleas be answered with a measure of
kindness, salvation, and compassion.

Torah Reader (or Gabbai):

Help, shield, and save all who trust in You, God.
And let us say: *Amen.*
Let us all declare the greatness of God and give honor to the
Torah as (*the first to be called to the Torah*) comes forward. Praised is
God who gave the Torah to Israel in holiness.

Congregation and Torah Reader:

You who cling to ADONAI your God have been sustained to
this day.
V'attem ha-d'veikim badonai eloheikhem ḥayyim kull'khem ha-yom.

B'RAKHOT RECITED BY ONE CALLED UP TO THE TORAH
*The person who is honored with an aliyah recites the following
before the Torah is read:*

Praise ADONAI, to whom all prayer is directed.

Barkhu et Adonai ha-m'vorakh.

The congregation responds:

Praise ADONAI, to whom all prayer is directed forever and ever.

Barukh Adonai ha-m'vorakh l'olam va·ed.

The person repeats the above response, then continues:

Barukh atah ADONAI, our God, ruler of time and space, who
has chosen us from among all peoples, giving us the Torah.
Barukh atah ADONAI, who gives the Torah.

*Barukh atah Adonai eloheinu melekh ha-olam,
asher baḥar banu mi-kol ha-amim,
v'natan lanu et torato.
Barukh atah Adonai, notein ha-torah.*

The person who is honored recites the following after the Torah is read:

Barukh atah ADONAI, our God, ruler of time and space, who
has given us a teaching of truth, planting eternal life in our
midst. *Barukh atah ADONAI,* who gives the Torah.

*Barukh atah Adonai eloheinu melekh ha-olam,
asher natan lanu torat emet,
v'ḥayyei olam nata b'tokheinu.
Barukh atah Adonai, notein ha-torah.*

On the second day, turn to page 103.

בְּרֵאשִׁית כא

רִאשׁוֹן א וַיהוָה פָּקַד אֶת־שָׂרָה כַּאֲשֶׁר אָמָר וַיַּעַשׂ יהוָה לְשָׂרָה כַּאֲשֶׁר דִּבֵּר: ב וַתַּהַר וַתֵּלֶד שָׂרָה לְאַבְרָהָם בֵּן לִזְקֻנָיו לַמּוֹעֵד אֲשֶׁר־דִּבֶּר אֹתוֹ אֱלֹהִים: ג וַיִּקְרָא אַבְרָהָם אֶת־שֶׁם־בְּנוֹ הַנּוֹלַד־לוֹ אֲשֶׁר־יָלְדָה־לּוֹ שָׂרָה יִצְחָק: ד וַיָּמָל אַבְרָהָם אֶת־יִצְחָק בְּנוֹ בֶּן־שְׁמֹנַת יָמִים כַּאֲשֶׁר צִוָּה אֹתוֹ אֱלֹהִים:

שֵׁנִי ה וְאַבְרָהָם בֶּן־מְאַת שָׁנָה בְּהִוָּלֶד לוֹ אֵת יִצְחָק בְּנוֹ: ו וַתֹּאמֶר שָׂרָה צְחֹק עָשָׂה לִי אֱלֹהִים כָּל־הַשֹּׁמֵעַ יִצְחַק־לִי: ז וַתֹּאמֶר מִי מִלֵּל לְאַבְרָהָם הֵינִיקָה בָנִים שָׂרָה כִּי־יָלַדְתִּי בֵן לִזְקֻנָיו: ח וַיִּגְדַּל הַיֶּלֶד וַיִּגָּמַל וַיַּעַשׂ אַבְרָהָם מִשְׁתֶּה גָדוֹל בְּיוֹם הִגָּמֵל אֶת־יִצְחָק: [בשבת שלישי] ט וַתֵּרֶא שָׂרָה אֶת־בֶּן־הָגָר הַמִּצְרִית אֲשֶׁר־יָלְדָה לְאַבְרָהָם מְצַחֵק: י וַתֹּאמֶר לְאַבְרָהָם גָּרֵשׁ הָאָמָה הַזֹּאת וְאֶת־בְּנָהּ כִּי לֹא יִירַשׁ בֶּן־הָאָמָה הַזֹּאת עִם־בְּנִי עִם־יִצְחָק: יא וַיֵּרַע הַדָּבָר מְאֹד בְּעֵינֵי אַבְרָהָם עַל אוֹדֹת בְּנוֹ: יב וַיֹּאמֶר אֱלֹהִים

TORAH READING, DAY 1. Although Rosh Hashanah commemorates the anniversary of the creation of the world, the Rabbis did not select the opening passage of Genesis as a reading for the first day; instead, they chose the story of the birth of Isaac, focusing on a particular human story rather than the creation of the whole world.

The Rabbis may have wanted to stress the continuity of the Jewish people: the birth of a second Jewish generation after the founding generation of Abraham and Sarah.

The Torah does not present us with an idealized heroic family but rather, offers us a domestic scene with clashing personalities and motives that can be variously interpreted as selfless or selfish. This ambiguity allows us to consider the complexity of our own motivations and how difficult it is to understand ourselves and others. In any given year, we may identify with Abraham or Sarah or Hagar or the children, Ishmael and Isaac; as we change, so may our sympathies with the different characters.

ALIYOT. The Rabbis of the ancient synagogue differentiated between Shabbat and festivals by assigning a different number of *aliyot*—the divisions of the Torah reading—to each. On Rosh Hashanah there are five; on Yom Kippur, six; and on Shabbat, seven. When a holy day falls on Shabbat, the reading is subdivided into seven *aliyot*.

VERSE 1. TOOK NOTE OF SARAH פָּקַד אֶת־שָׂרָה. The Torah reading opens with God taking note of Sarah and on her behalf acting according to the divine promise. Sarah, introduced first in this reading, and Hagar will be the central characters in this chapter.

VERSE 6. GOD HAS BROUGHT ME LAUGHTER צְחֹק עָשָׂה לִי. The root צחק (tz-ḥ-k), used here and in verse 9, can convey two opposite understandings of Sarah's words: she may be saying, "When people hear the news that I have given birth, they will rejoice with me," or she may be saying, ". . . they will laugh at me." Similarly, the word מְצַחֵק (verse 9), used when Sarah sees the son of Hagar "playing," can mean either "to have fun with" or "to make fun of." In the first interpretation, one might simply see two children at play and argue that Sarah's judgment is harsh; in the second, those who read Sarah's judgment as wise might look at the way the children played together and see Ishmael's bullying of Isaac as the cause of Sarah's displeasure.

VERSE 8. WAS WEANED וַיִּגָּמַל. Weaning at about age three marked the completion of the first significant stage in a child's life.

TORAH READING, FIRST DAY

On the second day, turn to page 103.

Liturgical Practice

The Ashkenazic rite is unique in prescribing a special chant for the High Holy Day Torah reading. Solemn and meditative, its use may be explained by the Zohar's statement that all who listen to Leviticus chapter 16—the portion for Yom Kippur in which the sudden death of Aaron's children is mentioned—should shed tears. From Yom Kippur the custom of using this special melody extended to Rosh Hashanah as well.

— ABRAHAM TZVI IDELSOHN *(adapted)*

God Took Note of Sarah

The idea of "remembrance" is a primary theme of Rosh Hashanah, ordained in the Torah in connection with the day (Leviticus 23:24). It is featured in one of the three main sections of the Rosh Hashanah Musaf Amidah. The Rabbis designated Rosh Hashanah as Yom Ha-zikaron (the Day of Remembrance), a phrase used repeatedly in the liturgy. Remembrance is a mental act; the word used here, *pakad*, refers to an act of remembrance that is realized in deed and not only in thought—and is therefore translated by the stronger expression, "took note of...." By choosing to begin the Torah reading here, the Rabbis may be expressing the hope that God will similarly remember us for good on Rosh Hashanah, and act accordingly.

God Has Brought Me Laughter

Before God there are yet other languages than those of words: melody, weeping, and laughter. They are the possession of all who are alive. . . . They are the manifestations of the very deep levels of our being. — ḤAYIM NAḤMAN BIALIK

Listen to Sarah's Voice

Sarah was superior to Abraham in prophecy. — MIDRASH TANḤUMA

GENESIS 21

First Aliyah 1 ADONAI took note of Sarah as promised, and ADONAI did for Sarah what had been announced. 2 Sarah conceived and bore a son to Abraham in his old age, at the set time of which God had spoken. 3 Abraham gave his newborn son, whom Sarah had borne him, the name of Isaac. 4 And when his son Isaac was eight days old, Abraham circumcised him, as God had commanded him.

Second Aliyah 5 Now Abraham was one hundred years old when his son Isaac was born to him. 6 Sarah said, "God has brought me laughter; everyone who hears will laugh with me." 7 And she added,

"Who would have said to Abraham
that Sarah would suckle children!
Yet I have borne a son in his old age."

8 The child grew up and was weaned, and Abraham held a great feast on the day that Isaac was weaned.

[*Third Aliyah on Shabbat*] 9 Sarah saw the son whom Hagar the Egyptian had borne to Abraham playing. 10 She said to Abraham, "Cast out that slave-woman and her son, for the son of that slave shall not share in the inheritance with my son Isaac." 11 The matter distressed Abraham greatly, for it concerned a son of his. 12 But God said to Abraham,

אֶל־אַבְרָהָם אַל־יֵרַע בְּעֵינֶיךָ עַל־הַנַּעַר וְעַל־אֲמָתֶךָ כֹּל אֲשֶׁר תֹּאמַר אֵלֶיךָ שָׂרָה שְׁמַע בְּקֹלָהּ כִּי בְיִצְחָק יִקָּרֵא לְךָ זָרַע:

שלישי [בשבת רביעי] יג וְגַם אֶת־בֶּן־הָאָמָה לְגוֹי אֲשִׂימֶנּוּ כִּי זַרְעֲךָ הוּא: יד וַיַּשְׁכֵּם אַבְרָהָם | בַּבֹּקֶר וַיִּקַּח־לֶחֶם וְחֵמַת מַיִם וַיִּתֵּן אֶל־הָגָר שָׂם עַל־שִׁכְמָהּ וְאֶת־הַיֶּלֶד וַיְשַׁלְּחֶהָ וַתֵּלֶךְ וַתֵּתַע בְּמִדְבַּר בְּאֵר שָׁבַע: טו וַיִּכְלוּ הַמַּיִם מִן־הַחֵמֶת וַתַּשְׁלֵךְ אֶת־הַיֶּלֶד תַּחַת אַחַד הַשִּׂיחִם: טז וַתֵּלֶךְ וַתֵּשֶׁב לָהּ מִנֶּגֶד הַרְחֵק כִּמְטַחֲוֵי קֶשֶׁת כִּי אָמְרָה אַל־אֶרְאֶה בְּמוֹת הַיָּלֶד וַתֵּשֶׁב מִנֶּגֶד וַתִּשָּׂא אֶת־קֹלָהּ וַתֵּבְךְּ: יז וַיִּשְׁמַע אֱלֹהִים אֶת־קוֹל הַנַּעַר וַיִּקְרָא מַלְאַךְ אֱלֹהִים | אֶל־הָגָר מִן־הַשָּׁמַיִם וַיֹּאמֶר לָהּ מַה־לָּךְ הָגָר אַל־תִּירְאִי כִּי־שָׁמַע אֱלֹהִים אֶל־קוֹל הַנַּעַר בַּאֲשֶׁר הוּא־שָׁם: [בשבת חמישי] יח קוּמִי שְׂאִי אֶת־הַנַּעַר וְהַחֲזִיקִי אֶת־יָדֵךְ בּוֹ כִּי־לְגוֹי גָּדוֹל אֲשִׂימֶנּוּ: יט וַיִּפְקַח אֱלֹהִים אֶת־עֵינֶיהָ וַתֵּרֶא בְּאֵר מָיִם וַתֵּלֶךְ וַתְּמַלֵּא אֶת־הַחֵמֶת מַיִם וַתַּשְׁקְ אֶת־הַנָּעַר: כ וַיְהִי אֱלֹהִים אֶת־הַנַּעַר וַיִּגְדָּל וַיֵּשֶׁב בַּמִּדְבָּר וַיְהִי רֹבֶה קַשָּׁת: כא וַיֵּשֶׁב בְּמִדְבַּר פָּארָן וַתִּקַּח־לוֹ אִמּוֹ אִשָּׁה מֵאֶרֶץ מִצְרָיִם:

VERSE 16. LET ME NOT LOOK ON AS THE CHILD DIES אַל־אֶרְאֶה בְּמוֹת הַיָּלֶד. We may see Hagar as a passive person, unable to act and finally deserting her child, or we may sympathize with her as a mother who feels utterly hopeless and does not want to see the death of her child.

VERSE 17. GOD HEARD THE CRY OF THE BOY וַיִּשְׁמַע אֱלֹהִים אֶת־קוֹל הַנַּעַר. Rabbi Mendel of Vorki, a Hasidic master, remarks: "But we never read that Ishmael cried aloud! Thus we learn that God can hear the silent cries of the anguished heart, even when no words are uttered."

A MESSENGER OF GOD CALLED TO HAGAR וַיִּקְרָא מַלְאַךְ אֱלֹהִים אֶל־הָגָר. The chapter opens with the birth of Isaac, fulfilling the promise made to Sarah, and ends with God's listening to Ishmael's cry and speaking to Hagar.

VERSE 19. GOD OPENED HER EYES וַיִּפְקַח אֱלֹהִים אֶת־עֵינֶיהָ. Does the well now appear miraculously, in answer to the prayer of a mother who is deeply distressed, or had it been there all along and Hagar had failed to see it?

VERSE 20. AND BECAME SKILLED WITH A BOW וַיְהִי רֹבֶה קַשָּׁת. The midrash interprets this verse to mean that Ishmael became a desert brigand (Genesis Rabbah 45:9); the biblical wording points to someone who supports himself through violence. Could it have been because of how he was treated as a child? Or was this the personality that Sarah observed from the beginning? Or might it relate to his mother's desertion of him as she sits a "bowshot away"?

VERSE 21. HIS MOTHER GOT A WIFE FOR HIM FROM THE LAND OF EGYPT וַתִּקַּח־לוֹ אִמּוֹ אִשָּׁה מֵאֶרֶץ מִצְרָיִם. The Egyptian connection is not incidental. Later in the Book of Genesis, it is the Ishmaelites who sell Joseph into slavery in Egypt. The descendants of the slave boy who was sent out of Abraham's house played a critical role in the Egyptian enslavement of Abraham's descendants (Genesis 37:25–28).

Sarah

Sarah, like Rebecca who
comes after her, plays the
role of "heavy" in our
male-oriented Scriptures
. . . Here it is Sarah who
carries the moral burden
of sending Ishmael and
Hagar away against Abra-
ham's wishes, leaving his
character unblemished . . .
The impression we get
from the text is that
Sarah, like other strong
women of the Bible, has
a clear image of her son's
destiny. "Sarah saw,"
Scripture says when she
observes Ishmael playing
with Isaac . . . Abraham
had lost sight of the
promise, had actually
shrugged it off when it
was given, concerned
only about Ishmael. But
Sarah saw and, in seeing,
knew she had to act.
Motherhood focused her
vision.

And God Opened Her Eyes

"Do not be distressed over the boy or your slave; whatever Sarah tells you, do as she says, for it is through Isaac that off-spring shall be continued for you."

Third Aliyah [Fourth Aliyah on Shabbat] 13 As for the son of the slave-woman, I will make a nation of him, too, for he is your seed."

14 Early next morning Abraham took some bread and a skin of water, and gave them to Hagar. He placed them over her shoulder, together with the child, and sent her away. She wandered about in the wilderness of Beer-sheba. 15 When the water was gone from the skin, she left the child under one of the bushes, 16 and went and sat down at a distance, a bowshot away; for she thought, "Let me not look on as the child dies." And sitting thus afar, she burst into tears.

17 God heard the cry of the boy, and a messenger of God called to Hagar from heaven and said to her, "What troubles you, Hagar? Fear not, for God has heeded the cry of the boy where he is. *[Fifth Aliyah on Shabbat]* 18 Come, lift up the boy and hold him by the hand, for I will make a great nation of him." 19 Then God opened her eyes and she saw a well of water. She went and filled the skin with water, and let the boy drink. 20 God was with the boy and he grew up; he dwelt in the wilderness and became skilled with a bow. 21 He lived in the wilderness of Paran; and his mother got a wife for him from the land of Egypt.

רביעי [בשבת ששי] כב וַיְהִי בָּעֵת הַהִוא וַיֹּאמֶר אֲבִימֶלֶךְ
וּפִיכֹל שַׂר־צְבָאוֹ אֶל־אַבְרָהָם לֵאמֹר אֱלֹהִים עִמְּךָ בְּכֹל
אֲשֶׁר־אַתָּה עֹשֶׂה: כג וְעַתָּה הִשָּׁבְעָה לִי בֵאלֹהִים הֵנָּה
אִם־תִּשְׁקֹר לִי וּלְנִינִי וּלְנֶכְדִּי כַּחֶסֶד אֲשֶׁר־עָשִׂיתִי עִמְּךָ
תַּעֲשֶׂה עִמָּדִי וְעִם־הָאָרֶץ אֲשֶׁר־גַּרְתָּה בָּהּ: כד וַיֹּאמֶר
אַבְרָהָם אָנֹכִי אִשָּׁבֵעַ: כה וְהוֹכִחַ אַבְרָהָם אֶת־אֲבִימֶלֶךְ
עַל־אֹדוֹת בְּאֵר הַמַּיִם אֲשֶׁר גָּזְלוּ עַבְדֵי אֲבִימֶלֶךְ:
כו וַיֹּאמֶר אֲבִימֶלֶךְ לֹא יָדַעְתִּי מִי עָשָׂה אֶת־הַדָּבָר הַזֶּה
וְגַם־אַתָּה לֹא־הִגַּדְתָּ לִּי וְגַם אָנֹכִי לֹא שָׁמַעְתִּי בִּלְתִּי
הַיּוֹם: כז וַיִּקַּח אַבְרָהָם צֹאן וּבָקָר וַיִּתֵּן לַאֲבִימֶלֶךְ וַיִּכְרְתוּ
שְׁנֵיהֶם בְּרִית:

חמישי [בשבת שביעי] כח וַיַּצֵּב אַבְרָהָם אֶת־שֶׁבַע כִּבְשֹׂת הַצֹּאן
לְבַדְּהֶן: כט וַיֹּאמֶר אֲבִימֶלֶךְ אֶל־אַבְרָהָם מָה הֵנָּה שֶׁבַע
כְּבָשֹׂת הָאֵלֶּה אֲשֶׁר הִצַּבְתָּ לְבַדָּנָה: ל וַיֹּאמֶר כִּי אֶת־
שֶׁבַע כְּבָשֹׂת תִּקַּח מִיָּדִי בַּעֲבוּר תִּהְיֶה־לִּי לְעֵדָה כִּי
חָפַרְתִּי אֶת־הַבְּאֵר הַזֹּאת: לא עַל־כֵּן קָרָא לַמָּקוֹם הַהוּא
בְּאֵר שָׁבַע כִּי שָׁם נִשְׁבְּעוּ שְׁנֵיהֶם: לב וַיִּכְרְתוּ בְרִית
בִּבְאֵר שָׁבַע וַיָּקָם אֲבִימֶלֶךְ וּפִיכֹל שַׂר־צְבָאוֹ וַיָּשֻׁבוּ אֶל־
אֶרֶץ פְּלִשְׁתִּים: לג וַיִּטַּע אֶשֶׁל בִּבְאֵר שָׁבַע וַיִּקְרָא־שָׁם
בְּשֵׁם יְהֹוָה אֵל עוֹלָם: לד וַיָּגָר אַבְרָהָם בְּאֶרֶץ פְּלִשְׁתִּים
יָמִים רַבִּים:

The Torah Service continues with Ḥatzi Kaddish on page 106.

The Torah Service continues with Ḥatzi Kaddish on page 106.

VERSES 22–27. In contrast to the first part of the reading, which describes the separation of families, this next story is one of reconciliation: two tribes at war come together and agree to a covenant. The Torah may be deliberately contrasting two different ways of resolving conflict. In the first, the response to conflict is separation; in the second, a covenant is created by Abimelech and Abraham. Similarly, in the first story there is no extended conversation between the offended parties. Sarah says nothing directly to Hagar; Hagar speaks silently to herself. In contrast, here are two parties with significant grievances toward each other: they face each other, manage to communicate, and conclude a peace treaty.

VERSE 22. ABIMELECH. Earlier in Genesis (20:2), Abimelech was introduced to us as the King of Gerar, a city in the Negev.

VERSE 26. I DO NOT KNOW... NOT ... NOR לֹא יָדַעְתִּי... וְגַם... וְגַם. Abimelech responds defensively to Abraham's accusation. When Abimelech critiqued Abraham's behavior earlier in Genesis, Abraham reacted with similarly self-justifying words (Genesis 20:10–13). Yet somehow they soon proceed to settle their differences. Perhaps each one suddenly perceives his own defensiveness as mirrored by the other—a mutual recognition that enables them to forge a covenant.

VERSE 33. THE EVERLASTING GOD אֵל עוֹלָם. This appellation for God is unique in the entire Bible. The Torah reading began with God taking note of Sarah, and with this mention of God, our reading ends. While the human actors behave in quite human ways, God's presence always hovers in the background.

Then Abraham Reproached Abimelech

Rabbi Yose the son of Rabbi Ḥanina said: "Reproof leads to love, as it says, 'Reprove a wise man, and he will love you'" (Proverbs 9:8). Such indeed is Rabbi Yose's view, for he said: "Love unaccompanied by reproof is not love." Resh Lakish added: "Reproof leads to peace; hence, 'And Abraham reproved Abimelech.'" Such indeed is his view, for he said: "Peace unaccompanied by reproof is not peace."

—MIDRASH GENESIS RABBAH

Fourth Aliyah [Sixth Aliyah on Shabbat] 22 At that time Abimelech and Phicol, chief of his troops, said to Abraham, "God is with you in everything that you do. 23 Therefore swear to me here by God that you will not deal falsely with me or my kith and kin, but will deal with me and with the land in which you have sojourned as loyally as I have dealt with you." 24 And Abraham said, "I swear it."

25 Then Abraham reproached Abimelech for the well of water which the servants of Abimelech had seized. 26 But Abimelech said, "I do not know who did this; you did not tell me, nor have I heard of it until today." 27 Abraham took sheep and oxen and gave them to Abimelech, and the two of them made a pact.

Fifth Aliyah [Seventh Aliyah on Shabbat] 28 Abraham then set seven ewes of the flock by themselves, 29 and Abimelech said to Abraham, "What mean these seven ewes which you have set apart?" 30 He replied, "You are to accept these seven ewes from me as proof that I dug this well." 31 Hence that place was called Beer-sheba, for there the two of them swore an oath. 32 When they had concluded the pact at Beer-sheba, Abimelech and Phicol, chief of his troops, departed and returned to the land of the Philistines. 33 [Abraham] planted a tamarisk at Beer-sheba, and invoked there the name of ADONAI, the Everlasting God. 34 And Abraham resided in the land of the Philistines a long time.

The Torah Service continues with Ḥatzi Kaddish on page 106.

בְּרֵאשִׁית כב

רִאשׁוֹן א וַיְהִי אַחַר הַדְּבָרִים הָאֵלֶּה וְהָאֱלֹהִים נִסָּה אֶת־אַבְרָהָם וַיֹּאמֶר אֵלָיו אַבְרָהָם וַיֹּאמֶר הִנֵּנִי: ב וַיֹּאמֶר קַח־נָא אֶת־בִּנְךָ אֶת־יְחִידְךָ אֲשֶׁר־אָהַבְתָּ אֶת־יִצְחָק וְלֶךְ־לְךָ אֶל־אֶרֶץ הַמֹּרִיָּה וְהַעֲלֵהוּ שָׁם לְעֹלָה עַל אַחַד הֶהָרִים אֲשֶׁר אֹמַר אֵלֶיךָ: ג וַיַּשְׁכֵּם אַבְרָהָם בַּבֹּקֶר וַיַּחֲבֹשׁ אֶת־חֲמֹרוֹ וַיִּקַּח אֶת־שְׁנֵי נְעָרָיו אִתּוֹ וְאֵת יִצְחָק בְּנוֹ וַיְבַקַּע עֲצֵי עֹלָה וַיָּקָם וַיֵּלֶךְ אֶל־הַמָּקוֹם אֲשֶׁר־אָמַר־לוֹ הָאֱלֹהִים:

TORAH READING, DAY 2. An overarching theme of the Torah readings on Rosh Hashanah is life's fragility. Yesterday's selection celebrated the birth of Isaac, but later Hagar and Ishmael faced death in the desert. Conversely, today's reading begins with the binding of Isaac—which the Rabbis called "the Akedah"; it ends with the birth of his future mate. Once again, God intervenes with the gift of life.

The Akedah is one of the most enigmatic of biblical texts. It has been seen as emblematic of Jewish experience, of faithfulness and martyrdom. It has also been the subject of radically different interpretations; for example, some modern interpreters criticize Abraham for not protesting God's demand, seeing Isaac as enduringly wounded, even though his life is saved at the conclusion of the tale. Some ancient rabbinic readings, troubled by the moral questions found in the binding of Isaac, see Satan lurking in the background, testing Abraham much like Job, and some rabbis even put Job's protests into Abraham's mouth. What then is the nature of the test? Perhaps the question was not of Abraham's faithfulness, but of whether Abraham would ultimately protest an unjust command. Do we then read this passage on Rosh Hashanah because it records obedience to God's will, or is the underlying message one of God's faithfulness—that God never desires the sacrifice of any human, or the death of Abraham's descendants? Is Abraham a humble person of faith to be admired, or someone whose certainty in the truth of his vision almost led to tragic violence? Is Isaac's willingness to die in faithfulness a model for what may be asked of us? What demands does God make of us? To what are we willing to submit ourselves? In calling forth the association of the binding of Isaac and the ram that is substituted, the reading prepares us for the blowing of the ram's horn, which raises the question: To what does the shofar blast call us?

VERSE 1. SOME TIME AFTERWARD וַיְהִי אַחַר הַדְּבָרִים הָאֵלֶּה. The phrase indicates an indefinite connection with previous events. It may refer back to the immediate past scene (the agreement between Abraham and Abimelech) or it may refer back to the banishment of Hagar and Ishmael. No specific age is given for Isaac, but he is now old enough to carry a load of firewood and to ask an intelligent question based on experience and observation. Some commentators even picture Isaac as an adult, fully complicit in all that is taking place.

GOD PUT ABRAHAM TO THE TEST וְהָאֱלֹהִים נִסָּה אֶת־אַבְרָהָם. This information is divulged to the reader, although not to Abraham, to remove any possible misunderstanding by the reader of God's intent.

HERE I AM הִנֵּנִי. There is no adequate English equivalent for the Hebrew הִנֵּנִי (hineini), here translated as "Here I am." The term indicates readiness, attentiveness, receptivity, and responsiveness to instructions. It serves as a kind of refrain throughout the Akedah. Here, Abraham employs it in answer to God; later in verse 7, to Isaac (where it is rendered "Yes"), and then again in response to the angel of Adonai in verse 11. (*The Jewish Study Bible*)

VERSE 2. The descriptive terms "son," "favored one," "Isaac," and "whom you love" are listed in ascending order of endearment, emphasizing the enormity of God's request and the agonizing nature of the decision Abraham must make.

THAT I WILL POINT OUT TO YOU אֲשֶׁר אֹמַר אֵלֶיךָ. Not immediately specifying the place where the binding of Isaac is to take place adds to the sense of Abraham's willingness to blindly follow God's command. Later tradition identified the mountain as the site of the Temple.

TORAH READING, SECOND DAY

The Akedah/Binding of Isaac and Its Interpreters

For the most part, rabbinic literature praises Abraham for his faithful obedience to God's command, though some rabbinic texts indicate ambivalence regarding Abraham's unqualified acquiescence. This was also the perspective of the 19th-century Christian theologian Søren Kierkegaard, who understood Abraham's action as a "teleological suspension of the ethical," a demonstration of such unwavering faith that it superseded a father's love for his son as well as the prohibition of murder. But many post-Holocaust Jewish writers are increasingly reticent even to appear to validate violence in the name of religious faith, and instead suggest that Abraham failed the test and should have raised a protest against God's instruction, just as he raised a protest against the destruction of the cities of Sodom and Gomorrah (Genesis 18).

GENESIS 22

First Aliyah 1 Some time afterward, God put Abraham to the test, saying to him, "Abraham." He answered, "Here I am."

2 "Take your son, your favored one, Isaac, whom you love, and go to the land of Moriah, and offer him there as a burnt offering on one of the heights that I will point out to you."

3 So early next morning, Abraham saddled his ass and took with him two of his servants and his son Isaac. He split the wood for the burnt offering, and he set out for the place of which God had told him.

שני ד בַּיּוֹם הַשְּׁלִישִׁי וַיִּשָּׂא אַבְרָהָם אֶת־עֵינָיו וַיַּרְא אֶת־
הַמָּקוֹם מֵרָחֹק: ה וַיֹּאמֶר אַבְרָהָם אֶל־נְעָרָיו שְׁבוּ־לָכֶם
פֹּה עִם־הַחֲמוֹר וַאֲנִי וְהַנַּעַר נֵלְכָה עַד־כֹּה וְנִשְׁתַּחֲוֶה
וְנָשׁוּבָה אֲלֵיכֶם: ו וַיִּקַּח אַבְרָהָם אֶת־עֲצֵי הָעֹלָה וַיָּשֶׂם
עַל־יִצְחָק בְּנוֹ וַיִּקַּח בְּיָדוֹ אֶת־הָאֵשׁ וְאֶת־הַמַּאֲכֶלֶת
וַיֵּלְכוּ שְׁנֵיהֶם יַחְדָּו: ז וַיֹּאמֶר יִצְחָק אֶל־אַבְרָהָם אָבִיו
וַיֹּאמֶר אָבִי וַיֹּאמֶר הִנֶּנִּי בְנִי וַיֹּאמֶר הִנֵּה הָאֵשׁ וְהָעֵצִים
וְאַיֵּה הַשֶּׂה לְעֹלָה: ח וַיֹּאמֶר אַבְרָהָם אֱלֹהִים יִרְאֶה־לּוֹ
הַשֶּׂה לְעֹלָה בְּנִי וַיֵּלְכוּ שְׁנֵיהֶם יַחְדָּו:

שלישי ט וַיָּבֹאוּ אֶל־הַמָּקוֹם אֲשֶׁר אָמַר־לוֹ הָאֱלֹהִים וַיִּבֶן
שָׁם אַבְרָהָם אֶת־הַמִּזְבֵּחַ וַיַּעֲרֹךְ אֶת־הָעֵצִים וַיַּעֲקֹד
אֶת־יִצְחָק בְּנוֹ וַיָּשֶׂם אֹתוֹ עַל־הַמִּזְבֵּחַ מִמַּעַל לָעֵצִים:
י וַיִּשְׁלַח אַבְרָהָם אֶת־יָדוֹ וַיִּקַּח אֶת־הַמַּאֲכֶלֶת לִשְׁחֹט
אֶת־בְּנוֹ: יא וַיִּקְרָא אֵלָיו מַלְאַךְ יהוה מִן־הַשָּׁמַיִם וַיֹּאמֶר
אַבְרָהָם | אַבְרָהָם וַיֹּאמֶר הִנֵּנִי: יב וַיֹּאמֶר אַל־תִּשְׁלַח יָדְךָ
אֶל־הַנַּעַר וְאַל־תַּעַשׂ לוֹ מְאוּמָה כִּי | עַתָּה יָדַעְתִּי כִּי־יְרֵא
אֱלֹהִים אַתָּה וְלֹא חָשַׂכְתָּ אֶת־בִּנְךָ אֶת־יְחִידְךָ מִמֶּנִּי:

VERSE 5. THEN ABRAHAM SAID TO HIS SERVANTS, "YOU STAY HERE" וַיֹּאמֶר אַבְרָהָם אֶל־נְעָרָיו שְׁבוּ־לָכֶם פֹּה. Abraham may be concealing the truth from his servants (lest they prevent him from carrying out God's instruction), from Isaac (lest he flee), and from himself (lest the frank acknowledgment of his real intention cause his resolve to break). (*The Jewish Study Bible*)

VERSES 6, 8. THE TWO WALKED OFF TOGETHER ... THE TWO OF THEM WALKED ON TOGETHER וַיֵּלְכוּ שְׁנֵיהֶם יַחְדָּו. The text repeats this phrase within the space of a few verses. This leads Rashi to raise the question of whether what is hinted at here is ironic—though they walked together they were of two minds—or whether it is to be understood as meaning that they were truly "together"—that is, Isaac sensed what was intended and accorded with Abraham's resolve.

VERSE 11. A MESSENGER מַלְאַךְ. Originally God addressed Abraham directly; now, it is an angel. Some interpret this shift as implying that Abraham has failed the test by not protesting but rather raising the knife against his child. Indeed, God never again appears to Abraham, and similarly Abraham never again talks to Sarah, his wife. There seems to be total alienation—both human and divine. In contrast, Job, who classically protests against needless suffering, in the end is directly addressed by God.

ABRAHAM! ABRAHAM! אַבְרָהָם אַבְרָהָם. This repetition of the name can convey either urgency or a special relationship between the one addressed and the One who calls.

VERSE 12. DO NOT RAISE YOUR HAND AGAINST THE BOY אַל־תִּשְׁלַח יָדְךָ אֶל־הַנַּעַר. Some commentators remark that the true test was whether Abraham would desist from the slaughter. Would he trust this second voice? Others note that in the ancient world, where the sacrifice of children was practiced among some peoples, the instruction not to sacrifice would have been seen as unique.

YOUR SON, YOUR FAVORED ONE אֶת־בִּנְךָ אֶת־יְחִידְךָ. These two phrases are repetitions of God's initial call, although this time the phrase "whom you love" is left out.

And the Two Walked Together

Later Jewish tradition saw the binding of Isaac as a symbolic precedent for all Jewish martyrdom. In accord with this thinking, Isaac is portrayed as a willing participant in his own sacrifice; in one version of the story, Isaac is understood to have died on the altar and been restored to life by the angel. Later Jewish martyrs could not believe that their own sacrifice was greater than that of the forebears of the people.

"Do Not Raise Your Hand Against the Boy"

Abraham Joshua Heschel describes how he studied the Akedah, the story of the binding of Isaac, with his ḥeder rebbe (teacher) in Poland.

Here is the experience of a child of seven who was reading in school the chapter which tells of the sacrifice of Isaac on the way to Mt. Moriah with his father. "He lay on the altar, bound, waiting to be sacrificed. My heart began to beat even faster; it actually sobbed with pity for Isaac. Behold, Abraham now lifted the knife. And now my heart froze within me with fright. Suddenly the voice of the angel was heard: 'Abraham, lay not your hand upon the lad, for now I know that you fear God.' And here I broke out in tears and wept aloud. 'Why are you crying?' asked the rabbi. 'You know that Isaac was not killed.' And I said to him, still weeping, 'But, Rabbi, supposing the angel had come a second too late?' The rabbi comforted me and calmed me by telling me that an angel cannot come late."

An angel cannot be late, but man, made of flesh and blood, may be.

Second Aliyah 4 On the third day Abraham looked up and saw the place from afar. 5 Then Abraham said to his servants, "You stay here with the ass. The boy and I will go up there; we will worship and we will return to you."

6 Abraham took the wood for the burnt offering and put it on his son Isaac. He himself took the firestone and the knife; and the two walked off together. 7 Then Isaac said to his father Abraham, "Father!" And he answered, "Yes, my son." And he said, "Here are the firestone and the wood; but where is the sheep for the burnt offering?" 8 And Abraham said, "It is God who will see to the sheep for this burnt offering, my son." And the two of them walked on together.

Third Aliyah 9 They arrived at the place of which God had told him. Abraham built an altar there; he laid out the wood; he bound his son Isaac; he laid him on the altar, on top of the wood. 10 And Abraham picked up the knife to slay his son. 11 Then a messenger of ADONAI called to him from heaven: "Abraham! Abraham!" And he answered, "Here I am."

12 "Do not raise your hand against the boy, or do anything to him. For now I know that you fear God, since you have not withheld your son, your favored one, from Me."

יג וַיִּשָּׂא אַבְרָהָם אֶת־עֵינָיו וַיַּרְא וְהִנֵּה־אַיִל אַחַר נֶאֱחַז בַּסְּבַךְ בְּקַרְנָיו וַיֵּלֶךְ אַבְרָהָם וַיִּקַּח אֶת־הָאַיִל וַיַּעֲלֵהוּ לְעֹלָה תַּחַת בְּנוֹ: יד וַיִּקְרָא אַבְרָהָם שֵׁם־הַמָּקוֹם הַהוּא יְהֹוָה | יִרְאֶה אֲשֶׁר יֵאָמֵר הַיּוֹם בְּהַר יְהֹוָה יֵרָאֶה:

רביעי טו וַיִּקְרָא מַלְאַךְ יְהֹוָה אֶל־אַבְרָהָם שֵׁנִית מִן־הַשָּׁמָיִם: טז וַיֹּאמֶר בִּי נִשְׁבַּעְתִּי נְאֻם־יְהֹוָה כִּי יַעַן אֲשֶׁר עָשִׂיתָ אֶת־הַדָּבָר הַזֶּה וְלֹא חָשַׂכְתָּ אֶת־בִּנְךָ אֶת־יְחִידֶךָ: יז כִּי־בָרֵךְ אֲבָרֶכְךָ וְהַרְבָּה אַרְבֶּה אֶת־זַרְעֲךָ כְּכוֹכְבֵי הַשָּׁמַיִם וְכַחוֹל אֲשֶׁר עַל־שְׂפַת הַיָּם וְיִרַשׁ זַרְעֲךָ אֵת שַׁעַר אֹיְבָיו: יח וְהִתְבָּרְכוּ בְזַרְעֲךָ כֹּל גּוֹיֵי הָאָרֶץ עֵקֶב אֲשֶׁר שָׁמַעְתָּ בְּקֹלִי: יט וַיָּשָׁב אַבְרָהָם אֶל־נְעָרָיו וַיָּקֻמוּ וַיֵּלְכוּ יַחְדָּו אֶל־בְּאֵר שָׁבַע וַיֵּשֶׁב אַבְרָהָם בִּבְאֵר שָׁבַע:

חמישי כ וַיְהִי אַחֲרֵי הַדְּבָרִים הָאֵלֶּה וַיֻּגַּד לְאַבְרָהָם לֵאמֹר הִנֵּה יָלְדָה מִלְכָּה גַם־הִוא בָּנִים לְנָחוֹר אָחִיךָ: כא אֶת־עוּץ בְּכֹרוֹ וְאֶת־בּוּז אָחִיו וְאֶת־קְמוּאֵל אֲבִי אֲרָם: כב וְאֶת־כֶּשֶׂד וְאֶת־חֲזוֹ וְאֶת־פִּלְדָּשׁ וְאֶת־יִדְלָף וְאֵת בְּתוּאֵל: כג וּבְתוּאֵל יָלַד אֶת־רִבְקָה שְׁמֹנָה אֵלֶּה יָלְדָה מִלְכָּה לְנָחוֹר אֲחִי אַבְרָהָם: כד וּפִילַגְשׁוֹ וּשְׁמָהּ רְאוּמָה וַתֵּלֶד גַּם־הִוא אֶת־טֶבַח וְאֶת־גַּחַם וְאֶת־תַּחַשׁ וְאֶת־מַעֲכָה:

VERSE 13. ABRAHAM LOOKED UP וַיִּשָּׂא אַבְרָהָם. This is strikingly similar to the situation of Hagar, who also lifts up her eyes and is suddenly capable of perceiving. Rashi quotes an older midrash that the *ayil*, the ram, is one of the ten things in existence before creation; i.e., the *ayil* was always there and Abraham never saw it—just like Hagar and the well. Could it be that Abraham has missed something central about the very nature of the world around him?

A RAM אַיִל אַחַר. The Jewish Publication Society translation used here reads *ehad*, following many Hebrew manuscripts and ancient versions; the traditional Masoretic text reads *ahar*, "after."

VERSE 14. ADONAI, THERE IS VISION יהוה יִרְאֶה. The Hebrew may be read as "God is seen" or as "the supplicant is seen."

VERSE 19. The Torah reports that Abraham and his servants returned to Beer-sheba, but where is Isaac? Rabbinic midrash offers many different responses: some say that Isaac dwelled in the Garden of Eden for the next three years (see, for instance, Midrash Hagadol), remarking that Isaac died and was resurrected; some say that he went to study in the yeshiva led by Eber, Noah's grandson, much as children now go off to university. Some modern commentators note that this is quite different from the description of father and son walking "together" toward the binding and see this verse as indicating Isaac's alienation from his father; Abraham and Isaac never appear together again in the biblical text.

VERSE 23. REBECCA אֶת־רִבְקָה. After the almost tragic narrative of the Akedah, the reading ends with the joyous announcement of births and an assurance that there will be future generations.

Where Is Sarah?

Where is Sarah? The Rabbis answer: after Abraham and Isaac leave, Sarah goes to Hebron, looking for them. Satan—the tempter, the Adversary, the Alter Ego—appears to her and reveals that Abraham intends to sacrifice her son; hearing this, her heart breaks from sorrow and she dies, as it is written: "Sarah died in Kiryat Arba—now Hebron" (23:2). But others teach that Satan reveals to her that Abraham has spared her son from his knife; and her heart bursts with joy. Such is the anatomy of a mother's heart.

—ELLEN FRANKEL

Heritage

The ram came last of all. And Abraham did not know that it came to answer the boy's question—first of his strength when his day was on the wane.

The old man raised his head. Seeing that it was no dream and that the angel stood there—the knife slipped from his hand.

The boy, released from his bonds, saw his father's back.

Isaac, as the story goes, was not sacrificed. He lived for many years, saw what life's pleasures had to offer, until his eyesight dimmed.

But he bequeathed that hour to his offspring. They are born with a knife in their hearts.

—ḤAYIM GOURI

13 When Abraham looked up, his eye fell upon a ram, caught in the thicket by its horns. So Abraham went and took the ram and offered it up as a burnt offering in place of his son. 14 And Abraham named that site *Adonai-yireh*, whence the present saying, "On the mount of ADONAI, there is vision."

Fourth Aliyah 15 The messenger of ADONAI called to Abraham a second time from heaven, 16 and said, "By Myself I swear," ADONAI declares: "Because you have done this and have not withheld your son, your favored one, 17 I will bestow My blessing upon you and make your descendants as numerous as the stars of heaven and the sands on the seashore; and your descendants shall seize the gates of their foes. 18 All the nations of the earth shall bless themselves by your descendants, because you have obeyed My command." 19 Abraham then returned to his servants, and they departed together for Beer-sheba; and Abraham stayed in Beer-sheba.

Fifth Aliyah 20 Some time later, Abraham was told, "Milcah too has borne sons to your brother Nahor: 21 Uz the first-born, and Buz his brother, and Kemuel the father of Aram; 22 and Chesed, Hazo, Pildash, Jidlaph, and Bethuel"— 23 Bethuel being the father of Rebecca. These eight Milcah bore to Nahor, Abraham's brother. 24 And his concubine, whose name was Reumah, also bore [sons]— Tebah, Gaham, and Tahash—and [a daughter,] Maacah.

Both Torah scrolls are placed on the Reader's desk.

יִתְגַּדַּל וְיִתְקַדַּשׁ שְׁמֵהּ רַבָּא, בְּעָלְמָא דִּי בְרָא, כִרְעוּתֵהּ,
וְיַמְלִיךְ מַלְכוּתֵהּ בְּחַיֵּיכוֹן וּבְיוֹמֵיכוֹן וּבְחַיֵּי דְכָל־בֵּית
יִשְׂרָאֵל, בַּעֲגָלָא וּבִזְמַן קָרִיב, וְאִמְרוּ אָמֵן.

יְהֵא שְׁמֵהּ רַבָּא מְבָרַךְ לְעָלַם וּלְעָלְמֵי עָלְמַיָּא.

יִתְבָּרַךְ וְיִשְׁתַּבַּח וְיִתְפָּאַר וְיִתְרוֹמַם וְיִתְנַשֵּׂא וְיִתְהַדָּר
וְיִתְעַלֶּה וְיִתְהַלָּל שְׁמֵהּ דְּקֻדְשָׁא, בְּרִיךְ הוּא, לְעֵלָּא לְעֵלָּא
מִכָּל־בִּרְכָתָא וְשִׁירָתָא תֻּשְׁבְּחָתָא וְנֶחֱמָתָא דַּאֲמִירָן
בְּעָלְמָא, וְאִמְרוּ אָמֵן.

הַגְבָּהַת הַתּוֹרָה

*A Magbiah and Golel are called to raise and tie each Sefer Torah after it is read.
As the Torah is lifted, we recite:*

וְזֹאת הַתּוֹרָה אֲשֶׁר־שָׂם מֹשֶׁה לִפְנֵי בְּנֵי יִשְׂרָאֵל,
עַל־פִּי יהוה בְּיַד־מֹשֶׁה.

מַפְטִיר לְרֹאשׁ הַשָּׁנָה

בְּמִדְבַּר כט

א וּבַחֹדֶשׁ הַשְּׁבִיעִי בְּאֶחָד לַחֹדֶשׁ מִקְרָא־קֹדֶשׁ יִהְיֶה לָכֶם
כָּל־מְלֶאכֶת עֲבֹדָה לֹא תַעֲשׂוּ יוֹם תְּרוּעָה יִהְיֶה לָכֶם:
ב וַעֲשִׂיתֶם עֹלָה לְרֵיחַ נִיחֹחַ לַיהוה פַּר בֶּן־בָּקָר אֶחָד
אַיִל אֶחָד כְּבָשִׂים בְּנֵי־שָׁנָה שִׁבְעָה תְּמִימִם: ג וּמִנְחָתָם
סֹלֶת בְּלוּלָה בַשֶּׁמֶן שְׁלֹשָׁה עֶשְׂרֹנִים לַפָּר שְׁנֵי עֶשְׂרֹנִים
לָאָיִל: ד וְעִשָּׂרוֹן אֶחָד לַכֶּבֶשׂ הָאֶחָד לְשִׁבְעַת הַכְּבָשִׂים:
ה וּשְׂעִיר־עִזִּים אֶחָד חַטָּאת לְכַפֵּר עֲלֵיכֶם: ו מִלְּבַד
עֹלַת הַחֹדֶשׁ וּמִנְחָתָהּ וְעֹלַת הַתָּמִיד וּמִנְחָתָהּ וְנִסְכֵּיהֶם
כְּמִשְׁפָּטָם לְרֵיחַ נִיחֹחַ אִשֶּׁה לַיהוה:

THIS IS THE TORAH וְזֹאת הַתּוֹרָה. The Rabbis combined Deuteronomy 4:44 and Numbers 9:23, underscoring that our entire Torah came from Moses as dictated by God. This theological claim is not made in the Bible itself. As this passage conflates two biblical verses, the 20th-century Orthodox Jewish thinker Joseph Ber Soloveitchik, for instance, did not recite it.

When reciting this passage, some people hold up or kiss the *tzitzit* of their *tallit*, to affirm their own active fulfillment of the Torah.

VERSE 1. IN THE SEVENTH MONTH וּבַחֹדֶשׁ הַשְּׁבִיעִי. Many scholars speculate that in biblical times, the southern kingdom of Judah celebrated its new year in the spring and the northern kingdom of Israel in the fall; the first month for one was the seventh for the other. Later Judaism, inheriting a variety of dates marking a new year, assigned each one a different function. The Rabbis reckoned historical events, including the annual pilgrimage festivals, from the first of Nisan (in the spring). Meanwhile, they associated the first day of the seventh month, Tishrei (in the fall) with the creation story, Adam and Eve's sin, and God's annual judgment of the world.

YOU SHALL NOT WORK AT YOUR OCCUPATIONS כָּל־מְלֶאכֶת עֲבֹדָה לֹא תַעֲשׂוּ. Other "work" is allowed. Unlike for Shabbat, the Rabbis allowed cooking and carrying in celebration of the holy day.

A DAY WHEN THE HORN IS SOUNDED יוֹם תְּרוּעָה. Maimonides cites this verse as the source for the commandment to listen to the shofar blasts (Mishneh Torah, Laws of Shofar 1:1).

¶ The following may be sung as the Torah is tied.

תּוֹרָה צִוָּה לָנוּ מֹשֶׁה,
מוֹרָשָׁה קְהִלַּת יַעֲקֹב.

Moses commanded the observance of Torah; it is the inheritance of the community of Jacob.

Torah tzivvah lanu moshe, morashah k'hillat ya·akov.

The Holy Day Sacrifice

Said Abraham to the Holy One: "Should the people Israel sin against You, Heaven forbid, You might treat them as the generation that perished in the flood!"

Said God: "No."

Said Abraham: "Give me a sign."

God directed Abraham to offer animal sacrifices and Abraham came to understand the atoning power of that ritual act. And he was able to envision that atonement would be gained for the people Israel through the ritual of sacrifice at the Temple in Jerusalem.

Said Abraham: "That will suffice while the Temple is standing. But when there is no Temple, what will become of the people Israel?"

Said God: "I have already arranged for these passages concerning the sacrifices. Whenever they read about the sacrifices I shall consider them as having offered sacrifices in My Presence, and I shall forgive them all their sins."

—BABYLONIAN TALMUD, MEGILLAH
(trans. Jules Harlow)

Ḥatzi Kaddish

Both Torah scrolls are placed on the Reader's desk.

May God's great name be exalted and hallowed throughout the created world, as is God's wish. May God's sovereignty soon be established, in your lifetime and in your days, and in the days of all the House of Israel. And respond with: *Amen.*

May God's great name be acknowledged forever and ever!
Y'hei sh'meih rabba m'varakh l'alam u-l'almei almayya.

May the name of the Holy One be acknowledged and celebrated, lauded and worshipped, exalted and honored, extolled and acclaimed—though God, who is blessed, *b'rikh hu,* is truly far beyond all acknowledgment and praise, or any expressions of gratitude or consolation ever spoken in the world. And respond with: *Amen.*

Lifting the Torah

A Magbiah and Golel are called to raise and tie each Sefer Torah after it is read. As the Torah is lifted, we recite:

This is the Torah, God's word by Moses' hand, which Moses set before the people Israel.

V'zot ha-torah asher sam mosheh lifnei b'nei yisra·el al pi Adonai b'yad mosheh.

Maftir for Rosh Hashanah

NUMBERS 29

1 In the seventh month, on the first day of the month, you shall observe a sacred occasion: you shall not work at your occupations. You shall observe it as a day when the horn is sounded. 2 You shall present a burnt offering of pleasing odor to ADONAI: one bull of the herd, one ram, and seven yearling lambs, without blemish. 3 The grain offering with them— choice flour with oil mixed in—shall be: three-tenths of a measure for a bull, two-tenths for a ram, 4 and one-tenth for each of the seven lambs. 5 And there shall be one goat for a purification offering, to make expiation in your behalf— 6 in addition to the burnt offering of the new moon with its meal offering and the regular burnt offering with its grain offering, each with its libation as prescribed, gifts of pleasing odor to ADONAI.

A male:

מִי שֶׁבֵּרַךְ אֲבוֹתֵינוּ אַבְרָהָם יִצְחָק וְיַעֲקֹב, [וְאִמּוֹתֵינוּ] שָׂרָה רִבְקָה רָחֵל וְלֵאָה,
הוּא יְבָרֵךְ אֶת _____ בֶּן _____ שֶׁעָלָה הַיּוֹם לִכְבוֹד הַמָּקוֹם וְלִכְבוֹד
הַתּוֹרָה וְלִכְבוֹד יוֹם הַדִּין. הַקָּדוֹשׁ בָּרוּךְ הוּא יִשְׁמֹר אוֹתוֹ וְאֶת־כָּל־מִשְׁפַּחְתּוֹ,
וְיִשְׁלַח בְּרָכָה וְהַצְלָחָה בְּכָל־מַעֲשֵׂה יָדָיו, וְיִכְתְּבֵהוּ וְיַחְתְּמֵהוּ לְחַיִּים טוֹבִים בְּזֶה
יוֹם הַדִּין עִם כָּל־יִשְׂרָאֵל אֶחָיו וְאַחְיוֹתָיו, וְנֹאמַר אָמֵן.

A female:

מִי שֶׁבֵּרַךְ אֲבוֹתֵינוּ אַבְרָהָם יִצְחָק וְיַעֲקֹב, [וְאִמּוֹתֵינוּ] שָׂרָה רִבְקָה רָחֵל וְלֵאָה,
הוּא יְבָרֵךְ אֶת _____ בַּת _____ שֶׁעָלְתָה הַיּוֹם לִכְבוֹד הַמָּקוֹם וְלִכְבוֹד
הַתּוֹרָה וְלִכְבוֹד יוֹם הַדִּין. הַקָּדוֹשׁ בָּרוּךְ הוּא יִשְׁמֹר אוֹתָהּ וְאֶת־כָּל־מִשְׁפַּחְתָּהּ,
וְיִשְׁלַח בְּרָכָה וְהַצְלָחָה בְּכָל־מַעֲשֵׂה יָדֶיהָ, וְיִכְתְּבֶהָ וְיַחְתְּמָהּ לְחַיִּים טוֹבִים בְּזֶה
יוֹם הַדִּין עִם כָּל־יִשְׂרָאֵל אַחֶיהָ וְאַחְיוֹתֶיהָ, וְנֹאמַר אָמֵן.

Plural:

מִי שֶׁבֵּרַךְ אֲבוֹתֵינוּ אַבְרָהָם יִצְחָק וְיַעֲקֹב, [וְאִמּוֹתֵינוּ] שָׂרָה רִבְקָה רָחֵל וְלֵאָה,
הוּא יְבָרֵךְ אֶת _____ וְאֶת _____ , אֲשֶׁר עָלוּ הַיּוֹם לִכְבוֹד הַמָּקוֹם וְלִכְבוֹד
הַתּוֹרָה וְלִכְבוֹד יוֹם הַדִּין. הַקָּדוֹשׁ בָּרוּךְ הוּא יִשְׁמֹר אוֹתָם וְאֶת־כָּל־
מִשְׁפְּחוֹתֵיהֶם, וְיִשְׁלַח בְּרָכָה וְהַצְלָחָה בְּכָל־מַעֲשֵׂה יְדֵיהֶם וְיִכְתְּבֵם
וְיַחְתְּמֵם לְחַיִּים טוֹבִים בְּזֶה יוֹם הַדִּין עִם כָּל־יִשְׂרָאֵל אֲחֵיהֶם
וְאַחְיוֹתֵיהֶם, וְנֹאמַר אָמֵן.

בִּרְכַּת הַגּוֹמֵל

*This b'rakhah is recited by one who has recovered from a serious illness
or survived a life-threatening crisis.*

בָּרוּךְ אַתָּה יהוה אֱלֹהֵינוּ מֶלֶךְ הָעוֹלָם, הַגּוֹמֵל לְחַיָּבִים
טוֹבוֹת, שֶׁגְּמָלַנִי כָּל־טוֹב.

We respond:

מִי
שֶׁגְּמָלֵךְ *for a group:* שֶׁגְּמָלְכֶם / *for a female:* שֶׁגְּמָלֵךְ / *for a male:* שֶׁגְּמָלְךָ
כָּל־טוֹב,
הוּא (יִגְמָלְךָ / יִגְמְלֵךְ / יִגְמָלְכֶם) כָּל־טוֹב, סֶלָה.

BIRKAT HA-GOMEL בִּרְכַּת
הַגּוֹמֵל. In thanking God for
having been saved from
danger and calamity, we are
conscious of the fragility of
our lives and the gratitude
with which we should meet
each day of our lives. Ellen
Frankel, a contemporary
writer, remarks further that
through the recitation of
this b'rakhah, we summon
support from all those who
care about our welfare.

Mi-she-beirakh: Blessing for Those Called to the Torah

A male:

May the One who blessed our ancestors Abraham, Isaac, and Jacob, Sarah, Rebecca, Rachel, and Leah bless _____, who has ascended today to honor God, the Torah, and the Day of Judgment. May the Holy Blessed One protect him and his entire family, bring blessing and success to all the works of his hands, and inscribe and seal him for a good life on this Day of Judgment, together with all his fellow Jews, and let us say: *Amen.*

A female:

May the One who blessed our ancestors Abraham, Isaac, and Jacob, Sarah, Rebecca, Rachel, and Leah bless _____, who has ascended today to honor God, the Torah, and the Day of Judgment. May the Holy Blessed One protect her and her entire family, bring blessing and success to all the works of her hands, and inscribe and seal her for a good life on this Day of Judgment, together with all her fellow Jews, and let us say: *Amen.*

Plural:

May the One who blessed our ancestors Abraham, Isaac, and Jacob, Sarah, Rebecca, Rachel, and Leah bless _____, who have ascended today to honor God, the Torah, and the Day of Judgment. May the Holy Blessed One protect them and their entire families, bring blessing and success to all the works of their hands, and inscribe and seal them for a good life on this Day of Judgment, together with all their fellow Jews, and let us say: *Amen.*

Birkat Ha-gomel

This b'rakhah is recited by one who has recovered from a serious illness or survived a life-threatening crisis.

Barukh atah ADONAI, our God, ruler of time and space, who bestows goodness on us despite our imperfections, and who has treated me so favorably.

Barukh atah Adonai eloheinu melekh ha-olam,
ha-gomel l'ḥayyavim tovot, she-g'malani kol tov.

We respond:

May the One who has shown such favor to you continue to bestow all that is good upon you, *selah.*

Mi
(for a male: she-g'mal'kha / for a female: she-g'maleikh / for a group: she-g'malkhem)
kol tov,
hu (for a male: yigmal'kha / for a female: yigm'leikh / for a group: yigmalkhem)
kol tov, selah.

הפטרה ליום ראשון

On the second day, we continue on page 111.

בְּרָכָה שֶׁלִּפְנֵי הַהַפְטָרָה

בָּרוּךְ אַתָּה יהוה אֱלֹהֵינוּ מֶלֶךְ הָעוֹלָם, אֲשֶׁר בָּחַר
בִּנְבִיאִים טוֹבִים, וְרָצָה בְדִבְרֵיהֶם הַנֶּאֱמָרִים בֶּאֱמֶת.
בָּרוּךְ אַתָּה יהוה, הַבּוֹחֵר בַּתּוֹרָה וּבְמֹשֶׁה עַבְדּוֹ
וּבְיִשְׂרָאֵל עַמּוֹ וּבִנְבִיאֵי הָאֱמֶת וָצֶדֶק.

שְׁמוּאֵל א א

א וַיְהִי אִישׁ אֶחָד מִן־הָרָמָתַיִם צוֹפִים מֵהַר אֶפְרָיִם וּשְׁמוֹ
אֶלְקָנָה בֶּן־יְרֹחָם בֶּן־אֱלִיהוּא בֶּן־תֹּחוּ בֶן־צוּף אֶפְרָתִי׃
ב וְלוֹ שְׁתֵּי נָשִׁים שֵׁם אַחַת חַנָּה וְשֵׁם הַשֵּׁנִית פְּנִנָּה וַיְהִי
לִפְנִנָּה יְלָדִים וּלְחַנָּה אֵין יְלָדִים׃ ג וְעָלָה הָאִישׁ הַהוּא
מֵעִירוֹ מִיָּמִים | יָמִימָה לְהִשְׁתַּחֲוֺת וְלִזְבֹּחַ לַיהוה צְבָאוֹת
בְּשִׁלֹה וְשָׁם שְׁנֵי בְנֵי־עֵלִי חָפְנִי וּפִנְחָס כֹּהֲנִים לַיהוה׃
ד וַיְהִי הַיּוֹם וַיִּזְבַּח אֶלְקָנָה וְנָתַן לִפְנִנָּה אִשְׁתּוֹ וּלְכָל־בָּנֶיהָ
וּבְנוֹתֶיהָ מָנוֹת׃ ה וּלְחַנָּה יִתֵּן מָנָה אַחַת אַפָּיִם כִּי אֶת־
חַנָּה אָהֵב וַיהוה סָגַר רַחְמָהּ׃ ו וְכִעֲסַתָּה צָרָתָהּ גַּם־כַּעַס
בַּעֲבוּר הַרְעִמָהּ כִּי־סָגַר יהוה בְּעַד רַחְמָהּ׃ ז וְכֵן יַעֲשֶׂה
שָׁנָה בְשָׁנָה מִדֵּי עֲלֹתָהּ בְּבֵית יהוה כֵּן תַּכְעִסֶנָּה וַתִּבְכֶּה
וְלֹא תֹאכַל׃ ח וַיֹּאמֶר לָהּ אֶלְקָנָה אִישָׁהּ חַנָּה לָמֶה תִבְכִּי
וְלָמֶה לֹא תֹאכְלִי וְלָמֶה יֵרַע לְבָבֵךְ הֲלוֹא אָנֹכִי טוֹב לָךְ
מֵעֲשָׂרָה בָּנִים׃ ט וַתָּקָם חַנָּה אַחֲרֵי אָכְלָה בְשִׁלֹה וְאַחֲרֵי
שָׁתֹה וְעֵלִי הַכֹּהֵן יֹשֵׁב עַל־הַכִּסֵּא עַל־מְזוּזַת הֵיכַל יהוה׃

HAFTARAH, DAY 1. The Haftarah readings taken from the prophetic books of the Bible often complement the Torah reading by adding a different layer of understanding. Like the Torah reading, this Haftarah features a couple struggling with infertility, as well as a fertile "other" woman who disdains the barren wife. Characteristically in the Bible, infertility is a sign of the chosenness of both the woman and the child to be born to her. It is also emblematic of the way in which life's most difficult and painful challenges, particularly in areas which seem to come easily to others, may also be moments of deepening one's relationship with God. Additionally, Hannah's giving up of Samuel to the work of God anticipates, albeit in a milder fashion, Abraham's giving up of Isaac, the subject of tomorrow's Torah reading.

Thus, the Haftarah for the first day picks up on themes in the Torah readings of both days. But the motives and behaviors of the characters are quite different: Sarah sends Ishmael away in order to keep Isaac close, while Hannah willingly gives up her own child. Isaac is bound as sacrifice and lives life in his father's shadow, whereas Samuel will be an active prophet, crowning and dethroning. Some congregations conclude the Haftarah at the end of the narrative (1:1–28), others conclude with the Song of Hannah (2:1–10), and some read only the Song.

VERSE 3. SHILOH. שִׁלֹה. Joshua had established Shiloh as the resting place of the Ark.

VERSE 8. AM I NOT MORE DEVOTED TO YOU THAN TEN SONS? הֲלוֹא אָנֹכִי טוֹב לָךְ מֵעֲשָׂרָה בָּנִים. Elkanah's well-meaning effort to comfort Hannah is unsuccessful because, rather than listening to and addressing the root of Hannah's sadness, he imposes his own understanding of why she is sad. Later on, the priest Eli also makes incorrect assumptions about the reasons for Hannah's behavior (verses 13–14); he prays on Hannah's behalf only after he is able to listen to her. On Rosh Hashanah, as we pray for God to listen to our prayers, this passage highlights the importance of deep empathic listening, especially at times of personal crisis—and how frequently our listening is less than perceptive.

HAFTARAH READING, FIRST DAY

On the second day, we continue on page 111.

Blessing before the Haftarah

Barukh atah ADONAI, our God, ruler of time and space, who chose worthy prophets; and who was pleased by their words, spoken in truth. *Barukh atah* ADONAI, who has chosen the Torah, Moses Your servant, Your people Israel, and the prophets of truth and justice.

I SAMUEL 1

1 There was a man from Ramathaim of the Zuphites, in the hill country of Ephraim, whose name was Elkanah son of Jeroham son of Elihu son of Tohu son of Zuph, an Ephraimite. 2 He had two wives, one named Hannah and the other Peninnah; Peninnah had children, but Hannah was childless. 3 This man used to go up from his town every year to worship and to offer sacrifice to *Adonai Tz'va·ot* at Shiloh.—Hophni and Phinehas, the two sons of Eli, were priests of ADONAI there.

4 One such day, Elkanah offered a sacrifice. He used to give portions to his wife Peninnah and to all her sons and daughters; 5 but to Hannah he would give one portion only—though Hannah was his favorite—for ADONAI had closed her womb. 6 Moreover, her rival, to make her miserable, would taunt her that ADONAI had closed her womb. 7 This happened year after year: Every time she went up to the House of ADONAI, the other would taunt her, so that she wept and would not eat. 8 Her husband Elkanah said to her, "Hannah, why are you crying and why aren't you eating? Why are you so sad? Am I not more devoted to you than ten sons?"

9 After they had eaten and drunk at Shiloh, Hannah rose.—The priest Eli was sitting on the seat near the doorpost of the temple of ADONAI.—

י וְהִיא מָרַת נָפֶשׁ וַתִּתְפַּלֵּל עַל־יהוה וּבָכֹה תִבְכֶּה:
יא וַתִּדֹּר נֶדֶר וַתֹּאמַר יהוה צְבָאוֹת אִם־רָאֹה תִרְאֶה |
בָּעֳנִי אֲמָתֶךָ וּזְכַרְתַּנִי וְלֹא־תִשְׁכַּח אֶת־אֲמָתֶךָ וְנָתַתָּה
לַאֲמָתְךָ זֶרַע אֲנָשִׁים וּנְתַתִּיו לַיהוה כָּל־יְמֵי חַיָּיו וּמוֹרָה
לֹא־יַעֲלֶה עַל־רֹאשׁוֹ: יב וְהָיָה כִּי הִרְבְּתָה לְהִתְפַּלֵּל לִפְנֵי
יהוה וְעֵלִי שֹׁמֵר אֶת־פִּיהָ: יג וְחַנָּה הִיא מְדַבֶּרֶת עַל־
לִבָּהּ רַק שְׂפָתֶיהָ נָּעוֹת וְקוֹלָהּ לֹא יִשָּׁמֵעַ וַיַּחְשְׁבֶהָ עֵלִי
לְשִׁכֹּרָה: יד וַיֹּאמֶר אֵלֶיהָ עֵלִי עַד־מָתַי תִּשְׁתַּכָּרִין הָסִירִי
אֶת־יֵינֵךְ מֵעָלָיִךְ: טו וַתַּעַן חַנָּה וַתֹּאמֶר לֹא אֲדֹנִי אִשָּׁה
קְשַׁת־רוּחַ אָנֹכִי וְיַיִן וְשֵׁכָר לֹא שָׁתִיתִי וָאֶשְׁפֹּךְ אֶת־
נַפְשִׁי לִפְנֵי יהוה: טז אַל־תִּתֵּן אֶת־אֲמָתְךָ לִפְנֵי בַּת־
בְּלִיָּעַל כִּי־מֵרֹב שִׂיחִי וְכַעְסִי דִּבַּרְתִּי עַד־הֵנָּה: יז וַיַּעַן עֵלִי
וַיֹּאמֶר לְכִי לְשָׁלוֹם וֵאלֹהֵי יִשְׂרָאֵל יִתֵּן אֶת־שֵׁלָתֵךְ אֲשֶׁר
שָׁאַלְתְּ מֵעִמּוֹ: יח וַתֹּאמֶר תִּמְצָא שִׁפְחָתְךָ חֵן בְּעֵינֶיךָ
וַתֵּלֶךְ הָאִשָּׁה לְדַרְכָּהּ וַתֹּאכַל וּפָנֶיהָ לֹא־הָיוּ־לָהּ עוֹד:
יט וַיַּשְׁכִּמוּ בַבֹּקֶר וַיִּשְׁתַּחֲווּ לִפְנֵי יהוה וַיָּשֻׁבוּ וַיָּבֹאוּ
אֶל־בֵּיתָם הָרָמָתָה וַיֵּדַע אֶלְקָנָה אֶת־חַנָּה אִשְׁתּוֹ וַיִּזְכְּרֶהָ
יהוה: כ וַיְהִי לִתְקֻפוֹת הַיָּמִים וַתַּהַר חַנָּה וַתֵּלֶד בֵּן
וַתִּקְרָא אֶת־שְׁמוֹ שְׁמוּאֵל כִּי מֵיהוה שְׁאִלְתִּיו: כא וַיַּעַל
הָאִישׁ אֶלְקָנָה וְכָל־בֵּיתוֹ לִזְבֹּחַ לַיהוה אֶת־זֶבַח הַיָּמִים
וְאֶת־נִדְרוֹ: כב וְחַנָּה לֹא עָלָתָה כִּי־אָמְרָה לְאִישָׁהּ עַד
יִגָּמֵל הַנַּעַר וַהֲבִאֹתִיו וְנִרְאָה אֶת־פְּנֵי יהוה וְיָשַׁב שָׁם
עַד־עוֹלָם: כג וַיֹּאמֶר לָהּ אֶלְקָנָה אִישָׁהּ עֲשִׂי הַטּוֹב
בְּעֵינַיִךְ שְׁבִי עַד־גָּמְלֵךְ אֹתוֹ אַךְ יָקֵם יהוה אֶת־דְּבָרוֹ
וַתֵּשֶׁב הָאִשָּׁה וַתֵּינֶק אֶת־בְּנָהּ עַד־גָּמְלָהּ אֹתוֹ:
כד וַתַּעֲלֵהוּ עִמָּהּ כַּאֲשֶׁר גְּמָלַתּוּ בְּפָרִים שְׁלֹשָׁה וְאֵיפָה
אַחַת קֶמַח וְנֵבֶל יַיִן וַתְּבִאֵהוּ בֵית־יהוה שִׁלוֹ וְהַנַּעַר
נָעַר: כה וַיִּשְׁחֲטוּ אֶת־הַפָּר וַיָּבִאוּ אֶת־הַנַּעַר אֶל־עֵלִי:
כו וַתֹּאמֶר בִּי אֲדֹנִי חֵי נַפְשְׁךָ אֲדֹנִי אֲנִי הָאִשָּׁה הַנִּצֶּבֶת
עִמְּכָה בָּזֶה לְהִתְפַּלֵּל אֶל־יהוה: כז אֶל־הַנַּעַר הַזֶּה
הִתְפַּלָּלְתִּי וַיִּתֵּן יהוה לִי אֶת־שְׁאֵלָתִי אֲשֶׁר שָׁאַלְתִּי
מֵעִמּוֹ: כח וְגַם אָנֹכִי הִשְׁאִלְתִּהוּ לַיהוה כָּל־הַיָּמִים אֲשֶׁר
הָיָה הוּא שָׁאוּל לַיהוה וַיִּשְׁתַּחוּ שָׁם לַיהוה:

VERSE 13. Hannah became a model of prayer for the Rabbis, who based much of our practice regarding recitation of the Amidah, the silent prayer, on this chapter in the Book of Samuel.

VERSE 17. Remarkably, Eli not only attends to Hannah's explanation, but also recants his prior harsh judgment and blesses Hannah.

VERSES 27–28. Forms of the verb שאל, "to ask," "borrow," "lend," are repeated several times in these verses. On Rosh Hashanah we ask for life. What we may come to understand is that our lives are lent to us by God. And God borrows us for—asks us to do—God's service.

Reversals and
renewals hold
special power on
Rosh Hashanah.
Contemporary
families struggling
with the problems
of infertility may
find themselves
identifying with
the stories of Sarah
and Hannah and
inspired by them. Or
they may find these
stories difficult for
them, when their
own dreams are
unrealized. But these
narratives encom-
pass more than the
birth of children,
as basic as that is to
them. Sarah's song
of laughter and
Hannah's prayer of
success alert us to
the unexpected, the
changes and won-
ders that can spark
our lives as a new
year and new season
come upon us.

—FRANCINE
KLAGSBRUN

10 In her wretchedness, she prayed to ADONAI, weeping all the while. 11 And she made this vow: "O *Adonai Tz'va·ot*, if You will look upon the suffering of Your maidservant and will remember me and not forget Your maidservant, and if You will grant Your maidservant a male child, I will dedicate him to ADONAI for all the days of his life; and no razor shall ever touch his head."

12 As she kept on praying before ADONAI, Eli watched her mouth. 13 Now Hannah was praying in her heart; only her lips moved, but her voice could not be heard. So Eli thought she was drunk. 14 Eli said to her, "How long will you make a drunken spectacle of your-self? Sober up!" 15 And Hannah replied, "Oh no, my lord! I am a very unhappy woman. I have drunk no wine or other strong drink, but I have been pouring out my heart to ADONAI. 16 Do not take your maidservant for a worthless woman; I have only been speak-ing all this time out of my great anguish and distress." 17 "Then go in peace," said Eli, "and may the God of Israel grant you what you have asked." 18 She answered, "You are most kind to your handmaid." So the woman left, and she ate, and was no longer downcast. 19 Early the next morning, they bowed low before ADONAI, and they went back home to Ramah.

Elkanah knew his wife Hannah and ADONAI remembered her. 20 Hannah conceived, and at the turn of the year bore a son. She named him Samuel, meaning, "I asked ADONAI for him." 21 And when the man Elkanah and all his household were going up to offer to ADONAI the annual sacrifice and his votive sacrifice, 22 Hannah did not go up. She said to her husband, "When the child is weaned, I will bring him. For when he has appeared before ADONAI, he must remain there for good." 23 Her husband Elkanah said to her, "Do as you think best. Stay home until you have weaned him. May ADONAI's word be fulfilled." So the woman stayed home and nursed her son until she had weaned him.

24 When she had weaned him, she took him up with her, along with three bulls, one *ephah* of flour, and a jar of wine. And though the boy was still very young, she brought him to the House of ADONAI at Shiloh. 25 After slaughtering the bull, they brought the boy to Eli. 26 She said, "Please, my lord! As you live, my lord, I am the woman who stood here beside you and prayed to ADONAI. 27 It was this boy I prayed for; and ADONAI has granted me what I asked. 28 I, in turn, hereby lend him to ADONAI. For as long as he lives he is lent to ADONAI." And they bowed low there before ADONAI.

Some congregations end here. For concluding b'rakhot, turn to page 114.

VERSE 1. AND HANNAH PRAYED וַתִּתְפַּלֵּל חַנָּה. A late medieval tradition observed: "This teaches that women are obligated to pray, for Hannah used to pray eighteen b'rakhot" (Yalkut Shimoni, 1 Samuel 2.80). The Hebrew word for "eighteen" (sh'moneh esreih) designates the weekday Amidah.

א וַתִּתְפַּלֵּל חַנָּה וַתֹּאמַר
עָלַץ לִבִּי בַּיהוָה רָמָה קַרְנִי בַּיהוָה
רָחַב פִּי עַל־אוֹיְבַי כִּי שָׂמַחְתִּי בִּישׁוּעָתֶךָ:
ב אֵין־קָדוֹשׁ כַּיהוָה כִּי אֵין בִּלְתֶּךָ
וְאֵין צוּר כֵּאלֹהֵינוּ:
ג אַל־תַּרְבּוּ תְדַבְּרוּ גְּבֹהָה גְבֹהָה
יֵצֵא עָתָק מִפִּיכֶם
כִּי אֵל דֵּעוֹת יְהוָֹה וְלוֹ נִתְכְּנוּ עֲלִלוֹת:
ד קֶשֶׁת גִּבֹּרִים חַתִּים וְנִכְשָׁלִים אָזְרוּ חָיִל:
ה שְׂבֵעִים בַּלֶּחֶם נִשְׂכָּרוּ וּרְעֵבִים חָדֵלּוּ
עַד־עֲקָרָה יָלְדָה שִׁבְעָה וְרַבַּת בָּנִים אֻמְלָלָה:
ו יְהוָה מֵמִית וּמְחַיֶּה מוֹרִיד שְׁאוֹל וַיָּעַל:
ז יְהוָה מוֹרִישׁ וּמַעֲשִׁיר מַשְׁפִּיל אַף־מְרוֹמֵם:
ח מֵקִים מֵעָפָר דָּל מֵאַשְׁפֹּת יָרִים אֶבְיוֹן
לְהוֹשִׁיב עִם־נְדִיבִים וְכִסֵּא כָבוֹד יַנְחִלֵם:
כִּי לַיהוָה מְצֻקֵי אֶרֶץ וַיָּשֶׁת עֲלֵיהֶם תֵּבֵל:
ט רַגְלֵי חֲסִידָיו יִשְׁמֹר וּרְשָׁעִים בַּחֹשֶׁךְ יִדָּמּוּ
כִּי־לֹא בְכֹחַ יִגְבַּר־אִישׁ:
י יְהוָֹה יֵחַתּוּ מְרִיבָיו עָלָיו בַּשָּׁמַיִם יַרְעֵם:
יְהוָה יָדִין אַפְסֵי־אָרֶץ
וְיִתֶּן־עֹז לְמַלְכּוֹ וְיָרֵם קֶרֶן מְשִׁיחוֹ:

B'rakhot that follow the Haftarah may be found on page 114.

VERSE 6. SHEOL שְׁאוֹל. In the biblical age, most Israelites believed that the dead continued to exist in the netherworld called Sheol.

VERSE 10. AND TRIUMPH TO THE ONE WHOM [GOD] ANOINTS וְיָרֵם קֶרֶן מְשִׁיחוֹ. Literally, "raise the horn of God's anointed one." The song opens and closes on this specific image of triumph. In context, it anticipates Samuel's anointing David with a horn of oil (I Samuel 16:13). As the Rosh Hashanah Haftarah reading, these concluding references to spiritual victory, divine judgment, and God's anointed one take on a messianic tone of promise.

Michael Fishbane (commenting in *Etz Hayim*) points out other Rosh Hashanah themes that are present in this Haftarah. The birth of a child is a microcosmic allusion to the birth of all of creation, which we celebrate on this day. In verse 3 of Hannah's prayer, she describes God as all-knowing. In verse 6, she refers to God as the One who determines our birth and death. And in verse 8, she speaks of the One who raises up and brings low.

What Do We Pray For?

Eli thought Hannah was drunk with wine. As High Priest, the divine spirit rested upon him and he was able to see within the hearts of men and women. Yet, he saw Hannah as a drunkard—drunk with a worldly desire, a desire for a child so she would no longer suffer the shame and ridicule afforded her by Peninnah.

But Hannah answered, "No, it is not wine but my soul that pours out to God. For my desire for a child has purpose and meaning beyond the pursuits and follies of human beings. I have already promised my child to God."

So it is with our prayers: We pray for material things, but it is not the material, but the spiritual within them, that our soul desires.

The mission of every human being is to bring the many things of this chaotic world into harmony with their inner purpose and the oneness that underlies them. To do this, each of us must have those things related to our mission: our family, our health, our homes, our income. We pray for these things from the innermost of our hearts; our soul pours out for them—because our soul knows that without them she cannot fulfill her mission in this world.

And God listens. Because God wishes to dwell within our mundane world.

—ZVI FREEMAN (adapted)

I SAMUEL 2

1 And Hannah prayed:

My heart exults in ADONAI;
I have triumphed through ADONAI.
I gloat over my enemies;
I rejoice in Your deliverance.

2 There is no holy one like ADONAI,
truly, there is none beside You;
there is no rock like our God.

3 Talk no more with lofty pride,
let no arrogance cross your lips!
For ADONAI is an all-knowing God
who measures all actions.
4 The bows of the mighty are broken,
and the faltering are girded with strength.
5 Those once sated must hire out for bread;
those once hungry hunger no more.
While the barren woman bears seven,
the mother of many is forlorn.
6 ADONAI deals death and gives life,
casts down into Sheol and raises up.
7 ADONAI makes poor and makes rich,
casts down, and also lifts high—
8 raising the poor from the dust,
lifting up the needy from the dunghill,
setting them with nobles,
granting them seats of honor.
For the pillars of the earth are ADONAI's,
who has set the world upon them.
9 [God] guards the steps of the faithful,
but the wicked perish in darkness—
for none shall prevail by strength.

10 The foes of ADONAI shall be shattered;
[God] will thunder against them in the heavens.
ADONAI will judge the ends of the earth.
[God] will give power to the king,
And triumph to the one whom [God] anoints.

B'rakhot that follow the Haftarah may be found on page 114.

בְּרָכָה שֶׁלִּפְנֵי הַהַפְטָרָה

בָּרוּךְ אַתָּה יהוה אֱלֹהֵינוּ מֶלֶךְ הָעוֹלָם, אֲשֶׁר בָּחַר
בִּנְבִיאִים טוֹבִים, וְרָצָה בְדִבְרֵיהֶם הַנֶּאֱמָרִים בֶּאֱמֶת.
בָּרוּךְ אַתָּה יהוה, הַבּוֹחֵר בַּתּוֹרָה וּבְמֹשֶׁה עַבְדּוֹ
וּבְיִשְׂרָאֵל עַמּוֹ וּבִנְבִיאֵי הָאֱמֶת וָצֶדֶק.

יִרְמְיָה לא

בֹּ כֹּה אָמַר יהוה
מָצָא חֵן בַּמִּדְבָּר
עַם שְׂרִידֵי חָרֶב
הָלוֹךְ לְהַרְגִּיעוֹ יִשְׂרָאֵל:
גּ מֵרָחוֹק יהוה נִרְאָה לִי
וְאַהֲבַת עוֹלָם אֲהַבְתִּיךְ
עַל־כֵּן מְשַׁכְתִּיךְ חָסֶד:
דּ עוֹד אֶבְנֵךְ וְנִבְנֵית
בְּתוּלַת יִשְׂרָאֵל
עוֹד תַּעְדִּי תֻפַּיִךְ
וְיָצָאת בִּמְחוֹל מְשַׂחֲקִים:
הּ עוֹד תִּטְּעִי כְרָמִים
בְּהָרֵי שֹׁמְרוֹן
נָטְעוּ נֹטְעִים וְחִלֵּלוּ:
וּ כִּי יֶשׁ־יוֹם
קָרְאוּ נֹצְרִים בְּהַר אֶפְרָיִם
קוּמוּ וְנַעֲלֶה צִיּוֹן
אֶל־יהוה אֱלֹהֵינוּ:
זּ כִּי־כֹה | אָמַר יהוה
רָנּוּ לְיַעֲקֹב שִׂמְחָה
וְצַהֲלוּ בְּרֹאשׁ הַגּוֹיִם

HAFTARAH, DAY 2. The Haftarah expands the theme of redemption begun in our Torah reading, when Isaac was not sacrificed because of God's saving hand. Jeremiah prophesied that God would bring the people back from exile and comfort them, emphasizing not exile but redemption. Thus, the Haftarah asks us to understand the Torah portion not from Abraham's original perspective but backward, from the point of view of the saving moment at the story's end. Similarly, Jeremiah focuses on the theme of God's saving or redeeming, as he speaks to the people Israel, now in exile. These so-called "ten lost tribes," collectively referred to as "Ephraim," were exiled by Assyria in the 8th century B.C.E. (well before Jeremiah was born), but the prophet promises that they will return.

VERSE 3. ETERNAL LOVE I CONCEIVED FOR YOU THEN. וְאַהֲבַת עוֹלָם אֲהַבְתִּיךְ In the mystical tradition, Isaac is seen as the one who has awe of God (yir·at ha-shem). Indeed, many may experience the Torah reading for this day as conveying awe and fear. The Haftarah emphasizes the opposite, the love of God (ahavat ha-shem). Indeed, much of the imagery in these verses is of marriage: the wedding of God and Israel. Jeremiah idealizes the time of wandering in the desert as a moment when God and Israel were alone with each other, in love.

HAFTARAH READING, SECOND DAY

Blessing before the Haftarah

Barukh atah ADONAI, our God, ruler of time and space, who chose worthy prophets; and who was pleased by their words, spoken in truth. *Barukh atah* ADONAI, who has chosen the Torah, Moses Your servant, Your people Israel, and the prophets of truth and justice.

JEREMIAH 31

2 Thus said ADONAI:
The people escaped from the sword
found favor in the wilderness,
when Israel was marching homeward.
3 ADONAI appeared to me of old:
Eternal love I conceived for you then;
therefore I continue My grace to you.
4 I will build you firmly again,
O Maiden Israel!
Again you shall take up your hand-drums
and go forth to the rhythm of the dancers.
5 Again you shall plant vineyards
on the hills of Samaria;
growers shall plant and live to enjoy them.
6 For the day is coming when sentries
shall proclaim on the heights of Ephraim:
Come, let us go up to Zion,
to our God ADONAI!

7 For thus said ADONAI:
Cry out in joy for Jacob,
shout at the crossroads of the nations!

הַשְׁמִ֧יעוּ הַֽלְל֣וּ וְאִמְר֗וּ
הוֹשַׁ֤ע יְהֹוָה֙ אֶֽת־עַמְּךָ֔
אֵ֖ת שְׁאֵרִ֥ית יִשְׂרָאֵֽל:
ח הִנְנִי֩ מֵבִ֨יא אוֹתָ֜ם מֵאֶ֣רֶץ צָפ֗וֹן
וְקִבַּצְתִּים֮ מִיַּרְכְּתֵי־אָ֒רֶץ֒
בָּ֣ם עִוֵּ֤ר וּפִסֵּ֙חַ֙ הָרָ֣ה וְיֹלֶ֣דֶת יַחְדָּ֑ו
קָהָ֥ל גָּד֖וֹל יָשׁ֥וּבוּ הֵֽנָּה:
ט בִּבְכִ֣י יָבֹ֗אוּ
וּֽבְתַחֲנוּנִים֮ אֽוֹבִילֵם֒
אֽוֹלִיכֵם֙ אֶל־נַ֣חֲלֵי מַ֔יִם
בְּדֶ֣רֶךְ יָשָׁ֔ר לֹ֥א יִכָּֽשְׁל֖וּ בָּ֑הּ
כִּֽי־הָיִ֤יתִי לְיִשְׂרָאֵל֙ לְאָ֔ב
וְאֶפְרַ֖יִם בְּכֹ֥רִי הֽוּא:
י שִׁמְע֤וּ דְבַר־יְהֹוָה֙ גּוֹיִ֔ם
וְהַגִּ֥ידוּ בָֽאִיִּ֖ים מִמֶּרְחָ֑ק
וְאִמְר֗וּ מְזָרֵ֤ה יִשְׂרָאֵל֙ יְקַבְּצֶ֔נּוּ
וּשְׁמָר֖וֹ כְּרֹעֶ֥ה עֶדְרֽוֹ:
יא כִּֽי־פָדָ֥ה יְהֹוָ֖ה אֶֽת־יַעֲקֹ֑ב
וּגְאָל֕וֹ מִיַּ֖ד חָזָ֥ק מִמֶּֽנּוּ:
יב וּבָ֙אוּ֙ וְרִנְּנ֣וּ בִמְרוֹם־צִיּ֔וֹן
וְנָהֲר֞וּ אֶל־ט֣וּב יְהֹוָ֗ה
עַל־דָּגָן֙ וְעַל־תִּירֹ֣שׁ וְעַל־יִצְהָ֔ר
וְעַל־בְּנֵי־צֹ֖אן וּבָקָ֑ר
וְהָיְתָ֤ה נַפְשָׁם֙ כְּגַ֣ן רָוֶ֔ה
וְלֹא־יוֹסִ֥יפוּ לְדַאֲבָ֖ה עֽוֹד:
יג אָ֣ז תִּשְׂמַ֤ח בְּתוּלָה֙ בְּמָח֔וֹל
וּבַחֻרִ֥ים וּזְקֵנִ֖ים יַחְדָּ֑ו
וְהָפַכְתִּ֨י אֶבְלָ֤ם לְשָׂשׂוֹן֙
וְנִ֣חַמְתִּ֔ים וְשִׂמַּחְתִּ֖ים מִֽיגוֹנָֽם:
יד וְרִוֵּיתִ֛י נֶ֥פֶשׁ הַכֹּהֲנִ֖ים דָּ֑שֶׁן
וְעַמִּ֛י אֶת־טוּבִ֥י יִשְׂבָּ֖עוּ
נְאֻם־יְהֹוָֽה:

VERSE 8. FROM THE NORTHLAND מֵאֶרֶץ צָפוֹן. The Assyrians conquered the northern kingdom of Israel in 722 B.C.E. and deported much of the populace. Some 97 years later, Assyria was itself conquered by Babylonia, in 625 B.C.E. Preaching around this time, Jeremiah does not name the country of exile but uses the less specific term, "northern lands," which can mean either Assyria or Babylonia.

Sing aloud in praise, and say:
Save, O ADONAI, Your people,
the remnant of Israel.
8 I will bring them in from the northland,
gather them from the ends of the earth—
the blind and the lame among them,
those with child and those in labor—
in a vast throng they shall return here.
9 They shall come with weeping,
and with compassion will I guide them.
I will lead them to streams of water,
by a level road where they will not stumble.
For I am ever a Father to Israel,
Ephraim is My first-born.

10 Hear the word of ADONAI, O nations,
and tell it in the isles afar.
Say:
The One who scattered Israel will gather them,
and will guard them as a shepherd [guards] the flock.
11 For ADONAI will ransom Jacob,
redeem him from one too strong for him.
12 They shall come and shout on the heights of Zion,
radiant over the bounty of ADONAI—
over new grain and wine and oil,
and over sheep and cattle.
They shall fare like a watered garden;
they shall never languish again.
13 Then shall maidens dance gaily,
young men and old alike.
I will turn their mourning to joy,
I will comfort them and cheer them in their grief.
14 I will give the priests their fill of fatness,
and My people shall enjoy My full bounty
                              —declares ADONAI.

טו כֹּה ׀ אָמַר יְהֹוָה
קוֹל בְּרָמָה נִשְׁמָע
נְהִי בְּכִי תַמְרוּרִים
רָחֵל מְבַכָּה עַל־בָּנֶיהָ
מֵאֲנָה לְהִנָּחֵם
עַל־בָּנֶיהָ כִּי אֵינֶנּוּ:
טז כֹּה ׀ אָמַר יְהֹוָה
מִנְעִי קוֹלֵךְ מִבֶּכִי
וְעֵינַיִךְ מִדִּמְעָה
כִּי יֵשׁ שָׂכָר לִפְעֻלָּתֵךְ
נְאֻם־יְהֹוָה
וְשָׁבוּ מֵאֶרֶץ אוֹיֵב:
יז וְיֵשׁ־תִּקְוָה לְאַחֲרִיתֵךְ
נְאֻם־יְהֹוָה
וְשָׁבוּ בָנִים לִגְבוּלָם:
יח שָׁמוֹעַ שָׁמַעְתִּי אֶפְרַיִם מִתְנוֹדֵד
יִסַּרְתַּנִי וָאִוָּסֵר
כְּעֵגֶל לֹא לֻמָּד
הֲשִׁיבֵנִי וְאָשׁוּבָה
כִּי אַתָּה יְהֹוָה אֱלֹהָי:
יט כִּי־אַחֲרֵי שׁוּבִי נִחַמְתִּי
וְאַחֲרֵי הִוָּדְעִי סָפַקְתִּי עַל־יָרֵךְ
בֹּשְׁתִּי וְגַם־נִכְלַמְתִּי
כִּי נָשָׂאתִי חֶרְפַּת נְעוּרָי:
כ הֲבֵן יַקִּיר לִי אֶפְרַיִם
אִם יֶלֶד שַׁעֲשֻׁעִים
כִּי־מִדֵּי דַבְּרִי בּוֹ
זָכֹר אֶזְכְּרֶנּוּ עוֹד
עַל־כֵּן הָמוּ מֵעַי לוֹ
רַחֵם אֲרַחֲמֶנּוּ
נְאֻם־יְהֹוָה:

ROSH HASHANAH AND THE MESSAGE OF THE HAFTARAH. The first verse of the Haftarah thematically connects this Haftarah reading to the Akedah. Every year "the people escape from the sword," just as every year Isaac escapes the knife. The end of the Haftarah strikes another note: the message of repentance. No matter what our misdeeds, no matter the nature of our mistakes, God will receive us back if we are truly contrite, and if we choose to return to God. Indeed, the prophet uses some of the most loving language to describe the wayward sinner who regrets what has been done and is welcomed back to the fold. In this Haftarah, as in the prophetic readings for the first day of Rosh Hashanah, a woman serves as a source of national redemption. First we read of Hannah, the mother of Samuel, who guided the Jewish people from anarchy to monarchy; and now of Rachel, whose weeping moved God to return her people to their land.

15 Thus said ADONAI:
A cry is heard in Ramah—
wailing, bitter weeping—
Rachel weeping for her children.
She refuses to be comforted
for her children, who are gone.
16 Thus said ADONAI:
Restrain your voice from weeping,
your eyes from shedding tears;
for there is a reward for your labor
                              —declares ADONAI:
They shall return from the enemy's land.
17 And there is hope for your future
                              —declares ADONAI:
Your children shall return to their country.

18 I can hear Ephraim lamenting:
You have chastised me, and I am chastised
like a calf that has not been broken.
Receive me back, let me return,
for You, O ADONAI, are my God.
19 Now that I have turned back, I am filled with remorse;
Now that I am made aware, I strike my thigh.
I am ashamed and humiliated,
for I bear the disgrace of my youth.
20 Truly, Ephraim is a dear son to Me,
a child that is dandled!
Whenever I have turned against him,
My thoughts would dwell on him still.
That is why My heart yearns for him;
I will receive him back in love
                              —declares ADONAI.

הַבְּרָכוֹת שֶׁלְּאַחַר הַהַפְטָרָה

בָּרוּךְ אַתָּה יהוה אֱלֹהֵינוּ מֶלֶךְ הָעוֹלָם, צוּר כָּל־הָעוֹלָמִים, צַדִּיק בְּכָל־הַדּוֹרוֹת, הָאֵל הַנֶּאֱמָן הָאוֹמֵר וְעֹשֶׂה, הַמְדַבֵּר וּמְקַיֵּם, שֶׁכָּל־דְּבָרָיו אֱמֶת וָצֶדֶק. נֶאֱמָן אַתָּה הוּא יהוה אֱלֹהֵינוּ וְנֶאֱמָנִים דְּבָרֶיךָ, וְדָבָר אֶחָד מִדְּבָרֶיךָ אָחוֹר לֹא יָשׁוּב רֵיקָם, כִּי אֵל מֶלֶךְ נֶאֱמָן וְרַחֲמָן אָתָּה. בָּרוּךְ אַתָּה יהוה, הָאֵל הַנֶּאֱמָן בְּכָל־דְּבָרָיו.

רַחֵם עַל צִיּוֹן כִּי הִיא בֵּית חַיֵּינוּ. וְלַעֲלוּבַת נֶפֶשׁ תּוֹשִׁיעַ בִּמְהֵרָה בְיָמֵינוּ. בָּרוּךְ אַתָּה יהוה, מְשַׂמֵּחַ צִיּוֹן בְּבָנֶיהָ.

שַׂמְּחֵנוּ, יהוה אֱלֹהֵינוּ בְּאֵלִיָּהוּ הַנָּבִיא עַבְדֶּךָ וּבְמַלְכוּת בֵּית דָּוִד מְשִׁיחֶךָ. בִּמְהֵרָה יָבֹא וְיָגֵל לִבֵּנוּ, עַל כִּסְאוֹ לֹא יֵשֶׁב זָר וְלֹא יִנְחֲלוּ עוֹד אֲחֵרִים אֶת־כְּבוֹדוֹ, כִּי בְשֵׁם קָדְשְׁךָ נִשְׁבַּעְתָּ לּוֹ שֶׁלֹּא יִכְבֶּה נֵרוֹ לְעוֹלָם וָעֶד. בָּרוּךְ אַתָּה יהוה, מָגֵן דָּוִד.

עַל הַתּוֹרָה וְעַל הָעֲבוֹדָה וְעַל הַנְּבִיאִים [וְעַל יוֹם הַשַּׁבָּת הַזֶּה] וְעַל יוֹם הַזִּכָּרוֹן הַזֶּה שֶׁנָּתַתָּ לָּנוּ יהוה אֱלֹהֵינוּ [לִקְדֻשָּׁה וְלִמְנוּחָה,] לְכָבוֹד וּלְתִפְאָרֶת. עַל הַכֹּל יהוה אֱלֹהֵינוּ אֲנַחְנוּ מוֹדִים לָךְ, וּמְבָרְכִים אוֹתָךְ. יִתְבָּרַךְ שִׁמְךָ בְּפִי כָּל־חַי תָּמִיד לְעוֹלָם וָעֶד, וּדְבָרְךָ אֱמֶת וְקַיָּם לָעַד. בָּרוּךְ אַתָּה יהוה, מֶלֶךְ עַל כָּל־הָאָרֶץ מְקַדֵּשׁ [הַשַּׁבָּת וְ] יִשְׂרָאֵל וְיוֹם הַזִּכָּרוֹן.

B'RAKHOT AFTER THE HAFTARAH. A series of *b'rakhot* concludes the reading from the Prophets. The earliest synagogue services may have centered on the public reading of biblical passages and the prayers concluding the reading may have originally formed the core of the synagogue service. Thus, the prayers concluding our reading mention the sanctity of the day and express messianic longing, two themes also included in the Amidah. In ancient times, a reading from the Writings, the third division of the Hebrew Bible, was also included in the public biblical reading.

WHO ACCOMPLISHES WHAT IS SPOKEN הַמְדַבֵּר וּמְקַיֵּם. At the opening of Genesis, God's word effectuates all that is created: "God said… and it was so." Our liturgy asserts that God will likewise carry out the promises recorded in the scriptural passages that we have just read aloud and studied.

MAY YOUR PROMISE PROVE TRUE וּדְבָרְךָ אֱמֶת. On the Days of Awe we talk of God's teaching as an everlasting truth and we then conclude by declaring God's sovereignty over all the earth. God's sovereignty is identified here with the truthful and eternal teaching of Torah.

B'rakhot after the Haftarah

Barukh atah ADONAI, our God, ruler of time and space, eternal protector, righteous in all generations, the faithful God who fulfills what is promised, who accomplishes what is spoken, whose every word is true and just. Faithful are You, ADONAI, and Your words are trustworthy; not one of Your words will prove empty, for You are a faithful and compassionate sovereign. *Barukh atah* ADONAI, God who faithfully fulfills all Your words.

Show compassion to Zion, our true home, and speedily, in our time, bring redemption to those sad in spirit. *Barukh atah* ADONAI, who makes Zion happy with her children.

Make us joyful, ADONAI our God, with Elijah the prophet, Your servant, and with the kingdom of David, Your anointed—may he soon come and make our hearts rejoice. May no stranger sit on his throne and may no other inherit his glory, for You have promised him, by Your holy name, that his light shall never be extinguished. *Barukh atah* ADONAI, Shield of David.

For all this we thank You and praise You, ADONAI our God: for the Torah, for the ability to worship, for the prophets, [for the Shabbat,] and for this Day of Remembrance, which You have given us, ADONAI our God, [for holiness and for rest,] for honor and glory. May Your name be blessed by all that is living, always and forever, and may Your promise prove true and everlasting. *Barukh atah* ADONAI, ruler of all the earth, who makes [Shabbat,] the people Israel and the Day of Remembrance holy.

תפילות על שבר ושלימות
PRAYERS OF BROKENNESS AND WHOLENESS

Congregations may recite any or all of these prayers. Some may choose to do so immediately before or after the Maftir reading (page 106). Others may substitute this section for the more traditional prayers for our country and for the State of Israel (page 117). On Shabbat, some may also recite the traditional prayers for the congregation and those who serve the community (page 288).

BROKENNESS AND WHOLENESS (*shever u-sh'leimut*). A shofar is sounded in two distinct ways. One is a tragic cry. The Talmud debates whether it resembles wailing (*t'ru·ot*), or gasps from pain (*sh'varim*). Further, the Talmud likens this shofar cry to the sound uttered by the mother of the Canaanite general Sisera when she learned of her son's death (at the hands of Jael; Judges 5). In that view, the shofar's call reminds us of the world's suffering and pain, even within the families of our enemies. In contrast, the shofar's other sound— a long, single shout (*t'ki·ah*)—is a cry of triumph.

MY VOICE קוֹלִי. Psalm 142:2–4,8. The word *kol* (קוֹל), "voice," can refer also to the shofar's call. (The *b'rakhah* for hearing a shofar concludes: *kol shofar*, "the sound of the shofar.")

Prayers for Healing and Caregivers

א

I raise my voice in cries to God.
I raise my voice pleading for help.
My words tumble out
when I speak to God of my troubles,
as my spirit is faint within me.
Free me from all that confines my soul, that I might gratefully acknowledge Your name.

Psalm 142:2–4, 8

קוֹלִי אֶל־יהוה אֶזְעָק
קוֹלִי אֶל־יהוה אֶתְחַנָּן.
אֶשְׁפֹּךְ לְפָנָיו שִׂיחִי
צָרָתִי לְפָנָיו אַגִּיד
בְּהִתְעַטֵּף עָלַי רוּחִי.
הוֹצִיאָה מִמַּסְגֵּר נַפְשִׁי
לְהוֹדוֹת אֶת־שְׁמֶךָ.

תהלים קמב ב-ד, ח

Merciful Sovereign, we stand before You today, grateful for the wonderful gift of life with which You have blessed us, but also mindful of its fragility. Some of us are in good health, yet aware of our family and friends who are not as fortunate; some among us are ill, and in pain.

As we contemplate the sounds of the shofar we think of its rending cry, calling to mind cries of brokenness and suffering. In the midst of turmoil, we turn to You at this moment of prayer. God of healing, may we find comfort under Your protecting wings.

ב

May the One who blessed our ancestors Abraham, Isaac, and Jacob, Sarah, Rebecca, Rachel, and Leah bless all who are ill and remove from them any sickness; send complete healing, both in body and in spirit; and send blessing and good fortune to all the work of their hands—and to all the people Israel. And let us say: *Amen.*

מִי שֶׁבֵּרַךְ אֲבוֹתֵינוּ אַבְרָהָם יִצְחָק
וְיַעֲקֹב, וְאִמּוֹתֵינוּ שָׂרָה רִבְקָה רָחֵל
וְלֵאָה, הוּא יְבָרֵךְ אֶת־כָּל־הַחוֹלִים,
וְיָסִיר מֵהֶם כָּל־מַחֲלָה, וְיִשְׁלַח
בִּמְהֵרָה רְפוּאָה שְׁלֵמָה, רְפוּאַת
הַנֶּפֶשׁ וּרְפוּאַת הַגּוּף, וְיִשְׁלַח בְּרָכָה
וְהַצְלָחָה בְּכָל מַעֲשֵׂה יְדֵיהֶם, עִם כָּל־
יִשְׂרָאֵל, וְנֹאמַר אָמֵן.

Some among us are caregivers of friends and family members who are ill; our hearts ache for their pain, our minds are sometimes filled with fear.

Some of us are doctors, therapists, nurses, aides, working each day to repair injury, cure disease, alleviate pain, and we are sometimes called upon to attend those who are close to death.

Help us and them to have strength to face others' suffering and to be healers of body and soul.

ג

May the One who blessed our ancestors Abraham, Isaac, and Jacob, Sarah, Rebecca, Rachel, and Leah, bless all who engage in acts of healing and all who visit the sick. May the Holy One justly reward them and bless them with wisdom and understanding, strength and openness, as they faithfully engage in their tasks. May all their works be blessed and successful, along with those of all the people Israel, and let us say: *Amen.*

מִי שֶׁבֵּרַךְ אֲבוֹתֵינוּ אַבְרָהָם יִצְחָק וְיַעֲקֹב, וְאִמּוֹתֵינוּ שָׂרָה רִבְקָה רָחֵל וְלֵאָה, הוּא יְבָרֵךְ אֶת־כָּל־מִי שֶׁעוֹסְקִים בִּרְפוּאַת חוֹלִים, וְכָל־מִי שֶׁמְּבַקְּרִים אוֹתָם. הַקָּדוֹשׁ בָּרוּךְ הוּא יְשַׁלֵּם שְׂכָרָם, יִתֵּן לָהֶם חָכְמָה, הֲבָנָה, כֹּחַ, וְלֵב שׁוֹמֵעַ לַעֲסוֹק בַּעֲבוֹדָתָם בֶּאֱמוּנָה, וְיִשְׁלַח בְּרָכָה וְהַצְלָחָה בְּכָל־מַעֲשֵׂה יְדֵיהֶם, עִם כָּל־יִשְׂרָאֵל, וְנֹאמַר אָמֵן.

Mi she-beirakh avoteinu
m'kor ha-b'rakhah l'immoteinu.
May the Source of strength
who blessed the ones before us
help us find the courage
to make our lives a blessing,
   and let us say: Amen.

Mi she-beirakh immoteinu
m'kor ha-b'rakhah la-avoteinu.
Bless those in need of healing
with r'fu·ah sh'leimah:
a renewal of body,
a renewal of spirit,
   and let us say: Amen.
—DEBBIE FRIEDMAN

I lift my eyes to the mountains,
 from where shall my help come?
My help is from God,
 the Creator of heaven and earth.
Psalm 121:12

Essa einai el he-harim, mei-ayin yavo ezri.
Ezri me'im Adonai, oseih shamayim va'aretz.

אֶשָּׂא עֵינַי אֶל־הֶהָרִים מֵאַיִן יָבֹא עֶזְרִי. עֶזְרִי מֵעִם יהוה עֹשֵׂה שָׁמַיִם וָאָרֶץ.
תהלים קכא א-ב

Prayers for Our Community's Welfare

As we contemplate the sounds of the shofar calling to us,
we are summoned by the knowledge of suffering in our midst.
Some in our community live in loneliness; some worry about daily
sustenance; some struggle to get through each day.
The shofar calls us to hear the cries of those among whom we live,
the cries of people whom we may not even see.
Help us to become instruments of redemption; teach us to hear the
silent crying of those in need. Wake us from our self-absorption.
As the shofar curves from narrowness to breadth,
so too may You bring all people from affliction to ease.
Help those who cannot care for themselves; bless those who accompany
the lonely and those who help feed, clothe, and house the poor.
Bless the leaders of our community and our country,
that we may walk on the path of righteousness and compassion.

May the One who blessed our ancestors
Abraham, Isaac and Jacob, Sarah, Rebecca,
Rachel, and Leah, bless all who faithfully
work in our community to feed the hungry,
give *tz'dakah* to the poor, help the weak,
and raise up those who are fallen. May the
Holy One justly reward them and send
blessing and success to all the work of their
hands, along with that of all the people
Israel, and let us say: *Amen.*

Out of narrow straits I've called out to God;
God answered me with abundance.

Psalm 118:5

Min ha-meitzar karati Yah, anani va-merḥav Yah.

מִי שֶׁבֵּרַךְ אֲבוֹתֵינוּ אַבְרָהָם יִצְחָק
וְיַעֲקֹב, וְאִמּוֹתֵינוּ שָׂרָה רִבְקָה רָחֵל
וְלֵאָה, הוּא יְבָרֵךְ אֶת־כָּל־מִי
שֶׁעוֹסְקִים בְּצָרְכֵי צִבּוּר בֶּאֱמוּנָה,
וְנוֹתְנִים פַּת לָאוֹרְחִים וּצְדָקָה
לָעֲנִיִּים, וְעוֹזְרִים דַּלִּים, וּמַגְבִּיהִים
שְׁפָלִים. הַקָּדוֹשׁ בָּרוּךְ הוּא יְשַׁלֵּם
שְׂכָרָם, וְיִשְׁלַח בְּרָכָה וְהַצְלָחָה בְּכָל־
מַעֲשֵׂה יְדֵיהֶם, עִם כָּל־יִשְׂרָאֵל,
וְנֹאמַר אָמֵן.

מִן־הַמֵּצַר קָרָאתִי יָּה,
עָנָנִי בַמֶּרְחָב יָהּ. תהלים קיח ה

Prayers for the Whole House of Israel and for the World

When we hear the piercing cries of the shofar [*on Shabbat say:* As we await
the sounds of the shofar], let us have the courage to open our ears to
the cries of our blood-soaked earth, to the weeping of a world in pain,
ravaged by hatred, ignorance, war, and greed.
Help us to hear the shouts and voiceless cries of humanity throughout
the world living in fear, injustice, deprivation, and indignity.
We thank You, God, for those courageous souls who devote their lives to
the work of *tikkun olam*, the repair of the world. Strengthen their faith

and their will; bless the work of their hands. Above the noisy clamor of hate and ignorance may their voices ascend, bright and clear, calling us all to build a world of harmony, a world filled with compassion.

As the shattered sh'varim and weeping t'ru·ot give way to the full, whole sounds of t'ki·ah, may our broken-hearted prayers today strengthen our faith, arouse our hopes, and unify our will to work toward a world redeemed.

Bless Your holy land, our beloved Eretz Yisrael—too often rent by war, misunderstanding, intolerance, and fear. Be with those on whose shoulders Israel's safety depends and defend them from all harm. Grant them the physical might to protect all its citizens and the spiritual strength, wisdom, and understanding so that justice and righteousness reign in the land.

Grant good judgment and strength to the leaders of the State of Israel, and to all the leaders of the House of Israel, that all who dwell in Your holy land may find peace, that all may grow ever nearer to fulfilling the vision of Your prophet, "nation shall not lift up sword against nation, neither shall they learn war anymore."

[OMIT ON SHABBAT:] As we rise to hear the sound of the shofar, may we all rise to our calling to be instruments of Your holy work. Save us from cynicism, paralysis and despair. Help us to turn from selfishness to concern, and from apathy to care.

May we move from narrowness to expanse, from brokenness to wholeness, from degradation to beauty, from woundedness to healing, from war to peace, and from hatred to love.

The sound of your brother's blood cries out to Me from the ground. Genesis 4:10

קוֹל דְּמֵי אָחִיךָ צֹעֲקִים אֵלַי מִן־הָאֲדָמָה: בראשית ד י

May the One who brings harmony on high, bring harmony to us and to all Israel [and to all who dwell on earth]. And respond with: *Amen.*

Oseh shalom bi-m'romav, hu ya·aseh shalom aleinu v'al kol yisrael [v'al kol yosh'vei teiveil], v'imru: amen.

עֹשֶׂה שָׁלוֹם בִּמְרוֹמָיו, הוּא יַעֲשֶׂה שָׁלוֹם עָלֵינוּ וְעַל כָּל־יִשְׂרָאֵל [וְעַל כָּל־יוֹשְׁבֵי תֵבֵל] וְאִמְרוּ אָמֵן.

Thus says ADONAI: Stop your voice from weeping and your eyes from shedding tears, for surely your work will be rewarded. Thus has ADONAI spoken.

Jeremiah 31:16

כֹּה אָמַר יהוה מִנְעִי קוֹלֵךְ מִבֶּכִי וְעֵינַיִךְ מִדִּמְעָה, כִּי יֵשׁ שָׂכָר לִפְעֻלָּתֵךְ, נְאֻם־יהוה. ירמיה לא טז

A PRAYER FOR OUR COUNTRY

אֱלֹהֵינוּ וֵאלֹהֵי אֲבוֹתֵינוּ [וְאִמּוֹתֵינוּ], קַבֶּל־נָא בְּרַחֲמִים
אֶת־תְּפִלָּתֵנוּ בְּעַד אַרְצֵנוּ וּמֶמְשַׁלְתָּהּ. הָרֵק אֶת־בִּרְכָתְךָ
עַל הָאָרֶץ הַזֹּאת, עַל רָאשֶׁיהָ, שׁוֹפְטֶיהָ, וּפְקִידֶיהָ
הָעוֹסְקִים בְּצָרְכֵי צִבּוּר בֶּאֱמוּנָה. הוֹרֵם מֵחֻקֵּי תוֹרָתֶךָ,
הֲבִינֵם מִשְׁפְּטֵי צִדְקֶךָ לְמַעַן לֹא יָסוּרוּ מֵאַרְצֵנוּ שָׁלוֹם
וְשַׁלְוָה, אֹשֶׁר וָחֹפֶשׁ כָּל־הַיָּמִים. אָנָּא יהוה אֱלֹהֵי
הָרוּחוֹת לְכָל־בָּשָׂר, שְׁלַח רוּחֲךָ עַל כָּל־תּוֹשְׁבֵי אַרְצֵנוּ.
עֲקֹר מִלִּבָּם שִׂנְאָה וְאֵיבָה, קִנְאָה וְתַחֲרוּת, וְטַע בֵּין בְּנֵי
הָאֻמּוֹת וְהָאֱמוּנוֹת הַשּׁוֹנוֹת הַשּׁוֹכְנִים בָּהּ, אַהֲבָה
וְאַחֲוָה, שָׁלוֹם וְרֵעוּת. וּבְכֵן יְהִי רָצוֹן מִלְּפָנֶיךָ שֶׁתְּהִי
אַרְצֵנוּ בְּרָכָה לְכָל־יוֹשְׁבֵי תֵבֵל, וְתַשְׁרֶה בֵּינֵיהֶם רֵעוּת
וְחֵרוּת, וְקַיֵּם בִּמְהֵרָה חֲזוֹן נְבִיאֶיךָ: לֹא יִשָּׂא גוֹי אֶל גּוֹי
חֶרֶב וְלֹא יִלְמְדוּ עוֹד מִלְחָמָה. וְנֶאֱמַר: כִּי כוּלָּם יֵדְעוּ
אוֹתִי לְמִקְּטַנָּם וְעַד גְּדוֹלָם, וְנֹאמַר אָמֵן.

A PRAYER FOR THE STATE OF ISRAEL

אָבִינוּ שֶׁבַּשָּׁמַיִם, צוּר יִשְׂרָאֵל וְגוֹאֲלוֹ, בָּרֵךְ אֶת־מְדִינַת
יִשְׂרָאֵל, [שֶׁתְּהֵא] רֵאשִׁית צְמִיחַת גְּאֻלָּתֵנוּ. הָגֵן עָלֶיהָ
בְּאֶבְרַת חַסְדֶּךָ, וּפְרֹשׂ עָלֶיהָ סֻכַּת שְׁלוֹמֶךָ. וּשְׁלַח אוֹרְךָ
וַאֲמִתְּךָ לְרָאשֶׁיהָ, שָׂרֶיהָ וְיוֹעֲצֶיהָ, וְתַקְּנֵם בְּעֵצָה
טוֹבָה מִלְּפָנֶיךָ. חַזֵּק אֶת־יְדֵי מְגִנֵּי אֶרֶץ קָדְשֵׁנוּ, וְהַנְחִילֵם
אֱלֹהֵינוּ יְשׁוּעָה, וַעֲטֶרֶת נִצָּחוֹן תְּעַטְּרֵם. וְנָתַתָּ שָׁלוֹם
בָּאָרֶץ וְשִׂמְחַת עוֹלָם לְיוֹשְׁבֶיהָ, וְנֹאמַר אָמֵן.

PRAYER FOR OUR COUNTRY. It has been customary since medieval times to include in the liturgy a prayer for the welfare of the government. Secure governments were seen as providing safety for the Jewish community, and a biblical warrant for such prayers was found in the verse instructing Israel to "seek the welfare of the city to which I have exiled you and pray to Adonai in its behalf; for in its prosperity you shall prosper" (Jeremiah 29:7). Early versions of this prayer referred to God as "the One who gives dominion to kings" and reflected the anxiety that Jews felt as a beleaguered minority. The text here was composed in the 1920s expressly for a democratic government by Professor Louis Ginzberg, who served as rector of the Jewish Theological Seminary. (The version of his prayer as edited in *Siddur Sim Shalom* is presented as an alternative.) Ginzberg's prayer transforms what was formerly "A Prayer for the Government" into "A Prayer for Our Country" and for its people, the source of authority in a democracy. Whereas earlier prayers asked that the monarch be compassionate to the Jewish people, this prayer expresses the hope that the leaders of the country will be fair and just to all and help to bring the world closer to a vision of peace and justice.

THE VISION OF YOUR PROPHETS חֲזוֹן נְבִיאֶיךָ. Isaiah 2:4 and Jeremiah 31:34.

PRAYER FOR THE STATE OF ISRAEL. Upon Israel's independence in 1948, many prayers were circulated for the well-being of the new state. This one was probably composed by Israel's Chief Rabbis and may have been edited by the writer S. Y. Agnon. Some congregations add the bracketed term, which modulates the prayer's messianic language from an expression of certainty to one of hope. The additional phrase implies our need to realize in the State our ideal vision.

A PRAYER FOR OUR COUNTRY

Our God and God of our ancestors, with mercy accept our prayer on behalf of our country and its government. Pour out Your blessings upon this land, upon its leader, its judges, officers, and officials, who are devoted in good faith to the needs of the public. Instruct them with the laws of Your Torah and help them understand Your rules of justice, so that peace and security, happiness and freedom, will never depart from our land. We pray, ADONAI, God whose spirit is in all creatures, awaken that spirit within all the inhabitants of our land. Uproot from their hearts hatred and malice, jealousy and strife. Plant among those of different nationalities and faiths who dwell in our nation, love and companionship, peace and friendship. May it therefore be Your will that our land be a blessing to all who dwell on earth and cause them to dwell in friendship and freedom. Speedily fulfill the vision of Your prophets: "Nation shall not lift up sword against nation, neither shall they learn war any more"; "For all of them, from the least of them to the greatest, shall know Me." And let us say: Amen.

An Alternative Prayer for Our Country

Our God and God of our ancestors: We ask Your blessings for our country—for its government, for its leaders and advisors, and for all who exercise just and rightful authority. Teach them insights from Your Torah, that they may administer all affairs of state fairly, that peace and security, happiness and prosperity, justice and freedom may forever abide in our midst.

Creator of all flesh, bless all the inhabitants of our country with Your spirit. May citizens of all races and creeds forge a common bond in true harmony, to banish hatred and bigotry, and to safeguard the ideals and free institutions that are the pride and glory of our country.

May this land, under Your providence, be an influence for good throughout the world, uniting all people in peace and freedom—helping them to fulfill the vision of Your prophet: "Nation shall not lift up sword against nation, neither shall they experience war any more." And let us say: Amen.

A PRAYER FOR THE STATE OF ISRAEL

Avinu she-ba-shamayim, Stronghold and Redeemer of the people Israel: Bless the State of Israel, [that it may be] the beginning of our redemption. Shield it with Your love; spread over it the shelter of Your peace. Guide its leaders and advisors with Your light and Your truth. Help them with Your good counsel. Strengthen the hands of those who defend our Holy Land. Deliver them; crown their efforts with triumph. Bless the Land with peace and its inhabitants with lasting joy. And let us say: Amen.

An Alternative Prayer for the State of Israel

רִבּוֹן הָעוֹלָם, קַבֵּל נָא בְּרַחֲמִים וּבְרָצוֹן אֶת־תְּפִלָּתֵנוּ לְמַעַן מְדִינַת יִשְׂרָאֵל.

Sovereign of the universe, accept in lovingkindness and with favor our prayers for the State of Israel, her government, and all who dwell within her boundaries and under her authority. Open our eyes and our hearts to the wonder of Israel and strengthen our faith in Your power to work redemption in every human soul. Grant us also the fortitude to keep ever before us those ideals upon which the State of Israel was founded. Grant courage, wisdom, and strength to those entrusted with guiding Israel's destiny to do Your will. Be with those on whose shoulders Israel's safety depends and defend them from all harm. Spread over Israel and all the world Your shelter of peace, and may the vision of Your prophet soon be fulfilled: "Nation shall not lift up sword against nation, neither shall they learn war any more" (Isaiah 2:4). לֹא

יִשָּׂא גוֹי אֶל גּוֹי חֶרֶב לֹא יִלְמְדוּ עוֹד מִלְחָמָה.

סדר תקיעת שופר

THE SHOFAR IS TRADITIONALLY NOT BLOWN ON SHABBAT.

Meditations before Shofar Blowing

א

Soundless, no outward signs or tokens: this, indeed, is how time passes, often escaping notice altogether. Unaware of time passing, we are part of nature; aware of time passing, we are apart from nature.

Discovering that time is short, the task long, and the Task-Assigner demanding (Avot 2:15), small wonder that we arrange a blare of trumpets, a blast of the shofar, to awaken us to the passage of that precious, finite, irreversible measure of our lives.

According to Maimonides, the message of the shofar is precisely this:

"Awake, O you sleepers, awake from your sleep!
O you slumberers, awake from your slumber!"

Hence only we mortals, aware of our perishing, proclaim the passage of time; only we mortals, ringing bells and sounding alarms, startle ourselves awake.

Happy, indeed, are those who comprehend in wakefulness the shofar's sound!

ב

The shofar exclaims: Wake up from your slumber!

Examine your deeds and turn in repentance, remembering your Creator. You sleepers who forget the truth while caught up in the fads and follies of the time, frittering away your years in vanity and emptiness which cannot help: take a good look at yourselves. Improve your ways. Let everyone abandon their bad deeds and their wicked thoughts.

When the Holy One, on judgment day, begins to judge, God ascends the throne of strict judgment, as it is written, "The God of judgment has ascended with acclamation." But when the people Israel, standing in judgment, sound the shofar, the Holy One is filled with mercy, and moves to the throne of compassion.

BLOWING THE SHOFAR. The Torah describes Rosh Hashanah as the day on which the shofar is to be sounded (Numbers 29:1). In the Bible, the sounding of the shofar is associated with a call to war, the cessation of war, and the assembly of the people. Quintessentially, God's descent on Sinai was accompanied by shofar blasts.

Later Jewish tradition saw the call of the shofar as God's call for us to return in t'shuvah (repentance).

SOUNDLESS. This passage was written by Everett Gendler, a contemporary rabbi.

THE SHOFAR EXCLAIMS. The first paragraphs of this reading are a translation of Maimonides' interpretation of the meaning of the blowing of the shofar (Mishneh Torah, Hilkhot Teshuvah 3:4). The final paragraph is from Leviticus Rabbah 29:3. The translation is by Jules Harlow.

MAY THE CRY. Adapted from a prayer written by Hershel J. Matt (Mahzor Hadash).

IN YOUR GREAT MERCY. Written by Jules Harlow.

ראש השנה · סדר קריאת התורה · תקיעת שופר 118

SERVICE OF BLOWING THE SHOFAR

Listening

The ten days of returning are meant to reawaken our inner understanding, for it has fallen asleep and needs to be aroused. It is roused through the sound of the shofar. True understanding derives from hearing, for its source is the listening that is accomplished with our inner ear.

—THE NAZIR, DAVID HACOHEN
(trans. Aubrey L. Glazer)

¶ The Shofar

The voice of the shofar calls,
    rises up
from the straits.
It rises from among the hats,
    the murmurs,
the lockets, the children's
    wide eyes,
the rickety air conditioner.
Hastily, snack bags pass from
    a large hand
to a little one, the rustle of
    cellophane,
to quiet the infants.

T'ki·ah, Sh'varim, T'ru·ah
Sing ye praises in a skillful
    song

Sing praises to our Sovereign
    sing praises,
with the groans of the
    wounded beast
whose voice is inscrutable:
A naked voice, parched,
    insistent.
May its blow
break the locks of my heart.

—ESTHER ETTINGER

True Hearing

On Rosh Hashanah before he blew the shofar, the Rabbi of Kobryn would call out: "Little brothers, do not depend upon me! Everyone had better take their own part!" —A ḤASIDIC TALE

ג

¶ May the cry of the shofar shatter our complacency.
    May the cry of the shofar penetrate our souls.
May the cry of the shofar break the bonds of all that enslaves us.
    May the cry of the shofar destroy the idols we have placed at the forefront of our lives.
May the cry of the shofar awaken us to how we have sinned.
    May the cry of the shofar summon us to a life of responsibility.
May the cry of the shofar elicit the response, "Here I am."
    May the cry of the shofar remind us that we can be instruments of redemption.
May the cry of the shofar penetrate our hearts.
    May the cry of the shofar bring blessing to us, the people who hear its call.

ד

¶ In Your great mercy, ADONAI,
bring us near to Your Presence.
Help us to break down the barriers
that keep us far from You:

falsehood and faithlessness,
callousness and selfishness,
injustice and hard-heartedness.

Our hope is in You,
for You respond in mercy
when we sound the shofar.

עָלָה אֱלֹהִים בִּתְרוּעָה,
יהוה בְּקוֹל שׁוֹפָר.
זַמְּרוּ אֱלֹהִים זַמֵּרוּ,
זַמְּרוּ לְמַלְכֵּנוּ זַמֵּרוּ.
כִּי מֶלֶךְ כָּל־הָאָרֶץ אֱלֹהִים,
זַמְּרוּ מַשְׂכִּיל.
מָלַךְ אֱלֹהִים עַל גּוֹיִם,
אֱלֹהִים יָשַׁב עַל כִּסֵּא קָדְשׁוֹ.

We rise. Some congregations repeat each poetic line after the leader.

מִן הַמֵּצַר קָרָאתִי יָּה, עָנָנִי בַמֶּרְחָב יָהּ.
קוֹלִי שָׁמָעְתָּ, אַל תַּעְלֵם אָזְנְךָ לְרַוְחָתִי לְשַׁוְעָתִי.
רֹאשׁ דְּבָרְךָ אֱמֶת, וּלְעוֹלָם כָּל־מִשְׁפַּט צִדְקֶךָ.
עֲרֹב עַבְדְּךָ לְטוֹב, אַל יַעַשְׁקֻנִי זֵדִים.
שָׂשׂ אָנֹכִי עַל אִמְרָתֶךָ, כְּמוֹצֵא שָׁלָל רָב.
טוּב טַעַם וָדַעַת לַמְּדֵנִי, כִּי בְמִצְוֹתֶיךָ הֶאֱמָנְתִּי.
נִדְבוֹת פִּי רְצֵה נָא יהוה, וּמִשְׁפָּטֶיךָ לַמְּדֵנִי.

The ba'al t'ki·ah (the person blowing the shofar) recites the following b'rakhot.

בָּרוּךְ אַתָּה יהוה, אֱלֹהֵינוּ מֶלֶךְ הָעוֹלָם,
אֲשֶׁר קִדְּשָׁנוּ בְּמִצְוֹתָיו וְצִוָּנוּ לִשְׁמוֹעַ קוֹל שׁוֹפָר. אָמֵן.
בָּרוּךְ אַתָּה יהוה, אֱלֹהֵינוּ מֶלֶךְ הָעוֹלָם,
שֶׁהֶחֱיָנוּ וְקִיְּמָנוּ וְהִגִּיעָנוּ לַזְּמַן הַזֶּה. אָמֵן.

תְּקִיעָה שְׁבָרִים-תְּרוּעָה תְּקִיעָה
תְּקִיעָה שְׁבָרִים-תְּרוּעָה תְּקִיעָה
תְּקִיעָה שְׁבָרִים-תְּרוּעָה תְּקִיעָה

תְּקִיעָה שְׁבָרִים תְּקִיעָה
תְּקִיעָה שְׁבָרִים תְּקִיעָה
תְּקִיעָה שְׁבָרִים תְּקִיעָה

תְּקִיעָה תְּרוּעָה תְּקִיעָה
תְּקִיעָה תְּרוּעָה תְּקִיעָה
תְּקִיעָה תְּרוּעָה תְּקִיעָה גְדוֹלָה

The Service of Blowing the Shofar offers us a glimpse of the high drama and sounds of the ancient Temple service. In many places, the shofar blower appears out of the congregation, often hiding the shofar out of sight, to give voice to the three blasts: *t'k·iah, sh'varim, t'ru·ah*, while the congregation stands in rapt attention. However, the *b'rakhah* reminds us that our focus should be on ourselves and our fellow congregants, not on the shofar blower. We recite the words *tzivvanu lishmo·a kol shofar*—we are instructed to heed the call of the shofar. The blasts might be strong and sustained or weak and hesitant, but they still have the potential to evoke a response in us. This year, what will our inner ear hear?

One expression of the transformative potential of the shofar service is the tradition that negative forces (named Satan) may disrupt the effectiveness of the shofar's call. Although there are many forces at work within us, resisting any change of direction, the call of the shofar asks us to face the variety of forces at work within us and to choose those that accord to the true calling of our soul.

God has ascended with acclamation,
Adonai ascends with the shofar blast.
Sing to our God, sing!
Sing to our sovereign, sing!
For God is sovereign of all the earth.
Sing with all your skill.
God is sovereign over all nations.
God reigns upon a holy throne.

We rise. Some congregations repeat each poetic line after the leader.

Out of narrow straits, I've called out to God;
God answered me with abundance.
Hear my voice! Do not close Your ear to my cry, my plea.
Truth is the essence of Your speech; Your just laws are eternal.
Surround Your servant with good;
do not let evildoers oppress me.
I rejoice in Your word, as one who has found great treasure.
Grant me discernment and wisdom;
I have faith in Your commandments.
May the words I utter be acceptable;
Adonai, instruct me in Your just laws.

Min ha-meitzar karati Yah anani va-merḥav Yah.
Koli shamata al taleim ozn'kha l'ravḥati l'shavati.
Rosh d'var'kha emet u-l'olam kol mishpat tzidkekha.
Arov avd'kha l'tov al ya·ashkuni zeidim.
Sas anokhi al imratekha k'motzei shalal rav.
Tuv ta·am va-da·at lam'deini ki v'mitzvotekha he·emanti.
Nidvot pi r'tzeih na Adonai u-mishpatekha lam'deini.

The ba'al t'ki·ah (the person blowing the shofar) recites the following b'rakhot.

Barukh atah Adonai, our God, ruler of time and space, who has made us holy through mitzvot and instructed us to hear the sound of the shofar. Amen.

Barukh atah Adonai, our God, ruler of time and space, for granting us life, for sustaining us, and for bringing us to this moment. Amen.

T'ki·ah	sh'varim-t'ru·ah	t'ki·ah	T'ki·ah	sh'varim	t'ki·ah
T'ki·ah	sh'varim-t'ru·ah	t'ki·ah	T'ki·ah	sh'varim	t'ki·ah
T'ki·ah	sh'varim-t'ru·ah	t'ki·ah	T'ki·ah	sh'varim	t'ki·ah

T'ki·ah t'ru·ah t'ki·ah
T'ki·ah t'ru·ah t'ki·ah
T'ki·ah t'ru·ah t'ki·ah g'dolah

יְהִי רָצוֹן מִלְּפָנֶיךָ, יהוה אֱלֹהֵינוּ וֵאלֹהֵי אֲבוֹתֵינוּ [וְאִמּוֹתֵנוּ],
שֶׁהַתְּקִיעוֹת וְהַקּוֹלוֹת הַיּוֹצְאִים מִן הַשּׁוֹפָר שֶׁאָנוּ תּוֹקְעִים,
יַעֲלוּ לִפְנֵי כִּסֵּא כְבוֹדֶךָ, וִיכַפְּרוּ עַל כָּל־חַטֹּאתֵינוּ. בָּרוּךְ אַתָּה,
בַּעַל הָרַחֲמִים.

אַשְׁרֵי הָעָם יֹדְעֵי תְרוּעָה, יהוה בְּאוֹר־פָּנֶיךָ יְהַלֵּכוּן.
בְּשִׁמְךָ יְגִילוּן כָּל־הַיּוֹם, וּבְצִדְקָתְךָ יָרוּמוּ.

We are seated.

אַשְׁרֵי יוֹשְׁבֵי בֵיתֶךָ, עוֹד יְהַלְלוּךָ סֶּלָה.
אַשְׁרֵי הָעָם שֶׁכָּכָה לּוֹ, אַשְׁרֵי הָעָם שֶׁיהוה אֱלֹהָיו.

תְּהִלָּה לְדָוִד.

אֲרוֹמִמְךָ אֱלוֹהַי הַמֶּלֶךְ, וַאֲבָרְכָה שִׁמְךָ לְעוֹלָם וָעֶד.
בְּכָל־יוֹם אֲבָרְכֶךָּ, וַאֲהַלְלָה שִׁמְךָ לְעוֹלָם וָעֶד.
גָּדוֹל יהוה וּמְהֻלָּל מְאֹד, וְלִגְדֻלָּתוֹ אֵין חֵקֶר.
דּוֹר לְדוֹר יְשַׁבַּח מַעֲשֶׂיךָ, וּגְבוּרֹתֶיךָ יַגִּידוּ.
הֲדַר כְּבוֹד הוֹדֶךָ, וְדִבְרֵי נִפְלְאֹתֶיךָ אָשִׂיחָה.
וֶעֱזוּז נוֹרְאוֹתֶיךָ יֹאמֵרוּ, וּגְדֻלָּתְךָ אֲסַפְּרֶנָּה.
זֵכֶר רַב־טוּבְךָ יַבִּיעוּ, וְצִדְקָתְךָ יְרַנֵּנוּ.
חַנּוּן וְרַחוּם יהוה, אֶרֶךְ אַפַּיִם וּגְדָל־חָסֶד.
טוֹב־יהוה לַכֹּל, וְרַחֲמָיו עַל־כָּל־מַעֲשָׂיו.
יוֹדוּךָ יהוה כָּל־מַעֲשֶׂיךָ, וַחֲסִידֶיךָ יְבָרְכוּכָה.
כְּבוֹד מַלְכוּתְךָ יֹאמֵרוּ, וּגְבוּרָתְךָ יְדַבֵּרוּ.
לְהוֹדִיעַ לִבְנֵי הָאָדָם גְּבוּרֹתָיו, וּכְבוֹד הֲדַר מַלְכוּתוֹ.
מַלְכוּתְךָ מַלְכוּת כָּל־עוֹלָמִים, וּמֶמְשַׁלְתְּךָ בְּכָל־דּוֹר וָדֹר.
סוֹמֵךְ יהוה לְכָל־הַנֹּפְלִים, וְזוֹקֵף לְכָל־הַכְּפוּפִים.
עֵינֵי־כֹל אֵלֶיךָ יְשַׂבֵּרוּ, וְאַתָּה נוֹתֵן־לָהֶם אֶת־אָכְלָם בְּעִתּוֹ.
פּוֹתֵחַ אֶת־יָדֶךָ, וּמַשְׂבִּיעַ לְכָל־חַי רָצוֹן.
צַדִּיק יהוה בְּכָל־דְּרָכָיו, וְחָסִיד בְּכָל־מַעֲשָׂיו.
קָרוֹב יהוה לְכָל־קֹרְאָיו, לְכֹל אֲשֶׁר יִקְרָאֻהוּ בֶאֱמֶת.
רְצוֹן־יְרֵאָיו יַעֲשֶׂה, וְאֶת־שַׁוְעָתָם יִשְׁמַע וְיוֹשִׁיעֵם.
שׁוֹמֵר יהוה אֶת־כָּל־אֹהֲבָיו, וְאֵת כָּל־הָרְשָׁעִים יַשְׁמִיד.
◁ תְּהִלַּת יהוה יְדַבֶּר־פִּי,
וִיבָרֵךְ כָּל־בָּשָׂר שֵׁם קָדְשׁוֹ לְעוֹלָם וָעֶד. תהלים קמה
וַאֲנַחְנוּ נְבָרֵךְ יָהּ, מֵעַתָּה וְעַד־עוֹלָם. הַלְלוּ־יָהּ.

JOYOUS ARE THE PEOPLE
אַשְׁרֵי הָעָם. Psalm 89:16–17.
Though we may have
entered this moment with
trepidation, once awakened
by the call of the shofar
to God's presence, we can
emerge joyful.

ASHREI. According to
Rabbi Elazar (Babylonia,
3rd century) speaking in
the name of Rabbi Abina,
the thrice-daily recita-
tion of Psalm 145 (which,
with the addition of three
other verses from psalms, is
known as the Ashrei) opens
a pathway to eternity.
The Talmud explains that
Ashrei is an alphabetical
acrostic that symbolically
encompasses the variety of
praises of God, and that it
contains an especially appropriate description of the
thankfulness with which we
are to approach God: "You
open Your hand, satisfying
all the living with contentment" (Babylonian Talmud,
Berakhot 4b).
  For synagogue use, two
verses were added to the
opening, both of which
begin with the word ashrei,
"joyous" (Psalms 84:5 and
144:15). Additionally, Psalm
115:18 was appended to
the end, referring to those
assembled in prayer.

MEDITATION AFTER THE BLOWING OF THE SHOFAR

May it be Your will, our God, and God of our ancestors, that the cries of this shofar rise up to Your throne, and that they serve as atonement for all our sins. *Barukh atah*, Master of mercy.

Joyous are the people who experience the calling of the shofar;
ADONAI, they walk by the light of Your presence.
They continuously rejoice in Your name, and are exalted through Your righteousness.

We are seated.

ASHREI

Joyous are they who dwell in Your house; they shall praise You forever.
　Joyous the people who are so favored; joyous the people whose God is ADONAI.

PSALM 145

A PSALM OF DAVID.

I exalt You, my God, my sovereign; I praise Your name, always.
　Every day I praise You, glorifying Your name, always.
Great is ADONAI, greatly to be praised, though God's greatness is unfathomable.
　One generation praises Your works to another, telling of Your mighty deeds.
I would speak of Your majestic glory and of Your wondrous acts.
　People speak of Your awe-inspiring deeds; I, too, shall recount Your greatness.
They recount Your great goodness, and sing of Your righteousness.
　ADONAI is merciful and compassionate, patient, and abounding in love.
ADONAI is good to all, and God's mercy embraces all of creation.
　All of creation acknowledges You, and the faithful bless You.
They speak of the glory of Your sovereignty; and tell of Your might,
　proclaiming to humanity Your mighty deeds,
　and the glory of Your majestic sovereignty.
Your sovereignty is eternal; Your dominion endures through each generation.
　ADONAI supports all who falter, and lifts up all who are bent down.
The eyes of all look hopefully to You,
and You provide them nourishment in due time.
　You open Your hand, satisfying all the living with contentment.
ADONAI is righteous in all that is done, faithful to all creation.
　ADONAI is near to all who call, to all who sincerely call.
God fulfills the desire of those who are faithful,
listening to their cries, rescuing them.
　ADONAI watches over all those who love the Holy One,
　but will destroy all the wicked.
My mouth shall utter praise of ADONAI.
May all that is mortal praise God's name forever and ever.
　We shall praise ADONAI now and always. Halleluyah!

We rise. Leader:

יְהַלְלוּ אֶת־שֵׁם יהוה, כִּי־נִשְׂגָּב שְׁמוֹ לְבַדּוֹ.

Congregation:

הוֹדוֹ עַל־אֶרֶץ וְשָׁמֵיִם. וַיֵּרֶם קֶרֶן לְעַמּוֹ,
תְּהִלָּה לְכָל־חֲסִידָיו, לִבְנֵי יִשְׂרָאֵל עַם קְרֹבוֹ, הַלְלוּ־יָהּ.

ON SHABBAT, WE RECITE THIS PSALM:

מִזְמוֹר לְדָוִד.

הָבוּ לַיהוה בְּנֵי אֵלִים, הָבוּ לַיהוה כָּבוֹד וָעֹז.
הָבוּ לַיהוה כְּבוֹד שְׁמוֹ, הִשְׁתַּחֲווּ לַיהוה בְּהַדְרַת־קֹדֶשׁ.
קוֹל יהוה עַל־הַמָּיִם,
אֵל־הַכָּבוֹד הִרְעִים, יהוה עַל־מַיִם רַבִּים.
קוֹל־יהוה בַּכֹּחַ, קוֹל יהוה בֶּהָדָר.
קוֹל־יהוה שֹׁבֵר אֲרָזִים, וַיְשַׁבֵּר יהוה אֶת־אַרְזֵי הַלְּבָנוֹן.
וַיַּרְקִידֵם כְּמוֹ־עֵגֶל, לְבָנוֹן וְשִׂרְיֹן כְּמוֹ בֶן־רְאֵמִים.
קוֹל־יהוה חֹצֵב לַהֲבוֹת אֵשׁ.
קוֹל יהוה יָחִיל מִדְבָּר,
יָחִיל יהוה מִדְבַּר קָדֵשׁ.
קוֹל יהוה יְחוֹלֵל אַיָּלוֹת
וַיֶּחֱשֹׂף יְעָרוֹת, וּבְהֵיכָלוֹ כֻּלּוֹ אֹמֵר כָּבוֹד.
יהוה לַמַּבּוּל יָשָׁב, וַיֵּשֶׁב יהוה מֶלֶךְ לְעוֹלָם.
יהוה עֹז לְעַמּוֹ יִתֵּן, יהוה יְבָרֵךְ אֶת־עַמּוֹ בַשָּׁלוֹם. תהלים כט

PSALM 29. Psalm 29 was chosen to accompany the procession of the Torah as it is returned to the ark on Shabbat morning because of the predominant image of the voice of God. The phrase *kol Adonai* ("the voice of God") is repeated seven times—which was identified by the ancient Rabbis with the revelation of God's word on Sinai. The thunder and lightning described here evokes the scene of the revelation at Sinai in the Book of Exodus; the Bible identifies Kadesh with the Sinai desert.

Biblical scholars see the psalm as a depiction of a storm coming in from the Mediterranean, passing over the mountains of Lebanon—cedars top those high mountains and are among the world's sturdiest and longest-lived trees—moving over the fertile land and then through the desert. A similarly worded poem was found among the remains of the pre-Israelite Canaanite people of Ugarit. That poem is a paean to Baal, the pagan storm-god.

Our psalm begins with reference to the waters of the Mediterranean Sea and ends with God enthroned above the primal waters of creation. It also begins with an angelic chorus praising God and toward the end mentions the human chorus praising God in the Temple. Thus earth and heaven, the human and the divine, are joined. Similarly, Torah is that which ties heaven and earth together.

RETURNING THE TORAH

We rise. Leader:

Extol the name of ADONAI, for God's name alone is exalted.

Congregation:

God's glory encompasses heaven and earth; God extols the faithful—
raising up Israel, the people God keeps close. Halleluyah!

Hodo al eretz v'shamayim, va-yarem keren l'ammo;
t'hillah l'khol ḥasidav, liv'nei yisra·el am k'rovo. Hal'luyah!

ON SHABBAT, WE RECITE THIS PSALM:

PSALM 29

A SONG OF DAVID.

Acclaim ADONAI, O exalted creatures;
acclaim ADONAI, with glory and strength.
Acclaim ADONAI, for God's name is glorious;
pay homage to ADONAI in the splendor of the sanctuary.
The voice of ADONAI is stronger than the voice of the sea;
God is exalted above the rushing waters.
The voice of ADONAI is powerful;
the voice of ADONAI is glorious.
The voice of ADONAI shatters majestic cedars,
the very cedars of Lebanon.
The trees skip like calves;
the mountains, like wild oxen.
The voice of ADONAI flashes fire, splitting rocks;
the voice of ADONAI convulses the desert,
the very desert of Kadesh.
The voice of ADONAI makes hinds calve;
the voice of ADONAI strips the forest bare,
while in God's sanctuary all acknowledge God's glory.
ADONAI was enthroned above the primal waters;
ADONAI sat enthroned, the eternal sovereign.
ADONAI will grant strength to God's people, blessing them with peace.

Havu ladonai b'nei eilim, havu ladonai kavod va-oz.
Havu ladonai k'vod sh'mo, hishtaḥavu ladonai b'hadrat kodesh.

Kol Adonai ba-ko·aḥ, kol Adonai be-hadar,
kol Adonai shoveir arazim, va-y'shabbeir Adonai et arzei ha-l'vanon.

Kol Adonai ḥotzeiv lahavot eish, kol Adonai yaḥil midbar,
yaḥil Adonai midbar kadeish. Kol Adonai y'ḥoleil ayyalot

Adonai la-mabbul yashav, va-yeishev Adonai melekh l'olam.
Adonai oz l'ammo yittein, Adonai y'vareikh et ammo va-shalom.

לְדָוִד מִזְמוֹר.

לַיהוה הָאָרֶץ וּמְלוֹאָהּ, תֵּבֵל וְיֹשְׁבֵי בָהּ.

כִּי־הוּא עַל־יַמִּים יְסָדָהּ, וְעַל־נְהָרוֹת יְכוֹנְנֶהָ.

מִי־יַעֲלֶה בְהַר־יהוה, וּמִי־יָקוּם בִּמְקוֹם קָדְשׁוֹ.

נְקִי כַפַּיִם וּבַר־לֵבָב, אֲשֶׁר לֹא־נָשָׂא לַשָּׁוְא נַפְשִׁי,
וְלֹא נִשְׁבַּע לְמִרְמָה.

יִשָּׂא בְרָכָה מֵאֵת יהוה, וּצְדָקָה מֵאֱלֹהֵי יִשְׁעוֹ.

זֶה דּוֹר דֹּרְשָׁו, מְבַקְשֵׁי פָנֶיךָ יַעֲקֹב, סֶלָה.

שְׂאוּ שְׁעָרִים רָאשֵׁיכֶם, וְהִנָּשְׂאוּ פִּתְחֵי עוֹלָם,
וְיָבוֹא מֶלֶךְ הַכָּבוֹד.

מִי זֶה מֶלֶךְ הַכָּבוֹד,

יהוה עִזּוּז וְגִבּוֹר, יהוה גִּבּוֹר מִלְחָמָה.

שְׂאוּ שְׁעָרִים רָאשֵׁיכֶם, וּשְׂאוּ פִּתְחֵי עוֹלָם,
וְיָבֹא מֶלֶךְ הַכָּבוֹד.

מִי הוּא זֶה מֶלֶךְ הַכָּבוֹד,

יהוה צְבָאוֹת הוּא מֶלֶךְ הַכָּבוֹד, סֶלָה. תהלים כד

PSALM 24. This psalm's dramatic imagery of gates that open for God's symbolic entrance to the Temple explains why it accompanies our Torah's return to the ark. Yet the psalm focuses first of all on the state of the worshipper: purity of action—especially verbal honesty—must characterize those who would enter this holy place and receive its blessing. This develops a theme of the *b'rakhah* recited just after each Torah reading, describing the Torah as "a teaching of truth": in order to live in accord with Torah, we must exemplify inner truthfulness while also pursuing truth in the world.

A Song of David

Each of the two psalms recited as the Torah is carried around the congregation (one on Shabbat, one on weekdays) begins with the same Hebrew words—but in a different order. Psalm 24 begins לְדָוִד מִזְמוֹר, literally "to David a psalm," and Psalm 29 begins מִזְמוֹר לְדָוִד, "a psalm to David." The Midrash comments on this difference, saying that sometimes David would be so inspired that he immediately began writing, but at other times he had to struggle to find inspiration.

On weekdays:

PSALM 24

A SONG OF DAVID.

The earth is ADONAI's in all its fullness,
the land and all who dwell on it.
For it was God who founded it upon the seas,
and set it firm upon the flowing streams.
Who may ascend the mount of ADONAI?
Who may come forward in God's sanctuary?
One who has clean hands and a pure heart,
who has not taken God's name in vain, nor sworn deceitfully.
One such as this will receive ADONAI's blessing,
a just reward from God, the deliverer.
This generation searches for You;
like Jacob, seeks Your presence, *selah.*
Open up, arched gateways—open up, doors of the world;
may the sovereign who is exalted enter.
Who is the sovereign who is exalted?
ADONAI, mighty and triumphant, triumphant in battle.
Open up, arched gateways—open up, doors of the world;
may the sovereign who is exalted enter.
Who is the sovereign who is exalted?
Adonai Tz'va·ot is the sovereign who is exalted. *Selah.*

Ladonai ha-aretz u-m'lo·ah, teiveil v'yosh'vei vah.
   Ki hu al yammim y'sadah, v'al n'harot y'khon'neha.
Mi ya·aleh v'har Adonai, u-mi yakum bi-m'kom kodsho.
   N'ki khappayim u-var leivav, asher lo nasa la-shav nafshi,
   v'lo nishba l'mirmah.
Yissa v'rakhah mei-eit Adonai, u-tz'dakah mei-elohei yisho.
   Zeh dor dor'shav m'vakshei fanekha ya·akov, selah.
S'u sh'arim rasheikhem, v'hinnas'u pithei olam,
v'yavo melekh ha-kavod.
   Mi zeh melekh ha-kavod, Adonai izzuz v'gibbor,
   Adonai gibbor milhamah.
S'u sh'arim rasheikhem, v'hinnas'u pithei olam,
v'yavo melekh ha-kavod.
   Mi hu zeh melekh ha-kavod,
   Adonai Tz'va·ot hu melekh ha-kavod, selah.

The Torah scrolls are placed in the ark.

וּבְנֻחֹה יֹאמַר: שׁוּבָה יהוה רִבְבוֹת אַלְפֵי יִשְׂרָאֵל.
קוּמָה יהוה לִמְנוּחָתֶֽךָ, אַתָּה וַאֲרוֹן עֻזֶּֽךָ.
כֹּהֲנֶֽיךָ יִלְבְּשׁוּ־צֶֽדֶק, וַחֲסִידֶֽיךָ יְרַנֵּֽנוּ.
בַּעֲבוּר דָּוִד עַבְדֶּֽךָ, אַל־תָּשֵׁב פְּנֵי מְשִׁיחֶֽךָ.
◁ כִּי לֶֽקַח טוֹב נָתַֽתִּי לָכֶם, תּוֹרָתִי אַל־תַּעֲזֹֽבוּ.
עֵץ־חַיִּים הִיא לַמַּחֲזִיקִים בָּהּ, וְתֹמְכֶֽיהָ מְאֻשָּׁר.
דְּרָכֶֽיהָ דַרְכֵי־נֹֽעַם, וְכָל־נְתִיבוֹתֶֽיהָ שָׁלוֹם.
הֲשִׁיבֵֽנוּ יהוה אֵלֶֽיךָ וְנָשֽׁוּבָה, חַדֵּשׁ יָמֵֽינוּ כְּקֶֽדֶם.

The ark is closed.

חֲצִי קַדִּישׁ

יִתְגַּדַּל וְיִתְקַדַּשׁ שְׁמֵהּ רַבָּא, בְּעָלְמָא דִּי בְרָא, כִרְעוּתֵהּ,
וְיַמְלִיךְ מַלְכוּתֵהּ בְּחַיֵּיכוֹן וּבְיוֹמֵיכוֹן וּבְחַיֵּי דְכָל־בֵּית
יִשְׂרָאֵל, בַּעֲגָלָא וּבִזְמַן קָרִיב, וְאִמְרוּ אָמֵן.

יְהֵא שְׁמֵהּ רַבָּא מְבָרַךְ לְעָלַם וּלְעָלְמֵי עָלְמַיָּא.

יִתְבָּרַךְ וְיִשְׁתַּבַּח וְיִתְפָּאַר וְיִתְרוֹמַם וְיִתְנַשֵּׂא וְיִתְהַדָּר
וְיִתְעַלֶּה וְיִתְהַלָּל שְׁמֵהּ דְּקֻדְשָׁא, בְּרִיךְ הוּא,
לְעֵֽלָּא לְעֵֽלָּא מִכָּל־בִּרְכָתָא וְשִׁירָתָא תֻּשְׁבְּחָתָא וְנֶחֱמָתָא
דַּאֲמִירָן בְּעָלְמָא, וְאִמְרוּ אָמֵן.

WHENEVER THE ARK WAS SET DOWN וּבְנֻחֹה יֹאמַר. Numbers 10:36. As the Torah completes its circuit through the synagogue, we recall Moses' words when the people finished a stage in their journey through the wilderness and came to rest in a new camp. This verse and the ones that follow (Psalm 132:8–10; Proverbs 4:2; 3:18, 3:17; Lamentations 5:21) can also serve to refer to our own inner journey—accompanied by Torah.

IT IS A TREE OF LIFE FOR THOSE WHO GRASP IT עֵץ חַיִּים הִיא לַמַּחֲזִיקִים בָּהּ This verse (Proverbs 3:18) is the source of the custom of holding onto the *atzei ḥayyim*, the Torah handles, while reciting the *b'rakhot* over the Torah—thus grasping the "tree of life" both physically and figuratively.

ITS WAYS ARE PLEASANT WAYS, AND ALL ITS PATHS ARE PEACE, דְּרָכֶֽיהָ דַרְכֵי־נֹֽעַם, וְכָל־נְתִיבוֹתֶֽיהָ שָׁלוֹם. Proverbs 3:17. As we put away the Torah, we pray that our study should promote actions that lead to pleasantness and peace.

*Make Our Days
Seem Fresh*

"Make our days seem fresh" should not be seen as a plea for restoration of a formerly perfect condition; we were never perfect. Rather, it is a plea for resilience, a plea for the ability to renew ourselves after moments of crisis and dislocation. As Elie Wiesel remarks, "God gave Adam a secret—and that secret was not how to begin, but how to begin again."

The Torah scrolls are placed in the ark.

Whenever the Ark was set down, Moses would say:
ADONAI, may You dwell among the myriad families of the people Israel.
> Return, ADONAI, to Your sanctuary,
> You and Your glorious Ark.
Let Your priests be robed in righteousness,
and Your faithful sing for joy.
> For the sake of David, Your servant,
> do not turn away from Your anointed.
I have given you a precious inheritance:
Do not forsake My teaching.
> It is a tree of life for those who grasp it,
> and all who hold onto it are blessed.
Its ways are pleasant ways, and all its paths are peace.
> Turn us toward You, ADONAI, and we will return to You;
> make our days seem fresh, as they once were.

Eitz ḥayyim hi la-maḥazikim bah, v'tom'kheha m'ushar.
D'rakheha darkhei no·am, v'khol n'tivoteha shalom.
Hashiveinu Adonai eilekha v'nashuvah, ḥaddeish yameinu k'kedem.

The ark is closed.

Ḥatzi Kaddish

May God's great name be exalted and hallowed throughout the created world, as is God's wish. May God's sovereignty soon be established, in your lifetime and in your days, and in the days of all the House of Israel. And respond with: *Amen.*
b'ḥayyeikhon u-v'yomeikhon u-v'ḥayyei d'khol beit yisra·el,
ba-agala u-viz'man kariv, v'imru amen.

May God's great name be acknowledged forever and ever!
Y'hei sh'meih rabba m'varakh l'alam u-l'almei almayya. Yitbarakh

May the name of the Holy One be acknowledged and celebrated, lauded and worshipped, exalted and honored, extolled and acclaimed—though God, who is blessed, is truly far beyond all acknowledgment and praise, or any expressions of gratitude or consolation ever spoken in the world. And respond with: *Amen.*
b'rikh hu, l'eilla l'eilla mi-kol birkhata v'shirata
tushb'ḥata v'neḥamata da-amiran b'alma, v'imru amen.

מוסף לראש השנה   MUSAF SERVICE OF ROSH HASHANAH

Before the Amidah begins, it is customary to take three steps backward, as if we are leaving our familiar surroundings, and then three steps forward, as we approach God's presence.

When reciting the words בָּרוּךְ אַתָּה on this page, we customarily bend the knees and bow, standing up straight by the time we reach the word יהוה. We repeat these motions at the end of the first b'rakhah when we come to the words "barukh atah Adonai." The sign ↑ indicates the places to bow.

AMIDAH. The Amidah, literally "the prayer said while standing," is the moment of personal meditation. It always contains three introductory b'rakhot. The first mentions our ancestors and their relation to God; the second describes God's continuing presence in the world; the third emphasizes God's uniqueness and the path to God: holiness. Similarly, every Amidah ends with three b'rakhot. The first looks toward the restoration of God's presence to Zion; the next thanks God for all the gifts we experience in life; and the final one asks for peace. In the Musaf Amidah for Rosh Hashanah, three special sections are added in the middle, each expressing the themes of the day: Malkhuyot, prayers celebrating God's sovereignty; Zikhronot, prayers of remembrance (since today is called "the day of remembrance"); and Shofarot, prayers describing the central symbol of the day. Some congregations blow the shofar after the silent recitation of each of these sections, while others pray the Amidah and wait for the leader's repetition to hear the blowing the shofar.

אֲדֹנָי שְׂפָתַי תִּפְתָּח וּפִי יַגִּיד תְּהִלָּתֶךָ.

Version with Patriarchs and Matriarchs:

↑ **בָּרוּךְ** אַתָּה יהוה,
אֱלֹהֵינוּ וֵאלֹהֵי אֲבוֹתֵינוּ
[וְאִמּוֹתֵינוּ], אֱלֹהֵי אַבְרָהָם,
אֱלֹהֵי יִצְחָק, וֵאלֹהֵי יַעֲקֹב,
אֱלֹהֵי שָׂרָה, אֱלֹהֵי רִבְקָה,
אֱלֹהֵי רָחֵל, וֵאלֹהֵי לֵאָה,
הָאֵל הַגָּדוֹל הַגִּבּוֹר וְהַנּוֹרָא,
אֵל עֶלְיוֹן, גּוֹמֵל חֲסָדִים
טוֹבִים, וְקוֹנֵה הַכֹּל, וְזוֹכֵר
חַסְדֵי אָבוֹת [וְאִמָּהוֹת],
וּמֵבִיא גוֹאֵל לִבְנֵי בְנֵיהֶם
לְמַעַן שְׁמוֹ בְּאַהֲבָה.

Version with Patriarchs:

↑ **בָּרוּךְ** אַתָּה יהוה,
אֱלֹהֵינוּ וֵאלֹהֵי אֲבוֹתֵינוּ,
אֱלֹהֵי אַבְרָהָם, אֱלֹהֵי
יִצְחָק, וֵאלֹהֵי יַעֲקֹב, הָאֵל
הַגָּדוֹל הַגִּבּוֹר וְהַנּוֹרָא,
אֵל עֶלְיוֹן, גּוֹמֵל חֲסָדִים
טוֹבִים, וְקוֹנֵה הַכֹּל, וְזוֹכֵר
חַסְדֵי אָבוֹת, וּמֵבִיא גוֹאֵל
לִבְנֵי בְנֵיהֶם לְמַעַן שְׁמוֹ
בְּאַהֲבָה.

ADONAI, OPEN MY LIPS אֲדֹנָי שְׂפָתַי תִּפְתָּח. Psalm 51:17. Every Amidah begins with this request asking God to afford us the appropriate attitude and words for prayer. Perhaps the phrase conveys a mystical sense that prayer originates in our soul, the part of God within us all.

GOD OF ABRAHAM, GOD OF ISAAC, AND GOD OF JACOB, אֱלֹהֵי אַבְרָהָם, אֱלֹהֵי יִצְחָק, וֵאלֹהֵי יַעֲקֹב. God began the conversation with Moses at the burning bush with this self-description (Exodus 3:6). Perhaps the quotation of these words expresses the hope that we too might feel the presence of God.

GREAT, MIGHTY, AWE-INSPIRING, TRANSCENDENT GOD הָאֵל הַגָּדוֹל הַגִּבּוֹר וְהַנּוֹרָא. Deuteronomy 10:17. The next two verses in the Torah continue, "who upholds the cause of the fatherless and the widow and befriends the stranger, providing him with food and clothing. You too must befriend the stranger, for you were strangers in the land of Egypt."

THE SILENT AMIDAH

An Alternate Rendering

Some may want to engage in silent prayer by reading through the prayers and meditations in this column through p. 139. The alternate renderings of the opening and closing blessings are by André Ungar. Meditations on the themes of the day by other authors are found in the middle of the Amidah.

Help me, O God,
to pray. Our ancestors worshipped You.
Abraham and Sarah,
Rebecca and Isaac,
Jacob, Rachel, and Leah
stood in awe before You.
We, too, reach for You,
infinite, awe-inspiring,
transcendent God,
source of all being, whose
truth shines through our
ancestors' lives. We, their
distant descendants, draw
strength from their lives
and from Your redeeming
love. Be our help and our
shield, as You were theirs.
We praise You, God,
Guardian of Abraham.

O sovereign God who
   delights in life,
make our lives worthy to
   be remembered.
Out of Your love for us,
   O living God,
enter our names in the
   Ledger of Life.

Before the Amidah begins, it is customary to take three steps backward, as if we are leaving our familiar surroundings, and then three steps forward, as we approach God's presence.
   When reciting the words "barukh atah" on this page, we customarily bend the knees and bow, standing up straight by the time we reach the word "Adonai." We repeat these motions at the end of the first b'rakhah when we come to the words "barukh atah Adonai." The sign ʄ indicates the places to bow.

ADONAI, open my lips that my mouth may speak Your praise.

First B'rakhah: Our Ancestors

Version with Patriarchs:

ʄ *Barukh atah* ADONAI,
our God and God of our
   ancestors,
God of Abraham, God of
   Isaac, and God of Jacob,
great, mighty, awe-inspiring,
   transcendent God,
who acts with lovingkindness
   and creates all things,
who remembers the loving
   deeds of our ancestors,
and who will send a redeemer
   to their children's children
   with love
   for the sake of divine honor.

Version with Patriarchs and Matriarchs:

ʄ *Barukh atah* ADONAI,
our God and God of our
   ancestors,
God of Abraham, God of
   Isaac, and God of Jacob,
God of Sarah, God of
   Rebecca, God of Rachel,
   and God of Leah,
great, mighty, awe-inspiring,
   transcendent God,
who acts with lovingkindness
   and creates all things,
who remembers the loving
   deeds of our ancestors,
and who will send a redeemer
   to their children's children
   with love
   for the sake of divine honor.

זָכְרֵנוּ לְחַיִּים, מֶלֶךְ חָפֵץ בַּחַיִּים,
וְכָתְבֵנוּ בְּסֵפֶר הַחַיִּים, לְמַעַנְךָ אֱלֹהִים חַיִּים.

Version with Patriarchs and Matriarchs: *Version with Patriarchs:*

מֶלֶךְ עוֹזֵר וּפוֹקֵד מֶלֶךְ עוֹזֵר וּמוֹשִׁיעַ וּמָגֵן.
וּמוֹשִׁיעַ וּמָגֵן. ‡ בָּרוּךְ אַתָּה יהוה, מָגֵן
‡ בָּרוּךְ אַתָּה יהוה, מָגֵן אַבְרָהָם.
אַבְרָהָם וּפוֹקֵד שָׂרָה.

אַתָּה גִבּוֹר לְעוֹלָם, אֲדֹנָי, מְחַיֵּה מֵתִים אַתָּה,
רַב לְהוֹשִׁיעַ.

מְכַלְכֵּל חַיִּים בְּחֶסֶד, מְחַיֵּה מֵתִים בְּרַחֲמִים רַבִּים, סוֹמֵךְ
נוֹפְלִים, וְרוֹפֵא חוֹלִים, וּמַתִּיר אֲסוּרִים, וּמְקַיֵּם אֱמוּנָתוֹ
לִישֵׁנֵי עָפָר. מִי כָמְוֹךָ בַּעַל גְּבוּרוֹת, וּמִי דּוֹמֶה לָּךְ, מֶלֶךְ
מֵמִית וּמְחַיֶּה וּמַצְמִיחַ יְשׁוּעָה.

מִי כָמְוֹךָ אַב הָרַחֲמִים, זוֹכֵר יְצוּרָיו לְחַיִּים בְּרַחֲמִים.

וְנֶאֱמָן אַתָּה לְהַחֲיוֹת מֵתִים.
בָּרוּךְ אַתָּה יהוה, מְחַיֵּה הַמֵּתִים.

אַתָּה קָדוֹשׁ וְשִׁמְךָ קָדוֹשׁ וּקְדוֹשִׁים בְּכָל־יוֹם יְהַלְלוּךָ, סֶּלָה.

וּבְכֵן תֵּן פַּחְדְּךָ יהוה אֱלֹהֵינוּ עַל כָּל־מַעֲשֶׂיךָ
וְאֵימָתְךָ עַל כָּל־מַה־שֶּׁבָּרָאתָ,
וְיִירָאוּךָ כָּל־הַמַּעֲשִׂים
וְיִשְׁתַּחֲווּ לְפָנֶיךָ כָּל־הַבְּרוּאִים,
וְיֵעָשׂוּ כֻלָּם אֲגֻדָּה אַחַת לַעֲשׂוֹת רְצוֹנְךָ בְּלֵבָב שָׁלֵם,
כְּמוֹ שֶׁיָּדַעְנוּ יהוה אֱלֹהֵינוּ שֶׁהַשִּׁלְטוֹן לְפָנֶיךָ,
עֹז בְּיָדְךָ וּגְבוּרָה בִּימִינֶךָ,
וְשִׁמְךָ נוֹרָא עַל כָּל־מַה־שֶּׁבָּרָאתָ.

REMEMBER US זָכְרֵנוּ. This brief anonymous and ancient poem, added at each service during the High Holy Day season, stresses the theme that God treasures life; on this day, we pray for another year of life.

YOU ARE MIGHTY אַתָּה גִבּוֹר. This b'rakhah, which describes God's presence and activity in the world, centers on the kindness and care of God for the incapacitated—even the dead are in God's care.

GIVE LIFE TO THE DEAD מְחַיֵּה מֵתִים. To be sure, the primary meaning of this phrase was understood to refer to the afterlife, but the Rabbis also understood that the phrase referred to a spiritual revival in this world. Thus the b'rakhah one makes on greeting a friend whom one has not seen for a year utilizes this phrase, "who gives life to the dead."

WHO IS LIKE YOU, SOURCE OF COMPASSION? מִי כָמְוֹךָ אַב הָרַחֲמִים. A second piyyut inserted at each of the services in the High Holy Day season, emphasizing God's kindness.

U-V'KHEIN וּבְכֵן. These three paragraphs, which are introduced by the same word, וּבְכֵן (u-v'khein), are ascribed by many scholars to the 3rd century, and may constitute the earliest poetic additions to the Amidah. Stages of redemption are described in this series of prayers. Reuven Hammer, a modern commentator, remarks that the first paragraph implores God to cause the entire world to live with reverence for God. The next paragraph discusses not the universal, but the particular: the return of Israel to its land (and specifically to Jerusalem) and the kingship of David. The third paragraph describes the rejoicing that will come to the righteous "when You remove the tyranny of arrogance from the earth" and God will rule alone over the entire world from Zion and Jerusalem.

Your power sustains the universe. You breathe life into dead matter. With compassion You care for all who live. Your limitless love lets life triumph over death, heals the sick, upholds the exhausted, frees the enslaved, keeps faith even with the dead. Who is like You, God of splendor and power incomparable?

As a tender parent, You nurture our souls that we may grow into a life of compassion.

You govern both life and death; Your presence brings our souls to blossom. We praise You, God, who wrests life from death.

Sacred are You, sacred Your mystery. Seekers of holiness worship You all their lives.

Remember us for life, Sovereign who delights in life, and inscribe us in the Book of Life, for Your sake, God of life.

Version with Patriarchs:
You are the Sovereign who helps and saves and shields.

ʄ *Barukh atah* ADONAI, Shield of Abraham.

Version with Patriarchs and Matriarchs:
You are the Sovereign who helps and guards, saves and shields.

ʄ *Barukh atah* ADONAI, Shield of Abraham and Guardian of Sarah.

Second B'rakhah: God's Saving Care

You are mighty forever, ADONAI,
You give life to the dead; great is Your saving power.

You sustain the living through love,
    and with great mercy give life to the dead.
You support the falling,
    heal the sick,
    loosen the chains of the bound,
    and keep faith with those who sleep in the dust.
Who is like You, Almighty,
    and who can be compared to You?—
    Sovereign, who brings death and life,
    and causes salvation to flourish.

Who is like You, source of compassion,
    who remembers with compassion Your creatures for life?

You are faithful in bringing life to the dead.
Barukh atah ADONAI, who gives life to the dead.

Third B'rakhah: God's Holiness

Holy are You and holy is Your name;
holy ones praise You each day.

U-v'khein—ADONAI our God,
instill Your awe in all You have made,
and fear of You in all You have created,
so that all You have fashioned revere You,
all You have created bow in recognition,
and all be bound together, carrying out Your will wholeheartedly.
For we know that true sovereignty is Yours,
power and strength are in Your hands,
and Your name is to be revered beyond any of Your creations.

ADONAI WILL REIGN
FOREVER יִמְלֹךְ יהוה לְעוֹלָם.
Psalm 146:10.

ADONAI TZ'VA·OT WILL
BE EXALTED וַיִּגְבַּה יהוה
צְבָאוֹת. Isaiah 5:16.

RECALLING THE EXODUS
FROM EGYPT זֵכֶר לִיצִיאַת
מִצְרָיִם. On each Shabbat
and holy day we recall the
Exodus as the formative
moment of our history.
Our freedom, which we
celebrate, obligates us ethi-
cally and religiously. The
holy day marks both our
joy and our understanding
that we are responsible to
serve God and repair the
world.

וּבְכֵן תֵּן כָּבוֹד יהוה לְעַמֶּךָ,
תְּהִלָּה לִירֵאֶיךָ וְתִקְוָה לְדוֹרְשֶׁיךָ,
וּפִתְחוֹן פֶּה לַמְיַחֲלִים לָךְ,
שִׂמְחָה לְאַרְצֶךָ וְשָׂשׂוֹן לְעִירֶךָ,
וּצְמִיחַת קֶרֶן לְדָוִד עַבְדֶּךָ,
וַעֲרִיכַת נֵר לְבֶן־יִשַׁי מְשִׁיחֶךָ, בִּמְהֵרָה בְיָמֵינוּ.

וּבְכֵן צַדִּיקִים יִרְאוּ וְיִשְׂמָחוּ
וִישָׁרִים יַעֲלֹזוּ,
וַחֲסִידִים בְּרִנָּה יָגִילוּ,
וְעוֹלָתָה תִּקְפָּץ־פִּיהָ
וְכָל־הָרִשְׁעָה כֻּלָּהּ כְּעָשָׁן תִּכְלֶה,
כִּי תַעֲבִיר מֶמְשֶׁלֶת זָדוֹן מִן הָאָרֶץ.

וְתִמְלֹךְ, אַתָּה יהוה לְבַדֶּךָ, עַל כָּל־מַעֲשֶׂיךָ, בְּהַר צִיּוֹן
מִשְׁכַּן כְּבוֹדֶךָ, וּבִירוּשָׁלַיִם עִיר קָדְשֶׁךָ, כַּכָּתוּב בְּדִבְרֵי
קָדְשֶׁךָ: יִמְלֹךְ יהוה לְעוֹלָם, אֱלֹהַיִךְ צִיּוֹן לְדֹר וָדֹר,
הַלְלוּ־יָהּ.

קָדוֹשׁ אַתָּה וְנוֹרָא שְׁמֶךָ, וְאֵין אֱלוֹהַּ מִבַּלְעָדֶיךָ, כַּכָּתוּב:
וַיִּגְבַּה יהוה צְבָאוֹת בַּמִּשְׁפָּט, וְהָאֵל הַקָּדוֹשׁ נִקְדַּשׁ
בִּצְדָקָה. בָּרוּךְ אַתָּה יהוה, הַמֶּלֶךְ הַקָּדוֹשׁ.

אַתָּה בְחַרְתָּנוּ מִכָּל־הָעַמִּים,
אָהַבְתָּ אוֹתָנוּ וְרָצִיתָ בָּנוּ,
וְרוֹמַמְתָּנוּ מִכָּל־הַלְּשׁוֹנוֹת,
וְקִדַּשְׁתָּנוּ בְּמִצְוֹתֶיךָ,
וְקֵרַבְתָּנוּ מַלְכֵּנוּ לַעֲבוֹדָתֶךָ,
וְשִׁמְךָ הַגָּדוֹל וְהַקָּדוֹשׁ עָלֵינוּ קָרָאתָ.

וַתִּתֶּן לָנוּ, יהוה אֱלֹהֵינוּ,
בְּאַהֲבָה אֶת־יוֹם [הַשַּׁבָּת הַזֶּה וְאֶת־יוֹם] הַזִּכָּרוֹן הַזֶּה,
יוֹם [זִכְרוֹן] תְּרוּעָה [בְּאַהֲבָה]
מִקְרָא קֹדֶשׁ, זֵכֶר לִיצִיאַת מִצְרָיִם.

Let all creation stand in
     awe of You;
let all humankind sense
     Your mystery.
May all people be united
     in doing Your will
     whole-heartedly.
We know that You judge
     those who govern,
that ultimate power is
     Yours alone,
that Your care embraces
     all Your creatures.

Make us all people of
     honor.
Smile on all who serve
     You.
Give hope to those who
     seek You,
courage to those who
     await the fulfillment of
     the messianic dream,
soon in our lifetime.

May the righteous wit-
     ness it and be happy,
may good people be filled
     with joy—
when at last all jeering
     stops and evil evapo-
     rates,
when the reign of vio-
     lence vanishes from
     Earth.

And You, You alone,
     will rule over all Your
     creation
from Mount Zion, Your
     glorious dwelling place,
from Jerusalem, Your
     holy city,
as sacred Scripture pro-
     claims: "God will reign
     throughout the world,
     your God, O Zion,
     forever and ever.
Halleluyah!"

Sacred are You, and
     sacred Your mystery.
Seekers of holiness wor-
     ship You all their lives.
We praise You, God, ulti-
     mate sacred mystery.

U-v'khein—Bestow honor to Your people, Adonai,
praise to those who revere You,
hope to those who seek You,
recognition to those who await You,
joy to Your land, and gladness to Your city.
May the light of David, Your servant, dawn,
and the lamp of the son of Jesse, Your anointed, be kindled
speedily in our day.

U-v'khein—The righteous, beholding this, will rejoice,
the upright will be glad,
the pious will celebrate with song, evil will be silenced,
and all wickedness will disappear like smoke,
when You remove the tyranny of arrogance from the earth.

You alone, Adonai, will rule all Your creation,
from Mount Zion, the dwelling-place of Your glory,
and from Jerusalem, Your holy city.
As it is written in the Book of Psalms:
"Adonai will reign forever;
your God, O Zion, from generation to generation. Halleluyah!"

You are holy, and Your name is revered,
     for there is no God but You.
As Your prophet Isaiah wrote: "*Adonai Tz'va·ot* will be exalted
through justice, the holy God sanctified through righteousness."
Barukh atah Adonai, the Holy Sovereign.

Fourth B'rakhah: The Holiness of Rosh Hashanah
You have chosen us among all peoples, loving us, wanting us.
You have distinguished us among all nations, making us holy
through Your commandments, drawing us close to Your
service, and calling us by Your great and holy name.

With love, You have bestowed on us, Adonai our God, [this
Shabbat and] this Day of Remembrance, a day for [recalling]
the shofar sound [with love], a day for holy assembly and for
recalling the Exodus from Egypt.

Some recite this traditional version; others continue on the next page with A Prayer for Jewry in Distress.

וּמִפְּנֵי חֲטָאֵינוּ גָּלִינוּ מֵאַרְצֵנוּ וְנִתְרַחַקְנוּ מֵעַל אַדְמָתֵנוּ
וְאֵין אֲנַחְנוּ יְכוֹלִים לַעֲשׂוֹת חוֹבוֹתֵינוּ בְּבֵית בְּחִירָתֶךָ,
בַּבַּֽיִת הַגָּדוֹל וְהַקָּדוֹשׁ שֶׁנִּקְרָא שִׁמְךָ עָלָיו, מִפְּנֵי הַיָּד
שֶׁנִּשְׁתַּלְּחָה בְּמִקְדָּשֶׁךָ.

יְהִי רָצוֹן מִלְּפָנֶֽיךָ, יְהוה אֱלֹהֵֽינוּ וֵאלֹהֵי אֲבוֹתֵֽינוּ
[וְאִמּוֹתֵֽינוּ], מֶֽלֶךְ רַחֲמָן הַמֵּשִׁיב בָּנִים לִגְבוּלָם, שֶׁתָּשׁוּב
וּתְרַחֵם עָלֵֽינוּ וְעַל מִקְדָּשְׁךָ בְּרַחֲמֶֽיךָ הָרַבִּים, וְתִבְנֵֽהוּ
מְהֵרָה וּתְגַדֵּל כְּבוֹדוֹ. אָבִֽינוּ מַלְכֵּֽנוּ, גַּלֵּה כְּבוֹד מַלְכוּתְךָ
עָלֵֽינוּ מְהֵרָה, וְהוֹפַע וְהִנָּשֵׂא עָלֵֽינוּ לְעֵינֵי כָּל־חָי, וְקָרֵב
פְּזוּרֵֽינוּ מִבֵּין הַגּוֹיִם וּנְפוּצוֹתֵֽינוּ כַּנֵּס מִיַּרְכְּתֵי־אָֽרֶץ.
וַהֲבִיאֵֽנוּ לְצִיּוֹן עִירְךָ בְּרִנָּה, וְלִירוּשָׁלַֽיִם בֵּית מִקְדָּשְׁךָ
בְּשִׂמְחַת עוֹלָם, שֶׁשָּׁם עָשׂוּ אֲבוֹתֵֽינוּ [וְאִמּוֹתֵֽינוּ] לְפָנֶֽיךָ
אֶת־קָרְבְּנוֹת חוֹבוֹתֵיהֶם, תְּמִידִים כְּסִדְרָם וּמוּסָפִים
כְּהִלְכָתָם, וְאֶת־מוּסְפֵי [יוֹם הַשַּׁבָּת הַזֶּה וְ] יוֹם הַזִּכָּרוֹן
הַזֶּה עָשׂוּ וְהִקְרִֽיבוּ לְפָנֶֽיךָ בְּאַהֲבָה כְּמִצְוַת רְצוֹנֶֽךָ כַּכָּתוּב
בְּתוֹרָתֶֽךָ, עַל יְדֵי מֹשֶׁה עַבְדֶּֽךָ מִפִּי כְבוֹדֶֽךָ כָּאָמוּר:

The Sephardic rite continues on page 130.
On Shabbat, those reciting the traditional sacrificial list add this paragraph:

וּבְיוֹם הַשַּׁבָּת שְׁנֵי כְבָשִׂים בְּנֵי שָׁנָה תְּמִימִם, וּשְׁנֵי
עֶשְׂרֹנִים סֹֽלֶת מִנְחָה בְּלוּלָה בַשֶּֽׁמֶן וְנִסְכּוֹ. עֹלַת שַׁבַּת
בְּשַׁבַּתּוֹ, עַל עֹלַת הַתָּמִיד וְנִסְכָּהּ. במדבר כח ט-י

וּבַחֹֽדֶשׁ הַשְּׁבִיעִי, בְּאֶחָד לַחֹֽדֶשׁ, מִקְרָא קֹֽדֶשׁ יִהְיֶה לָכֶם
כָּל מְלֶֽאכֶת עֲבֹדָה לֹא תַעֲשׂוּ, יוֹם תְּרוּעָה יִהְיֶה לָכֶם.
וַעֲשִׂיתֶם עֹלָה לְרֵֽיחַ נִיחֹֽחַ לַיהוה, פַּר בֶּן־בָּקָר אֶחָד, אַֽיִל
אֶחָד, כְּבָשִׂים בְּנֵי שָׁנָה שִׁבְעָה, תְּמִימִם. במדבר כט א-ב
וּמִנְחָתָם וְנִסְכֵּיהֶם כִּמְדֻבָּר: שְׁלֹשָׁה עֶשְׂרֹנִים לַפָּר, וּשְׁנֵי
עֶשְׂרֹנִים לָאַֽיִל, וְעִשָּׂרוֹן לַכֶּֽבֶשׂ, וְיַֽיִן כְּנִסְכּוֹ, וּשְׁנֵי שְׂעִירִים
לְכַפֵּר, וּשְׁנֵי תְמִידִים כְּהִלְכָתָם. מִלְּבַד עֹלַת הַחֹֽדֶשׁ
וּמִנְחָתָהּ, וְעֹלַת הַתָּמִיד וּמִנְחָתָהּ, וְנִסְכֵּיהֶם כְּמִשְׁפָּטָם,
לְרֵֽיחַ נִיחֹֽחַ אִשֶּׁה לַיהוה. במדבר כט ג-ו

BECAUSE OF OUR SINS
מִפְּנֵי חֲטָאֵֽינוּ. The first of the middle b'rakhot of the Amidah is called קְדֻשַּׁת הַיּוֹם (k'dushat ha-yom), the expression of the holiness of the day. The content of this b'rakhah is not prescribed in the Talmud. During the first millennium, the prayers concerning the holiness of the day came to be centered on the Temple and its offerings, as if the utterance of the words substituted for the missing sacrifices. Recently, some have begun reciting alternate prayers, which understand the rebuilding of the Temple as a metaphor for the repair of the world in which we all need to engage. (See the following page.)

Our Sacrifice

Our worship is one of prayer and praise. But when we think of the piety of our ancestors, who from their meager store of cattle and grain, the yield of the shepherd's care and the farmer's toil, offered their best in the service of God, can we be content with a gift of mere words that costs us neither labor nor privation? Shall we not feel impelled to devote of our substance to the service of God? Shall we not give of our store to the relief of suffering, the healing of sickness, the dispelling of ignorance and error, the righting of wrongs and the strengthening of faith?

—MORDECAI KAPLAN
AND EUGENE KOHN
(adapted)

Some recite this traditional version; others continue on the next page with A Prayer for Jewry in Distress.

Because of our sins we have been exiled from our land and removed from our soil. And so, because of the hand that was set against Your sanctuary, we are unable to fulfill our obligations in the great and holy place that You chose to carry Your name.

May it be Your will, ADONAI our God and God of our ancestors, compassionate sovereign who restores their descendants to their promised land, that You may once again have compassion on us and return in Your great mercy to Your sanctuary. May You speedily rebuild it and renew its glory. *Avinu Malkeinu,* speedily manifest the glory of Your dominion, revealing to all humanity that You are our sovereign. Welcome back our dispersed from among the nations, and gather those scattered to the ends of the earth. Bring us exultantly to Zion, Your city, and with everlasting joy to Jerusalem, Your sanctuary, where our ancestors once offered to You their obligatory daily and holy day sacrifices, each as prescribed. The [Shabbat and] New Year sacrifices were offered there in love, as You commanded, as it is written in Your Torah by Moses, Your servant, by Your instruction:

The Sephardic rite continues on page 130.

On Shabbat, those reciting the traditional sacrificial list add this paragraph:

On Shabbat: two yearling lambs without blemish, together with two-tenths of a measure of choice flour with oil mixed in as a grain offering, and with the proper libation. A burnt offering for every Shabbat, in addition to the regular burnt offering and its libation. Numbers 28:9–10

In the seventh month, on the first day of the month, you shall observe a sacred occasion: you shall not work at your occupations. You shall observe it as a day when the horn is sounded. You shall present a burnt offering of pleasing odor to ADONAI: one bull of the herd, one ram, and seven yearling lambs, without blemish. Numbers 29:1–2

As ordained, they shall be accompanied by grain offerings and by libations: three-tenths of a measure for the bull, two-tenths for the ram, one-tenth for each lamb, wine for its libation, two goats for expiation, and the two daily offerings as is their custom. This is in addition to the burnt offering of the new moon with its meal offering and the regular burnt offering with its grain offering, each with its libation as prescribed, gifts of pleasing odor to ADONAI. Numbers 29:3–6

A PRAYER FOR JEWRY IN DISTRESS

אֱלֹהֵינוּ וֵאלֹהֵי אֲבוֹתֵינוּ [וְאִמּוֹתֵינוּ], רַחֵם עַל אַחֵינוּ
בֵּית יִשְׂרָאֵל הַנְּתוּנִים בְּצָרָה וְהוֹצִיאֵם מֵאֲפֵלָה לְאוֹרָה.
וְקַבֵּל בְּרַחֲמִים אֶת־תְּפִלַּת עַמְּךָ בְּנֵי יִשְׂרָאֵל, בְּכָל־
מְקוֹמוֹת מוֹשְׁבוֹתֵיהֶם, הַשּׁוֹפְכִים אֶת־לִבָּם לְפָנֶיךָ בְּיוֹם
[הַשַּׁבָּת הַזֶּה וּבְיוֹם] הַזִּכָּרוֹן הַזֶּה.

Those who recited the traditional sacrificial list do not recite this paragraph:

יְהִי רָצוֹן מִלְּפָנֶיךָ, יהוה אֱלֹהֵינוּ וֵאלֹהֵי אֲבוֹתֵינוּ
[וְאִמּוֹתֵינוּ], שֶׁיִּבָּנֶה בֵּית הַמִּקְדָּשׁ בִּמְהֵרָה בְיָמֵינוּ,
כְּפִי שֶׁהִבְטַחְתָּנוּ עַל יְדֵי נְבִיאֶךָ, כַּכָּתוּב:
וְהָיָה בְּאַחֲרִית הַיָּמִים,
נָכוֹן יִהְיֶה הַר בֵּית יהוה בְּרֹאשׁ הֶהָרִים וְנִשָּׂא מִגְּבָעוֹת,
וְנָהֲרוּ אֵלָיו כָּל־הַגּוֹיִם.
וְהָלְכוּ עַמִּים רַבִּים וְאָמְרוּ,
לְכוּ וְנַעֲלֶה אֶל הַר יהוה, אֶל בֵּית אֱלֹהֵי יַעֲקֹב,
וְיֹרֵנוּ מִדְּרָכָיו, וְנֵלְכָה בְּאֹרְחֹתָיו.
כִּי מִצִּיּוֹן תֵּצֵא תוֹרָה וּדְבַר יהוה מִירוּשָׁלָיִם.
וְשָׁפַט בֵּין הַגּוֹיִם וְהוֹכִיחַ לְעַמִּים רַבִּים,
וְכִתְּתוּ חַרְבוֹתָם לְאִתִּים וַחֲנִיתוֹתֵיהֶם לְמַזְמֵרוֹת,
לֹא יִשָּׂא גוֹי אֶל גּוֹי חֶרֶב וְלֹא יִלְמְדוּ עוֹד מִלְחָמָה.

ON SHABBAT, WE RECITE THIS PARAGRAPH:

יִשְׂמְחוּ בְמַלְכוּתְךָ שׁוֹמְרֵי שַׁבָּת וְקוֹרְאֵי עֹנֶג, עַם מְקַדְּשֵׁי
שְׁבִיעִי, כֻּלָּם יִשְׂבְּעוּ וְיִתְעַנְּגוּ מִטּוּבֶךָ. וּבַשְּׁבִיעִי רָצִיתָ
בּוֹ וְקִדַּשְׁתּוֹ, חֶמְדַּת יָמִים אוֹתוֹ קָרָאתָ, זֵכֶר לְמַעֲשֵׂה
בְרֵאשִׁית.

MAY IT BE YOUR WILL יְהִי רָצוֹן. This prayer was first published in *Siddur Va'ani Tefilati*, the prayerbook of the Masorti (Conservative) movement in Israel. It substitutes for the traditional prayer, which speaks of the exile, our inability to perform the Temple sacrifices, and the hope of return. The prayer acknowledges the new condition of the Jewish people having returned to the Land of Israel and it includes the prophetic hope that Israel may become a land of peace and justice and a signpost of world peace.

AND IT SHALL COME TO PASS וְהָיָה בְּאַחֲרִית הַיָּמִים. Isaiah 2:2–4. Isaiah's vision of universal peace has become the dream of a world community and is inscribed as the watchword of the United Nations. This phrase is subject to different interpretations. Most contemporary biblical scholars think that it simply points to a future time, perhaps at some slight distance from the present. Classical exegetes thought of it as referring to a messianic end-time.

LET US GO UP לְכוּ וְנַעֲלֶה. Isaiah 2:2–4, the prophet's vision of universal religious unity.

The exile of the nation is connected by a very strong tie with the exile of the world, and the redemption of the nation with the redemption of the individual soul. Both the exile of the nation and its redemption are to be thought of not by themselves, but only in relation to the destiny of the world and to the destiny of the soul.

—MARTIN BUBER

A PRAYER FOR JEWRY IN DISTRESS

Our God and God of our ancestors, show compassion to our brothers and sisters of the House of Israel, who suffer persecution; deliver them from darkness to light. Accept with compassion the prayers of Your people Israel who cry out to You on this [Shabbat and this] Day of Remembrance, wherever they dwell.

Those who recited the traditional sacrificial list do not recite this paragraph:

May it be Your will, ADONAI our God and God of our ancestors, that the Holy Temple be rebuilt speedily in our time, as You promised, in the words of Your prophet Isaiah: "And it shall come to pass, in the end of days, that the House of ADONAI will be firmly established at the top of the mountain, raised high above all other hills. All peoples shall flow toward it, and nations shall say, 'Let us go up to the mountain of ADONAI to the house of the God of Jacob, and we shall learn from God's ways and walk in God's paths.' For instruction shall go forth from Zion and the word of ADONAI from Jerusalem. God will provide proper judgment among nations and admonish many peoples. They shall beat their swords into plowshares, and spears into pruning hooks. Nation shall not take up sword against nation, neither shall they learn war anymore."

ON SHABBAT, WE RECITE THIS PARAGRAPH:

Those who observe Shabbat and call it a delight rejoice in Your sovereignty. May the people who sanctify the seventh day be fulfilled and delighted with Your abundant goodness. You have loved the seventh day and sanctified it, calling it the treasured day, a sign of creation.

מַלְכֻיּוֹת

עָלֵינוּ לְשַׁבֵּחַ לַאֲדוֹן הַכֹּל,
לָתֵת גְּדֻלָּה לְיוֹצֵר בְּרֵאשִׁית,
שֶׁלֹּא עָשָׂנוּ כְּגוֹיֵי הָאֲרָצוֹת,
וְלֹא שָׂמָנוּ כְּמִשְׁפְּחוֹת הָאֲדָמָה,
שֶׁלֹּא שָׂם חֶלְקֵנוּ כָּהֶם,
וְגֹרָלֵנוּ כְּכָל־הֲמוֹנָם.
יּ וַאֲנַחְנוּ כּוֹרְעִים וּמִשְׁתַּחֲוִים וּמוֹדִים,
לִפְנֵי מֶלֶךְ, מַלְכֵי הַמְּלָכִים,
הַקָּדוֹשׁ בָּרוּךְ הוּא.
שֶׁהוּא נוֹטֶה שָׁמַיִם וְיֹסֵד אָרֶץ,
וּמוֹשַׁב יְקָרוֹ בַּשָּׁמַיִם מִמַּעַל,
וּשְׁכִינַת עֻזּוֹ בְּגָבְהֵי מְרוֹמִים,
הוּא אֱלֹהֵינוּ אֵין עוֹד.
אֱמֶת מַלְכֵּנוּ אֶפֶס זוּלָתוֹ,
כַּכָּתוּב בְּתוֹרָתוֹ:
וְיָדַעְתָּ הַיּוֹם וַהֲשֵׁבֹתָ אֶל־לְבָבֶךָ,
כִּי יהוה הוּא הָאֱלֹהִים בַּשָּׁמַיִם מִמַּעַל
וְעַל הָאָרֶץ מִתָּחַת, אֵין עוֹד.

MALKHUYOT. The first of the special sections of Musaf is entitled Malkhuyot—prayers and biblical verses celebrating God's sovereignty. All appellations of God are metaphors, but the image of God as sovereign had particular power for medieval and rabbinic Judaism. (The Torah has few references to God as sovereign, but there are many in prophetic writings and in Psalms.) It represents a rejection of earthly authority as the arbiter of ultimate values. Additionally, the metaphor of God as sovereign expresses the common human experience of a transcendent power both glorious and terrifying, as well as the corresponding sense of vulnerability and dependence evoked by this image. Lastly, biblical narratives depict the earthly sovereign as functioning as a judge, so by employing the metaphor of sovereignty in reference to God we focus on Rosh Hashanah as Yom Ha-Din, the Day of Judgment, when God is said to ascend the throne of judgment. The Malkhuyot section concludes with the fourth *b'rakhah* on the holiness of Rosh Hashanah, to which is added the phrase *melekh al kol ha-aretz*, "ruler of all the earth." These words join the standard holy day Amidah *b'rakhah* that describes God as sanctifying the people Israel and the holy day—in this case specified as *Yom Ha-zikkaron*, the Day of Remembrance.

IT IS FOR US עָלֵינוּ. Aleinu, originally written for the Rosh Hashanah service, is one of the best-known and oft-repeated prayers. Its central theme is a proclamation of God's sovereignty, an appropriate introduction to this section. It is traditionally attributed to Rav, a 3rd-century rabbi. Although this may not be historically accurate, it is certainly one of the oldest prayers.

The beginning of faith is
... not a feeling for the
mystery of living or a
sense of awe, wonder and
amazement. The root of
religion is the question
what to do with the
feeling for the mystery of
living, what to do with
awe, wonder and amaze-
ment. Religion begins
with a consciousness that
something is asked of us.
—ABRAHAM JOSHUA
HESCHEL

How to Serve God

Rabbi Baer of Radoshitz,
who later became a
Ḥasidic master, once
asked of his teacher, the
Seer of Lublin, "Show
me one general way to
the service of God." The
seer replied, "It is impossible to tell people what
way they should take.
One way to serve God is
through the teachings;
another, through prayer;
another, through fast-
ing; and still another is
through eating. Everyone
should carefully observe
what way the heart pulls,
and then choose that way
with all the strength of
one's being."
—MARTIN BUBER

Malkhuyot—God's Sovereignty
PRAYERS AND BIBLICAL VERSES ON GOD'S SOVEREIGNTY

ALEINU—GOD, WHOM WE WORSHIP
It is for us to praise the Ruler of all,
to acclaim the Creator,
who has not made us merely a nation,
nor formed us as all earthly families,
nor given us an ordinary destiny.
ʕ And so we bow,
acknowledging the supreme sovereign,
the Holy One, who is praised—
the One who spreads out the heavens and establishes the earth,
whose glorious abode is in the highest heaven,
whose powerful presence is in the loftiest heights.
This is our God, none else;
ours is the true sovereign, there is no other.
As it is written in the Torah:
"Know this day and take it to heart,
that ADONAI is God in heaven above and on earth below;
there is no other."

עַל כֵּן נְקַוֶּה לְּךָ יהוה אֱלֹהֵינוּ, לִרְאוֹת מְהֵרָה בְּתִפְאֶרֶת
עֻזֶּךָ, לְהַעֲבִיר גִּלּוּלִים מִן הָאָרֶץ וְהָאֱלִילִים כָּרוֹת יִכָּרֵתוּן,
לְתַקֵּן עוֹלָם בְּמַלְכוּת שַׁדַּי, וְכָל־בְּנֵי בָשָׂר יִקְרְאוּ בִשְׁמֶךָ,
לְהַפְנוֹת אֵלֶיךָ כָּל־רִשְׁעֵי אָרֶץ. יַכִּירוּ וְיֵדְעוּ כָּל־יוֹשְׁבֵי
תֵבֵל, כִּי לְךָ תִּכְרַע כָּל־בֶּרֶךְ, תִּשָּׁבַע כָּל־לָשׁוֹן. לְפָנֶיךָ יהוה
אֱלֹהֵינוּ יִכְרְעוּ וְיִפְּלוּ, וְלִכְבוֹד שִׁמְךָ יְקָר יִתֵּנוּ. וִיקַבְּלוּ
כֻלָּם אֶת־עֹל מַלְכוּתֶךָ, וְתִמְלֹךְ עֲלֵיהֶם מְהֵרָה לְעֹלָם
וָעֶד. כִּי הַמַּלְכוּת שֶׁלְּךָ הִיא, וּלְעוֹלְמֵי עַד תִּמְלוֹךְ בְּכָבוֹד.

כַּכָּתוּב בְּתוֹרָתֶךָ:

א יהוה יִמְלֹךְ לְעֹלָם וָעֶד. שמות טו יח

ב וְנֶאֱמַר: לֹא־הִבִּיט אָוֶן בְּיַעֲקֹב, וְלֹא רָאָה עָמָל
בְּיִשְׂרָאֵל, יהוה אֱלֹהָיו עִמּוֹ וּתְרוּעַת מֶלֶךְ בּוֹ. במדבר כג כא

ג וְנֶאֱמַר: וַיְהִי בִישֻׁרוּן מֶלֶךְ, בְּהִתְאַסֵּף רָאשֵׁי עָם, יַחַד
שִׁבְטֵי יִשְׂרָאֵל. דברים לג ה

וּבְדִבְרֵי קָדְשְׁךָ כָּתוּב לֵאמֹר:

א כִּי לַיהוה הַמְּלוּכָה וּמֹשֵׁל בַּגּוֹיִם. תהלים כב כט

ב וְנֶאֱמַר: יהוה מָלָךְ גֵּאוּת לָבֵשׁ, לָבֵשׁ יהוה עֹז הִתְאַזָּר,
אַף תִּכּוֹן תֵּבֵל בַּל־תִּמּוֹט. תהלים צג א

ג וְנֶאֱמַר: שְׂאוּ שְׁעָרִים רָאשֵׁיכֶם וְהִנָּשְׂאוּ פִּתְחֵי עוֹלָם,
וְיָבוֹא מֶלֶךְ הַכָּבוֹד. מִי זֶה מֶלֶךְ הַכָּבוֹד, יהוה עִזּוּז וְגִבּוֹר,
יהוה גִּבּוֹר מִלְחָמָה. שְׂאוּ שְׁעָרִים רָאשֵׁיכֶם, וּשְׂאוּ פִּתְחֵי
עוֹלָם, וְיָבֹא מֶלֶךְ הַכָּבוֹד. מִי הוּא זֶה מֶלֶךְ הַכָּבוֹד, יהוה
צְבָאוֹת הוּא מֶלֶךְ הַכָּבוֹד, סֶלָה. תהלים כד ז-י

ESTABLISHING IN THE WORLD THE SOVEREIGNTY OF THE ALMIGHTY לְתַקֵּן עוֹלָם. *Tikkun olam*, which means "mending the world," is an ancient Hebrew phrase that has acquired additional resonance in modern times. In its setting in this prayer, *l'takken olam* means "to establish the world in the kingdom of the Almighty [*Shaddai*]," or to bring about God's rule on earth. In contemporary usage it refers to the betterment of the world, including the relief of human suffering, the achievement of peace and mutual respect among peoples, and protection of the planet itself from destruction.
(*adapted from Arthur Green*)

THE BIBLICAL VERSES OF MALKHUYOT/SOVEREIGNTY. Whereas the Book of Psalms, some books of the Prophets, and the later rabbinic tradition take for granted that God is naturally referred to as King, these three verses are the only verses in the entire Five Books of Moses that expressly connect God to kingship. Perhaps this omission reflects a desire to further distance Judaism from the surrounding idolatrous nations, in which the human monarch was often seen as a manifestation of the deity.

A NOTE ON THE TRANSLATION OF BIBLICAL VERSES. The meanings and emphases of the verses of Malkhuyot, Zikhronot, and Shofarot in their liturgical settings sometimes differ from their meanings in their biblical contexts. The translations here reflect that shift—varying, when appropriate, from some of the familiar English renditions, such as the JPS translation used in *Etz Hayim*, the Conservative movement's Torah commentary.

LIFT UP HIGH, O YOU GATES; LIFT UP THE ETERNAL DOORS שְׂאוּ שְׁעָרִים רָאשֵׁיכֶם וְהִנָּשְׂאוּ פִּתְחֵי עוֹלָם. Classically, "Jerusalem" refers to both the city on earth and a "heavenly city," each reflective of the other. "Gates" and "doors" refer not only to the gates of Jerusalem or the Temple, but also to "cosmic doors," through which the presence of God enters the world.

We all worship idols. We
make our transitory needs
into ultimate concerns. We
are caught up in the busy-
ness of our lives and then
do not see beyond these
concerns. But from time to
time we can be reminded
that there is a perspective
in which these matters that
are so important to us now
will, one way or another,
pass away.

There are essential ques-
tions which should never
be too distant from us:
What gives our lives meaning? How do we effectuate
good? How do we care for
those we love? How do
we tend to those in need?
How do we not close our-
selves off to the cries of
pain in the world?

Facing these questions,
we are opened to greater
concerns than our own
neediness. In creating that
opening we clear a space
for divine instruction as to
how to live our lives, how
to establish the kingdom
of God.

And so, ADONAI our God, we await You, that soon we may behold Your strength revealed in full glory, sweeping away the abominations of the earth, obliterating idols, establishing in the world the sovereignty of the Almighty. All flesh will call out Your name—even the wicked will turn toward You. Then all who live on earth will recognize and understand that to You alone knees must bend and allegiance be sworn. All will bow down and prostrate themselves before You, ADONAI our God, honor Your glorious name, and accept the obligation of Your sovereignty. May You soon rule over them forever and ever, for true dominion is Yours; You will rule in glory until the end of time.

As it is written in Your Torah:

א ADONAI will be *Sovereign* forever and ever. Exodus 15:18

ב God does not gaze upon the errors of Jacob,
nor look upon the sins of Israel;
ADONAI their God is with them,
their *Sovereign's* acclaim is in their midst. Numbers 23:21

ג God became *Sovereign* in Jeshurun,
as the leaders of the people gathered
with the tribes of Israel. Deuteronomy 33:5

And it is also written in Psalms:

א For *sovereignty* is ADONAI's;
God rules over the nations. Psalm 22:29

ב ADONAI is *sovereign*, robed in splendor, girded in strength.
So the earth is established on sure foundation. Psalm 93:1

ג Lift up high, O you gates; lift up the eternal doors,
so that the *Sovereign* of Glory may enter.
Who is the *Sovereign* of Glory?
ADONAI, mighty and valiant,
ADONAI, mighty in battle.
Lift up high, O you gates;
lift up the eternal doors, so that the *Sovereign* of Glory
    may enter.
Who is the *Sovereign* of Glory?
Adonai Tz'va·ot is the *Sovereign* of Glory, forever. Psalm 24:7–10

וְעַל יְדֵי עֲבָדֶיךָ הַנְּבִיאִים כָּתוּב לֵאמֹר:

א כֹּה אָמַר יהוה, מֶֽלֶךְ יִשְׂרָאֵל וְגֹאֲלוֹ יהוה צְבָאוֹת, אֲנִי רִאשׁוֹן וַאֲנִי אַחֲרוֹן, וּמִבַּלְעָדַי אֵין אֱלֹהִים. ישעיה מד ו

ב וְנֶאֱמַר: וְעָלוּ מוֹשִׁעִים בְּהַר צִיּוֹן לִשְׁפֹּט אֶת־הַר עֵשָׂו, וְהָיְתָה לַיהוה הַמְּלוּכָה. עבדיה א כא

ג וְנֶאֱמַר: וְהָיָה יהוה לְמֶֽלֶךְ עַל כָּל־הָאָֽרֶץ, בַּיּוֹם הַהוּא יִהְיֶה יהוה אֶחָד וּשְׁמוֹ אֶחָד. זכריה יד ט

וּבְתוֹרָתְךָ כָּתוּב לֵאמֹר:

שְׁמַע יִשְׂרָאֵל, יהוה אֱלֹהֵֽינוּ, יהוה אֶחָד. דברים ו ד

אֱלֹהֵֽינוּ וֵאלֹהֵי אֲבוֹתֵֽינוּ [וְאִמּוֹתֵֽינוּ], מְלוֹךְ עַל כָּל־הָעוֹלָם כֻּלּוֹ בִּכְבוֹדֶֽךָ, וְהִנָּשֵׂא עַל כָּל־הָאָֽרֶץ בִּיקָרֶֽךָ, וְהוֹפַע בַּהֲדַר גְּאוֹן עֻזֶּֽךָ עַל כָּל־יוֹשְׁבֵי תֵבֵל אַרְצֶֽךָ, וְיֵדַע כָּל־פָּעוּל כִּי אַתָּה פְעַלְתּוֹ, וְיָבִין כָּל־יְצוּר כִּי אַתָּה יְצַרְתּוֹ, וְיֹאמַר כֹּל אֲשֶׁר נְשָׁמָה בְאַפּוֹ, יהוה אֱלֹהֵי יִשְׂרָאֵל מֶֽלֶךְ, וּמַלְכוּתוֹ בַּכֹּל מָשָֽׁלָה. אֱלֹהֵֽינוּ וֵאלֹהֵי אֲבוֹתֵֽינוּ [וְאִמּוֹתֵֽינוּ] [רְצֵה בִמְנוּחָתֵֽנוּ] קַדְּשֵֽׁנוּ בְּמִצְוֹתֶֽיךָ, וְתֵן חֶלְקֵֽנוּ בְּתוֹרָתֶֽךָ, שַׂבְּעֵֽנוּ מִטּוּבֶֽךָ, וְשַׂמְּחֵֽנוּ בִּישׁוּעָתֶֽךָ. [וְהַנְחִילֵֽנוּ, יהוה אֱלֹהֵֽינוּ, בְּאַהֲבָה וּבְרָצוֹן שַׁבַּת קָדְשֶֽׁךָ, וְיָנֽוּחוּ בָהּ יִשְׂרָאֵל מְקַדְּשֵׁי שְׁמֶֽךָ.] וְטַהֵר לִבֵּֽנוּ לְעָבְדְּךָ בֶּאֱמֶת, כִּי אַתָּה אֱלֹהִים אֱמֶת, וּדְבָרְךָ אֱמֶת וְקַיָּם לָעַד. בָּרוּךְ אַתָּה יהוה, מֶֽלֶךְ עַל כָּל־הָאָֽרֶץ, מְקַדֵּשׁ [הַשַּׁבָּת וְ] יִשְׂרָאֵל וְיוֹם הַזִּכָּרוֹן.

In some communities, at the conclusion of each special section of the Silent Amidah, the shofar is blown. (The shofar is traditionally not blown on Shabbat.)

תְּקִיעָה שְׁבָרִים־תְּרוּעָה תְּקִיעָה
תְּקִיעָה שְׁבָרִים תְּקִיעָה
תְּקִיעָה תְּרוּעָה תְּקִיעָה

ADONAI SHALL BE AC-KNOWLEDGED SOVEREIGN וְהָיָה יהוה לְמֶֽלֶךְ עַל כָּל־הָאָֽרֶץ. Zechariah 14:9. This verse is also quoted at the conclusion of the Aleinu. In it, we recognize that God's Oneness is not yet fully realized, and we express our hope that our prayers and actions will contribute to achieving that ideal. Here, the verse is followed directly by the first line of the Sh'ma (Deuteronomy 6:4), which is our declaration that God is, indeed, One, although the Sh'ma itself does not contain any form of the word *melekh*. The ancient Rabbis understood the recitation of the Sh'ma as *kabbalat ol malkhut shamayim*, the acceptance of the yoke of God's sovereignty. Therefore it was deemed appropriate to recite the Sh'ma as the tenth verse of Malkhuyot.

OUR GOD AND GOD OF OUR ANCESTORS אֱלֹהֵֽינוּ וֵאלֹהֵי אֲבוֹתֵֽינוּ. This paragraph concludes the fourth *b'rakhah* of the Amidah; the text is nearly identical to the liturgy of Shabbat and Festivals. It includes a prayer to purify our hearts so that our service to God may be *emet*, "truth" (וְטַהֵר לִבֵּֽנוּ לְעָבְדְּךָ בֶּאֱמֶת). The Hebrew word *emet* implies more than mere honesty or absence of falsehood: it connotes also faithfulness, wholeness, and integrity. Thus, we express our longing to be constant and consistent in our prayer and to liberate our relationship with God from the mixed motives and inner conflicts that generally characterize human behavior. The prayer's penultimate sentence—unique to the High Holy Days—takes up this theme of truth, applying the attribute to God and God's word, and emphasizing it as an essential quality of the Divine.

And Your servants the prophets further wrote:
א Thus said ADONAI, *Sovereign* and Redeemer of Israel,
Adonai Tz'va·ot: I am the first and I am the last, and there is no
God but Me. Isaiah 44:6
ב Liberators shall ascend Mount Zion to judge Mount Esau;
then *sovereignty* shall be ADONAI's. Obadiah 1:21
ג ADONAI shall be acknowledged *sovereign* of all the earth;
on that day ADONAI shall be One, and the name of God,
One. Zechariah 14:9

And it is written in Your Torah:
Hear, O Israel, ADONAI is our God, ADONAI alone.

Deuteronomy 6:4

Our God, our ancestors' God, consecrate us with Your mitzvot, give us a share in Your truth. Sate us with Your goodness, delight us with Your help. Make our hearts worthy to serve You truly. May we possess [Your holy Shabbat and] this Day of Remembrance with love and eagerness. We praise You O God, whose [Shabbat,] people Israel and whose Day of Remembrance are sacred.

Our God and God of our ancestors: in Your glory, rule over the entire universe; in Your splendor, be exalted over all the earth; in the majestic beauty of Your overwhelming presence, appear to all the inhabitants of Your world. Then, all that You have made will recognize You as their maker, all that You created will understand that You are their creator, and all living beings will say: ADONAI, the God of Israel, is sovereign, ruling over all.

Our God and God of our ancestors: [embrace our rest,] make us holy through Your commandments and let the Torah be our portion. Fill our lives with Your goodness and gladden us with Your triumph. [ADONAI our God, grant that we inherit Your holy Shabbat, lovingly and willingly, so that the people Israel, who sanctify Your name, may find rest on this day.] Purify our hearts to serve You truly, for You are the God of truth, and Your word is true, eternal, and unchanging. *Barukh atah ADONAI,* ruler of all the earth, who makes [Shabbat,] the people Israel and the Day of Remembrance holy.

In some communities, at the conclusion of each special section of the Silent Amidah, the shofar is blown. (The shofar is traditionally not blown on Shabbat.)

T'ki·ah sh'varim-t'ru·ah t'ki·ah
T'ki·ah sh'varim t'ki·ah
T'ki·ah t'ru·ah t'ki·ah

זִכְרוֹנוֹת

אַתָּה זוֹכֵר מַעֲשֵׂה עוֹלָם, וּפוֹקֵד כָּל־יְצוּרֵי קֶדֶם.
לְפָנֶיךָ נִגְלוּ כָּל־תַּעֲלוּמוֹת, וַהֲמוֹן נִסְתָּרוֹת שֶׁמִּבְּרֵאשִׁית.
אֵין שִׁכְחָה לִפְנֵי כִסֵּא כְבוֹדֶךָ, וְאֵין נִסְתָּר מִנֶּגֶד עֵינֶיךָ.
אַתָּה זוֹכֵר אֶת־כָּל־הַמִּפְעָל, וְגַם כָּל־הַיְצוּר לֹא
נִכְחָד מִמֶּךָּ.
הַכֹּל גָּלוּי וְיָדוּעַ לְפָנֶיךָ, יהוה אֱלֹהֵינוּ,
צוֹפֶה וּמַבִּיט עַד סוֹף כָּל־הַדּוֹרוֹת.
כִּי תָבִיא חֹק זִכָּרוֹן, לְהִפָּקֵד כָּל־רוּחַ וָנָפֶשׁ,
לְהִזָּכֵר מַעֲשִׂים רַבִּים, וַהֲמוֹן בְּרִיּוֹת לְאֵין תַּכְלִית.
מֵרֵאשִׁית כָּזֹאת הוֹדַעְתָּ, וּמִלְּפָנִים אוֹתָהּ גִּלִּיתָ.

זֶה הַיּוֹם תְּחִלַּת מַעֲשֶׂיךָ, זִכָּרוֹן לְיוֹם רִאשׁוֹן,
כִּי חֹק לְיִשְׂרָאֵל הוּא, מִשְׁפָּט לֵאלֹהֵי יַעֲקֹב.
וְעַל הַמְּדִינוֹת בּוֹ יֵאָמֵר:
אֵיזוֹ לַחֶרֶב, וְאֵיזוֹ לַשָּׁלוֹם, אֵיזוֹ לָרָעָב, וְאֵיזוֹ לַשֹּׂבַע.
וּבְרִיּוֹת בּוֹ יִפָּקֵדוּ, לְהַזְכִּירָם לַחַיִּים וְלַמָּוֶת.
מִי לֹא נִפְקָד כְּהַיּוֹם הַזֶּה, כִּי זֵכֶר כָּל־הַיְצוּר לְפָנֶיךָ בָּא,
מַעֲשֵׂה אִישׁ וּפְקֻדָּתוֹ, וַעֲלִילוֹת מִצְעֲדֵי גֶבֶר,
מַחְשְׁבוֹת אָדָם וְתַחְבּוּלוֹתָיו, וְיִצְרֵי מַעַלְלֵי אִישׁ.

אַשְׁרֵי אִישׁ שֶׁלֹּא יִשְׁכָּחֶךָּ, וּבֶן־אָדָם יִתְאַמֶּץ־בָּךְ.
כִּי דוֹרְשֶׁיךָ לְעוֹלָם לֹא יִכָּשֵׁלוּ, וְלֹא יִכָּלְמוּ לָנֶצַח
כָּל־הַחוֹסִים בָּךְ.
כִּי זֵכֶר כָּל־הַמַּעֲשִׂים לְפָנֶיךָ בָּא, וְאַתָּה דוֹרֵשׁ
מַעֲשֵׂה כֻלָּם.

וְגַם אֶת־נֹחַ בְּאַהֲבָה זָכַרְתָּ, וַתִּפְקְדֵהוּ בִּדְבַר יְשׁוּעָה
וְרַחֲמִים,
בַּהֲבִיאֲךָ אֶת־מֵי הַמַּבּוּל, לְשַׁחֵת כָּל־בָּשָׂר מִפְּנֵי רֹעַ
מַעַלְלֵיהֶם.
עַל כֵּן זִכְרוֹנוֹ בָּא לְפָנֶיךָ, יהוה אֱלֹהֵינוּ,
לְהַרְבּוֹת זַרְעוֹ כְּעַפְרוֹת תֵּבֵל, וְצֶאֱצָאָיו כְּחוֹל הַיָּם.

ZIKHRONOT shifts the prism through which we view Rosh Hashanah to Yom Ha-Zikkaron (the Day of Remembrance), highlighting the covenantal relationship between God and humanity. The metaphor of God as remembering captures the intimate concern and engagement of God with each individual person and creature, as well as our corresponding sense of accountability for our deeds.

YOU REMEMBER אַתָּה זוֹכֵר. The introductory poem to this section is the earliest liturgical addition to this section.

RITE OF REMEMBRANCE חֹק זִכָּרוֹן. The "rite" is Rosh Hashanah, the Day of Remembrance.

REMEMBER. In the Bible, God is described as remembering far more often than are humans. Memory is, primarily, a divine quality, representing God's ability to overcome the limitations of a particular time, to see the part as one segment of a far greater whole. When humans remember, therefore, we are imitating God, overcoming our own limits and, in God-like fashion, identifying with the breadth of history. Remembering is essential, because memory is divine. It is part of what makes us all images of God. Fundamentally, our memory is who we are. (*David Kraemer*)

What ought we to try to remember? Jewish tradition asks us to hold on to those memories that will guide us in the future, those that have the power to give direction to our lives. What have we done, or heard, that might instruct us? Which memories of events in our lives, which behavior of ours has something to teach us: about the care with which we relate to others, about our truthfulness, about our doing what is right, or of our using our talents to bring about a better world? We are asked to see our lives as not only a celebration of freedom but also as an acceptance of responsibility.

To direct our lives, the High Holy Day liturgy asks that we contemplate two things. We are asked to examine ourselves, to make a checklist of what we have done right and what we have done wrong. We may not remember each incident— just one or two may stand out. But we can determine the direction of our lives: our jealousies, our self-indulgence, our passivity, our fears of acting at our best. If we do not examine our lives, we will remain morally stagnant, and a year from now we will yet again feel less than proud of our behavior.

The liturgy also asks us—and God—to remember the covenant. The world was not

(continued)

Fifth B'rakhah: Zikhronot — Remembrances

PRAYERS AND BIBLICAL VERSES ON REMEMBRANCE

You remember the deeds of the world and You are mindful of Your creatures since the beginning of time.

Before You stands revealed all that is hidden, and every mystery from the moment of creation.

Nothing is forgotten in Your awe-inspiring presence, nothing concealed from Your gaze;

You remember every deed, and nothing in creation can be hidden from You.

Everything is revealed and known to You, ADONAI our God; You see to the end of time.

It is You who established a rite of remembrance, to take account of every being, every soul, to recall the multitude of deeds, and call to mind countless creations.

From the beginning You made this known, and from of old You revealed it.

This day, which You, God of Jacob, established as a ritual for the people Israel, and as a day of judgment, marks the beginning of Your creation, a reminder of the very first day.

And this is a day of decree for all nations: war or peace, famine or abundance. Every creature is called to account: reckoned for life or death. Who is not remembered this day?

Everyone's record is set before You: each individual's actions and their consequences, all that people do, all that humans think and plan, and all that each of us intends.

Blessed is the person who does not forget You, the one who draws strength from You; for those who seek You will never stumble, and those who trust in You will never be shamed.

Surely, the record of every deed is before You; You probe everyone's acts.

Did You not lovingly remember Noah, when You brought the flood waters, destroying all flesh because of their evil deeds?

Did You not assure him with words of salvation and compassion?

So his memory, ADONAI our God, came before You and his descendants became as numerous as the dust of the earth, and his children like the sand of the sea.

כַּכָּתוּב בְּתוֹרָתֶךָ:

א **וַיִּזְכֹּר** אֱלֹהִים אֶת־נֹחַ, וְאֵת כָּל־הַחַיָּה וְאֶת־כָּל־הַבְּהֵמָה
אֲשֶׁר אִתּוֹ בַּתֵּבָה, וַיַּעֲבֵר אֱלֹהִים רוּחַ עַל־הָאָרֶץ, וַיָּשֹׁכּוּ
הַמָּיִם. בראשית ח א

ב וְנֶאֱמַר: וַיִּשְׁמַע אֱלֹהִים אֶת־נַאֲקָתָם, וַיִּזְכֹּר אֱלֹהִים
אֶת־בְּרִיתוֹ אֶת־אַבְרָהָם אֶת־יִצְחָק וְאֶת־יַעֲקֹב. שמות ב כד

ג וְנֶאֱמַר: וְזָכַרְתִּי אֶת־בְּרִיתִי יַעֲקוֹב, וְאַף אֶת־בְּרִיתִי
יִצְחָק, וְאַף אֶת־בְּרִיתִי אַבְרָהָם אֶזְכֹּר, וְהָאָרֶץ אֶזְכֹּר.
ויקרא כו מב

וּבְדִבְרֵי קָדְשְׁךָ כָּתוּב לֵאמֹר:

א זֵכֶר עָשָׂה לְנִפְלְאֹתָיו, חַנּוּן וְרַחוּם יְהוָה. תהלים קיא ד

ב וְנֶאֱמַר: טֶרֶף נָתַן לִירֵאָיו, יִזְכֹּר לְעוֹלָם בְּרִיתוֹ. תהלים קיא ה

ג וְנֶאֱמַר: וַיִּזְכֹּר לָהֶם בְּרִיתוֹ, וַיִּנָּחֵם כְּרֹב חֲסָדָיו. תהלים קו מה

וְעַל יְדֵי עֲבָדֶיךָ הַנְּבִיאִים כָּתוּב לֵאמֹר:

א הָלֹךְ וְקָרָאתָ בְאָזְנֵי יְרוּשָׁלִַם לֵאמֹר, כֹּה אָמַר יְהוָה,
זָכַרְתִּי לָךְ חֶסֶד נְעוּרַיִךְ, אַהֲבַת כְּלוּלֹתָיִךְ, לֶכְתֵּךְ אַחֲרַי
בַּמִּדְבָּר, בְּאֶרֶץ לֹא זְרוּעָה. ירמיהו ב ב

ב וְנֶאֱמַר: וְזָכַרְתִּי אֲנִי אֶת־בְּרִיתִי אוֹתָךְ בִּימֵי נְעוּרָיִךְ,
וַהֲקִימוֹתִי לָךְ בְּרִית עוֹלָם. יחזקאל טז ס

ג וְנֶאֱמַר: הֲבֵן יַקִּיר לִי אֶפְרַיִם, אִם יֶלֶד שַׁעֲשׁוּעִים, כִּי־
מִדֵּי דַבְּרִי בּוֹ זָכֹר אֶזְכְּרֶנּוּ עוֹד, עַל כֵּן הָמוּ מֵעַי לוֹ, רַחֵם
אֲרַחֲמֶנּוּ, נְאֻם יְהוָה. ירמיהו לא כ

אֱלֹהֵינוּ וֵאלֹהֵי אֲבוֹתֵינוּ [וְאִמּוֹתֵינוּ], זָכְרֵנוּ בְּזִכָּרוֹן טוֹב
לְפָנֶיךָ, וּפָקְדֵנוּ בִּפְקֻדַּת יְשׁוּעָה וְרַחֲמִים מִשְּׁמֵי שְׁמֵי קֶדֶם.
וּזְכָר־לָנוּ, יְהוָה אֱלֹהֵינוּ, אֶת־הַבְּרִית וְאֶת־הַחֶסֶד וְאֶת־
הַשְּׁבוּעָה אֲשֶׁר נִשְׁבַּעְתָּ לְאַבְרָהָם אָבִינוּ בְּהַר הַמֹּרִיָּה.
וְתֵרָאֶה לְפָנֶיךָ עֲקֵדָה שֶׁעָקַד אַבְרָהָם אָבִינוּ אֶת־יִצְחָק
בְּנוֹ עַל גַּבֵּי הַמִּזְבֵּחַ, וְכָבַשׁ רַחֲמָיו לַעֲשׂוֹת רְצוֹנְךָ בְּלֵבָב
שָׁלֵם. כֵּן יִכְבְּשׁוּ רַחֲמֶיךָ אֶת־כַּעַסְךָ מֵעָלֵינוּ, וּבְטוּבְךָ

THEN I WILL REMEMBER MY COVENANT וְזָכַרְתִּי אֶת־בְּרִיתִי. Leviticus 26:42. This follows a discussion of future generations of Israel humbling themselves and atoning for sin. God's "remembrance" thus follows Israel's t'shuvah.

GOD REMEMBERED THE COVENANT וַיִּזְכֹּר לָהֶם בְּרִיתוֹ. Psalm 106:45. The act of remembering causes even God to act differently. So, too, our remembering on this day should lead us to change who we are and how we behave.

OUR GOD אֱלֹהֵינוּ. This prayer evokes the Binding of Isaac, noting that Abraham subdued his mercy in order to do God's will. In return, we ask God to do the reverse: to allow divine mercy to subdue the divine will to anger. We thus echo God's own prayer. "What does God pray? Rav Zutra ben Tobi said in the name of Rav: 'May it be My will that My mercy may suppress My anger, and that My mercy may prevail over My [other] attributes, so that I may deal with My children in the attribute of mercy and, on their behalf, stop short of the limit of strict justice'" (Babylonian Talmud, Berakhot 7a).

THE HIGHEST HEAVENS ABOVE מִשְּׁמֵי שְׁמֵי קֶדֶם. The phrase, from Psalm 68:34, has both a spatial and a temporal connotation. Like the Hebrew word olam, which can refer to both infinite space and eternal time, kedem can refer either to the east, where the sun rises, or to ancient times.

(continued from previous page) created to be a place of destruction, but rather as a realm in which each of us can hear a "yes" resounding in our being: an affirmation that existence has meaning, that God's love can overcome the coldness and indifference we sometimes experience. We can enter into the world with a sense of gratitude and responsibility that God may bless the work of our hands.

When we remember that life is given to us as a blessing and that we can be a blessing, our lives can be transformed. Regretful memories can inspire us to change. Recollections of love and holiness in our lives can nourish and renew us. Remembering the covenant can help us find our place in this world.

As it is written in Your Torah:

א God *remembered* Noah and all the beasts and all the cattle that were with him in the ark, and God caused a wind to blow across the earth and the waters subsided. Genesis 8:1

ב God heard their agonized cry, and God *remembered* the covenant with Abraham and Isaac and Jacob. Exodus 2:24

ג Then will I *remember* My covenant with Jacob; I will *remember* also my covenant with Isaac, and also My covenant with Abraham; and I will *remember* the land. Leviticus 26:42

And it is also written in the Book of Psalms:

א God has made wondrous works to be *remembered*; ADONAI is gracious and compassionate. Psalm 111:4

ב God always *remembers* the covenant, providing sustenance for those in awe of the Divine. Psalm 111:5

ג God *remembered* the covenant and, with great love, relented.
Psalm 106:45

And Your servants the prophets further wrote:

א Go proclaim to Jerusalem: Thus said ADONAI: I *remember* the affection of your youth, your love when we were betrothed when you followed Me in the wilderness, a barren land. Jeremiah 2:2

ב I will always *remember* the covenant I made with you in the days of your youth, and establish it with you as a covenant that will last forever. Ezekiel 16:60

ג Is not Ephraim My dear son, My precious child, whom I *remember* fondly even when I speak against him? So my heart reaches out to him, and I always feel compassion for him, declares ADONAI. Jeremiah 31:20

Our God and God of our ancestors, remember us favorably, and from the highest heavens above fulfill Your promise of compassion and deliverance. For our sake, remember Your loving relationship with us, the covenant and the promise that You made to Abraham on Mount Moriah. Hold before You the image of our ancestor Abraham binding his son Isaac on the altar, when he overcame his compassion in order to obey Your command wholeheartedly. Now, allow Your compassion to overcome Your anger at us, and in Your great goodness,

הַגָּדוֹל יָשׁוּב חֲרוֹן אַפְּךָ מֵעַמְּךָ וּמֵעִירְךָ וּמִנַּחֲלָתֶךָ. וְקַיֶּם־
לָנוּ, יהוה אֱלֹהֵינוּ, אֶת־הַדָּבָר שֶׁהִבְטַחְתָּנוּ בְּתוֹרָתֶךָ, עַל
יְדֵי מֹשֶׁה עַבְדֶּךָ, מִפִּי כְבוֹדֶךָ, כָּאָמוּר:

וְזָכַרְתִּי לָהֶם בְּרִית רִאשֹׁנִים, אֲשֶׁר הוֹצֵאתִי־אֹתָם מֵאֶרֶץ
מִצְרַיִם לְעֵינֵי הַגּוֹיִם לִהְיוֹת לָהֶם לֵאלֹהִים, אֲנִי יהוה.

ויקרא כו מה

כִּי זוֹכֵר כָּל־הַנִּשְׁכָּחוֹת אַתָּה הוּא מֵעוֹלָם, וְאֵין שִׁכְחָה
לִפְנֵי כִסֵּא כְבוֹדֶךָ. וַעֲקֵדַת יִצְחָק לְזַרְעוֹ הַיּוֹם בְּרַחֲמִים
תִּזְכֹּר. בָּרוּךְ אַתָּה יהוה, זוֹכֵר הַבְּרִית.

*In some communities, at the conclusion of each special section of the Silent
Amidah, the shofar is blown. (The shofar is traditionally not blown on Shabbat.)*

תקיעה שברים־תרועה תקיעה
תקיעה שברים תקיעה
תקיעה תרועה תקיעה

שׁוֹפָרוֹת

אַתָּה נִגְלֵיתָ בַּעֲנַן כְּבוֹדֶךָ, עַל עַם קָדְשְׁךָ, לְדַבֵּר עִמָּם.
מִן הַשָּׁמַיִם הִשְׁמַעְתָּם קוֹלֶךָ, וְנִגְלֵיתָ עֲלֵיהֶם בְּעַרְפְלֵי טֹהַר.
גַּם כָּל־הָעוֹלָם כֻּלּוֹ חָל מִפָּנֶיךָ, וּבְרִיּוֹת בְּרֵאשִׁית חָרְדוּ מִמֶּךָּ,
בְּהִגָּלוֹתְךָ מַלְכֵּנוּ עַל הַר סִינַי, לְלַמֵּד לְעַמְּךָ תּוֹרָה וּמִצְוֹת,
וַתַּשְׁמִיעֵם אֶת־הוֹד קוֹלֶךָ, וְדִבְּרוֹת קָדְשְׁךָ מִלַּהֲבוֹת אֵשׁ.
בְּקֹלֹת וּבְרָקִים עֲלֵיהֶם נִגְלֵיתָ, וּבְקוֹל שׁוֹפָר עֲלֵיהֶם הוֹפָעְתָּ.

כַּכָּתוּב בְּתוֹרָתֶךָ:

א וַיְהִי בַיּוֹם הַשְּׁלִישִׁי בִּהְיֹת הַבֹּקֶר, וַיְהִי קֹלֹת וּבְרָקִים,
וְעָנָן כָּבֵד עַל הָהָר, וְקֹל שֹׁפָר חָזָק מְאֹד, וַיֶּחֱרַד כָּל־הָעָם
אֲשֶׁר בַּמַּחֲנֶה. שמות יט טז

ב וְנֶאֱמַר: וַיְהִי קוֹל הַשׁוֹפָר הוֹלֵךְ וְחָזֵק מְאֹד, מֹשֶׁה יְדַבֵּר
וְהָאֱלֹהִים יַעֲנֶנּוּ בְקוֹל. שמות יט יט

ג וְנֶאֱמַר: וְכָל־הָעָם רֹאִים אֶת־הַקּוֹלֹת וְאֶת־הַלַּפִּידִם,
וְאֵת קוֹל הַשֹׁפָר וְאֶת־הָהָר עָשֵׁן, וַיַּרְא הָעָם וַיָּנֻעוּ
וַיַּעַמְדוּ מֵרָחֹק. שמות כ טו

YOU REVEALED YOUR-SELF אַתָּה נִגְלֵיתָ. Like the introductory poems to Malkhuyot and Shofarot, this poem dates back to the 5th century or earlier and exhibits some of the features that characterize the transition from early post-biblical to medieval liturgical poetry. There are four stresses in each line, the same rhythm as in Aleinu, the prayer with which the special sections of Musaf began.

TO YOUR HOLY PEOPLE עַל עַם קָדְשֶׁךָ. The preposition here is עַל, literally "upon," as opposed to the more usual אֶל, "to." The implication could be that Israel is no mere recipient of revelation, but the vehicle upon which God's word is carried into the world.

ALLOWING THEM TO HEAR YOUR VOICE מִן הַשָּׁמַיִם הִשְׁמַעְתָּם קוֹלֶךָ. Deuteronomy 4:36.

YOUR SACRED WORDS וְדִבְּרוֹת קָדְשֶׁךָ. A reference to the Decalogue, which was revealed to the people Israel at Sinai, accompanied by the sound of the shofar.

ON THE THIRD DAY. All three verses from the Torah are taken from the description in Exodus of the revelation on Mount Sinai. The last verse, with its confusion of sight and sound—"the people saw the thunder and lightning"—conveys the full depth of the transformative experience of revelation.

מוסף לראש השנה · תפילת העמידה בלחש **135**

reconcile Yourself to Your people, Your city, and Your land. Fulfill for us the words of Your promise contained in Your Torah transmitted by Your servant Moses from Your glorious Presence, as it is written:

For their sake, I will *remember* the covenant with that first generation whom I brought out of the land of Egypt in the sight of the nations, to be their God; I am ADONAI. Leviticus 26:45

You have always remembered that which has been forgotten, for there is no forgetting in Your realm. So on this day, in Your great mercy, remember the binding of Isaac for the sake of his descendants. *Barukh atah* ADONAI, who remembers the covenant.

In some communities, at the conclusion of each special section of the Silent Amidah, the shofar is blown. (The shofar is traditionally not blown on Shabbat.)

T'ki·ah sh'varim-t'ru·ah t'ki·ah
T'ki·ah sh'varim t'ki·ah
T'ki·ah t'ru·ah t'ki·ah

Sixth B'rakhah: Shofarot

PRAYERS AND BIBLICAL VERSES ON THE SHOFAR

You revealed Yourself in a cloud of glory
to speak to Your holy people,
allowing them to hear Your voice from the heavens.
Through a pure mist You disclosed Yourself,
and the whole world—everything—quivered in Your presence.
All of creation trembled in awe,
as You, our sovereign, made Yourself known on Mount Sinai,
teaching Your people Torah and mitzvot.
You spoke to them from amidst fiery flames,
allowing them to hear Your majestic voice and Your sacred words,
revealed Yourself to them amidst thunder and lightning,
and appeared to them with the sounding of the shofar.

As it is written in Your Torah:
א On the third day, as morning dawned, there was thunder and lightning, a dense cloud covering the mountain, and the powerful sound of the *shofar*; all the people who were in the camp trembled. Exodus 19:16
ב The sound of the *shofar* grew ever more powerful; as Moses spoke, God's response thundered. Exodus 19:19
ג All the people saw the thunder and lightning, the blare of the *shofar* and the mountain smoking; as the people saw it, they fell back and stood at a distance. Exodus 20:15

Meditations on Redemption

The kingdom of God is not a kingdom above the world or opposed to it or even side by side with it. . . . It is not a future of miracle for which human beings can only wait, but a future of commandment which always has its present and ever demands a beginning and decision from each human being.

—LEO BAECK

וּבְדִבְרֵי קָדְשְׁךָ כָּתוּב לֵאמֹר:

א עָלָה אֱלֹהִים בִּתְרוּעָה, יהוה בְּקוֹל **שׁוֹפָר.** תהלים מז ו

ב וְנֶאֱמַר: בַּחֲצֹצְרוֹת וְקוֹל **שׁוֹפָר** הָרִיעוּ לִפְנֵי הַמֶּלֶךְ יהוה. תהלים צח ו

ג וְנֶאֱמַר: תִּקְעוּ בַחֹדֶשׁ **שׁוֹפָר,** בַּכֶּסֶה לְיוֹם חַגֵּנוּ. כִּי חֹק לְיִשְׂרָאֵל הוּא, מִשְׁפָּט לֵאלֹהֵי יַעֲקֹב. תהלים פא ד-ה

וְנֶאֱמַר: הַלְלוּ יָהּ, הַלְלוּ־אֵל בְּקָדְשׁוֹ, הַלְלוּהוּ בִּרְקִיעַ עֻזּוֹ. הַלְלוּהוּ בִגְבוּרֹתָיו, הַלְלוּהוּ כְּרֹב גֻּדְלוֹ. הַלְלוּהוּ בְּתֵקַע **שׁוֹפָר,** הַלְלוּהוּ בְּנֵבֶל וְכִנּוֹר. הַלְלוּהוּ בְתֹף וּמָחוֹל, הַלְלוּהוּ בְּמִנִּים וְעוּגָב. הַלְלוּהוּ בְצִלְצְלֵי שָׁמַע, הַלְלוּהוּ בְּצִלְצְלֵי תְרוּעָה. כֹּל הַנְּשָׁמָה תְּהַלֵּל יָהּ, הַלְלוּיָהּ. תהלים קנ א-ו

וְעַל יְדֵי עֲבָדֶיךָ הַנְּבִיאִים כָּתוּב לֵאמֹר:

א כָּל־יֹשְׁבֵי תֵבֵל וְשֹׁכְנֵי אָרֶץ, כִּנְשֹׂא נֵס הָרִים תִּרְאוּ, וְכִתְקֹעַ **שׁוֹפָר** תִּשְׁמָעוּ. ישעיה יח ג

ב וְנֶאֱמַר: וְהָיָה בַּיּוֹם הַהוּא יִתָּקַע **בְּשׁוֹפָר** גָּדוֹל, וּבָאוּ הָאֹבְדִים בְּאֶרֶץ אַשּׁוּר וְהַנִּדָּחִים בְּאֶרֶץ מִצְרָיִם, וְהִשְׁתַּחֲווּ לַיהוה בְּהַר הַקֹּדֶשׁ בִּירוּשָׁלָיִם. ישעיה כז יג

ג וְנֶאֱמַר: וַיהוה עֲלֵיהֶם יֵרָאֶה, וְיָצָא כַבָּרָק חִצּוֹ, וַאדֹנָי אֱלֹהִים **בַּשּׁוֹפָר** יִתְקָע, וְהָלַךְ בְּסַעֲרוֹת תֵּימָן. יהוה צְבָאוֹת יָגֵן עֲלֵיהֶם. זכריה ט יד-טו

כֵּן תָּגֵן עַל עַמְּךָ יִשְׂרָאֵל בִּשְׁלוֹמֶךָ.

VERSES FROM PSALMS. The verses from the Book of Psalms speak of the shofar as the instrument announcing the day of judgment, as God ascends the divine throne.

GOD ASCENDS AMIDST THE CRY עָלָה אֱלֹהִים בִּתְרוּעָה. According to the midrash (Leviticus Rabbah 29:3), this verse's use of the two names of God—*Elohim* (associated with strict justice) and *Adonai* (associated with compassion and loving-kindness)—reflects how God's relationship with us changes over the course of Rosh Hashanah. At the beginning, God ascends and sits on the Throne of Justice, as it is said, "*Elohim* ascends with the *t'ru∙ah* [shofar alarm-call]." But when the people Israel blow the shofar, God's compassion is aroused and God moves from the Throne of Justice to the Throne of Compassion, and truly becomes *Adonai*, as the verse says, "With the shofar's sound, *Adonai* is enthroned."

SOUND THE SHOFAR ON

OUR FEAST DAY תִּקְעוּ בַחֹדֶשׁ שׁוֹפָר. Rosh Hashanah is the only festival that occurs on the new moon. This verse, with its reference to when the moon is hidden, בַּכֶּסֶה (*ba-keseh*), is used in the Babylonian Talmud as the prooftext for God's judgment taking place on this day (Rosh Hashanah, 8a-b).

PSALM 150. Although there are already three verses from Psalms, Psalm 150 has been added to the service of Shofarot. This is pursuant to the Babylonian Talmud (Rosh Hashanah 32a), where the Sages state that the ten verses each in Malkhuyot, Zikhronot, and Shofarot correspond to the ten references to the word הַלְלוּ (*hal'lu*), "praise [God]," in Psalm 150. There are also a total of thirteen references to "praise" in the psalm, corresponding to the Thirteen Attributes of God.

VERSES FROM THE PROPHETS. The final three verses from the Prophets refer to the shofar as God's instrument of redemption. The ram was substituted for Isaac as a sacrifice, and the ram's horn announces that God does not wish the death of Isaac's descendants. The horn of that ram is destined to be sounded in the world that is to come (Pirkei D'Rabbi Eliezer, chapter 30).

AND SO, TOO, PROTECT YOUR PEOPLE ISRAEL כֵּן תָּגֵן. Following these Shofarot verses is a brief liturgical coda that amplifies the plea for redemption just quoted in Zechariah 9:15.

Revelation is of the past, but it has no meaning unless and until it becomes operative in the present. The Bible is simply a closed book until it is read with an open heart and a ready will. Scripture is not a body of abstract propositions. It is God's summons to human beings, and only when it is heard in the context of present experience can it become an active force in life once more and impel people to make themselves the means whereby the redemptive history which it records is carried one step further, according to the purposes of God. Revelation is a call to present decision and a guide to present action.

—WILL HERBERG

And it is also written in Psalms:

א God ascends amidst the cry of the *shofar*; with its sound Adonai is enthroned. Psalm 47:6

ב Sound the trumpet and *shofar* before the Sovereign, Adonai. Psalm 98:6

ג Sound the *shofar* on our feast day, on the new moon, when it is hidden. For it is Israel's law, a decree of the God of Jacob. Psalm 81:4–5

Halleluyah! Praise God in the sanctuary,
praise God in the powerful heavens.
  Praise God for the mighty deeds,
  praise God for infinite greatness.
Praise God with the *shofar* call,
praise God with harp and lyre.
  Praise God with drum and dance,
  praise God with flute and strings.
Praise God with crashing cymbals,
praise God with resounding cymbals.
  Let every breath of life praise Adonai. Halleluyah! Psalm 150:1–6

And Your servants the prophets further wrote:

א All you inhabitants of the world and dwellers on earth: when a banner is raised on the mountains, look! When the *shofar* is sounded, listen! Isaiah 18:3

ב For on that day, a great *shofar* will be sounded: those lost in the land of Assyria and those cast away in the land of Egypt shall come back and worship Adonai on the holy mountain in Jerusalem. Isaiah 27:13

ג Adonai will appear to them, shooting arrows like lightning; the lord, God, will sound the *shofar*, advancing in a stormy south wind. *Adonai Tz'va·ot* will protect them. Zechariah 9:14–15

And so, too, protect Your people Israel with Your peace.

אֱלֹהֵינוּ וֵאלֹהֵי אֲבוֹתֵינוּ [וְאִמוֹתֵינוּ],
תְּקַע בְּשׁוֹפָר גָּדוֹל לְחֵרוּתֵנוּ,
וְשָׂא נֵס לְקַבֵּץ גָּלֻיּוֹתֵינוּ,
וְקָרֵב פְּזוּרֵינוּ מִבֵּין הַגּוֹיִם,
וּנְפוּצוֹתֵינוּ כַּנֵּס מִיַּרְכְּתֵי אָרֶץ.
וַהֲבִיאֵנוּ לְצִיּוֹן עִירְךָ בְּרִנָּה,
וְלִירוּשָׁלַיִם בֵּית מִקְדָּשְׁךָ בְּשִׂמְחַת עוֹלָם.
שָׁם עָשׂוּ אֲבוֹתֵינוּ [וְאִמוֹתֵינוּ] לְפָנֶיךָ אֶת־עוֹלוֹתֵיהֶם
וְאֶת־שַׁלְמֵיהֶם. וְכֵן כָּתוּב בְּתוֹרָתֶךָ:
וּבְיוֹם שִׂמְחַתְכֶם וּבְמוֹעֲדֵיכֶם וּבְרָאשֵׁי חָדְשֵׁיכֶם,
וּתְקַעְתֶּם בַּחֲצֹצְרֹת עַל עֹלֹתֵיכֶם וְעַל זִבְחֵי שַׁלְמֵיכֶם,
וְהָיוּ לָכֶם לְזִכָּרוֹן לִפְנֵי אֱלֹהֵיכֶם, אֲנִי יהוה אֱלֹהֵיכֶם.

במדבר י י

כִּי אַתָּה שׁוֹמֵעַ קוֹל שׁוֹפָר, וּמַאֲזִין תְּרוּעָה וְאֵין דּוֹמֶה לָּךְ.
בָּרוּךְ אַתָּה יהוה, שׁוֹמֵעַ קוֹל תְּרוּעַת עַמּוֹ יִשְׂרָאֵל
בְּרַחֲמִים.

In some communities, at the conclusion of each special section of the Silent Amidah, the shofar is blown. (The shofar is traditionally not blown on Shabbat.)

תקיעה שברים־תרועה תקיעה
תקיעה שברים תקיעה
תקיעה תרועה תקיעה גדולה

רְצֵה יהוה אֱלֹהֵינוּ, בְּעַמְּךָ יִשְׂרָאֵל וּבִתְפִלָּתָם, וְהָשֵׁב
אֶת־הָעֲבוֹדָה לִדְבִיר בֵּיתֶךָ, [וְאִשֵּׁי יִשְׂרָאֵל]
וּתְפִלָּתָם בְּאַהֲבָה תְקַבֵּל בְּרָצוֹן, וּתְהִי לְרָצוֹן תָּמִיד
עֲבוֹדַת יִשְׂרָאֵל עַמֶּךָ.

וְתֶחֱזֶינָה עֵינֵינוּ בְּשׁוּבְךָ לְצִיּוֹן בְּרַחֲמִים.
בָּרוּךְ אַתָּה יהוה, הַמַּחֲזִיר שְׁכִינָתוֹ לְצִיּוֹן.

TRUMPETS חֲצֹצְרֹת. The Mishnah prescribes that trumpets are to accompany the sounding of the shofar (Rosh Hashanah 3:3–4). Trumpets are depicted on the Arch of Titus in Rome as some of the booty brought home after the capture of Jerusalem in 70 C.E. They were probably blown only by the priests and levites, and so have dropped out of our own ritual performance. The Bible records that the trumpets were sounded at the time of the festival sacrifice.

WHO LISTENS . . . TO THE . . . SPLINTERED CALL OF YOUR PEOPLE ISRAEL שׁוֹמֵעַ קוֹל תְּרוּעַת עַמּוֹ יִשְׂרָאֵל בְּרַחֲמִים. After all the repetitions of the word "shofar," the closing b'rakhah of the service of Shofarot omits the word. Instead, we praise God as the One who hears the t'ru·ah—the staccato call—of the people Israel. Our collective cries have themselves become a kind of shofar.

RESTORE WORSHIP TO YOUR SANCTUARY וְהָשֵׁב אֶת־הָעֲבוֹדָה לִדְבִיר בֵּיתֶךָ. An essential motif of Jewish theology is that we are in exile and that our collective relationship with God cannot be fulfilled. Yearning for the restoration of the Temple expresses the wish to have a direct relationship with God.

FIERY OFFERINGS וְאִשֵּׁי יִשְׂרָאֵל. The reference to the "fiery offerings" originally referred to the Temple sacrifices, but was understood by many Hasidic commentators as referring to the fervor of true prayer.

YOUR DIVINE PRESENCE שְׁכִינָתוֹ. The Hebrew word *shekhinah* has been used for centuries to refer to God's immanence, the presence of God that is felt in the world. The word *shekhinah* is grammatically feminine. Accordingly, the Jewish mystical tradition generally describes the Divine Presence—known as the Shekhinah—in feminine imagery.

The shofar has revelatory power for us today, as it did in accompanying the revelation at Sinai. We must be careful, however, never to confuse the tool of revelation with the content of revelation. Just as the shofar announced God's revelation at Sinai, demanding our attention, so today, the shofar is intended to clear a path, to open our ears. The question then is, what will we hear? What is being revealed to us today? —JAN UHRBACH

The blasts of the shofar on Rosh Hashanah revitalize the soul and mind of every Jew. Each one receives a new soul and a new level of understanding, all according to their own level. This new soul and vision are drawn from the inner countenance of God.
—NAḤMAN OF BRATZLAV

Our God and God of our ancestors, sound the great shofar proclaiming our freedom, raise up the banner signaling the ingathering of our exiles, draw near those scattered amidst the nations, and from the ends of the earth assemble our dispersed. Bring us with song and boundless joy to Zion, Your city, to Jerusalem the site of Your Temple, where our ancestors brought their sacrifices and their offerings, as is written in Your Torah: On your joyous occasions—your fixed festivals and new moons—you shall sound the trumpets over your sacrifices and offerings. They shall be a remembrance of you before your God; I, ADONAI, am your God.   Numbers 10:10

For You hear the sound of the shofar, and attend to its splintered call—You are beyond compare. *Barukh atah ADONAI*, who listens with compassion to the sounds of the splintered call of Your people Israel.

In some communities, at the conclusion of each special section of the Silent Amidah, the shofar is blown. (The shofar is traditionally not blown on Shabbat.)

T'ki·ah sh'varim-t'ru·ah t'ki·ah
T'ki·ah sh'varim t'ki·ah
T'ki·ah t'ru·ah t'ki·ah g'dolah

Seventh B'rakhah: The Restoration of Zion

ADONAI our God, embrace Your people Israel and their prayer. Restore worship to Your sanctuary. May the [fiery offerings and] prayers of the people Israel be lovingly accepted by You, and may our service always be pleasing.

Let our eyes behold Your merciful return to Zion.
Barukh atah ADONAI, who restores Your Divine Presence to Zion.

מוֹדִים אֲנַחְנוּ לָךְ, שָׁאַתָּה הוּא יהוה אֱלֹהֵינוּ
וֵאלֹהֵי אֲבוֹתֵינוּ [וְאִמּוֹתֵינוּ] לְעוֹלָם וָעֶד,
צוּר חַיֵּינוּ מָגֵן יִשְׁעֵנוּ אַתָּה הוּא.
לְדוֹר וָדוֹר נוֹדֶה לְךָ וּנְסַפֵּר תְּהִלָּתֶךָ עַל חַיֵּינוּ הַמְּסוּרִים
בְּיָדֶךָ, וְעַל נִשְׁמוֹתֵינוּ הַפְּקוּדוֹת לָךְ, וְעַל נִסֶּיךָ שֶׁבְּכָל־יוֹם
עִמָּנוּ, וְעַל נִפְלְאוֹתֶיךָ וְטוֹבוֹתֶיךָ שֶׁבְּכָל־עֵת,
עֶרֶב וָבֹקֶר וְצָהֳרָיִם.
הַטּוֹב, כִּי לֹא כָלוּ רַחֲמֶיךָ, וְהַמְרַחֵם, כִּי לֹא תַמּוּ חֲסָדֶיךָ,
מֵעוֹלָם קִוִּינוּ לָךְ.

וְעַל כֻּלָּם יִתְבָּרַךְ וְיִתְרוֹמַם שִׁמְךָ מַלְכֵּנוּ תָּמִיד
לְעוֹלָם וָעֶד.

וּכְתוֹב לְחַיִּים טוֹבִים כָּל־בְּנֵי בְרִיתֶךָ.

INSCRIBE וּכְתוֹב. This is the
third of the four special
insertions in the Amidah
for the Ten Days of Repentance.

וְכֹל הַחַיִּים יוֹדוּךָ סֶּלָה, וִיהַלְלוּ אֶת־שִׁמְךָ בֶּאֱמֶת הָאֵל
יְשׁוּעָתֵנוּ וְעֶזְרָתֵנוּ סֶלָה.
בָּרוּךְ אַתָּה יהוה, הַטּוֹב שִׁמְךָ וּלְךָ נָאֶה לְהוֹדוֹת.

שִׂים שָׁלוֹם בָּעוֹלָם טוֹבָה וּבְרָכָה חֵן וָחֶסֶד וְרַחֲמִים
עָלֵינוּ וְעַל כָּל־יִשְׂרָאֵל עַמֶּךָ. בָּרְכֵנוּ אָבִינוּ, כֻּלָּנוּ כְּאֶחָד
בְּאוֹר פָּנֶיךָ, כִּי בְאוֹר פָּנֶיךָ נָתַתָּ לָנוּ, יהוה אֱלֹהֵינוּ, תּוֹרַת
חַיִּים וְאַהֲבַת חֶסֶד, וּצְדָקָה וּבְרָכָה וְרַחֲמִים וְחַיִּים
וְשָׁלוֹם. וְטוֹב בְּעֵינֶיךָ לְבָרֵךְ אֶת־עַמְּךָ יִשְׂרָאֵל, בְּכָל־עֵת
וּבְכָל־שָׁעָה בִּשְׁלוֹמֶךָ.

GRANT PEACE שִׂים שָׁלוֹם.
Every Jewish prayer service
ends with a prayer for
peace. The midrash says
that peace is one of the
names of God.

(continued)

Alternate Rendering of the Final B'rakhot of the Amidah

Would that Your people at prayer gained delight in You. Would that we were aflame with the passionate piety of our ancestors' worship. Would that You found our worship acceptable, and forever cherished Your people. If only our eyes could see Your glory perennially renewed in Jerusalem. We praise You, God whose presence forever radiates from Zion.

You are our God today as You were our ancestors' God throughout the ages; firm foundation of our lives, we are Yours in gratitude and love. Our lives are safe in Your hand, our souls entrusted to Your care. Our sense of wonder and our praise of Your miracles and kindnesses greet You daily at dawn, noon, and dusk. O Gentle One, Your caring is endless; O Compassionate One, Your love is eternal. You are forever our hope. Let all the living confront You with thankfulness, delight, and truth. Help us, O God; sustain us. We praise You, God whose touchstone is goodness.

May a life of goodness await all of us, children of Your covenant.

To pray to You is joy.

(continued)

Eighth B'rakhah: Gratitude for Life and Its Blessings

ℓ We thank You,

You who are our God and the God of our ancestors through all
     time, protector of our lives, shield of our salvation.
From one generation to the next we thank You
and sing Your praises—
          for our lives that are in Your hands,
          for our souls that are under Your care,
          for Your miracles that accompany us each day,
          and for Your wonders and Your gifts that are
          with us each moment—
evening, morning, and noon.
You are the One who is good,
whose mercy is never-ending;
the One who is compassionate,
whose love is unceasing.
We have always placed our hope in You.

For all these blessings may Your name be praised and exalted,
our sovereign, always and forever.

And inscribe all the people of Your covenant for a good life.

May all that lives thank You always, and praise Your name
faithfully forever, God of our deliverance and help.
ℓ *Barukh atah* ADONAI, whose name is goodness and
to whom praise is fitting.

Ninth B'rakhah: Prayer for Peace

Grant peace to the world: goodness and blessing, grace, love,
and compassion to us and all Your people Israel. Bless us, our
creator, united as one in the light of Your countenance; by that
light, ADONAI our God, You gave us a guide to life: the love of
kindness, righteousness, blessing, compassion, life, and peace.
May it please You to bless Your people Israel at every season
and at all times with Your gift of peace.

בְּסֵפֶר חַיִּים,
בְּרָכָה וְשָׁלוֹם וּפַרְנָסָה טוֹבָה,
נִזָּכֵר וְנִכָּתֵב לְפָנֶיךָ,
אֲנַחְנוּ וְכָל־עַמְּךָ בֵּית יִשְׂרָאֵל,
לְחַיִּים טוֹבִים וּלְשָׁלוֹם.
בָּרוּךְ אַתָּה יהוה, עוֹשֵׂה הַשָּׁלוֹם.

On the first day, the following may be added:

אֱלֹהַי, נְצוֹר לְשׁוֹנִי מֵרָע, וּשְׂפָתַי מִדַּבֵּר מִרְמָה, וְלִמְקַלְלַי
נַפְשִׁי תִדֹּם, וְנַפְשִׁי כֶּעָפָר לַכֹּל תִּהְיֶה. פְּתַח לִבִּי
בְּתוֹרָתֶךָ, וּבְמִצְוֹתֶיךָ תִּרְדּוֹף נַפְשִׁי. וְכָל־הַחוֹשְׁבִים עָלַי
רָעָה, מְהֵרָה הָפֵר עֲצָתָם וְקַלְקֵל מַחֲשַׁבְתָּם. עֲשֵׂה לְמַעַן
שְׁמֶךָ, עֲשֵׂה לְמַעַן יְמִינֶךָ, עֲשֵׂה לְמַעַן קְדֻשָּׁתֶךָ, עֲשֵׂה
לְמַעַן תּוֹרָתֶךָ. לְמַעַן יֵחָלְצוּן יְדִידֶיךָ, הוֹשִׁיעָה יְמִינְךָ
וַעֲנֵנִי. יִהְיוּ לְרָצוֹן אִמְרֵי פִי וְהֶגְיוֹן לִבִּי לְפָנֶיךָ, יהוה צוּרִי
וְגוֹאֲלִי. עֹשֶׂה שָׁלוֹם בִּמְרוֹמָיו, הוּא יַעֲשֶׂה שָׁלוֹם עָלֵינוּ,
וְעַל כָּל־יִשְׂרָאֵל [וְעַל כָּל־יוֹשְׁבֵי תֵבֵל] וְאִמְרוּ: אָמֵן.

On the second day, the following may be added:

יְהִי רָצוֹן מִלְּפָנֶיךָ יהוה אֱלֹהַי וֵאלֹהֵי אֲבוֹתַי [וְאִמּוֹתַי],
יוֹצֵר בְּרֵאשִׁית, כְּשֵׁם שֶׁהַמְצֵאתָ עוֹלָמְךָ בְּיוֹם זֶה
וְנִתְיַחַדְתָּ בְּעוֹלָמֶךָ וְתָלִיתָ בּוֹ עֶלְיוֹנִים וְתַחְתּוֹנִים
בְּמַאֲמָרֶיךָ, כֵּן בְּרַחֲמֶיךָ הָרַבִּים תְּיַחֵד לְבָבִי וּלְבַב כָּל־
עַמְּךָ בֵּית יִשְׂרָאֵל לְאַהֲבָה וּלְיִרְאָה אֶת־שְׁמֶךָ. וְהָאֵר
עֵינֵינוּ בִּמְאוֹר תּוֹרָתֶךָ, כִּי עִמְּךָ מְקוֹר חַיִּים, בְּאוֹרְךָ
נִרְאֶה אוֹר. וְזַכֵּנוּ לִרְאוֹת בָּאוֹר הַצָּפוּן לַצַּדִּיקִים
לֶעָתִיד לָבוֹא. יִהְיוּ לְרָצוֹן אִמְרֵי־פִי וְהֶגְיוֹן לִבִּי לְפָנֶיךָ,
יהוה צוּרִי וְגֹאֲלִי.

INSCRIBED FOR LIFE לְחַיִּים טוֹבִים (l'ḥayyim tovim). A final plea for a year of life, a good life.

MY GOD אֱלֹהַי. The Babylonian Talmud says that every Amidah must be accompanied by a personal prayer (Berakhot 17a). The prayer that is printed here for the first day is one of the Talmud's exemplars; it is attributed to Mar son of Ravina (5th century). The prayer for the second day appears in the Prague prayerbook *Sha'arei Tziyon* (1662); its English rendering is by Jules Harlow. Both prayers are distinguished by their use of the first-person singular ("I," "me," "my"), whereas almost all other prayers are in the first-person plural ("we," "us," "our").

MAY THE WORDS יִהְיוּ לְרָצוֹן. Psalm 19:15.

(continued from previous page)
O God, from whom all peace flows, grant serenity to Your people, with love and mercy, life and goodness for all. Shelter us with kindness, bless us with tranquility at all times and all seasons.

May we, and all Your people, the House of Israel, be deserving of a year of life, blessing, peace, and an honorable livelihood.

We praise You, God whose blessing is peace.

Concluding Meditation

May my tongue be innocent of malice and my lips free from lies. When confronted by enemies may my soul stay calm, truly humble to all. Open my heart with Your teachings, that I may be guided by You. May all who plan evil against me abandon their schemes. Hear my words and help me, God, because You are loving, because You reveal Your Torah. May You find delight in the words of my mouth and in the emotions of my heart, God my strength and my salvation. As You maintain harmony in the heavens, give peace to us and to the whole Jewish people. Amen.

May we and the entire House of Israel be called to mind and inscribed for life, blessing, sustenance, and peace in the Book of Life.

Barukh atah ADONAI, who brings peace.

Personal Prayers Concluding the Amidah

On the first day, the following may be added:

My God, keep my tongue from evil, my lips from lies. Help me ignore those who would slander me. Let me be humble before all. Open my heart to Your Torah, that I may pursue Your mitzvot. Frustrate the designs of those who plot evil against me; make nothing of their schemes. Act for the sake of Your name, Your power, Your holiness, and Your Torah. Answer my prayer for the deliverance of Your people. May the words of my mouth and the meditations of my heart be acceptable to You, ADONAI, my rock and my redeemer. May the One who brings peace to the universe bring peace to us and to all the people Israel [and to all who dwell on earth]. Amen.

On the second day, the following may be added:

Creator of beginnings, as You created Your world on this day, uniting fragments into a universe, so may it be Your will to help unite my fragmented heart and the heart of all Your people Israel to love and revere You. Illumine our lives with the light of Your Torah, for in Your light do we see light. Grant us this year a hint of the light of redemption, the light of healing and of peace. May the words of my mouth and the meditations of my heart be acceptable to You, ADONAI, my rock and my redeemer. Amen.

HIN'NI: THE PRAYER OF A MALE LEADER:

הִנְנִי הֶעָנִי מִמַּעַשׂ, נִרְעָשׁ וְנִפְחָד מִפַּחַד יוֹשֵׁב תְּהִלּוֹת
יִשְׂרָאֵל, בָּאתִי לַעֲמֹד וּלְהִתְחַנֵּן לְפָנֶיךָ עַל עַמְּךָ יִשְׂרָאֵל
אֲשֶׁר שְׁלָחוּנִי, אַף עַל פִּי שֶׁאֵינִי כְדַאי וְהָגוּן לְכָךְ.
לָכֵן אֲבַקֵּשׁ מִמְּךָ, אֱלֹהֵי אַבְרָהָם, אֱלֹהֵי יִצְחָק, וֵאלֹהֵי
יַעֲקֹב, אֱלֹהֵי שָׂרָה, אֱלֹהֵי רִבְקָה, אֱלֹהֵי רָחֵל, וֵאלֹהֵי לֵאָה,
יְהוָה יְהוָה, אֵל רַחוּם וְחַנּוּן, אֱלֹהֵי יִשְׂרָאֵל, שַׁדַּי אָיוֹם
וְנוֹרָא, הֱיֵה נָא מַצְלִיחַ דַּרְכִּי אֲשֶׁר אֲנִי הוֹלֵךְ, לַעֲמֹד
וּלְבַקֵּשׁ רַחֲמִים עָלַי וְעַל שׁוֹלְחָי.

וְנָא אַל תַּפְשִׁיעֵם בְּחַטֹּאתַי וְאַל תְּחַיְּבֵם בַּעֲוֹנוֹתַי, כִּי
חוֹטֵא וּפוֹשֵׁעַ אָנִי. וְאַל יִכָּלְמוּ בִּפְשָׁעַי וְאַל יֵבוֹשׁוּ בִּי
וְאַל אֵבוֹשָׁה בָּהֶם. וְקַבֵּל תְּפִלָּתִי כִּתְפִלַּת רָגִיל וְקוֹלוֹ
נָעִים וּפִרְקוֹ נָאֶה וּמְעֹרָב בְּדַעַת עִם הַבְּרִיּוֹת. וְתִגְעַר
בְּשָׂטָן לְבַל יַשְׂטִינֵנִי. וִיהִי נָא דִגְלֵנוּ עָלֶיךָ אַהֲבָה וְעַל
כָּל־פְּשָׁעִים תְּכַסֶּה בְּאַהֲבָה. וְכָל־צָרוֹת וְרָעוֹת הֲפָךְ־לָנוּ
וּלְכָל־יִשְׂרָאֵל לְשָׂשׂוֹן וּלְשִׂמְחָה לְחַיִּים וּלְשָׁלוֹם. הָאֱמֶת
וְהַשָּׁלוֹם אֱהָבוּ, וְלֹא יְהִי שׁוּם מִכְשׁוֹל בִּתְפִלָּתִי.

וִיהִי רָצוֹן מִלְּפָנֶיךָ, יְהוָה, אֱלֹהֵי אַבְרָהָם יִצְחָק וְיַעֲקֹב,
שָׂרָה רִבְקָה רָחֵל וְלֵאָה, הָאֵל הַגָּדוֹל הַגִּבּוֹר וְהַנּוֹרָא,
אֵל עֶלְיוֹן, אֶהְיֶה אֲשֶׁר אֶהְיֶה, שֶׁתָּבוֹא תְפִלָּתִי לִפְנֵי
כִסֵּא כְבוֹדֶךָ, בַּעֲבוּר כָּל־הַצַּדִּיקִים וְהַחֲסִידִים הַתְּמִימִים
וְהַיְשָׁרִים, וּבַעֲבוּר כְּבוֹד שִׁמְךָ הַגָּדוֹל וְהַנּוֹרָא, כִּי אַתָּה
שׁוֹמֵעַ תְּפִלַּת עַמְּךָ יִשְׂרָאֵל בְּרַחֲמִים. בָּרוּךְ אַתָּה שׁוֹמֵעַ
תְּפִלָּה.

HIN'NI הִנְנִי. The responsibility of the leader in the High Holy Day services is especially weighty, for unlike Shabbat and festival prayers, the prayers of these days, occurring as they do only once a year, are less familiar to the congregation. In the Middle Ages, when most of the congregation did not possess a prayerbook, leading the congregation in prayer was an even weightier task. Thus, there developed the tradition of the leader privately praying that the service might be conducted properly: that the people be inspired and that God be moved by the pleas of the congregation. There are many such prayers, called r'shuyot—the particular r'shut printed here was one most often recited in Eastern Europe. It was composed in the 16th century and its author is unknown. Originally the prayer was recited silently by the leader; and even today, when it has become a public statement in musical form, some portion of it is recited meditatively and quietly.

ONE WORTHY OF THIS TASK רָגִיל. An early citation in the Talmud declares that the person leading the congregation in prayer on a solemn day ought to be someone who is *ragil*. The Talmud then lists the qualities that a *ragil* should have, and the poet has included many of these here (Babylonian Talmud, Taanit 16a).

GOOD REPUTE וּפִרְקוֹ נָאֶה. This unusual Hebrew phrase is defined in the Talmud by Abbaye (late 3rd century, Babylonia) as one about whom nothing bad has been said (Babylonian Talmud, Taanit 16a).

Hin'ni: Here I Stand

HIN'NI: *THE PRAYER OF A FEMALE LEADER:*

הִנְנִי הֶעָנִיָּה מִמַּעַשׂ, נִרְעֶשֶׁת וְנִפְחֶדֶת מִפַּחַד יוֹשֵׁב תְּהִלּוֹת
יִשְׂרָאֵל, בָּאתִי לַעֲמֹד וּלְהִתְחַנֵּן לְפָנֶיךָ עַל עַמְּךָ יִשְׂרָאֵל
אֲשֶׁר שְׁלָחוּנִי, אַף עַל פִּי שֶׁאֵינִי כְדָאִית וַהֲגוּנָה לְכָךְ.
לָכֵן אֲבַקֵּשׁ מִמְּךָ, אֱלֹהֵי אַבְרָהָם, אֱלֹהֵי יִצְחָק, וֵאלֹהֵי
יַעֲקֹב, אֱלֹהֵי שָׂרָה, אֱלֹהֵי רִבְקָה, אֱלֹהֵי רָחֵל, וֵאלֹהֵי לֵאָה,
יהוה יהוה, אֵל רַחוּם וְחַנּוּן, אֱלֹהֵי יִשְׂרָאֵל, שַׁדַּי אָיוֹם
וְנוֹרָא, הֱיֵה נָא מַצְלִיחַ דַּרְכִּי אֲשֶׁר אֲנִי הוֹלֶכֶת, לַעֲמֹד
וּלְבַקֵּשׁ רַחֲמִים עָלַי וְעַל שׁוֹלְחָי.

וְנָא אַל תַּפְשִׁיעֵם בְּחַטֹּאתִי וְאַל תְּחַיְּבֵם בַּעֲוֹנוֹתַי, כִּי
חוֹטֵאת וּפוֹשַׁעַת אָנִי. וְאַל יִכָּלְמוּ בִּפְשָׁעַי וְאַל יֵבֹשׁוּ בִּי
וְאַל אֵבוֹשָׁה בָּהֶם. וְקַבֵּל תְּפִלָּתִי כִּתְפִלַּת רְגִילָה וְקוֹלָהּ
נָעִים וּפִרְקָהּ נָאֶה וּמְעֹרֶבֶת בְּדַעַת עִם הַבְּרִיּוֹת. וְתִגְעַר
בְּשָׂטָן לְבַל יַשְׂטִינֵנִי. וִיהִי נָא דִגְלֵנוּ עָלֶיךָ אַהֲבָה וְעַל
כָּל־פְּשָׁעִים תְּכַסֶּה בְּאַהֲבָה. וְכָל־צָרוֹת וְרָעוֹת הֲפָךְ־לָנוּ
וּלְכָל־יִשְׂרָאֵל לְשָׂשׂוֹן וּלְשִׂמְחָה לְחַיִּים וּלְשָׁלוֹם. הָאֱמֶת
וְהַשָּׁלוֹם אֱהָבוּ, וְלֹא יְהִי שׁוּם מִכְשׁוֹל בִּתְפִלָּתִי.

וִיהִי רָצוֹן מִלְּפָנֶיךָ, יהוה, אֱלֹהֵי אַבְרָהָם יִצְחָק וְיַעֲקֹב,
שָׂרָה רִבְקָה רָחֵל וְלֵאָה, הָאֵל הַגָּדוֹל הַגִּבּוֹר וְהַנּוֹרָא,
אֵל עֶלְיוֹן, אֶהְיֶה אֲשֶׁר אֶהְיֶה, שֶׁתָּבוֹא תְפִלָּתִי לִפְנֵי כִסֵּא
כְבוֹדֶךָ, בַּעֲבוּר כָּל־הַצַּדִּיקִים וְהַחֲסִידִים הַתְּמִימִים
וְהַיְשָׁרִים, וּבַעֲבוּר כְּבוֹד שִׁמְךָ הַגָּדוֹל וְהַנּוֹרָא, כִּי אַתָּה
שׁוֹמֵעַ תְּפִלַּת עַמְּךָ יִשְׂרָאֵל בְּרַחֲמִים. בָּרוּךְ אַתָּה שׁוֹמֵעַ
תְּפִלָּה.

Here I stand, impoverished in merit, trembling in the presence of the One who hears the prayers of Israel. Even though I am unfit and unworthy for the task, I come to represent Your people Israel and plead on their behalf. Therefore, gracious and merciful ADONAI, awe-inspiring God of Abraham, Isaac, and Jacob, of Sarah, Rebecca, Rachel, and Leah, I pray that I might successfully seek compassion for myself and those who send me.

Charge them not with my sins and let them not bear the guilt of my transgressions, though I have sinned and transgressed. May they not be shamed for my deeds, and may their deeds cause me no shame. Accept my prayer as if it were uttered by one worthy of this task, a person of good repute, whose voice is sweet and whose nature is pleasing to all. Quiet what might trouble me. May our faith in You be accepted lovingly and may Your love cover over our sins. Transform our afflictions and those of all Israel to joy and gladness, life and peace. Love integrity and peace and may there be no obstacles confronting my prayer.

May it be Your will, ADONAI, God of Abraham, Isaac, and Jacob, Sarah, Rebecca, Rachel, and Leah, great, mighty, awe-inspiring, transcendent God, who responded to Moses, saying, "I will be there with you, in the way that I will be there with you," that my prayer reach Your throne, through the merit of all honest, righteous, and devout people, and for the sake of Your glory. Praised are You, merciful God, who hears prayer.

כִּי שֵׁם יהוה אֶקְרָא, הָבוּ גֹדֶל לֵאלֹהֵינוּ.
אֲדֹנָי שְׂפָתַי תִּפְתָּח וּפִי יַגִּיד תְּהִלָּתֶךָ.

The ark is opened.

Version with Patriarchs and Matriarchs:

בָּרוּךְ אַתָּה יהוה,
אֱלֹהֵינוּ וֵאלֹהֵי אֲבוֹתֵינוּ
[וְאִמּוֹתֵינוּ], אֱלֹהֵי אַבְרָהָם,
אֱלֹהֵי יִצְחָק, וֵאלֹהֵי יַעֲקֹב,
אֱלֹהֵי שָׂרָה, אֱלֹהֵי רִבְקָה,
אֱלֹהֵי רָחֵל, וֵאלֹהֵי לֵאָה,
הָאֵל הַגָּדוֹל הַגִּבּוֹר וְהַנּוֹרָא,
אֵל עֶלְיוֹן, גּוֹמֵל חֲסָדִים
טוֹבִים, וְקוֹנֵה הַכֹּל, וְזוֹכֵר
חַסְדֵי אָבוֹת [וְאִמָּהוֹת],
וּמֵבִיא גוֹאֵל לִבְנֵי בְנֵיהֶם
לְמַעַן שְׁמוֹ בְּאַהֲבָה.

Version with Patriarchs:

בָּרוּךְ אַתָּה יהוה,
אֱלֹהֵינוּ וֵאלֹהֵי אֲבוֹתֵינוּ,
אֱלֹהֵי אַבְרָהָם, אֱלֹהֵי
יִצְחָק, וֵאלֹהֵי יַעֲקֹב, הָאֵל
הַגָּדוֹל הַגִּבּוֹר וְהַנּוֹרָא,
אֵל עֶלְיוֹן, גּוֹמֵל חֲסָדִים
טוֹבִים, וְקוֹנֵה הַכֹּל, וְזוֹכֵר
חַסְדֵי אָבוֹת, וּמֵבִיא גוֹאֵל
לִבְנֵי בְנֵיהֶם לְמַעַן שְׁמוֹ
בְּאַהֲבָה.

מְסוֹד חֲכָמִים וּנְבוֹנִים,
וּמִלֶּמֶד דַּעַת מְבִינִים,
אֶפְתְּחָה פִי בִּתְפִלָּה וּבְתַחֲנוּנִים,
לְחַלּוֹת וּלְחַנֵּן פְּנֵי מֶלֶךְ מַלְכֵי הַמְּלָכִים וַאֲדוֹנֵי הָאֲדוֹנִים.

The ark is closed.

זָכְרֵנוּ לְחַיִּים, מֶלֶךְ חָפֵץ בַּחַיִּים,
וְכָתְבֵנוּ בְּסֵפֶר הַחַיִּים, לְמַעַנְךָ אֱלֹהִים חַיִּים.

AS I PROCLAIM כִּי שֵׁם יהוה אֶקְרָא. This verse, taken from Moses' final speech to the children of Israel (Deuteronomy 32:3), was probably originally inserted as an instructional phrase, to be recited by the leader, asking the congregation to respond by answering "Amen" to the *b'rakhot* that follow. Thus it would mean: "When I proclaim God's name, Adonai, you should respond by acknowledging God as well."

ADONAI, OPEN MY LIPS אֲדֹנָי שְׂפָתַי תִּפְתָּח. Psalm 51:17. Every Amidah begins with this request asking God to afford us the appropriate attitude and words for prayer. Perhaps the phrase conveys a mystical sense that prayer originates in our soul, the part of God within us all.

GOD OF ABRAHAM, GOD OF ISAAC, AND GOD OF JACOB אֱלֹהֵי אַבְרָהָם, אֱלֹהֵי יִצְחָק, וֵאלֹהֵי יַעֲקֹב. God begins the conversation with Moses at the burning bush with this self-description (Exodus 3:6). We understand the world of prayer through the experience of those who came before us—both in our immediate and our ancient past. Perhaps the quotation of these words expresses the hope that we too might feel the presence of God. Moses saw only a burning bush, but his inner ear heard so much more.

GREAT, MIGHTY, AWE-INSPIRING הַגָּדוֹל הַגִּבּוֹר וְהַנּוֹרָא. This phrase is a quotation from Deuteronomy 10:17–18, where God's might is characterized by the befriending of the stranger, the widow, and the orphan.

REMEMBER US זָכְרֵנוּ. This brief anonymous and ancient poem, added at each service during the High Holy Day season, stresses the theme that God treasures life.

INSPIRED BY THE INSIGHT מְסוֹד חֲכָמִים. These lines serve to introduce *piyyutim*, poetic additions to the Amidah, that address the holy day's themes. The reference to "sages" and "those who acquired wisdom" is a relic of the era when adding *piyyutim* was a matter of controversy, which prompted this appeal to the authority of those sages who permitted them. This introduction proclaimed that the Amidah's *piyyutim* are faithful to tradition, in that they are saturated with biblical and midrashic quotations.

REPETITION OF THE AMIDAH

The Individual Worshipper and Public Prayer

The individual worshipper prays according to what is written in the prayer book, but at the same time a person's thoughts and words give to each phrase a unique interpretation formed by the personal and private overtones which a singular personality lends to a fixed text. The community in which a person prays adds its own contribution, whether of harmony or discord, elevating or diminishing the spirit of each individual worshipper praying with the congregation.

The prayer of the individual worshipping within a congregation may be compared to a musical performance. Each musician gives a composition his or her own individual personal interpretation, but the orchestra constructs and gives an ensemble tone to the piece. Notwithstanding the fixed notation, each performance expresses the musician and the community of that time and place as much as it does the composer.

—ADIN STEINSALTZ
(adapted)

As I proclaim God's name, ADONAI, exalt our God.
ADONAI, open my lips that my mouth may speak Your praise.
The ark is opened.

First B'rakhah: Our Ancestors

Version with Patriarchs:

Barukh atah ADONAI,
our God and God of our
    ancestors,
God of Abraham, God of
    Isaac, and God of Jacob,
great, mighty, awe-inspiring,
    transcendent God,
who acts with lovingkindness
    and creates all things,
who remembers the loving
    deeds of our ancestors,
and who will send a redeemer
    to their children's children
    with love
    for the sake of divine honor.

Version with Patriarchs and Matriarchs:

Barukh atah ADONAI,
our God and God of our
    ancestors,
God of Abraham, God of
    Isaac, and God of Jacob,
God of Sarah, God of
    Rebecca, God of Rachel,
    and God of Leah,
great, mighty, awe-inspiring,
    transcendent God,
who acts with lovingkindness
    and creates all things,
who remembers the loving
    deeds of our ancestors,
and who will send a redeemer
    to their children's children
    with love
    for the sake of divine honor.

Inspired by the insight of sages
and the teachings of those who acquired wisdom,
I open my lips in prayer and supplication
to entreat the sovereign of all sovereigns,
the supreme ruler.

The ark is closed.

Remember us for life, Sovereign who delights in life,
and inscribe us in the Book of Life, for Your sake, God of life.
*Zokhreinu l'ḥayyim, melekh ḥafeitz ba-ḥayyim,
v'khotveinu b'seifer ha-ḥayyim, l'ma·ankha Elohim ḥayyim.*

מֶֽלֶךְ עוֹזֵר וּפוֹקֵד
וּמוֹשִׁיעַ וּמָגֵן.
בָּרוּךְ אַתָּה יהוה,
מָגֵן אַבְרָהָם וּפוֹקֵד שָׂרָה.

מֶֽלֶךְ עוֹזֵר וּמוֹשִׁיעַ וּמָגֵן.
בָּרוּךְ אַתָּה יהוה,
מָגֵן אַבְרָהָם.

אַתָּה גִּבּוֹר לְעוֹלָם, אֲדֹנָי, מְחַיֵּה מֵתִים אַתָּה,
רַב לְהוֹשִׁיעַ.

מְכַלְכֵּל חַיִּים בְּחֶֽסֶד, מְחַיֵּה מֵתִים בְּרַחֲמִים רַבִּים, סוֹמֵךְ
נוֹפְלִים, וְרוֹפֵא חוֹלִים, וּמַתִּיר אֲסוּרִים, וּמְקַיֵּם אֱמוּנָתוֹ
לִישֵׁנֵי עָפָר. מִי כָמֽוֹךָ בַּֽעַל גְּבוּרוֹת, וּמִי דּֽוֹמֶה לָּךְ, מֶֽלֶךְ
מֵמִית וּמְחַיֵּה וּמַצְמִיחַ יְשׁוּעָה.

מִי כָמֽוֹךָ אַב הָרַחֲמִים, זוֹכֵר יְצוּרָיו לְחַיִּים בְּרַחֲמִים.

וְנֶאֱמָן אַתָּה לְהַחֲיוֹת מֵתִים. בָּרוּךְ אַתָּה יהוה, מְחַיֵּה
הַמֵּתִים.

MIGHTY FOREVER אַתָּה גִּבּוֹר. This b'rakhah, which describes God's presence and activity in the world, centers on the kindness and care of God for the incapacitated—even the dead are in God's care.

GIVE LIFE TO THE DEAD מְחַיֵּה מֵתִים. To be sure, the primary meaning of this phrase was understood to refer to the afterlife, but the Rabbis also understood that the phrase referred to a spiritual revival in this world. Thus the b'rakhah one makes on greeting a friend whom one has not seen for a year utilizes the phrase "who gives life to the dead."

WHO IS LIKE YOU, SOURCE OF COMPASSION מִי כָמֽוֹךָ אַב הָרַחֲמִים. A second insertion at each of the services in the High Holy Day season. The gift of life is an expression of God's kindness.

Version with Patriarchs:

You are the Sovereign
who helps and saves and
shields.

Barukh atah ADONAI,
Shield of Abraham.

Version with Patriarchs and Matriarchs:

You are the Sovereign who
helps and guards, saves and
shields.

Barukh atah ADONAI,
Shield of Abraham and
Guardian of Sarah.

Second B'rakhah: God's Saving Care

You are mighty forever, ADONAI,
You give life to the dead;
great is Your saving power.

You sustain the living through love,
give life to the dead with great mercy.
You support the falling,
heal the sick,
loosen the chains of the bound,
and keep faith with those who sleep in the dust.
Who is like You, Almighty,
and who can be compared to You?—
Sovereign, who brings death and life,
and causes salvation to flourish.

M'khalkeil ḥayyim b'ḥesed, m'ḥayyeih meitim b'raḥamim rabbim,
someikh nof'lim, v'rofei ḥolim, u-mattir asurim, u-m'kayyeim emunato
li-sheinei afar. Mi khamokha ba·al g'vurot u-mi domeh lakh, melekh
meimit u-m'ḥayyeh u-matzmi·aḥ y'shu·ah.

Who is like You, source of compassion,
who remembers with compassion Your creatures for life?
Mi khamokha av ha-raḥamim, zokheir y'tzurav l'ḥayyim b'raḥamim.

Faithful are You in bringing life to the dead.
Barukh atah ADONAI, who gives life to the dead.

וּבְכֵן וּלְךָ תַעֲלֶה קְדֻשָּׁה, כִּי אַתָּה אֱלֹהֵינוּ מֶלֶךְ.

The ark is opened.

וּנְתַנֶּה תֹּקֶף קְדֻשַּׁת הַיּוֹם, כִּי הוּא נוֹרָא וְאָיוֹם. וּבוֹ תִנָּשֵׂא מַלְכוּתֶךָ, וְיִכּוֹן בְּחֶסֶד כִּסְאֶךָ, וְתֵשֵׁב עָלָיו בֶּאֱמֶת. אֱמֶת כִּי אַתָּה הוּא דַיָּן וּמוֹכִיחַ, וְיוֹדֵעַ וָעֵד, וְכוֹתֵב וְחוֹתֵם, וְסוֹפֵר וּמוֹנֶה, וְתִזְכּוֹר כָּל־הַנִּשְׁכָּחוֹת. וְתִפְתַּח אֶת־סֵפֶר הַזִּכְרוֹנוֹת, וּמֵאֵלָיו יִקָּרֵא, וְחוֹתָם יַד כָּל־אָדָם בּוֹ.

וּבְשׁוֹפָר גָּדוֹל יִתָּקַע, וְקוֹל דְּמָמָה דַקָּה יִשָּׁמַע. וּמַלְאָכִים יֵחָפֵזוּן, וְחִיל וּרְעָדָה יֹאחֵזוּן, וְיֹאמְרוּ הִנֵּה יוֹם הַדִּין, לִפְקוֹד עַל צְבָא מָרוֹם בַּדִּין, כִּי לֹא יִזְכּוּ בְעֵינֶיךָ בַּדִּין. וְכָל־בָּאֵי עוֹלָם יַעַבְרוּן לְפָנֶיךָ כִּבְנֵי מָרוֹן. כְּבַקָּרַת רוֹעֶה עֶדְרוֹ, מַעֲבִיר צֹאנוֹ תַּחַת שִׁבְטוֹ, כֵּן תַּעֲבִיר וְתִסְפּוֹר וְתִמְנֶה, וְתִפְקוֹד נֶפֶשׁ כָּל־חַי, וְתַחְתּוֹךְ קִצְבָה לְכָל־בְּרִיָּה, וְתִכְתּוֹב אֶת־גְּזַר דִּינָם.

בְּרֹאשׁ הַשָּׁנָה יִכָּתֵבוּן, וּבְיוֹם צוֹם כִּפּוּר יֵחָתֵמוּן.

כַּמָּה יַעַבְרוּן וְכַמָּה יִבָּרֵאוּן.
מִי יִחְיֶה, וּמִי יָמוּת.
מִי בְקִצּוֹ, וּמִי לֹא בְקִצּוֹ.
מִי בָאֵשׁ, וּמִי בַמַּיִם.
מִי בַחֶרֶב, וּמִי בַחַיָּה.
מִי בָרָעָב, וּמִי בַצָּמָא.
מִי בָרַעַשׁ, וּמִי בַמַּגֵּפָה.
מִי בַחֲנִיקָה, וּמִי בַסְּקִילָה.
מִי יָנוּחַ, וּמִי יָנוּעַ.
מִי יִשָּׁקֵט, וּמִי יִטָּרֵף.
מִי יִשָּׁלֵו, וּמִי יִתְיַסָּר.
מִי יֵעָנִי, וּמִי יֵעָשִׁיר.
מִי יִשָּׁפֵל, וּמִי יָרוּם.

THE "GREAT SHOFAR" WILL BE SOUNDED וּבְשׁוֹפָר גָּדוֹל יִתָּקַע. In a remarkable exercise of poetic license, the anonymous author of this treasured High Holy Day prayer has transformed the prophetic image of the end of days to today. Isaiah, preaching in Jerusalem in the eighth century B.C.E., had predicted (27:13) that those exiled from the northern kingdom of Israel—the ten lost tribes—would return, and all the nations would gather on God's holy mountain. Later interpreters, from Second Temple times on, understood this as a vision of final redemption, a time of final judgment. In this prayer, judgment is not of an end time but in the present—now, even as we pray.

ON ROSH HASHANAH IT IS WRITTEN בְּרֹאשׁ הַשָּׁנָה יִכָּתֵבוּן. This image of God writing each person's fate in a book appears already in the Jerusalem Talmud (Rosh Hashanah 1:3).

WHEN WE REALLY BEGIN. Written by Stanley Rabinowitz and adapted by Shamai Kanter and Jack Riemer.

¶ When we really begin a
new year it is decided,
*and when we actually repent
it is determined:*
who shall be truly alive and
who shall merely exist;
*who shall be happy and who
shall be miserable;*
who shall attain fulfillment
in their day and who shall
not attain fulfillment in
their day;
*who shall be tormented by
the fire of ambition and
who shall be overcome by
the waters of failure;*
who shall be pierced by the
sharp sword of envy and
who shall be torn by the
wild beast of resentment;
*who shall hunger for compan-
ionship and who shall thirst
for approval;*
who shall be shattered by
the earthquake of social
change and who shall be
plagued by the pressures
of conformity;
*who shall be strangled by
insecurity and who shall be
stoned into submission;*
who shall be content and
who shall wander in
search of satisfaction;
*who shall be serene and who
shall be distraught;*
who shall be at ease and
who shall be afflicted with
anxiety;
*who shall be poor in their
own eyes and who shall be
rich in tranquility;*
who shall be brought low
with futility and who
shall be exalted through
achievement.
*But repentance, prayer, and
good deeds have the power
to change the character of
our lives.*
Let us resolve to repent, to
pray, and to do good deeds
so that we may begin a
truly new year.

Third B'rakhah: God's Holiness

May our sanctification ascend to You,
for You are our Sovereign, God.

U-NETANEH TOKEF—THE SACRED POWER OF THE DAY
The ark is opened.

Let us speak of the sacred power of this day—profound and
awe-inspiring. On it, Your sovereignty is celebrated, and Your
throne, from which You rule in truth, is established with love.
Truly, You are Judge and Prosecutor, Expert, and Witness,
completing the indictment, bringing the case, and enumerating the counts. You recall all that is forgotten, and will open
the book of remembrance, which speaks for itself, for our own
hands have signed the page.

The great shofar will be sounded and the still small voice will
be heard.
Angels will be alarmed, seized with fear and trembling, declaring, "This very day is the Day of Judgment"—for even the
hosts of heaven are judged; no one is innocent in Your sight.
All that lives on earth will pass before You like a flock of sheep.
As a shepherd examines the flock, making each sheep pass
under the staff, so You will review and number and count,
judging each living being, determining the fate of everything
in creation, inscribing their destiny.

On Rosh Hashanah it is written, and on the Fast of the Day of
Atonement it is sealed!—
B'rosh ha-shanah yikkateivun, u-v'yom tzom kippur yeiḥateimun.

How many will pass on, and how many will be born;
who will live and who will die;
who will live a long life and who will come to an untimely end;
who will perish by fire and who by water; who by sword and
who by beast; who by hunger and who by thirst; who by
earthquake and who by plague.
who will be strangled and who will be stoned;
who will be at peace and who will be troubled;
who will be serene and who will be disturbed;
who will be tranquil and who will be tormented;
who will be impoverished and who will be enriched;
who will be brought low, and who will be raised up.

וּתְשׁוּבָה וּתְפִלָּה וּצְדָקָה מַעֲבִירִין אֶת־רֹעַ הַגְּזֵרָה.

כִּי כְּשִׁמְךָ כֵּן תְּהִלָּתֶךָ, קָשֶׁה לִכְעוֹס וְנֽוֹחַ לִרְצוֹת.
כִּי לֹא תַחְפֹּץ בְּמוֹת הַמֵּת, כִּי אִם בְּשׁוּבוֹ מִדַּרְכּוֹ וְחָיָה.
וְעַד יוֹם מוֹתוֹ תְּחַכֶּה לּוֹ, אִם יָשׁוּב מִיַּד תְּקַבְּלוֹ.
אֱמֶת כִּי אַתָּה הוּא יוֹצְרָם, וְאַתָּה יוֹדֵעַ יִצְרָם,
כִּי הֵם בָּשָׂר וָדָם.

אָדָם יְסוֹדוֹ מֵעָפָר וְסוֹפוֹ לֶעָפָר. בְּנַפְשׁוֹ יָבִיא לַחְמוֹ.
מָשׁוּל כְּחֶֽרֶס הַנִּשְׁבָּר, כְּחָצִיר יָבֵשׁ, וּכְצִיץ נוֹבֵל, כְּצֵל
עוֹבֵר, וּכְעָנָן כָּלָה, וּכְרֽוּחַ נוֹשָֽׁבֶת, וּכְאָבָק פּוֹרֵֽחַ,
וְכַחֲלוֹם יָעוּף.
וְאַתָּה הוּא מֶֽלֶךְ אֵל חַי וְקַיָּם.

אֵין קִצְבָּה לִשְׁנוֹתֶֽיךָ, וְאֵין קֵץ לְאֹֽרֶךְ יָמֶֽיךָ. וְאֵין שִׁעוּר
לְמַרְכְּבוֹת כְּבוֹדֶֽךָ, וְאֵין פֵּרוּשׁ לְעֵילוֹם שְׁמֶֽךָ. שִׁמְךָ נָאֶה
לְךָ וְאַתָּה נָאֶה לִשְׁמֶֽךָ, וּשְׁמֵֽנוּ קָרָֽאתָ בִּשְׁמֶֽךָ.

The ark is closed and we remain standing.

עֲשֵׂה לְמַֽעַן שְׁמֶֽךָ, וְקַדֵּשׁ אֶת־שִׁמְךָ עַל מַקְדִּישֵׁי שְׁמֶֽךָ,
בַּעֲבוּר כְּבוֹד שִׁמְךָ הַנַּעֲרָץ וְהַנִּקְדָּשׁ.

T'SHUVAH תְּשׁוּבָה. From the root שׁוּב (shov), this noun can mean "repentance" or "turning." It involves self-critique and a resolve to act more in accord with one's principles.

T'FILLAH תְּפִלָּה. From the root פלל (palal) and often translated as "prayer," this noun also implies self-judgment. Moments of t'fillah can bring insight and affirm primary religious commitments.

TZ'DAKAH צְדָקָה. From the root צדק (tzadak), this noun derives from the word for "righteousness" or "justice." It refers to all acts treating others with care and respect. In that sense, our gifts to the needy fulfill a divine obligation.

TRANSFORM THE HARSHNESS OF OUR DESTINY מַעֲבִירִין אֶת־רֹעַ הַגְּזֵרָה. We do not know how our regret may influence what God writes in the Books of Life and

Death. Yet we can transform our experience—however harsh—through how we see ourselves and deal with others—that is, through t'shuvah, t'fillah, and tz'dakah.

SCRIPTURE COMPARES מָשׁוּל. What follows is a poetic cascade of imagery drawn from the Bible. Its staccato formulation underscores the brevity and fragility of life.

A BROKEN SHARD חֶֽרֶס הַנִּשְׁבָּר. Jeremiah 18 develops the image of the potter shattering an ill-formed clay bowl, an image used as well in a prominent Kol Nidrei *piyyut*.

WITHERING GRASS, A SHRIVELED FLOWER חָצִיר יָבֵשׁ, צִיץ נוֹבֵל. Isaiah 40:7.

A PASSING SHADOW צֵל עוֹבֵר. Psalm 144:4.

A FADING CLOUD עָנָן כָּלָה. Based on Job 7:9.

A FLEETING BREEZE רֽוּחַ נוֹשָֽׁבֶת. Isaiah (in 40:7) is referring to God's life-giving breath, which quickly passes through a person, who in the end withers.

SCATTERED DUST אָבָק פּוֹרֵֽחַ. Based on Isaiah 5:24.

A VANISHING DREAM חֲלוֹם יָעוּף. Job 20:8.

YOU HAVE LINKED OUR NAME WITH YOURS וּשְׁמֵֽנוּ קָרָֽאתָ בִּשְׁמֶֽךָ. God has many names, so which one is this phrase referring to? Some say the line alludes to the Thirteen Attributes describing God's graciousness. More likely it refers to the unpronounceable four-letter name of God (yod, heh, vav, heh) which is a play on the verb "to be," and thus may refer to God's eternal being, mentioned in the previous line of this prayer. The ending of the word "Israel" is yet another name for God, *El*. By being linked to God's name, Israel becomes the "eternal people," and partakes of the mystery of God's timeless nature.

Piyyut for Musaf of Rosh Hashanah

וְאֵיךְ אַתָּה מַבִּיט מִלְמַעְלָה? פּוֹתֵחַ עוֹד שָׁנָה?
And just how are You looking down from on high? Beginning another year?

וְאֵיךְ אַתָּה סוֹפֵר אוֹתָנוּ, כְּמוֹ כְּבָשִׂים פּוֹעִים,
And just how do You take account of us, as bleating sheep,

קְרֵבִים אֵלֶיךָ, לַבָּמָה?
approaching You, on the platform?

וּמָה אַתָּה אוֹמֵר עָלֵינוּ,
And what are You saying about us,

עַל הָעֵץ, וְעַל הַפְּרִי, וְעַל הָעוֹף,
about the tree, the fruit, the bird,

עַל הַחַיָּה, וְהַבְּהֵמָה?
the animal, and the beast?

וְאֵיךְ אַתָּה מוֹנֶה אוֹתָנוּ לְפָנֶיךָ בַּחַגִּים שֶׁל הַשָּׁנָה?
And just how is it that You measure us front and center on the holidays of the year?

עַל אֵיזֶה תַּעֲרִיף דִּבַּרְתָּ?! וְכַמָּה תְּבַקֵּשׁ?!
Just what tax were You talking about?! How much will You ask?!

וְאֵיךְ אַתָּה מַדְלִיק אוֹתָנוּ? אֶת־מִי תִּזְרֹק לַמַּיִם קֹדֶם? וּמִי רִאשׁוֹן יִפֹּל לָאֵשׁ??
And just how will You burn us? Who will You throw into the water first? And who will be the first to fall into the fire??

וּמַה כָּתוּב לְךָ לְמַעְלָה, בְּמַטּוּתָא, עַל שִׁבְעִים מִיתוֹת בֵּית־דִּין?
What have You written above—please tell me—about the seventy types of death sentences?

וּמָה הַפַּעַם תְּחַדֵּשׁ??
What new forms will You create this time??

תִּשְׁמַע אַתָּה לְבַד אֶחָד שֶׁשָּׁט לְמַעְלָה. אַתָּה גִּבּוֹר, מַדְהִים, אַדִּיר.
Listen, You alone are the One that hovers above. You—Valiant, Dumbfounding, Impressive.

אֲנַחְנוּ צִיץ עוֹבֵר. אֲנַחְנוּ עֵדֶר צֹאן פּוֹעֶה בַּדִּיר,
We are a withering bud. We are a flock of sheep bleating in the pen.

אַתָּה מוֹנֶה, סוֹפֵר.
You measure and count.

אֲנַחְנוּ קַשׁ נִדָּף, פָּרוּעַ, עַל גַּרְגִּיר־הָעֲרֵמָה.
We—straws in the wind, tossed wildly, upon the grain heap.

וְרַק אַתָּה מֵשִׁיב הָרוּחַ,
Yet only You stir the spirit

עַל קְלִפַּת־הָאֲדָמָה.
on the earth's crust.

—ADMIEL KOSMAN
(trans. Aubrey L. Glazer)

But T'shuvah, T'fillah, and Tz'dakah have the power to transform the harshness of our destiny.

U-t'shuvah u-t'fillah u-tz'dakah ma·avirin et ro·a ha-g'zeirah.

Our praise of You accords with Your essential nature: slow to anger and easily appeased.
You do not desire the death of the sinner, but rather that we change our ways and live.
You wait until the day of death, and if one returns, You accept that person back immediately.
Truly, You are their Creator, and know the nature of Your creatures, that they are only flesh and blood.

Each person's origin is dust, and each person will return to the earth having spent life seeking sustenance. Scripture compares human beings to a broken shard,
withering grass,
a shriveled flower,
a passing shadow,
a fading cloud,
a fleeting breeze,
scattered dust,
a vanishing dream.
And You—You are the Sovereign, living God, ever-present.

V'atah hu melekh El ḥai v'kayyam.

Your years never end,
Your time has no measure,
the extent of Your glory can never be imagined,
for there is no understanding of the mystery of Your nature.
Your name befits You,
as You befit Your name,
and You have linked our name with Yours.

The ark is closed and we remain standing.

Act kindly for the sake of Your name,
and sanctify Your name with those who hallow Your name.
Do so for the honor of Your revered and holy name.

קְדֻשָּׁה

The Kedushah is recited while standing. The tradition recommends standing like angels, with feet together.

כְּסוֹד שִׂיחַ שַׂרְפֵי קֹדֶשׁ, הַמַּקְדִּישִׁים שִׁמְךָ בַּקֹּדֶשׁ, דָּרֵי מַעְלָה עִם דָּרֵי מַטָּה, כַּכָּתוּב עַל יַד נְבִיאֶךָ: וְקָרָא זֶה אֶל זֶה וְאָמַר:

קָדוֹשׁ, קָדוֹשׁ, קָדוֹשׁ יהוה צְבָאוֹת, מְלֹא כָל־הָאָרֶץ כְּבוֹדוֹ.

כְּבוֹדוֹ מָלֵא עוֹלָם, מְשָׁרְתָיו שׁוֹאֲלִים זֶה לָזֶה אַיֵּה מְקוֹם כְּבוֹדוֹ, לְעֻמָּתָם בָּרוּךְ יֹאמֵרוּ:

בָּרוּךְ כְּבוֹד יהוה מִמְּקוֹמוֹ.

מִמְּקוֹמוֹ הוּא יִפֶן בְּרַחֲמִים, וְיָחֹן עַם הַמְיַחֲדִים שְׁמוֹ עֶרֶב וָבֹקֶר, בְּכָל־יוֹם תָּמִיד, פַּעֲמַיִם בְּאַהֲבָה שְׁמַע אוֹמְרִים:

שְׁמַע יִשְׂרָאֵל, יהוה אֱלֹהֵינוּ, יהוה אֶחָד.

הוּא אֱלֹהֵינוּ, הוּא אָבִינוּ, הוּא מַלְכֵּנוּ, הוּא מוֹשִׁיעֵנוּ, וְהוּא יַשְׁמִיעֵנוּ בְּרַחֲמָיו שֵׁנִית לְעֵינֵי כָּל־חָי, לִהְיוֹת לָכֶם לֵאלֹהִים

אֲנִי יהוה אֱלֹהֵיכֶם.

אַדִּיר אַדִּירֵנוּ, יהוה אֲדֹנֵינוּ, מָה אַדִּיר שִׁמְךָ בְּכָל־הָאָרֶץ. וְהָיָה יהוה לְמֶלֶךְ עַל כָּל־הָאָרֶץ, בַּיּוֹם הַהוּא יִהְיֶה יהוה אֶחָד וּשְׁמוֹ אֶחָד.

וּבְדִבְרֵי קָדְשְׁךָ כָּתוּב לֵאמֹר: יִמְלֹךְ יהוה לְעוֹלָם, אֱלֹהַיִךְ צִיּוֹן לְדֹר וָדֹר, הַלְלוּיָהּ.

THE KEDUSHAH is composed of an interweaving of two prophetic visions: that of Isaiah, who saw the angels singing "holy, holy, holy," and that of Ezekiel, whose vision of heavenly forces descending to earth concludes with the phrase "praise God's glory." The form of the Kedushah is antiphonal: in heaven, one chorus of angels responds to another; on earth, leader and congregation respond to each other. In this version, recited at each Musaf service, Israel's recitation of the Sh'ma is offered as a counterpoint to the angelic praise. Ultimately, our prayer brings heaven and earth into conversation: just as the angels affirm God's universal presence, so too the congregation proclaims God's unity. The quotation from Isaiah, remarking that "one calls to the other," thus has a dual meaning in the liturgy: one chorus of angels responds to the other, and we and the angels respond to each other.

GLORY כָּבוֹד. The Kedushah combines several different senses of God's glory: God's creation (the world), God's presence, and the honor and praise we offer God. By placing biblical verses side by side with these several meanings, the *Kedushah* expresses both God's immanence and palpable presence, and God's transcendence, the sense that the Divine is beyond our understanding.

WHEREVER GOD DWELLS מִמְּקוֹמוֹ. The Rabbis said that the word "place" (מָקוֹם, makom) is one of the names of God. "God is the place of the world, but the world is not God's place" (Genesis Rabbah 68:10). The fact that God is everywhere allows us to recite the Kedushah outside of heaven and outside the Temple. Every synagogue filled with prayer becomes God's place.

WILL PROCLAIM וְהוּא יַשְׁמִיעֵנוּ. God and humanity exist in a call and response. God calls to us and we respond to that calling. We turn to God and God brings redemption.

AGAIN שֵׁנִית. Literally, "a second time." The first time was the Exodus. Jewish history exists between the promise of freedom at the Exodus and its fulfillment in the messianic era.

The Kedushah

The Kedushah is recited while standing. The tradition recommends standing like angels, with feet together.

Where Is the Dwelling of God?

"Where is the dwelling of God?"

This was the question with which the Rabbi of Kotzk surprised a number of learned ḥasidim who happened to be visiting him.

They laughed at him: "What a thing to ask! Is not the whole world full of God's glory?"

Then he answered his own question: "God dwells wherever a person lets God in."

—A ḤASIDIC TALE

Those who dwell on earth now add their sanctification of Your name to the mystic utterance of those on high, as Your prophet Isaiah described:
Each cried out to the other:
"Holy, holy, holy is *Adonai Tz'va·ot*, the whole world is filled with God's glory!"
Kadosh, kadosh, kadosh Adonai Tz'va·ot, m'lo khol ha-aretz k'vodo.

God's glory fills the universe. As one angelic chorus asks, "Where is the place of God's glory?" another responds:
"Praised is ADONAI's glory wherever God dwells."
Barukh k'vod Adonai mi-m'komo.

From where God dwells, may God turn with compassion toward the people who twice each day, evening and morning, lovingly proclaim God's oneness, reciting the Sh'ma: "Hear, O Israel, ADONAI is our God, ADONAI alone."
Sh'ma yisra·el, Adonai eloheinu, Adonai eḥad.

The Holy One is our God, our creator, our sovereign, our redeemer. Yet again, God will in mercy proclaim to us before all that lives:
Hu eloheinu, hu avinu, hu malkeinu, hu moshi·einu, v'hu yashmi·einu b'raḥamav
sheinit l'einei kol ḥai, lihyot lakhem leilohim.
"I, ADONAI, am your God."
Ani Adonai eloheikhem.

Majesty, our majesty, ADONAI, our master, how majestic is Your name throughout the world!

ADONAI shall be acknowledged sovereign of all the earth.
On that day ADONAI shall be one, and the name of God, one.

As the psalmist sang:
ADONAI will reign forever; your God, O Zion, from generation to generation. Halleluyah!
Yimlokh Adonai l'olam, elohayikh tziyyon l'dor va-dor, hal'luyah.

לְדוֹר וָדוֹר נַגִּיד גָּדְלֶךָ, וּלְנֵצַח נְצָחִים קְדֻשָּׁתְךָ נַקְדִּישׁ,
וְשִׁבְחֲךָ אֱלֹהֵינוּ מִפִּינוּ לֹא יָמוּשׁ לְעוֹלָם וָעֶד, כִּי אֵל מֶלֶךְ
גָּדוֹל וְקָדוֹשׁ אָתָּה.

We are seated.

חֲמוֹל עַל מַעֲשֶׂיךָ,
וְתִשְׂמַח בְּמַעֲשֶׂיךָ,
וְיֹאמְרוּ לְךָ חוֹסֶיךָ,
בְּצַדֶּקְךָ עֲמוּסֶיךָ,
תֻּקְדַּשׁ אָדוֹן עַל כָּל־מַעֲשֶׂיךָ.

א

הָאוֹחֵז בְּיַד מִדַּת מִשְׁפָּט.
וְכֹל מַאֲמִינִים שֶׁהוּא אֵל אֱמוּנָה,
הַבּוֹחֵן וּבוֹדֵק גִּנְזֵי נִסְתָּרוֹת.
וְכֹל מַאֲמִינִים שֶׁהוּא בּוֹחֵן כְּלָיוֹת,
הַגּוֹאֵל מִמָּוֶת וּפוֹדֶה מִשַּׁחַת.
וְכֹל מַאֲמִינִים שֶׁהוּא גּוֹאֵל חָזָק,

ב

הַדָּן יְחִידִי לְבָאֵי עוֹלָם.
וְכֹל מַאֲמִינִים שֶׁהוּא דַּיָּן אֱמֶת,
הֶהָגוּי בְּאֶהְיֶה אֲשֶׁר אֶהְיֶה.
וְכֹל מַאֲמִינִים שֶׁהוּא הָיָה וְהֹוֶה וְיִהְיֶה,
הַוַּדַּאי שְׁמוֹ כֵּן תְּהִלָּתוֹ.
וְכֹל מַאֲמִינִים שֶׁהוּא וְאֵין בִּלְתּוֹ,

HAVE COMPASSION חֲמוֹל.
The three paragraphs that
follow are a pastiche of
stanzas taken from a variety of different *piyyutim*.
All traditional maḥzorim
arrange them as here.

WE BELIEVE וְכֹל מַאֲמִינִים.
This *piyyut* is 1500 years
old, having been com-
posed by one of the
earliest liturgical poets,
Yannai, who lived in the
Land of Israel some time
between the 5th and 7th
century. The poem is a
double alphabetical acrostic: the first line states an
attribute of God, and the
second uses the same let-
ter to describe the human
perspective. As much as he
can, the poet alliterates an
entire line, thus emphasizing the particular quality.

**KNOWS OUR DEEPEST FEEL-
INGS** בּוֹחֵן כְּלָיוֹת. Literally,
"examines our kidneys." In
the ancient world, priests
would examine the innards
of sacrificed animals to
determine the future or to
interpret messages from
God.

THE STEADFAST REDEEMER
גּוֹאֵל חָזָק. The poet is paraphrasing Jeremiah 50:34,
where the prophet asserts
that only God—no earthly
nation—will redeem Israel.

**SOLE JUDGE OF ALL THAT
LIVES ON EARTH** הַדָּן יְחִידִי לְבָאֵי עוֹלָם. This phrase, taken from
the Mishnah, is echoed in *U-netaneh Tokef*: all that lives on earth
passes before God, the sole Judge on this judgment day.

A PROMISE OF THE FUTURE בְּאֶהְיֶה אֲשֶׁר אֶהְיֶה. In God's revelation
to Moses at the burning bush, God replies to Moses' question,
"Who shall I say sent me?" with the phrase quoted here, explicating the name of God: יהוה. The phrase has been variously translated as "I am that which I am," "I will be that which I will be," or "I
will be there with you in the way that I will be there with you."

From one generation to another we will declare Your greatness, and forever sanctify You with words of holiness. Your praise will never leave our lips, for You are God and Sovereign, great and holy.

We are seated.

Have compassion on Your creation
and rejoice in Your handiwork.
As You pardon Your people,
all who trust in You will declare:
"Be sanctified, Lord, throughout Your creation."

GOD'S QUALITIES: A PIYYUT

א

God upholds the standard of justice.
   We believe that God is faithful.
God examines the store of our hidden thoughts.
   We believe that God knows our deepest feelings.
God redeems us from death, saves us from the grave.
   We believe that God is the steadfast redeemer.

Ha-oḥeiz b'yad middat mishpat.
V'khol ma·aminim she-hu El emunah,
ha-boḥein u-vodeik ginzei nistarot.
V'khol ma·aminim she-hu boḥein k'layot,
ha-go·el mi-mavet u-fodeh mi-shaḥat.
V'khol ma·aminim she-hu go·el ḥazak,

ב

God is the sole judge of all that lives on earth.
   We believe that God is the judge of truth.
God's name is a promise of the future.
   We believe that God is eternal.
God is unwavering; so is God known and such is God's glory.
   We believe that there is none beside God.

ha-dan y'ḥidi l'va·ei olam.
V'khol ma·aminim she-hu dayyan emet,
he-haguy b'ehyeh asher ehyeh.
V'khol ma·aminim she-hu hayah hoveh v'yihyeh,
ha-vaddai sh'mo kein t'hillato.
V'khol ma·aminim she-hu v'ein bilto,

ג

הַזּוֹכֵר לְמַזְכִּירָיו טוֹבוֹת זִכְרוֹנוֹת.
וְכֹל מַאֲמִינִים שֶׁהוּא זוֹכֵר הַבְּרִית,
הַחוֹתֵךְ חַיִּים לְכָל־חָי.
וְכֹל מַאֲמִינִים שֶׁהוּא חַי וְקַיָּם,
הַטּוֹב וּמֵטִיב לָרָעִים וְלַטּוֹבִים.
וְכֹל מַאֲמִינִים שֶׁהוּא טוֹב לַכֹּל,

ד

הַיּוֹדֵעַ יֵצֶר כָּל־יְצוּרִים.
וְכֹל מַאֲמִינִים שֶׁהוּא יוֹצְרָם בַּבֶּטֶן,
הַכֹּל יָכוֹל וְכוֹלְלָם יַחַד.
וְכֹל מַאֲמִינִים שֶׁהוּא כֹּל יָכוֹל,
הַלָּן בְּסֵתֶר בְּצֵל, שַׁדָּי.
וְכֹל מַאֲמִינִים שֶׁהוּא לְבַדּוֹ הוּא,

ה

הַמַּמְלִיךְ מְלָכִים וְלוֹ הַמְּלוּכָה.
וְכֹל מַאֲמִינִים שֶׁהוּא מֶלֶךְ עוֹלָם,
הַנּוֹהֵג בְּחַסְדּוֹ כָּל־דּוֹר.
וְכֹל מַאֲמִינִים שֶׁהוּא נוֹצֵר חֶסֶד,
הַסּוֹבֵל וּמַעֲלִים עַיִן מִסּוֹרְרִים.
וְכֹל מַאֲמִינִים שֶׁהוּא סוֹלֵחַ סֶלָה,

MINDFUL OF THE COVENANT זוֹכֵר הַבְּרִית. The phrase is used in the Torah when God promises Noah that the world will never again be destroyed and points to the rainbow as a symbol of that eternal covenant.

GOD'S DWELLING PLACE IS HIDDEN הַלָּן בְּסֵתֶר בְּצֵל, שַׁדָּי. The poet plays on a verse from Psalms (91:1) which refers to humans resting in the mystery of God's protecting love, in the hidden places, in God's shadow. The poet cleverly places a comma before the Hebrew word "God" and thus transforms the meaning of the verse, making God the subject, not the object. Thus it is God, not the devotee, who resides in secret places.

GOD'S LOVE IS SURE נוֹצֵר חֶסֶד. The phrase is from the Thirteen Attributes, where God is described as "reassuring love to thousands of generations" (Exodus 34:7).

Doubt

God is the Unseen One —no image can capture God. Equally, then, God is the One about whom no descriptive words can truly be uttered—that may be the secret of the Jewish sensibility which makes the name of God unpronounceable.

There are moments— singular or common, depending perhaps on our personality— when we might feel the presence of God, and certainly others when our reality—tragic, joyous, uneventful—is so overwhelmingly with us that even the idea of God seems distant, perhaps ludicrous. And then there are those moments of aloneness when the world seems barren and the idea of God seems distant, even absurd. The person of faith knows that presence and absence are equally true of the experience of God. Sometimes God feels so close that one experiences the presence of an intimate companion, but the obverse is also true. And in those moments of absence, we question whether the experience of presence was only a delusion.

To have faith is equally to know doubt. The person of faith knows that the atheist is not a person who is bullheaded, unseeing, but rather someone who has exclusively experienced the absence which is the lot of even the person of faith. Both faithfulness to God and denial tell of our human reality. When the person of faith is in touch with the depth of his or her spiritual and rational consciousness, one knows that one's heart contains both truths. What are we to do, then, other than to live faithfully, with doubt?

ג

God considers the good of all those who keep God in mind.
We believe that God is mindful of the covenant.
God carves out the lifespan of all that is alive.
We believe that God is living and eternal.
God's goodness flows to the deserving and to the undeserving.
We believe that God is good to all.
ha-zokheir l'mazkirav tovot zikhronot.
V'khol ma·aminim she-hu zokheir ha-b'rit,
ha-ḥoteikh ḥayyim l'khol ḥai.
V'khol ma·aminim she-hu ḥai v'kayyam,
ha-tov u-meitiv la-ra·im v'la-tovim.
V'khol ma·aminim she-hu tov la-kol.

ד

God knows the nature of all creatures.
We believe that God fashioned us in the womb.
God's power is limitless, fashioning all that is.
We believe that God is infinitely powerful.
God's dwelling place is hidden, beyond the heavens.
We believe that God is incomparable,
ha-yodei·a yeitzer kol y'tzurim.
V'khol ma·aminim she-hu yotz'ram ba-baten,
ha-kol yakhol v'khol'lam yaḥad.
V'khol ma·aminim she-hu kol yakhol,
ha-lan b'seiter b'tzeil shaddai.
V'khol ma·aminim she-hu l'vado hu,

ה

God is the supreme Ruler of all.
We believe that God is the Sovereign of time
and space.
God acts with love in each generation.
We believe that God's love is sure.
God is patient, even overlooking the sins of those who are rebellious.
We believe that God is constantly forgiving.
ha-mamlikh m'lakhim v'lo ha-m'lukhah.
V'khol ma·aminim she-hu melekh olam,
ha-noheig b'ḥasdo kol dor.
V'khol ma·aminim she-hu notzeir ḥased,
ha-soveil u-ma·lim ayin mi-sor'rim.
V'khol ma·aminim she-hu solei·aḥ selah,

הָעֶלְיוֹן וְעֵינוֹ אֶל יְרֵאָיו.

וְכֹל מַאֲמִינִים שֶׁהוּא עוֹנֶה לַחַשׁ,

הַפּוֹתֵחַ שַׁעַר לְדוֹפְקֵי בִּתְשׁוּבָה.

וְכֹל מַאֲמִינִים שֶׁהוּא פְּתוּחָה יָדוֹ,

הַצּוֹפֶה לָרָשָׁע וְחָפֵץ בְּהִצָּדְקוֹ.

וְכֹל מַאֲמִינִים שֶׁהוּא צַדִּיק וְיָשָׁר,

ז

הַקָּצָר בְּזַעַם וּמַאֲרִיךְ אַף.

וְכֹל מַאֲמִינִים שֶׁהוּא קָשֶׁה לִכְעוֹס,

הָרַחוּם וּמַקְדִּים רַחֲמִים לָרֹגֶז.

וְכֹל מַאֲמִינִים שֶׁהוּא רַךְ לִרְצוֹת,

הַשָּׁוֶה וּמַשְׁוֶה קָטֹן וְגָדוֹל.

וְכֹל מַאֲמִינִים שֶׁהוּא שׁוֹפֵט צֶדֶק,

הַתָּם וּמִתַּמָּם עִם תְּמִימִים.

וְכֹל מַאֲמִינִים שֶׁהוּא תָּמִים פָּעֳלוֹ.

תִּשְׂגַּב לְבַדֶּךָ, וְתִמְלֹךְ עַל כֹּל בְּיִחוּד, כַּכָּתוּב עַל יַד
נְבִיאֶךָ: וְהָיָה יהוה לְמֶלֶךְ עַל כָּל־הָאָרֶץ, בַּיּוֹם הַהוּא
יִהְיֶה יהוה אֶחָד וּשְׁמוֹ אֶחָד.

MAY YOU BE SOVEREIGN
וְהָיָה יהוה לְמֶלֶךְ. Zechariah
14:9.

I Believe

I assert with absolute
faith
that prayers preceded
God.
Prayers created God.
God created humans.
Humans create prayers
that create God who cre-
ates humanity.

—YEHUDA AMICHAI
(trans. Edward Feld)

Belief

Sometimes the atheist
looking out the window
sees more of God than all
who pray in the syna-
gogue or church.

—MARTIN BUBER

ו

God looks down from above, watching over the faithful.
We believe that God responds even to our silent prayers.
God opens a gate for those who approach in repentance.
We believe that God's arms are always open.
God awaits the repentance of those who have been sinful.
We believe that God is just and upright.

ha-elyon v'eino el y'rei·av.
V'khol ma·aminim she-hu oneh laḥash,
ha-potei·aḥ sha·ar l'dof'kei bi-t'shuvah.
V'khol ma·aminim she-hu p'tuḥah yado,
ha-tzofeh la-rasha v'ḥafeitz b'hitzad'ko.
V'khol ma·aminim she-hu tzaddik v'yashar,

ז

God is patient, holding back wrath.
We believe that it is difficult to arouse God's fury.
God is kind, replacing anger with love.
We believe that it is easy to secure God's favor.
God is the One before whom all are equal.
We believe that God is a righteous judge.
God is blameless and deals righteously with the faithful.
We believe that God's ways are perfect.

ha-katzar b'za·am u-ma·arikh af.
V'khol ma·aminim she-hu kasheh likh·os,
ha-raḥum u-makdim raḥamim la-rogez.
V'khol ma·aminim she-hu rakh lirtzot,
ha-shaveh u-mashveh katon v'gadol.
V'khol ma·aminim she-hu shofeit tzedek,
ha-tam u-mittameim im t'mimim.
V'khol ma·aminim she-hu tamim po·alo.

Alone, exalted, may You rule over a united humanity, as the
prophet Zechariah said, "ADONAI shall be acknowledged sovereign over all the earth. On that day, ADONAI shall be one and
the name of God, one."

וּבְכֵן תֵּן פַּחְדְּךָ יהוה אֱלֹהֵינוּ, עַל כָּל־מַעֲשֶׂיךָ
וְאֵימָתְךָ עַל כָּל־מַה־שֶּׁבָּרָאתָ,
וְיִירָאוּךָ כָּל־הַמַּעֲשִׂים
וְיִשְׁתַּחֲווּ לְפָנֶיךָ כָּל־הַבְּרוּאִים,
וְיֵעָשׂוּ כֻלָּם אֲגֻדָּה אֶחָת
לַעֲשׂוֹת רְצוֹנְךָ בְּלֵבָב שָׁלֵם,
כְּמוֹ שֶׁיָּדַעְנוּ יהוה אֱלֹהֵינוּ, שֶׁהַשִּׁלְטוֹן לְפָנֶיךָ,
עֹז בְּיָדְךָ וּגְבוּרָה בִּימִינֶךָ,
וְשִׁמְךָ נוֹרָא עַל כָּל־מַה־שֶּׁבָּרָאתָ.

וּבְכֵן תֵּן כָּבוֹד יהוה לְעַמֶּךָ,
תְּהִלָּה לִירֵאֶיךָ
וְתִקְוָה לְדוֹרְשֶׁיךָ
וּפִתְחוֹן פֶּה לַמְיַחֲלִים לָךְ,
שִׂמְחָה לְאַרְצֶךָ
וְשָׂשׂוֹן לְעִירֶךָ
וּצְמִיחַת קֶרֶן לְדָוִד עַבְדֶּךָ
וַעֲרִיכַת נֵר לְבֶן־יִשַׁי מְשִׁיחֶךָ, בִּמְהֵרָה בְיָמֵינוּ.

וּבְכֵן צַדִּיקִים יִרְאוּ וְיִשְׂמָחוּ
וִישָׁרִים יַעֲלֹזוּ
וַחֲסִידִים בְּרִנָּה יָגִילוּ,
וְעוֹלָתָה תִּקְפָּץ־פִּיהָ,
וְכָל־הָרִשְׁעָה כֻּלָּהּ כְּעָשָׁן תִּכְלֶה
כִּי תַעֲבִיר מֶמְשֶׁלֶת זָדוֹן מִן הָאָרֶץ.

U-V'KHEIN וּבְכֵן. These three paragraphs, which are introduced by the same word, וּבְכֵן (u-v'khein), are ascribed by many scholars to the 3rd century, and may constitute the earliest poetic additions to the Amidah.

Stages of redemption are described in this series of prayers. The first paragraph implores God to cause the entire world to live with reverence for God. The next paragraph discusses not the universal, but the particular: the return of Israel to its land (and specifically to Jerusalem) and the kingship of David. The third paragraph describes the rejoicing that will come to the righteous "when You remove the tyranny of arrogance from the earth" and God will rule alone over the entire world from Zion and Jerusalem. (adapted from Reuven Hammer)

U-v'khein—ADONAI our God,
instill Your awe in all You have made,
and fear of You in all You have created,
so that all You have fashioned revere You,
all You have created bow in recognition,
and all be bound together, carrying out Your will wholeheartedly.
For we know that true sovereignty is Yours,
power and strength are in Your hands,
and Your name is to be revered beyond any of Your creations.

U-v'khein—Bestow honor to Your people, ADONAI,
praise to those who revere You,
hope to those who seek You,
recognition to those who await You,
joy to Your land, and gladness to Your city.
Simḥah l'artzekha v'sason l'irekha
May the light of David, Your servant, dawn,
and the lamp of the son of Jesse, Your anointed,
be kindled speedily in our day.

U-v'khein—The righteous, beholding this, will rejoice,
the upright will be glad,
the pious will celebrate with song,
evil will be silenced,
and all wickedness will disappear like smoke,
when You remove the tyranny of arrogance from the earth.

וְיֶאֱתָיוּ כֹל לְעָבְדֶךָ,
וִיבָרְכוּ שֵׁם כְּבוֹדֶךָ,
וְיַגִּֽידוּ בָאִיִּים צִדְקֶךָ,
וְיִדְרְשֽׁוּךָ עַמִּים לֹא יְדָעֽוּךָ,
וִיהַלְלֽוּךָ כָּל־אַפְסֵי אָֽרֶץ,
וְיֹאמְרוּ תָמִיד יִגְדַּל יהוה.
וְיִזְבְּחוּ אֶת־עֲצַבֵּיהֶם,
וְיַחְפְּרוּ עִם פְּסִילֵיהֶם.
וְיַטּוּ שְׁכֶם אֶחָד לְעָבְדֶךָ,
וְיִירָאֽוּךָ עִם שֶֽׁמֶשׁ מְבַקְשֵׁי פָנֶֽיךָ,
וְיַכִּֽירוּ כֹּחַ מַלְכוּתֶֽךָ,
וִילַמְּדוּ תוֹעִים בִּינָה.
וִימַלְלוּ אֶת־גְּבוּרָתֶֽךָ,
וִינַשְּׂאֽוּךָ מִתְנַשֵּׂא לְכֹל לְרֹאשׁ,
וִיסַלְּדוּ בְחִילָה פָנֶֽיךָ,
וִיעַטְּרֽוּךָ נֵֽזֶר תִּפְאָרָה.
וְיִפְצְחוּ הָרִים רִנָּה,
וְיִצְהֲלוּ אִיִּים בְּמָלְכֶֽךָ,
וִיקַבְּלוּ עֹל מַלְכוּתְךָ עֲלֵיהֶם,
וִירוֹמְמֽוּךָ בִּקְהַל עָם.
וְיִשְׁמְעוּ רְחוֹקִים וְיָבֹֽאוּ,
וְיִתְּנוּ לְךָ כֶּֽתֶר מְלוּכָה.

AND ALL SHALL COME TO SERVE YOU וְיֶאֱתָיוּ כֹל לְעָבְדֶךָ. This alphabetic *piyyut* elaborates the theme that will be spelled out in the next paragraph of this b'rakhah, looking toward God's exclusive reign in the messianic era. It plays on biblical verses which foretell the praise of God in the end of days. Some see in it references to the Roman iconoclastic uprising of the 7th century (e.g., "their idols overthrown"), which must have struck the Jews as a partial fulfillment of biblical prophecies." Solomon Schechter (1847–1915) wrote: "How one would like to catch a glimpse of that early hymnologist to whom we owe the well-known *piyyut, V'ye·etayu.* In its iconoclastic victory of monotheism over all kinds of idolatries, ancient as well as modern, it might best be described as the Marseillaise of the people of the Lord of Hosts—a Marseillaise which is not followed by a reign of terror but by the Kingdom of God on earth, when the upright shall exult and the saints triumphantly rejoice."

Israel Zangwill composed this poetic adaptation of the piyyut, published in the British United Synagogue Maḥzor, 1909.

¶ All the world shall come to serve Thee
   and praise Thy glorious name,
and Thy righteousness triumphant
      the islands shall acclaim.
And nations shall give Thee homage
   who knew Thee not before,
and the ends of earth shall praise Thee,
   Thy name they shall adore.
They shall build for Thee their altars,
      their idols overthrown;
and their hands shall clasp in friendship
   as they turn to Thee alone.
They shall bow before Thy grandeur,
 and know Thy kingdom's might;
they shall walk in under-standing,
   who are astray in night.
They shall exult in Thy greatness,
   and of Thy power speak,
and extol Thee, shrined, uplifted
   beyond man's highest peak.
And with reverential homage,
   of love and wonder born,
with the ruler's crown of beauty
   Thy head they shall adorn.
With the coming of Thy kingdom
   the hills shall break into song,
and the islands laugh exultant
   that they to God belong.
All their congregations
   so loud Thy praise shall sing,
that faraway peoples, hearing,
   shall come and hail Thee King.

THE DREAM OF UNIVERSAL REDEMPTION: A PIYYUT

And all shall come to serve You,
praise Your honored name,
proclaiming Your just rule in every island.
Nations that knew You not will seek You,
even those that live at the ends of the earth will laud You,
constantly proclaiming, "God is great."
They shall put away their idols,
bury their icons,
and come as one to serve You.
At the rising of the sun,
those who seek You will be inspired with awe,
and those in error will recognize the power of
   Your sovereignty
and learn wisdom.
They will speak of Your salvation,
exalting You above all.
Trembling, they shall greet You,
crowning You with a crown of glory.
Acceding to Your rule,
mountains will burst with song,
and islands rejoice in Your sovereignty.
You will be extolled in the gathering of nations,
as distant people will journey
to crown You as Sovereign.

V'ye·etayu kol l'ovdekha,
vivar'khu sheim k'vodekha,
v'yaggidu va-iyyim tzidkekha,
v'yidr'shukha ammim lo y'da·ukha,
vihal'lukha kol afsei aretz,
v'yom'ru tamid yigdal Adonai.
V'yizn'ḥu et-atzabeihem,
v'yaḥp'ru im p'sileihem.
V'yattu sh'khem eḥad l'ovdekha,
v'yira·ukha im shemesh m'vakshei fanekha,
V'yakkiru ko·aḥ malkhutekha,
vilam'du to·im binah.
Vimal'lu et-g'vuratekha, vinas'ukha mitnassei l'khol l'rosh,
visal'du v'ḥilah fanekha, vi·at'rukha neizer tifarah.
V'yiftz'ḥu harim rinnah, v'yitzhalu i'yyim v'molkhekha,
vikab'lu ol malkhut'kha aleihem, virom'mukha bi-k'hal am.
V'yishm·u r'ḥokim v'yavo·u, v'yit'nu l'kha keter m'lukhah.

וְתִמְלֹךְ, אַתָּה יהוה לְבַדֶּךָ, עַל כָּל־מַעֲשֶׂיךָ, בְּהַר צִיּוֹן מִשְׁכַּן
כְּבוֹדֶךָ, וּבִירוּשָׁלַיִם עִיר קָדְשֶׁךָ, כַּכָּתוּב בְּדִבְרֵי קָדְשֶׁךָ:
יִמְלֹךְ יהוה לְעוֹלָם, אֱלֹהַיִךְ צִיּוֹן לְדֹר וָדֹר, הַלְלוּ־יָהּ.

קָדוֹשׁ אַתָּה וְנוֹרָא שְׁמֶךָ, וְאֵין אֱלוֹהַּ מִבַּלְעָדֶיךָ, כַּכָּתוּב:
וַיִּגְבַּהּ יהוה צְבָאוֹת בַּמִּשְׁפָּט, וְהָאֵל הַקָּדוֹשׁ נִקְדָּשׁ
בִּצְדָקָה. בָּרוּךְ אַתָּה יהוה, הַמֶּלֶךְ הַקָּדוֹשׁ.

אַתָּה בְחַרְתָּנוּ מִכָּל־הָעַמִּים, אָהַבְתָּ אוֹתָנוּ וְרָצִיתָ בָּנוּ,
וְרוֹמַמְתָּנוּ מִכָּל־הַלְּשׁוֹנוֹת, וְקִדַּשְׁתָּנוּ בְּמִצְוֹתֶיךָ,
וְקֵרַבְתָּנוּ מַלְכֵּנוּ לַעֲבוֹדָתֶךָ,
וְשִׁמְךָ הַגָּדוֹל וְהַקָּדוֹשׁ עָלֵינוּ קָרָאתָ.

וַתִּתֶּן לָנוּ, יהוה אֱלֹהֵינוּ, בְּאַהֲבָה אֶת־יוֹם [הַשַּׁבָּת הַזֶּה
וְאֶת־יוֹם] הַזִּכָּרוֹן הַזֶּה, יוֹם [זִכְרוֹן] תְּרוּעָה [בְּאַהֲבָה]
מִקְרָא קֹדֶשׁ, זֵכֶר לִיצִיאַת מִצְרָיִם.

Some congregations recite this traditional version; others continue on the next page
with A Prayer for Jewry in Distress.

וּמִפְּנֵי חֲטָאֵינוּ גָּלִינוּ מֵאַרְצֵנוּ וְנִתְרַחַקְנוּ מֵעַל אַדְמָתֵנוּ
וְאֵין אֲנַחְנוּ יְכוֹלִים לַעֲשׂוֹת חוֹבוֹתֵינוּ בְּבֵית בְּחִירָתֶךָ, בַּבַּיִת
הַגָּדוֹל וְהַקָּדוֹשׁ שֶׁנִּקְרָא שִׁמְךָ עָלָיו, מִפְּנֵי הַיָּד שֶׁנִּשְׁתַּלְּחָה
בְּמִקְדָּשֶׁךָ.

יְהִי רָצוֹן מִלְּפָנֶיךָ, יהוה אֱלֹהֵינוּ וֵאלֹהֵי אֲבוֹתֵינוּ [וְאִמּוֹתֵינוּ],
מֶלֶךְ רַחֲמָן הַמֵּשִׁיב בָּנִים לִגְבוּלָם, שֶׁתָּשׁוּב וּתְרַחֵם עָלֵינוּ
וְעַל מִקְדָּשְׁךָ בְּרַחֲמֶיךָ הָרַבִּים, וְתִבְנֵהוּ מְהֵרָה וּתְגַדֵּל כְּבוֹדוֹ.
אָבִינוּ מַלְכֵּנוּ, גַּלֵּה כְּבוֹד מַלְכוּתְךָ עָלֵינוּ מְהֵרָה, וְהוֹפַע
וְהִנָּשֵׂא עָלֵינוּ לְעֵינֵי כָּל־חָי, וְקָרֵב פְּזוּרֵינוּ מִבֵּין הַגּוֹיִם
וּנְפוּצוֹתֵינוּ כַּנֵּס מִיַּרְכְּתֵי־אָרֶץ.

וַהֲבִיאֵנוּ לְצִיּוֹן עִירְךָ בְּרִנָּה, וְלִירוּשָׁלַיִם בֵּית מִקְדָּשְׁךָ
בְּשִׂמְחַת עוֹלָם, שֶׁשָּׁם עָשׂוּ אֲבוֹתֵינוּ [וְאִמּוֹתֵינוּ] לְפָנֶיךָ
אֶת־קָרְבְּנוֹת חוֹבוֹתֵיהֶם, תְּמִידִים כְּסִדְרָם וּמוּסָפִים
כְּהִלְכָתָם, וְאֶת־מוּסְפֵי [יוֹם הַשַּׁבָּת הַזֶּה וְ] יוֹם הַזִּכָּרוֹן
הַזֶּה עָשׂוּ וְהִקְרִיבוּ לְפָנֶיךָ בְּאַהֲבָה כְּמִצְוַת רְצוֹנֶךָ, כַּכָּתוּב
בְּתוֹרָתֶךָ, עַל יְדֵי מֹשֶׁה עַבְדֶּךָ מִפִּי כְבוֹדֶךָ כָּאָמוּר:

ADONAI WILL REIGN
FOREVER יִמְלֹךְ יהוה
לְעוֹלָם. Psalm 146:10.

ADONAI TZV'VA·OT
WILL BE EXALTED וַיִּגְבַּהּ
יהוה צְבָאוֹת בַּמִּשְׁפָּט.
Isaiah 5:16.

BECAUSE OF OUR SINS
מִפְּנֵי חֲטָאֵינוּ. The first
of the middle b'rakhot
of the Amidah is called
קְדֻשַּׁת הַיּוֹם (k'dushat
ha-yom), the expres-
sion of the holiness of
the day. The content
of this b'rakhah is
not prescribed in the
Talmud. During the first
millennium, the prayer
concerning the holiness
of the day came to be
centered on the Temple
and its offerings, as if
the utterance of the
words substituted for
the missing sacrifices.
Recently, some have
begun reciting alternate
prayers, which under-
stand the rebuilding
of the Temple as a
metaphor for the repair
of the world in which
we all need to engage.
(See the following page.)

You alone, ADONAI, will rule all Your creation,
from Mount Zion, the dwelling-place of Your glory,
and from Jerusalem, Your holy city.
As it is written in the Book of Psalms:
"ADONAI will reign forever; your God, O Zion, from generation
to generation. Halleluyah!"
Yimlokh Adonai l'olam, elohayikh tziyyon l'dor va-dor hal'luyah.

You are holy, and Your name is revered, for there is no God but You.
As Your prophet Isaiah wrote: "*Adonai Tz'va·ot* will be exalted through
justice, the holy God sanctified through righteousness."
Barukh atah ADONAI, the Holy Sovereign.

Fourth B'rakhah: The Holiness of Rosh Hashanah

You have chosen us among all peoples, loving us, wanting us.
You have distinguished us among all nations, making us holy through Your
commandments, drawing us close to Your service, and calling us
by Your great and holy name.

With love, You have bestowed on us, ADONAI our God, [this Shabbat and]
this Day of Remembrance, a day for [recalling] the shofar sound [with
love], a day for holy assembly and for recalling the Exodus from Egypt.

*Some congregations recite this traditional version; others continue on the next page with
A Prayer for Jewry in Distress.*

Because of our sins we have been exiled from our land and removed
from our soil. And so, because of the hand which was set against Your
sanctuary, we are unable to fulfill our obligations in that great and holy
place which You chose to carry Your name. May it be Your will, ADONAI
our God and God of our ancestors, compassionate sovereign who restores
their descendants to their promised land, that You may once again have
compassion on us and return in Your great mercy to Your sanctuary. May
You speedily rebuild it and renew its glory. *Avinu Malkeinu*, speedily
manifest the glory of Your dominion, revealing to all humanity that You
are our sovereign, gather our dispersed people from among the nations,
and bring back those scattered to the ends of the earth.

Bring us exultantly to Zion, Your city, and with everlasting joy to
Jerusalem, Your sanctuary, where our ancestors once offered to You
their obligatory, daily, and holy day sacrifices, each as prescribed. The
[Shabbat and] New Year sacrifices were offered there in love, as You
commanded, as it is written in Your Torah by Moses, Your servant, by
Your instruction:

The Sephardic rite continues on page 153.

On Shabbat, those reciting the traditional sacrificial list add this paragraph:

וּבְיוֹם הַשַּׁבָּת שְׁנֵי כְבָשִׂים בְּנֵי שָׁנָה תְּמִימִם, וּשְׁנֵי
עֶשְׂרוֹנִים סְלֶת מִנְחָה בְּלוּלָה בַשֶּׁמֶן וְנִסְכּוֹ: עֹלַת שַׁבַּת
בְּשַׁבַּתּוֹ, עַל עֹלַת הַתָּמִיד וְנִסְכָּהּ: במדבר כח ט-י

וּבַחֹדֶשׁ הַשְּׁבִיעִי, בְּאֶחָד לַחֹדֶשׁ, מִקְרָא קֹדֶשׁ יִהְיֶה לָכֶם
כָּל מְלֶאכֶת עֲבֹדָה לֹא תַעֲשׂוּ, יוֹם תְּרוּעָה יִהְיֶה לָכֶם.
וַעֲשִׂיתֶם עֹלָה לְרֵיחַ נִיחֹחַ לַיהוה, פַּר בֶּן־בָּקָר אֶחָד, אַיִל
אֶחָד, כְּבָשִׂים בְּנֵי שָׁנָה שִׁבְעָה, תְּמִימִם. במדבר כט א-ב
וּמִנְחָתָם וְנִסְכֵּיהֶם כִּמְדֻבָּר: שְׁלֹשָׁה עֶשְׂרֹנִים לַפָּר, וּשְׁנֵי
עֶשְׂרֹנִים לָאַיִל, וְעִשָּׂרוֹן לַכֶּבֶשׂ, וְיַיִן כְּנִסְכּוֹ, וּשְׁנֵי שְׂעִירִים
לְכַפֵּר, וּשְׁנֵי תְמִידִים כְּהִלְכָתָם. מִלְּבַד עֹלַת הַחֹדֶשׁ
וּמִנְחָתָהּ, וְעֹלַת הַתָּמִיד וּמִנְחָתָהּ, וְנִסְכֵּיהֶם כְּמִשְׁפָּטָם,
לְרֵיחַ נִיחֹחַ אִשֶּׁה לַיהוה: במדבר כט ג-ו

A PRAYER FOR JEWRY IN DISTRESS

אֱלֹהֵינוּ וֵאלֹהֵי אֲבוֹתֵינוּ [וְאִמּוֹתֵינוּ], רַחֵם עַל אַחֵינוּ
בֵּית יִשְׂרָאֵל הַנְּתוּנִים בְּצָרָה וְהוֹצִיאֵם מֵאֲפֵלָה לְאוֹרָה.
וְקַבֵּל בְּרַחֲמִים אֶת־תְּפִלַּת עַמְּךָ בְּנֵי יִשְׂרָאֵל, בְּכָל־
מְקוֹמוֹת מוֹשְׁבוֹתֵיהֶם, הַשּׁוֹפְכִים אֶת־לִבָּם לְפָנֶיךָ בְּיוֹם
[הַשַּׁבָּת הַזֶּה וּבְיוֹם] הַזִּכָּרוֹן הַזֶּה.

Those who recited the traditional sacrificial list now continue on the next page.

יְהִי רָצוֹן מִלְּפָנֶיךָ, יהוה אֱלֹהֵינוּ וֵאלֹהֵי אֲבוֹתֵינוּ
[וְאִמּוֹתֵינוּ], שֶׁיִּבָּנֶה בֵּית הַמִּקְדָּשׁ בִּמְהֵרָה בְיָמֵינוּ,
כְּפִי שֶׁהִבְטַחְתָּנוּ עַל יְדֵי נְבִיאָךְ, כַּכָּתוּב: וְהָיָה בְּאַחֲרִית
הַיָּמִים, נָכוֹן יִהְיֶה הַר בֵּית יהוה בְּרֹאשׁ הֶהָרִים וְנִשָּׂא
מִגְּבָעוֹת, וְנָהֲרוּ אֵלָיו כָּל־הַגּוֹיִם. וְהָלְכוּ עַמִּים רַבִּים
וְאָמְרוּ, לְכוּ וְנַעֲלֶה אֶל הַר יהוה, אֶל בֵּית אֱלֹהֵי יַעֲקֹב,
וְיֹרֵנוּ מִדְּרָכָיו, וְנֵלְכָה בְּאֹרְחֹתָיו. כִּי מִצִּיּוֹן תֵּצֵא תוֹרָה
וּדְבַר יהוה מִירוּשָׁלָיִם. וְשָׁפַט בֵּין הַגּוֹיִם וְהוֹכִיחַ לְעַמִּים
רַבִּים, וְכִתְּתוּ חַרְבוֹתָם לְאִתִּים וַחֲנִיתוֹתֵיהֶם לְמַזְמֵרוֹת,
לֹא יִשָּׂא גוֹי אֶל גּוֹי חֶרֶב וְלֹא יִלְמְדוּ עוֹד מִלְחָמָה.

MAY IT BE YOUR WILL יְהִי
רָצוֹן. From *Siddur Va'ani
Tefilati*, the prayerbook of
the Masorti (Conservative)
movement in Israel. This
acknowledges the Jewish
people's having returned
to the Land of Israel. (The
more traditional wording
speaks of the exile, our
inability to perform the
Temple sacrifices, and the
hope of return.)

**AND IT SHALL COME TO
PASS** וְהָיָה בְּאַחֲרִית הַיָּמִים.
Isaiah 2:2–4. Most contemporary biblical scholars
think that this phrase
points to the indefinite
future. Classical exegetes
thought of it as referring to
a messianic end-time. This
vision of universal peace is
inscribed as the watchword
of the United Nations.

LET US GO UP לְכוּ וְנַעֲלֶה.
Isaiah's vision of universal
religious unity.

**INSTRUCTION SHALL GO
FORTH** תֵּצֵא תוֹרָה. The
word *torah*, translated here
as "instruction," can be
understood in its wid-
est sense: all that is right
and true. Jewish mystics
understood the verse as
referring to a future divine
revelation.

Our Sacrifice

Our worship is one of prayer and praise. But when we think of the piety of our ancestors, who from their meager store of cattle and grain, the yield of the shepherd's care and the farmer's toil, offered their best in the service of God, can we be content with a gift of mere words that costs us neither labor nor privation? Shall we not feel impelled to devote of our substance to the service of God? Shall we not give of our store to the relief of suffering, the healing of sickness, the dispelling of ignorance and error, the righting of wrongs and the strengthening of faith?

—MORDECAI KAPLAN
AND EUGENE KOHN
(*adapted*)

"The sacrifices of God are a broken spirit; a contrite and broken heart" (Psalm 51:19). Rabbi Abba bar Judan said: What God regards as unfit for sacrifice in an animal, God holds as fit in a human being. An animal that is blind or broken or maimed is unfit for sacrifice (Leviticus 22:22), but a human being who has a broken and contrite heart is a fit offering to God.

—PESIKTA OF
RAV KAHANA

The Sephardic rite continues on page 153.

On Shabbat, those reciting the traditional sacrificial list add this paragraph:

On Shabbat: two yearling lambs without blemish, together with two-tenths of a measure of choice flour with oil mixed in as a grain offering, and with the proper libation. A burnt offering for every Shabbat, in addition to the regular burnt offering and its libation. Numbers 28:9–10

In the seventh month, on the first day of the month, you shall observe a sacred occasion: you shall not work at your occupations. You shall observe it as a day when the horn is sounded.
You shall present a burnt offering of pleasing odor to ADONAI: one bull of the herd, one ram, and seven yearling lambs, without blemish. Numbers 29:1–2 As ordained, they shall be accompanied by grain offerings and by libations: three-tenths of a measure for the bull, two-tenths for the ram, one-tenth for each lamb, wine for its libation, two goats for expiation, and the two daily offerings as is their custom. This is in addition to the burnt offering of the new moon with its meal offering and the regular burnt offering with its grain offering, each with its libation as prescribed, gifts of pleasing odor to ADONAI. Numbers 29:3–6

A PRAYER FOR JEWRY IN DISTRESS

Our God and God of our ancestors, show compassion to our brothers and sisters of the House of Israel, who suffer persecution; deliver them from darkness to light. Accept with compassion the prayers of Your people Israel who cry out to You on this [Shabbat and this] Day of Remembrance, wherever they dwell.

Those who recited the traditional sacrificial list now continue on the next page.

May it be Your will, ADONAI our God and God of our ancestors, that the Holy Temple be rebuilt speedily in our time, as You promised, in the words of Your prophet Isaiah: "And it shall come to pass, in the end of days, that the House of ADONAI will be firmly established at the top of the mountain, raised high above all other hills. All peoples shall flow toward it, and nations shall say, 'Let us go up to the mountain of ADONAI to the house of the God of Jacob, and we shall learn from God's ways and walk in God's paths.' For instruction shall go forth from Zion and the word of ADONAI from Jerusalem. God will provide proper judgment among nations and admonish many peoples. They shall beat their swords into plowshares, and spears into pruning hooks. Nation shall not take up sword against nation, neither shall they learn war anymore."

יִשְׂמְחוּ בְמַלְכוּתְךָ שׁוֹמְרֵי שַׁבָּת וְקוֹרְאֵי עֹנֶג, עַם מְקַדְּשֵׁי שְׁבִיעִי, כֻּלָּם יִשְׂבְּעוּ וְיִתְעַנְּגוּ מִטּוּבֶךָ, וּבַשְּׁבִיעִי רָצִיתָ בּוֹ וְקִדַּשְׁתּוֹ, חֶמְדַּת יָמִים אוֹתוֹ קָרָאתָ, זֵכֶר לְמַעֲשֵׂה בְרֵאשִׁית.

Congregation recites:

אֱלֹהֵינוּ וֵאלֹהֵי אֲבוֹתֵינוּ [וְאִמּוֹתֵינוּ], הֱיֵה עִם פִּיפִיּוֹת שְׁלוּחֵי עַמְּךָ בֵּית יִשְׂרָאֵל, הָעוֹמְדִים לְבַקֵּשׁ תְּפִלָּה וְתַחֲנוּנִים מִלְּפָנֶיךָ עַל עַמְּךָ בֵּית יִשְׂרָאֵל.

הָבִינֵם מַה שֶּׁיְּדַבֵּרוּ,	הוֹרֵם מַה שֶּׁיֹּאמֵרוּ,
יְדָעֵם אֵיךְ יְפָאֲרוּ.	הֲשִׁיבֵם מַה שֶּׁיִּשְׁאָלוּ,
בֶּרֶךְ לְךָ יִכְרָעוּן,	בְּאוֹר פָּנֶיךָ יְהַלֵּכוּן,
וּמִבִּרְכוֹת פִּיךָ כֻּלָּם יִתְבָּרֵכוּן.	עַמְּךָ בְּפִיהֶם יְבָרְכוּן,

Reader responds:

אוֹחִילָה לָאֵל, אֲחַלֶּה פָנָיו, אֶשְׁאֲלָה מִמֶּנּוּ מַעֲנֵה לָשׁוֹן. אֲשֶׁר בִּקְהַל עָם אָשִׁירָה עֻזּוֹ, אַבִּיעָה רְנָנוֹת בְּעַד מִפְעָלָיו. לְאָדָם מַעַרְכֵי לֵב, וּמֵיהוה מַעֲנֵה לָשׁוֹן. יהוה שְׂפָתַי תִּפְתָּח, וּפִי יַגִּיד תְּהִלָּתֶךָ. יִהְיוּ לְרָצוֹן אִמְרֵי פִי וְהֶגְיוֹן לִבִּי לְפָנֶיךָ, יהוה, צוּרִי וְגוֹאֲלִי.

THE SPECIAL SECTIONS OF MUSAF: MALKHUYOT, ZIKHRONOT, AND SHOFAROT.

The distinctive feature of the Rosh Hashanah Musaf Amidah is the insertion of Malkhuyot, Zikhronot, and Shofarot (verses relating to God's sovereignty, to remembrance, and to the sounding of the shofar) into the typical seven-b'rakhah structure of the holy day Amidah.

The verses of Malkhuyot, Zikhronot, and Shofarot highlight the complex, interrelated themes of Rosh Hashanah. The new year is a time to recognize what is of ultimate value for us, what of the past we wish to recall and carry with us into the future, and what of the past we would like God to recall. It is a day to meditate on our behavior in the world: What are we called to? From a religious perspective, what goals are worth striving toward?

In each of the three sections, a poetic introduction is followed by ten biblical verses (three from the Five Books of the Torah, three from Psalms, three from the Prophets, and then another verse from the Torah). Each verse contains the key word for that section: a reference to sovereignty, memory, or the shofar. Additional poetic material introduces the last verse of each section. The section then concludes with a b'rakhah, the blowing of the shofar, and two brief prayers, one announcing this day as the birthday of the world, הַיּוֹם הֲרַת עוֹלָם, and the second a plea that our prayers be heard, אֲרֶשֶׁת שְׂפָתֵינוּ.

The recitation of biblical verses is mandated in the Mishnah and Talmud (Babylonian Talmud, Rosh Hashanah 32a), which provide guidelines for their selection. However, the number of verses required was the subject of debate. (The predominant opinion is ten, while the minority holds that three is sufficient—one from each of the major biblical divisions.)

BE WITH THE MESSENGER הֱיֵה עִם פִּיפִיּוֹת. This paragraph is a prayer by the congregation that the Shekhinah be present as inspiration to the prayer leader. It is a complement to the meditation of the prayer leader which follows.

I PRAY TO YOU, GOD אוֹחִילָה לָאֵל. On Rosh Hashanah and Yom Kippur, the unique additions to the Musaf Amidah are introduced by a personal prayer of the leader asking for God's help in offering prayer that is effective in reaching both the congregation and God. This meditation was written in the first millennium and appears not only in the Ashkenazic tradition but in the Sephardic as well, where it precedes the entire repetition of the Amidah.

Every year there descends and radiates a new and renewed light which has never yet shone. For the light of every year withdraws to its source in the Infinite One who is beyond time . . . but through the sounding of the shofar and by means of the prayers we utter, a new and superior light is elicited . . . a new and more sublime light that has never yet shone since the beginning of the world. Its manifestation, however, depends on the actions of those below, and on their merits and penitence during the Ten Days of T'shuvah.

—SCHNEUR ZALMAN
OF LIADI

ON SHABBAT, WE RECITE THIS PARAGRAPH:

Those who observe Shabbat and call it a delight rejoice in Your sovereignty. May the people who sanctify the seventh day be fulfilled and delighted with Your abundant goodness. You have loved the seventh day and sanctified it, calling it the treasured day, a sign of creation.

Yism'ḥu v'malkhut'kha shom'rei shabbat v'kor'ei oneg, am m'kad'shei sh'vi·i, kullam yisb'u v'yit·an'gu mi-tuvekha, u-va-sh'vi·i ratzita bo v'kiddashto, ḥemdat yamim oto karata, zeikher l'ma·aseih v'reishit.

Introduction to the Three Special Sections of Musaf

Congregation recites:

Our God and God of our ancestors, be with the messengers of Your people Israel as they stand praying for the ability to plead before You, on our behalf.
Teach them what to say,
inspire them in their speech,
respond to their requests,
instruct them how to properly glorify You.
May they walk in the light of Your presence,
and bend their knees to You.
May Your people be blessed through the
words of their mouths, and may all find
blessing through the blessings of Your mouth.

Reader responds:

I pray to You, God, that I may come into Your presence.
Grant me proper speech, for I would sing of Your strength amidst the congregation of Your people and utter praises describing Your deeds.
A person may have the best of intentions, but it is God who grants the ability of expression.
ADONAI, open my lips that my mouth may declare Your glory.
And may the words of my mouth and the thoughts in my heart be acceptable to You, ADONAI, my stronghold and my redeemer.

מַלְכֻיּוֹת

The ark is opened.

עָלֵינוּ לְשַׁבֵּחַ לַאֲדוֹן הַכֹּל,
לָתֵת גְּדֻלָּה לְיוֹצֵר בְּרֵאשִׁית,
שֶׁלֹּא עָשָׂנוּ כְּגוֹיֵי הָאֲרָצוֹת,
וְלֹא שָׂמָנוּ כְּמִשְׁפְּחוֹת הָאֲדָמָה,
שֶׁלֹּא שָׂם חֶלְקֵנוּ כָּהֶם,
וְגֹרָלֵנוּ כְּכָל־הֲמוֹנָם.
↑ וַאֲנַחְנוּ כּוֹרְעִים וּמִשְׁתַּחֲוִים וּמוֹדִים,
לִפְנֵי מֶלֶךְ, מַלְכֵי הַמְּלָכִים,
הַקָּדוֹשׁ בָּרוּךְ הוּא.
שֶׁהוּא נוֹטֶה שָׁמַיִם וְיֹסֵד אָרֶץ,
וּמוֹשַׁב יְקָרוֹ בַּשָּׁמַיִם מִמַּעַל,
וּשְׁכִינַת עֻזּוֹ בְּגָבְהֵי מְרוֹמִים,
הוּא אֱלֹהֵינוּ אֵין עוֹד.
אֱמֶת מַלְכֵּנוּ אֶפֶס זוּלָתוֹ,
כַּכָּתוּב בְּתוֹרָתוֹ:
וְיָדַעְתָּ הַיּוֹם וַהֲשֵׁבֹתָ אֶל־לְבָבֶךָ,
כִּי יהוה הוּא הָאֱלֹהִים בַּשָּׁמַיִם מִמַּעַל
וְעַל הָאָרֶץ מִתַּחַת, אֵין עוֹד.

The ark is closed.

MALKHUYOT. The first of the special sections of Musaf is entitled Malkhuyot—prayers and biblical verses celebrating God's sovereignty. All appellations of God are metaphors, but the image of God as sovereign had particular power for medieval and rabbinic Judaism. (The Torah has few references to God as sovereign, but there are many in prophetic writings and in Psalms.) It represents a rejection of earthly authority as the arbiter of ultimate values. Additionally, the metaphor of God as sovereign expresses the common human experience of a transcendent power both glorious and terrifying, as well as the corresponding sense of vulnerability and dependence evoked by this image. Lastly, biblical narratives depict the earthly sovereign as functioning as a judge, so by employing the metaphor of sovereignty in reference to God we focus on Rosh Hashanah as Yom Ha-Din, the Day of Judgment, when God is said to ascend the throne of judgment. The Malkhuyot section concludes with the fourth b'rakhah on the holiness of Rosh Hashanah, to which is added the phrase *melekh al kol ha-aretz*, "ruler of all the earth." These words join the standard holy day Amidah b'rakhah that describes God as sanctifying the people Israel and the holy day—in this case specified as *Yom Ha-zikkaron*, the Day of Remembrance.

IT IS FOR US עָלֵינוּ. Aleinu, originally written for the Rosh Hashanah service, is one of the best-known and oft-repeated prayers. Its central theme is a proclamation of God's sovereignty, an appropriate introduction to this section. It is traditionally attributed to Rav, a 3rd-century rabbi. Although this may not be historically accurate, it is certainly one of the oldest prayers.

AND SO WE BOW וַאֲנַחְנוּ כּוֹרְעִים וּמִשְׁתַּחֲוִים וּמוֹדִים. Throughout the year, we bow at the waist when praying this line. On Rosh Hashanah, it is customary for the prayer leader—and in many communities, members of the congregation as well—to prostrate themselves entirely. The Torah contains several references to "falling on the face" in supplicatory prayer, most often in connection with a request for forgiveness. Prostration commonly accompanied prayer in the Temple and in the early synagogue, but it was de-emphasized in order to distinguish Judaism from its sister religions, and was retained only on Rosh Hashanah and Yom Kippur. Here, we prostrate ourselves as an expression of our humility and as an acknowledgment of God's absolute power and sovereignty. In some congregations two people help the prayer leader stand up while keeping their feet together, as the angels are said to do.

Tikkun Olam—The Repair of the World

If you see what needs to be repaired and how to repair it, then you have found a piece of the world that God has left for you to complete. But if you only see what is wrong and what is ugly in the world, then it is you yourself that needs repair.

—MENACHEM
MENDEL SCHNEERSON

Humility Before God

The essence of t'shuvah is achieved through humility, for one must make oneself like ayin/nothing—like a wilderness to be tread upon.

—NAḤMAN OF BRATZLAV

Malkhuyot—God's Sovereignty
PRAYERS AND BIBLICAL VERSES ON GOD'S SOVEREIGNTY

ALEINU—GOD, WHOM WE WORSHIP
The ark is opened.

It is for us to praise the Ruler of all,
to acclaim the Creator,
who has not made us merely a nation,
nor formed us as all earthly families,
nor given us an ordinary destiny.
ɼ And so we bow,
acknowledging the supreme sovereign,
the Holy One, who is praised—
the One who spreads out the heavens and establishes the earth,
whose glorious abode is in the highest heaven,
whose powerful presence is in the loftiest heights.
This is our God, none else;
ours is the true sovereign, there is no other.
As it is written in the Torah:
"Know this day and take it to heart,
that ADONAI is God in heaven above and on earth below;
there is no other."

The ark is closed.

Meditations on Malkhuyot

The ark is opened.

מֶלֶךְ עֶלְיוֹן

אֵל דָּר בַּמָּרוֹם, אַדִּיר בַּמָּרוֹם, אָמֵץ יָדוֹ תָּרוּם,
לַעֲדֵי עַד יִמְלֹךְ

מֶלֶךְ עֶלְיוֹן

הַמְדַבֵּר בִּצְדָקָה, הַלּוֹבֵשׁ צְדָקָה, הַמַּאֲזִין צְעָקָה,
לַעֲדֵי עַד יִמְלֹךְ

מֶלֶךְ עֶלְיוֹן

טוֹב שׁוֹכֵן עַד, טוּבוֹ לָעַד, טִפַּח שְׁמֵי עַד,
לַעֲדֵי עַד יִמְלֹךְ

מֶלֶךְ עֶלְיוֹן

מֶלֶךְ עוֹלָמִים, מְפַעְנֵחַ נֶעְלָמִים, מֵשִׂיחַ אִלְּמִים,
לַעֲדֵי עַד יִמְלֹךְ

מֶלֶךְ עֶלְיוֹן

שָׁנָה אֵין לְפָנָיו, שֶׁקֶט בִּפְנִינָיו, שֶׁבַח טוֹב בְּמַצְפּוּנָיו,
לַעֲדֵי עַד יִמְלֹךְ

The ark is closed.

מֶלֶךְ אֶבְיוֹן

תְּנוּמָה תְעוּפֶנּוּ, תַּרְדֵּמָה תְּעוֹפְפֶנּוּ, תֹּהוּ יְשׁוּפֶנּוּ,
עַד מָתַי יִמְלֹךְ

The ark is opened.

אֲבָל מֶלֶךְ עֶלְיוֹן

תָּקְפּוֹ לָעַד, תִּפְאַרְתּוֹ עֲדֵי עַד, תְּהִלָּתוֹ עוֹמֶדֶת לָעַד,
לַעֲדֵי עַד יִמְלֹךְ.

The ark is closed.

THE SOVEREIGN ON HIGH
מֶלֶךְ עֶלְיוֹן. In the Middle Ages, Jews were under the sway of kings and nobles. The fickle rule of these sovereigns often had terrible consequences for the Jewish communities beholden to them. This *piyyut*, which describes the ideals of divine rule and contrasts them with the corruption of human sovereignty, had, in its context, a subversive quality. In its original form, each stanza describing God's attributes alternated with a stanza describing the failure of human royalty. The *piyyut* was shortened later—probably for reasons of time—and almost all of the stanzas describing earthly rule were removed. While human kings might proclaim that their rule was justified by divine right, Jews, praying in the synagogue, declared that only God's rule had true legitimacy. They thus understood the central meaning of the Malkhuyot portion of the Musaf service to be the acknowledgment that no earthly person or object can lay claim to absolute authority. As we meditate on this section of the service, we, too, might contemplate which values have ultimate claim on our lives.

The Bible describes the experience of God's presence in two different ways. At Sinai the experience is earth-shattering, filled with the sounds and sights of thunder and lightning; but the prophet Elijah returns to Sinai and only hears "the thin silent sound" of God's presence. Denise Levertov's poem suggests that latter sense.

⁋ The Thread

Something is very gently,
invisibly, silently,
pulling at me—a thread
or net of threads
finer than cobweb and as
elastic. I haven't tried
the strength of it. No
   barbed hook
pierced and tore me. Was it
not long ago this thread
began to draw me? Or
way back? Was I
born with its knot
   about my
neck, a bridle? Not fear
but a stirring
of wonder makes me
catch my breath when I feel
the tug of it when I thought
it had loosened itself
   and gone.
                —DENISE LEVERTOV

Meditations on Malkhuyot

The ark is opened.

The *Sovereign* on High,
God, who dwells in the heights,
and is wondrous in the heavens,
will display the power of the Divine, and
will rule forever and ever.   *La-adei ad yimlokh melekh elyon*

The *Sovereign* on High
speaks with righteousness,
is clothed in justice,
listens to those who cry out and
will rule forever and ever.   *La-adei ad yimlokh melekh elyon*

The *Sovereign* on High
who is good,
whose goodness is everlasting,
and who fashioned the infinite heavens
will rule forever and ever.   *La-adei ad yimlokh melekh elyon*

The *Sovereign* on High,
the eternal Sovereign,
perceives all that is hidden,
gives speech to the mute, and
will rule forever and ever.   *La-adei ad yimlokh melekh elyon*

The *Sovereign* on High
never sleeps,
is surrounded by tranquility,
holds out a treasured reward for the righteous, and
will rule forever and ever.   *La-adei ad yimlokh*

The ark is closed.

The impoverished earthly sovereign
is chased by exhaustion,
falls into a deep sleep,
and is enveloped in chaos.
How long can that rule last?   *Ad matai yimlokh*

The ark is opened.

But—the *Sovereign* on High   *Aval melekh elyon*
whose power is eternal,
who is glorious forever,
and who is justly praised forever,
will rule forever and ever.   *La-adei ad yimlokh*

The ark is closed.

עַל כֵּן נְקַוֶּה לְּךָ יהוה אֱלֹהֵינוּ, לִרְאוֹת מְהֵרָה
בְּתִפְאֶרֶת עֻזֶּךָ, לְהַעֲבִיר גִּלּוּלִים מִן הָאָרֶץ וְהָאֱלִילִים
כָּרוֹת יִכָּרֵתוּן, לְתַקֵּן עוֹלָם בְּמַלְכוּת שַׁדַּי, וְכָל־בְּנֵי בָשָׂר
יִקְרְאוּ בִשְׁמֶךָ, לְהַפְנוֹת אֵלֶיךָ כָּל־רִשְׁעֵי אָרֶץ. יַכִּירוּ
וְיֵדְעוּ כָּל־יוֹשְׁבֵי תֵבֵל, כִּי לְךָ תִּכְרַע כָּל־בֶּרֶךְ, תִּשָּׁבַע כָּל־
לָשׁוֹן. לְפָנֶיךָ יהוה אֱלֹהֵינוּ יִכְרְעוּ וְיִפֹּלוּ, וְלִכְבוֹד שִׁמְךָ
יְקָר יִתֵּנוּ. וִיקַבְּלוּ כֻלָּם אֶת־עוֹל מַלְכוּתֶךָ, וְתִמְלֹךְ עֲלֵיהֶם
מְהֵרָה לְעוֹלָם וָעֶד. כִּי הַמַּלְכוּת שֶׁלְּךָ הִיא, וּלְעוֹלְמֵי עַד
תִּמְלוֹךְ בְּכָבוֹד.

כַּכָּתוּב בְּתוֹרָתֶךָ:

א יהוה יִמְלֹךְ לְעֹלָם וָעֶד. שמות טו יח

ב וְנֶאֱמַר: לֹא־הִבִּיט אָוֶן בְּיַעֲקֹב, וְלֹא רָאָה עָמָל
בְּיִשְׂרָאֵל, יהוה אֱלֹהָיו עִמּוֹ וּתְרוּעַת מֶלֶךְ בּוֹ. במדבר כג כא

ג וְנֶאֱמַר: וַיְהִי בִישֻׁרוּן מֶלֶךְ, בְּהִתְאַסֵּף רָאשֵׁי עָם, יַחַד
שִׁבְטֵי יִשְׂרָאֵל. דברים לג ה

וּבְדִבְרֵי קָדְשְׁךָ כָּתוּב לֵאמֹר:

א כִּי לַיהוה הַמְּלוּכָה וּמֹשֵׁל בַּגּוֹיִם. תהלים כב כט

ב וְנֶאֱמַר: יהוה מָלָךְ גֵּאוּת לָבֵשׁ, לָבֵשׁ יהוה עֹז הִתְאַזָּר,
אַף תִּכּוֹן תֵּבֵל בַּל־תִּמּוֹט. תהלים צג א

ג וְנֶאֱמַר: שְׂאוּ שְׁעָרִים רָאשֵׁיכֶם וְהִנָּשְׂאוּ פִּתְחֵי עוֹלָם,
וְיָבוֹא מֶלֶךְ הַכָּבוֹד. מִי זֶה מֶלֶךְ הַכָּבוֹד, יהוה עִזּוּז וְגִבּוֹר,
יהוה גִּבּוֹר מִלְחָמָה. שְׂאוּ שְׁעָרִים רָאשֵׁיכֶם, וּשְׂאוּ פִּתְחֵי
עוֹלָם, וְיָבֹא מֶלֶךְ הַכָּבוֹד. מִי הוּא זֶה מֶלֶךְ הַכָּבוֹד, יהוה
צְבָאוֹת הוּא מֶלֶךְ הַכָּבוֹד, סֶלָה. תהלים כד ז־י

ESTABLISHING IN THE WORLD THE SOVEREIGNTY OF THE ALMIGHTY לְתַקֵּן עוֹלָם. *Tikkun olam*, which means "mending the world," is an ancient Hebrew phrase that has acquired additional resonance in modern times. In its setting in this prayer, *l'takken olam* means "to establish the world in the kingdom of the Almighty [*Shaddai*]," or to bring about God's rule on earth. In contemporary usage it refers to the betterment of the world, including the relief of human suffering, the achievement of peace and mutual respect among peoples, and protection of the planet itself from destruction.
(adapted from Arthur Green)

THE BIBLICAL VERSES OF MALKHUYOT/SOVEREIGNTY. Whereas the Book of Psalms, some books of the Prophets, and the later rabbinic tradition take for granted that God is naturally referred to as King, these three verses are the only verses in the entire Five Books of Moses that expressly connect God to kingship. Perhaps this omission reflects a desire to further distance Judaism from the surrounding idolatrous nations, in which the human monarch was often seen as a manifestation of the deity.

A NOTE ON THE TRANSLATION OF BIBLICAL VERSES. The meanings and emphases of the verses of Malkhuyot, Zikhronot, and Shofarot in their liturgical settings sometimes differ from their meanings in their biblical contexts. The translations here reflect that shift— varying, when appropriate, from some of the familiar English renditions, such as the JPS translation used in *Etz Hayim*, the Conservative movement's Torah commentary.

LIFT UP HIGH, O YOU GATES; LIFT UP THE ETERNAL DOORS שְׂאוּ שְׁעָרִים רָאשֵׁיכֶם וְהִנָּשְׂאוּ פִּתְחֵי עוֹלָם. Classically, "Jerusalem" refers to both the city on earth and a "heavenly city," each reflective of the other. "Gates" and "doors" refer not only to the gates of Jerusalem or the Temple, but also to "cosmic doors," through which the presence of God enters the world.

Shofar and the Soul

The Torah teaches us וּתְרוּעַת מֶלֶךְ בּוֹ, "their Sovereign's acclaim is in their midst" (Numbers 23:21), a reminder that just as a trumpet blast announces a mortal king, so the shofar is blown to announce the coronation of God. According to the Midrash, the verse can be understood as "the shofar blast of kingship is within the person [Israel]." That is, the true shofar—the true power to crown God as sovereign—is found within the heart of each and every Jew. The physical shofar does no more than amplify the soul's yearning to exalt the Divine.

And so, ADONAI our God, we await You, that soon we may behold Your strength revealed in full glory, sweeping away the abominations of the earth, obliterating idols, establishing in the world the sovereignty of the Almighty, when all flesh will call out Your name—even the wicked will turn toward You. Then all who live on earth will recognize and understand that to You alone knees must bend and allegiance be sworn. All will bow down and prostrate themselves before You, ADONAI our God, honor Your glorious name, and accept the obligation of Your sovereignty. May You soon rule over them forever and ever, for true dominion is Yours; You will rule in glory until the end of time.

As it is written in Your Torah:
א ADONAI will be *sovereign* forever and ever. Exodus 15:18
ב God does not gaze upon the sins of Jacob,
nor look upon the errors of Israel;
ADONAI their God is with them,
their *sovereign's* acclaim is in their midst. Numbers 23:21
ג God became *sovereign* in Jeshurun,
as the leaders of the people gathered
with the tribes of Israel. Deuteronomy 33:5

And it is also written in Psalms:
א For *sovereignty* is ADONAI's;
God rules over the nations. Psalm 22:29
ב ADONAI is *sovereign*, robed in splendor, girded in strength.
So the earth is established on sure foundation. Psalm 93:1
ג Lift up high, O you gates; lift up the eternal doors, so that
the *Sovereign* of Glory may enter. Who is the
Sovereign of Glory? ADONAI, mighty and valiant,
ADONAI, mighty in battle. Lift up high, O you gates; lift up
the eternal doors, so that the *Sovereign* of Glory
may enter. Who is the *Sovereign* of Glory? *Adonai Tz'va·ot*
is the *Sovereign* of Glory, forever. Psalm 24:7–10

וְעַל יְדֵי עֲבָדֶיךָ הַנְּבִיאִים כָּתוּב לֵאמֹר:

א כֹּה אָמַר יהוה, מֶלֶךְ יִשְׂרָאֵל וְגֹאֲלוֹ יהוה צְבָאוֹת, אֲנִי רִאשׁוֹן וַאֲנִי אַחֲרוֹן, וּמִבַּלְעָדַי אֵין אֱלֹהִים. ישעיה מד ו

ב וְנֶאֱמַר: וְעָלוּ מוֹשִׁעִים בְּהַר צִיּוֹן לִשְׁפֹּט אֶת־הַר עֵשָׂו, וְהָיְתָה לַיהוה הַמְּלוּכָה. עבדיה א כא

ג וְנֶאֱמַר: וְהָיָה יהוה לְמֶלֶךְ עַל כָּל־הָאָרֶץ, בַּיּוֹם הַהוּא יִהְיֶה יהוה אֶחָד וּשְׁמוֹ אֶחָד. זכריה יד ט

וּבְתוֹרָתְךָ כָּתוּב לֵאמֹר:

שְׁמַע יִשְׂרָאֵל, יהוה אֱלֹהֵינוּ, יהוה אֶחָד. דברים ו ד

אֱלֹהֵינוּ וֵאלֹהֵי אֲבוֹתֵינוּ [וְאִמּוֹתֵינוּ],
מְלוֹךְ עַל כָּל־הָעוֹלָם כֻּלּוֹ בִּכְבוֹדֶךָ,
וְהִנָּשֵׂא עַל כָּל־הָאָרֶץ בִּיקָרֶךָ,
וְהוֹפַע בַּהֲדַר גְּאוֹן עֻזֶּךָ עַל כָּל־יוֹשְׁבֵי תֵבֵל אַרְצֶךָ,
וְיֵדַע כָּל־פָּעוּל כִּי אַתָּה פְעַלְתּוֹ,
וְיָבִין כָּל־יְצוּר כִּי אַתָּה יְצַרְתּוֹ,
וְיֹאמַר כֹּל אֲשֶׁר נְשָׁמָה בְאַפּוֹ,
יהוה אֱלֹהֵי יִשְׂרָאֵל מֶלֶךְ, וּמַלְכוּתוֹ בַּכֹּל מָשָׁלָה.

אֱלֹהֵינוּ וֵאלֹהֵי אֲבוֹתֵינוּ [וְאִמּוֹתֵינוּ] [רְצֵה בִמְנוּחָתֵנוּ]
קַדְּשֵׁנוּ בְּמִצְוֹתֶיךָ, וְתֵן חֶלְקֵנוּ בְּתוֹרָתֶךָ,
שַׂבְּעֵנוּ מִטּוּבֶךָ, וְשַׂמְּחֵנוּ בִּישׁוּעָתֶךָ. [וְהַנְחִילֵנוּ, יהוה אֱלֹהֵינוּ, בְּאַהֲבָה וּבְרָצוֹן שַׁבַּת קָדְשֶׁךָ, וְיָנוּחוּ בָהּ יִשְׂרָאֵל מְקַדְּשֵׁי שְׁמֶךָ.]
וְטַהֵר לִבֵּנוּ לְעָבְדְּךָ בֶּאֱמֶת, כִּי אַתָּה אֱלֹהִים אֱמֶת,
וּדְבָרְךָ אֱמֶת וְקַיָּם לָעַד.
בָּרוּךְ אַתָּה יהוה, מֶלֶךְ עַל כָּל־הָאָרֶץ,
מְקַדֵּשׁ [הַשַּׁבָּת וְ] יִשְׂרָאֵל וְיוֹם הַזִּכָּרוֹן.

ADONAI SHALL BE ACKNOWLEDGED SOVEREIGN וְהָיָה יהוה לְמֶלֶךְ עַל כָּל־הָאָרֶץ. Zechariah 14:9. This verse is also quoted at the conclusion of the Aleinu. In it, we recognize that God's Oneness is not yet fully realized, and we express our hope that our prayers and actions will contribute to achieving that ideal. Here, the verse is followed directly by the first line of the Sh'ma (Deuteronomy 6:4), which is our declaration that God is, indeed, One, although the Sh'ma itself does not contain any form of the word *melekh*. The ancient Rabbis understood the recitation of the Sh'ma as *kabbalat ol malkhut shamayim*, the acceptance of the yoke of God's sovereignty. Therefore it was deemed appropriate to recite the Sh'ma as the tenth verse of Malkhuyot.

OUR GOD AND GOD OF OUR ANCESTORS אֱלֹהֵינוּ וֵאלֹהֵי אֲבוֹתֵינוּ. This paragraph concludes the fourth *b'rakhah* of the Amidah; the text is nearly identical to the liturgy of Shabbat and Festivals. It includes a prayer to purify our hearts so that our service to God may be *emet*, "truth" (וְטַהֵר לִבֵּנוּ לְעָבְדְּךָ בֶּאֱמֶת). The Hebrew word *emet* implies more than mere honesty or absence of falsehood: it connotes also faithfulness, wholeness, and integrity. Thus, we express our longing to be constant and consistent in our prayer and to liberate our relationship with God from the mixed motives and inner conflicts that generally characterize human behavior. The prayer's penultimate sentence—unique to the High Holy Days—takes up this theme of truth, applying the attribute to God and God's word, and emphasizing it as an essential quality of the Divine.

Rabbi Kalonymous Kal-
mish Shapira, the Rebbe
of the Warsaw Ghetto,
wrote on Rosh Hashanah
5702/1941 (*Esh Kodesh*):
"The time for repentance
is Rosh Hashanah, the
anniversary of the cre-
ation of the world. This
is because repentance . . .
is also a kind of creativity." The Hebrew word
t'shuvah means repen-
tance and return. How-
ever, as a creative act,
t'shuvah is not a simple
return. We return to who
we are meant to be, but
have not yet become.
We return to growth and
possibility that has lain
dormant within us and
not yet flourished, much
as a sculpture lies hidden
within a brute block
of stone. That is why
the process of *t'shuvah*,
as painful and even
humiliating as it can be,
is in fact very joyous and
hopeful.

*(Adapted and translated
by Jan Uhrbach)*

And Your servants the prophets further wrote:

א Thus said ADONAI, *sovereign* and redeemer of Israel,
Adonai Tz'va·ot: I am the first and I am the last, and there is no
God but Me.   Isaiah 44:6

ב Liberators shall ascend Mount Zion to judge Mount Esau;
then *sovereignty* shall be ADONAI's.   Obadiah 1:21

ג ADONAI shall be acknowledged *sovereign* of all the earth.
On that day ADONAI shall be one, and the name of God, one.

Zechariah 14:9

And it is written in Your Torah:
Hear, O Israel, ADONAI is our God, ADONAI alone.

Deuteronomy 6:4

Our God and God of our ancestors: in Your glory, rule over the
entire universe; in Your splendor, be exalted over all the earth;
in the majestic beauty of Your overwhelming presence, appear
to all the inhabitants of Your world. Then, all that You have
made will recognize You as their maker, all that You created will
understand that You are their creator, and all living beings will
say: ADONAI, the God of Israel, is sovereign, ruling over all.

Our God and God of our ancestors: [embrace our rest,] make
us holy through Your commandments and let the Torah be our
portion. Fill our lives with Your goodness and gladden us with
Your triumph. [ADONAI our God, grant that we inherit Your
holy Shabbat, lovingly and willingly, so that the people Israel,
who sanctify Your name, may find rest on this day.] Purify our
hearts to serve You truly, for You are the God of truth, and Your
word is true, eternal, and unchanging. *Barukh atah ADONAI,*
ruler of all the earth, who makes [Shabbat,] the people Israel
and the Day of Remembrance holy.

[*Leader: Barukh atah Adonai,*] *Congregation: melekh al kol ha-aretz,
m'kaddeish [ha-shabbat v'] yisra·el [Leader: v'yom ha-zikkaron].*

(The shofar is traditionally not blown on Shabbat.)

תְּקִיעָה שְׁבָרִים־תְּרוּעָה תְּקִיעָה
תְּקִיעָה שְׁבָרִים תְּקִיעָה
תְּקִיעָה תְּרוּעָה תְּקִיעָה

הַיּוֹם הֲרַת עוֹלָם, הַיּוֹם יַעֲמִיד בַּמִּשְׁפָּט כָּל־יְצוּרֵי
עוֹלָמִים, אִם כְּבָנִים אִם כַּעֲבָדִים. אִם כְּבָנִים, רַחֲמֵנוּ
כְּרַחֵם אָב עַל בָּנִים. וְאִם כַּעֲבָדִים עֵינֵינוּ לְךָ תְלוּיוֹת,
עַד שֶׁתְּחָנֵּנוּ וְתוֹצִיא כָאוֹר מִשְׁפָּטֵנוּ, אָיֹם קָדוֹשׁ.

WE OMIT THIS PARAGRAPH ON SHABBAT:

אֲרֶשֶׁת שְׂפָתֵינוּ יֶעֱרַב לְפָנֶיךָ, אֵל רָם וְנִשָּׂא,
מֵבִין וּמַאֲזִין, מַבִּיט וּמַקְשִׁיב לְקוֹל תְּקִיעָתֵנוּ,
וּתְקַבֵּל בְּרַחֲמִים וּבְרָצוֹן סֵדֶר מַלְכִיּוֹתֵינוּ.

TODAY THE WORLD STANDS AS AT BIRTH הַיּוֹם הֲרַת עוֹלָם. The ancient Rabbis debated whether Rosh Hashanah marks either the first day of the creation of the world or the sixth day, when humanity was formed. The liturgical emphasis on the word "today" suggests that this is no mere anniversary celebration; rather, all humanity—and all creation—are re-created anew today.

AWE-INSPIRING AND HOLY ONE אָיֹם קָדוֹשׁ. In the original version of this prayer, the last two words were *ha-yom kadosh*, "on this holy day." The language was changed to *ayom kadosh*, "awe-inspiring and Holy One," because final judgment is actually suspended until Yom Kippur.

T'ki·ah sh'varim-t'ru·ah t'ki·ah
T'ki·ah sh'varim t'ki·ah
T'ki·ah t'ru·ah t'ki·ah

Today the world stands as at birth. Today all creation is called to judgment, whether as Your children or as Your servants. If as Your children, be compassionate with us as a parent is compassionate with children. If as Your servants, we look to You expectantly, waiting for You to be gracious to us and, as day emerges from night, to bring forth a favorable judgment on our behalf, awe-inspiring and Holy One.

Ha-yom harat olam, ha-yom ya·amid ba-mishpat kol y'tzurei olamim, im k'vanim im ka-avadim. Im k'vanim, raḥameinu k'raḥem av al banim. V'im ka-avadim eineinu l'kha t'luyot, ad she-t'ḥonneinu v'totzi kha-or mishpateinu, ayom kadosh.

WE OMIT THIS PARAGRAPH ON SHABBAT:

May the words of our lips be pleasing to You, exalted God, who listens, discerns, considers, and attends to the sound of our shofar blast. Lovingly accept our prayerful offering that proclaims Your sovereignty.

Areshet s'fateinu ye·erav l'fanekha, El ram v'nissa, meivin u-ma·azin, mabbit u-makshiv l'kol t'ki·ateinu. U-t'kabbeil b'raḥamim u-v'ratzon seder malkhuyyoteinu.

Meditations on Zikhronot

אֶפְחַד בְּמַעֲשַׂי אֶדְאַג בְּכָל־עֵת אִירָא
מִיּוֹם־דִּין בְּבוֹאִי לְזִכָּרוֹן.
אֶדְרֹשׁ לְחַנּוּן אֲחַלֶּה לְרַחוּם אֲחַנֵּן
לְחָק־לִי יוֹם זִכָּרוֹן.
בְּבוֹאִי לַמִּשְׁפָּט בְּמִי אֶשָּׁעֵן וּמִי יְחַפֵּשׂ
לִי צֶדֶק לְזִכָּרוֹן.
גֶּבֶר אִם יַעֲמָד לְפָנָיו הֲיוֹעִיל בְּעֵת יְבַקֵּשׁ
מֶנִּי זְכוּת לְזִכָּרוֹן.
מַעֲלָלֵי גֶבֶר וּמִסְפָּר צְעָדָיו נִשְׁכְּחוּ
מֵאֱנוֹשׁ וְלָאֵל לְזִכָּרוֹן.
שִׂיחוּ מִזְמוֹת אֶל יַחַד כָּל־בְּנֵי אִישׁ
עוֹבְרֵי תַחַת שֵׁבֶט כַּצֹּאן לְזִכָּרוֹן.
פְּנֵה אֱלֹהִים בְּיוֹשְׁבֵי גַנִּים מַקְשִׁיב
לְנִדְבָּרֵימוֹ בְּדָת לְזִכָּרוֹן.

I WORRY אֶפְחַד. This *piyyut*, written for this section of the Musaf service, is ascribed to Yose ben Yose (5th century) and is thus among the earliest liturgical texts. In the original it is a double acrostic, with every line ending with the word *zikkaron*, "remember." As the poem progresses, the biblical verses that we recite later in this section are woven into the poem.

LISTENING TO EACH OTHER מַקְשִׁיב לְנִדְבָּרֵימוֹ. The poet bases this image on a series of midrashim interpreting the verse in the Song of Songs, "O you who sit in the garden, friends are listening to your voice; let me hear your voice" (8:13). These midrashim understand the garden to be either the synagogue or the study hall, and the voices that are heard are those engaged in study or prayer. Given the liturgical context, the poet may well have especially had the latter activity in mind.

The Broken Tablets

The broken tablets were
also carried in an ark.
Insofar as they repre-
    sented everything
    shattered
everything lost, they
    were the law of broken
    things,
the leaf torn from the
    stem in a storm, a
    cheek touched
in fondness once but now
    the name forgotten.
How they must have
    rumbled, clattered on
    the way even carried so
    carefully through the
    waste land,
how they must have
    rattled around until
    the pieces
broke into pieces, the
    edges softened
crumbling, dust collected
    at the bottom of the
    ark
ghosts of old letters, old
    laws. Insofar
as a law broken is still
    remembered
these laws were obeyed.
    And insofar as
    memory
preserves the pattern of
    broken things
these bits of stone were
    preserved
through many journeys
    and ruined days
even, they say, into the
    promised land.
    —RODGER KAMENETZ

Meditations on Zikhronot

I fear for what I have done, always anxious of the Day of
Judgment, as *memory* rushes in,
    I would seek out the One who is merciful, pray to the One
    who is compassionate, who ordained for me this Day of
    Remembrance,
As I come to judgment, who would support me? Who would
find me innocent when my deeds are *recalled*?
    Should someone arise and argue my case, could they justify
    me, as all is *recalled*?
Though a person's very footsteps and deeds are forgotten in
this world, God *remembers.*
    Tell us God's thoughts as each person passes as sheep under
    God's staff, and God *remembers* them.
O turn, God, to those who sit in Your garden, listening to each
other address prayers to You, now *recalled.*

BIBLICAL RECOLLECTIONS OF GOD'S REMEMBRANCE
As You remembered Noah and with the wind dispersed the
waters of the flood,
So too remember us upon the flood of cruelty that threatens
    this frail ark, our world, and send the spirit of Your care and
    goodness to calm the sea.

As in Egypt you heard our screaming, and remembered there
    Your pact with Abraham, Isaac, and Jacob, Sarah, Rebecca,
    Rachel and Leah,
So too remember us—
Enslaved to our ways of living that we dare not change,
Oppressed by fears of Pharaohs who turn living waters into
        blood.

As You instructed Jeremiah:
Whisper in the ear of Jerusalem how I remember your youthful
    passion, so too remember now
To whisper in her ear again
The words and acts that will establish justice, mercy, and peace.

זִכְרוֹנוֹת

אַתָּה זוֹכֵר מַעֲשֵׂה עוֹלָם, וּפוֹקֵד כָּל־יְצוּרֵי קֶדֶם.
לְפָנֶיךָ נִגְלוּ כָּל־תַּעֲלוּמוֹת, וַהֲמוֹן נִסְתָּרוֹת שֶׁמִּבְּרֵאשִׁית.
אֵין שִׁכְחָה לִפְנֵי כִסֵּא כְבוֹדֶךָ, וְאֵין נִסְתָּר מִנֶּגֶד עֵינֶיךָ.
אַתָּה זוֹכֵר אֶת־כָּל־הַמִּפְעָל, וְגַם כָּל־הַיְצוּר לֹא
נִכְחָד מִמֶּךָ.
הַכֹּל גָּלוּי וְיָדוּעַ לְפָנֶיךָ, יהוה אֱלֹהֵינוּ,
צוֹפֶה וּמַבִּיט עַד סוֹף כָּל־הַדּוֹרוֹת.
כִּי תָבִיא חֹק זִכָּרוֹן, לְהִפָּקֵד כָּל־רוּחַ וָנָפֶשׁ,
לְהִזָּכֵר מַעֲשִׂים רַבִּים, וַהֲמוֹן בְּרִיּוֹת לְאֵין תַּכְלִית.
מֵרֵאשִׁית כָּזֹאת הוֹדָעְתָּ, וּמִלְּפָנִים אוֹתָהּ גִּלִּיתָ.

זֶה הַיּוֹם תְּחִלַּת מַעֲשֶׂיךָ, זִכָּרוֹן לְיוֹם רִאשׁוֹן:
כִּי חֹק לְיִשְׂרָאֵל הוּא, מִשְׁפָּט לֵאלֹהֵי יַעֲקֹב.
וְעַל הַמְּדִינוֹת בּוֹ יֵאָמֵר:
אֵיזוֹ לַחֶרֶב, וְאֵיזוֹ לַשָּׁלוֹם, אֵיזוֹ לָרָעָב, וְאֵיזוֹ לַשָּׂבַע.
וּבְרִיּוֹת בּוֹ יִפָּקֵדוּ, לְהַזְכִּירָם לַחַיִּים וְלַמָּוֶת.
מִי לֹא נִפְקַד כְּהַיּוֹם הַזֶּה, כִּי זֵכֶר כָּל־הַיְצוּר לְפָנֶיךָ בָּא,
מַעֲשֵׂה אִישׁ וּפְקֻדָּתוֹ, וַעֲלִילוֹת מִצְעֲדֵי גָבֶר,
מַחְשְׁבוֹת אָדָם וְתַחְבּוּלוֹתָיו, וְיִצְרֵי מַעַלְלֵי אִישׁ.

אַשְׁרֵי אִישׁ שֶׁלֹּא יִשְׁכָּחֶךָ, וּבֶן־אָדָם יִתְאַמֶּץ־בָּךְ.
כִּי דוֹרְשֶׁיךָ לְעוֹלָם לֹא יִכָּשֵׁלוּ, וְלֹא יִכָּלְמוּ לָנֶצַח
כָּל־הַחוֹסִים בָּךְ.
כִּי זֵכֶר כָּל־הַמַּעֲשִׂים לְפָנֶיךָ בָּא, וְאַתָּה דוֹרֵשׁ
מַעֲשֵׂה כֻלָּם.

וְגַם אֶת־נֹחַ בְּאַהֲבָה זָכַרְתָּ, וַתִּפְקְדֵהוּ בִּדְבַר יְשׁוּעָה
וְרַחֲמִים,
בַּהֲבִיאֲךָ אֶת־מֵי הַמַּבּוּל, לְשַׁחֵת כָּל־בָּשָׂר מִפְּנֵי רֹעַ
מַעַלְלֵיהֶם.
עַל כֵּן זִכְרוֹנוֹ בָּא לְפָנֶיךָ, יהוה אֱלֹהֵינוּ,
לְהַרְבּוֹת זַרְעוֹ כְּעַפְרוֹת תֵּבֵל, וְצֶאֱצָאָיו כְּחוֹל הַיָּם.

ZIKHRONOT. The Bible refers to Rosh Hashanah as Yom Ha-Zikkaron (the Day of Remembrance), highlighting the covenantal relationship between God and humanity. The metaphor of God as remembering captures the intimate concern and engagement of God with each individual person and creature, as well as our corresponding sense of accountability for our deeds.

YOU REMEMBER אַתָּה זוֹכֵר. The introductory poem to this section is from the first half of the first millennium.

RITE OF REMEMBRANCE חֹק זִכָּרוֹן. The "rite" is Rosh Hashanah, the Day of Remembrance.

"REMEMBER" In the Bible, God is described as remembering far more often than are humans. Memory is, primarily, a divine quality, representing God's ability to overcome the limitations of a particular time, to see the part as one segment of a far greater whole. When humans remember, therefore, we are imitating God, overcoming our own limits and, in God-like fashion, identifying with the breadth of history. Remembering is essential, because memory is divine. It is part of what makes us all images of God. Fundamentally, our memory is who we are. (David Kraemer)

The authentic individual
is neither an end nor a
beginning but a link be-
tween ages, both memory
and expectation. . . .

To us, recollection is a
holy act; we sanctify the
present by remember-
ing the past. To us Jews,
the essence of faith is
memory. To believe is to
remember.

—ABRAHAM JOSHUA
HESCHEL

Fifth B'rakhah: Zikhronot — Remembrances
PRAYERS AND BIBLICAL VERSES ON REMEMBRANCE

You remember the deeds of the world and You are mindful
of Your creatures since the beginning of time.
Before You stands revealed all that is hidden, and every
mystery from the moment of creation.
Nothing is forgotten in Your awe-inspiring presence, nothing
concealed from Your gaze;
You remember every deed, and nothing in creation can be
hidden from You.
Everything is revealed and known to You, ADONAI our God;
You see to the end of time.
It is You who established a rite of remembrance, to take
account of every being, every soul, to recall the multitude
of deeds, and call to mind countless creations.
From the beginning You made this known, and from of old You
revealed it.

This day which You, God of Jacob, established as a ritual
for the people Israel, and as a day of judgment, marks the
beginning of Your creation, a reminder of the very first day.
And this is a day of decree for all nations: war or peace, famine
or abundance. Every creature is called to account: reckoned
for life or death. Who is not remembered this day?
Everyone's record is set before You: each individual's actions
and their consequences, all that people do, all that humans
think and plan, and all that each of us intends.

Blessed is the person who does not forget You, the one who
draws strength from You; for those who seek You will never
stumble, and those who trust in You will never be shamed.
Surely, the record of every deed is before You; You probe
everyone's acts.

Did You not lovingly remember Noah, when You brought the
flood waters, destroying all flesh because of their evil deeds?
Did You not assure him with words of salvation and
compassion?
So his memory, ADONAI our God, came before You and his
descendants became as numerous as the dust of the earth,
and his children like the sand of the sea.

כַּכָּתוּב בְּתוֹרָתֶךָ:

א וַיִּזְכֹּר אֱלֹהִים אֶת־נֹחַ, וְאֵת כָּל־הַחַיָּה וְאֶת־כָּל־הַבְּהֵמָה אֲשֶׁר אִתּוֹ בַּתֵּבָה, וַיַּעֲבֵר אֱלֹהִים רוּחַ עַל־הָאָרֶץ, וַיָּשֹׁכּוּ הַמָּיִם. בראשית ח א

ב וְנֶאֱמַר: וַיִּשְׁמַע אֱלֹהִים אֶת־נַאֲקָתָם, וַיִּזְכֹּר אֱלֹהִים אֶת־בְּרִיתוֹ אֶת־אַבְרָהָם אֶת־יִצְחָק וְאֶת־יַעֲקֹב. שמות ב כד

ג וְנֶאֱמַר: וְזָכַרְתִּי אֶת־בְּרִיתִי יַעֲקוֹב, וְאַף אֶת־בְּרִיתִי יִצְחָק, וְאַף אֶת־בְּרִיתִי אַבְרָהָם אֶזְכֹּר, וְהָאָרֶץ אֶזְכֹּר. ויקרא כו מב

וּבְדִבְרֵי קָדְשְׁךָ כָּתוּב לֵאמֹר:

א זֵכֶר עָשָׂה לְנִפְלְאוֹתָיו, חַנּוּן וְרַחוּם יהוה. תהלים קיא ד

ב וְנֶאֱמַר: טֶרֶף נָתַן לִירֵאָיו, יִזְכֹּר לְעוֹלָם בְּרִיתוֹ. תהלים קיא ה

ג וְנֶאֱמַר: וַיִּזְכֹּר לָהֶם בְּרִיתוֹ, וַיִּנָּחֵם כְּרֹב חֲסָדָיו. תהלים קו מה

וְעַל יְדֵי עֲבָדֶיךָ הַנְּבִיאִים כָּתוּב לֵאמֹר:

א הָלֹךְ וְקָרָאתָ בְאָזְנֵי יְרוּשָׁלַיִם לֵאמֹר, כֹּה אָמַר יהוה, זָכַרְתִּי לָךְ חֶסֶד נְעוּרַיִךְ, אַהֲבַת כְּלוּלֹתָיִךְ, לֶכְתֵּךְ אַחֲרַי בַּמִּדְבָּר, בְּאֶרֶץ לֹא זְרוּעָה. ירמיהו ב ב

ב וְנֶאֱמַר: וְזָכַרְתִּי אֲנִי אֶת־בְּרִיתִי אוֹתָךְ בִּימֵי נְעוּרָיִךְ, וַהֲקִימוֹתִי לָךְ בְּרִית עוֹלָם. יחזקאל טז ס

ג וְנֶאֱמַר: הֲבֵן יַקִּיר לִי אֶפְרַיִם, אִם יֶלֶד שַׁעֲשׁוּעִים, כִּי־מִדֵּי דַבְּרִי בּוֹ זָכֹר אֶזְכְּרֶנּוּ עוֹד, עַל כֵּן הָמוּ מֵעַי לוֹ, רַחֵם אֲרַחֲמֶנּוּ, נְאֻם יהוה. ירמיהו לא כ

אֱלֹהֵינוּ וֵאלֹהֵי אֲבוֹתֵינוּ [וְאִמּוֹתֵינוּ], זָכְרֵנוּ בְּזִכָּרוֹן טוֹב לְפָנֶיךָ, וּפָקְדֵנוּ בִּפְקֻדַּת יְשׁוּעָה וְרַחֲמִים מִשְּׁמֵי שְׁמֵי קֶדֶם. וּזְכָר־לָנוּ, יהוה אֱלֹהֵינוּ, אֶת־הַבְּרִית וְאֶת־הַחֶסֶד, וְאֶת־הַשְּׁבוּעָה אֲשֶׁר נִשְׁבַּעְתָּ לְאַבְרָהָם אָבִינוּ בְּהַר הַמֹּרִיָּה. וְתֵרָאֶה לְפָנֶיךָ עֲקֵדָה שֶׁעָקַד אַבְרָהָם אָבִינוּ אֶת־יִצְחָק בְּנוֹ עַל גַּבֵּי הַמִּזְבֵּחַ, וְכָבַשׁ רַחֲמָיו לַעֲשׂוֹת רְצוֹנְךָ בְּלֵבָב שָׁלֵם. כֵּן יִכְבְּשׁוּ רַחֲמֶיךָ אֶת־כַּעַסְךָ מֵעָלֵינוּ, וּבְטוּבְךָ

LEVITICUS 26:42. In the Torah, this verse is preceded by a reference to future generations of Israel humbling themselves and atoning for sin. God's "remembrance" thus follows Israel's t'shuvah.

PSALM 106:45. The act of remembering causes even God—who is enduring and unchanging—to act differently with Israel. So, too, our remembering on Rosh Hashanah should lead us to change who we are and how we behave.

OUR GOD אֱלֹהֵינוּ. This prayer evokes the Binding of Isaac, noting that Abraham subdued his mercy in order to do God's will. In return, we ask God to do the reverse: to allow mercy to subdue the divine will to anger. We thus echo God's own prayer, as our Sages said, "What does God pray? Rav Zutra ben Tobi said in the name of Rab: 'May it be My will that My mercy may suppress My anger, and that My mercy may prevail over My [other] attributes, so that I may deal with My children in the attribute of mercy and, on their behalf, stop short of the limit of strict justice'" (Babylonian Talmud, Berakhot 7a).

THE HIGHEST HEAVENS ABOVE מִשְּׁמֵי שְׁמֵי קֶדֶם. The phrase, from Psalm 68:34, has both a spatial and a temporal connotation. Like the Hebrew word olam, which can refer to both infinite space and eternal time, kedem can refer either to the east, whence the sun (which was imagined to come from heaven) rises, or to ancient times.

Forgetting and
Remembering

א
Forgetfulness leads to
exile, while remem-
brance is the secret of
redemption.
—BAAL SHEM TOV

ב
Rabbi Sh'lomo of
Karlin asked: "What is
the worst thing the Evil
Urge can achieve?" And
he answered: "To make
a person forget that one
is the child of a king."
—A HASIDIC TALE

ג
God does not forget
those who have been
abandoned by others.
Some of the key verses
in this section are taken
from the story of the
flood, when God re-
members those who are
left when the world has
come undone, and from
the story of the Israel-
ites as slaves in Egypt,
when God hears their
cries. God remembers
us even when we think
that we are disgraced or
abandoned.
—RACHEL KAHN-TROSTER

As it is written in Your Torah:

א God *remembered* Noah and all the beasts and all the cattle that were with him in the ark, and God caused a wind to blow across the earth and the waters subsided. Genesis 8:1

ב God heard their agonized cry, and God *remembered* the covenant with Abraham and Isaac and Jacob. Exodus 2:24

ג Then will I *remember* My covenant with Jacob; I will remember also my covenant with Isaac, and also My covenant with Abraham; and I will remember the land. Leviticus 26:42

And it is also written in the Book of Psalms:

א God has made wondrous works to be *remembered*; ADONAI is gracious and compassionate. Psalm 111:4

ב God always *remembers* the covenant, providing sustenance for those in awe of the Divine. Psalm 111:5

ג God *remembered* the covenant and, with great love, relented.
Psalm 106:45

And Your servants the prophets further wrote:

א Go proclaim to Jerusalem: Thus said ADONAI: I *remember* the affection of your youth, your love when we were betrothed when you followed Me in the wilderness, a barren land. Jeremiah 2:2

ב I will always *remember* the covenant I made with you in the days of your youth, and establish it with you as a covenant that will last forever. Ezekiel 16:60

ג Is not Ephraim My dear son, My precious child, whom I *remember* fondly even when I speak against him? So my heart reaches out to him, and I always feel compassion for him, declares ADONAI. Jeremiah 31:20

Our God and God of our ancestors, remember us favorably, and from the highest heavens above fulfill Your promise of compassion and deliverance. For our sake, remember Your loving relationship with us, the covenant and the promise that You made to Abraham on Mount Moriah. Hold before You the image of our ancestor Abraham binding his son Isaac on the altar, when he overcame his compassion in order to obey Your command wholeheartedly. Now, allow Your compassion

הַגָּדוֹל יָשׁוּב חֲרוֹן אַפְּךָ מֵעַמְּךָ וּמֵעִירְךָ וּמִנַּחֲלָתֶךָ. וְקַיֶּם־לָנוּ, יְהוה אֱלֹהֵינוּ, אֶת־הַדָּבָר שֶׁהִבְטַחְתָּנוּ בְּתוֹרָתֶךָ, עַל יְדֵי מֹשֶׁה עַבְדֶּךָ, מִפִּי כְבוֹדֶךָ, כָּאָמוּר:

וְזָכַרְתִּי לָהֶם בְּרִית רִאשֹׁנִים, אֲשֶׁר הוֹצֵאתִי־אֹתָם מֵאֶרֶץ מִצְרַיִם לְעֵינֵי הַגּוֹיִם לִהְיוֹת לָהֶם לֵאלֹהִים, אֲנִי יְהוה. ויקרא כו מה

כִּי זוֹכֵר כָּל־הַנִּשְׁכָּחוֹת אַתָּה הוּא מֵעוֹלָם, וְאֵין שִׁכְחָה לִפְנֵי כִסֵּא כְבוֹדֶךָ. וַעֲקֵדַת יִצְחָק לְזַרְעוֹ הַיּוֹם בְּרַחֲמִים תִּזְכֹּר. בָּרוּךְ אַתָּה יְהוה, זוֹכֵר הַבְּרִית.

(The shofar is traditionally not blown on Shabbat.)

תקיעה שברים־תרועה תקיעה
תקיעה שברים תקיעה
תקיעה תרועה תקיעה

הַיּוֹם הֲרַת עוֹלָם, הַיּוֹם יַעֲמִיד בַּמִּשְׁפָּט כָּל־יְצוּרֵי עוֹלָמִים, אִם כְּבָנִים אִם כַּעֲבָדִים. אִם כְּבָנִים, רַחֲמֵנוּ כְּרַחֵם אָב עַל בָּנִים. וְאִם כַּעֲבָדִים עֵינֵינוּ לְךָ תְלוּיוֹת, עַד שֶׁתְּחָנֵּנוּ וְתוֹצִיא כָאוֹר מִשְׁפָּטֵנוּ, אָיוֹם קָדוֹשׁ.

WE OMIT THIS PARAGRAPH ON SHABBAT:

אֲרֶשֶׁת שְׂפָתֵינוּ יֶעֱרַב לְפָנֶיךָ, אֵל רָם וְנִשָּׂא,
מֵבִין וּמַאֲזִין, מַבִּיט וּמַקְשִׁיב לְקוֹל תְּקִיעָתֵנוּ,
וּתְקַבֵּל בְּרַחֲמִים וּבְרָצוֹן
סֵדֶר זִכְרוֹנוֹתֵינוּ.

to overcome Your anger at us, and in Your great goodness, reconcile Yourself to Your people, Your city, and Your land. Fulfill for us the words of Your promise contained in Your Torah transmitted by Your servant Moses from Your glorious Presence, as it is written:

For their sake, I will remember the covenant with that first generation whom I brought out of the land of Egypt in the sight of the nations, to be their God; I am ADONAI.   Leviticus 26:45

You have always remembered that which has been forgotten, for there is no forgetting in Your realm. So on this day, in Your great mercy, remember the binding of Isaac for the sake of his descendants. *Barukh atah ADONAI*, who remembers the covenant.

(The shofar is traditionally not blown on Shabbat.)
T'ki·ah sh'varim-t'ru·ah t'ki·ah
T'ki·ah sh'varim t'ki·ah
T'ki·ah t'ru·ah t'ki·ah

Today the world stands as at birth. Today all creation is called to judgment, whether as Your children or as Your servants. If as Your children, be compassionate with us as a parent is compassionate with children. If as Your servants, we look to You expectantly, waiting for You to be gracious to us, and as day emerges from night bring forth a favorable judgment on our behalf, awe-inspiring and Holy One.

Ha-yom harat olam, ha-yom ya·amid ba-mishpat kol y'tzurei olamim, im k'vanim im ka-avadim. Im k'vanim, raḥameinu k'raḥem av al banim. V'im ka-avadim eineinu l'kha t'luyot, ad she-t'ḥonneinu v'totzi kha-or mishpateinu, ayom kadosh.

WE OMIT THIS PARAGRAPH ON SHABBAT:

May the words of our lips be pleasing to You, exalted God, who listens, discerns, considers, and attends to the sound of our shofar blast. Lovingly accept our offering of verses proclaiming Your remembrance.

Areshet s'fateinu ye·erav l'fanekha, El ram v'nissa, meivin u-ma·azin, mabbit u-makshiv l'kol t'ki·ateinu. U-t'kabbel b'raḥamim u-v'ratzon seder zikhronoteinu.

Meditations on Shofarot

אָנוּסָה לְעֶזְרָה אֶמְצָא אַמְצָא נֶגְדִּי אֵל קָרוֹב
לִי בְּעֵת קָרְאִי בְּקוֹל.
אֲשֶׁר בַּעֲדַת אֵל בְּקִרְבִּי נִצָּב פֹּה בְּמִקְדָּשׁ
מְעַט אֲצַפְצֵף לוֹ בְּקוֹל.
בְּקַרְנֵי דָרְשֵׁנִי שֶׂה פְזוּרָה אֲנִי נִגְזַזְתִּי
וְנֶאֱלַמְתִּי בְּלִי לְהָרִים קוֹל.
נָא הַבֵּט וּרְאֵה עָנְיִי וּמְרוּדִי אֵין לִי
מַכִּיר לְמִי אֶשָּׂא קוֹל.
נֵצַח אֲקַוֶּה כִּי לֹא יִפֹּל דָּבָר מִמַּקְשִׁיבֵי
דְמָמָה וְקוֹל.
שׂוֹשׂ יָשִׂישׂ לִבִּי בְקִרְבִּי בְּשָׁמְעִי דוֹדִי
דוֹפֵק עַל פְּתָחַי בְּקוֹל.
רְאוּ נֵס בֶּהָרִים וְקוֹל שׁוֹפָר בָּאָרֶץ
לְהַשְׁמִיעַ רֶנֶן מִדְמוּמֵי קוֹל.
תְּהִלָּה יִתְּנוּ אָז לַכֹּל הִשְׁמִיעַ לָאֵל
מוֹשֵׁל בַּכֹּל יַמְתִּיקוּ קוֹל.

הַאָמְנָם עוֹד יָבוֹאוּ יָמִים בִּסְלִיחָה וּבְחֶסֶד,
וְתֵלְכִי בַּשָּׂדֶה, תֵּלְכִי בּוֹ כַּהֵלֶךְ הַתָּם,
וּמַחֲשׂוֹף כַּף־רַגְלֵךְ יְלַטֵּף בַּעֲלֵי הָאַסְפֶּסֶת,
אוֹ שִׁלְפֵי־שִׁבֳּלִים יִדְקְרוּךְ וְתִמְתַּק דְּקִירָתָם.
אוֹ מָטָר יַשִּׂיגֵךְ בַּעֲדַת טִפּוֹתָיו הַדּוֹפֶקֶת
עַל כְּתֵפַיִךְ, חָזֵךְ, צַוָּארֵךְ, וְרֹאשֵׁךְ רַעֲנָן.
וְתֵלְכִי בַּשָּׂדֶה הָרָטֹב וְיִרְחַב בָּךְ הַשֶּׁקֶט
כָּאוֹר בְּשׁוּלֵי הֶעָנָן. (continued)

SHOFAROT. The Bible calls Rosh Hashanah "the day of the shofar call/yom t'ru·ah" (Numbers 29:1). The sounding of the shofar awakens us to a calling, a divine calling. It accompanied the revelation of the Torah on Mount Sinai, and it has the power to arouse us from our own self-absorption and make us aware of the needs of the world beyond us. Equally, the shofar is the symbol of the announcement of messianic time; for the prophets, its sound was the harbinger of divine redemption.

RUNNING FOR HELP אָנוּסָה לְעֶזְרָה. This piyyut is ascribed to Yose ben Yose (5th century, Land of Israel) and is therefore thought to be one of the first liturgical additions to this section of the service. The unabridged original is a double acrostic with each line ending with the word kol, "voice." Towards the end, the biblical verses which we recite later on are worked into the poem.

SILENT ONES מִדְמוּמֵי. There are many possible layers of meaning to this phrase. One interpretation is that even the dead, those who lie silently in the earth, are roused by God's calling.

WILL FORGIVING AND GRACEFUL DAYS YET COME הַאָמְנָם עוֹד. Shofarot calls us to walk with righteousness and wholeness in the world, but our going out to the world need not be boisterous or grand like the sound of the shofar itself. Rather, our discovery of the gifts of life and the revelation of our path can come while we quietly make our way. It is this quiet ecstasy which the modern Hebrew poet Leah Goldberg describes in this poem: a time of peace that can descend on us when we are through with our wars.

The sounding of the shofar is a call, a call demanding a response from each of us. It is a call that asks us to listen to the shouted and muffled cries of the world, and equally to attend to the beauty of the world which calls out to us. The sound of the shofar is a signal to join in the progress to redemption. Kadya Molodowsky's poem reminds us of what we have shut out and what we need to be open to.

Night Visitors

At night, a bird arrived at
  my door,
Knocked with its wings
On my window and
  door.
—Come right in, fiddle-
  bird, musician of my
  youth,
I still put aside bread and
  water for you.
Come right in, and be my
  honored guest.
We've both been decreed
  this life and this death.

And then a cat strayed in
  from the night,
Scratched with its claws,
Scratched and scraped.
—Come right in, dread
  childhood beast,
  kitty-cat,
I've never, not once,
  grabbed a broom and
  said, "Scat!"
Come right in, and be my
  honored guest,
We've been given the
  fate to be homeless and
  lost.

A goat came next, with
  its pointy goatee,
Knocked with its hooves,
Ground with its horns.
—Come in, goaty-bloaty,
  beard, milk from a ladle.

(continued)

Meditations on Shofarot

If I ran for help, I would find God close by, when I cried out and *called*.

  Now, in the the midst of God's congregation, as I stand on this holy ground, I sing out and *call*.

Meet me, seek me, I am a sheep that has strayed; I am shorn, mute, unable to raise my voice and *call*.

  Gaze upon my overwhelmed and impoverished existence, no one knows me; to whom can I *call*?

I always trust that no one will be forsaken as they listen to God's silence and *call*.

  My heart will be overjoyed when I hear my beloved knocking at my door *calling*.

Then I would see the banner over the mountain, and the sound of the shofar on earth, when even the silent ones will voice joyful song and *call*,

  And, praise will be given to all who cried out to God, the ruler of all; how sweet that *call*.

WILL FORGIVING AND GRACEFUL DAYS YET COME
Will forgiving and graceful days yet come,
when you walk in the field as the innocent walk
and the soles of your feet caress the clover leaves,
or pricked by stubble the sting will feel sweet?
Or rain will overtake you, congregating drops tapping
on your shoulder, your chest, your throat, your head, refreshed.
And you walk in the wet field, the quiet expanding within
like light peeking out of a cloud. *(continued)*

וְנָשַׁמְתְּ אֶת־רֵיחוֹ שֶׁל הַתֶּלֶם נָשֹׁם וְרָגוֹעַ,
וְרָאִית אֶת־הַשֶּׁמֶשׁ בִּרְאִי־הַשְּׁלוּלִית הַזָּהֹב,
וּפְשׁוּטִים הַדְּבָרִים וְחַיִּים, וּמֻתָּר בָּם לִנְגֹּעַ,
וּמֻתָּר, וּמֻתָּר לֶאֱהֹב.

אַתְּ תֵּלְכִי בַּשָּׂדֶה. לְבַדֵּךְ. לֹא נִצְרֶבֶת בְּלַהַט
הַשְּׂרֵפוֹת, בַּדְּרָכִים שֶׁסָּמְרוּ מֵאֵימָה וּמִדָּם.
וּבְיֹשֶׁר־לֵבָב שׁוּב תִּהְיִי עֲנָוָה וְנִכְנַעַת
כְּאַחַד הַדְּשָׁאִים, כְּאַחַד הָאָדָם.

שׁוֹפָרוֹת

אַתָּה נִגְלֵיתָ בַּעֲנַן כְּבוֹדֶךָ, עַל עַם קָדְשְׁךָ, לְדַבֵּר עִמָּם.
מִן הַשָּׁמַיִם הִשְׁמַעְתָּם קוֹלֶךָ, וְנִגְלֵיתָ עֲלֵיהֶם בְּעַרְפְּלֵי טֹהַר.
גַּם כָּל־הָעוֹלָם כֻּלּוֹ חָל מִפָּנֶיךָ, וּבְרִיּוֹת בְּרֵאשִׁית חָרְדוּ מִמֶּךָּ,
בְּהִגָּלוֹתְךָ מַלְכֵּנוּ עַל הַר סִינַי, לְלַמֵּד לְעַמְּךָ תּוֹרָה וּמִצְוֹת,
וַתַּשְׁמִיעֵם אֶת־הוֹד קוֹלֶךָ, וְדִבְּרוֹת קָדְשְׁךָ מִלַּהֲבוֹת אֵשׁ.
בְּקֹלֹת וּבְרָקִים עֲלֵיהֶם נִגְלֵיתָ, וּבְקוֹל שׁוֹפָר עֲלֵיהֶם הוֹפָעְתָּ.

כַּכָּתוּב בְּתוֹרָתֶךָ:

א וַיְהִי בַיּוֹם הַשְּׁלִישִׁי בִּהְיֹת הַבֹּקֶר, וַיְהִי קֹלֹת וּבְרָקִים,
וְעָנָן כָּבֵד עַל הָהָר, וְקֹל **שֹׁפָר** חָזָק מְאֹד, וַיֶּחֱרַד כָּל־הָעָם
אֲשֶׁר בַּמַּחֲנֶה. שמות יט טז

ב וַנֶּאֱמַר: וַיְהִי קוֹל **הַשּׁוֹפָר** הוֹלֵךְ וְחָזֵק מְאֹד, מֹשֶׁה
יְדַבֵּר וְהָאֱלֹהִים יַעֲנֶנּוּ בְקוֹל. שמות יט יט

ג וַנֶּאֱמַר: וְכָל־הָעָם רֹאִים אֶת־הַקּוֹלֹת וְאֶת־הַלַּפִּידִם,
וְאֵת קוֹל הַ**שֹּׁפָר**, וְאֶת־הָהָר עָשֵׁן, וַיַּרְא הָעָם וַיָּנֻעוּ
וַיַּעַמְדוּ מֵרָחֹק. שמות כ טו

ALLOWING THEM TO HEAR YOUR VOICE מִן הַשָּׁמַיִם הִשְׁמַעְתָּם קוֹלֶךָ. Deuteronomy 4:36.

YOUR SACRED WORDS וְדִבְּרוֹת קָדְשְׁךָ. A reference to the Decalogue, which was revealed to the people Israel at Sinai, accompanied by the sound of the shofar.

ON THE THIRD DAY. All three verses from the Torah are taken from the description in Exodus of the revelation on Mount Sinai. The first two (Exodus 19:16, 19) occur before the giving of the Decalogue, and the last (Exodus 20:15) after. This last verse, with its conflation of sight and sound—"the people saw the thunder and lightning"—conveys the full depth of the transformative experience of revelation.

YOU REVEALED YOURSELF אַתָּה נִגְלֵיתָ. Like the introductory poems to Malkhuyot and Zikhronot, this poem dates back to the fifth century (or earlier) and exhibits some of the features that characterize the transition from early post-Biblical to medieval liturgical poetry. There are four stresses in each line, the same rhythm as in Aleinu, the prayer with which the special sections of Musaf began.

TO YOUR HOLY PEOPLE עַל עַם קָדְשְׁךָ. The preposition here is עַל, literally "upon," as opposed to the more usual אֶל, "to." The implication could be that Israel is no mere recipient of revelation, but the vehicle upon which God's word is carried into the world.

(continued from previous page)
To this day, your song
   transforms bed into
   cradle.
Come in, and be my
   honored guest,
We've both been decreed
   a schoolteacher's lot.

At night a person came,
   stood by my door,
And I was befallen with
Such anxious fear.
—Who are you? Are you
   holding a knife in your
   hand?
Are you hiding betrayal?
   Do you hold smolder-
   ing brands?
And I slammed the door
   shut, turned the lock,
   threw the bolt,
Fell to the floor, put my
   face in my hands.
The night grew dark,
   then, as blindness is
   dark.
My floor became hard as
   stone,
And he stood on the
   other side of the door.
From the other side, I
   heard sobs and a moan.
   —KADYA MOLODOWSKY
   (trans. Kathryn Hellerstein)

And you will breathe the odor of the ridge, breathing, quiet,
and you will see the sun mirrored in the golden puddle,
and daily affairs and life will seem simple, easy to touch,
easy, easy to love.

You will walk in the field. Alone. Not scorched by the flames
of conflagrations, on roads that bristled with horror and blood.
With a heart at peace, you will once again be humble, and bend
like a blade of grass, like a human being. —LEAH GOLDBERG

Sixth B'rakhah: Shofarot
PRAYERS AND BIBLICAL VERSES ON THE SHOFAR
You revealed Yourself in a cloud of glory
to speak to Your holy people,
allowing them to hear Your voice from the heavens.
Through a pure mist You disclosed Yourself,
and the whole world—everything—quivered in Your presence.
All of creation trembled in awe,
as You, our sovereign, made Yourself known on Mount Sinai,
teaching Your people Torah and mitzvot.
You spoke to them from amidst fiery flames,
allowing them to hear Your majestic voice and Your sacred words,
revealed Yourself to them amidst thunder and lightning,
and appeared to them with the sounding of the shofar.

As it is written in Your Torah:
א On the third day, as morning dawned, there was thunder
and lightning, a dense cloud covering the mountain, and the
powerful sound of the *shofar*; all the people who were in the
camp trembled.   Exodus 19:16
ב The sound of the *shofar* grew ever more powerful; as Moses
spoke, God's response thundered.   Exodus 19:19
ג All the people saw the thunder and lightning, the blare of the
shofar and the mountain smoking; as the people saw it, they
fell back and stood at a distance.   Exodus 20:15

 וּבְדִבְרֵי קָדְשְׁךָ כָּתוּב לֵאמֹר:

א עָלָה אֱלֹהִים בִּתְרוּעָה, יהוה בְּקוֹל **שׁוֹפָר**. תהלים מז ו

ב וְנֶאֱמַר: בַּחֲצֹצְרוֹת וְקוֹל **שׁוֹפָר** הָרִיעוּ לִפְנֵי הַמֶּלֶךְ יהוה. תהלים צח ו

ג וְנֶאֱמַר: תִּקְעוּ בַחֹדֶשׁ **שׁוֹפָר**, בַּכֶּסֶה לְיוֹם חַגֵּנוּ. כִּי חֹק לְיִשְׂרָאֵל הוּא, מִשְׁפָּט לֵאלֹהֵי יַעֲקֹב. תהלים פא ד-ה

וְנֶאֱמַר: הַלְלוּ יָהּ, הַלְלוּ־אֵל בְּקָדְשׁוֹ, הַלְלוּהוּ בִּרְקִיעַ עֻזּוֹ. הַלְלוּהוּ בִגְבוּרֹתָיו, הַלְלוּהוּ כְּרֹב גֻּדְלוֹ. הַלְלוּהוּ בְּתֵקַע שׁוֹפָר, הַלְלוּהוּ בְּנֵבֶל וְכִנּוֹר. הַלְלוּהוּ בְּתֹף וּמָחוֹל, הַלְלוּהוּ בְּמִנִּים וְעֻגָב. הַלְלוּהוּ בְצִלְצְלֵי שָׁמַע, הַלְלוּהוּ בְּצִלְצְלֵי תְרוּעָה. כֹּל הַנְּשָׁמָה תְּהַלֵּל יָהּ, הַלְלוּיָהּ. תהלים קנ א-ו

וְעַל יְדֵי עֲבָדֶיךָ הַנְּבִיאִים כָּתוּב לֵאמֹר:

א כָּל־יֹשְׁבֵי תֵבֵל וְשֹׁכְנֵי אָרֶץ, כִּנְשֹׂא נֵס הָרִים תִּרְאוּ, וְכִתְקֹעַ **שׁוֹפָר** תִּשְׁמָעוּ. ישעיה יח ג

ב וְנֶאֱמַר: וְהָיָה בַּיּוֹם הַהוּא יִתָּקַע **בְּשׁוֹפָר** גָּדוֹל, וּבָאוּ הָאֹבְדִים בְּאֶרֶץ אַשּׁוּר וְהַנִּדָּחִים בְּאֶרֶץ מִצְרָיִם, וְהִשְׁתַּחֲווּ לַיהוה בְּהַר הַקֹּדֶשׁ בִּירוּשָׁלָיִם. ישעיה כז יג

ג וְנֶאֱמַר: וַיהוה עֲלֵיהֶם יֵרָאֶה, וְיָצָא כַבָּרָק חִצּוֹ, וַאדֹנָי אֱלֹהִים **בַּשּׁוֹפָר** יִתְקָע, וְהָלַךְ בְּסַעֲרוֹת תֵּימָן. יהוה צְבָאוֹת יָגֵן עֲלֵיהֶם. זכריה ט יד-טו

כֵּן תָּגֵן עַל עַמְּךָ יִשְׂרָאֵל בִּשְׁלוֹמֶךָ.

VERSES FROM PSALMS. The verses from the Book of Psalms speak of the shofar as the instrument announcing the day of judgment, as God ascends the divine throne.

GOD ASCENDS AMIDST THE CRY עָלָה אֱלֹהִים בִּתְרוּעָה. According to the midrash (Leviticus Rabbah 29:3), this verse's use of the two names of God—*Elohim* (associated with strict justice) and *Adonai* (associated with compassion and loving-kindness)—reflects how God's relationship with us changes over the course of Rosh Hashanah. At the beginning, God ascends and sits on the Throne of Justice, as it is said, "*Elohim* ascends with the *t'ru·ah* [shofar alarm-call]." But when the people Israel blow the shofar, God's compassion is aroused and God moves from the Throne of Justice to the Throne of Compassion, and truly becomes Adonai, as the verse says, "With the shofar's sound, Adonai is enthroned."

SOUND THE SHOFAR ON OUR FEAST DAY תִּקְעוּ בַחֹדֶשׁ שׁוֹפָר. Rosh Hashanah is the only festival that occurs on the new moon. This verse, with its reference to when the moon is hidden, בַּכֶּסֶה (*ba-keseh*), is used in the Babylonian Talmud as the prooftext for God's judgment taking place on this day (Rosh Hashanah 8a–b).

AND SO, TOO, PROTECT YOUR PEOPLE ISRAEL כֵּן תָּגֵן. Following these Shofarot verses is a brief liturgical coda that amplifies the plea for redemption just quoted in Zechariah 9:15.

And it is also written in Psalms:

א God ascends amidst the cry of the *shofar*; with its sound Adonai is enthroned. Psalm 47:6

ב Sound the trumpet and *shofar* before the Sovereign, Adonai. Psalm 98:6

ג Sound the *shofar* on our feast day, on the new moon, when it is hidden. For it is Israel's law, a decree of the God of Jacob. Psalm 81:4–5

Halleluyah! Praise God in the sanctuary,
Praise God in the powerful heavens.
Praise God for the mighty deeds,
Praise God for infinite greatness.
Praise God with the *shofar* call,
Praise God with harp and lyre.
Praise God with drum and dance,
Praise God with flute and strings.
Praise God with crashing cymbals,
Praise God with resounding cymbals.
Let every breath of life praise Adonai. Halleluyah! Psalm 150:1–6

Hal'luyah.
Hal'lu El b'kodsho, hal'luhu bi-r'ki·a uzzo.
Hal'luhu vi-g'vurotav, hal'luhu k'rov gudlo.
Hal'luhu b'teika shofar, hal'luhu b'neiveil v'khinnor.
Hal'luhu b'tof u-maḥol, hal'luhu b'minnim v'ugav.
Hal'luhu v'tziltz'lei shama, hal'luhu b'tziltz'lei t'ru·ah.
Kol ha-n'shamah t'hallel yah, hal'luyah.

And Your servants the prophets further wrote:

א All you inhabitants of the world and dwellers on earth: when a banner is raised on the mountains, look! When the *shofar* is sounded, listen! Isaiah 18:3

ב For on that day, a great *shofar* will be sounded: those lost in the land of Assyria and those cast away in the land of Egypt shall come back and worship Adonai on the holy mountain in Jerusalem. Isaiah 27:13

ג Adonai will appear to them, shooting arrows like lightning; the lord, God, will sound the *shofar*, advancing in a stormy south wind. *Adonai Tz'va·ot* will protect them. Zechariah 9:14–15

And so, too, protect Your people Israel with Your peace.

אֱלֹהֵינוּ וֵאלֹהֵי אֲבוֹתֵינוּ [וְאִמּוֹתֵינוּ],
תְּקַע בְּשׁוֹפָר גָּדוֹל לְחֵרוּתֵנוּ,
וְשָׂא נֵס לְקַבֵּץ גָּלֻיּוֹתֵינוּ,
וְקָרֵב פְּזוּרֵינוּ מִבֵּין הַגּוֹיִם,
וּנְפוּצוֹתֵינוּ כַּנֵּס מִיַּרְכְּתֵי אָרֶץ.
וַהֲבִיאֵנוּ לְצִיּוֹן עִירְךָ בְּרִנָּה,
וְלִירוּשָׁלַיִם בֵּית מִקְדָּשְׁךָ בְּשִׂמְחַת עוֹלָם.
שָׁשָׁם עָשׂוּ אֲבוֹתֵינוּ [וְאִמּוֹתֵינוּ] לְפָנֶיךָ אֶת־עוֹלוֹתֵיהֶם
וְאֶת־שַׁלְמֵיהֶם. וְכֵן כָּתוּב בְּתוֹרָתֶךָ:
וּבְיוֹם שִׂמְחַתְכֶם וּבְמוֹעֲדֵיכֶם וּבְרָאשֵׁי חָדְשֵׁיכֶם,
וּתְקַעְתֶּם בַּחֲצֹצְרֹת עַל עֹלֹתֵיכֶם וְעַל זִבְחֵי שַׁלְמֵיכֶם,
וְהָיוּ לָכֶם לְזִכָּרוֹן לִפְנֵי אֱלֹהֵיכֶם, אֲנִי יהוה אֱלֹהֵיכֶם.

במדבר י׳

כִּי אַתָּה שׁוֹמֵעַ קוֹל שׁוֹפָר, וּמַאֲזִין תְּרוּעָה וְאֵין דּוֹמֶה לָךְ.
בָּרוּךְ אַתָּה יהוה, שׁוֹמֵעַ קוֹל תְּרוּעַת עַמּוֹ יִשְׂרָאֵל
בְּרַחֲמִים.

(The shofar is traditionally not blown on Shabbat.)

תקיעה שברים־תרועה תקיעה
תקיעה שברים תקיעה
תקיעה תרועה תקיעה גדולה

הַיּוֹם הֲרַת עוֹלָם, הַיּוֹם יַעֲמִיד בַּמִּשְׁפָּט כָּל־יְצוּרֵי
עוֹלָמִים, אִם כְּבָנִים אִם כַּעֲבָדִים. אִם כְּבָנִים, רַחֲמֵנוּ
כְּרַחֵם אָב עַל בָּנִים. וְאִם כַּעֲבָדִים עֵינֵינוּ לְךָ תְלוּיוֹת,
עַד שֶׁתְּחָנֵּנוּ וְתוֹצִיא כָאוֹר מִשְׁפָּטֵנוּ, אָיֹם קָדוֹשׁ.

WE OMIT THIS PARAGRAPH ON SHABBAT:

אֲרֶשֶׁת שְׂפָתֵינוּ יֶעֱרַב לְפָנֶיךָ, אֵל רָם וְנִשָּׂא,
מֵבִין וּמַאֲזִין, מַבִּיט וּמַקְשִׁיב לְקוֹל תְּקִיעָתֵנוּ,
וּתְקַבֵּל בְּרַחֲמִים וּבְרָצוֹן סֵדֶר שׁוֹפְרוֹתֵינוּ.

TRUMPETS חֲצֹצְרֹת. The Mishnah prescribes that trumpets are to accompany the sounding of the shofar (Rosh Hashanah 3:3–4). Trumpets are depicted on the Arch of Titus in Rome as some of the booty brought home after the capture of Jerusalem in 70 C.E. They were probably blown only by the priests and levites, and so have dropped out of our own ritual performance. The Bible records that the trumpets are to be sounded at the time of the festival sacrifice.

WHO LISTENS WITH COMPASSION TO THE SOUNDS OF THE SPLINTERED CALL OF YOUR PEOPLE ISRAEL שׁוֹמֵעַ קוֹל תְּרוּעַת עַמּוֹ יִשְׂרָאֵל בְּרַחֲמִים. After all these many repetitions of the word "shofar," the closing *b'rakhah* of the service of Shofarot omits the word. Instead, we praise God as the One who hears the *t'ru·ah*—the staccato call—of the people Israel. Our collective cries have themselves become a kind of shofar.

Our God and God of our ancestors, sound the great *shofar* proclaiming our freedom, raise up the banner signaling the ingathering of our exiles, draw near those scattered amidst the nations, and from the ends of the earth assemble our dispersed. Bring us with song and boundless joy to Zion, Your city, to Jerusalem the site of Your Temple, where our ancestors brought their sacrifices and their offerings, as is written in Your Torah: On your joyous occasions—your fixed festivals and new moons—you shall sound the trumpets over your sacrifices and offerings. They shall be a remembrance of you before your God; I, ADONAI, am your God. Numbers 10:10

For You hear the sound of the shofar, and attend to its splintered call—You are beyond compare. *Barukh atah ADONAI*, who listens with compassion to the sounds of the splintered call of Your people Israel.

(The shofar is traditionally not blown on Shabbat.)

T'ki·ah sh'varim-t'ru·ah t'ki·ah
T'ki·ah sh'varim t'ki·ah
T'ki·ah t'ru·ah t'ki·ah g'dolah

Today the world stands as at birth. Today all creation is called to judgment, whether as Your children or as Your servants. If as Your children, be compassionate with us as a parent is compassionate with children. If as Your servants, we look to You expectantly, waiting for You to be gracious to us, and as day emerges from night bring forth a favorable judgment on our behalf, awe-inspiring and Holy One.

Ha-yom harat olam, ha-yom ya·amid ba-mishpat kol y'tzurei olamim, im k'vanim im ka-avadim. Im k'vanim, rahameinu k'rahem av al banim. V'im ka-avadim eineinu l'kha t'luyot, ad she-t'honneinu v'totzi kha-or mishpateinu, ayom kadosh.

WE OMIT THIS PARAGRAPH ON SHABBAT:

May the words of our lips be pleasing to You, exalted God, who listens, discerns, considers, and attends to the sound of our shofar blast. Lovingly accept our service of the shofar.

Areshet s'fateinu ye·erav l'fanekha, El ram v'nissa, mevin u-ma·azin, mabbit u-makshiv l'kol t'ki·ateinu. U-t'kabbel b'rahamim u-v'ratzon seder shof'roteinu.

רְצֵה יהוה אֱלֹהֵינוּ, בְּעַמְּךָ יִשְׂרָאֵל, וּבִתְפִלָּתָם, וְהָשֵׁב אֶת־הָעֲבוֹדָה לִדְבִיר בֵּיתֶךָ, [וְאִשֵּׁי יִשְׂרָאֵל] וּתְפִלָּתָם בְּאַהֲבָה תְקַבֵּל בְּרָצוֹן, וּתְהִי לְרָצוֹן תָּמִיד עֲבוֹדַת יִשְׂרָאֵל עַמֶּךָ.

If the kohanim will be reciting the Priestly Blessing, this b'rakhah continues:

וְתֶעֱרַב עָלֶיךָ עֲתִירָתֵנוּ. וְתֶחֱזֶינָה עֵינֵינוּ בְּשׁוּבְךָ לְצִיּוֹן בְּרַחֲמִים, וְשָׁם נַעֲבָדְךָ בְּיִרְאָה כִּימֵי עוֹלָם וּכְשָׁנִים קַדְמוֹנִיּוֹת. בָּרוּךְ אַתָּה יהוה, שֶׁאוֹתְךָ לְבַדְּךָ בְּיִרְאָה נַעֲבוֹד.

If the kohanim will not be blessing the congregation, we proceed here:

וְתֶחֱזֶינָה עֵינֵינוּ בְּשׁוּבְךָ לְצִיּוֹן בְּרַחֲמִים. בָּרוּךְ אַתָּה יהוה, הַמַּחֲזִיר שְׁכִינָתוֹ לְצִיּוֹן.

While reciting the first words, by custom we remain seated while bowing our head.

Congregation recites:

¶ **מוֹדִים אֲנַחְנוּ לָךְ** שָׁאַתָּה הוּא יהוה אֱלֹהֵינוּ וֵאלֹהֵי אֲבוֹתֵינוּ [וְאִמּוֹתֵינוּ] אֱלֹהֵי כָל־בָּשָׂר, יוֹצְרֵנוּ, יוֹצֵר בְּרֵאשִׁית. בְּרָכוֹת וְהוֹדָאוֹת לְשִׁמְךָ הַגָּדוֹל וְהַקָּדוֹשׁ, עַל שֶׁהֶחֱיִיתָנוּ וְקִיַּמְתָּנוּ. כֵּן תְּחַיֵּנוּ וּתְקַיְּמֵנוּ, וְתֶאֱסוֹף גָּלֻיּוֹתֵינוּ לְחַצְרוֹת קָדְשֶׁךָ, לִשְׁמוֹר חֻקֶּיךָ וְלַעֲשׂוֹת רְצוֹנֶךָ, וּלְעָבְדְּךָ בְּלֵבָב שָׁלֵם, עַל שֶׁאֲנַחְנוּ מוֹדִים לָךְ. בָּרוּךְ אֵל הַהוֹדָאוֹת.

Leader recites:

מוֹדִים אֲנַחְנוּ לָךְ שָׁאַתָּה הוּא יהוה אֱלֹהֵינוּ וֵאלֹהֵי אֲבוֹתֵינוּ [וְאִמּוֹתֵינוּ] לְעוֹלָם וָעֶד, צוּר חַיֵּינוּ מָגֵן יִשְׁעֵנוּ אַתָּה הוּא לְדוֹר וָדוֹר. נוֹדֶה לְּךָ וּנְסַפֵּר תְּהִלָּתֶךָ, עַל חַיֵּינוּ הַמְּסוּרִים בְּיָדֶךָ וְעַל נִשְׁמוֹתֵינוּ הַפְּקוּדוֹת לָךְ, וְעַל נִסֶּיךָ שֶׁבְּכָל־יוֹם עִמָּנוּ וְעַל נִפְלְאוֹתֶיךָ וְטוֹבוֹתֶיךָ שֶׁבְּכָל־עֵת, עֶרֶב וָבֹקֶר וְצָהֳרָיִם. ◁ הַטּוֹב, כִּי לֹא כָלוּ רַחֲמֶיךָ, וְהַמְרַחֵם כִּי לֹא תַמּוּ חֲסָדֶיךָ מֵעוֹלָם קִוִּינוּ לָךְ.

imperative of thanking God for the gifts of life. The central idea in this version is *modim anaḥnu lakh. . . . al she-anaḥnu modim lakh*, "we thank You for the ability to thank You." The prayer may be understood as an expression of appreciation for being part of a religious tradition that values reflection and gratitude. More radically, this prayer may be understood as expressing the thought that our prayers may be addressed to God, but God is the source of all—even the words of holiness we speak. The very ability to thank is thus a manifestation of the presence of God within us.

RESTORE WORSHIP TO YOUR SANCTUARY וְהָשֵׁב אֶת־הָעֲבוֹדָה לִדְבִיר בֵּיתֶךָ. A motif of Jewish theology is that we are in exile and that our collective relationship with God cannot be fulfilled. Yearning for the restoration of the Temple expresses the wish to have a direct relationship with God.

THE FIERY OFFERINGS וְאִשֵּׁי יִשְׂרָאֵל. The reference to the "fiery offerings," originally referring to the sacrifices that took place in the Temple, was understood by many Ḥasidic commentators as referring to the intensity of religious fervor in true prayer.

YOUR DIVINE PRESENCE שְׁכִינָתוֹ. The Hebrew word *shekhinah* has been used for centuries to refer to God's immanence, the presence of God that is felt in the world. The word *shekhinah* is grammatically feminine. Accordingly, the Jewish mystical tradition generally describes the Divine Presence—known as the Shekhinah—in feminine imagery.

WE THANK YOU מוֹדִים. A second version of the Modim b'rakhah was created by the Sages to be recited by the congregation while the leader chants the official prayer (Babylonian Talmud, Sotah 40a). In this way, each of us fulfills in a personal manner the

Seventh B'rakhah: The Restoration of Zion

ADONAI our God, embrace Your people Israel and their prayer. Restore worship to Your sanctuary. May the [fiery offerings and] prayers of the people Israel be lovingly accepted by You, and may our service always be pleasing.

If the kohanim will be reciting the Priestly Blessing, this b'rakhah continues:

May our prayers be pleasing to You and may our eyes behold Your merciful return to Zion so that we may worship there as in days of old. *Barukh atah* ADONAI, for You alone shall we worship in awe.

If the kohanim will not be blessing the congregation, we proceed here:

Let our eyes behold Your merciful return to Zion. *Barukh atah* ADONAI, who restores Your Divine Presence to Zion.

Eighth B'rakhah: Gratitude for Life and Its Blessings

While reciting the first words, by custom we remain seated while bowing our head.

Leader recites:

We thank You, You who are our God and the God of our ancestors through all time, protector of our lives, shield of our salvation. From one generation to the next we thank You and sing Your praises—
for our lives that are in Your hands,
for our souls that are under Your care,
for Your miracles that accompany us each day,
and for Your wonders and Your gifts that are with us each moment—
evening, morning, and noon. You are the One who is good, whose mercy is never-ending; the One who is compassionate, whose love is unceasing. We have always placed our hope in You.

Congregation recites:

ʄ We thank You for the ability to acknowledge You. You are our God and the God of our ancestors, the God of all flesh, our creator, and the creator of all. We offer praise and blessing to Your holy and great name, for granting us life and for sustaining us. May You continue to grant us life and sustenance. Gather our dispersed to Your holy courtyards, that we may fulfill Your mitzvot and serve You wholeheartedly, carrying out Your will. May God, the source of gratitude, be praised.

וְעַל כֻּלָּם יִתְבָּרַךְ וְיִתְרוֹמַם שִׁמְךָ מַלְכֵּנוּ תָּמִיד לְעוֹלָם וָעֶד.

We recite the following paragraph, which the leader then repeats:

אָבִינוּ מַלְכֵּנוּ, זְכוֹר רַחֲמֶיךָ וּכְבוֹשׁ כַּעַסְךָ, וְכַלֵּה דֶּבֶר
וְחֶרֶב, וְרָעָב וּשְׁבִי, וּמַשְׁחִית וְעָוֹן, וּשְׁמַד, וּמַגֵּפָה,
וּפֶגַע רַע וְכָל־מַחֲלָה, וְכָל־תַּקָלָה, וְכָל־קְטָטָה, וְכָל־מִינֵי
פֻּרְעָנִיּוֹת, וְכָל־גְּזֵרָה רָעָה וְשִׂנְאַת חִנָּם, מֵעָלֵינוּ, וּמֵעַל
כָּל־בְּנֵי בְרִיתֶךָ, וּמֵעַל כָּל־הָעוֹלָם.

וּכְתוֹב לְחַיִּים טוֹבִים כָּל־בְּנֵי בְרִיתֶךָ.

וְכָל הַחַיִּים יוֹדוּךָ סֶּלָה, וִיהַלְלוּ אֶת־שִׁמְךָ בֶּאֱמֶת הָאֵל
יְשׁוּעָתֵנוּ וְעֶזְרָתֵנוּ סֶלָה.
בָּרוּךְ אַתָּה יהוה, הַטּוֹב שִׁמְךָ וּלְךָ נָאֶה לְהוֹדוֹת.

If the kohanim do not bless the congregation, we continue on page 169.

בִּרְכַּת כֹּהֲנִים

We rise. The kohanim recite quietly:

יְהִי רָצוֹן מִלְּפָנֶיךָ יהוה אֱלֹהֵינוּ וֵאלֹהֵי אֲבוֹתֵינוּ [וְאִמּוֹתֵינוּ],
שֶׁתְּהֵא הַבְּרָכָה הַזֹּאת שֶׁצִּוִּיתָנוּ לְבָרֵךְ אֶת־עַמְּךָ יִשְׂרָאֵל בְּרָכָה
שְׁלֵמָה, וְלֹא יִהְיֶה בָּהּ שׁוּם מִכְשׁוֹל וְעָוֹן מֵעַתָּה וְעַד עוֹלָם.

Leader (quietly):

אֱלֹהֵינוּ וֵאלֹהֵי אֲבוֹתֵינוּ [וְאִמּוֹתֵינוּ], בָּרְכֵנוּ בַבְּרָכָה
הַמְשֻׁלֶּשֶׁת, בַּתּוֹרָה הַכְּתוּבָה עַל יְדֵי מֹשֶׁה עַבְדֶּךָ,
הָאֲמוּרָה מִפִּי אַהֲרֹן וּבָנָיו כֹּהֲנִים—עַם קְדוֹשֶׁךָ כָּאָמוּר:

The kohanim recite:

בָּרוּךְ אַתָּה יהוה, אֱלֹהֵינוּ מֶלֶךְ הָעוֹלָם, אֲשֶׁר קִדְּשָׁנוּ
בִּקְדֻשָּׁתוֹ שֶׁל אַהֲרֹן, וְצִוָּנוּ לְבָרֵךְ אֶת־עַמּוֹ יִשְׂרָאֵל
בְּאַהֲבָה.   **אָמֵן**

אָמֵן   יְבָרֶכְךָ יהוה וְיִשְׁמְרֶךָ.
אָמֵן   יָאֵר יהוה פָּנָיו אֵלֶיךָ וִיחֻנֶּךָּ.
אָמֵן   יִשָּׂא יהוה פָּנָיו אֵלֶיךָ וְיָשֵׂם לְךָ שָׁלוֹם.

שָׁלוֹם שָׁלוֹם לָרָחוֹק וְלַקָּרוֹב, אָמַר יהוה, וּרְפָאתִיו.

We are seated.

FOR ALL THESE וְעַל כֻּלָּם. In the language of the Bible and the prayerbook, "God's name is exalted" when we acknowledge God, recognize God's goodness in creation, and act to enable God's justice and compassion to be visible in the world.

AND INSCRIBE וּכְתוֹב. This is the third of the four special insertions in the Amidah for the Ten Days of Repentance.

BIRKAT KOHANIM. This blessing (Numbers 6:24–26) is known as the Birkat Kohanim, the Priestly Blessing, as the Torah prescribes that it is to be recited by Aaron and his descendants, the *kohanim* (priests), to bring God's blessing upon the people Israel. Its words are the only biblical verses that have been found in archaeological digs of biblical times. In most synagogues in Israel, this blessing is recited every day by the *kohanim* in each community, who come to the front of the synagogue after preparing themselves ritually, and extend their hands toward the community in a traditional gesture that serves as a conduit of blessing. In many synagogues in the Diaspora, the *kohanim* reenact this ancient blessing only during the Musaf service on High Holy Days and festivals. At other times, and at all times in many congregations, the blessing is recited by the service leader.

For all these blessings may Your name be praised and exalted, our sovereign, always and forever.

We recite the following paragraph, which the leader then repeats:
Avinu Malkeinu, remember Your compassion and subdue Your anger. Bring an end to pestilence, sword, and hunger; captivity and destruction, sin and oppression, plague and calamity; every illness, misfortune, and quarrel; all kinds of danger, every evil decree, and causeless hatred. Bring an end to these for us and for all the people of Your covenant.

And inscribe all the people of Your covenant for a good life.
U-kh'tov l'ḥayyim tovim kol b'nei v'ritekha.

May all that lives thank You always, and praise Your name faithfully forever, God of our deliverance and help.
Barukh atah ADONAI, whose name is goodness and to whom praise is fitting.

If the kohanim do not bless the congregation, we continue on page 169.
The Priestly Blessing
We rise. The kohanim recite quietly:
May it be Your will, ADONAI our God and God of our ancestors, that this blessing with which You have instructed us to bless Your people Israel be perfect and complete, and that it not be diminished by any error or sin, now or ever.

Leader (quietly):
Our God and God of our ancestors: Bless us with the threefold blessing written in the Torah by the hand of Moses Your servant, recited by Aaron and his descendants, the *kohanim*, the consecrated priests of Your people: *am k'doshekha ka-amur.*

The kohanim recite:
Barukh atah ADONAI, our God, ruler of time and space, who has made us holy with the sanctity of Aaron and has instructed us to bless the people Israel with love.   *Amen*
May ADONAI bless and protect you.   *Amen*
May ADONAI's countenance shine upon you and grant you kindness.

Amen

May ADONAI's countenance be lifted toward you and grant you peace.

Amen

Shalom, shalom—shalom to those who are far off, shalom to those who are near, says ADONAI, and I shall heal them.

We are seated.

אֱלֹהֵינוּ וֵאלֹהֵי אֲבוֹתֵינוּ [וְאִמּוֹתֵינוּ], בָּרְכֵנוּ בַּבְּרָכָה
הַמְשֻׁלֶּשֶׁת בַּתּוֹרָה הַכְּתוּבָה עַל יְדֵי מֹשֶׁה עַבְדֶּךָ,
הָאֲמוּרָה מִפִּי אַהֲרֹן וּבָנָיו, כֹּהֲנִים, עַם קְדוֹשֶׁךָ, כָּאָמוּר:

כֵּן יְהִי רָצוֹן.   יְבָרֶכְךָ יהוה וְיִשְׁמְרֶךָ.

כֵּן יְהִי רָצוֹן.   יָאֵר יהוה פָּנָיו אֵלֶיךָ וִיחֻנֶּךָּ.

כֵּן יְהִי רָצוֹן.   יִשָּׂא יהוה פָּנָיו אֵלֶיךָ וְיָשֵׂם לְךָ שָׁלוֹם.

AND GRANT YOU KIND-NESS וִיחֻנֶּךָּ (vi-ḥuneka). This phrase is open to at least two interpretations: that God be kind to you, or that God grant you the capacity for kindness. The latter interpretation is attested to by the midrash: "God grant you the understanding to be kind to one another" (Numbers Rabbah 11:6).

שִׂים שָׁלוֹם בָּעוֹלָם, טוֹבָה וּבְרָכָה, חֵן וָחֶסֶד וְרַחֲמִים
עָלֵינוּ וְעַל כָּל־יִשְׂרָאֵל עַמֶּךָ. בָּרְכֵנוּ אָבִינוּ כֻּלָּנוּ כְּאֶחָד
בְּאוֹר פָּנֶיךָ, כִּי בְאוֹר פָּנֶיךָ נָתַתָּ לָּנוּ, יהוה אֱלֹהֵינוּ, תּוֹרַת
חַיִּים וְאַהֲבַת חֶסֶד, וּצְדָקָה וּבְרָכָה וְרַחֲמִים וְחַיִּים,
וְשָׁלוֹם. וְטוֹב בְּעֵינֶיךָ לְבָרֵךְ אֶת־עַמְּךָ יִשְׂרָאֵל, בְּכָל־עֵת
וּבְכָל־שָׁעָה בִּשְׁלוֹמֶךָ.

בְּסֵפֶר חַיִּים, בְּרָכָה וְשָׁלוֹם וּפַרְנָסָה טוֹבָה, נִזָּכֵר וְנִכָּתֵב
לְפָנֶיךָ, אֲנַחְנוּ וְכָל־עַמְּךָ בֵּית יִשְׂרָאֵל, לְחַיִּים טוֹבִים
וּלְשָׁלוֹם.

וְנֶאֱמַר: כִּי בִי יִרְבּוּ יָמֶיךָ, וְיוֹסִיפוּ לְךָ שְׁנוֹת חַיִּים.
לְחַיִּים טוֹבִים תִּכְתְּבֵנוּ, אֱלֹהִים חַיִּים.
כָּתְבֵנוּ בְּסֵפֶר הַחַיִּים,
כַּכָּתוּב: וְאַתֶּם הַדְּבֵקִים בַּיהוה אֱלֹהֵיכֶם, חַיִּים
כֻּלְּכֶם הַיּוֹם.

GRANT PEACE שִׂים שָׁלוֹם. Every Jewish prayer service ends with a prayer for peace. The midrash says that peace is one of the names of God. The words of Sim Shalom, "grant peace," are related directly to the conclusion of Birkat Kohanim, the priestly blessing: "May God grant You peace." Additionally, the paragraph uses the metaphor of the light of God's face as bestowing blessing. Thus, this *b'rakhah* is traditionally recited at all services at which Birkat Kohanim is recited. On fast days such as Yom Kippur, Birkat Kohanim is recited at all services throughout the day.

INSCRIBE US FOR A GOOD LIFE לְחַיִּים טוֹבִים תִּכְתְּבֵנוּ (l'ḥayyim tovim tikht'veinu). A final plea for a year of life, a good life.

Ninth B'rakhah: Prayer for Peace

If the kohanim do not bless the congregation, we continue here:

Our God and God of our ancestors,
bless us with the threefold blessing of the Torah
written by Moses Your servant,
recited by Aaron and his descendants, the kohanim,
the consecrated priests of Your people:

May ADONAI bless and protect you.

> *So may it be God's will. Kein y'hi ratzon.*

May ADONAI's countenance shine upon you
and grant you kindness.

> *So may it be God's will. Kein y'hi ratzon.*

May ADONAI's countenance be lifted toward you
and grant you peace.

> *So may it be God's will. Kein y'hi ratzon.*

All services continue here:

Grant peace to the world, goodness and blessing, grace, love,
and compassion, for us and for all the people Israel. Bless us,
our creator, united as one with the light of Your presence; by
that light, ADONAI our God, You gave us a guide to life, the
love of kindness, generosity, blessing, compassion, life, and
peace. May it please You to bless Your people Israel at all times
with Your gift of peace.

May we and the entire House of Israel be called to mind and
inscribed for life, blessing, sustenance, and peace in the Book
of Life.

*B'sefer ḥayyim b'rakhah v'shalom u-farnasah tovah,
nizzakher v'nikkatev l'fanekha, anaḥnu v'khol am'kha beit yisra·el,
l'ḥayyim tovim u-l'shalom.*

As it is written: "Through Me shall your days be increased, and
years be added to your life."
Inscribe us for a good life,
You who are the God of life; write us in the Book of Life,
as is written in Your Torah: "And those of you who cling to God
on this day are truly alive today."

הַיּוֹם תְּאַמְּצֵנוּ, אָמֵן.

הַיּוֹם תְּבָרְכֵנוּ, אָמֵן.

הַיּוֹם תְּגַדְּלֵנוּ, אָמֵן.

הַיּוֹם תִּדְרְשֵׁנוּ לְטוֹבָה, אָמֵן.

הַיּוֹם תִּכְתְּבֵנוּ לְחַיִּים טוֹבִים, אָמֵן.

הַיּוֹם תְּקַבֵּל בְּרַחֲמִים וּבְרָצוֹן אֶת־תְּפִלָּתֵנוּ, אָמֵן.

הַיּוֹם תִּשְׁמַע שַׁוְעָתֵנוּ, אָמֵן.

הַיּוֹם תִּתְמְכֵנוּ בִּימִין צִדְקֶךָ, אָמֵן.

The ark is closed.

TODAY הַיּוֹם. The *piyyut* is an alphabetical acrostic, though it has become common to recite only the first four verses, a verse in the middle, and three concluding ones.

ON A DAY LIKE THIS כְּהַיּוֹם. Presumably at a moment like this, when our sins have been forgiven, we face God, the congregation, and the world in purity.

I SHALL BRING YOU וַהֲבִיאוֹתִים. Isaiah 56:7.

כְּהַיּוֹם הַזֶּה תְּבִיאֵנוּ שָׂשִׂים וּשְׂמֵחִים בְּבִנְיַן שָׁלֵם, כַּכָּתוּב עַל יַד נְבִיאֶךָ: וַהֲבִיאוֹתִים אֶל הַר קָדְשִׁי, וְשִׂמַּחְתִּים בְּבֵית תְּפִלָּתִי, כִּי בֵיתִי בֵּית תְּפִלָּה יִקָּרֵא לְכָל־הָעַמִּים. וּצְדָקָה וּבְרָכָה וְרַחֲמִים וְחַיִּים וְשָׁלוֹם יִהְיֶה לָנוּ לְכָל־יִשְׂרָאֵל וּלְכָל־יוֹשְׁבֵי תֵבֵל עַד הָעוֹלָם. בָּרוּךְ אַתָּה יהוה, עוֹשֶׂה הַשָּׁלוֹם.

HA-YOM—THIS DAY: A PIYYUT

The ark is opened.

Strengthen us—today. *Amen.*

Bless us—today. *Amen.*

Exalt us—today. *Amen.*

Seek our well-being—today. *Amen.*

Inscribe us for a good life—today. *Amen.*

Lovingly accept our prayers—today. *Amen.*

Hear our plea—today. *Amen.*

Sustain us with the power of Your righteousness—today. *Amen.*

Ha-yom t'am'tzeinu. Amen.
Ha-yom t'var'kheinu. Amen.
Ha-yom t'gad'leinu. Amen.
Ha-yom tidr'sheinu l'tovah. Amen.
Ha-yom tikht'veinu l'ḥayyim tovim. Amen.
Ha-yom t'kabbel b'raḥamim u-v'ratzon et t'fillateinu. Amen.
Ha-yom tishma shavateinu. Amen.
Ha-yom titm'kheinu bimin tzidkekha. Amen.

The ark is closed.

On a day like this, bring us joyfully to the fullness of redemption. As Your prophet Isaiah said, "I shall bring you to My holy mountain and make you joyous in My house of prayer, for My house shall be called a house of prayer for all people." May we, the entire people Israel and all humanity, be granted justice, blessing, compassion, life, and peace forever. *Barukh atah ADONAI,* who brings peace.

KADDISH SHALEM. The
Kaddish Shalem (literally
"Full Kaddish") ends the
Musaf service. It is called
the "Full Kaddish" because
it includes a plea that the
prayers we have offered be
acceptable.

יִתְגַּדַּל וְיִתְקַדַּשׁ שְׁמֵהּ רַבָּא, בְּעָלְמָא דִּי בְרָא,
כִרְעוּתֵהּ, וְיַמְלִיךְ מַלְכוּתֵהּ בְּחַיֵּיכוֹן וּבְיוֹמֵיכוֹן וּבְחַיֵּי
דְכָל־בֵּית יִשְׂרָאֵל, בַּעֲגָלָא וּבִזְמַן קָרִיב, וְאִמְרוּ אָמֵן.

יְהֵא שְׁמֵהּ רַבָּא מְבָרַךְ לְעָלַם וּלְעָלְמֵי עָלְמַיָּא.

יִתְבָּרַךְ וְיִשְׁתַּבַּח וְיִתְפָּאַר וְיִתְרוֹמַם וְיִתְנַשֵּׂא וְיִתְהַדָּר
וְיִתְעַלֶּה וְיִתְהַלָּל שְׁמֵהּ דְּקֻדְשָׁא, בְּרִיךְ הוּא לְעֵלָּא לְעֵלָּא
מִכָּל־בִּרְכָתָא וְשִׁירָתָא תֻּשְׁבְּחָתָא וְנֶחֱמָתָא דַּאֲמִירָן
בְּעָלְמָא, וְאִמְרוּ אָמֵן.

In some communities, the shofar is blown.
(The shofar is traditionally not blown on Shabbat.)

תקיעה שברים-תרועה תקיעה
תקיעה שברים תקיעה
תקיעה תרועה תקיעה גדולה

תִּתְקַבַּל צְלוֹתְהוֹן וּבָעוּתְהוֹן דְּכָל־יִשְׂרָאֵל קֳדָם אֲבוּהוֹן
דִּי בִשְׁמַיָּא, וְאִמְרוּ אָמֵן.

יְהֵא שְׁלָמָא רַבָּא מִן שְׁמַיָּא וְחַיִּים עָלֵינוּ וְעַל כָּל־
יִשְׂרָאֵל, וְאִמְרוּ אָמֵן.

עֹשֶׂה שָׁלוֹם בִּמְרוֹמָיו הוּא יַעֲשֶׂה שָׁלוֹם עָלֵינוּ וְעַל כָּל־
יִשְׂרָאֵל [וְעַל כָּל־יוֹשְׁבֵי תֵבֵל], וְאִמְרוּ אָמֵן.

Kaddish Shalem

May God's great name be exalted and hallowed throughout the created world, as is God's wish. May God's sovereignty soon be established, in your lifetime and in your days, and in the days of all the House of Israel. And respond with: *Amen.*

May God's great name be acknowledged forever and ever!
Y'hei sh'meih rabba m'varakh l'alam u-l'almei almayya.

May the name of the Holy One be acknowledged and celebrated, lauded and worshipped, exalted and honored, extolled and acclaimed— though God, who is blessed, *b'rikh hu*, is truly far beyond all acknowledgment and praise, or any expressions of gratitude or consolation ever spoken in the House of Israel. And respond with: *Amen.*

In some communities, the shofar is blown.
(The shofar is traditionally not blown on Shabbat.)

T'ki·ah sh'varim-t'ru·ah t'ki·ah
T'ki·ah sh'varim t'ki·ah
T'ki·ah t'ru·ah t'ki·ah g'dolah

May the prayers and pleas of all Israel be accepted by their Creator in heaven. And respond with: *Amen.*

May abundant peace from heaven, and life, come to us and to all Israel. And respond with: *Amen.*

May the One who brings harmony on high, bring harmony to us and to all Israel [and to all who dwell on earth].
And respond with: *Amen.*

Oseh shalom bi-m'romav hu ya·aseh shalom aleinu v'al kol yisra·el
[v'al kol yosh'vei teiveil], v'imru amen.

אֵין כֵּאלֹהֵינוּ, אֵין כַּאדוֹנֵינוּ,
אֵין כְּמַלְכֵּנוּ, אֵין כְּמוֹשִׁיעֵנוּ.
מִי כֵאלֹהֵינוּ, מִי כַאדוֹנֵינוּ,
מִי כְמַלְכֵּנוּ, מִי כְמוֹשִׁיעֵנוּ.
נוֹדֶה לֵאלֹהֵינוּ, נוֹדֶה לַאדוֹנֵינוּ,
נוֹדֶה לְמַלְכֵּנוּ, נוֹדֶה לְמוֹשִׁיעֵנוּ.
בָּרוּךְ אֱלֹהֵינוּ, בָּרוּךְ אֲדוֹנֵינוּ,
בָּרוּךְ מַלְכֵּנוּ, בָּרוּךְ מוֹשִׁיעֵנוּ.
אַתָּה הוּא אֱלֹהֵינוּ, אַתָּה הוּא אֲדוֹנֵינוּ,
אַתָּה הוּא מַלְכֵּנוּ, אַתָּה הוּא מוֹשִׁיעֵנוּ.
אַתָּה הוּא שֶׁהִקְטִירוּ אֲבוֹתֵינוּ לְפָנֶיךָ אֶת־קְטֹרֶת
הַסַּמִּים.

אָמַר רַבִּי אֶלְעָזָר אָמַר רַבִּי חֲנִינָא: תַּלְמִידֵי חֲכָמִים
מַרְבִּים שָׁלוֹם בָּעוֹלָם, שֶׁנֶּאֱמַר: וְכָל־בָּנַיִךְ לִמּוּדֵי יהוה,
וְרַב שְׁלוֹם בָּנָיִךְ, אַל תִּקְרָא בָּנַיִךְ אֶלָּא בּוֹנָיִךְ. שָׁלוֹם רָב
לְאֹהֲבֵי תוֹרָתֶךָ, וְאֵין לָמוֹ מִכְשׁוֹל. יְהִי שָׁלוֹם בְּחֵילֵךְ,
שַׁלְוָה בְּאַרְמְנוֹתָיִךְ. ◁ לְמַעַן אַחַי וְרֵעָי, אֲדַבְּרָה־נָּא
שָׁלוֹם בָּךְ. לְמַעַן בֵּית יהוה אֱלֹהֵינוּ, אֲבַקְשָׁה טוֹב לָךְ.
יהוה עֹז לְעַמּוֹ יִתֵּן, יהוה יְבָרֵךְ אֶת־עַמּוֹ בַשָּׁלוֹם.

In some congregations, the service continues with Kaddish D'rabbanan, page 41.

NONE COMPARES אֵין
כֵּאלֹהֵינוּ. This first-
millennium prayer was
originally composed as
a mystic meditation: the
repetitions served to bring
the devotee to an ecstatic
visionary state. Because of
its simplicity and ease of
recall it became a favorite
prayer with which to
conclude a service. The first
three verses spell out the
acrostic "amen," the last
two *barukh atah*. Note, as
well, that the poem begins
with aleph and ends with
aleph.

RABBI ELAZAR TAUGHT אָמַר
רַבִּי אֶלְעָזָר. The concluding
teaching of the service, one
that is quoted extensively
in the Talmud, expresses
the hope that the teach-
ing and learning we have
experienced today will help
create a world of peace and
that our children will follow
in this path.

**WHEN ALL OF YOUR CHILD-
REN ARE TAUGHT OF THE
LORD,** וְכָל־בָּנַיִךְ לִמּוּדֵי יהוה
וְרַב שְׁלוֹם בָּנָיִךְ. Isaiah 54:13.

**THOSE WHO LOVE YOUR
TORAH HAVE GREAT PEACE**
שָׁלוֹם רָב לְאֹהֲבֵי תוֹרָתֶךָ.
This verse begins a series
of verses all containing a
prayer for peace, offering
a fitting conclusion to this
teaching on peace (Psalms
119:165, 122:7–9, 29:11).

CONCLUDING PRAYERS

Ein Keiloheinu

None compares to our God, to our master.

None compares to our sovereign, to our deliverer.

Who compares to our God, to our master?

Who compares to our sovereign, to our deliverer?

Let us thank our God, our master.

Let us thank our sovereign, our deliverer.

You are our God, our master.

You are our sovereign, our deliverer.

You are the one to whom our ancestors offered fragrant incense.

Ein keiloheinu, ein kadoneinu,
Ein k'malkeinu, ein k'moshi·einu.
Mi kheiloheinu, mi khadoneinu,
Mi kh'malkeinu, mi kh'moshi·einu.
Nodeh leiloheinu, nodeh ladoneinu.
Nodeh l'malkeinu, nodeh l'moshi·einu.
Barukh eloheinu, barukh adoneinu,
Barukh malkeinu, barukh moshi·einu.
Atah hu eloheinu, atah hu adoneinu,
Atah hu malkeinu, atah hu moshi·einu.
Atah hu she-hiktiru avoteinu l'fanekha et k'toret ha-sammim.

A Final Teaching

Rabbi Elazar taught in the name of Rabbi Ḥanina: Disciples of the Sages increase peace in the world, as it was said by the prophet Isaiah: "When all of your children are instructed by ADONAI, great will be the peace of your children." The second mention of "your children" (*banayikh*) means all who have true understanding (*bonayikh*), like disciples of the Sages; they too are taught of ADONAI, serving and blessed with peace. And thus it is written in the Book of Psalms: "Those who love Your Torah have great peace; nothing makes them stumble." And it is also written: "May there be peace within your walls, security within your gates. For the sake of my brethren and companions I say: May peace reside within you. For the sake of the House of ADONAI I will seek your welfare." "May ADONAI grant God's people dignity; may ADONAI bless God's people with peace."

In some congregations, the service continues with Kaddish D'rabbanan, page 41.

We rise.

עָלֵינוּ לְשַׁבֵּחַ לַאֲדוֹן הַכֹּל, לָתֵת גְּדֻלָּה לְיוֹצֵר
בְּרֵאשִׁית, שֶׁלֹּא עָשָׂנוּ כְּגוֹיֵי הָאֲרָצוֹת, וְלֹא שָׂמָנוּ
כְּמִשְׁפְּחוֹת הָאֲדָמָה, שֶׁלֹּא שָׂם חֶלְקֵנוּ כָּהֶם, וְגֹרָלֵנוּ
כְּכָל־הֲמוֹנָם.

‹ וַאֲנַחְנוּ כּוֹרְעִים וּמִשְׁתַּחֲוִים וּמוֹדִים,
לִפְנֵי מֶלֶךְ, מַלְכֵי הַמְּלָכִים, הַקָּדוֹשׁ בָּרוּךְ הוּא.
שֶׁהוּא נוֹטֶה שָׁמַיִם וְיוֹסֵד אָרֶץ, וּמוֹשַׁב יְקָרוֹ בַּשָּׁמַיִם
מִמַּעַל, וּשְׁכִינַת עֻזּוֹ בְּגָבְהֵי מְרוֹמִים, הוּא אֱלֹהֵינוּ אֵין
עוֹד. אֱמֶת מַלְכֵּנוּ אֶפֶס זוּלָתוֹ, כַּכָּתוּב בְּתוֹרָתוֹ:
וְיָדַעְתָּ הַיּוֹם וַהֲשֵׁבֹתָ אֶל־לְבָבֶךָ, כִּי יהוה הוּא
הָאֱלֹהִים בַּשָּׁמַיִם מִמַּעַל, וְעַל הָאָרֶץ מִתַּחַת, אֵין עוֹד.

עַל כֵּן נְקַוֶּה לְךָ יהוה אֱלֹהֵינוּ, לִרְאוֹת מְהֵרָה בְּתִפְאֶרֶת
עֻזֶּךָ, לְהַעֲבִיר גִּלּוּלִים מִן הָאָרֶץ וְהָאֱלִילִים כָּרוֹת יִכָּרֵתוּן,
לְתַקֵּן עוֹלָם בְּמַלְכוּת שַׁדַּי, וְכָל־בְּנֵי בָשָׂר יִקְרְאוּ בִשְׁמֶךָ,
לְהַפְנוֹת אֵלֶיךָ כָּל־רִשְׁעֵי אָרֶץ.
יַכִּירוּ וְיֵדְעוּ כָּל־יוֹשְׁבֵי תֵבֵל, כִּי לְךָ תִּכְרַע כָּל־בֶּרֶךְ,
תִּשָּׁבַע כָּל־לָשׁוֹן. לְפָנֶיךָ יהוה אֱלֹהֵינוּ יִכְרְעוּ וְיִפֹּלוּ,
וְלִכְבוֹד שִׁמְךָ יְקָר יִתֵּנוּ. וִיקַבְּלוּ כֻלָּם אֶת־עֹל מַלְכוּתֶךָ.
וְתִמְלֹךְ עֲלֵיהֶם מְהֵרָה לְעוֹלָם וָעֶד. כִּי הַמַּלְכוּת
שֶׁלְּךָ הִיא, וּלְעוֹלְמֵי עַד תִּמְלוֹךְ בְּכָבוֹד. ‹ כַּכָּתוּב
בְּתוֹרָתֶךָ: יהוה יִמְלֹךְ לְעֹלָם וָעֶד. וְנֶאֱמַר: וְהָיָה יהוה
לְמֶלֶךְ עַל כָּל־הָאָרֶץ, בַּיּוֹם הַהוּא יִהְיֶה יהוה אֶחָד,
וּשְׁמוֹ אֶחָד.

ALEINU עָלֵינוּ. This prayer was originally written for and recited during the *Malkhuyot* מַלְכֻיּוֹת (Sovereignty) section of the Rosh Hashanah Musaf service. Since the late Middle Ages, it has acquired a special pride of place in Ashkenazic liturgy and is recited as part of the conclusion of every service. It is customary to physically bow when we recite the line "And so we bow" וַאֲנַחְנוּ כּוֹרְעִים (*Va-anaḥnu kor'im*).

ESTABLISHING IN THE WORLD THE SOVEREIGNTY OF THE ALMIGHTY לְתַקֵּן עוֹלָם בְּמַלְכוּת שַׁדַּי. Beginning in the nineteenth century, this phrase came to be seen as similar to Isaiah's call to be a light unto the nations, and was interpreted as a call to universal justice. In this vein, the phrase *l'takken olam* לְתַקֵּן עוֹלָם was understood to mean "to repair the world," to be partners with God in achieving a time of peace and righteousness. Even earlier, Maimonides (12th century) had argued that the single most important characteristic of God's sovereignty would be an end to one people dominating another.

ADONAI WILL REIGN FOREVER AND EVER יהוה יִמְלֹךְ לְעֹלָם וָעֶד. Exodus 15:18.

ON THAT DAY ADONAI SHALL BE ONE בַּיּוֹם הַהוּא יִהְיֶה יהוה אֶחָד. Zechariah 14:9. In reciting the Sh'ma, we declare that God is one. Through our prayer we hope to make God one with the world.

We rise.

Aleinu

It is for us to praise the ruler of all, to acclaim the Creator, who has not made us merely a nation, nor formed us as all earthly families, nor given us an ordinary destiny.

ʃ And so we bow, acknowledging the supreme sovereign, the Holy One, who is praised—the One who spreads out the heavens and establishes the earth, whose glorious abode is in the highest heaven, whose powerful presence is in the loftiest heights. This is our God, none else; ours is the true sovereign, there is no other. As it is written in the Torah: "Know this day and take it to heart, that ADONAI is God in heaven above and on earth below; there is no other."

Aleinu l'shabbei·aḥ la-adon ha-kol, la-teit g'dullah l'yotzeir b'reishit,
she-lo asanu k'goyei ha-aratzot, v'lo samanu k'mishp'ḥot ha-adamah,
she-lo sam ḥelkeinu ka-hem, v'goraleinu k'khol hamonam.
ʃ Va-anaḥnu kor'im u-mishtaḥavim u-modim,
lifnei melekh malkhei ha-m'lakhim, ha-kadosh barukh hu.
She-hu noteh shamayim v'yoseid aretz, u-moshav y'karo ba-shamayim mi-ma·al,
u-sh'khinat uzzo b'govhei m'romim, hu eloheinu ein od. Emet malkeinu efes zulato,
ka-katuv b'torato: v'yadata ha-yom va-hasheivota el l'vavekha, ki Adonai hu ha-Elohim
ba-shamayim mi-ma·al, v'al ha-aretz mi-taḥat, ein od.

And so, ADONAI our God, we await You, that soon we may behold Your strength revealed in full glory, sweeping away the abominations of the earth, obliterating idols, establishing in the world the sovereignty of the Almighty. All flesh will call out Your name—even the wicked will turn toward You. Then all who live on earth will recognize and understand that to You alone all knees must bend and allegiance be sworn. All will bow down and prostrate themselves before You, ADONAI our God, honor Your glorious name, and accept the obligation of Your sovereignty. May You soon rule over them forever and ever, for true dominion is Yours; You will rule in glory until the end of time.

As is written in Your Torah: "ADONAI will reign forever and ever." And as the prophet said: "ADONAI shall be acknowledged sovereign of all the earth. On that day ADONAI shall be one, and the name of God, one."

V'ne·emar: v'hayah Adonai l'melekh al kol ha-aretz,
ba-yom ha-hu yihyeh Adonai eḥad, u-sh'mo eḥad.

קַדִּישׁ יָתוֹם

יִתְגַּדַּל וְיִתְקַדַּשׁ שְׁמֵהּ רַבָּא, בְּעָלְמָא דִּי בְרָא, כִּרְעוּתֵהּ, וְיַמְלִיךְ מַלְכוּתֵהּ בְּחַיֵּיכוֹן וּבְיוֹמֵיכוֹן וּבְחַיֵּי דְכָל־בֵּית יִשְׂרָאֵל, בַּעֲגָלָא וּבִזְמַן קָרִיב, וְאִמְרוּ אָמֵן.

יְהֵא שְׁמֵהּ רַבָּא מְבָרַךְ לְעָלַם וּלְעָלְמֵי עָלְמַיָּא.

יִתְבָּרַךְ וְיִשְׁתַּבַּח וְיִתְפָּאַר וְיִתְרוֹמַם וְיִתְנַשֵּׂא וְיִתְהַדָּר וְיִתְעַלֶּה וְיִתְהַלָּל שְׁמֵהּ דְּקֻדְשָׁא, **בְּרִיךְ הוּא**, לְעֵלָּא לְעֵלָּא מִכָּל־בִּרְכָתָא וְשִׁירָתָא תֻּשְׁבְּחָתָא וְנֶחֱמָתָא דַּאֲמִירָן בְּעָלְמָא, וְאִמְרוּ אָמֵן.

יְהֵא שְׁלָמָא רַבָּא מִן שְׁמַיָּא וְחַיִּים עָלֵינוּ וְעַל כָּל־יִשְׂרָאֵל, וְאִמְרוּ אָמֵן.

עֹשֶׂה שָׁלוֹם בִּמְרוֹמָיו הוּא יַעֲשֶׂה שָׁלוֹם עָלֵינוּ וְעַל כָּל־יִשְׂרָאֵל [וְעַל כָּל־יוֹשְׁבֵי תֵבֵל], וְאִמְרוּ אָמֵן.

A Kavvanah for Kaddish

Grant that the memories of those who have gone before us be a source of strength for me and for everyone of the House of Israel. May the souls of our departed find peace in Your sheltering care, and may we all be blessed with peace, tranquility, and the fullness of life.

Mourner's Kaddish

May God's great name be exalted and hallowed throughout the created world, as is God's wish. May God's sovereignty soon be established, in your lifetime and in your days, and in the days of all the House of Israel. And respond with: *Amen.*

May God's great name be acknowledged forever and ever!

May the name of the Holy One be acknowledged and celebrated, lauded and worshipped, exalted and honored, extolled and acclaimed—though God, who is blessed, *b'rikh hu*, is truly far beyond all acknowledgment and praise, or any expressions of gratitude or consolation ever spoken in the world. And respond with: *Amen.*

May abundant peace from heaven, and life, come to us and to all Israel. And respond with: *Amen.*

May the One who brings harmony on high, bring harmony to us and to all Israel [and to all who dwell on earth]. And respond with: *Amen.*

Mourners and those observing Yahrzeit:
Yitgaddal v'yitkaddash sh'meih rabba b'alma di v'ra ki-r'uteih
v'yamlikh malkhuteih b'ḥayyeikhon u-v'yomeikhon u-v'ḥayyei d'khol
beit yisra·el ba-agala u-viz'man kariv v'imru amen.

Congregation and mourners:
Y'hei sh'meih rabba m'varakh l'alam u-l'almei almayya.

Mourners:
Yitbarakh v'yishtabaḥ v'yitpa·ar v'yitromam v'yitnassei v'yit·haddar
v'yit·alleh v'yit·hallal sh'meih d'kudsha b'rikh hu l'eilla l'eilla mi-kol
birkhata v'shirata tushb'ḥata v'neḥamata da-amiran b'alma v'imru
amen.

Y'hei sh'lama rabba min sh'mayya v'ḥayyim aleinu v'al kol yisra·el
v'imru amen.

Oseh shalom bi-m'romav hu ya·aseh shalom aleinu v'al kol yisra·el [v'al
kol yosh'vei teiveil], v'imru amen.

ADON OLAM אֲדוֹן עוֹלָם. It is unclear who authored this thousand-year-old poem, but it appears in the beginning of the morning service, at the conclusion of Musaf (additional) services, and also at the end of evening services in both the Ashkenazic and Sephardic liturgies. The latter version contains several more verses than are found in the former.

אֲדוֹן עוֹלָם אֲשֶׁר מָלַךְ,   בְּטֶרֶם כָּל־יְצִיר נִבְרָא.

לְעֵת נַעֲשָׂה בְחֶפְצוֹ כֹּל,   אֲזַי מֶלֶךְ שְׁמוֹ נִקְרָא.

וְאַחֲרֵי כִּכְלוֹת הַכֹּל,   לְבַדּוֹ יִמְלוֹךְ נוֹרָא.

וְהוּא הָיָה, וְהוּא הֹוֶה,   וְהוּא יִהְיֶה, בְּתִפְאָרָה.

וְהוּא אֶחָד וְאֵין שֵׁנִי,   לְהַמְשִׁיל לוֹ לְהַחְבֵּירָה.

בְּלִי רֵאשִׁית בְּלִי תַכְלִית,   וְלוֹ הָעֹז וְהַמִּשְׂרָה.

וְהוּא אֵלִי וְחַי גֹּאֲלִי,   וְצוּר חֶבְלִי בְּעֵת צָרָה.

וְהוּא נִסִּי וּמָנוֹס לִי,   מְנָת כּוֹסִי בְּיוֹם אֶקְרָא.

בְּיָדוֹ אַפְקִיד רוּחִי,   בְּעֵת אִישַׁן וְאָעִירָה.

וְעִם רוּחִי גְּוִיָּתִי,   יְהֹוָה לִי וְלֹא אִירָא.

בִּרְכַּת פְּרֵידָה
לְשָׁנָה טוֹבָה תִּכָּתֵבוּ וְתֵחָתֵמוּ.

Adon Olam

This poem is the statement of an individual—written in the first-person singular—and is the expression of a person's feelings about God. Beginning with the exalted God of eternity, the Creator of all—majestic and inspiring—the poet moves to the personal God of the individual who cares for human beings at times of woe and into whose hand we can commit our lives, bodies, and souls, and thus have no fear. God the transcendent and the exalted is also God the immanent, who cares for each individual. The poet seems to have created an entire poem based upon an idea expressed in the Book of Psalms:

"Who is like ADONAI
  our God,
Who though enthroned
  on high,
Yet bends to see what is
  below" (Psalm 113:5–6).
  —REUVEN HAMMER
        (adapted)

ADON OLAM

Before creation shaped the world,
    eternally God reigned alone,
But only with creation done
    could God as Sovereign be known.
When all is ended, God alone
    will reign in awe-inspiring majesty.
God was, God is, always will be
    glorious in eternity.
God is unique and without peer,
    with none at all to be compared.
Without beginning, endlessly,
    God's vast dominion is not shared.
But still—my God, my only hope,
    my one true refuge in distress,
My shelter sure, my cup of life,
    with goodness real and limitless.
I place my spirit in God's care;
    my body too can feel God near.
When I sleep, as when I wake,
    God is with me, I have no fear.

Adon olam asher malakh   b'terem kol y'tzir nivra
L'et na·asah v'heftzo kol   azai melekh sh'mo nikra.
V'aharei ki-kh'lot ha-kol   l'vaddo yimlokh nora
V'hu hayah v'hu hoveh   v'hu yihyeh b'tifarah.
V'hu ehad v'ein sheni   l'hamshil lo l'hahbirah.
B'li reishit b'li takhlit   v'lo ha-oz v'ha-misrah.
V'hu eli v'hai go·ali   v'tzur hevli b'et tzarah.
V'hu nissi u-manos li   m'nat kosi b'yom ekra.
B'yado afkid ruhi   b'et ishan v'a·irah
V'im ruhi g'viyyati   Adonai li v'lo ira.

Traditional High Holy Day Greeting
May you be inscribed and sealed for a good year.
L'shanah tovah tikkateivu v'teihateimu.

תשליך TASHLIKH

תשליך

INTRODUCTION. Tashlikh is a ceremony performed near a body of water, preferably one that flows into a larger body of water. It takes place on the first day of Rosh Hashanah, except when the first day falls on Shabbat, in which case it takes place on the second day. The origin of Tashlikh is shrouded in mystery. The first direct mention can be found in the halakhic work of Rabbi Jacob Moellin (Maharil, 15th century), who approved of the custom of going to the water to recite particular biblical verses and prayers on Rosh Hashanah, but specified that it is inappropriate to throw bread in the water to represent the sins that are being cast away. Clearly, both the custom and the bread-throwing preceded him; but we do not know when this tradition began.

The ceremony of Tashlikh survived and grew in popularity, despite significant rabbinic opposition. Some rabbis opposed Tashlikh because it makes the complex process of separating sin from our lives seem too facile, as if it is simply a matter of casting bread from our hands. But Tashlikh survived because it fulfilled a popular need. Most of what we do on Rosh Hashanah depends on verbal expression or on listening. Tashlikh, the symbolic casting away of our sins, constitutes one of the few active rituals of the day.

Tashlikh has been understood in a variety of ways. Throwing bread into the water can be understood as a symbolic casting away of our sins, marking the purification that takes place on these days. Moreover, just as fish eat our bread and what is cast away becomes nourishment, so we pray that even our sins will eventually be turned to good effect in the world. Lastly, just as the waters of the sea go around the world, so too can we, at this moment, become conscious of how we are connected to all that is around us.

Before the bread is cast into the water, the following may be recited:

מִי־אֵל כָּמוֹךָ נֹשֵׂא עָוֹן וְעֹבֵר עַל־פֶּשַׁע לִשְׁאֵרִית נַחֲלָתוֹ,
לֹא־הֶחֱזִיק לָעַד אַפּוֹ כִּי־חָפֵץ חֶסֶד הוּא. יָשׁוּב יְרַחֲמֵנוּ
יִכְבֹּשׁ עֲוֹנֹתֵינוּ וְתַשְׁלִיךְ בִּמְצֻלוֹת יָם כָּל־חַטֹּאתָם. תִּתֵּן
אֱמֶת לְיַעֲקֹב חֶסֶד לְאַבְרָהָם אֲשֶׁר־נִשְׁבַּעְתָּ לַאֲבֹתֵינוּ
מִימֵי קֶדֶם. מיכה ז יח-כ

The following may be added:

קָרָאתִי מִצָּרָה לִי אֶל־יהוה וַיַּעֲנֵנִי מִבֶּטֶן שְׁאוֹל שִׁוַּעְתִּי
שָׁמַעְתָּ קוֹלִי. וַתַּשְׁלִיכֵנִי מְצוּלָה בִּלְבַב יַמִּים וְנָהָר
יְסֹבְבֵנִי כָּל־מִשְׁבָּרֶיךָ וְגַלֶּיךָ עָלַי עָבָרוּ. וַאֲנִי אָמַרְתִּי
נִגְרַשְׁתִּי מִנֶּגֶד עֵינֶיךָ אַךְ אוֹסִיף לְהַבִּיט אֶל־הֵיכַל קָדְשֶׁךָ.
אֲפָפוּנִי מַיִם עַד־נֶפֶשׁ תְּהוֹם יְסֹבְבֵנִי סוּף חָבוּשׁ לְרֹאשִׁי.
לְקִצְבֵי הָרִים יָרַדְתִּי הָאָרֶץ בְּרִחֶיהָ בַעֲדִי לְעוֹלָם וַתַּעַל
מִשַּׁחַת חַיַּי יהוה אֱלֹהָי. בְּהִתְעַטֵּף עָלַי נַפְשִׁי אֶת־יהוה
זָכָרְתִּי וַתָּבוֹא אֵלֶיךָ תְּפִלָּתִי אֶל־הֵיכַל קָדְשֶׁךָ. יונה ב ג-ח

After the bread is cast into the water, one of the following may be recited:

א

לֹא־יָרֵעוּ וְלֹא־יַשְׁחִיתוּ בְּכָל־הַר קָדְשִׁי כִּי־מָלְאָה הָאָרֶץ
דֵּעָה אֶת־יהוה כַּמַּיִם לַיָּם מְכַסִּים. ישעיה יא ט

ב

כִּי־מֵי נֹחַ זֹאת לִי אֲשֶׁר נִשְׁבַּעְתִּי מֵעֲבֹר מֵי־נֹחַ עוֹד עַל־
הָאָרֶץ כֵּן נִשְׁבַּעְתִּי מִקְּצֹף עָלַיִךְ וּמִגְּעָר־בָּךְ. כִּי הֶהָרִים
יָמוּשׁוּ וְהַגְּבָעוֹת תְּמוּטֶינָה וְחַסְדִּי מֵאִתֵּךְ לֹא־יָמוּשׁ
וּבְרִית שְׁלוֹמִי לֹא תָמוּט אָמַר מְרַחֲמֵךְ יהוה. ישעיה נד ט-י

TASHLIKH

The Sea

Throwing bread into the water and reciting the biblical passage mentioning "the deep" is a reminder of the deep out of which the days of creation were formed. Thus, by going to the sea on Rosh Hashanah, we celebrate creation and are led to think of our own place in God's scheme of creation. When we contemplate these matters and repent from our sins, then they are truly thrown away, into the water, and we feel renewed on this Day of Judgment.

—MOSES ISSERLES

Before the bread is cast into the water, the following may be recited:

Is there any divinity save You who forgives the sins and pardons the transgressions of the remnant, Your people? You do not maintain anger forever, for You delight in love. You will return to us compassionately, overcoming the consequences of our sin, hurling our sins into the depths of the sea. You will keep faith with Jacob, showing enduring love to Abraham, as You promised our ancestors in days of old. Micah 7:18-20

The following may be added:

In my trouble I called to ADONAI, who answered me; from the belly of Sheol I cried out, and You heard my voice. You cast me into the depths, into the heart of the sea, the floods engulfed me; all Your breakers and billows swept over me. I thought I was driven away out of Your sight: Would I ever gaze again upon Your holy Temple? The waters closed in over me, the deep engulfed me. Weeds twined around my head. I sank to the base of the mountains; the bars of the earth closed upon me forever. Yet You brought my life up from the pit, O my God ADONAI! When my life was ebbing away, I called ADONAI to mind; and my prayer came before You, into Your holy Temple. Jonah 2:3-8

After the bread is cast into the water, one of the following may be recited:

א

None shall hurt or destroy in all My holy mountain, for the love of ADONAI shall fill the earth as the waters fill the sea.

Isaiah 11:9

ב

For this is like the waters of Noah to Me; for just as I have sworn that the waters of Noah should no more flood the earth; so have I sworn that I will not be angry with you, nor rebuke you. For the mountains may move and the hills shake; but My kindness shall not depart from you, nor shall my covenant of peace be taken away—says ADONAI, who has taken you back in love. Isaiah 54:9–10

מנחה לראש השנה   AFTERNOON SERVICE OF ROSH HASHANAH

אַשְׁרֵי יוֹשְׁבֵי בֵיתֶךָ, עוֹד יְהַלְלוּךָ סֶּלָה.
אַשְׁרֵי הָעָם שֶׁכָּכָה לוֹ, אַשְׁרֵי הָעָם שֶׁיהוה אֱלֹהָיו.

תְּהִלָּה לְדָוִד.

אֲרוֹמִמְךָ אֱלוֹהַי הַמֶּלֶךְ, וַאֲבָרְכָה שִׁמְךָ לְעוֹלָם וָעֶד.
בְּכָל־יוֹם אֲבָרְכֶךָּ, וַאֲהַלְלָה שִׁמְךָ לְעוֹלָם וָעֶד.
גָּדוֹל יהוה וּמְהֻלָּל מְאֹד, וְלִגְדֻלָּתוֹ אֵין חֵקֶר.
דּוֹר לְדוֹר יְשַׁבַּח מַעֲשֶׂיךָ, וּגְבוּרֹתֶיךָ יַגִּידוּ.
הֲדַר כְּבוֹד הוֹדֶךָ, וְדִבְרֵי נִפְלְאֹתֶיךָ אָשִׂיחָה.
וֶעֱזוּז נוֹרְאֹתֶיךָ יֹאמֵרוּ, וּגְדֻלָּתְךָ אֲסַפְּרֶנָּה.
זֵכֶר רַב־טוּבְךָ יַבִּיעוּ, וְצִדְקָתְךָ יְרַנֵּנוּ.
חַנּוּן וְרַחוּם יהוה, אֶרֶךְ אַפַּיִם וּגְדָל־חָסֶד.
טוֹב־יהוה לַכֹּל, וְרַחֲמָיו עַל־כָּל־מַעֲשָׂיו.
יוֹדוּךָ יהוה כָּל־מַעֲשֶׂיךָ, וַחֲסִידֶיךָ יְבָרְכוּכָה.
כְּבוֹד מַלְכוּתְךָ יֹאמֵרוּ, וּגְבוּרָתְךָ יְדַבֵּרוּ.
לְהוֹדִיעַ לִבְנֵי הָאָדָם גְּבוּרֹתָיו, וּכְבוֹד הֲדַר מַלְכוּתוֹ.
מַלְכוּתְךָ מַלְכוּת כָּל־עוֹלָמִים, וּמֶמְשַׁלְתְּךָ בְּכָל־דּוֹר וָדֹר.
סוֹמֵךְ יהוה לְכָל־הַנֹּפְלִים, וְזוֹקֵף לְכָל־הַכְּפוּפִים.
עֵינֵי־כֹל אֵלֶיךָ יְשַׂבֵּרוּ, וְאַתָּה נוֹתֵן לָהֶם אֶת־אָכְלָם בְּעִתּוֹ.
פּוֹתֵחַ אֶת־יָדֶךָ, וּמַשְׂבִּיעַ לְכָל־חַי רָצוֹן.

MINHAH, the afternoon service, is centered on the Amidah. Preparatory prayers—Ashrei (Psalm 145) and U-va L'tziyyon Go-eil ("Adonai has assured a redeemer for Zion")—precede the recitation of the Amidah. When Rosh Hashanah falls on Shabbat, the Torah is removed from the ark and the beginning of the Torah portion for the following Shabbat is read. Avinu Malkeinu is recited after the Amidah (except on Shabbat).

PSALM 145. This psalm, which was treasured by the Rabbis, is recited thrice daily. It was in liturgical use during the Second Temple period. For synagogue use, a verse (Psalm 115:18) was appended to the end, referring to those who are praying in the synagogue. Two additional verses (Psalms 84:5 and 144:15) were added to the opening, both of which begin with the word אַשְׁרֵי (ashrei), "joyous," which has given this psalm its popular name, though the word does not appear in Psalm 145 itself. The psalm begins and ends with personal verses of praise. In the middle verses, the author affirms God's sovereignty, and then immediately connects that affirmation to verses describing God's love and compassion. Ashrei is an alphabetical acrostic and thus easy to remember. Many readers relate to individual verses more than to the literary flow of the whole poem.

MY GOD, MY SOVEREIGN אֱלוֹהַי הַמֶּלֶךְ. The psalmist addresses God directly, establishing a feeling of closeness. On the other hand, the psalmist speaks to God as הַמֶּלֶךְ (ha-melekh), "sovereign." This tension is one that classical Jewish thinkers constantly seek to maintain.

ADONAI IS MERCIFUL AND COMPASSIONATE חַנּוּן וְרַחוּם יהוה. Confirmed by the proclamation of God's attributes to Moses: "A God compassionate and merciful" (Exodus 34:6). This psalm paints a picture of a loving God, who cares for all creatures.

ADONAI SUPPORTS ALL WHO FALTER סוֹמֵךְ יהוה לְכָל־הַנֹּפְלִים. Until now, the poet has praised God's greatness and splendor; with this verse, the focus shifts to God's concern for those in need. Here, God's sovereignty is primarily manifest in love and care.

PREPARATORY PRAYERS

*You Satisfy Each
Person's Will*

Day in, day out
I swallow
the beauty of the world
this hungering beauty

My God
open windows within me
to let the world enter
calmly and peacefully
that more of the world
enter

the world that I love
cry over
and love again and again
—MIRIAM BARUCH HALFI

ASHREI

Joyous are they who dwell in Your house;
they shall praise You forever.
> *Joyous the people who are so favored;*
> *joyous the people whose God is ADONAI.*

PSALM 145
A PSALM OF DAVID.

I exalt You, my God, my sovereign;
I praise Your name, always.
> *Every day I praise You, glorifying Your name, always.*

Great is ADONAI, greatly to be praised,
though God's greatness is unfathomable.
> *One generation praises Your works to another,*
> *telling of Your mighty deeds.*

I would speak of Your majestic glory
and of Your wondrous acts.
> *People speak of Your awe-inspiring deeds;*
> *I, too, shall recount Your greatness.*

They recount Your great goodness,
and sing of Your righteousness.
> *ADONAI is merciful and compassionate,*
> *patient, and abounding in love.*

ADONAI is good to all,
and God's mercy embraces all of creation.
> *All of creation acknowledges You,*
> *and the faithful bless You.*

They speak of the glory of Your sovereignty;
and tell of Your might,
> *proclaiming to humanity Your mighty deeds,*
> *and the glory of Your majestic sovereignty.*

Your sovereignty is eternal,
Your dominion endures through each generation.
> *ADONAI supports all who falter,*
> *and lifts up all who are bent down.*

The eyes of all look hopefully to You,
and You provide them nourishment in due time.
> *You open Your hand,*
> *satisfying all the living with contentment.*

ALL THAT IS MORTAL כָּל־בָּשָׂר. Unlike many other psalms that concentrate on Israel, this psalm is universal. There are no references to the Temple, to Israel, or to historical events. God is depicted as the sovereign of the world who cares for all creatures.

WE SHALL PRAISE וַאֲנַחְנוּ נְבָרֵךְ יָהּ. Psalm 115:18.

ADONAI HAS ASSURED A REDEEMER וּבָא לְצִיּוֹן. This collection of biblical verses is known as the Kedushah D'sidra, most likely because it was recited after Torah study (sidra, the weekly Torah portion). It is part of the concluding section of the weekday morning service, but is recited at the afternoon service on Shabbat and festivals.

Kedushah D'sidra consists of four sections: verses of comfort from the prophet Isaiah (59:20–21); a statement of God's holiness (Psalm 22:40), followed by verses of holiness that are included in all versions of the Kedushah of the Amidah (Isaiah 6:3, Ezekiel 3:12, and Exodus 15:18), together with their Aramaic translation (shown here in gray type); verses about God's forgiving nature (1 Chronicles 29:18; Psalms 78:38, 86:5, 119:142; Micah 7:20; Psalms 68:20, 46:8, 84:13, 20:10); and a passage about the truth of Torah (found on the following page), which concludes with additional verses.

Unlike other versions of the Kedushah, this version includes quotations from

(continued)

צַדִּיק יהוה בְּכָל־דְּרָכָיו, וְחָסִיד בְּכָל־מַעֲשָׂיו.

קָרוֹב יהוה לְכָל־קֹרְאָיו, לְכֹל אֲשֶׁר יִקְרָאֻהוּ בֶאֱמֶת.

רְצוֹן־יְרֵאָיו יַעֲשֶׂה, וְאֶת־שַׁוְעָתָם יִשְׁמַע וְיוֹשִׁיעֵם.

שׁוֹמֵר יהוה אֶת־כָּל־אֹהֲבָיו, וְאֵת כָּל־הָרְשָׁעִים יַשְׁמִיד.

◁ תְּהִלַּת יהוה יְדַבֶּר־פִּי,

וִיבָרֵךְ כָּל־בָּשָׂר שֵׁם קָדְשׁוֹ לְעוֹלָם וָעֶד. תהלים קמה.

וַאֲנַחְנוּ נְבָרֵךְ יָהּ, מֵעַתָּה וְעַד־עוֹלָם. הַלְלוּ־יָהּ.

וּבָא לְצִיּוֹן גּוֹאֵל וּלְשָׁבֵי פֶשַׁע בְּיַעֲקֹב, נְאֻם יהוה.

וַאֲנִי זֹאת בְּרִיתִי אוֹתָם, אָמַר יהוה, רוּחִי אֲשֶׁר עָלֶיךָ,

וּדְבָרַי אֲשֶׁר־שַׂמְתִּי בְּפִיךָ, לֹא־יָמוּשׁוּ מִפִּיךָ וּמִפִּי זַרְעֲךָ

וּמִפִּי זֶרַע זַרְעֲךָ, אָמַר יהוה, מֵעַתָּה וְעַד־עוֹלָם.

◁ וְאַתָּה קָדוֹשׁ, יוֹשֵׁב תְּהִלּוֹת יִשְׂרָאֵל.

וְקָרָא זֶה אֶל־זֶה וְאָמַר: **קָדוֹשׁ קָדוֹשׁ קָדוֹשׁ יהוה צְבָאוֹת, מְלֹא כָל־הָאָרֶץ כְּבוֹדוֹ.** וּמְקַבְּלִין דֵּין מִן דֵּין וְאָמְרִין: קַדִּישׁ בִּשְׁמֵי מְרוֹמָא עִלָּאָה בֵּית שְׁכִינְתֵּהּ, קַדִּישׁ עַל אַרְעָא עוֹבַד גְּבוּרְתֵּהּ, קַדִּישׁ לְעָלַם וּלְעָלְמֵי עָלְמַיָּא, יהוה צְבָאוֹת, מַלְיָא כָל־אַרְעָא זִיו יְקָרֵהּ.

◁ וַתִּשָּׂאֵנִי רוּחַ, וָאֶשְׁמַע אַחֲרַי קוֹל רַעַשׁ גָּדוֹל: **בָּרוּךְ כְּבוֹד יהוה מִמְּקוֹמוֹ.** וּנְטָלַתְנִי רוּחָא, וְשִׁמְעֵת בַּתְרַי קָל זִיעַ סַגִּיא, דִּמְשַׁבְּחִין וְאָמְרִין: בְּרִיךְ יְקָרָא דַיהוה מֵאֲתַר בֵּית שְׁכִינְתֵּהּ.

◁ **יהוה יִמְלֹךְ לְעֹלָם וָעֶד.** יהוה מַלְכוּתֵהּ קָאֵם לְעָלַם וּלְעָלְמֵי עָלְמַיָּא.

יהוה אֱלֹהֵי אַבְרָהָם יִצְחָק וְיִשְׂרָאֵל אֲבֹתֵינוּ, שָׁמְרָה־זֹּאת לְעוֹלָם לְיֵצֶר מַחְשְׁבוֹת לְבַב עַמֶּךָ, וְהָכֵן לְבָבָם אֵלֶיךָ.

וְהוּא רַחוּם יְכַפֵּר עָוֺן וְלֹא יַשְׁחִית, וְהִרְבָּה לְהָשִׁיב אַפּוֹ, וְלֹא־יָעִיר כָּל־חֲמָתוֹ.

כִּי אַתָּה אֲדֹנָי טוֹב וְסַלָּח, וְרַב חֶסֶד לְכָל־קֹרְאֶיךָ.

צִדְקָתְךָ צֶדֶק לְעוֹלָם, וְתוֹרָתְךָ אֱמֶת.

ADONAI is righteous in all that is done, faithful to all creation.
ADONAI is near to all who call, to all who sincerely call.
God fulfills the desire of those who are faithful,
listening to their cries, rescuing them.
ADONAI watches over all those who love the Holy One,
but will destroy all the wicked.
My mouth shall utter praise of ADONAI.
May all that is mortal praise God's name forever and ever.

We shall praise ADONAI now and always. Halleluyah!

ADONAI has assured a redeemer for Zion, for those of the House of
Jacob who turn from sin. ADONAI has said: "This is My covenant
with them: My spirit shall remain with you and with your descen-
dants. My words shall be upon your lips and upon the lips of your
children and your children's children, now and forever."
And You, O Holy One, are enthroned through the praises of the people
Israel.
The angels on high called out one to another: "Holy, holy, holy is *Adonai
Tz'va·ot*, the whole world is filled with God's glory."
Kadosh, kadosh, kadosh Adonai Tz'va·ot, m'lo khol ha-aretz k'vodo.

They receive sanction from one another, saying: "*Adonai Tz'va·ot* is holy
in the highest heavens, holy on the earth, and holy forever, through-
out all time; the radiance of God's glory fills the whole world."
Then a wind lifted me up and I heard the sound of a great rushing
behind me, saying: "Praised is ADONAI's glory wherever God dwells."
Barukh k'vod Adonai mi-m'komo.
ADONAI will reign forever and ever.
Adonai yimlokh l'olam va·ed.

ADONAI, God of our ancestors Abraham, Isaac, and Israel, impress this
always upon Your people, and direct our hearts toward You.
God, being merciful, grants atonement for sin and does not destroy.
Time and again God restrains wrath, refusing to let rage be all-
consuming.
You, ADONAI, are kind and forgiving, loving to all who call upon You.
Your righteousness is everlasting; Your Torah is truth.

תִּתֵּן אֱמֶת לְיַעֲקֹב, חֶסֶד לְאַבְרָהָם, אֲשֶׁר נִשְׁבַּעְתָּ
לַאֲבֹתֵינוּ מִימֵי קֶדֶם.
בָּרוּךְ אֲדֹנָי, יוֹם יוֹם יַעֲמָס־לָנוּ, הָאֵל יְשׁוּעָתֵנוּ סֶלָה.
יהוה צְבָאוֹת עִמָּנוּ, מִשְׂגָּב־לָנוּ אֱלֹהֵי יַעֲקֹב סֶלָה.
יהוה צְבָאוֹת, אַשְׁרֵי אָדָם בֹּטֵחַ בָּךְ.
יהוה הוֹשִׁיעָה, הַמֶּלֶךְ יַעֲנֵנוּ בְיוֹם־קָרְאֵנוּ.

בָּרוּךְ הוּא אֱלֹהֵינוּ, שֶׁבְּרָאָנוּ לִכְבוֹדוֹ, וְהִבְדִּילָנוּ מִן
הַתּוֹעִים, וְנָתַן לָנוּ תּוֹרַת אֱמֶת, וְחַיֵּי עוֹלָם נָטַע בְּתוֹכֵנוּ.
הוּא יִפְתַּח לִבֵּנוּ בְּתוֹרָתוֹ וְיָשֵׂם בְּלִבֵּנוּ אַהֲבָתוֹ וְיִרְאָתוֹ,
וְלַעֲשׂוֹת רְצוֹנוֹ וּלְעָבְדוֹ בְּלֵבָב שָׁלֵם, לְמַעַן לֹא נִיגַע
לָרִיק, וְלֹא נֵלֵד לַבֶּהָלָה.
יְהִי רָצוֹן מִלְּפָנֶיךָ, יהוה אֱלֹהֵינוּ וֵאלֹהֵי אֲבוֹתֵינוּ
[וְאִמּוֹתֵינוּ], שֶׁנִּשְׁמֹר חֻקֶּיךָ בָּעוֹלָם הַזֶּה, וְנִזְכֶּה
וְנִחְיֶה וְנִרְאֶה, וְנִירַשׁ טוֹבָה וּבְרָכָה, לִשְׁנֵי יְמוֹת
הַמָּשִׁיחַ, וּלְחַיֵּי הָעוֹלָם הַבָּא.

לְמַעַן יְזַמֶּרְךָ כָבוֹד וְלֹא יִדֹּם, יהוה אֱלֹהַי לְעוֹלָם אוֹדֶךָּ.
בָּרוּךְ הַגֶּבֶר אֲשֶׁר יִבְטַח בַּיהוה, וְהָיָה יהוה מִבְטַחוֹ.
בִּטְחוּ בַיהוה עֲדֵי־עַד, כִּי בְּיָהּ יהוה צוּר עוֹלָמִים.
◁ וְיִבְטְחוּ בְךָ יוֹדְעֵי שְׁמֶךָ, כִּי לֹא־עָזַבְתָּ דֹרְשֶׁיךָ יהוה.
יהוה חָפֵץ לְמַעַן צִדְקוֹ, יַגְדִּיל תּוֹרָה וְיַאְדִּיר.

חֲצִי קַדִּישׁ

יִתְגַּדַּל וְיִתְקַדַּשׁ שְׁמֵהּ רַבָּא, בְּעָלְמָא דִּי בְרָא, כִּרְעוּתֵהּ,
וְיַמְלִיךְ מַלְכוּתֵהּ בְּחַיֵּיכוֹן וּבְיוֹמֵיכוֹן וּבְחַיֵּי דְכָל־בֵּית
יִשְׂרָאֵל, בַּעֲגָלָא וּבִזְמַן קָרִיב, וְאִמְרוּ אָמֵן.

יְהֵא שְׁמֵהּ רַבָּא מְבָרַךְ לְעָלַם וּלְעָלְמֵי עָלְמַיָּא.

יִתְבָּרַךְ וְיִשְׁתַּבַּח וְיִתְפָּאַר וְיִתְרוֹמַם וְיִתְנַשֵּׂא וְיִתְהַדָּר
וְיִתְעַלֶּה וְיִתְהַלָּל שְׁמֵהּ דְּקֻדְשָׁא, בְּרִיךְ הוּא, לְעֵלָּא
לְעֵלָּא מִכָּל־בִּרְכָתָא וְשִׁירָתָא תֻּשְׁבְּחָתָא וְנֶחֱמָתָא
דַּאֲמִירָן בְּעָלְמָא, וְאִמְרוּ אָמֵן.

On days other than Shabbat, we continue with the Amidah on page 187.

(continued from previous page)
Ezekiel's description of his personal experience of God. The prayer may be expressing the hope that we too may partake of that profound experience.
(adapted from Reuven Hammer)

PRAISED IS OUR GOD בָּרוּךְ הוּא אֱלֹהֵינוּ. This sentence begins the prayerful ending of this passage. The phrase "not labor in vain, nor shall our children suffer confusion" is taken from Isaiah 65:23, but in its context here it may also be understood as "that we may not act meaninglessly or sow confusion."

THUS I WILL SING לְמַעַן יְזַמֶּרְךָ. Psalm 30:13.

BLESSED IS THE ONE בָּרוּךְ הַגֶּבֶר. Jeremiah 17:7.

TRUST IN ADONAI בִּטְחוּ בַיהוה. Isaiah 26:4.

THOSE WHO LOVE YOU וְיִבְטְחוּ בְךָ. Psalm 9:11.

ADONAI . . . EXALTS יהוה חָפֵץ. Isaiah 42:21.

MAY GOD'S GREAT NAME יְהֵא שְׁמֵהּ. Whenever the people Israel enter the synagogue and house of study and proclaim: יְהֵא שְׁמֵהּ רַבָּא מְבָרַךְ לְעָלַם וּלְעָלְמֵי עָלְמַיָּא (Y'hei sh'meih rabba m'varakh l'alam u-l'almei almayya), "May God's great name be acknowledged forever and ever," the Holy One nods and says: "Happy is the sovereign in whose house such praise is spoken" (Babylonian Talmud, Berakhot 3a).

You will be faithful to Jacob and merciful to Abraham, fulfilling the promise You made to our ancestors.

> *Praised is* ADONAI, *the God of our deliverance, who sustains us day after day.*

Adonai Tz'va·ot is with us; the God of Jacob is our refuge.

> *Adonai Tz'va·ot, blessed is the one who trusts in You.*

ADONAI, help us; answer us, Sovereign, when we call.

> *Praised is our God who created us for the divine glory, setting us apart from those who go astray, giving us the Torah, which is truth, and planting within us eternal life.*

May God open our hearts to the Torah—inspiring us to love, revere, and wholeheartedly serve God. Thus shall we not labor in vain, nor shall our children suffer confusion.

> ADONAI, *our God and God of our ancestors, may we fulfill Your precepts in this world, to be worthy of happiness and blessing in the messianic era and in the world to come.*

Thus I will sing Your praise unceasingly; thus I will exalt You, ADONAI my God, forever.

> *Blessed is the one who trusts in* ADONAI.

Trust in ADONAI forever and ever; ADONAI is an unfailing stronghold.

> *Those who love You trust in You; You never forsake those who seek You,* ADONAI.

ADONAI, through divine righteousness, exalts the Torah with greatness and glory.

Ḥatzi Kaddish

May God's great name be exalted and hallowed throughout the created world, as is God's wish. May God's sovereignty soon be established, in your lifetime and in your days, and in the days of all the House of Israel. And respond with: *Amen.*

May God's great name be acknowledged forever and ever!
Y'hei sh'meih rabba m'varakh l'alam u-l'almei almayya.

May the name of the Holy One be acknowledged and celebrated, lauded and worshipped, exalted and honored, extolled and acclaimed— though God, who is blessed, *b'rikh hu,* is truly far beyond all acknowledgment and praise, or any expressions of gratitude or consolation ever spoken in the world. And respond with: *Amen.*

On days other than Shabbat, we continue with the Amidah on page 187.

סֵדֶר קְרִיאַת הַתּוֹרָה לְשַׁבָּת

הוֹצָאַת הַתּוֹרָה

וַאֲנִי תְפִלָּתִי־לְךָ יהוה עֵת רָצוֹן, אֱלֹהִים בְּרׇב־חַסְדֶּךָ עֲנֵנִי בֶּאֱמֶת יִשְׁעֶךָ.

We rise as the ark is opened.

וַיְהִי בִּנְסֹעַ הָאָרֹן וַיֹּאמֶר מֹשֶׁה:
קוּמָה יהוה וְיָפֻצוּ אֹיְבֶיךָ, וְיָנֻסוּ מְשַׂנְאֶיךָ מִפָּנֶיךָ.

כִּי מִצִּיּוֹן תֵּצֵא תוֹרָה, וּדְבַר יהוה מִירוּשָׁלָיִם.
בָּרוּךְ שֶׁנָּתַן תּוֹרָה לְעַמּוֹ יִשְׂרָאֵל בִּקְדֻשָּׁתוֹ.

Leader:

גַּדְּלוּ לַיהוה אִתִּי, וּנְרוֹמְמָה שְׁמוֹ יַחְדָּו.

Congregation and leader:

לְךָ יהוה הַגְּדֻלָּה וְהַגְּבוּרָה וְהַתִּפְאֶרֶת וְהַנֵּצַח וְהַהוֹד,
כִּי־כֹל בַּשָּׁמַיִם וּבָאָרֶץ,
לְךָ יהוה הַמַּמְלָכָה וְהַמִּתְנַשֵּׂא לְכֹל לְרֹאשׁ.
רוֹמְמוּ יהוה אֱלֹהֵינוּ וְהִשְׁתַּחֲווּ לַהֲדֹם רַגְלָיו,
קָדוֹשׁ הוּא.
רוֹמְמוּ יהוה אֱלֹהֵינוּ וְהִשְׁתַּחֲווּ לְהַר קָדְשׁוֹ,
כִּי־קָדוֹשׁ יהוה אֱלֹהֵינוּ.

TORAH READING. Each week in the synagogue, the coming week's Torah portion is begun on the previous Shabbat afternoon. By preserving this tradition on Rosh Hashanah, we connect our observance of the New Year with the weekly Shabbat cycle that forms the ongoing rhythm of Jewish life. When Rosh Hashanah falls on Shabbat, the Torah portion that is read on the following Shabbat (called Shabbat Shuvah) is always Ha·azinu, which consists of Deuteronomy 32.

AS THE ARK WAS CARRIED FORWARD וַיְהִי בִּנְסֹעַ. Numbers 10:35. Reciting this verse evokes a period of special closeness between God and Israel, both at Sinai and in their journey through the desert. This verse is from a description of how the people moved from one encampment to another. It depicts the Ark as the seat of divine protection, leading the march and warding off the fledgling nation's enemies.

TORAH SHALL GO FORTH FROM ZION כִּי מִצִּיּוֹן. Isaiah 2:3. As the ark is opened, we express our belief that Torah contains ideals appropriate to all humanity. Isaiah envisioned all the nations of the world coming to Mount Zion and worshipping one God.

ACCLAIM גַּדְּלוּ *gad'lu.* Psalm 34:4.

YOURS, ADONAI לְךָ יהוה (*l'kha Adonai*). 1 Chronicles 29:11. According to the Chronicler, these verses were part of David's last speech to the people Israel.

EXALT ADONAI רוֹמְמוּ יהוה (*rom'mu Adonai*). Two verses with the same opening words, taken from Psalm 99:5, 9.

TORAH SERVICE FOR SHABBAT

Taking Out the Torah

May this be an auspicious time, ADONAI, for my prayer.
God, in Your abundant mercy,
answer me with Your faithful deliverance.
Va-ani t'fillati l'kha, Adonai, eit ratzon.
Elohim b'rov ḥasdekha, aneini be-emet yish·ekha.

We rise as the ark is opened.
As the Ark was carried forward, Moses would say:
ADONAI! Scatter Your foes, so that Your enemies flee Your Presence.

Torah shall go forth from Zion,
and the word of ADONAI from Jerusalem.
Praised is the One who gave Torah to the people Israel
in holiness.
Ki mi-tziyyon teitzei torah, u-d'var Adonai mi-rushalayim.
Barukh she-natan torah l'ammo yisra·el bi-k'dushato.

Leader:
ʄ Acclaim ADONAI with me; let us exalt God's name together.

Congregation and leader:
Yours, ADONAI, is the greatness, the power, the splendor, the triumph,
and the majesty—for all in heaven and on earth is Yours. Yours is the sovereignty, above all else. Exalt ADONAI our God, and bow down at God's
throne, for our God is holy. Exalt ADONAI our God, bow toward God's
holy mountain, for ADONAI our God is holy.
L'kha Adonai ha-g'dullah v'ha-g'vurah
v'ha-tiferet v'ha-neitzaḥ v'ha-hod,
ki khol ba-shamayim u-va-aretz.
L'kha Adonai ha-mamlakhah v'ha-mitnassei l'khol l'rosh.
Rom'mu Adonai eloheinu v'hishtaḥavu la-hadom raglav,
kadosh hu.
Rom'mu Adonai eloheinu v'hishtaḥavu l'har kodsho,
ki kadosh Adonai eloheinu.

אַב הָרַחֲמִים הוּא יְרַחֵם עַם עֲמוּסִים, וְיִזְכֹּר בְּרִית אֵיתָנִים, וְיַצִּיל נַפְשׁוֹתֵינוּ מִן הַשָּׁעוֹת הָרָעוֹת, וְיִגְעַר בְּיֵצֶר הָרַע מִן הַנְּשׂוּאִים, וְיָחֹן אוֹתָנוּ לִפְלֵיטַת עוֹלָמִים, וִימַלֵּא מִשְׁאֲלוֹתֵינוּ בְּמִדָּה טוֹבָה יְשׁוּעָה וְרַחֲמִים.

Torah Reader (or Gabbai):

וְתִגָּלֶה וְתֵרָאֶה מַלְכוּתוֹ עָלֵינוּ בִּזְמַן קָרוֹב, וְיָחֹן פְּלֵיטָתֵנוּ וּפְלֵיטַת עַמּוֹ בֵּית יִשְׂרָאֵל לְחֵן וּלְחֶסֶד לְרַחֲמִים וּלְרָצוֹן, וְנֹאמַר אָמֵן. הַכֹּל הָבוּ גֹדֶל לֵאלֹהֵינוּ, וּתְנוּ כָבוֹד לַתּוֹרָה.

(כֹּהֵן, קְרָב: יַעֲמֹד _____ בֶּן _____ הַכֹּהֵן.)

(בַּת כֹּהֵן, קָרְבִי: תַּעֲמֹד _____ בַּת _____ הַכֹּהֵן.)

(יַעֲמֹד _____ בֶּן _____ רִאשׁוֹן.)

(תַּעֲמֹד _____ בַּת _____ רִאשׁוֹנָה.)

בָּרוּךְ שֶׁנָּתַן תּוֹרָה לְעַמּוֹ יִשְׂרָאֵל בִּקְדֻשָּׁתוֹ.

Congregation and Torah Reader:

וְאַתֶּם הַדְּבֵקִים בַּיהוה אֱלֹהֵיכֶם, חַיִּים כֻּלְּכֶם הַיּוֹם.

The person who is honored with an aliyah recites the following before the Torah is read:

בָּרְכוּ אֶת־יהוה הַמְבֹרָךְ.

The congregation responds:

בָּרוּךְ יהוה הַמְבֹרָךְ לְעוֹלָם וָעֶד.

The person repeats the above response, then continues:

בָּרוּךְ אַתָּה יהוה אֱלֹהֵינוּ מֶלֶךְ הָעוֹלָם, אֲשֶׁר בָּחַר בָּנוּ מִכָּל־הָעַמִּים וְנָתַן לָנוּ אֶת־תּוֹרָתוֹ. בָּרוּךְ אַתָּה יהוה, נוֹתֵן הַתּוֹרָה.

The person who is honored recites the following after the Torah is read:

בָּרוּךְ אַתָּה יהוה אֱלֹהֵינוּ מֶלֶךְ הָעוֹלָם, אֲשֶׁר נָתַן לָנוּ תּוֹרַת אֱמֶת, וְחַיֵּי עוֹלָם נָטַע בְּתוֹכֵנוּ. בָּרוּךְ אַתָּה יהוה, נוֹתֵן הַתּוֹרָה.

HAS CHOSEN US בָּחַר בָּנוּ. At the moment of approaching the Torah, one may feel especially chosen and may also experience the moment as being directly commanded.

GIVING US THE TORAH . . . WHO GIVES THE TORAH נוֹתֵן הַתּוֹרָה . . . וְנָתַן לָנוּ אֶת־תּוֹרָתוֹ. In Hebrew, the *b'rakhah* uses both the present and the past tense. God not only gave us the Torah in the past, but also we receive it anew whenever we devote ourselves to studying it.

ALIYOT. During the talmudic era, each person called to the Torah would chant the assigned passage directly from the scroll. The first person would recite the opening *b'rakhah*, while the last recited the closing one. Over time, the practice evolved. Today, each person called to the Torah recites both *b'rakhot*, and the Torah is chanted by a designated reader.

The Rabbis instituted a practice of calling a *kohen* for the first aliyah and a *levi* for the second, in order to mitigate arguments about who deserved the opening honors. Some modern congregations retain this traditional practice; others call their congregants to *aliyot* without regard to priestly status.

Each person called to the Torah uses either the corner of the *tallit* or the Torah binder to touch the scroll at the starting place (indicated by the reader) and then kisses the *tallit* or binder, reciting the *b'rakhah* while holding the handles of the Torah. When the reading is completed, that person repeats the kissing gesture at the ending place, rolls the Torah closed, and, holding the handles of the Torah, recites the final *b'rakhah*.

When I read Torah, I am a link in a very long chain that shapes my identity; it is a ritual of personal and communal self-definition, as well as a reenactment of the first public reading of the Torah by Ezra and the scribes rededicating the Temple. I enunciate the words, and add my own meaning to the centuries of interpretation that preceded me; thus they serve both as a key to my own inner life and as a form of historical identification.

—RAYMOND SCHEINDLIN

May the One who is the source of compassion, who has always sustained us, have mercy on us, and remember the covenant with our ancestors. May God save us in difficult times, restrain the impulse to evil within us, and grace our lives with enduring deliverance. May our pleas be answered with a measure of kindness, salvation, and compassion.

Torah Reader (or Gabbai):

May God's sovereignty be revealed to us soon. May God favor the remnant of the people Israel with grace and kindness, with compassion and love.
And let us say: *Amen.*
Let us all declare the greatness of God and give honor to the Torah as (*the first to be called to the Torah*) comes forward. Praised is God who gave the Torah to Israel in holiness.

Congregation and Torah Reader:

You who cling to Adonai your God have been sustained to this day.
V'attem ha-d'veikim badonai eloheikhem ḥayyim kull'khem ha-yom.

B'RAKHOT RECITED BY ONE CALLED UP TO THE TORAH
The person who is honored with an aliyah recites the following before the Torah is read:

Praise Adonai, to whom all prayer is directed.

The congregation responds:

Praise Adonai, to whom all prayer is directed forever and ever.
Barukh Adonai ha-m'vorakh l'olam va·ed.

The person repeats the above response, then continues:

Barukh atah Adonai, our God, ruler of time and space, who has chosen us from among all peoples, giving us the Torah. *Barukh atah Adonai,* who gives the Torah.

The person who is honored recites the following after the Torah is read:

Barukh atah Adonai, our God, ruler of time and space, who has given us a teaching of truth, planting eternal life in our midst. *Barukh atah Adonai,* who gives the Torah.

קְרִיאַת הַתּוֹרָה

דְּבָרִים לב

ראשון א הַאֲזִינוּ הַשָּׁמַיִם וַאֲדַבֵּרָה וְתִשְׁמַע הָאָרֶץ אִמְרֵי־
פִי: ב יַעֲרֹף כַּמָּטָר לִקְחִי תִּזַּל כַּטַּל אִמְרָתִי כִּשְׂעִירִם
עֲלֵי־דֶשֶׁא וְכִרְבִיבִים עֲלֵי־עֵשֶׂב: ג כִּי שֵׁם יהוה אֶקְרָא
הָבוּ גֹדֶל לֵאלֹהֵינוּ:

שני ד הַצּוּר תָּמִים פָּעֳלוֹ כִּי כָל־דְּרָכָיו מִשְׁפָּט אֵל אֱמוּנָה
וְאֵין עָוֶל צַדִּיק וְיָשָׁר הוּא: ה שִׁחֵת לוֹ לֹא בָּנָיו מוּמָם
דּוֹר עִקֵּשׁ וּפְתַלְתֹּל: ו הֲלַיהוה תִּגְמְלוּ־זֹאת עַם נָבָל וְלֹא
חָכָם הֲלוֹא־הוּא אָבִיךָ קָּנֶךָ הוּא עָשְׂךָ וַיְכֹנְנֶךָ:

שלישי ז זְכֹר יְמוֹת עוֹלָם בִּינוּ שְׁנוֹת דֹּר־וָדֹר שְׁאַל אָבִיךָ
וְיַגֵּדְךָ זְקֵנֶיךָ וְיֹאמְרוּ לָךְ: ח בְּהַנְחֵל עֶלְיוֹן גּוֹיִם בְּהַפְרִידוֹ
בְּנֵי אָדָם יַצֵּב גְּבֻלֹת עַמִּים לְמִסְפַּר בְּנֵי יִשְׂרָאֵל: ט כִּי
חֵלֶק יהוה עַמּוֹ יַעֲקֹב חֶבֶל נַחֲלָתוֹ: י יִמְצָאֵהוּ בְּאֶרֶץ
מִדְבָּר וּבְתֹהוּ יְלֵל יְשִׁמֹן יְסֹבְבֶנְהוּ יְבוֹנְנֵהוּ יִצְּרֶנְהוּ
כְּאִישׁוֹן עֵינוֹ: יא כְּנֶשֶׁר יָעִיר קִנּוֹ עַל־גּוֹזָלָיו יְרַחֵף יִפְרֹשׂ
כְּנָפָיו יִקָּחֵהוּ יִשָּׂאֵהוּ עַל־אֶבְרָתוֹ: יב יהוה בָּדָד יַנְחֶנּוּ
וְאֵין עִמּוֹ אֵל נֵכָר:

TORAH READING. The Torah reading is taken from Deuteronomy 32, Moses' speech to Israel before his death. It poetically describes the consequences of Israel's anticipated betrayal of the covenant with God, while acknowledging the divine might and favor that have blessed Israel in the past. Some of the themes, especially those of God as judge and of God as a caring parent, connect to themes of Rosh Hashanah.

VERSE 1. The instruments of God's creation are witnesses to God's word. "Heaven and earth" function here as objective onlookers, who serve as witnesses to the poem's charges and the fairness of God's punishment of Israel. **VERSE 4.** This verse introduces the first theme of the poem: God has treated Israel justly. **ROCK** צוּר. *Tzur*; this term for God expresses the idea that the deity is a source of refuge, a protector. Protecting forts were located on high rocky hills. **VERSE 5. UNWORTHY CHILDREN** לֹא בָּנָיו מוּמָם. The poem uses a parent-child metaphor to express God's relationship with Israel. Israel, in contrast to God, is faithless and perfidious, a "crooked, perverse generation." There is a dual edge to this metaphor: a child's sinfulness against a parent is especially wrongful, but the parent, loving the child, will certainly take the child back when the child is ready to return. The translation of this verse is a paraphrase because the text is difficult and the meaning of the Hebrew is uncertain. **VERSE 6.** Continuing with the parent-child metaphor, the poem now addresses the Israelites directly. They are charged with responding to God's benefactions with ingratitude and rebellion. **VERSE 8. MOST HIGH** עֶלְיוֹן. *Elyon* is frequently used in the Bible (primarily in poetic passages) as a title of God. Here it emphasizes God's supremacy over all beings that Israel may have considered divine. The demand that Israel worship only God connects the reading to a major theme of Rosh Hashanah: God's sovereignty. **VERSE 11.** God led Israel safely through the desert in the manner of an eagle, who is said to train its young to fly and catches them on its back when they tire or fall.

Torah Reading DEUTERONOMY 32

First aliyah 1 Give ear, O heavens, let me speak;
　　　let the earth hear the words I utter!
2 May my discourse come down as the rain,
　　　my speech distill as the dew,
like showers on young growth,
　　　like droplets on the grass.
3 For the name of ADONAI I proclaim;
　　　give glory to our God!

Second aliyah 4 The Rock!—whose deeds are perfect,
　　　yea, all God's ways are just;
A faithful God, never false,
　　　true and upright indeed.
5 Unworthy children—
　　　that crooked, perverse generation—
　　　their baseness has played God false.
6 Do you thus requite ADONAI,
　　　O dull and witless people?
Is not this the Father who created you—
　　　fashioned you and made you endure!

Third aliyah 7 Remember the days of old,
　　　consider the years of ages past;
Ask your parent, who will inform you,
　　　your elders, who will tell you:
8 When the Most High gave nations their homes
　　　and set the divisions of humanity,
[God] fixed the boundaries of peoples
　　　in relation to Israel's numbers.
9 For ADONAI's portion is this people;
　　　Jacob, God's own allotment.

10 [God] found them in a desert region,
　　　in an empty howling waste.
[God] engirded them, watched over them,
　　　guarded them as the pupil of God's eye.
11 Like an eagle who rouses its nestlings,
　　　gliding down to its young,
so did [God] spread wings and take them,
　　　bear them along on pinions;
12 ADONAI alone did guide them,
　　　no alien god alongside.

הַגְבָּהַת הַתּוֹרָה

A Magbiah and Golel are called to raise and tie the Sefer Torah.
As the Torah is lifted, we rise and recite:

וְזֹאת הַתּוֹרָה אֲשֶׁר־שָׂם מֹשֶׁה לִפְנֵי בְּנֵי יִשְׂרָאֵל,
עַל־פִּי יהוה בְּיַד־מֹשֶׁה.

הַכְנָסַת הַתּוֹרָה

Leader:

יְהַלְלוּ אֶת־שֵׁם יהוה, כִּי־נִשְׂגָּב שְׁמוֹ לְבַדּוֹ.

Congregation:

הוֹדוֹ עַל־אֶרֶץ וְשָׁמָיִם. וַיָּרֶם קֶרֶן לְעַמּוֹ,
תְּהִלָּה לְכָל־חֲסִידָיו, לִבְנֵי יִשְׂרָאֵל עַם קְרֹבוֹ, הַלְלוּ־יָהּ.

לְדָוִד מִזְמוֹר.
לַיהוה הָאָרֶץ וּמְלוֹאָהּ, תֵּבֵל וְיֹשְׁבֵי בָהּ.
כִּי־הוּא עַל־יַמִּים יְסָדָהּ, וְעַל־נְהָרוֹת יְכוֹנְנֶהָ.
מִי־יַעֲלֶה בְהַר־יהוה, וּמִי־יָקוּם בִּמְקוֹם קָדְשׁוֹ.
נְקִי כַפַּיִם וּבַר־לֵבָב, אֲשֶׁר לֹא־נָשָׂא לַשָּׁוְא נַפְשִׁי,
וְלֹא נִשְׁבַּע לְמִרְמָה.
יִשָּׂא בְרָכָה מֵאֵת יהוה, וּצְדָקָה מֵאֱלֹהֵי יִשְׁעוֹ.
זֶה דּוֹר דֹּרְשָׁו, מְבַקְשֵׁי פָנֶיךָ יַעֲקֹב, סֶלָה.
שְׂאוּ שְׁעָרִים רָאשֵׁיכֶם, וְהִנָּשְׂאוּ פִּתְחֵי עוֹלָם,
וְיָבוֹא מֶלֶךְ הַכָּבוֹד.
מִי זֶה מֶלֶךְ הַכָּבוֹד,
יהוה עִזּוּז וְגִבּוֹר, יהוה גִּבּוֹר מִלְחָמָה.
שְׂאוּ שְׁעָרִים רָאשֵׁיכֶם, וּשְׂאוּ פִּתְחֵי עוֹלָם,
וְיָבֹא מֶלֶךְ הַכָּבוֹד.
מִי הוּא זֶה מֶלֶךְ הַכָּבוֹד,
יהוה צְבָאוֹת הוּא מֶלֶךְ הַכָּבוֹד, סֶלָה. תהלים כד

PSALM 24. This psalm's dramatic imagery of gates that open for God's symbolic entrance to the Temple explains why it accompanies our Torah's return to the ark. Yet the psalm focuses first of all on the state of the worshipper: purity of action—especially verbal honesty—must characterize those who would enter this holy place and receive its blessing. This develops a theme of the *b'rakhah* recited just after each Torah reading, describing the Torah as "a teaching of truth": in order to live in accord with Torah, we must exemplify inner truthfulness while also pursuing truth in the world.

Lifting the Torah

*A Magbiah and Golel are called to raise and tie the Sefer Torah.
As the Torah is lifted, we rise and recite:*

This is the Torah, God's word by Moses' hand,
which Moses set before the people Israel.

*V'zot ha-torah asher sam mosheh lifnei b'nei yisra·el al pi Adonai
b'yad mosheh.*

Returning the Torah

Leader:

Extol the name of Adonai, for God's name alone is exalted.

Congregation:

God's glory encompasses heaven and earth; God extols the faithful—
raising up Israel, the people God keeps close. Halleluyah!

*Hodo al eretz v'shamayim, va-yarem keren l'ammo;
t'hillah l'khol ḥasidav, liv'nei yisra·el am k'rovo. Hal'luyah!*

PSALM 24

A SONG OF DAVID.

The earth is Adonai's in all its fullness, the land and all who dwell on it.
For it was God who founded it upon the seas, and set it firm upon the
flowing streams. Who may ascend the mount of Adonai? Who may
come forward in God's sanctuary? One who has clean hands and a pure
heart, who has not taken God's name in vain, nor sworn deceitfully.
One such as this will receive Adonai's blessing, a just reward from
God, the deliverer. This generation searches for You; like Jacob, seeks
Your presence, *selah*. Open up, arched gateways—open up, doors of the
world; may the sovereign who is exalted enter. Who is the sovereign
who is exalted? Adonai, mighty and triumphant, triumphant in battle.
Open up, arched gateways—open up, doors of the world; may the
sovereign who is exalted enter. Who is the sovereign who is exalted?
Adonai Tz'va·ot is the sovereign who is exalted. *Selah.*

*Ladonai ha-aretz u-m'lo·ah, teiveil v'yosh'vei vah.
Ki hu al yammim y'sadah, v'al n'harot y'khon'neha.
Mi ya·aleh v'har Adonai, u-mi yakum bi-m'kom kodsho.
N'ki khappayim u-var leivav, asher lo nasa la-shav nafshi, v'lo nishba l'mirmah.
Yissa v'rakhah mei-eit Adonai, u-tz'dakah mei-elohei yisho.
Zeh dor dor'shav m'vakshei fanekha ya·akov, selah.
S'u sh'arim rasheikhem, v'hinnas'u pithei olam, v'yavo melekh ha-kavod.
Mi zeh melekh ha-kavod, Adonai izzuz v'gibbor, Adonai gibbor milḥamah.
S'u sh'arim rasheikhem, v'hinnas'u pithei olam, v'yavo melekh ha-kavod.
Mi hu zeh melekh ha-kavod, Adonai Tz'va·ot hu melekh ha-kavod, selah.*

The Sefer Torah is placed in the ark.

וּבְנֻחֹה יֹאמַר: שׁוּבָה יהוה רִבְבוֹת אַלְפֵי יִשְׂרָאֵל.

קוּמָה יהוה לִמְנוּחָתֶךָ, אַתָּה וַאֲרוֹן עֻזֶּךָ.

כֹּהֲנֶיךָ יִלְבְּשׁוּ־צֶדֶק, וַחֲסִידֶיךָ יְרַנֵּנוּ.

בַּעֲבוּר דָּוִד עַבְדֶּךָ, אַל־תָּשֵׁב פְּנֵי מְשִׁיחֶךָ.

◁ כִּי לֶקַח טוֹב נָתַתִּי לָכֶם, תּוֹרָתִי אַל־תַּעֲזֹבוּ.

עֵץ־חַיִּים הִיא לַמַּחֲזִיקִים בָּהּ, וְתֹמְכֶיהָ מְאֻשָּׁר.

דְּרָכֶיהָ דַרְכֵי־נֹעַם, וְכָל־נְתִיבוֹתֶיהָ שָׁלוֹם.

הֲשִׁיבֵנוּ יהוה אֵלֶיךָ וְנָשׁוּבָה, חַדֵּשׁ יָמֵינוּ כְּקֶדֶם.

The ark is closed.

חֲצִי קַדִּישׁ

יִתְגַּדַּל וְיִתְקַדַּשׁ שְׁמֵהּ רַבָּא, בְּעָלְמָא דִּי בְרָא, כִּרְעוּתֵהּ,

וְיַמְלִיךְ מַלְכוּתֵהּ בְּחַיֵּיכוֹן וּבְיוֹמֵיכוֹן וּבְחַיֵּי דְכָל־בֵּית

יִשְׂרָאֵל, בַּעֲגָלָא וּבִזְמַן קָרִיב, וְאִמְרוּ אָמֵן.

יְהֵא שְׁמֵהּ רַבָּא מְבָרַךְ לְעָלַם וּלְעָלְמֵי עָלְמַיָּא.

יִתְבָּרַךְ וְיִשְׁתַּבַּח וְיִתְפָּאַר וְיִתְרוֹמַם וְיִתְנַשֵּׂא וְיִתְהַדָּר

וְיִתְעַלֶּה וְיִתְהַלָּל שְׁמֵהּ דְּקֻדְשָׁא, בְּרִיךְ הוּא, לְעֵלָּא לְעֵלָּא

מִכָּל־בִּרְכָתָא וְשִׁירָתָא תֻּשְׁבְּחָתָא וְנֶחֱמָתָא דַּאֲמִירָן

בְּעָלְמָא, וְאִמְרוּ אָמֵן.

WHENEVER THE ARK WAS SET DOWN וּבְנֻחֹה יֹאמַר. Numbers 10:36. As the Torah completes its circuit through the synagogue, we recall Moses' words when the people finished a stage in their journey through the wilderness and came to rest in a new camp. This verse and the ones that follow (Psalm 132:8–10; Proverbs 4:2; 3:18, 3:17; Lamentations 5:21) can also serve to refer to our own inner journey—accompanied by Torah.

IT IS A TREE OF LIFE FOR THOSE WHO GRASP IT עֵץ־חַיִּים הִיא לַמַּחֲזִיקִים בָּהּ This verse (Proverbs 3:18) is the source of the custom of holding onto the *atzei ḥayyim*, the Torah handles, while reciting the *b'rakhot* over the Torah—thus grasping the "tree of life" both physically and figuratively.

ITS WAYS ARE PLEASANT WAYS, AND ALL ITS PATHS ARE PEACE דְּרָכֶיהָ דַרְכֵי־נֹעַם, וְכָל־נְתִיבוֹתֶיהָ שָׁלוֹם. Proverbs 3:17. As we put away the Torah, we pray that our study should promote actions that lead to pleasantness and peace.

The Sefer Torah is placed in the ark.

Whenever the Ark was set down, Moses would say:

ADONAI, may You dwell among the myriad families of the people Israel.

> Return, ADONAI, to Your sanctuary,
> You and Your glorious Ark.

Let Your priests be robed in righteousness,
and Your faithful sing for joy.

> For the sake of David, Your servant,
> do not turn away from Your anointed.

I have given you a precious inheritance:
Do not forsake My teaching.

> It is a tree of life for those who grasp it,
> and all who hold onto it are blessed.

Its ways are pleasant ways, and all its paths are peace.

> Turn us toward You, ADONAI, and we will return to You;
> make our days seem fresh, as they once were.

Eitz ḥayyim hi la-maḥazikim bah, v'tom'kheha m'ushar.
D'rakheha darkhei no·am, v'khol n'tivoteha shalom.
Hashiveinu Adonai eilekha v'nashuvah, ḥaddeish yameinu k'kedem.

The ark is closed.

Ḥatzi Kaddish

May God's great name be exalted and hallowed throughout the created world, as is God's wish. May God's sovereignty soon be established, in your lifetime and in your days, and in the days of all the House of Israel. And respond with: *Amen.*

May God's great name be acknowledged forever and ever!
Y'hei sh'meih rabba m'varakh l'alam u-l'almei almayya.

May the name of the Holy One be acknowledged and celebrated, lauded and worshipped, exalted and honored, extolled and acclaimed—though God, who is blessed, *b'rikh hu*, is truly far beyond all acknowledgment and praise, or any expressions of gratitude or consolation ever spoken in the world. And respond with: *Amen.*

כִּי שֵׁם יהוה אֶקְרָא, הָבוּ גֹדֶל לֵאלֹהֵינוּ.
אֲדֹנָי שְׂפָתַי תִּפְתָּח, וּפִי יַגִּיד תְּהִלָּתֶךָ.

Version with Patriarchs and Matriarchs:	*Version with Patriarchs:*

בָּרוּךְ אַתָּה יהוה،
אֱלֹהֵינוּ וֵאלֹהֵי אֲבוֹתֵינוּ
[וְאִמּוֹתֵינוּ]، אֱלֹהֵי אַבְרָהָם،
אֱלֹהֵי יִצְחָק، וֵאלֹהֵי יַעֲקֹב،
אֱלֹהֵי שָׂרָה، אֱלֹהֵי רִבְקָה،
אֱלֹהֵי רָחֵל، וֵאלֹהֵי לֵאָה،
הָאֵל הַגָּדוֹל הַגִּבּוֹר וְהַנּוֹרָא،
אֵל עֶלְיוֹן، גּוֹמֵל חֲסָדִים
טוֹבִים، וְקוֹנֵה הַכֹּל، וְזוֹכֵר
חַסְדֵי אָבוֹת [וְאִמָּהוֹת]،
וּמֵבִיא גוֹאֵל לִבְנֵי בְנֵיהֶם
לְמַעַן שְׁמוֹ בְּאַהֲבָה.

בָּרוּךְ אַתָּה יהוה،
אֱלֹהֵינוּ וֵאלֹהֵי אֲבוֹתֵינוּ،
אֱלֹהֵי אַבְרָהָם، אֱלֹהֵי
יִצְחָק، וֵאלֹהֵי יַעֲקֹב، הָאֵל
הַגָּדוֹל הַגִּבּוֹר וְהַנּוֹרָא،
אֵל עֶלְיוֹן، גּוֹמֵל חֲסָדִים
טוֹבִים، וְקוֹנֵה הַכֹּל، וְזוֹכֵר
חַסְדֵי אָבוֹת، וּמֵבִיא גוֹאֵל
לִבְנֵי בְנֵיהֶם לְמַעַן שְׁמוֹ
בְּאַהֲבָה.

זָכְרֵנוּ לְחַיִּים، מֶלֶךְ חָפֵץ בַּחַיִּים،
וְכָתְבֵנוּ בְּסֵפֶר הַחַיִּים،
לְמַעַנְךָ אֱלֹהִים חַיִּים.

Version with Patriarchs and Matriarchs:	*Version with Patriarchs:*

מֶלֶךְ עוֹזֵר וּפוֹקֵד
וּמוֹשִׁיעַ וּמָגֵן.
בָּרוּךְ אַתָּה יהוה، מָגֵן
אַבְרָהָם וּפוֹקֵד שָׂרָה.

מֶלֶךְ עוֹזֵר וּמוֹשִׁיעַ וּמָגֵן.
בָּרוּךְ אַתָּה יהוה، מָגֵן
אַבְרָהָם.

GOD OF ABRAHAM . . . GOD OF SARAH . . . אֱלֹהֵי אַבְרָהָם . . . אֱלֹהֵי שָׂרָה. The tradition of reciting the names of each patriarch originates with God's own speech: at the burning bush, God begins addressing Moses by saying, "I am the God of Abraham, the God of Isaac, and the God of Jacob." Some congregations add the names of the four matriarchs at the beginning of this *b'rakhah*, because of their significance as founders of our people, and as part of our effort to reclaim women's voices and to honor women's experiences.

REMEMBER US זָכְרֵנוּ. This brief anonymous and ancient poem, added at each service during the High Holy Day season, stresses the theme that God treasures life.

SHIELD OF ABRAHAM מָגֵן אַבְרָהָם. After Genesis 15:1.

GUARDIAN OF SARAH פוֹקֵד שָׂרָה. Or: "the One who remembered Sarah" (after Genesis 21:1). We, who stand here today, are the fruit of God's promise to Abraham and Sarah.

THE AMIDAH

As I proclaim God's name, ADONAI, exalt our God.
ADONAI, open my lips that my mouth may speak Your praise.

Meditation on Prayer
In the Bible, God speaks
to us, and we listen. At
the moment of prayer,
we speak to God and
God listens.

—ISAAC ARAMA

God of Abraham,
God of Isaac,
and God of Jacob
Why is the word "God"
repeated each time?
We might more easily
have said it once. The
repeated use of the word
"God" highlights that
each patriarch—and
matriarch—knew God
personally and sought a
distinct relationship
with God.

First B'rakhah: Our Ancestors

Version with Patriarchs:

ʄ *Barukh atah* ADONAI,
our God and God of our
   ancestors,
God of Abraham, God of
   Isaac, and God of Jacob,
great, mighty, awe-inspiring,
   transcendent God,
who acts with lovingkindness
   and creates all things,
who remembers the loving
   deeds of our ancestors,
and who will send a redeemer
   to their children's children
   with love
   for the sake of divine honor.

Version with Patriarchs and Matriarchs:

ʄ *Barukh atah* ADONAI,
our God and God of our
   ancestors,
God of Abraham, God of
   Isaac, and God of Jacob,
God of Sarah, God of
   Rebecca, God of Rachel,
   and God of Leah,
great, mighty, awe-inspiring,
   transcendent God,
who acts with lovingkindness
   and creates all things,
who remembers the loving
   deeds of our ancestors,
and who will send a redeemer
   to their children's children
   with love
   for the sake of divine honor.

Remember us for life, Sovereign who delights in life,
and inscribe us in the Book of Life, for Your sake, God of life.
Zokhreinu l'hayyim, melekh hafeitz ba-hayyim,
v'khotveinu b'seifer ha-hayyim, l'ma·ankha Elohim hayyim.

Version with Patriarchs:

You are the Sovereign
who helps and saves and
shields.

ʄ *Barukh atah* ADONAI,
Shield of Abraham.

Version with Patriarchs and Matriarchs:

You are the Sovereign who
helps and guards, saves and
shields.

ʄ *Barukh atah* ADONAI,
Shield of Abraham and
Guardian of Sarah.

אַתָּה גִבּוֹר לְעוֹלָם אֲדֹנָי, מְחַיֵּה מֵתִים אַתָּה,
רַב לְהוֹשִׁיעַ.

מְכַלְכֵּל חַיִּים בְּחֶסֶד,
מְחַיֵּה מֵתִים בְּרַחֲמִים רַבִּים,
סוֹמֵךְ נוֹפְלִים, וְרוֹפֵא חוֹלִים,
וּמַתִּיר אֲסוּרִים,
וּמְקַיֵּם אֱמוּנָתוֹ לִישֵׁנֵי עָפָר.
מִי כָמוֹךָ בַּעַל גְּבוּרוֹת,
וּמִי דוֹמֶה לָּךְ,
מֶלֶךְ מֵמִית וּמְחַיֶּה וּמַצְמִיחַ יְשׁוּעָה.

מִי כָמוֹךָ אַב הָרַחֲמִים, זוֹכֵר יְצוּרָיו לְחַיִּים בְּרַחֲמִים.

וְנֶאֱמָן אַתָּה לְהַחֲיוֹת מֵתִים. בָּרוּךְ אַתָּה יהוה,
מְחַיֵּה הַמֵּתִים.

*When the Amidah is recited together in a minyan, we continue below
with the Kedushah.*

אַתָּה קָדוֹשׁ וְשִׁמְךָ קָדוֹשׁ, וּקְדוֹשִׁים בְּכָל־יוֹם
יְהַלְלוּךָ, סֶּלָה.

When the Amidah is recited silently, we continue on the next page.

קְדֻשָּׁה

נְקַדֵּשׁ אֶת־שִׁמְךָ בָּעוֹלָם, כְּשֵׁם שֶׁמַּקְדִּישִׁים אוֹתוֹ בִּשְׁמֵי
מָרוֹם, כַּכָּתוּב עַל יַד נְבִיאֶךָ, וְקָרָא זֶה אֶל זֶה וְאָמַר:

קָדוֹשׁ, קָדוֹשׁ, קָדוֹשׁ יהוה צְבָאוֹת,
מְלֹא כָל־הָאָרֶץ כְּבוֹדוֹ.

SUPPORT THE FALLING
סוֹמֵךְ נוֹפְלִים. After Psalm
145:14.

HEAL THE SICK רוֹפֵא חוֹלִים.
After Exodus 15:26.

LOOSEN THE CHAINS OF
THE BOUND מַתִּיר אֲסוּרִים
Psalm 146:7.

BRINGS DEATH AND LIFE
מֵמִית וּמְחַיֶּה. 1 Samuel 2:6.

WHO IS LIKE YOU, SOURCE
OF COMPASSION מִי כָמוֹךָ
אַב הָרַחֲמִים. Jewish mystical tradition highlights
the theological tension
between God's qualities of
power and strict judg-
ment, גְּבוּרָה (g'vurah), and
God's qualities of mercy
and lovingkindness, חֶסֶד
(ḥesed). Throughout the
year, this b'rakhah reminds
us that God is unsurpassed
in power. At this season
of judgment, we add this
line to remind us—and
God—that God is also
unsurpassed in mercy.

GIVES LIFE TO THE DEAD
מְחַיֵּה הַמֵּתִים. Over the
millennia, many Jewish
perspectives on the afterlife have been proposed.
Many sages (including
Saadiah Gaon, 10th cen-
tury, and Maimonides, 12th
century) caution against
speculation about the
specific implications of
the doctrine of bodily
resurrection of the dead. They understand it to be an articulation of God's supreme power: God cares for
even the dead.

THE KEDUSHAH. The Kedushah always includes the vision of Isaiah (6:3) of the heavenly chorus reciting
God's praise, "Holy, holy, holy…," as well as Ezekiel's vision (3:12) of the angels responding "Praised is Adonai's
glory…." It concludes with an affirmation of God's sovereignty, "Adonai will reign forever" (Psalm 146:10). We
join with the angels in enunciating God's praise. While doing so, our custom is to imitate an angel—whom
Ezekiel described as having a single leg—by standing with one's feet together.

HOLY קָדוֹשׁ. We become holy when we imitate God's qualities: "As God is called 'merciful' so should you
be merciful. . . . as God is called 'righteous' and 'loving,' so should you be righteous and loving" (Babylonian
Talmud, Sotah 14a).

Immortality

Each morning You restore consciousness to my sleep-filled body, and I awake.

Each spring You restore vitality to trees, plants, and animals that have hibernated through the winter, and they grow once more.

Each day I remember those who have died; they live on beyond the grave.

Each moment I contemplate the rebirth of our people; I recall that You put the breath of life into dry bones.

Praised are You, Adonai, for planting immortality in my soul, in my people, and in our world.

—ROBERT SCHEINBERG

Second B'rakhah: God's Saving Care

You are mighty forever, ADONAI—
You give life to the dead;
great is Your saving power.

You sustain the living through love,
    and with great mercy give life to the dead.
You support the falling,
    heal the sick,
    loosen the chains of the bound,
    and keep faith with those who sleep in the dust.
Who is like You, Almighty,
    and who can be compared to You?—
    Sovereign, who brings death and life,
    and causes salvation to flourish.

M'khalkeil ḥayyim b'ḥesed, m'ḥayyeih meitim b'raḥamim rabbim, someikh nof'lim, v'rofei ḥolim, u-mattir asurim, u-m'kayyeim emunato li-sheinei afar. Mi khamokha ba·al g'vurot u-mi domeh lakh, melekh meimit u-m'ḥayyeih u-matzmi·aḥ y'shu·ah.

Who is like You, source of compassion,
who remembers with compassion Your creatures for life?
Mi khamokha av ha-raḥamim, zokheir y'tzurav l'ḥayyim b'raḥamim.

You are faithful in bringing life to the dead.
Barukh atah ADONAI, who gives life to the dead.

Third B'rakhah: God's Holiness

When the Amidah is recited together in a minyan, we continue below with the Kedushah.

Holy are You and holy is Your name;
    holy ones praise You each day.

When the Amidah is recited silently, we continue on the next page.

THE KEDUSHAH

Let us hallow Your name in this world as it is hallowed in the high heavens, as Isaiah wrote of his vision,
Each cried out to the other:
"Holy, holy, holy is *Adonai Tz'va·ot;* the whole world is filled with God's glory!"
Kadosh, kadosh, kadosh Adonai Tz'va·ot, m'lo khol ha-aretz k'vodo.

לְעֻמָּתָם בָּרוּךְ יֹאמֵרוּ:
בָּרוּךְ כְּבוֹד־יהוה מִמְּקוֹמוֹ.
וּבְדִבְרֵי קָדְשְׁךָ כָּתוּב לֵאמֹר:

יִמְלֹךְ יהוה לְעוֹלָם, אֱלֹהַיִךְ צִיּוֹן לְדֹר וָדֹר, הַלְלוּ־יָהּ.
לְדוֹר וָדוֹר נַגִּיד גָּדְלֶךָ, וּלְנֵצַח נְצָחִים קְדֻשָּׁתְךָ נַקְדִּישׁ,
וְשִׁבְחֲךָ אֱלֹהֵינוּ מִפִּינוּ לֹא יָמוּשׁ לְעוֹלָם וָעֶד, כִּי אֵל מֶלֶךְ
גָּדוֹל וְקָדוֹשׁ אָתָּה.

All services continue here:

וּבְכֵן תֵּן פַּחְדְּךָ יהוה אֱלֹהֵינוּ עַל כָּל־מַעֲשֶׂיךָ,
וְאֵימָתְךָ עַל כָּל־מַה־שֶּׁבָּרָאתָ,
וְיִירָאוּךָ כָּל־הַמַּעֲשִׂים
וְיִשְׁתַּחֲווּ לְפָנֶיךָ כָּל־הַבְּרוּאִים,
וְיֵעָשׂוּ כֻלָּם אֲגֻדָּה אַחַת לַעֲשׂוֹת רְצוֹנְךָ בְּלֵבָב שָׁלֵם,
כְּמוֹ שֶׁיָּדַעְנוּ יהוה אֱלֹהֵינוּ
שֶׁהַשִּׁלְטוֹן לְפָנֶיךָ, עֹז בְּיָדְךָ וּגְבוּרָה בִּימִינֶךָ,
וְשִׁמְךָ נוֹרָא עַל כָּל־מַה־שֶּׁבָּרָאתָ.

וּבְכֵן תֵּן כָּבוֹד יהוה לְעַמֶּךָ
תְּהִלָּה לִירֵאֶיךָ וְתִקְוָה לְדוֹרְשֶׁיךָ,
וּפִתְחוֹן פֶּה לַמְיַחֲלִים לָךְ,
שִׂמְחָה לְאַרְצֶךָ וְשָׂשׂוֹן לְעִירֶךָ,
וּצְמִיחַת קֶרֶן לְדָוִד עַבְדֶּךָ
וַעֲרִיכַת נֵר לְבֶן־יִשַׁי מְשִׁיחֶךָ, בִּמְהֵרָה בְיָמֵינוּ.

וּבְכֵן צַדִּיקִים יִרְאוּ וְיִשְׂמָחוּ,
וִישָׁרִים יַעֲלֹזוּ,
וַחֲסִידִים בְּרִנָּה יָגִילוּ,
וְעוֹלָתָה תִּקְפָּץ־פִּיהָ
וְכָל־הָרִשְׁעָה כֻּלָּהּ כְּעָשָׁן תִּכְלֶה,
כִּי תַעֲבִיר מֶמְשֶׁלֶת זָדוֹן מִן הָאָרֶץ.

U-V'KHEIN וּבְכֵן. These three paragraphs, which are introduced by the same word, וּבְכֵן (u-v'khein), are ascribed by many scholars to the 2nd or 3rd century, and may constitute the earliest poetical additions to the High Holy Day Amidah.

Stages of redemption are described in this series of prayers. The first paragraph implores God to cause the entire world to live with reverence for God. The next paragraph discusses not the universal, but the particular: the return of the people Israel to its land and specifically to Jerusalem, and the kingship of David. The third paragraph describes the rejoicing that will come to the righteous "when You remove the tyranny of arrogance from the earth" and God will rule alone over the entire world from Zion and Jerusalem. *(adapted from Reuven Hammer)*

AWE . . . FEAR . . . פַּחְדְּךָ . . . וְאֵימָתְךָ. These emotions are meant to induce obedience to God's will and inspire us to bring sanctity to the world.

THE LIGHT OF DAVID קֶרֶן לְדָוִד. See Psalm 132:17.

May All Be
Bound Together

The purpose of creation is not division, nor separation. The purpose of the human race is not a struggle to the death between classes, between nations. Humanity is meant to become a single body. . . . Our purpose is the great upbuilding of unity and peace. And when all nations are bound together in one association living in justice and righteousness, they atone for each other.

—MARTIN BUBER

All Wickedness
Will Disappear

There were once some lawless men who caused Rabbi Meir a great deal of trouble. Rabbi Meir accordingly prayed that they should die. His wife, Beruriah, said to him: "How can you think that such a prayer is permitted? . . . When sin ceases there shall be no more wicked people. Therefore pray for them that they turn from their ways, and there will be no more wicked people." Then he prayed on their behalf.

—BABYLONIAN TALMUD,
BERAKHOT

Others respond with praise:
"Praised is ADONAI's glory wherever God dwells."
Barukh k'vod Adonai mi-m'komo.
And in Your holy scripture it is further declared:
ADONAI will reign forever;
your God, O Zion, from generation to generation. Halleluyah!
Yimlokh Adonai l'olam, elohayikh tziyyon l'dor va-dor, hal'luyah.

From one generation to another we will declare Your greatness, and forever sanctify You with words of holiness. Your praise will never leave our lips, for You are God and Sovereign, great and holy.

All services continue here:
U-v'khein—ADONAI our God,
instill Your awe in all You have made,
and fear of You in all You have created,
so that all You have fashioned revere You,
all You have created bow in recognition,
and all be bound together, carrying out Your will
wholeheartedly.
For we know that true sovereignty is Yours,
power and strength are in Your hands,
and Your name is to be revered beyond any of Your creations.

U-v'khein—Bestow honor to Your people, ADONAI,
praise to those who revere You,
hope to those who seek You,
recognition to those who await You,
joy to Your land, and gladness to Your city.
Simḥah l'artzekha v'sason l'irekha
May the light of David, Your servant, dawn,
and the lamp of the son of Jesse, Your anointed, be kindled
speedily in our day.

U-v'khein—The righteous, beholding this, will rejoice,
the upright will be glad,
the pious will celebrate with song,
evil will be silenced,
and all wickedness will disappear like smoke,
when You remove the tyranny of arrogance from the earth.

וְתִמְלֹךְ אַתָּה יהוה לְבַדֶּךָ, עַל כָּל־מַעֲשֶׂיךָ,
בְּהַר צִיּוֹן מִשְׁכַּן כְּבוֹדֶךָ
וּבִירוּשָׁלַיִם עִיר קָדְשֶׁךָ,
כַּכָּתוּב בְּדִבְרֵי קָדְשֶׁךָ:
יִמְלֹךְ יהוה לְעוֹלָם, אֱלֹהַיִךְ צִיּוֹן לְדֹר וָדֹר, הַלְלוּ־יָהּ.

קָדוֹשׁ אַתָּה וְנוֹרָא שְׁמֶךָ, וְאֵין אֱלוֹהַּ מִבַּלְעָדֶיךָ,
כַּכָּתוּב: וַיִּגְבַּהּ יהוה צְבָאוֹת בַּמִּשְׁפָּט, וְהָאֵל הַקָּדוֹשׁ
נִקְדַּשׁ בִּצְדָקָה. בָּרוּךְ אַתָּה יהוה, הַמֶּלֶךְ הַקָּדוֹשׁ.

אַתָּה בְחַרְתָּנוּ מִכָּל־הָעַמִּים,
אָהַבְתָּ אוֹתָנוּ וְרָצִיתָ בָּנוּ,
וְרוֹמַמְתָּנוּ מִכָּל־הַלְּשׁוֹנוֹת,
וְקִדַּשְׁתָּנוּ בְּמִצְוֹתֶיךָ,
וְקֵרַבְתָּנוּ מַלְכֵּנוּ לַעֲבוֹדָתֶךָ,
וְשִׁמְךָ הַגָּדוֹל וְהַקָּדוֹשׁ עָלֵינוּ קָרָאתָ.

וַתִּתֶּן־לָנוּ, יהוה אֱלֹהֵינוּ בְּאַהֲבָה אֶת־יוֹם [הַשַּׁבָּת הַזֶּה
וְאֶת־יוֹם] הַזִּכָּרוֹן הַזֶּה, יוֹם [זִכְרוֹן] תְּרוּעָה [בְּאַהֲבָה]
מִקְרָא קֹדֶשׁ, זֵכֶר לִיצִיאַת מִצְרָיִם.

אֱלֹהֵינוּ וֵאלֹהֵי אֲבוֹתֵינוּ [וְאִמּוֹתֵינוּ], יַעֲלֶה וְיָבֹא, וְיַגִּיעַ
וְיֵרָאֶה, וְיֵרָצֶה וְיִשָּׁמַע, וְיִפָּקֵד וְיִזָּכֵר זִכְרוֹנֵנוּ וּפִקְדוֹנֵנוּ,
וְזִכְרוֹן אֲבוֹתֵינוּ [וְאִמּוֹתֵינוּ], וְזִכְרוֹן מָשִׁיחַ בֶּן־דָּוִד עַבְדֶּךָ,
וְזִכְרוֹן יְרוּשָׁלַיִם עִיר קָדְשֶׁךָ, וְזִכְרוֹן כָּל־עַמְּךָ בֵּית יִשְׂרָאֵל
לְפָנֶיךָ לִפְלֵיטָה לְטוֹבָה, לְחֵן וּלְחֶסֶד וּלְרַחֲמִים, לְחַיִּים
וּלְשָׁלוֹם, בְּיוֹם הַזִּכָּרוֹן הַזֶּה.
זָכְרֵנוּ יהוה אֱלֹהֵינוּ בּוֹ לְטוֹבָה,   אָמֵן.
וּפָקְדֵנוּ בוֹ לִבְרָכָה,   אָמֵן.
וְהוֹשִׁיעֵנוּ בוֹ לְחַיִּים,   אָמֵן.
וּבִדְבַר יְשׁוּעָה וְרַחֲמִים חוּס וְחָנֵּנוּ, וְרַחֵם עָלֵינוּ
וְהוֹשִׁיעֵנוּ, כִּי אֵלֶיךָ עֵינֵינוּ, כִּי אֵל מֶלֶךְ חַנּוּן וְרַחוּם אָתָּה.

YOU ALONE ... WILL RULE
וְתִמְלֹךְ אַתָּה לְבַדֶּךָ. God's
sovereignty is always envisioned as the rule of justice,
and therefore a time of
peace. It is the ultimate
conclusion of history.

**ADONAI WILL REIGN
FOREVER** יִמְלֹךְ יהוה לְעוֹלָם.
Psalm 146:10.

**ADONAI TZ'VA·OT WILL BE
EXALTED** וַיִּגְבַּהּ יהוה צְבָאוֹת.
Isaiah 5:16. In concluding
the b'rakhah, this verse
highlights its themes as
expanded on the High
Holy Days: We await the
day when earthly powers
become subservient to the
divine ideals of justice and
righteousness.

THE HOLY SOVEREIGN הַמֶּלֶךְ
הַקָּדוֹשׁ. The rest of the year,
this b'rakhah concludes
with the words הָאֵל הַקָּדוֹשׁ
"the Holy God." The High
Holy Days, though, empha-
size God's sovereignty.

**CALLING US BY YOUR GREAT
AND HOLY NAME** וְשִׁמְךָ
הַגָּדוֹל וְהַקָּדוֹשׁ עָלֵינוּ קָרָאתָ.
The name "Israel" means
"wrestling with God" (Genesis 32:28). Our relationship
with God is part of our
self-definition as Jews.

**MAY THE THOUGHT OF US
RISE UP AND REACH YOU**
יַעֲלֶה וְיָבֹא. This paragraph
is recited on every festival
and new moon, though
some scholars think that it
was originally written for
the Rosh Hashanah liturgy
since it emphasizes re-
membrance. The objects of
remembrance move from
the present to the past
(our ancestors) and then to
future hope.

In Maimonides' view chosenness does not imply superiority or inherent sanctity, since the correct reading of the Bible in fact implies conditional chosenness. The election is one of duty, not of rights or attributes. Superiority and sanctity do not belong to historical Israel, to concrete individuals, but to a mythical Israel, held up as a model and ideal, defined by submission to God's commandments and respect for the covenant. . . . Judaism avoided being drawn into a universalistic, proselytizing monotheism through its interpretation of election as a duty, the particular relation between a people and its God in its social and historical reality.

—HENRI ATLAN

You alone, ADONAI, will rule all Your creation,
from Mount Zion, the dwelling-place of Your glory,
and from Jerusalem, Your holy city.
As it is written in the Book of Psalms:
"ADONAI will reign forever;
your God, O Zion, from generation to generation. Halleluyah!"

You are holy, and Your name is revered, for there is no God but You. As Your prophet Isaiah wrote: "*Adonai Tz'va·ot* will be exalted through justice, the holy God sanctified through righteousness."
Barukh atah ADONAI, the Holy Sovereign.

Fourth B'rakhah: The Holiness of Rosh Hashanah
You have chosen us among all peoples,
loving us, wanting us.
You have distinguished us among all nations,
making us holy through Your commandments,
drawing us close to Your service,
and calling us by Your great and holy name.

With love, You have bestowed on us, ADONAI our God, [this Shabbat and] this Day of Remembrance, a day for [recalling] the shofar sound [with love], a day for holy assembly and for recalling the Exodus from Egypt.

Our God and God of our ancestors, may the thought of us rise up and reach You. Attend to us and accept us; hear us and respond to us. Keep us in mind, and keep in mind the thought of our ancestors, as well as the Messiah, the descendant of David; Jerusalem, Your holy city; and all Your people, the House of Israel. On this Day of Remembrance respond to us with deliverance, goodness, compassion, love, life, and peace.

Remember us for good;	*Amen.*
respond to us with blessing;	*Amen.*
redeem us with life.	*Amen.*

Show us compassion and care with words of salvation and kindness; have mercy on us and redeem us. Our eyes are turned to You, for You are a compassionate and loving sovereign.

אֱלֹהֵינוּ וֵאלֹהֵי אֲבוֹתֵינוּ [וְאִמּוֹתֵינוּ],
מְלֹךְ עַל כָּל־הָעוֹלָם כֻּלּוֹ בִּכְבוֹדֶךָ,
וְהִנָּשֵׂא עַל כָּל־הָאָרֶץ בִּיקָרֶךָ,
וְהוֹפַע בַּהֲדַר גְּאוֹן עֻזֶּךָ
עַל כָּל־יוֹשְׁבֵי תֵבֵל אַרְצֶךָ.
וְיֵדַע כָּל־פָּעוּל כִּי אַתָּה פְעַלְתּוֹ
וְיָבִין כָּל־יָצוּר כִּי אַתָּה יְצַרְתּוֹ,
וְיֹאמַר כֹּל אֲשֶׁר נְשָׁמָה בְאַפּוֹ:
יְהֹוָה אֱלֹהֵי יִשְׂרָאֵל מֶלֶךְ, וּמַלְכוּתוֹ בַּכֹּל מָשָׁלָה.

אֱלֹהֵינוּ וֵאלֹהֵי אֲבוֹתֵינוּ [וְאִמּוֹתֵינוּ], [רְצֵה בִמְנוּחָתֵנוּ]
קַדְּשֵׁנוּ בְּמִצְוֹתֶיךָ, וְתֵן חֶלְקֵנוּ בְּתוֹרָתֶךָ, שַׂבְּעֵנוּ מִטּוּבֶךָ
וְשַׂמְּחֵנוּ בִּישׁוּעָתֶךָ [וְהַנְחִילֵנוּ, יְהֹוָה אֱלֹהֵינוּ, בְּאַהֲבָה
וּבְרָצוֹן שַׁבַּת קָדְשֶׁךָ, וְיָנוּחוּ בָהּ יִשְׂרָאֵל מְקַדְּשֵׁי שְׁמֶךָ]
וְטַהֵר לִבֵּנוּ לְעָבְדְּךָ בֶּאֱמֶת, כִּי אַתָּה אֱלֹהִים אֱמֶת,
וּדְבָרְךָ אֱמֶת וְקַיָּם לָעַד. בָּרוּךְ אַתָּה יְהֹוָה, מֶלֶךְ עַל כָּל־
הָאָרֶץ, מְקַדֵּשׁ [הַשַּׁבָּת וְ] יִשְׂרָאֵל וְיוֹם הַזִּכָּרוֹן.

רְצֵה, יְהֹוָה אֱלֹהֵינוּ, בְּעַמְּךָ יִשְׂרָאֵל וּבִתְפִלָּתָם, וְהָשֵׁב
אֶת־הָעֲבוֹדָה לִדְבִיר בֵּיתֶךָ, [וְאִשֵּׁי יִשְׂרָאֵל]
וּתְפִלָּתָם בְּאַהֲבָה תְקַבֵּל בְּרָצוֹן, וּתְהִי לְרָצוֹן תָּמִיד
עֲבוֹדַת יִשְׂרָאֵל עַמֶּךָ.

וְתֶחֱזֶינָה עֵינֵינוּ בְּשׁוּבְךָ לְצִיּוֹן בְּרַחֲמִים. בָּרוּךְ אַתָּה
יְהֹוָה, הַמַּחֲזִיר שְׁכִינָתוֹ לְצִיּוֹן.

RESTORE WORSHIP TO YOUR SANCTUARY וְהָשֵׁב אֶת־הָעֲבוֹדָה לִדְבִיר בֵּיתֶךָ. According to the Babylonian Talmud, "Ever since the day when the Temple was destroyed, there has been an iron barrier separating Israel from God" (Berakhot 32b). Each destruction of the Temple in Jerusalem (first by the Babylonians in 586 B.C.E., then by the Romans in 70 C.E.) was a cataclysmic event in early Jewish history. In praying for the restoration of the Temple, we express our wish both for the sense of immediate connection with God that is believed to have characterized the Temple service, and for the common sense of purpose and religious community that was experienced there.

FIERY OFFERINGS וְאִשֵּׁי יִשְׂרָאֵל. The phrase "fiery offerings" originally referred to the sacrifices in the Temple, but later medieval and Ḥasidic commentators understood it as a description of the intensity of religious fervor required of true prayer. It is as if to say, "May our prayers have the same meaning and effect as burnt offerings once did for our ancestors."

YOUR DIVINE PRESENCE שְׁכִינָתוֹ. The Hebrew word *shekhinah* has been used for centuries to refer to God's immanence, the presence of God that is felt in the world. The word *shekhinah* is grammatically feminine. Accordingly, Jewish mystical tradition has tended to personify as female the Divine Presence, who is known as the Shekhinah.

Our God and God of our ancestors:
May You rule over the entire universe in Your glory,
may You be raised up over all the earth in Your splendor,
and may You manifest Yourself
to all the inhabitants of the world
in the majestic beauty of Your strength.
Then all creatures will know that You created them;
all living things will understand that You gave them life;
and everything that breathes will proclaim:
ADONAI, the God of Israel, is sovereign, ruling over all.

Our God and God of our ancestors, [embrace our rest,] make us holy through Your mitzvot and let the Torah be our portion. Fill our lives with Your goodness and gladden us with Your triumph. [ADONAI our God, grant that we inherit Your holy Shabbat, lovingly and willingly, so that the people Israel, who sanctify Your name, may find rest on this day.] Purify our hearts to serve You truly, for You are the God of truth, and Your word is true, eternal, and unchanging. *Barukh atah* ADONAI, ruler of all the earth, who makes [Shabbat,] the people Israel and the Day of Remembrance holy.

[*Leader: Barukh atah Adonai,*] Congregation: *melekh al kol ha-aretz, m'kaddeish [ha-shabbat v'] yisra·el* [*Leader: v'yom ha-zikkaron*].

Fifth B'rakhah: The Restoration of Zion
ADONAI our God, embrace Your people Israel and their prayer. Restore worship to Your sanctuary. May the [fiery offerings and] prayers of the people Israel be lovingly accepted by You, and may our service always be pleasing.

Let our eyes behold Your merciful return to Zion. *Barukh atah* ADONAI, who restores Your Divine Presence to Zion.

SILENT AMIDAH: *We recite the paragraph on the right; while reciting its first words, we bow.*

REPETITION OF THE AMIDAH: *While reciting the first words, by custom we remain seated while bowing our head.*

We recite quietly:

מוֹדִים אֲנַחְנוּ לָךְ שָׁאַתָּה הוּא יהוה אֱלֹהֵינוּ וֵאלֹהֵי אֲבוֹתֵינוּ [וְאִמּוֹתֵינוּ], אֱלֹהֵי כָל־בָּשָׂר, יוֹצְרֵנוּ, יוֹצֵר בְּרֵאשִׁית. בְּרָכוֹת וְהוֹדָאוֹת לְשִׁמְךָ הַגָּדוֹל וְהַקָּדוֹשׁ, עַל שֶׁהֶחֱיִיתָנוּ וְקִיַּמְתָּנוּ. כֵּן תְּחַיֵּנוּ וּתְקַיְּמֵנוּ, וְתֶאֱסוֹף גָּלֻיּוֹתֵינוּ לְחַצְרוֹת קָדְשֶׁךָ, לִשְׁמוֹר חֻקֶּיךָ וְלַעֲשׂוֹת רְצוֹנֶךָ, וּלְעָבְדְּךָ בְּלֵבָב שָׁלֵם, עַל שֶׁאֲנַחְנוּ מוֹדִים לָךְ. בָּרוּךְ אֵל הַהוֹדָאוֹת.

Leader recites:

מוֹדִים אֲנַחְנוּ לָךְ שָׁאַתָּה הוּא יהוה אֱלֹהֵינוּ וֵאלֹהֵי אֲבוֹתֵינוּ [וְאִמּוֹתֵינוּ] לְעוֹלָם וָעֶד, צוּר חַיֵּינוּ מָגֵן יִשְׁעֵנוּ אַתָּה הוּא. לְדוֹר וָדוֹר נוֹדֶה לְּךָ וּנְסַפֵּר תְּהִלָּתֶךָ, עַל חַיֵּינוּ הַמְּסוּרִים בְּיָדֶךָ וְעַל נִשְׁמוֹתֵינוּ הַפְּקוּדוֹת לָךְ, וְעַל נִסֶּיךָ שֶׁבְּכָל־יוֹם עִמָּנוּ וְעַל נִפְלְאוֹתֶיךָ וְטוֹבוֹתֶיךָ שֶׁבְּכָל־עֵת, עֶרֶב וָבֹקֶר וְצָהֳרָיִם. ◁ הַטּוֹב, כִּי לֹא כָלוּ רַחֲמֶיךָ, וְהַמְרַחֵם, כִּי לֹא תַמּוּ חֲסָדֶיךָ מֵעוֹלָם קִוִּינוּ לָךְ.

וְעַל כֻּלָּם יִתְבָּרַךְ וְיִתְרוֹמַם שִׁמְךָ מַלְכֵּנוּ תָּמִיד לְעוֹלָם וָעֶד.

וּכְתוֹב לְחַיִּים טוֹבִים כָּל־בְּנֵי בְרִיתֶךָ.

וְכֹל הַחַיִּים יוֹדוּךָ סֶּלָה, וִיהַלְלוּ אֶת־שִׁמְךָ בֶּאֱמֶת, הָאֵל יְשׁוּעָתֵנוּ וְעֶזְרָתֵנוּ סֶלָה. ◁ בָּרוּךְ אַתָּה יהוה, הַטּוֹב שִׁמְךָ וּלְךָ נָאֶה לְהוֹדוֹת.

THE CONGREGATIONAL RESPONSE. A second version of Modim (the b'rakhah of thanksgiving) was created by the Sages to be recited by the congregation while the leader chants the official prayer (Babylonian Talmud, Sotah 40a). In this way, we each fulfill the imperative of acknowledging God. The central idea expressed in this version is *modim anaḥnu lakh… al she-anaḥnu modim lakh*, "we thank You for the ability to thank You." In this formulation, gratitude is seen as a special gift of our humanity—the expression of thankfulness connects us to the world with a sense of humility and a joyful spirit of openness.

FOR ALL THESE BLESSINGS וְעַל כֻּלָּם. In the language of the Bible and the prayerbook, "God's name is exalted" when we acknowledge God, recognize God's goodness in creation, and act to enable God's justice and compassion to be visible in the world.

AND INSCRIBE וּכְתוֹב. This is the third of the four special insertions in the Amidah for the Ten Days of Repentance. At the beginning of the Amidah, we simply asked for "life"; as we reach the close of the Amidah, the adjective "good" is added to our prayer for life.

Sixth B'rakhah: Gratitude for Life and Its Blessings

SILENT AMIDAH: We recite the paragraph on the left; while reciting its first words, we bow.

REPETITION OF THE AMIDAH: While reciting the first words, by custom we remain seated while bowing our head.

Leader recites:

We thank You, You who are our God and the God of our ancestors through all time, protector of our lives, shield of our salvation. From one generation to the next we thank You and sing Your praises—

for our lives that are in Your hands,

for our souls that are under Your care,

for Your miracles that accompany us each day,

and for Your wonders and Your gifts that are with us each moment—

evening, morning, and noon. You are the One who is good, whose mercy is never-ending; the One who is compassionate, whose love is unceasing. We have always placed our hope in You.

We recite quietly:

ↄ We thank You for the ability to acknowledge You. You are our God and the God of our ancestors, the God of all flesh, our creator, and the creator of all. We offer praise and blessing to Your holy and great name, for granting us life and for sustaining us. May You continue to grant us life and sustenance. Gather our dispersed to Your holy courtyards that we may fulfill Your mitzvot and serve You wholeheartedly, carrying out Your will. May God, the source of gratitude, be praised.

For all these blessings may Your name be praised and exalted, our sovereign, always and forever.

And inscribe all the people of Your covenant for a good life. *U-kh'tov l'ḥayyim tovim kol b'nei v'ritekha.*

May all that lives thank You always, and praise Your name faithfully forever, God of our deliverance and help.
ↄ *Barukh atah* ADONAI, whose name is goodness and to whom praise is fitting.

שָׁלוֹם רָב עַל יִשְׂרָאֵל עַמְּךָ וְעַל כָּל־יוֹשְׁבֵי תֵבֵל תָּשִׂים לְעוֹלָם, כִּי אַתָּה הוּא מֶלֶךְ אָדוֹן לְכָל־הַשָּׁלוֹם. וְטוֹב בְּעֵינֶיךָ לְבָרֵךְ אֶת־עַמְּךָ יִשְׂרָאֵל בְּכָל־עֵת וּבְכָל־שָׁעָה בִּשְׁלוֹמֶךָ.

בְּסֵפֶר חַיִּים, בְּרָכָה וְשָׁלוֹם וּפַרְנָסָה טוֹבָה, נִזָּכֵר וְנִכָּתֵב לְפָנֶיךָ, אֲנַחְנוּ וְכָל־עַמְּךָ בֵּית יִשְׂרָאֵל, לְחַיִּים טוֹבִים וּלְשָׁלוֹם.

בָּרוּךְ אַתָּה יהוה, עוֹשֵׂה הַשָּׁלוֹם.

When the Amidah is recited silently, personal prayers are added here.
The following may also be recited:

אֱלֹהַי, נְצוֹר לְשׁוֹנִי מֵרָע, וּשְׂפָתַי מִדַּבֵּר מִרְמָה, וְלִמְקַלְלַי נַפְשִׁי תִדֹּם, וְנַפְשִׁי כֶּעָפָר לַכֹּל תִּהְיֶה. פְּתַח לִבִּי בְּתוֹרָתֶךָ, וּבְמִצְוֹתֶיךָ תִּרְדּוֹף נַפְשִׁי. וְכָל־הַחוֹשְׁבִים עָלַי רָעָה, מְהֵרָה הָפֵר עֲצָתָם וְקַלְקֵל מַחֲשַׁבְתָּם. עֲשֵׂה לְמַעַן שְׁמֶךָ, עֲשֵׂה לְמַעַן יְמִינֶךָ, עֲשֵׂה לְמַעַן קְדֻשָּׁתֶךָ. עֲשֵׂה לְמַעַן תּוֹרָתֶךָ. לְמַעַן יֵחָלְצוּן יְדִידֶיךָ, הוֹשִׁיעָה יְמִינְךָ וַעֲנֵנִי. יִהְיוּ לְרָצוֹן אִמְרֵי פִי וְהֶגְיוֹן לִבִּי לְפָנֶיךָ, יהוה צוּרִי וְגוֹאֲלִי. עֹשֶׂה שָׁלוֹם בִּמְרוֹמָיו, הוּא יַעֲשֶׂה שָׁלוֹם עָלֵינוּ, וְעַל כָּל־יִשְׂרָאֵל [וְעַל כָּל־יוֹשְׁבֵי תֵבֵל] וְאִמְרוּ: אָמֵן.

ON SHABBAT, WE CONTINUE WITH KADDISH SHALEM ON PAGE 195.

IN THE BOOK OF LIFE בְּסֵפֶר חַיִּים. This is the fourth of the special insertions in the Amidah of the High Holy Days. This final addition expands the theme of goodness enunciated in the previous addition. In the end, we pray not only for life but also for blessing, peace, and prosperity.

WHO BRINGS PEACE עוֹשֵׂה הַשָּׁלוֹם. In the words of the Midrash, "Great is peace, for all the prayers conclude with pleas for peace" (Sifrei Numbers 42). In addition to the Amidah, the Grace after Meals, Priestly Blessing, Kaddish Shalem, Mourner's Kaddish, and evening Sh'ma and Its Blessings all conclude with prayers for peace.

MY GOD אֱלֹהַי. The Babylonian Talmud says that every Amidah must be accompanied by a personal prayer. This private prayer, attributed to Mar son of Ravina, is among the Talmud's exemplars (Berakhot 17a). It was so admired that it entered the formal liturgy. Distinctively, it uses the first-person singular ("I"), whereas almost all other prayers are in the first-person plural ("we").

MAY THE WORDS יִהְיוּ לְרָצוֹן Psalm 19:15.

Seventh B'rakhah: Prayer for Peace

Grant abundant and lasting peace to Your people Israel and all who dwell on earth, for You are the sovereign master of all the ways of peace. May it please You to bless Your people Israel at all times with Your gift of peace.

May we and the entire House of Israel be called to mind and inscribed for life, blessing, sustenance, and peace in the Book of Life.

B'seifer ḥayyim b'rakhah v'shalom u-farnasah tovah, nizzakheir v'nikkateiv l'fanekha, anaḥnu v'khol am'kha beit yisra·el, l'ḥayyim tovim u-l'shalom.

Barukh atah ADONAI, who brings peace.

When the Amidah is recited silently, personal prayers are added here. The following may also be recited:

My God, keep my tongue from evil, my lips from lies. Help me ignore those who would slander me. Let me be humble before all. Open my heart to Your Torah, that I may pursue Your mitzvot. Frustrate the designs of those who plot evil against me; make nothing of their schemes. Act for the sake of Your name, Your power, Your holiness, and Your Torah. Answer my prayer for the deliverance of Your people. May the words of my mouth and the meditations of my heart be acceptable to You, ADONAI, my rock and my redeemer. May the One who brings peace to the universe bring peace to us and to all the people Israel [and to all who dwell on earth]. Amen.

ON SHABBAT, WE CONTINUE WITH KADDISH SHALEM ON PAGE 195.

We rise as the ark is opened. An alternative version begins on page 93.
Avinu Malkeinu is not recited on Shabbat.

אָבִינוּ מַלְכֵּנוּ! חָטָאנוּ לְפָנֶיךָ.

אָבִינוּ מַלְכֵּנוּ! אֵין לָנוּ מֶלֶךְ אֶלָּא אָתָּה.

אָבִינוּ מַלְכֵּנוּ! עֲשֵׂה עִמָּנוּ לְמַעַן שְׁמֶךָ.

אָבִינוּ מַלְכֵּנוּ! חַדֵּשׁ עָלֵינוּ שָׁנָה טוֹבָה.

אָבִינוּ מַלְכֵּנוּ! בַּטֵּל מֵעָלֵינוּ כָּל־גְּזֵרוֹת קָשׁוֹת.

אָבִינוּ מַלְכֵּנוּ! בַּטֵּל מַחְשְׁבוֹת שׂוֹנְאֵינוּ.

אָבִינוּ מַלְכֵּנוּ! הָפֵר עֲצַת אוֹיְבֵינוּ.

אָבִינוּ מַלְכֵּנוּ! כַּלֵּה כָּל־צַר וּמַשְׂטִין מֵעָלֵינוּ.

אָבִינוּ מַלְכֵּנוּ! כַּלֵּה דֶּבֶר וְחֶרֶב וְרָעָב וּשְׁבִי וּמַשְׁחִית וְעָוֹן
וּשְׁמַד מִבְּנֵי בְרִיתֶךָ.

אָבִינוּ מַלְכֵּנוּ! סְלַח וּמְחַל לְכָל־עֲוֹנוֹתֵינוּ.

אָבִינוּ מַלְכֵּנוּ! מְחֵה וְהַעֲבֵר פְּשָׁעֵינוּ וְחַטֹּאתֵינוּ מִנֶּגֶד עֵינֶיךָ.

After the leader has recited each of these lines, we repeat it:

◁ אָבִינוּ מַלְכֵּנוּ! הַחֲזִירֵנוּ בִּתְשׁוּבָה שְׁלֵמָה לְפָנֶיךָ.

אָבִינוּ מַלְכֵּנוּ! שְׁלַח רְפוּאָה שְׁלֵמָה לְחוֹלֵי עַמֶּךָ.

אָבִינוּ מַלְכֵּנוּ! זָכְרֵנוּ בְּזִכָּרוֹן טוֹב לְפָנֶיךָ.

אָבִינוּ מַלְכֵּנוּ! כָּתְבֵנוּ בְּסֵפֶר חַיִּים טוֹבִים.

אָבִינוּ מַלְכֵּנוּ! כָּתְבֵנוּ בְּסֵפֶר גְּאֻלָּה וִישׁוּעָה.

אָבִינוּ מַלְכֵּנוּ! כָּתְבֵנוּ בְּסֵפֶר פַּרְנָסָה וְכַלְכָּלָה.

אָבִינוּ מַלְכֵּנוּ! כָּתְבֵנוּ בְּסֵפֶר זְכֻיּוֹת.

אָבִינוּ מַלְכֵּנוּ! כָּתְבֵנוּ בְּסֵפֶר סְלִיחָה וּמְחִילָה.

אָבִינוּ מַלְכֵּנוּ! הַצְמַח לָנוּ יְשׁוּעָה בְּקָרוֹב.

אָבִינוּ מַלְכֵּנוּ! הָרֵם קֶרֶן יִשְׂרָאֵל עַמֶּךָ.

אָבִינוּ מַלְכֵּנוּ! הָרֵם קֶרֶן מְשִׁיחֶךָ.

אָבִינוּ מַלְכֵּנוּ! שְׁמַע קוֹלֵנוּ, חוּס וְרַחֵם עָלֵינוּ.

אָבִינוּ מַלְכֵּנוּ! קַבֵּל בְּרַחֲמִים וּבְרָצוֹן אֶת־תְּפִלָּתֵנוּ.

אָבִינוּ מַלְכֵּנוּ! נָא אַל תְּשִׁיבֵנוּ רֵיקָם מִלְּפָנֶיךָ.

אָבִינוּ מַלְכֵּנוּ! זְכוֹר כִּי עָפָר אֲנָחְנוּ.

אָבִינוּ מַלְכֵּנוּ! חֲמוֹל עָלֵינוּ וְעַל עוֹלָלֵינוּ וְטַפֵּנוּ.

אָבִינוּ מַלְכֵּנוּ! עֲשֵׂה לְמַעַן הֲרוּגִים עַל שֵׁם קָדְשֶׁךָ.

אָבִינוּ מַלְכֵּנוּ! עֲשֵׂה לְמַעַן טְבוּחִים עַל יַחוּדֶךָ.

AVINU MALKEINU אָבִינוּ מַלְכֵּנוּ. The Babylonian Talmud reports: "It once happened that Rabbi Eliezer led the congregation and recited twenty-four b'rakhot, but his prayers were not answered. Then Rabbi Akiva followed him and led the congregation in prayer, saying, 'Our father, our sovereign, You are truly our father. Our father, our sovereign, we have no ruler but You. Our father, our sovereign, we have sinned before You. Our father, our sovereign, have mercy on us. Our father, our sovereign, do it for Your name's sake,' and his prayers were answered" (Taanit 25b). Generations have added many more verses to this prayer. The verses mentioning the martyrs were added after the Crusades.

Avinu Malkeinu was first introduced as a prayer for material blessing. It then took on an added layer of pleas against devastation by human enemies, and finally, special prayers for the High Holy Days (for instance, "inscribe us in the Book of Life").

The image of God as "father" represents relatedness and closeness; that of God as Ruler conveys authority and greater distance. Jewish theology has always talked of transcendence and immanence, God as ineffable and God as close at hand. The appeal here brings together both aspects of God.

Avinu Malkeinu

We rise as the ark is opened. An alternative version begins on page 93. Avinu Malkeinu is not recited on Shabbat.

Avinu Malkeinu, we have sinned in Your presence.
Avinu Malkeinu, we have no sovereign but You.
Avinu Malkeinu, act toward us kindly in accord with Your name.
Avinu Malkeinu, make this a good new year for us.
Avinu Malkeinu, annul every harsh decree against us.
Avinu Malkeinu, nullify the designs of our foes.
Avinu Malkeinu, frustrate the plots of our enemies.
Avinu Malkeinu, rid us of every oppressor and adversary.
Avinu Malkeinu, rid Your covenanted people of disease, war, hunger, captivity, and destruction.
Avinu Malkeinu, forgive and pardon all our sins.
Avinu Malkeinu, do not look toward our sins and transgressions; blot them out.
Avinu Malkeinu, return us to Your presence, fully penitent.
Avinu Malkeinu, send complete healing to the sick among Your people.
Avinu Malkeinu, remember us favorably.
Avinu Malkeinu, inscribe us for good in the Book of Life.
Avinu Malkeinu, inscribe us in the Book of Redemption.
Avinu Malkeinu, inscribe us in the Book of Sustenance.
Avinu Malkeinu, inscribe us in the Book of Merit.
Avinu Malkeinu, inscribe us in the Book of Forgiveness.

Avinu malkeinu, haḥazireinu bi-t'shuvah sh'leimah l'fanekha.
Avinu malkeinu, sh'laḥ r'fu·ah sh'leimah l'ḥolei ammekha.
Avinu malkeinu, zokhreinu b'zikkaron tov l'fanekha.
Avinu malkeinu, kotveinu b'seifer ḥayyim tovim.
Avinu malkeinu, kotveinu b'seifer g'ullah vi-shu·ah.
Avinu malkeinu, kotveinu b'seifer parnasah v'khalkalah.
Avinu malkeinu, kotveinu b'seifer z'khuyyot.
Avinu malkeinu, kotveinu b'seifer s'liḥah u-m'ḥilah.

Avinu Malkeinu, cause our salvation to flourish soon.
Avinu Malkeinu, cause Your people Israel to be exalted.
Avinu Malkeinu, raise up Your anointed with strength.
Avinu Malkeinu, hear our voice, be kind, sympathize with us.
Avinu Malkeinu, accept our prayer, willingly and lovingly.
Avinu Malkeinu, do not turn us away empty-handed.
Avinu Malkeinu, remember that we are but dust.
Avinu Malkeinu, have compassion for us, our infants, and our children.
Avinu Malkeinu, do this for the sake of those who were martyred for Your holy name.
Avinu Malkeinu, do this for the sake of those who were slaughtered for their exclusive devotion to You.

אָבִינוּ מַלְכֵּנוּ! עֲשֵׂה לְמַעַן בָּאֵי בָאֵשׁ וּבַמַּיִם עַל קִדּוּשׁ שְׁמֶךָ.

אָבִינוּ מַלְכֵּנוּ! עֲשֵׂה לְמַעַנְךָ אִם לֹא לְמַעֲנֵנוּ.

אָבִינוּ מַלְכֵּנוּ! חָנֵּנוּ וַעֲנֵנוּ, כִּי אֵין בָּנוּ מַעֲשִׂים, עֲשֵׂה עִמָּנוּ צְדָקָה וָחֶסֶד וְהוֹשִׁיעֵנוּ.

קַדִּישׁ שָׁלֵם

יִתְגַּדַּל וְיִתְקַדַּשׁ שְׁמֵהּ רַבָּא, בְּעָלְמָא דִּי בְרָא, כִּרְעוּתֵהּ, וְיַמְלִיךְ מַלְכוּתֵהּ בְּחַיֵּיכוֹן וּבְיוֹמֵיכוֹן וּבְחַיֵּי דְכָל־בֵּית יִשְׂרָאֵל, בַּעֲגָלָא וּבִזְמַן קָרִיב, וְאִמְרוּ אָמֵן.

יְהֵא שְׁמֵהּ רַבָּא מְבָרַךְ לְעָלַם וּלְעָלְמֵי עָלְמַיָּא.

יִתְבָּרַךְ וְיִשְׁתַּבַּח וְיִתְפָּאַר וְיִתְרוֹמַם וְיִתְנַשֵּׂא וְיִתְהַדָּר וְיִתְעַלֶּה וְיִתְהַלָּל שְׁמֵהּ דְּקֻדְשָׁא, בְּרִיךְ הוּא, לְעֵלָּא לְעֵלָּא מִכָּל־בִּרְכָתָא וְשִׁירָתָא תֻּשְׁבְּחָתָא וְנֶחֱמָתָא דַּאֲמִירָן בְּעָלְמָא, וְאִמְרוּ אָמֵן.

תִּתְקַבַּל צְלוֹתְהוֹן וּבָעוּתְהוֹן דְּכָל־יִשְׂרָאֵל קֳדָם אֲבוּהוֹן דִּי בִשְׁמַיָּא, וְאִמְרוּ אָמֵן.

יְהֵא שְׁלָמָא רַבָּא מִן שְׁמַיָּא וְחַיִּים עָלֵינוּ וְעַל כָּל־יִשְׂרָאֵל, וְאִמְרוּ אָמֵן.

עֹשֶׂה שָׁלוֹם בִּמְרוֹמָיו הוּא יַעֲשֶׂה שָׁלוֹם עָלֵינוּ וְעַל כָּל־יִשְׂרָאֵל [וְעַל כָּל־יוֹשְׁבֵי תֵבֵל], וְאִמְרוּ אָמֵן.

KADDISH SHALEM קַדִּישׁ שָׁלֵם is recited at the end of every worship service that features an Amidah. Its distinguishing sentence is the line תִּתְקַבַּל צְלוֹתְהוֹן, "May the prayers . . . of all Israel be accepted."

PEACE . . . HARMONY שְׁלָמָא שָׁלוֹם. Like many traditional Jewish prayers, this one ends with thoughts of peace.

Said the Holy One to
Israel: "My children,
if you turn this day,
changing your bad ways,
you will become new
creatures, not the same
people as before. Then
will I consider you as if
I had created you anew.
And then shall you,
newborn, be as the new
heavens and the new
earth that I shall create."

Avinu Malkeinu, do this for the sake of those who went
through fire and water to sanctify Your holy name.
 Avinu Malkeinu, do this for Your sake if not for ours.

Avinu Malkeinu, have mercy on us, answer us, for our deeds are
insufficient; deal with us charitably and lovingly, and redeem us.

*Avinu Malkeinu, honneinu va-aneinu ki ein banu ma·asim,
aseih immanu tz'dakah va-hesed v'hoshi·einu.*

Kaddish Shalem

May God's great name be exalted and hallowed throughout the
created world, as is God's wish. May God's sovereignty soon be
established, in your lifetime and in your days, and in the days of
all the House of Israel. And respond with: *Amen.*

May God's great name be acknowledged forever and ever!
Y'hei sh'meih rabba m'varakh l'alam u-l'almei almayya.

May the name of the Holy One be acknowledged and celebrated, lauded and worshipped, exalted and honored, extolled
and acclaimed—though God, who is blessed, *b'rikh hu,* is truly
far beyond all acknowledgment and praise, or any expressions
of gratitude or consolation ever spoken in the world. And
respond with: *Amen.*

May the prayers and pleas of all Israel be accepted by their
creator in heaven. And respond with: *Amen.*

May abundant peace from heaven, and life, come to us and to
all Israel. And respond with: *Amen.*

May the One who brings harmony on high, bring harmony to
us and to all Israel [and to all who dwell on earth]. And respond
with: *Amen.*

*Oseh shalom bi-m'romav hu ya·aseh shalom aleinu v'al kol yisra·el [v'al
kol yosh'vei teiveil], v'imru amen.*

עָלֵינוּ לְשַׁבֵּחַ לַאֲדוֹן הַכֹּל, לָתֵת גְּדֻלָּה לְיוֹצֵר בְּרֵאשִׁית, שֶׁלֹּא עָשָׂנוּ כְּגוֹיֵי הָאֲרָצוֹת, וְלֹא שָׂמָנוּ כְּמִשְׁפְּחוֹת הָאֲדָמָה, שֶׁלֹּא שָׂם חֶלְקֵנוּ כָּהֶם, וְגֹרָלֵנוּ כְּכָל-הֲמוֹנָם.

וַאֲנַחְנוּ כּוֹרְעִים וּמִשְׁתַּחֲוִים וּמוֹדִים, לִפְנֵי מֶלֶךְ מַלְכֵי הַמְּלָכִים, הַקָּדוֹשׁ בָּרוּךְ הוּא, שֶׁהוּא נוֹטֶה שָׁמַיִם וְיֹסֵד אָרֶץ, וּמוֹשַׁב יְקָרוֹ בַּשָּׁמַיִם מִמַּעַל, וּשְׁכִינַת עֻזּוֹ בְּגָבְהֵי מְרוֹמִים, הוּא אֱלֹהֵינוּ אֵין עוֹד. אֱמֶת מַלְכֵּנוּ אֶפֶס זוּלָתוֹ, כַּכָּתוּב בְּתוֹרָתוֹ: וְיָדַעְתָּ הַיּוֹם וַהֲשֵׁבֹתָ אֶל-לְבָבֶךָ, כִּי יְהוה הוּא הָאֱלֹהִים בַּשָּׁמַיִם מִמַּעַל, וְעַל הָאָרֶץ מִתָּחַת, אֵין עוֹד.

עַל כֵּן נְקַוֶּה לְּךָ יְהוה אֱלֹהֵינוּ, לִרְאוֹת מְהֵרָה בְּתִפְאֶרֶת עֻזֶּךָ, לְהַעֲבִיר גִּלּוּלִים מִן הָאָרֶץ וְהָאֱלִילִים כָּרוֹת יִכָּרֵתוּן, לְתַקֵּן עוֹלָם בְּמַלְכוּת שַׁדַּי, וְכָל-בְּנֵי בָשָׂר יִקְרְאוּ בִשְׁמֶךָ, לְהַפְנוֹת אֵלֶיךָ כָּל-רִשְׁעֵי אָרֶץ. יַכִּירוּ וְיֵדְעוּ כָּל-יוֹשְׁבֵי תֵבֵל, כִּי לְךָ תִּכְרַע כָּל-בֶּרֶךְ, תִּשָּׁבַע כָּל-לָשׁוֹן. לְפָנֶיךָ יְהוה אֱלֹהֵינוּ יִכְרְעוּ וְיִפֹּלוּ, וְלִכְבוֹד שִׁמְךָ יְקָר יִתֵּנוּ. וִיקַבְּלוּ כֻלָּם אֶת-עֹל מַלְכוּתֶךָ. וְתִמְלֹךְ עֲלֵיהֶם מְהֵרָה לְעוֹלָם וָעֶד. כִּי הַמַּלְכוּת שֶׁלְּךָ הִיא, וּלְעוֹלְמֵי עַד תִּמְלֹךְ בְּכָבוֹד.

◁ כַּכָּתוּב בְּתוֹרָתֶךָ: יְהוה יִמְלֹךְ לְעוֹלָם וָעֶד.

וְנֶאֱמַר: וְהָיָה יְהוה לְמֶלֶךְ עַל כָּל-הָאָרֶץ, בַּיּוֹם הַהוּא יִהְיֶה יְהוה אֶחָד, וּשְׁמוֹ אֶחָד.

ALEINU עָלֵינוּ. This prayer was originally composed for the Malkhuyot מַלְכֻיּוֹת ("Sovereignty") section of the Rosh Hashanah Musaf service. Since the late Middle Ages, it has acquired a special pride of place in Ashkenazic liturgy and is recited as part of the conclusion of every service.

It is customary to physically bow when we recite the line "And so we bow" וַאֲנַחְנוּ כּוֹרְעִים (Va-anaḥnu kor'im).

KNOW THIS DAY וְיָדַעְתָּ הַיּוֹם. Deuteronomy 4:39, Moses' speech enunciating the meaning of God's revelation at Sinai.

ESTABLISHING IN THE WORLD THE SOVEREIGNTY OF THE ALMIGHTY לְתַקֵּן עוֹלָם בְּמַלְכוּת שַׁדַּי. Beginning in the 19th century, this phrase came to be seen as similar to Isaiah's call to be "a light unto the nations," and it was reinterpreted as a call to universal justice. In this vein, the phrase l'takken olam לְתַקֵּן עוֹלָם was understood to mean "to repair the world," to be partners with God in achieving a time of peace and righteousness. Even earlier, Maimonides (12th century) had argued that the single most important characteristic of God's sovereignty would be an end to one people dominating another. This paragraph emphasizes God's saving hand.

ADONAI WILL REIGN FOREVER AND EVER יְהוה יִמְלֹךְ לְעוֹלָם וָעֶד. From the Song at the Sea, Exodus 15:18.

ON THAT DAY ADONAI SHALL BE ONE בַּיּוֹם הַהוּא יִהְיֶה יְהוה אֶחָד. Zechariah 14:9. In reciting the Sh'ma, we declare that God is one. Through our prayer we hope to make the world at one with God.

CONCLUDING PRAYERS

Aleinu

It is for us to praise the ruler of all, to acclaim the Creator, who has not made us merely a nation, nor formed us as all earthly families, nor given us an ordinary destiny.

ʄ And so we bow, acknowledging the supreme sovereign, the Holy One, who is praised—the One who spreads out the heavens and establishes the earth, whose glorious abode is in the highest heaven, whose powerful presence is in the loftiest heights. This is our God, none else; ours is the true sovereign, there is no other. As it is written in the Torah: "Know this day and take it to heart, that ADONAI is God in heaven above and on earth below, there is no other."

Aleinu l'shabbei·aḥ la-adon ha-kol, la-teit g'dullah l'yotzeir b'reishit,
she-lo asanu k'goyei ha-aratzot, v'lo samanu k'mishp'ḥot ha-adamah,
she-lo sam ḥelkeinu ka-hem, v'goraleinu k'khol hamonam.
ʄ Va-anaḥnu kor'im u-mishtaḥavim u-modim,
lifnei melekh malkhei ha-m'lakhim, ha-kadosh barukh hu.
She-hu noteh shamayim v'yoseid aretz, u-moshav y'karo ba-shamayim
mi-ma·al, u-sh'khinat uzzo b'govhei m'romim, hu eloheinu ein od.
Emet malkeinu efes zulato, ka-katuv b'torato: v'yadata ha-yom
va-hasheivota el l'vavekha, ki Adonai hu ha-Elohim
ba-shamayim mi-ma·al, v'al ha-aretz mi-taḥat, ein od.

And so, ADONAI our God, we await You, that soon we may behold Your strength revealed in full glory, sweeping away the abominations of the earth, obliterating idols, establishing in the world the sovereignty of the Almighty. All flesh will call out Your name—even the wicked will turn toward You. Then all who live on earth will recognize and understand that to You alone knees must bend and allegiance be sworn. All will bow down and prostrate themselves before You, ADONAI our God, honor Your glorious name, and accept the obligation of Your sovereignty. May You soon rule over them forever and ever, for true dominion is Yours; You will rule in glory until the end of time.

As is written in Your Torah: "ADONAI will reign forever and ever." And as the prophet said: "ADONAI shall be acknowledged sovereign of all the earth. On that day ADONAI shall be one, and the name of God, one."

V'ne·emar: v'hayah Adonai l'melekh al kol ha-aretz,
ba-yom ha-hu yihyeh Adonai eḥad, u-sh'mo eḥad.

קַדִּישׁ יָתוֹם

Mourners and those observing Yahrzeit:

יִתְגַּדַּל וְיִתְקַדַּשׁ שְׁמֵהּ רַבָּא, בְּעָלְמָא דִּי בְרָא, כִּרְעוּתֵהּ,
וְיַמְלִיךְ מַלְכוּתֵהּ בְּחַיֵּיכוֹן וּבְיוֹמֵיכוֹן וּבְחַיֵּי דְכָל־בֵּית
יִשְׂרָאֵל, בַּעֲגָלָא וּבִזְמַן קָרִיב, וְאִמְרוּ אָמֵן.

Congregation and mourners:

יְהֵא שְׁמֵהּ רַבָּא מְבָרַךְ לְעָלַם וּלְעָלְמֵי עָלְמַיָּא.

Mourners:

יִתְבָּרַךְ וְיִשְׁתַּבַּח וְיִתְפָּאַר וְיִתְרוֹמַם וְיִתְנַשֵּׂא
וְיִתְהַדָּר וְיִתְעַלֶּה וְיִתְהַלָּל שְׁמֵהּ דְּקֻדְשָׁא, **בְּרִיךְ הוּא,**
לְעֵלָּא לְעֵלָּא מִכָּל־בִּרְכָתָא וְשִׁירָתָא, תֻּשְׁבְּחָתָא
וְנֶחָמָתָא דַּאֲמִירָן בְּעָלְמָא, וְאִמְרוּ אָמֵן.

יְהֵא שְׁלָמָא רַבָּא מִן שְׁמַיָּא וְחַיִּים עָלֵינוּ
וְעַל כָּל־יִשְׂרָאֵל, וְאִמְרוּ אָמֵן.

עֹשֶׂה שָׁלוֹם בִּמְרוֹמָיו הוּא יַעֲשֶׂה שָׁלוֹם עָלֵינוּ
וְעַל כָּל־יִשְׂרָאֵל [וְעַל כָּל־יוֹשְׁבֵי תֵבֵל], וְאִמְרוּ אָמֵן.

Mourner's Kaddish

For an explanation of Kaddish, see page 26.

May God's great name be exalted and hallowed throughout the created world, as is God's wish. May God's sovereignty soon be established, in your lifetime and in your days, and in the days of all the House of Israel. And respond with: *Amen.*

May God's great name be acknowledged forever and ever!

May the name of the Holy One be acknowledged and celebrated, lauded and worshipped, exalted and honored, extolled and acclaimed—though God, who is blessed, *b'rikh hu,* is truly far beyond all acknowledgment and praise, or any expressions of gratitude or consolation ever spoken in the House of Israel. And respond with: *Amen.*

May abundant peace from heaven, and life, come to us and to all Israel. And respond with: *Amen.*

May the One who brings harmony on high, bring harmony to us and to all Israel [and to all who dwell on earth]. And respond with: *Amen.*

Mourners and those observing Yahrzeit:
Yitgaddal v'yitkaddash sh'meih rabba, b'alma di v'ra, ki-r'uteih,
v'yamlikh malkhuteih b'ḥayyeikhon u-v'yomeikhon u-v'ḥayyei d'khol beit yisra·el,
ba-agala u-viz'man kariv,
v'imru amen.

Congregation and mourners:
Y'hei sh'meih rabba m'varakh l'alam u-l'almei almayya.

Mourners:
Yitbarakh v'yishtabbaḥ v'yitpa·ar v'yitromam v'yitnassei v'yit·haddar
v'yit·alleh v'yit·hallal sh'meih d'kudsha, b'rikh hu,
l'eilla l'eilla mi-kol birkhata v'shirata tushb'ḥata v'neḥamata da-amiran b'alma,
v'imru amen.

Y'hei sh'lama rabba min sh'mayya v'ḥayyim aleinu v'al kol yisra·el,
v'imru amen.

Oseh shalom bi-m'romav hu ya·aseh shalom aleinu
v'al kol yisra·el [v'al kol yosh'vei teiveil],
v'imru amen.

ערב יום כיפור בבית   EREV YOM KIPPUR AT HOME

Before sitting down to the last meal before the beginning of Yom Kippur, it is customary to pray the afternoon service and recite the confession (page 430).

Kapparot כַּפָּרוֹת

Holding the money to be given to tz'dakah in one's hand:

זֶה חֲלִיפָתִי, זֶה תְּמוּרָתִי, זֶה כַּפָּרָתִי. זֶה הַכֶּסֶף יֵלֵךְ לִצְדָקָה, וַאֲנִי אֵלֵךְ וְאֶכָּנֵס לְחַיִּים טוֹבִים אֲרֻכִּים וּלְשָׁלוֹם.

This is in my stead. May this be my substitute; may this be my atonement. This money will go to tz'dakah, that I may enter the path to a good, long life, and to peace.

Zeh ḥalifati, zeh t'murati, zeh kapparati.
Zeh ha-kesef yeileikh li-tz'dakah,
va-ani eileikh v'ekkaneis l'ḥayyim tovim arukkim u-l'shalom.

After concluding the meal, before leaving for synagogue:

Lighting a Memorial Candle

Upon lighting a memorial candle, the following may be recited:

"A light from God is a human soul" (Proverbs 20:27). At this moment of solemn reflection, I call to mind memories of
_____. May _____'s soul enjoy eternal life, together with the souls of Sarah, Rebecca, Rachel, and Leah; Abraham, Isaac, and Jacob; and all righteous women and men. May I be inspired to acts of justice and kindness in _____'s memory. Amen.

KAPPAROT כַּפָּרוֹת. The ritual of Kapparot symbolizes the transfer of sins from the sinner to some other object or being. In this respect, it is like the ritual of Tashlikh on Rosh Hashanah, or the ancient Yom Kippur ceremony of the scapegoat (Leviticus 16). Whereas this ceremony has been performed using a chicken—later eaten at the meal—today it is more common to use a small sum of money, bundled into a cloth and circled over the head of the individual as the words of the ritual are recited. The money is then contributed to tz'dakah, in fulfillment of the ancient promise that acts of charity can save us from the severity of any decree against us.

THE MEAL סְעוּדָה מַפְסֶקֶת. Before we leave for the synagogue and the fast of Yom Kippur begins, we eat a סְעוּדָה מַפְסֶקֶת, *s'udah mafseket*, a concluding meal, to prepare us for the fast ahead. The meal is eaten with a spirit of joy for having arrived at this time. There is no Kiddush for Yom Kippur, though the normal rituals for a meal—handwashing, *motzi*, and Grace after Meals—are observed (see page 32). We light candles before leaving for synagogue. Our mood becomes more solemn as we contemplate the day's themes. At this time it is especially appropriate to ask forgiveness from those we have wronged.

MEMORIAL CANDLE. Before we leave for synagogue and before we light the Holy Day candles, it is customary to light a *yizkor* candle, a memorial candle, which will burn throughout Yom Kippur for immediate family members whom we remember now. Some light one candle for each person in the family who has died. There is no traditional *b'rakhah* for this candlelighting—it is a moment of private meditation.

Kapparot

Every act of charity and
every deed of kindness
that the people Israel do
is vital in making peace—
and is an important
intercessor for the
people Israel with God in
heaven.

—BABYLONIAN TALMUD,
BAVA BATRA

Lighting the
Yahrzeit Candle

A new year beginning,
and I can't call you to say,
"I'm bursting with
wonderful news!"
Your arms won't
encircle me
when I grieve,
when I mourn,
you'll never know now
the unexpected
achievements,
the abiding sorrows.

And yet, as I stand here
with this candle,
I allow myself
some quiet moments,
until, once again,
your face shines
in my memory,
until, once again,
I feel you
blessing me.

—MERLE FELD

Candlelighting

הַדְלָקַת נֵרוֹת

בָּרוּךְ אַתָּה יהוה אֱלֹהֵינוּ מֶלֶךְ הָעוֹלָם, אֲשֶׁר קִדְּשָׁנוּ בְּמִצְוֹתָיו וְצִוָּנוּ לְהַדְלִיק נֵר שֶׁל [שַׁבָּת וְשֶׁל] יוֹם הַכִּפּוּרִים.

Barukh atah ADONAI, our God, ruler of time and space, who
has made us holy through mitzvot and instructed us to light the
[Shabbat and] Yom Kippur candles.

Barukh atah Adonai eloheinu melekh ha-olam,
asher kid'shanu b'mitzvotav v'tzivvanu
l'hadlik neir shel [Shabbat v'shel] yom ha-kippurim.

בָּרוּךְ אַתָּה יהוה אֱלֹהֵינוּ מֶלֶךְ הָעוֹלָם, שֶׁהֶחֱיָנוּ וְקִיְּמָנוּ וְהִגִּיעָנוּ לַזְּמַן הַזֶּה.

Barukh atah ADONAI, our God, ruler of time and space, for
granting us life, for sustaining us, and for bringing us to this
moment.

Barukh atah Adonai eloheinu melekh ha-olam,
she-heḥeyanu v'kiy'manu v'higgi·anu la-z'man ha-zeh.

Blessing the Children

בִּרְכַּת הַבָּנִים וְהַבָּנוֹת

It is a custom to add the following prayers before Yom Kippur:

For a son:

יְשִׂימְךָ אֱלֹהִים כְּאֶפְרַיִם וְכִמְנַשֶּׁה.

May God make you like Ephraim and Manasseh.

Y'sim'kha elohim k'efrayim v'khi-m'nasheh.

For a daughter:

יְשִׂימֵךְ אֱלֹהִים כְּשָׂרָה רִבְקָה רָחֵל וְלֵאָה.

May God make you like Sarah, Rebecca, Rachel, and Leah.

Y'simeikh elohim k'sarah, rivkah, raheil, v'lei·ah.

Recited for all:

יְבָרֶכְךָ יהוה וְיִשְׁמְרֶךָ.
יָאֵר יהוה פָּנָיו אֵלֶיךָ וִיחֻנֶּךָּ.
יִשָּׂא יהוה פָּנָיו אֵלֶיךָ וְיָשֵׂם לְךָ שָׁלוֹם.

May ADONAI bless and protect you.
May ADONAI's countenance shine upon you
　　and grant you kindness.
May ADONAI's countenance be lifted toward you
　　and grant you peace.

Y'varekh'kha Adonai v'yishm'rekha.
Ya·eir Adonai panav eilekha vi-hunnekka.
Yissa Adonai panav eilekha v'yaseim l'kha shalom.

BLESSING THE CHILDREN.
After lighting the candles, it is customary to bless the family using biblical verses that express our hopes for peace and protection during the year ahead. For sons, we fulfill Jacob's blessing to his grandsons Manasseh and Ephraim, in which he told them, "By you shall the people Israel invoke blessings, saying: 'May God make you like Ephraim and Manasseh'" (Genesis 48:20). For daughters, Jews have long recited a parallel blessing naming the four matriarchs. We follow that with a recitation of the Priestly Blessing (Numbers 6:24–26). Finally, the blessing "May your eyes look straight ahead…" is traditionally invoked only on this occasion, just before Yom Kippur.

Meditation before Yom Kippur for One Who Cannot Fast

Ribbono shel olam/Master of the Universe,
Creator of all, Source of all Life,
who knows what is deep in human hearts,
who nurtures every living being:

As you know, God,
Yom Kippur is upon us, and because of my condition,
I am not able to keep the traditional fast—
I cannot abstain totally from eating.

You know, God, that it is not my intent
to be apart from our people and our tradition.
My current state of health makes it unsuitable for me to fast.

So, God, I turn to You now in sincerity and openness.
Help me in the coming year to do my best in guarding my health.
Help us, Your children, learn how to protect our bodies from harm.
Help us support others in caring for their *tzelem Elohim*, the divine image within all of us.

Guide caring family and all caregivers in their partnering with You
to bring healing, if not cure; support and strength, if not an end to symptoms.
Grant them the ability to do this mitzvah with love and devotion.

Rofei khol basar/Healer of all living creatures:
I thank You for the breath that is in me,
which lives for the possibilities of today and tomorrow.

—SIMKHA Y. WEINTRAUB
(adapted)

For a son:

עֵינֶיךָ לְנֹכַח יַבִּיטוּ,
פִּיךָ יְדַבֵּר חָכְמוֹת,
וְלִבְּךָ יֶהְגֶּה אֵימוֹת,
יָדֶיךָ יַעַסְקוּ בְּמִצְוֹת,
רַגְלֶיךָ יָרוּצוּ לַעֲשׂוֹת
רְצוֹן אָבִיךָ שֶׁבַּשָּׁמַיִם,
וְתִכָּתֵב וְתֵחָתֵם
לְחַיִּים טוֹבִים וַאֲרֻכִּים
בְּתוֹךְ כָּל־יִשְׂרָאֵל. אָמֵן.

For a daughter:

עֵינַיִךְ לְנֹכַח יַבִּיטוּ,
פִּיךְ יְדַבֵּר חָכְמוֹת,
וְלִבֵּךְ יֶהְגֶּה אֵימוֹת,
יָדַיִךְ יַעַסְקוּ בְּמִצְוֹת,
רַגְלַיִךְ יָרוּצוּ לַעֲשׂוֹת
רְצוֹן אָבִיךְ שֶׁבַּשָּׁמַיִם,
וְתִכָּתְבִי וְתֵחָתְמִי
לְחַיִּים טוֹבִים וַאֲרֻכִּים
בְּתוֹךְ כָּל־יִשְׂרָאֵל. אָמֵן.

May your eyes look straight ahead,
your mouth speak wisdom,
your heart meditate with awe and wonder,
your hands busy themselves with mitzvot,
your legs run to do the will of your Father in heaven,
and may you be inscribed and sealed for a good, long life
among all of the people Israel. Amen.

כל־נדרי וערבית ליום כיפור   KOL NIDREI AND EVENING SERVICE OF YOM KIPPUR

SHALOM שָׁלוֹם. Isaiah
57:19. This verse from the
Haftarah for Yom Kippur
morning is used here to welcome everyone to the
synagogue. The welcome will be developed further
when the liturgy declares that we are permitted
tonight "to pray with those who have transgressed."

שָׁלוֹם **שָׁלוֹם** לָרָחוֹק וְלַקָּרוֹב אָמַר יהוה.

KITTEL קִיטֶל. Originally a
Yiddish term, the word *kittel*
refers to a white garment
traditionally worn on Yom
Kippur as well as at sacred
moments of life transition,
including at a wedding and
as a burial shroud. Why do
the rabbi and cantor and some members of the
congregation wear white robes tonight? One explanation is that the priestly garments were white, and
the High Priest wore white rather than gold when
entering the Holy of Holies on Yom Kippur.

לִבִישַׁת קִיטֶל

כְּשֵׁם שֶׁאֲנִי מִתְלַבֵּשׁ/מִתְלַבֶּשֶׁת בְּבֶגֶד לָבָן, כֵּן תַּלְבִּין
אֶת־נִשְׁמָתִי וְגוּפָתִי, כַּכָּתוּב: אִם־יִהְיוּ חֲטָאֵיכֶם
כַּשָּׁנִים כַּשֶּׁלֶג יַלְבִּינוּ.

EVEN IF YOUR SINS אִם יִהְיוּ. Isaiah 1:18.

TALLIT טַלִּית. Kol Nidrei,
which we begin while there
is still daylight, is the only
evening service at which
a *tallit* is worn by congregants. We seek to come
before God on this day fully attired in garments
of holiness, just as the priests entered the Temple
Court in holy garments.

עֲטִיפַת טַלִּית

בָּרוּךְ אַתָּה יהוה אֱלֹהֵינוּ מֶלֶךְ הָעוֹלָם, אֲשֶׁר קִדְּשָׁנוּ
בְּמִצְוֹתָיו, וְצִוָּנוּ לְהִתְעַטֵּף בַּצִּיצִת.

WEARING A TALLIT. In most communities the *tallit*
is worn after the age of thirteen, though in some it
is not worn until one has married.

Women have traditionally been considered
exempt from this command, although the Talmud
records that the Rabbis taught that women were
required to wear *tzitzit*, with only one authority,
Rabbi Shimon, disagreeing (Babylonian Talmud,
Menaḥot 43a). It also records that such a prominent authority as Rabbi Yehudah required the
women in his household to wear them. It is becoming more and more common today for women to
wear a *tallit*. (*after Reuven Hammer*)

PREPARATORY PRAYERS

The Meaning of the Day

One day a year we make a journey in the company of the whole community of Israel— all of us together, each of us alone. That day is "The Day," the Day of Atonement, the day that is deathlike. It is the day we wear the *kittel*, the white gown that will one day be our shroud. It is the day when eating and drinking cease. It is a day when the world recedes and we are set free to uncover the true meaning of our lives.

—JONATHAN MAGONET
(adapted)

Entering Community

Prayer recited in community has a special

Shalom: shalom to those who are far off, shalom to those who are near, says ADONAI.

Meditation for Putting on the Kittel

Just as I clothe myself in this white garment, so may You purify my soul and my body, as the prophet Isaiah said,

> "Even if your sins are like crimson,
> they will turn snow-white."

K'shem she-ani mitlabbeish/mitlabbeshet b'veged lavan, kein talbin et nishmati v'gufati, ka-katuv: im yihyu hata·eikhem ka-shanim ka-sheleg yalbinu.

B'rakhah for Putting on the Tallit

Barukh atah ADONAI, our God, ruler of time and space, who has made us holy through mitzvot and instructed us to wrap ourselves in *tzitzit*.

Barukh atah Adonai eloheinu melekh ha-olam, asher kid'shanu b'mitzvotav v'tzivvanu l'hitattef ba-tzitzit.

dimension. Individuals may pray alone and keenly experience God. Judaism recognizes this and does not discourage solitary prayer. But Judaism is wary lest such aloneness become the norm and the permanent condition of the human being. Religion is not simply what we do with our aloneness, but what we do with others. Prayer should not isolate us, it should not lead us to believe that we need only God and ourselves, but prayer should lead us outward toward the love and care of the world we meet. Through prayer we discover how important the community is for sustaining our own salvation.

—REUVEN HAMMER (adapted)

God of the faithless and God of the faithful, with doubt, we come in loneliness, we wait silently, we pray expecting nothing, wanting everything.

God of the faithful and God of the faithless, You, who speak in whispered silence, You, whose reason is mystery— Your order is infinite; remember, we are finite and need words and reason.

God of the faithless and God of the faithful God in all forms and formless who was, and is, and will be, hear us and turn.

—EDWARD FELD
(after Myriam Kubovy)

רִבּוֹן כָּל־הָעוֹלָמִים, אֵין צַדִּיק בָּאָרֶץ אֲשֶׁר לֹא יֶחֱטָא. בָּשָׂר וָדָם אָנֹכִי, וְהַרְבֵּה הָלַכְתִּי בַּעֲצַת יֵצֶר הָרַע וּבְדַרְכֵי לִבִּי.

בָּרֵאתָ בִּי אָזְנַיִם לִשְׁמוֹעַ בָּהֶן לְעוֹלָמֶךָ וּלְתוֹרָתֶךָ, וַאֲנִי הִקְשַׁבְתִּי לִרְכִילוּת, לְשׁוֹן הָרַע, וְדִבְרֵי שִׂנְאָה, וַאֲפִלּוּ יוֹתֵר, הִתְנַהַגְתִּי כְּאִלּוּ אֲנִי שׁוֹמֵעַ לַאֲחֵרִים וְלֹא שָׁמְעָתִּי.

בָּרֵאתָ בִּי פֶּה וְלָשׁוֹן וְנָתַתָּ בָּהֶם כֹּחַ לְדַבֵּר בָּהֶם הָאוֹתִיּוֹת הַקְּדוֹשׁוֹת אֲשֶׁר בָּהֶן בָּרֵאתָ שָׁמַיִם וָאָרֶץ וּמְלוֹאָהּ, וּבְכֹחַ הַדִּבּוּר הִבְדַּלְתָּ אֶת־הָאָדָם מִן הַבְּהֵמָה, וַאֲנִי טִמֵּאתִי אֶת־פִּי בִּלְשׁוֹן הָרַע, בִּשְׁקָרִים, בְּלֵיצָנוּת, בִּרְכִילוּת, בְּמַחֲלֹקֶת, וּבְהַלְבָּנַת פָּנִים.

בָּרֵאתָ בִּי יָדַיִם וְחוּשׁ הַמִּשּׁוּשׁ לְהַבִּיעַ בָּהֶן אַהֲבָה וַעֲדִינוּת, וַאֲנִי הִכֵּיתִי וּפָגַעְתִּי בָּהֶן.

בָּרֵאתָ בִּי רַגְלַיִם לַהֲלוֹךְ לְכָל־דְּבַר מִצְוָה, וַאֲנִי רַצְתִּי לַעֲשׂוֹת דִּבְרֵי הֶבֶל וּבַטָּלָה.

בָּרֵאתָ בִּי אֶבְרֵי־מִין לְהַבִּיעַ בָּהֶן אַהֲבָה, וַאֲנִי הִשְׁתַּמַּשְׁתִּי בָּהֶן לַשֶּׁקֶר.

מִשַּׁשְׁתִּי אֶת־כָּל־אֵבָרַי וּמְצָאתִי אוֹתָם בַּעֲלֵי מוּמִין, אֵין בִּי מְתֹם.

לָכֵן אֲנִי מְקַבֵּל/מְקַבֶּלֶת עָלַי קְדֻשַּׁת יוֹם הַכִּפּוּרִים, חֲמִשָּׁה עִנּוּיִים שֶׁצִּוִּיתָ לָנוּ עַל יְדֵי מֹשֶׁה עַבְדְּךָ בְּתוֹרָתְךָ הַקְּדוֹשָׁה: אֲכִילָה וּשְׁתִיָּה, רְחִיצָה, סִיכָה, נְעִילַת הַסַּנְדָּל, תַּשְׁמִישׁ הַמִּטָּה, וְלִשְׁבּוֹת בַּיּוֹם הַקָּדוֹשׁ הַזֶּה מִכָּל־מְלָאכָה, לְבַקֵּשׁ סְלִיחָתְךָ עַל שִׁמּוּשֵׁי הַגָּרוּעַ בְּכָל־מַתְּנוֹתֶיךָ הַטּוֹבוֹת בַּשָּׁנָה שֶׁעָבְרָה, וְלִלְמוֹד מֵחָדָשׁ עַל קְדֻשַּׁת גּוּפִי.

A PRAYER FOR PURITY
תְּפִלָּה זַכָּה. This medita-tion on our imperfections, composed by Rabbi Abra-ham Danziger (1748–1820), author of *Ḥayyei Adam*, precedes the formal ser-vice. Danziger's words are deeply personal, and have been incorporated into most Ashkenazic maḥ-zorim. The prayer is a medi-tation on the five types of abstention discussed below, as well as the restriction against work on the holy day. The original medita-tion has been adapted.

ABSTENTION. Regarding Yom Kippur, Numbers 29:7 instructs וְעִנִּיתֶם אֶת־נַפְשֹׁתֵיכֶם, "afflict your-selves." Interpreting this verse, the Rabbis specified the following five absten-tions (Mishnah Yoma, chapter 8). First, we avoid eating and drinking. Second, we do not bathe, recognizing that even cleanliness is a luxury. We also avoid two other luxu-ries: wearing leather shoes, and using cosmetics. Lastly, we refrain from sexual relations.

Yom Kippur provides the opportunity to atone for sins against God. Yom Kippur does not automatically atone for sins against another human being until one has placated the person offended.

—MISHNAH YOMA

¶ A Meditation before Yom Kippur

I hereby forgive all who have hurt me, all who have done me wrong, whether deliberately or by accident, whether by word or by deed. May no one be punished on my account.

As I forgive and pardon fully those who have done me wrong, may those whom I have harmed by word or by deed forgive and pardon me, whether I acted deliberately or by accident.

May the words of my mouth and the meditations of my heart be acceptable to You, my rock and my redeemer.

Forgiveness Is Not Forgetting

We forgive, not because we believe that what was done was unimportant, but because we are prepared to put aside our anger long enough to hear words which reflect remorse and regret, long enough to begin to believe that people have the potential to grow.

—CHARLES KLEIN

A PRAYER FOR PURITY

Master of the Universe:
Is there a person anywhere who never sins?
I am but flesh and blood, often yielding to temptation;
I am human, often torn by conflicts.

You created me with ears
so I could listen to Your world and Your word,
but instead I have listened to gossip and words of hatred.
Worse, I have also given the impression of hearing
while I was not really listening.

You created me with a tongue and a mouth
and gave them the ability to speak the words
with which You formed heaven and earth;
with this power of speech You distinguished between
    human beings and animals.
But I made my mouth impure by embarrassing people,
by laughing at others, by gossiping, by lying,
by causing arguments.

You created me with hands, with the sense of touch,
with the ability to transmit tenderness and comfort,
but I have often used my hands for hurting others.

You created me with legs to walk in the paths of holiness,
but I have used them to run to do frivolous things.

You created me with sexual organs to express love,
but I have used them falsely.

I have looked over all my body from my head to my feet,
and I have been found wanting.

Therefore I come to You on this Yom Kippur—this Day of Atonement—and have taken on myself the mitzvah not to eat or drink, not to bathe or perfume myself, not to wear leather shoes or engage in acts of physical intimacy, and to stop all work, in order to devote this day to asking forgiveness for the misuse of Your gifts during this past year, and to learn once again the holiness of my body.

הוֹצָאַת הַתּוֹרָה לְכָל־נִדְרֵי

We rise as the ark is opened.
A meditation while the Torah scrolls are taken out of the ark:

שְׁגִיאוֹת מִי־יָבִין מִנִּסְתָּרוֹת נַקֵּנִי.
גַּם מִזֵּדִים חֲשֹׂךְ עַבְדֶּךָ
אַל־יִמְשְׁלוּ־בִי
אָז אֵיתָם
וְנִקֵּיתִי מִפֶּשַׁע רָב.
יִהְיוּ לְרָצוֹן אִמְרֵי־פִי
וְהֶגְיוֹן לִבִּי לְפָנֶיךָ
יהוה צוּרִי וְגֹאֲלִי.

In some congregations, a procession carrying the Torah scrolls marches around the synagogue while we recite repeatedly as needed:

אוֹר זָרֻעַ לַצַּדִּיק וּלְיִשְׁרֵי־לֵב שִׂמְחָה.

This affirmation is traditionally recited three times:

בִּישִׁיבָה שֶׁל מַעְלָה וּבִישִׁיבָה שֶׁל מַטָּה,
עַל דַּעַת הַמָּקוֹם וְעַל דַּעַת הַקָּהָל,
אָנוּ מַתִּירִין לְהִתְפַּלֵּל עִם הָעֲבַרְיָנִים.

TORAH SCROLLS הוֹצָאַת הַתּוֹרָה. A Jewish court is composed of three judges, tonight represented by the sh'li·aḥ tzibbur (prayer leader) and two communal leaders. At least two Torah scrolls are taken from the ark and held next to the leader to constitute the court, perhaps signifying that the heavenly court witnesses our liturgical affirmation of Kol Nidrei.

WHO CAN UNDERSTAND שְׁגִיאוֹת מִי יָבִין. Psalm 19:13–15.

LIGHT IS SOWN אוֹר זָרֻעַ. Psalm 97:11.

WE GRANT PERMISSION TO PRAY WITH THOSE WHO HAVE TRANSGRESSED אָנוּ מַתִּירִין לְהִתְפַּלֵּל עִם הָעֲבַרְיָנִים. Yom Kippur begins with the affirmation that whatever our faults and doubts on this night, everyone is welcome in the synagogue. While the origins of this preface to Kol Nidrei are obscure, during the late Middle Ages it took on special meaning. Conversos, Spanish and Portugese Jews who had kept their religious identity secret, wanted to rejoin their communities on Yom Kippur. The formula "By authority of the court" assured them that they had permission both from heaven above and from the community here on earth to pray with their fellow Jews. This affirmation can welcome all of us who feel burdened by guilt and the sense of being unworthy to join with our community. The Talmud says that, on a fast day, no prayer will be accepted unless sinners join in.

THE MELODY. The opening melodic phrase of Kol Nidrei—at least 1300 years old—bears a remarkable similarity to the French-Sephardic and Iraqi (Babylonian) chant for the beginning of Genesis, בְּרֵאשִׁית בָּרָא אֱלֹהִים. We know that some Babylonian Jews migrated to Spain, and their manner of singing the liturgy spread from there to southern France, and then eastward. While the early Babylonian chant of the Torah was not preserved in Europe, the use of this melody for Kol Nidrei preserves this ancient melody. The contrast between the pleading melody of the traditional Kol Nidrei and the somber legalism of the words points to a larger confrontation we encounter tonight: the sadness of recognizing our own imperfection and finitude, and the gap between what is required of us and our achievements.

❡ A Meditation on Kol Nidrei

All the vows on our lips,
the burdens in our hearts,
the pent-up regrets about
which we brooded and spoke
through prayers without end
on last Atonement Day
did not change our way of
life,
did not bring deliverance
in the year that has gone.
From mountain peaks of
fervor
we fell to common ways
at the close of the fast.
Will You hear our regret?
Will You open our prison,
release us from shackles of
habit?
Will You accept our prayers,
forgive our wrongs,
though we sin again and
again?
In moments of weakness
we do not remember
promises of Atonement Day.
Recall that we easily forget;
take only our heart's intent.
Forgive us, pardon us.

—ZE'EV FALK
(trans. Stanley Schachter)

Kol Nidrei

I am grateful for this,
a moment of truth,
grateful to stand before You
in judgment.

You know me as a liar
and I am flooded with relief
to have my darkest self
exposed at last.

Every day I break my vows—
to be the dutiful child,
selfless parent, caring friend,
responsible citizen of the
world.

No one sees, no one knows,
how often I take the easy way,
I let myself off the hook,
give myself the benefit of
the doubt—
every day, every day.

On this day, this one day,
I stand before You naked,
without disguise, without
embellishment, naked,
shivering, ridiculous.

I implore You—
let me try again.

—MERLE FELD

Taking out the Torah Scrolls

We rise as the ark is opened.
A meditation while the Torah scrolls are taken out of the ark:

Who can understand the source of our errors?

Cleanse me of secret faults, and restrain Your servant
from willful sins; may they not control me.

Then shall I be innocent of wrongdoing, wholly clear
of transgression.

May the words of my mouth and the meditations of
my heart be acceptable to You, ADONAI, my rock
and my redeemer.

In some congregations, a procession carrying the Torah scrolls marches around the synagogue while we recite repeatedly as needed:

Light is sown for the righteous, and joy for those whose
hearts are true.

Or zaru·a la-tzaddik u-l'yishrei lev simḥah.

THE EARTHLY AND HEAVENLY COURTS
This affirmation is traditionally recited three times:

By the authority of the court on high and by the
authority of this court below, with divine consent
and with the consent of this congregation, we grant
permission to pray with those who have transgressed.

Bi-shivah shel malah u-vi-shivah shel mattah,
al da·at ha-makom v'al da·at ha-kahal,
anu mattirin l'hitpalleil im ha-avaryanim.

YOM KIPPUR · EVENING SERVICE · KOL NIDREI

Recited three times:

כָּל־נִדְרֵי וֶאֱסָרֵי וַחֲרָמֵי, וְקוֹנָמֵי וְכִנּוּיֵי, וְקִנּוּסֵי
וּשְׁבוּעוֹת, דִּנְדַרְנָא וּדְאִשְׁתַּבַּעְנָא, וּדְאַחֲרִימְנָא
וְדַאֲסַרְנָא עַל נַפְשָׁתָנָא, מִיּוֹם כִּפּוּרִים זֶה עַד יוֹם
כִּפּוּרִים הַבָּא עָלֵינוּ לְטוֹבָה, כֻּלְּהוֹן אִחֲרַטְנָא בְהוֹן,
כֻּלְּהוֹן יְהוֹן שָׁרָן, שְׁבִיקִין שְׁבִיתִין, בְּטֵלִין וּמְבֻטָּלִין,
לָא שְׁרִירִין וְלָא קַיָּמִין. נִדְרָנָא לָא נִדְרֵי, וֶאֱסָרָנָא לָא
אֱסָרֵי, וּשְׁבוּעָתָנָא לָא שְׁבוּעוֹת.

Leader and congregation; some congregations recite this verse three times:

וְנִסְלַח לְכָל־עֲדַת בְּנֵי יִשְׂרָאֵל וְלַגֵּר הַגָּר בְּתוֹכָם,
כִּי לְכָל־הָעָם בִּשְׁגָגָה.

Leader:

סְלַח־נָא לַעֲוֹן הָעָם הַזֶּה כְּגֹדֶל חַסְדֶּךָ, וְכַאֲשֶׁר נָשָׂאתָה
לָעָם הַזֶּה מִמִּצְרַיִם וְעַד־הֵנָּה. וְשָׁם נֶאֱמַר:

Leader and congregation; some congregations recite this verse three times:

וַיֹּאמֶר יהוה סָלַחְתִּי כִּדְבָרֶךָ.

בָּרוּךְ אַתָּה יהוה אֱלֹהֵינוּ מֶלֶךְ הָעוֹלָם, שֶׁהֶחֱיָנוּ
וְקִיְּמָנוּ וְהִגִּיעָנוּ לַזְּמַן הַזֶּה:

The Torah scrolls are returned to the ark.
On days other than Shabbat, the service continues on page 207.

KOL NIDREI כָּל־נִדְרֵי. The Kol Nidrei is an Aramaic legal formula created in response to a widely felt need to nullify unfulfilled personal vows, a desire to enter the new year with a clean slate. In the 9th century, Babylonian Jewish leaders opposed its recitation. Therefore, Rabbenu Tam (France, 12th century) changed the language from past tense to future, a change that was widely adopted. Most of all, Kol Nidrei expresses our fear that even our best intentions for the new year will not be fulfilled. At the same time, it expresses how much we regret what was not accomplished in the past year. Kol Nidrei mentions seven types of promises and uses seven verbs expressing nullification. Seven symbolizes completion.

THE ENTIRE CONGREGATION . . . SHALL BE FORGIVEN וְנִסְלַח לְכָל־עֲדַת בְּנֵי יִשְׂרָאֵל. Numbers 15:26. In the Bible, this verse follows the command to bring a sacrifice when the entire people have sinned in error. Here it is removed from its biblical context and adopted as a statement of God's forgiveness, implying that all of our sins are really errors of judgment and so surely are to be forgiven when we express regret. Thus, the story of Yom Kippur is as much one of God's forgiveness as it is of human failing.

I HAVE FORGIVEN סָלַחְתִּי. Numbers 14:20. In the story of the scouts and the recalcitrance of the Israelites in the desert, the Bible assures us that even when the entire community acts against God's wishes, God forgives. Moses prays for the people, and God responds, "I have forgiven you as you have asked." So too, God forgives each of us when we approach this day regretting our acts.

FOR GRANTING US LIFE שֶׁהֶחֱיָנוּ. We recite this *b'rakhah*, offered on all occasions when we experience a moment of joyful newness, to remind us that Yom Kippur is a time of blessing. We stand together as a community and express thanks that we are here together after another year.

KOL NIDREI

A Deathless Prayer

Pain and . . . fear . . . kept us awake. A cloudless sky, thickly set with glittering stars, looked in upon our grief-filled prison. The moon shone through the window. Its light was dazzling that night and gave the pale, wasted faces of the prisoners a ghostly appearance. It was as if all the life had ebbed out of them. I shuddered with dread, for it suddenly occurred to me that I was the only living man among the corpses.

All at once the oppressive silence was broken by a mournful tune. It was the plaintive tones of the ancient Kol Nidrei prayer. I raised myself up to see whence it came. There, close to the wall, the moonlight caught the uplifted face of an old man, who, in self-forgetful, pious absorption, was singing softly to himself. . . . His prayer brought the ghostly group of seemingly insensible human beings back to life. Little by little, they all roused themselves and all eyes were fixed on the moonlight-flooded face. We sat up very quietly, so as not to disturb the old man, and he did not notice that we were listening. . . .

When at last he was silent, there was exaltation among us, an exaltation which people can experience when they have fallen as low as we had fallen and then, through the mystic power of a deathless prayer, have awakened once more to the world of the spirit.

—LEON SZALET, *a concentration camp survivor*
(trans. Catherine Bland Williams)

Recited three times:

All vows, renunciations, bans, oaths, formulas of obligation, pledges, and promises that we vow or promise to ourselves and to God from this Yom Kippur to the next—may it approach us for good—we hereby retract. May they all be undone, repealed, cancelled, voided, annulled, and regarded as neither valid nor binding. Our vows shall not be considered vows; our renunciations shall not be considered renunciations; and our promises shall not be considered promises.

Kol nidrei ve-esarei va-ḥaramei, v'konamei v'khinnuyei, v'kinnusei u-sh'vu-ot, dindarna u-d'ishtabbana, u-d'aḥarimna v'da-asarna al nafshatana, mi-yom kippurim zeh ad yom kippurim ha-ba aleinu l'tovah, kul'hon iḥaratna v'hon, kul'hon y'hon sh'ran, sh'vikin sh'vitin, b'teilin u-m'vuttalin, la sharirin v'la kayyamin. Nidrana la nidrei, ve-esarana la esarei, u-sh'vu·atana la sh'vu·ot.

ASSURANCE OF FORGIVENESS

Leader and congregation; some congregations recite this verse three times:
"The entire congregation of the people Israel shall be forgiven, as well as the stranger who dwells among them, for all have erred."

V'nislaḥ l'khol adat b'nei yisra·el v'la-ger ha-gar b'tokham, ki l'khol ha-am bi-sh'gagah.

Leader:

[Moses prayed:] "As befits Your abundant love, please forgive this people's sin, just as You have always forgiven this people from the time of the Exodus from Egypt until now." And there it further says:

Leader and congregation; some congregations recite this verse three times:
ADONAI replied, "I have forgiven, as you have asked."
Va-yomer Adonai, salaḥti ki-d'varekha.

Barukh atah ADONAI, our God, ruler of time and space, for granting us life, for sustaining us, and for bringing us to this moment.

Barukh atah Adonai eloheinu melekh ha-olam, she-heḥeyanu v'kiy'manu v'higi·anu la-z'man ha-zeh.

The Torah scrolls are returned to the ark.

On days other than Shabbat, the service continues on page 207.

שַׁבָּת

מִזְמוֹר שִׁיר לְיוֹם הַשַּׁבָּת.

טוֹב לְהֹדוֹת לַיהוה, וּלְזַמֵּר לְשִׁמְךָ עֶלְיוֹן.

לְהַגִּיד בַּבֹּקֶר חַסְדֶּךָ, וֶאֱמוּנָתְךָ בַּלֵּילוֹת.

עֲלֵי־עָשׂוֹר וַעֲלֵי־נָבֶל, עֲלֵי הִגָּיוֹן בְּכִנּוֹר.

כִּי שִׂמַּחְתַּנִי יהוה בְּפָעֳלֶךָ, בְּמַעֲשֵׂי יָדֶיךָ אֲרַנֵּן.

מַה־גָּדְלוּ מַעֲשֶׂיךָ יהוה, מְאֹד עָמְקוּ מַחְשְׁבֹתֶיךָ.

אִישׁ־בַּעַר לֹא יֵדָע וּכְסִיל לֹא־יָבִין אֶת־זֹאת.

בִּפְרֹחַ רְשָׁעִים כְּמוֹ עֵשֶׂב וַיָּצִיצוּ כָּל־פֹּעֲלֵי אָוֶן,
לְהִשָּׁמְדָם עֲדֵי־עַד.

וְאַתָּה מָרוֹם לְעֹלָם יהוה.

כִּי הִנֵּה אֹיְבֶיךָ יהוה, כִּי הִנֵּה אֹיְבֶיךָ יֹאבֵדוּ,
יִתְפָּרְדוּ כָּל־פֹּעֲלֵי אָוֶן.

וַתָּרֶם כִּרְאֵים קַרְנִי, בַּלֹּתִי בְּשֶׁמֶן רַעֲנָן.

וַתַּבֵּט עֵינִי בְּשׁוּרָי, בַּקָּמִים עָלַי מְרֵעִים, תִּשְׁמַעְנָה אָזְנָי.

◁ צַדִּיק כַּתָּמָר יִפְרָח, כְּאֶרֶז בַּלְּבָנוֹן יִשְׂגֶּה.

שְׁתוּלִים בְּבֵית יהוה, בְּחַצְרוֹת אֱלֹהֵינוּ יַפְרִיחוּ.

עוֹד יְנוּבוּן בְּשֵׂיבָה, דְּשֵׁנִים וְרַעֲנַנִּים יִהְיוּ.

לְהַגִּיד כִּי־יָשָׁר יהוה, צוּרִי וְלֹא־עַוְלָתָה בּוֹ. תהלים צב

יהוה מָלָךְ גֵּאוּת לָבֵשׁ, לָבֵשׁ יהוה עֹז הִתְאַזָּר,
אַף־תִּכּוֹן תֵּבֵל בַּל־תִּמּוֹט.

נָכוֹן כִּסְאֲךָ מֵאָז, מֵעוֹלָם אָתָּה.

נָשְׂאוּ נְהָרוֹת יהוה, נָשְׂאוּ נְהָרוֹת קוֹלָם,
יִשְׂאוּ נְהָרוֹת דָּכְיָם.

◁ מִקֹּלוֹת מַיִם רַבִּים, אַדִּירִים מִשְׁבְּרֵי־יָם,
אַדִּיר בַּמָּרוֹם יהוה.

עֵדֹתֶיךָ נֶאֶמְנוּ מְאֹד לְבֵיתְךָ נַאֲוָה־קֹדֶשׁ, יהוה,
לְאֹרֶךְ יָמִים. תהלים צג

In many congregations, Mourner's Kaddish (page 247) is recited here.

SHABBAT. While fasting on Shabbat is normally discouraged, the Rabbis ruled that Yom Kippur (שַׁבָּת שַׁבָּתוֹן, *shabbat shabbaton*), the holiest day of the year, overrides Shabbat. When any holy day falls on Friday night, the evening service begins with an abridged Kabbalat Shabbat, including only traces of the Shabbat liturgy.

PSALM 92. This psalm includes themes appropriate to Shabbat. Contemplating creation, the poet begins with an expression of wonder and ends with hope: a vision of a future peace and wholeness, described as "being transplanted in God's house." Shabbat is both a remembrance of creation and a foretaste of redemption, both a looking back to the seven days of creation and a looking toward the culmination of all time.

LIKE THE PALM TREE... CEDAR. כְּאֶרֶז... כַּתָּמָר. Palm trees grow in the Jericho Valley, one of the lowest places on earth; cedars grow on the mountaintops of Lebanon, the highest in the Middle East. Palm trees grow straight up and bear dates, discarding their leaves each year; cedars, which bear no fruit though their wood is precious, grow wide and are evergreens. Both will be planted in God's house, for all difference is united in the God who is one.

PSALM 93. This psalm describes God's enthronement as Sovereign. It may have become associated with Shabbat because it is only with rest, peace, and the sense of completion on Shabbat that God can be seen as truly enthroned.

Yom Kippur and Shabbat

When Yom Kippur would fall on Shabbat, the pious Rabbi Leib would prepare all the Shabbat necessities according to his custom for every other Shabbat during the year, and set the table. When he came home after the Kol Nidrei service, he would sit down at the table and say, "Master of the universe, the obstacle to observing the Shabbat is not on my part. I would like to delight in the Shabbat as You have commanded. But You have said that we must afflict ourselves on this day, and so, since that is Your will, Leib is leaving everything on the table, according to Your holy will."   —OR HA-MEIR
(trans. S.Y. Agnon)

The Angelic Song

These two psalms inspired a legend that on the first Shabbat, at the end of creation, God sat in heaven on a throne of joy, while the angels gathered around to sing songs of praise. Adam, and then the Shabbat itself, joined in the song, reciting these psalms.

¶ Psalm 93: An Interpretive Translation

Entwined in worlds, enwrapped in glory,
  You are.
So has it been, and so it is—
  eternally You are.
Waves pounding out their song reach up to God from their depths,
  for the song of the sea, beaten to the sound of the breakers, tells of the God within.
These are proof enough for the faithful—that You are the lord of time.
—EDWARD FELD and ARTHUR GOULD

ON SHABBAT, WE RECITE THESE PSALMS:

PSALM 92: A SONG FOR SHABBAT

It is good to thank You, ADONAI,
to sing Your praise, exalted God,
  to speak of Your love each morning,
  and of Your faithfulness at night,
  to the music of the lute and the melody of the harp.
Your creation, ADONAI, gives me joy; I sing of Your handiwork.
  How vast Your works, ADONAI,
  how intricate Your designs.
The thoughtless cannot comprehend,
the foolish cannot fathom this:
  the wicked flourish like grass, those who commit evil blossom,
  only to be destroyed in the end.
But You, ADONAI, are supreme forever.
  Surely, Your enemies, ADONAI, surely, Your enemies shall perish;
  those who commit evil shall crumble.
And You will raise my head high, like the horn of the ox,
anointing me with fragrant oil.
  Were enemies to gather against me, my gaze would remain
  steady, for my ears would hear:
The righteous shall flourish like the palm tree; they shall endure like a cedar in Lebanon, transplanted in the house of ADONAI, thriving in our God's courtyard.
  In old age, they are yet fruitful, always fresh and fragrant,
  proclaiming that ADONAI is flawless, my stronghold, never unjust.

Tzaddik ka-tamar yifrah, k'erez ba-l'vanon yisgeh. Sh'tulim b'veit Adonai, b'hatzrot eloheinu yafrihu. Od y'nuvun b'seivah, d'sheinim v'ra·anannim yihyu, l'haggid ki yashar Adonai, tzuri v'lo avlatah bo.

PSALM 93

ADONAI is sovereign, robed in splendor, girded in strength.
Surely the earth stands firm; it will not be shaken.
Your kingdom stands from earliest time, You are eternal.
The rivers rise to You, ADONAI, the rivers raise their voices,
the rivers raise up their waves,
from the roaring of the deep, and the mighty breakers of
  the sea: "ADONAI is supreme."
Your teaching, ADONAI, never fails.
Holiness befits Your house, ADONAI, until the end of time.

Mi-kolot mayim rabbim addirim mishb'rei yam, addir ba-marom Adonai. Eidotekha ne·emnu m'od l'veit'kha na·avah kodesh, Adonai l'orekh yamim.

In many congregations, Mourner's Kaddish (page 247) is recited here.

We rise. Leader:

בָּרְכוּ אֶת־יהוה הַמְבֹרָךְ.

Congregation, then the leader repeats:

↑ בָּרוּךְ יהוה הַמְבֹרָךְ לְעוֹלָם וָעֶד.

We are seated.

בָּרוּךְ אַתָּה יהוה אֱלֹהֵינוּ מֶלֶךְ הָעוֹלָם,
אֲשֶׁר בִּדְבָרוֹ מַעֲרִיב עֲרָבִים,
בְּחָכְמָה פּוֹתֵחַ שְׁעָרִים,
וּבִתְבוּנָה מְשַׁנֶּה עִתִּים,
וּמַחֲלִיף אֶת־הַזְּמַנִּים,
וּמְסַדֵּר אֶת־הַכּוֹכָבִים בְּמִשְׁמְרוֹתֵיהֶם בָּרָקִיעַ כִּרְצוֹנוֹ.
בּוֹרֵא יוֹם וָלָיְלָה,
גּוֹלֵל אוֹר מִפְּנֵי חֹשֶׁךְ, וְחֹשֶׁךְ מִפְּנֵי אוֹר.
◁ וּמַעֲבִיר יוֹם וּמֵבִיא לָיְלָה,
וּמַבְדִּיל בֵּין יוֹם וּבֵין לָיְלָה,
יהוה צְבָאוֹת שְׁמוֹ.
אֵל חַי וְקַיָּם, תָּמִיד יִמְלוֹךְ עָלֵינוּ לְעוֹלָם וָעֶד.
בָּרוּךְ אַתָּה יהוה, הַמַּעֲרִיב עֲרָבִים.

THE SH'MA AND ITS BLESSINGS קְרִיאַת שְׁמַע וּבְרְכוֹתֶיהָ. The evening service (Arvit) always includes two climactic moments: the Sh'ma and the Amidah, the silent personal prayer. On Yom Kippur, Kol Nidrei precedes this core, while S'liḥot and Viddui, prayers of forgiveness and confession, follow it.

B'rakhot surround the Sh'ma and serve to interpret the themes enunciated in the biblical verses that make up the Sh'ma itself. Two b'rakhot precede the Sh'ma: the first reflects on God's presence in the cycles of the day and seasons, and the second acknowledges God's love, represented by the gift of Torah, God's instruction as to how we should live. Two b'rakhot also follow the Sh'ma: the first acknowledges the Exodus from Egypt, which has set us on the path of freedom and responsibility; the last speaks to our concrete concerns for safety in the darkness of night. The three paragraphs of the Sh'ma stand in the middle of these four b'rakhot. The recitation of the Sh'ma preceded and followed by a b'rakhah is mentioned in the very earliest rabbinic description of the priestly service in the Second Temple (Mishnah Tamid 5:1).

BARUKH ATAH ADONAI יהוה אַתָּה בָּרוּךְ. This first b'rakhah before the Sh'ma acknowledges the experience of God through witnessing the natural cycles of time. Now, at this first touch of darkness, we are asked to attend to the rhythms of time, to day and night, to cycles of life, and to the flow of time. Some of our liturgical texts reflect the biblical and rabbinic understandings of the universe, which include a flat earth and gates in heaven for the entrance and exiting of the sun. These ancient images may remind us of the sense of awe we feel when we contemplate the wonders of the universe.

CREATES בּוֹרֵא. The word בּוֹרֵא, "creates," is used as a verb in the Bible only when the subject is God, for ultimately creation of the world is a mystery.

ADONAI TZ'VA·OT צְבָאוֹת יהוה. In the ancient world, the sun, the moon, and the stars were all seen as divine powers. Biblical monotheism demolished these ancient gods and they were then depicted as handmaidens of God, God's army. Thus this term alludes to God's mastery of all the forces of the universe.

EVENING SERVICE
THE SH'MA AND ITS BLESSINGS

¶ God and Nature: An
Interpretive Translation
Beloved are You,
   eternal God,
by whose design the
   evening falls,
by whose command
   dimensions open up
and eons pass away and
   stars spin in their orbits.
You set the rhythms of
   day and night;
the alternation of light
   and darkness
sings Your creating word.
In rising sun and in
   spreading dusk,
Creator of all, You are
   made manifest.
Eternal, everlasting God,
may we always be aware
   of Your dominion.
Beloved are You,
   Adonai, for this hour
   of nightfall.

—ANDRÉ UNGAR

Community
We begin this service
amidst our community.
Rabbi Ḥayim of Tzanz
used to tell this parable:
A man, wandering lost
in the forest for several
days, finally encountered
another. He called out:
"Brother, show me the
way of this forest." The
man replied: "Brother,
I too am lost. I can only
tell you this: The ways I have tried
lead nowhere; they have only led
me astray. Take my hand, and let us
search for the way together." Rabbi
Ḥayim would add: "So it is with us.
When we go our separate ways, we
may go astray. Let us join hands and
look for the way together."

—A HASIDIC TALE

Bar'khu: The Call to Worship Together
*We rise as we are called by the leader's words of invitation to prayer.
The leader bows when saying the word "bar'khu" (praise) and stands
straight when reciting the name of God. Similarly, the congregation
bows at the word "barukh" (praise) and straightens to full height at
the recitation of God's name.*

We rise. Leader:

Praise ADONAI, to whom all prayer is directed.

Congregation, then the leader repeats:

ʃ Praise ADONAI, to whom all prayer is directed
forever and ever.

Barukh Adonai ha-m'vorakh l'olam va·ed.

We are seated.

First B'rakhah before the Sh'ma:
The Evening Light

Barukh atah ADONAI, our God, ruler of time and space,
whose word brings the evening dusk,
whose wisdom opens the gates of dawn,
whose understanding changes the day's division,
whose will sets the succession of seasons and arranges the
   stars in their places in the sky,
who creates day and night,
who rolls light before darkness and darkness from light,
who makes day pass into night,
who distinguishes day from night;
Adonai Tz'va·ot is Your name.
Living and ever-present God,
May Your rule be with us, forever and ever.
Barukh atah ADONAI, who brings each evening's dusk.

אַהֲבַת עוֹלָם בֵּית יִשְׂרָאֵל עַמְּךָ אָהֵבְתָּ, תּוֹרָה וּמִצְוֹת, חֻקִּים וּמִשְׁפָּטִים אוֹתֵנוּ לִמַּדְתָּ. עַל כֵּן יהוה אֱלֹהֵינוּ, בְּשָׁכְבֵנוּ וּבְקוּמֵנוּ נָשִׂיחַ בְּחֻקֵּיךָ, וְנִשְׂמַח בְּדִבְרֵי תוֹרָתֶךָ וּבְמִצְוֹתֶיךָ לְעוֹלָם וָעֶד. ◁ כִּי הֵם חַיֵּינוּ וְאֹרֶךְ יָמֵינוּ, וּבָהֶם נֶהְגֶּה יוֹמָם וָלֵיְלָה, וְאַהֲבָתְךָ אַל תָּסִיר מִמֶּנּוּ לְעוֹלָמִים. בָּרוּךְ אַתָּה יהוה, אוֹהֵב עַמּוֹ יִשְׂרָאֵל.

קְרִיאַת שְׁמַע

Some people may wish to pause here for a moment. Some may close their eyes; others place a hand over their eyes. The intention is to concentrate on the One-ness of God. These words are added in the absence of a minyan: אֵל מֶלֶךְ נֶאֱמָן

שְׁמַע יִשְׂרָאֵל יהוה אֱלֹהֵינוּ יהוה אֶחָד:
בָּרוּךְ שֵׁם כְּבוֹד מַלְכוּתוֹ לְעוֹלָם וָעֶד:

וְאָהַבְתָּ אֵת יהוה אֱלֹהֶיךָ בְּכָל-לְבָבְךָ וּבְכָל-נַפְשְׁךָ וּבְכָל-מְאֹדֶךָ: וְהָיוּ הַדְּבָרִים הָאֵלֶּה אֲשֶׁר אָנֹכִי מְצַוְּךָ הַיּוֹם עַל-לְבָבֶךָ: וְשִׁנַּנְתָּם לְבָנֶיךָ וְדִבַּרְתָּ בָּם בְּשִׁבְתְּךָ בְּבֵיתֶךָ וּבְלֶכְתְּךָ בַדֶּרֶךְ וּבְשָׁכְבְּךָ וּבְקוּמֶךָ: וּקְשַׁרְתָּם לְאוֹת עַל-יָדֶךָ וְהָיוּ לְטֹטָפֹת בֵּין עֵינֶיךָ: וּכְתַבְתָּם עַל-מְזֻזוֹת בֵּיתֶךָ וּבִשְׁעָרֶיךָ: דברים ו ד-ט

TORAH AND GOD'S LOVE אַהֲבַת עוֹלָם. The Sh'ma is our affirmation of God as well as a statement of our obligation to God. In the b'rakhot before the Sh'ma, we affirm God's gifts to us—first as the creator of the universe, and second by giving us instruction as to how to live, the Torah. Similarly, since the Sh'ma commands that we love God "with all our hearts," this b'rakhah emphasizes God's antecedent love of human beings and the people Israel. Jewish tradition teaches that God's love for us and our own love of each human being ("Love your neighbor as yourself," Leviticus 19:18) live in our hearts side by side.

THE SH'MA. The Sh'ma is recited twice daily: morning and evening. It is a קְרִיאָה (k'ri·ah), a reading or declaration. The three paragraphs from the Torah that comprise the Sh'ma were selected because they express basic aspects of Jewish belief. According to the Rabbis, the first of the three paragraphs proclaims allegiance to the sovereignty of heaven, עֹל מַלְכוּת שָׁמַיִם (ol malkhut shamayim); the second proclaims allegiance to the commandments, עֹל מִצְוֹת (ol mitzvot); and the third reminds us of the Exodus, יְצִיאַת מִצְרַיִם (y'tzia·at mitzrayim), our primary sacred story.

HEAR שְׁמַע. To hear is to emphasize the nonmaterial over the physical, to internalize the sense of God.

ALONE אֶחָד. The word *eḥad* literally means "one." As an affirmation about God, it can be understood in multiple ways. The present rendering emphasizes the monotheistic claims of Jewish faith. Others translate *eḥad* as "unique," emphasizing God's otherness. Mystic commentators interpret "oneness" as a unity of heaven and earth, saying that we are ultimately all connected to the One.

PRAISED BE THE NAME בָּרוּךְ שֵׁם. According to the Mishnah, when God's name was pronounced by the High Priest on Yom Kippur, the people would respond, "Praised be the name . . ." (Yoma 3:8). Since this is a response but not part of the biblical text, it is normally not recited out loud, in order not to interrupt the flow of biblical verses. On Yom Kippur, however, we imitate our ancestors in the Temple courtyard and recite it aloud.

Faith

Faith is not something that we acquire once and for all. Faith is an insight that must be acquired at every single moment. Those who honestly search, those who yearn and fail, we did not presume to judge. Let them pray to be able to pray, and if they do not succeed, if they have no tears to shed, let them yearn for tears, let them try to discover their heart, and let them take strength from the certainty that this too is prayer.

—ABRAHAM JOSHUA HESCHEL

⁋ Sh'ma: Declaration of Faith

Loving life
and its mysterious source
with all our heart
and all our spirit,
all our senses and strength,
we take upon ourselves
and into ourselves
these promises:
to care for the earth
and those who live upon it,
to pursue justice and peace,
to love kindness and
  compassion.
We will teach this to our
  children
throughout the passage of
  the day—
as we dwell in our homes
and as we go on our
  journeys,
from the time we rise
until we fall asleep.
And may our actions
be faithful to our words
that our children's children
may live to know:
Truth and kindness
have embraced,
peace and justice have
  kissed
and are one.

—MARCIA FALK

Second B'rakhah before the Sh'ma: Torah and God's Love

You have loved Your people, the House of Israel, with infinite love; You taught us Torah and mitzvot, statutes and laws. Therefore, ADONAI our God, as we lie down or rise up, we shall think of Your laws and speak of them, rejoicing in Your words of Torah and Your mitzvot forever and ever. For they are our life and the fullness of our days, and on them we will meditate day and night. May You never withdraw Your love from us. *Barukh atah* ADONAI, who loves the people Israel.

Ahavat olam beit yisra·el am'kha ahavta. Torah u-mitzvot, ḥukkim u-mishpatim otanu limmadta. Al kein Adonai eloheinu, b'shokhveinu u-v'kumeinu nasi·aḥ b'ḥukkekha, v'nismaḥ b'divrei toratekha u-v'mitzvotekha l'olam va·ed. Ki heim ḥayyeinu v'orekh yameinu, u-va-hem nehgeh yomam va-lailah.

Recitation of the Sh'ma

Some people may wish to pause here for a moment. Some may close their eyes; others place a hand over their eyes. The intention is to concentrate on the oneness of God. These words are added in the absence of a minyan:

God is a faithful sovereign.

Hear, O Israel, ADONAI is our God, ADONAI alone. Praised be the name of the One whose glorious sovereignty is forever and ever.

Sh'ma yisra·el Adonai eloheinu Adonai eḥad.
Barukh shem k'vod malkhuto l'olam va·ed.

You shall love ADONAI your God with all your heart, with all your soul, and with all that is yours. These words that I command you this day shall be taken to heart. Teach them again and again to your children, and speak of them when you sit in your home, when you walk on your way, when you lie down, and when you rise up. Bind them as a sign upon your hand and as a symbol above your eyes. Inscribe them upon the doorposts of your home and on your gates. Deuteronomy 6:4–9

V'ahavta eit Adonai elohekha b'khol l'vav'kha u-v'khol nafsh'kha u-v'khol m'odekha. V'hayu ha-d'varim ha-eilleh asher anokhi m'tzav'kha ha-yom al l'vavekha. V'shinnantam l'vanekha v'dibbarta bam, b'shivt'kha b'veitekha u-v'lekht'kha va-derekh u-v'shokhb'kha u-v'kumekha. U-k'shartam l'ot al yadekha v'hayu l'totafot bein einekha. U-kh'tavtam al m'zuzot beitekha u-vi-sh'arekha.

וְהָיָה אִם־שָׁמֹעַ תִּשְׁמְעוּ אֶל־מִצְוֹתַי אֲשֶׁר אָנֹכִי מְצַוֶּה אֶתְכֶם הַיּוֹם לְאַהֲבָה אֶת־יהוה אֱלֹהֵיכֶם וּלְעָבְדוֹ בְּכָל־לְבַבְכֶם וּבְכָל־נַפְשְׁכֶם: וְנָתַתִּי מְטַר־אַרְצְכֶם בְּעִתּוֹ יוֹרֶה וּמַלְקוֹשׁ וְאָסַפְתָּ דְגָנֶךָ וְתִירֹשְׁךָ וְיִצְהָרֶךָ: וְנָתַתִּי עֵשֶׂב בְּשָׂדְךָ לִבְהֶמְתֶּךָ וְאָכַלְתָּ וְשָׂבָעְתָּ: הִשָּׁמְרוּ לָכֶם פֶּן־יִפְתֶּה לְבַבְכֶם וְסַרְתֶּם וַעֲבַדְתֶּם אֱלֹהִים אֲחֵרִים וְהִשְׁתַּחֲוִיתֶם לָהֶם: וְחָרָה אַף־יהוה בָּכֶם וְעָצַר אֶת־הַשָּׁמַיִם וְלֹא־יִהְיֶה מָטָר וְהָאֲדָמָה לֹא תִתֵּן אֶת־יְבוּלָהּ וַאֲבַדְתֶּם מְהֵרָה מֵעַל הָאָרֶץ הַטֹּבָה אֲשֶׁר יהוה נֹתֵן לָכֶם: וְשַׂמְתֶּם אֶת־דְּבָרַי אֵלֶּה עַל־לְבַבְכֶם וְעַל־נַפְשְׁכֶם וּקְשַׁרְתֶּם אֹתָם לְאוֹת עַל־יֶדְכֶם וְהָיוּ לְטוֹטָפֹת בֵּין עֵינֵיכֶם: וְלִמַּדְתֶּם אֹתָם אֶת־בְּנֵיכֶם לְדַבֵּר בָּם בְּשִׁבְתְּךָ בְּבֵיתֶךָ וּבְלֶכְתְּךָ בַדֶּרֶךְ וּבְשָׁכְבְּךָ וּבְקוּמֶךָ: וּכְתַבְתָּם עַל־מְזוּזוֹת בֵּיתֶךָ וּבִשְׁעָרֶיךָ: לְמַעַן יִרְבּוּ יְמֵיכֶם וִימֵי בְנֵיכֶם עַל הָאֲדָמָה אֲשֶׁר נִשְׁבַּע יהוה לַאֲבֹתֵיכֶם לָתֵת לָהֶם כִּימֵי הַשָּׁמַיִם עַל־הָאָרֶץ:

דברים יא יג-כא

וַיֹּאמֶר יהוה אֶל־מֹשֶׁה לֵּאמֹר: דַּבֵּר אֶל־בְּנֵי יִשְׂרָאֵל וְאָמַרְתָּ אֲלֵהֶם וְעָשׂוּ לָהֶם צִיצִת עַל־כַּנְפֵי בִגְדֵיהֶם לְדֹרֹתָם וְנָתְנוּ עַל־צִיצִת הַכָּנָף פְּתִיל תְּכֵלֶת: וְהָיָה לָכֶם לְצִיצִת וּרְאִיתֶם אֹתוֹ וּזְכַרְתֶּם אֶת־כָּל־מִצְוֹת יהוה וַעֲשִׂיתֶם אֹתָם וְלֹא־תָתוּרוּ אַחֲרֵי לְבַבְכֶם וְאַחֲרֵי עֵינֵיכֶם אֲשֶׁר־אַתֶּם זֹנִים אַחֲרֵיהֶם: לְמַעַן תִּזְכְּרוּ וַעֲשִׂיתֶם אֶת־כָּל־מִצְוֹתָי וִהְיִיתֶם קְדֹשִׁים לֵאלֹהֵיכֶם: אֲנִי יהוה אֱלֹהֵיכֶם אֲשֶׁר הוֹצֵאתִי אֶתְכֶם מֵאֶרֶץ מִצְרַיִם לִהְיוֹת לָכֶם לֵאלֹהִים אֲנִי ◁ יהוה אֱלֹהֵיכֶם:

במדבר טו לז-מא

אֱמֶת

וֶאֱמוּנָה כָּל־זֹאת, וְקַיָּם עָלֵינוּ, כִּי הוּא יהוה אֱלֹהֵינוּ וְאֵין זוּלָתוֹ, וַאֲנַחְנוּ יִשְׂרָאֵל עַמּוֹ. הַפּוֹדֵנוּ מִיַּד מְלָכִים, מַלְכֵּנוּ הַגּוֹאֲלֵנוּ מִכַּף כָּל־הֶעָרִיצִים. הָאֵל הַנִּפְרָע לָנוּ מִצָּרֵינוּ, וְהַמְשַׁלֵּם גְּמוּל לְכָל־אֹיְבֵי נַפְשֵׁנוּ,

IF YOU WILL HEAR וְהָיָה אִם שָׁמֹעַ. This passage, like many in the Torah, reflects the tradition's insistence that moral coherence underlies the world. The text's plain meaning describes a very literal form of the idea of divine reward and punishment, one with which every generation of Jews since biblical times has struggled theologically. Some Reform and Reconstructionist liturgists have gone so far as to remove this paragraph from their recitation of the Sh'ma. Traditional Jewish prayer, however, has retained it, reflecting a deep belief that in a way we may not grasp, the consequences of our moral and immoral behavior resound in the world.

ADONAI SAID TO MOSES וַיֹּאמֶר יהוה אֶל־מֹשֶׁה. The Rabbis emphasized the last words of this paragraph as the prime reason for its inclusion in the Sh'ma: the remembrance of the Exodus from Egypt. In Jewish theology, the historical Exodus anticipates the redemption in the future: true freedom. The means of achieving redemption, we are taught, is remembering our responsibility to live lives that are holy.

TRULY—THIS IS OUR FAITHFUL AFFIRMATION אֱמֶת וֶאֱמוּנָה. So closely was the Sh'ma linked with this next b'rakhah, the blessing of redemption, that the Rabbis insisted that the first word—truly—be recited along with the very last words of the Sh'ma, so we always read the two

(continued)

¶ Faithfulness: An
Interpretive Translation

*If you faithfully obey
My laws today, and love
Me, I shall give you your
livelihood in good time
and in full measure. You
shall work and reap the
results of your labor,
satisfied with what you
have achieved. Be care-
ful, however. Let not
your heart be seduced,
lured after false goals,
seeking alien ideals, lest
God's image depart from
you and you sink into
dissoluteness and lose
your joyous God-given
heritage.*

—ANDRÉ UNGAR

If you will hear and obey the mitzvot that I command you this day, to love and serve ADONAI your God with all your heart and all your soul, then I will grant the rain for your land in season, rain in autumn and rain in spring. You shall gather in your grain and wine and oil—I will also provide grass in your fields for cattle—and you shall eat and be satisfied. Take care lest your heart be tempted, and you stray to serve other gods and bow to them. Then ADONAI's anger will flare up against you, and God will close up the sky so that there will be no rain and the earth will not yield its produce. You will quickly disappear from the good land that ADONAI is giving you.

Therefore, impress these words of mine upon your heart and upon your soul. Bind them as a sign upon your hand and as a symbol above your eyes; teach them to your children, speaking of them when you sit in your home, when you walk on your way, when you lie down and when you rise up; inscribe them upon the doorposts of your home and on your gates.

Then the length of your days and the days of your children, on the land that ADONAI swore to give to your ancestors, will be as the days of the heavens over the earth.
Deuteronomy 11:13–21

ADONAI said to Moses: Speak to the people Israel, and instruct them that in every generation they shall put *tzitzit* on the corners of their garments, placing a thread of blue on the *tzitzit*, the fringe of each corner. That shall be your *tzitzit* and you shall look at it, and remember all the mitzvot of ADONAI, and fulfill them, and not be seduced by your heart and eyes as they lead you astray. Then you will remember and fulfill all My mitzvot, and be holy before your God. I am ADONAI your God, who brought you out of the land of Egypt to be your God. I am ADONAI your God—
Numbers 15:37–41

Truly—
This is our faithful affirmation, binding on us: That ADONAI is our God and there is none other, and we, Israel, are God's people.
God redeems us from earthly rulers,
Our sovereign delivers us from the hand of all tyrants,
*God brings judgment upon our oppressors, retribution
upon all our mortal enemies,*

הָעֹשֶׂה גְדֹלוֹת עַד אֵין חֵקֶר, וְנִפְלָאוֹת עַד אֵין מִסְפָּר. הַשָּׂם נַפְשֵׁנוּ בַּחַיִּים, וְלֹא נָתַן לַמּוֹט רַגְלֵנוּ, הַמַּדְרִיכֵנוּ עַל בָּמוֹת אוֹיְבֵינוּ, וַיָּרֶם קַרְנֵנוּ עַל כָּל־שׂוֹנְאֵינוּ. הָעֹשֶׂה לָּנוּ נִסִּים וּנְקָמָה בְּפַרְעֹה, אוֹתוֹת וּמוֹפְתִים בְּאַדְמַת בְּנֵי חָם. הַמַּכֶּה בְעֶבְרָתוֹ כָּל־בְּכוֹרֵי מִצְרָיִם, וַיּוֹצֵא אֶת־עַמּוֹ יִשְׂרָאֵל מִתּוֹכָם לְחֵרוּת עוֹלָם. הַמַּעֲבִיר בָּנָיו בֵּין גִּזְרֵי יַם סוּף, אֶת־רוֹדְפֵיהֶם וְאֶת־שׂוֹנְאֵיהֶם בִּתְהוֹמוֹת טִבַּע, וְרָאוּ בָנָיו גְּבוּרָתוֹ, שִׁבְּחוּ וְהוֹדוּ לִשְׁמוֹ.

◁ וּמַלְכוּתוֹ בְּרָצוֹן קִבְּלוּ עֲלֵיהֶם, מֹשֶׁה וּמִרְיָם וּבְנֵי יִשְׂרָאֵל לְךָ עָנוּ שִׁירָה בְּשִׂמְחָה רַבָּה, וְאָמְרוּ כֻלָּם:

מִי־כָמֹכָה בָּאֵלִם יהוה, מִי כָּמֹכָה נֶאְדָּר בַּקֹּדֶשׁ, נוֹרָא תְהִלֹּת, עֹשֵׂה פֶלֶא.

מַלְכוּתְךָ רָאוּ בָנֶיךָ, בּוֹקֵעַ יָם לִפְנֵי מֹשֶׁה, זֶה אֵלִי עָנוּ וְאָמְרוּ:

יהוה יִמְלֹךְ לְעוֹלָם וָעֶד.

וְנֶאֱמַר: כִּי־פָדָה יהוה אֶת־יַעֲקֹב, וּגְאָלוֹ מִיַּד חָזָק מִמֶּנּוּ. בָּרוּךְ אַתָּה יהוה, גָּאַל יִשְׂרָאֵל.

(continued from previous page)
יהוה אֱלֹהֵיכֶם together: אֱמֶת (Adonai eloheikhem emet). It is as if we say, "the Holy One, Your God, is true (or truth)," and, for a moment, while saying אֱמֶת (emet), we have a brief taste of that truth. The world as it is normally presented to us is a world in which truth is hidden: its full revelation constitutes redemption. When we recite the Sh'ma and affirm God's oneness, we may have a token of that redemption.

GOD SMOTE הַמַּכֶּה. The reality is that the cost of achieving freedom may be violence. America, for instance, won its independence through revolution. In the Italian liturgical tradition, this sentence is omitted on Shabbat, since it is not considered to be in keeping with the peaceful mood of the day.

MIRIAM מִרְיָם. After the deliverance at the Sea, we are told that Moses led the men in song and Miriam led the women in response, joyously singing מִי כָמֹכָה "Who is like You . . ."

WHO IS LIKE YOU מִי כָמֹכָה. Exodus 15:11.

ADONAI WILL REIGN יהוה יִמְלֹךְ. Exodus 15:18.

ADONAI HAS RESCUED כִּי פָדָה יהוה. Jeremiah 31:11.

REDEEMED גָּאַל. The 20th-century Jewish philosopher Franz Rosenzweig remarks that the verb is in the past tense, unlike all the other b'rakhot of the Sh'ma, which are in the present tense. It is as if a community that truly is able to recite the Sh'ma together must already have been redeemed.

God performs wonders beyond understanding,
marvels beyond all reckoning.
God places us among the living,
not allowing our steps to falter,
and leads us past the false altars of our enemies.
God exalted us above all those who hated us,
avenged us with miracles before Pharaoh,
offered signs and wonders in the land of Egypt.
God smote, in anger, all of Egypt's firstborn,
brought Israel from its midst to lasting freedom,
led them through the divided water of the Sea of Reeds.
As their pursuing enemies drowned in the depths,
God's children beheld the power of the Divine;
they praised and acknowledged God's name,
willingly accepting God's rule.
Then Moses, Miriam, and the people Israel joyfully sang this
song to You:

"*Who is like You, ADONAI, among the mighty! Who is like You,*
adorned in holiness, revered in praise, working wonders!"
Mi khamokha ba-eilim Adonai, mi kamokha ne·dar ba-kodesh,
nora t'hillot, oseih fele.

Your children recognized Your sovereignty, as You split the sea
before Moses. "This is my God," they responded, and
they said:

"*ADONAI will reign forever and ever.*"
Adonai yimlokh l'olam va·ed.

And so it is written: "ADONAI has rescued Jacob and redeemed
him from the hand of those more powerful than he."
Barukh atah ADONAI, who redeemed the people Israel.

הַשְׁכִּיבֵנוּ יהוה אֱלֹהֵינוּ לְשָׁלוֹם,

וְהַעֲמִידֵנוּ מַלְכֵּנוּ לְחַיִּים,

וּפְרוֹשׂ עָלֵינוּ סֻכַּת שְׁלוֹמֶךָ,

וְתַקְּנֵנוּ בְּעֵצָה טוֹבָה מִלְּפָנֶיךָ,

וְהוֹשִׁיעֵנוּ לְמַעַן שְׁמֶךָ,

וְהָגֵן בַּעֲדֵנוּ,

וְהָסֵר מֵעָלֵינוּ אוֹיֵב, דֶּבֶר, וְחֶרֶב, וְרָעָב וְיָגוֹן,

וְהָסֵר שָׂטָן מִלְּפָנֵינוּ וּמֵאַחֲרֵינוּ,

וּבְצֵל כְּנָפֶיךָ תַּסְתִּירֵנוּ.

כִּי אֵל שׁוֹמְרֵנוּ וּמַצִּילֵנוּ אָתָּה,

כִּי אֵל מֶלֶךְ חַנּוּן וְרַחוּם אָתָּה,

וּשְׁמֹר צֵאתֵנוּ וּבוֹאֵנוּ, לְחַיִּים וּלְשָׁלוֹם, מֵעַתָּה וְעַד עוֹלָם.

◁ וּפְרֹשׂ עָלֵינוּ סֻכַּת שְׁלוֹמֶךָ.

בָּרוּךְ אַתָּה יהוה, הַפּוֹרֵשׂ סֻכַּת שָׁלוֹם עָלֵינוּ וְעַל כָּל־עַמּוֹ יִשְׂרָאֵל וְעַל יְרוּשָׁלָיִם.

ALLOW US . . . TO SLEEP הַשְׁכִּיבֵנוּ. Nighttime may provoke fear: Who will protect us as we sleep? Will we wake up? We beseech God to protect us from those threatening forces that we can see, as well as from those we cannot observe. Ten verbs are enunciated in this prayer, creating a powerful drama of motion and movement, an expression of the will to live.

EVIL FORCES שָׂטָן. "Satan," in the Bible, is a term generally used to refer either to evil impulses or to an adversary, but never to a fallen angel.

CANOPY OF PEACE סֻכַּת שָׁלוֹם. This phrase is not found in the Bible but may allude either to Amos 9:11, where the prophet sees the rebuilding of the fallen *sukkah* of David as an image of redemption, or to Psalm 27:5, where the poet prays to be hidden in God's *sukkah*, protected from enemies, while gazing peacefully at God's countenance.

JERUSALEM יְרוּשָׁלָיִם. In Jewish thought, the peace of Jerusalem symbolizes universal peace.

God's Presence
What a stark contrast
between the verses at the
Sea, where we were gath-
ered together as a people,
as a multitude, and saw
the power of our Warrior
God—and then the first
verses of this prayer,
where we are vulnerable
and alone, looking to a
more tender, personal
side of the same God.

—MERLE FELD

Second B'rakhah after the Sh'ma: Peace in the Night

Allow us, ADONAI our God, to sleep peacefully
and to awaken again to life, our sovereign.

Spread over us Your canopy of peace,
restore us with Your good counsel,
and save us for the sake of Your name.

Shield us: Remove from us enemies and pestilence, sword,
starvation, and sorrow, and remove the evil forces that
surround us.

Shelter us in the shadow of Your wings,
for You, God, watch over and deliver us,
and You are the Sovereign, merciful and compassionate.

Ensure our going and coming for life and peace, now and
forever.

May You spread over us Your canopy of peace.

Barukh atah ADONAI, who spreads the canopy of peace
over us, and over all the people Israel, and over Jerusalem.

We rise.

ON SHABBAT, WE RECITE THE FOLLOWING PARAGRAPH:

וְשָׁמְרוּ בְנֵי־יִשְׂרָאֵל אֶת־הַשַּׁבָּת, לַעֲשׂוֹת אֶת־הַשַּׁבָּת
לְדֹרֹתָם בְּרִית עוֹלָם. בֵּינִי וּבֵין בְּנֵי יִשְׂרָאֵל אוֹת הִיא
לְעֹלָם, כִּי־שֵׁשֶׁת יָמִים עָשָׂה יהוה אֶת־הַשָּׁמַיִם וְאֶת־
הָאָרֶץ, וּבַיּוֹם הַשְּׁבִיעִי שָׁבַת וַיִּנָּפַשׁ.

For Yom Kippur:

כִּי־בַיּוֹם הַזֶּה יְכַפֵּר עֲלֵיכֶם לְטַהֵר אֶתְכֶם מִכֹּל
חַטֹּאתֵיכֶם, לִפְנֵי יהוה תִּטְהָרוּ.

חֲצִי קַדִּישׁ

יִתְגַּדַּל וְיִתְקַדַּשׁ שְׁמֵהּ רַבָּא, בְּעָלְמָא דִּי בְרָא, כִּרְעוּתֵהּ,
וְיַמְלִיךְ מַלְכוּתֵהּ בְּחַיֵּיכוֹן וּבְיוֹמֵיכוֹן וּבְחַיֵּי דְכָל־בֵּית
יִשְׂרָאֵל, בַּעֲגָלָא וּבִזְמַן קָרִיב, וְאִמְרוּ אָמֵן.

יְהֵא שְׁמֵהּ רַבָּא מְבָרַךְ לְעָלַם וּלְעָלְמֵי עָלְמַיָּא.

יִתְבָּרַךְ וְיִשְׁתַּבַּח וְיִתְפָּאַר וְיִתְרוֹמַם וְיִתְנַשֵּׂא וְיִתְהַדָּר
וְיִתְעַלֶּה וְיִתְהַלָּל שְׁמֵהּ דְּקֻדְשָׁא, בְּרִיךְ הוּא, לְעֵלָּא לְעֵלָּא
מִכָּל־בִּרְכָתָא וְשִׁירָתָא תֻּשְׁבְּחָתָא וְנֶחֱמָתָא דַּאֲמִירָן
בְּעָלְמָא, וְאִמְרוּ אָמֵן.

THE PEOPLE ISRAEL SHALL OBSERVE וְשָׁמְרוּ בְנֵי־יִשְׂרָאֵל. Exodus 31:16–17.

AND RESTED וַיִּנָּפַשׁ. Or: "was refreshed." The basic root meaning of this verb is "to breathe" and it is related to the noun נֶפֶשׁ (*nefesh*), "life" or "soul" (i.e., that which breathes). When one rests, one infuses oneself with a new breath of life. The peculiarity of the phrasing of this verse gave birth to the idea of the נְשָׁמָה יְתֵרָה (*n'shamah y'teirah*), the "additional soul" granted us on Shabbat. (Reuven Hammer)

FOR ON THIS DAY כִּי בַיּוֹם הַזֶּה. Leviticus 16:30. Each Shabbat and holy day, an appropriate verse from the Bible is inserted just before the Amidah in the evening service—the beginning of the Jewish day—proclaiming the central purpose of the sacred occasion.

KADDISH קַדִּישׁ. This Kaddish marks the break between the recitation of the Sh'ma and Its Blessings, the public declaration of our faith, and the more private, introspective part of our liturgy, the Amidah.

MAY GOD'S GREAT NAME יְהֵא שְׁמֵהּ רַבָּא. The seven words of this response are an almost exact Aramaic translation of the Hebrew refrain commonly used in the ancient Temple in Jerusalem, בָּרוּךְ שֵׁם כְּבוֹד מַלְכוּתוֹ לְעוֹלָם וָעֶד "Praised be the name of the One whose glorious sovereignty is forever and ever." This is familiar to us today as the response following the first verse of the Sh'ma.

TRULY FAR BEYOND לְעֵלָּא לְעֵלָּא. Distinctively during the High Holy Day period, Ashkenazic versions of the Kaddish emphasize God's sovereignty by repeating the word *l'eilla*, "beyond." Evidently that was already an alternate version of this prayer, given that some Jewish communities, including those of Rome and Yemen, repeat the word *l'eilla* all year long. Ashkenazim preserved both versions—reciting one year round, the other from Rosh Hashanah through Yom Kippur.

Shabbat

We are obsessed with work. During the week we rest so we can go back to work. We play so that we can go back to work. We love so that we can go back to work. One ulterior motive after another. Worrying over the past, living in the future. But one day each week there is a day devoted to being present, the seventh day. On that day, we do not have to go anywhere or do anything. Everything is done and we are already here.

—LAWRENCE KUSHNER
(adapted)

Atonement

According to Rabbi Elazar ben Azariah, this verse teaches that Yom Kippur can atone only for sins "before God." Sins against other people can be atoned only by approaching the one who has been harmed.

—MISHNAH YOMA

May God's Great Name Be Acknowledged

Whenever the people Israel enter the synagogue and house of study and proclaim: יְהֵא שְׁמֵהּ רַבָּא מְבָרַךְ לְעָלַם וּלְעָלְמֵי עָלְמַיָּא, "May God's great name be acknowledged forever and ever," the Holy One nods and says: "Happy is the sovereign in whose house such praise is spoken!"

—BABYLONIAN TALMUD, BERAKHOT

Biblical Sanctification of the Day

We rise.

ON SHABBAT, WE RECITE THE FOLLOWING PARAGRAPH:

The people Israel shall observe the Shabbat, to maintain it as an everlasting covenant throughout all generations. It is a sign between Me and the people Israel for all time, that in six days ADONAI made the heavens and the earth, and on the seventh day, ceased from work and rested.

V'sham'ru v'nei yisra·el et ha-shabbat,
la·asot et ha-shabbat l'dorotam b'rit olam.
Beini u-vein b'nei yisra·el ot hi l'olam,
ki sheishet yamim asah Adonai et ha-shamayim v'et ha-aretz,
u-va-yom ha-sh'vi·i shavat va-yinnafash.

For Yom Kippur:

For on this day, atonement shall be made for you to purify you from all your transgressions. In the presence of ADONAI you shall be pure.

Ki va-yom ha-zeh y'khapper aleikhem
l'taheir etkhem mi-kol ḥattoteikhem,
lifnei Adonai tit·haru.

Ḥatzi Kaddish

May God's great name be exalted and hallowed throughout the created world, as is God's wish. May God's sovereignty soon be established, in your lifetime and in your days, and in the days of all the House of Israel. And respond with: *Amen.*

May God's great name be acknowledged forever and ever!
Y'hei sh'meih rabba m'varakh l'alam u-l'almei almayya.

May the name of the Holy One be acknowledged and celebrated, lauded and worshipped, exalted and honored, extolled and acclaimed—though God, who is blessed, *b'rikh hu*, is truly far beyond all acknowledgment and praise, or any expressions of gratitude or consolation ever spoken in the world. And respond with: *Amen.*

We recite this Silent Amidah at the evening, morning, and afternoon services of Yom Kippur.

Before the Amidah begins, it is customary to take three steps backward, as if we are leaving our familiar surroundings, and then three steps forward, as we approach God's presence.

When reciting the words בָּרוּךְ אַתָּה on this page, we customarily bend the knees and bow, standing up straight by the time we reach the word יהוה. We repeat these motions at the end of the first b'rakhah when we come to the words בָּרוּךְ אַתָּה יהוה. The sign ﭏ indicates the places to bow.

אֲדֹנָי שְׂפָתַי תִּפְתָּח, וּפִי יַגִּיד תְּהִלָּתֶךָ.

Version with Patriarchs and Matriarchs:

ﭏ בָּרוּךְ אַתָּה יהוה,
אֱלֹהֵינוּ וֵאלֹהֵי אֲבוֹתֵינוּ
[וְאִמּוֹתֵינוּ], אֱלֹהֵי אַבְרָהָם,
אֱלֹהֵי יִצְחָק, וֵאלֹהֵי יַעֲקֹב,
אֱלֹהֵי שָׂרָה, אֱלֹהֵי רִבְקָה,
אֱלֹהֵי רָחֵל, וֵאלֹהֵי לֵאָה,
הָאֵל הַגָּדוֹל הַגִּבּוֹר וְהַנּוֹרָא,
אֵל עֶלְיוֹן, גּוֹמֵל חֲסָדִים
טוֹבִים, וְקוֹנֵה הַכֹּל, וְזוֹכֵר
חַסְדֵי אָבוֹת [וְאִמָּהוֹת],
וּמֵבִיא גוֹאֵל לִבְנֵי בְנֵיהֶם
לְמַעַן שְׁמוֹ בְּאַהֲבָה.

Version with Patriarchs:

ﭏ בָּרוּךְ אַתָּה יהוה,
אֱלֹהֵינוּ וֵאלֹהֵי אֲבוֹתֵינוּ,
אֱלֹהֵי אַבְרָהָם, אֱלֹהֵי
יִצְחָק, וֵאלֹהֵי יַעֲקֹב, הָאֵל
הַגָּדוֹל הַגִּבּוֹר וְהַנּוֹרָא,
אֵל עֶלְיוֹן, גּוֹמֵל חֲסָדִים
טוֹבִים, וְקוֹנֵה הַכֹּל, וְזוֹכֵר
חַסְדֵי אָבוֹת, וּמֵבִיא גוֹאֵל
לִבְנֵי בְנֵיהֶם לְמַעַן שְׁמוֹ
בְּאַהֲבָה.

AMIDAH. Amidah literally means "standing" and is the moment of personal prayer recited quietly, as if standing before God. Every Amidah contains three introductory b'rakhot. The first recalls our ancestors and their relation to God; the second describes God's continuing presence in the world; the third emphasizes God's uniqueness and the path to God: holiness. Similarly, every Amidah ends with three b'rakhot. The first looks toward the restoration of God's presence to Zion; the next thanks God for all the gifts we experience in life; and the final one asks for peace. On Yom Kippur—as on Shabbat and holy days—there is only one intermediate b'rakhah, which describes the holiness of the day.

BENDING THE KNEES AND BOWING. The Talmud encourages us to pay attention to the movement of each of our vertebrae as we bow, enabling us to focus on the miracle of our bodies' construction. We stand up straight when we reach God's name, for we speak to God face to face. The Talmud confined the bowing to the beginning and end of this first b'rakhah, and to the beginning and end of the next to last b'rakhah, thanking God for the gift of life.

ADONAI, OPEN MY LIPS אֲדֹנָי שְׂפָתַי תִּפְתָּח. Psalm 51:17, where prayer is exalted over sacrifice.

GOD OF ABRAHAM אֱלֹהֵי אַבְרָהָם. Why don't we say *eloheinu melekh ha-olam,* "ruler of time and space," as part of the opening b'rakhah as we do with every opening b'rakhah, but immediately proceed to "God of Abraham"? Because Abraham was the first to discover that God is the ruler of the entire universe, by mentioning him we also acknowledge God.

GOD OF SARAH אֱלֹהֵי שָׂרָה. Many congregations add the names of the four matriarchs at the beginning of this b'rakhah, because of their significance as founders of our people, and as part of our effort to reclaim women's voices and to honor women's experiences.

GREAT, MIGHTY, AWE-INSPIRING הַגָּדוֹל הַגִּבּוֹר וְהַנּוֹרָא. This phrase is a quotation from Deuteronomy 10:17–18, where God's might is characterized by the befriending of the stranger, the widow, and the orphan.

REDEEMER גוֹאֵל. Judaism's messianic impulse reminds us that the world, as broken as it sometimes appears, is ultimately perfectible; God's teachings, carried out by us, will help the world achieve such perfection. Some prefer to use the word גְּאֻלָּה (g'ullah), "redemption," in place of "redeemer," to de-emphasize the role of any single individual in facilitating the world's healing.

THE SILENT AMIDAH

Meditation on Prayer

In the Bible, God speaks to us, and we listen. At the moment of prayer, we speak to God and God listens.

—ISAAC ARAMA

We recite this Silent Amidah at the evening, morning, and afternoon services of Yom Kippur.

Before the Amidah begins, it is customary to take three steps backward, as if we are leaving our familiar surroundings, and then three steps forward, as we approach God's presence.

When reciting the words "barukh atah" on this page, we customarily bend the knees and bow, standing up straight by the time we reach the word "Adonai." We repeat these motions at the end of the first b'rakhah when we come to the words "barukh atah Adonai." The sign ſ indicates the places to bow.

God of Abraham, God of Isaac, and God of Jacob

Why is the word "God" repeated each time? We might more easily have said it once. The repeated use of the word "God" highlights that each patriarch—and matriarch—knew God personally and sought a distinct relationship with God.

ADONAI, open my lips that my mouth may speak Your praise.

First B'rakhah: Our Ancestors

Version with Patriarchs:

ſ Barukh atah ADONAI,
our God and God of our
  ancestors,
God of Abraham, God of
  Isaac, and God of Jacob,
great, mighty, awe-inspiring,
  transcendent God,
who acts with lovingkindness
  and creates all things,
who remembers the loving
  deeds of our ancestors,
and who will send a redeemer
  to their children's children
  with love
  for the sake of divine honor.

Version with Patriarchs and Matriarchs:

ſ Barukh atah ADONAI,
our God and God of our
  ancestors,
God of Abraham, God of
  Isaac, and God of Jacob,
God of Sarah, God of
  Rebecca, God of Rachel,
  and God of Leah,
great, mighty, awe-inspiring,
  transcendent God,
who acts with lovingkindness
  and creates all things,
who remembers the loving
  deeds of our ancestors,
and who will send a redeemer
  to their children's children
  with love
  for the sake of divine honor.

זָכְרֵנוּ לְחַיִּים, מֶלֶךְ חָפֵץ בַּחַיִּים,
וְכָתְבֵנוּ בְּסֵפֶר הַחַיִּים, לְמַעַנְךָ אֱלֹהִים חַיִּים.

Version with Patriarchs and Matriarchs: *Version with Patriarchs:*

מֶלֶךְ עוֹזֵר וּפוֹקֵד   מֶלֶךְ עוֹזֵר וּמוֹשִׁיעַ וּמָגֵן.
וּמוֹשִׁיעַ וּמָגֵן.   ↑ בָּרוּךְ אַתָּה יהוה, מָגֵן
↑ בָּרוּךְ אַתָּה יהוה, מָגֵן   אַבְרָהָם.
אַבְרָהָם וּפוֹקֵד שָׂרָה.

אַתָּה גִבּוֹר לְעוֹלָם אֲדֹנָי, מְחַיֵּה מֵתִים אַתָּה,
רַב לְהוֹשִׁיעַ.

מְכַלְכֵּל חַיִּים בְּחֶסֶד, מְחַיֵּה מֵתִים בְּרַחֲמִים רַבִּים,
סוֹמֵךְ נוֹפְלִים, וְרוֹפֵא חוֹלִים, וּמַתִּיר אֲסוּרִים, וּמְקַיֵּם
אֱמוּנָתוֹ לִישֵׁנֵי עָפָר. מִי כָמוֹךָ בַּעַל גְּבוּרוֹת וּמִי דּוֹמֶה
לָּךְ, מֶלֶךְ מֵמִית וּמְחַיֶּה וּמַצְמִיחַ יְשׁוּעָה.

מִי כָמוֹךָ אַב הָרַחֲמִים, זוֹכֵר יְצוּרָיו לְחַיִּים בְּרַחֲמִים.

וְנֶאֱמָן אַתָּה לְהַחֲיוֹת מֵתִים. בָּרוּךְ אַתָּה יהוה,
מְחַיֵּה הַמֵּתִים.

אַתָּה קָדוֹשׁ וְשִׁמְךָ קָדוֹשׁ, וּקְדוֹשִׁים בְּכָל־יוֹם
יְהַלְלוּךָ, סֶּלָה.

REMEMBER US זָכְרֵנוּ. This brief prayer is the first of four that are added on the ten days of the High Holy Day season. All four of the additions center on the prayer for חַיִּים (hayyim), "life."

SHIELD OF ABRAHAM מָגֵן אַבְרָהָם. After Genesis 15:1.

GUARDIAN OF SARAH פוֹקֵד שָׂרָה. Or: "the One who remembered Sarah" (after Genesis 21:1). We, who stand here today, are the fruit of God's promise to Abraham and Sarah.

SUPPORT THE FALLING סוֹמֵךְ נוֹפְלִים. After Psalm 145:14.

HEAL THE SICK רוֹפֵא חוֹלִים. After Exodus 15:26.

LOOSEN THE CHAINS OF THE BOUND מַתִּיר אֲסוּרִים. Psalm 146:7.

BRINGS DEATH AND LIFE מֵמִית וּמְחַיֶּה. 1 Samuel 2:6.

WHO IS LIKE YOU, SOURCE OF COMPASSION מִי כָמוֹךָ אַב הָרַחֲמִים. Jewish mystical tradition highlights the theological tension between God's qualities of power and strict judgment, גְּבוּרָה (g'vurah), and God's qualities of mercy and lovingkindness, חֶסֶד (ḥesed). Throughout the year, this b'rakhah reminds us that God is unsurpassed in power. At this season of judgment, we add this line to remind us—and God—that God is also unsurpassed in mercy.

GIVES LIFE TO THE DEAD מְחַיֵּה הַמֵּתִים. Over the millennia, many Jewish perspectives on the afterlife have been proposed. While many Jewish thinkers (including Saadiah Gaon, 10th century, and Maimonides, 12th century) express caution about the specific implications of bodily resurrection of the dead, they understand this doctrine to express an important aspect of God's supreme power. God's power extends even to the dead.

HOLY קָדוֹשׁ. We become holy when we imitate God's qualities: "As God is called 'merciful' so should you be merciful. . . . as God is called 'righteous' and 'loving,' so should you be righteous and loving" (Babylonian Talmud, Sotah 14a).

Immortality

Each morning You restore consciousness to my sleep-filled body, and I awake.

Each spring You restore vitality to trees, plants, and animals that have hibernated through the winter, and they grow once more.

Each day I remember those who have died; they live on beyond the grave.

Each moment I contemplate the rebirth of our people; I recall that You put the breath of life into dry bones.

Praised are You, Adonai, for planting immortality in my soul, in my people, and in our world.

—ROBERT SCHEINBERG

Remember us for life,
Sovereign who delights in life,
and inscribe us in the Book of Life,
for Your sake, God of life.

Version with Patriarchs:	*Version with Patriarchs and Matriarchs:*
You are the sovereign who helps and saves and shields.	You are the sovereign who helps and guards, saves and shields.
ſ *Barukh atah* ADONAI, Shield of Abraham.	ſ *Barukh atah* ADONAI, Shield of Abraham and Guardian of Sarah.

Second B'rakhah: God's Saving Care

You are mighty forever, ADONAI—
You give life to the dead;
great is Your saving power.

You sustain the living through love,
    and with great mercy give life to the dead.
You support the falling,
    heal the sick,
    loosen the chains of the bound,
    and keep faith with those who sleep in the dust.
Who is like You, Almighty,
    and who can be compared to You?—
    Sovereign, who brings death and life,
    and causes salvation to flourish.

Who is like You, source of compassion,
    who remembers with compassion Your creatures for life?

You are faithful in bringing life to the dead.
Barukh atah ADONAI, who gives life to the dead.

Third B'rakhah: God's Holiness

Holy are You and holy is Your name;
    holy ones praise You each day.

וּבְכֵן תֵּן פַּחְדְּךָ יהוה אֱלֹהֵינוּ עַל כָּל־מַעֲשֶׂיךָ

וְאֵימָתְךָ עַל כָּל־מַה־שֶּׁבָּרָאתָ,

וְיִירָאוּךָ כָּל־הַמַּעֲשִׂים

וְיִשְׁתַּחֲווּ לְפָנֶיךָ כָּל־הַבְּרוּאִים,

וְיֵעָשׂוּ כֻלָּם אֲגֻדָּה אַחַת לַעֲשׂוֹת רְצוֹנְךָ בְּלֵבָב שָׁלֵם,

כְּמוֹ שֶׁיָּדַעְנוּ יהוה אֱלֹהֵינוּ שֶׁהַשִּׁלְטוֹן לְפָנֶיךָ,

עֹז בְּיָדְךָ וּגְבוּרָה בִּימִינֶךָ,

וְשִׁמְךָ נוֹרָא עַל כָּל־מַה־שֶּׁבָּרָאתָ.

וּבְכֵן תֵּן כָּבוֹד יהוה לְעַמֶּךָ,

תְּהִלָּה לִירֵאֶיךָ וְתִקְוָה לְדוֹרְשֶׁיךָ,

וּפִתְחוֹן פֶּה לַמְיַחֲלִים לָךְ,

שִׂמְחָה לְאַרְצֶךָ וְשָׂשׂוֹן לְעִירֶךָ

וּצְמִיחַת קֶרֶן לְדָוִד עַבְדֶּךָ,

וַעֲרִיכַת נֵר לְבֶן־יִשַׁי מְשִׁיחֶךָ, בִּמְהֵרָה בְיָמֵינוּ.

וּבְכֵן צַדִּיקִים יִרְאוּ וְיִשְׂמָחוּ

וִישָׁרִים יַעֲלֹזוּ,

וַחֲסִידִים בְּרִנָּה יָגִילוּ,

וְעוֹלָתָה תִּקְפָּץ־פִּיהָ

וְכָל־הָרִשְׁעָה כֻּלָּהּ כְּעָשָׁן תִּכְלֶה,

כִּי תַעֲבִיר מֶמְשֶׁלֶת זָדוֹן מִן הָאָרֶץ.

וְתִמְלֹךְ אַתָּה יהוה לְבַדֶּךָ עַל כָּל־מַעֲשֶׂיךָ

בְּהַר צִיּוֹן מִשְׁכַּן כְּבוֹדֶךָ

וּבִירוּשָׁלַיִם עִיר קָדְשֶׁךָ,

כַּכָּתוּב בְּדִבְרֵי קָדְשֶׁךָ:

יִמְלֹךְ יהוה לְעוֹלָם, אֱלֹהַיִךְ צִיּוֹן לְדֹר וָדֹר, הַלְלוּ־יָהּ.

קָדוֹשׁ אַתָּה וְנוֹרָא שְׁמֶךָ, וְאֵין אֱלוֹהַּ מִבַּלְעָדֶיךָ,

כַּכָּתוּב: וַיִּגְבַּהּ יהוה צְבָאוֹת בַּמִּשְׁפָּט, וְהָאֵל הַקָּדוֹשׁ

נִקְדַּשׁ בִּצְדָקָה. בָּרוּךְ אַתָּה יהוה, הַמֶּלֶךְ הַקָּדוֹשׁ.

U-V'KHEIN וּבְכֵן. These three paragraphs, which are introduced by the same word, וּבְכֵן (u-v'khein), are ascribed by many scholars to the 2nd or 3rd century, and may constitute the earliest poetic additions to the High Holy Day Amidah.

Stages of redemption are described in this series of prayers. The first paragraph implores God to cause the entire world to live with reverence for God. The next paragraph discusses not the universal, but the particular: the return of the people Israel to its land and specifically to Jerusalem, and the kingship of David. The third paragraph describes the rejoicing that will come to the righteous "when You remove the tyranny of arrogance from the earth" and God will rule alone over the entire world from Zion and Jerusalem.
(adapted from Reuven Hammer)

AWE . . . FEAR . . . פַּחְדְּךָ . . . וְאֵימָתְךָ. These emotions are meant to induce obedience to God's will and inspire us to bring sanctity to the world.

THE LIGHT OF DAVID קֶרֶן לְדָוִד. See Psalm 132:17.

YOU ALONE . . . WILL RULE וְתִמְלֹךְ אַתָּה לְבַדֶּךָ. God's sovereignty is always envisioned as the rule of justice, and therefore a time of peace. It is the ultimate conclusion of history.

ADONAI WILL REIGN FOREVER יִמְלֹךְ יהוה לְעוֹלָם. Psalm 146:10.

ADONAI TZ'VA·OT WILL BE EXALTED וַיִּגְבַּהּ יהוה צְבָאוֹת. Isaiah 5:16. This verse, with which the b'rakhah concludes, highlights the themes of this b'rakhah, as it has been expanded on the High Holy Days: We await the day when earthly powers become subservient to the divine ideals of justice and righteousness.

THE HOLY SOVEREIGN הַמֶּלֶךְ הַקָּדוֹשׁ. The rest of the year, this b'rakhah concludes with the words הָאֵל הַקָּדוֹשׁ "the Holy God." God's sovereignty is a central theme of the High Holy Days.

The purpose of creation is not division, nor separation. The purpose of the human race is not a struggle to the death between classes, between nations. Humanity is meant to become a single body. . . . Our purpose is the great upbuilding of unity and peace. And when all nations are bound together in one association living in justice and righteousness, they atone for each other. —MARTIN BUBER

All Wickedness Will Disappear

There were once some lawless men who caused Rabbi Meir a great deal of trouble. Rabbi Meir accordingly prayed that they should die. His wife, Beruriah, said to him: "How can you think that such a prayer is permitted? . . . When sin ceases there shall be no more wicked people. Therefore pray for them that they turn from their ways, and there will be no more wicked people." Then he prayed on their behalf.

—BABYLONIAN TALMUD, BERAKHOT

U-v'khein—ADONAI our God,
instill Your awe in all You have made,
and fear of You in all You have created,
so that all You have fashioned revere You,
all You have created bow in recognition,
and all be bound together, carrying out Your will wholeheartedly.
For we know that true sovereignty is Yours,
power and strength are in Your hands,
and Your name is to be revered beyond any of Your creations.

U-v'khein—Bestow honor to Your people, ADONAI,
praise to those who revere You,
hope to those who seek You,
recognition to those who await You,
joy to Your land, and gladness to Your city.
May the light of David, Your servant, dawn,
and the lamp of the son of Jesse, Your anointed, be kindled
speedily in our day.

U-v'khein—The righteous, beholding this, will rejoice,
the upright will be glad,
the pious will celebrate with song,
evil will be silenced,
and all wickedness will disappear like smoke,
when You remove the tyranny of arrogance from the earth.

You alone, ADONAI, will rule all Your creation,
from Mount Zion, the dwelling-place of Your glory,
and from Jerusalem, Your holy city.
As it is written in the Book of Psalms:
"ADONAI will reign forever;
your God, O Zion, from generation to generation. Halleluyah!"

You are holy, and Your name is revered,
for there is no God but You.
As Your prophet Isaiah wrote: "*Adonai Tz'va·ot* will be exalted
through justice, the holy God sanctified through righteousness."
Barukh atah ADONAI, the Holy Sovereign.

CALLING US BY YOUR GREAT
AND HOLY NAME וְשִׁמְךָ
הַגָּדוֹל וְהַקָּדוֹשׁ עָלֵינוּ קָרָאתָ.
The name "Israel" means
"wrestling with God" (Genesis 32:28). Our relationship
with God is part of our self-
definition as a people.

אַתָּה בְחַרְתָּנוּ מִכָּל־הָעַמִּים,
אָהַבְתָּ אוֹתָנוּ וְרָצִיתָ בָּנוּ,
וְרוֹמַמְתָּנוּ מִכָּל־הַלְּשׁוֹנוֹת,
וְקִדַּשְׁתָּנוּ בְּמִצְוֹתֶיךָ,
וְקֵרַבְתָּנוּ מַלְכֵּנוּ לַעֲבוֹדָתֶךָ,
וְשִׁמְךָ הַגָּדוֹל וְהַקָּדוֹשׁ עָלֵינוּ קָרָאתָ.

וַתִּתֶּן־לָנוּ, יהוה אֱלֹהֵינוּ, בְּאַהֲבָה אֶת־יוֹם [הַשַּׁבָּת הַזֶּה
לִקְדֻשָּׁה וְלִמְנוּחָה וְאֶת־יוֹם] הַכִּפֻּרִים הַזֶּה, לִמְחִילָה
וְלִסְלִיחָה וּלְכַפָּרָה, וְלִמְחָל־בּוֹ אֶת־כָּל־עֲוֹנוֹתֵינוּ
[בְּאַהֲבָה] מִקְרָא קֹדֶשׁ, זֵכֶר לִיצִיאַת מִצְרָיִם.

אֱלֹהֵינוּ וֵאלֹהֵי אֲבוֹתֵינוּ [וְאִמּוֹתֵינוּ], יַעֲלֶה וְיָבֹא, וְיַגִּיעַ
וְיֵרָאֶה, וְיֵרָצֶה וְיִשָּׁמַע, וְיִפָּקֵד וְיִזָּכֵר זִכְרוֹנֵנוּ וּפִקְדוֹנֵנוּ,
וְזִכְרוֹן אֲבוֹתֵינוּ [וְאִמּוֹתֵינוּ], וְזִכְרוֹן מָשִׁיחַ בֶּן־דָּוִד עַבְדֶּךָ,
וְזִכְרוֹן יְרוּשָׁלַיִם עִיר קָדְשֶׁךָ, וְזִכְרוֹן כָּל־עַמְּךָ בֵּית יִשְׂרָאֵל
לְפָנֶיךָ לִפְלֵיטָה לְטוֹבָה, לְחֵן וּלְחֶסֶד וּלְרַחֲמִים, לְחַיִּים
וּלְשָׁלוֹם, בְּיוֹם הַכִּפֻּרִים הַזֶּה.
זָכְרֵנוּ יהוה אֱלֹהֵינוּ בּוֹ לְטוֹבָה,
וּפָקְדֵנוּ בוֹ לִבְרָכָה,
וְהוֹשִׁיעֵנוּ בוֹ לְחַיִּים,
וּבִדְבַר יְשׁוּעָה וְרַחֲמִים חוּס וְחָנֵּנוּ, וְרַחֵם עָלֵינוּ
וְהוֹשִׁיעֵנוּ, כִּי אֵלֶיךָ עֵינֵינוּ, כִּי אֵל מֶלֶךְ חַנּוּן וְרַחוּם אָתָּה.

אֱלֹהֵינוּ וֵאלֹהֵי אֲבוֹתֵינוּ [וְאִמּוֹתֵינוּ], מְחַל לַעֲוֹנוֹתֵינוּ
בְּיוֹם [הַשַּׁבָּת הַזֶּה וּבְיוֹם] הַכִּפֻּרִים הַזֶּה. מְחֵה וְהַעֲבֵר
פְּשָׁעֵינוּ וְחַטֹּאתֵינוּ מִנֶּגֶד עֵינֶיךָ, כָּאָמוּר: אָנֹכִי אָנֹכִי הוּא
מֹחֶה פְשָׁעֶיךָ לְמַעֲנִי, וְחַטֹּאתֶיךָ לֹא אֶזְכֹּר. וְנֶאֱמַר:
מָחִיתִי כָעָב פְּשָׁעֶיךָ וְכֶעָנָן חַטֹּאותֶיךָ, שׁוּבָה אֵלַי כִּי
גְאַלְתִּיךָ. וְנֶאֱמַר: כִּי־בַיּוֹם הַזֶּה יְכַפֵּר עֲלֵיכֶם לְטַהֵר
אֶתְכֶם מִכֹּל חַטֹּאתֵיכֶם, לִפְנֵי יהוה תִּטְהָרוּ.

I, SURELY I אָנֹכִי אָנֹכִי. Isaiah
43:25.

I SWEEP ASIDE YOUR SINS
LIKE A MIST מָחִיתִי כָעָב
פְּשָׁעֶיךָ. Isaiah 44:22.

FOR ON THIS DAY כִּי־בַיּוֹם
הַזֶּה. Leviticus 16:30.

A difficult task was assigned this people in its history. It is so easy to listen to the voices of idols, and it is so hard to receive the word of the One God into oneself. It is so easy to remain a slave, and it is so difficult to become a free person. But this people can only exist in the full seriousness of its task. It can only exist in this freedom which reaches beyond all other freedoms. Its history began when it heard the word, rising out of the mystery, and emerging into clarity: "I am the One-Who-Is thy God, who brought you out of the land of Egypt, out of the House of Bondage. . ." This people traveled through the history of humanity, century after century, millennium after millennium. Its very history became divine guidance for it.

—LEO BAECK

What Do I Want?

You know what is for my good. If I recite my wants, it is not to remind You of them, but so that I may better understand how great is my dependence on You. If, then, I ask You for the things that may not be for my well-being, it is because I am ignorant; Your choice is better than mine and I submit myself to Your unalterable decree and Your supreme direction.

—BAHYA IBN PAKUDA

Fourth B'rakhah: The Holiness of Yom Kippur

You have chosen us among all peoples, loving us, wanting us. You have distinguished us among all nations, making us holy through Your commandments, drawing us close to Your service, and calling us by Your great and holy name.

With love, You have bestowed on us, ADONAI our God, this [Shabbat, for sanctity and rest, and this] Yom Kippur for pardon, forgiveness, and atonement, that all our sins be forgiven [through Your love], a sacred time, recalling the Exodus from Egypt.

Our God and God of our ancestors,
may the thought of us rise up and reach You.
Attend to us and accept us;
hear us and respond to us.
Keep us in mind,
and keep in mind the thought of our ancestors,
as well as the Messiah, the descendant of David;
Jerusalem, Your holy city;
and all Your people, the House of Israel.
On this Yom Kippur respond to us with deliverance, goodness,
compassion, love, life, and peace.
Remember us for good;
respond to us with blessing;
redeem us with life.
Show us compassion and care with words of salvation and
kindness; have mercy on us and redeem us. Our eyes are turned
to You, for You are a compassionate and loving sovereign.

Our God and God of our ancestors, forgive our sins on this [Shabbat and this] Yom Kippur. Blot out and disregard them, as the prophet Isaiah says in Your name: "I, surely I, am the One who wipes away sin, for this is My nature; I will not recall your errors," and the prophet adds: "I sweep aside your sins like a mist, and disperse your transgressions like a cloud. Turn back to Me, for I will redeem you." And in Your Torah it is written: "For on this day, atonement shall be made for you to purify you from all your transgressions. In the presence of ADONAI you shall be pure."

אֱלֹהֵינוּ וֵאלֹהֵי אֲבוֹתֵינוּ [וְאִמּוֹתֵינוּ], [רְצֵה בִמְנוּחָתֵנוּ]
קַדְּשֵׁנוּ בְּמִצְוֹתֶיךָ וְתֵן חֶלְקֵנוּ בְּתוֹרָתֶךָ, שַׂבְּעֵנוּ מִטּוּבֶךָ
וְשַׂמְּחֵנוּ בִּישׁוּעָתֶךָ, [וְהַנְחִילֵנוּ יהוה אֱלֹהֵינוּ בְּאַהֲבָה
וּבְרָצוֹן שַׁבַּת קָדְשֶׁךָ, וְיָנוּחוּ בָהּ יִשְׂרָאֵל מְקַדְּשֵׁי שְׁמֶךָ]
וְטַהֵר לִבֵּנוּ לְעָבְדְּךָ בֶּאֱמֶת, כִּי אַתָּה סָלְחָן לְיִשְׂרָאֵל
וּמָחֳלָן לְשִׁבְטֵי יְשֻׁרוּן בְּכָל־דּוֹר וָדוֹר, וּמִבַּלְעָדֶיךָ אֵין
לָנוּ מֶלֶךְ מוֹחֵל וְסוֹלֵחַ אֶלָּא אָתָּה. בָּרוּךְ אַתָּה יהוה,
מֶלֶךְ מוֹחֵל וְסוֹלֵחַ לַעֲוֹנוֹתֵינוּ וְלַעֲוֹנוֹת עַמּוֹ בֵּית יִשְׂרָאֵל,
וּמַעֲבִיר אַשְׁמוֹתֵינוּ בְּכָל־שָׁנָה וְשָׁנָה, מֶלֶךְ עַל כָּל־הָאָרֶץ
מְקַדֵּשׁ [הַשַּׁבָּת וְ] יִשְׂרָאֵל וְיוֹם הַכִּפּוּרִים.

רְצֵה, יהוה אֱלֹהֵינוּ, בְּעַמְּךָ יִשְׂרָאֵל וּבִתְפִלָּתָם, וְהָשֵׁב
אֶת־הָעֲבוֹדָה לִדְבִיר בֵּיתֶךָ [וְאִשֵּׁי יִשְׂרָאֵל]
וּתְפִלָּתָם בְּאַהֲבָה תְקַבֵּל בְּרָצוֹן, וּתְהִי לְרָצוֹן תָּמִיד
עֲבוֹדַת יִשְׂרָאֵל עַמֶּךָ.

וְתֶחֱזֶינָה עֵינֵינוּ בְּשׁוּבְךָ לְצִיּוֹן בְּרַחֲמִים.
בָּרוּךְ אַתָּה יהוה, הַמַּחֲזִיר שְׁכִינָתוֹ לְצִיּוֹן.

☙ מוֹדִים אֲנַחְנוּ לָךְ, שָׁאַתָּה הוּא יהוה אֱלֹהֵינוּ
וֵאלֹהֵי אֲבוֹתֵינוּ [וְאִמּוֹתֵינוּ] לְעוֹלָם וָעֶד,
צוּר חַיֵּינוּ מָגֵן יִשְׁעֵנוּ אַתָּה הוּא.
לְדוֹר וָדוֹר נוֹדֶה לְּךָ וּנְסַפֵּר תְּהִלָּתֶךָ,
עַל חַיֵּינוּ הַמְּסוּרִים בְּיָדֶךָ,
וְעַל נִשְׁמוֹתֵינוּ הַפְּקוּדוֹת לָךְ,
וְעַל נִסֶּיךָ שֶׁבְּכָל־יוֹם עִמָּנוּ,
וְעַל נִפְלְאוֹתֶיךָ וְטוֹבוֹתֶיךָ שֶׁבְּכָל־עֵת,
עֶרֶב וָבֹקֶר וְצָהֳרָיִם.
הַטּוֹב, כִּי לֹא כָלוּ רַחֲמֶיךָ,
וְהַמְרַחֵם, כִּי לֹא תַמּוּ חֲסָדֶיךָ,
מֵעוֹלָם קִוִּינוּ לָךְ.

YOU FORGIVE אַתָּה סָלְחָן. The grammatical form of the nouns סָלְחָן (solhan) and מָחֳלָן (moholan) indicate an essential personal quality. For example, when one לוֹמֵד (lomed), "studies," until becoming a scholar, one is then called a לַמְדָן (lamdan). The use of this form reflects the poet's belief that God's forgiving nature is, in fact, God's essence.

RESTORE WORSHIP TO YOUR SANCTUARY וְהָשֵׁב אֶת־הָעֲבוֹדָה לִדְבִיר בֵּיתֶךָ. According to the Babylonian Talmud, "Ever since the day when the Temple was destroyed, there has been an iron barrier separating Israel from God" (Berakhot 32b). Each destruction of the Temple in Jerusalem (first by the Babylonians in 586 B.C.E. and then by the Romans in 70 C.E.) was a cataclysmic event in early Jewish history. In the exile, amidst the brokenness that surrounds us, we can never know whether our service to God is appropriate or not. The prayer for the restoration of the Temple carries with it the hope that we might someday be assured that our service to God is proper.

YOUR DIVINE PRESENCE שְׁכִינָתוֹ. The Hebrew word shekhinah has been used for centuries to refer to God's immanence, the presence of God that is felt in the world. The word

shekhinah is grammatically feminine. Accordingly, the Jewish mystical tradition generally describes the Divine Presence—known as the Shekhinah—in feminine imagery.

PROTECTOR OF OUR LIVES צוּר חַיֵּינוּ. God is our source of support and stability.

FROM ONE GENERATION TO THE NEXT לְדוֹר וָדוֹר. After Psalm 79:13. In a world where nations, values, and ideals rise and fall, our relationship with God is a constant truth.

The fire that was on the altar entered into the hearts of the priests and worshippers so that their song was full of passion, and the power of prayer filled their beings.

—THE ZOHAR

Your Miracles
That Accompany Us
Each Day
The 20th-century Ḥasidic master, the Netivot Shalom, remarks that each day we are confronted with new tasks of repair of the world, but each day God renews creation and so there is new energy that we may call on for the new day.

Our God and God of our ancestors: [embrace our rest,] make us holy through Your mitzvot and let the Torah be our portion. Fill our lives with Your goodness and gladden us with Your triumph. [ADONAI our God, grant that we inherit Your holy Shabbat, lovingly and willingly, so that the people Israel, who sanctify Your name, may find rest on this day.] Purify our hearts to serve You faithfully, for You forgive the people Israel and pardon the tribes of Jeshurun in every generation. Beside You, we have no sovereign who pardons and forgives. *Barukh atah ADONAI*, sovereign who pardons and forgives our sins and those of the people, the House of Israel, each year sweeping away our guilt—ruler of all the earth, who makes [Shabbat,] the people Israel and the Day of Atonement holy.

Fifth B'rakhah: The Restoration of Zion

ADONAI our God, embrace Your people Israel and their prayer. Restore worship to Your sanctuary. May the [fiery offerings and] prayers of Israel be lovingly accepted by You, and may our service always be pleasing.

Let our eyes behold Your merciful return to Zion. *Barukh atah ADONAI*, who restores Your Divine Presence to Zion.

Sixth B'rakhah: Gratitude for Life and Its Blessings

ſ We thank You,
You who are our God and the God of our ancestors through all
     time, protector of our lives, shield of our salvation.
From one generation to the next we thank You
and sing Your praises—
     for our lives that are in Your hands,
     for our souls that are under Your care,
     for Your miracles that accompany us each day,
     and for Your wonders and Your gifts that are
     with us each moment—
evening, morning, and noon.
You are the One who is good,
whose mercy is never-ending;
the One who is compassionate,
whose love is unceasing.
We have always placed our hope in You.

וְעַל כֻּלָּם יִתְבָּרַךְ וְיִתְרוֹמַם שִׁמְךָ מַלְכֵּנוּ תָּמִיד לְעוֹלָם וָעֶד.

וּכְתוֹב לְחַיִּים טוֹבִים כָּל־בְּנֵי בְרִיתֶךָ.

וְכֹל הַחַיִּים יוֹדוּךָ סֶּלָה,
וִיהַלְלוּ אֶת־שִׁמְךָ בֶּאֱמֶת,
הָאֵל יְשׁוּעָתֵנוּ וְעֶזְרָתֵנוּ סֶלָה.
בָּרוּךְ אַתָּה יהוה, הַטּוֹב שִׁמְךָ וּלְךָ נָאֶה לְהוֹדוֹת.

In the evening, we say:

שָׁלוֹם רָב עַל יִשְׂרָאֵל עַמְּךָ וְעַל כָּל־יוֹשְׁבֵי תֵבֵל תָּשִׂים לְעוֹלָם, כִּי אַתָּה הוּא מֶלֶךְ אָדוֹן לְכָל־הַשָּׁלוֹם. וְטוֹב בְּעֵינֶיךָ לְבָרֵךְ אֶת־עַמְּךָ יִשְׂרָאֵל בְּכָל־עֵת וּבְכָל־שָׁעָה בִּשְׁלוֹמֶךָ.

In the morning or afternoon, we say:

שִׂים שָׁלוֹם בָּעוֹלָם, טוֹבָה וּבְרָכָה, חֵן וָחֶסֶד וְרַחֲמִים עָלֵינוּ וְעַל כָּל־יִשְׂרָאֵל עַמֶּךָ. בָּרְכֵנוּ אָבִינוּ כֻּלָּנוּ כְּאֶחָד בְּאוֹר פָּנֶיךָ, כִּי בְאוֹר פָּנֶיךָ נָתַתָּ לָנוּ, יהוה אֱלֹהֵינוּ, תּוֹרַת חַיִּים וְאַהֲבַת חֶסֶד, וּצְדָקָה וּבְרָכָה וְרַחֲמִים וְחַיִּים, וְשָׁלוֹם. וְטוֹב בְּעֵינֶיךָ לְבָרֵךְ אֶת־עַמְּךָ יִשְׂרָאֵל, בְּכָל־עֵת וּבְכָל־שָׁעָה בִּשְׁלוֹמֶךָ.

All services continue here:

בְּסֵפֶר חַיִּים, בְּרָכָה וְשָׁלוֹם וּפַרְנָסָה טוֹבָה, נִזָּכֵר וְנִכָּתֵב לְפָנֶיךָ, אֲנַחְנוּ וְכָל־עַמְּךָ בֵּית יִשְׂרָאֵל, לְחַיִּים טוֹבִים וּלְשָׁלוֹם.

בָּרוּךְ אַתָּה יהוה, עוֹשֶׂה הַשָּׁלוֹם.

וידוי

אֱלֹהֵינוּ וֵאלֹהֵי אֲבוֹתֵינוּ [וְאִמּוֹתֵינוּ],
תָּבֹא לְפָנֶיךָ תְּפִלָּתֵנוּ, וְאַל תִּתְעַלַּם מִתְּחִנָּתֵנוּ,
שֶׁאֵין אֲנַחְנוּ עַזֵּי פָנִים וּקְשֵׁי עֹרֶף לוֹמַר לְפָנֶיךָ,
יהוה אֱלֹהֵינוּ וֵאלֹהֵי אֲבוֹתֵינוּ [וְאִמּוֹתֵינוּ],
צַדִּיקִים אֲנַחְנוּ וְלֹא חָטָאנוּ,
אֲבָל אֲנַחְנוּ וַאֲבוֹתֵינוּ [וְאִמּוֹתֵינוּ] חָטָאנוּ.

MAY YOUR NAME BE PRAISED AND EXALTED יִתְבָּרַךְ וְיִתְרוֹמַם שִׁמְךָ. In the language of the Bible and the prayerbook, "God's name is exalted" when we acknowledge God, recognize God's goodness in creation, and act to enable God's justice and compassion to be visible in the world.

AND INSCRIBE וּכְתוֹב. This is the third of the four special insertions in the Amidah for the Ten Days of Repentance. With the first two insertions, we prayed for God's mercy that we may live another year; now we pray that the life we are granted be good.

IN THE BOOK OF LIFE בְּסֵפֶר חַיִּים. This is the last of the four special insertions in the Amidah, added for the Ten Days of Repentance. In this final addition, the theme of a "good life" is expanded to include peace and prosperity.

WHO BRINGS PEACE עוֹשֶׂה הַשָּׁלוֹם. In the words of the Midrash, "Great is peace, for all the prayers conclude with pleas for peace" (Sifrei Numbers 42). In addition to the Amidah, the Grace after Meals, Priestly Blessing, Kaddish Shalem, Mourner's Kaddish, and evening Sh'ma and Its Blessings all conclude with prayers for peace.

A full commentary on the Confession appears with the public recitation on page 234.

The Blessing of Shalom

When the blessing of *shalom* is lacking, however much we have of other blessings—wealth or power, fame or family, even health—these all appear as nothing. But when *shalom* is present, however little else we have somehow seems sufficient.

Shalom means "peace," of course, but it means so much more as well:
wholeness, fullness, and
    completion;
integrity and perfection;
healing, health, and
    harmony;
utter tranquility;
loving and being loved;
consummation;
forgiveness and reconciliation;
totality of well-being.

And even all of these together do not spell out sufficiently the meaning of *shalom*. But though we cannot accurately translate or adequately define *shalom*, we can experience it.

—HERSHEL J. MATT

For all these blessings may Your name be praised and exalted, our sovereign, always and forever.

And inscribe all the people of Your covenant for a good life.

May all that lives thank You always, and praise Your name faithfully forever, God of our deliverance and help.
ſ *Barukh atah* ADONAI, whose name is goodness and to whom praise is fitting.

Seventh B'rakhah: Prayer for Peace

In the evening, we say:

Grant abundant and lasting peace to Your people Israel and all who dwell on earth, for You are the sovereign master of all the ways of peace. May it please You to bless Your people Israel at all times with Your gift of peace.

In the morning or afternoon, we say:

Grant peace to the world: goodness and blessing, grace, love, and compassion, for us and for all the people Israel. Bless us, our creator, united as one with the light of Your presence; by that light, ADONAI our God, You gave us a guide to life, the love of kindness, generosity, blessing, compassion, life, and peace. May it please You to bless Your people Israel at all times with Your peace.

All services continue here:

May we and the entire House of Israel be called to mind and inscribed for life, blessing, sustenance, and peace in the Book of Life.

Barukh atah ADONAI, who brings peace.

VIDDUI — PRAYERS OF CONFESSION

Because confession is an essential aspect of Yom Kippur, we add this liturgical confession each time that we recite the Amidah.

INTRODUCTION TO THE CONFESSION

Our God and God of our ancestors,
hear our prayer; do not ignore our plea.
Our God and God of our ancestors,
we are neither so insolent nor so obstinate
as to claim in Your presence
that we are righteous, without sin;
for we, like our ancestors who came before us, have sinned.

Customarily, we each strike our heart as we recite every phrase of this confession.

אָשַׁמְנוּ, בָּגַדְנוּ, גָּזַלְנוּ, דִּבַּרְנוּ דְפִי. הֶעֱוִינוּ, וְהִרְשַׁעְנוּ, זַדְנוּ, חָמַסְנוּ,
טָפַלְנוּ שֶׁקֶר. יָעַצְנוּ רָע, כִּזַּבְנוּ, לַצְנוּ, מָרַדְנוּ, נִאַצְנוּ. סָרַרְנוּ, עָוִינוּ, פָּשַׁעְנוּ,
צָרַרְנוּ, קִשִּׁינוּ עֹרֶף. רָשַׁעְנוּ, שִׁחַתְנוּ, תִּעַבְנוּ, תָּעִינוּ, תִּעְתָּעְנוּ.

סַרְנוּ מִמִּצְוֹתֶיךָ וּמִמִּשְׁפָּטֶיךָ הַטּוֹבִים, וְלֹא שָׁוָה לָנוּ. וְאַתָּה צַדִּיק עַל
כָּל־הַבָּא עָלֵינוּ, כִּי אֱמֶת עָשִׂיתָ וַאֲנַחְנוּ הִרְשָׁעְנוּ. מַה נֹּאמַר לְפָנֶיךָ
יוֹשֵׁב מָרוֹם, וּמַה נְּסַפֵּר לְפָנֶיךָ שׁוֹכֵן שְׁחָקִים, הֲלֹא כָּל־הַנִּסְתָּרוֹת
וְהַנִּגְלוֹת אַתָּה יוֹדֵעַ.

אַתָּה יוֹדֵעַ רָזֵי עוֹלָם, וְתַעֲלוּמוֹת סִתְרֵי כָל־חָי. אַתָּה חוֹפֵשׂ כָּל־חַדְרֵי
בָטֶן, וּבוֹחֵן כְּלָיוֹת וָלֵב. אֵין דָּבָר נֶעְלָם מִמֶּךָּ, וְאֵין נִסְתָּר מִנֶּגֶד עֵינֶיךָ.
וּבְכֵן יְהִי רָצוֹן מִלְּפָנֶיךָ, יהוה אֱלֹהֵינוּ וֵאלֹהֵי אֲבוֹתֵינוּ [וְאִמּוֹתֵינוּ],
שֶׁתִּסְלַח לָנוּ עַל כָּל־חַטֹּאתֵינוּ,
וְתִמְחַל לָנוּ עַל כָּל־עֲוֹנוֹתֵינוּ,
וּתְכַפֵּר לָנוּ עַל כָּל־פְּשָׁעֵינוּ.

Customarily, we each strike our heart as we recite the words עַל חֵטְא שֶׁחָטָאנוּ.

עַל חֵטְא שֶׁחָטָאנוּ לְפָנֶיךָ בְּאֹנֶס וּבְרָצוֹן,
וְעַל חֵטְא שֶׁחָטָאנוּ לְפָנֶיךָ בְּאִמּוּץ הַלֵּב.
עַל חֵטְא שֶׁחָטָאנוּ לְפָנֶיךָ בִּבְלִי דָעַת,
וְעַל חֵטְא שֶׁחָטָאנוּ לְפָנֶיךָ בְּבִטּוּי שְׂפָתָיִם.
עַל חֵטְא שֶׁחָטָאנוּ לְפָנֶיךָ בְּגִלּוּי עֲרָיוֹת,
וְעַל חֵטְא שֶׁחָטָאנוּ לְפָנֶיךָ בַּגָּלוּי וּבַסָּתֶר.
עַל חֵטְא שֶׁחָטָאנוּ לְפָנֶיךָ בְּדַעַת וּבְמִרְמָה,
וְעַל חֵטְא שֶׁחָטָאנוּ לְפָנֶיךָ בְּדִבּוּר פֶּה.
עַל חֵטְא שֶׁחָטָאנוּ לְפָנֶיךָ בְּהוֹנָאַת רֵעַ,
וְעַל חֵטְא שֶׁחָטָאנוּ לְפָנֶיךָ בְּהִרְהוֹר הַלֵּב.
עַל חֵטְא שֶׁחָטָאנוּ לְפָנֶיךָ בִּוְעִידַת זְנוּת,
וְעַל חֵטְא שֶׁחָטָאנוּ לְפָנֶיךָ בְּוִדּוּי פֶּה.
עַל חֵטְא שֶׁחָטָאנוּ לְפָנֶיךָ בְּזִלְזוּל הוֹרִים וּמוֹרִים,
וְעַל חֵטְא שֶׁחָטָאנוּ לְפָנֶיךָ בְּזָדוֹן וּבִשְׁגָגָה.

The Shorter Confession—Ashamnu

Customarily, we each strike our heart as we recite every phrase of this confession.

We abuse, we betray, we are cruel, we destroy, we embitter, we falsify, we gossip, we hate, we insult, we jeer, we kill, we lie, we mock, we neglect, we oppress, we pervert, we quarrel, we rebel, we steal, we transgress, we are unkind, we are violent, we are wicked, we are extremists, we yearn to do evil, we are zealous for bad causes.

Ashamnu, bagadnu, gazalnu, dibbarnu dofi,
he·evinu, v'hirshanu, zadnu, ḥamasnu, tafalnu sheker,
ya·atznu ra, kizzavnu, latznu, maradnu, ni·atznu,
sararnu, avinu, pashanu, tzararnu, kishinu oref,
rashanu, shiḥatnu, ti·avnu, ta·inu, titanu.

PRAYER ACCOMPANYING THE CONFESSION

We have turned from Your goodly laws and commandments, but it has not profited us. Surely, You are in the right with respect to all that comes upon us, for You have acted faithfully, but we have been in the wrong. What can we say to You who sit on high, and what can we tell You who dwell in heaven, for You know all that is hidden as well as all that is revealed.

You know the mysteries of the universe, the deepest secrets of everyone alive. You probe our innermost depths; You examine our thoughts and feelings. Nothing escapes You; nothing is secret from You. Therefore, may it be Your will, our God and God of our ancestors, to forgive us for all our sins, to pardon us for all our iniquities, and to grant us atonement for all our transgressions.

The Longer Confession—Al Ḥet

Customarily, we each strike our heart as we recite the words "We have sinned."

We have sinned against You unwillingly and willingly,
    and we have sinned against You through hardening our hearts.
We have sinned against You thoughtlessly,
    and we have sinned against You in idle chatter.
We have sinned against You through sexual immorality,
    and we have sinned against You openly and in private.
We have sinned against You knowingly and deceitfully,
    and we have sinned against You by the way we talk.
We have sinned against You by defrauding others,
    and we have sinned against You in our innermost thoughts.
We have sinned against You through forbidden trysts,
    and we have sinned against You through empty confession.
We have sinned against You by scorning parents and teachers,
    and we have sinned against You purposely and by mistake.

עַל חֵטְא שֶׁחָטָאנוּ לְפָנֶיךָ בְּחֹזֶק יָד,

וְעַל חֵטְא שֶׁחָטָאנוּ לְפָנֶיךָ בְּחִלּוּל הַשֵּׁם.

עַל חֵטְא שֶׁחָטָאנוּ לְפָנֶיךָ בְּטֻמְאַת שְׂפָתָיִם,

וְעַל חֵטְא שֶׁחָטָאנוּ לְפָנֶיךָ בְּטִפְשׁוּת פֶּה.

עַל חֵטְא שֶׁחָטָאנוּ לְפָנֶיךָ בְּיֵצֶר הָרָע,

וְעַל חֵטְא שֶׁחָטָאנוּ לְפָנֶיךָ בְּיוֹדְעִים וּבְלֹא יוֹדְעִים.

וְעַל כֻּלָּם, אֱלוֹהַּ סְלִיחוֹת, סְלַח לָנוּ, מְחַל לָנוּ, כַּפֶּר־לָנוּ.

עַל חֵטְא שֶׁחָטָאנוּ לְפָנֶיךָ בְּכַחַשׁ וּבְכָזָב,

וְעַל חֵטְא שֶׁחָטָאנוּ לְפָנֶיךָ בְּכַפַּת שֹׁחַד.

עַל חֵטְא שֶׁחָטָאנוּ לְפָנֶיךָ בְּלָצוֹן,

וְעַל חֵטְא שֶׁחָטָאנוּ לְפָנֶיךָ בְּלָשׁוֹן הָרָע.

עַל חֵטְא שֶׁחָטָאנוּ לְפָנֶיךָ בְּמַשָּׂא וּבְמַתָּן,

וְעַל חֵטְא שֶׁחָטָאנוּ לְפָנֶיךָ בְּמַאֲכָל וּבְמִשְׁתֶּה.

עַל חֵטְא שֶׁחָטָאנוּ לְפָנֶיךָ בְּנֶשֶׁךְ וּבְמַרְבִּית,

וְעַל חֵטְא שֶׁחָטָאנוּ לְפָנֶיךָ בִּנְטִיַּת גָּרוֹן.

עַל חֵטְא שֶׁחָטָאנוּ לְפָנֶיךָ בְּשִׂיחַ שִׂפְתוֹתֵינוּ,

וְעַל חֵטְא שֶׁחָטָאנוּ לְפָנֶיךָ בְּשִׁקּוּר עָיִן.

עַל חֵטְא שֶׁחָטָאנוּ לְפָנֶיךָ בְּעֵינַיִם רָמוֹת,

וְעַל חֵטְא שֶׁחָטָאנוּ לְפָנֶיךָ בְּעַזּוּת מֵצַח.

וְעַל כֻּלָּם, אֱלוֹהַּ סְלִיחוֹת, סְלַח לָנוּ, מְחַל לָנוּ, כַּפֶּר־לָנוּ.

עַל חֵטְא שֶׁחָטָאנוּ לְפָנֶיךָ בִּפְרִיקַת עֹל,

וְעַל חֵטְא שֶׁחָטָאנוּ לְפָנֶיךָ בִּפְלִילוּת.

עַל חֵטְא שֶׁחָטָאנוּ לְפָנֶיךָ בִּצְדִיַּת רֵעַ,

וְעַל חֵטְא שֶׁחָטָאנוּ לְפָנֶיךָ בְּצָרוּת עָיִן.

עַל חֵטְא שֶׁחָטָאנוּ לְפָנֶיךָ בְּקַלּוּת רֹאשׁ,

וְעַל חֵטְא שֶׁחָטָאנוּ לְפָנֶיךָ בְּקַשְׁיוּת עֹרֶף.

עַל חֵטְא שֶׁחָטָאנוּ לְפָנֶיךָ בְּרִיצַת רַגְלַיִם לְהָרַע,

וְעַל חֵטְא שֶׁחָטָאנוּ לְפָנֶיךָ בִּרְכִילוּת.

עַל חֵטְא שֶׁחָטָאנוּ לְפָנֶיךָ בִּשְׁבוּעַת שָׁוְא,

וְעַל חֵטְא שֶׁחָטָאנוּ לְפָנֶיךָ בְּשִׂנְאַת חִנָּם.

עַל חֵטְא שֶׁחָטָאנוּ לְפָנֶיךָ בִּתְשׂוּמֶת־יָד,

וְעַל חֵטְא שֶׁחָטָאנוּ לְפָנֶיךָ בְּתִמְהוֹן לֵבָב.

וְעַל כֻּלָּם, אֱלוֹהַּ סְלִיחוֹת, סְלַח לָנוּ, מְחַל לָנוּ, כַּפֶּר־לָנוּ.

We have sinned against You by resorting to violence,
  and we have sinned against You by public desecration of Your name.
We have sinned against You through foul speech,
  and we have sinned against You through foolish talk.
We have sinned against You through pursuing the impulse to evil,
  and we have sinned against You wittingly and unwittingly.

For all these sins, forgiving God, forgive us, pardon us, grant us atonement.

We have sinned against You through denial and deceit,
  and we have sinned against You by taking bribes.
We have sinned against You by clever cynicism,
  and we have sinned against You by speaking ill of others.
We have sinned against You by the way we do business,
  and we have sinned against You in our eating and drinking.
We have sinned against You by greed and oppressive interest,
  and we have sinned against You through arrogance.
We have sinned against You in everyday conversation,
  and we have sinned against You through conspiratorial glances.
We have sinned against You through condescension,
  and we have sinned against You through stubbornness.

For all these sins, forgiving God, forgive us, pardon us, grant us atonement.

We have sinned against You by throwing off all restraint,
  and we have sinned against You by rashly judging others.
We have sinned against You by plotting against others,
  and we have sinned against You through selfishness.
We have sinned against You through superficiality,
  and we have sinned against You through stubbornness.
We have sinned against You by rushing to do evil,
  and we have sinned against You through gossip.
We have sinned against You through empty promises,
  and we have sinned against You through baseless hatred.
We have sinned against You by betraying trust,
  and we have sinned against You by succumbing to confusion.

For all these sins, forgiving God, forgive us, pardon us, grant us atonement.

וְעַל מִצְוֺת עֲשֵׂה וְעַל מִצְוֺת לֹא תַעֲשֶׂה. בֵּין שֶׁיֵּשׁ בָּהּ
קוּם עֲשֵׂה, וּבֵין שֶׁאֵין בָּהּ קוּם עֲשֵׂה, אֶת־הַגְּלוּיִּים לָנוּ
וְאֶת־שֶׁאֵינָם גְּלוּיִּים לָנוּ. אֶת־הַגְּלוּיִּים לָנוּ כְּבָר אֲמַרְנוּם
לְפָנֶיךָ וְהוֹדִינוּ לְךָ עֲלֵיהֶם, וְאֶת־שֶׁאֵינָם גְּלוּיִּים
לָנוּ, לְפָנֶיךָ הֵם גְּלוּיִּים וִידוּעִים, כַּדָּבָר שֶׁנֶּאֱמַר:
הַנִּסְתָּרֹת לַיהוה אֱלֹהֵינוּ, וְהַנִּגְלֹת לָנוּ וּלְבָנֵינוּ עַד־
עוֹלָם, לַעֲשׂוֹת אֶת־כָּל־דִּבְרֵי הַתּוֹרָה הַזֹּאת.

SECRET MATTERS הַנִּסְתָּרֹת.
Deuteronomy 29:28.

אֱלֹהַי, עַד שֶׁלֹּא נוֹצַרְתִּי אֵינִי כְדַאי, וְעַכְשָׁו שֶׁנּוֹצַרְתִּי כְּאִלּוּ
לֹא נוֹצַרְתִּי. עָפָר אֲנִי בְּחַיַּי, קַל וָחֹמֶר בְּמִיתָתִי. הֲרֵי אֲנִי
לְפָנֶיךָ כִּכְלִי מָלֵא בוּשָׁה וּכְלִמָּה. יְהִי רָצוֹן מִלְּפָנֶיךָ, יהוה
אֱלֹהַי וֵאלֹהֵי אֲבוֹתַי [וְאִמּוֹתַי], שֶׁלֹּא אֶחֱטָא עוֹד. וּמַה
שֶּׁחָטָאתִי לְפָנֶיךָ מָרֵק בְּרַחֲמֶיךָ הָרַבִּים, אֲבָל לֹא עַל יְדֵי
יִסּוּרִים וָחֳלָיִים רָעִים.

MY GOD אֱלֹהַי. The Baby-
lonian Talmud says that
every Amidah must be
accompanied by a personal
prayer. These two private
prayers, the first attributed
to Rava and the second
to Mar son of Ravina, are
among the Talmud's exem-
plars (Berakhot 17a). They
were so admired that they
entered the formal liturgy.
Both prayers distinctively
use the first-person singular
("I"), whereas almost all
other prayers—including
the confessions—are in the
first-person plural ("we").

אֱלֹהַי, נְצוֹר לְשׁוֹנִי מֵרָע, וּשְׂפָתַי מִדַּבֵּר מִרְמָה, וְלִמְקַלְלַי
נַפְשִׁי תִדּוֹם, וְנַפְשִׁי כֶּעָפָר לַכֹּל תִּהְיֶה. פְּתַח לִבִּי בְּתוֹרָתֶךָ,
וּבְמִצְוֺתֶיךָ תִּרְדּוֹף נַפְשִׁי. וְכָל־הַחוֹשְׁבִים עָלַי רָעָה, מְהֵרָה
הָפֵר עֲצָתָם וְקַלְקֵל מַחֲשַׁבְתָּם. עֲשֵׂה לְמַעַן שְׁמֶךָ, עֲשֵׂה
לְמַעַן יְמִינֶךָ, עֲשֵׂה לְמַעַן קְדֻשָּׁתֶךָ, עֲשֵׂה לְמַעַן תּוֹרָתֶךָ.
לְמַעַן יֵחָלְצוּן יְדִידֶיךָ, הוֹשִׁיעָה יְמִינְךָ וַעֲנֵנִי. יִהְיוּ לְרָצוֹן
אִמְרֵי פִי וְהֶגְיוֹן לִבִּי לְפָנֶיךָ, יהוה צוּרִי וְגֹאֲלִי. עֹשֶׂה שָׁלוֹם
בִּמְרוֹמָיו, הוּא יַעֲשֶׂה שָׁלוֹם עָלֵינוּ, וְעַל כָּל־יִשְׂרָאֵל
[וְעַל כָּל־יוֹשְׁבֵי תֵבֵל] וְאִמְרוּ: אָמֵן.

MAY THE WORDS יִהְיוּ לְרָצוֹן.
Psalm 19:15.

On Yom Kippur morning, continue on page 252.
On Yom Kippur afternoon, continue on page 374.

And forgive us the breach of all commandments and prohibitions, whether involving deeds or not, whether known to us or not. The sins known to us we have acknowledged, and those unknown to us are surely known to You, as the Torah states: "Secret matters are the concern of ADONAI our God; but in matters that are revealed, it is for us and our children to apply all teachings of the Torah till the end of time."

Personal Prayers Concluding the Amidah

My God, before I was created I was entirely lacking in substance; and now that I have been created, it is as if I never was. Dust and ashes am I in life, all the more so in death. I stand before You as a vessel full of embarrassment and shame. May it be Your will, ADONAI my God and God of my ancestors, that I sin no more, and that in Your great mercy You erase the sins I have sinned before You, but not through great pain and suffering.

My God, keep my tongue from evil, my lips from lies. Help me ignore those who would slander me. Let me be humble before all. Open my heart to Your Torah, that I may pursue Your mitzvot. Frustrate the designs of those who plot evil against me; make nothing of their schemes. Act for the sake of Your name, Your power, Your holiness, and Your Torah. Answer my prayer for the deliverance of Your people. May the words of my mouth and the meditations of my heart be acceptable to You, ADONAI, my rock and my redeemer. May the One who brings peace to the universe bring peace to us and to all the people Israel [and to all who dwell on earth]. Amen.

On Yom Kippur morning, continue on page 252.
On Yom Kippur afternoon, continue on page 374.

שַׁבָּת

וַיְכֻלּוּ הַשָּׁמַיִם וְהָאָרֶץ וְכָל־צְבָאָם.
וַיְכַל אֱלֹהִים בַּיּוֹם הַשְּׁבִיעִי מְלַאכְתּוֹ אֲשֶׁר עָשָׂה,
וַיִּשְׁבֹּת בַּיּוֹם הַשְּׁבִיעִי, מִכָּל־מְלַאכְתּוֹ אֲשֶׁר עָשָׂה.
וַיְבָרֶךְ אֱלֹהִים אֶת יוֹם הַשְּׁבִיעִי וַיְקַדֵּשׁ אֹתוֹ,
כִּי בוֹ שָׁבַת מִכָּל־מְלַאכְתּוֹ, אֲשֶׁר בָּרָא אֱלֹהִים לַעֲשׂוֹת.

THE HEAVENS AND THE EARTH וַיְכֻלּוּ הַשָּׁמַיִם וְהָאָרֶץ. Genesis 2:1–3.

PROTECTION TO OUR ANCESTORS מָגֵן אָבוֹת. Literally, "shield of our ancestors." The evening service contains no repetition of the Amidah. This paragraph, which includes the themes of each of the seven b'rakhot of the Shabbat Amidah, is added on Shabbat eve. As elsewhere in the High Holy Day liturgy, the word מֶלֶךְ (melekh), "sovereign," is substituted for the word אֵל (El), "God" (which is recited in the year-round version of this prayer), to emphasize the metaphor of God's sovereignty on this day.

Version with Patriarchs and Matriarchs:

◁ בָּרוּךְ אַתָּה יהוה, אֱלֹהֵינוּ
וֵאלֹהֵי אֲבוֹתֵינוּ [וְאִמּוֹתֵינוּ],
אֱלֹהֵי אַבְרָהָם, אֱלֹהֵי יִצְחָק,
וֵאלֹהֵי יַעֲקֹב, אֱלֹהֵי שָׂרָה,
אֱלֹהֵי רִבְקָה, אֱלֹהֵי רָחֵל,
וֵאלֹהֵי לֵאָה, הָאֵל הַגָּדוֹל
הַגִּבּוֹר וְהַנּוֹרָא, אֵל עֶלְיוֹן,
קוֹנֵה שָׁמַיִם וָאָרֶץ.

Version with Patriarchs:

◁ בָּרוּךְ אַתָּה יהוה, אֱלֹהֵינוּ
וֵאלֹהֵי אֲבוֹתֵינוּ, אֱלֹהֵי
אַבְרָהָם, אֱלֹהֵי יִצְחָק, וֵאלֹהֵי
יַעֲקֹב, הָאֵל הַגָּדוֹל הַגִּבּוֹר
וְהַנּוֹרָא, אֵל עֶלְיוֹן,
קוֹנֵה שָׁמַיִם וָאָרֶץ.

מָגֵן אָבוֹת בִּדְבָרוֹ, מְחַיֵּה מֵתִים בְּמַאֲמָרוֹ, הַמֶּלֶךְ הַקָּדוֹשׁ
שֶׁאֵין כָּמוֹהוּ, הַמֵּנִיחַ לְעַמּוֹ בְּיוֹם שַׁבַּת קָדְשׁוֹ, כִּי בָם רָצָה
לְהָנִיחַ לָהֶם. לְפָנָיו נַעֲבוֹד בְּיִרְאָה וָפַחַד, וְנוֹדֶה לִשְׁמוֹ
בְּכָל־יוֹם תָּמִיד. מְעוֹן הַבְּרָכוֹת, אֵל הַהוֹדָאוֹת, אֲדוֹן הַשָּׁלוֹם,
מְקַדֵּשׁ הַשַּׁבָּת וּמְבָרֵךְ שְׁבִיעִי, וּמֵנִיחַ בִּקְדֻשָּׁה לְעַם מְדֻשְּׁנֵי־
עֹנֶג, זֵכֶר לְמַעֲשֵׂה בְרֵאשִׁית.

◁ אֱלֹהֵינוּ וֵאלֹהֵי אֲבוֹתֵינוּ [וְאִמּוֹתֵינוּ], רְצֵה בִמְנוּחָתֵנוּ.
קַדְּשֵׁנוּ בְּמִצְוֹתֶיךָ, וְתֵן חֶלְקֵנוּ בְּתוֹרָתֶךָ,
שַׂבְּעֵנוּ מִטּוּבֶךָ, וְשַׂמְּחֵנוּ בִּישׁוּעָתֶךָ,
וְטַהֵר לִבֵּנוּ לְעָבְדְּךָ בֶּאֱמֶת,
וְהַנְחִילֵנוּ יהוה אֱלֹהֵינוּ בְּאַהֲבָה וּבְרָצוֹן שַׁבַּת קָדְשֶׁךָ,
וְיָנוּחוּ בָהּ יִשְׂרָאֵל מְקַדְּשֵׁי שְׁמֶךָ.
בָּרוּךְ אַתָּה יהוה, מְקַדֵּשׁ הַשַּׁבָּת.

The heavens and the earth, and all they contain, were completed. On the seventh day God finished the work, ceasing from all work on the seventh day. Then God blessed the seventh day, making it holy, because on it, God had ceased from all the work of creation.

Va-y'khullu ha-shamayim v'ha-aretz v'khol tz'va·am. Va-y'khal Elohim ba-yom ha-sh'vi·i m'lakhto asher asah, va-yishbot ba-yom ha-sh'vi·i mi-kol m'lakhto asher asah. Va-y'varekh Elohim et yom ha-sh'vi·i va-y'kaddeish oto, ki vo shavat mi-kol m'lakhto, asher bara Elohim la·asot.

Version with Patriarchs:

Barukh atah ADONAI, our God and God of our ancestors, God of Abraham, God of Isaac, and God of Jacob, great, mighty, awe-inspiring, transcendent God, Creator of heaven and earth.

Version with Patriarchs and Matriarchs:

Barukh atah ADONAI, our God and God of our ancestors, God of Abraham, God of Isaac, and God of Jacob, God of Sarah, God of Rebecca, God of Rachel, and God of Leah, great, mighty, awe-inspiring, transcendent God, Creator of heaven and earth.

God, who promised protection to our ancestors and assures life to the dead, the incomparable holy sovereign, desired to give rest to the people Israel and so provided them with the holy Shabbat. We worship in awe and reverence in God's presence and offer thanks, each day, always, to God. The source of blessings, the master of peace, God, whom we praise, sanctifies Shabbat, blesses the seventh day, and provides sacred rest to a people overflowing with joy, as a symbol of the work of creation.

Magein avot bi-d'varo, m'ḥayyeih meitim b'ma·amaro, ha-melekh ha-kadosh she-ein kamohu, ha-meini·aḥ l'ammo b'yom shabbat kodsho, ki vam ratzah l'hani·aḥ la-hem. L'fanav na·avod b'yir·ah va-faḥad, v'nodeh li-sh'mo b'khol yom tamid. M'on ha-b'rakhot, El ha-hoda·ot, adon ha-shalom, m'kaddeish ha-shabbat u-m'vareikh sh'vi·i, u-meini·aḥ bi-k'dushah l'am m'dush'nei oneg, zeikher l'ma·aseih v'reishit.

Our God and God of our ancestors,
embrace our rest.
Make us holy through Your mitzvot
and let the Torah be our portion.
Fill our lives with Your goodness
and gladden us with Your triumph.
Purify our hearts to serve You faithfully.
ADONAI our God, grant that we inherit Your holy Shabbat, lovingly and willingly, so that the people Israel, who sanctify Your name, may find rest on this day. *Barukh atah ADONAI,* who makes Shabbat holy.

יַעֲלֶה תַּחֲנוּנֵנוּ מֵעֶרֶב,
וְיָבֹא שַׁוְעָתֵנוּ מִבֹּקֶר,
וְיֵרָאֶה רִנּוּנֵנוּ עַד עָרֶב.

יַעֲלֶה קוֹלֵנוּ מֵעֶרֶב,
וְיָבֹא צִדְקָתֵנוּ מִבֹּקֶר,
וְיֵרָאֶה פִּדְיוֹנֵנוּ עַד עָרֶב.

יַעֲלֶה עִנּוּיֵנוּ מֵעֶרֶב,
וְיָבֹא סְלִיחָתֵנוּ מִבֹּקֶר,
וְיֵרָאֶה נַאֲקָתֵנוּ עַד עָרֶב.

יַעֲלֶה מְנוּסֵנוּ מֵעֶרֶב,
וְיָבֹא לְמַעֲנוֹ מִבֹּקֶר,
וְיֵרָאֶה כִּפּוּרֵנוּ עַד עָרֶב.

יַעֲלֶה יִשְׁעֵנוּ מֵעֶרֶב,
וְיָבֹא טָהֳרֵנוּ מִבֹּקֶר,
וְיֵרָאֶה חִנּוּנֵנוּ עַד עָרֶב.

יַעֲלֶה זִכְרוֹנֵנוּ מֵעֶרֶב,
וְיָבֹא וְעוּדֵנוּ מִבֹּקֶר,
וְיֵרָאֶה הַדְרָתֵנוּ עַד עָרֶב.

יַעֲלֶה דָפְקֵנוּ מֵעֶרֶב,
וְיָבֹא גִּילֵנוּ מִבֹּקֶר,
וְיֵרָאֶה בַּקָּשָׁתֵנוּ עַד עָרֶב.

יַעֲלֶה אַנְקָתֵנוּ מֵעֶרֶב,
וְיָבֹא אֵלֶיךָ מִבֹּקֶר,
וְיֵרָאֶה אֵלֵינוּ עַד עָרֶב.

S'LIḤAH AND VIDDUI (Forgiveness and Confession) stand in a complementary relationship to one another: *Viddui* (confession) is the human realization that we have sinned and failed—that our lives are imperfect. *S'liḥah* (forgiveness) is the divine assurance that our confession (repeated ten times on Yom Kippur) is received in love. Note that the assurance of God's forgiveness now precedes our confession.

YA·ALEH יַעֲלֶה. is the overture to these special sections in the evening service. It is an anonymous medieval poem, which describes Yom Kippur as a progression from Kol Nidrei to Ne·ilah. Each verse includes *ya·aleh* יַעֲלֶה (rise) in the evening, *yavo* יָבֹא (arrive) in the morning, and *yeira·eh* יֵרָאֶה (appear) at the end of the day. The author expresses the anxiety at the beginning of this day of self-examination with its pleas for forgiveness, as well as the hope for purification at the fast's completion.

The poem is a reverse acrostic at the first letter of the middle word in each clause. It is as if, throughout the day, we move back in our recollections, allowing the events of the year to pass before our mind's eye. This day is set aside for introspection: at different hours, in different light, we may see different aspects of our lives; and as we move inward, we can be in touch with the ways our lives might be renewed, until we arrive at א (*alef*), the point of origin.

Two differing translations appear here, one that attempts to imitate the play on letters embedded in the Hebrew poem, the other that captures the Hebrew rhythms. This juxtaposition illustrates the choices that need be made in translating medieval poetry.

S'LIḤOT

Let our yearning rise to
  You in the evening,
our exclamations come to
  You in the morning,
then wondrous joy shall
  appear by evening.
  Let our voices rise to You
    in the evening,
  our unsung deeds come to
    You in the morning,
  so our true redemption
    shall appear by evening.
Let our sufferings rise to
  You in the evening,
our remorse come to You
  in the morning,
then our pardon shall
  appear by evening.
  Let our outcries rise
    to You in the evening,
  take note of them for Your
    sake in the morning,
  pour Your mercy upon us
    by evening.
Let our lament rise to You
  in the evening,
and may You know the
  purity of our spirit in the
  morning,
that the joy of forgiveness
  appear by evening.
  Let intimations of regret
    rise to You in the evening,
  and hopefulness in our
    gathering come to You
    in the morning,
  then our glory, reflective
    of You, shall appear by
    evening.
Let our fervent knocking at
  the gates rise to You
  in the evening,
our entreaties come to You
  in the morning,
and Your forgiveness
  delight us by evening.
  Let our confession rise up
    to You in the evening,
  may it blaze across the
    skies in the morning,
  so the forgiveness of all
    appear by evening.

Following the silent Amidah, the most important themes of Yom Kippur are the subject of these two special sections, S'liḥot and Viddui, which begin here and are repeated throughout the day. The entire liturgy of Yom Kippur rests upon these two pillars: God is merciful and forgiving, and confession brings forgiveness and atonement.

THE UNFOLDING OF THE DAY: A PIYYUT

May our supplications rise up at evening,
our pleas arrive with the dawn,
our songs transform the dusk.
  May our voices rise up at evening,
    our righteous acts arrive with the dawn,
    our redemption transform the dusk.
May our suffering rise up at evening,
our forgiveness arrive with the dawn,
our purity transform the dusk.
  May our prayers rise up at evening,
    coming to You with the dawn,
    transforming us at dusk.

Ya·aleh taḥanuneinu mei-erev,
  v'yavo shav·ateinu mi-boker,
    v'yeira·eh rinnuneinu ad arev.
Ya·aleh koleinu mei-erev,
  v'yavo tzidkateinu mi-boker,
    v'yeira·eh pidyoneinu ad arev.
Ya·aleh innuyeinu mei-erev,
  v'yavo s'liḥateinu mi-boker,
    v'yeira·eh na·akateinu ad arev.
Ya·aleh m'nuseinu mei-erev,
  v'yavo l'ma·ano mi-boker,
    v'yeira·eh kippureinu ad arev.
Ya·aleh yish·einu mei-erev,
  v'yavo tohoreinu mi-boker,
    v'yeira·eh ḥinnuneinu ad arev.
Ya·aleh zikhroneinu mei-erev,
  v'yavo vi·udeinu mi-boker,
    v'yeira·eh hadrateinu ad arev.
Ya·aleh dofkeinu mei-erev,
  v'yavo gileinu mi-boker,
    v'yeira·eh bakkashateinu ad arev.
Ya·aleh enkateinu mei-erev,
  v'yavo eilekha mi-boker,
    v'yeira·eh eileinu ad arev.

שְׁמַע תְּפִלָּה, עָדֶיךָ כָּל־בָּשָׂר יָבֹאוּ.
יָבוֹא כָל־בָּשָׂר לְהִשְׁתַּחֲוֹת לְפָנֶיךָ יהוה.
יָבְוֹאוּ וְיִשְׁתַּחֲווּ לְפָנֶיךָ אֲדֹנָי, וִיכַבְּדוּ לִשְׁמֶךָ.
לְכוּ נְרַנְּנָה לַיהוה, נָרִיעָה לְצוּר יִשְׁעֵנוּ.
נְקַדְּמָה פָנָיו בְּתוֹדָה, בִּזְמִרוֹת נָרִיעַ לוֹ.
אֲשֶׁר־לוֹ הַיָּם וְהוּא עָשָׂהוּ, וְיַבֶּשֶׁת יָדָיו יָצָרוּ.
אֲשֶׁר בְּיָדוֹ נֶפֶשׁ כָּל־חָי, וְרוּחַ כָּל־בְּשַׂר־אִישׁ.

כִּי יֵשׁ לַכֶּסֶף מוֹצָא, וּמָקוֹם לַזָּהָב יָזֹקּוּ.
וְהַחָכְמָה מֵאַיִן תִּמָּצֵא, וְאֵי זֶה מְקוֹם בִּינָה.

תְּהוֹם אָמַר לֹא בִי־הִיא, וְיָם אָמַר אֵין עִמָּדִי.
לֹא־יֻתַּן סְגוֹר תַּחְתֶּיהָ, וְלֹא יִשָּׁקֵל כֶּסֶף מְחִירָהּ.
לֹא־יְעַרְכֶנָּה זָהָב וּזְכוֹכִית, וּתְמוּרָתָהּ כְּלִי־פָז.
רָאמוֹת וְגָבִישׁ לֹא יִזָּכֵר.
וְהַחָכְמָה מֵאַיִן תִּמָּצֵא, וְאֵי זֶה מְקוֹם בִּינָה.

אֱלֹהִים הֵבִין דַּרְכָּהּ, וְהוּא יָדַע אֶת־מְקוֹמָהּ.
כִּי־הוּא לִקְצוֹת־הָאָרֶץ יַבִּיט, תַּחַת כָּל־הַשָּׁמַיִם יִרְאֶה.
לַעֲשׂוֹת לָרוּחַ מִשְׁקָל, וּמַיִם תִּכֵּן בְּמִדָּה.
בַּעֲשֹׂתוֹ לַמָּטָר חֹק, וְדֶרֶךְ לַחֲזִיז קֹלוֹת.
אָז רָאָהּ וַיְסַפְּרָהּ, הֱכִינָהּ וְגַם־חֲקָרָהּ.
וַיֹּאמֶר לָאָדָם:
הֵן יִרְאַת אֲדֹנָי הִיא חָכְמָה, וְסוּר מֵרָע בִּינָה. אִיּוֹב כח

S'LIHOT consists of selections of biblical verses or a *piyyut*, culminating in a declaration of the Thirteen Attributes of God. Different rites and traditions repeat this cycle up to thirteen times. In this maḥzor, we have three repetitions.

Following the Ashkenazic rite, we begin with a medley of biblical verses, known as "verses of mercy." The selected verses are Psalm 65:3; Isaiah 66:23 (adapted); Psalms 86:9, 95:1–2, 5; and Job 12:10.

Then following the Sephardic tradition, we have included verses from the Book of Job. The Sephardic custom of reciting that biblical book on Kol Nidrei evening was inspired by the Mishnah, which says that the High Priest would study it during the night of Yom Kippur (Yoma 1:6). Invoking the Book of Job may also imply that on this day we question not only our own performance during the year but also the state of the world, and God's justice as well. (This theme will be further explored during the Musaf service tomorrow.)

These particular verses evoke a sense of the mystery of existence. Repentance may begin with a realization of the limitations of our knowledge—whether of ourselves or of the world.

¶ בְּאוֹתוֹ עֶרֶב מוּזָר
מִישֶׁהוּ שָׁאַל:
הַאִם אֶפְשָׁר לְשַׁנּוֹת אֶת הֶעָבָר?
וְהָאִשָּׁה הַחוֹלָנִית עָנְתָה בְּזַעַף:
הֶעָבָר אֵינֶנּוּ תַּכְשִׁיט
חָתוּם בְּתוֹךְ קֻפְסָה שֶׁל בְּדֹלַח
גַּם אֵינֶנּוּ
נָחָשׁ בְּתוֹךְ צִנְצֶנֶת שֶׁל כֹּהַל –
הֶעָבָר מִתְנוֹעֵעַ
בְּתוֹךְ הַהֹוֶה
וְכַאֲשֶׁר הַהֹוֶה נוֹפֵל לְתוֹךְ בּוֹר
נוֹפֵל אִתּוֹ הֶעָבָר –
כַּאֲשֶׁר הֶעָבָר מַבִּיט הַשָּׁמַיְמָה
זוֹ הֲרָמַת הַחַיִּים כֻּלָּם,
גַּם חַיֵּי עָבָר רָחוֹק עַד מְאֹד.

אַךְ הָאִישׁ הַגַּלְמוּד מִלְמֵל:
וַהֲלֹא הָיָה פַּעַם אַבְרָהָם בַּתֵּבֵל
זֶה שֶׁלֹּא לָקַח אֲפִלּוּ חוּט
מִנֶּפֶשׁ מוֹלִידוֹ.

In that strange night
someone asked:
Can you change the past?
And the woman who was
ill angrily responded:
The past is not a piece of
jewelry
sealed in a crystal box
nor is it a snake preserved
in a bottle of formalde-
hyde—
The past trembles
within the present
and when the present
falls into a pit
the past goes with it—
when the past looks
toward heaven
all of life is upraised,
even the distant past.

But the lonely man
muttered:
Did not Abraham once
stride the earth,
he who did not seem
attached to even the
cord
of the one who gave him
birth?

—ZELDA
(trans. Edward Feld)

First Cycle of S'liḥot Prayers: Pleas of Mercy

All flesh comes to You, You who hear prayer.
All flesh shall come to worship You, ADONAI.
They shall come to bow down before You, ADONAI,
and they will pay honor to Your name.
Come, let us sing to ADONAI;
and cry out to the stronghold of our deliverance.
Let us greet God with thanks,
and sing songs of praise.
The sea belongs to God, God made it;
the land was created by God's hands.
In God's hand is every living soul
and the breath of all human flesh.

SELECTIONS FROM THE BOOK OF JOB

We know there is a place where gold is found,
and somewhere there is silver for refining.
But wisdom—where can it be found?
Where is the place of true knowledge?
V'ha-ḥokhmah mei-ayin timmatzei, v'ei zeh m'kom binah.
The deep declares, "It is not in me!"
The ocean echoes, "Neither is it here!"
Yet it has no match in gold or glass,
it cannot be traded for precious trinkets,
not even for corals or crystal.
But wisdom—where can it be found?
Where is the place of true knowledge?
God perceives its path.
God knows its place.
While peering to the ends of the earth,
inspecting everything under the heavens,
weighing out the winds,
apportioning the water,
setting quotas for the rain,
fixing routes for the thunderstorms,
God saw it and appraised it,
examined it and plumbed it,
and then God said to human beings:
"The fear of ADONAI—that is wisdom;
departing from sin—that is true knowledge." Job 28

הַנְּשָׁמָה לָךְ וְהַגּוּף פָּעֳלָךְ, חוּסָה עַל עֲמָלָךְ.

הַנְּשָׁמָה לָךְ וְהַגּוּף שֶׁלָּךְ, יהוה עֲשֵׂה לְמַעַן שְׁמֶךָ.

אָתָאנוּ עַל שִׁמְךָ יהוה, עֲשֵׂה לְמַעַן שְׁמֶךָ.

בַּעֲבוּר כְּבוֹד שִׁמְךָ, כִּי אֵל חַנּוּן וְרַחוּם שְׁמֶךָ.

לְמַעַן שִׁמְךָ יהוה, וְסָלַחְתָּ לַעֲוֺנֵנוּ, כִּי רַב הוּא.

We repeat after the leader:

דַּרְכְּךָ אֱלֹהֵינוּ לְהַאֲרִיךְ אַפֶּךָ
לָרָעִים וְלַטּוֹבִים, וְהִיא תְהִלָּתֶךָ.

לְמַעַנְךָ אֱלֹהֵינוּ עֲשֵׂה וְלֹא לָנוּ,
רְאֵה עֲמִידָתֵנוּ דַּלִּים וְרֵיקִים.

תַּעֲלֶה אֲרוּכָה לְעָלֶה נִדָּף,
תְּנַחֵם עַל עָפָר וָאֵפֶר.

תַּשְׁלִיךְ חֲטָאֵינוּ וְתָחֹן בְּמַעֲשֶׂיךָ,
תֵּרֶא כִּי אֵין אִישׁ עָשָׂה עִמָּנוּ צְדָקָה.

THE SOUL IS YOURS הַנְּשָׁמָה לָךְ. These are fragments of two anonymous poems, which appear in fragmentary form in a variety of versions of the printed Ashkenazic maḥzor. The verse beginning with א must have been taken from one *piyyut*, and the one beginning with ת from another one.

YOUR NATURE שְׁמֶךָ. Literally, "Your name." Reference is made to God's "name" six times, as if to say that God's "reputation" for kindness depends on God's exercising forgiveness on this day.

FORGIVE, THEN, OUR SIN וְסָלַחְתָּ לַעֲוֺנֵנוּ. In Psalm 25:11, the verse reads "forgive my sin." Here it is changed to first person plural, as in much of our liturgy.

PATIENT WITH SINNERS, NOT ONLY WITH THE RIGHTEOUS לְהַאֲרִיךְ אַפֶּךָ. This insight is based on a passage in the Babylonian Talmud (Eruvin 22a) which asks why the Torah refers to God's patience in the plural as אֶרֶךְ אַפַּיִם (*erekh appayim*) and not the singular, אֶרֶךְ אַף (*erekh af*). The response is that God is patient with sinners as much as with the righteous, and therefore the plural.

DRIVEN LEAF עָלֶה נִדָּף. Leviticus 26:36 describes the punishment of Israel for their sins as being so fearful that even "the sound of a driven leaf shall put them (Israel) to flight." The poet reverses that image and prays that even though we may be in exile, may we still experience God's love.

NO HUMAN BEING כִּי אֵין אִישׁ. A phrase recalling the biblical story of Moses' looking around and seeing that "there was no human being" watching him, then killing the Egyptian taskmaster (Exodus 2:12). Today, we have no Moses to protect us; only God can redeem us.

Body and Soul

Originally the holy (*kadosh*) meant that which is set apart, isolated, segregated. In Jewish piety it assumed a new meaning, denoting a quality that is involved, immersed in common and earthly endeavors; carried primarily by individual, private, simple deeds rather than public ceremonies.

—ABRAHAM JOSHUA HESCHEL

The soul is Yours, the body is Your creation.
Have compassion on Your handiwork.
The soul is Yours, the body is Yours.
Deal with us according to Your nature.
Ha-n'shamah lakh v'ha-guf po·olakh, ḥusah al amalakh.
Ha-n'shamah lakh v'ha-guf she-lakh, Adonai, aseih l'ma·an sh'mekha.
Atanu al shimkha, Adonai, aseih l'ma·an sh'mekha.

We come before You relying on who You are.
According to Your glorious nature, help us.
You are known as "gracious, compassionate God."
Forgive, then, our sin, though it is great.
Your way is to be patient with sinners,
not only with the righteous.
That is the source of our praise for You.
For Your sake, not ours, God, help us.
See how we stand before You, humbled and empty-handed.
Grant relief to this driven leaf.
Have compassion on that which is but dust and ashes.
Cast away our sins; be kind to Your creations.
No human being can plead for us; have mercy on us.

Dark'kha eloheinu l'ha·arikh appekha
la-ra·im v'la-tovim,
v'hi t'hillatekha.

L'ma·ankha eloheinu aseih v'lo lanu,
r'eih amidateinu dallim v'reikim.

Ta·aleh arukhah l'aleh niddaf, tinnaḥeim al afar va-eifer.
Tashlikh ḥata·einu v'taḥon b'ma·asekha.
Teireh ki ein ish, aseih immanu tz'dakah.

אֵל, אֶרֶךְ אַפַּיִם אַתָּה,
וּבַעַל הָרַחֲמִים נִקְרֵאתָ,
וְדֶרֶךְ תְּשׁוּבָה הוֹרֵיתָ.
גְּדֻלַּת רַחֲמֶיךָ וַחֲסָדֶיךָ תִּזְכֹּר הַיּוֹם
וּבְכָל־יוֹם לְזֶרַע יְדִידֶיךָ.
תֵּפֶן אֵלֵינוּ בְּרַחֲמֶיךָ,
כִּי אַתָּה הוּא בַּעַל הָרַחֲמִים.

בְּתַחֲנוּן וּבִתְפִלָּה פָּנֶיךָ נְקַדֵּם,
כְּהוֹדַעְתָּ לֶעָנָו מִקֶּדֶם.
מֵחֲרוֹן אַפְּךָ שׁוּב,
כְּמוֹ בְּתוֹרָתְךָ כָּתוּב,
וּבְצֵל כְּנָפֶיךָ נֶחֱסֶה וְנִתְלוֹנָן,
כְּיוֹם וַיֵּרֶד יהוה בֶּעָנָן.
◁ תַּעֲבֹר עַל פֶּשַׁע וְתִמְחֶה אָשָׁם,
כְּיוֹם וַיִּתְיַצֵּב עִמּוֹ שָׁם.
תַּאֲזִין שַׁוְעָתֵנוּ וְתַקְשִׁיב מֶנּוּ מַאֲמָר,
כְּיוֹם וַיִּקְרָא בְשֵׁם יהוה.

וַיַּעֲבֹר יהוה עַל־פָּנָיו וַיִּקְרָא:

יהוה יהוה, אֵל רַחוּם וְחַנּוּן, אֶרֶךְ אַפַּיִם, וְרַב־חֶסֶד
וֶאֱמֶת. נֹצֵר חֶסֶד לָאֲלָפִים, נֹשֵׂא עָוֹן וָפֶשַׁע וְחַטָּאָה,
וְנַקֵּה.

וְסָלַחְתָּ לַעֲוֹנֵנוּ וּלְחַטָּאתֵנוּ וּנְחַלְתָּנוּ.

Some customarily strike their heart when asking God to forgive and pardon:

סְלַח לָנוּ אָבִינוּ כִּי חָטָאנוּ, מְחַל לָנוּ מַלְכֵּנוּ כִּי פָשָׁעְנוּ,
כִּי־אַתָּה אֲדֹנָי טוֹב וְסַלָּח, וְרַב־חֶסֶד לְכָל־קוֹרְאֶיךָ.

GOD, YOU ARE PATIENT אֵל, אֶרֶךְ אַפַּיִם. Following on the heels of the very moment when Israel was closest to God, standing at Sinai, having heard God utter the Ten Commandments, the Torah pictures the people sinking from the greatest heights to terrible depths. Israel committed the greatest breach against God: constructing a golden calf and worshiping it. But Moses prayed and God forgave. It is this quintessence of sin and forgiveness that is the basis of Yom Kippur. God does not wish to punish us for our sins, but desires that we return on the path to God. If the sin of the golden calf could be forgiven, so can any sin.

After praying for Israel, Moses asked to see God's face. God replied that no one can see God directly, but human beings can experience the Divine indirectly. God passed before Moses and Moses heard the words of the Thirteen Attributes (Exodus 34:6–7), which speak of God's love. The message of the liturgy is that God is experienced in the moment of forgiveness and love.

It is the experience of forgiveness, not the wallowing in the overwhelming nature of our sinfulness, which is the object of this day. Therefore, the liturgy places the promise of God's forgiveness before the confession of our sins. Ashkenazic tradition offers a variety of introductions to the Thirteen Attributes, and this maḥzor uses a different one for each time the passage is recited in this service.

ABOUT THE DAY . . . AS ON THE DAY כְּיוֹם. The phrases that follow are from Exodus 34:5, the scene of Moses on Mount Sinai following the shattering of the tablets. When Moses was on the mountain, he did not eat or drink. Yom Kippur can be like that day of Sinai, when Moses discovered God's love and forgiveness.

GRANTING PARDON וְנַקֵּה. The text in the Torah (Exodus 34:7) continues לֹא יְנַקֶּה lo y'nakkeih, "God does not remit all punishment." By ending the quote with וְנַקֵּה v'nakkeih, the liturgist reverses the meaning of the biblical text, emphasizing only God's mercy.

THE THIRTEEN ATTRIBUTES

God, You are patient.
You are known as the source of mercy.
You taught the way of repentance.
Today, and every day, call to mind the wonder of Your compassion
and mercy toward the children of those You loved. Turn toward us in
mercy, for You are the source of mercy.

We approach Your presence with supplication and prayer, and with the
words You revealed to Moses, the humble one,
    long ago.
Turn away from wrath and let us nestle under Your wings,
as it is written in Your Torah,
    about the day "God descended in a cloud."
Overlook sin, blot out guilt,
    as on the day "God stood beside him."
Hear our cry, attend to our plea,
    as on the day "he called the name ADONAI."

    And ADONAI passed before him and called:
    ADONAI, ADONAI, God, merciful and compassionate, patient,
    abounding in love and faithfulness, assuring love for thousands of
    generations, forgiving iniquity, transgression, and sin, and granting
    pardon.
    Adonai, Adonai, El raḥum v'ḥannun, erekh appayim v'rav ḥesed ve-emet.
    Notzeir ḥesed la-alafim, nosei avon va-fesha v'ḥatta·ah v'nakkeih.

Forgive our transgressions and our sins; claim us for Your own.

Some customarily strike their heart when asking God to forgive and pardon:
Forgive us, our creator, for we have sinned;
pardon us, our sovereign, for we have transgressed—
for You, ADONAI, are kind and forgiving;
You act generously to all who call on You.
S'laḥ lanu avinu ki ḥatanu,
m'ḥal lanu malkeinu ki fashanu,
ki atah Adonai tov v'sallaḥ
v'rav ḥesed l'khol kor'ekha.

Some congregations repeat each verse after the leader recites it.

כִּי הִנֵּה כַחֹמֶר בְּיַד הַיּוֹצֵר,
בִּרְצוֹתוֹ מַרְחִיב וּבִרְצוֹתוֹ מְקַצֵּר,
כֵּן אֲנַחְנוּ בְיָדְךָ חֶסֶד נוֹצֵר,
לַבְּרִית הַבֵּט וְאַל תֵּפֶן לַיֵּצֶר.

כִּי הִנֵּה כָאֶבֶן בְּיַד הַמְסַתֵּת,
בִּרְצוֹתוֹ אוֹחֵז וּבִרְצוֹתוֹ מְכַתֵּת,
כֵּן אֲנַחְנוּ בְיָדְךָ מְחַיֶּה וּמְמוֹתֵת,
לַבְּרִית הַבֵּט וְאַל תֵּפֶן לַיֵּצֶר.

כִּי הִנֵּה כַגַּרְזֶן בְּיַד הֶחָרָשׁ,
בִּרְצוֹתוֹ דִּבֵּק לָאוּר וּבִרְצוֹתוֹ פֵּרַשׁ,
כֵּן אֲנַחְנוּ בְיָדְךָ תּוֹמֵךְ עָנִי וָרָשׁ,
לַבְּרִית הַבֵּט וְאַל תֵּפֶן לַיֵּצֶר.

כִּי הִנֵּה כַהֶגֶה בְּיַד הַמַּלָּח,
בִּרְצוֹתוֹ אוֹחֵז וּבִרְצוֹתוֹ שִׁלַּח,
כֵּן אֲנַחְנוּ בְיָדְךָ אֵל טוֹב וְסַלָּח,
לַבְּרִית הַבֵּט וְאַל תֵּפֶן לַיֵּצֶר.

כִּי הִנֵּה כַזְּכוּכִית בְּיַד הַמְזַגֵּג,
בִּרְצוֹתוֹ חוֹגֵג וּבִרְצוֹתוֹ מְמוֹגֵג,
כֵּן אֲנַחְנוּ בְיָדְךָ מוֹחֵל זָדוֹן וְשָׁגֵג,
לַבְּרִית הַבֵּט וְאַל תֵּפֶן לַיֵּצֶר.

כִּי הִנֵּה כַיְרִיעָה בְּיַד הָרוֹקֵם,
בִּרְצוֹתוֹ מְיַשֵּׁר וּבִרְצוֹתוֹ מְעַקֵּם,
כֵּן אֲנַחְנוּ בְיָדְךָ אֵל קַנָּא וְנוֹקֵם,
לַבְּרִית הַבֵּט וְאַל תֵּפֶן לַיֵּצֶר.

כִּי הִנֵּה כַכֶּסֶף בְּיַד הַצּוֹרֵף,
בִּרְצוֹתוֹ מְסַגְסֵג וּבִרְצוֹתוֹ מְצָרֵף,
כֵּן אֲנַחְנוּ בְיָדְךָ מַמְצִיא לְמָזוֹר תֶּרֶף,
לַבְּרִית הַבֵּט וְאַל תֵּפֶן לַיֵּצֶר.

AS CLAY IN THE HAND OF THE POTTER כִּי הִנֵּה כַחֹמֶר בְּיַד הַיּוֹצֵר. This *piyyut* of unknown authorship is based on the verse from Jeremiah, "Like clay in the hand of the potter, so are you in My hand, O House of Israel" (18:6). The poet takes up this theme and compares God with various types of artisans—masons, glaziers, and weavers. Humans are compared to the materials that artisans use—stone, glass, or cloth. The poet reflects on the fragility of human existence and pleads that God use us creatively, not destructively.

RECALL YOUR COVENANT לַבְּרִית הַבֵּט. Based on Psalm 74:20: "Look to the covenant! For the dark places of the land are full of the haunts of lawlessness."

THE ACCUSER יֵצֶר. The word יֵצֶר (*yeitzer*) means "impulse," and the Rabbis used it to refer to the יֵצֶר הָרַע (*yeitzer ha-ra*), the "evil impulse," which leads human beings to sin. In biblical and rabbinic mythology, this impulse was depicted as one of the angels who had the duty of acting as prosecutor. In the Book of Job this angel, a member of God's court, is designated הַשָּׂטָן (*ha-satan*). There is no notion of a "fallen" or "rebellious" angel in Jewish mythology.

Second Cycle of S'liḥot Prayers: Human Vulnerability

Some congregations repeat each verse after the leader recites it.

As clay in the hand of the potter, who thickens or thins it
at will, so are we in Your hand, Guardian of love;
  Recall Your covenant; do not heed the accuser.
La-b'rit habbeit v'al teifen la-yeitzer.

As stone in the hand of the mason, who preserves or breaks it
at will, so are we in Your hand, God of life and death;
  Recall Your covenant; do not heed the accuser.
La-b'rit habbeit v'al teifen la-yeitzer.

As iron in the hand of the blacksmith, who forges or withdraws it
at will, so are we in Your hand, Support of the poor;
  Recall Your covenant; do not heed the accuser.
La-b'rit habbeit v'al teifen la-yeitzer.

As the helm in the hand of the sailor, who holds the course or abandons it
at will, so are we in Your hand, good and forgiving God.
  Recall Your covenant; do not heed the accuser.
La-b'rit habbeit v'al teifen la-yeitzer.

As glass in the hand of the glazier, who shapes or melts it
at will, so are we in Your hand, pardoner of sin and transgression;
  Recall Your covenant; do not heed the accuser.
La-b'rit habbeit v'al teifen la-yeitzer.

As cloth in the hand of the draper, who drapes or twists it
at will, so are we in Your hand, righteous God;
  Recall Your covenant; do not heed the accuser.
La-b'rit habbeit v'al teifen la-yeitzer.

As silver in the hand of the smelter, who alloys or refines it
at will, so are we in Your hand, Healer of wounds,
  Recall Your covenant; do not heed the accuser.
La-b'rit habbeit v'al teifen la-yeitzer.

הוֹדִיעֵנִי יהוה קִצִּי, וּמִדַּת יָמַי מַה־הִיא,
אֵדְעָה מֶה־חָדֵל אָנִי.
אַךְ־בְּצֶלֶם יִתְהַלֶּךְ־אִישׁ אַךְ־הֶבֶל יֶהֱמָיוּן,
יִצְבֹּר וְלֹא־יֵדַע מִי־אֹסְפָם.
וְעַתָּה מַה־קִּוִּיתִי אֲדֹנָי, תּוֹחַלְתִּי לְךָ הִיא.
מִכָּל־פְּשָׁעַי הַצִּילֵנִי, חֶרְפַּת נָבָל אַל־תְּשִׂימֵנִי.
יהוה חֲקַרְתַּנִי וַתֵּדָע.
אַתָּה יָדַעְתָּ שִׁבְתִּי וְקוּמִי, בַּנְתָּה לְרֵעִי מֵרָחוֹק.
כִּי אֵין מִלָּה בִּלְשׁוֹנִי, הֵן יהוה יָדַעְתָּ כֻלָּהּ.
אָנָה אֵלֵךְ מֵרוּחֶךָ, וְאָנָה מִפָּנֶיךָ אֶבְרָח.
לֹא־נִכְחַד עָצְמִי מִמֶּךָּ, אֲשֶׁר־עֻשֵּׂיתִי בַסֵּתֶר
רֻקַּמְתִּי בְּתַחְתִּיּוֹת אָרֶץ.
גָּלְמִי רָאוּ עֵינֶיךָ וְעַל־סִפְרְךָ כֻּלָּם יִכָּתֵבוּ,
יָמִים יֻצָּרוּ וְלוֹ אֶחָד בָּהֶם.
כִּי־אַתָּה קָנִיתָ כִלְיֹתָי, תְּסֻכֵּנִי בְּבֶטֶן אִמִּי.
חָקְרֵנִי אֵל וְדַע לְבָבִי, בְּחָנֵנִי וְדַע שַׂרְעַפָּי.
וּרְאֵה אִם־דֶּרֶךְ־עֹצֶב בִּי, וּנְחֵנִי בְּדֶרֶךְ עוֹלָם.
◁ שִׁמְעָה תְפִלָּתִי יהוה וְשַׁוְעָתִי הַאֲזִינָה אֶל־דִּמְעָתִי
אַל־תֶּחֱרַשׁ כִּי גֵר אָנֹכִי עִמָּךְ, תּוֹשָׁב כְּכָל־אֲבוֹתָי.
הָשַׁע מִמֶּנִּי וְאַבְלִיגָה, בְּטֶרֶם אֵלֵךְ וְאֵינֶנִּי.

FROM PSALMS. From earliest times, the S'liḥot liturgy for the evening included a series of biblical verses chosen for the way they illustrate the themes of the day. Each cantor would select verses that often were connected only through the repetition of a key word. Congregations, familiar with the Bible, were able to repeat each verse, or complete them, following the cantor.

This meditation on creation, the meaning of our humanity, and the consciousness of our finitude, combines verses from Psalms 39 and 139.

MAKE ME AN INSTRUMENT OF YOUR SALVATION הָשַׁע מִמֶּנִּי. Traditional commentators and modern scholars have argued over the meaning of this phrase. One possibility is that the verb is related to שִׁעְשׁוּעַ (shishu·a), "that which is full of play and gives delight." The translation would be: "Delight in me and I would recover, before I die and am no more." Others have understood it to come from the root ישע, meaning "victory" or "salvation."

REFLECTIONS FROM PSALMS

Tell me, God, my end—the measure of my days—
that I would know how fleeting my life is.

We walk about like empty shells,
all our efforts add up to little;
we pile up possessions,
but don't know how to account for our lives.

What then should I hope for, God?
Only that You save me from the consequences of my sin.

You observe my walking and lying down;
You are familiar with all my ways.

There is no word on my tongue but that You, God, know it well.

Where can I escape from Your spirit?
Where can I flee from Your presence?

I was never concealed from You,
even as I was being shaped in hidden places,
knit together in the recesses of the earth.

Your eyes saw my unformed limbs;
they were recorded in Your book;
fashioned over days, they all belonged to You.

It was You who created my innermost ability to feel;
You fashioned me in my mother's womb.

Examine me now, God;
look into my heart,
probe me, and know my secrets.

If You see within me cause for sadness, guide me toward eternal truths.

Hear my prayer, God, give ear to my cry;
do not disregard my tears;
like all my forebears I am a wanderer,
a guest in Your house.

Make me an instrument of Your salvation
that I might be redeemed,
before I go away and am no more.

אֵל, מֶלֶךְ יוֹשֵׁב עַל כִּסֵּא רַחֲמִים,
מִתְנַהֵג בַּחֲסִידוּת, מוֹחֵל עֲוֹנוֹת עַמּוֹ,
מַעֲבִיר רִאשׁוֹן רִאשׁוֹן,
מַרְבֶּה מְחִילָה לְחַטָּאִים, וּסְלִיחָה לְפוֹשְׁעִים,
עוֹשֶׂה צְדָקוֹת עִם כָּל־בָּשָׂר וָרוּחַ, לֹא כְרָעָתָם תִּגְמוֹל.
◁ אֵל, הוֹרֵיתָ לָּנוּ לוֹמַר שְׁלֹשׁ עֶשְׂרֵה,
זְכָר־לָנוּ הַיּוֹם בְּרִית שְׁלֹשׁ עֶשְׂרֵה,
כְּמוֹ שֶׁהוֹדַעְתָּ לֶעָנָו מִקֶּדֶם,
כְּמוֹ שֶׁכָּתוּב: וַיֵּרֶד יהוה בֶּעָנָן, וַיִּתְיַצֵּב עִמּוֹ שָׁם,
וַיִּקְרָא בְשֵׁם יהוה.

וַיַּעֲבֹר יהוה עַל־פָּנָיו וַיִּקְרָא:

יהוה יהוה, אֵל רַחוּם וְחַנּוּן, אֶרֶךְ אַפַּיִם, וְרַב־חֶסֶד
וֶאֱמֶת. נֹצֵר חֶסֶד לָאֲלָפִים, נֹשֵׂא עָוֹן וָפֶשַׁע וְחַטָּאָה,
וְנַקֵּה.

וְסָלַחְתָּ לַעֲוֹנֵנוּ וּלְחַטָּאתֵנוּ וּנְחַלְתָּנוּ.

Some customarily strike their heart when asking God to forgive and pardon:

סְלַח לָנוּ אָבִינוּ כִּי חָטָאנוּ,
מְחַל לָנוּ מַלְכֵּנוּ כִּי פָשָׁעְנוּ,
כִּי־אַתָּה אֲדֹנָי טוֹב וְסַלָּח
וְרַב־חֶסֶד לְכָל־קֹרְאֶיךָ.

THRONE OF MERCY כִּסֵּא רַחֲמִים. Mythically, God is said to have two thrones: the seat of judgment and the seat of mercy. On Rosh Hashanah, God sits in judgment; on Yom Kippur, God moves to the throne of mercy.

GOD, YOU TAUGHT US אֵל הוֹרֵיתָ לָּנוּ. The biblical verse is ambiguous as to whether it was Moses or God who recited the Thirteen Attributes of God. Rabbi Yoḥanan describes God as wearing a *tallit* like a cantor and showing Moses how to pray. God said to Moses: "Whenever Israel sins, they should recite this passage and I will forgive them." And then God spoke the words of the Thirteen Attributes (Babylonian Talmud, Rosh Hashanah 17b).

Finding Forgiveness

Rabba the son of Hani-
nah the Elder said in the
name of Rav: if one sins
and is embarrassed by
what was done, all one's
sins are forgiven.
—BABYLONIAN TALMUD,
BERAKHOT

THE THIRTEEN ATTRIBUTES

God, Sovereign who sits on a throne of mercy,
acting with unbounded grace,
forgiving the sins of Your people, one by one,
as each comes before You,
generously forgiving sinners and pardoning transgressors,
acting charitably with every living thing:
do not repay them for their misdeeds.

God, You taught us how to recite
the thirteen attributes of Your name;
remember the promise implied in these thirteen attributes,
which You first revealed to Moses, the humble one,
as it is written: God descended in a cloud
and stood beside him,
and he called the name ADONAI.

And ADONAI passed before him and called:
ADONAI, ADONAI, God, merciful and compassionate,
patient, abounding in love and faithfulness, assuring love for
thousands of generations, forgiving iniquity, transgression,
and sin, and granting pardon.
Va-ya·avor Adonai al panav va-yikra:
Adonai, Adonai, El raḥum v'ḥannun, erekh appayim v'rav ḥesed
ve-emet. Notzeir ḥesed la-alafim, nosei avon va-fesha v'ḥatta·ah
v'nakkeih.

Forgive our transgressions and our sins; claim us for Your own.
V'salaḥta la-avoneinu u-l'ḥattateinu u-n'ḥaltanu.

Some customarily strike their heart when asking God to forgive and pardon:
Forgive us, our creator, for we have sinned;
pardon us, our sovereign, for we have transgressed—
for You, ADONAI, are kind and forgiving;
You act generously to all who call on You.
S'laḥ lanu avinu ki ḥatanu,
m'ḥal lanu malkeinu ki fashanu,
ki atah Adonai tov v'sallaḥ
v'rav ḥesed l'khol kor'ekha.

Some congregations repeat each verse after the leader recites it.

בָּרוּךְ אֱלֹהֵי עֶלְיוֹן מֵרֹאשׁ אַחֲרִית חוֹזֶה
שׁוֹמֵעַ אֶל אֶבְיוֹן וְעֵנוּתוֹ לֹא תִבְזֶה
מְכַפֵּר כָּל־שְׁגָיוֹ בְּיוֹם הֶעָשׂוֹר הַזֶּה
מָחָר יַעֲשֶׂה יהוה אֶת־הַדָּבָר הַזֶּה.

נַפְשִׁי לְךָ עוֹרֶגֶת כְּאַיָּל עַל אֲפִיקִים
וּמִיּוֹם דִּין חוֹרֶגֶת בְּעַד מַעֲשֶׂיהָ רֵיקִים
בְּאֵין חַטָּאת נוֹהֶגֶת וְלֹא עוֹלוֹת מַצְדִּיקִים
לְבַד בָּךְ רוֹגֶגֶת קְדֻשַּׁת שְׁמְךָ לְהָקִים
תִּרְצֵנָה כְּאִישׁ לִפְנֵי הַכַּפֹּרֶת יֶזֶה.
מָחָר יַעֲשֶׂה יהוה אֶת־הַדָּבָר הַזֶּה.

יוֹם נִקְרֵאתִי לָבֹא בַדִּין עִם הַמֶּלֶךְ
לְבָבִי כָּלָה בְּחֻבּוֹ כְּטַל מַשְׁכִּים הוֹלֵךְ
לֹא יוֹעִיל בִּזְהָבוֹ וְלֹא דַלּוּת וָהֵלֶךְ
לְבַעֲבוּר כְּבוֹדְךָ שׁוֹבְבוּ בְּאַרְצוֹת חַיִּים לְהָלֵךְ
וּלְמַעַנְךָ סְלַח נָא לַעֲוֹן הָעָם הַזֶּה.
מָחָר יַעֲשֶׂה יהוה אֶת־הַדָּבָר הַזֶּה.

מַלְכִי אֱלֹהִים צַוֵּה יְשׁוּעוֹת יַעֲקֹב וְקָרֵב
וּרְצֵה תַּעֲנִית דָּוֶה מֵעֶרֶב עַד עֶרֶב
וְגִשְׁמֵי נְדָבוֹת רַוֵּה צְמֵאוֹנוֹ וְטַל עֶרֶב
צוּר יִשְׂרָאֵל מִקְוֵה מֶחֱטָא לְטַהֲרִי תֶרֶב
עֻזִּי וְזִמְרָת יָהּ הִנֵּה אֱלֹהֵינוּ זֶה
מָחָר יַעֲשֶׂה יהוה אֶת־הַדָּבָר הַזֶּה.

נְקֵה חֲטָאַי קוֹרֵא בְּבֵית מִקְדָּשׁ הַקֹּדֶשׁ
בְּמוֹרֶךְ לֵבָב יָרֵא שְׂאֵת חַטֹּאתָיו גֻּדָּשׁ
אִם בִּירְאָה יִבָּרֵא לֵב חָדָשׁ לְהִתְחַדֵּשׁ
כַּאֲשֶׁר בִּשֵּׂר מוֹרֵה צֶדֶק בְּמִשְׁפַּט קֹדֶשׁ
בֶּעָשׂוֹר לַחֹדֶשׁ הַשְּׁבִיעִי הַזֶּה.
מָחָר יַעֲשֶׂה יהוה אֶת־הַדָּבָר הַזֶּה.

בָּרוּךְ אֱלֹהֵי עֶלְיוֹן. This *piyyut* is recited in the Italian rite for Kol Nidrei evening. It has been ascribed to Benjamin ben Abraham min Ha-anavim, who lived in Italy in the 13th century. The liturgy of Yom Kippur is filled with memories of the pageantry of the day when the Temple stood in Jerusalem and the High Priest entered the Holy of Holies to pray for the people Israel. By entwining our own practice with memories of the biblical drama, the poet hopes we can achieve a sense of purity that our ancestors experienced through the Temple ritual.

SURELY YOU WILL DO SO TOMORROW מָחָר יַעֲשֶׂה יהוה אֶת־הַדָּבָר הַזֶּה. This chorus is based on Exodus 9:5, Moses' warning to Pharaoh that God will surely bring a pestilence on Egypt—but that the Israelites will not be harmed.

THE RIGHTEOUS TEACHER מוֹרֵה צֶדֶק. During the Second Temple period, this phrase was widely used. Here it refers to Moses.

Third Cycle of S'liḥot Prayers: Yearning for God

Some congregations repeat each verse after the leader recites it.

To You we pray, above us all, beyond all time and space.
Understand us—mortal beings, poor in spirit, weak of flesh—
for You turn toward the humble, the broken, the weak.
Forgive us on this special day.
> *Surely You will do so tomorrow.*

Maḥar ya·aseh Adonai et ha-davar ha-zeh.

> *My soul yearns for You, though I am afraid of Your judgment.*
> *Our ritual is imperfect,*
> *we can no longer follow the prescribed form,*
> *yet we depend on You.*
> *Turn to us as if we were High Priests standing before Your Ark.*
> *Surely You will do so tomorrow.*

Maḥar ya·aseh Adonai et ha-davar ha-zeh.

My heart is caught in the web it has spun,
and I am conscious of how short my life is.
We depart like dew that may shine for a morning;
not saved by its lowly state, it quickly fades.
On this day when we are summoned before the judge of all,
turn to us for Your honor's sake; allow us to walk in the land of the living.
Forgive the sins of Your people.
> *Surely You will do so tomorrow.*

Maḥar ya·aseh Adonai et ha-davar ha-zeh.

> *My sovereign, redeem the children of Jacob*
> *and accept our fasting from one evening to the next.*
> *Rain down on us the redemption we have prayed for,*
> *and quench our thirst.*
> *Tzur Yisra·el, Stronghold of Israel, bathe me in Your purifying waters,*
> *and purify me as I sing to You: Surely this is our God!*
> *Surely You will do so tomorrow.*

Maḥar ya·aseh Adonai et ha-davar ha-zeh.

Wipe away my sins as I call to You, filled with awe, in Your holy sanctuary.
Form me anew, granting me a heart freshly born,
as the righteous teacher foretold in Your holy law
regarding this special day.
> *Surely You will do so tomorrow.*

Maḥar ya·aseh Adonai et ha-davar ha-zeh.

טֶרֶם הֱיוֹתִי חַסְדְּךָ בָאֲנִי,
הַשָּׁם לְיֵשׁ אַיִן וְהִמְצִיאַנִי.
מִי הוּא אֲשֶׁר רֶקֶם תְּמוּנָתִי?
וּמִי עַצְמִי בְכוּר יָצַק וְהִקְפִּאַנִי?
מִי הוּא אֲשֶׁר נָפַח נְשָׁמָה בִי?
וּמִי בֶטֶן שְׁאוֹל פָּתַח וְהוֹצִיאַנִי?
מִי נִהֲגַנִי מִנְּעוּרַי עַד הֲלֹם?
מִי לִמְּדַנִי בִין וְהִפְלִיאַנִי?
אָמְנָם אֲנִי חֹמֶר בְּקֶרֶב יָדְךָ,
אַתָּה עֲשִׂיתַנִי, אֱמֶת, לֹא אֲנִי.
אוֹדֶה עֲלֵי פְשָׁעַי וְלֹא אֹמַר לְךָ
כִּי הֶעָרִים נָחָשׁ וְהִשִּׁיאַנִי.
אֵיכָה אֲכַחֵד מִמְּךָ חֶטְאַי?
הֲלֹא

טֶרֶם הֱיוֹתִי חַסְדְּךָ בָאֲנִי!

FROM NOTHING, YOU FORMED ME הַשָּׁם לְיֵשׁ אַיִן וְהִמְצִיאַנִי. Solomon ibn Gabirol (1020–1057) was among the most important of the Spanish-Jewish poets and the originator of many of this poetry's genres. In this poem, he sees the pure soul—that part of the human which is constituted by the image of God—as the instrument of redemption. However we may have sinned, there is some aspect of who we are that is a reflection of the Divine. Allowing ourselves to feel God's presence within can be the source of our overcoming despair at our own imperfection. Ibn Gabirol believes that as much as we have sinned, the Divine is always present within us.

יָהּ אָנָה אֶמְצָאֲךָ
מְקוֹמְךָ נַעֲלֶה וְנֶעְלָם
וְאָנָה לֹא אֶמְצָאֲךָ

כְּבוֹדְךָ מָלֵא עוֹלָם

דְּרַשְׁתִּי קִרְבָתְךָ
בְּכָל-לִבִּי קְרָאתִיךָ
וּבְצֵאתִי לִקְרָאתְךָ
לִקְרָאתִי מְצָאתִיךָ

ADONAI, WHERE SHALL I FIND YOU יָהּ אָנָה אֶמְצָאֲךָ. Yehudah Halevi (1075–1141) is perhaps the most famous of the Spanish poets. Like Ibn Gabirol, he excelled not only in poetry but in philosophy, as well. His religious poetry frequently expresses intense yearning and love. This yearning was also manifested in his personal life—it impelled him to leave Spain and journey to the Land of Israel, where he died. This fragment of a longer poem is a beautiful expression of the encounter with God as a mutual meeting.

YOUR KINDNESS ACCOMPANIED ME: A PIYYUT

Even before I came to be, Your kindness accompanied me.
For from nothing, You formed me.
Who was it who fashioned me? Spun the clay?
Fired the kiln? Hardened me?
Who breathed life into me?
Opened the belly of the deep? Pulled me out?
Who guided me from childhood to today?
Gave me understanding? Filled me with wonder?
Though I am but clay in Your hands,
was it not You who made me? Truly, You, not me.
Yet, I confess my sins, and I do not say
that I was fooled by another, who beguiled me.
Why would I try to hide my sin from You?
For even before I came to be, Your kindness accompanied me.

Terem heyoti, ḥasd'kha va·ani.

THE WORLD IS FULL OF YOUR GLORY: A PIYYUT

Adonai, where shall I find You?
High and hidden is Your place.
And where shall I not find You?
The world is full of Your glory.

I sought Your closeness,
I called to You with all my heart,
And going out to meet You
I found You coming toward me.

Yah, ana emtza·akha
m'kom'kha na·aleh v'ne·lam
v'ana lo emtza·akha
k'vod'kha malei olam

Darashti kirvat'kha
b'khol libbi k'ra·tikha
u-v'tzeiti li-k'rat'kha
li-k'rati m'tzatikha.

אֵל, מֶלֶךְ יוֹשֵׁב עַל כִּסֵּא רַחֲמִים, מִתְנַהֵג בַּחֲסִידוּת, מוֹחֵל עֲוֹנוֹת עַמּוֹ, מַעֲבִיר רִאשׁוֹן רִאשׁוֹן, מַרְבֶּה מְחִילָה לְחַטָּאִים, וּסְלִיחָה לְפוֹשְׁעִים, עוֹשֶׂה צְדָקוֹת עִם כָּל־בָּשָׂר וָרוּחַ, לֹא כְרָעָתָם תִּגְמוֹל.

◁ אֵל, הוֹרֵיתָ לָּנוּ לוֹמַר שְׁלֹשׁ עֶשְׂרֵה, זְכָר־לָנוּ הַיּוֹם בְּרִית שְׁלֹשׁ עֶשְׂרֵה, כְּמוֹ שֶׁהוֹדַעְתָּ לֶעָנָו מִקֶּדֶם, כְּמוֹ שֶׁכָּתוּב: וַיֵּרֶד יהוה בֶּעָנָן, וַיִּתְיַצֵּב עִמּוֹ שָׁם, וַיִּקְרָא בְשֵׁם יהוה.

וַיַּעֲבֹר יהוה עַל־פָּנָיו וַיִּקְרָא:

יהוה יהוה, אֵל רַחוּם וְחַנּוּן, אֶרֶךְ אַפַּיִם, וְרַב־חֶסֶד וֶאֱמֶת. נֹצֵר חֶסֶד לָאֲלָפִים, נֹשֵׂא עָוֹן וָפֶשַׁע וְחַטָּאָה, וְנַקֵּה.

וְסָלַחְתָּ לַעֲוֹנֵנוּ וּלְחַטָּאתֵנוּ וּנְחַלְתָּנוּ.

Some customarily strike their heart when asking God to forgive and pardon:

סְלַח לָנוּ אָבִינוּ כִּי חָטָאנוּ, מְחַל לָנוּ מַלְכֵּנוּ כִּי פָשָׁעְנוּ, כִּי אַתָּה אֲדֹנָי טוֹב וְסַלָּח, וְרַב־חֶסֶד לְכָל־קוֹרְאֶיךָ.

הַאֲזִינָה יהוה תְּפִלָּתֵנוּ, וְהַקְשִׁיבָה בְּקוֹל תַּחֲנוּנוֹתֵינוּ. הַקְשִׁיבָה לְקוֹל שַׁוְעֵנוּ, מַלְכֵּנוּ וֵאלֹהֵינוּ, כִּי־אֵלֶיךָ נִתְפַּלָּל. תְּהִי נָא אָזְנְךָ־קַשֶּׁבֶת וְעֵינֶיךָ פְתוּחוֹת אֶל־תְּפִלַּת עֲבָדֶיךָ עַמְּךָ יִשְׂרָאֵל. וְשָׁמַעְתָּ מִן הַשָּׁמַיִם, מִמְּכוֹן שִׁבְתְּךָ, אֶת־תְּפִלָּתָם וְאֶת־תְּחִנּוֹתֵיהֶם, וְעָשִׂיתָ מִשְׁפָּטָם. וְסָלַחְתָּ לְעַמְּךָ אֲשֶׁר חָטְאוּ־לָךְ.

כְּרַחֵם אָב עַל־בָּנִים, כֵּן תְּרַחֵם יהוה עָלֵינוּ. לַיהוה הַיְשׁוּעָה, עַל־עַמְּךָ בִרְכָתֶךָ סֶּלָה. יהוה צְבָאוֹת עִמָּנוּ, מִשְׂגָּב־לָנוּ אֱלֹהֵי יַעֲקֹב, סֶלָה. יהוה צְבָאוֹת, אַשְׁרֵי אָדָם בֹּטֵחַ בָּךְ. יהוה הוֹשִׁיעָה, הַמֶּלֶךְ יַעֲנֵנוּ בְיוֹם־קָרְאֵנוּ.

◁ סְלַח־נָא לַעֲוֹן הָעָם הַזֶּה כְּגֹדֶל חַסְדֶּךָ, וְכַאֲשֶׁר נָשָׂאתָה לָעָם הַזֶּה מִמִּצְרַיִם וְעַד־הֵנָּה. וְשָׁם נֶאֱמַר: וַיֹּאמֶר יהוה סָלַחְתִּי כִּדְבָרֶךָ.

ONE BY ONE רִאשׁוֹן רִאשׁוֹן. According to the Babylonian Talmud, God counts only one sin at a time, for if the totality of our sins were counted altogether, we might be judged negatively; each sin is forgiven individually (Rosh Hashanah 17a).

LISTEN TO OUR PRAYERS הַאֲזִינָה יהוה תְּפִלָּתֵנוּ. The words come from Psalm 86:6, though the liturgist has changed the first person singular "my" to the first personal plural "our." The same change is made in the next two verses.

OUR SOVEREIGN, OUR GOD מַלְכֵּנוּ וֵאלֹהֵינוּ. Psalm 5:3.

MAY YOUR EAR HEAR תְּהִי נָא אָזְנְךָ קַשֶּׁבֶת. Nehemiah 1:6.

IN YOUR HEAVENLY ABODE וְשָׁמַעְתָּ מִן הַשָּׁמַיִם. 1 Kings 8:49–50.

AS A PARENT אָב. Psalm 103:13 has "May You, God look kindly on your faithful ones." The liturgist did not presume that we are all faithful, but we can still pray that God should turn toward each of us.

SALVATION IS ADONAI'S ALONE לַיהוה הַיְשׁוּעָה. Psalm 3:9.

ADONAI TZ'VA·OT יהוה צְבָאוֹת. Psalm 46:8.

BLESSED IS THE ONE אַשְׁרֵי אָדָם. Psalm 84:13. God moves to the throne of mercy.

ADONAI SAVE US יהוה הוֹשִׁיעָה. Psalm 20:10.

FORGIVE סְלַח. Numbers 14:19–20.

The Thirteen Attributes

The liturgy for Yom Kippur is filled with the image of God's mercy and love overcoming harsh judgment. The Rabbis taught that human behavior should imitate God. Our admission of our inadequacy to stand up to absolute standards of judgment and our expectation of God's forgiveness teach us about the kindness we need in approaching others.

I Forgive as You Asked

The S'liḥot section ends with God's response to Moses, announcing forgiveness. Jewish tradition wants us to hear the echo of these words as we recite the confession; forgiveness, while assured, is dependent on our asking.

THE THIRTEEN ATTRIBUTES

God, Sovereign who sits on a throne of mercy, acting with unbounded grace, forgiving the sins of Your people, one by one, as each comes before You, generously forgiving sinners and pardoning transgressors, acting charitably with every living thing: do not repay them for their misdeeds.

God, You taught us how to recite the Thirteen Attributes of Your name; remember the promise implied in these Thirteen Attributes, which You first revealed to Moses, the humble one, as it is written: God descended in a cloud and stood beside him, and he called the name ADONAI:

And ADONAI passed before him and called:

ADONAI, ADONAI, God, merciful and compassionate, patient, abounding in love and faithfulness, assuring love for thousands of generations, forgiving iniquity, transgression, and sin, and granting pardon.

Adonai, Adonai, El raḥum v'ḥannun, erekh appayim v'rav ḥesed ve-emet. Notzeir ḥesed la-alafim, nosei avon va-fesha v'ḥatta·ah v'nakkeih.

Forgive our transgressions and our sins; claim us for Your own.

Some customarily strike their heart when asking God to forgive and pardon:

Forgive us, our creator, for we have sinned; pardon us, our sovereign, for we have transgressed—for You, ADONAI, are kind and forgiving; You act generously to all who call on You.

S'laḥ lanu avinu ki ḥatanu, m'ḥal lanu malkeinu ki fashanu,
ki atah Adonai tov v'sallaḥ, v'rav ḥesed l'khol kor'ekha.

Listen to our prayers, God, hear our pleading, our sorrow-filled voices.
Our sovereign, our God, it is to You we pray.
May Your ear hear, and Your eyes open to the prayers of Your servants, the people Israel.
In Your heavenly abode, may You hear their pleas and prayers, and respond to what they ask.
May You forgive Your people who have sinned against You.
As a parent looks kindly on a child, may You, God, look kindly on us.
Salvation is ADONAI's alone—pour blessings on Your people forever.
Adonai Tz'va·ot is with us, our support, the God of Jacob, forever.
Blessed is the one who trusts in You, Adonai Tz'va·ot.
ADONAI, save us! Surely the Sovereign One will respond to us on the day we call out.
"As befits Your abundant love, please forgive this people's sin, just as You have always forgiven this people from the time of the Exodus from Egypt until now." When Moses recited this prayer it is recorded:
ADONAI said, "I forgive, as you asked."
Va-yomer Adonai: salaḥti ki-d'varekha.

כַּפֵּר חַטָּאֵינוּ בַּיּוֹם הַזֶּה וְטַהֲרֵנוּ, כְּמָה שֶׁכָּתוּב: כִּי בַיּוֹם הַזֶּה יְכַפֵּר עֲלֵיכֶם לְטַהֵר אֶתְכֶם, מִכֹּל חַטֹּאתֵיכֶם לִפְנֵי יהוה תִּטְהָרוּ. הֲבִיאֵנוּ אֶל־הַר קָדְשֶׁךָ, וְשַׂמְּחֵנוּ בְּבֵית תְּפִלָּתֶךָ, כְּמָה שֶׁכָּתוּב: כִּי בֵיתִי בֵּית־תְּפִלָּה יִקָּרֵא לְכָל־הָעַמִּים.

We rise as the ark is opened. After the leader recites each verse, we repeat it.

שְׁמַע קוֹלֵנוּ, יהוה אֱלֹהֵינוּ, חוּס וְרַחֵם עָלֵינוּ, וְקַבֵּל בְּרַחֲמִים וּבְרָצוֹן אֶת־תְּפִלָּתֵנוּ.

הֲשִׁיבֵנוּ יהוה אֵלֶיךָ וְנָשׁוּבָה, חַדֵּשׁ יָמֵינוּ כְּקֶדֶם.

אַל־תַּשְׁלִיכֵנוּ מִלְּפָנֶיךָ, וְרוּחַ קָדְשְׁךָ אַל־תִּקַּח מִמֶּנּוּ.

אַל־תַּשְׁלִיכֵנוּ לְעֵת זִקְנָה, כִּכְלוֹת כֹּחֵנוּ אַל־תַּעַזְבֵנוּ.

Said quietly:

אַל־תַּעַזְבֵנוּ, יהוה אֱלֹהֵינוּ, אַל־תִּרְחַק מִמֶּנּוּ.
עֲשֵׂה־עִמָּנוּ אוֹת לְטוֹבָה, וְיִרְאוּ שׂוֹנְאֵינוּ וְיֵבֹשׁוּ,
כִּי־אַתָּה יהוה עֲזַרְתָּנוּ וְנִחַמְתָּנוּ.
אֲמָרֵינוּ הַאֲזִינָה יהוה, בִּינָה הֲגִיגֵנוּ.
יִהְיוּ לְרָצוֹן אִמְרֵי־פִינוּ וְהֶגְיוֹן לִבֵּנוּ לְפָנֶיךָ, יהוה צוּרֵנוּ וְגֹאֲלֵנוּ.
כִּי־לְךָ יהוה הוֹחָלְנוּ, אַתָּה תַעֲנֶה, אֲדֹנָי אֱלֹהֵינוּ.

The ark is closed.

אֱלֹהֵינוּ וֵאלֹהֵי אֲבוֹתֵינוּ [וְאִמּוֹתֵינוּ],
אַל תַּעַזְבֵנוּ וְאַל תִּטְּשֵׁנוּ,
וְאַל תַּכְלִימֵנוּ וְאַל תָּפֵר בְּרִיתְךָ אִתָּנוּ.
קָרְבֵנוּ לְתוֹרָתֶךָ, לַמְּדֵנוּ מִצְוֹתֶיךָ, הוֹרֵנוּ דְּרָכֶיךָ,
הַט לִבֵּנוּ לְיִרְאָה אֶת־שְׁמֶךָ, וּמוֹל אֶת־לְבָבֵנוּ לְאַהֲבָתֶךָ,
וְנָשׁוּב אֵלֶיךָ בֶּאֱמֶת וּבְלֵב שָׁלֵם. ◁ וּלְמַעַן שִׁמְךָ הַגָּדוֹל
תִּמְחַל וְתִסְלַח לַעֲוֹנֵנוּ, כַּכָּתוּב בְּדִבְרֵי קָדְשֶׁךָ:
לְמַעַן־שִׁמְךָ יהוה, וְסָלַחְתָּ לַעֲוֹנִי כִּי רַב־הוּא.

CONCLUDING BIBLICAL VERSES. Just as the S'liḥot began with a series of biblical verses, it now moves to its conclusion with a similar series. Likewise, just as the evening service began by permitting sinners to pray along with the righteous, it now climaxes with the announcement, "My house shall be called a house of prayer for all people." The quotations are from Leviticus 16:30 and Isaiah 56:7.

HEAR OUR VOICE שְׁמַע קוֹלֵנוּ. Sh'ma Koleinu is a supplication that seeks to penetrate the silence that surrounds us, to evoke God's response, and to draw God into our prayer. "Hear our voice" may be among the most poignant words spoken in prayer. This prayer's first sentence is from the concluding prayer of personal petition in the daily Amidah. (In Jewish liturgy, a general plea that God hear our prayer typically precedes or follows a set of specific requests.) It then quotes Lamentations 5:21; Psalms 51:13; 71:9; 38:22; 86:17; 19:15; 5:2; 38:16.

The Babylonian Talmud records an argument as to whether personal prayers should be recited in the plural (Berakhot 29b–30a). When most Jewish liturgy quotes biblical verses that were phrased in the first person singular, it recasts them as plural. (The authors of the prayerbook felt free to emend the Bible's wording in this way.) Some scholars believe that this liturgical transformation took place around the turn of the first millennium. In this view, all prayers of confession were originally phrased in the first person singular: "my" sin rather than "our" sin. The triumph of the communal over the individual is the contribution of the Middle Ages. Thus only the last verse on this page, Psalm 25:11, is left in the singular, as if each of us must finally confront our own sinfulness. Some editions of the maḥzor change even that verse to the plural.

DO NOT ABANDON US אַל־תַּעַזְבֵנוּ. This verse is only whispered, for we do not want to assert out loud even the possibility of abandonment. The whispering then extends to what follows—personal prayers that our plea may be heard.

As an owl in the desert
screens in the night, so
I want to be heard, my
God.

*As a thrush cries as
danger nears its nest,
so we plead that You
attend us.*

The eagle circles round
and round, higher and
higher, to protect its
young; carry us on
eagle's wings and guard
us from danger.

*A dove hovers constantly
over its young, never
tiring of its task, so
let me be nestled in
Your care.*

Spread Your wings, carry
me, watch over me.
Bring me to Your holy
house on eagle's wings.

—EDWARD FELD

CONCLUDING BIBLICAL VERSES

Grant atonement and purify us this day, as it is written in the
Torah, "For on this day, atonement shall be made for you to
purify you from all your transgressions; in the presence of
ADONAI you shall be pure." Bring us to Your holy mountain and
make us joyful in Your house of prayer, as Isaiah prophesied,
"For My house shall be called a house of prayer for all people."

CULMINATION OF S'LIHOT: HEAR OUR VOICE

We rise as the ark is opened. After the leader recites each verse, we repeat it.

Hear our voice, ADONAI our God, be kind, and have compassion
for us. Willingly and lovingly accept our prayer.

> *Turn us toward You, ADONAI, and we will return to You;*
> *make our days seem fresh, as they once were.*

Do not cast us away from You;
take not Your holy presence from us.

> *Do not cast us away as we grow old;*
> *do not desert us as our energy wanes.*

*Sh'ma koleinu, Adonai eloheinu, hus v'raheim aleinu,
v'kabbeil b'rahamim u-v'ratzon et t'fillateinu.
Hashiveinu Adonai eilekha v'nashuvah, haddeish yameinu k'kedem.
Al tashlikheinu mi-l'fanekha, v'ru·ah kodsh'kha al tikkah mimmennu.
Al tashlikheinu l'eit ziknah, ki-kh'lot koheinu al ta·azveinu.*

Said quietly:

Do not abandon us, ADONAI our God, do not distance Yourself
from us.

> *Give us a signal of hope, so that our enemies will understand*
> *and hesitate, knowing that You have been our help and comfort.*

Hear our words, ADONAI, and consider our innermost thoughts.

> *May the words of our mouths and the meditations of our*
> *hearts be acceptable to You, ADONAI, our rock and redeemer.*

It is for You we wait; surely You will respond, ADONAI our God.
The ark is closed.

Our God and God of our ancestors, do not abandon us, do not
forsake us, do not shame us, do not annul Your covenant with us.
Draw us close to Your Torah, teach us Your mitzvot, show us Your
ways. Open our hearts to revere Your name, circumcise our hearts
to love You; then, we will turn to You, faithfully, with a perfect
heart. And as befits Your own great name, pardon and forgive
our sins, as the psalmist wrote: "For the sake of Your own name,
forgive my sin, though it be great."

V'salahta la-avoni ki rav hu.

אֱלֹהֵֽינוּ וֵאלֹהֵי אֲבוֹתֵֽינוּ [וְאִמּוֹתֵֽינוּ],
סְלַח לָֽנוּ, מְחַל לָֽנוּ, כַּפֶּר־לָֽנוּ.

כִּי

וְאַתָּה אֱלֹהֵֽינוּ,	אָֽנוּ עַמֶּֽךָ
וְאַתָּה אָבִֽינוּ.	אָֽנוּ בָנֶֽיךָ
וְאַתָּה אֲדוֹנֵֽנוּ,	אָֽנוּ עֲבָדֶֽיךָ
וְאַתָּה חֶלְקֵֽנוּ.	אָֽנוּ קְהָלֶֽךָ
וְאַתָּה גוֹרָלֵֽנוּ,	אָֽנוּ נַחֲלָתֶֽךָ
וְאַתָּה רוֹעֵֽנוּ.	אָֽנוּ צֹאנֶֽךָ
וְאַתָּה נוֹטְרֵֽנוּ,	אָֽנוּ כַרְמֶֽךָ
וְאַתָּה יוֹצְרֵֽנוּ.	אָֽנוּ פְעֻלָּתֶֽךָ
וְאַתָּה דוֹדֵֽנוּ,	אָֽנוּ רַעְיָתֶֽךָ
וְאַתָּה קְרוֹבֵֽנוּ.	אָֽנוּ סְגֻלָּתֶֽךָ
וְאַתָּה מַלְכֵּֽנוּ,	אָֽנוּ עַמֶּֽךָ
וְאַתָּה מַאֲמִירֵֽנוּ.	אָֽנוּ מַאֲמִירֶֽךָ

וידוי

וְאַתָּה רַחוּם וְחַנּוּן.	אָֽנוּ עַזֵּי פָנִים
וְאַתָּה אֶֽרֶךְ אַפַּֽיִם.	אָֽנוּ קְשֵׁי עֹֽרֶף
וְאַתָּה מָלֵא רַחֲמִים.	אָֽנוּ מְלֵאֵי עָוֺן
וְאַתָּה הוּא וּשְׁנוֹתֶֽיךָ לֹא יִתָּֽמּוּ.	אָֽנוּ יָמֵֽינוּ כְּצֵל עוֹבֵר

אֱלֹהֵֽינוּ וֵאלֹהֵי אֲבוֹתֵֽינוּ [וְאִמּוֹתֵֽינוּ],
תָּבֹא לְפָנֶֽיךָ תְּפִלָּתֵֽנוּ, וְאַל תִּתְעַלַּם מִתְּחִנָּתֵֽנוּ,
שֶׁאֵין אֲנַֽחְנוּ עַזֵּי פָנִים וּקְשֵׁי עֹֽרֶף לוֹמַר לְפָנֶֽיךָ,
יהוה אֱלֹהֵֽינוּ וֵאלֹהֵי אֲבוֹתֵֽינוּ [וְאִמּוֹתֵֽינוּ],
צַדִּיקִים אֲנַֽחְנוּ וְלֹא חָטָֽאנוּ,
אֲבָל אֲנַֽחְנוּ וַאֲבוֹתֵֽינוּ [וְאִמּוֹתֵֽינוּ] חָטָֽאנוּ.

WE ARE YOUR PEOPLE כִּי אָֽנוּ עַמֶּֽךָ. An early medieval poem, which expands on the verse from Song of Songs: "I am for my beloved and my beloved is mine" (2:16). It completes the S'lihot/Forgiveness section and forms the transition to the confession. Here we end in joyous song, then move to a meditative melody, as we begin the Viddui/Confession. In this poem we emphasize our relatedness to God, whereas in the next we emphasize the stark difference between the human and the Divine.

VIDDUI—PRAYERS OF CONFESSION וִדּוּי. In addition to fasting and otherwise afflicting oneself, the central mitzvah that must be performed on Yom Kippur is *viddui* (confession). The rabbinic requirement to confess is based on the biblical passage that describes the confession of the High Priest when performing the Temple ceremony. Following the destruction of the Temple, greater emphasis was placed on synagogue ritual and individual prayer, and it fell upon each person to make confession on Yom Kippur.

A PASSING SHADOW כְּצֵל עוֹבֵר. Psalm 144:4.

FOR TIME WITHOUT END וּשְׁנוֹתֶֽיךָ לֹא יִתָּֽמּוּ. "Of old You established the earth; / the heavens are the work of Your hands. / They shall perish, but You shall endure; / they shall all wear out like a garment; / You change them like clothing and they pass away. / But You are the same, and Your years never end" (Psalm 102:26–28).

WE, LIKE OUR ANCESTORS אֲנַֽחְנוּ וַאֲבוֹתֵֽינוּ. In the Babylonian Talmud, Mar Zutra remarked that anyone who says "we have sinned" has understood the meaning of confession (Yoma 87b). Every human being is imperfect. Even previous generations—whom we may idealize—contained sinners. As the Rabbis taught: no one has walked the earth and not sinned. In ascribing sin to our ancestors, the liturgist is quoting Psalm 106:6.

Our God and God of our ancestors, forgive us, pardon us, grant us atonement.

For—

We are Your people,	and You are our God;
we are Your children	and You are our parent.
We are Your servants,	and You are our master;
we are Your congregation,	and You are our portion.
We are Your heritage,	and You are our destiny;
we are Your flock,	and You are our shepherd.
We are Your vineyard,	and You are our guardian;
we are Your creatures,	and You are our creator.
We are Your spouse,	and You are our beloved;
we are Your cherished ones,	and You are near to us.
We are Your people,	and You are our sovereign;
we are the ones You address,	and You are the One to whom we speak.

Ki

Anu ammekha,	*v'atah eloheinu,*
anu vanekha	*v'atah avinu.*
Anu avadekha	*v'atah adoneinu,*
anu k'halekha	*v'atah ḥelkeinu.*
Anu naḥalatekha	*v'atah goraleinu,*
anu tzonekha	*v'atah ro·einu.*
Anu kharmekha	*v'atah not'reinu,*
anu f'ullatekha,	*v'atah yotz'reinu.*
Anu ra·yatekha	*v'atah dodeinu,*
anu s'gullatekha	*v'atah k'roveinu.*
Anu ammekha	*v'atah malkeinu,*
anu ma·amirekha	*v'atah ma·amireinu.*

VIDDUI — PRAYERS OF CONFESSION

We are insolent;	You are gracious and compassionate.
We are obstinate;	You are patient.
We are sinful;	You are merciful.
Our days are a passing shadow,	but You are the One who truly is, for time without end.

Our God and God of our ancestors, hear our prayer; do not ignore our plea. Our God and God of our ancestors, we are neither so insolent nor so obstinate as to claim in Your presence that we are righteous, without sin; for we, like our ancestors who came before us, have sinned.

Sin and Repentance
No sin is so light that it may be overlooked; no sin is so heavy that it may not be repented of.
—MOSES IBN EZRA

אָשַׁמְנוּ, בָּגַדְנוּ, גָּזַלְנוּ, דִּבַּרְנוּ דְפִי.
הֶעֱוִינוּ, וְהִרְשַׁעְנוּ, זַדְנוּ, חָמַסְנוּ, טָפַלְנוּ שֶׁקֶר.
יָעַצְנוּ רָע, כִּזַּבְנוּ, לַצְנוּ, מָרַדְנוּ, נִאַצְנוּ.
סָרַרְנוּ, עָוִינוּ, פָּשַׁעְנוּ, צָרַרְנוּ, קִשִּׁינוּ עֹרֶף.
רָשַׁעְנוּ, שִׁחַתְנוּ, תִּעַבְנוּ, תָּעִינוּ, תִּעְתָּעְנוּ.

סַרְנוּ מִמִּצְוֹתֶיךָ וּמִמִּשְׁפָּטֶיךָ הַטּוֹבִים, וְלֹא שָׁוָה לָנוּ.
וְאַתָּה צַדִּיק עַל כָּל־הַבָּא עָלֵינוּ, כִּי אֱמֶת עָשִׂיתָ
וַאֲנַחְנוּ הִרְשָׁעְנוּ.

One or more of the following penitential prayers may be included.

א

הִרְשַׁעְנוּ וּפָשַׁעְנוּ, לָכֵן לֹא נוֹשָׁעְנוּ. וְתֵן בְּלִבֵּנוּ לַעֲזוֹב דֶּרֶךְ
רֶשַׁע וְחִישׁ לָנוּ יֶשַׁע, כַּכָּתוּב עַל יַד נְבִיאֶךָ: יַעֲזֹב רָשָׁע דַּרְכּוֹ,
וְאִישׁ אָוֶן מַחְשְׁבֹתָיו, וְיָשֹׁב אֶל־יהוה וִירַחֲמֵהוּ, וְאֶל־אֱלֹהֵינוּ
כִּי־יַרְבֶּה לִסְלוֹחַ.

ב

אֱלֹהֵינוּ וֵאלֹהֵי אֲבוֹתֵינוּ [וְאִמּוֹתֵינוּ],
סְלַח וּמְחַל לַעֲוֹנוֹתֵינוּ
בְּיוֹם [הַשַּׁבָּת הַזֶּה וּבְיוֹם] הַכִּפּוּרִים הַזֶּה.
מְחֵה וְהַעֲבֵר פְּשָׁעֵינוּ וְחַטֹּאתֵינוּ מִנֶּגֶד עֵינֶיךָ,
וְכֹף אֶת־יִצְרֵנוּ לְהִשְׁתַּעְבֶּד־לָךְ,
וְהַכְנַע עָרְפֵּנוּ לָשׁוּב אֵלֶיךָ,
וְחַדֵּשׁ כִּלְיוֹתֵינוּ לִשְׁמוֹר פִּקּוּדֶיךָ,
וּמוֹל אֶת־לְבָבֵנוּ לְאַהֲבָה וּלְיִרְאָה אֶת־שְׁמֶךָ,
כַּכָּתוּב בְּתוֹרָתֶךָ: וּמָל יהוה אֱלֹהֶיךָ אֶת־לְבָבְךָ,
וְאֶת־לְבַב זַרְעֶךָ, לְאַהֲבָה אֶת־יהוה אֱלֹהֶיךָ
בְּכָל־לְבָבְךָ וּבְכָל־נַפְשְׁךָ
לְמַעַן חַיֶּיךָ.

STRIKE OUR HEART. The custom of striking our heart while confessing our sins is first mentioned in a midrash on Ecclesiastes 7:2 ("the living will lay it to heart"): "Rabbi Meir said: 'Why do people strike their hearts [in remorse for their sins]? Because the heart is the seat and source of sin'" (Ecclesiastes Rabbah).

WE ABUSE אָשַׁמְנוּ. The liturgical list is alphabetical, with the hope that it will help us find our own words to name our transgressions. We might concentrate on one particular failing in our lives.

WE DESTROY שִׁחַתְנוּ. In this bilingual alphabetical list, the English word that represents the letter D means roughly the same as the Hebrew word that represents the letter ש (shin). The sin of בַּל תַּשְׁחִית (bal tash·hit), "not destroying anything needlessly," was enumerated by the Rabbis among the 613 commandments of the Torah. To destroy any part of creation is to undo God's work, to reject God's gift.

YOU HAVE ACTED FAITHFULLY וְאַתָּה צַדִּיק. Nehemiah 9:33. The prayer of the Levites at the rededication of the Temple, upon the return from the Babylonian Exile.

LET THE WICKED FORSAKE יַעֲזֹב רָשָׁע. Isaiah 55:7.

BLOT OUT AND DISREGARD מְחֵה וְהַעֲבֵר. Both inner and outer parts of the body are mentioned in this prayer. Body and soul are intimately bound, as we seek to behave differently. It is as if we simultaneously ask the Creator to fashion for us a less sinful body as the home for our newly purified self.

CIRCUMCISE וּמָל. Deuteronomy 30:6. Circumcision is an act of completion and perfection. Removing the flesh—our sins, which mask our essential nature—reveals the true function of the heart: to lead us to a life of love, righteousness, and peace.

When we sin, we betray our true selves; when we repent, we rediscover the purity of our souls—and find, once again, that God dwells within us. As the 20th-century Jewish thinker and rabbi Joseph Ber Soloveitchik remarked, it is because we ourselves are God's temple that repentance and forgiveness are possible.

Repentance

Penitence can transform all our past sins into spiritual assets. From every error we can derive an important lesson, and from every lowly fall we can derive the inspiration to climb to spiritual heights.

Who Are We

Emotions ebb and flow throughout these holy days. Paradoxes swim in the stream of prayer. At one moment, we believe our deeds to be of such import that the world stands still so that we may take account of them. At another moment, we imagine ourselves so small, so insignificant that our lives are like a passing breath. We are great; we are small. We are the center of the universe; we are nothing at all. And yet, no matter how large we imagine our sins to be, and no matter how puny we imagine ourselves to be, God will never forsake us.

—NINA BETH CARDIN

The Shorter Confession—Ashamnu

Customarily, we each strike our heart as we recite every phrase of this confession.

We abuse, we betray, we are cruel, we destroy, we embitter, we falsify, we gossip, we hate, we insult, we jeer, we kill, we lie, we mock, we neglect, we oppress, we pervert, we quarrel, we rebel, we steal, we transgress, we are unkind, we are violent, we are wicked, we are extremists, we yearn to do evil, we are zealous for bad causes.

Ashamnu, bagadnu, gazalnu, dibbarnu dofi;
he·evinu, v'hirshanu, zadnu, hamasnu, tafalnu sheker;
ya·atznu ra, kizzavnu, latznu, maradnu, ni·atznu;
sararnu, avinu, pashanu, tzararnu, kishinu oref;
rashanu, shihatnu, ti·avnu, ta·inu, titanu.

We have turned from Your goodly laws and commandments, but it has not profited us. Surely, You are in the right with respect to all that comes upon us, for You have acted faithfully, but we have been in the wrong.

PENITENTIAL PRAYERS BEFORE THE GREAT CONFESSION
One or more of the following penitential prayers may be included.

א

We have done wrong and transgressed, and so we have not triumphed. Inspire our hearts to abandon the path of evil, and hasten our redemption. And so Your prophet Isaiah declared: "Let the wicked forsake their path, and the sinful their design. Let them return to ADONAI, who will show them compassion. Let them return to our God, who will surely forgive them."

ב

Our God and God of our ancestors,
forgive and pardon our sins
[on this Shabbat and] on this Day of Atonement.
Blot out and disregard our sins and errors;
subdue our instincts so that they may serve You.
Bend our stiffness so that we turn to You;
renew our passion for observing Your ordinances.
Circumcise our hearts to love and revere Your name,
as it is written in Your Torah: "Then ADONAI your God
will circumcise your heart and the hearts of your offspring
to love ADONAI your God with all your heart and all your soul,
that you may live."

הַזְּדוֹנוֹת וְהַשְּׁגָגוֹת אַתָּה מַכִּיר, הָרָצוֹן וְהָאֹנֶס,
הַגְּלוּיִם וְהַנִּסְתָּרִים, לְפָנֶיךָ הֵם גְּלוּיִם וִידוּעִים.
מָה אָנוּ, מֶה חַיֵּינוּ, מֶה חַסְדֵּנוּ, מַה צִּדְקֵנוּ,
מַה יִּשְׁעֵנוּ, מַה כֹּחֵנוּ, מַה גְּבוּרָתֵנוּ.
מַה נֹּאמַר לְפָנֶיךָ, יהוה אֱלֹהֵינוּ
וֵאלֹהֵי אֲבוֹתֵינוּ [וְאִמּוֹתֵינוּ].
הֲלֹא כָּל־הַגִּבּוֹרִים כְּאַיִן לְפָנֶיךָ,
וְאַנְשֵׁי הַשֵּׁם כְּלֹא הָיוּ,
וַחֲכָמִים כִּבְלִי מַדָּע,
וּנְבוֹנִים כִּבְלִי הַשְׂכֵּל,
כִּי רֹב מַעֲשֵׂיהֶם תֹּהוּ,
וִימֵי חַיֵּיהֶם הֶבֶל לְפָנֶיךָ.
וּמוֹתַר הָאָדָם מִן הַבְּהֵמָה אָיִן,
כִּי הַכֹּל הָבֶל.

מַה־נֹּאמַר לְפָנֶיךָ יוֹשֵׁב מָרוֹם,
וּמַה־נְּסַפֵּר לְפָנֶיךָ שׁוֹכֵן שְׁחָקִים.
הֲלֹא כָּל־הַנִּסְתָּרוֹת וְהַנִּגְלוֹת אַתָּה יוֹדֵעַ.

שִׁמְךָ מֵעוֹלָם עוֹבֵר עַל פֶּשַׁע,
שַׁוְעָתֵנוּ תַּאֲזִין בְּעָמְדֵנוּ לְפָנֶיךָ בִּתְפִלָּה.
תַּעֲבוֹר עַל פֶּשַׁע לְעַם שָׁבֵי פֶשַׁע,
תִּמְחֶה פְּשָׁעֵינוּ מִנֶּגֶד עֵינֶיךָ.

אַתָּה יוֹדֵעַ רָזֵי עוֹלָם, וְתַעֲלוּמוֹת סִתְרֵי כָל־חָי.
אַתָּה חוֹפֵשׂ כָּל־חַדְרֵי בָטֶן, וּבוֹחֵן כְּלָיוֹת וָלֵב.
אֵין דָּבָר נֶעְלָם מִמֶּךָּ, וְאֵין נִסְתָּר מִנֶּגֶד עֵינֶיךָ.
וּבְכֵן יְהִי רָצוֹן מִלְּפָנֶיךָ
יהוה אֱלֹהֵינוּ וֵאלֹהֵי אֲבוֹתֵינוּ [וְאִמּוֹתֵינוּ]
שֶׁתִּסְלַח לָנוּ עַל כָּל־חַטֹּאתֵינוּ
וְתִמְחַל לָנוּ עַל כָּל־עֲוֹנוֹתֵינוּ
וּתְכַפֶּר־לָנוּ עַל כָּל־פְּשָׁעֵינוּ.

YOU RECOGNIZE אַתָּה מַכִּיר. Our confession is not to enlighten the High Court; God already knows all that we have done. Rather, we recite these words to proclaim in our own voice that we acknowledge and take responsibility for our deeds.

WHAT ARE WE מָה אָנוּ. This prayer, which originated here in the Yom Kippur liturgy, is now included in the daily prayerbook, as part of the introductory morning service throughout the year.

YOU HAVE ALWAYS BEEN KNOWN שִׁמְךָ מֵעוֹלָם. From a double alphabetical acrostic piyyut by Elijah the Elder (ca. 1040). It begins אַתָּה מֵבִין תַּעֲלֻמוֹת לֵב (atah meivin ta·alumot lev), "You understand the secrets of the heart." Almost all rites preserve only these final lines, corresponding to the Hebrew alphabet's last two letters.

YOU KNOW THE MYSTERIES OF THE UNIVERSE אַתָּה יוֹדֵעַ רָזֵי עוֹלָם. The Babylonian Talmud, Yoma 87b, presents various liturgies that fulfill the obligation of confession. This one is offered by Rav (3rd century, Babylonia).

¶ *All Our Secrets*

All our secrets are known to You, Adonai; we cannot even fool ourselves. Lying is a vain exercise; help us not even to try.

How could we deceive You, within us, at once forming and knowing our most secret thoughts?

We live in a world of illusion. We each think we are separate, alone, cut off, misunderstood, unwanted. We forget we are part of Your glory, each of us a unique ray of Your light.

As we live our lives, rent asunder, each in our own small world, help us to remember what we often forget: We need one another; we each are part of the other; and in some place, so well known, yet so secret, we may find our true solace in You.

—JULES HARLOW
(*adapted*)

ג

You recognize both our sins and our mistakes, acts of will and
those committed under compulsion; public acts and private
ones are equally revealed and known to You.
What are we? What is our life? Our goodness? Our
righteousness? Our achievement? Our power? Our victories?
What shall we say in Your presence,
Adonai our God and God of our ancestors?
Heroes count as nothing in Your presence,
famous people are as if they never existed,
the wise seem ignorant,
and clever ones as if they lack reason.
The sum of their acts is chaos;
in Your presence the days of their lives are futile.
Human beings have no superiority over beasts;
all life is vanity.

What can we say before You, You who live in the transcendent?
And what can we tell about ourselves to You who dwell on high?
You surely know both the secret and the revealed.

ד

You have always been known as the one who overlooks
transgression.
Hear our cry, as we stand before You, in prayer.
Overlook the transgressions of a people turning from
transgression.
Wipe away our transgressions from Your sight.

ה

You know the mysteries of the universe,
the deepest secrets of everyone alive.
You probe our innermost depths;
You examine our thoughts and feelings.
Nothing escapes You;
nothing is secret from You.
Therefore, may it be Your will, our God and God of our ancestors,
to forgive us for all our sins,
to pardon us for all our iniquities,
and to grant us atonement for all our transgressions.

It is customary to strike one's heart when the words עַל חֵטְא are recited.

עַל חֵטְא שֶׁחָטָאנוּ לְפָנֶיךָ בְּאֹנֶס וּבְרָצוֹן,
וְעַל חֵטְא שֶׁחָטָאנוּ לְפָנֶיךָ בְּאִמּוּץ הַלֵּב.
עַל חֵטְא שֶׁחָטָאנוּ לְפָנֶיךָ בִּבְלִי דָעַת,
וְעַל חֵטְא שֶׁחָטָאנוּ לְפָנֶיךָ בְּבִטּוּי שְׂפָתָיִם.
עַל חֵטְא שֶׁחָטָאנוּ לְפָנֶיךָ בְּגִלּוּי עֲרָיוֹת,
וְעַל חֵטְא שֶׁחָטָאנוּ לְפָנֶיךָ בַּגָּלוּי וּבַסֵּתֶר.
עַל חֵטְא שֶׁחָטָאנוּ לְפָנֶיךָ בְּדַעַת וּבְמִרְמָה,
וְעַל חֵטְא שֶׁחָטָאנוּ לְפָנֶיךָ בְּדִבּוּר פֶּה.
עַל חֵטְא שֶׁחָטָאנוּ לְפָנֶיךָ בְּהוֹנָאַת רֵעַ,
וְעַל חֵטְא שֶׁחָטָאנוּ לְפָנֶיךָ בְּהִרְהוֹר הַלֵּב.
עַל חֵטְא שֶׁחָטָאנוּ לְפָנֶיךָ בִּוְעִידַת זְנוּת,
וְעַל חֵטְא שֶׁחָטָאנוּ לְפָנֶיךָ בְּוִדּוּי פֶּה.
עַל חֵטְא שֶׁחָטָאנוּ לְפָנֶיךָ בְּזִלְזוּל הוֹרִים וּמוֹרִים,
וְעַל חֵטְא שֶׁחָטָאנוּ לְפָנֶיךָ בְּזָדוֹן וּבִשְׁגָגָה.
עַל חֵטְא שֶׁחָטָאנוּ לְפָנֶיךָ בְּחֹזֶק יָד,
וְעַל חֵטְא שֶׁחָטָאנוּ לְפָנֶיךָ בְּחִלּוּל הַשֵּׁם.
עַל חֵטְא שֶׁחָטָאנוּ לְפָנֶיךָ בְּטֻמְאַת שְׂפָתָיִם,
וְעַל חֵטְא שֶׁחָטָאנוּ לְפָנֶיךָ בְּטִפְּשׁוּת פֶּה.
◁ עַל חֵטְא שֶׁחָטָאנוּ לְפָנֶיךָ בְּיֵצֶר הָרָע,
וְעַל חֵטְא שֶׁחָטָאנוּ לְפָנֶיךָ בְּיוֹדְעִים וּבְלֹא יוֹדְעִים.

וְעַל כֻּלָּם, אֱלֹוהַּ סְלִיחוֹת, סְלַח לָנוּ, מְחַל לָנוּ, כַּפֶּר־לָנוּ.

עַל חֵטְא שֶׁחָטָאנוּ לְפָנֶיךָ בְּכַחַשׁ וּבְכָזָב,
וְעַל חֵטְא שֶׁחָטָאנוּ לְפָנֶיךָ בְּכַפַּת שֹׁחַד.
עַל חֵטְא שֶׁחָטָאנוּ לְפָנֶיךָ בְּלָצוֹן,
וְעַל חֵטְא שֶׁחָטָאנוּ לְפָנֶיךָ בְּלָשׁוֹן הָרָע.
עַל חֵטְא שֶׁחָטָאנוּ לְפָנֶיךָ בְּמַשָּׂא וּבְמַתָּן,
וְעַל חֵטְא שֶׁחָטָאנוּ לְפָנֶיךָ בְּמַאֲכָל וּבְמִשְׁתֶּה.

THE LONGER CONFESSION. Despite the double alphabetical acrostic in which the sins are enumerated, the Al Het is not simply a formal list. The sins it enumerates are the stuff of daily life, and they point to our repeated moral failures. It makes almost no specific reference to violations of the rituals of Judaism. Such infractions as the desecration of Shabbat and festivals, and the failure to abide by the disciplines that invest our daily life with sacred significance, are categorized by the Talmud as "sins between people and God." It is taken for granted that only sins "between one person and another" need to be detailed (Babylonian Talmud, Yoma 86b).

Amidst a community of imperfect humans, we gain the courage to confess our sins to God. Knowing that it is God whom we are facing, we are called to a level of honesty and truthfulness that is greater than any intermediary would demand.

The forty-four lines included in the Al Het are an expansion of the six lines that appear in Saadiah Gaon's prayerbook (10th century), the twelve in Amram Gaon's (9th century), and the twenty-two in Maimonides' (12th century).

DEFRAUDING OTHERS
הוֹנָאַת רֵעַ. Or, "oppressing others" (materially or spiritually), for so the Rabbis understood the related verb in Leviticus 19:33.

SPEAKING BADLY OF OTHERS בְּלָשׁוֹן הָרָע. The tradition distinguished between לָשׁוֹן הָרָע (l'shon ha-ra) and רְכִילוּת (r'khilut), both enumerated here. The first is the spreading of truthful yet damaging statements, even without intending any harm. The latter is the telling of outright falsehoods about another.

Embarrassment not only precedes religious commitment; it is the touchstone of religious existence. . . .

What is the truth of being human? The lack of pretension, the acknowledgment of opaqueness, shortsightedness, inadequacy. But truth also demands rising, striving, for the goal is both within and beyond us. The truth of being human is gratitude; its secret is appreciation.

—ABRAHAM JOSHUA HESCHEL

The Longer Confession—Al Ḥet

It is customary to strike one's heart when the words "We have sinned" are recited.

We have sinned against You unwillingly and willingly,
and we have sinned against You through hardening our hearts.
We have sinned against You thoughtlessly,
and we have sinned against You in idle chatter.
We have sinned against You through sexual immorality,
and we have sinned against You openly and in private.
We have sinned against You knowingly and deceitfully,
and we have sinned against You by the way we talk.
We have sinned against You by defrauding others,
and we have sinned against You in our innermost thoughts.
We have sinned against You through forbidden trysts,
and we have sinned against You through empty confession.
We have sinned against You by scorning parents and teachers,
and we have sinned against You purposely and by mistake.
We have sinned against You by resorting to violence,
and we have sinned against You by public desecration of Your name.
We have sinned against You through foul speech,
and we have sinned against You through foolish talk.
We have sinned against You through pursuing the impulse to evil,
and we have sinned against You wittingly and unwittingly.

For all these sins, forgiving God, forgive us, pardon us, grant us atonement.

V'al kullam, elo·ah s'liḥot, s'laḥ lanu, m'ḥal lanu, kapper lanu.

We have sinned against You through denial and deceit,
and we have sinned against You by taking bribes.
We have sinned against You by clever cynicism,
and we have sinned against You by speaking ill of others.
We have sinned against You by the way we do business,
And we have sinned against You in our eating and drinking.

עַל חֵטְא שֶׁחָטָאנוּ לְפָנֶיךָ בְּנֶשֶׁךְ וּבְמַרְבִּית,
וְעַל חֵטְא שֶׁחָטָאנוּ לְפָנֶיךָ בִּנְטִיַּת גָּרוֹן.
עַל חֵטְא שֶׁחָטָאנוּ לְפָנֶיךָ בְּשִׂיחַ שִׂפְתוֹתֵינוּ,
וְעַל חֵטְא שֶׁחָטָאנוּ לְפָנֶיךָ בְּשִׂקּוּר עָיִן.
◁ עַל חֵטְא שֶׁחָטָאנוּ לְפָנֶיךָ בְּעֵינַיִם רָמוֹת,
וְעַל חֵטְא שֶׁחָטָאנוּ לְפָנֶיךָ בְּעַזּוּת מֵצַח.

וְעַל כֻּלָּם, אֱלוֹהַּ סְלִיחוֹת, סְלַח לָנוּ, מְחַל לָנוּ, כַּפֶּר־לָנוּ.

עַל חֵטְא שֶׁחָטָאנוּ לְפָנֶיךָ בִּפְרִיקַת עֹל,
וְעַל חֵטְא שֶׁחָטָאנוּ לְפָנֶיךָ בִּפְלִילוּת.
עַל חֵטְא שֶׁחָטָאנוּ לְפָנֶיךָ בִּצְדִיַּת רֵעַ,
וְעַל חֵטְא שֶׁחָטָאנוּ לְפָנֶיךָ בְּצָרוּת עָיִן.
עַל חֵטְא שֶׁחָטָאנוּ לְפָנֶיךָ בְּקַלּוּת רֹאשׁ,
וְעַל חֵטְא שֶׁחָטָאנוּ לְפָנֶיךָ בְּקַשְׁיוּת עֹרֶף.
עַל חֵטְא שֶׁחָטָאנוּ לְפָנֶיךָ בְּרִיצַת רַגְלַיִם לְהָרַע,
וְעַל חֵטְא שֶׁחָטָאנוּ לְפָנֶיךָ בִּרְכִילוּת.
עַל חֵטְא שֶׁחָטָאנוּ לְפָנֶיךָ בִּשְׁבוּעַת שָׁוְא,
וְעַל חֵטְא שֶׁחָטָאנוּ לְפָנֶיךָ בְּשִׂנְאַת חִנָּם.
◁ עַל חֵטְא שֶׁחָטָאנוּ לְפָנֶיךָ בִּתְשׂוּמֶת־יָד,
וְעַל חֵטְא שֶׁחָטָאנוּ לְפָנֶיךָ בְּתִמְהוֹן לֵבָב.

וְעַל כֻּלָּם, אֱלוֹהַּ סְלִיחוֹת, סְלַח לָנוּ, מְחַל לָנוּ, כַּפֶּר־לָנוּ.

וְעַל מִצְוֹת עֲשֵׂה וְעַל מִצְוֹת לֹא תַעֲשֶׂה, בֵּין שֶׁיֵּשׁ בָּהּ קוּם
עֲשֵׂה, וּבֵין שֶׁאֵין בָּהּ קוּם עֲשֵׂה, אֶת־הַגְּלוּיִים לָנוּ וְאֶת־
שֶׁאֵינָם גְּלוּיִים לָנוּ. אֶת־הַגְּלוּיִים לָנוּ כְּבָר אֲמַרְנוּם לְפָנֶיךָ
וְהוֹדִינוּ לְךָ עֲלֵיהֶם, וְאֶת־שֶׁאֵינָם גְּלוּיִים לָנוּ, לְפָנֶיךָ הֵם
גְּלוּיִים וִידוּעִים, כַּדָּבָר שֶׁנֶּאֱמַר: הַנִּסְתָּרֹת לַיהוה אֱלֹהֵינוּ,
וְהַנִּגְלֹת לָנוּ וּלְבָנֵינוּ עַד־עוֹלָם, לַעֲשׂוֹת אֶת־כָּל־דִּבְרֵי
הַתּוֹרָה הַזֹּאת.

וְאַתָּה רַחוּם מְקַבֵּל שָׁבִים,
וְעַל הַתְּשׁוּבָה מֵרֹאשׁ הִבְטַחְתָּנוּ,
וְעַל הַתְּשׁוּבָה עֵינֵינוּ מְיַחֲלוֹת לָךְ.

CONSPIRATORIAL GLANCES
בְּשִׂקּוּר עָיִן. Many sins in this section and the next refer to attitudes that we hold in relationships. The Hebrew speaks in terms of the way that we "see" the world. We confess to שִׂקּוּר עָיִן (*sikkur ayin*), "conspiratorial glances"; עֵינַיִם רָמוֹת (*einayim ramot*), literally "eyes raised high," which we translate as "condescension"; צָרוּת עָיִן (*tzarut ayin*), "selfishness," literally, "narrow vision."

SUPERFICIALITY בְּקַלּוּת רֹאשׁ. Literally, "lightheadedness." The Rabbis used this term to refer to a state of mind in which we are unable to exercise sound judgment. Many Jewish legal authorities oppose the use of mind-altering drugs if they deny us the ability to make reasoned judgments.

SECRET MATTERS הַנִּסְתָּרֹת. Deuteronomy 29:28.

Enumerating Sins

No list of sins can ever be complete. By beginning with *alef* and ending with *tav*, we express our intention to include in our confession everything of which we are guilty, from A to Z. However, this form of the Al Ḥet does not relieve us of our individual obligation to confess the particular sins of which we are each personally responsible. And we are also called upon to contemplate those sins which are especially prevalent in our world today.

Of Anger and of Peace

Bear in mind that life is short, and that with every passing day you are nearer to the end of your life. Therefore, how can you waste your time on petty quarrels and discords? Restrain your anger; hold your temper in check, and enjoy peace with everyone.

—NAḤMAN OF BRATZLAV

We have sinned against You by greed and oppressive interest,
and we have sinned against You through arrogance.
We have sinned against You in everyday conversation,
and we have sinned against You through conspiratorial glances.
We have sinned against You through condescension,
and we have sinned against You through stubbornness.

For all these sins, forgiving God, forgive us, pardon us, grant us atonement.

V'al kullam, elo·ah s'liḥot, s'laḥ lanu, m'ḥal lanu, kapper lanu.

We have sinned against You by throwing off all restraint,
and we have sinned against You by rashly judging others.
We have sinned against You by plotting against others,
and we have sinned against You through selfishness.
We have sinned against You through superficiality,
and we have sinned against You through stubbornness.
We have sinned against You by rushing to do evil,
and we have sinned against You through gossip.
We have sinned against You through empty promises,
and we have sinned against You through baseless hatred.
We have sinned against You by betraying trust,
and we have sinned against You by succumbing to confusion.

For all these sins, forgiving God, forgive us, pardon us, grant us atonement.

V'al kullam, elo·ah s'liḥot, s'laḥ lanu, m'ḥal lanu, kapper lanu.

And forgive us the breach of all commandments and prohibitions, whether involving deeds or not, whether known to us or not. The sins known to us we have acknowledged, and those unknown to us are surely known to You, as the Torah states: "Secret matters are the concern of ADONAI our God; but in matters that are revealed, it is for us and our children to apply all teachings of the Torah till the end of time."

You are compassionate, welcoming those who turn back to You. You have promised, since the dawn of creation, that repentance would be received. Now our eyes look toward You, to accept our repentance.

One or more of the following meditations may be selected as endings for the Viddui.

א

חַנָּה, מָרַת רוּחַ הִתְפַּלְלָה לְפָנֶיךָ, וַיִּמָּלֵא לִבָּהּ בֶּכִי, וְקוֹלָהּ לֹא יִשָּׁמַע, אַךְ בְּחַנְתָּ אֶת־לִבָּהּ וַתִּפֶן אֵלֶיהָ. עֲנֵה לָנוּ בְּעֵת בַּקָּשָׁתֵנוּ כְּשֶׁעָנִיתָ לְתַחְנַת הָאִשָּׁה בְּשִׁילֹה וְנִזְכֶּה לָשִׁיר כְּמוֹתָהּ: יהוה מַשְׁפִּיל אַף־מְרוֹמֵם, מֵקִים מֵעָפָר דָּל.

וְדָוִד עַבְדְּךָ אָמַר לְפָנֶיךָ: שְׁגִיאוֹת מִי־יָבִין, מִנִּסְתָּרוֹת נַקֵּנִי. נַקֵּנוּ יהוה אֱלֹהֵינוּ מִכָּל־פְּשָׁעֵינוּ, וְטַהֲרֵנוּ מִכָּל־טֻמְאוֹתֵינוּ, וּזְרוֹק עָלֵינוּ מַיִם טְהוֹרִים וְטַהֲרֵנוּ, כַּכָּתוּב עַל יַד נְבִיאֶךָ: וְזָרַקְתִּי עֲלֵיכֶם מַיִם טְהוֹרִים וּטְהַרְתֶּם, מִכֹּל טֻמְאוֹתֵיכֶם וּמִכָּל־גִּלּוּלֵיכֶם אֲטַהֵר אֶתְכֶם.

מִיכָה עַבְדְּךָ אָמַר לְפָנֶיךָ: מִי אֵל כָּמוֹךָ נֹשֵׂא עָוֹן וְעֹבֵר עַל־פֶּשַׁע לִשְׁאֵרִית נַחֲלָתוֹ, לֹא־הֶחֱזִיק לָעַד אַפּוֹ, כִּי־חָפֵץ חֶסֶד הוּא. יָשׁוּב יְרַחֲמֵנוּ, יִכְבֹּשׁ עֲוֹנֹתֵינוּ, וְתַשְׁלִיךְ בִּמְצֻלוֹת יָם כָּל־חַטֹּאתָם. תִּתֵּן אֱמֶת לְיַעֲקֹב, חֶסֶד לְאַבְרָהָם, אֲשֶׁר־נִשְׁבַּעְתָּ לַאֲבוֹתֵינוּ מִימֵי קֶדֶם.

דָּנִיֵּאל אִישׁ חֲמוּדוֹת שִׁוַּע לְפָנֶיךָ: הַטֵּה אֱלֹהַי אָזְנְךָ וּשְׁמָע, פְּקַח עֵינֶיךָ וּרְאֵה שֹׁמְמֹתֵינוּ, וְהָעִיר אֲשֶׁר־נִקְרָא שִׁמְךָ עָלֶיהָ. כִּי לֹא עַל־צִדְקֹתֵינוּ אֲנַחְנוּ מַפִּילִים תַּחֲנוּנֵינוּ לְפָנֶיךָ, כִּי עַל־רַחֲמֶיךָ הָרַבִּים. אֲדֹנָי שְׁמָעָה, אֲדֹנָי סְלָחָה, אֲדֹנָי הַקְשִׁיבָה וַעֲשֵׂה אַל־תְּאַחַר, לְמַעַנְךָ אֱלֹהַי, כִּי־שִׁמְךָ נִקְרָא עַל־עִירְךָ וְעַל־עַמֶּךָ.

אַל תַּעַזְבֵנוּ אָבִינוּ,
וְאַל תִּטְּשֵׁנוּ בּוֹרְאֵנוּ,
וְאַל תַּזְנִיחֵנוּ יוֹצְרֵנוּ,
וְאַל תַּעַשׂ עִמָּנוּ כָּלָה כְּחַטֹּאתֵינוּ.
וְקַיֶּם־לָנוּ יהוה אֱלֹהֵינוּ אֶת־הַדָּבָר שֶׁהִבְטַחְתָּנוּ בְּקַבָּלָה עַל יְדֵי יִרְמְיָהוּ חוֹזֶךָ, כָּאָמוּר: בַּיָּמִים הָהֵם וּבָעֵת הַהִיא, נְאֻם־יהוה,

HANNAH חַנָּה. The listing of biblical figures who prayed to God for forgiveness places our own plea for forgiveness in an ongoing history of prayer. Hannah became, for the Rabbis, the model of proper prayer; David, the psalmist, is the master of prayer. Micah's prayer is appended to the prophetic reading on Shabbat Shuvah—the Shabbat that precedes the Day of Atonement. The Rabbis saw Daniel as a biblical embodiment of their own sense of dutiful prayer, since the Bible records that he prayed facing toward Jerusalem three times a day (Daniel 6:11).

WHO CAN BE AWARE OF ERROR שְׁגִיאוֹת מִי יָבִין Psalm 19:13. The paragraph ends with a quotation from Ezekiel 36:25.

IS THERE ANY DIVINITY SAVE YOU מִי אֵל כָּמוֹךָ Micah 7:18–20. The passage is recited also on Rosh Hashanah at Tashlikh.

MY GOD, TURN YOUR EAR הַטֵּה אֱלֹהַי אָזְנְךָ Daniel 9:18–19.

IN THOSE DAYS בַּיָּמִים הָהֵם Jeremiah 50:20.

Throughout the long
hours of prayer, we speak
of all the reasons why
God should care for
us and forgive us: our
remorse, our atonement,
our acknowledgment
of wrongdoing, God's
own promise of mercy,
God's wish to be known
in the world as loving.
In this prayer, we call on
our association with our
ancestors who were cared
for by God. We subtly
imply that since we are
their children, we have
inherited their spiritual
legacy. In placing our
own prayer in the context
of theirs, perhaps what
is implied as well is that
we seek to live our lives
in accordance with that
which gave them honor.
—NINA BETH CARDIN

Concluding Prayers of Confession

One or more of the following five meditations may be selected as endings for the Viddui.

א

Hannah, sad and depressed, prayed to You, her heart overflowing with tears, her voice inaudible. But You understood her heartfelt cry and turned to her. Answer us in our time of need, as You responded to the plea of the woman in Shiloh, that like her we may sing: Adonai "brings down and lifts up, raises up the poor from the dust of the earth."

Your servant David pleaded before You: "Who can be aware of error? Cleanse me of my most secret sins." Cleanse us, Adonai our God, of all our transgressions; purify us of all our foulness; pour over us purifying water that we may be cleansed, as the prophet Ezekiel wrote: "I will sprinkle purifying water upon you and you shall be cleansed; I will cleanse you of all your impurities and your idolatries."

Your servant Micah declared: "Is there any divinity save You who forgives the sins and pardons the transgressions of the remnant, Your people? You do not maintain anger forever, for You delight in love. You will return to us compassionately, overcoming the consequences of our sin, hurling our sins into the depths of the sea. You will keep faith with Jacob, showing enduring love to Abraham, as You promised our ancestors in days of old."

Your beloved Daniel prayed to You: "My God, turn Your ear toward us, listen, open Your eyes and see our desolation and that of the city known by Your name." Not because of our own merit do we cast our plea before You. Rather, we depend on the generosity of Your compassion. Adonai, hear! Adonai, forgive! Adonai, listen! Do not delay. For Your sake, O my God; for Your city and Your people are known by Your name.

Do not forsake us—You, who formed us;
do not abandon us—You, who created us;
do not cast us away—You, who fashioned us;
do not destroy us, as You would our sins.
Adonai our God, fulfill for us the promise that You made
to Jeremiah, the visionary, kept alive in our tradition, as it is
written: "In those days and in that time, this will be the word
of Adonai:

MAY THE ONE WHO AN-
SWERED מִי שֶׁעָנָה. We do
not stand alone on this
day, but within a tradition
of prayer and forgive-
ness. Lines of this prayer
are mentioned as early as
Mishnah Taanit (ca. 200
C.E.). Over time, more
names and more biblical
allusions were added. Here
we include responses to
biblical women along with
the traditional listing. An
extant Ḥasidic version offers
a similarly inclusive list.

SINAI חֹרֵב. In the Torah,
ḥorev (Horeb) is another
name for Sinai.

HER WELL בִּבְאֵרָה. According to the Midrash, a well
accompanied Israel in the
desert and supplied the
camp with water because of
the merit of Miriam.

EACH OF US HAS A NAME
לְכָל־אִישׁ יֵשׁ שֵׁם. This poem
by Zelda (Zelda Schneerson
Mishkovsky, a 20th-century
Hebrew poet), translated
from the Hebrew by Marcia
Falk, is an extended meditation on the names we are
given by fathers, mothers,
others, and on the names
we acquire for ourselves.
On this day, we ponder the
various names by which we
are known, and the names
by which we wish to be
known.

יְבַקֵּשׁ אֶת־עֲוֹן יִשְׂרָאֵל וְאֵינֶנּוּ,
וְאֶת־חַטֹּאת יְהוּדָה וְלֹא תִמָּצֶאנָה,
כִּי אֶסְלַח לַאֲשֶׁר אַשְׁאִיר.
עַמְּךָ וְנַחֲלָתְךָ רְעֵבֵי טוּבְךָ,
צְמֵאֵי חַסְדֶּךָ,
תְּאֵבֵי יִשְׁעֶךָ,
יַכִּירוּ וְיֵדְעוּ כִּי לַיהוה אֱלֹהֵינוּ הָרַחֲמִים וְהַסְּלִיחוֹת.

ב

מִי שֶׁעָנָה לְשָׂרָה אִמֵּנוּ בְּזִקְנָתָהּ,   הוּא יַעֲנֵנוּ.
מִי שֶׁעָנָה לְאַבְרָהָם אָבִינוּ בְּהַר הַמּוֹרִיָּה,   הוּא יַעֲנֵנוּ.
מִי שֶׁעָנָה לְיִצְחָק בְּנָם כְּשֶׁנֶּעֱקַד עַל גַּבֵּי הַמִּזְבֵּחַ,   הוּא יַעֲנֵנוּ.
מִי שֶׁעָנָה לְרִבְקָה בְּהֵרָיוֹנָהּ,   הוּא יַעֲנֵנוּ.
מִי שֶׁעָנָה לְיַעֲקֹב בְּבֵית אֵל,   הוּא יַעֲנֵנוּ.
מִי שֶׁעָנָה לְלֵאָה בְּעֶנְיָהּ,   הוּא יַעֲנֵנוּ.
מִי שֶׁעָנָה לְרָחֵל בְּעִצְבוֹנָהּ,   הוּא יַעֲנֵנוּ.
מִי שֶׁעָנָה לְיוֹסֵף בְּבֵית הָאֲסוּרִים,   הוּא יַעֲנֵנוּ.
מִי שֶׁעָנָה לַמְיַלְּדוֹת הָעִבְרִיּוֹת עַל הָאָבְנָיִם,   הוּא יַעֲנֵנוּ.
מִי שֶׁעָנָה לְיוֹכֶבֶד עַל שְׂפַת הַיְאֹר,   הוּא יַעֲנֵנוּ.
מִי שֶׁעָנָה לַאֲבוֹתֵינוּ וּלְאִמּוֹתֵינוּ עַל יַם סוּף,   הוּא יַעֲנֵנוּ.
מִי שֶׁעָנָה לְמֹשֶׁה בְּחוֹרֵב,   הוּא יַעֲנֵנוּ.
מִי שֶׁעָנָה לְמִרְיָם בִּבְאֵרָהּ,   הוּא יַעֲנֵנוּ.
מִי שֶׁעָנָה לְאַהֲרֹן בְּמַחְתָּתוֹ,   הוּא יַעֲנֵנוּ.
מִי שֶׁעָנָה לְפִנְחָס בְּקוּמוֹ מִתּוֹךְ הָעֵדָה,   הוּא יַעֲנֵנוּ.
מִי שֶׁעָנָה לִבְנוֹת צְלָפְחָד בְּעָמְדָן פֶּתַח
אֹהֶל מוֹעֵד,   הוּא יַעֲנֵנוּ.
מִי שֶׁעָנָה לְכָל־הַצַּדִּיקִים וְהַצַּדִּיקוֹת וְהַחֲסִידִים
וְהַחֲסִידוֹת וְהַתְּמִימִים וְהַתְּמִימוֹת וְהַיְשָׁרִים
וְהַיְשָׁרוֹת וְהָרַחֲמָנִים וְהָרַחֲמָנִיּוֹת,   הוּא יַעֲנֵנוּ.

ג

לְכָל־אִישׁ יֵשׁ שֵׁם
שֶׁנָּתַן לוֹ אֱלֹהִים
וְנָתְנוּ לוֹ אָבִיו וְאִמּוֹ
לְכָל־אִישׁ יֵשׁ שֵׁם
שֶׁנָּתְנוּ לוֹ קוֹמָתוֹ וְאֹפֶן חִיּוּכוֹ
וְנָתַן לוֹ הָאָרִיג

Answer Us
What would constitute
an answer to our prayers?
We do not truly expect
nature to overturn its
course, or others to
suddenly change their
plans, because we have
expressed our hope
that the future bend to
our desires. Rather, if
our prayer succeeds,
we can experience
closeness to the Divine,
an appreciation of God's
bounty, connection
with the rest of creation,
discovery of meaning in
our lives, and an inner
feeling of wholeness and
peace. For a moment, we
may experience ourselves
as held fast in God's
invisible arms. Perhaps
this is what the ancient
pilgrims themselves
experienced when
they heard the priests
pronounce the final word
of blessing: "... *shalom,*
peace."

Iniquity shall be sought in Israel, but there shall be none;
and sin shall be sought in Judah, but none shall be found.
For I will pardon those whom I leave as a remnant."
Your people hunger for Your goodness,
thirst for Your love,
and long for Your salvation.
May they know that compassion and forgiveness come from
ADONAI our God.

ב

May the One who answered:

SARAH past the time of her youth,	*hu ya·aneinu*
ABRAHAM on Mount Moriah,	*hu ya·aneinu*
ISAAC, their son, bound on the altar,	*hu ya·aneinu*
REBECCA as her sons struggled within her,	*hu ya·aneinu*
JACOB at Beth El,	*hu ya·aneinu*
LEAH in her loneliness,	*hu ya·aneinu*
RACHEL, desperate for a child,	*hu ya·aneinu*
JOSEPH, abandoned in prison,	*hu ya·aneinu*
the HEBREW MIDWIVES as they stood at the birthing place,	*hu ya·aneinu*
JOCHEBED having faith on the bank of the Nile,	*hu ya·aneinu*
the PEOPLE ISRAEL on the shores of the Sea,	*hu ya·aneinu*
MOSES standing on the slopes of Sinai,	*hu ya·aneinu*
MIRIAM with her well of water,	*hu ya·aneinu*
AARON offering incense to God,	*hu ya·aneinu*
PHINEAS seeking his place above the crowd,	*hu ya·aneinu*
the DAUGHTERS OF ZELOPHEHAD standing their ground,	*hu ya·aneinu*
and those who are righteous, upright, decent, and compassionate—answer us.	*hu ya·aneinu*

ג

Each of us has a name
given by the Source of Life
and given by our parents

Each of us has a name
given by our stature and our smile
and given by what we wear

לְכָל־אִישׁ יֵשׁ שֵׁם
שֶׁנָּתְנוּ לוֹ הֶהָרִים
וְנָתְנוּ לוֹ כְּתָלָיו

לְכָל־אִישׁ יֵשׁ שֵׁם
שֶׁנָּתְנוּ לוֹ הַמַּזָּלוֹת
וְנָתְנוּ לוֹ שְׁכֵנָיו

לְכָל־אִישׁ יֵשׁ שֵׁם
שֶׁנָּתְנוּ לוֹ חֲטָאָיו
וְנָתְנָה לוֹ כְּמִיהָתוֹ

לְכָל־אִישׁ יֵשׁ שֵׁם
שֶׁנָּתְנוּ לוֹ שׂוֹנְאָיו
וְנָתְנָה לוֹ אַהֲבָתוֹ

לְכָל־אִישׁ יֵשׁ שֵׁם
שֶׁנָּתְנוּ לוֹ חַגָּיו
וְנָתְנָה לוֹ מְלַאכְתּוֹ

לְכָל־אִישׁ יֵשׁ שֵׁם
שֶׁנָּתְנוּ לוֹ תְּקוּפוֹת הַשָּׁנָה
וְנָתַן לוֹ עִוְרוֹנוֹ

לְכָל־אִישׁ יֵשׁ שֵׁם
שֶׁנָּתַן לוֹ הַיָּם
וְנָתַן לוֹ
מוֹתוֹ.

ד

לֵידָה הִיא מוֹצָא
וּמָוֶת הוּא יַעַד
וְהַחַיִּים הֵם נְסִיעָה:
מִיַּלְדוּת לְבַגְרוּת
מִנַּעֲרוּת לְזִקְנוּת
מִתְּמִימוּת לְהַכָּרָה
וּמִבּוּרוּת לִידִיעָה;
מִסִּכְלוּת לְבִינָה
וְאָז, אוּלַי, לְחָכְמָה;

BIRTH IS A BEGINNING לֵידָה הִיא מוֹצָא. This prayer, written by Alvin Fine, has been reprinted in numerous prayerbooks. It reflects on the human condition and understands that each moment constitutes a stage in a journey, at best a pilgrimage—images that are descriptive of a contemporary religious stance for many people. We are on the way to holiness, to the experience of the Divine, but we can never claim a full achievement of the religious life. The Viddui/Confession that we have just recited makes us aware of our failings and of our vulnerabilities, but we can emerge with renewed dedication to finding our way, to discovering our own particular path to holiness.

The prayer appears here in a slightly adapted version and with a Hebrew translation by Alan Lettofsky.

Each of us has a name
given by the mountains
and given by our walls

Each of us has a name
given by the stars
and given by our neighbors

Each of us has a name
given by our sins
and given by our longing

Each of us has a name
given by our enemies
and given by our love

Each of us has a name
given by our celebrations
and given by our work

Each of us has a name
given by the seasons
and given by our blindness

Each of us has a name
given by the sea
and given by
our death

ד

Birth is a beginning
and death a destination.
And life is a journey:
From childhood to maturity
And youth to age;
From innocence to awareness
And ignorance to knowing;
From foolishness to discretion,
And then, perhaps, to wisdom;

מֵחוּלְשָׁה לִגְבוּרָה

אוֹ גְּבוּרָה לְחוּלְשָׁה –

וּלְעִתִּים, בַּחֲזָרָה;

מִבְּרִיאוּת לְמַחֲלָה

נִתְפַּלֵּל בַּחֲזָרָה לַבְּרִיאוּת;

מִפֶּשַׁע לִסְלִיחָה

מִבְּדִידוּת לְאַהֲבָה

מִשִּׂמְחָה לְתוֹדָה

מִכְּאֵב לְרַחֲמִים

וְיָגוֹן לַהֲבָנָה

מִפַּחַד לֶאֱמוּנָה;

מִכִּשָּׁלוֹן לְכִשָּׁלוֹן לְכִשָּׁלוֹן

עַד בְּהִסְתַּכְּלוּת אֲחוֹרָה אוֹ לְפָנִים

אָנוּ רוֹאִים שֶׁנִּצָּחוֹן נִמְצָא

לֹא בְּאֵיזוֹ בָּמָה גְּבוֹהָה בַּדֶּרֶךְ

אֶלָּא בִּנְסִיעָה עַצְמָהּ, תַּחֲנָה אַחַר תַּחֲנָה

עֲלִיַּת רֶגֶל קְדוֹשָׁה.

לֵידָה הִיא מוֹצָא

וּמָוֶת הוּא יַעַד

וְהַחַיִּים הֵם נְסִיעָה,

עֲלִיַּת רֶגֶל קְדוֹשָׁה . . .

ה

רַחֲמָנָא דְעָנֵי לַעֲנִיֵּי עֲנֵינָא.

רַחֲמָנָא דְעָנֵי לְמַכִּיכֵי־רוּחָא עֲנֵינָא.

רַחֲמָנָא דְעָנֵי לִתְבִירֵי־לִבָּא עֲנֵינָא.

רַחֲמָנָא עֲנֵינָא,

רַחֲמָנָא חוּס,

רַחֲמָנָא פְּרָק,

רַחֲמָנָא שֵׁזֵב,

רַחֲמָנָא רַחֵם עֲלָן, הַשְׁתָּא בַּעֲגָלָא וּבִזְמַן קָרִיב.

GOD OF MERCY רַחֲמָנָא.
This is an Aramaic prayer
written in the late first millennium, similar to "May
the One who answered,"
מִי שֶׁעָנָה, on p. 240. Here,
though, the movement
from ancestors to the self
is more insistent. The first
three lines contain four
words each; and then the
rhythm breaks entirely
and the remaining lines
simply plead for God to
act speedily. The pace gets
faster; the lines get shorter; the
words more urgent. We are pleading then for our lives, nothing
less. With this brokenhearted cry,
the confession traditionally ends.

From weakness to strength
Or strength to weakness —
And often, back again;
From health to sickness
And back, we pray, to health again;
From offense to forgiveness,
From loneliness to love,
From joy to gratitude,
From pain to compassion,
And grief to understanding —
From fear to faith;
From defeat to defeat to defeat —
Until, looking backward or ahead,
We see that victory lies
Not at some high place along the way,
But in having made the journey, stage by stage,
A sacred pilgrimage.
Birth is a beginning
And death a destination.
And life is a journey,
A sacred pilgrimage . . .

ה

God of Mercy, who answers the poor, answer us.
  May the Merciful One, who answers the
  downtrodden, answer us.
God of Mercy, who answers the broken-hearted, answer us.
  May the Merciful One answer us.
God of Mercy, pity us.
  May the Merciful One redeem us.
God of Mercy, save us.
  May the Merciful One have compassion upon us, speedily,
  now and in time to come.

Raḥamana d'anei la-aniyyei aneina.
Raḥamana d'anei l'makkikhei ruḥa aneina.
Raḥamana d'anei li-t'virei libba aneina.
Raḥamana aneina, Raḥamana ḥus,
Raḥamana p'ruk, Raḥamana shazzeiv,
Raḥamana raḥem alan, hashta ba-agala u-viz'man kariv.

We rise as the ark is opened. An alternate version appears on the next page.
Avinu Malkeinu is not recited on Shabbat.

אָבִינוּ מַלְכֵּנוּ! חָטָאנוּ לְפָנֶיךָ.

אָבִינוּ מַלְכֵּנוּ! אֵין לָנוּ מֶלֶךְ אֶלָּא אָתָּה.

אָבִינוּ מַלְכֵּנוּ! עֲשֵׂה עִמָּנוּ לְמַעַן שְׁמֶךָ.

אָבִינוּ מַלְכֵּנוּ! חַדֵּשׁ עָלֵינוּ שָׁנָה טוֹבָה.

אָבִינוּ מַלְכֵּנוּ! בַּטֵּל מֵעָלֵינוּ כָּל־גְּזֵרוֹת קָשׁוֹת.

אָבִינוּ מַלְכֵּנוּ! בַּטֵּל מַחְשְׁבוֹת שׂוֹנְאֵינוּ.

אָבִינוּ מַלְכֵּנוּ! הָפֵר עֲצַת אוֹיְבֵינוּ.

אָבִינוּ מַלְכֵּנוּ! כַּלֵּה כָּל־צַר וּמַשְׂטִין מֵעָלֵינוּ.

אָבִינוּ מַלְכֵּנוּ! כַּלֵּה דֶּבֶר וְחֶרֶב וְרָעָב וּשְׁבִי וּמַשְׁחִית וְעָוֹן

וּשְׁמַד מִבְּנֵי בְרִיתֶךָ.

אָבִינוּ מַלְכֵּנוּ! סְלַח וּמְחַל לְכָל־עֲוֹנוֹתֵינוּ.

אָבִינוּ מַלְכֵּנוּ! מְחֵה וְהַעֲבֵר פְּשָׁעֵינוּ וְחַטֹּאתֵינוּ מִנֶּגֶד עֵינֶיךָ.

After the leader has recited each of these lines, we repeat it:

◁ אָבִינוּ מַלְכֵּנוּ! הַחֲזִירֵנוּ בִּתְשׁוּבָה שְׁלֵמָה לְפָנֶיךָ.

אָבִינוּ מַלְכֵּנוּ! שְׁלַח רְפוּאָה שְׁלֵמָה לְחוֹלֵי עַמֶּךָ.

אָבִינוּ מַלְכֵּנוּ! זָכְרֵנוּ בְּזִכָּרוֹן טוֹב לְפָנֶיךָ.

אָבִינוּ מַלְכֵּנוּ! כָּתְבֵנוּ בְּסֵפֶר חַיִּים טוֹבִים.

אָבִינוּ מַלְכֵּנוּ! כָּתְבֵנוּ בְּסֵפֶר גְּאֻלָּה וִישׁוּעָה.

אָבִינוּ מַלְכֵּנוּ! כָּתְבֵנוּ בְּסֵפֶר פַּרְנָסָה וְכַלְכָּלָה.

אָבִינוּ מַלְכֵּנוּ! כָּתְבֵנוּ בְּסֵפֶר זְכֻיּוֹת.

אָבִינוּ מַלְכֵּנוּ! כָּתְבֵנוּ בְּסֵפֶר סְלִיחָה וּמְחִילָה.

אָבִינוּ מַלְכֵּנוּ! הַצְמַח לָנוּ יְשׁוּעָה בְּקָרוֹב.

אָבִינוּ מַלְכֵּנוּ! הָרֵם קֶרֶן יִשְׂרָאֵל עַמֶּךָ.

אָבִינוּ מַלְכֵּנוּ! הָרֵם קֶרֶן מְשִׁיחֶךָ.

אָבִינוּ מַלְכֵּנוּ! שְׁמַע קוֹלֵנוּ, חוּס וְרַחֵם עָלֵינוּ.

אָבִינוּ מַלְכֵּנוּ! קַבֵּל בְּרַחֲמִים וּבְרָצוֹן אֶת־תְּפִלָּתֵנוּ.

אָבִינוּ מַלְכֵּנוּ! נָא אַל תְּשִׁיבֵנוּ רֵיקָם מִלְּפָנֶיךָ.

אָבִינוּ מַלְכֵּנוּ! זְכוֹר כִּי עָפָר אֲנָחְנוּ.

אָבִינוּ מַלְכֵּנוּ! חֲמוֹל עָלֵינוּ וְעַל עוֹלָלֵינוּ וְטַפֵּנוּ.

אָבִינוּ מַלְכֵּנוּ! עֲשֵׂה לְמַעַן הֲרוּגִים עַל שֵׁם קָדְשֶׁךָ.

אָבִינוּ מַלְכֵּנוּ! עֲשֵׂה לְמַעַן טְבוּחִים עַל יִחוּדֶךָ.

AVINU MALKEINU אָבִינוּ מַלְכֵּנוּ. The Talmud reports: "It once happened that Rabbi Eliezer led the congregation and recited twenty-four *b'rakhot*, but his prayers were not answered. Then Rabbi Akiva followed him and led the congregation in prayer, saying, 'Our father, our sovereign, You are truly our father. Our father, our sovereign, we have no ruler but You. Our father, our sovereign, we have sinned before You. Our father, our sovereign, have mercy on us. Our father, our sovereign, do it for Your name's sake,' and his prayers were answered" (Babylonian Talmud, Taanit 25b). Generations have added many more verses to this prayer. The verses mentioning the martyrs were added after the Crusades.

Avinu Malkeinu was first introduced as a prayer for material blessing. To this were added several pleas against devastation through natural disaster and human enemies, and finally, special prayers for the High Holy Days (for instance, "inscribe us in the Book of Life").

The image of God as father represents relatedness and closeness; that of God as sovereign conveys authority and greater distance. Jewish theology has always talked of transcendence and immanence, God as inscrutable and God as close at hand: this prayer brings together both aspects of God, which is one reason it has been so powerful in the Jewish imagination.

Avinu Malkeinu

We rise as the ark is opened. An alternate version appears on the next page.
Avinu Malkeinu is not recited on Shabbat.

Avinu Malkeinu, we have sinned in Your presence.
Avinu Malkeinu, we have no sovereign but You.
Avinu Malkeinu, act toward us kindly in accord with Your name.
Avinu Malkeinu, make this a good new year for us.
Avinu Malkeinu, annul every harsh decree against us.
Avinu Malkeinu, nullify the designs of our foes.
Avinu Malkeinu, frustrate the plots of our enemies.
Avinu Malkeinu, rid us of every oppressor and adversary.
Avinu Malkeinu, rid Your covenanted people of disease, war, hunger, captivity, and destruction.
Avinu Malkeinu, forgive and pardon all our sins.
Avinu Malkeinu, do not look toward our sins and transgressions; blot them out.
Avinu Malkeinu, return us to Your presence, fully penitent.
Avinu Malkeinu, send complete healing to the sick among Your people.
Avinu Malkeinu, remember us favorably.

Avinu Malkeinu, inscribe us for good in the Book of Life.
Avinu Malkeinu, inscribe us in the Book of Redemption.
Avinu Malkeinu, inscribe us in the Book of Sustenance.
Avinu Malkeinu, inscribe us in the Book of Merit.
Avinu Malkeinu, inscribe us in the Book of Forgiveness.

Avinu malkeinu, haḥazireinu bi-t'shuvah sh'leimah l'fanekha.
Avinu malkeinu, sh'laḥ r'fu·ah sh'leimah l'ḥolei ammekha.
Avinu malkeinu, zokhreinu b'zikkaron tov l'fanekha.
Avinu malkeinu, kotveinu b'seifer ḥayyim tovim.
Avinu malkeinu, kotveinu b'seifer g'ullah vi-shu·ah.
Avinu malkeinu, kotveinu b'seifer parnasah v'khalkalah.
Avinu malkeinu, kotveinu b'seifer z'khuyyot.
Avinu malkeinu, kotveinu b'seifer s'liḥah u-m'ḥilah.

Avinu Malkeinu, cause our salvation to flourish soon.
Avinu Malkeinu, cause Your people Israel to be exalted.
Avinu Malkeinu, raise up Your anointed with strength.
Avinu Malkeinu, hear our voice, be kind, sympathize with us.
Avinu Malkeinu, accept our prayer, willingly and lovingly.
Avinu Malkeinu, do not turn us away empty-handed.
Avinu Malkeinu, remember that we are but dust.
Avinu Malkeinu, have compassion for us, our infants, and our children.
Avinu Malkeinu, do this for the sake of those who were martyred for Your holy name.
Avinu Malkeinu, do this for the sake of those who were slaughtered for their exclusive devotion to You.

אָבִֽינוּ מַלְכֵּֽנוּ! עֲשֵׂה לְמַֽעַן בָּאֵי בָאֵשׁ וּבַמַּֽיִם עַל קִדּוּשׁ שְׁמֶֽךָ.

אָבִֽינוּ מַלְכֵּֽנוּ! עֲשֵׂה לְמַעַנְךָ אִם לֹא לְמַעֲנֵֽנוּ.

אָבִֽינוּ מַלְכֵּֽנוּ! חָנֵּֽנוּ וַעֲנֵֽנוּ, כִּי אֵין בָּֽנוּ מַעֲשִׂים, עֲשֵׂה עִמָּֽנוּ צְדָקָה וָחֶֽסֶד וְהוֹשִׁיעֵֽנוּ.

אָבִֽינוּ מַלְכֵּֽנוּ! חָטָֽאנוּ לְפָנֶֽיךָ.

בּוֹרְאֵֽנוּ מְבָרְכֵֽנוּ, אֵין לָֽנוּ מֶֽלֶךְ אֶלָּא אָֽתָּה.

גּוֹאֲלֵֽנוּ מִשְׁמְרֵֽנוּ, עֲשֵׂה עִמָּֽנוּ לְמַֽעַן שְׁמֶֽךָ.

דּוֹרְשֵֽׁנוּ מְפַרְנְסֵֽנוּ, חַדֵּשׁ עָלֵֽינוּ שָׁנָה טוֹבָה.

הוֹדִיעֵֽנוּ מוֹשִׁיעֵֽנוּ, בַּטֵּל מֵעָלֵֽינוּ כָּל־גְּזֵרוֹת קָשׁוֹת.

וָתִיקֵֽנוּ מְפַלְּטֵֽנוּ, בַּטֵּל מַחְשְׁבוֹת שׂוֹנְאֵֽינוּ.

זָנֵֽנוּ מְנוּסֵֽנוּ, כַּלֵּה דֶּֽבֶר וְחֶֽרֶב וְרָעָב וּשְׁבִי וּמַשְׁחִית וְעָוֹן וּשְׁמַד מִבְּנֵי בְרִיתֶֽךָ.

חוֹסֵֽנוּ מְחַיֵּֽינוּ, הָפֵר עֲצַת אוֹיְבֵֽינוּ.

טַהֲרֵֽנוּ מְרַחֲמֵֽנוּ, סְלַח וּמְחַל לְכָל־עֲוֹנוֹתֵֽינוּ.

יוֹצְרֵֽנוּ מְלַמְּדֵֽנוּ, הַחֲזִירֵֽנוּ בִּתְשׁוּבָה שְׁלֵמָה לְפָנֶֽיךָ.

כּוֹנְנֵֽנוּ מְכַלְכְּלֵֽנוּ, שְׁלַח רְפוּאָה שְׁלֵמָה לְחוֹלֵי עַמֶּֽךָ.

לְבוּבֵֽנוּ מְגַדְּלֵֽנוּ, זָכְרֵֽנוּ בְּזִכָּרוֹן טוֹב לְפָנֶֽיךָ.

אָבִֽינוּ מַלְכֵּֽנוּ, כָּתְבֵֽנוּ בְּסֵֽפֶר חַיִּים טוֹבִים.

אָבִֽינוּ מַלְכֵּֽנוּ, כָּתְבֵֽנוּ בְּסֵֽפֶר גְּאֻלָּה וִישׁוּעָה.

אָבִֽינוּ מַלְכֵּֽנוּ, כָּתְבֵֽנוּ בְּסֵֽפֶר פַּרְנָסָה וְכַלְכָּלָה.

אָבִֽינוּ מַלְכֵּֽנוּ, כָּתְבֵֽנוּ בְּסֵֽפֶר זְכֻיּוֹת.

אָבִֽינוּ מַלְכֵּֽנוּ, כָּתְבֵֽנוּ בְּסֵֽפֶר סְלִיחָה וּמְחִילָה.

AVINU MALKEINU אָבִֽינוּ מַלְכֵּֽנוּ. The images of God as "our father" (*avinu*) and "our sovereign" (*malkeinu*) are central to much of the High Holy Day liturgy. Yet these images may not have the same resonance for us as they once did for our ancestors. At the same time, the tradition is filled with many different metaphors for God. Therefore we offer this alternative version, featuring a variety of imagery. Its synonyms and metaphors for God are mostly taken from usages in other parts of the liturgy. Its alphabetical listing conveys the idea that we grasp the ineffable God through an infinite number of images.

Avinu Malkeinu, do this for the sake of those who went through fire and water to sanctify Your holy name.

    Avinu Malkeinu, do this for Your sake if not for ours.

Avinu Malkeinu, have mercy on us, answer us, for our deeds are insufficient; deal with us charitably and lovingly, and redeem us.

Avinu malkeinu, honneinu va-aneinu, ki ein banu ma·asim,
aseih immanu tz'dakah va-ḥesed v'hoshi·einu.

God's Names

God, we speak of You using a thousand images, trying to discover Your truth behind them. When we acknowledge the power that underlies creation, we address You as a sovereign. When we feel Your nearness and wonder that touch us, we know You as a parent. Help us as we use these names we give You to reach beyond them, and find Your presence in our lives.

—JONATHAN MAGONET

AVINU MALKEINU: ALTERNATE VERSION

Avinu Malkeinu, we have sinned in Your presence.

    Our creator, who blesses us, we have no sovereign but You.

Our redeemer, who guards us, act kindly, in keeping with Your name.

    You who seek us out and sustain us, make this new year a good one for us.

You who are our glory, our savior, annul every harsh decree against us.

    Ancient One, our rescuer, nullify the designs of our foes.

Provider, our refuge, rid Your covenanted people of disease, war, hunger, captivity, and destruction.

    You who are our strength, who gives us life, rid us of every oppressor and adversary.

You, who purify us, and have mercy on us, forgive and pardon all our sins.

    You who form us and instruct us, return us to Your presence, fully penitent.

You, who establish us, and provide for us, send complete healing to the sick among Your people.

    You, our beloved, who raised us, remember us favorably.

Avinu Malkeinu, inscribe us for good in the Book of Life.

Avinu Malkeinu, inscribe us in the Book of Redemption.

Avinu Malkeinu, inscribe us in the Book of Sustenance.

Avinu Malkeinu, inscribe us in the Book of Merit.

Avinu Malkeinu, inscribe us in the Book of Forgiveness.

Avinu malkeinu, kotveinu b'seifer ḥayyim tovim.
Avinu malkeinu, kotveinu b'seifer g'ullah vi-shu·ah.
Avinu malkeinu, kotveinu b'seifer parnasah v'khalkalah.
Avinu malkeinu, kotveinu b'seifer z'khuyyot.
Avinu malkeinu, kotveinu b'seifer s'liḥah u-m'ḥilah.

נוֹטְרֵנוּ מִפַּלְּטֵנוּ, הַצְמַח לָנוּ יְשׁוּעָה בְּקָרוֹב.

סוֹמְכֵנוּ מַצִּילֵנוּ, הָרֵם קֶרֶן יִשְׂרָאֵל עַמֶּךָ.

עֶזְרֵנוּ מַקְשִׁיבֵנוּ שְׁמַע קוֹלֵנוּ, חוּס וְרַחֵם עָלֵינוּ.

פּוֹדֵנוּ מְשַׁמְּרֵנוּ, קַבֵּל בְּרַחֲמִים וּבְרָצוֹן אֶת־תְּפִלָּתֵנוּ.

צוּרֵנוּ מְנוּסֵנוּ, נָא אַל תְּשִׁיבֵנוּ רֵיקָם מִלְּפָנֶיךָ.

קְדוֹשֵׁנוּ מַצְדִּיקֵנוּ, זְכוֹר כִּי עָפָר אֲנָחְנוּ.

רַחֲמֵנוּ מְחַיֵּינוּ, חֲמוֹל עָלֵינוּ וְעַל עוֹלָלֵינוּ וְטַפֵּינוּ.

שׁוֹמְרֵנוּ מוֹשִׁיעֵנוּ, עֲשֵׂה לְמַעַן הַהֲרוּגִים עַל שֵׁם קָדְשֶׁךָ.

תּוֹמְכֵנוּ מְסַעֲדֵנוּ, עֲשֵׂה לְמַעַנְךָ אִם לֹא לְמַעֲנֵנוּ.

אָבִינוּ מַלְכֵּנוּ, חָנֵּנוּ וַעֲנֵנוּ, כִּי אֵין בָּנוּ מַעֲשִׂים,

עֲשֵׂה עִמָּנוּ צְדָקָה וָחֶסֶד וְהוֹשִׁיעֵנוּ.

The ark is closed.

קַדִּישׁ שָׁלֵם

יִתְגַּדַּל וְיִתְקַדַּשׁ שְׁמֵהּ רַבָּא, בְּעָלְמָא דִּי בְרָא, כִּרְעוּתֵהּ, וְיַמְלִיךְ מַלְכוּתֵהּ בְּחַיֵּיכוֹן וּבְיוֹמֵיכוֹן וּבְחַיֵּי דְכָל־בֵּית יִשְׂרָאֵל, בַּעֲגָלָא וּבִזְמַן קָרִיב, וְאִמְרוּ אָמֵן.

יְהֵא שְׁמֵהּ רַבָּא מְבָרַךְ לְעָלַם וּלְעָלְמֵי עָלְמַיָּא.

יִתְבָּרַךְ וְיִשְׁתַּבַּח וְיִתְפָּאַר וְיִתְרוֹמַם וְיִתְנַשֵּׂא וְיִתְהַדָּר וְיִתְעַלֶּה וְיִתְהַלָּל שְׁמֵהּ דְּקֻדְשָׁא, בְּרִיךְ הוּא, לְעֵלָּא לְעֵלָּא מִכָּל־בִּרְכָתָא וְשִׁירָתָא תֻּשְׁבְּחָתָא וְנֶחָמָתָא דַּאֲמִירָן בְּעָלְמָא, וְאִמְרוּ אָמֵן.

תִּתְקַבֵּל צְלוֹתְהוֹן וּבָעוּתְהוֹן דְּכָל־יִשְׂרָאֵל קֳדָם אֲבוּהוֹן דִּי בִשְׁמַיָּא, וְאִמְרוּ אָמֵן.

יְהֵא שְׁלָמָא רַבָּא מִן שְׁמַיָּא וְחַיִּים עָלֵינוּ וְעַל כָּל־ יִשְׂרָאֵל, וְאִמְרוּ אָמֵן.

עֹשֶׂה שָׁלוֹם בִּמְרוֹמָיו הוּא יַעֲשֶׂה שָׁלוֹם עָלֵינוּ וְעַל כָּל־ יִשְׂרָאֵל [וְעַל כָּל־יוֹשְׁבֵי תֵבֵל], וְאִמְרוּ אָמֵן.

KADDISH SHALEM קַדִּישׁ שָׁלֵם is recited at the end of every worship service that features an Amidah. Its distinguishing sentence is the line תִּתְקַבֵּל צְלוֹתְהוֹן, "May the prayers . . . of all Israel be accepted."

PEACE . . . HARMONY שְׁלָמָא שָׁלוֹם. Like many traditional Jewish prayers, this one ends with thoughts of peace.

AND TO ALL WHO DWELL ON EARTH וְעַל כָּל־יוֹשְׁבֵי תֵבֵל. Our maḥzor follows the liturgical practice begun in some earlier Conservative movement prayerbooks by adding these words after mentioning Israel. (See, for example, the Shalom Rav prayer just recited at the end of the Amidah, page 218 above.)

At many moments in the liturgy, prayers focus on "Israel" or "the people Israel." The 20th-century philosopher Emmanuel Levinas pointed out that the designation "Israel" focuses our attention outward into the broader world of humanity, toward all those to whom we owe an ethical obligation of caring. In our prayers, we may move among various understandings of "Israel": Israel as Jewish community, Israel as national home, and Israel as symbolic of all those who uphold an ethical universe.

Our protector and savior, cause our salvation to flourish soon.
Our support and rescuer, cause Your people Israel to be exalted.
Our helper, who listens to us, hear our voice, be kind, sympathize with us.
Our redeemer, who watches over us, accept our prayer, willingly and lovingly.
Our fortress, who is our refuge, do not send us away empty-handed.
Holy One, who justifies us, remember that we are but dust.
Merciful One, who gives us life, have compassion for us, our infants, and our children.
Guardian, who grants us victory, do this for the sake of those who were martyred for Your holy name.
Benefactor, who provides for our welfare, do this for Your sake if not for ours.
Avinu Malkeinu, have mercy on us, answer us, for our deeds are insufficient; deal with us charitably and lovingly, and redeem us.

Avinu malkeinu, ḥonneinu va-aneinu, ki ein banu ma·asim, aseih immanu tz'dakah va-ḥesed v'hoshi·einu.

The ark is closed.

Kaddish Shalem

May God's great name be exalted and hallowed throughout the created world, as is God's wish. May God's sovereignty soon be established, in your lifetime and in your days, and in the days of all the House of Israel. And respond with: *Amen.*

May God's great name be acknowledged forever and ever!
Y'hei sh'meih rabba m'varakh l'alam u-l'almei almayya.

May the name of the Holy One be acknowledged and celebrated, lauded and worshipped, exalted and honored, extolled and acclaimed—though God, who is blessed, *b'rikh hu*, is truly far beyond all acknowledgment and praise, or any expressions of gratitude or consolation ever spoken in the world.
And respond with: *Amen.*

May the prayers and pleas of all Israel be accepted by their creator in heaven.
And respond with: *Amen.*

May abundant peace from heaven, and life, come to us and to all Israel.
And respond with: *Amen.*

May the One who brings harmony on high, bring harmony to us and to all Israel [and to all who dwell on earth]. And respond with: *Amen.*
Oseh shalom bi-m'romav hu ya·aseh shalom aleinu v'al kol yisra·el [v'al kol yosh'vei teiveil], v'imru amen.

עָלֵינוּ לְשַׁבֵּחַ לַאֲדוֹן הַכֹּל,
לָתֵת גְּדֻלָּה לְיוֹצֵר בְּרֵאשִׁית,
שֶׁלֹּא עָשָׂנוּ כְּגוֹיֵי הָאֲרָצוֹת,
וְלֹא שָׂמָנוּ כְּמִשְׁפְּחוֹת הָאֲדָמָה,
שֶׁלֹּא שָׂם חֶלְקֵנוּ כָּהֶם,
וְגֹרָלֵנוּ כְּכָל־הֲמוֹנָם.
וַאֲנַחְנוּ כּוֹרְעִים וּמִשְׁתַּחֲוִים וּמוֹדִים,
לִפְנֵי מֶלֶךְ מַלְכֵי הַמְּלָכִים, הַקָּדוֹשׁ בָּרוּךְ הוּא.
שֶׁהוּא נוֹטֶה שָׁמַיִם וְיֹסֵד אָרֶץ, וּמוֹשַׁב יְקָרוֹ בַּשָּׁמַיִם
מִמַּעַל, וּשְׁכִינַת עֻזּוֹ בְּגָבְהֵי מְרוֹמִים, הוּא אֱלֹהֵינוּ אֵין
עוֹד. אֱמֶת מַלְכֵּנוּ אֶפֶס זוּלָתוֹ, כַּכָּתוּב בְּתוֹרָתוֹ:
וְיָדַעְתָּ הַיּוֹם וַהֲשֵׁבֹתָ אֶל־לְבָבֶךָ, כִּי יהוה הוּא הָאֱלֹהִים
בַּשָּׁמַיִם מִמַּעַל, וְעַל הָאָרֶץ מִתָּחַת, אֵין עוֹד.

עַל כֵּן נְקַוֶּה לְּךָ יהוה אֱלֹהֵינוּ, לִרְאוֹת מְהֵרָה בְּתִפְאֶרֶת
עֻזֶּךָ, לְהַעֲבִיר גִּלּוּלִים מִן הָאָרֶץ וְהָאֱלִילִים כָּרוֹת יִכָּרֵתוּן,
לְתַקֵּן עוֹלָם בְּמַלְכוּת שַׁדַּי, וְכָל־בְּנֵי בָשָׂר יִקְרְאוּ בִשְׁמֶךָ,
לְהַפְנוֹת אֵלֶיךָ כָּל־רִשְׁעֵי אָרֶץ. יַכִּירוּ וְיֵדְעוּ כָּל־יוֹשְׁבֵי תֵבֵל,
כִּי לְךָ תִּכְרַע כָּל־בֶּרֶךְ, תִּשָּׁבַע כָּל־לָשׁוֹן. לְפָנֶיךָ יהוה
אֱלֹהֵינוּ יִכְרְעוּ וְיִפֹּלוּ, וְלִכְבוֹד שִׁמְךָ יְקָר יִתֵּנוּ. וִיקַבְּלוּ
כֻלָּם אֶת־עֹל מַלְכוּתֶךָ, וְתִמְלוֹךְ עֲלֵיהֶם מְהֵרָה לְעוֹלָם וָעֶד.
כִּי הַמַּלְכוּת שֶׁלְּךָ הִיא, וּלְעוֹלְמֵי עַד תִּמְלוֹךְ בְּכָבוֹד.
כַּכָּתוּב בְּתוֹרָתֶךָ: יהוה יִמְלֹךְ לְעֹלָם וָעֶד.
וְנֶאֱמַר: וְהָיָה יהוה לְמֶלֶךְ עַל כָּל־הָאָרֶץ,
בַּיּוֹם הַהוּא יִהְיֶה יהוה אֶחָד, וּשְׁמוֹ אֶחָד.

ALEINU עָלֵינוּ. This prayer was originally composed for, and recited during, the Malkhuyot/ מַלְכֻיּוֹת ("Sovereignty") section of the Rosh Hashanah Musaf service. Since the late Middle Ages, it has acquired a special pride of place in Ashkenazic liturgy and is recited as part of the conclusion of every service. It is customary to physically bow when we recite the line וַאֲנַחְנוּ כּוֹרְעִים (va-anaḥnu kor'im), "And so we bow."

KNOW THIS DAY וְיָדַעְתָּ הַיּוֹם. Deuteronomy 4:39, Moses' speech enunciating the meaning of God's revelation at Sinai.

ESTABLISHING IN THE WORLD THE SOVEREIGNTY OF THE ALMIGHTY לְתַקֵּן עוֹלָם בְּמַלְכוּת שַׁדַּי. Beginning in the 19th century, this phrase came to be seen as similar to Isaiah's call to be "a light unto the nations," and it was reinterpreted as a call to universal justice. In this vein, the phrase l'takken olam לְתַקֵּן עוֹלָם was understood to mean "to repair the world," to be partners with God in achieving a time of peace and righteousness. Even earlier, Maimonides (12th century) had argued that the single most important characteristic of God's sovereignty would be an end to one people dominating another. This paragraph emphasizes God's saving hand.

ADONAI WILL REIGN FOREVER AND EVER יהוה יִמְלֹךְ לְעֹלָם וָעֶד. From the Song at the Sea, Exodus 15:18.

ON THAT DAY ADONAI SHALL BE ONE בַּיּוֹם הַהוּא יִהְיֶה יהוה אֶחָד. Zechariah 14:9. In reciting the Sh'ma, we declare that God is one. Through our prayer we hope to make the world at one with God.

CONCLUDING PRAYERS

Aleinu

It is for us to praise the ruler of all, to acclaim the Creator, who has not made us merely a nation, nor formed us as all earthly families, nor given us an ordinary destiny.

ʄ And so we bow, acknowledging the supreme sovereign, the Holy One, who is praised—the One who spreads out the heavens and establishes the earth, whose glorious abode is in the highest heaven, whose powerful presence is in the loftiest heights. This is our God, none else; ours is the true sovereign, there is no other. As it is written in the Torah: "Know this day and take it to heart, that ADONAI is God in heaven above and on earth below; there is no other."

Aleinu l'shabbei·aḥ la-adon ha-kol, la-teit g'dullah l'yotzeir b'reishit,
she-lo asanu k'goyei ha-aratzot, v'lo samanu k'mishp'ḥot ha-adamah,
she-lo sam ḥelkeinu ka-hem, v'goraleinu k'khol hamonam.
ʄ Va-anaḥnu kor'im u-mishtaḥavim u-modim,
lifnei melekh malkhei ha-m'lakhim, ha-kadosh barukh hu.
She-hu noteh shamayim v'yoseid aretz, u-moshav y'karo ba-shamayim mi-ma·al,
u-sh'khinat uzzo b'govhei m'romim, hu eloheinu ein od. Emet malkeinu efes zulato,
ka-katuv b'torato: v'yadata ha-yom va-hasheivota el l'vavekha, ki Adonai hu ha-Elohim
ba-shamayim mi-ma·al, v'al ha-aretz mi-taḥat, ein od.

And so, ADONAI our God, we await You, that soon we may behold Your strength revealed in full glory, sweeping away the abominations of the earth, obliterating idols, establishing in the world the sovereignty of the Almighty. All flesh will call out Your name—even the wicked will turn toward You. Then all who live on earth will recognize and understand that to You alone knees must bend and allegiance be sworn. All will bow down and prostrate themselves before You, ADONAI our God, honor Your glorious name, and accept the obligation of Your sovereignty. May You soon rule over them forever and ever, for true dominion is Yours; You will rule in glory until the end of time.

As is written in Your Torah: "ADONAI will reign forever and ever." And as the prophet said: "ADONAI shall be acknowledged sovereign of all the earth. On that day ADONAI shall be one, and the name of God, one."

V'ne·emar: v'hayah Adonai l'melekh al kol ha-aretz,
ba-yom ha-hu yihyeh Adonai eḥad, u-sh'mo eḥad.

Some congregations recite Mourner's Kaddish after Aleinu; some, after the recitation of Psalm 27 on the next page.

קַדִּישׁ יָתוֹם

Mourners and those observing Yahrzeit:

יִתְגַּדַּל וְיִתְקַדַּשׁ שְׁמֵהּ רַבָּא,

בְּעָלְמָא דִּי בְרָא, כִּרְעוּתֵהּ,

וְיַמְלִיךְ מַלְכוּתֵהּ בְּחַיֵּיכוֹן וּבְיוֹמֵיכוֹן

וּבְחַיֵּי דְכָל־בֵּית יִשְׂרָאֵל,

בַּעֲגָלָא וּבִזְמַן קָרִיב,

וְאִמְרוּ אָמֵן.

Congregation and mourners:

יְהֵא שְׁמֵהּ רַבָּא מְבָרַךְ לְעָלַם וּלְעָלְמֵי עָלְמַיָּא.

Mourners:

יִתְבָּרַךְ וְיִשְׁתַּבַּח

וְיִתְפָּאַר וְיִתְרוֹמַם

וְיִתְנַשֵּׂא וְיִתְהַדָּר

וְיִתְעַלֶּה וְיִתְהַלָּל

שְׁמֵהּ דְּקֻדְשָׁא, בְּרִיךְ הוּא,

לְעֵלָּא לְעֵלָּא מִכָּל־בִּרְכָתָא וְשִׁירָתָא

תֻּשְׁבְּחָתָא וְנֶחֱמָתָא

דַּאֲמִירָן בְּעָלְמָא,

וְאִמְרוּ אָמֵן.

יְהֵא שְׁלָמָא רַבָּא מִן שְׁמַיָּא וְחַיִּים

עָלֵינוּ וְעַל כָּל־יִשְׂרָאֵל,

וְאִמְרוּ אָמֵן.

עֹשֶׂה שָׁלוֹם בִּמְרוֹמָיו

הוּא יַעֲשֶׂה שָׁלוֹם

עָלֵינוּ וְעַל כָּל־יִשְׂרָאֵל

[וְעַל כָּל־יוֹשְׁבֵי תֵבֵל],

וְאִמְרוּ אָמֵן.

KADDISH. The custom of mourners reciting Kaddish began sometime after the 11th century. Though its origin is obscure, it has become an essential element of Jewish prayer. It is not a private prayer; rather, it is recited in community with a minyan present. In that context the mourner affirms that tragedy has not separated him or her from God or the Jewish people, and, in turn, the communal response then constitutes a way of acknowledging the mourner.

Grant that the memories of those who have gone before us be a source of strength for me and for everyone of the House of Israel. May the souls of our departed find peace in Your sheltering care, and may we all be blessed with peace, tranquility, and the fullness of life.

The Blessing of Memory

It is hard to sing of oneness when our world is not complete, when those who once brought wholeness to our life have gone, and nothing but memory can fill the emptiness their passing leaves behind.

But memory can tell us only what we were, in company with those we loved; it cannot help us find what each of us, alone, must now become. Yet no one is really alone; those who live no more echo still within our thoughts and words, and what they did is part of what we have become.

We do best homage to our dead when we live our lives most fully, even in the shadow of our loss. For each of our lives is worth the life of the whole world; in each one is the breath of the Divine. In affirming God we affirm the worth of each one whose life, now ended, brought us closer to the source of life, in whose unity no one is alone and every life finds purpose.

—CHAIM STERN

Some congregations recite Mourner's Kaddish after Aleinu; some, after the recitation of Psalm 27 on the next page.

Mourner's Kaddish

May God's great name be exalted and hallowed throughout the created world, as is God's wish. May God's sovereignty soon be established, in your lifetime and in your days, and in the days of all the House of Israel. And respond with: *Amen.*

May God's great name be acknowledged forever and ever!

May the name of the Holy One be acknowledged and celebrated, lauded and worshipped, exalted and honored, extolled and acclaimed—though God, who is blessed, *b'rikh hu*, is truly far beyond all acknowledgment and praise, or any expressions of gratitude or consolation ever spoken in the world. And respond with: *Amen.*

May abundant peace from heaven, and life, come to us and to all Israel. And respond with: *Amen.*

May the One who brings harmony on high, bring harmony to us and to all Israel [and to all who dwell on earth]. And respond with: *Amen.*

Mourners and those observing Yahrzeit:
Yitgaddal v'yitkaddash sh'meih rabba, b'alma di v'ra, ki-r'uteih, v'yamlikh malkhuteih b'ḥayyeikhon u-v'yomeikhon u-v'ḥayyei d'khol beit yisra·el, ba-agala u-viz'man kariv, v'imru amen.

Congregation and mourners:
Y'hei sh'meih rabba m'varakh l'alam u-l'almei almayya.

Mourners:
Yitbarakh v'yishtabbaḥ v'yitpa·ar v'yitromam v'yitnassei v'yit·haddar v'yit·alleh v'yit·hallal sh'meih d'kudsha, b'rikh hu, l'eilla l'eilla mi-kol birkhata v'shirata tushb'ḥata v'neḥamata da-amiran b'alma, v'imru amen.

Y'hei sh'lama rabba min sh'mayya v'ḥayyim aleinu v'al kol yisra·el, v'imru amen.

Oseh shalom bi-m'romav hu ya·aseh shalom aleinu v'al kol yisra·el [v'al kol yosh'vei teiveil], v'imru amen.

לְדָוִד.

יהוה אוֹרִי וְיִשְׁעִי מִמִּי אִירָא,
יהוה מָעוֹז־חַיַּי מִמִּי אֶפְחָד.
בִּקְרֹב עָלַי מְרֵעִים לֶאֱכֹל אֶת־בְּשָׂרִי,
צָרַי וְאֹיְבַי לִי הֵמָּה כָשְׁלוּ וְנָפָלוּ.
אִם־תַּחֲנֶה עָלַי מַחֲנֶה לֹא־יִירָא לִבִּי,
אִם־תָּקוּם עָלַי מִלְחָמָה בְּזֹאת אֲנִי בוֹטֵחַ.
אַחַת שָׁאַלְתִּי מֵאֵת־יהוה, אוֹתָהּ אֲבַקֵּשׁ,
שִׁבְתִּי בְּבֵית־יהוה, כָּל־יְמֵי חַיַּי
לַחֲזוֹת בְּנֹעַם־יהוה וּלְבַקֵּר בְּהֵיכָלוֹ.
כִּי יִצְפְּנֵנִי בְּסֻכֹּה בְּיוֹם רָעָה,
יַסְתִּרֵנִי בְּסֵתֶר אָהֳלוֹ, בְּצוּר יְרוֹמְמֵנִי.
וְעַתָּה יָרוּם רֹאשִׁי עַל אֹיְבַי סְבִיבוֹתַי
וְאֶזְבְּחָה בְאָהֳלוֹ זִבְחֵי תְרוּעָה,
אָשִׁירָה וַאֲזַמְּרָה לַיהוה.
שְׁמַע־יהוה קוֹלִי אֶקְרָא, וְחָנֵּנִי וַעֲנֵנִי.
לְךָ אָמַר לִבִּי בַּקְּשׁוּ פָנָי, אֶת־פָּנֶיךָ יהוה אֲבַקֵּשׁ.
אַל־תַּסְתֵּר פָּנֶיךָ מִמֶּנִּי,
אַל תַּט־בְּאַף עַבְדֶּךָ, עֶזְרָתִי הָיִיתָ,
אַל־תִּטְּשֵׁנִי וְאַל־תַּעַזְבֵנִי אֱלֹהֵי יִשְׁעִי.
כִּי־אָבִי וְאִמִּי עֲזָבוּנִי, וַיהוה יַאַסְפֵנִי.
הוֹרֵנִי יהוה דַּרְכֶּךָ, וּנְחֵנִי בְּאֹרַח מִישׁוֹר, לְמַעַן שׁוֹרְרָי.
אַל־תִּתְּנֵנִי בְּנֶפֶשׁ צָרָי,
כִּי קָמוּ־בִי עֵדֵי־שֶׁקֶר וִיפֵחַ חָמָס.
◁ לוּלֵא הֶאֱמַנְתִּי, לִרְאוֹת בְּטוּב־יהוה בְּאֶרֶץ חַיִּים.
קַוֵּה אֶל־יהוה, חֲזַק וְיַאֲמֵץ לִבֶּךָ וְקַוֵּה אֶל־יהוה. תהלים כז

Some congregations recite Mourner's Kaddish (previous page) after the recitation of this psalm.

PSALM 27 is recited on each of the ten days from Rosh Hashanah to Yom Kippur. It has also become customary to recite it during the entire month before Rosh Hashanah, in preparation for the High Holy Days. In mystical Jewish tradition, the days of judgment are extended through the seventh day of Sukkot, known as Hoshana Rabbah, and so the psalm is recited until then.

Psalm 27 expresses two opposite feelings, each of which may be felt on this day. From the very beginning, the psalmist expresses absolute faith in God, culminating in the striking sentence: "Though my father and mother abandon me, Adonai will gather me in." But at the same time, the psalmist experiences God's absence—the speaker longs to "see God," yet receives no response to this longing. The poem's last line leaves us with a thin, consoling thread of hope, making us realize, perhaps, how much our lives depend faith.

DO NOT HIDE YOUR FACE FROM ME אַל־תַּסְתֵּר פָּנֶיךָ מִמֶּנִּי. "Face" suggests "presence"; the concrete metaphor serving the poet more than the abstract sense behind it. The speaker desperately seeks God's face (a privilege denied Moses). The practical manifestation of God's turning away would be the abandonment of the person to the enemies gathered about. (*adapted from Robert Alter*)

IF I COULD ONLY TRUST לוּלֵא הֶאֱמַנְתִּי. This is the only verse in the psalm that has no parallel. It is as if the speaker's voice simply trails off and then hears an inner voice calling: קַוֵּה אֶל־יהוה, "place your hope in Adonai." Or, perhaps someone else, in turn, urges the despairing supplicant to continue trusting that God will respond and asks that the person not lose faith.

Seeking God

"One thing I ask of Adonai—this I seek"
—The Hebrew pronoun *oto* can either mean "this" or it can refer back to "Adonai," making the seeking of God the object of the sentence. That is how the Ḥasidic master Levi Yitzḥak of Berditchev understood this verse. He would take it to mean, "One thing I ask of Adonai: to be able to seek Adonai all the days of my life and to sit in God's *sukkah*." Rabbi Levi Yitzḥak's teaching is that all the days of our lives should be constituted by a searching for God. Through the continuous search and passion manifested in a life of holiness, we can have a taste of what it means to dwell in God's house, to behold God's splendor, and to be with God in God's sanctuary.

A Psalm for the Season of Repentance—Psalm 27

A PSALM OF DAVID.

ADONAI is my light and my help. Whom shall I fear?
ADONAI is the stronghold of my life. Whom shall I dread?
When evil people assail me to devour my flesh
it is they, my enemies and those who besiege me,
who stumble and fall.
Should an armed camp be arrayed against me,
my heart would show no fear;
should they war against me, of this I would be sure.

One thing I ask of ADONAI—this I seek:
to dwell in the House of God all the days of my life,
to behold God's beauty and visit in God's sanctuary.

Aḥat sha·alti mei·eit Adonai, otah avakkeish
shivti b'veit Adonai, kol y'mei ḥayyai
la-ḥazot b'no·am Adonai u-l'vakkeir b'heikhalo.

Were God to hide me in God's *sukkah* on the calamitous day,
were God to enfold me in the secret recesses of God's tent,
I would be raised up in a protecting fort.
Now, I raise my head above the enemies that surround me,
and come with offerings, amidst trumpet blasts, to God's tent,
chanting and singing praise to ADONAI.
ADONAI, hear my voice as I cry out;
be gracious to me, and answer me.
It is You of whom my heart said, "Seek my face!"
It is Your presence that I seek, ADONAI.
Do not hide Your face from me; do not act angrily toward me.
You have always been my help; do not forsake me;
do not abandon me, my God, my deliverer.
Though my father and mother abandon me,
ADONAI will gather me in.
Show me Your way, ADONAI, and lead me on a straight path
despite those arrayed against me.
Do not hand me over to the grasp of those who besiege me;
for false witnesses and those who seek ill have risen against me.

If only I could trust that I would see God's goodness
in the land of the living . . .
Place your hope in ADONAI.
Be strong, take courage, and place your hope in ADONAI.

Some congregations recite Mourner's Kaddish (previous page) after the recitation of this psalm.

בְּטֶרֶם כָּל־יְצִיר נִבְרָא.   אֲדוֹן עוֹלָם אֲשֶׁר מָלַךְ,

אֲזַי מֶלֶךְ שְׁמוֹ נִקְרָא.   לְעֵת נַעֲשָׂה בְחֶפְצוֹ כֹּל,

לְבַדּוֹ יִמְלוֹךְ נוֹרָא.   וְאַחֲרֵי כִּכְלוֹת הַכֹּל,

וְהוּא יִהְיֶה, בְּתִפְאָרָה.   וְהוּא הָיָה, וְהוּא הֹוֶה,

לְהַמְשִׁיל לוֹ לְהַחְבִּירָה.   וְהוּא אֶחָד וְאֵין שֵׁנִי,

וְלוֹ הָעֹז וְהַמִּשְׂרָה.   בְּלִי רֵאשִׁית בְּלִי תַכְלִית,

וְצוּר חֶבְלִי בְּעֵת צָרָה.   וְהוּא אֵלִי וְחַי גֹּאֲלִי,

מְנָת כּוֹסִי בְּיוֹם אֶקְרָא.   וְהוּא נִסִּי וּמָנוֹס לִי,

בְּעֵת אִישָׁן וְאָעִירָה.   בְּיָדוֹ אַפְקִיד רוּחִי,

יְהֹוָה לִי וְלֹא אִירָא.   וְעִם רוּחִי גְוִיָּתִי,

ADON OLAM אֲדוֹן עוֹלָם. It is unclear who authored this thousand-year-old poem, but it appears in the beginning of the morning service, at the conclusion of Musaf (additional) services, and also at the end of evening services in both the Ashkenazic and Sephardic liturgies. The latter version contains several more verses than are found in the former, which is presented here.

Adon Olam

This poem is the statement of an individual—all of it is written in the first-person singular—and is the expression of a person's feelings about God. Beginning with the exalted God of eternity, the Creator of all—majestic and inspiring—the poet moves to the personal God of the individual who cares for human beings at times of woe and into whose hand we can commit our lives, bodies, and souls, and thus have no fear. God the transcendent and the exalted is also God the immanent, who cares for each individual. The poet seems to have created an entire poem based upon an idea expressed in the Book of Psalms:

"Who is like Adonai our God,
who though enthroned on high,
yet bends to see what is below" (Psalm 113:5–6).
—REUVEN HAMMER
(adapted)

ADON OLAM

Before creation shaped the world,
 eternally God reigned alone;
but only with creation done
 could God as Sovereign be known.
When all is ended, God alone
 will reign in awesome majesty.
God was, God is, always will be
 glorious in eternity.
God is unique and without peer,
 with none at all to be compared.
Without beginning, endlessly,
 God's vast dominion is not shared.
But still—my God, my only hope,
 my one true refuge in distress,
my shelter sure, my cup of life,
 with goodness real and limitless.
I place my spirit in God's care;
 my body too can feel God near.
When I sleep, as when I wake,
 God is with me, I have no fear.

Adon olam asher malakh   b'terem kol y'tzir nivra.
L'eit na·asah v'ḥeftzo kol   azai melekh sh'mo nikra.
V'aḥarei ki-kh'lot ha-kol   l'vaddo yimlokh nora
V'hu hayah v'hu hoveh   v'hu yihyeh b'tifarah.
V'hu eḥad v'ein sheni   l'hamshil lo l'haḥbirah.
B'li reishit b'li takhlit   v'lo ha-oz v'ha-misrah.
V'hu eli v'ḥai go·ali   v'tzur ḥevli b'eit tzarah.
V'hu nissi u-manos li   m'nat kosi b'yom ekra.
B'yado afkid ruḥi   b'eit ishan v'a·irah
V'im ruḥi g'viyyati   Adonai li v'lo ira.

יִגְדַּל אֱלֹהִים חַי וְיִשְׁתַּבַּח,
נִמְצָא וְאֵין עֵת אֶל מְצִיאוּתוֹ.
אֶחָד וְאֵין יָחִיד כְּיִחוּדוֹ,
נֶעְלָם, וְגַם אֵין סוֹף לְאַחְדּוּתוֹ.

אֵין לוֹ דְּמוּת הַגּוּף וְאֵינוֹ גוּף,
לֹא נַעֲרוֹךְ אֵלָיו קְדֻשָּׁתוֹ.
קַדְמוֹן לְכָל־דָּבָר אֲשֶׁר נִבְרָא,
רִאשׁוֹן וְאֵין רֵאשִׁית לְרֵאשִׁיתוֹ.

הִנּוֹ אֲדוֹן עוֹלָם וְכָל־נוֹצָר
יוֹרֶה גְדֻלָּתוֹ וּמַלְכוּתוֹ.
שֶׁפַע נְבוּאָתוֹ נְתָנוֹ
אֶל אַנְשֵׁי סְגֻלָּתוֹ וְתִפְאַרְתּוֹ.

לֹא קָם בְּיִשְׂרָאֵל כְּמֹשֶׁה עוֹד
נָבִיא וּמַבִּיט אֶת־תְּמוּנָתוֹ.
תּוֹרַת אֱמֶת נָתַן לְעַמּוֹ אֵל,
עַל יַד נְבִיאוֹ נֶאֱמַן בֵּיתוֹ.

לֹא יַחֲלִיף הָאֵל וְלֹא יָמִיר דָּתוֹ
לְעוֹלָמִים לְזוּלָתוֹ.
צוֹפֶה וְיוֹדֵעַ סְתָרֵינוּ,
מַבִּיט לְסוֹף דָּבָר בְּקַדְמָתוֹ.

גּוֹמֵל לְאִישׁ חֶסֶד כְּמִפְעָלוֹ,
נוֹתֵן לְרָשָׁע רַע כְּרִשְׁעָתוֹ.
יִשְׁלַח לְקֵץ יָמִין מְשִׁיחֵנוּ,
לִפְדּוֹת מְחַכֵּי קֵץ יְשׁוּעָתוֹ.

מֵתִים יְחַיֶּה אֵל בְּרוֹב חַסְדּוֹ,
בָּרוּךְ עֲדֵי עַד שֵׁם תְּהִלָּתוֹ.

YIGDAL יִגְדַּל. This song was written by Daniel ben Yehudah of Rome in the 14th century. It is a poetic summary of Maimonides' thirteen articles of faith.

Although it has become a popular hymn, recited both before the morning *b'rakhot* and at the conclusion of many services, there have always been objections to its use since many have argued that Judaism cannot be reduced to thirteen articles of faith. Some have altered the last lines, objecting to the affirmation of the resurrection of the dead.

In at least one of the cities of Hungary, the Hevra Kaddisha (Burial Society) would proceed from house to house on the seventh day of Adar, the legendary anniversary of the birth and death of Moses, and would sing *Yigdal*, repeating the last line declaiming the resurrection of the dead. (*Macy Nulman*)

בִּרְכַּת פְּרֵידָה
לְשָׁנָה טוֹבָה תֵּחָתֵמוּ.

God is Creator.
God is one, unique, eternal.
God is incomparable, with
   neither body nor form.
God precedes all and is
   beyond all.
Only God is to be
   worshiped.
The words of the prophets
   are true.
Moses was the spiritual
   ancestor of all the prophets.
The Torah was given to
   Moses.
The Torah is immutable.
God, as Creator, knows our
   deeds and thoughts.
Reward and punishment
   issue from God.
The Messiah will come.
God, in God's own time,
   will give life to the dead.

YIGDAL

Revere the living God, sing praises to God's name,
   both immanent and timeless, through eternity.
God's oneness is unique, no other can compare;
   unlimited and boundless is God's majesty.
No image can be seen, no form or body known;
   no mortal mind can fathom God's totality.
Before creation's start, the world as yet unformed,
   the living God endured in endless mystery.
The ruler of the world, whose creatures all declare
   the glory and the greatness of God's sovereignty.
God chose devoted servants, wise and faithful seers,
   and showered on each one the gift of prophecy.
In Israel none arose like Moses—touched by God—
   whose visions probed the limits of humanity.
The Torah, in its truth, God granted to us all,
   which loyal servant Moses taught us faithfully.
Our God will neither change nor modify God's law,
   its place remains established for eternity.
God penetrates our minds, the promptings of our hearts,
   anticipating actions that are yet to be.
God grants reward to those who lead a noble life,
   while punishing transgressors sinning wantonly.
Our Messiah, God will send, to greet the end of days,
   redeeming all who long for God to make them free.
In love our God restores the life to all our souls—
   may God be ever praised until eternity.

Yigdal Elohim ḥai v'yishtabbaḥ   *nimtza v'ein et el m'tzi·uto.*
   Eḥad v'ein yaḥid k'yiḥudo   *ne·lam, v'gam ein sof l'aḥduto.*
Ein lo d'mut ha-guf v'eino guf   *lo na·arokh eilav k'dushato.*
   Kadmon l'khol davar asher nivra   *rishon v'ein reishit l'reishito.*
Hinno adon olam, v'khol notzar   *yoreh g'dullato u-malkhuto.*
   Shefa n'vu·ato n'tano el   *anshei s'gullato v'tifarto.*
Lo kam b'yisra·el k'mosheh od   *navi u-mabbit et t'munato.*
   Torat emet natan l'ammo El   *al yad n'vi·o ne·eman beito.*
Lo yaḥalif ha-El v'lo yamir dato   *l'olamim l'zulato.*
   Tzofeh v'yodei·a s'tareinu   *mabbit l'sof davar b'kadmato.*
Gomel l'ish ḥesed k'mif·alo   *notein l'rasha ra k'rish·ato.*
   Yishlaḥ l'keitz yamin m'shiḥeinu   *lifdot m'ḥakkei keitz y'shu·ato.*
Meitim y'ḥayyeh El b'rov ḥasdo   *barukh adei ad shem t'hillato.*

Traditional High Holy Day Greeting

May you be sealed for a good year. *L'shanah tovah teiḥateimu.*

CONTINUATION OF THE

שחרית MORNING SERVICE
ליום כיפור OF YOM KIPPUR

We rise as the ark is opened.

כִּי שֵׁם יהוה אֶקְרָא, הָבוּ גֹדֶל לֵאלֹהֵינוּ.
אֲדֹנָי שְׂפָתַי תִּפְתָּח וּפִי יַגִּיד תְּהִלָּתֶךָ.

THE READER'S REPETITION OF THE AMIDAH. In the ancient and medieval synagogue, the silent Amidah was repeated aloud by the service leader since individual prayerbooks were virtually unknown through the first millennium. Even as manuscript copies became more available in the latter half of the Middle Ages, they were largely the possession of the wealthy, and most people still did not have access to their own. In that context, the reader's repetition was especially important and became the occasion for poetic embellishments of the standard prayer. Additions that are unique to Yom Kippur include the series of S'liḥot (Forgiveness) prayers and Viddui (Confession) prayers.

GOD OF SARAH . . . REBECCA . . . RACHEL AND . . . LEAH אֱלֹהֵי שָׂרָה, אֱלֹהֵי רִבְקָה, אֱלֹהֵי רָחֵל, וֵאלֹהֵי לֵאָה. Some congregations add the names of the four matriarchs at the beginning of this b'rakhah

Version with Patriarchs and Matriarchs:

בָּרוּךְ אַתָּה יהוה,
אֱלֹהֵינוּ וֵאלֹהֵי אֲבוֹתֵינוּ
[וְאִמּוֹתֵינוּ], אֱלֹהֵי אַבְרָהָם,
אֱלֹהֵי יִצְחָק, וֵאלֹהֵי יַעֲקֹב,
אֱלֹהֵי שָׂרָה, אֱלֹהֵי רִבְקָה,
אֱלֹהֵי רָחֵל, וֵאלֹהֵי לֵאָה,
הָאֵל הַגָּדוֹל הַגִּבּוֹר וְהַנּוֹרָא,
אֵל עֶלְיוֹן, גּוֹמֵל חֲסָדִים
טוֹבִים, וְקוֹנֵה הַכֹּל, וְזוֹכֵר
חַסְדֵי אָבוֹת [וְאִמָּהוֹת],
וּמֵבִיא גוֹאֵל לִבְנֵי בְנֵיהֶם
לְמַעַן שְׁמוֹ בְּאַהֲבָה.

Version with Patriarchs:

בָּרוּךְ אַתָּה יהוה,
אֱלֹהֵינוּ וֵאלֹהֵי אֲבוֹתֵינוּ,
אֱלֹהֵי אַבְרָהָם, אֱלֹהֵי
יִצְחָק, וֵאלֹהֵי יַעֲקֹב, הָאֵל
הַגָּדוֹל הַגִּבּוֹר וְהַנּוֹרָא,
אֵל עֶלְיוֹן, גּוֹמֵל חֲסָדִים
טוֹבִים, וְקוֹנֵה הַכֹּל, וְזוֹכֵר
חַסְדֵי אָבוֹת, וּמֵבִיא גוֹאֵל
לִבְנֵי בְנֵיהֶם לְמַעַן שְׁמוֹ
בְּאַהֲבָה.

מְסוֹד חֲכָמִים וּנְבוֹנִים,
וּמִלֶּמֶד דַּעַת מְבִינִים,
אֶפְתְּחָה פִּי בִּתְפִלָּה וּבְתַחֲנוּנִים,
לְחַלּוֹת וּלְחַנֵּן פְּנֵי מֶלֶךְ מָלֵא רַחֲמִים
מוֹחֵל וְסוֹלֵחַ לַעֲוֹנִים.

The ark is closed.

because of their significance as founders of our people, and as part of our effort to reclaim women's voices and to honor women as role models of faith.

INSPIRED BY THE INSIGHT מְסוֹד חֲכָמִים. These lines serve to introduce *piyyutim*, poetic additions to the Amidah, that address the holy day's themes. The reference to "sages" and "those who acquired wisdom" is a relic of the era when adding *piyyutim* was a matter of controversy, which prompted this appeal to the authority of those sages who permitted them. This introduction proclaimed that the Amidah's *piyyutim* are faithful to tradition, in that they are saturated with biblical and midrashic quotations. Its words continue to have meaning as the leader's personal plea for inspiration to guide the congregation appropriately—a poignant reminder of the responsibility that the leader takes on in representing the congregation before God.

REPETITION OF THE AMIDAH

Prayer of the Heart

The Ḥasidic master Mendel of Rymanov used to say that during the time he prayed the Amidah, all the people who had ever asked him to pray to God on their behalf would pass through his mind. Someone once asked how that was possible, since there was surely not enough time. Rabbi Mendel replied: "The need of every single one leaves a trace in my heart. In the hour of prayer I open my heart and say: 'Master of the universe, read what is written here!'"

God of Our Ancestors

As Jews on a religious quest, we recognize that we are, first of all, inheritors. Our spiritual vocabulary, our values, the lives that we lead are pathways built on markers laid down by those who came before us. Beginning on the roads that they surveyed, we are each able to proceed on our own religious journey. Surely, if we grow at all religiously, we will end up in a different place than they; but as we look back, we will always be reminded that it was possible for us to begin on our way because of the journey they undertook.

We rise as the ark is opened.

As I proclaim God's name, Adonai, exalt our God.

Adonai, open my lips that my mouth may speak Your praise.

First B'rakhah: Our Ancestors

Version with Patriarchs:

Barukh atah Adonai,
our God and God of our
   ancestors,
God of Abraham, God of
   Isaac, and God of Jacob,
great, mighty, awe-inspiring,
   transcendent God,
who acts with lovingkindness
   and creates all things,
who remembers the loving
   deeds of our ancestors,
and who will send a redeemer
   to their children's children
   with love
   for the sake of divine honor.

Version with Patriarchs and Matriarchs:

Barukh atah Adonai,
our God and God of our
   ancestors,
God of Abraham, God of
   Isaac, and God of Jacob,
God of Sarah, God of
   Rebecca, God of Rachel,
   and God of Leah,
great, mighty, awe-inspiring,
   transcendent God,
who acts with lovingkindness
   and creates all things,
who remembers the loving
   deeds of our ancestors,
and who will send a redeemer
   to their children's children
   with love
   for the sake of divine honor.

Inspired by the insight of sages
and the teachings of those who acquired wisdom,
I open my lips in prayer and supplication
to entreat the Merciful Sovereign,
who forgives and pardons sin.

The ark is closed.

זָכְרֵנוּ לְחַיִּים,
מֶלֶךְ חָפֵץ בַּחַיִּים,
וְכָתְבֵנוּ בְּסֵפֶר הַחַיִּים,
לְמַעַנְךָ אֱלֹהִים חַיִּים.

Version with Patriarchs and Matriarchs:	*Version with Patriarchs:*
מֶלֶךְ עוֹזֵר וּפוֹקֵד	מֶלֶךְ עוֹזֵר וּמוֹשִׁיעַ וּמָגֵן.
וּמוֹשִׁיעַ וּמָגֵן.	בָּרוּךְ אַתָּה יהוה, מָגֵן
בָּרוּךְ אַתָּה יהוה, מָגֵן	אַבְרָהָם.
אַבְרָהָם וּפוֹקֵד שָׂרָה.	

REMEMBER US זָכְרֵנוּ. This brief prayer is the first of four Amidah insertions which are added on the ten days of the High Holy Day season. Each of the four phrases of this short addition ends with the word חַיִּים (*hayyim*), "life." (This same word characterizes the three subsequent insertions, too.)

SHIELD OF ABRAHAM מָגֵן אַבְרָהָם. After Genesis 15:1.

GUARDIAN OF SARAH וּפוֹקֵד שָׂרָה. Or: "the One who remembered Sarah" (see Genesis 21:1). The Jewish people who stand here today are the fruit of the promise of God to Abraham and Sarah.

אַתָּה גִבּוֹר לְעוֹלָם אֲדֹנָי, מְחַיֵּה מֵתִים אַתָּה,
רַב לְהוֹשִׁיעַ.

מְכַלְכֵּל חַיִּים בְּחֶסֶד,
מְחַיֵּה מֵתִים בְּרַחֲמִים רַבִּים,
סוֹמֵךְ נוֹפְלִים, וְרוֹפֵא חוֹלִים,
וּמַתִּיר אֲסוּרִים,
וּמְקַיֵּם אֱמוּנָתוֹ לִישֵׁנֵי עָפָר.
מִי כָמוֹךָ בַּעַל גְּבוּרוֹת,
וּמִי דּוֹמֶה לָּךְ,
מֶלֶךְ מֵמִית וּמְחַיֶּה וּמַצְמִיחַ יְשׁוּעָה.

מִי כָמוֹךָ אַב הָרַחֲמִים, זוֹכֵר יְצוּרָיו לְחַיִּים בְּרַחֲמִים.

וְנֶאֱמָן אַתָּה לְהַחֲיוֹת מֵתִים. בָּרוּךְ אַתָּה יהוה, מְחַיֵּה
הַמֵּתִים.

Remember us for life,
Sovereign who delights in life,
and inscribe us in the Book of Life,
for Your sake, God of life.

Zokhreinu l'ḥayyim, melekh ḥafeitz ba-ḥayyim,
v'khotveinu b'seifer ha-ḥayyim, l'ma·ankha Elohim ḥayyim.

Version with Patriarchs:
You are the Sovereign who helps and saves and shields.
Barukh atah ADONAI,
Shield of Abraham.

Version with Patriarchs and Matriarchs:
You are the Sovereign who helps and guards, saves and shields.
Barukh atah ADONAI,
Shield of Abraham and Guardian of Sarah.

Second B'rakhah: God's Saving Care

You are mighty forever, ADONAI—
You give life to the dead;
great is Your saving power.

You sustain the living through love,
and with great mercy give life to the dead.
You support the falling, heal the sick,
loosen the chains of the bound,
and keep faith with those who sleep in the dust.
Who is like You, Almighty,
and who can be compared to You?—
Sovereign, who brings death and life,
and causes salvation to flourish.

M'khalkeil ḥayyim b'ḥesed, m'ḥayyeih meitim b'raḥamim rabbim,
someikh nof'lim, v'rofei ḥolim, u-mattir asurim, u-m'kayyeim emunato
li-sheinei afar. Mi khamokha ba·al g'vurot u-mi domeh lakh, melekh
meimit u-m'ḥayyeih u-matzmi·aḥ y'shu·ah.

Who is like You, source of compassion,
who remembers with compassion Your creatures for life?
Mi khamokha av ha-raḥamim, zokheir y'tzurav l'ḥayyim b'raḥamim.

You are faithful in bringing life to the dead. *Barukh atah*
ADONAI, who gives life to the dead.

יִמְלֹךְ יהוה לְעוֹלָם אֱלֹהַיִךְ צִיּוֹן לְדֹר וָדֹר, הַלְלוּ־יָהּ.
וְאַתָּה קָדוֹשׁ, יוֹשֵׁב תְּהִלּוֹת יִשְׂרָאֵל.

אֵל נָא:

א

אַתָּה הוּא אֱלֹהֵינוּ

בַּשָּׁמַיִם וּבָאָרֶץ   גִּבּוֹר וְנַעֲרָץ.
דָּגוּל מֵרְבָבָה   הוּא שָׂח וַיֶּהִי.
וְצִוָּה וְנִבְרָאוּ   זִכְרוֹ לָנֶצַח.
חַי עוֹלָמִים   טְהוֹר עֵינַיִם.
יוֹשֵׁב סֵתֶר   כִּתְרוֹ יְשׁוּעָה.
לְבוּשׁוֹ צְדָקָה   מַעֲטֵהוּ קִנְאָה.
נֶאְפָּד נְקָמָה   סִתְרוֹ יֹשֶׁר.
עֲצָתוֹ אֱמוּנָה   פְּעֻלָּתוֹ אֱמֶת.
צַדִּיק וְיָשָׁר   קָרוֹב לְקוֹרְאָיו בֶּאֱמֶת.
רָם וּמִתְנַשֵּׂא   שׁוֹכֵן שְׁחָקִים.
תּוֹלֶה אֶרֶץ עַל בְּלִימָה.
חַי וְקַיָּם נוֹרָא וּמָרוֹם וְקָדוֹשׁ.

ADONAI WILL REIGN יִמְלֹךְ יהוה. Psalm 146:10. After stating God's care for the poor, the psalmist concludes with this verse, describing God's eternal majesty.

AND YOU, O HOLY ONE, ARE ENTHRONED THROUGH THE PRAISES OF ISRAEL וְאַתָּה קָדוֹשׁ, יוֹשֵׁב תְּהִלּוֹת יִשְׂרָאֵל. Psalm 22:4. A midrash provocatively implies that God's dominion in the world is dependent on human activity: "'You are My witnesses,' says Adonai, 'and I am God' (Isaiah 43:12)—when you are My witnesses, I am God, but when you are not My witnesses, it is as if I am not God" (Sifrei Deuteronomy 346).

GOD, PLEASE HEAR US אֵל נָא (literally: "God, may it please You!"). These two words, *El na*, have served as an introduction to heartfelt prayer since biblical times, beginning with Moses' prayer for his sister, Miriam, when she was ill (Numbers 12:13), אֵל נָא רְפָא נָא לָהּ (*El na r'fa na lah*), "God, please heal her." Here, they serve as an introduction to the series of *piyyutim* that leads up to the Kedushah.

YOU ARE ADONAI OUR GOD אַתָּה הוּא אֱלֹהֵינוּ. This alphabetical *piyyut* is attributed to Elazar Kallir, the most well-known of the early masters of liturgical poetry, believed to have lived in the Land of Israel in the 5th or 6th century C.E.

IN HEAVEN AND ON EARTH בַּשָּׁמַיִם וּבָאָרֶץ. This *piyyut* juxtaposes God's closeness to us and God's distance from us. God is dramatically more powerful than any earthly entity, but at the same time, God showers constant attention on the world, without which it would cease to exist.

CROWNED WITH SALVATION כִּתְרוֹ יְשׁוּעָה. This line and the next three lines, all using the metaphor of God's clothing, are based on Isaiah 59:17.

SUSPEND THE EARTH IN SPACE תּוֹלֶה אֶרֶץ עַל בְּלִימָה. This reference to Job 26:7 notes the traditional belief that in the absence of God's sustaining care, the earth would tumble into the abyss. Even with our sophisticated understanding of astrophysics today, the religious person continues to be amazed by the complexity of the forces holding the earth in its orbit.

Third B'rakhah: God's Holiness

ADONAI will reign forever; your God, O Zion, from generation to generation. Halleluyah!

Yimlokh Adonai l'olam, elohayikh tziyyon l'dor va-dor, hal'luyah.

And You, O Holy One, are enthroned through the praises of the people Israel.

THREE PIYYUTIM INTRODUCE THE KEDUSHAH
God, please hear us.

א

Many congregations recite this piyyut responsively:

You are our God	*in heaven and on earth—*
powerful and revered,	*celebrated by multitudes.*
You spoke, and the world	
came to be,	*commanded, and it was created.*
Your name endures forever;	*You are eternal.*
Perceiving perfectly	*You dwell in secret.*
Crowned with salvation,	*You are attired in righteousness,*
wrapped in zeal,	*and armed with retribution.*
Urging uprightness,	*You counsel faithfulness.*
Your actions are truthful,	*righteous and just.*
You are close to those who	
call honestly.	*Though elevated and exalted,*
You dwell in the heavens	*and suspend the earth in space.*
You live and endure,	*revered, exalted, and holy.*

El na.
Atah hu eloheinu
Ba-shamayim u-va-aretz   gibbor v'na·aratz.
Dagul mei-r'vavah   hu saḥ va-yehi.
V'tzivvah v'nivra·u   zikhro la-netzaḥ.
Ḥai olamim   t'hor einayim.
Yosheiv seiter   kitro y'shu·ah.
L'vusho tz'dakah   ma·ateihu kin·ah.
Nepad n'kamah   sitro yosher.
Atzato emunah   p'ullato emet.
Tzaddik v'yashar   karov l'kor'av be-emet.
Ram u-mitnassei   shokhein sh'ḥakim.
Toleh eretz al b'limah.   Ḥai v'kayyam nora u-marom v'kadosh.

ב

חַי עוֹלָמִים.	וּבְכֵן נְאַדֶּרְךָ
לְחַי עוֹלָמִים,	הָאַדֶּרֶת וְהָאֱמוּנָה
לְחַי עוֹלָמִים,	הַבִּינָה וְהַבְּרָכָה
לְחַי עוֹלָמִים,	הַגַּאֲוָה וְהַגְּדֻלָּה
לְחַי עוֹלָמִים,	הַדֵּעָה וְהַדִּבּוּר
לְחַי עוֹלָמִים,	הַהוֹד וְהֶהָדָר
לְחַי עוֹלָמִים,	הַוַּעַד וְהַוָּתִיקוּת
לְחַי עוֹלָמִים,	הַזֹּךְ וְהַזֹּהַר
לְחַי עוֹלָמִים,	הַחַיִל וְהַחֹסֶן
לְחַי עוֹלָמִים,	הַטֶּכֶס וְהַטֹּהַר
לְחַי עוֹלָמִים,	הַיִּחוּד וְהַיִּרְאָה
לְחַי עוֹלָמִים,	הַכֶּתֶר וְהַכָּבוֹד
לְחַי עוֹלָמִים,	הַלֶּקַח וְהַלִּבּוּב
לְחַי עוֹלָמִים,	הַמְּלוּכָה וְהַמֶּמְשָׁלָה
לְחַי עוֹלָמִים,	הַנּוֹי וְהַנֵּצַח
לְחַי עוֹלָמִים,	הַשִּׂגּוּי וְהַשֶּׂגֶב
לְחַי עוֹלָמִים,	הָעֹז וְהָעֲנָוָה
לְחַי עוֹלָמִים,	הַפְּדוּת וְהַפְּאֵר
לְחַי עוֹלָמִים,	הַצְּבִי וְהַצֶּדֶק
לְחַי עוֹלָמִים,	הַקְּרִיאָה וְהַקְּדֻשָּׁה
לְחַי עוֹלָמִים,	הָרֹן וְהָרוֹמֵמוּת
לְחַי עוֹלָמִים,	הַשִּׁיר וְהַשֶּׁבַח
לְחַי עוֹלָמִים.	הַתְּהִלָּה וְהַתִּפְאֶרֶת

AND SO וּבְכֵן (u-v'khein). This word serves to introduce piyyutim in a series.

TO THE ONE WHO GIVES LIFE TO THE WORLD לְחַי עוֹלָמִים. This piyyut, first found in the 6th-century mystical text Heikhalot Rabbati, exemplifies the style of the early Jewish mystics of the merkavah ("chariot") school of mysticism. These ecstatics used hymns such as this one to achieve a meditative state through which they could journey through the celestial sphere, to commune with God's presence and perceive God's chariot (as described by the prophet Ezekiel). This poem, referred to as the "Song of the Angels," utilizes numerous synonyms, arranged alphabetically. We presume that religious poems of this genre functioned as a mantra-like meditative device rather than conveying a precise meaning. In fact, the simplest meaning of this poem is not clear: are all the alphabetical attributes characteristics of God, or aspects of humanity that we dedicate to God? Perhaps the attributes fall into both categories—the best of our own characteristics are representations of the divine. In many Sephardic and Ḥasidic communities, this piyyut is recited every Shabbat.

And so, we will exalt You, the One who gives life to the world, by dedicating

power and faith	to the One who gives life to the world,
understanding and blessing	to the One who gives life to the world,
greatness and pride	to the One who gives life to the world,
knowledge and speech	to the One who gives life to the world,
splendor and magnificence	to the One who gives life to the world,
counsel and truth	to the One who gives life to the world,
luster and brilliance	to the One who gives life to the world,
vigor and might	to the One who gives life to the world,
purity and order	to the One who gives life to the world,
unity and awe	to the One who gives life to the world,
sovereignty and honor	to the One who gives life to the world,
wisdom and fascination	to the One who gives life to the world,
dominion and sovereignty	to the One who gives life to the world,
beauty and permanence	to the One who gives life to the world,
greatness and sublimity	to the One who gives life to the world,
strength and humility	to the One who gives life to the world,
redemption and glory	to the One who gives life to the world,
esteem and righteousness	to the One who gives life to the world,
holiness and calling	to the One who gives life to the world,
elevation and exultation	to the One who gives life to the world,
song and praise	to the One who gives life to the world,
adoration and grandeur	to the One who gives life to the world.

U-v'khein n'adderkha ḥai olamim.
Ha-adderet v'ha-emunah l'ḥai olamim.
Ha-ga·avah v'ha-g'dullah l'ḥai olamim.
Ha-hod v'he-hadar l'ḥai olamim.
Ha-zokh v'ha-zohar l'ḥai olamim.
Ha-tekhes v'ha-tohar l'ḥai olamim.
Ha-keter v'ha-kavod l'ḥai olamim.
Ha-m'lukhah v'ha-memshalah l'ḥai olamim.
Ha-siggui v'ha-segev l'ḥai olamim.
Ha-p'dut v'ha-p'er l'ḥai olamim.
Ha-k'ri·ah v'ha-k'dushah l'ḥai olamim.
Ha-shir v'ha-shevah l'ḥai olamim.

Ha-binah v'ha-b'rakhah l'ḥai olamim,
Ha-de·ah v'ha-dibbur l'ḥai olamim,
Ha-va·ad v'ha-vatikut l'ḥai olamim,
Ha-ḥayil v'ha-ḥosen l'ḥai olamim,
Ha-yiḥud v'ha-yir·ah l'ḥai olamim,
Ha-lekaḥ v'ha-libbuv l'ḥai olamim,
Ha-noy v'ha-netzaḥ l'ḥai olamim,
Ha-oz v'ha-anavah l'ḥai olamim,
Ha-tz'vi v'ha-tzedek l'ḥai olamim,
Ha-ron v'ha-romeimut l'ḥai olamim,
Ha-t'hillah v'ha-tif·eret l'ḥai olamim.

We recite each line and the leader repeats it.

ג

וּבְכֵן לְךָ הַכֹּל יַכְתִּירוּ
לְאֵל עוֹרֵךְ דִּין

לְבוֹחֵן לְבָבוֹת בְּיוֹם דִּין,   לְגוֹלֶה עֲמֻקוֹת בַּדִּין.

לְדוֹבֵר מֵישָׁרִים בְּיוֹם דִּין,   לְהוֹגֶה דֵעוֹת בַּדִּין.

לְוָתִיק וְעוֹשֶׂה חֶסֶד בְּיוֹם דִּין,   לְזוֹכֵר בְּרִיתוֹ בַּדִּין.

לְחוֹמֵל מַעֲשָׂיו בְּיוֹם דִּין,   לְטַהֵר חוֹסָיו בַּדִּין.

לְיוֹדֵעַ מַחֲשָׁבוֹת בְּיוֹם דִּין,   לְכוֹבֵשׁ כַּעֲסוֹ בַּדִּין.

לְלוֹבֵשׁ צְדָקוֹת בְּיוֹם דִּין,   לְמוֹחֵל עֲוֹנוֹת בַּדִּין.

לְנוֹרָא תְהִלּוֹת בְּיוֹם דִּין,   לְסוֹלֵחַ לַעֲמוּסָיו בַּדִּין.

לְעוֹנֶה לְקוֹרְאָיו בְּיוֹם דִּין,   לְפוֹעֵל רַחֲמָיו בַּדִּין.

לְצוֹפֶה נִסְתָּרוֹת בְּיוֹם דִּין,   לְקוֹנֶה עֲבָדָיו בַּדִּין.

לְרַחֵם עַמּוֹ בְּיוֹם דִּין,   לְשׁוֹמֵר אוֹהֲבָיו בַּדִּין.

לְתוֹמֵךְ תְּמִימָיו בְּיוֹם דִּין.

ARBITER OF JUSTICE עוֹרֵךְ דִּין. This short *piyyut* by Elazar Kallir (the Land of Israel, 5th–6th century) contains the first enunciation in the liturgy of the major High Holy Day theme of God as the judge of the world.

VOICE OF RIGHTEOUSNESS לְדוֹבֵר מֵישָׁרִים Isaiah 33:15, where the phrase refers to a righteous person (and not God). In the mind of the poet, righteous behavior is godly behavior.

WHO IS WISE AND ACTS LOVINGLY ON THE DAY OF JUDGMENT לְוָתִיק וְעוֹשֶׂה חֶסֶד בְּיוֹם דִּין. The Hebrew word *din*, translated here as "judgment" or "justice" depending on the context, is one of the most heavily weighted words in the Jewish tradition. It usually connotes God's quality of strict judgment and the insistence on holding us to high standards of behavior. Indeed, this *piyyut* begins with an imposing, even intimidating tone, but soon the theme of God's compassion enters. God's judgment is then depicted as tempered with love and therefore redemptive.

WHO REMEMBERS THE COVENANT WHILE DISPENSING JUSTICE לְזוֹכֵר בְּרִיתוֹ בַּדִּין. In the Book of Exodus, when God is enraged at the people Israel after the golden calf episode and declares an intention to destroy them, Moses reminds God of the covenant that God had established with Abraham, Isaac, and Jacob—and God relents (Exodus 32:13). Thus, reminding God of the covenant supports the argument that the people Israel must be judged for life in the coming year.

EXONERATES US לְסוֹלֵחַ לַעֲמוּסָיו. Literally, "forgives the carried ones." This is a reference to Isaiah 46:3, which uses a maternal image to describe God's relationship with Israel ("carried since the womb").

HOLDS CLOSE THOSE WHO SERVE GOD WITH JUSTICE לְקוֹנֶה עֲבָדָיו בַּדִּין. More literally, "who acquires servants via justice." When we act justly, we serve the Divine.

Angels and Humans

If God is continually surrounded by and praised by the perfect ministering angels, why would God delight in imperfect and mortal human beings? As the psalmist asked: "What are mortals, that You should be mindful of them?" (Psalm 8).

One answer, especially appropriate for the Days of Awe, is that God delights in human imperfection even more than in the perfection of divine beings, since only human beings have free will and can grow, develop, and change. It is our need to do *t'shuvah*, and our capacity for *t'shuvah*, that set us apart from the angelic realm and that earn us God's interest and admiration.

ג

We recite each line and the leader repeats it.

And so, let all crown You, Sovereign—
the ultimate arbiter of justice,

who probes all hearts on the Day of Judgment,
and reveals what is hidden, with justice;
> *who is the voice of truth on the Day of Judgment,*
> *and pronounces rules of justice;*

who is wise and acts lovingly on the Day of Judgment,
and remembers the covenant, while dispensing justice;
> *who has compassion for all creation on the Day of Judgment,*
> *and purifies the faithful with justice;*

who knows our thoughts on the Day of Judgment,
and overcomes anger with justice;
> *who is clothed in righteousness on the Day of Judgment,*
> *and whose forgiveness of wrongdoing is a hallmark of justice;*

who is revered in praises on the Day of Judgment,
and exonerates us as an exercise of justice;
> *who responds to those who cry out on the Day of Judgment,*
> *and demonstrates mercy in justice;*

who discerns all mysteries on the Day of Judgment,
and holds close those who serve God with justice;
> *who has compassion for the people Israel on the*
> *Day of Judgment,*
> *and guards those who love God, with justice;*

and who upholds those who trust wholeheartedly in the Divine,
on the Day of Judgment.

L'vokhein l'vavot b'yom din	*l'goleh amukkot ba-din.*
L'doveir meisharim b'yom din	*l'hogeh dei·ot ba-din.*
L'vatik v'oseh ḥesed b'yom din	*l'zokheir b'rito ba-din.*
L'ḥomeil ma·asav b'yom din	*l'taheir ḥosav ba-din.*
L'yodei·a maḥashavot b'yom din	*l'khoveish ka·aso ba-din.*
L'loveish tz'dakot b'yom din	*l'moḥeil avonot ba-din.*
L'nora t'hillot b'yom din	*l'solei·aḥ la-amusav ba-din.*
L'oneh l'kor'av b'yom din	*l'fo·eil raḥamav ba-din.*
L'tzofeh nistarot b'yom din	*l'koneh avadav ba-din.*
L'raḥeim ammo b'yom din	*l'shomeir ohavav ba-din.*
L'tomeikh t'mimav b'yom din.	

קְדֻשָּׁה

וּבְכֵן וּלְךָ תַעֲלֶה קְדֻשָּׁה,
כִּי אַתָּה אֱלֹהֵינוּ מֶלֶךְ מוֹחֵל וְסוֹלֵחַ.

נַעֲרִיצְךָ וְנַקְדִּישְׁךָ כְּסוֹד שִׂיחַ שַׂרְפֵי־קֹדֶשׁ הַמַּקְדִּישִׁים
שִׁמְךָ בַּקֹּדֶשׁ, כַּכָּתוּב עַל יַד נְבִיאֶךָ, וְקָרָא זֶה אֶל זֶה וְאָמַר:
**קָדוֹשׁ, קָדוֹשׁ, קָדוֹשׁ יהוה צְבָאוֹת,
מְלֹא כָל־הָאָרֶץ כְּבוֹדוֹ.**

כְּבוֹדוֹ מָלֵא עוֹלָם, מְשָׁרְתָיו שׁוֹאֲלִים זֶה לָזֶה אַיֵּה מְקוֹם
כְּבוֹדוֹ. לְעֻמָּתָם בָּרוּךְ יֹאמֵרוּ:
בָּרוּךְ כְּבוֹד־יהוה מִמְּקוֹמוֹ.

מִמְּקוֹמוֹ הוּא יִפֶן בְּרַחֲמִים, וְיָחֹן עַם הַמְיַחֲדִים שְׁמוֹ עֶרֶב
וָבֹקֶר בְּכָל־יוֹם תָּמִיד, פַּעֲמַיִם בְּאַהֲבָה שְׁמַע אוֹמְרִים:
שְׁמַע יִשְׂרָאֵל יהוה אֱלֹהֵינוּ יהוה אֶחָד.

הוּא אֱלֹהֵינוּ, הוּא אָבִינוּ, הוּא מַלְכֵּנוּ, הוּא מוֹשִׁיעֵנוּ,
וְהוּא יַשְׁמִיעֵנוּ בְּרַחֲמָיו שֵׁנִית לְעֵינֵי כָּל־חָי, לִהְיוֹת לָכֶם
לֵאלֹהִים:
אֲנִי יהוה אֱלֹהֵיכֶם.

אַדִּיר אַדִּירֵנוּ, יהוה אֲדֹנֵנוּ מָה־אַדִּיר שִׁמְךָ בְּכָל־הָאָרֶץ.
וְהָיָה יהוה לְמֶלֶךְ עַל כָּל־הָאָרֶץ, בַּיּוֹם הַהוּא יִהְיֶה יהוה
אֶחָד, וּשְׁמוֹ אֶחָד. וּבְדִבְרֵי קָדְשְׁךָ כָּתוּב לֵאמֹר:
יִמְלֹךְ יהוה לְעוֹלָם, אֱלֹהַיִךְ צִיּוֹן לְדֹר וָדֹר, הַלְלוּ־יָהּ.

לְדוֹר וָדוֹר נַגִּיד גָּדְלֶךָ, וּלְנֵצַח נְצָחִים קְדֻשָּׁתְךָ נַקְדִּישׁ.
וְשִׁבְחֲךָ אֱלֹהֵינוּ מִפִּינוּ לֹא יָמוּשׁ לְעוֹלָם וָעֶד, כִּי אֵל מֶלֶךְ
גָּדוֹל וְקָדוֹשׁ אָתָּה.

We are seated.

KEDUSHAH. The Kedushah is a poetic elaboration of the third b'rakhah of the Amidah, in which the congregation and the leader proclaim God's holiness responsively. Antiphonal proclamations of God's holiness such as this are referred to as *d'varim she-bik'dushah*, "sections of holiness," and are recited only in the presence of a minyan. In this ancient mystic prayer, we pattern our praise after the angelic glorification of God. The Kedushah occurs in many different versions, but always contains three biblical quotations: "Holy, holy, holy" (Isaiah 6:3), "Praised is Adonai's glory wherever God dwells" (Ezekiel 3:12), and "Adonai will reign forever" (Psalm 146:10). The prayers surrounding these verses vary. On weekdays, they are brief. On Shabbat and holy days, they are more elaborate. On Yom Kippur, the Kedushah at all services is recited in its most elaborate version, which during the year is reserved for the Musaf service on Shabbat and festivals.
(adapted from Reuven Hammer)

HOLY קָדוֹשׁ. These are the words uttered by the angels, which Isaiah recorded when he had an overwhelming experience of being in the very presence of God. Holiness is God's essential quality, of which we can partake when we dedicate ourselves to God and undertake to imitate the divine qualities of mercy, love, and justice.

ADONAI, OUR MASTER יהוה אֲדֹנֵנוּ. Psalm 8:2.

ADONAI SHALL BE ACKNOWLEDGED וְהָיָה יהוה לְמֶלֶךְ. Zechariah 14:9.

ADONAI SHALL REIGN FOREVER יִמְלֹךְ יהוה לְעוֹלָם. Psalm 146:10.

The Kedushah

Now, may our sanctification rise up to You,
for You, our God, are a forgiving and merciful sovereign.

Let us revere and hallow You with the mystic language of the heavenly
chorus who sanctify Your name in Your holy realm, as in Isaiah's vision,
Each cried out to the other:
"Holy, holy, holy is *Adonai Tz'va·ot*, the whole world is filled with God's
glory!"

Kadosh, kadosh, kadosh Adonai Tz'va·ot, m'lo khol ha-aretz k'vodo.

God's glory fills the universe. As one angelic chorus asks, "Where is the
place of God's glory?" another responds:
"Praised is Adonai's glory wherever God dwells."

Barukh k'vod Adonai mi-m'komo.

From where God dwells, may God turn with compassion toward the
people who twice each day, evening and morning, lovingly proclaim God's
oneness, reciting the Sh'ma: "Hear, O Israel, Adonai is our God, Adonai
alone."

Sh'ma yisra·el, Adonai eloheinu, Adonai eḥad.

The Holy One is our God, our creator, our sovereign, our redeemer. Yet
again, God will in mercy proclaim to us before all that lives:

*Hu eloheinu, hu avinu, hu malkeinu, hu moshi·einu, v'hu yashmi·einu b'raḥamav
sheinit l'einei kol ḥai, lihyot lakhem leilohim.*

"I, Adonai, am your God."

Ani Adonai eloheikhem.

Majesty, our majesty, Adonai, our master, how majestic is Your name
throughout the world!

Adonai shall be acknowledged sovereign of all the earth. On that day
Adonai shall be one, and the name of God, one.

As the psalmist sang:
Adonai will reign forever; your God, O Zion, from generation to
generation. Halleluyah!

Yimlokh Adonai l'olam, elohayikh tziyyon l'dor va-dor, hal'luyah.

From one generation to another we will declare Your greatness, and forever
sanctify You with words of holiness. Your praise will never leave our lips,
for You are God and Sovereign, great and holy.

We are seated.

חֲמֹל עַל מַעֲשֶׂיךָ
וְתִשְׂמַח בְּמַעֲשֶׂיךָ,
וְיֹאמְרוּ לְךָ חוֹסֶיךָ
בְּצַדֶּקְךָ עֲמוּסֶיךָ,
תִּקְדַּשׁ אָדוֹן עַל כָּל־מַעֲשֶׂיךָ.

וּבְכֵן תֵּן פַּחְדְּךָ יהוה אֱלֹהֵינוּ עַל כָּל־מַעֲשֶׂיךָ
וְאֵימָתְךָ עַל כָּל־מַה־שֶּׁבָּרֵאתָ,
וְיִירָאוּךָ כָּל־הַמַּעֲשִׂים
וְיִשְׁתַּחֲווּ לְפָנֶיךָ כָּל־הַבְּרוּאִים,
וְיֵעָשׂוּ כֻלָּם אֲגֻדָּה אֶחָת
לַעֲשׂוֹת רְצוֹנְךָ בְּלֵבָב שָׁלֵם,
כְּמוֹ שֶׁיָּדַעְנוּ יהוה אֱלֹהֵינוּ שֶׁהַשִּׁלְטוֹן לְפָנֶיךָ,
עֹז בְּיָדְךָ וּגְבוּרָה בִּימִינֶךָ,
וְשִׁמְךָ נוֹרָא עַל כָּל־מַה־שֶּׁבָּרֵאתָ.

וּבְכֵן תֵּן כָּבוֹד יהוה לְעַמֶּךָ
תְּהִלָּה לִירֵאֶיךָ וְתִקְוָה לְדוֹרְשֶׁיךָ
וּפִתְחוֹן פֶּה לַמְיַחֲלִים לָךְ,
שִׂמְחָה לְאַרְצֶךָ וְשָׂשׂוֹן לְעִירֶךָ,
וּצְמִיחַת קֶרֶן לְדָוִד עַבְדֶּךָ
וַעֲרִיכַת נֵר לְבֶן־יִשַׁי מְשִׁיחֶךָ,
בִּמְהֵרָה בְיָמֵינוּ.

וּבְכֵן צַדִּיקִים יִרְאוּ וְיִשְׂמָחוּ
וִישָׁרִים יַעֲלֹזוּ,
וַחֲסִידִים בְּרִנָּה יָגִילוּ,
וְעוֹלָתָה תִּקְפָּץ־פִּיהָ
וְכָל־הָרִשְׁעָה כֻּלָּהּ כְּעָשָׁן תִּכְלֶה,
כִּי תַעֲבִיר מֶמְשֶׁלֶת זָדוֹן מִן הָאָרֶץ.

U-V'KHEIN וּבְכֵן. These three paragraphs, which are all introduced by the same word, וּבְכֵן (u-v'khein), are ascribed by many scholars to the 2nd or 3rd century, and may constitute the earliest poetic additions to the Amidah.

Stages of redemption are described in this series of prayers. The first paragraph implores God to cause the entire world to live with reverence for God.

The second paragraph discusses not the universal, but the particular: the return of the people Israel to its land (and specifically to Jerusalem), and the kingship of David.

The third paragraph describes the rejoicing that will come to the righteous "when You remove the tyranny of arrogance from the earth" and God will rule alone over the entire world from Zion and Jerusalem. (adapted from Reuven Hammer)

God's Rule

And it shall come to pass in the end of days
that the mountain of the house of Adonai shall be firmly established
at the head of all the mountains;
it shall tower above the hills
and people shall flow to it.
And many nations shall go, and say, "Come, let us go up to the mountain of Adonai,
to the house of the God of Jacob
that God may teach us God's ways,
and that we may walk in God's paths;
for instruction shall go forth from Zion,
and the word of Adonai from Jerusalem."
God shall judge among many peoples,
and shall instruct the great nations however distant,
and they shall beat their swords into plowshares,
and their spears into pruning hooks;
nation shall not lift up sword against nation,
neither shall they learn war any more.
But all will sit under their vine and under their fig tree,
and none shall make them afraid;
for it it is *Adonai Tz'va·ot* who has spoken.
Though all nations may walk in the name of their gods,
we will walk in the name of Adonai our God,
forever and ever.

—MICAH 4:1–5

Have compassion on Your creation;
and rejoice in Your handiwork.
As You vindicate Your people,
all who trust in You will declare:
"Be sanctified, Lord, throughout Your creation."

U-v'khein—ADONAI our God,
instill Your awe in all You have made,
and fear of You in all You have created,
so that all You have fashioned revere You,
all You have created bow in recognition,
and all be bound together, carrying out Your will
   wholeheartedly.
For we know that true sovereignty is Yours,
power and strength are in Your hands,
and Your name is to be revered beyond any of Your creations.

U-v'khein—Bestow honor to Your people, ADONAI,
praise to those who revere You,
hope to those who seek You,
recognition to those who await You,
joy to Your land, and gladness to Your city.
Simḥah l'artzekha v'sason l'irekha
May the light of David, Your servant, dawn,
and the lamp of the son of Jesse, Your anointed,
be kindled speedily in our day.

U-v'khein—The righteous, beholding this, will rejoice,
the upright will be glad,
the pious will celebrate with song,
evil will be silenced,
and all wickedness will disappear like smoke,
when You remove the tyranny of arrogance from the earth.

וְתִמְלֹךְ אַתָּה יהוה לְבַדֶּךָ עַל כָּל־מַעֲשֶׂיךָ
בְּהַר צִיּוֹן מִשְׁכַּן כְּבוֹדֶךָ
וּבִירוּשָׁלַיִם עִיר קָדְשֶׁךָ,
כַּכָּתוּב בְּדִבְרֵי קָדְשֶׁךָ:
יִמְלֹךְ יהוה לְעוֹלָם, אֱלֹהַיִךְ צִיּוֹן לְדֹר וָדֹר, הַלְלוּ־יָהּ.

קָדוֹשׁ אַתָּה וְנוֹרָא שְׁמֶךָ
וְאֵין אֱלוֹהַּ מִבַּלְעָדֶיךָ,
כַּכָּתוּב: וַיִּגְבַּהּ יהוה צְבָאוֹת בַּמִּשְׁפָּט, וְהָאֵל הַקָּדוֹשׁ
נִקְדַּשׁ בִּצְדָקָה. בָּרוּךְ אַתָּה יהוה, הַמֶּלֶךְ הַקָּדוֹשׁ.

אַתָּה בְחַרְתָּנוּ מִכָּל־הָעַמִּים,
אָהַבְתָּ אוֹתָנוּ וְרָצִיתָ בָּנוּ,
וְרוֹמַמְתָּנוּ מִכָּל־הַלְּשׁוֹנוֹת,
וְקִדַּשְׁתָּנוּ בְּמִצְוֹתֶיךָ,
וְקֵרַבְתָּנוּ מַלְכֵּנוּ לַעֲבוֹדָתֶךָ,
וְשִׁמְךָ הַגָּדוֹל וְהַקָּדוֹשׁ עָלֵינוּ קָרָאתָ.

וַתִּתֶּן־לָנוּ יהוה אֱלֹהֵינוּ בְּאַהֲבָה אֶת־יוֹם [הַשַּׁבָּת הַזֶּה
לִקְדֻשָּׁה וְלִמְנוּחָה וְאֶת־יוֹם] הַכִּפּוּרִים הַזֶּה לִמְחִילָה
וְלִסְלִיחָה וּלְכַפָּרָה וְלִמְחָל־בּוֹ אֶת־כָּל־עֲוֹנוֹתֵינוּ
[בְּאַהֲבָה] מִקְרָא קֹדֶשׁ, זֵכֶר לִיצִיאַת מִצְרָיִם.

אֱלֹהֵינוּ וֵאלֹהֵי אֲבוֹתֵינוּ [וְאִמּוֹתֵינוּ], יַעֲלֶה וְיָבֹא, וְיַגִּיעַ
וְיֵרָאֶה, וְיֵרָצֶה וְיִשָּׁמַע, וְיִפָּקֵד וְיִזָּכֵר זִכְרוֹנֵנוּ וּפִקְדוֹנֵנוּ,
וְזִכְרוֹן אֲבוֹתֵינוּ [וְאִמּוֹתֵינוּ], וְזִכְרוֹן מָשִׁיחַ בֶּן־דָּוִד
עַבְדֶּךָ, וְזִכְרוֹן יְרוּשָׁלַיִם עִיר קָדְשֶׁךָ, וְזִכְרוֹן כָּל־עַמְּךָ בֵּית
יִשְׂרָאֵל לְפָנֶיךָ לִפְלֵיטָה לְטוֹבָה, לְחֵן וּלְחֶסֶד וּלְרַחֲמִים,
לְחַיִּים וּלְשָׁלוֹם, בְּיוֹם הַכִּפּוּרִים הַזֶּה.
זָכְרֵנוּ יהוה אֱלֹהֵינוּ בּוֹ לְטוֹבָה,   אָמֵן.
וּפָקְדֵנוּ בוֹ לִבְרָכָה,   אָמֵן.
וְהוֹשִׁיעֵנוּ בוֹ לְחַיִּים,   אָמֵן.
וּבִדְבַר יְשׁוּעָה וְרַחֲמִים חוּס וְחָנֵּנוּ, וְרַחֵם
עָלֵינוּ וְהוֹשִׁיעֵנוּ, כִּי אֵלֶיךָ עֵינֵינוּ, כִּי אֵל מֶלֶךְ
חַנּוּן וְרַחוּם אָתָּה.

ADONAI TZ'VA·OT WILL BE EXALTED וַיִּגְבַּהּ יהוה צְבָאוֹת, Isaiah 5:16. Isaiah depicts the terror of God's judgment, but in this liturgical context God's strict justice is seen as an element of awe-inspiring holiness.

HOLY SOVEREIGN הַמֶּלֶךְ הַקָּדוֹשׁ. This is one of several changes made to the text of the Amidah during the High Holy Day season. Throughout the year, the Kedushah concludes with the b'rakhah "Praised are You, Adonai, the holy God." On Rosh Hashanah, Yom Kippur, and the days between them, we substitute the word melekh, literally "King," for the word El, "God." Symbolically, Rosh Hashanah is the day of God's coronation—God became sovereign as the world came into being.

MAY THE THOUGHT OF US RISE UP AND REACH YOU יַעֲלֶה וְיָבֹא. This paragraph is added to the Amidah on Rosh Ḥodesh (the new moon), the pilgrimage festivals, Rosh Hashanah, and Yom Kippur, and the name of the festival is inserted in the prayer at the appropriate point. One mystical commentary (Etz Yosef, 19th-century Poland) suggests that the eight verbs that begin this section, and which ask that remembrance of us rise and be received, correspond to the seven heavenly realms through which we pray that our prayer penetrate, plus the highest realm where God dwells.

You alone, ADONAI, will rule all Your creation,
from Mount Zion, the dwelling-place of Your glory,
and from Jerusalem, Your holy city.
As it is written in the Book of Psalms:
"ADONAI will reign forever;
your God, O Zion, from generation to generation. Halleluyah!"

You are holy, and Your name is revered, for there is no God but You.
As Your prophet Isaiah wrote: "*Adonai Tz'va·ot* will be exalted through
justice, the holy God sanctified through righteousness."
Barukh atah ADONAI, the Holy Sovereign.

Fourth B'rakhah: The Holiness of Yom Kippur

You have chosen us among all peoples, loving us, wanting us.
You have distinguished us among all nations, making us holy through
Your commandments, drawing us close to Your service, and calling us
by Your great and holy name.

With love, You have bestowed on us, ADONAI our God, this [Shabbat,
for sanctity and rest, and this] Yom Kippur for pardon, forgiveness, and
atonement, that all our sins be forgiven [through Your love], a sacred
time, recalling the Exodus from Egypt.

Our God and God of our ancestors,
may the thought of us rise up and reach You.
Attend to us and accept us;
hear us and respond to us.
Keep us in mind,
and keep in mind the thought of our ancestors,
as well as the Messiah, the descendant of David;
Jerusalem, Your holy city;
and all Your people, the House of Israel.
On this Yom Kippur respond to us
with deliverance, goodness, compassion, love, life, and peace.

Remember us for good;   *Amen.*

respond to us with blessing;   *Amen.*

redeem us with life.   *Amen.*

Show us compassion and care with words of salvation and kindness;
have mercy on us and redeem us. Our eyes are turned to You, for You
are a compassionate and loving sovereign.

Some congregations omit S'liḥot in Shaḥarit and turn to Sh'ma Koleinu, page 262.

אֱלֹהֵינוּ וֵאלֹהֵי אֲבוֹתֵינוּ [וְאִמּוֹתֵינוּ]

אִם תָּעִינוּ לֹא תַתְעֵנוּ,

אִם שָׁגַגְנוּ לֹא תַשְׁלֵנוּ.

אִם רִחַקְנוּ קָרֵב נָא,

אִם קֵרַבְנוּ לֹא תִרְחָק.

אִם צָעַקְנוּ לֹא תַעְלִים,

אִם פָּשַׁעְנוּ לֹא תִפְרַע.

אִם עָוִינוּ לֹא תַסְתִּיר,

אִם סָרַרְנוּ לֹא תָסוּר.

אִם נָקַמְנוּ לֹא תִטֹּר,

אִם מָרִינוּ לֹא כִּמְרֵינוּ.

אִם לַצְנוּ לֹא תִלְחַם,

אִם כִּחַשְׁנוּ לֹא תְכַלֶּה.

אִם יָרַדְנוּ לֹא תַטְבִּיעַ,

אִם טָעִינוּ לֹא תְטַאטְאֵנוּ.

אִם חָבַלְנוּ לֹא תַחְבּוֹל,

אִם זַדְנוּ לֹא תִזְכּוֹר.

אִם וִכַּחְנוּ לֹא תוֹכִיחַ,

אִם הִרְשַׁעְנוּ לֹא תֶהְדּוֹף.

אִם דָּפַקְנוּ לֹא תִדְחֶה,

אִם גָּעַלְנוּ לֹא תִגְעַל.

אִם בָּאנוּ לֹא תִמְאַס,

אִם אָשַׁמְנוּ לֹא תְאַבֵּד.

IF WE HAVE ERRED אִם תָּעִינוּ. The form of this poem—with its repetitions, meter, and reverse alphabetical acrostic—gives this *piyyut* a decisive energy. So does the use of the stronger Hebrew expression לֹא *lo* ("do not") instead of the more natural אַל *al* (which would indicate a request, "please do not . . ."). The poem contains central themes of the S'liḥah: though we have sinned, God's mercy will overcome God's harsh judgment. The last line incorporates the word אָשַׁמְנוּ (*ashamnu*), "we have sinned," which is the first word of the confession we are about to recite.

S'LIḤOT: PRAYERS OF FORGIVENESS

S'liḥah

I expect nothing in return
—I love tranquility.
Even windswept chaff of
  quarrels
will weigh upon me
like a heavy oil press's
  plank.

But I'm open to everyone
and I can admit that I've
  erred
and by way of truth's light
  I rejoice in it.

I want to receive the
  truth from everyone—
and it is not my nature to
  hold on, but to listen.
After all, what is a
  human being but a
  misjudgment.
  —THE HAZON ISH
  (trans. Aubrey L. Glazer)

Some congregations omit S'liḥot in Shaḥarit and turn to Sh'ma Koleinu, page 262.

Our God and God of our ancestors:
If we have erred, do not send us away;
  if we have made mistakes, do not abandon us.
If we have distanced ourselves, come close;
  if we dare come close, do not be distant.
If we cry out, do not shut Your ears;
  if we have trespassed, do not punish us.
If we have transgressed, do not hide Yourself;
  if we have strayed, do not turn away from us.
If we have been vengeful, do not bear a grudge;
  if we have rebelled, do not deem us traitors.
If we have been insolent, do not battle us;
  if we have been quarrelsome, do not wipe us out.
If we have sunk to the depths, do not cause us to drown;
  if we have fallen short, do not sweep us aside.
If we have done harm, do not harm us;
  if we have acted with malice, do not recall it.
If we have been combative, do not upbraid us;
  if we have done evil, do not cast us to the wind.
If we call upon You, do not push us aside;
  if we are impure, do not abhor us.
If we approach You, do not disdain us;
  if we have sinned, do not do away with us.

אֵל, מֶלֶךְ יוֹשֵׁב עַל כִּסֵּא רַחֲמִים, מִתְנַהֵג בַּחֲסִידוּת, מוֹחֵל עֲוֹנוֹת עַמּוֹ, מַעֲבִיר רִאשׁוֹן רִאשׁוֹן, מַרְבֶּה מְחִילָה לְחַטָּאִים, וּסְלִיחָה לְפוֹשְׁעִים, עוֹשֶׂה צְדָקוֹת עִם כָּל־בָּשָׂר וָרוּחַ, לֹא כְרָעָתָם תִּגְמוֹל.

◁ אֵל, הוֹרֵיתָ לָּנוּ לוֹמַר שְׁלֹשׁ עֶשְׂרֵה, זְכָר־לָנוּ הַיּוֹם בְּרִית שְׁלֹשׁ עֶשְׂרֵה, כְּמוֹ שֶׁהוֹדַעְתָּ לֶעָנָו מִקֶּדֶם, כְּמוֹ שֶׁכָּתוּב: וַיֵּרֶד יהוה בֶּעָנָן, וַיִּתְיַצֵּב עִמּוֹ שָׁם, וַיִּקְרָא בְשֵׁם יהוה.

וַיַּעֲבֹר יהוה עַל־פָּנָיו וַיִּקְרָא:

יהוה יהוה, אֵל רַחוּם וְחַנּוּן, אֶרֶךְ אַפַּיִם, וְרַב־חֶסֶד וֶאֱמֶת. נֹצֵר חֶסֶד לָאֲלָפִים, נֹשֵׂא עָוֹן וָפֶשַׁע וְחַטָּאָה, וְנַקֵּה.

וְסָלַחְתָּ לַעֲוֹנֵנוּ וּלְחַטָּאתֵנוּ וּנְחַלְתָּנוּ.

Some customarily strike their heart when asking God to forgive and pardon:

סְלַח לָנוּ אָבִינוּ כִּי חָטָאנוּ,
מְחַל לָנוּ מַלְכֵּנוּ כִּי פָשָׁעְנוּ,
כִּי אַתָּה אֲדֹנָי טוֹב וְסַלָּח
וְרַב חֶסֶד לְכָל־קוֹרְאֶיךָ.

כַּפֵּר חֲטָאֵינוּ בַּיּוֹם הַזֶּה וְטַהֲרֵנוּ, כְּמָה שֶׁכָּתוּב: כִּי־בַיּוֹם הַזֶּה יְכַפֵּר עֲלֵיכֶם לְטַהֵר אֶתְכֶם, מִכֹּל חַטֹּאתֵיכֶם לִפְנֵי יהוה תִּטְהָרוּ. שַׂמְּחֵנוּ בְּבֵית תְּפִלָּתֶךָ, כְּמָה שֶׁכָּתוּב: כִּי בֵיתִי בֵּית־תְּפִלָּה יִקָּרֵא לְכָל־הָעַמִּים.

THE THIRTEEN ATTRIBUTES. God's forgiveness of the sin of the Golden Calf is highlighted in the Bible by God's revealing to Moses the fundamental attributes of God's nature: kindness and compassion. The forgiveness of Israel's terrible sin at the birth of the nation forms the basis of the liturgical appeal for God's forgiveness of the people Israel's sins today.

ONE BY ONE מַעֲבִיר רִאשׁוֹן רִאשׁוֹן. According to the Babylonian Talmud, God counts only one sin at a time (Rosh Hashanah 17a). If the totality of our sins were all counted together, we might be judged negatively; and so God forgives each sin, one by one.

FOR ON THIS DAY כִּי בַיּוֹם הַזֶּה. The quotations are from Leviticus 16:30 and Isaiah 56:7.

צָעַקְנוּ וְעָנִיתָ
לָחַשְׁנוּ וְשָׁמַעְתָּ
קִוִּינוּ וְהוֹשַׁעְתָּ
הֶחֱרַשְׁנוּ וְנִלְחַמְתָּ
הִמְרִינוּ וְנֶעֱלַמְתָּ

We cried out and You
  answered,
We meditated and You
  heard,
We hoped and You
  saved us,
We were silent and You
  fought our battles,
We rebelled and You
  disappeared.

—YANNAI

God, Sovereign who sits on a throne of mercy, acting with unbounded grace, forgiving the sins of Your people, one by one, as each comes before You, generously forgiving sinners and pardoning transgressors, acting charitably with every living thing: do not repay them for their misdeeds.

God, You taught us how to recite the thirteen attributes of Your name; remember the promise implied in these thirteen attributes, which You first revealed to Moses, the humble one, as it is written: God descended in a cloud and stood beside him, and he called the name ADONAI.

And ADONAI passed before him and called:

ADONAI, ADONAI, God, merciful and compassionate, patient, abounding in love and faithfulness, assuring love for thousands of generations, forgiving iniquity, transgression, and sin, and granting pardon.

Adonai, Adonai, El raḥum v'ḥannun, erekh appayim v'rav ḥesed ve-emet. Notzeir ḥesed la-alafim, nosei avon va-fesha v'ḥatta·ah v'nakkeih.

Forgive our transgressions and our sins; claim us for Your own.

Some customarily strike their heart when asking God to forgive and pardon:

Forgive us, our creator, for we have sinned;
pardon us, our sovereign, for we have transgressed—
for You, ADONAI, are kind and forgiving;
You act generously to all who call on You.

S'laḥ lanu avinu ki ḥatanu,
m'ḥal lanu malkeinu ki fashanu,
ki atah Adonai tov v'sallaḥ
v'rav ḥesed l'khol kor'ekha.

Grant atonement and purify us this day, as it is written in the Torah, "For on this day, atonement shall be made for you to purify you from all your transgressions. In the presence of ADONAI you shall be pure."
Make us joyful in Your house of prayer, as Isaiah prophesied, "For My house shall be called a house of prayer for all people."

שְׁמַע קוֹלֵנוּ, יהוה אֱלֹהֵינוּ, חוּס וְרַחֵם עָלֵינוּ,
וְקַבֵּל בְּרַחֲמִים וּבְרָצוֹן אֶת־תְּפִלָּתֵנוּ.

הֲשִׁיבֵנוּ יהוה אֵלֶיךָ וְנָשׁוּבָה, חַדֵּשׁ יָמֵינוּ כְּקֶדֶם.

אַל־תַּשְׁלִיכֵנוּ מִלְּפָנֶיךָ, וְרוּחַ קָדְשְׁךָ אַל־תִּקַּח מִמֶּנּוּ.

אַל־תַּשְׁלִיכֵנוּ לְעֵת זִקְנָה, כִּכְלוֹת כֹּחֵנוּ אַל־תַּעַזְבֵנוּ.

Said quietly:

אַל־תַּעַזְבֵנוּ, יהוה אֱלֹהֵינוּ, אַל־תִּרְחַק מִמֶּנּוּ.
עֲשֵׂה־עִמָּנוּ אוֹת לְטוֹבָה, וְיִרְאוּ שׂוֹנְאֵינוּ וְיֵבֹשׁוּ,
כִּי־אַתָּה יהוה עֲזַרְתָּנוּ וְנִחַמְתָּנוּ.

◁ אֲמָרֵינוּ הַאֲזִינָה יהוה, בִּינָה הֲגִיגֵנוּ. יִהְיוּ לְרָצוֹן
אִמְרֵי־פִינוּ וְהֶגְיוֹן לִבֵּנוּ לְפָנֶיךָ, יהוה צוּרֵנוּ וְגֹאֲלֵנוּ.
כִּי־לְךָ יהוה הוֹחַלְנוּ, אַתָּה תַעֲנֶה, אֲדֹנָי אֱלֹהֵינוּ.

The ark is closed.

אֱלֹהֵינוּ וֵאלֹהֵי אֲבוֹתֵינוּ [וְאִמּוֹתֵינוּ],
אַל תַּעַזְבֵנוּ
וְאַל תִּטְּשֵׁנוּ,
וְאַל תַּכְלִימֵנוּ
וְאַל תָּפֵר בְּרִיתְךָ אִתָּנוּ.
קָרְבֵנוּ לְתוֹרָתֶךָ,
לַמְּדֵנוּ מִצְוֹתֶיךָ,
הוֹרֵנוּ דְּרָכֶיךָ,
הַט לִבֵּנוּ לְיִרְאָה אֶת־שְׁמֶךָ,
וּמוֹל אֶת־לְבָבֵנוּ לְאַהֲבָתֶךָ,
וְנָשׁוּב אֵלֶיךָ בֶּאֱמֶת וּבְלֵב שָׁלֵם.
◁ וּלְמַעַן שִׁמְךָ הַגָּדוֹל תִּמְחַל וְתִסְלַח לַעֲוֹנֵנוּ,
כַּכָּתוּב בְּדִבְרֵי קָדְשֶׁךָ:
לְמַעַן־שִׁמְךָ יהוה,
וְסָלַחְתָּ לַעֲוֹנִי כִּי רַב־הוּא.

HEAR OUR VOICE שְׁמַע
קוֹלֵנוּ. The first sentence in this set of verses is a quotation from the concluding prayer of personal petition in the daily Amidah. It is typical of Jewish liturgy that before or after the main body of requests, there is a generalized plea that God hear our prayer. Sh'ma Koleinu ("Hear our voice") is a supplication that seeks to penetrate the silence surrounding us, to evoke a response from God, and to draw God into our prayer. "Hear our voice" may be among the most poignant words spoken in prayer.

The verses quoted here are Lamentations 5:21; Psalms 51:13; 71:9; 38:22; 86:17; 19:15; 5:2; 38:16. A millennium ago, the maḥzor's editors adapted the biblical text by changing singular wording to plural.

DO NOT ABANDON US
אַל־תַּעַזְבֵנוּ. This verse is only whispered, for we do not want to assert out loud even the possibility of abandonment. The whispering then extends to what follows—personal prayers that our plea may be heard.

MY SIN עֲוֹנִי. Though this entire prayer speaks in the plural, the verse from Psalm 25:11 is in the singular, as if to say that we each must eventually confront our own sinfulness. Some editions of the maḥzor change even this verse to the plural.

CULMINATION OF S'LIḤOT: HEAR OUR VOICE

The ark is opened. After the leader recites each verse, we repeat it.

Hear our voice, ADONAI our God, be kind, and have compassion for us.
Willingly and lovingly accept our prayer.

Turn us toward You, ADONAI, and we will return to You;
make our days seem fresh, as they once were.

Do not cast us away from You;
take not Your holy presence from us.

Do not cast us away as we grow old;
do not desert us as our energy wanes.

Sh'ma koleinu, Adonai eloheinu, ḥus v'raḥeim aleinu,
v'kabbeil b'raḥamim u-v'ratzon et t'fillateinu.
Hashiveinu Adonai eilekha v'nashuvah,
ḥaddeish yameinu k'kedem.
Al tashlikheinu mi-l'fanekha,
v'ru·aḥ kodsh'kha al tikkaḥ mimmenu.
Al tashlikheinu l'eit ziknah,
ki-kh'lot koḥeinu al ta·azveinu.

Said quietly:

Do not abandon us, ADONAI our God, do not distance Yourself from us.

Give us a signal of hope, so that our enemies will understand
and hesitate, knowing that You have been our help and comfort.

Hear our words, ADONAI, and consider our innermost thoughts.

May the words of our mouths and the meditations of our
hearts be acceptable to You, ADONAI, our rock and redeemer.

It is for You we wait; surely You will respond, ADONAI our God.

The ark is closed.

Our God and God of our ancestors, do not abandon us, do not forsake us, do not shame us, do not annul Your covenant with us. Draw us close to Your Torah, teach us Your mitzvot, show us Your ways. Open our hearts to revere Your name, circumcise our hearts to love You; then, we will turn to You, faithfully, with a perfect heart. And as befits Your own great name, pardon and forgive our sins, as the psalmist wrote: "For the sake of Your own name, forgive my sin, though it be great."

V'salaḥta la-avoni ki rav hu.

אֱלֹהֵינוּ וֵאלֹהֵי אֲבוֹתֵינוּ [וְאִמּוֹתֵינוּ],
סְלַח לָנוּ, מְחַל לָנוּ, כַּפֶּר־לָנוּ.

כִּי

אָנוּ עַמֶּךָ,   וְאַתָּה אֱלֹהֵינוּ,

אָנוּ בָנֶיךָ,   וְאַתָּה אָבִינוּ.

אָנוּ עֲבָדֶיךָ,   וְאַתָּה אֲדוֹנֵנוּ,

אָנוּ קְהָלֶךָ,   וְאַתָּה חֶלְקֵנוּ.

אָנוּ נַחֲלָתֶךָ,   וְאַתָּה גוֹרָלֵנוּ,

אָנוּ צֹאנֶךָ,   וְאַתָּה רוֹעֵנוּ.

אָנוּ כַרְמֶךָ,   וְאַתָּה נוֹטְרֵנוּ,

אָנוּ פְעֻלָּתֶךָ,   וְאַתָּה יוֹצְרֵנוּ.

אָנוּ רַעְיָתֶךָ,   וְאַתָּה דוֹדֵנוּ,

אָנוּ סְגֻלָּתֶךָ,   וְאַתָּה קְרוֹבֵנוּ.

אָנוּ עַמֶּךָ,   וְאַתָּה מַלְכֵּנוּ,

אָנוּ מַאֲמִירֶךָ,   וְאַתָּה מַאֲמִירֵנוּ.

וידוי

אָנוּ עַזֵּי פָנִים   וְאַתָּה רַחוּם וְחַנּוּן.

אָנוּ קְשֵׁי עֹרֶף   וְאַתָּה אֶרֶךְ אַפַּיִם.

אָנוּ מְלֵאֵי עָוֹן   וְאַתָּה מָלֵא רַחֲמִים.

אָנוּ יָמֵינוּ כְּצֵל עוֹבֵר   וְאַתָּה הוּא וּשְׁנוֹתֶיךָ לֹא יִתָּמּוּ.

אֱלֹהֵינוּ וֵאלֹהֵי אֲבוֹתֵינוּ [וְאִמּוֹתֵינוּ], תָּבוֹא לְפָנֶיךָ
תְּפִלָּתֵנוּ וְאַל תִּתְעַלַּם מִתְּחִנָּתֵנוּ, שֶׁאֵין אֲנַחְנוּ עַזֵּי פָנִים
וּקְשֵׁי עֹרֶף לוֹמַר לְפָנֶיךָ, יהוה אֱלֹהֵינוּ וֵאלֹהֵי אֲבוֹתֵינוּ
[וְאִמּוֹתֵינוּ], צַדִּיקִים אֲנַחְנוּ וְלֹא חָטָאנוּ,
אֲבָל אֲנַחְנוּ וַאֲבוֹתֵינוּ [וְאִמּוֹתֵינוּ] חָטָאנוּ.

WE ARE YOUR PEOPLE כִּי אָנוּ עַמֶּךָ. An early medieval poem, which expands on the verse from Song of Songs (2:16), "I am for my beloved and my beloved is mine." In this poem we emphasize our relatedness to God; in the next, we emphasize the utter difference between the human and the Divine.

A PASSING SHADOW כְּצֵל עוֹבֵר. Psalm 144:4.

FOR TIME WITHOUT END וּשְׁנוֹתֶיךָ לֹא יִתָּמּוּ. "Of old You established the earth; / the heavens are the work of Your hands. / They shall perish, but You shall endure; / they shall all wear out like a garment; / You change them like clothing and they pass away. / But You are the same, and Your years never end" (Psalm 102:26–28).

FOR WE, LIKE OUR ANCESTORS . . . HAVE SINNED אֲבָל אֲנַחְנוּ וַאֲבוֹתֵינוּ [וְאִמּוֹתֵינוּ] חָטָאנוּ aval anaḥnu va-avoteinu [v'immoteinu] ḥatanu. Some medieval commentators note that there is a measure of solace in remembering that our ancestors were imperfect but they were forgiven. Others object to the mention that our ancestors sinned, and so in some editions that phrase is omitted.

Sin and Repentance

No sin is so light that it may be overlooked; no sin is so heavy that one cannot repent of it.

—MOSES IBN EZRA

Facing Ourselves

There is a law which states, "You should not deceive your fellow" (Leviticus 19:11), but to be faithful to God is to go beyond the law— not even to deceive one's self.

—JULES HARLOW

Our God and God of our ancestors, forgive us, pardon us, grant us atonement.

For—

We are Your people,	and You are our God;
we are Your children	and You are our parent.
We are Your servants,	and You are our master;
we are Your congregation,	and You are our portion.
We are Your heritage,	and You are our destiny;
we are Your flock,	and You are our shepherd.
We are Your vineyard,	and You are our guardian;
we are Your creatures,	and You are our creator.
We are Your spouse,	and You are our beloved;
we are Your cherished ones,	and You are near to us.
We are Your people,	and You are our sovereign;
we are the ones You address,	and You are the One to whom we speak.

Ki

Anu ammekha,	*v'atah eloheinu,*
anu vanekha	*v'atah avinu.*
Anu avadekha	*v'atah adoneinu,*
anu k'halekha	*v'atah ḥelkeinu.*
Anu naḥalatekha	*v'atah goraleinu,*
anu tzonekha	*v'atah ro·einu.*
Anu kharmekha	*v'atah not'reinu,*
anu f'ullatekha,	*v'atah yotz'reinu.*
Anu ra·yatekha	*v'atah dodeinu,*
anu s'gullatekha	*v'atah k'roveinu.*
Anu ammekha	*v'atah malkeinu,*
anu ma·amirekha	*v'atah ma·amireinu.*

VIDDUI — PRAYERS OF CONFESSION

We are insolent,
    You are gracious and compassionate.
We are obstinate,
    You are patient.
We are sinful,
    You are merciful.
Our days are a passing shadow,
    but You are the One who truly is, for time without end.

Our God and God of our ancestors, hear our prayer, do not ignore our plea. Our God and God of our ancestors, we are neither so insolent nor so obstinate as to claim in Your presence that we are righteous, without sin; for we, like our ancestors who came before us, have sinned.

Customarily, we each strike our heart as we recite every phrase of this confession.

אָשַׁמְנוּ, בָּגַדְנוּ, גָּזַלְנוּ, דִּבַּרְנוּ דְפִי.
הֶעֱוִינוּ, וְהִרְשַׁעְנוּ, זַדְנוּ, חָמַסְנוּ, טָפַלְנוּ שֶׁקֶר.
יָעַצְנוּ רָע, כִּזַּבְנוּ, לַצְנוּ, מָרַדְנוּ, נִאַצְנוּ.
סָרַרְנוּ, עָוִינוּ, פָּשַׁעְנוּ, צָרַרְנוּ, קִשִּׁינוּ עְרֶף.
רָשַׁעְנוּ, שִׁחַתְנוּ, תִּעַבְנוּ, תָּעִינוּ, תִּעְתָּעְנוּ.

סַרְנוּ מִמִּצְוֹתֶיךָ וּמִמִּשְׁפָּטֶיךָ הַטּוֹבִים, וְלֹא שָׁוָה לָנוּ. וְאַתָּה צַדִּיק עַל כָּל־הַבָּא עָלֵינוּ, כִּי אֱמֶת עָשִׂיתָ וַאֲנַחְנוּ הִרְשָׁעְנוּ.

One or more of the following penitential prayers may be included.

א

הִרְשַׁעְנוּ וּפָשַׁעְנוּ, לָכֵן לֹא נוֹשָׁעְנוּ. וְתֵן בְּלִבֵּנוּ לַעֲזֹב דֶּרֶךְ רֶשַׁע וְחִישׁ לָנוּ יֶשַׁע, כַּכָּתוּב עַל יַד נְבִיאֶךָ: יַעֲזֹב רָשָׁע דַּרְכּוֹ, וְאִישׁ אָוֶן מַחְשְׁבֹתָיו, וְיָשֹׁב אֶל־יהוה וִירַחֲמֵהוּ, וְאֶל־אֱלֹהֵינוּ כִּי־יַרְבֶּה לִסְלוֹחַ.

ב

אֱלֹהֵינוּ וֵאלֹהֵי אֲבוֹתֵינוּ [וְאִמּוֹתֵינוּ], סְלַח וּמְחַל לַעֲוֹנוֹתֵינוּ בְּיוֹם [הַשַּׁבָּת הַזֶּה וּבְיוֹם] הַכִּפּוּרִים הַזֶּה. מְחֵה וְהַעֲבֵר פְּשָׁעֵינוּ וְחַטֹּאתֵינוּ מִנֶּגֶד עֵינֶיךָ, וְכֹף אֶת־ יִצְרֵנוּ לְהִשְׁתַּעְבֶּד־לָךְ, וְהַכְנַע עָרְפֵּנוּ לָשׁוּב אֵלֶיךָ, וְחַדֵּשׁ כִּלְיוֹתֵינוּ לִשְׁמוֹר פִּקּוּדֶיךָ, וּמוֹל אֶת־לְבָבֵנוּ לְאַהֲבָה וּלְיִרְאָה אֶת־שְׁמֶךָ, כַּכָּתוּב בְּתוֹרָתֶךָ: וּמָל יהוה אֱלֹהֶיךָ אֶת־לְבָבְךָ וְאֶת־לְבַב זַרְעֶךָ, לְאַהֲבָה אֶת־יהוה אֱלֹהֶיךָ בְּכָל־לְבָבְךָ וּבְכָל־נַפְשְׁךָ לְמַעַן חַיֶּיךָ.

STRIKE OUR HEART. The custom of striking our heart while confessing our sins is first mentioned in a midrash on Ecclesiastes 7:2 ("the living will lay it to heart"): "Rabbi Meir said: 'Why do people strike their hearts [in remorse for their sins]? Because the heart is the seat and source of sin'" (Ecclesiastes Rabbah).

ASHAMNU אָשַׁמְנוּ. The list is alphabetical, with the hope that it will jog our own processes of association and will help us find our own words to name our transgressions. We might concentrate on one particular fault in our lives.

WE BETRAY בָּגַדְנוּ. A sin is considered betrayal of God.

LET THE WICKED FORSAKE יַעֲזֹב רָשָׁע דַּרְכּוֹ. Isaiah 55:7.

BLOT OUT AND DISREGARD מְחֵה וְהַעֲבֵר. Both inner and outer parts of the body are mentioned in this prayer. Body and soul are intimately bound, as we seek to behave differently. It is as if we simultaneously ask the Creator to fashion for us a less sinful body as the home for our newly purified self.

CIRCUMCISE וּמָל. Deuteronomy 30:6. Circumcision is an act of completion and perfection. Removing the flesh—our sins, which mask our essential nature— reveals the true function of the heart: to lead us to a life of love, righteousness, and peace.

Jewish tradition requires a verbal confession— a confession in words— as part of the process of repentance. It is not enough simply to feel repentant or contrite, or to think thoughts of repentance. . . . But you can't confess in words without language, and there is no language without some kind of form, even if it's as rudimentary as a grammar or an alphabet. In this sense, the Ashamnu is language in its most pared-down, astringent form; the naked alphabet, as it were; the barest, most elemental expression of language. It is a list of sins whittled down to single words, and those single words go from *alef* to *tav*, relentlessly and inexorably. . . . The Viddui is alphabetical because it is about the confession of the totality of one's sins from *alef* to *tav*, from *alpha* to *omega*. . . . [You cannot] hide any sins or forget them or inadvertently skip one sin or another, just as in reciting the alphabet you cannot leave out a letter.

—DAVID STERN

The Shorter Confession—Ashamnu

Customarily, we each strike our heart as we recite every phrase of this confession.

We abuse, we betray, we are cruel, we destroy, we embitter, we falsify, we gossip, we hate, we insult, we jeer, we kill, we lie, we mock, we neglect, we oppress, we pervert, we quarrel, we rebel, we steal, we transgress, we are unkind, we are violent, we are wicked, we are extremists, we yearn to do evil, we are zealous for bad causes.

Ashamnu, bagadnu, gazalnu, dibbarnu dofi;
he·evinu, v'hirshanu, zadnu, ḥamasnu, tafalnu sheker;
ya·atznu ra, kizzavnu, latznu, maradnu, ni·atznu;
sararnu, avinu, pashanu, tzararnu, kishinu oref;
rashanu, shiḥatnu, ti·avnu, ta·inu, titanu.

We have turned from Your goodly laws and commandments, but it has not profited us. Surely, You are in the right with respect to all that comes upon us, for You have acted faithfully, but we have been in the wrong.

PENITENTIAL PRAYERS BEFORE THE GREAT CONFESSION

One or more of the following penitential prayers may be included.

א

We have done wrong and transgressed, and so we have not triumphed. Inspire our hearts to abandon the path of evil, and hasten our redemption. And so Your prophet Isaiah declared: "Let the wicked forsake their path, and the sinful their design. Let them return to ADONAI, who will show them compassion. Let them return to our God, who will surely forgive them."

ב

Our God and God of our ancestors,
forgive and pardon our sins
[on this Shabbat and] on this Day of Atonement.
Blot out and disregard our sins and errors;
subdue our instincts so that they may serve You.
Bend our stiffness so that we turn to You;
renew our passion for observing Your ordinances.
Circumcise our hearts to love and revere Your name,
as it is written in Your Torah: "Then ADONAI your God
will circumcise your heart and the hearts of your offspring
to love ADONAI your God with all your heart and all your soul,
that you may live."

ג

הַזְּדוֹנוֹת וְהַשְּׁגָגוֹת אַתָּה מַכִּיר. הָרָצוֹן וְהָאֹנֶס,
הַגְּלוּיִים וְהַנִּסְתָּרִים, לְפָנֶיךָ הֵם גְּלוּיִים וִידוּעִים.
מָה אָנוּ, מֶה חַיֵּינוּ, מֶה חַסְדֵּנוּ, מַה צִּדְקֵנוּ,
מַה יְשׁוּעֵנוּ, מַה כֹּחֵנוּ, מַה גְּבוּרָתֵנוּ.
מַה נֹּאמַר לְפָנֶיךָ יהוה אֱלֹהֵינוּ
וֵאלֹהֵי אֲבוֹתֵינוּ [וְאִמּוֹתֵינוּ].
הֲלֹא כָּל־הַגִּבּוֹרִים כְּאַיִן לְפָנֶיךָ,
וְאַנְשֵׁי הַשֵּׁם כְּלֹא הָיוּ,
וַחֲכָמִים כִּבְלִי מַדָּע,
וּנְבוֹנִים כִּבְלִי הַשְׂכֵּל,
כִּי רֹב מַעֲשֵׂיהֶם תֹּהוּ,
וִימֵי חַיֵּיהֶם הֶבֶל לְפָנֶיךָ.
וּמוֹתַר הָאָדָם מִן הַבְּהֵמָה אָיִן,
כִּי הַכֹּל הָבֶל.
מַה־נֹּאמַר לְפָנֶיךָ יוֹשֵׁב מָרוֹם,
וּמַה־נְּסַפֵּר לְפָנֶיךָ שׁוֹכֵן שְׁחָקִים.
הֲלֹא כָּל־הַנִּסְתָּרוֹת וְהַנִּגְלוֹת אַתָּה יוֹדֵעַ.

ד

שִׁמְךָ מֵעוֹלָם עוֹבֵר עַל פֶּשַׁע.
שַׁוְעָתֵנוּ תַּאֲזִין בְּעָמְדֵנוּ לְפָנֶיךָ בִּתְפִלָּה.
תַּעֲבֹר עַל פֶּשַׁע לְעַם שָׁבֵי פֶשַׁע.
תִּמְחֶה פְּשָׁעֵינוּ מִנֶּגֶד עֵינֶיךָ.

ה

אַתָּה יוֹדֵעַ רָזֵי עוֹלָם, וְתַעֲלוּמוֹת סִתְרֵי כָל־חָי.
אַתָּה חוֹפֵשׂ כָּל־חַדְרֵי בָטֶן, וּבוֹחֵן כְּלָיוֹת וָלֵב.
אֵין דָּבָר נֶעְלָם מִמֶּךָּ, וְאֵין נִסְתָּר מִנֶּגֶד עֵינֶיךָ.
וּבְכֵן יְהִי רָצוֹן מִלְּפָנֶיךָ יהוה אֱלֹהֵינוּ
וֵאלֹהֵי אֲבוֹתֵינוּ [וְאִמּוֹתֵינוּ]
שֶׁתִּסְלַח לָנוּ עַל כָּל־חַטֹּאתֵינוּ
וְתִמְחַל לָנוּ עַל כָּל־עֲוֹנוֹתֵינוּ
וּתְכַפֶּר־לָנוּ עַל כָּל־פְּשָׁעֵינוּ.

YOU RECOGNIZE אַתָּה מַכִּיר.
Our confession is not to
enlighten the High Court;
God already knows all
that we have done. Rather,
we recite these words to
proclaim in our own voice
that we acknowledge and
take responsibility for our
deeds.

WHAT ARE WE מָה אָנוּ. This
prayer, which originated
here in the Yom Kippur
liturgy, is now included in
the daily prayerbook, as
part of the introductory
morning service through-
out the year.

Our Sins

If I had to reduce the essential meaning of the vast religious panorama of the High Holy Days to just one word, I would select the word "responsibility." . . . The prayers, the sounding of the shofar, the fasting and the confession—all of it is based on the belief that we are responsible for our actions, accountable for our deeds, and judged for the things we do or fail to do.

This is one of the central, basic teachings of Judaism. You are a responsible human being. First and always, you are responsible for yourself.... What you do with your life, with your body and soul, your mind, your intelligence, your creative talents, all these are charged to your account. It is the height of irresponsibility— a sin—to neglect one's health and physical well-being; to disregard the nurture and cultivation of one's mind and spirit; to be indifferent to the needs of the soul and to deprive it of the nourishment which the religious life can provide. *V'al kullam*—for all these things a person is judged.

Judaism further teaches us that a person does not live alone in the world. . . . You are a part of a group, a people; you are part of humanity. You are therefore responsible for the welfare of your neighbor, whether the person is next door or a continent away. You are responsible for the well-being of your fellow Jews, wherever they may be . . . and charged to your account is your treatment of all human beings . . . the advantaged and the disadvantaged. *V'al kullam*—for all these things a person is judged.

—MAX ROUTTENBERG

ג

You recognize both our sins and our mistakes, acts of will
 and those committed under compulsion; public acts and
 private ones are equally revealed and known to You.
What are we? What is our life? Our goodness? Our righteousness? Our achievement? Our power? Our victories?
What shall we say in Your presence,
 ADONAI our God and God of our ancestors?
Heroes count as nothing in Your presence,
 famous people are as if they never existed,
 the wise seem ignorant,
 and clever ones as if they lack reason.
The sum of their acts is chaos;
 in Your presence the days of their lives are futile.
Human beings have no superiority over beasts;
 all life is vanity.
What can we say before You, You who live in the
 transcendent?
And what can we tell about ourselves to You who dwell
 on high?
You surely know both the secret and the revealed.

ד

You have always been known as the One who overlooks
 transgression.
Hear our cry, as we stand before You, in prayer.
Overlook the transgressions of a people turning from
 transgression.
Wipe away our transgressions from Your sight.

ה

You know the mysteries of the universe,
the deepest secrets of everyone alive.
You probe our innermost depths;
You examine our thoughts and feelings.
Nothing escapes You;
nothing is secret from You.
Therefore, may it be Your will,
our God and God of our ancestors,
to forgive us for all our sins,
to pardon us for all our iniquities,
and to grant us atonement for all our transgressions.

It is customary to strike one's heart when we say the words עַל חֵטְא שֶׁחָטָאנוּ.

עַל חֵטְא שֶׁחָטָאנוּ לְפָנֶיךָ בְּאֹנֶס וּבְרָצוֹן,

וְעַל חֵטְא שֶׁחָטָאנוּ לְפָנֶיךָ בְּאִמּוּץ הַלֵּב.

עַל חֵטְא שֶׁחָטָאנוּ לְפָנֶיךָ בִּבְלִי דָעַת,

וְעַל חֵטְא שֶׁחָטָאנוּ לְפָנֶיךָ בְּבִטּוּי שְׂפָתָיִם.

עַל חֵטְא שֶׁחָטָאנוּ לְפָנֶיךָ בְּגִלּוּי עֲרָיוֹת,

וְעַל חֵטְא שֶׁחָטָאנוּ לְפָנֶיךָ בְּגָלוּי וּבַסָּתֶר.

עַל חֵטְא שֶׁחָטָאנוּ לְפָנֶיךָ בְּדַעַת וּבְמִרְמָה,

וְעַל חֵטְא שֶׁחָטָאנוּ לְפָנֶיךָ בְּדִבּוּר פֶּה.

עַל חֵטְא שֶׁחָטָאנוּ לְפָנֶיךָ בְּהוֹנָאַת רֵעַ,

וְעַל חֵטְא שֶׁחָטָאנוּ לְפָנֶיךָ בְּהִרְהוֹר הַלֵּב.

עַל חֵטְא שֶׁחָטָאנוּ לְפָנֶיךָ בִּוְעִידַת זְנוּת,

וְעַל חֵטְא שֶׁחָטָאנוּ לְפָנֶיךָ בְּוִדּוּי פֶּה.

עַל חֵטְא שֶׁחָטָאנוּ לְפָנֶיךָ בְּזִלְזוּל הוֹרִים וּמוֹרִים,

וְעַל חֵטְא שֶׁחָטָאנוּ לְפָנֶיךָ בְּזָדוֹן וּבִשְׁגָגָה.

עַל חֵטְא שֶׁחָטָאנוּ לְפָנֶיךָ בְּחֹזֶק יָד,

וְעַל חֵטְא שֶׁחָטָאנוּ לְפָנֶיךָ בְּחִלּוּל הַשֵּׁם.

עַל חֵטְא שֶׁחָטָאנוּ לְפָנֶיךָ בְּטֻמְאַת שְׂפָתָיִם,

וְעַל חֵטְא שֶׁחָטָאנוּ לְפָנֶיךָ בְּטִפְּשׁוּת פֶּה.

◁ עַל חֵטְא שֶׁחָטָאנוּ לְפָנֶיךָ בְּיֵצֶר הָרָע,

וְעַל חֵטְא שֶׁחָטָאנוּ לְפָנֶיךָ בְּיוֹדְעִים וּבְלֹא יוֹדְעִים.

וְעַל כֻּלָּם, אֱלוֹהַּ סְלִיחוֹת, סְלַח לָנוּ, מְחַל לָנוּ, כַּפֶּר־לָנוּ.

עַל חֵטְא שֶׁחָטָאנוּ לְפָנֶיךָ בְּכַחַשׁ וּבְכָזָב,

וְעַל חֵטְא שֶׁחָטָאנוּ לְפָנֶיךָ בְּכַפַּת שֹׁחַד.

עַל חֵטְא שֶׁחָטָאנוּ לְפָנֶיךָ בְּלָצוֹן,

וְעַל חֵטְא שֶׁחָטָאנוּ לְפָנֶיךָ בִּלְשׁוֹן הָרָע.

עַל חֵטְא שֶׁחָטָאנוּ לְפָנֶיךָ בְּמַשָּׂא וּבְמַתָּן,

וְעַל חֵטְא שֶׁחָטָאנוּ לְפָנֶיךָ בְּמַאֲכָל וּבְמִשְׁתֶּה.

עַל חֵטְא שֶׁחָטָאנוּ לְפָנֶיךָ בְּנֶשֶׁךְ וּבְמַרְבִּית,

וְעַל חֵטְא שֶׁחָטָאנוּ לְפָנֶיךָ בִּנְטִיַּת גָּרוֹן.

THE LONGER CONFESSION.
Despite the double alpha-
betical acrostic in which
the sins are enumerated,
the Al Ḥet is not simply
a formal list. The sins it
enumerates are the stuff
of daily life, and they point
to our repeated moral
failures. It makes almost
no specific reference to
violations of the rituals of
Judaism. Such infractions as
the desecration of Shabbat
and festivals, and the failure
to abide by the disciplines
that invest our daily life
with sacred significance,
are categorized by the
Talmud as "sins between
people and God." It is taken
for granted that only sins
"between one person and
another" need to be de-
tailed (Babylonian Talmud,
Yoma 86b).

Amidst a community of
fellow imperfect humans,
we gain the courage to
confess our sins to God.
Knowing that it is God
whom we are facing, we are
called to a level of honesty
and truthfulness that is
greater than any inter-
mediary would demand.

The forty-four lines
included in the Al Ḥet
are an expansion of the
six lines that appear in
Saadiah Gaon's prayerbook
(10th century), the twelve
in Amram Gaon's (9th
century), and the twenty-
two in Maimonides' (12th
century).

The Longer Confession—Al Ḥet

It is customary to strike one's heart when we say the words "We have sinned."

Embarrassment not
only precedes religious
commitment; it is the
touchstone of religious
existence. . . . What the
world needs is a sense of
embarrassment. . . . We
are guilty of misunder-
standing the meaning of
existence; we are guilty
of distorting our goals
and misrepresenting our
souls. We are better than
our assertions, more
intricate, more pro-
found than our theories
maintain.

What is the truth
of being human? The
lack of pretension, the
acknowledgment of
opaqueness, shortsight-
edness, inadequacy.
But truth also demands
rising, striving, for the
goal is both within and
beyond us. The truth of
being human is gratitude;
its secret is appreciation.

—ABRAHAM JOSHUA
HESCHEL

We have sinned against You unwillingly and willingly,
   and we have sinned against You through hardening our hearts.
We have sinned against You thoughtlessly,
   and we have sinned against You in idle chatter.
We have sinned against You through sexual immorality,
   and we have sinned against You openly and in private.
We have sinned against You knowingly and deceitfully,
   and we have sinned against You by the way we talk.
We have sinned against You by defrauding others,
   and we have sinned against You in our innermost thoughts.
We have sinned against You through forbidden trysts,
   and we have sinned against You through empty confession.
We have sinned against You by scorning parents and teachers,
   and we have sinned against You purposely and by mistake.
We have sinned against You by resorting to violence,
   *and we have sinned against You by public desecration of
   Your name.*
We have sinned against You through foul speech,
   and we have sinned against You through foolish talk.
We have sinned against You through pursuing the impulse
to evil,
   and we have sinned against You wittingly and unwittingly.

*For all these sins, forgiving God, forgive us, pardon us,
grant us atonement.*

V'al kullam, elo·ah s'liḥot, s'laḥ lanu, m'ḥal lanu, kapper lanu.

We have sinned against You through denial and deceit,
   and we have sinned against You by taking bribes.
We have sinned against You by clever cynicism,
   and we have sinned against You by speaking ill of others.
We have sinned against You by the way we do business,
   and we have sinned against You in our eating and drinking.
We have sinned against You by greed and oppressive interest,
   and we have sinned against You through arrogance.

עַל חֵטְא שֶׁחָטָאנוּ לְפָנֶיךָ בְּשִׂיחַ שִׂפְתוֹתֵינוּ,
וְעַל חֵטְא שֶׁחָטָאנוּ לְפָנֶיךָ בְּשִׁקּוּר עָיִן.
▷ עַל חֵטְא שֶׁחָטָאנוּ לְפָנֶיךָ בְּעֵינַיִם רָמוֹת,
וְעַל חֵטְא שֶׁחָטָאנוּ לְפָנֶיךָ בְּעַזּוּת מֵצַח.

וְעַל כֻּלָּם, אֱלוֹהַּ סְלִיחוֹת, סְלַח לָנוּ, מְחַל לָנוּ, כַּפֶּר־לָנוּ.

עַל חֵטְא שֶׁחָטָאנוּ לְפָנֶיךָ בִּפְרִיקַת עֹל,
וְעַל חֵטְא שֶׁחָטָאנוּ לְפָנֶיךָ בִּפְלִילוּת.
עַל חֵטְא שֶׁחָטָאנוּ לְפָנֶיךָ בִּצְדִיַּת רֵעַ,
וְעַל חֵטְא שֶׁחָטָאנוּ לְפָנֶיךָ בְּצָרוּת עָיִן.
עַל חֵטְא שֶׁחָטָאנוּ לְפָנֶיךָ בְּקַלּוּת רֹאשׁ,
וְעַל חֵטְא שֶׁחָטָאנוּ לְפָנֶיךָ בְּקַשְׁיוּת עֹרֶף.
עַל חֵטְא שֶׁחָטָאנוּ לְפָנֶיךָ בְּרִיצַת רַגְלַיִם לְהָרַע,
וְעַל חֵטְא שֶׁחָטָאנוּ לְפָנֶיךָ בִּרְכִילוּת.
עַל חֵטְא שֶׁחָטָאנוּ לְפָנֶיךָ בִּשְׁבוּעַת שָׁוְא,
וְעַל חֵטְא שֶׁחָטָאנוּ לְפָנֶיךָ בְּשִׂנְאַת חִנָּם.
▷ עַל חֵטְא שֶׁחָטָאנוּ לְפָנֶיךָ בִּתְשׂוּמֶת־יָד,
וְעַל חֵטְא שֶׁחָטָאנוּ לְפָנֶיךָ בְּתִמְהוֹן לֵבָב.

וְעַל כֻּלָּם, אֱלוֹהַּ סְלִיחוֹת, סְלַח לָנוּ, מְחַל לָנוּ, כַּפֶּר־לָנוּ.

SELFISHNESS צָרוּת עָיִן, tzarut ayin. Literally, "narrowness of vision." Each of us is different and sees the world differently. Seeing the world through the perspective of the "other" is often the beginning of ethical wisdom.

CONFUSION תִּמָּהוֹן לֵבָב, timhon leivav. The formal confession of sins ends with a note about our internal confusion—and how that prevents us from acting properly. What we seek from the day is clarity about the direction of our lives.

אֱלֹהֵי עוֹלָם אַתָּה בָּרֵאתָ שָׁמַיִם
וָאֶרֶץ בְּאַהֲבָה,
יָצַרְתָּ צְמָחִים וְחַיּוֹת, וְנָפַחְתָּ נִשְׁמַת
חַיִּים בִּבְנֵי אָדָם.
נִבְרָאנוּ בְּקֶרֶב עוֹלָם נָקִי וְטָהוֹר,
וְכָעֵת הוּא נֶחֱרַס עַל־יָדֵינוּ.
לֹא עַל צִדְקוֹתֵינוּ אֲנַחְנוּ מַפִּילִים
תַּחֲנוּנֵינוּ לְפָנֶיךָ יְהֹוָה אֱלֹהֵינוּ,
כִּי אָשַׁמְנוּ, בִּזְבַּזְנוּ, וְגָרַמְנוּ נֶזֶק כַּבִּיר:
עַל חֵטְא שֶׁמִּלֵּאנוּ אֶרֶץ וְיַמִּים
בְּזֶבֶל וּבְאַשְׁפָּה,
עַל חֵטְא שֶׁהִשְׁמַדְנוּ לָנֶצַח חַיּוֹת
נִפְלָאוֹת שֶׁהִצַּלְתָּ מִמֵּי הַמַּבּוּל,
וְעַל חֵטְא שֶׁהִכְרַתְנוּ יְעָרוֹת
עֵצִים הַמְקַיְּמִים נֶפֶשׁ כָּל־חַי.
אָנָּא יְהֹוָה פְּקַח עֵינֵינוּ וְנִרְאֶה אֶת־
הוֹד יְצִירְתֶךָ,
אָז נְשַׁבֵּחֲךָ כְּמוֹ שֶׁכָּתוּב: מָה־רַבּוּ
מַעֲשֶׂיךָ יְהֹוָה, כֻּלָּם בְּחָכְמָה עָשִׂיתָ
מָלְאָה הָאָרֶץ קִנְיָנֶךָ.
הָסֵר אֶת־לֵב הָאֶבֶן מִבְּשָׂרֵנוּ, וְתֵן לֵב
בָּשָׂר בְּקִרְבֵּנוּ.
תֶּן לָנוּ חָכְמָה וְאֹמֶץ־לֵב לִשְׁמוֹר עַל
הָאָרֶץ מִתַּחַת הַשָּׁמַיִם.

Eternal God, You created the
heavens and earth in love.
You fashioned plants and
animals, breathing Your spirit
into humanity.
We were created amidst a clean and pure world, but it is now
degraded in our grasp.
Not on our own merits do we beseech You, Adonai our God,
for we have sinned, we have wasted, we have caused vast damage:

For the sin of filling the sea and land with filth and garbage;
for the sin of destroying species that You saved from the flood;
and for the sin of laying bare the forests and habitats that sustain life.

Please, God, open our eyes that we might see the splendor of Your
creation. Then we shall praise You, as it is written: "How great are
Your works, Adonai! You have made them all with wisdom; the earth
is filled with Your creations" (Psalm 104:24).

Remove the heart of stone from our flesh, and give us a feeling heart.
Grant us wisdom and determination to safeguard the earth beneath
the heavens.
—DANIEL NEVINS

We have sinned against You in everyday conversation,
*and we have sinned against You through conspiratorial
glances.*
We have sinned against You through condescension,
and we have sinned against You through stubbornness.

*For all these sins, forgiving God, forgive us, pardon us,
grant us atonement.*
V'al kullam, elo·ah s'liḥot, s'laḥ lanu, m'ḥal lanu, kapper lanu.

We have sinned against You by throwing off all restraint,
*and we have sinned against You by rashly judging
others.*
We have sinned against You by plotting against others,
and we have sinned against You through selfishness.
We have sinned against You through superficiality,
and we have sinned against You through stubbornness.
We have sinned against You by rushing to do evil,
and we have sinned against You through gossip.
We have sinned against You through empty promises,
*and we have sinned against You through baseless
hatred.*
We have sinned against You by betraying trust,
*and we have sinned against You by succumbing to
confusion.*

*For all these sins, forgiving God, forgive us, pardon us,
grant us atonement.*
V'al kullam, elo·ah s'liḥot, s'laḥ lanu, m'ḥal lanu, kapper lanu.

וְעַל מִצְוֹת עֲשֵׂה וְעַל מִצְוֹת לֹא תַעֲשֶׂה. בֵּין שֶׁיֵּשׁ־בָּהּ
קוּם עֲשֵׂה וּבֵין שֶׁאֵין בָּהּ קוּם עֲשֵׂה, אֶת־הַגְּלוּיִים לָנוּ וְאֶת־
שֶׁאֵינָם גְּלוּיִים לָנוּ. אֶת־הַגְּלוּיִים לָנוּ כְּבָר אֲמַרְנוּם
לְפָנֶיךָ וְהוֹדִינוּ לְךָ עֲלֵיהֶם, וְאֶת־שֶׁאֵינָם גְּלוּיִים לָנוּ לְפָנֶיךָ
הֵם גְּלוּיִים וִידוּעִים, כַּדָּבָר שֶׁנֶּאֱמַר: ◁ הַנִּסְתָּרֹת לַיהוה
אֱלֹהֵינוּ, וְהַנִּגְלֹת לָנוּ וּלְבָנֵינוּ עַד־עוֹלָם לַעֲשׂוֹת אֶת־כָּל־
דִּבְרֵי הַתּוֹרָה הַזֹּאת.

חַנָּה, מָרַת רוּחַ הִתְפַּלְלָה לְפָנֶיךָ, וַיִּמָּלֵא לִבָּהּ בֶּכִי, וְקוֹלָהּ
לֹא יִשָּׁמֵע, אַךְ בָּחַנְתָּ אֶת־לִבָּהּ וַתִּפֶן אֵלֶיהָ. עֲנֵה לָנוּ
בְּעֵת בַּקָּשָׁתֵנוּ כְּשֶׁעָנִיתָ לִתְחִנַּת הָאִשָּׁה בְּשִׁילֹה וְנִזְכֶּה
לָשִׁיר כְּמוֹתָהּ: יהוה מַשְׁפִּיל אַף־מְרוֹמֵם, מֵקִים מֵעָפָר דָּל.
וְנֶאֱמַר: שׁוּבָה יִשְׂרָאֵל עַד יהוה אֱלֹהֶיךָ, כִּי כָשַׁלְתָּ בַּעֲוֹנֶךָ.
קְחוּ עִמָּכֶם דְּבָרִים וְשׁוּבוּ אֶל־יהוה.

וְאַתָּה רַחוּם מְקַבֵּל שָׁבִים, וְעַל הַתְּשׁוּבָה מֵרֹאשׁ
הִבְטַחְתָּנוּ, וְעַל הַתְּשׁוּבָה עֵינֵינוּ מְיַחֲלוֹת לָךְ.

אֱלֹהֵינוּ וֵאלֹהֵי אֲבוֹתֵינוּ [וְאִמּוֹתֵינוּ], מְחַל לַעֲוֹנוֹתֵינוּ
בְּיוֹם [הַשַּׁבָּת הַזֶּה וּבְיוֹם] הַכִּפּוּרִים הַזֶּה. מְחֵה וְהַעֲבֵר
פְּשָׁעֵינוּ וְחַטֹּאתֵינוּ מִנֶּגֶד עֵינֶיךָ, כָּאָמוּר: אָנֹכִי אָנֹכִי הוּא
מֹחֶה פְשָׁעֶיךָ לְמַעֲנִי, וְחַטֹּאתֶיךָ לֹא אֶזְכֹּר. וְנֶאֱמַר: מָחִיתִי
כָעָב פְּשָׁעֶיךָ וְכֶעָנָן חַטֹּאותֶיךָ, שׁוּבָה אֵלַי כִּי גְאַלְתִּיךָ.
וְנֶאֱמַר: כִּי־בַיּוֹם הַזֶּה יְכַפֵּר עֲלֵיכֶם לְטַהֵר אֶתְכֶם מִכֹּל
חַטֹּאתֵיכֶם, לִפְנֵי יהוה תִּטְהָרוּ.

אֱלֹהֵינוּ וֵאלֹהֵי אֲבוֹתֵינוּ [וְאִמּוֹתֵינוּ], [רְצֵה בִמְנוּחָתֵנוּ]
קַדְּשֵׁנוּ בְּמִצְוֹתֶיךָ וְתֵן חֶלְקֵנוּ בְּתוֹרָתֶךָ, שַׂבְּעֵנוּ מִטּוּבֶךָ
וְשַׂמְּחֵנוּ בִּישׁוּעָתֶךָ [וְהַנְחִילֵנוּ יהוה אֱלֹהֵינוּ בְּאַהֲבָה
וּבְרָצוֹן שַׁבַּת קָדְשֶׁךָ, וְיָנוּחוּ בָהּ יִשְׂרָאֵל מְקַדְּשֵׁי שְׁמֶךָ]
וְטַהֵר לִבֵּנוּ לְעָבְדְּךָ בֶּאֱמֶת, כִּי אַתָּה סָלְחָן לְיִשְׂרָאֵל וּמָחֳלָן
לְשִׁבְטֵי יְשֻׁרוּן בְּכָל־דּוֹר וָדוֹר, וּמִבַּלְעָדֶיךָ אֵין לָנוּ מֶלֶךְ מוֹחֵל
וְסוֹלֵחַ אֶלָּא אָתָּה. בָּרוּךְ אַתָּה יהוה, מֶלֶךְ מוֹחֵל וְסוֹלֵחַ
לַעֲוֹנוֹתֵינוּ וְלַעֲוֹנוֹת עַמּוֹ בֵּית יִשְׂרָאֵל, וּמַעֲבִיר אַשְׁמוֹתֵינוּ
בְּכָל־שָׁנָה וְשָׁנָה, מֶלֶךְ עַל כָּל־הָאָרֶץ, מְקַדֵּשׁ [הַשַּׁבָּת וְ]
יִשְׂרָאֵל וְיוֹם הַכִּפּוּרִים.

SECRET MATTERS
הַנִּסְתָּרֹת. Deuteronomy 29:28.

HANNAH חַנָּה. The Bible's depiction of her request for a child became, for the Rabbis, the model of proper prayer. We orient our own prayer accordingly, as we plead for forgiveness.

ADONAI BRINGS יהוה מַשְׁפִּיל. I Samuel 2:7–8.

TAKE WORDS WITH YOU קְחוּ עִמָּכֶם דְּבָרִים. Hosea 14:3. That is, speak your confession.

I, SURELY I אָנֹכִי אָנֹכִי. Isaiah 43:25.

I SWEEP ASIDE YOUR SINS LIKE A MIST מָחִיתִי כָעָב פְּשָׁעֶיךָ. Isaiah 44:22.

FOR ON THIS DAY כִּי בַיּוֹם הַזֶּה. Leviticus 16:30.

YOU FORGIVE אַתָּה סָלְחָן. The grammatical form of the nouns סָלְחָן (solhan) and מָחֳלָן (moholan) indicate an essential personal quality. For example, when one לוֹמֵד (lomed), "studies," until becoming a scholar, one is then called a לַמְדָּן (lamdan). The use of this form reflects the poet's belief that God's forgiving nature is, in fact, God's essence.

And forgive us the breach of all commandments and prohibitions, whether involving deeds or not, whether known to us or not. The sins known to us we have acknowledged, and those unknown to us are surely known to You, as the Torah states: "Secret matters are the concern of ADONAI our God; but in matters that are revealed, it is for us and our children to apply all teachings of the Torah till the end of time."

Hannah, sad and depressed, prayed to You, her heart overflowing with tears, her voice inaudible. But You understood her heartfelt cry and turned to her. Answer us in our time of need, as You responded to the plea of the woman in Shiloh, that we may sing like her: ADONAI "brings down and lifts up, raises up the poor from the dust of the earth."

Your prophet Hosea declared: "Return, O Israel, to ADONAI your God, for you have stumbled because of your sin. Take words with you and return to ADONAI."

You are compassionate, welcoming those who turn back to You. You have promised, since the dawn of creation, that repentance would be received. Now our eyes look toward You, to accept our repentance.

Our God and God of our ancestors, forgive our sins on this [Shabbat and this] Yom Kippur. Blot out and disregard them, as the prophet Isaiah says in Your name: "I, surely I, am the One who wipes away sin, for this is My nature; I will not recall your errors," and the prophet adds: "I sweep aside your sins like a mist, and disperse your transgressions like a cloud. Turn back to Me, for I will redeem you." And in Your Torah it is written: "For on this day, atonement shall be made for you to purify you from all your transgressions. In the presence of ADONAI you shall be pure."

Our God and God of our ancestors: [embrace our rest,] make us holy through Your mitzvot and let the Torah be our portion. Fill our lives with Your goodness and gladden us with Your triumph. [ADONAI our God, grant that we inherit Your holy Shabbat, lovingly and willingly, so that the people Israel, who sanctify Your name, may find rest on this day.] Purify our hearts to serve You faithfully, for You forgive the people Israel and pardon the tribes of Jeshurun in every generation. Beside You, we have no sovereign who pardons and forgives. *Barukh atah ADONAI*, sovereign who pardons and forgives our sins and those of the people, the House of Israel, each year sweeping away our guilt—ruler of all the earth, who makes [Shabbat,] the people Israel and the Day of Atonement holy.
melekh al kol ha-aretz, m'kaddeish [ha-shabbat v'] yisra·el

רְצֵה יהוה אֱלֹהֵינוּ, בְּעַמְּךָ יִשְׂרָאֵל וּבִתְפִלָּתָם, וְהָשֵׁב אֶת־הָעֲבוֹדָה לִדְבִיר בֵּיתֶךָ, [וְאִשֵּׁי יִשְׂרָאֵל] וּתְפִלָּתָם בְּאַהֲבָה תְקַבֵּל בְּרָצוֹן, וּתְהִי לְרָצוֹן תָּמִיד עֲבוֹדַת יִשְׂרָאֵל עַמֶּךָ.

וְתֶחֱזֶינָה עֵינֵינוּ בְּשׁוּבְךָ לְצִיּוֹן בְּרַחֲמִים. בָּרוּךְ אַתָּה יהוה, הַמַּחֲזִיר שְׁכִינָתוֹ לְצִיּוֹן.

While reciting the first words, by custom we remain seated while bowing our head.

Congregation recites:

↱ **מוֹדִים** אֲנַחְנוּ לָךְ שָׁאַתָּה הוּא יהוה אֱלֹהֵינוּ וֵאלֹהֵי אֲבוֹתֵינוּ [וְאִמּוֹתֵינוּ] אֱלֹהֵי כָל־בָּשָׂר, יוֹצְרֵנוּ, יוֹצֵר בְּרֵאשִׁית. בְּרָכוֹת וְהוֹדָאוֹת לְשִׁמְךָ הַגָּדוֹל וְהַקָּדוֹשׁ, עַל שֶׁהֶחֱיִיתָנוּ וְקִיַּמְתָּנוּ. כֵּן תְּחַיֵּנוּ וּתְקַיְּמֵנוּ, וְתֶאֱסוֹף גָּלֻיּוֹתֵינוּ לְחַצְרוֹת קָדְשֶׁךָ, לִשְׁמוֹר חֻקֶּיךָ וְלַעֲשׂוֹת רְצוֹנֶךָ, וּלְעָבְדְּךָ בְּלֵבָב שָׁלֵם, עַל שֶׁאֲנַחְנוּ מוֹדִים לָךְ. בָּרוּךְ אֵל הַהוֹדָאוֹת.

Leader recites:

מוֹדִים אֲנַחְנוּ לָךְ שָׁאַתָּה הוּא יהוה אֱלֹהֵינוּ וֵאלֹהֵי אֲבוֹתֵינוּ [וְאִמּוֹתֵינוּ] לְעוֹלָם וָעֶד, צוּר חַיֵּינוּ מָגֵן יִשְׁעֵנוּ אַתָּה הוּא. לְדוֹר וָדוֹר נוֹדֶה לְךָ וּנְסַפֵּר תְּהִלָּתֶךָ, עַל חַיֵּינוּ הַמְּסוּרִים בְּיָדֶךָ וְעַל נִשְׁמוֹתֵינוּ הַפְּקוּדוֹת לָךְ, וְעַל נִסֶּיךָ שֶׁבְּכָל־יוֹם עִמָּנוּ וְעַל נִפְלְאוֹתֶיךָ וְטוֹבוֹתֶיךָ שֶׁבְּכָל־עֵת, עֶרֶב וָבֹקֶר וְצָהֳרָיִם. ◁ הַטּוֹב, כִּי לֹא כָלוּ רַחֲמֶיךָ, וְהַמְרַחֵם כִּי לֹא תַמּוּ חֲסָדֶיךָ, מֵעוֹלָם קִוִּינוּ לָךְ.

וְעַל כֻּלָּם יִתְבָּרַךְ וְיִתְרוֹמַם שִׁמְךָ מַלְכֵּנוּ תָּמִיד לְעוֹלָם וָעֶד.

RESTORE WORSHIP TO YOUR SANCTUARY וְהָשֵׁב אֶת־הָעֲבוֹדָה לִדְבִיר בֵּיתֶךָ. According to the Babylonian Talmud, "Ever since the day when the Temple was destroyed, there has been an iron barrier separating Israel from God" (Berakhot 32b). Each destruction of the Temple in Jerusalem (first by the Babylonians in 586 B.C.E. and then by the Romans in 70 C.E.) was a cataclysmic event in early Jewish history. We pray for the restoration of the sense of immediate connection with God that is believed to have characterized the Temple service.

YOUR DIVINE PRESENCE שְׁכִינָתוֹ. The Hebrew word *shekhinah* has been used for centuries to refer to God's immanence, the presence of God that is felt in the world. The word *shekhinah* is grammatically feminine. Accordingly, Jewish mystical tradition has tended to personify as female the Divine Presence, who is known as the Shekhinah.

THE CONGREGATIONAL RESPONSE. A second version of Modim (the *b'rakhah* of thanksgiving) was created by the Sages to be recited by the congregation while the leader chants the official prayer (Babylonian Talmud, Sotah 40a). In this way, we each fulfill the imperative of acknowledging God. The central idea in this version is *modim anaḥnu lakh . . . al she-anaḥnu modim lakh*, "we thank You for the ability to thank You." Our prayers may be addressed to God, but God is also their source.

FOR ALL THESE BLESSINGS וְעַל כֻּלָּם. In the language of the Bible and the prayerbook, "God's name is exalted" when we acknowledge God, recognize God's goodness in creation, and act to enable God's justice and compassion to be visible in the world.

Fifth B'rakhah: The Restoration of Zion

ADONAI our God, embrace Your people Israel and their prayer. Restore worship to Your sanctuary. May the [fiery offerings and] prayers of the people Israel be lovingly accepted by You, and may our service always be pleasing.

Let our eyes behold Your merciful return to Zion. *Barukh atah* ADONAI, who restores Your Divine Presence to Zion.

Sixth B'rakhah: Gratitude for Life and Its Blessings

While reciting the first words, by custom we remain seated while bowing our head.

Thankfulness
It is gratefulness which makes the soul great.
—ABRAHAM JOSHUA HESCHEL

Leader recites:

We thank You, You who are our God and the God of our ancestors through all time, protector of our lives, shield of our salvation. From one generation to the next we thank You and sing Your praises—
for our lives that are in Your hands,
for our souls that are under Your care,
for Your miracles that accompany us each day,
and for Your wonders and Your gifts that are with us each moment—
evening, morning, and noon. You are the One who is good, whose mercy is never-ending; the One who is compassionate, whose love is unceasing. We have always placed our hope in You.

Congregation recites:

ʄ We thank You for the ability to acknowledge You. You are our God and the God of our ancestors, the God of all flesh, our creator, and the creator of all. We offer praise and blessing to Your holy and great name, for granting us life and for sustaining us. May You continue to grant us life and sustenance. Gather our dispersed to Your holy courtyards, that we may fulfill Your mitzvot and serve You wholeheartedly, carrying out Your will. May God, the source of gratitude, be praised.

For all these blessings may Your name be praised and exalted, our sovereign, always and forever.

אָבִינוּ מַלְכֵּנוּ, זְכֹר רַחֲמֶיךָ וּכְבֹשׁ כַּעַסְךָ, וְכַלֵּה דֶּבֶר וְחֶרֶב וְרָעָב וּשְׁבִי וּמַשְׁחִית וְעָוֹן וּשְׁמָד וּמַגֵּפָה וּפֶגַע רַע וְכָל־מַחֲלָה, וְכָל־תְּקָלָה וְכָל־קְטָטָה, וְכָל־מִינֵי פֻרְעָנִיּוֹת וְכָל־גְּזֵרָה רָעָה וְשִׂנְאַת חִנָּם, מֵעָלֵינוּ וּמֵעַל כָּל־בְּנֵי בְרִיתֶךָ.

וּכְתֹב לְחַיִּים טוֹבִים כָּל־בְּנֵי בְרִיתֶךָ.

וְכֹל הַחַיִּים יוֹדוּךָ סֶּלָה, וִיהַלְלוּ אֶת־שִׁמְךָ בֶּאֱמֶת, הָאֵל יְשׁוּעָתֵנוּ וְעֶזְרָתֵנוּ סֶלָה. בָּרוּךְ אַתָּה יהוה, הַטּוֹב שִׁמְךָ וּלְךָ נָאֶה לְהוֹדוֹת.

אֱלֹהֵינוּ וֵאלֹהֵי אֲבוֹתֵינוּ [וְאִמּוֹתֵינוּ], בָּרְכֵנוּ בַּבְּרָכָה הַמְשֻׁלֶּשֶׁת בַּתּוֹרָה הַכְּתוּבָה עַל יְדֵי מֹשֶׁה עַבְדֶּךָ, הָאֲמוּרָה מִפִּי אַהֲרֹן וּבָנָיו, כֹּהֲנִים, עַם קְדוֹשֶׁךָ, כָּאָמוּר:

יְבָרֶכְךָ יהוה וְיִשְׁמְרֶךָ.   כֵּן יְהִי רָצוֹן.
יָאֵר יהוה פָּנָיו אֵלֶיךָ וִיחֻנֶּךָּ.   כֵּן יְהִי רָצוֹן.
יִשָּׂא יהוה פָּנָיו אֵלֶיךָ וְיָשֵׂם לְךָ שָׁלוֹם.   כֵּן יְהִי רָצוֹן.

שִׂים שָׁלוֹם בָּעוֹלָם, טוֹבָה וּבְרָכָה, חֵן וָחֶסֶד וְרַחֲמִים עָלֵינוּ וְעַל כָּל־יִשְׂרָאֵל עַמֶּךָ. בָּרְכֵנוּ אָבִינוּ כֻּלָּנוּ כְּאֶחָד בְּאוֹר פָּנֶיךָ, כִּי בְאוֹר פָּנֶיךָ נָתַתָּ לָּנוּ, יהוה אֱלֹהֵינוּ, תּוֹרַת חַיִּים וְאַהֲבַת חֶסֶד, וּצְדָקָה וּבְרָכָה וְרַחֲמִים וְחַיִּים וְשָׁלוֹם. וְטוֹב בְּעֵינֶיךָ לְבָרֵךְ אֶת־עַמְּךָ יִשְׂרָאֵל, בְּכָל־עֵת וּבְכָל־שָׁעָה בִּשְׁלוֹמֶךָ.

בְּסֵפֶר חַיִּים, בְּרָכָה וְשָׁלוֹם וּפַרְנָסָה טוֹבָה, נִזָּכֵר וְנִכָּתֵב לְפָנֶיךָ, אֲנַחְנוּ וְכָל־עַמְּךָ בֵּית יִשְׂרָאֵל, לְחַיִּים טוֹבִים וּלְשָׁלוֹם.

בָּרוּךְ אַתָּה יהוה, עוֹשֶׂה הַשָּׁלוֹם.

ON SHABBAT, WE CONTINUE WITH KADDISH SHALEM ON PAGE 272.

ON SHABBAT, WE CONTINUE WITH KADDISH SHALEM ON PAGE 272.

AND INSCRIBE וּכְתֹב. This is the third of the four special insertions in the Amidah for the Ten Days of Repentance. With the first two insertions, we prayed for God's mercy that we may live another year; now we pray that the life we are granted be good.

MAY ADONAI BLESS YOU AND PROTECT YOU יְבָרֶכְךָ יהוה וְיִשְׁמְרֶךָ. This blessing (Numbers 6:24–26) is known as Birkat Kohanim, the "Priestly Blessing," as the Torah prescribes that it is to be recited by Aaron and his descendants, the *kohanim* (priests), to bring God's blessing upon the people Israel. In most Israeli synagogues, this blessing is recited every day. The *kohanim*, who come to the front of the synagogue after preparing themselves ritually, extend their hands toward the community in a traditional gesture, thus serving as a conduit of blessing. In many synagogues in the Diaspora, the *kohanim* re-enact this ancient blessing during the Musaf service on High Holy Days and festivals.

GRANT PEACE שִׂים שָׁלוֹם. Generally in the Ashkenazic liturgy, the *b'rakhah* Sim Shalom is recited only during the morning (Shaḥarit and Musaf) services, whereas a similar *b'rakhah*, Shalom Rav ("abundant peace"), is used instead at afternoon and evening services. However, on fast days such as Yom Kippur, Sim Shalom is said at every service. The words of Sim Shalom are related directly to the conclusion of Birkat Kohanim (*v'yasem l'kha shalom*, "may God grant you peace"); thus Sim Shalom is traditionally recited at all services at which the Birkat Kohanim is recited. On fast days, Birkat Kohanim is recited at all services throughout the day (but not the evening).

Great is peace, for the
  only vessel that can contain blessings is peace.
Great is peace, for all the
  prayers conclude with
  pleas for peace.
Great is peace, for we
  must seek it even in time
  of war.
Great is peace, for it is the
  reward of the righteous.
Great is peace, for it is
  bestowed upon those
  who love the Torah.
Great is peace, for it is
  bestowed upon the
  humble.
Great is peace, for it is
  bestowed upon those
  who act justly.
Great is peace, for it is
  equal to all of the work
  of creation.
Great is peace, for even
  those who dwell on high
  need peace, as it is said,
  עֹשֶׂה שָׁלוֹם בִּמְרוֹמָיו "God
  imposes peace in God's
  heights" (Job 25:2). If
  in a place where there
  is no hatred and envy,
  enmity or malice, peace
  is needed, how much
  more so in a place where
  all these qualities are
  lacking!
Great is peace, for the
  name of the Holy One
  is Peace.

—MIDRASH
SIFREI NUMBERS
(trans. Reuven Hammer, adapted)

Avinu Malkeinu, remember Your compassion and subdue Your anger. Bring an end to pestilence, sword, and hunger; captivity and destruction, sin and oppression, plague and calamity; every illness, misfortune, and quarrel; all kinds of danger, every evil decree, and causeless hatred. Bring an end to these for us and for all the people of Your covenant.

And inscribe all the people of Your covenant for a good life.
U-kh'tov l'ḥayyim tovim kol b'nei v'ritekha.

May all that lives thank You always, and praise Your name faithfully forever, God of our deliverance and help.
Barukh atah ADONAI, whose name is goodness and to whom praise is fitting.

Seventh B'rakhah: Prayer for Peace

Our God and God of our ancestors, bless us with the three-fold blessing of the Torah written by Moses Your servant, recited by Aaron and his descendants, the *kohanim*, the consecrated priests of Your people:

May ADONAI bless and protect you.
　　　　　　　　　So may it be God's will. *Kein y'hi ratzon.*
May ADONAI's countenance shine upon you and
　grant you kindness.　*So may it be God's will.* *Kein y'hi ratzon.*
May ADONAI's countenance be lifted toward you and
　grant you peace.　　*So may it be God's will.* *Kein y'hi ratzon.*

Grant peace to the world: goodness and blessing, grace, love, and compassion to us and all the people Israel. Bless us, our creator, united as one in the light of Your countenance; by that light, ADONAI our God, You gave us a guide to life: the love of kindness, righteousness, blessing, compassion, life, and peace. May it please You to bless Your people Israel at every season and at all times with Your gift of peace.

May we and the entire House of Israel be called to mind and inscribed for life, blessing, sustenance, and peace in the Book of Life.

B'seifer ḥayyim b'rakhah v'shalom u-farnasah tovah, nizzakheir v'nikkateiv l'fanekha, anaḥnu v'khol am'kha beit yisra·el, l'ḥayyim tovim u-l'shalom.

Barukh atah ADONAI, who brings peace.

ON SHABBAT, WE CONTINUE WITH KADDISH SHALEM ON PAGE 272.

We rise as the ark is opened. An alternate version begins on page 244.
Avinu Malkeinu is not recited on Shabbat.

אָבִינוּ מַלְכֵּנוּ! חָטָאנוּ לְפָנֶיךָ.

אָבִינוּ מַלְכֵּנוּ! אֵין לָנוּ מֶלֶךְ אֶלָּא אָתָּה.

אָבִינוּ מַלְכֵּנוּ! עֲשֵׂה עִמָּנוּ לְמַעַן שְׁמֶךָ.

אָבִינוּ מַלְכֵּנוּ! חַדֵּשׁ עָלֵינוּ שָׁנָה טוֹבָה.

אָבִינוּ מַלְכֵּנוּ! בַּטֵּל מֵעָלֵינוּ כָּל־גְּזֵרוֹת קָשׁוֹת.

אָבִינוּ מַלְכֵּנוּ! בַּטֵּל מַחְשְׁבוֹת שׂוֹנְאֵינוּ.

אָבִינוּ מַלְכֵּנוּ! הָפֵר עֲצַת אוֹיְבֵינוּ.

אָבִינוּ מַלְכֵּנוּ! כַּלֵּה כָּל־צַר וּמַשְׂטִין מֵעָלֵינוּ.

אָבִינוּ מַלְכֵּנוּ! כַּלֵּה דֶּבֶר וְחֶרֶב וְרָעָב וּשְׁבִי וּמַשְׁחִית
וְעָוֺן וּשְׁמַד מִבְּנֵי בְרִיתֶךָ.

אָבִינוּ מַלְכֵּנוּ! סְלַח וּמְחַל לְכָל־עֲוֺנוֹתֵינוּ.

אָבִינוּ מַלְכֵּנוּ! מְחֵה וְהַעֲבֵר פְּשָׁעֵינוּ וְחַטֹּאתֵינוּ מִנֶּגֶד עֵינֶיךָ.

After the leader has recited each of these lines, we repeat it:

◁ אָבִינוּ מַלְכֵּנוּ! הַחֲזִירֵנוּ בִּתְשׁוּבָה שְׁלֵמָה לְפָנֶיךָ.

אָבִינוּ מַלְכֵּנוּ! שְׁלַח רְפוּאָה שְׁלֵמָה לְחוֹלֵי עַמֶּךָ.

אָבִינוּ מַלְכֵּנוּ! זָכְרֵנוּ בְּזִכָּרוֹן טוֹב לְפָנֶיךָ.

אָבִינוּ מַלְכֵּנוּ! כָּתְבֵנוּ בְּסֵפֶר חַיִּים טוֹבִים.

אָבִינוּ מַלְכֵּנוּ! כָּתְבֵנוּ בְּסֵפֶר גְּאֻלָּה וִישׁוּעָה.

אָבִינוּ מַלְכֵּנוּ! כָּתְבֵנוּ בְּסֵפֶר פַּרְנָסָה וְכַלְכָּלָה.

אָבִינוּ מַלְכֵּנוּ! כָּתְבֵנוּ בְּסֵפֶר זְכֻיּוֹת.

אָבִינוּ מַלְכֵּנוּ! כָּתְבֵנוּ בְּסֵפֶר סְלִיחָה וּמְחִילָה.

אָבִינוּ מַלְכֵּנוּ! הַצְמַח לָנוּ יְשׁוּעָה בְּקָרוֹב.

אָבִינוּ מַלְכֵּנוּ! הָרֵם קֶרֶן יִשְׂרָאֵל עַמֶּךָ.

אָבִינוּ מַלְכֵּנוּ! הָרֵם קֶרֶן מְשִׁיחֶךָ.

אָבִינוּ מַלְכֵּנוּ! שְׁמַע קוֹלֵנוּ, חוּס וְרַחֵם עָלֵינוּ.

אָבִינוּ מַלְכֵּנוּ! קַבֵּל בְּרַחֲמִים וּבְרָצוֹן אֶת־תְּפִלָּתֵנוּ.

אָבִינוּ מַלְכֵּנוּ! נָא אַל תְּשִׁיבֵנוּ רֵיקָם מִלְּפָנֶיךָ.

אָבִינוּ מַלְכֵּנוּ! זְכוֹר כִּי עָפָר אֲנָחְנוּ.

אָבִינוּ מַלְכֵּנוּ! חֲמוֹל עָלֵינוּ וְעַל עוֹלָלֵינוּ וְטַפֵּנוּ.

אָבִינוּ מַלְכֵּנוּ! עֲשֵׂה לְמַעַן הֲרוּגִים עַל שֵׁם קָדְשֶׁךָ.

אָבִינוּ מַלְכֵּנוּ! עֲשֵׂה לְמַעַן טְבוּחִים עַל יִחוּדֶךָ.

AVINU MALKEINU אָבִינוּ מַלְכֵּנוּ. The Babylonian Talmud reports that Rabbi Akiva prayed with the words *avinu malkeinu* and his prayers were accepted (Taanit 25b). Originally, this was a prayer for material blessing. In time, verses were added asking for deliverance from natural and human devastation. References to martyrdom, as well as meditations on the new year, were also added.

Avinu malkeinu literally means "our father, our king." The image of God as "father" represents relatedness and closeness. (In the ancient world the term "father" is associated with the one who gives life, and so many modern prayerbooks reflect this nuance by translating the word as "creator" or "source.") The figure of God as king, or sovereign, conveys authority, particularly that of judge, and so connotes greater distance. Jewish theology has always recognized this paradoxical sense of God, speaking both of God's being close at hand, and also as distant and inscrutable—similarly of God's kindness and caring as well as God's punishing hand for sinful behavior.

Avinu Malkeinu

We rise as the ark is opened. An alternate version begins on page 244.
Avinu Malkeinu is not recited on Shabbat.

Avinu Malkeinu, we have sinned in Your presence.
  Avinu Malkeinu, we have no sovereign but You.
Avinu Malkeinu, act toward us kindly in accord with Your name.
  Avinu Malkeinu, make this a good new year for us.
Avinu Malkeinu, annul every harsh decree against us.
  Avinu Malkeinu, nullify the designs of our foes.
Avinu Malkeinu, frustrate the plots of our enemies.
  Avinu Malkeinu, rid us of every oppressor and adversary.
Avinu Malkeinu, rid Your covenanted people of disease, war, hunger, captivity,
and destruction.
  Avinu Malkeinu, forgive and pardon all our sins.
Avinu Malkeinu, do not look toward our sins and transgressions; blot them out.
  Avinu Malkeinu, return us to Your presence, fully penitent.
Avinu Malkeinu, send complete healing to the sick among Your people.
  Avinu Malkeinu, remember us favorably.
Avinu Malkeinu, inscribe us for good in the Book of Life.
  Avinu Malkeinu, inscribe us in the Book of Redemption.
Avinu Malkeinu, inscribe us in the Book of Sustenance.
  Avinu Malkeinu, inscribe us in the Book of Merit.
Avinu Malkeinu, inscribe us in the Book of Forgiveness.

Avinu malkeinu, haḥazireinu bi-t'shuvah sh'leimah l'fanekha.
Avinu malkeinu, sh'laḥ r'fu·ah sh'leimah l'ḥolei ammekha.
Avinu malkeinu, zokhreinu b'zikkaron tov l'fanekha.
Avinu malkeinu, kotveinu b'seifer ḥayyim tovim.
Avinu malkeinu, kotveinu b'seifer g'ullah vi-shu·ah.
Avinu malkeinu, kotveinu b'seifer parnasah v'khalkalah.
Avinu malkeinu, kotveinu b'seifer z'khuyyot.
Avinu malkeinu, kotveinu b'seifer s'liḥah u-m'ḥilah.

Avinu Malkeinu, cause our salvation to flourish soon.
  Avinu Malkeinu, cause Your people Israel to be exalted.
Avinu Malkeinu, raise up Your anointed with strength.
  Avinu Malkeinu, hear our voice, be kind, sympathize with us.
Avinu Malkeinu, accept our prayer, willingly and lovingly.
  Avinu Malkeinu, do not turn us away empty-handed.
Avinu Malkeinu, remember that we are but dust.
  Avinu Malkeinu, have compassion for us, our infants, and our children.
Avinu Malkeinu, do this for the sake of those who were martyred for Your holy name.
  Avinu Malkeinu, do this for the sake of those who were slaughtered for their
  exclusive devotion to You.

אָבִינוּ מַלְכֵּנוּ! עֲשֵׂה לְמַעַן בָּאֵי בָאֵשׁ וּבַמַּיִם עַל
קִדּוּשׁ שְׁמֶךָ.
אָבִינוּ מַלְכֵּנוּ! עֲשֵׂה לְמַעַנְךָ אִם לֹא לְמַעֲנֵנוּ.
אָבִינוּ מַלְכֵּנוּ! חָנֵּנוּ וַעֲנֵנוּ, כִּי אֵין בָּנוּ מַעֲשִׂים,
עֲשֵׂה עִמָּנוּ צְדָקָה וָחֶסֶד וְהוֹשִׁיעֵנוּ.

The ark is closed.

קַדִּישׁ שָׁלֵם

יִתְגַּדַּל וְיִתְקַדַּשׁ שְׁמֵהּ רַבָּא, בְּעָלְמָא דִּי בְרָא, כִּרְעוּתֵהּ,
וְיַמְלִיךְ מַלְכוּתֵהּ בְּחַיֵּיכוֹן וּבְיוֹמֵיכוֹן וּבְחַיֵּי דְּכָל־בֵּית
יִשְׂרָאֵל, בַּעֲגָלָא וּבִזְמַן קָרִיב, וְאִמְרוּ אָמֵן.

יְהֵא שְׁמֵהּ רַבָּא מְבָרַךְ לְעָלַם וּלְעָלְמֵי עָלְמַיָּא.

יִתְבָּרַךְ וְיִשְׁתַּבַּח וְיִתְפָּאַר וְיִתְרוֹמַם וְיִתְנַשֵּׂא וְיִתְהַדָּר
וְיִתְעַלֶּה וְיִתְהַלָּל שְׁמֵהּ דְּקֻדְשָׁא, בְּרִיךְ הוּא, לְעֵלָּא לְעֵלָּא
מִכָּל־בִּרְכָתָא וְשִׁירָתָא תֻּשְׁבְּחָתָא וְנֶחָמָתָא דַּאֲמִירָן
בְּעָלְמָא, וְאִמְרוּ אָמֵן.

תִּתְקַבֵּל צְלוֹתְהוֹן וּבָעוּתְהוֹן דְּכָל־יִשְׂרָאֵל קֳדָם אֲבוּהוֹן
דִּי בִשְׁמַיָּא, וְאִמְרוּ אָמֵן.

יְהֵא שְׁלָמָא רַבָּא מִן שְׁמַיָּא וְחַיִּים עָלֵינוּ וְעַל כָּל־
יִשְׂרָאֵל, וְאִמְרוּ אָמֵן.

עֹשֶׂה שָׁלוֹם בִּמְרוֹמָיו הוּא יַעֲשֶׂה שָׁלוֹם עָלֵינוּ וְעַל כָּל־
יִשְׂרָאֵל [וְעַל כָּל־יוֹשְׁבֵי תֵבֵל], וְאִמְרוּ אָמֵן.

KADDISH SHALEM. Every service that features an Amidah is brought to a close with Kaddish Shalem, the complete Kaddish, so called because in addition to the words of the Kaddish recited at other times in the service, it adds a line asking God to accept our prayers: "May the prayers and pleas of all Israel be accepted by their creator in heaven." Here, the placement of Kaddish Shalem marks the end of the morning Shaḥarit prayers. The liturgy now moves on to the Torah service. In a formal sense, though introduced and followed by *b'rakhot* and prayers, the reading of the Torah and the Haftarah constitutes study, not prayer. For the ancient Rabbis, prayer was quintessentially defined by the Amidah, which we have now completed.

Avinu Malkeinu, do this for the sake of those who went through fire and water to sanctify Your holy name.

Avinu Malkeinu, do this for Your sake if not for ours.

Avinu Malkeinu, have mercy on us, answer us, for our deeds are insufficient; deal with us charitably and lovingly, and redeem us.

Avinu malkeinu, ḥonneinu va-aneinu, ki ein banu ma·asim,
aseih immanu tz'dakah va-ḥesed v'hoshi·einu.

The ark is closed.

Kaddish Shalem

May God's great name be exalted and hallowed throughout the created world, as is God's wish. May God's sovereignty soon be established, in your lifetime and in your days, and in the days of all the House of Israel. And respond with: *Amen.*

May God's great name be acknowledged forever and ever!
Y'hei sh'meih rabba m'varakh l'alam u-l'almei almayya.

May the name of the Holy One be acknowledged and celebrated, lauded and worshipped, exalted and honored, extolled and acclaimed—though God, who is blessed, *b'rikh hu,* is truly far beyond all acknowledgment and praise, or any expressions of gratitude or consolation ever spoken in the world. And respond with: *Amen.*

May the prayers and pleas of all Israel be accepted by their creator in heaven. And respond with: *Amen.*

May abundant peace from heaven, and life, come to us and to all Israel. And respond with: *Amen.*

May the One who brings harmony on high, bring harmony to us and to all Israel [and to all who dwell on earth]. And respond with: *Amen.*

Oseh shalom bi-m'romav hu ya·aseh shalom aleinu v'al kol yisra·el [v'al kol yosh'vei teiveil],
v'imru amen.

TORAH SERVICE
OF YOM KIPPUR

סדר קריאת התורה
ליום כיפור

אֵין־כָּמֽוֹךָ בָאֱלֹהִים, אֲדֹנָי, וְאֵין כְּמַעֲשֶֽׂיךָ.
מַלְכוּתְךָ מַלְכוּת כָּל־עוֹלָמִים, וּמֶמְשַׁלְתְּךָ בְּכָל־דּוֹר וָדֹר.
יהוה מֶֽלֶךְ, יהוה מָלָךְ, יהוה יִמְלֹךְ לְעֹלָם וָעֶד.
יהוה עֹז לְעַמּוֹ יִתֵּן, יהוה יְבָרֵךְ אֶת־עַמּוֹ בַשָּׁלוֹם.

אַב הָרַחֲמִים, הֵיטִֽיבָה בִרְצוֹנְךָ אֶת־צִיּוֹן, תִּבְנֶה חוֹמוֹת
יְרוּשָׁלָֽיִם. כִּי בְךָ לְבַד בָּטָֽחְנוּ, מֶֽלֶךְ אֵל רָם וְנִשָּׂא, אֲדוֹן
עוֹלָמִים.

We rise as the ark is opened.

וַיְהִי בִּנְסֹֽעַ הָאָרֹן וַיֹּֽאמֶר מֹשֶׁה:
קוּמָה יהוה וְיָפֻֽצוּ אֹיְבֶֽיךָ, וְיָנֻֽסוּ מְשַׂנְאֶֽיךָ מִפָּנֶֽיךָ.
כִּי מִצִּיּוֹן תֵּצֵא תוֹרָה, וּדְבַר־יהוה מִירוּשָׁלָֽיִם.
בָּרוּךְ שֶׁנָּתַן תּוֹרָה לְעַמּוֹ יִשְׂרָאֵל בִּקְדֻשָּׁתוֹ.

סֵֽדֶר **THE TORAH SERVICE**
קְרִיאַת הַתּוֹרָה. In Jewish thought, a widespread view is that since the Temple's destruction, our most direct connection to the divine will is through Torah. Thus, the opening of the ark, the Torah's procession through the congregation, and the reading aloud from the scroll are all symbolic moments when the presence and will of the Divine may be most closely felt. It is as if with the opening of the ark, the doorway to heaven itself is opened. Over time, taking out the Torah came to be seen as a royal procession. The Torah was adorned with a crown, and its cover's hem was kissed as the scroll passed through the congregation. Additionally, the Torah is dressed with accoutrements of the High Priest, including a breastplate and bells (originally used to signal his presence). In short, our way of treating the Torah scroll combines the three "crowns" about which our Rabbis spoke: the crown of sovereignty, the crown of priesthood, and the crown of Torah.

NONE COMPARES TO YOU אֵין כָּמֽוֹךָ. As etiquette in Europe's royal courts became more elaborate (14th century), the Ashkenazic rite incorporated verses emphasizing God's sovereignty, as if to say that God alone—and no earthly ruler—is the true sovereign.

ADONAI IS SOVEREIGN יהוה מֶֽלֶךְ. This sentence is a compilation of biblical phrases referring to God's sovereignty. Stitched together, they form a creed: God has ruled the world since before creation and will continue to rule eternally. The other verses in this passage are from Psalms 86:8, 145:13, and 29:11.

COMPASSIONATE CREATOR אַב הָרַחֲמִים. Literally, "merciful father." This address, followed by a verse that calls for Jerusalem's reconstruction (Psalm 51:20), is all that remains from prayers for forgiveness that were recited here in an earlier era.

AS THE ARK WAS CARRIED FORWARD וַיְהִי בִנְסֹֽעַ. Numbers 10:35. Reciting this verse evokes a period of special closeness between God and Israel, both at Sinai and in their journey through the desert. This verse is from a description of how the people moved from one encampment to another. It depicts the Ark as the seat of divine protection, leading the march and warding off the fledgling nation's enemies.

TORAH SHALL GO FORTH FROM ZION כִּי מִצִּיּוֹן. Isaiah 2:3. As the ark is opened, we express our belief that Torah contains ideals appropriate to all humanity. Isaiah envisioned all the nations of the world coming to Mount Zion and worshipping one God.

TAKING OUT THE TORAH

Meditations on the Meaning of Torah

א

Open my eyes, that through the study of Your Torah I may see wondrous things.

—PSALM 119:18

ב

What Torah means to us depends on what God means to us.

—JACOB PETUCHOWSKI

ג

The custom of our ancestors has the status of Torah.

—TOSAFOT TO BABYLONIAN TALMUD, MENAHOT

ד

The people Israel, the Torah, and the Holy One are all one. —THE ZOHAR

None compares to You, ADONAI,
and nothing is like Your works.
Your sovereignty is everlasting;
Your rule endures through all generations.
ADONAI is sovereign, ADONAI has always been sovereign,
ADONAI will be sovereign forever and ever.
ADONAI, give strength to Your people;
ADONAI, bless Your people with peace.

Malkhut'kha malkhut kol-olamim, u-memshalt'kha b'khol dor va-dor.
Adonai melekh, Adonai malakh, Adonai yimlokh l'olam va·ed.
Adonai oz l'ammo yittein, Adonai y'vareikh et-ammo va-shalom.

Compassionate Creator, may it please You that Zion flourish;
build the walls of Jerusalem. For in You alone do we put our
trust, transcendent Sovereign—Master of all time.

Av ha-rahamim, hetivah virtzon'kha et tziyyon,
tivneh homot y'rushalayim.
Ki v'kha l'vad batahnu, melekh El ram v'nissa, adon olamim.

We rise as the ark is opened.
As the Ark was carried forward, Moses would say:
ADONAI! Scatter Your foes,
so that Your enemies flee Your Presence.

Kumah Adonai v'yafutzu oy'vekha,
v'yanusu m'san·ekha mi-panekha.

Torah shall go forth from Zion,
and the word of ADONAI from Jerusalem.
Praised is the One who gave Torah to the people Israel
in holiness.

Ki mi-tziyyon teitzei torah, u-d'var Adonai mirushalayim.
Barukh she-natan Torah l'ammo yisra·el bi-k'dushato.

ON SHABBAT, CONTINUE AT THE BOTTOM OF THIS PAGE.
We recite three times:

יהוה יהוה, אֵל רַחוּם וְחַנּוּן, אֶרֶךְ אַפַּיִם וְרַב חֶסֶד וֶאֱמֶת,
נֹצֵר חֶסֶד לָאֲלָפִים, נֹשֵׂא עָוֹן וָפֶשַׁע וְחַטָּאָה, וְנַקֵּה.

אָבִינוּ מַלְכֵּנוּ, אֲדוֹן הַשָּׁלוֹם, עָזְרֵנוּ וְהוֹשִׁיעֵנוּ שֶׁנִּזְכֶּה תָּמִיד
לֶאֱחֹז בְּמִדַּת הַשָּׁלוֹם. וְיִהְיֶה שָׁלוֹם בֵּין כָּל־אָדָם לַחֲבֵרוֹ וּבֵין
אִישׁ לְאִשְׁתּוֹ, וְלֹא תִהְיֶה שׁוּם מַחֲלֹקֶת בֵּין כָּל־בְּנֵי מִשְׁפַּחְתִּי.
אַתָּה עוֹשֶׂה שָׁלוֹם בִּמְרוֹמֶיךָ, כֵּן תַּמְשִׁיךְ שָׁלוֹם עָלֵינוּ וְעַל
כָּל־הָעוֹלָם כֻּלּוֹ, נִתְקָרֵב אֵלֶיךָ וּלְתוֹרָתְךָ בֶּאֱמֶת וְנַעֲשֶׂה כֻלָּנוּ
אֲגֻדָּה אַחַת לַעֲשׂוֹת רְצוֹנְךָ בְּלֵבָב שָׁלֵם. אֲדוֹן הַשָּׁלוֹם, בָּרְכֵנוּ
בַשָּׁלוֹם. אָמֵן.

יִהְיוּ לְרָצוֹן אִמְרֵי־פִי וְהֶגְיוֹן לִבִּי לְפָנֶיךָ יהוה צוּרִי וְגוֹאֲלִי.

Some recite the following three times:

וַאֲנִי תְפִלָּתִי־לְךָ, יהוה, עֵת רָצוֹן.
אֱלֹהִים בְּרָב־חַסְדֶּךָ, עֲנֵנִי בֶּאֱמֶת יִשְׁעֶךָ.

ON SHABBAT, WE MEDITATE AS FOLLOWS:

בְּרִיךְ שְׁמֵהּ דְּמָרֵא עָלְמָא, בְּרִיךְ כִּתְרָךְ וְאַתְרָךְ. יְהֵא
רְעוּתָךְ עִם עַמָּךְ יִשְׂרָאֵל לְעָלַם, וּפֻרְקַן יְמִינָךְ אַחֲזֵי לְעַמָּךְ
בְּבֵית מִקְדְּשָׁךְ, וּלְאַמְטוּיֵי לָנָא מִטּוּב נְהוֹרָךְ וּלְקַבֵּל צְלוֹתָנָא
בְּרַחֲמִין. יְהֵא רַעֲוָא קֳדָמָךְ דְּתוֹרִיךְ לָן חַיִּין בְּטִיבוּתָא, וְלֶהֱוֵי
אֲנָא פְקִידָא בְּגוֹ צַדִּיקַיָּא, לְמִרְחַם עָלַי, וּלְמִנְטַר יָתִי וְיָת כָּל־
דִּי לִי וְדִי לְעַמָּךְ יִשְׂרָאֵל. אַנְתְּ הוּא זָן לְכֹלָּא, וּמְפַרְנֵס לְכֹלָּא.
אַנְתְּ הוּא שַׁלִּיט עַל כֹּלָּא. אַנְתְּ הוּא דְּשַׁלִּיט עַל מַלְכַיָּא,
וּמַלְכוּתָא דִּי לָךְ הִיא. אֲנָא עַבְדָּא דְּקֻדְשָׁא בְּרִיךְ הוּא
דְּסָגֵדְנָא קַמֵּהּ וּמִקַּמָּא דִּיקַר אוֹרַיְתֵהּ בְּכָל־עִדָּן וְעִדָּן.

BEFORE THE OPEN ARK. The sight of the Torah in the opened ark evokes a sense of reverence, inspiring reflection and meditation. Over time, various personal prayers have been added to the Torah service. Rabbi Isaac Luria (1534–1572, Egypt and the Land of Israel) suggested that the Thirteen Attributes be recited before the open ark, as a communal plea for forgiveness.

AVINU MALKEINU אָבִינוּ מַלְכֵּנוּ. Adapted by Jules Harlow from a meditation written by Rabbi Nathan Sternharz (1780–1845), the chief recorder of the teachings of the Ḥasidic master Naḥman of Bratzlav.

MAY THIS BE . . . FOR MY PRAYER וַאֲנִי תְפִלָּתִי־לְךָ. Psalm 69:14. This poetic phrase can be literally translated as: "And I, I am a prayer to You…" Our lives may be seen as prayers offered to God.

PRAISED BE YOUR NAME בְּרִיךְ שְׁמֵהּ. From the Zohar (part 2, 206a), the central text of Jewish mysticism, composed in Aramaic. A translation of the Zohar's introduction to this meditation appears in the leftmost column.

As soon as the Torah scroll is placed on [the reading desk] the whole congregation below should assume an attitude of awe and fear, of trembling and quaking, as though they were at that moment standing at Mount Sinai to receive the Torah, and should pay attention and listen carefully; for it is not permitted then to open one's mouth, even for discussing the Torah, still less other subjects. All must be in awe and fear, as though they were speechless, as it is written: "And when he opened it, all the people stood up," and also, "And the ears of all the people were attentive to the Torah scroll" (Nehemiah 8:5 and 8:3). Rabbi Shimon said: "When the Torah scroll is taken out to be read before the congregation, the heavenly gates of mercy are opened and the attribute of love is stirred up, and each one should then recite the following prayer: "Ruler of the universe, praised be Your name and Your sovereignty. . . ."

—THE ZOHAR

ON SHABBAT, CONTINUE AT THE BOTTOM OF THIS PAGE.
We recite three times:

ADONAI, ADONAI, God merciful and compassionate, patient, abounding in love and faithfulness, assuring love for thousands of generations, forgiving iniquity, transgression, and sin, and granting pardon.

Adonai, Adonai, El raḥum v'ḥannun, erekh appayim v'rav ḥesed ve-emet. Notzeir ḥesed la-alafim, nosei avon va-fesha v'ḥatta·ah v'nakkeih.

PRIVATE MEDITATION

Avinu Malkeinu, Master of peace, help us and strengthen us so that we always strive for peace. May there be harmony among all people, their companions, and friends. May there be no discord among the members of my family. You who establish peace above, extend peace upon us and the whole world. May we draw close to You and Your Torah in truth and may we all be bound together, carrying out Your will wholeheartedly. Master of peace, bless us with peace. Amen.

May the words of my mouth and the meditations of my heart be acceptable to You, ADONAI, my rock and my redeemer.

Some recite the following three times:

May this be an auspicious time, ADONAI, for my prayer. God, in Your abundant mercy, answer me with Your faithful deliverance.

Va-ani t'fillati l'kha, Adonai, eit ratzon. Elohim b'rov ḥasdekha, aneini be-emet yish·ekha.

ON SHABBAT, WE MEDITATE AS FOLLOWS:

Ruler of the universe, praised be Your name and Your sovereignty. May Your favor abide with Your people Israel forever, and may Your liberating power be revealed to them in Your sanctuary. Extend to us the goodness of Your light and with compassion accept our prayers. May it be Your will to grant us long life and well-being; may I be counted among the righteous, and in Your compassion protect me, my family, and all the people Israel. You are the One who nourishes and sustains all life. You rule over all—even kings—for true sovereignty is Yours. I am a servant of the Holy One, whom I revere and whose precious Torah I revere in every time and place. Not on

לָא עַל אֱנָשׁ רָחִצְנָא, וְלָא עַל בַּר אֱלָהִין סָמְכְנָא, אֶלָּא
בֶּאֱלָהָא דִשְׁמַיָּא, דְּהוּא אֱלָהָא קְשׁוֹט, וְאוֹרַיְתֵהּ קְשׁוֹט,
וּנְבִיאוֹהִי קְשׁוֹט, וּמַסְגֵּא לְמֶעְבַּד טַבְוָן וּקְשׁוֹט.

◁ בֵּהּ אֲנָא רָחִץ וְלִשְׁמֵהּ קַדִּישָׁא יַקִּירָא אֲנָא אֲמַר
תֻּשְׁבְּחָן. יְהֵא רַעֲוָא קֳדָמָךְ דְּתִפְתַּח לִבִּי בְּאוֹרַיְתָא,
וְתַשְׁלִים מִשְׁאֲלִין דְּלִבִּי וְלִבָּא דְכָל־עַמָּךְ יִשְׂרָאֵל, לְטָב
וּלְחַיִּין וְלִשְׁלָם. אָמֵן.

Two scrolls of the Torah are taken from the ark.
We repeat each of these lines after the leader has recited it:

שְׁמַע יִשְׂרָאֵל יהוה אֱלֹהֵינוּ יהוה אֶחָד.

אֶחָד אֱלֹהֵינוּ גָּדוֹל אֲדוֹנֵנוּ קָדוֹשׁ וְנוֹרָא שְׁמוֹ.

Leader:

𝄐 גַּדְּלוּ לַיהוה אִתִּי, וּנְרוֹמְמָה שְׁמוֹ יַחְדָּו.

The Torah is carried in a circuit around the congregation.

לְךָ יהוה הַגְּדֻלָּה וְהַגְּבוּרָה וְהַתִּפְאֶרֶת וְהַנֵּצַח וְהַהוֹד,
כִּי־כֹל בַּשָּׁמַיִם וּבָאָרֶץ,
לְךָ יהוה הַמַּמְלָכָה וְהַמִּתְנַשֵּׂא לְכֹל לְרֹאשׁ.
רוֹמְמוּ יהוה אֱלֹהֵינוּ וְהִשְׁתַּחֲווּ לַהֲדֹם רַגְלָיו, קָדוֹשׁ הוּא.
רוֹמְמוּ יהוה אֱלֹהֵינוּ, וְהִשְׁתַּחֲווּ לְהַר קָדְשׁוֹ,
כִּי קָדוֹשׁ יהוה אֱלֹהֵינוּ.

HEAR, O ISRAEL שְׁמַע
יִשְׂרָאֵל. Taking out the
Torah becomes a moment
of affirming Israel's most
fundamental creed, as if
we are standing before our
sovereign, God, and affirming our loyalty.

AWE-INSPIRING וְנוֹרָא.
This word is appropriately
added on the High Holy
Days.

ACCLAIM גַּדְּלוּ gad'lu. Psalm
34:4.

YOURS, ADONAI לְךָ יהוה
(l'kha Adonai). 1 Chronicles
29:11. According to the
Chronicler, these verses
were part of David's last
speech to the people Israel.

EXALT ADONAI רוֹמְמוּ
יהוה (rom'mu Adonai).
Two verses with the same
opening words, taken from
Psalm 99:5, 9.

A Personal Meditation

Avinu Malkeinu, bless
my family with peace.
Teach me to appreciate
the treasures of my life
and help us always to
find contentment in one
another. Save us from
dissension and jealousy;
shield us from pettiness
and rivalry. May selfish
pride not divide us; may
pride in one another
unite us. Help us to
renew our love for one
another continually. In
the light of Your Torah
grant us, the people
Israel, and all humanity,
Your handiwork, health
and fulfillment, harmony,
peace, and joy in the new
year. Amen.

—NAVAH HARLOW

mortals nor on angels do I rely, but rather on the God of heav-
en, the God of truth, whose Torah is truth and whose prophets
are true and who abounds in deeds of goodness and truth.

I put my trust in God and I utter praise to God's holy, precious name. May it be Your will that You open my heart to
Your Torah, and that You fulfill the desires of my heart and the
hearts of all Your people Israel, for goodness, for life, and for
peace. Amen.

Beih ana raḥeitz,
v'li-shmeih kaddisha yakkira ana eimar tushb'ḥan.
Y'heih ra·ava kodamakh d'tiftaḥ libbi b'oraita,
v'tashlim mishalin d'libbi v'libba d'khol ammakh yisra·el,
l'tav u-l'ḥayyin v'lish'lam. Amen.

Two scrolls of the Torah are taken from the ark.
We repeat each of these lines after the leader has recited it:
Hear, O Israel, ADONAI is our God, ADONAI alone.
Sh'ma yisra·el, Adonai eloheinu, Adonai eḥad.

Our God is one; great is our sovereign; holy and awe-inspiring
is God's name.
Eḥad eloheinu, gadol adoneinu, kadosh v'nora sh'mo.

Leader:
ʄ Acclaim ADONAI with me; let us exalt God's name together.

The Torah is carried in a circuit around the congregation.
Yours, ADONAI, is the greatness, the power, the splendor, the
triumph, and the majesty—for all in heaven and on earth is
Yours. Yours is the sovereignty, above all else. Exalt ADONAI
our God, and bow down at God's throne, for our God is holy.
Exalt ADONAI our God, bow toward God's holy mountain, for
ADONAI our God is holy.

L'kha Adonai ha-g'dullah v'ha-g'vurah
v'ha-tiferet v'ha-neitzaḥ v'ha-hod,
ki khol ba-shamayim u-va-aretz.
L'kha Adonai ha-mamlakhah v'ha-mitnassei l'khol l'rosh.
Rom'mu Adonai eloheinu v'hishtaḥavu la-hadom raglav,
kadosh hu.
Rom'mu Adonai eloheinu v'hishtaḥavu l'har kodsho,
ki kadosh Adonai eloheinu.

אַב הָרַחֲמִים הוּא יְרַחֵם עַם עֲמוּסִים, וְיִזְכֹּר בְּרִית
אֵיתָנִים, וְיַצִּיל נַפְשׁוֹתֵינוּ מִן הַשָּׁעוֹת הָרָעוֹת, וְיִגְעַר
בְּיֵצֶר הָרָע מִן הַנְּשׂוּאִים, וְיָחֹן אוֹתָנוּ לִפְלֵיטַת עוֹלָמִים,
וִימַלֵּא מִשְׁאֲלוֹתֵינוּ בְּמִדָּה טוֹבָה יְשׁוּעָה וְרַחֲמִים.

Torah Reader (or Gabbai):

וְיַעֲזֹר וְיָגֵן וְיוֹשִׁיעַ לְכָל הַחוֹסִים בּוֹ, וְנֹאמַר **אָמֵן.**
הַכֹּל הָבוּ גֹדֶל לֵאלֹהֵינוּ, וּתְנוּ כָבוֹד לַתּוֹרָה.
(כֹּהֵן, קְרַב: יַעֲמֹד _____ בֶּן _____ הַכֹּהֵן.)
(בַּת כֹּהֵן, קְרִבִי: תַּעֲמֹד _____ בַּת _____ הַכֹּהֵן.)
(יַעֲמֹד _____ בֶּן _____ רִאשׁוֹן.)
(תַּעֲמֹד _____ בַּת _____ רִאשׁוֹנָה.)
בָּרוּךְ שֶׁנָּתַן תּוֹרָה לְעַמּוֹ יִשְׂרָאֵל בִּקְדֻשָּׁתוֹ.

Congregation and Torah Reader:

וְאַתֶּם הַדְּבֵקִים בַּיהוה אֱלֹהֵיכֶם, חַיִּים כֻּלְּכֶם הַיּוֹם.

The person who is honored with an aliyah recites the following
before the Torah is read:

בָּרְכוּ אֶת־יהוה הַמְבֹרָךְ.

The congregation responds:

בָּרוּךְ יהוה הַמְבֹרָךְ לְעוֹלָם וָעֶד.

The person repeats the above response, then continues:

בָּרוּךְ אַתָּה יהוה אֱלֹהֵינוּ מֶלֶךְ הָעוֹלָם,
אֲשֶׁר בָּחַר בָּנוּ מִכָּל־הָעַמִּים וְנָתַן לָנוּ אֶת־תּוֹרָתוֹ.
בָּרוּךְ אַתָּה יהוה, נוֹתֵן הַתּוֹרָה.

The person who is honored recites the following after the Torah is read:

בָּרוּךְ אַתָּה יהוה אֱלֹהֵינוּ מֶלֶךְ הָעוֹלָם,
אֲשֶׁר נָתַן לָנוּ תּוֹרַת אֱמֶת, וְחַיֵּי עוֹלָם נָטַע בְּתוֹכֵנוּ.
בָּרוּךְ אַתָּה יהוה, נוֹתֵן הַתּוֹרָה.

ALIYOT. During the talmudic era, each person called to the Torah would chant the assigned passage directly from the scroll. The first person would recite the opening *b'rakhah*, while the last recited the closing one. Over time, the practice evolved. Today, each person called to the Torah recites both *b'rakhot*, and the Torah is chanted by a designated reader.

The Rabbis instituted a practice of calling a *kohen* for the first aliyah and a *levi* for the second, in order to mitigate arguments about who deserved the opening honors. Some modern congregations retain this traditional practice; others call their congregants to *aliyot* without regard to priestly status.

Each person called to the Torah uses either the corner of the *tallit* or the Torah binder to touch the scroll at the starting place (indicated by the reader) and then kisses the *tallit* or binder, reciting the *b'rakhah* while holding the handles of the Torah. When the reading is completed, that person repeats the kissing gesture at the ending place, rolls the Torah closed, and, holding the handles of the Torah, recites the final *b'rakhah*.

WHO HAS CHOSEN US בָּחַר בָּנוּ. At the moment of approaching the Torah, one may feel especially chosen and may also experience the moment as being directly commanded.

GIVING US THE TORAH . . . WHO GIVES THE TORAH וְנָתַן לָנוּ אֶת־ תּוֹרָתוֹ . . . נוֹתֵן הַתּוֹרָה. In Hebrew, the *b'rakhah* uses both the present and the past tense. God not only gave us the Torah in the past, but also we receive it anew whenever we devote ourselves to studying it.

When I read Torah, I
am a link in a very long
chain that shapes my
identity; it is a ritual of
personal and communal
self-definition, as well
as a reenactment of the
first public reading of the
Torah by Ezra and the
scribes rededicating the
Temple. I enunciate the
words, and add my own
meaning to the centuries
of interpretation that
preceded me; thus they
serve both as a key to my
own inner life and as a
form of historical identification.

—RAYMOND SCHEINDLIN

May the One who is the source of compassion, who has always
sustained us, have mercy on us, and remember the covenant
with our ancestors. May God save us in difficult times, restrain
the impulse to evil within us, and grace our lives with enduring deliverance. May our pleas be answered with a measure of
kindness, salvation, and compassion.

Torah Reader (or Gabbai):
Help, shield, and save all who trust in You, God.
And let us say: *Amen.*
Let us all declare the greatness of God and give honor to the
Torah as (*the first to be called to the Torah*) comes forward. Praised is
God who gave the Torah to Israel in holiness.

Congregation and Torah Reader:
You who cling to ADONAI your God have been sustained to
this day.
V'attem ha-d'veikim badonai eloheikhem ḥayyim kull'khem ha-yom.

B'RAKHOT RECITED BY ONE CALLED UP TO THE TORAH
The person who is honored with an aliyah recites the following
before the Torah is read:
Praise ADONAI, to whom all prayer is directed.
Barkhu et Adonai ha-m'vorakh.

The congregation responds:
Praise ADONAI, to whom all prayer is directed forever and ever.
Barukh Adonai ha-m'vorakh l'olam va·ed.

The person repeats the above response, then continues:
Barukh atah ADONAI, our God, ruler of time and space, who
has chosen us from among all peoples, giving us the Torah.
Barukh atah ADONAI, who gives the Torah.
*Barukh atah Adonai eloheinu melekh ha-olam,
asher baḥar banu mi-kol ha-amim,
v'natan lanu et torato.
Barukh atah Adonai, notein ha-torah.*

The person who is honored recites the following after the Torah is read:
Barukh atah ADONAI, our God, ruler of time and space, who
has given us a teaching of truth, planting eternal life in our
midst. *Barukh atah* ADONAI, who gives the Torah.
*Barukh atah Adonai eloheinu melekh ha-olam,
asher natan lanu torat emet,
v'ḥayyei olam nata b'tokheinu.
Barukh atah Adonai, notein ha-torah.*

וַיִּקְרָא טז

LEVITICUS 16. The Torah reading for Yom Kippur Morning consists of instructions for the service of atonement performed by the High Priest in the tabernacle on Yom Kippur, a marked shift from the Rosh Hashanah readings, which contain narratives of the lives of the patriarchs and matriarchs. The focus on ritual observance highlights a theme of Yom Kippur: the relationship between the ethical and the ritual. The Torah reading reminds us that, even when we have done all we can do to cleanse ourselves—physically, emotionally, and morally—something more is

ראשון א וַיְדַבֵּ֨ר יהוה֙ אֶל־מֹשֶׁ֔ה אַחֲרֵ֣י מ֔וֹת שְׁנֵ֖י בְּנֵ֣י אַהֲרֹ֑ן בְּקׇרְבָתָ֥ם לִפְנֵי־יהו֖ה וַיָּמֻֽתוּ: ב וַיֹּ֨אמֶר יהוה֜ אֶל־מֹשֶׁ֗ה דַּבֵּר֮ אֶל־אַהֲרֹ֣ן אָחִ֒יךָ֒ וְאַל־יָבֹ֤א בְכׇל־עֵת֙ אֶל־הַקֹּ֔דֶשׁ מִבֵּ֖ית לַפָּרֹ֑כֶת אֶל־פְּנֵ֨י הַכַּפֹּ֜רֶת אֲשֶׁ֤ר עַל־הָֽאָרֹן֙ וְלֹ֣א יָמ֔וּת כִּ֚י בֶּֽעָנָ֔ן אֵרָאֶ֖ה עַל־הַכַּפֹּֽרֶת: ג בְּזֹ֛את יָבֹ֥א אַהֲרֹ֖ן אֶל־הַקֹּ֑דֶשׁ בְּפַ֧ר בֶּן־בָּקָ֛ר לְחַטָּ֖את וְאַ֥יִל לְעֹלָֽה: [בשבת שני] ד כְּתֹֽנֶת־בַּ֨ד קֹ֜דֶשׁ יִלְבָּ֗שׁ וּמִֽכְנְסֵי־בַד֮ יִהְי֣וּ עַל־בְּשָׂרוֹ֒ וּבְאַבְנֵ֥ט בַּד֙ יַחְגֹּ֔ר וּבְמִצְנֶ֥פֶת בַּ֖ד יִצְנֹ֑ף בִּגְדֵי־קֹ֣דֶשׁ הֵ֔ם וְרָחַ֥ץ בַּמַּ֛יִם אֶת־בְּשָׂר֖וֹ וּלְבֵשָֽׁם: ה וּמֵאֵ֗ת עֲדַת֙ בְּנֵ֣י יִשְׂרָאֵ֔ל יִקַּ֛ח שְׁנֵֽי־שְׂעִירֵ֥י עִזִּ֖ים לְחַטָּ֑את וְאַ֥יִל אֶחָ֖ד לְעֹלָֽה: ו וְהִקְרִ֧יב אַהֲרֹ֛ן אֶת־פַּ֥ר הַחַטָּ֖את אֲשֶׁר־ל֑וֹ וְכִפֶּ֥ר בַּעֲד֖וֹ וּבְעַ֥ד בֵּיתֽוֹ:

required: the dramatic rituals of Yom Kippur. The morning's Haftarah addresses the same issue but from the opposite perspective, reminding us that ritual alone is also insufficient. The Haftarah challenges us to examine the way in which our rituals do, or do not, lead to ethical behavior and a refinement of our moral sensibilities. Taken together, the Torah reading and the Haftarah present us with the interdependence of ethics and ritual, of human effort and divine aid, of regret and forgiveness.

VERSE 1. AFTER THE DEATH OF THE TWO SONS OF AARON אַחֲרֵי מוֹת שְׁנֵי בְּנֵי אַהֲרֹן. Aaron's two sons had died while bringing a "foreign fire" to the Temple precincts, an act described here as coming too close to the Divine Presence. Jewish scholars and biblical commentators disagree as to what constituted the sons' sin, or even if they actually sinned. Nevertheless, when this verse—which introduces the day's ritual—pointedly mentions their death, it prompts us to approach the holy with awe and trembling. From the Torah's perspective, we are dealing with matters of life and death. (The Yom Kippur liturgy underscores this theme.)

VERSE 2. FOR I APPEAR IN THE CLOUD OVER THE COVER כִּי בֶּעָנָן אֵרָאֶה עַל־הַכַּפֹּרֶת. Only once during the year would the High Priest enter the Holy of Holies. A cloud covered the ark, and a voice could be heard from between the cherubim. In biblical priestly thought, it was here that the divine was perceptible.

VERSE 4. A LINEN TUNIC כְּתֹנֶת־בַּד. On this day, the High Priest put aside his elaborate, regal daily garments and conducted the ritual of purification in simple white clothing. One midrashic interpretation is that the usual gold vestments might evoke the sin of the golden calf. Leaders of the Yom Kippur service customarily wear white, as do some congregants, in imitation of the service of the High Priest.

VERSE 6. TO MAKE EXPIATION FOR HIMSELF AND FOR HIS HOUSEHOLD וְכִפֶּר בַּעֲדוֹ וּבְעַד בֵּיתוֹ. Before atoning for the community, Aaron must atone for himself and his household. The priest must liberate himself from his own and his family's transgressions before he can effectuate atonement for anyone else. Aaron sprinkles blood all around himself, making himself a symbolic sacrifice, and once he is cleansed, he emerges symbolically reborn.

TORAH READING

The Torah reading for Yom Kippur has six aliyot, one more than on festivals, to indicate its special character. On Shabbat, the reading is divided into seven aliyot, as is the practice every Shabbat.

Ritual Then and Now

Ritual fills the human need for completeness. It speaks to the depths of human emotion by giving a specific expression and form to work through diverse emotions. Ritual also offers us the hope and comfort that, having followed prescribed rules, we will have done everything possible to attain forgiveness and even to preserve our lives with an inner sense of security.

The rituals we observe on Yom Kippur are designed to effect inner and outer cleansing in conjunction with our religious and ethical work. First, we read these passages in the Torah, remembering and studying the laws given by God to Moses for Aaron's performance of the ritual of atonement in the tabernacle. Later in the day, we ourselves dramatically reenact this service, using the Mishnaic version, composed many centuries later. Finally, we observe the command at the end of the Torah reading to "afflict" ourselves, through abstaining from food, drink, and sexual intimacy. All these elements and more are designed to give us a sense that our sins have been wiped away.

At the same time, the rituals of Yom Kippur are no substitute for the work of repentance, תְּשׁוּבָה (*teshuvah*); rather, they are the culmination of a long process of self-examination, repentance, and repair inaugurated forty days earlier on the first of Elul. After we have sought and granted forgiveness from each other, it is the day of Yom Kippur itself that gives us a sense of closure, of accomplishment. It can give us a sense of transcendence, and of transformation.

Liturgical Practice

The Ashkenazic rite is unique in prescribing a special chant for High Holy Day Torah reading. Solemn and meditative, its use may be explained by the Zohar's statement that all who listen to Leviticus chapter 16—the portion for Yom Kippur in which the sudden death of Aaron's children is mentioned—should shed tears. The custom of using this special melody extended to Rosh Hashanah as well.

—*after* ABRAHAM ZVI IDELSOHN

LEVITICUS 16

First aliyah

1 ADONAI spoke to Moses after the death of the two sons of Aaron who died when they drew too close to the presence of ADONAI. 2 ADONAI said to Moses: Tell your brother Aaron that he is not to come at will into the Shrine behind the curtain, in front of the cover that is upon the ark, lest he die; for I appear in the cloud over the cover. 3 Thus only shall Aaron enter the Shrine: with a bull of the herd for a purification offering and a ram for a burnt offering.— [*Second aliyah on Shabbat*] 4 He shall be dressed in a sacral linen tunic, with linen breeches next to his flesh, and be girt with a linen sash, and he shall wear a linen turban. They are sacral vestments; he shall bathe his body in water and then put them on.— 5 And from the Israelite community he shall take two he-goats for a purification offering and a ram for a burnt offering.

6 Aaron is to offer his own bull of purification offering, to make expiation for himself and for his household.

שני [בשבת שלישי] ז וְלָקַח אֶת־שְׁנֵי הַשְּׂעִירִם וְהֶעֱמִיד אֹתָם
לִפְנֵי יְהֹוָה פֶּתַח אֹהֶל מוֹעֵד: ח וְנָתַן אַהֲרֹן עַל־שְׁנֵי
הַשְּׂעִירִם גֹּרָלוֹת גּוֹרָל אֶחָד לַיהֹוָה וְגוֹרָל אֶחָד לַעֲזָאזֵל:
ט וְהִקְרִיב אַהֲרֹן אֶת־הַשָּׂעִיר אֲשֶׁר עָלָה עָלָיו הַגּוֹרָל
לַיהֹוָה וְעָשָׂהוּ חַטָּאת: י וְהַשָּׂעִיר אֲשֶׁר עָלָה עָלָיו הַגּוֹרָל
לַעֲזָאזֵל יׇעֳמַד־חַי לִפְנֵי יְהֹוָה לְכַפֵּר עָלָיו לְשַׁלַּח אֹתוֹ
לַעֲזָאזֵל הַמִּדְבָּרָה: יא וְהִקְרִיב אַהֲרֹן אֶת־פַּר הַחַטָּאת
אֲשֶׁר־לוֹ וְכִפֶּר בַּעֲדוֹ וּבְעַד בֵּיתוֹ וְשָׁחַט אֶת־פַּר הַחַטָּאת
אֲשֶׁר־לוֹ:

שלישי [בשבת רביעי] יב וְלָקַח מְלֹא־הַמַּחְתָּה גַּחֲלֵי־אֵשׁ מֵעַל
הַמִּזְבֵּחַ מִלִּפְנֵי יְהֹוָה וּמְלֹא חׇפְנָיו קְטֹרֶת סַמִּים דַּקָּה
וְהֵבִיא מִבֵּית לַפָּרֹכֶת: יג וְנָתַן אֶת־הַקְּטֹרֶת עַל־הָאֵשׁ
לִפְנֵי יְהֹוָה | וְכִסָּה עֲנַן הַקְּטֹרֶת אֶת־הַכַּפֹּרֶת אֲשֶׁר עַל־
הָעֵדוּת וְלֹא יָמוּת: יד וְלָקַח מִדַּם הַפָּר וְהִזָּה בְאֶצְבָּעוֹ
עַל־פְּנֵי הַכַּפֹּרֶת קֵדְמָה וְלִפְנֵי הַכַּפֹּרֶת יַזֶּה שֶׁבַע־פְּעָמִים
מִן־הַדָּם בְּאֶצְבָּעוֹ: טו וְשָׁחַט אֶת־שְׂעִיר הַחַטָּאת אֲשֶׁר

גּוֹרָל אֶחָד לַיהוה וְגוֹרָל אֶחָד לַעֲזָאזֵל. Aaron makes a selection by lottery to determine which of two goats will be sacrificed and which will be burdened with the sins of all Israel and flung into the wilderness as a scapegoat. The rituals are designed to return Israel to a pristine condition free of sin to start the new year. The scapegoat ritual, however, reminds us that our control is limited and that our destiny is a mystery. The Rabbis insisted that the two goats had to be exactly the same—in color, age, and so on. What differentiated their fate? Only the chance designation of the lottery.

The scapegoat is sent to Azazel, later in this chapter designated as "the wilderness," a place devoid of human or animal existence and therefore perhaps biblically understood as the dwelling place of demonic forces, or that which is barren—the opposite of God, the giver of life. The meaning of the word Azazel has been lost. Some, like the medieval commentator Abraham Ibn Ezra, think it is the name of a demon; others, like the ancient Rabbis, a place name: the place where the goat was sent away (ez, goat; azal, went away). The sending away of the scapegoat is a visible representation of the human wish to be rid of sin.

VERSE 12. AND BRING THIS BEHIND THE CURTAIN וְהֵבִיא מִבֵּית לַפָּרֹכֶת. Once a year, the High Priest—and only the High Priest—entered the Holy of Holies. In that moment, the connection between heaven and earth was made real. The loss of that moment created a crisis for the generations following the Temple's destruction. Some Jews believed that by their being in exile, God was no longer perceptible. Others argued that even without the Temple's rituals, they could evoke God's presence via gathering in prayer as a community, studying sacred texts together, and performing kind deeds.

VERSE 13. THE CLOUD FROM THE INCENSE SCREENS THE COVER וְכִסָּה עֲנַן הַקְּטֹרֶת אֶת־הַכַּפֹּרֶת. The smoke cloud created by the incense now covers the ark, allowing the Divine to enter but not be seen. The cloud cover becomes a symbolic indication of the hiddenness of God.

VERSE 14. Blood represents life; members of the animal kingdom cannot exist without blood. The blood of the sacrifice offered on the altar is the "life" of the sacrifice. God accepts it in place of human life, grants expiation, and refrains from punishment and wrath. In recognition of the special power of blood, care is taken to remove blood from meat before it is fit (kasher) for eating.

God's Prayer

Rabbi Yoḥanan said in the name of Rabbi Yose: "How do we know that the Holy One says prayers? Because Scripture says: 'I shall bring them to My holy mountain and make them joyful in My house of prayer (*beit t'fillati*)' (Isaiah 56:7). It is not said 'their prayer' (*t'fillatam*) but 'My prayer' (*t'fillati*); hence you learn that the Holy One says prayers.

What does the Holy One pray? Rabbi Zutra ben Tobi said in the name of Rav: "May it be My will that My mercy suppress My anger, and that My mercy prevail over My other attributes, so that I deal with My children via the attribute of mercy and, on their behalf, not be constrained by strict justice!"

It was taught: Rabbi Ishmael ben Elisha said: "I once entered into the innermost part of the Temple to offer incense, and I saw—seated upon a high and exalted throne— *Akatriel Yah Adonai Tz'va·ot*, who said to me: 'My son Ishmael, bless Me!' I replied: 'May it be Your will that Your mercy suppress Your anger, and that Your mercy prevail over Your other attributes, so that You deal with Your children via the attribute of mercy and, on their behalf, not be constrained by strict justice!' *Akatriel Yah Adonai Tz'va·ot* nodded to me." —BABYLONIAN TALMUD, BERAKHOT

Second aliyah [Third aliyah on Shabbat]

7 Aaron shall take the two he-goats and let them stand before ADONAI at the entrance of the Tent of Meeting; 8 and he shall place lots upon the two goats, one marked for ADONAI and the other marked for Azazel. 9 Aaron shall bring forward the goat designated by lot for ADONAI, which he is to offer as a purification offering; 10 while the goat designated by lot for Azazel shall be left standing alive before ADONAI, to make expiation with it and to send it off to the wilderness for Azazel. 11 Aaron shall then offer his bull of purification offering, to make expiation for himself and his household. He shall slaughter his bull of purification offering.

Third aliyah [Fourth aliyah on Shabbat]

12 Then he shall take a panful of glowing coals scooped from the altar before ADONAI, and two handfuls of finely ground aromatic incense, and bring this behind the curtain. 13 He shall put the incense on the fire before ADONAI, so that the cloud from the incense screens the cover that is over [the Ark of] the Pact, lest he die. 14 He shall take some of the blood of the bull and sprinkle it with his finger over the cover on the east side; and in front of the cover he shall sprinkle some of the blood with his finger seven times. 15 He shall then slaughter the

לָעָם וְהֵבִיא אֶת־דָּמוֹ אֶל־מִבֵּית לַפָּרֹכֶת וְעָשָׂה אֶת־דָּמוֹ
כַּאֲשֶׁר עָשָׂה לְדַם הַפָּר וְהִזָּה אֹתוֹ עַל־הַכַּפֹּרֶת וְלִפְנֵי
הַכַּפֹּרֶת: יז וְכִפֶּר עַל־הַקֹּדֶשׁ מִטֻּמְאֹת בְּנֵי יִשְׂרָאֵל
וּמִפִּשְׁעֵיהֶם לְכָל־חַטֹּאתָם וְכֵן יַעֲשֶׂה לְאֹהֶל מוֹעֵד
הַשֹּׁכֵן אִתָּם בְּתוֹךְ טֻמְאֹתָם: יז וְכָל־אָדָם לֹא־יִהְיֶה |
בְּאֹהֶל מוֹעֵד בְּבֹאוֹ לְכַפֵּר בַּקֹּדֶשׁ עַד־צֵאתוֹ וְכִפֶּר בַּעֲדוֹ
וּבְעַד בֵּיתוֹ וּבְעַד כָּל־קְהַל יִשְׂרָאֵל:

רביעי [בשבת חמישי] יח וְיָצָא אֶל־הַמִּזְבֵּחַ אֲשֶׁר לִפְנֵי־יְהוָה
וְכִפֶּר עָלָיו וְלָקַח מִדַּם הַפָּר וּמִדַּם הַשָּׂעִיר וְנָתַן עַל־
קַרְנוֹת הַמִּזְבֵּחַ סָבִיב: יט וְהִזָּה עָלָיו מִן־הַדָּם בְּאֶצְבָּעוֹ
שֶׁבַע פְּעָמִים וְטִהֲרוֹ וְקִדְּשׁוֹ מִטֻּמְאֹת בְּנֵי יִשְׂרָאֵל:
כ וְכִלָּה מִכַּפֵּר אֶת־הַקֹּדֶשׁ וְאֶת־אֹהֶל מוֹעֵד וְאֶת־הַמִּזְבֵּחַ
וְהִקְרִיב אֶת־הַשָּׂעִיר הֶחָי: כא וְסָמַךְ אַהֲרֹן אֶת־שְׁתֵּי יָדָיו
עַל רֹאשׁ הַשָּׂעִיר הַחַי וְהִתְוַדָּה עָלָיו אֶת־כָּל־עֲוֺנֹת בְּנֵי
יִשְׂרָאֵל וְאֶת־כָּל־פִּשְׁעֵיהֶם לְכָל־חַטֹּאתָם וְנָתַן אֹתָם עַל־
רֹאשׁ הַשָּׂעִיר וְשִׁלַּח בְּיַד־אִישׁ עִתִּי הַמִּדְבָּרָה: כב וְנָשָׂא
הַשָּׂעִיר עָלָיו אֶת־כָּל־עֲוֺנֹתָם אֶל־אֶרֶץ גְּזֵרָה וְשִׁלַּח אֶת־
הַשָּׂעִיר בַּמִּדְבָּר:
כג וּבָא אַהֲרֹן אֶל־אֹהֶל מוֹעֵד וּפָשַׁט אֶת־בִּגְדֵי הַבָּד
אֲשֶׁר לָבַשׁ בְּבֹאוֹ אֶל־הַקֹּדֶשׁ וְהִנִּיחָם שָׁם: כד וְרָחַץ
אֶת־בְּשָׂרוֹ בַמַּיִם בְּמָקוֹם קָדוֹשׁ וְלָבַשׁ אֶת־בְּגָדָיו וְיָצָא
וְעָשָׂה אֶת־עֹלָתוֹ וְאֶת־עֹלַת הָעָם וְכִפֶּר בַּעֲדוֹ וּבְעַד הָעָם:

VERSE 16. THE IMPURITY AND TRANSGRESSION OF THE ISRAELITES, WHATEVER THEIR SINS מִטֻּמְאֹת בְּנֵי יִשְׂרָאֵל וּמִפִּשְׁעֵיהֶם לְכָל־חַטֹּאתָם. The understanding here is that both the sinner and the sanctuary need atonement. The Bible includes various views regarding ritual impurity. The prophets stressed that unethical behavior created impurity. Priestly writings are more often concerned with impurity created through contact with the dead or other objects considered impure, lest that impurity be brought into the sanctuary.

VERSE 21. AND CONFESS OVER IT וְהִתְוַדָּה עָלָיו. The ritual does not suffice without a spoken confession. Such spoken confession, known as וִדּוּי (viddui), becomes a central part of Yom Kippur liturgy, repeated ten times during the day. The number ten may not be accidental: the High Priest had bathed himself ten times during the Temple's atonement ritual. After the Temple's destruction, the rite of confession, which had been only one small element in the atonement ritual, soon became its central feature. The Viddui, repeated again and again, is more than a mere acknowledgement of sin: it serves as a ritual act of cleansing.

DESIGNATED AGENT אִישׁ עִתִּי. This part of the ritual could be performed by anyone, priest or layperson.

people's goat of purification offering, bring its blood behind the curtain, and do with its blood as he has done with the blood of the bull: he shall sprinkle it over the cover and in front of the cover.

16 Thus he shall purge the Shrine of the impurity and transgression of the Israelites, whatever their sins; and he shall do the same for the Tent of Meeting, which abides with them in the midst of their impurity. 17 When he goes in to make expiation in the Shrine, nobody else shall be in the Tent of Meeting until he comes out—to make expiation for himself and his household, and for the whole congregation of Israel.

Fourth aliyah [Fifth aliyah on Shabbat]

18 Then he shall go out to the altar that is before ADONAI and purge it: he shall take some of the blood of the bull and of the goat and apply it to each of the horns of the altar; 19 and the rest of the blood he shall sprinkle on it with his finger seven times. Thus he shall purify it of the impurity of the Israelites and consecrate it.

20 When he has finished purging the Shrine, the Tent of Meeting, and the altar, the live goat shall be brought forward. 21 Aaron shall lay both his hands upon the head of the live goat and confess over it all the iniquities and transgressions of the Israelites, whatever their sins, putting them on the head of the goat; and it shall be sent off to the wilderness through a designated agent. 22 Thus the goat shall carry on it all their iniquities to an inaccessible region; and the goat shall be set free in the wilderness.

23 And Aaron shall go into the Tent of Meeting, take off the linen vestments that he put on when he entered the Shrine, and leave them there. 24 He shall bathe his body in water in the holy precinct and put on his vestments; then he shall come out and offer his burnt offering and the burnt offering of the people, making expiation for himself and for the people.

חמישי [בשבת שישי] כה וְאֵת חֵלֶב הַחַטָּאת יַקְטִיר הַמִּזְבֵּחָה: כו וְהַמְשַׁלֵּחַ אֶת־הַשָּׂעִיר לַעֲזָאזֵל יְכַבֵּס בְּגָדָיו וְרָחַץ אֶת־בְּשָׂרוֹ בַּמָּיִם וְאַחֲרֵי־כֵן יָבוֹא אֶל־הַמַּחֲנֶה: כז וְאֵת פַּר הַחַטָּאת וְאֵת | שְׂעִיר הַחַטָּאת אֲשֶׁר הוּבָא אֶת־דָּמָם לְכַפֵּר בַּקֹּדֶשׁ יוֹצִיא אֶל־מִחוּץ לַמַּחֲנֶה וְשָׂרְפוּ בָאֵשׁ אֶת־עֹרֹתָם וְאֶת־בְּשָׂרָם וְאֶת־פִּרְשָׁם: כח וְהַשֹּׂרֵף אֹתָם יְכַבֵּס בְּגָדָיו וְרָחַץ אֶת־בְּשָׂרוֹ בַּמָּיִם וְאַחֲרֵי־כֵן יָבוֹא אֶל־הַמַּחֲנֶה: כט וְהָיְתָה לָכֶם לְחֻקַּת עוֹלָם בַּחֹדֶשׁ הַשְּׁבִיעִי בֶּעָשׂוֹר לַחֹדֶשׁ תְּעַנּוּ אֶת־נַפְשֹׁתֵיכֶם וְכָל־מְלָאכָה לֹא תַעֲשׂוּ הָאֶזְרָח וְהַגֵּר הַגָּר בְּתוֹכְכֶם: ל כִּי־בַיּוֹם הַזֶּה יְכַפֵּר עֲלֵיכֶם לְטַהֵר אֶתְכֶם מִכֹּל חַטֹּאתֵיכֶם לִפְנֵי יְהוָה תִּטְהָרוּ:

שישי [בשבת שביעי] לא שַׁבַּת שַׁבָּתוֹן הִיא לָכֶם וְעִנִּיתֶם אֶת־נַפְשֹׁתֵיכֶם חֻקַּת עוֹלָם: לב וְכִפֶּר הַכֹּהֵן אֲשֶׁר־יִמְשַׁח אֹתוֹ וַאֲשֶׁר יְמַלֵּא אֶת־יָדוֹ לְכַהֵן תַּחַת אָבִיו וְלָבַשׁ אֶת־בִּגְדֵי הַבָּד בִּגְדֵי הַקֹּדֶשׁ: לג וְכִפֶּר אֶת־מִקְדַּשׁ הַקֹּדֶשׁ וְאֶת־אֹהֶל מוֹעֵד וְאֶת־הַמִּזְבֵּחַ יְכַפֵּר וְעַל הַכֹּהֲנִים וְעַל־כָּל־עַם הַקָּהָל יְכַפֵּר: לד וְהָיְתָה־זֹּאת לָכֶם לְחֻקַּת עוֹלָם לְכַפֵּר עַל־בְּנֵי יִשְׂרָאֵל מִכָּל־חַטֹּאתָם אַחַת בַּשָּׁנָה וַיַּעַשׂ כַּאֲשֶׁר צִוָּה יְהוָה אֶת־מֹשֶׁה:

VERSE 29. The customs and rituals we follow on Yom Kippur are based on this verse. The seventh month is the month of Tishrei, counting from Nisan, the month in which Passover occurs. The phrase "afflict yourselves," תְּעַנּוּ אֶת־נַפְשֹׁתֵיכֶם, was interpreted by the Rabbis to mean abstaining from both food and drink. They added three other restrictions: not anointing oneself, not wearing solid leather shoes, and not engaging in sexual intercourse.

VERSE 30. This verse speaks of purity and atonement, which are states that we can achieve only after God has granted forgiveness. The ritual returns the sanctuary to its pristine condition; thus, the ritual of Yom Kippur allows us to start again, fresh.

Sacrifices

We should imagine the emotion of an ancient Israelite in offering sacrifices. Animals were rarely slaughtered—one might own only one or two, certainly just a few. Thus the offering was truly an economic sacrifice. In biblical Temple practice, the part of the animal which is offered to God is totally burnt on the altar. In the view of some biblical scholars this made it clear to the participant that the animal was not being offered as food for the Divine. Rather, as the smoke rose to the sky, it represented a symbolic enactment of the attempt to reach the divine resident in the heavens. The offering may have been made in complete silence, adding to the awe of the moment. We no longer have a system of sacrifice, but we do have the memory of our ancestors who sought to come close to the Divine.

Fifth aliyah [Sixth aliyah on Shabbat]

25 The fat of the purification offering he shall turn into smoke on the altar.

26 The one who set the Azazel-goat free shall wash those clothes and bathe the body in water—and after that may reenter the camp.

27 The bull of purification offering and the goat of purification offering whose blood was brought in to purge the Shrine shall be taken outside the camp; and their hides, flesh, and dung shall be consumed in fire. 28 The one who burned them shall wash those clothes and bathe the body in water—and after that may re-enter the camp.

29 And this shall be to you a law for all time: In the seventh month, on the tenth day of the month, you shall practice self-denial; and you shall do no manner of work, neither the citizen nor the alien who resides among you. 30 For on this day expiation shall be made for you to purify you of all your sins; you shall be pure before ADONAI.

Sixth aliyah [Seventh aliyah on Shabbat]

31 It shall be a sabbath of complete rest for you, and you shall practice self-denial; it is a law for all time. 32 The priest who has been anointed and ordained to serve as priest in place of his father shall make expiation. He shall put on the linen vestments, the sacral vestments. 33 He shall purge the innermost Shrine; he shall purge the Tent of Meeting and the altar; and he shall make expiation for the priests and for all the people of the congregation.

34 This shall be to you a law for all time: to make expiation for the Israelites for all their sins once a year.

And Moses did as ADONAI had commanded him.

Both Torah scrolls are placed on the Reader's desk.

יִתְגַּדַּל וְיִתְקַדַּשׁ שְׁמֵהּ רַבָּא, בְּעָלְמָא דִּי בְרָא, כִּרְעוּתֵהּ,
וְיַמְלִיךְ מַלְכוּתֵהּ בְּחַיֵּיכוֹן וּבְיוֹמֵיכוֹן וּבְחַיֵּי דְכָל־בֵּית
יִשְׂרָאֵל, בַּעֲגָלָא וּבִזְמַן קָרִיב, וְאִמְרוּ אָמֵן.

יְהֵא שְׁמֵהּ רַבָּא מְבָרַךְ לְעָלַם וּלְעָלְמֵי עָלְמַיָּא.

יִתְבָּרַךְ וְיִשְׁתַּבַּח וְיִתְפָּאַר וְיִתְרוֹמַם וְיִתְנַשֵּׂא וְיִתְהַדָּר
וְיִתְעַלֶּה וְיִתְהַלָּל שְׁמֵהּ דְּקֻדְשָׁא, בְּרִיךְ הוּא, לְעֵלָּא לְעֵלָּא
מִכָּל־בִּרְכָתָא וְשִׁירָתָא תֻּשְׁבְּחָתָא וְנֶחֱמָתָא דַּאֲמִירָן
בְּעָלְמָא, וְאִמְרוּ אָמֵן.

הַגְבָּהַת הַתּוֹרָה

A Magbiah and Golel are called to raise and tie each Sefer Torah after it is read.
As the Torah is lifted, we recite:

וְזֹאת הַתּוֹרָה אֲשֶׁר־שָׂם מֹשֶׁה לִפְנֵי בְּנֵי יִשְׂרָאֵל,
עַל־פִּי יהוה בְּיַד־מֹשֶׁה.

מַפְטִיר

בְּמִדְבַּר כט

ז וּבֶעָשׂוֹר לַחֹדֶשׁ הַשְּׁבִיעִי הַזֶּה מִקְרָא־קֹדֶשׁ יִהְיֶה
לָכֶם וְעִנִּיתֶם אֶת־נַפְשֹׁתֵיכֶם כָּל־מְלָאכָה לֹא תַעֲשׂוּ:
ח וְהִקְרַבְתֶּם עֹלָה לַיהוה רֵיחַ נִיחֹחַ פַּר בֶּן־בָּקָר אֶחָד
אַיִל אֶחָד כְּבָשִׂים בְּנֵי־שָׁנָה שִׁבְעָה תְּמִימִם יִהְיוּ לָכֶם:
ט וּמִנְחָתָם סֹלֶת בְּלוּלָה בַשֶּׁמֶן שְׁלֹשָׁה עֶשְׂרֹנִים לַפָּר שְׁנֵי
עֶשְׂרֹנִים לָאַיִל הָאֶחָד: י עִשָּׂרוֹן עִשָּׂרוֹן לַכֶּבֶשׂ הָאֶחָד
לְשִׁבְעַת הַכְּבָשִׂים: יא שְׂעִיר־עִזִּים אֶחָד חַטָּאת מִלְּבַד
חַטַּאת הַכִּפֻּרִים וְעֹלַת הַתָּמִיד וּמִנְחָתָהּ וְנִסְכֵּיהֶם:

THIS IS THE TORAH וְזֹאת הַתּוֹרָה. The Rabbis combined Deuteronomy 4:44 and Numbers 9:23, underscoring that our entire Torah came from Moses as dictated by God. This theological claim is not made in the Bible itself. As this passage conflates two biblical verses, the 20th-century Orthodox Jewish thinker Joseph Ber Soloveitchik, for instance, did not recite it.

When reciting this passage, some people hold up or kiss the *tzitzit* of their *tallit*, to affirm their own daily fulfillment of the Torah's instructions.

MAFTIR מַפְטִיר. On each festival, following the main Torah reading, we bring a second Torah scroll to the reading table, and from it we read the appropriate passage in the Book of Numbers for that festival, enumerating the sacrifices offered on that day. This passage, regarding Yom Kippur, is prefaced by the same exhortation with which our main Torah reading concluded: on this day, we must afflict ourselves.

VERSE 8. The instructions call for each type of common farm animal to be offered as a sacrifice: oxen, sheep, and (in verse 11) goats. The most numerous are the sheep: one adult ram and seven yearling rams. Compared to the requirements for other sacred occasions, the number of animals called for is minimal. This holy day's essential drama lies elsewhere.

VERSE 9. Every animal sacrifice was accompanied by offerings of ground grain and olive oil.

¶ *The following may be sung as the Torah is tied.*

תּוֹרָה צִוָּה לָנוּ מֹשֶׁה,
מוֹרָשָׁה קְהִלַּת יַעֲקֹב.

Moses commanded the observance of Torah; it is the inheritance of the community of Jacob.

Torah tzivvah lanu moshe, morashah k'hillat ya·akov.

The Holy Day Sacrifice

Said Abraham to the Holy One: "Should the people Israel sin against You, Heaven forbid, You might treat them as the generation that perished in the flood!"

Said God: "No."

Said Abraham: "Give me a sign."

God directed Abraham to offer animal sacrifices and Abraham came to understand the atoning power of that ritual act. And he was able to envision that atonement would be gained for the people Israel through the ritual of sacrifice at the Temple in Jerusalem.

Said Abraham: "That will suffice while the Temple is standing. But when there is no Temple, what will become of the people Israel?"

Said God: "I have already arranged for these passages concerning the sacrifices. Whenever they read about the sacrifices I shall consider them as having offered sacrifices in My Presence, and I shall forgive them all their sins."

—BABYLONIAN TALMUD, MEGILLAH
(trans. Jules Harlow)

Ḥatzi Kaddish

Both Torah scrolls are placed on the Reader's desk.

May God's great name be exalted and hallowed throughout the created world, as is God's wish. May God's sovereignty soon be established, in your lifetime and in your days, and in the days of all the House of Israel. And respond with: *Amen.*

May God's great name be acknowledged forever and ever!
Y'hei sh'meih rabba m'varakh l'alam u-l'almei almayya.

May the name of the Holy One be acknowledged and celebrated, lauded and worshipped, exalted and honored, extolled and acclaimed—though God, who is blessed, *b'rikh hu,* is truly far beyond all acknowledgment and praise, or any expressions of gratitude or consolation ever spoken in the world. And respond with: *Amen.*

Lifting the Torah

A Magbiah and Golel are called to raise and tie each Sefer Torah after it is read. As the Torah is lifted, we recite:

This is the Torah, God's word by Moses' hand, which Moses set before the people Israel.

V'zot ha-torah asher sam mosheh lifnei b'nei yisra·el al pi Adonai b'yad mosheh.

Maftir

NUMBERS 29

7 On the tenth day of the same seventh month you shall observe a sacred occasion when you shall practice self-denial. You shall do no work. 8 You shall present to ADONAI a burnt offering of pleasing odor: one bull of the herd, one ram, seven yearling lambs; see that they are without blemish. 9 The grain offering with them—of choice flour with oil mixed in—shall be: three-tenths of a measure for a bull, two-tenths for the one ram, 10 one-tenth for each of the seven lambs. 11 And there shall be one goat for a purification offering, in addition to the purification offering of expiation and the regular burnt offering with its grain offering, each with its libation.

For those called to the Torah:
A male:

מִי שֶׁבֵּרַךְ אֲבוֹתֵינוּ אַבְרָהָם יִצְחָק וְיַעֲקֹב, [וְאִמּוֹתֵינוּ] שָׂרָה רִבְקָה רָחֵל וְלֵאָה,
הוּא יְבָרֵךְ אֶת _____ בֶּן _____ שֶׁעָלָה הַיּוֹם לִכְבוֹד הַמָּקוֹם וְלִכְבוֹד
הַתּוֹרָה וְלִכְבוֹד יוֹם הַדִּין. הַקָּדוֹשׁ בָּרוּךְ הוּא יִשְׁמֹר אוֹתוֹ וְאֶת־כָּל־מִשְׁפַּחְתּוֹ,
וְיִשְׁלַח בְּרָכָה וְהַצְלָחָה בְּכָל־מַעֲשֵׂה יָדָיו, וְיִכְתְּבֵהוּ וְיַחְתְּמֵהוּ לְחַיִּים טוֹבִים בְּזֶה
יוֹם הַדִּין עִם כָּל־יִשְׂרָאֵל אֶחָיו וְאַחְיוֹתָיו, וְנֹאמַר אָמֵן.

A female:

מִי שֶׁבֵּרַךְ אֲבוֹתֵינוּ אַבְרָהָם יִצְחָק וְיַעֲקֹב, [וְאִמּוֹתֵינוּ] שָׂרָה רִבְקָה רָחֵל וְלֵאָה,
הוּא יְבָרֵךְ אֶת _____ בַּת _____ שֶׁעָלְתָה הַיּוֹם לִכְבוֹד הַמָּקוֹם וְלִכְבוֹד
הַתּוֹרָה וְלִכְבוֹד יוֹם הַדִּין. הַקָּדוֹשׁ בָּרוּךְ הוּא יִשְׁמֹר אוֹתָהּ וְאֶת־כָּל־מִשְׁפַּחְתָּהּ,
וְיִשְׁלַח בְּרָכָה וְהַצְלָחָה בְּכָל־מַעֲשֵׂה יָדֶיהָ וְיִכְתְּבֶהָ וְיַחְתְּמָהּ לְחַיִּים טוֹבִים בְּזֶה
יוֹם הַדִּין עִם כָּל־יִשְׂרָאֵל אַחֶיהָ וְאַחְיוֹתֶיהָ, וְנֹאמַר אָמֵן.

Plural:

מִי שֶׁבֵּרַךְ אֲבוֹתֵינוּ אַבְרָהָם יִצְחָק וְיַעֲקֹב, [וְאִמּוֹתֵינוּ] שָׂרָה רִבְקָה רָחֵל וְלֵאָה,
הוּא יְבָרֵךְ אֶת _____ וְאֶת _____, וְאֶת־כָּל־הַקְּרוּאִים אֲשֶׁר עָלוּ הַיּוֹם
לִכְבוֹד הַמָּקוֹם וְלִכְבוֹד הַתּוֹרָה וְלִכְבוֹד יוֹם הַדִּין. הַקָּדוֹשׁ בָּרוּךְ הוּא יִשְׁמֹר
אוֹתָם וְאֶת־כָּל־מִשְׁפְּחוֹתֵיהֶם, וְיִשְׁלַח בְּרָכָה וְהַצְלָחָה בְּכָל־מַעֲשֵׂה יְדֵיהֶם
וְיִכְתְּבֵם וְיַחְתְּמֵם לְחַיִּים טוֹבִים בְּזֶה יוֹם הַדִּין עִם כָּל־יִשְׂרָאֵל אֲחֵיהֶם
וְאַחְיוֹתֵיהֶם, וְנֹאמַר אָמֵן.

Prayer for those who are ill:

מִי שֶׁבֵּרַךְ אֲבוֹתֵינוּ אַבְרָהָם יִצְחָק וְיַעֲקֹב, [וְאִמּוֹתֵינוּ] שָׂרָה רִבְקָה רָחֵל וְלֵאָה,
הוּא יְבָרֵךְ אֶת־כָּל־הַחוֹלִים _____ וְיָסִיר מֵהֶם כָּל־מַחֲלָה, וְיִרְפָּא לְכָל־גּוּפָם,
וְיִסְלַח לְכָל־עֲוֹנָם, וְיִשְׁלַח בְּרָכָה וְהַצְלָחָה בְּכָל־מַעֲשֵׂה יְדֵיהֶם, עִם כָּל־יִשְׂרָאֵל
אֲחֵיהֶם וְאַחְיוֹתֵיהֶם, וְנֹאמַר אָמֵן.

בִּרְכַּת הַגּוֹמֵל

*This b'rakhah is recited by one who has recovered from a serious illness
or survived a life-threatening crisis.*

בָּרוּךְ אַתָּה יהוה אֱלֹהֵינוּ מֶלֶךְ הָעוֹלָם, הַגּוֹמֵל לְחַיָּבִים
טוֹבוֹת, שֶׁגְּמָלַנִי כָּל־טוֹב.

The congregation responds:

מִי
for a group: שֶׁגְּמָלְכֶם / *for a female:* שֶׁגְּמָלֵךְ / *for a male:* שֶׁגְּמָלְךָ
כָּל־טוֹב, הוּא (יִגְמָלְךָ / יִגְמָלֵךְ / יִגְמָלְכֶם) כָּל־טוֹב, סֶלָה.

בִּרְכַּת **BIRKAT HA-GOMEL**
הַגּוֹמֵל. In thanking God for
having been saved from
danger and calamity, we are
conscious of the fragility of
our lives and the gratitude
with which we should meet
each day of our lives. Ellen
Frankel, a contemporary
writer, remarks further that
through the recitation of
this b'rakhah, we summon
support from all those who
care about our welfare.

Blessings for Those Called to the Torah and for Those Who Are Ill

For those called to the Torah:

A male:

May the One who blessed our ancestors Abraham, Isaac, and Jacob, Sarah, Rebecca, Rachel, and Leah bless _____, who has ascended today to honor God, the Torah, and the Day of Judgment. May the Holy Blessed One protect him and his entire family, bring blessing and success to all the works of his hands, and inscribe and seal him for a good life on this Day of Judgment, together with all his fellow Jews, and let us say: *Amen.*

A female:

May the One who blessed our ancestors Abraham, Isaac, and Jacob, Sarah, Rebecca, Rachel, and Leah bless _____, who has ascended today to honor God, the Torah, and the Day of Judgment. May the Holy Blessed One protect her and her entire family, bring blessing and success to all the works of her hands, and inscribe and seal her for a good life on this Day of Judgment, together with all her fellow Jews, and let us say: *Amen.*

Plural:

May the One who blessed our ancestors Abraham, Isaac, and Jacob, Sarah, Rebecca, Rachel, and Leah bless _____, who have ascended today to honor God, the Torah, and the Day of Judgment. May the Holy Blessed One protect them and their entire families, bring blessing and success to all the works of their hands, and inscribe and seal them for a good life on this Day of Judgment, together with all their fellow Jews, and let us say: *Amen.*

Prayer for all those who are ill:

May the One who blessed our ancestors Abraham, Isaac and Jacob, Sarah, Rebecca, Rachel, and Leah bless all who are ill _____ and remove from them any sickness. Heal their bodies, forgive their transgressions, send blessing and good fortune to all the work of their hands, as well as to all their brothers and sisters, the people Israel, and let us say: *Amen.*

BIRKAT HA-GOMEL
This b'rakhah is recited by one who has recovered from a serious illness or survived a life-threatening crisis.

Barukh atah ADONAI, our God, ruler of time and space, who bestows goodness on us despite our imperfections, and who has treated me so favorably.

Barukh atah Adonai, eloheinu melekh ha-olam, ha-gomel l'ḥayyavim tovot, she-g'malani kol tov.

The congregation responds:

May the One who has shown such favor to you continue to bestow all that is good upon you, *selah.*

Mi

(for a male: she-g'mal'kha / for a female: she-g'maleikh / for a group: she-g'malkhem)

kol tov,

hu (for a male: yigmal'kha / for a female: yigm'leikh / for a group: yigmalkhem) kol tov, selah.

הַפְטָרָה. In 539 B.C.E., Cyrus led the Persians in the conquest of Babylonia. Two years later, he issued a decree allowing conquered peoples to return to their lands. The news stirred the Jewish exiles in Babylonia, and the prophet reflects that excitement. The Haftarah begins with the announcement that the road to return has now been cleared: God has opened the highway from Babylonia to the Land of Israel. The prophet then expresses a fear that moral corruption—which he views as the cause of the exile—will soon rear its head again. The thought of return, with its promise of rebuilding the Temple, launches the prophet into an attack on religious hypocrisy. Ritual devotion, he asserts, must be accompanied by ethical behavior.

This morning's Torah reading focused on an elaborate ritual for purifying the sanctuary. Now the Haftarah emphasizes that the aim of ritual is to transform our behavior. In juxtaposing these two biblical passages, the Rabbis have provided us with a telling measure of their understanding of Judaism.

VERSE 15. The prophet employs contrasting imagery: though God is on high, divine concern is focused on the most lowly.

בְּרָכָה שֶׁלִּפְנֵי הַהַפְטָרָה

בָּרוּךְ אַתָּה יהוה אֱלֹהֵינוּ מֶלֶךְ הָעוֹלָם, אֲשֶׁר בָּחַר
בִּנְבִיאִים טוֹבִים, וְרָצָה בְדִבְרֵיהֶם הַנֶּאֱמָרִים בֶּאֱמֶת.
בָּרוּךְ אַתָּה יהוה, הַבּוֹחֵר בַּתּוֹרָה וּבְמֹשֶׁה עַבְדּוֹ
וּבְיִשְׂרָאֵל עַמּוֹ וּבִנְבִיאֵי הָאֱמֶת וָצֶדֶק.

יְשַׁעְיָהוּ נז

יד וְאָמַר סֹלּוּ־סֹלּוּ
פַּנּוּ־דָרֶךְ
הָרִימוּ מִכְשׁוֹל
מִדֶּרֶךְ עַמִּי:
טו כִּי כֹה אָמַר רָם וְנִשָּׂא
שֹׁכֵן עַד וְקָדוֹשׁ שְׁמוֹ
מָרוֹם וְקָדוֹשׁ אֶשְׁכּוֹן
וְאֶת־דַּכָּא וּשְׁפַל־רוּחַ
לְהַחֲיוֹת רוּחַ שְׁפָלִים
וּלְהַחֲיוֹת לֵב נִדְכָּאִים:
טז כִּי לֹא לְעוֹלָם אָרִיב
וְלֹא לָנֶצַח אֶקְצוֹף
כִּי־רוּחַ מִלְּפָנַי יַעֲטוֹף
וּנְשָׁמוֹת אֲנִי עָשִׂיתִי:
יז בַּעֲוֹן בִּצְעוֹ קָצַפְתִּי
וְאַכֵּהוּ הַסְתֵּר וְאֶקְצֹף
וַיֵּלֶךְ שׁוֹבָב בְּדֶרֶךְ לִבּוֹ:
יח דְּרָכָיו רָאִיתִי וְאֶרְפָּאֵהוּ
וְאַנְחֵהוּ וַאֲשַׁלֵּם נִחֻמִים לוֹ וְלַאֲבֵלָיו:
יט בּוֹרֵא נִיב שְׂפָתָיִם
שָׁלוֹם | שָׁלוֹם לָרָחוֹק וְלַקָּרוֹב
אָמַר יהוה וּרְפָאתִיו:
כ וְהָרְשָׁעִים כַּיָּם נִגְרָשׁ
כִּי הַשְׁקֵט לֹא יוּכָל
וַיִּגְרְשׁוּ מֵימָיו רֶפֶשׁ וָטִיט:
כא אֵין שָׁלוֹם אָמַר אֱלֹהַי לָרְשָׁעִים:

HAFTARAH

B'rakhah before the Haftarah

Barukh atah ADONAI, our God, ruler of time and space, who chose worthy prophets; and who was pleased by their words, spoken in truth. *Barukh atah* ADONAI, who has chosen the Torah, Moses Your servant, Your people Israel, and the prophets of truth and justice.

ISAIAH 57

14 [ADONAI] says:
Build up, build up a highway!
Clear a road!
Remove all obstacles
from the road of My people!
15 For thus said the One who high aloft
forever dwells, whose name is holy:
I dwell on high, in holiness;
yet with the contrite and the lowly in spirit—
Reviving the spirits of the lowly,
reviving the hearts of the contrite.
16 For I will not always contend,
I will not be angry forever:
Nay, I who make spirits flag,
also create the breath of life.
17 For their sinful greed I was angry;
I struck them and turned away in My wrath.
Though stubborn, they follow the way of their hearts,
18 I note how they fare and will heal them:
I will guide them and mete out solace to them,
and to the mourners among them 19 heartening, comforting words:
It shall be well,
well with the far and the near   —said ADONAI—
And I will heal them.
20 But the wicked are like the troubled sea
which cannot rest,
whose waters toss up mire and mud.
21 There is no safety   —said my God—
for the wicked.

VERSE 1. RAISE YOUR VOICE LIKE A RAM'S HORN כַּשּׁוֹפָר הָרֵם קוֹלֶךָ. God tells the prophet to be like a shofar in trumpeting the people's misdeeds, and in calling upon them to care for those in need. The mention both of shofar and of fasting (verse 3) verbally links this Haftarah with Yom Kippur.

VERSE 3. WHY, WHEN WE FASTED, DID YOU NOT SEE? לָמָּה צַּמְנוּ וְלֹא רָאִיתָ. This passage's precise historical setting is uncertain. Clearly, the prophet is responding to the people's disappointment that though they have engaged in acts of piety, their downtrodden state has not improved. Perhaps the prophet is addressing those who returned to Jerusalem after the exile in Babylonia—that is, after 537 B.C.E.—for their discouragement would have been understandable, given that those who came back found a society in ruins and continued to live under foreign domination. (Indeed, foreign rule would last through most of the Second Temple's existence.) In the prophet's time, the First Temple's remembered glory did not seem to be reflected in the circumstances of return.

א קְרָא בְגָרוֹן אַל־תַּחְשֹׂךְ
כַּשּׁוֹפָר הָרֵם קוֹלֶךָ
וְהַגֵּד לְעַמִּי פִּשְׁעָם
וּלְבֵית יַעֲקֹב חַטֹּאתָם:
ב וְאוֹתִי יוֹם יוֹם יִדְרֹשׁוּן
וְדַעַת דְּרָכַי יֶחְפָּצוּן
כְּגוֹי אֲשֶׁר־צְדָקָה עָשָׂה
וּמִשְׁפַּט אֱלֹהָיו לֹא עָזָב
יִשְׁאָלוּנִי מִשְׁפְּטֵי־צֶדֶק
קִרְבַת אֱלֹהִים יֶחְפָּצוּן:
ג לָמָּה צַּמְנוּ וְלֹא רָאִיתָ
עִנִּינוּ נַפְשֵׁנוּ וְלֹא תֵדָע
הֵן בְּיוֹם צֹמְכֶם
תִּמְצְאוּ־חֵפֶץ
וְכָל־עַצְּבֵיכֶם תִּנְגֹּשׂוּ:
ד הֵן לְרִיב וּמַצָּה תָּצוּמוּ
וּלְהַכּוֹת בְּאֶגְרֹף רֶשַׁע
לֹא־תָצוּמוּ כַיּוֹם
לְהַשְׁמִיעַ בַּמָּרוֹם קוֹלְכֶם:
ה הֲכָזֶה יִהְיֶה צוֹם אֶבְחָרֵהוּ
יוֹם עַנּוֹת אָדָם נַפְשׁוֹ
הֲלָכֹף כְּאַגְמֹן רֹאשׁוֹ
וְשַׂק וָאֵפֶר יַצִּיעַ
הֲלָזֶה תִּקְרָא־צוֹם
וְיוֹם רָצוֹן לַיהוָה:
ו הֲלוֹא זֶה צוֹם אֶבְחָרֵהוּ
פַּתֵּחַ חַרְצֻבּוֹת רֶשַׁע
הַתֵּר אֲגֻדּוֹת מוֹטָה
וְשַׁלַּח רְצוּצִים חָפְשִׁים
וְכָל־מוֹטָה תְּנַתֵּקוּ:
ז הֲלוֹא פָרֹס לָרָעֵב לַחְמֶךָ
וַעֲנִיִּים מְרוּדִים תָּבִיא בָיִת

ISAIAH 58:1–12

1 Cry with full throat, without restraint;
raise your voice like a ram's horn!
Declare to My people their transgression,
to the House of Jacob their sin.

2 To be sure, they seek Me daily,
eager to learn My ways.
Like a nation that does what is right,
that has not abandoned the laws of its God,
they ask Me for the right way,
they are eager for the nearness of God:
3 "Why, when we fasted, did You not see?
When we starved our bodies, did You pay no heed?"
Because on your fast day
you see to your business
and oppress all your laborers!
4 Because you fast in strife and contention,
and you strike with a wicked fist!
Your fasting today is not such
as to make your voice heard on high.
5 Is such the fast I desire,
a day for people to starve their bodies?
Is it bowing the head like a bulrush
and lying in sackcloth and ashes?
Do you call that a fast,
a day when Adonai is favorable?
6 No, this is the fast I desire:
to unlock fetters of wickedness,
and untie the cords of the yoke
to let the oppressed go free;
to break off every yoke.
7 It is to share your bread with the hungry,
and to take the wretched poor into your home;
when you see the naked, to clothe them,
and do not ignore your own flesh.

8 Then shall your light burst through like the dawn
and your healing spring up quickly;

כִּי־תִרְאֶה עָרֹם וְכִסִּיתוֹ
וּמִבְּשָׂרְךָ לֹא תִתְעַלָּם:
ח אָז יִבָּקַע כַּשַּׁחַר אוֹרֶךָ
וַאֲרֻכָתְךָ מְהֵרָה תִצְמָח
וְהָלַךְ לְפָנֶיךָ צִדְקֶךָ
כְּבוֹד יהוה יַאַסְפֶךָ:
ט אָז תִּקְרָא וַיהוה יַעֲנֶה
תְּשַׁוַּע וְיֹאמַר הִנֵּנִי
אִם־תָּסִיר מִתּוֹכְךָ מוֹטָה
שְׁלַח אֶצְבַּע וְדַבֶּר־אָוֶן:
י וְתָפֵק לָרָעֵב נַפְשֶׁךָ
וְנֶפֶשׁ נַעֲנָה תַּשְׂבִּיעַ
וְזָרַח בַּחֹשֶׁךְ אוֹרֶךָ
וַאֲפֵלָתְךָ כַּצָּהֳרָיִם:
יא וְנָחֲךָ יהוה תָּמִיד
וְהִשְׂבִּיעַ בְּצַחְצָחוֹת נַפְשֶׁךָ
וְעַצְמֹתֶיךָ יַחֲלִיץ
וְהָיִיתָ כְּגַן רָוֶה
וּכְמוֹצָא מַיִם אֲשֶׁר לֹא־יְכַזְּבוּ מֵימָיו:
יב וּבָנוּ מִמְּךָ חָרְבוֹת עוֹלָם
מוֹסְדֵי דוֹר־וָדוֹר תְּקוֹמֵם
וְקֹרָא לְךָ גֹּדֵר פֶּרֶץ
מְשׁוֹבֵב נְתִיבוֹת לָשָׁבֶת:
יג אִם־תָּשִׁיב מִשַּׁבָּת רַגְלֶךָ
עֲשׂוֹת חֲפָצֶיךָ בְּיוֹם קָדְשִׁי
וְקָרָאתָ לַשַּׁבָּת עֹנֶג
לִקְדוֹשׁ יהוה מְכֻבָּד
וְכִבַּדְתּוֹ מֵעֲשׂוֹת דְּרָכֶיךָ
מִמְּצוֹא חֶפְצְךָ וְדַבֵּר דָּבָר:
יד אָז תִּתְעַנַּג עַל־יהוה
וְהִרְכַּבְתִּיךָ עַל־בָּמֳתֵי אָרֶץ
וְהַאֲכַלְתִּיךָ נַחֲלַת יַעֲקֹב אָבִיךָ
כִּי פִּי יהוה דִּבֵּר:

**VERSE 13. IF YOU CALL
SHABBAT "DELIGHT"** וְקָרָאתָ
לַשַּׁבָּת עֹנֶג. This is the origin
of the term *Oneg Shabbat*.
For the Jew who enters
into a life of observance of
the mitzvot, ritual involves
moments of joy, of sadness,
of serious reflection, and
of meditation. These com-
prise the range of human
emotion, allowing us to
experience the fullness of
our humanity.

"Then when you call, Adonai will answer; when you cry, [God] will say *hineini*, here I am" (Isaiah 58:9). On Rosh Hashanah, in the story of the binding of Isaac, we read of God's call to Abraham and Abraham's response, "*Hineini*, here I am." Today, on Yom Kippur, it is we who call and God who responds, "*Hineini*, here I am." Through our acts of righteousness, compassion, and repair of the world, we have the potential to bring the Divine Presence into the world.

your Vindicator shall march before you,
the Presence of Adonai shall be your rear guard.
9 Then, when you call, Adonai will answer;
when you cry, [God] will say: Here I am.
If you banish the yoke from your midst,
the menacing hand, and evil speech,
10 and you offer your compassion to the hungry
and satisfy the famished creature—
then shall your light shine in darkness,
and your gloom shall be like noonday.
11 Adonai will guide you always,
slaking your thirst in parched places
and give strength to your bones.
You shall be like a watered garden,
like a spring whose waters do not fail.
12 Some from your midst shall rebuild ancient ruins,
you shall restore foundations laid long ago.
And you shall be called
"Repairer of fallen walls,
Restorer of lanes for habitation."
13 If you refrain from trampling Shabbat,
from pursuing your affairs on My holy day;
if you call Shabbat "delight,"
Adonai's holy day "honored";
and if you honor it and go not your ways
nor look to your affairs, nor strike bargains—
14 then you can seek the favor of Adonai.
I will set you astride the heights of the earth,
and let you enjoy the heritage of your father Jacob—
for the mouth of Adonai has spoken.

הַבְּרָכוֹת שֶׁלְּאַחַר הַהַפְטָרָה

בָּרוּךְ אַתָּה יהוה אֱלֹהֵינוּ מֶלֶךְ הָעוֹלָם, צוּר כָּל־
הָעוֹלָמִים, צַדִּיק בְּכָל־הַדּוֹרוֹת, הָאֵל הַנֶּאֱמָן הָאוֹמֵר
וְעֹשֶׂה, הַמְדַבֵּר וּמְקַיֵּם, שֶׁכָּל־דְּבָרָיו אֱמֶת וָצֶדֶק. נֶאֱמָן
אַתָּה הוּא יהוה אֱלֹהֵינוּ וְנֶאֱמָנִים דְּבָרֶיךָ, וְדָבָר אֶחָד
מִדְּבָרֶיךָ אָחוֹר לֹא יָשׁוּב רֵיקָם, כִּי אֵל מֶלֶךְ נֶאֱמָן וְרַחֲמָן
אָתָּה. בָּרוּךְ אַתָּה יהוה, הָאֵל הַנֶּאֱמָן בְּכָל־דְּבָרָיו.

רַחֵם עַל צִיּוֹן כִּי הִיא בֵּית חַיֵּינוּ. וְלַעֲלוּבַת נֶפֶשׁ תּוֹשִׁיעַ
בִּמְהֵרָה בְיָמֵינוּ. בָּרוּךְ אַתָּה יהוה, מְשַׂמֵּחַ צִיּוֹן בְּבָנֶיהָ.

שַׂמְּחֵנוּ, יהוה אֱלֹהֵינוּ בְּאֵלִיָּהוּ הַנָּבִיא עַבְדֶּךָ וּבְמַלְכוּת
בֵּית דָּוִד מְשִׁיחֶךָ. בִּמְהֵרָה יָבֹא וְיָגֵל לִבֵּנוּ, עַל כִּסְאוֹ לֹא
יֵשֵׁב זָר וְלֹא יִנְחֲלוּ עוֹד אֲחֵרִים אֶת־כְּבוֹדוֹ, כִּי בְשֵׁם
קָדְשְׁךָ נִשְׁבַּעְתָּ לּוֹ שֶׁלֹּא יִכְבֶּה נֵרוֹ לְעוֹלָם וָעֶד. בָּרוּךְ
אַתָּה יהוה, מָגֵן דָּוִד.

עַל הַתּוֹרָה וְעַל הָעֲבוֹדָה וְעַל הַנְּבִיאִים [וְעַל יוֹם הַשַּׁבָּת
הַזֶּה] וְעַל יוֹם הַכִּפּוּרִים הַזֶּה שֶׁנָּתַתָּ לָּנוּ יהוה אֱלֹהֵינוּ
[לִקְדֻשָּׁה וְלִמְנוּחָה,] לִמְחִילָה וְלִסְלִיחָה וּלְכַפָּרָה, לְכָבוֹד
וּלְתִפְאָרֶת. עַל הַכֹּל יהוה אֱלֹהֵינוּ אֲנַחְנוּ מוֹדִים לָךְ,
וּמְבָרְכִים אוֹתָךְ. יִתְבָּרַךְ שִׁמְךָ בְּפִי כָּל־חַי תָּמִיד לְעוֹלָם
וָעֶד. וּדְבָרְךָ אֱמֶת וְקַיָּם לָעַד. בָּרוּךְ אַתָּה יהוה, מֶלֶךְ
מוֹחֵל וְסוֹלֵחַ לַעֲוֹנוֹתֵינוּ וְלַעֲוֹנוֹת עַמּוֹ בֵּית יִשְׂרָאֵל,
וּמַעֲבִיר אַשְׁמוֹתֵינוּ בְּכָל־שָׁנָה וְשָׁנָה, מֶלֶךְ עַל כָּל־הָאָרֶץ
מְקַדֵּשׁ [הַשַּׁבָּת וְ]יִשְׂרָאֵל וְיוֹם הַכִּפּוּרִים.

**B'RAKHOT AFTER THE HAF-
TARAH.** A series of *b'rakhot*
concludes the reading from
the Prophets. The earliest
synagogue services may
have centered on the public
reading of biblical passages,
and the prayers concluding
the reading may well have
formed the original core
of the synagogue service.
For example, the prayers
concluding our reading
mention the sanctity of the
day and express messi-
anic longing—two themes
likewise featured in the
Amidah. In ancient times,
the public biblical reading
also included a selection
from the third division of
the Hebrew Bible, known as
the Writings.

**WHO ACCOMPLISHES WHAT
IS SPOKEN** הַמְדַבֵּר וּמְקַיֵּם.
At the opening of Genesis,
God's word effectuates all
that is created: "God said…
and it was so." Our liturgy
asserts that God will likewise carry out the promises
recorded in the scriptural
passages that we have just
read aloud and studied.

**MAY YOUR PROMISE PROVE
TRUE** וּדְבָרְךָ אֱמֶת. On
the Days of Awe we talk
of God's teaching as an
everlasting truth and we
then conclude by declaring
God's sovereignty over all
the earth. God's sovereignty
is identified here with the
truthful and eternal teaching of Torah.

B'rakhot after the Haftarah

Barukh atah ADONAI, our God, ruler of time and space, eternal protector, righteous in all generations, the faithful God who fulfills what is promised, who accomplishes what is spoken, whose every word is true and just. Faithful are You, ADONAI, and Your words are trustworthy; not one of Your words will prove empty, for You are a faithful and compassionate sovereign. *Barukh atah* ADONAI, God who faithfully fulfills all Your words.

Show compassion to Zion, our true home, and speedily, in our time, bring redemption to those sad in spirit. *Barukh atah* ADONAI, who makes Zion happy with her children.

Make us joyful, ADONAI our God, with Elijah the prophet, Your servant, and with the Kingdom of David, Your anointed—may he soon come and make our hearts rejoice. May no stranger sit on his throne, and may no other inherit his glory, for You have promised him, by Your holy name, that his light shall never be extinguished. *Barukh atah* ADONAI, Shield of David.

For all this we thank You and praise You, ADONAI our God: for the Torah, for the ability to worship, for the prophets, [for Shabbat,] and for this Day of Atonement, which You have given us, ADONAI our God, [for holiness and for rest,] for pardon, forgiveness, and atonement, for honor and glory. May Your name be blessed by all that is living, always and forever, and may Your promise prove true and everlasting. *Barukh atah* ADONAI, sovereign who pardons and forgives our sins and those of the people, the House of Israel, each year sweeping away our guilt—ruler of all the earth, who makes [Shabbat,] the people Israel and the Day of Atonement holy.

ON SHABBAT, WE RECITE THE FOLLOWING TWO PARAGRAPHS:

A PRAYER FOR THE CONGREGATION

יְקוּם פֻּרְקָן מִן שְׁמַיָּא, חִנָּא וְחִסְדָּא וְרַחֲמֵי וְחַיֵּי אֲרִיכֵי
וּמְזוֹנֵי רְוִיחֵי, וְסִיַּעְתָּא דִשְׁמַיָּא, וּבַרְיוּת גּוּפָא וּנְהוֹרָא
מְעַלְיָא, זַרְעָא חַיָּא וְקַיָּמָא, זַרְעָא דִי לָא יִפְסֹק, וְדִי
לָא יִבְטַל מִפִּתְגָּמֵי אוֹרַיְתָא, לְכָל־קְהָלָא קַדִּישָׁא הָדֵין,
רַבְרְבַיָּא עִם זְעֵרַיָּא, טַפְלָא וּנְשַׁיָּא. מַלְכָּא דְעָלְמָא יְבָרֵךְ
יָתְכוֹן, יַפִּישׁ חַיֵּיכוֹן, וְיַסְגֵּא יוֹמֵיכוֹן וְיִתֵּן אַרְכָא לִשְׁנֵיכוֹן,
וְתִתְפָּרְקוּן וְתִשְׁתֵּזְבוּן, מִן כָּל־עָקָא, וּמִן כָּל־מַרְעִין
בִּישִׁין. ◁ מָרַן דִּי בִשְׁמַיָּא יְהֵא בְּסַעְדְּכוֹן כָּל־זְמַן וְעִדָּן,
וְנֹאמַר אָמֵן.

A PRAYER FOR THOSE WHO SERVE THE COMMUNITY

מִי שֶׁבֵּרַךְ אֲבוֹתֵינוּ אַבְרָהָם יִצְחָק וְיַעֲקֹב, וְאִמּוֹתֵינוּ
שָׂרָה רִבְקָה רָחֵל וְלֵאָה, הוּא יְבָרֵךְ אֶת־כָּל־הַקָּהָל
הַקָּדוֹשׁ הַזֶּה, עִם כָּל־קְהִלּוֹת הַקֹּדֶשׁ, הֵם וּמִשְׁפְּחוֹתֵיהֶם
וְכֹל אֲשֶׁר לָהֶם, וּמִי שֶׁמְּיַחֲדִים בָּתֵּי כְנֵסִיּוֹת לִתְפִלָּה, וּמִי
שֶׁבָּאִים בְּתוֹכָם לְהִתְפַּלֵּל, וּמִי שֶׁנּוֹתְנִים נֵר לַמָּאוֹר וְיַיִן
לְקִדּוּשׁ וּלְהַבְדָּלָה, וּפַת לָאוֹרְחִים וּצְדָקָה לָעֲנִיִּים,
◁ וְכָל־מִי שֶׁעוֹסְקִים בְּצָרְכֵי צִבּוּר וּבְבִנְיַן אֶרֶץ יִשְׂרָאֵל
בֶּאֱמוּנָה. הַקָּדוֹשׁ בָּרוּךְ הוּא יְשַׁלֵּם שְׂכָרָם וְיָסִיר מֵהֶם
כָּל־מַחֲלָה. וְיִרְפָּא לְכָל־גּוּפָם, וְיִסְלַח לְכָל־עֲוֹנָם, וְיִשְׁלַח
בְּרָכָה וְהַצְלָחָה בְּכָל־מַעֲשֵׂה יְדֵיהֶם, עִם כָּל־יִשְׂרָאֵל
אֲחֵיהֶם וְאַחְיוֹתֵיהֶם, וְנֹאמַר אָמֵן.

On all days:
A PRAYER FOR OUR COUNTRY

אֱלֹהֵינוּ וֵאלֹהֵי אֲבוֹתֵינוּ [וְאִמּוֹתֵינוּ], קַבֶּל־נָא בְּרַחֲמִים
אֶת־תְּפִלָּתֵנוּ בְּעַד אַרְצֵנוּ וּמֶמְשַׁלְתָּהּ. הָרֵק אֶת־בִּרְכָתְךָ
עַל הָאָרֶץ הַזֹּאת, עַל רֹאשָׁהּ, שׁוֹפְטֶיהָ, וּפְקִידֶיהָ
הָעוֹסְקִים בְּצָרְכֵי צִבּוּר בֶּאֱמוּנָה. הוֹרֵם מֵחֻקֵּי תוֹרָתֶךָ,
הֲבִינֵם מִשְׁפְּטֵי צִדְקֶךָ לְמַעַן לֹא יָסוּרוּ מֵאַרְצֵנוּ שָׁלוֹם
וְשַׁלְוָה, אֹשֶׁר וְחֹפֶשׁ כָּל־הַיָּמִים. אָנָּא יהוה אֱלֹהֵי
הָרוּחוֹת לְכָל־בָּשָׂר, שְׁלַח רוּחֲךָ עַל כָּל־תּוֹשָׁבֵי אַרְצֵנוּ.

COMMUNITY CONCERNS.
Classically, the Torah service became a moment of expressing community concerns. יְקוּם פֻּרְקָן (Y'kum Purkan), "May the blessings of heaven," is a prayer written in the common language of the time: Aramaic. It petitions God on behalf of the local synagogue community, and is followed by a Hebrew prayer of similar purpose. The first prayer expresses the hope that all members of the community may enjoy long, prosperous lives; the second singles out those people who give of their own means and time to support Jewish communal institutions and needy individuals.

PRAYER FOR OUR COUNTRY.
It has been customary since medieval times to include in the liturgy a prayer for the welfare of the government. Secure governments were seen as providing safety for the Jewish community, and a biblical warrant for such prayers was found in the verse instructing Israel to "seek the welfare of the city to which I have exiled you and pray to Adonai in its behalf; for in its prosperity you shall prosper" (Jeremiah 29:7). Early versions of this prayer referred to God as "the One who gives dominion to kings" and reflected the anxiety that Jews felt as a beleaguered minority. The text here was composed in the 1920s expressly for a democratic government by Professor Louis Ginzberg, who served as rector of the Jewish Theological
(continued)

An Alternative Prayer for Our Country

Our God and God of our ancestors: We ask Your blessings for our country—for its government, for its leaders and advisors, and for all who exercise just and rightful authority. Teach them insights from Your Torah, that they may administer all affairs of state fairly, that peace and security, happiness and prosperity, justice and freedom may forever abide in our midst.

Creator of all flesh, bless all the inhabitants of our country with Your spirit. May citizens of all races and creeds forge a common bond in true harmony, to banish hatred and bigotry, and to safeguard the ideals and free institutions that are the pride and glory of our country.

May this land, under Your providence, be an influence for good throughout the world, uniting all people in peace and freedom—helping them to fulfill the vision of Your prophet: "Nation shall not lift up sword against nation, neither shall they experience war any more." And let us say: Amen.

ON SHABBAT, WE RECITE THE FOLLOWING TWO PARAGRAPHS:

A PRAYER FOR THE CONGREGATION

May the blessings of heaven—kindness and compassion, long life, ample sustenance, well-being, and healthy offspring devoted to Torah—be granted to all members of this congregation. May the Sovereign of the universe bless you, adding to your days and your years. May you be spared all distress and disease. May our Protector in heaven be your help at all times. And let us all say: Amen.

A PRAYER FOR THOSE WHO SERVE THE COMMUNITY

May God who blessed our ancestors, Abraham, Isaac, and Jacob, Sarah, Rebecca, Rachel, and Leah, bless this entire congregation together with all holy congregations: them, their sons and daughters, their families, and all that is theirs; along with those who unite to establish synagogues for prayer, and those who enter them to pray, and those who give funds for heat and light, and wine for Kiddush and Havdalah, bread to the wayfarer and charity to the poor; and all who devotedly involve themselves with the needs of this community and the Land of Israel. May the Holy One reward them, remove sickness from them, heal them, and forgive their sins. May God bless them by making all their worthy endeavors prosper, as well as those of the entire people Israel. And let us say: Amen.

On all days:

A PRAYER FOR OUR COUNTRY

Our God and God of our ancestors, with mercy accept our prayer on behalf of our country and its government. Pour out Your blessings upon this land, upon its leader, its judges, officers, and officials, who are devoted in good faith to the needs of the public. Instruct them with the laws of Your Torah and help them understand Your rules of justice, so that peace and security, happiness and freedom, will never depart from our land. We pray, ADONAI, God whose spirit is in all creatures, awaken that spirit within all the inhabitants of our land. Uproot from

עֲקֹר מִלִּבָּם שִׂנְאָה וְאֵיבָה, קִנְאָה וְתַחֲרוּת, וְטַע בֵּין בְּנֵי הָאֻמּוֹת וְהָאֱמוּנוֹת הַשּׁוֹנוֹת הַשּׁוֹכְנִים בָּהּ, אַהֲבָה וְאַחֲוָה, שָׁלוֹם וְרֵעוּת. וּבְכֵן יְהִי רָצוֹן מִלְּפָנֶיךָ שֶׁתְּהִי אַרְצֵנוּ בְּרָכָה לְכָל־יוֹשְׁבֵי תֵבֵל, וְתַשְׁרֶה בֵּינֵיהֶם רֵעוּת וְחֵרוּת, וְקַיֵּם בִּמְהֵרָה חֲזוֹן נְבִיאֶיךָ: לֹא יִשָּׂא גוֹי אֶל גּוֹי חֶרֶב וְלֹא יִלְמְדוּ עוֹד מִלְחָמָה. וְנֶאֱמַר: כִּי כֻלָּם יֵדְעוּ אוֹתִי לְמִקְּטַנָּם וְעַד גְּדוֹלָם, וְנֹאמַר אָמֵן.

A PRAYER FOR THE STATE OF ISRAEL

אָבִינוּ שֶׁבַּשָּׁמַיִם, צוּר יִשְׂרָאֵל וְגוֹאֲלוֹ, בָּרֵךְ אֶת־מְדִינַת יִשְׂרָאֵל, [שֶׁתְּהֵא] רֵאשִׁית צְמִיחַת גְּאֻלָּתֵנוּ. הָגֵן עָלֶיהָ בְּאֶבְרַת חַסְדֶּךָ, וּפְרֹשׂ עָלֶיהָ סֻכַּת שְׁלוֹמֶךָ. וּשְׁלַח אוֹרְךָ וַאֲמִתְּךָ לְרָאשֶׁיהָ, שָׂרֶיהָ וְיוֹעֲצֶיהָ, וְתַקְּנֵם בְּעֵצָה טוֹבָה מִלְּפָנֶיךָ. חַזֵּק אֶת־יְדֵי מְגִנֵּי אֶרֶץ קָדְשֵׁנוּ, וְהַנְחִילֵם אֱלֹהֵינוּ יְשׁוּעָה, וַעֲטֶרֶת נִצָּחוֹן תְּעַטְּרֵם. וְנָתַתָּ שָׁלוֹם בָּאָרֶץ וְשִׂמְחַת עוֹלָם לְיוֹשְׁבֶיהָ, וְנֹאמַר אָמֵן.

A PRAYER FOR PEACE

יְהִי רָצוֹן מִלְּפָנֶיךָ יהוה אֱלֹהֵינוּ וֵאלֹהֵי אֲבוֹתֵינוּ [וְאִמּוֹתֵינוּ] שֶׁתְּבַטֵּל מִלְחָמוֹת וּשְׁפִיכוּת דָּמִים מִן הָעוֹלָם וְתַשְׁכִּין שָׁלוֹם גָּדוֹל בָּעוֹלָם וְלֹא יִשָּׂא גוֹי אֶל גּוֹי חֶרֶב וְלֹא יִלְמְדוּ עוֹד מִלְחָמָה.

יַכִּירוּ וְיֵדְעוּ כָּל־יוֹשְׁבֵי תֵבֵל שֶׁלֹּא בָּאנוּ לָעוֹלָם בִּשְׁבִיל רִיב וּמַחֲלֹקֶת וְלֹא בִּשְׁבִיל שִׂנְאָה וְקִנְאָה וְקִנְטוּר וּשְׁפִיכוּת דָּמִים. רַק בָּאנוּ לָעוֹלָם כְּדֵי לְהַכִּיר אוֹתְךָ, תִּתְבָּרֵךְ לָנֶצַח.

וּבְכֵן תְּרַחֵם עָלֵינוּ וִיקֻיַּם בָּנוּ מִקְרָא שֶׁכָּתוּב: וְנָתַתִּי שָׁלוֹם בָּאָרֶץ וּשְׁכַבְתֶּם וְאֵין מַחֲרִיד וְהִשְׁבַּתִּי חַיָּה רָעָה מִן הָאָרֶץ וְחֶרֶב לֹא תַעֲבֹר בְּאַרְצְכֶם. וְיִגַּל כַּמַּיִם מִשְׁפָּט, וּצְדָקָה כְּנַחַל אֵיתָן. כִּי מָלְאָה הָאָרֶץ דֵּעָה אֶת־יהוה כַּמַּיִם לַיָּם מְכַסִּים.

(continued from previous page)
Seminary. (The version of his prayer as edited in *Siddur Sim Shalom* is presented as an alternative.) Ginzberg's prayer transforms what was formerly "A Prayer for the Government" into "A Prayer for Our Country" and for its people, the source of authority in a democracy. Whereas earlier prayers asked that the monarch be compassionate to the Jewish people, this prayer expresses the hope that the leaders of the country will be fair and just to all and help to bring the world closer to a vision of peace and justice.

PRAYER FOR THE STATE OF ISRAEL. Upon Israel's independence in 1948, many prayers were circulated for the well-being of the new state. This one was probably composed by Israel's Chief Rabbis and may have been edited by the writer S.Y. Agnon.

THAT IT MAY BE שֶׁתְּהֵא. The Hebrew word was added by the Chief Rabbi of England, Immanuel Jakobovits, turning the phrase "the beginning of the redemption" into an expression of hope, rather than a statement of fact.

A PRAYER FOR PEACE. Rabbi Nathan Sternharz, student of the Hasidic master Naḥman of Bratzlav, recorded this prayer. Adapted and translated by Jules Harlow.

רִבּוֹן הָעוֹלָם, קַבֶּל נָא
בְּרַחֲמִים וּבְרָצוֹן אֶת־
תְּפִלָּתֵנוּ לְמַעַן מְדִינַת
יִשְׂרָאֵל

Sovereign of the universe, accept in lovingkindness and with favor our prayers for the State of Israel, her government, and all who dwell within her boundaries and under her authority. Open our eyes and our hearts to the wonder of Israel and strengthen our faith in Your power to work redemption in every human soul. Grant us also the fortitude to keep ever before us those ideals upon which the State of Israel was founded.

Grant courage, wisdom, and strength to those entrusted with guiding Israel's destiny to do Your will. Be with those on whose shoulders Israel's safety depends and defend them from all harm.

Spread over Israel and all the world Your shelter of peace, and may the vision of Your prophet soon be fulfilled: "Nation shall not lift up sword against nation, neither shall they learn war any more" (Isaiah 2:4).

לֹא יִשָּׂא גוֹי אֶל גּוֹי חֶרֶב
לֹא יִלְמְדוּ עוֹד מִלְחָמָה.

their hearts hatred and malice, jealousy and strife. Plant among those of different nationalities and faiths who dwell in our nation, love and companionship, peace and friendship. May it therefore be Your will that our land be a blessing to all who dwell on earth and cause them to dwell in friendship and freedom. Speedily fulfill the vision of Your prophets: "Nation shall not lift up sword against nation, neither shall they learn war any more"; "For all of them, from the least of them to the greatest, shall know Me." And let us say: Amen.

A PRAYER FOR THE STATE OF ISRAEL

Avinu she-ba-shamayim, Stronghold and Redeemer of the people Israel: Bless the State of Israel, [that it may be] the beginning of our redemption. Shield it with Your love; spread over it the shelter of Your peace. Guide its leaders and advisors with Your light and Your truth. Help them with Your good counsel. Strengthen the hands of those who defend our Holy Land. Deliver them; crown their efforts with triumph. Bless the Land with peace and its inhabitants with lasting joy. And let us say: Amen.

A PRAYER FOR PEACE

May we see the day when war and bloodshed cease,
when a great peace will embrace the whole world.
> *Then nation will not threaten nation,*
> *and mankind will not again know war.*
For all who live on earth shall realize
we have not come into being to hate or to destroy.
We have come into being to praise, to labor, and to love.
> *Compassionate God, bless the leaders of all nations*
> *with the power of compassion.*
Fulfill the promise conveyed in Scripture:
I will bring peace to the land,
and you shall lie down and no one shall terrify you.
> *I will rid the land of vicious beasts*
> *and it shall not be ravaged by war.*
Let love and justice flow like a mighty stream.
Let peace fill the earth as the waters fill the sea.
And let us say: Amen.

Some people whose parents are living have a custom of leaving the service at this time, but even those who do not yet need to say the personal prayers of remembrance might remain and recite prayers for others as well as join in the communal prayers (beginning on page 292, below).

(beginning on page 292, below)

Adonai, what are human beings
    that You take account of them,
    mortals that You care for them?
Humans are as a breath, their
    days like a passing shadow.
In the morning they flourish
    anew, in the evening they
    shrivel and die.
Teach us to count each day,
    that we may acquire a heart of
    wisdom.

יהוה, מָה־אָדָם וַתֵּדָעֵהוּ,
בֶּן־אֱנוֹשׁ וַתְּחַשְּׁבֵהוּ.
אָדָם לַהֶבֶל דָּמָה,
יָמָיו כְּצֵל עוֹבֵר.
בַּבֹּקֶר יָצִיץ וְחָלָף,
לָעֶרֶב יְמוֹלֵל וְיָבֵשׁ.
לִמְנוֹת יָמֵינוּ כֵּן הוֹדַע
וְנָבִיא לְבַב חָכְמָה.

On this solemn day we each make judgments about the quality of our life.
We re-examine our deeds and relationships with our community and with others.
We express our yearnings for a new year, a new beginning, a year during which we commit ourselves to work toward bringing health and peace to all.
We long for a year when individually and communally we shall strive to live in a way that is more reflective of the ideals that we cherish.
Now, in the midst of looking at our life and assessing its quality, we pause to reflect and to remember, and to dedicate ourselves anew.

God is always before me, at my
    right hand, lest I fall.
Therefore I am glad, made
    happy, though I know that
    my flesh will lie in the ground
    forever.

שִׁוִּיתִי יהוה לְנֶגְדִּי תָמִיד,
כִּי מִימִינִי בַּל־אֶמּוֹט.
לָכֵן שָׂמַח לִבִּי וַיָּגֶל
כְּבוֹדִי, אַף בְּשָׂרִי יִשְׁכֹּן
לָבֶטַח.

The deaths of those we now remember left holes in our lives. But we are grateful for the gift of their lives and we are strengthened by the blessings that they left us and the precious memories that comfort and sustain us as we recall them this day.

INTRODUCTION. Yizkor is a time set aside to formally include in our thoughts and prayers family and friends who have passed away. Though Yizkor is recited on each of the festivals, on the High Holy Days we may feel a special connection to those who have played a significant role in our life's journey. The themes and somber ambience of the Yom Kippur service make this day especially appropriate for contemplating life and death. Thus, in reciting Yizkor, the veil between the worlds of the living and the dead becomes more transparent, less opaque. May the memory of those we recall be a blessing in our lives.

WHAT ARE HUMAN BEINGS מָה־אָדָם. The verses in this passage come from Psalms 144:3–4, 90:6, and 90:12.

GOD IS ALWAYS שִׁוִּיתִי יהוה. Psalm 16:8–9.

YIZKOR

When I stray from You,
Adonai, my life is as death;
but when I cleave to You,
even in death I have life.

You embrace the souls of the
living and the dead.

The earth inherits that
which perishes.

The dust returns to dust; but
the soul, which is God's, is
eternal.

Adonai is compassionate to
all creation, granting us a
share in unending life.

God redeems our life from
the grave, joining us forever in the unending chain
of life.

May we preserve the memo-
ry of those we love and are
now gone, through charity
in deed and thought.

May we live unselfishly, in
truth and love and peace,
so that we will be remem-
bered as a blessing, as we
lovingly remember, this
day, those who live on in
our hearts.

—JULES HARLOW

Backwards and Forwards

Yizkor:

Looking backward, we recall
our ancestry.

Looking forward, we con-
front our destiny.

Looking backward, we
reflect on our origins.

Looking forward, we choose
our path.

Remembering that we are a
tree of life, not letting go,
holding on, and holding to,
we walk into an unknown,
beckoning future,
with our past beside us.

—HAROLD SCHULWEIS
(adapted)

WE RECALL

Some of us recall parents who watched over us, nursed us, guided us, and sacrificed for us.

Some of us lovingly call to mind a wife, husband, or partner with whom we were truly united—in our hopes and our pains, in our failures and our achievements, in our joys and our sorrows.

Some of us remember brothers and sisters, who grew up together with us, sharing in the play of childhood, in the youthful adventure of discovering life's possibilities, bound to us by a heritage of family tradition and by years of togetherness and love.

Some of us call to mind children, entrusted to us too briefly, to whom we gave our loving care and from whom we received a trust that enriched our lives.

So many of us recall beloved relatives and friends whose affection and devotion enhanced our lives, and whose visible presence will never return to cheer, encourage, or support us.

Though they are gone, we are grateful for the blessings they brought to our lives. We are sustained and comforted by the thought that their presence in our lives remains an enduring blessing that we can bequeath to others.

We can show our devotion to them by our devotion to those ideas that they cherished.

O God of love, make us worthy of the love we have received by teaching us to love You with all our heart and with all our soul and with all our might, and to spread the light of Your divine love on all whose lives touch ours.

Give us strength to live faithfully, for we are cheered by our confidence that You will not permit our lives to be wasted, but will bring all our worthy strivings to live on, even as we may not see their fulfillment.

—MORDECAI M. KAPLAN, EUGENE KOHN, AND IRA EISENSTEIN
(adapted from Mahzor Hadash)

We each continue in private meditation, selecting from among the following and adding appropriate names as indicated. Personal prayers may be added.

We rise.

In memory of male relatives or friends:

יִזְכֹּר אֱלֹהִים אֶת נִשְׁמַת

(for a father) _____ אָבִי מוֹרִי

(for a husband) _____ אִישִׁי

(for a partner) _____ בֶּן זוּגִי

(for a brother) _____ אָחִי

(for a son) _____ בְּנִי

(for other relative) _____ קְרוֹבִי

(for a friend) _____ חֲבֵרִי

(others) _____

שֶׁהָלַךְ לְעוֹלָמוֹ [שֶׁהָלְכוּ לְעוֹלָמָם]. הִנְנִי נוֹדֵב/נוֹדֶבֶת
צְדָקָה בְּעַד הַזְכָּרַת נִשְׁמָתוֹ [נִשְׁמוֹתֵיהֶם]. אָנָּא תְּהִי
[תִּהְיֶינָה] נַפְשׁוֹ צְרוּרָה [נַפְשָׁם צְרוּרוֹת] בִּצְרוֹר הַחַיִּים
וּתְהִי מְנוּחָתוֹ [מְנוּחָתָם] כָּבוֹד, שְׂבַע שְׂמָחוֹת אֶת־
פָּנֶיךָ, נְעִימוֹת בִּימִינְךָ נֶצַח. אָמֵן.

In memory of female relatives or friends:

יִזְכֹּר אֱלֹהִים אֶת נִשְׁמַת

(for a mother) _____ אִמִּי מוֹרָתִי

(for a wife) _____ אִשְׁתִּי

(for a partner) _____ בַּת זוּגִי

(for a sister) _____ אֲחוֹתִי

(for a daughter) _____ בִּתִּי

(for other relative) _____ קְרוֹבָתִי

(for a friend) _____ חֲבֵרָתִי

(others) _____

שֶׁהָלְכָה לְעוֹלָמָהּ [שֶׁהָלְכוּ לְעוֹלָמָן]. הִנְנִי נוֹדֵב/נוֹדֶבֶת
צְדָקָה בְּעַד הַזְכָּרַת נִשְׁמָתָהּ [נִשְׁמוֹתֵיהֶן]. אָנָּא תְּהִי
[תִּהְיֶינָה] נַפְשָׁהּ צְרוּרָה [נַפְשָׁן צְרוּרוֹת] בִּצְרוֹר הַחַיִּים
וּתְהִי מְנוּחָתָהּ [מְנוּחָתָן] כָּבוֹד, שְׂבַע שְׂמָחוֹת אֶת־פָּנֶיךָ,
נְעִימוֹת בִּימִינְךָ נֶצַח. אָמֵן.

צְדָקָה **TZ'DAKAH/CHARITY**.
The Yizkor service was called *seder matnat yad*, the service of expressing generosity on behalf of those who have died. That name comes from the closing line of the Torah reading for the final day of the pilgrimage festivals (when Yizkor is recited): "Every person giving a gift according to the blessing they have received from Adonai" (Deuteronomy 16:17). Offering charitable gifts and performing acts of justice, love, and care in memory of those who have died provide us with ways of honoring their memory and continuing their influence for good.

Though I stared earnestly at my fingernail

Yesterday when I was on
the #7 bus
I happened to look
at the cuticle
of my right forefinger
and for a moment
I thought not that it
was mine
but that it was
my father's—

the same small
confusion I have
from time to time
when I catch sight
of my daughter
in her denim skirt, size 3,
and I feel lean, willowy,
in her clothes.

So there I was
on the #7 bus
overtaken by a longing
very close to love
staring at the cuticle
of my right forefinger.

I remembered how clean
and short he kept his
nails
and suddenly there was
the whole man
reconstituted
from a fingernail
standing before me,
smiling broadly,
his face flushed
with pleasure.

But then just as suddenly
he was gone
and though I stared
earnestly
at my fingernail
I failed to bring him back.
—MERLE FELD

We each continue in private meditation, selecting from among the following and adding appropriate names as indicated. Personal prayers may be added.

We rise.

In memory of male relatives or friends:

May God remember the soul of
    my father _____
    my husband _____
    my partner _____
    my brother _____
    my son _____
    my relative _____
    my friend _____
    (others) _____

who has [have] gone to his [their] eternal home. In loving testimony to his life [their lives], I pledge *tz'dakah* to help perpetuate ideals important to him [them]. Through such deeds, and through prayer and remembrance, may his [their] soul[s] be bound up in the bond of life. May I prove myself worthy of the many gifts with which he [they] blessed me. May these moments of meditation strengthen the ties that link me to his [their] memory. May he [they] rest in peace forever in God's presence. Amen.

In memory of female relatives or friends:

May God remember the soul of
    my mother _____
    my wife _____
    my partner _____
    my sister _____
    my daughter _____
    my relative _____
    my friend _____
    (others) _____

who has [have] gone to her [their] eternal home. In loving testimony to her life [their lives], I pledge *tz'dakah* to help perpetuate ideals important to her [them]. Through such deeds, and through prayer and remembrance, may her [their] soul[s] be bound up in the bond of life. May I prove myself worthy of the many gifts with which she [they] blessed me. May these moments of meditation strengthen the ties that link me to her [their] memory. May she [they] rest in peace forever in God's presence. Amen.

IN MEMORY OF MARTYRS:

יִזְכּוֹר אֱלֹהִים נִשְׁמוֹת כָּל־אַחֵינוּ בְּנֵי יִשְׂרָאֵל שֶׁמָּסְרוּ
אֶת־נַפְשָׁם עַל קִדּוּשׁ הַשֵּׁם. הִנְנִי נוֹדֵב/נוֹדֶבֶת צְדָקָה
בְּעַד הַזְכָּרַת נִשְׁמָתָם. אָנָּא יִשָּׁמַע בְּחַיֵּינוּ הֵד גְּבוּרָתָם
וּמְסִירוּתָם וְיֵרָאֶה בְּמַעֲשֵׂינוּ טְהָר לִבָּם וְתִהְיֶינָה
נַפְשׁוֹתֵיהֶם צְרוּרוֹת בִּצְרוֹר הַחַיִּים וּתְהִי מְנוּחָתָם כָּבוֹד,
שֹׂבַע שְׂמָחוֹת אֶת־פָּנֶיךָ, נְעִימוֹת בִּימִינְךָ נֶצַח. אָמֵן.

IN MEMORY OF CONGREGANTS:

יִזְכּוֹר אֱלֹהִים נִשְׁמוֹת יְדִידֵינוּ חַבְרֵי הַקָּהָל הַקָּדוֹשׁ הַזֶּה
שֶׁהָלְכוּ לְעוֹלָמָם. אָנָּא תִּהְיֶינָה נַפְשׁוֹתֵיהֶם צְרוּרוֹת
בִּצְרוֹר הַחַיִּים וּתְהִי מְנוּחָתָם כָּבוֹד, שֹׂבַע שְׂמָחוֹת אֶת־
פָּנֶיךָ, נְעִימוֹת בִּימִינְךָ נֶצַח. אָמֵן.

IN MEMORY OF THE SIX MILLION:

אֵל מָלֵא רַחֲמִים, שׁוֹכֵן בַּמְּרוֹמִים, הַמְצֵא מְנוּחָה נְכוֹנָה
תַּחַת כַּנְפֵי הַשְּׁכִינָה, בְּמַעֲלוֹת קְדוֹשִׁים וּטְהוֹרִים, כְּזֹהַר
הָרָקִיעַ מַזְהִירִים, לְנִשְׁמוֹת כָּל־אַחֵינוּ בְּנֵי יִשְׂרָאֵל
שֶׁנִּטְבְּחוּ בַּשּׁוֹאָה, אֲנָשִׁים נָשִׁים וָטַף, שֶׁנֶּחְנְקוּ וְשֶׁנִּשְׂרְפוּ
וְשֶׁנֶּהֶרְגוּ, שֶׁמָּסְרוּ אֶת־נַפְשָׁם עַל קִדּוּשׁ הַשֵּׁם, בְּגַן עֵדֶן
תְּהִי מְנוּחָתָם. אָנָּא בַּעַל הָרַחֲמִים, הַסְתִּירֵם בְּסֵתֶר
כְּנָפֶיךָ לְעוֹלָמִים. וּצְרוֹר בִּצְרוֹר הַחַיִּים אֶת־נִשְׁמוֹתֵיהֶם.
יהוה הוּא נַחֲלָתָם. וְיָנוּחוּ בְשָׁלוֹם עַל מִשְׁכְּבוֹתֵיהֶם.
וְנֹאמַר אָמֵן.

IN PARADISE בְּגַן עֵדֶן. Literally, "in the Garden of Eden." We imagine that the soul, which connects all living beings with their divine source, returns, after the death of the body, to God's care.

A Yizkor Meditation in Memory of a Parent Who Was Hurtful

Dear God,

You know my heart. Indeed, You know me better than I know myself, so I turn to You before I rise for Kaddish.

My emotions swirl as I say this prayer. The parent I remember was not kind to me. His/her death left me with a legacy of unhealed wounds, of anger and of dismay that a parent could hurt a child as I was hurt.

I do not want to pretend to love, or to grief that I do not feel, but I do want to do what is right as a Jew and as a child.

Help me, O God, to subdue my bitter emotions that do me no good, and to find that place in myself where happier memories may lie hidden, and where grief for all that could have been, all that should have been, may be calmed by forgiveness, or at least soothed by the passage of time.

I pray that You, who raise up slaves to freedom, will liberate me from the oppression of my hurt and anger, and that You will lead me from this desert to Your holy place.

—ROBERT SAKS

IN MEMORY OF MARTYRS:

May God remember the souls of the martyrs of our people, who gave their lives for the sanctification of God's name. In their memory do I pledge *tz'dakah*. May their bravery, their dedication, and their purity be reflected in our lives. May their souls be bound up in the bond of life. May they rest in peace forever in God's presence. Amen.

IN MEMORY OF CONGREGANTS:

May God remember the souls of our friends, members of this holy congregation, who have gone to their eternal home. May their souls be bound up in the bond of life. May these moments of meditation strengthen the ties that link us to their memory. May they rest in peace forever in God's presence. Amen.

Exalted, compassionate God, comfort the bereaved families of this congregation. Help us to perpetuate everything that was worthy in the lives of those no longer with us, whom we remember this day. May their memory endure as a blessing. And let us say: Amen.

IN MEMORY OF THE SIX MILLION:

Exalted, compassionate God, grant perfect peace in Your sheltering presence, among the holy and the pure, whose radiance is like the heavens, to the souls of all the men, women, and children of the House of Israel who were slaughtered, strangled, and burned in the Shoah. May they rest in paradise. Master of mercy, may they find eternal shelter beneath Your sheltering wings, and may their souls be bound up in the bond of life. ADONAI is their portion. May they rest in peace. And let us say: *Amen.*

אֵל מָלֵא רַחֲמִים, שׁוֹכֵן בַּמְּרוֹמִים, הַמְצֵא מְנוּחָה נְכוֹנָה
תַּחַת כַּנְפֵי הַשְּׁכִינָה, בְּמַעֲלוֹת קְדוֹשִׁים וּטְהוֹרִים, כְּזֹהַר
הָרָקִיעַ מַזְהִירִים, לְנִשְׁמוֹת כָּל־אֵלֶּה שֶׁהִזְכַּרְנוּ הַיּוֹם לִבְרָכָה,
שֶׁהָלְכוּ לְעוֹלָמָם, בְּגַן עֵדֶן תְּהִי מְנוּחָתָם. אָנָּא בַּעַל
הָרַחֲמִים, הַסְתִּירֵם בְּסֵתֶר כְּנָפֶיךָ לְעוֹלָמִים. וּצְרוֹר בִּצְרוֹר
הַחַיִּים אֶת־נִשְׁמוֹתֵיהֶם. יהוה הוּא נַחֲלָתָם. וְיָנוּחוּ בְשָׁלוֹם
עַל מִשְׁכְּבוֹתֵיהֶם. וְנֹאמַר אָמֵן.

מִזְמוֹר לְדָוִד.

יהוה רֹעִי, לֹא אֶחְסָר.

בִּנְאוֹת דֶּשֶׁא יַרְבִּיצֵנִי,

עַל מֵי מְנֻחוֹת יְנַהֲלֵנִי.

נַפְשִׁי יְשׁוֹבֵב, יַנְחֵנִי בְמַעְגְּלֵי־צֶדֶק לְמַעַן שְׁמוֹ.

גַּם כִּי אֵלֵךְ בְּגֵיא צַלְמָוֶת לֹא אִירָא רָע כִּי אַתָּה עִמָּדִי.

שִׁבְטְךָ וּמִשְׁעַנְתֶּךָ הֵמָּה יְנַחֲמֻנִי.

תַּעֲרֹךְ לְפָנַי שֻׁלְחָן נֶגֶד צֹרְרָי,

דִּשַּׁנְתָּ בַשֶּׁמֶן רֹאשִׁי, כּוֹסִי רְוָיָה.

אַךְ טוֹב וָחֶסֶד יִרְדְּפוּנִי כָּל־יְמֵי חַיָּי,

וְשַׁבְתִּי בְּבֵית יהוה לְאֹרֶךְ יָמִים. תהלים כג

My Peace

My peace is tied by a thread
to yours.

And the beloved holidays
and glorious seasons of
the year—
with the wealth of
fragrances, flowers,
fruit, leaves, and winds,
the fog and the rain,
the sudden snow
and the dew—
are suspended on a thread
of longing.

I and you and the
Sabbath.
I and you and our lives
in the last incarnation.
I and you
and the lie.
And the fear.
And the breaches.
I and you
and the Creator
of the heavens that have
no shore.
I and you
and the riddle.
I and you
and death.

> —ZELDA
> (trans. Marcia Falk)

IN MEMORY OF ALL THE DEAD:

Exalted, compassionate God, grant perfect peace in Your sheltering presence, among the holy and the pure, whose radiance is like the heavens, to the souls of all those we have recalled today. May their memory be a blessing, and may they rest in paradise. Master of mercy, may they find eternal shelter beneath Your sheltering wings, and may their souls be bound up in the bond of life. ADONAI is their portion. May they rest in peace. And let us say: *Amen.*

PSALM 23

A PSALM OF DAVID.

ADONAI is my shepherd, I shall not want.
God gives me repose in green meadows,
and guides me over calm waters.
God will revive my spirit and direct me on the right path—
for that is God's way.
Though I walk in the valley of the shadow of death, I fear no
    harm, for You are at my side.
Your staff and Your rod comfort me.
You prepare a banquet for me in the presence of my foes:
You anoint my head with oil, my cup overflows.
Surely goodness and kindness shall be my portion all the
    days of my life,
And I shall dwell in the house of ADONAI in the fullness
    of time.

קַדִּישׁ יָתוֹם

Mourners:

יִתְגַּדַּל וְיִתְקַדַּשׁ שְׁמֵהּ רַבָּא,
בְּעָלְמָא דִּי בְרָא, כִּרְעוּתֵהּ,
וְיַמְלִיךְ מַלְכוּתֵהּ בְּחַיֵּיכוֹן וּבְיוֹמֵיכוֹן
וּבְחַיֵּי דְכָל־בֵּית יִשְׂרָאֵל,
בַּעֲגָלָא וּבִזְמַן קָרִיב,
וְאִמְרוּ אָמֵן.

Congregation and mourners:

יְהֵא שְׁמֵהּ רַבָּא מְבָרַךְ לְעָלַם וּלְעָלְמֵי עָלְמַיָּא.

Mourners:

יִתְבָּרַךְ וְיִשְׁתַּבַּח
וְיִתְפָּאַר וְיִתְרוֹמַם
וְיִתְנַשֵּׂא וְיִתְהַדָּר
וְיִתְעַלֶּה וְיִתְהַלָּל
שְׁמֵהּ דְּקֻדְשָׁא, בְּרִיךְ הוּא,
לְעֵלָּא לְעֵלָּא מִכָּל־בִּרְכָתָא וְשִׁירָתָא
תֻּשְׁבְּחָתָא וְנֶחֱמָתָא
דַּאֲמִירָן בְּעָלְמָא,
וְאִמְרוּ אָמֵן.

יְהֵא שְׁלָמָא רַבָּא מִן שְׁמַיָּא וְחַיִּים
עָלֵינוּ וְעַל כָּל־יִשְׂרָאֵל,
וְאִמְרוּ אָמֵן.

עֹשֶׂה שָׁלוֹם בִּמְרוֹמָיו
הוּא יַעֲשֶׂה שָׁלוֹם
עָלֵינוּ וְעַל כָּל־יִשְׂרָאֵל
[וְעַל כָּל־יוֹשְׁבֵי תֵבֵל],
וְאִמְרוּ אָמֵן.

Mourner's Kaddish

May God's great name be exalted and hallowed throughout the created world, as is God's wish. May God's sovereignty soon be established, in your lifetime and in your days, and in the days of all the House of Israel. And respond with: *Amen.*

May God's great name be acknowledged forever and ever!

May the name of the Holy One be acknowledged and celebrated, lauded and worshipped, exalted and honored, extolled and acclaimed—though God, who is blessed, *b'rikh hu,* is truly far beyond all acknowledgment and praise, or any expressions of gratitude or consolation ever spoken in the world. And respond with: *Amen.*

May abundant peace from heaven, and life, come to us and to all Israel. And respond with: *Amen.*

May the One who brings harmony on high, bring harmony to us and to all Israel [and to all who dwell on earth]. And respond with: *Amen.*

Mourners:
Yitgaddal v'yitkaddash sh'meih rabba, b'alma di v'ra, ki-r'uteih, v'yamlikh malkhuteih b'ḥayyeikhon u-v'yomeikhon u-v'ḥayyei d'khol beit yisra·el, ba-agala u-viz'man kariv, v'imru amen.

Congregation and mourners:
Y'hei sh'meih rabba m'varakh l'alam u-l'almei almayya.

Mourners:
Yitbarakh v'yishtabbaḥ v'yitpa·ar v'yitromam v'yitnassei v'yit·haddar v'yit·alleh v'yit·hallal sh'meih d'kudsha, b'rikh hu, l'eilla l'eilla mi-kol birkhata v'shirata tushb'ḥata v'neḥamata da-amiran b'alma, v'imru amen.

Y'hei sh'lama rabba min sh'mayya v'ḥayyim aleinu v'al kol yisra·el, v'imru amen.

Oseh shalom bi-m'romav hu ya·aseh shalom aleinu v'al kol yisra·el [v'al kol yosh'vei teiveil], v'imru amen.

ASHREI. According to
Rabbi Elazar (Babylonia,
3rd century) speaking in
the name of Rabbi Abina,
the thrice-daily recita-
tion of Psalm 145 (which,
with the addition of three
other verses from psalms, is
known as the Ashrei) opens
a pathway to eternity.
The Talmud explains that
Ashrei is an alphabetical
acrostic that symbolically
encompasses the variety of
praises of God, and that it
contains an especially appropriate description of the
thankfulness with which we
are to approach God: "You
open Your hand, satisfying
all the living with contentment" (Babylonian Talmud,
Berakhot 4b).

For synagogue use, two
verses were added to the
opening, both of which
begin with the word ashrei,
"joyous" (Psalms 84:5 and
144:15). Additionally, Psalm
115:18 was appended to
the end, referring to those
assembled in prayer.

אַשְׁרֵי יוֹשְׁבֵי בֵיתֶךָ, עוֹד יְהַלְלוּךָ סֶּלָה.
אַשְׁרֵי הָעָם שֶׁכָּכָה לּוֹ, אַשְׁרֵי הָעָם שֶׁיהוה אֱלֹהָיו.

תְּהִלָּה לְדָוִד.

אֲרוֹמִמְךָ אֱלוֹהַי הַמֶּלֶךְ, וַאֲבָרְכָה שִׁמְךָ לְעוֹלָם וָעֶד.
בְּכָל־יוֹם אֲבָרְכֶךָּ, וַאֲהַלְלָה שִׁמְךָ לְעוֹלָם וָעֶד.
גָּדוֹל יהוה וּמְהֻלָּל מְאֹד, וְלִגְדֻלָּתוֹ אֵין חֵקֶר.
דּוֹר לְדוֹר יְשַׁבַּח מַעֲשֶׂיךָ, וּגְבוּרֹתֶיךָ יַגִּידוּ.
הֲדַר כְּבוֹד הוֹדֶךָ, וְדִבְרֵי נִפְלְאֹתֶיךָ אָשִׂיחָה.
וֶעֱזוּז נוֹרְאוֹתֶיךָ יֹאמֵרוּ, וּגְדֻלָּתְךָ אֲסַפְּרֶנָּה.
זֵכֶר רַב־טוּבְךָ יַבִּיעוּ, וְצִדְקָתְךָ יְרַנֵּנוּ.
חַנּוּן וְרַחוּם יהוה, אֶרֶךְ אַפַּיִם וּגְדָל־חָסֶד.
טוֹב־יהוה לַכֹּל, וְרַחֲמָיו עַל־כָּל־מַעֲשָׂיו.
יוֹדוּךָ יהוה כָּל־מַעֲשֶׂיךָ, וַחֲסִידֶיךָ יְבָרְכוּכָה.
כְּבוֹד מַלְכוּתְךָ יֹאמֵרוּ, וּגְבוּרָתְךָ יְדַבֵּרוּ.
לְהוֹדִיעַ לִבְנֵי הָאָדָם גְּבוּרֹתָיו, וּכְבוֹד הֲדַר מַלְכוּתוֹ.
מַלְכוּתְךָ מַלְכוּת כָּל־עֹלָמִים, וּמֶמְשַׁלְתְּךָ בְּכָל־דּוֹר וָדֹר.
סוֹמֵךְ יהוה לְכָל־הַנֹּפְלִים, וְזוֹקֵף לְכָל־הַכְּפוּפִים.
עֵינֵי־כֹל אֵלֶיךָ יְשַׂבֵּרוּ, וְאַתָּה נוֹתֵן לָהֶם אֶת־אָכְלָם בְּעִתּוֹ.
פּוֹתֵחַ אֶת־יָדֶךָ, וּמַשְׂבִּיעַ לְכָל־חַי רָצוֹן.
צַדִּיק יהוה בְּכָל־דְּרָכָיו, וְחָסִיד בְּכָל־מַעֲשָׂיו.
קָרוֹב יהוה לְכָל־קֹרְאָיו, לְכֹל אֲשֶׁר יִקְרָאֻהוּ בֶאֱמֶת.
רְצוֹן־יְרֵאָיו יַעֲשֶׂה, וְאֶת־שַׁוְעָתָם יִשְׁמַע וְיוֹשִׁיעֵם.
שׁוֹמֵר יהוה אֶת־כָּל־אֹהֲבָיו, וְאֵת כָּל־הָרְשָׁעִים יַשְׁמִיד.
◁ תְּהִלַּת יהוה יְדַבֶּר־פִּי,
וִיבָרֵךְ כָּל־בָּשָׂר שֵׁם קָדְשׁוֹ לְעוֹלָם וָעֶד.
וַאֲנַחְנוּ נְבָרֵךְ יָהּ, מֵעַתָּה וְעַד עוֹלָם. הַלְלוּיָהּ. תהלים קמה

ASHREI

Joyous are they who dwell in Your house;
they shall praise You forever.

> *Joyous the people who are so favored;*
> *joyous the people whose God is ADONAI.*

PSALM 145

A PSALM OF DAVID.

I exalt You, my God, my sovereign;
I praise Your name, always.

> *Every day I praise You, glorifying Your name, always.*

Great is ADONAI, greatly to be praised,
though God's greatness is unfathomable.

> *One generation praises Your works to another,*
> *telling of Your mighty deeds.*

I would speak of Your majestic glory
and of Your wondrous acts.

> *People speak of Your awe-inspiring deeds; I, too, shall recount Your greatness.*

They recount Your great goodness, and sing of Your righteousness.

> *ADONAI is merciful and compassionate, patient, and abounding in love.*

ADONAI is good to all, and God's mercy embraces all of creation.

> *All of creation acknowledges You, and the faithful bless You.*

They speak of the glory of Your sovereignty; and tell of Your might,

> *proclaiming to humanity Your mighty deeds,*
> *and the glory of Your majestic sovereignty.*

Your sovereignty is eternal; Your dominion endures through each generation.

> *ADONAI supports all who falter, and lifts up all who are bent down.*

The eyes of all look hopefully to You,
and You provide them nourishment in due time.

> *You open Your hand, satisfying all the living with contentment.*

ADONAI is righteous in all that is done, faithful to all creation.

> *ADONAI is near to all who call, to all who sincerely call.*

God fulfills the desire of those who are faithful,
listening to their cries, rescuing them.

> *ADONAI watches over all those who love the Holy One,*
> *but will destroy all the wicked.*

My mouth shall utter praise of ADONAI.
May all that is mortal praise God's name forever and ever.

> *We shall praise ADONAI now and always. Halleluyah!*

We rise. Leader:

יְהַלְלוּ אֶת־שֵׁם יהוה, כִּי־נִשְׂגָּב שְׁמוֹ לְבַדּוֹ.

Congregation:

הוֹדוֹ עַל־אֶרֶץ וְשָׁמָיִם. וַיָּרֶם קֶרֶן לְעַמּוֹ,
תְּהִלָּה לְכָל־חֲסִידָיו, לִבְנֵי יִשְׂרָאֵל עַם קְרֹבוֹ, הַלְלוּ־יָהּ.

ON SHABBAT, WE RECITE THIS PSALM:

מִזְמוֹר לְדָוִד

הָבוּ לַיהוה בְּנֵי אֵלִים, הָבוּ לַיהוה כָּבוֹד וָעֹז.
הָבוּ לַיהוה כְּבוֹד שְׁמוֹ, הִשְׁתַּחֲווּ לַיהוה בְּהַדְרַת־קֹדֶשׁ.
קוֹל יהוה עַל־הַמָּיִם,
אֵל־הַכָּבוֹד הִרְעִים, יהוה עַל־מַיִם רַבִּים.
קוֹל־יהוה בַּכֹּחַ, קוֹל יהוה בֶּהָדָר.
קוֹל־יהוה שֹׁבֵר אֲרָזִים, וַיְשַׁבֵּר יהוה אֶת־אַרְזֵי הַלְּבָנוֹן.
וַיַּרְקִידֵם כְּמוֹ־עֵגֶל, לְבָנוֹן וְשִׂרְיֹן כְּמוֹ בֶן־רְאֵמִים.
קוֹל־יהוה חֹצֵב לַהֲבוֹת אֵשׁ.
קוֹל יהוה יָחִיל מִדְבָּר,
יָחִיל יהוה מִדְבַּר קָדֵשׁ.
קוֹל יהוה יְחוֹלֵל אַיָּלוֹת
וַיֶּחֱשֹׂף יְעָרוֹת, וּבְהֵיכָלוֹ כֻּלּוֹ אֹמֵר כָּבוֹד.
יהוה לַמַּבּוּל יָשָׁב, וַיֵּשֶׁב יהוה מֶלֶךְ לְעוֹלָם.
יהוה עֹז לְעַמּוֹ יִתֵּן, יהוה יְבָרֵךְ אֶת־עַמּוֹ בַשָּׁלוֹם. תהלים כט

GOD'S GLORY הוֹדוֹ. Psalm 148:13–14.

PSALM 29. Psalm 29 was chosen to accompany the procession of the Torah as it is returned to the ark on Shabbat morning because of the predominant image of the voice of God. The phrase *kol Adonai* ("the voice of God") is repeated seven times—which was identified by the ancient Rabbis with the revelation of God's word on Sinai. The thunder and lightning described here evokes the scene of the revelation at Sinai in the Book of Exodus; the Bible identifies Kadesh with the Sinai desert.

Biblical scholars see the psalm as a depiction of a storm coming in from the Mediterranean, passing over the mountains of Lebanon—cedars top those high mountains and are among the world's sturdiest and longest-lived trees—moving over the fertile land and then through the desert.

Our psalm begins with reference to the waters of the Mediterranean Sea and ends with God enthroned above the primal waters of creation. It also begins with an angelic chorus praising God and toward the end mentions the human chorus praising God in the Temple. Thus earth and heaven, the human and the divine, are joined. Similarly, Torah is that which ties heaven and earth together.

RETURNING THE TORAH

We rise. Leader:

Extol the name of ADONAI, for God's name alone is exalted.

Congregation:

God's glory encompasses heaven and earth; God extols the faithful—
raising up Israel, the people God keeps close. Halleluyah!

Hodo al eretz v'shamayim, va-yarem keren l'ammo;
t'hillah l'khol ḥasidav, liv'nei yisra·el am k'rovo. Hal'luyah!

ON SHABBAT, WE RECITE THIS PSALM:

PSALM 29

A SONG OF DAVID.

Acclaim ADONAI, O exalted creatures;
acclaim ADONAI, with glory and strength.
Acclaim ADONAI, for God's name is glorious;
pay homage to ADONAI in the splendor of the sanctuary.
The voice of ADONAI is stronger than the voice of the sea;
God is exalted above the rushing waters.
The voice of ADONAI is powerful;
the voice of ADONAI is glorious.
The voice of ADONAI shatters majestic cedars,
the very cedars of Lebanon.
The trees skip like calves;
the mountains, like wild oxen.
The voice of ADONAI flashes fire, splitting rocks;
the voice of ADONAI convulses the desert,
the very desert of Kadesh.
The voice of ADONAI makes hinds calve;
the voice of ADONAI strips the forest bare,
while in God's sanctuary all acknowledge God's glory.
ADONAI was enthroned above the primal waters;
ADONAI sat enthroned, the eternal sovereign.
ADONAI will grant strength to God's people, blessing them with peace.

Havu ladonai b'nei eilim, havu ladonai kavod va-oz.
Havu ladonai k'vod sh'mo, hishtaḥavu ladonai b'hadrat kodesh.

Kol Adonai ba-ko·aḥ, kol Adonai be-hadar,
kol Adonai shoveir arazim, va-y'shabbeir Adonai et arzei ha-l'vanon.

Kol Adonai ḥotzeiv lahavot eish, kol Adonai yaḥil midbar,
yaḥil Adonai midbar kadeish. Kol Adonai y'ḥoleil ayyalot

Adonai la-mabbul yashav, va-yeishev Adonai melekh l'olam.
Adonai oz l'ammo yittein, Adonai y'vareikh et ammo va-shalom.

לְדָוִד מִזְמוֹר.

לַיהוה הָאָרֶץ וּמְלוֹאָהּ, תֵּבֵל וְיֹשְׁבֵי בָהּ.

כִּי־הוּא עַל־יַמִּים יְסָדָהּ, וְעַל־נְהָרוֹת יְכוֹנְנֶהָ.

מִי־יַעֲלֶה בְהַר־יהוה, וּמִי־יָקוּם בִּמְקוֹם קָדְשׁוֹ.

נְקִי כַפַּיִם וּבַר־לֵבָב, אֲשֶׁר לֹא־נָשָׂא לַשָּׁוְא נַפְשִׁי,

וְלֹא נִשְׁבַּע לְמִרְמָה.

יִשָּׂא בְרָכָה מֵאֵת יהוה, וּצְדָקָה מֵאֱלֹהֵי יִשְׁעוֹ.

זֶה דּוֹר דֹּרְשָׁו, מְבַקְשֵׁי פָנֶיךָ יַעֲקֹב, סֶלָה.

שְׂאוּ שְׁעָרִים רָאשֵׁיכֶם, וְהִנָּשְׂאוּ פִּתְחֵי עוֹלָם,

וְיָבוֹא מֶלֶךְ הַכָּבוֹד.

מִי זֶה מֶלֶךְ הַכָּבוֹד,

יהוה עִזּוּז וְגִבּוֹר, יהוה גִּבּוֹר מִלְחָמָה.

שְׂאוּ שְׁעָרִים רָאשֵׁיכֶם, וּשְׂאוּ פִּתְחֵי עוֹלָם,

וְיָבֹא מֶלֶךְ הַכָּבוֹד.

מִי הוּא זֶה מֶלֶךְ הַכָּבוֹד,

יהוה צְבָאוֹת הוּא מֶלֶךְ הַכָּבוֹד, סֶלָה. תהלים כד

PSALM 24. This psalm's dramatic imagery of gates that open for God's symbolic entrance to the Temple explains why it accompanies our Torah's return to the ark. Yet the psalm focuses first of all on the state of the worshipper: purity of action—especially verbal honesty—must characterize those who would enter this holy place and receive its blessing. This develops a theme of the b'rakhah recited just after each Torah reading, describing the Torah as "a teaching of truth": in order to live in accord with Torah, we must exemplify inner truthfulness while also pursuing truth in the world.

A Song of David

Each of the two psalms recited as the Torah is carried around the congregation (one on Shabbat, one on weekdays) begins with the same Hebrew words—but in a different order. Psalm 24 begins לְדָוִד מִזְמוֹר, literally "to David a psalm," and Psalm 29 begins מִזְמוֹר לְדָוִד, "a psalm to David." The Midrash comments on this difference, saying that sometimes David would be so inspired that he immediately began writing, but at other times he had to struggle to find inspiration.

On weekdays:

PSALM 24

A SONG OF DAVID.

The earth is ADONAI's in all its fullness,
the land and all who dwell on it.
For it was God who founded it upon the seas,
and set it firm upon the flowing streams.
Who may ascend the mount of ADONAI?
Who may come forward in God's sanctuary?
One who has clean hands and a pure heart,
who has not taken God's name in vain, nor sworn deceitfully.
One such as this will receive ADONAI's blessing,
a just reward from God, the deliverer.
This generation searches for You;
like Jacob, seeks Your presence, *selah.*
Open up, arched gateways—open up, doors of the world;
may the sovereign who is exalted enter.
Who is the sovereign who is exalted?
ADONAI, mighty and triumphant, triumphant in battle.
Open up, arched gateways—open up, doors of the world;
may the sovereign who is exalted enter.
Who is the sovereign who is exalted?
Adonai Tz'va·ot is the sovereign who is exalted. Selah.

Ladonai ha-aretz u-m'lo·ah, teiveil v'yosh'vei vah.
    Ki hu al yammim y'sadah, v'al n'harot y'khon'neha.
Mi ya·aleh v'har Adonai, u-mi yakum bi-m'kom kodsho.
    N'ki khappayim u-var leivav, asher lo nasa la-shav nafshi,
        v'lo nishba l'mirmah.
Yissa v'rakhah mei-eit Adonai, u-tz'dakah mei-elohei yisho.
    Zeh dor dor'shav m'vakshei fanekha ya·akov, selah.
S'u sh'arim rasheikhem, v'hinnas'u pithei olam,
v'yavo melekh ha-kavod.
    Mi zeh melekh ha-kavod, Adonai izzuz v'gibbor,
    Adonai gibbor milhamah.
S'u sh'arim rasheikhem, v'hinnas'u pithei olam,
v'yavo melekh ha-kavod.
    Mi hu zeh melekh ha-kavod,
    Adonai Tz'va·ot hu melekh ha-kavod, selah.

The Torah scrolls are placed in the ark.

וּבְנֻחֹה יֹאמַר: שׁוּבָה יהוה רִבְבוֹת אַלְפֵי יִשְׂרָאֵל.

קוּמָה יהוה לִמְנוּחָתֶךָ, אַתָּה וַאֲרוֹן עֻזֶּךָ.

כֹּהֲנֶיךָ יִלְבְּשׁוּ־צֶדֶק, וַחֲסִידֶיךָ יְרַנֵּנוּ.

בַּעֲבוּר דָּוִד עַבְדֶּךָ, אַל־תָּשֵׁב פְּנֵי מְשִׁיחֶךָ.

◁ כִּי לֶקַח טוֹב נָתַתִּי לָכֶם, תּוֹרָתִי אַל־תַּעֲזֹבוּ.

עֵץ־חַיִּים הִיא לַמַּחֲזִיקִים בָּהּ, וְתֹמְכֶיהָ מְאֻשָּׁר.

דְּרָכֶיהָ דַרְכֵי־נֹעַם, וְכָל־נְתִיבוֹתֶיהָ שָׁלוֹם.

הֲשִׁיבֵנוּ יהוה אֵלֶיךָ וְנָשׁוּבָה, חַדֵּשׁ יָמֵינוּ כְּקֶדֶם.

The ark is closed.

חֲצִי קַדִּישׁ

יִתְגַּדַּל וְיִתְקַדַּשׁ שְׁמֵהּ רַבָּא, בְּעָלְמָא דִּי בְרָא, כִּרְעוּתֵהּ, וְיַמְלִיךְ מַלְכוּתֵהּ בְּחַיֵּיכוֹן וּבְיוֹמֵיכוֹן וּבְחַיֵּי דְכָל־בֵּית יִשְׂרָאֵל, בַּעֲגָלָא וּבִזְמַן קָרִיב, וְאִמְרוּ אָמֵן.

יְהֵא שְׁמֵהּ רַבָּא מְבָרַךְ לְעָלַם וּלְעָלְמֵי עָלְמַיָּא.

יִתְבָּרַךְ וְיִשְׁתַּבַּח וְיִתְפָּאַר וְיִתְרוֹמַם וְיִתְנַשֵּׂא וְיִתְהַדָּר וְיִתְעַלֶּה וְיִתְהַלָּל שְׁמֵהּ דְּקֻדְשָׁא, בְּרִיךְ הוּא, לְעֵלָּא לְעֵלָּא מִכָּל־בִּרְכָתָא וְשִׁירָתָא תֻּשְׁבְּחָתָא וְנֶחֱמָתָא דַּאֲמִירָן בְּעָלְמָא, וְאִמְרוּ אָמֵן.

WHENEVER THE ARK WAS SET DOWN וּבְנֻחֹה יֹאמַר.
Numbers 10:36. As the Torah completes its circuit through the synagogue, we recall Moses' words when the people finished a stage in their journey through the wilderness and came to rest in a new camp. This verse and the ones that follow can also refer to our own inner journey—accompanied by Torah. Thus we pray for God to remain with us even as we conclude the day's study.

RETURN קוּמָה. Psalm 132:8–10.

IT IS A TREE OF LIFE FOR THOSE WHO GRASP IT עֵץ חַיִּים הִיא לַמַּחֲזִיקִים בָּהּ This verse (Proverbs 3:18) is the source of the custom of holding onto the *atzei ḥayyim*, the Torah handles, while reciting the *b'rakhot* over the Torah— thus grasping the "tree of life" both physically and figuratively.

ITS WAYS ARE PLEASANT WAYS, AND ALL ITS PATHS ARE PEACE דְּרָכֶיהָ דַרְכֵי־נֹעַם, וְכָל־נְתִיבוֹתֶיהָ שָׁלוֹם. Proverbs 3:17. As we put away the Torah, we pray that our study should promote actions that lead to pleasantness and peace.

Make Our Days Seem Fresh

"Make our days seem fresh" should not be seen as a plea for restoration of a formerly perfect condition; we were never perfect. Rather, it is a plea for resilience, a plea for the ability to renew ourselves after moments of crisis and dislocation. As Elie Wiesel remarks, "God gave Adam a secret—and that secret was not how to begin, but how to begin again."

Whenever the Ark was set down, Moses would say:
ADONAI, may You dwell among the myriad families of the people Israel.

> Return, ADONAI, to Your sanctuary,
> You and Your glorious Ark.

Let Your priests be robed in righteousness,
and Your faithful sing for joy.

> For the sake of David, Your servant,
> do not turn away from Your anointed.

I have given you a precious inheritance:
Do not forsake My teaching.

> It is a tree of life for those who grasp it,
> and all who hold onto it are blessed.

Its ways are pleasant ways, and all its paths are peace.

> Turn us toward You, ADONAI, and we will return to You;
> make our days seem fresh, as they once were.

Eitz ḥayyim hi la-maḥazikim bah, v'tom'kheha m'ushar.
D'rakheha darkhei no·am, v'khol n'tivoteha shalom.
Hashiveinu Adonai eilekha v'nashuvah, ḥaddeish yameinu k'kedem.

The ark is closed.

Ḥatzi Kaddish

May God's great name be exalted and hallowed throughout the created world, as is God's wish. May God's sovereignty soon be established, in your lifetime and in your days, and in the days of all the House of Israel. And respond with: *Amen.*

b'ḥayyeikhon u-v'yomeikhon u-v'ḥayyei d'khol beit yisra·el,
ba-agala u-viz'man kariv, v'imru amen.

May God's great name be acknowledged forever and ever!
Y'hei sh'meih rabba m'varakh l'alam u-l'almei almayya. Yitbarakh

May the name of the Holy One be acknowledged and celebrated, lauded and worshipped, exalted and honored, extolled and acclaimed—though God, who is blessed, is truly far beyond all acknowledgment and praise, or any expressions of gratitude or consolation ever spoken in the world. And respond with: *Amen.*

b'rikh hu, l'eilla l'eilla mi-kol birkhata v'shirata
tushb'ḥata v'neḥamata da-amiran b'alma, v'imru amen.

מוסף ליום כיפור
MUSAF SERVICE OF YOM KIPPUR

Before the Amidah begins, it is customary to take three steps backward, as if we are leaving our familiar surroundings, and then three steps forward, as we approach God's presence.

When reciting the words בָּרוּךְ אַתָּה on this page, we customarily bend the knees and bow, standing up straight by the time we reach the word יהוה. We repeat these motions at the end of the first b'rakhah when we come to the words "barukh atah Adonai." The sign ⅂ indicates the places to bow.

אֲדֹנָי שְׂפָתַי תִּפְתָּח וּפִי יַגִּיד תְּהִלָּתֶךָ.

Version with Patriarchs and Matriarchs:

⅂ בָּרוּךְ אַתָּה יהוה,
אֱלֹהֵינוּ וֵאלֹהֵי אֲבוֹתֵינוּ
[וְאִמּוֹתֵינוּ], אֱלֹהֵי אַבְרָהָם,
אֱלֹהֵי יִצְחָק, וֵאלֹהֵי יַעֲקֹב,
אֱלֹהֵי שָׂרָה, אֱלֹהֵי רִבְקָה,
אֱלֹהֵי רָחֵל, וֵאלֹהֵי לֵאָה,
הָאֵל הַגָּדוֹל הַגִּבּוֹר וְהַנּוֹרָא,
אֵל עֶלְיוֹן, גּוֹמֵל חֲסָדִים
טוֹבִים, וְקוֹנֵה הַכֹּל, וְזוֹכֵר
חַסְדֵי אָבוֹת [וְאִמָּהוֹת],
וּמֵבִיא גוֹאֵל לִבְנֵי בְנֵיהֶם
לְמַעַן שְׁמוֹ בְּאַהֲבָה.

Version with Patriarchs:

⅂ בָּרוּךְ אַתָּה יהוה,
אֱלֹהֵינוּ וֵאלֹהֵי אֲבוֹתֵינוּ,
אֱלֹהֵי אַבְרָהָם, אֱלֹהֵי
יִצְחָק, וֵאלֹהֵי יַעֲקֹב, הָאֵל
הַגָּדוֹל הַגִּבּוֹר וְהַנּוֹרָא,
אֵל עֶלְיוֹן, גּוֹמֵל חֲסָדִים
טוֹבִים, וְקוֹנֵה הַכֹּל, וְזוֹכֵר
חַסְדֵי אָבוֹת, וּמֵבִיא גוֹאֵל
לִבְנֵי בְנֵיהֶם לְמַעַן שְׁמוֹ
בְּאַהֲבָה.

AMIDAH. The Amidah, literally "the prayer said while standing," is the moment of personal meditation. It always contains three introductory b'rakhot. The first mentions our ancestors and their relation to God; the second describes God's continuing presence in the world; the third emphasizes God's uniqueness and the path to God: holiness. Similarly, every Amidah ends with three b'rakhot. The first looks toward the restoration of God's presence to Zion; the next thanks God for all the gifts we experience in life; and the final one asks for peace. On Yom Kippur, a middle blessing is added, expressing the holiness of the day. The confession, the central liturgical element of Yom Kippur, is recited at the conclusion of the Amidah.

ADONAI, OPEN MY LIPS אֲדֹנָי שְׂפָתַי תִּפְתָּח. Psalm 51:17. Every Amidah begins with this request asking God to afford us the appropriate attitude and words for prayer. Perhaps the phrase conveys a mystical sense that prayer originates in our soul, the part of God within us all.

GOD OF ABRAHAM, GOD OF ISAAC, AND GOD OF JACOB אֱלֹהֵי אַבְרָהָם, אֱלֹהֵי יִצְחָק, וֵאלֹהֵי יַעֲקֹב. God begins the conversation with Moses at the burning bush with this self-description (Exodus 3:6). We understand the world of prayer, first of all, through the experience of those who came before us—both in our immediate and our ancient past. Perhaps the quotation of these words expresses the hope that we too might feel the presence of God. Moses saw only a burning bush, but his inner ear heard so much more.

GREAT, MIGHTY, AWE-INSPIRING הַגָּדוֹל הַגִּבּוֹר וְהַנּוֹרָא. This phrase is a quotation from Deuteronomy 10:17–18, where God's might is characterized by the befriending of the stranger, the widow, and the orphan.

THE SILENT AMIDAH

Rabbi Simeon taught:
When you pray, don't
only follow the form.
Rather, turn your prayer
into a personal plea;
and don't see yourself as
someone who is over-
whelmed by sin.

—MISHNAH AVOT

Before the Amidah begins, it is customary to take three steps backward, as if we are leaving our familiar surroundings, and then three steps forward, as we approach God's presence.

When reciting the words "barukh atah" on this page, we customarily bend the knees and bow, standing up straight by the time we reach the word "Adonai." We repeat these motions at the end of the first b'rakhah when we come to the words "barukh atah Adonai." The sign ʕ indicates the places to bow.

ADONAI, open my lips that my mouth may speak Your praise.

An Alternate Rendering

Some may want to engage in silent prayer by reading through the prayers and meditations in this column through page 357. The alternate renderings are by André Ungar. Meditations on sin and forgiveness by other authors are found in the middle of the Amidah.

Help me, O God,
to pray. Our ances-
tors worshipped You.
Abraham and Sarah,
Rebecca and Isaac,
Jacob, Rachel, and Leah
stood in awe before You.
We, too, reach for You,
infinite, awe-inspiring,
transcendent God,
source of all being whose
truth shines through our
ancestors' lives. We, their
distant descendants, draw
strength from their lives
and from Your redeeming
love. Be our help and our
shield, as You were theirs.
We praise You, God,
Guardian of Abraham.

O sovereign God who
delights in life,
make our lives worthy to
be remembered.
Out of Your love for us,
O living God,
Enter our names in the
Ledger of Life.

First B'rakhah: Our Ancestors

Version with Patriarchs:

ʕ *Barukh atah* ADONAI,
our God and God of our
ancestors,
God of Abraham, God of
Isaac, and God of Jacob,
great, mighty, awe-inspiring,
transcendent God,
who acts with lovingkindness
and creates all things,
who remembers the loving
deeds of our ancestors,
and who will send a redeemer
to their children's children
with love
for the sake of divine honor.

Version with Patriarchs and Matriarchs:

ʕ *Barukh atah* ADONAI,
our God and God of our
ancestors,
God of Abraham, God of
Isaac, and God of Jacob,
God of Sarah, God of
Rebecca, God of Rachel,
and God of Leah,
great, mighty, awe-inspiring,
transcendent God,
who acts with lovingkindness
and creates all things,
who remembers the loving
deeds of our ancestors,
and who will send a redeemer
to their children's children
with love
for the sake of divine honor.

זָכְרֵנוּ לְחַיִּים, מֶלֶךְ חָפֵץ בַּחַיִּים,
וְכָתְבֵנוּ בְּסֵפֶר הַחַיִּים, לְמַעַנְךָ אֱלֹהִים חַיִּים.

Version with Patriarchs and Matriarchs: *Version with Patriarchs:*

מֶלֶךְ עוֹזֵר וּפוֹקֵד   מֶלֶךְ עוֹזֵר וּמוֹשִׁיעַ וּמָגֵן.
וּמוֹשִׁיעַ וּמָגֵן.   ⟷ בָּרוּךְ אַתָּה יהוה, מָגֵן
⟷ בָּרוּךְ אַתָּה יהוה, מָגֵן   אַבְרָהָם.
אַבְרָהָם וּפוֹקֵד שָׂרָה.

אַתָּה גִבּוֹר לְעוֹלָם, אֲדֹנָי, מְחַיֵּה מֵתִים אַתָּה,
רַב לְהוֹשִׁיעַ.

מְכַלְכֵּל חַיִּים בְּחֶסֶד, מְחַיֵּה מֵתִים בְּרַחֲמִים רַבִּים, סוֹמֵךְ
נוֹפְלִים, וְרוֹפֵא חוֹלִים, וּמַתִּיר אֲסוּרִים, וּמְקַיֵּם אֱמוּנָתוֹ
לִישֵׁנֵי עָפָר. מִי כָמוֹךָ בַּעַל גְּבוּרוֹת, וּמִי דּוֹמֶה לָּךְ, מֶלֶךְ
מֵמִית וּמְחַיֶּה וּמַצְמִיחַ יְשׁוּעָה.

מִי כָמוֹךָ אַב הָרַחֲמִים, זוֹכֵר יְצוּרָיו לְחַיִּים בְּרַחֲמִים.

וְנֶאֱמָן אַתָּה לְהַחֲיוֹת מֵתִים.
בָּרוּךְ אַתָּה יהוה, מְחַיֵּה הַמֵּתִים.

אַתָּה קָדוֹשׁ וְשִׁמְךָ קָדוֹשׁ וּקְדוֹשִׁים בְּכָל־יוֹם יְהַלְלוּךָ,
סֶלָה.

וּבְכֵן תֵּן פַּחְדְּךָ יהוה אֱלֹהֵינוּ עַל כָּל־מַעֲשֶׂיךָ
וְאֵימָתְךָ עַל כָּל־מַה־שֶּׁבָּרָאתָ,
וְיִירָאוּךָ כָּל־הַמַּעֲשִׂים
וְיִשְׁתַּחֲווּ לְפָנֶיךָ כָּל־הַבְּרוּאִים,
וְיֵעָשׂוּ כֻלָּם אֲגֻדָּה אַחַת לַעֲשׂוֹת רְצוֹנְךָ בְּלֵבָב שָׁלֵם,
כְּמוֹ שֶׁיָּדַעְנוּ יהוה אֱלֹהֵינוּ,
שֶׁהַשָּׁלְטוֹן לְפָנֶיךָ, עֹז בְּיָדְךָ וּגְבוּרָה בִּימִינֶךָ,
וְשִׁמְךָ נוֹרָא עַל כָּל־מַה־שֶּׁבָּרָאתָ.

REMEMBER US זָכְרֵנוּ. This brief anonymous and ancient poem, added at each service during the High Holy Day season, stresses the theme that God treasures life.

MIGHTY FOREVER אַתָּה גִבּוֹר. This *b'rakhah*, which describes God's presence and activity in the world, centers on the kindness and care of God for the incapacitated—even the dead are in God's care.

GIVE LIFE TO THE DEAD מְחַיֵּה מֵתִים. To be sure, the primary meaning of this phrase was understood to refer to the afterlife, but the Rabbis also understood that the phrase referred to a spiritual revival in this world. Thus the *b'rakhah* one makes on greeting a friend whom one has not seen for a year utilizes the phrase "who gives life to the dead."

WHO IS LIKE YOU, SOURCE OF COMPASSION? מִי כָמוֹךָ אַב הָרַחֲמִים. A second *piyyut* inserted at each of the services in the High Holy Day season, emphasizing God's kindness.

U-V'KHEIN וּבְכֵן. These three paragraphs, which are introduced by the same word, וּבְכֵן (u-v'khein), are ascribed by many scholars to the 3rd century, and may constitute the earliest poetic additions to the Amidah. Stages of redemption are described in this series of prayers. Reuven Hammer, a modern commentator, remarks that the first paragraph implores God to cause the entire world to live with reverence for God. The next paragraph discusses not the universal, but the particular: the return of Israel to its land (and specifically to Jerusalem) and the kingship of David. The third paragraph describes the rejoicing that will come to the righteous "when You remove the tyranny of arrogance from the earth" and God will rule alone over the entire world from Zion and Jerusalem.

Your power sustains the universe. You breathe life into dead matter. With compassion You care for all who live. Your limitless love lets life triumph over death, heals the sick, upholds the exhausted, frees the enslaved, keeps faith even with the dead. Who is like You, God of splendor and power incomparable?

As a tender parent, You nurture our souls that we may grow into a life of compassion.

You govern both life and death; Your presence brings our souls to blossom. We praise You, God, who wrests life from death.

Remember us for life, Sovereign who delights in life, and inscribe us in the Book of Life, for Your sake, God of life.

Version with Patriarchs:
You are the Sovereign who helps and saves and shields.

ᚠ *Barukh atah* ADONAI, shield of Abraham.

Version with Patriarchs and Matriarchs:
You are the Sovereign who helps and guards, saves and shields.

ᚠ *Barukh atah* ADONAI, shield of Abraham and guardian of Sarah.

Second B'rakhah: God's Saving Care

You are mighty forever, ADONAI—
You give life to the dead; great is Your saving power.

You sustain the living through love,
    and with great mercy give life to the dead.
You support the falling, heal the sick,
    loosen the chains of the bound,
    and keep faith with those who sleep in the dust.
Who is like You, Almighty,
    and who can be compared to You?—
    Sovereign, who brings death and life,
    and causes salvation to flourish.

Who is like You, source of compassion,
who remembers with compassion Your creatures for life?

You are faithful in bringing life to the dead.
Barukh atah ADONAI, who gives life to the dead.

Third B'rakhah: God's Holiness

Holy are You and holy is Your name;
holy ones praise You each day.

U-v'khein—ADONAI our God,
instill Your awe in all You have made,
and fear of You in all You have created,
so that all You have fashioned revere You,
all You have created bow in recognition,
and all be bound together, carrying out Your will wholeheartedly.
For we know that true sovereignty is Yours,
power and strength are in Your hands,
and Your name is to be revered beyond any of Your creations.

וּבְכֵן תֵּן כָּבוֹד יהוה לְעַמֶּךָ,
תְּהִלָּה לִירֵאֶיךָ וְתִקְוָה לְדוֹרְשֶׁיךָ,
וּפִתְחוֹן פֶּה לַמְיַחֲלִים לָךְ,
שִׂמְחָה לְאַרְצֶךָ וְשָׂשׂוֹן לְעִירֶךָ,
וּצְמִיחַת קֶרֶן לְדָוִד עַבְדֶּךָ,
וַעֲרִיכַת נֵר לְבֶן־יִשַׁי מְשִׁיחֶךָ, בִּמְהֵרָה בְיָמֵינוּ.

וּבְכֵן צַדִּיקִים יִרְאוּ וְיִשְׂמָחוּ,
וִישָׁרִים יַעֲלֹזוּ,
וַחֲסִידִים בְּרִנָּה יָגִילוּ,
וְעוֹלָתָה תִּקְפָּץ־פִּיהָ,
וְכָל־הָרִשְׁעָה כֻּלָּהּ כְּעָשָׁן תִּכְלֶה,
כִּי תַעֲבִיר מֶמְשֶׁלֶת זָדוֹן מִן הָאָרֶץ.

וְתִמְלֹךְ, אַתָּה יהוה לְבַדֶּךָ, עַל כָּל־מַעֲשֶׂיךָ, בְּהַר צִיּוֹן
מִשְׁכַּן כְּבוֹדֶךָ, וּבִירוּשָׁלַיִם עִיר קָדְשֶׁךָ, כַּכָּתוּב בְּדִבְרֵי
קָדְשֶׁךָ: יִמְלֹךְ יהוה לְעוֹלָם, אֱלֹהַיִךְ צִיּוֹן לְדֹר וָדֹר, הַלְלוּ־יָהּ.

קָדוֹשׁ אַתָּה וְנוֹרָא שְׁמֶךָ, וְאֵין אֱלוֹהַּ מִבַּלְעָדֶיךָ, כַּכָּתוּב:
וַיִּגְבַּהּ יהוה צְבָאוֹת בַּמִּשְׁפָּט, וְהָאֵל הַקָּדוֹשׁ נִקְדַּשׁ
בִּצְדָקָה. בָּרוּךְ אַתָּה יהוה, הַמֶּלֶךְ הַקָּדוֹשׁ.

אַתָּה בְחַרְתָּנוּ מִכָּל־הָעַמִּים, אָהַבְתָּ אוֹתָנוּ וְרָצִיתָ בָּנוּ,
וְרוֹמַמְתָּנוּ מִכָּל־הַלְּשׁוֹנוֹת, וְקִדַּשְׁתָּנוּ בְּמִצְוֹתֶיךָ,
וְקֵרַבְתָּנוּ מַלְכֵּנוּ לַעֲבוֹדָתֶךָ,
וְשִׁמְךָ הַגָּדוֹל וְהַקָּדוֹשׁ עָלֵינוּ קָרָאתָ.

וַתִּתֶּן לָנוּ, יהוה אֱלֹהֵינוּ, בְּאַהֲבָה אֶת־יוֹם [הַשַּׁבָּת הַזֶּה
לִקְדֻשָּׁה וְלִמְנוּחָה וְאֶת־יוֹם] הַכִּפֻּרִים הַזֶּה לִמְחִילָה
וְלִסְלִיחָה וּלְכַפָּרָה, וְלִמְחָל־בּוֹ אֶת־כָּל־עֲוֹנוֹתֵינוּ
[בְּאַהֲבָה] מִקְרָא קֹדֶשׁ, זֵכֶר לִיצִיאַת מִצְרָיִם.

U-V'KHEIN וּבְכֵן. Although only the last paragraph in this series contains a formal quotation from the Bible, each of these paragraphs represents prayerful reworkings of biblical expressions of hope. For example, the phrase "recognition to those who await you" is based on Ezekiel 29:21, "and to you will I give recognition (פִּתְחוֹן־פֶּה) among them that all may know that I am Adonai." Similarly, the Book of Job (5:16) speaks of "evil being silenced" (וְעֹלָתָה קָפְצָה פִּיהָ). And the refrain of U-v'khein ("and so") is taken from Esther 4:16, in which Esther describes how she will unlawfully approach the king to plead for the lives of her people.

ADONAI WILL REIGN FOREVER יִמְלֹךְ יהוה לְעוֹלָם. Psalm 146:10.

ADONAI TZV'VA·OT WILL BE EXALTED וַיִּגְבַּהּ יהוה צְבָאוֹת בַּמִּשְׁפָּט. Isaiah 5:16.

Let all creation stand in
awe of You;
let all humankind sense
Your mystery.
May all people be united in
doing Your will whole-
heartedly.
We know that You judge
those who govern,
that ultimate power is
Yours alone,
that Your care embraces all
Your creatures.

Make us all people of
honor.
Smile on all who serve You.
Give hope to those who
seek You,
courage to those who await
the fulfillment of the
messianic dream,
soon in our lifetime.

May the righteous witness
it and be happy,
may good people be filled
with joy—
when at last all jeering
stops and evil evaporates,
when the reign of violence
vanishes from Earth.

And You, You alone, will
rule over all Your creation
from Mount Zion, Your
glorious dwelling place,
from Jerusalem, Your holy
city,
as sacred Scripture pro-
claims: "God will reign
throughout the world,
your God O Zion, forever
and ever.
Halleluyah!"

Sacred are You, and sacred
Your mystery. Seekers of
holiness worship You all
their lives.
We praise You, God, ulti-
mate sacred mystery.

U-v'khein—Bestow honor to Your people, ADONAI,
praise to those who revere You,
hope to those who seek You,
recognition to those who await You,
joy to Your land, and gladness to Your city.
May the light of David, Your servant, dawn,
and the lamp of the son of Jesse, Your anointed,
be kindled speedily in our day.

U-v'khein—The righteous, beholding this, will rejoice,
the upright will be glad,
the pious will celebrate with song,
evil will be silenced,
and all wickedness will disappear like smoke,
when You remove the tyranny of arrogance from the earth.

You alone, ADONAI, will rule all Your creation,
from Mount Zion, the dwelling-place of Your glory,
and from Jerusalem, Your holy city.
As it is written in the Book of Psalms:
"ADONAI will reign forever;
your God, O Zion, from generation to generation.
Halleluyah!" Psalm 146:10

You are holy, and Your name is revered,
    for there is no God but You.
As Your prophet Isaiah wrote: "*Adonai Tz'va·ot* will be
exalted through justice, the holy God sanctified through
righteousness." *Barukh atah* ADONAI, the Holy Sovereign.

Fourth B'rakhah: The Holiness of Yom Kippur

You have chosen us among all peoples, loving us, wanting us.
You have distinguished us among all nations, making us holy
through Your commandments, drawing us close to Your
service, and calling us by Your great and holy name.

With love, You have bestowed on us, ADONAI our God, this
[Shabbat, for sanctity and rest, and this] Yom Kippur for pardon, forgiveness, and atonement, that all our sins be forgiven
[through Your love], a sacred time, recalling the Exodus from
Egypt.

Some recite this traditional version; others continue on the next page with
A Prayer for Jewry in Distress.

וּמִפְּנֵי חֲטָאֵינוּ גָּלֽינוּ מֵאַרְצֵֽנוּ וְנִתְרַחַֽקְנוּ מֵעַל אַדְמָתֵֽנוּ
וְאֵין אֲנַֽחְנוּ יְכוֹלִים לַעֲשׂוֹת חוֹבוֹתֵֽינוּ בְּבֵית בְּחִירָתֶֽךָ, בַּבַּֽיִת
הַגָּדוֹל וְהַקָּדוֹשׁ שֶׁנִּקְרָא שִׁמְךָ עָלָיו, מִפְּנֵי הַיָּד שֶׁנִּשְׁתַּלְּחָה
בְּמִקְדָּשֶֽׁךָ.

יְהִי רָצוֹן מִלְּפָנֶֽיךָ, יְהוָה אֱלֹהֵֽינוּ וֵאלֹהֵי אֲבוֹתֵֽינוּ
[וְאִמּוֹתֵֽינוּ], מֶֽלֶךְ רַחֲמָן הַמֵּשִׁיב בָּנִים לִגְבוּלָם, שֶׁתָּשׁוּב
וּתְרַחֵם עָלֵֽינוּ וְעַל מִקְדָּשְׁךָ בְּרַחֲמֶֽיךָ הָרַבִּים, וְתִבְנֵֽהוּ
מְהֵרָה וּתְגַדֵּל כְּבוֹדוֹ. אָבִֽינוּ מַלְכֵּֽנוּ, גַּלֵּה כְּבוֹד מַלְכוּתְךָ
עָלֵֽינוּ מְהֵרָה, וְהוֹפַע וְהִנָּשֵׂא עָלֵֽינוּ לְעֵינֵי כָּל־חָי, וְקָרֵב
פְּזוּרֵֽינוּ מִבֵּין הַגּוֹיִם וּנְפוּצוֹתֵֽינוּ כַּנֵּס מִיַּרְכְּתֵי־אָֽרֶץ.

וַהֲבִיאֵֽנוּ לְצִיּוֹן עִירְךָ בְּרִנָּה, וְלִירוּשָׁלַֽיִם בֵּית מִקְדָּשְׁךָ
בְּשִׂמְחַת עוֹלָם, וְשָׁם עָשׂוּ אֲבוֹתֵֽינוּ [וְאִמּוֹתֵֽינוּ] לְפָנֶֽיךָ אֶת־
קָרְבְּנוֹת חוֹבוֹתֵיהֶם, תְּמִידִים כְּסִדְרָם וּמוּסָפִים כְּהִלְכָתָם,

ON SHABBAT: וְאֶת־מוּסְפֵי יוֹם הַשַּׁבָּת הַזֶּה וְיוֹם הַכִּפּוּרִים הַזֶּה

On other days: וְאֶת־מוּסַף יוֹם הַכִּפּוּרִים הַזֶּה

On all days: עָשׂוּ וְהִקְרִֽיבוּ לְפָנֶֽיךָ בְּאַהֲבָה כְּמִצְוַת רְצוֹנֶֽךָ
כַּכָּתוּב בְּתוֹרָתֶֽךָ, עַל יְדֵי מֹשֶׁה עַבְדֶּֽךָ מִפִּי כְבוֹדֶֽךָ כָּאָמוּר:

The Sephardic rite continues on page 305.
On Shabbat, those reciting the traditional sacrificial list add this paragraph:

וּבְיוֹם הַשַּׁבָּת שְׁנֵי כְבָשִׂים בְּנֵי שָׁנָה תְּמִימִם, וּשְׁנֵי
עֶשְׂרֹנִים סֹֽלֶת מִנְחָה בְּלוּלָה בַשֶּֽׁמֶן וְנִסְכּוֹ: עֹלַת שַׁבַּת
בְּשַׁבַּתּוֹ, עַל עֹלַת הַתָּמִיד וְנִסְכָּהּ: במדבר כח ט-י

וּבֶעָשׂוֹר לַחֹֽדֶשׁ הַשְּׁבִיעִי הַזֶּה מִקְרָא־קֹֽדֶשׁ יִהְיֶה לָכֶם
וְעִנִּיתֶם אֶת־נַפְשֹׁתֵיכֶם כָּל־מְלָאכָה לֹא תַעֲשׂוּ:
וְהִקְרַבְתֶּם עֹלָה לַיהוָה רֵֽיחַ נִיחֹֽחַ פַּר בֶּן־בָּקָר אֶחָד אַֽיִל
אֶחָד כְּבָשִׂים בְּנֵי־שָׁנָה שִׁבְעָה תְּמִימִם יִהְיוּ לָכֶם: במדבר כט ז-ח

וּמִנְחָתָם וְנִסְכֵּיהֶם כַּמְדֻבָּר, שְׁלֹשָׁה עֶשְׂרֹנִים לַפָּר וּשְׁנֵי
עֶשְׂרֹנִים לָאַֽיִל וְעִשָּׂרוֹן לַכֶּֽבֶשׂ, וְיַֽיִן כְּנִסְכּוֹ, וּשְׁנֵי שְׂעִירִים
לְכַפֵּר, וּשְׁנֵי תְמִידִים כְּהִלְכָתָם.

BECAUSE OF OUR SINS
וּמִפְּנֵי חֲטָאֵֽינוּ. The first
of the middle b'rakhot
of the Amidah is called
קְדֻשַּׁת הַיּוֹם (k'dushat
ha-yom), the expres-
sion of the holiness of
the day. The content
of this b'rakhah is
not prescribed in the
Talmud. During the first
millennium, the prayers
concerning the holiness
of the day came to be
centered on the Temple
and its offerings, as if
the utterance of the
words substituted for
the missing sacrifices.
Recently, some have
begun reciting alternate
prayers, which under-
stand the rebuilding of
the Temple as a meta-
phor for the repair of
the world in which we
all need to engage. (See
the following page.)

א

Behold, I set before you today life and goodness, death and evil. . . . Choose life.

—DEUTERONOMY 30:15, 19

ב

Our agony is that we are capable of acts which contradict God's great expectations of us. Our glory is that we are capable of achieving atonement and reconciliation.

—JULES HARLOW

ג

Each person has personal choice: if you desire to do good and be righteous, the capability is yours; and should you want to follow an evil path and be evil, that capability is also yours. That is the meaning of the verse in Genesis, "Behold the human has become like us knowing good and evil" (Genesis 3:22).

—MAIMONIDES, LAWS OF REPENTANCE

ד

Rabbi Elazar HaKapar teaches that jealousy, preoccupation with desire, and pursuit of honor deprive a human being of this world.

—MISHNAH AVOT

Some recite this traditional version; others continue on the next page with A Prayer for Jewry in Distress.

Because of our sins we have been exiled from our land and removed from our soil. And so, because of the hand which was set against Your sanctuary, we are unable to fulfill our obligations in that great and holy place which You chose to carry Your name.

May it be Your will, ADONAI our God and God of our ancestors, compassionate sovereign who restores their descendants to their promised land, that You may once again have compassion on us and return in Your great mercy to Your sanctuary. May You speedily rebuild it and renew its glory. *Avinu Malkeinu*, speedily manifest the glory of Your dominion, reveal to all humanity that You are our sovereign. Gather our dispersed people from among the nations, and bring back those scattered to the ends of the earth.

Welcome back our dispersed from among the nations, and gather those scattered to the ends of the earth. Bring us exultantly to Zion, Your city, and with everlasting joy to Jerusalem Your sanctuary, where our ancestors once offered to You their obligatory daily and holy day sacrifices, each as prescribed. The [Shabbat and] Yom Kippur sacrifices were offered there in love, as You commanded, as it is written in Your Torah by Moses, Your servant, by Your instruction:

The Sephardic rite continues on page 305.
On Shabbat, those reciting the traditional sacrificial list add this paragraph:

On Shabbat: two yearling lambs without blemish, together with two-tenths of a measure of choice flour with oil mixed in as a grain offering, and with the proper libation. A burnt offering for every Shabbat, in addition to the regular burnt offering and its libation. Numbers 28:9–10

On the tenth day of the seventh month, you shall observe a sacred occasion: when you shall practice self-denial; you shall not work at your occupations. You shall prepare a burnt offering as a pleasing odor to ADONAI: one bull of the herd, one ram, seven yearling lambs, without blemish. Numbers 29:7–8

As ordained, they shall be accompanied by grain offerings and by libations: three-tenths of a measure for the bull, two-tenths for the ram, one-tenth for each lamb, wine for its libation, two goats for expiation, and the two daily offerings as is their custom.

אֱלֹהֵינוּ וֵאלֹהֵי אֲבוֹתֵינוּ [וְאִמּוֹתֵינוּ], רַחֵם עַל אַחֵינוּ
בֵּית יִשְׂרָאֵל הַנְּתוּנִים בְּצָרָה וְהוֹצִיאֵם מֵאֲפֵלָה לְאוֹרָה.
וְקַבֵּל בְּרַחֲמִים אֶת־תְּפִלַּת עַמְּךָ בְּנֵי יִשְׂרָאֵל, בְּכָל־
מְקוֹמוֹת מוֹשְׁבוֹתֵיהֶם, הַשּׁוֹפְכִים אֶת־לִבָּם לְפָנֶיךָ בְּיוֹם
[הַשַּׁבָּת הַזֶּה וּבְיוֹם] הַכִּפּוּרִים הַזֶּה.

Those who recited the traditional sacrificial list now continue on the next page.

יְהִי רָצוֹן מִלְּפָנֶיךָ, יהוה אֱלֹהֵינוּ וֵאלֹהֵי אֲבוֹתֵינוּ
[וְאִמּוֹתֵינוּ], שֶׁיִּבָּנֶה בֵּית הַמִּקְדָּשׁ בִּמְהֵרָה בְיָמֵינוּ,
כְּפִי שֶׁהִבְטַחְתָּנוּ עַל יְדֵי נְבִיאֶךָ, כַּכָּתוּב:
וְהָיָה בְּאַחֲרִית הַיָּמִים,
נָכוֹן יִהְיֶה הַר בֵּית יהוה
בְּרֹאשׁ הֶהָרִים וְנִשָּׂא מִגְּבָעוֹת,
וְנָהֲרוּ אֵלָיו כָּל־הַגּוֹיִם.
וְהָלְכוּ עַמִּים רַבִּים וְאָמְרוּ,
לְכוּ וְנַעֲלֶה אֶל הַר יהוה, אֶל בֵּית אֱלֹהֵי יַעֲקֹב,
וְיֹרֵנוּ מִדְּרָכָיו, וְנֵלְכָה בְּאֹרְחֹתָיו.
כִּי מִצִּיּוֹן תֵּצֵא תוֹרָה וּדְבַר יהוה מִירוּשָׁלָיִם.
וְשָׁפַט בֵּין הַגּוֹיִם וְהוֹכִיחַ לְעַמִּים רַבִּים,
וְכִתְּתוּ חַרְבוֹתָם לְאִתִּים וַחֲנִיתוֹתֵיהֶם לְמַזְמֵרוֹת,
לֹא יִשָּׂא גוֹי אֶל גּוֹי חֶרֶב וְלֹא יִלְמְדוּ עוֹד מִלְחָמָה.

MAY IT BE YOUR WILL יְהִי רָצוֹן. From *Siddur Va'ani Tefilati*, the prayerbook of the Masorti (Conservative) movement in Israel. This acknowledges the Jewish people's having returned to the Land of Israel. (The more traditional wording speaks of the exile, our inability to perform the Temple sacrifices, and the hope of return.)

ה

The pathology of the self
will not be understood
unless the power that
evokes being human,
the ultimate evocation
of the self, is properly
understood. Boredom...
is a sickness of the self-
consciousness, the result
of one's inability to sense
that vital evocation.
Despair is due not to
failures but to the inability to hear deeply and
personally the challenge
that confronts us....
The self is inescapably
beset by the questions:
What shall I do with my
existence, with my being
here and now? What
does it mean to be alive?
What does being alive
imply for my will and in-
telligence? . . . The sense
of requiredness is not an
afterthought; it is given
with being human....
What is involved in
authentic living is not
only an intuition of
meaning but a sensitivity
to demand.
—ABRAHAM JOSHUA HESCHEL

A PRAYER FOR JEWRY IN DISTRESS

Our God and God of our ancestors, show compassion to our
brothers and sisters of the House of Israel, who suffer persecution; deliver them from darkness to light. Accept with compassion the prayers of Your people Israel who cry out to You
on [this Shabbat and] this Day of Atonement, wherever they
dwell.

Those who recited the traditional sacrificial list now continue on the next page.

May it be Your will, ADONAI our God and God of our ancestors, that the Holy Temple be rebuilt speedily in our time,
as You promised, in the words of Your prophet Isaiah: "And
it shall come to pass, in the end of days, that the House of
ADONAI will be firmly established at the top of the mountain,
raised high above all other hills. All peoples shall flow toward it,
and nations shall say, 'Let us go up to the mountain of ADONAI
to the house of the God of Jacob, and we shall learn from God's
ways and walk in God's paths.' For instruction shall go forth
from Zion and the word of ADONAI from Jerusalem. God
will provide proper judgment among nations and admonish
many peoples. They shall beat their swords into plowshares,
and spears into pruning hooks. Nation shall not take up sword
against nation, neither shall they learn war anymore."

ו

"The sacrifices of God are a broken spirit; a contrite and broken
heart" (Psalm 51:19). Rabbi Abba bar Judan said: What God
regards as unfit for sacrifice in an animal, God holds as fit in a
human being. An animal that is blind or broken or maimed is
unfit for sacrifice (Leviticus 22:22), but a human being who has
a broken and contrite heart is a fit offering to God.
—MIDRASH PESIKTA OF RAV KAHANA

ז

Rabbi Judah the Patriarch, citing Rabbi Judah the son of Rabbi
Simon, said: Ordinarily, if a person shot an arrow, how far will
it go? Over as much ground as an acre or two. But the power
of repentance is so great that it shoots straight up to heaven.
Rabbi Yose taught: God says, "Open to Me" (Song of Songs 5:2),
meaning: Make for Me an opening in you, an opening as narrow
as the eye of a needle, and I shall make the opening so wide that
camps full of soldiers and siege-engines could enter it.
—MIDRASH PESIKTA OF RAV KAHANA

ON SHABBAT, WE RECITE THIS PARAGRAPH:

יִשְׂמְחוּ בְמַלְכוּתְךָ שׁוֹמְרֵי שַׁבָּת וְקוֹרְאֵי עֹנֶג, עַם מְקַדְּשֵׁי
שְׁבִיעִי, כֻּלָּם יִשְׂבְּעוּ וְיִתְעַנְּגוּ מִטּוּבֶךָ, וּבַשְּׁבִיעִי רָצִיתָ בּוֹ
וְקִדַּשְׁתּוֹ, חֶמְדַּת יָמִים אוֹתוֹ קָרָאתָ, זֵכֶר לְמַעֲשֵׂה
בְרֵאשִׁית.

On all days:

אֱלֹהֵינוּ וֵאלֹהֵי אֲבוֹתֵינוּ [וְאִמּוֹתֵינוּ], מְחַל לַעֲוֹנוֹתֵינוּ
בְּיוֹם [הַשַּׁבָּת הַזֶּה וּבְיוֹם] הַכִּפֻּרִים הַזֶּה. מְחֵה וְהַעֲבֵר
פְּשָׁעֵינוּ וְחַטֹּאתֵינוּ מִנֶּגֶד עֵינֶיךָ, כָּאָמוּר: אָנֹכִי אָנֹכִי
הוּא מֹחֶה פְשָׁעֶיךָ לְמַעֲנִי, וְחַטֹּאתֶיךָ לֹא אֶזְכֹּר. וְנֶאֱמַר:
מָחִיתִי כָעָב פְּשָׁעֶיךָ וְכֶעָנָן חַטֹּאתֶיךָ, שׁוּבָה אֵלַי כִּי
גְאַלְתִּיךָ. וְנֶאֱמַר: כִּי בַיּוֹם הַזֶּה יְכַפֵּר עֲלֵיכֶם לְטַהֵר
אֶתְכֶם, מִכֹּל חַטֹּאתֵיכֶם לִפְנֵי יהוה תִּטְהָרוּ.

אֱלֹהֵינוּ וֵאלֹהֵי אֲבוֹתֵינוּ [וְאִמּוֹתֵינוּ], [רְצֵה בִמְנוּחָתֵנוּ]
קַדְּשֵׁנוּ בְּמִצְוֹתֶיךָ וְתֵן חֶלְקֵנוּ בְּתוֹרָתֶךָ, שַׂבְּעֵנוּ מִטּוּבֶךָ
וְשַׂמְּחֵנוּ בִּישׁוּעָתֶךָ [וְהַנְחִילֵנוּ יהוה אֱלֹהֵינוּ בְּאַהֲבָה
וּבְרָצוֹן שַׁבַּת קָדְשֶׁךָ, וְיָנוּחוּ בָהּ יִשְׂרָאֵל מְקַדְּשֵׁי שְׁמֶךָ]
וְטַהֵר לִבֵּנוּ לְעָבְדְּךָ בֶּאֱמֶת, כִּי אַתָּה סָלְחָן לְיִשְׂרָאֵל
וּמָחֳלָן לְשִׁבְטֵי יְשֻׁרוּן בְּכָל־דּוֹר וָדוֹר, וּמִבַּלְעָדֶיךָ אֵין
לָנוּ מֶלֶךְ מוֹחֵל וְסוֹלֵחַ אֶלָּא אָתָּה. בָּרוּךְ אַתָּה יהוה,
מֶלֶךְ מוֹחֵל וְסוֹלֵחַ לַעֲוֹנוֹתֵינוּ וְלַעֲוֹנוֹת עַמּוֹ בֵּית יִשְׂרָאֵל,
וּמַעֲבִיר אַשְׁמוֹתֵינוּ בְּכָל־שָׁנָה וְשָׁנָה, מֶלֶךְ עַל כָּל־הָאָרֶץ,
מְקַדֵּשׁ [הַשַּׁבָּת וְ] יִשְׂרָאֵל וְיוֹם הַכִּפֻּרִים.

I, SURELY I . . . אָנֹכִי אָנֹכִי.
Isaiah 43:25.

**I SWEEP ASIDE YOUR SINS
LIKE A MIST** מָחִיתִי כָעָב
פְּשָׁעֶיךָ. Isaiah 44:22.

FOR ON THIS DAY כִּי־בַיּוֹם
הַזֶּה. Leviticus 16:30.

YOU FORGIVE אַתָּה סָלְחָן.
The grammatical forms
מָחֳלָן / סָלְחָן (solhan) and
(moholan) indicate an
essential personal quality.
Similarly, לוֹמֵד (lomed)
means "study," but when
one becomes a scholar, one
is called a לַמְדָן (lamdan).
The use of this form reflects
the poet's belief that God's
forgiving nature is, in fact,
God's essence.

O our God, our ancestors' God, consecrate us with Your mitzvot, give us a share in Your truth. Sate us with Your goodness, delight us with Your help. Make our hearts worthy to serve You truly. May we possess [Your holy Shabbat and] this Day of Atonement with love and eagerness. We praise You, O God, whose [Shabbat,] people Israel and whose Day of Atonement are sacred.

ON SHABBAT, WE RECITE THIS PARAGRAPH:

Those who observe Shabbat and call it a delight rejoice in Your sovereignty. May the people who sanctify the seventh day be fulfilled and delighted with Your abundant goodness. You have loved the seventh day and sanctified it, calling it the treasured day, a sign of creation.

On all days:

Our God and God of our ancestors, forgive our sins on [this Shabbat and] this Yom Kippur. Blot out and disregard them, as the prophet Isaiah says in Your name: "I, surely I, am the One who wipes away sin, for this is My nature; I will not recall your errors," and the prophet adds: "I sweep aside your sins like a mist, and disperse your transgressions like a cloud. Turn back to Me, for I will redeem you." And in Your Torah it is written: "For on this day, atonement shall be made for you to purify you from all your transgressions. In the presence of ADONAI you shall be pure."

Our God and God of our ancestors: [embrace our rest,] make us holy through Your mitzvot and let the Torah be our portion. Fill our lives with Your goodness and gladden us with Your triumph. [ADONAI our God, grant that we inherit Your holy Shabbat, lovingly and willingly, so that the people Israel, who sanctify Your name, may find rest on this day.] Purify our hearts to serve You faithfully, for You forgive the people Israel and pardon the tribes of Jeshurun in every generation. Beside You, we have no sovereign who pardons and forgives. *Barukh atah ADONAI*, sovereign who pardons and forgives our sins and those of the people, the House of Israel, each year sweeping away our guilt—ruler of all the earth, who makes [Shabbat,] the people Israel and the Day of Atonement holy.

רְצֵה יהוה אֱלֹהֵינוּ, בְּעַמְּךָ יִשְׂרָאֵל וּבִתְפִלָּתָם, וְהָשֵׁב אֶת־הָעֲבוֹדָה לִדְבִיר בֵּיתֶךָ, [וְאִשֵּׁי יִשְׂרָאֵל] וּתְפִלָּתָם בְּאַהֲבָה תְקַבֵּל בְּרָצוֹן, וּתְהִי לְרָצוֹן תָּמִיד עֲבוֹדַת יִשְׂרָאֵל עַמֶּךָ.

וְתֶחֱזֶינָה עֵינֵינוּ בְּשׁוּבְךָ לְצִיּוֹן בְּרַחֲמִים. בָּרוּךְ אַתָּה יהוה, הַמַּחֲזִיר שְׁכִינָתוֹ לְצִיּוֹן.

◄ **מוֹדִים** אֲנַחְנוּ לָךְ שָׁאַתָּה הוּא יהוה אֱלֹהֵינוּ וֵאלֹהֵי אֲבוֹתֵינוּ [וְאִמּוֹתֵינוּ] לְעוֹלָם וָעֶד, צוּר חַיֵּינוּ מָגֵן יִשְׁעֵנוּ אַתָּה הוּא לְדוֹר וָדוֹר. נוֹדֶה לְּךָ וּנְסַפֵּר תְּהִלָּתֶךָ, עַל חַיֵּינוּ הַמְּסוּרִים בְּיָדֶךָ
וְעַל נִשְׁמוֹתֵינוּ הַפְּקוּדוֹת לָךְ,
וְעַל נִסֶּיךָ שֶׁבְּכָל־יוֹם עִמָּנוּ
וְעַל נִפְלְאוֹתֶיךָ וְטוֹבוֹתֶיךָ שֶׁבְּכָל־עֵת,
עֶרֶב וָבְקֶר וְצָהֳרָיִם.
הַטּוֹב, כִּי לֹא כָלוּ רַחֲמֶיךָ, וְהַמְרַחֵם כִּי לֹא תַמּוּ חֲסָדֶיךָ מֵעוֹלָם קִוִּינוּ לָךְ.

וְעַל כֻּלָּם יִתְבָּרַךְ וְיִתְרוֹמַם שִׁמְךָ מַלְכֵּנוּ תָּמִיד לְעוֹלָם וָעֶד.

RESTORE WORSHIP TO YOUR SANCTUARY וְהָשֵׁב אֶת־הָעֲבוֹדָה לִדְבִיר בֵּיתֶךָ. According to the Babylonian Talmud, "Ever since the day when the Temple was destroyed, there has been an iron barrier separating Israel from God" (Berakhot 32b). Each destruction of the Temple in Jerusalem (first by the Babylonians in 586 B.C.E., then by the Romans in 70 C.E.) was a cataclysmic event in early Jewish history. In praying for the restoration of the Temple, we express our wish both for the sense of immediate connection with God that is believed to have characterized the Temple service, and for the common sense of purpose and religious community that was experienced there.

THE FIERY OFFERINGS וְאִשֵּׁי יִשְׂרָאֵל. The reference to the "fiery offerings," originally referring specifically to the sacrifices that took place in the Temple, was understood by many Hasidic commentators as referring to the intensity of religious fervor in true prayer.

YOUR DIVINE PRESENCE שְׁכִינָתוֹ. The Hebrew word *shekhinah* has been used for centuries to refer to God's immanence, the presence of God that is felt in the world. The word *shekhinah* is grammatically feminine. Accordingly, Jewish mystical tradition has tended to personify as female the Divine Presence, who is known as the Shekhinah.

FOR ALL THESE וְעַל כֻּלָּם. In the language of the Bible and the prayerbook, "God's name is exalted" when we acknowledge God, recognize God's goodness in creation, and act to enable God's justice and compassion to be visible in the world.

Would that Your people
at prayer gained delight
in You. Would that we
were aflame with the
passionate piety of our
ancestors' worship.
Would that You found
our worship acceptable,
and forever cherished
Your people. If only our
eyes could see Your glory
perennially renewed in
Jerusalem. We praise
You, God whose pres-
ence forever radiates
from Zion.

You are our God today
as You were our ances-
tors' God throughout the
ages; firm foundation of
our lives, we are Yours
in gratitude and love.
Our lives are safe in Your
hand, our souls entrusted
to Your care. Our sense of
wonder and our praise of
Your miracles and kind-
nesses greet You daily at
dawn, dusk, and noon. O
Gentle One, Your caring
is endless; O Compas-
sionate One, Your love is
eternal. You are forever
our hope. Let all the living confront You with
thankfulness, delight, and
truth. Help us, O God;
sustain us. We praise You,
God whose touchstone is
goodness.

May a life of goodness
await all of us, children of
Your covenant.

To pray to You is joy.

(*continued*)

Fifth B'rakhah: The Restoration of Zion

ADONAI our God, embrace Your people Israel and their prayer.
Restore worship to Your sanctuary. May the [fiery offerings
and] prayers of the people Israel be lovingly accepted by You,
and may our service always be pleasing.

Let our eyes behold Your merciful return to Zion.
Barukh atah ADONAI, who restores Your Divine Presence
to Zion.

Sixth B'rakhah: Gratitude for Life and Its Blessings

ך We thank You,
You who are our God and the God of our ancestors through all
    time, protector of our lives, shield of our salvation.
From one generation to the next we thank You
and sing Your praises—
    for our lives that are in Your hands,
    for our souls that are under Your care,
    for Your miracles that accompany us each day,
    and for Your wonders and Your gifts that are
    with us each moment—
evening, morning, and noon.
You are the One who is good,
whose mercy is never-ending;
the One who is compassionate,
whose love is unceasing.
We have always placed our hope in You.

For all these blessings may Your name be praised and exalted,
our sovereign, always and forever.

INSCRIBE וּכְתוֹב. This is the third of the four special insertions in the Amidah for the Ten Days of Repentance.

GRANT PEACE שִׂים שָׁלוֹם. In the words of the Midrash, "Great is peace, for all prayers conclude with peace" (Sifre, Numbers 42).

IN THE BOOK OF LIFE בְּסֵפֶר חַיִּים. The last of the four special insertions in the Amidah added for the Ten Days of Repentance expands the plea for life to include peace and prosperity.

וּכְתוֹב לְחַיִּים טוֹבִים כָּל־בְּנֵי בְרִיתֶךָ.

וְכֹל הַחַיִּים יוֹדוּךָ סֶּלָה, וִיהַלְלוּ אֶת־שִׁמְךָ בֶּאֱמֶת, הָאֵל יְשׁוּעָתֵנוּ וְעֶזְרָתֵנוּ סֶלָה.

בָּרוּךְ אַתָּה יהוה, הַטּוֹב שִׁמְךָ וּלְךָ נָאֶה לְהוֹדוֹת.

שִׂים שָׁלוֹם בָּעוֹלָם טוֹבָה וּבְרָכָה חֵן וָחֶסֶד וְרַחֲמִים עָלֵינוּ וְעַל כָּל־יִשְׂרָאֵל עַמֶּךָ. בָּרְכֵנוּ אָבִינוּ, כֻּלָּנוּ כְּאֶחָד בְּאוֹר פָּנֶיךָ, כִּי בְאוֹר פָּנֶיךָ נָתַתָּ לָּנוּ, יהוה אֱלֹהֵינוּ, תּוֹרַת חַיִּים וְאַהֲבַת חֶסֶד, וּצְדָקָה וּבְרָכָה וְרַחֲמִים וְחַיִּים וְשָׁלוֹם. וְטוֹב בְּעֵינֶיךָ לְבָרֵךְ אֶת־עַמְּךָ יִשְׂרָאֵל, בְּכָל־עֵת וּבְכָל־שָׁעָה בִּשְׁלוֹמֶךָ.

בְּסֵפֶר חַיִּים,
בְּרָכָה וְשָׁלוֹם וּפַרְנָסָה טוֹבָה,
נִזָּכֵר וְנִכָּתֵב לְפָנֶיךָ,
אֲנַחְנוּ וְכָל־עַמְּךָ בֵּית יִשְׂרָאֵל,
לְחַיִּים טוֹבִים וּלְשָׁלוֹם.

בָּרוּךְ אַתָּה יהוה, עוֹשֵׂה הַשָּׁלוֹם.

וידוי

אֱלֹהֵינוּ וֵאלֹהֵי אֲבוֹתֵינוּ [וְאִמּוֹתֵינוּ],
תָּבֹא לְפָנֶיךָ תְּפִלָּתֵנוּ,
וְאַל תִּתְעַלַּם מִתְּחִנָּתֵנוּ,
שֶׁאֵין אֲנַחְנוּ עַזֵּי פָנִים וּקְשֵׁי עֹרֶף,
לוֹמַר לְפָנֶיךָ יהוה אֱלֹהֵינוּ וֵאלֹהֵי אֲבוֹתֵינוּ [וְאִמּוֹתֵינוּ],
צַדִּיקִים אֲנַחְנוּ וְלֹא חָטָאנוּ,
אֲבָל אֲנַחְנוּ וַאֲבוֹתֵינוּ [וְאִמּוֹתֵינוּ] חָטָאנוּ.

(continued from previous page)
O God, from whom all peace flows, grant serenity to Your Jewish people, with love and mercy, life and goodness for all. Shelter us with kindness, bless us with tranquility at all times and all seasons.

May we, and all Your people, the House of Israel, be deserving of a year of life, blessing, peace, and an honorable livelihood.

We praise You, God whose blessing is peace.

And inscribe all the people of Your covenant for a good life.

May all that lives thank You always, and praise Your name faithfully forever, God of our deliverance and help.
ℓ *Barukh atah* ADONAI, whose name is goodness and to whom praise is fitting.

Seventh B'rakhah: Prayer for Peace

Grant peace to the world: goodness and blessing, grace, love, and compassion to us and all Your people Israel. Bless us, our creator, united as one in the light of Your countenance; by that light, ADONAI our God, You gave us a guide to life: the love of kindness, righteousness, blessing, compassion, life, and peace. May it please You to bless Your people Israel at every season and at all times with Your gift of peace.

May we and the entire House of Israel be called to mind and inscribed for life, blessing, sustenance, and peace in the Book of Life.

Barukh atah ADONAI, who brings peace.

VIDDUI — PRAYERS OF CONFESSION

Because confession is an essential aspect of Yom Kippur, we add this liturgical confession each time that we recite the Amidah.

INTRODUCTION TO THE CONFESSION

Our God and God of our ancestors,
hear our prayer; do not ignore our plea.
Our God and God of our ancestors,
we are neither so insolent nor so obstinate
as to claim in Your presence
that we are righteous, without sin;
for we, like our ancestors who came before us, have sinned.

Customarily, we each strike our heart as we recite every phrase of this confession.

אָשַׁמְנוּ, בָּגַדְנוּ, גָּזַלְנוּ, דִּבַּרְנוּ דְפִי.

הֶעֱוִינוּ, וְהִרְשַׁעְנוּ, זַדְנוּ, חָמַסְנוּ, טָפַלְנוּ שֶׁקֶר.

יָעַצְנוּ רָע, כִּזַּבְנוּ, לַצְנוּ, מָרַדְנוּ, נִאַצְנוּ, סָרַרְנוּ,

עָוִינוּ, פָּשַׁעְנוּ, צָרַרְנוּ, קִשִּׁינוּ עְרֶף.

רָשַׁעְנוּ, שִׁחַתְנוּ, תִּעַבְנוּ, תָּעִינוּ, תִּעְתָּעְנוּ.

סַרְנוּ מִמִּצְוֹתֶיךָ וּמִמִּשְׁפָּטֶיךָ הַטּוֹבִים, וְלֹא שָׁוָה לָנוּ. וְאַתָּה צַדִּיק עַל כָּל־הַבָּא עָלֵינוּ, כִּי אֱמֶת עָשִׂיתָ וַאֲנַחְנוּ הִרְשָׁעְנוּ.

מַה נֹּאמַר לְפָנֶיךָ יוֹשֵׁב מָרוֹם?

וּמַה נְּסַפֵּר לְפָנֶיךָ שׁוֹכֵן שְׁחָקִים?

הֲלֹא כָּל־הַנִּסְתָּרוֹת וְהַנִּגְלוֹת אַתָּה יוֹדֵעַ.

אַתָּה יוֹדֵעַ רָזֵי עוֹלָם, וְתַעֲלוּמוֹת סִתְרֵי כָל־חָי.

אַתָּה חוֹפֵשׂ כָּל־חַדְרֵי בָטֶן, וּבוֹחֵן כְּלָיוֹת וָלֵב.

אֵין דָּבָר נֶעְלָם מִמֶּךָ, וְאֵין נִסְתָּר מִנֶּגֶד עֵינֶיךָ.

וּבְכֵן יְהִי רָצוֹן מִלְּפָנֶיךָ,

יהוה אֱלֹהֵינוּ וֵאלֹהֵי אֲבוֹתֵינוּ [וְאִמּוֹתֵינוּ],

שֶׁתִּסְלַח לָנוּ עַל כָּל־חַטֹּאתֵינוּ,

וְתִמְחַל לָנוּ עַל כָּל־עֲוֹנוֹתֵינוּ,

וּתְכַפֶּר־לָנוּ עַל כָּל־פְּשָׁעֵינוּ.

Customarily, we each strike our heart as we recite the words עַל חֵטְא שֶׁחָטָאנוּ.

עַל חֵטְא שֶׁחָטָאנוּ לְפָנֶיךָ בְּאֹנֶס וּבְרָצוֹן,

וְעַל חֵטְא שֶׁחָטָאנוּ לְפָנֶיךָ בְּאִמּוּץ הַלֵּב.

עַל חֵטְא שֶׁחָטָאנוּ לְפָנֶיךָ בִּבְלִי דָעַת,

וְעַל חֵטְא שֶׁחָטָאנוּ לְפָנֶיךָ בְּבִטּוּי שְׂפָתָיִם.

עַל חֵטְא שֶׁחָטָאנוּ לְפָנֶיךָ בְּגִלּוּי עֲרָיוֹת,

וְעַל חֵטְא שֶׁחָטָאנוּ לְפָנֶיךָ בַּגָּלוּי וּבַסָּתֶר.

The Shorter Confession—Ashamnu

Customarily, we each strike our heart as we recite every phrase of this confession.

We abuse, we betray, we are cruel, we destroy, we embitter, we falsify, we gossip, we hate, we insult, we jeer, we kill, we lie, we mock, we neglect, we oppress, we pervert, we quarrel, we rebel, we steal, we transgress, we are unkind, we are violent, we are wicked, we are extremists, we yearn to do evil, we are zealous for bad causes.

We have turned from Your goodly laws and commandments, but it has not profited us. Surely, You are in the right with respect to all that comes upon us, for You have acted faithfully, but we have been in the wrong.

What can we say before You, You who live in the transcendent?
And what can we tell about ourselves to You who dwell on high?
You surely know both the secret and the revealed.

You know the mysteries of the universe,
the deepest secrets of everyone alive.
You probe our innermost depths,
You examine our thoughts and feelings.
Nothing escapes You,
nothing is secret from You.
Therefore, may it be Your will, our God and God of our ancestors,
to forgive us for all our sins,
to pardon us for all our iniquities,
to grant us atonement for all our transgressions.

The Longer Confession—Al Ḥet

Customarily, we each strike our heart as we recite the words, "We have sinned."

We have sinned against You unwillingly and willingly,
    and we have sinned against You through hardening our hearts.
We have sinned against You thoughtlessly,
    and we have sinned against You in idle chatter.
We have sinned against You through sexual immorality,
    and we have sinned against You openly and in private.

עַל חֵטְא שֶׁחָטָאנוּ לְפָנֶיךָ בְּדַעַת וּבְמִרְמָה,
וְעַל חֵטְא שֶׁחָטָאנוּ לְפָנֶיךָ בְּדִבּוּר פֶּה.
עַל חֵטְא שֶׁחָטָאנוּ לְפָנֶיךָ בְּהוֹנָאַת רֵעַ,
וְעַל חֵטְא שֶׁחָטָאנוּ לְפָנֶיךָ בְּהַרְהוֹר הַלֵּב.
עַל חֵטְא שֶׁחָטָאנוּ לְפָנֶיךָ בּוְעִידַת זְנוּת,
וְעַל חֵטְא שֶׁחָטָאנוּ לְפָנֶיךָ בְּוִדּוּי פֶּה.
עַל חֵטְא שֶׁחָטָאנוּ לְפָנֶיךָ בְּזִלְזוּל הוֹרִים וּמוֹרִים,
וְעַל חֵטְא שֶׁחָטָאנוּ לְפָנֶיךָ בְּזָדוֹן וּבִשְׁגָגָה.
עַל חֵטְא שֶׁחָטָאנוּ לְפָנֶיךָ בְּחֹזֶק יָד,
וְעַל חֵטְא שֶׁחָטָאנוּ לְפָנֶיךָ בְּחִלּוּל הַשֵּׁם.
עַל חֵטְא שֶׁחָטָאנוּ לְפָנֶיךָ בְּטֻמְאַת שְׂפָתַיִם,
וְעַל חֵטְא שֶׁחָטָאנוּ לְפָנֶיךָ בְּטִפְּשׁוּת פֶּה.
עַל חֵטְא שֶׁחָטָאנוּ לְפָנֶיךָ בְּיֵצֶר הָרָע,
וְעַל חֵטְא שֶׁחָטָאנוּ לְפָנֶיךָ בְּיוֹדְעִים וּבְלֹא יוֹדְעִים.

וְעַל כֻּלָּם, אֱלוֹהַּ סְלִיחוֹת, סְלַח לָנוּ, מְחַל לָנוּ, כַּפֶּר־לָנוּ.

עַל חֵטְא שֶׁחָטָאנוּ לְפָנֶיךָ בְּכַחַשׁ וּבְכָזָב,
וְעַל חֵטְא שֶׁחָטָאנוּ לְפָנֶיךָ בְּכַפַּת שֹׁחַד.
עַל חֵטְא שֶׁחָטָאנוּ לְפָנֶיךָ בְּלָצוֹן,
וְעַל חֵטְא שֶׁחָטָאנוּ לְפָנֶיךָ בְּלָשׁוֹן הָרָע.
עַל חֵטְא שֶׁחָטָאנוּ לְפָנֶיךָ בְּמַשָּׂא וּבְמַתָּן,
וְעַל חֵטְא שֶׁחָטָאנוּ לְפָנֶיךָ בְּמַאֲכָל וּבְמִשְׁתֶּה.
עַל חֵטְא שֶׁחָטָאנוּ לְפָנֶיךָ בְּנֶשֶׁךְ וּבְמַרְבִּית,
וְעַל חֵטְא שֶׁחָטָאנוּ לְפָנֶיךָ בִּנְטִיַּת גָּרוֹן.
עַל חֵטְא שֶׁחָטָאנוּ לְפָנֶיךָ בְּשִׂיחַ שִׂפְתוֹתֵינוּ,
וְעַל חֵטְא שֶׁחָטָאנוּ לְפָנֶיךָ בְּשִׁקּוּר עָיִן.

We have sinned against You knowingly and deceitfully,
and we have sinned against You by the way we talk.
We have sinned against You by defrauding others,
and we have sinned against You in our innermost thoughts.
We have sinned against You through forbidden trysts,
and we have sinned against You through empty confession.
We have sinned against You by scorning parents and teachers,
and we have sinned against You purposely and by mistake.
We have sinned against You by resorting to violence,
and we have sinned against You by public desecration of Your name.
We have sinned against You through foul speech,
and we have sinned against You through foolish talk.
We have sinned against You through pursuing the impulse to evil,
and we have sinned against You wittingly and unwittingly.

For all these sins, forgiving God, forgive us, pardon us, grant us atonement.

We have sinned against You through denial and deceit,
and we have sinned against You by taking bribes.
We have sinned against You by clever cynicism,
and we have sinned against You by speaking ill of others.
We have sinned against You by the way we do business,
and we have sinned against You in our eating and drinking.
We have sinned against You by greed and oppressive interest,
and we have sinned against You through arrogance.
We have sinned against You in everyday conversation,
and we have sinned against You through conspiratorial glances.

עַל חֵטְא שֶׁחָטָאנוּ לְפָנֶיךָ בְּעֵינַיִם רָמוֹת,
וְעַל חֵטְא שֶׁחָטָאנוּ לְפָנֶיךָ בְּעַזּוּת מֵצַח.

וְעַל כֻּלָּם, אֱלוֹהַ סְלִיחוֹת, סְלַח לָנוּ, מְחַל לָנוּ, כַּפֶּר-לָנוּ.

עַל חֵטְא שֶׁחָטָאנוּ לְפָנֶיךָ בִּפְרִיקַת עֹל,
וְעַל חֵטְא שֶׁחָטָאנוּ לְפָנֶיךָ בִּפְלִילוּת.
עַל חֵטְא שֶׁחָטָאנוּ לְפָנֶיךָ בִּצְדִיַּת רֵעַ,
וְעַל חֵטְא שֶׁחָטָאנוּ לְפָנֶיךָ בְּצָרוּת עָיִן.
עַל חֵטְא שֶׁחָטָאנוּ לְפָנֶיךָ בְּקַלּוּת רֹאשׁ,
וְעַל חֵטְא שֶׁחָטָאנוּ לְפָנֶיךָ בְּקַשְׁיוּת עֹרֶף.
עַל חֵטְא שֶׁחָטָאנוּ לְפָנֶיךָ בְּרִיצַת רַגְלַיִם לְהָרַע,
וְעַל חֵטְא שֶׁחָטָאנוּ לְפָנֶיךָ בִּרְכִילוּת.
עַל חֵטְא שֶׁחָטָאנוּ לְפָנֶיךָ בִּשְׁבוּעַת שָׁוְא,
וְעַל חֵטְא שֶׁחָטָאנוּ לְפָנֶיךָ בְּשִׂנְאַת חִנָּם.
עַל חֵטְא שֶׁחָטָאנוּ לְפָנֶיךָ בִּתְשׂוּמֶת-יָד,
וְעַל חֵטְא שֶׁחָטָאנוּ לְפָנֶיךָ בְּתִמְהוֹן לֵבָב.

וְעַל כֻּלָּם, אֱלוֹהַ סְלִיחוֹת, סְלַח לָנוּ, מְחַל לָנוּ, כַּפֶּר-לָנוּ.

עַל מִצְוַת עֲשֵׂה וְעַל מִצְוַת לֹא תַעֲשֶׂה, בֵּין שֶׁיֵּשׁ בָּהּ
קוּם עֲשֵׂה, וּבֵין שֶׁאֵין בָּהּ קוּם עֲשֵׂה, אֶת-הַגְּלוּיִים לָנוּ
וְאֶת-שֶׁאֵינָם גְּלוּיִים לָנוּ. אֶת-הַגְּלוּיִים לָנוּ כְּבָר אֲמַרְנוּם
לְפָנֶיךָ, וְהוֹדִינוּ לְךָ עֲלֵיהֶם; וְאֶת-שֶׁאֵינָם גְּלוּיִים לָנוּ,
לְפָנֶיךָ הֵם גְּלוּיִים וִידוּעִים, כַּדָּבָר שֶׁנֶּאֱמַר: הַנִּסְתָּרֹת
לַיהוה אֱלֹהֵינוּ, וְהַנִּגְלֹת לָנוּ וּלְבָנֵינוּ עַד עוֹלָם, לַעֲשׂוֹת
אֶת-כָּל-דִּבְרֵי הַתּוֹרָה הַזֹּאת.

We have sinned against You through condescension,
and we have sinned against You through stubbornness.

For all these sins, forgiving God, forgive us, pardon us, grant us atonement.

We have sinned against You by throwing off all restraint,
and we have sinned against You by rashly judging others.
We have sinned against You by plotting against others,
and we have sinned against You through selfishness.
We have sinned against You through superficiality,
and we have sinned against You through stubbornness.
We have sinned against You by rushing to do evil,
and we have sinned against You through gossip.
We have sinned against You through empty promises,
and we have sinned against You through baseless hatred.
We have sinned against You by betraying trust,
and we have sinned against You by succumbing to confusion.

For all these sins, forgiving God, forgive us, pardon us, grant us atonement.

And forgive us the breach of all commandments and prohibitions, whether involving deeds or not, whether known to us or not. The sins known to us we have acknowledged, and those unknown to us are surely known to You, as the Torah states: "Secret matters are the concern of ADONAI our God; but in matters that are revealed, it is for us and our children to apply all teachings of the Torah till the end of time."

אֱלֹהַי, עַד שֶׁלֹּא נוֹצַרְתִּי אֵינִי כְדַאי, וְעַכְשָׁו שֶׁנּוֹצַרְתִּי
כְּאִלּוּ לֹא נוֹצַרְתִּי; עָפָר אֲנִי בְּחַיַּי, קַל וָחֹמֶר בְּמִיתָתִי;
הֲרֵי אֲנִי לְפָנֶיךָ כִּכְלִי מָלֵא בוּשָׁה וּכְלִמָּה. יְהִי רָצוֹן
מִלְּפָנֶיךָ, יהוה אֱלֹהַי וֵאלֹהֵי אֲבֹתַי [וְאִמּוֹתַי], שֶׁלֹּא
אֶחֱטָא עוֹד; וּמַה שֶּׁחָטָאתִי לְפָנֶיךָ מָרֵק בְּרַחֲמֶיךָ
הָרַבִּים, אֲבָל לֹא עַל יְדֵי יִסּוּרִים וָחֳלָיִים רָעִים.

אֱלֹהַי, נְצוֹר לְשׁוֹנִי מֵרָע, וּשְׂפָתַי מִדַּבֵּר מִרְמָה, וְלִמְקַלְלַי
נַפְשִׁי תִדֹּם, וְנַפְשִׁי כֶּעָפָר לַכֹּל תִּהְיֶה. פְּתַח לִבִּי
בְּתוֹרָתֶךָ, וּבְמִצְוֹתֶיךָ תִּרְדּוֹף נַפְשִׁי. וְכָל־הַחוֹשְׁבִים עָלַי
רָעָה, מְהֵרָה הָפֵר עֲצָתָם וְקַלְקֵל מַחֲשַׁבְתָּם. עֲשֵׂה לְמַעַן
שְׁמֶךָ, עֲשֵׂה לְמַעַן יְמִינֶךָ, עֲשֵׂה לְמַעַן קְדֻשָּׁתֶךָ. עֲשֵׂה
לְמַעַן תּוֹרָתֶךָ. לְמַעַן יֵחָלְצוּן יְדִידֶיךָ, הוֹשִׁיעָה יְמִינְךָ
וַעֲנֵנִי. יִהְיוּ לְרָצוֹן אִמְרֵי פִי וְהֶגְיוֹן לִבִּי לְפָנֶיךָ, יהוה צוּרִי
וְגֹאֲלִי. עֹשֶׂה שָׁלוֹם בִּמְרוֹמָיו, הוּא יַעֲשֶׂה שָׁלוֹם עָלֵינוּ,
וְעַל כָּל־יִשְׂרָאֵל [וְעַל כָּל־יוֹשְׁבֵי תֵבֵל] וְאִמְרוּ: אָמֵן.

MY GOD אֱלֹהַי. The Talmud says that every Amidah must be accompanied by a personal prayer. Note the use of the first person singular ("I"), while all other prayers, including the confessions, are in the first person plural ("we"). These prayers, the first attributed to Raba and the second to Mar son of Ravina, are quoted in the Talmud, and were so admired that they entered the formal liturgy (Babylonian Talmud, Berakhot 17a).

MAY THE WORDS יִהְיוּ לְרָצוֹן. Psalm 19:15.

Concluding Meditation
May my tongue be innocent of malice and my lips free from lies. When confronted by enemies may my soul stay calm, truly humble to all. Open my heart with Your teachings, that I may be guided by You. May all who plan evil against me abandon their schemes. Hear my words and help me, God, because You are loving, because You reveal Your Torah. May You find delight in the words of my mouth and in the emotions of my heart, God, my strength and my salvation. As You maintain harmony in the heavens, give peace to us and to the whole Jewish people. Amen.

Personal Prayers Concluding the Amidah

My God, before I was created I was entirely lacking in substance; and now that I have been created, it is as if I never was. Dust and ashes am I in life, all the more so in death. I stand before You as a vessel full of embarrassment and shame. May it be Your will, ADONAI my God and God of my ancestors, that I sin no more, and that in Your great mercy You erase the sins I have sinned before You, but not through great pain and suffering.

My God, keep my tongue from evil, my lips from lies. Help me ignore those who would slander me. Let me be humble before all. Open my heart to Your Torah, that I may pursue Your mitzvot. Frustrate the designs of those who plot evil against me; make nothing of their schemes. Act for the sake of Your power, Your holiness, and Your Torah. Answer my prayer for the deliverance of Your people. May the words of my mouth and the meditations of my heart be acceptable to You, ADONAI, my rock and my redeemer. May the One who brings peace to the universe bring peace to us and to all the people Israel [and to all who dwell on earth]. Amen.

הִנְנִי הֶעָנִי מִמַּעַשׂ, נִרְעָשׁ וְנִפְחָד מִפַּחַד יוֹשֵׁב תְּהִלּוֹת
יִשְׂרָאֵל, בָּאתִי לַעֲמֹד וּלְהִתְחַנֵּן לְפָנֶיךָ עַל עַמְּךָ יִשְׂרָאֵל
אֲשֶׁר שְׁלָחוּנִי, אַף עַל פִּי שֶׁאֵינִי כְּדַאי וְהָגוּן לְכָךְ. לָכֵן
אֲבַקֵּשׁ מִמְּךָ, אֱלֹהֵי אַבְרָהָם, אֱלֹהֵי יִצְחָק, וֵאלֹהֵי יַעֲקֹב,
אֱלֹהֵי שָׂרָה, אֱלֹהֵי רִבְקָה, אֱלֹהֵי רָחֵל, וֵאלֹהֵי לֵאָה, יהוה
יהוה, אֵל רַחוּם וְחַנּוּן, אֱלֹהֵי יִשְׂרָאֵל, שַׁדַּי אָיֹם וְנוֹרָא,
הֱיֵה נָא מַצְלִיחַ דַּרְכִּי אֲשֶׁר אֲנִי הוֹלֵךְ, לַעֲמֹד וּלְבַקֵּשׁ
רַחֲמִים עָלַי וְעַל שׁוֹלְחָי.

וְנָא אַל תַּפְשִׁיעֵם בְּחַטֹּאתַי וְאַל תְּחַיְּבֵם בַּעֲוֹנוֹתַי, כִּי
חוֹטֵא וּפוֹשֵׁעַ אָנִי. וְאַל יִכָּלְמוּ בִּפְשָׁעַי וְאַל יֵבוֹשׁוּ בִּי
וְאַל אֵבוֹשָׁה בָּהֶם. וְקַבֵּל תְּפִלָּתִי כִּתְפִלַּת רָגִיל וְקוֹלוֹ
נָעִים וּפִרְקוֹ נָאֶה וּמְעֹרָב בְּדַעַת עִם הַבְּרִיּוֹת. וְתִגְעַר
בַּשָּׂטָן לְבַל יַשְׂטִינֵנִי. וִיהִי נָא דִגְלֵנוּ עָלֶיךָ אַהֲבָה וְעַל
כָּל־פְּשָׁעִים תְּכַסֶּה בְּאַהֲבָה. וְכָל־צָרוֹת וְרָעוֹת הֲפָךְ־לָנוּ
וּלְכָל־יִשְׂרָאֵל לְשָׂשׂוֹן וּלְשִׂמְחָה לְחַיִּים וּלְשָׁלוֹם. הָאֱמֶת
וְהַשָּׁלוֹם אֱהָבוּ, וְלֹא יְהִי שׁוּם מִכְשׁוֹל בִּתְפִלָּתִי.

וִיהִי רָצוֹן מִלְּפָנֶיךָ, יהוה, אֱלֹהֵי אַבְרָהָם יִצְחָק וְיַעֲקֹב,
שָׂרָה רִבְקָה רָחֵל וְלֵאָה, הָאֵל הַגָּדוֹל הַגִּבּוֹר וְהַנּוֹרָא,
אֵל עֶלְיוֹן, אֶהְיֶה אֲשֶׁר אֶהְיֶה, שֶׁתָּבוֹא תְפִלָּתִי לִפְנֵי
כִסֵּא כְבוֹדֶךָ, בַּעֲבוּר כָּל־הַצַּדִּיקִים וְהַחֲסִידִים הַתְּמִימִים
וְהַיְשָׁרִים, וּבַעֲבוּר כְּבוֹד שִׁמְךָ הַגָּדוֹל וְהַנּוֹרָא, כִּי אַתָּה
שׁוֹמֵעַ תְּפִלַּת עַמְּךָ יִשְׂרָאֵל בְּרַחֲמִים. בָּרוּךְ אַתָּה שׁוֹמֵעַ
תְּפִלָּה.

HIN'NI הִנְנִי. The responsibility of the leader in the High Holy Day services is especially weighty, for unlike Shabbat and festival prayers, the prayers of these days, occurring as they do only once a year, are less familiar to the congregation. In the Middle Ages, when most of the congregation did not possess a prayerbook, leading the congregation in prayer was an even weightier task. Thus, there developed the tradition of the leader privately praying that the service might be conducted properly: that the people be inspired and that God be moved by the pleas of the congregation. There are many such prayers, called *r'shuyot*—the particular *r'shut* printed here was one most often recited in Eastern Europe. It was composed in the 16th century and its author is unknown. Originally the prayer was recited silently by the leader; and even today, when it has become a public statement in musical form, some portion of it is recited meditatively and quietly.

ONE WORTHY OF THIS TASK רָגִיל. An early citation in the Talmud declares that the person leading the congregation in prayer on a fast day ought to be someone who is *ragil*. The Talmud then lists the qualities that a *ragil* should have, and the poet has included many of these here (Babylonian Talmud, Taanit 16a).

GOOD REPUTE וּפִרְקוֹ נָאֶה. This unusual Hebrew phrase is defined in the Talmud by Abbaye (late 3rd century, Babylonia) as one about whom nothing bad has been said (Babylonian Talmud, Taanit 16a).

LOVE INTEGRITY AND PEACE הָאֱמֶת וְהַשָּׁלוֹם אֱהָבוּ. The prophet Zechariah (8:19) promises that if "you love integrity and peace," then fast days will be turned to days of joy.

Translation:

Hin'ni: Here I Stand

Here I stand, impoverished in merit, trembling in the presence of the One who hears the prayers of Israel. Even though I am unfit and unworthy for the task, I come to represent Your people Israel and plead on their behalf. Therefore, gracious and merciful ADONAI, awe-inspiring God of Abraham, Isaac, and Jacob, of Sarah, Rebecca, Rachel, and Leah, I pray that I might successfully seek compassion for myself and those who send me.

Charge them not with my sins and let them not bear the guilt of my transgressions, though I have sinned and transgressed. May they not be shamed for my deeds, and may their deeds cause me no shame. Accept my prayer as if it were uttered by one worthy of this task, a person of good repute, whose voice is sweet and whose nature is pleasing to all. Quiet what might trouble me. May our faith in You be accepted lovingly and may Your love cover over our sins. Transform our afflictions and those of all Israel to joy and gladness, life and peace. Love integrity and peace and may there be no obstacles confronting my prayer.

May it be Your will, ADONAI, God of Abraham, Isaac, and Jacob, Sarah, Rebecca, Rachel, and Leah, great, mighty, awe-inspiring, transcendent God, who responded to Moses, saying, "I will be there with you, in the way that I will be there with you," that my prayer reach Your throne, through the merit of all honest, righteous, and devout people, and for the sake of Your glory. Praised are You, merciful God, who hears prayer.

הִנְנִי הֶעָנִיָּה מִמַּעַשׂ, נִרְעֶשֶׁת וְנִפְחֶדֶת מִפַּחַד יוֹשֵׁב תְּהִלּוֹת יִשְׂרָאֵל, בָּאתִי לַעֲמֹד וּלְהִתְחַנֵּן לְפָנֶיךָ עַל עַמְּךָ יִשְׂרָאֵל אֲשֶׁר שְׁלָחוּנִי, אַף עַל פִּי שֶׁאֵינִי כְדַאִית וַהֲגוּנָה לְכָךְ. לָכֵן אֲבַקֵּשׁ מִמְּךָ, אֱלֹהֵי אַבְרָהָם, אֱלֹהֵי יִצְחָק, וֵאלֹהֵי יַעֲקֹב, אֱלֹהֵי שָׂרָה, אֱלֹהֵי רִבְקָה, אֱלֹהֵי רָחֵל, וֵאלֹהֵי לֵאָה, יהוה יהוה, אֵל רַחוּם וְחַנּוּן, אֱלֹהֵי יִשְׂרָאֵל, שַׁדַּי אָיוֹם וְנוֹרָא, הֱיֵה נָא מַצְלִיחַ דַּרְכִּי אֲשֶׁר אֲנִי הוֹלֶכֶת, לַעֲמֹד וּלְבַקֵּשׁ רַחֲמִים עָלַי וְעַל שׁוֹלְחַי.

וְנָא אַל תַּפְשִׁיעֵם בְּחַטֹּאתַי וְאַל תְּחַיְּבֵם בַּעֲוֹנוֹתַי, כִּי חוֹטֵאת וּפוֹשַׁעַת אָנִי. וְאַל יִכָּלְמוּ בִּפְשָׁעַי וְאַל יֵבוֹשׁוּ בִּי וְאַל אֵבוֹשָׁה בָּהֶם. וְקַבֵּל תְּפִלָּתִי כִּתְפִלַּת רְגִילָה וְקוֹלָהּ נָעִים וּפִרְקָהּ נָאֶה וּמְעֹרֶבֶת בְּדַעַת עִם הַבְּרִיּוֹת. וְתִגְעַר בְּשָׂטָן לְבַל יַשְׂטִינֵנִי. וִיהִי נָא דִגְלֵנוּ עָלֶיךָ אַהֲבָה וְעַל כָּל־פְּשָׁעִים תְּכַסֶּה בְּאַהֲבָה. וְכָל־צָרוֹת וְרָעוֹת הֲפָךְ־לָנוּ וּלְכָל־יִשְׂרָאֵל לְשָׂשׂוֹן וּלְשִׂמְחָה לְחַיִּים וּלְשָׁלוֹם. הָאֱמֶת וְהַשָּׁלוֹם אֱהָבוּ, וְלֹא יְהִי שׁוּם מִכְשׁוֹל בִּתְפִלָּתִי.

וִיהִי רָצוֹן מִלְּפָנֶיךָ, יהוה, אֱלֹהֵי אַבְרָהָם יִצְחָק וְיַעֲקֹב, שָׂרָה רִבְקָה רָחֵל וְלֵאָה, הָאֵל הַגָּדוֹל הַגִּבּוֹר וְהַנּוֹרָא, אֵל עֶלְיוֹן, אֶהְיֶה אֲשֶׁר אֶהְיֶה, שֶׁתָּבוֹא תְפִלָּתִי לִפְנֵי כִסֵּא כְבוֹדֶךָ, בַּעֲבוּר כָּל־הַצַּדִּיקִים וְהַחֲסִידִים הַתְּמִימִים וְהַיְשָׁרִים, וּבַעֲבוּר כְּבוֹד שִׁמְךָ הַגָּדוֹל וְהַנּוֹרָא, כִּי אַתָּה שׁוֹמֵעַ תְּפִלַּת עַמְּךָ יִשְׂרָאֵל בְּרַחֲמִים. בָּרוּךְ אַתָּה שׁוֹמֵעַ תְּפִלָּה.

We rise as the ark is opened.

כִּי שֵׁם יהוה אֶקְרָא, הָבוּ גֹדֶל לֵאלֹהֵינוּ.
אֲדֹנָי שְׂפָתַי תִּפְתָּח וּפִי יַגִּיד תְּהִלָּתֶךָ.

Version with Patriarchs and Matriarchs:	*Version with Patriarchs:*

בָּרוּךְ אַתָּה יהוה,
אֱלֹהֵינוּ וֵאלֹהֵי אֲבוֹתֵינוּ
[וְאִמּוֹתֵינוּ], אֱלֹהֵי אַבְרָהָם,
אֱלֹהֵי יִצְחָק, וֵאלֹהֵי יַעֲקֹב,
אֱלֹהֵי שָׂרָה, אֱלֹהֵי רִבְקָה,
אֱלֹהֵי רָחֵל, וֵאלֹהֵי לֵאָה,
הָאֵל הַגָּדוֹל הַגִּבּוֹר וְהַנּוֹרָא,
אֵל עֶלְיוֹן, גּוֹמֵל חֲסָדִים
טוֹבִים, וְקוֹנֵה הַכֹּל, וְזוֹכֵר
חַסְדֵי אָבוֹת [וְאִמָּהוֹת],
וּמֵבִיא גוֹאֵל לִבְנֵי בְנֵיהֶם
לְמַעַן שְׁמוֹ בְּאַהֲבָה.

בָּרוּךְ אַתָּה יהוה,
אֱלֹהֵינוּ וֵאלֹהֵי אֲבוֹתֵינוּ,
אֱלֹהֵי אַבְרָהָם, אֱלֹהֵי
יִצְחָק, וֵאלֹהֵי יַעֲקֹב, הָאֵל
הַגָּדוֹל הַגִּבּוֹר וְהַנּוֹרָא,
אֵל עֶלְיוֹן, גּוֹמֵל חֲסָדִים
טוֹבִים, וְקוֹנֵה הַכֹּל, וְזוֹכֵר
חַסְדֵי אָבוֹת, וּמֵבִיא גוֹאֵל
לִבְנֵי בְנֵיהֶם לְמַעַן שְׁמוֹ
בְּאַהֲבָה.

מְסוֹד חֲכָמִים וּנְבוֹנִים,
וּמִלֶּמֶד דַּעַת מְבִינִים,
אֶפְתְּחָה פִּי בִּתְפִלָּה וּבְתַחֲנוּנִים,
לְחַלּוֹת וּלְחַנֵּן פְּנֵי מֶלֶךְ מָלֵא רַחֲמִים
מוֹחֵל וְסוֹלֵחַ לַעֲוֹנִים.

The ark is closed.

זָכְרֵנוּ לְחַיִּים, מֶלֶךְ חָפֵץ בַּחַיִּים,
וְכָתְבֵנוּ בְּסֵפֶר הַחַיִּים, לְמַעַנְךָ אֱלֹהִים חַיִּים.

AS I PROCLAIM כִּי שֵׁם יהוה אֶקְרָא. This verse, taken from Moses' final speech to the children of Israel (Deuteronomy 32:3), was probably originally inserted as an instructional phrase, to be recited by the leader, asking the congregation to respond by answering "Amen" to the *b'rakhot* that follow. Thus it would mean: "When I proclaim God's name Adonai, you should respond by acknowledging God as well."

ADONAI, OPEN MY LIPS אֲדֹנָי שְׂפָתַי תִּפְתָּח. Psalm 51:17. Every Amidah begins with this request asking God to afford us the appropriate attitude and words for prayer. Perhaps the phrase conveys a mystical sense that prayer originates in our soul, the part of God within us all.

GOD OF ABRAHAM, GOD OF ISAAC, AND GOD OF JACOB אֱלֹהֵי אַבְרָהָם, אֱלֹהֵי יִצְחָק, וֵאלֹהֵי יַעֲקֹב. God begins the conversation with Moses at the burning bush with this self-description (Exodus 3:6). We understand the world of prayer through the experience of those who came before us—both in our immediate and our ancient past. Perhaps the quotation of these words expresses the hope that we too might feel the presence of God. Moses saw only a burning bush, but his inner ear heard so much more.

GREAT, MIGHTY, AWE-INSPIRING הַגָּדוֹל הַגִּבּוֹר וְהַנּוֹרָא. This phrase is a quotation from Deuteronomy 10:17–18, where God's might is characterized by the befriending of the stranger, the widow, and the orphan.

INSPIRED BY THE INSIGHT מְסוֹד חֲכָמִים. These lines serve to introduce *piyyutim*, poetic additions to the Amidah, that address the holy day's themes. The reference to "sages" and "those who acquired wisdom" is a relic of the era when adding *piyyutim* was a matter of controversy, which prompted this appeal to the authority of those sages who permitted them. This introduction proclaimed that the Amidah's *piyyutim* are faithful to tradition, in that they are saturated with biblical and midrashic quotations.

REMEMBER US זָכְרֵנוּ. This brief anonymous and ancient poem, added at each service during the High Holy Day season, stresses the theme that God treasures life.

REPETITION OF THE AMIDAH

We rise as the ark is opened.

As I proclaim God's name, ADONAI, exalt our God.
ADONAI, open my lips that my mouth may speak Your praise.

First B'rakhah: Our Ancestors

Our Ancestors

We create community through a sense of common ancestry. A convert to Judaism is traditionally called the child of Abraham and Sarah—all of us who call ourselves Jews take on a common past. In affirming that past, we are asked to take on the mythic qualities of the lives of these ancestors: to journey in the life of faith, to experience our lives as a calling, to engage in the struggle for justice and compassion in the world about us. Abraham and Sarah were promised that their children would not be lonely practitioners of faith but would find a community of people who acknowledged this heritage, and we, in joining in a moment of common prayer, in reciting their names, and in acknowledging them, begin to fulfill that promise.

Version with Patriarchs:

Barukh atah ADONAI,
our God and God of our
 ancestors,
God of Abraham, God of
 Isaac, and God of Jacob,
great, mighty, awe-inspiring,
 transcendent God,
who acts with lovingkindness
 and creates all things,
who remembers the loving
 deeds of our ancestors,
and who will send a redeemer
 to their children's children
 with love
 for the sake of divine honor.

Version with Patriarchs and Matriarchs:

Barukh atah ADONAI,
our God and God of our
 ancestors,
God of Abraham, God of
 Isaac, and God of Jacob,
God of Sarah, God of
 Rebecca, God of Rachel,
 and God of Leah,
great, mighty, awe-inspiring,
 transcendent God,
who acts with lovingkindness
 and creates all things,
who remembers the loving
 deeds of our ancestors,
and who will send a redeemer
 to their children's children
 with love
 for the sake of divine honor.

Inspired by the insight of sages
and the teachings of those who acquired wisdom,
I open my lips in prayer and supplication
to entreat the Merciful Sovereign,
who forgives and pardons sin.

The ark is closed.

Remember us for life, Sovereign who delights in life,
and inscribe us in the Book of Life, for Your sake, God of life.
Zokhreinu l'ḥayyim, melekh ḥafeitz ba-ḥayyim,
v'khotveinu b'seifer ha-ḥayyim, l'ma·ankha Elohim ḥayyim.

Version with Patriarchs and Matriarchs:	Version with Patriarchs:

Version with Patriarchs and Matriarchs:

מֶלֶךְ עוֹזֵר וּפוֹקֵד
וּמוֹשִׁיעַ וּמָגֵן.
בָּרוּךְ אַתָּה יהוה, מָגֵן
אַבְרָהָם וּפוֹקֵד שָׂרָה.

Version with Patriarchs:

מֶלֶךְ עוֹזֵר וּמוֹשִׁיעַ וּמָגֵן.
בָּרוּךְ אַתָּה יהוה, מָגֵן
אַבְרָהָם.

אַתָּה גִבּוֹר לְעוֹלָם, אֲדֹנָי, מְחַיֵּה מֵתִים אַתָּה,
רַב לְהוֹשִׁיעַ.

מְכַלְכֵּל חַיִּים בְּחֶסֶד, מְחַיֵּה מֵתִים בְּרַחֲמִים רַבִּים, סוֹמֵךְ
נוֹפְלִים, וְרוֹפֵא חוֹלִים, וּמַתִּיר אֲסוּרִים, וּמְקַיֵּם אֱמוּנָתוֹ
לִישֵׁנֵי עָפָר. מִי כָמוֹךָ בַּעַל גְּבוּרוֹת, וּמִי דּוֹמֶה לָּךְ, מֶלֶךְ
מֵמִית וּמְחַיֶּה וּמַצְמִיחַ יְשׁוּעָה.

מִי כָמוֹךָ אַב הָרַחֲמִים, זוֹכֵר יְצוּרָיו לְחַיִּים בְּרַחֲמִים.

וְנֶאֱמָן אַתָּה לְהַחֲיוֹת מֵתִים. בָּרוּךְ אַתָּה יהוה, מְחַיֵּה
הַמֵּתִים.

MIGHTY FOREVER אַתָּה גִבּוֹר. This b'rakhah, which describes God's presence and activity in the world, centers on the kindness and care of God for the incapacitated—even the dead are in God's care.

GIVE LIFE TO THE DEAD מְחַיֵּה מֵתִים. To be sure, the primary meaning of this phrase was understood to refer to the afterlife, but the Rabbis also understood that the phrase referred to a spiritual revival in this world. Thus the b'rakhah one makes on greeting a friend whom one has not seen for a year utilizes the phrase "who gives life to the dead."

WHO IS LIKE YOU, SOURCE OF COMPASSION מִי כָמוֹךָ אַב הָרַחֲמִים. A second insertion at each of the services in the High Holy Day season. The gift of life is an expression of God's kindness.

You are the Sovereign who helps and saves and shields.

Barukh atah ADONAI, shield of Abraham.

You are the Sovereign who helps and guards, saves and shields.

Barukh atah ADONAI, shield of Abraham and guardian of Sarah.

To Imitate God

Judaism is often depicted as believing in a stern and angry God of judgment. In fact, rabbinic Judaism portrays God as loving and caring, a deity whose essence is ethical concern. The liturgy of the Amidah quotes the psalmist in describing God as protecting the weakest members of society; even the dead remain present for God. Abraham Joshua Heschel pointed out that prophetic depictions of God's anger are expressions of God's sympathy for the oppressed and represents a negative judgment on those who would be part of a society that did not provide adequate care for the least powerful, its weakest members. For the ancient rabbis and for modern Jewish thinkers, to imitate God and to do God's will is to live a life marked by compassion.

Compassion

Abba Saul said: I can be like God: Just as God is merciful and compassionate, I too can act mercifully and compassionately.

—MEKHILTA OF
RABBI ISHMAEL

Second B'rakhah: God's Saving Care

You are mighty forever, ADONAI—
You give life to the dead;
great is Your saving power.

You sustain the living through love,
　　and with great mercy give life to the dead.
You support the falling, heal the sick,
　　loosen the chains of the bound,
　　and keep faith with those who sleep in the dust.
Who is like You, Almighty,
　　and who can be compared to You?—
　　Sovereign, who brings death and life,
　　and causes salvation to flourish.

M'khalkeil ḥayyim b'ḥesed, m'ḥayyeih meitim b'raḥamim rabbim, someikh nof'lim, v'rofei ḥolim, u-mattir asurim, u-m'kayyeim emunato li-sheinei afar. Mi khamokha ba·al g'vurot u-mi domeh lakh, melekh meimit u-m'ḥayyeh u-matzmi·aḥ y'shu·ah.

Who is like You, source of compassion,
who remembers with compassion Your creatures for life?
Mi khamokha av ha-raḥamim, zokheir y'tzurav l'ḥayyim b'raḥamim.

You are faithful in bringing life to the dead.
Barukh atah ADONAI, who gives life to the dead.

וּבְכֵן וּלְךָ תַעֲלֶה קְדֻשָּׁה, כִּי אַתָּה אֱלֹהֵינוּ מֶלֶךְ מוֹחֵל וְסוֹלֵחַ.

The ark is opened.

וּנְתַנֶּה תְּקֶף קְדֻשַּׁת הַיּוֹם, כִּי הוּא נוֹרָא וְאָיוֹם. וּבוֹ תִנָּשֵׂא מַלְכוּתֶךָ, וְיִכּוֹן בְּחֶסֶד כִּסְאֶךָ, וְתֵשֵׁב עָלָיו בֶּאֱמֶת. אֱמֶת כִּי אַתָּה הוּא דַיָּן וּמוֹכִיחַ, וְיוֹדֵעַ וָעֵד, וְכוֹתֵב וְחוֹתֵם, וְסוֹפֵר וּמוֹנֶה, וְתִזְכּוֹר כָּל־הַנִּשְׁכָּחוֹת. וְתִפְתַּח אֶת־סֵפֶר הַזִּכְרוֹנוֹת, וּמֵאֵלָיו יִקָּרֵא, וְחוֹתַם יַד כָּל־אָדָם בּוֹ.

וּבְשׁוֹפָר גָּדוֹל יִתָּקַע, וְקוֹל דְּמָמָה דַקָּה יִשָּׁמַע. וּמַלְאָכִים יֵחָפֵזוּן, וְחִיל וּרְעָדָה יֹאחֵזוּן, וְיֹאמְרוּ הִנֵּה יוֹם הַדִּין, לִפְקוֹד עַל צְבָא מָרוֹם בַּדִּין, כִּי לֹא יִזְכּוּ בְעֵינֶיךָ בַּדִּין. וְכָל־בָּאֵי עוֹלָם יַעַבְרוּן לְפָנֶיךָ כִּבְנֵי מָרוֹן. כְּבַקָּרַת רוֹעֶה עֶדְרוֹ, מַעֲבִיר צֹאנוֹ תַּחַת שִׁבְטוֹ, כֵּן תַּעֲבִיר וְתִסְפּוֹר וְתִמְנֶה, וְתִפְקוֹד נֶפֶשׁ כָּל־חָי, וְתַחְתּוֹךְ קִצְבָּה לְכָל־בְּרִיָּה, וְתִכְתּוֹב אֶת־גְּזַר דִּינָם.

בְּרֹאשׁ הַשָּׁנָה יִכָּתֵבוּן, וּבְיוֹם צוֹם כִּפּוּר יֵחָתֵמוּן.

כַּמָּה יַעַבְרוּן וְכַמָּה יִבָּרֵאוּן.
מִי יִחְיֶה, וּמִי יָמוּת.
מִי בְקִצּוֹ, וּמִי לֹא בְקִצּוֹ.
מִי בָאֵשׁ, וּמִי בַמַּיִם.
מִי בַחֶרֶב, וּמִי בַחַיָּה.
מִי בָרָעָב, וּמִי בַצָּמָא.
מִי בָרַעַשׁ, וּמִי בַמַּגֵּפָה.
מִי בַחֲנִיקָה, וּמִי בַסְּקִילָה.
מִי יָנוּחַ, וּמִי יָנוּעַ.
מִי יִשָּׁקֵט, וּמִי יִטָּרֵף.
מִי יִשָּׁלֵו, וּמִי יִתְיַסָּר.
מִי יֵעָנִי, וּמִי יֵעָשִׁיר.
מִי יִשָּׁפֵל, וּמִי יָרוּם.

THE "GREAT SHOFAR" WILL BE SOUNDED וּבְשׁוֹפָר גָּדוֹל יִתָּקַע. In a remarkable exercise of poetic license, the anonymous author of this treasured High Holy Day prayer has transformed the prophetic image of the end of days to today. Isaiah, preaching in Jerusalem in the eighth century B.C.E., had predicted (27:13) that those exiled from the northern kingdom of Israel—the ten lost tribes—would return, and all the nations would gather on God's holy mountain. Later interpreters, from Second Temple times on, understood this as a vision of final redemption, a time of final judgment. In this prayer, judgment is not of an end time but in the present—now, even as we pray.

ON ROSH HASHANAH IT IS WRITTEN בְּרֹאשׁ הַשָּׁנָה יִכָּתֵבוּן. This image of God writing each person's fate in a book appears already in the Jerusalem Talmud (Rosh Hashanah 1:3).

Most of us prefer to deny the unruliness of our fragility. But the facts on this list in Unetanah Tokef are inescapable: some will get sick; some will be born; there will be deaths by hunger and in wars. The liturgy begs us to pay attention to these plain facts. And we all know that if we haven't yet suffered an unbearable loss, one year, such a grief will permanently scar our hearts, or we will suffer yet another death that we cannot bear. We hope that we will live to see another year, but we know that without a doubt, certainly, definitely, and absolutely, a year will surely come that will break the pattern. That destiny is mysterious in its details, but death is our destiny, the fate of every person we know and love. Everyone dies, somehow and some time.

We are not praying to be spared an ending in death. We are not even asking that death be postponed. Rather, after reminding ourselves relentlessly of the many ways that life might end, we tell ourselves that the way to cope with ultimate vulnerability is through *t'shuvah*, *t'fillah*, and *tz'dakah*. Our goal is not security, but a life of meaning that recognizes our vulnerability but rises beyond it.

—LEONARD GORDON

Third B'rakhah: God's Holiness

May our sanctification ascend to You,
for You are our God, a forgiving sovereign.

U-NETANEH TOKEF—THE SACRED POWER OF THE DAY
The ark is opened.

Let us speak of the sacred power of this day—profound and awe-inspiring. On it, Your sovereignty is celebrated, and Your throne, from which You rule in truth, is established with love. Truly, You are Judge and Prosecutor, Expert, and Witness, completing the indictment, bringing the case, and enumerating the counts. You recall all that is forgotten, and will open the book of remembrance, which speaks for itself, for our own hands have signed the page.

The great shofar will be sounded and the still small voice will be heard.
Angels will be alarmed, seized with fear and trembling, declaring, "This very day is the Day of Judgment"—for even the hosts of heaven are judged; no one is innocent in Your sight.
All that lives on earth will pass before You like a flock of sheep.
As a shepherd examines the flock, making each sheep pass under the staff, so You will review and number and count, judging each living being, determining the fate of everything in creation, inscribing their destiny.

On Rosh Hashanah it is written, and on the Fast of the Day of Atonement it is sealed!—

B'rosh ha-shanah yikkateivun, u-v'yom tzom kippur yeiḥateimun.

How many will pass on, and how many will be born;
who will live and who will die;
who will live a long life and who will come to an untimely end;
who will perish by fire and who by water; who by sword and who by beast; who by hunger and who by thirst; who by earthquake and who by plague.
who will be strangled and who will be stoned;
who will be at peace and who will be troubled;
who will be serene and who will be disturbed;
who will be tranquil and who will be tormented;
who will be impoverished and who will be enriched;
who will be brought low, and who will be raised up.

וּתְשׁוּבָה וּתְפִלָּה וּצְדָקָה מַעֲבִירִין אֶת־רֹעַ הַגְּזֵרָה.

כִּי כְּשִׁמְךָ כֵּן תְּהִלָּתֶךָ, קָשֶׁה לִכְעֹס וְנוֹחַ לִרְצוֹת.
כִּי לֹא תַחְפֹּץ בְּמוֹת הַמֵּת, כִּי אִם בְּשׁוּבוֹ מִדַּרְכּוֹ וְחָיָה.
וְעַד יוֹם מוֹתוֹ תְּחַכֶּה לּוֹ, אִם יָשׁוּב מִיָּד תְּקַבְּלוֹ.
אֱמֶת כִּי אַתָּה הוּא יוֹצְרָם, וְאַתָּה יוֹדֵעַ יִצְרָם,
כִּי הֵם בָּשָׂר וָדָם.

אָדָם יְסוֹדוֹ מֵעָפָר וְסוֹפוֹ לֶעָפָר. בְּנַפְשׁוֹ יָבִיא לַחְמוֹ.
מָשׁוּל כַּחֶרֶס הַנִּשְׁבָּר, כְּחָצִיר יָבֵשׁ, וּכְצִיץ נוֹבֵל, כְּצֵל
עוֹבֵר, וּכְעָנָן כָּלָה, וּכְרוּחַ נוֹשָׁבֶת, וּכְאָבָק פּוֹרֵחַ,
וְכַחֲלוֹם יָעוּף.

וְאַתָּה הוּא מֶלֶךְ אֵל חַי וְקַיָּם.

אֵין קִצְבָה לִשְׁנוֹתֶיךָ, וְאֵין קֵץ לְאֹרֶךְ יָמֶיךָ. וְאֵין שִׁעוּר
לְמַרְכְּבוֹת כְּבוֹדֶךָ, וְאֵין פֵּרוּשׁ לְעֵילוֹם שְׁמֶךָ. שִׁמְךָ נָאֶה
לְךָ וְאַתָּה נָאֶה לִשְׁמֶךָ, וּשְׁמֵנוּ קָרֵאתָ בִּשְׁמֶךָ.

The ark is closed and we remain standing.

עֲשֵׂה לְמַעַן שְׁמֶךָ,
וְקַדֵּשׁ אֶת־שִׁמְךָ עַל מַקְדִּישֵׁי שְׁמֶךָ,
בַּעֲבוּר כְּבוֹד שִׁמְךָ הַנַּעֲרָץ וְהַנִּקְדָּשׁ.

T'SHUVAH תְּשׁוּבָה. From the root שׁוּב (shov), this noun can mean "repentance" or "turning." It involves self-critique and a resolve to act more in accord with one's principles.

T'FILLAH תְּפִלָּה. From the root פלל (palal) and often translated as "prayer," this noun also implies self-judgment. Moments of t'fillah can bring insight and affirm primary religious commitments.

TZ'DAKAH צְדָקָה. From the root צדק (tzadak), this noun derives from the word for "righteousness" or "justice." It refers to all acts treating others with care and respect. In that sense, our gifts to the needy fulfill a divine obligation.

TRANSFORM THE HARSHNESS OF OUR DESTINY מַעֲבִירִין אֶת־רֹעַ הַגְּזֵרָה. We do not know how our regret may influence what God writes in the Books of Life and Death. Yet we can transform our experience—however harsh—through how we see ourselves and deal with others—that is, through t'shuvah, t'fillah, and tz'dakah.

SCRIPTURE COMPARES מָשׁוּל. What follows is a poetic cascade of imagery drawn from the Bible. Its staccato formulation underscores the brevity and fragility of life. The images are drawn from Jeremiah 18 (a broken shard), Isaiah 40:7 (withering grass, a shriveled flower), Psalm 144:4 (a passing shadow), Job 7:9 (a fading cloud), Isaiah 40:7 (a fleeting breeze), Isaiah 5:24 (scattered dust), and Job 20:8 (a vanishing dream).

YOU HAVE LINKED OUR NAME WITH YOURS וּשְׁמֵנוּ קָרֵאתָ בִּשְׁמֶךָ. God has many names, so which one is this phrase referring to? Some say the line alludes to the Thirteen Attributes describing God's graciousness. More likely it refers to the unpronounceable four-letter name of God (yod, heh, vav, heh) which is a play on the verb "to be," and thus may refer to God's eternal being, mentioned in the previous line of this prayer. The ending of the word "Israel" is yet another name for God, El. By being linked to God's name, Israel becomes the "eternal people," and partakes of the mystery of God's timeless nature.

WHEN WE REALLY BEGIN. Written by Stanley Rabinowitz and adapted by Shamai Kanter and Jack Riemer.

¶ When we really begin a new year it is decided, *and when we actually repent it is determined:* who shall be truly alive and who shall merely exist; *who shall be happy and who shall be miserable;* who shall attain fulfillment in their day and who shall not attain fulfillment in their day; *who shall be tormented by the fire of ambition and who shall be overcome by the waters of failure;* who shall be pierced by the sharp sword of envy and who shall be torn by the wild beast of resentment; *who shall hunger for companionship and who shall thirst for approval;* who shall be shattered by the earthquake of social change and who shall be plagued by the pressures of conformity; *who shall be strangled by insecurity and who shall be stoned into submission;* who shall be content and who shall wander in search of satisfaction; *who shall be serene and who shall be distraught;* who shall be at ease and who shall be afflicted with anxiety; *who shall be poor in their own eyes and who shall be rich in tranquility;* who shall be brought low with futility and who shall be exalted through achievement. *But repentance, prayer, and good deeds have the power to change the character of our lives.* Let us resolve to repent, to pray, and to do good deeds so that we may begin a truly new year.

But *T'shuvah, T'fillah,* and *Tz'dakah* have the power to transform the harshness of our destiny.

U-t'shuvah u-t'fillah u-tz'dakah ma·avirin et ro·a ha-g'zerah.

Our praise of You accords with Your essential nature: slow to anger and easily appeased.

You do not desire the death of the sinner, but rather that we change our ways and live.

You wait until the day of death, and if one returns, You accept that person back immediately.

Truly, You are their Creator, and know the nature of Your creatures, that they are only flesh and blood.

Each person's origin is dust, and each person will return to the earth having spent life seeking sustenance. Scripture compares human beings to
a broken shard,
withering grass,
a shriveled flower,
a passing shadow,
a fading cloud,
a fleeting breeze,
scattered dust,
a vanishing dream.

And You—You are the Sovereign, living God, ever-present.

V'atah hu melekh El ḥai v'kayyam.

Your years never end,
Your time has no measure,
the extent of Your glory can never be imagined,
for there is no understanding of the mystery of Your nature.
Your name befits You,
as You befit Your name,
and You have linked our name with Yours.

The ark is closed and we remain standing.

Act kindly for the sake of Your name,
and sanctify Your name with those who hallow Your name.
Do so for the honor of Your revered and holy name.

קְדֻשָּׁה

The Kedushah is recited while standing. The tradition recommends standing like angels, with feet together.

כְּסוֹד שִׂיחַ שַׂרְפֵי קֹדֶשׁ, הַמַּקְדִּישִׁים שִׁמְךָ בַּקֹּדֶשׁ, דָּרֵי מַעְלָה עִם דָּרֵי מַטָּה, כַּכָּתוּב עַל יַד נְבִיאֶךָ: וְקָרָא זֶה אֶל זֶה וְאָמַר:

קָדוֹשׁ, קָדוֹשׁ, קָדוֹשׁ יהוה צְבָאוֹת, מְלֹא כָל־הָאָרֶץ כְּבוֹדוֹ.

כְּבוֹדוֹ מָלֵא עוֹלָם, מְשָׁרְתָיו שׁוֹאֲלִים זֶה לָזֶה אַיֵּה מְקוֹם כְּבוֹדוֹ, לְעֻמָּתָם בָּרוּךְ יֹאמֵרוּ:

בָּרוּךְ כְּבוֹד יהוה מִמְּקוֹמוֹ.

מִמְּקוֹמוֹ הוּא יִפֶן בְּרַחֲמִים, וְיָחֹן עַם הַמְיַחֲדִים שְׁמוֹ עֶרֶב וָבֹקֶר, בְּכָל־יוֹם תָּמִיד, פַּעֲמַיִם בְּאַהֲבָה שְׁמַע אוֹמְרִים:

שְׁמַע יִשְׂרָאֵל, יהוה אֱלֹהֵינוּ, יהוה אֶחָד.

הוּא אֱלֹהֵינוּ, הוּא אָבִינוּ, הוּא מַלְכֵּנוּ, הוּא מוֹשִׁיעֵנוּ, וְהוּא יַשְׁמִיעֵנוּ בְּרַחֲמָיו שֵׁנִית לְעֵינֵי כָּל־חָי, לִהְיוֹת לָכֶם לֵאלֹהִים

אֲנִי יהוה אֱלֹהֵיכֶם.

THE KEDUSHAH is composed of an interweaving of two prophetic visions: that of Isaiah, who saw the angels singing "holy, holy, holy," and that of Ezekiel, whose vision of heavenly forces descending to earth concludes with the phrase "praise God's glory." The form of the Kedushah is antiphonal: in heaven, one chorus of angels responds to another; on earth, leader and congregation respond to each other. In this version, recited at each Musaf service, Israel's recitation of the Sh'ma is offered as a counterpoint to the angelic praise. Ultimately, our prayer brings heaven and earth into conversation: just as the angels affirm God's universal presence, so too the congregation proclaims God's unity. The quotation from Isaiah, remarking that "one calls to the other," thus has a dual meaning in the liturgy: one chorus of angels responds to the other, and we and the angels respond to each other.

GLORY כְּבוֹד. The Kedushah combines several different senses of God's glory: God's creation (the world), God's presence, and the honor and praise we offer God. By placing biblical verses side by side with these several meanings, the *Kedushah* expresses both God's immanence and palpable presence, and God's transcendence, the sense that the Divine is beyond our understanding.

WHEREVER GOD DWELLS מִמְּקוֹמוֹ. The Rabbis said that the word "place" (מָקוֹם, *makom*) is one of the names of God. "God is the place of the world, but the world is not God's place" (Genesis Rabbah 68:10). The fact that God is everywhere allows us to recite the Kedushah outside of heaven and outside the Temple. Every synagogue filled with prayer becomes God's place.

WILL PROCLAIM וְהוּא יַשְׁמִיעֵנוּ. God and humanity exist in a call and response. God calls to us and we respond to that calling. We turn to God and God brings redemption.

AGAIN שֵׁנִית. Literally, "a second time." The first time was the Exodus. Jewish history exists between the promise of freedom at the Exodus and its fulfillment in the messianic era.

Where Is the Dwelling of God?

"Where is the dwelling of God?"

This was the question with which the Rabbi of Kotzk surprised a number of learned ḥasidim who happened to be visiting him.

They laughed at him: "What a thing to ask! Is not the whole world full of God's glory?"

Then he answered his own question: "God dwells wherever a person lets God in."

—A ḤASIDIC TALE

The Kedushah

The Kedushah is recited while standing. The tradition recommends standing like angels, with feet together.

Those who dwell on earth now add this sanctification of Your name to the mystic utterance of those on high, as Your prophet Isaiah described:

Each cried out to the other:
"Holy, holy, holy is *Adonai Tz'va·ot*, the whole world is filled with God's glory!"
Kadosh, kadosh, kadosh Adonai Tz'va·ot, m'lo khol ha-aretz k'vodo.

God's glory fills the universe. As one angelic chorus asks, "Where is the place of God's glory?" another responds: "Praised is ADONAI's glory wherever God dwells."
Barukh k'vod Adonai mi-m'komo.

From where God dwells, may God turn with compassion toward the people who twice each day, evening and morning, lovingly proclaim God's oneness, reciting the Sh'ma: "Hear, O Israel, ADONAI is our God, ADONAI alone."
Sh'ma yisra·el, Adonai eloheinu, Adonai eḥad.

The Holy One is our God, our creator, our sovereign, our redeemer. Yet again, God will in mercy proclaim to us before all that lives:
Hu eloheinu, hu avinu, hu malkeinu, hu moshi·einu, v'hu yashmi·einu b'raḥamav sheinit l'einei kol ḥai, lihyot lakhem leilohim.

"I, ADONAI, am your God."
Ani Adonai eloheikhem.

אַדִּיר אַדִּירֵנוּ, יהוה אֲדֹנֵינוּ, מָה אַדִּיר שִׁמְךָ בְּכָל־הָאָֽרֶץ.
וְהָיָה יהוה לְמֶֽלֶךְ עַל כָּל־הָאָֽרֶץ,
בַּיּוֹם הַהוּא יִהְיֶה יהוה אֶחָד וּשְׁמוֹ אֶחָד.

וּבְדִבְרֵי קָדְשְׁךָ כָּתוּב לֵאמֹר:
יִמְלֹךְ יהוה לְעוֹלָם, אֱלֹהַֽיִךְ צִיּוֹן לְדֹר וָדֹר, הַלְלוּ־יָהּ.

לְדוֹר וָדוֹר נַגִּיד גָּדְלֶֽךָ, וּלְנֵֽצַח נְצָחִים קְדֻשָּׁתְךָ נַקְדִּישׁ,
וְשִׁבְחֲךָ אֱלֹהֵֽינוּ מִפִּֽינוּ לֹא יָמוּשׁ לְעוֹלָם וָעֶד, כִּי אֵל מֶֽלֶךְ
גָּדוֹל וְקָדוֹשׁ אָֽתָּה.

We are seated.

חֲמוֹל עַל מַעֲשֶֽׂיךָ,
וְתִשְׂמַח בְּמַעֲשֶֽׂיךָ,
וְיֹאמְרוּ לְךָ חוֹסֶֽיךָ,
בְּצַדֶּקְךָ עֲמוּסֶֽיךָ,
תֻּקְדַּשׁ אָדוֹן עַל כָּל־מַעֲשֶֽׂיךָ.

עוֹד יִזְכָּר־לָֽנוּ, אַהֲבַת אֵיתָן, אֲדוֹנֵֽנוּ,
וּבַבֵּן הַנֶּעֱקַד יַשְׁבִּית מְדִינֵֽנוּ,
וּבִזְכוּת הַתָּם יוֹצִיא אָיוֹם לְצֶֽדֶק דִּינֵֽנוּ,
כִּי קָדוֹשׁ הַיּוֹם לַאֲדוֹנֵֽנוּ.

בְּאֵין מֵלִיץ יֹֽשֶׁר
מוּל מַגִּיד פֶּֽשַׁע,
תַּגִּיד לְיַעֲקֹב דְּבַר חֹק וּמִשְׁפָּט,
וְצַדְּקֵֽנוּ בַּמִּשְׁפָּט, הַמֶּֽלֶךְ הַמִּשְׁפָּט.

HAVE COMPASSION חֲמוֹל.
The three paragraphs that
follow are a pastiche of
stanzas taken from a variety of different *piyyutim*.
All traditional maḥzorim
arrange them as here.

THE INNOCENT ONE תָּם.
The word can also mean
"simple" or "whole." The
Bible describes Jacob as
"innocent" תָּם (*tam*), as
opposed to his brother,
Esau, the hunter. The
prayer is an appeal for
mercy on the basis of
the merits of the three
patriarchs.

**THE ONE WHO RECITES OUR
SIN** מַגִּיד פֶּֽשַׁע. Rather than
a fallen angel who opposes
God's will, both biblical
and rabbinic tradition de-
pict Satan as a prosecuting angel who
argues against the human cause.

YOU RECITE תַּגִּיד. With God as the
lawyer for the defense, the cause of the
people Israel will surely be vindicated.

Majesty, our majesty, ADONAI, our master, how majestic is Your name throughout the world!

ADONAI shall be acknowledged sovereign of all the earth. On that day ADONAI shall be one, and the name of God, one.

As the psalmist sang:
ADONAI will reign forever; your God, O Zion, from generation to generation. Halleluyah!
Yimlokh Adonai l'olam, elohayikh tziyyon l'dor va-dor, hal'luyah.

From one generation to another we will declare Your greatness, and forever sanctify You with words of holiness. Your praise will never leave our lips, for You are God and Sovereign, great and holy.
We are seated.

REMEMBER US FOR GOOD: THREE PIYYUTIM
Have compassion on Your creation
and rejoice in Your handiwork.
As You pardon Your people,
all who trust in You will declare:
"Be sanctified, Lord, throughout Your creation."

Lord, remember, for our sake, the love of Abraham of old.
May the binding of his son satisfy any guilt we may have
 incurred,
and may the merit of the innocent one serve to vindicate
 us this day,
for this day is holy to our Master.

As there is none fit to plead our case
against the one who recites our sin,
You recite for Jacob arguments of justice and law.
Vindicate our cause,
Sovereign Judge.

אָ

הָאוֹחֵז בְּיַד מִדַּת מִשְׁפָּט.

וְכֹל מַאֲמִינִים שֶׁהוּא אֵל אֱמוּנָה,

הַבּוֹחֵן וּבוֹדֵק גִּנְזֵי נִסְתָּרוֹת.

וְכֹל מַאֲמִינִים שֶׁהוּא בּוֹחֵן כְּלָיוֹת,

הַגּוֹאֵל מִמָּוֶת וּפוֹדֶה מִשַּׁחַת.

וְכֹל מַאֲמִינִים שֶׁהוּא גּוֹאֵל חָזָק,

בּ

הַדָּן יְחִידִי לְבָאֵי עוֹלָם.

וְכֹל מַאֲמִינִים שֶׁהוּא דַּיָּן אֱמֶת,

הֶהָגוּי בְּאֶהְיֶה אֲשֶׁר אֶהְיֶה.

וְכֹל מַאֲמִינִים שֶׁהוּא הָיָה וְהֹוֶה וְיִהְיֶה,

הַוַּדַּאי שְׁמוֹ כֵּן תְּהִלָּתוֹ.

וְכֹל מַאֲמִינִים שֶׁהוּא וְאֵין בִּלְתּוֹ,

גּ

הַזּוֹכֵר לְמַזְכִּירָיו טוֹבוֹת זִכְרוֹנוֹת.

וְכֹל מַאֲמִינִים שֶׁהוּא זוֹכֵר הַבְּרִית,

הַחוֹתֵךְ חַיִּים לְכָל־חָי.

וְכֹל מַאֲמִינִים שֶׁהוּא חַי וְקַיָּם,

הַטּוֹב וּמֵטִיב לָרָעִים וְלַטּוֹבִים.

וְכֹל מַאֲמִינִים שֶׁהוּא טוֹב לַכֹּל,

WE BELIEVE וְכֹל מַאֲמִינִים. This *piyyut* is 1500 years old, having been composed by one of the earliest liturgical poets, Yannai, who lived in the Land of Israel some time between the 5th and 7th century. The poem is a double alphabetical acrostic: the first line states an attribute of God, and the second uses the same letter to describe the human perspective. As much as he can, the poet alliterates an entire line, thus emphasizing the particular quality.

KNOWS OUR DEEPEST FEELINGS בּוֹחֵן כְּלָיוֹת. Literally, "examines our kidneys." Priests would examine the innards of sacrificed animals to determine the future or to interpret messages from God.

THE STEADFAST REDEEMER גּוֹאֵל חָזָק. The poet is paraphrasing Jeremiah 50:34, where the prophet asserts that only God—no earthly nation—will redeem Israel.

SOLE JUDGE OF ALL THAT LIVES ON EARTH הַדָּן יְחִידִי לְבָאֵי עוֹלָם. This phrase, taken from the Mishnah, is echoed in *U-netaneh Tokef*: all that lives on earth passes before God, the sole Judge on this judgment day.

A PROMISE OF THE FUTURE בְּאֶהְיֶה אֲשֶׁר אֶהְיֶה. In God's revelation to Moses at the burning bush, God replies to Moses' question, "Who shall I say sent me?" with the phrase quoted here, explicating the name of God: יהוה. The phrase has been variously translated as "I am that which I am," "I will be that which I will be," or "I will be there with you in the way that I will be there with you."

MINDFUL OF THE COVENANT זוֹכֵר הַבְּרִית. The phrase is used in the Torah when God promises Noah that the world will never again be destroyed and points to the rainbow as a symbol of that eternal covenant.

I Believe

I assert with absolute faith
that prayers preceded God.
Prayers created God.
God created humans.
Humans create prayers
that create God who creates humanity.

—YEHUDA AMICHAI
(trans. Edward Feld)

Belief

Sometimes the atheist looking out of the window sees more of God than all who pray in the synagogue or church.

—MARTIN BUBER

OUR BELIEF: A PIYYUT

א

God upholds the standard of justice.
We believe that God is faithful.
God examines the store of our hidden thoughts.
We believe that God knows our deepest feelings.
God redeems us from death, saves us from the grave.
We believe that God is the steadfast redeemer.

Ha-oḥeiz b'yad middat mishpat.
V'khol ma·aminim she-hu El emunah,
ha-boḥein u-vodeik ginzei nistarot.
V'khol ma·aminim she-hu boḥein k'layot,
ha-go·el mi-mavet u-fodeh mi-shaḥat.
V'khol ma·aminim she-hu go·el ḥazak,

ב

God is the sole judge of all that lives on earth.
We believe that God is the judge of truth.
God's name is a promise of the future.
We believe that God is eternal.
God is unwavering; so is God known and such is God's glory.
We believe that there is none beside God.

ha-dan y'ḥidi l'va·ei olam.
V'khol ma·aminim she-hu dayyan emet,
he-haguy b'ehyeh asher ehyeh.
V'khol ma·aminim she-hu hayah hoveh v'yihyeh,
ha-vaddai sh'mo kein t'hillato.
V'khol ma·aminim she-hu v'ein bilto,

ג

God considers the good of all those who keep God in mind.
We believe that God is mindful of the covenant.
God carves out the lifespan of all that is alive.
We believe that God is living and eternal.
God's goodness flows to the deserving and to the undeserving.
We believe that God is good to all.

ha-zokheir l'mazkirav tovot zikhronot.
V'khol ma·aminim she-hu zokheir ha-b'rit,
ha-ḥoteikh ḥayyim l'khol ḥai.
V'khol ma·aminim she-hu ḥai v'kayyam,
ha-tov u-meitiv la-ra·im v'la-tovim.
V'khol ma·aminim she-hu tov la-kol.

ד

הַיּוֹדֵעַ יֵצֶר כָּל־יְצוּרִים.

וְכֹל מַאֲמִינִים שֶׁהוּא יוֹצְרָם בַּבֶּטֶן,

הַכֹּל יָכוֹל וְכוֹלְלָם יָחַד.

וְכֹל מַאֲמִינִים שֶׁהוּא כֹּל יָכוֹל,

הַלָּן בְּסֵתֶר בְּצֵל, שַׁדַּי.

וְכֹל מַאֲמִינִים שֶׁהוּא לְבַדּוֹ הוּא,

ה

הַמַּמְלִיךְ מְלָכִים וְלוֹ הַמְּלוּכָה.

וְכֹל מַאֲמִינִים שֶׁהוּא מֶלֶךְ עוֹלָם,

הַנּוֹהֵג בְּחַסְדּוֹ כָּל־דּוֹר.

וְכֹל מַאֲמִינִים שֶׁהוּא נוֹצֵר חֶסֶד,

הַסּוֹבֵל וּמַעְלִים עַיִן מִסּוֹרְרִים.

וְכֹל מַאֲמִינִים שֶׁהוּא סוֹלֵחַ סֶלָה,

ו

הָעֶלְיוֹן וְעֵינוֹ אֶל יְרֵאָיו.

וְכֹל מַאֲמִינִים שֶׁהוּא עוֹנֶה לָחַשׁ,

הַפּוֹתֵחַ שַׁעַר לְדוֹפְקֵי בִתְשׁוּבָה.

וְכֹל מַאֲמִינִים שֶׁהוּא פְּתוּחָה יָדוֹ,

הַצּוֹפֶה לָרָשָׁע וְחָפֵץ בְּהִצָּדְקוֹ.

וְכֹל מַאֲמִינִים שֶׁהוּא צַדִּיק וְיָשָׁר,

GOD'S DWELLING PLACE IS HIDDEN הַלָּן בְּסֵתֶר בְּצֵל, שַׁדַּי. The poet plays on a verse from Psalms (91:1) which refers to humans resting in the mystery of God's protecting love, in the hidden places, in God's shadow. The poet cleverly places a comma before the Hebrew word "God" and thus transforms the meaning of the verse, making God the subject, not the object. Thus it is God, not the devotee, who resides in secret places.

GOD'S LOVE IS SURE נוֹצֵר חֶסֶד. The phrase is from the Thirteen Attributes, where God is described as "reassuring love to thousands of generations" (Exodus 34:7).

ADONAI SHALL BE ACKNOWLEDGED SOVEREIGN וְהָיָה יהוה לְמֶלֶךְ. Zechariah 14:9.

Doubt

God is the Unseen One —no image can capture God. Equally, then, God is the One about whom no descriptive words can truly be uttered—that may be the secret of the Jewish sensibility which makes the four-letter name of God unpronounceable.

There are moments—singular or common, depending perhaps on our personality—when we might feel the presence of God, and certainly others when our reality—tragic, joyous, uneventful—is so overwhelmingly with us that even the idea of God seems distant, perhaps ludicrous. And then there are those moments of aloneness when the world seems barren and the idea of God seems distant, even absurd. The person of faith knows that presence and absence are equally true of the experience of God. Sometimes God feels so close that one experiences the presence of an intimate companion, but the obverse is also true. And in those moments of absence, we question whether the experience of presence was only a delusion.

To have faith is also to know doubt. The person of faith knows that the atheist is not a person who is bullheaded, unseeing, but rather someone who has exclusively experienced the absence which is the lot of even the person of faith. Both faithfulness to God and denial tell of our human reality. When the person of faith is in touch with the depth of his or her spiritual and rational consciousness, one knows that one's heart contains both truths. What are we to do, then, other than to live faithfully, with doubt?

ד

God knows the nature of all creatures.
We believe that God fashioned us in the womb.
God's power is limitless, fashioning all that is.
We believe that God is infinitely powerful.
God's dwelling-place is hidden, beyond the heavens.
We believe that God is incomparable.

ha-yodei·a yeitzer kol y'tzurim.
V'khol ma·aminim she-hu yotz'ram ba-baten,
ha-kol yakhol v'khol'lam yaḥad.
V'khol ma·aminim she-hu kol yakhol,
ha-lan b'seiter b'tzeil shaddai.
V'khol ma·aminim she-hu l'vado hu,

ה

God is the supreme Ruler of all.
We believe that God is the Sovereign of time and space.
God acts with love in each generation.
We believe that God's love is sure.
God is patient, even overlooking the sins of those who are rebellious.
We believe that God is constantly forgiving.

ha-mamlikh m'lakhim v'lo ha-m'lukhah.
V'khol ma·aminim she-hu melekh olam,
ha-noheig b'ḥasdo kol dor.
V'khol ma·aminim she-hu notzeir ḥased,
ha-soveil u-ma·lim ayin mi-sor'rim.
V'khol ma·aminim she-hu solei·aḥ selah,

ו

God looks down from above, watching over the faithful.
We believe that God responds even to our silent prayers.
God opens a gate for those who approach in repentance.
We believe that God's arms are always open.
God awaits the repentance of those who have been sinful.
We believe that God is just and upright.

ha-elyon v'eino el y'rei·av.
V'khol ma·aminim she-hu oneh laḥash,
ha-potei·aḥ sha·ar l'dof'kei bi-t'shuvah.
V'khol ma·aminim she-hu p'tuḥah yado,
ha-tzofeh la-rasha v'ḥafeitz b'hitzad'ko.
V'khol ma·aminim she-hu tzaddik v'yashar,

הַקָּצָר בְּזַעַם וּמַאֲרִיךְ אַף.

וְכָל מַאֲמִינִים שֶׁהוּא קָשֶׁה לִכְעוֹס,

הָרַחוּם וּמַקְדִּים רַחֲמִים לָרְגֶז.

וְכָל מַאֲמִינִים שֶׁהוּא רַךְ לִרְצוֹת,

הַשָּׁוֶה וּמַשְׁוֶה קָטֹן וְגָדוֹל.

וְכָל מַאֲמִינִים שֶׁהוּא שׁוֹפֵט צֶדֶק,

הַתָּם וּמִתַּמֵּם עִם תְּמִימִים.

וְכָל מַאֲמִינִים שֶׁהוּא תָּמִים פָּעֳלוֹ.

תִּשְׂגַּב לְבַדֶּךָ, וְתִמְלֹךְ עַל כֹּל בְּיִחוּד, כַּכָּתוּב עַל יַד
נְבִיאֶךָ: וְהָיָה יהוה לְמֶלֶךְ עַל כָּל־הָאָרֶץ, בַּיּוֹם הַהוּא
יִהְיֶה יהוה אֶחָד וּשְׁמוֹ אֶחָד.

וּבְכֵן תֵּן פַּחְדְּךָ יהוה אֱלֹהֵינוּ עַל כָּל־מַעֲשֶׂיךָ,
וְאֵימָתְךָ עַל כָּל־מַה־שֶּׁבָּרָאתָ,
וְיִירָאוּךָ כָּל־הַמַּעֲשִׂים
וְיִשְׁתַּחֲווּ לְפָנֶיךָ כָּל־הַבְּרוּאִים,
וְיֵעָשׂוּ כֻלָּם אֲגֻדָּה אַחַת לַעֲשׂוֹת רְצוֹנְךָ בְּלֵבָב שָׁלֵם,
כְּמוֹ שֶׁיָּדַעְנוּ יהוה אֱלֹהֵינוּ,
שֶׁהַשִּׁלְטוֹן לְפָנֶיךָ, עֹז בְּיָדְךָ וּגְבוּרָה בִּימִינֶךָ,
וְשִׁמְךָ נוֹרָא עַל כָּל־מַה־שֶּׁבָּרָאתָ.

וּבְכֵן תֵּן כָּבוֹד יהוה לְעַמֶּךָ,
תְּהִלָּה לִירֵאֶיךָ וְתִקְוָה לְדוֹרְשֶׁיךָ,
וּפִתְחוֹן פֶּה לַמְיַחֲלִים לָךְ,
שִׂמְחָה לְאַרְצֶךָ וְשָׂשׂוֹן לְעִירֶךָ,
וּצְמִיחַת קֶרֶן לְדָוִד עַבְדֶּךָ,
וַעֲרִיכַת נֵר לְבֶן־יִשַׁי מְשִׁיחֶךָ, בִּמְהֵרָה בְיָמֵינוּ.

וּבְכֵן צַדִּיקִים יִרְאוּ וְיִשְׂמָחוּ,
וִישָׁרִים יַעֲלֹזוּ,
וַחֲסִידִים בְּרִנָּה יָגִילוּ,
וְעוֹלָתָה תִּקְפָּץ־פִּיהָ,
וְכָל־הָרִשְׁעָה כֻּלָּהּ כְּעָשָׁן תִּכְלֶה,
כִּי תַעֲבִיר מֶמְשֶׁלֶת זָדוֹן מִן הָאָרֶץ.

U-V'KHEIN וּבְכֵן. These three
paragraphs, which are
introduced by the same
word, וּבְכֵן (u-v'khein), are
ascribed by many scholars
to the 3rd century, and
may constitute the earliest
poetic additions to the
Amidah.

  Stages of redemption are
described in this series of
prayers. The first paragraph
implores God to cause the
entire world to live with
reverence for God. The
next paragraph discusses
not the universal, but the
particular: the return of
Israel to its land (and specifically to Jerusalem) and
the kingship of David. The
third paragraph describes
the rejoicing that will come
to the righteous "when You
remove the tyranny of arrogance from the earth" and
God will rule alone over the
entire world from Zion and
Jerusalem.
(adapted from Reuven Hammer)

Sin and Repentence

Every sin, even the least egregious, plants within a person a dislike or hatred for some aspect of existence. *T'shuvah* allows love to shine again. When a person sins, he or she enters the world of separation; reality is comprehended as a series of isolated moments. In that vision, evil is a thing in itself; it has a negative, destructive value. But when one does *t'shuvah* out of love, then immediately there sparks within that person the light of the world of unity, in which everything is seen as a single organism. In this transcendent vision, the sinful act becomes a motivation for good, an instrument of transformation. In this perspective, transgressions become virtues.

—ABRAHAM ISAAC KOOK
(*adapted*)

God is patient, holding back wrath.
We believe that it is difficult to arouse God's fury.
God is kind, replacing anger with love.
We believe that it is easy to secure God's favor.
God is the One before whom all are equal.
We believe that God is a righteous judge.
God is blameless and deals righteously with the faithful.
We believe that God's ways are perfect.

ha-katzar b'za·am u-ma·arikh af.
V'khol ma·aminim she-hu kasheh likh·os,
ha-rahum u-makdim rahamim la-rogez.
V'khol ma·aminim she-hu rakh lirtzot,
ha-shaveh u-mashveh katon v'gadol.
V'khol ma·aminim she-hu shofeit tzedek,
ha-tam u-mittameim im t'mimim.
V'khol ma·aminim she-hu tamim po·alo.

Alone, exalted, may You rule over a united humanity, as the prophet Zechariah said, "ADONAI shall be acknowledged sovereign of all the earth. On that day, ADONAI shall be one and the name of God, one."

U-v'khein—ADONAI our God, instill Your awe in all You have made, and fear of You in all You have created, so that all You have fashioned revere You, all You have created bow in recognition, and all be bound together, carrying out Your will wholeheartedly. For we know that true sovereignty is Yours, power and strength are in Your hands, and Your name is to be revered beyond any of Your creations.

U-v'khein—Bestow honor to Your people, ADONAI,
praise to those who revere You, hope to those who seek You,
recognition to those who await You, joy to Your land, and
gladness to Your city.
Simhah l'artzekha v'sason l'irekha
May the light of David, Your servant, dawn, and the lamp of the
son of Jesse, Your anointed, be kindled speedily in our day.

U-v'khein—The righteous, beholding this, will rejoice, the
upright will be glad, the pious will celebrate with song,
evil will be silenced, and all wickedness will disappear like
smoke, when You remove the tyranny of arrogance from the
earth.

וְיֶאֱתָיוּ כֹל לְעָבְדֶֽךָ,
וִיבָרְכוּ שֵׁם כְּבוֹדֶֽךָ,
וְיַגִּֽידוּ בָאִיִּים צִדְקֶֽךָ,
וְיִדְרְשֽׁוּךָ עַמִּים לֹא יְדָעֽוּךָ,
וִיהַלְלֽוּךָ כָּל־אַפְסֵי אָֽרֶץ,
וְיֹאמְרוּ תָמִיד יִגְדַּל יהוה.
וְיִזְנְחוּ אֶת־עֲצַבֵּיהֶם,
וְיַחְפְּרוּ עִם פְּסִילֵיהֶם.
וְיַטּֽוּ שְׁכֶם אֶחָד לְעָבְדֶֽךָ,
וְיִירָאֽוּךָ עִם שֶֽׁמֶשׁ מְבַקְשֵׁי פָנֶֽיךָ,
וְיַכִּֽירוּ כֹּֽחַ מַלְכוּתֶֽךָ,
וִילַמְּדוּ תוֹעִים בִּינָה.
וִימַלְלוּ אֶת־גְּבוּרָתֶֽךָ,
וִינַשְּׂאֽוּךָ מִתְנַשֵּׂא לְכֹל לְרֹאשׁ,
וִיסַלְּדוּ בְחִילָה פָנֶֽיךָ,
וִיעַטְּרֽוּךָ נֵֽזֶר תִּפְאָרָה.
וְיִפְצְחוּ הָרִים רִנָּה,
וְיִצְהֲלוּ אִיִּים בְּמָלְכֶֽךָ,
וִיקַבְּלוּ עֹל מַלְכוּתְךָ עֲלֵיהֶם,
וִירוֹמְמֽוּךָ בִּקְהַל עָם.
וְיִשְׁמְעוּ רְחוֹקִים וְיָבֹֽאוּ,
וְיִתְּנוּ לְךָ כֶּֽתֶר מְלוּכָה.

AND ALL SHALL COME TO SERVE YOU וְיֶאֱתָיוּ. This alphabetic *piyyut* further elaborates the theme spelled out in the next paragraph of this *b'rakhah*, looking toward God's exclusive reign in the messianic era. It plays on biblical verses which foretell the praise of God in the end of days. Some see in it references to the Roman iconoclastic uprising of the 7th century (e.g., "their idols overthrown"), which must have struck the Jews as a partial fulfillment of biblical prophecies. Solomon Schechter (1847–1915) wrote: "How one would like to catch a glimpse of that early hymnologist to whom we owe the well-known *piyyut*, *V'ye·etayu*. In its iconoclastic victory of monotheism over all kinds of idolatries, ancient as well as modern, it might best be described as the Marsellaise of the people of the Lord of Hosts—a Marsellaise which is not followed by a reign of terror but by the Kingdom of God on earth, when the upright shall exult and the saints triumphantly rejoice."

וְתִמְלֹךְ, אַתָּה יהוה לְבַדֶּֽךָ, עַל כָּל־מַעֲשֶֽׂיךָ,
בְּהַר צִיּוֹן מִשְׁכַּן כְּבוֹדֶֽךָ,
וּבִירוּשָׁלַֽיִם עִיר קָדְשֶֽׁךָ, כַּכָּתוּב בְּדִבְרֵי קָדְשֶֽׁךָ:
יִמְלֹךְ יהוה לְעוֹלָם, אֱלֹהַֽיִךְ צִיּוֹן לְדֹר וָדֹר, הַלְלוּ־יָהּ.

ADONAI WILL REIGN FOREVER יִמְלֹךְ יהוה לְעוֹלָם. Psalm 146:10.

Israel Zangwill composed this poetic adaptation of the piyyut, published in the British United Synagogue Maḥzor, 1909.

¶ All the world shall come to
serve Thee
   and praise Thy glorious name,
and Thy righteousness
triumphant
       the islands shall acclaim.
And nations shall give Thee
homage
      who knew Thee not before,
and the ends of earth shall
praise Thee,
      Thy name they shall adore.
They shall build for Thee their
altars,
       their idols overthrown;
and their hands shall clasp in
friendship
     as they turn to Thee alone.
They shall bow before Thy
grandeur,
 and know Thy kingdom's might;
they shall walk in under-
standing,
     who are astray in night.
They shall exult in Thy
greatness,
     and of Thy power speak,
and extol Thee, shrined,
uplifted
    beyond man's highest peak.
And with reverential homage,
   of love and wonder born,
with the ruler's crown of beauty
    Thy head they shall adorn.
With the coming of Thy
kingdom
   the hills shall break into song,
and the islands laugh exultant
    that they to God belong.
All their congregations
   so loud Thy praise shall sing,
that faraway peoples, hearing,
  shall come and hail Thee King.

THE DREAM OF UNIVERSAL REDEMPTION: A PIYYUT

And all shall come to serve You,
praising Your honored name,
proclaiming Your just rule in every island.
Nations that knew You not will seek You,
even those that live at the ends of the earth will laud You,
constantly proclaiming, "God is great."
They shall put away their idols,
bury their icons,
and come as one to serve You.
At the rising of the sun,
those who seek You will be inspired with awe,
and those in error will recognize the power of Your
   sovereignty
and learn wisdom.
They will speak of Your salvation,
exalting You above all.
Trembling, they shall greet You,
crowning You with a crown of glory.
Acceding to Your rule,
mountains will burst with song,
and islands rejoice in Your sovereignty.
You will be extolled in the gathering of nations,
as distant people will journey
to crown You as Sovereign.

V'ye·etayu kol l'ovdekha, vivar'khu shem k'vodekha,
v'yaggidu va-iyyim tzidkekha, v'yidr'shukha ammim lo y'da·ukha,
vihal'lukha kol afsei aretz, v'yom'ru tamid yigdal Adonai.
V'yizn'ḥu et-atzabeihem, v'yaḥp'ru im p'sileihem.
V'yattu sh'khem eḥad l'ovdekha, v'yira·ukha im
  shemesh m'vak'shei fanekha,
V'yakkiru ko·aḥ malkhutekha, vilam'du to·im binah.
Vimal'lu et-g'vuratekha, vinas'ukha mitnassei l'khol l'rosh,
visal'du v'ḥilah fanekha, vi·at'rukha nezer tifarah.
V'yiftz'ḥu harim rinnah, v'yitz'halu iyim v'molkhekha,
vikab'lu ol malkhut'kha aleihem, virom'mukha bi-k'hal am.
V'yishm'u r'ḥokim v'yavo·u, v'yit'nu l'kha keter m'lukhah.

You alone, ADONAI, will rule all Your creation, from Mount Zion, the dwelling-place of Your glory, and from Jerusalem, Your holy city. As it is written in the Book of Psalms: "ADONAI will reign forever; your God, O Zion, from generation to generation. Halleluyah!"

Yimlokh Adonai l'olam, elohayikh tziyyon l'dor va-dor hal'luyah.

ADONAI TZV'VA·OT WILL
BE VINDICATED וְיִגְבַּה
.יהוה צְבָאוֹת בַּמִּשְׁפָּט
Isaiah 5:16.

קָדוֹשׁ אַתָּה וְנוֹרָא שְׁמֶךָ, וְאֵין אֱלֽוֹהַּ מִבַּלְעָדֶֽיךָ, כַּכָּתוּב:
וַיִּגְבַּה יהוה צְבָאוֹת בַּמִּשְׁפָּט, וְהָאֵל הַקָּדוֹשׁ נִקְדַּשׁ
בִּצְדָקָה. בָּרוּךְ אַתָּה יהוה, הַמֶּֽלֶךְ הַקָּדוֹשׁ.

אַתָּה בְחַרְתָּנוּ מִכָּל־הָעַמִּים, אָהַבְתָּ אוֹתָֽנוּ וְרָצִֽיתָ בָּֽנוּ,
וְרוֹמַמְתָּֽנוּ מִכָּל־הַלְּשׁוֹנוֹת, וְקִדַּשְׁתָּֽנוּ בְּמִצְוֺתֶֽיךָ,
וְקֵרַבְתָּֽנוּ מַלְכֵּֽנוּ לַעֲבוֹדָתֶֽךָ,
וְשִׁמְךָ הַגָּדוֹל וְהַקָּדוֹשׁ עָלֵֽינוּ קָרָֽאתָ.

וַתִּתֶּן־לָֽנוּ, יהוה אֱלֹהֵֽינוּ, בְּאַהֲבָה אֶת־יוֹם [הַשַּׁבָּת הַזֶּה
לִקְדֻשָּׁה וְלִמְנוּחָה וְאֶת־יוֹם] הַכִּפּוּרִים הַזֶּה לִמְחִילָה
וְלִסְלִיחָה וּלְכַפָּרָה, וְלִמְחָל־בּוֹ אֶת־כָּל־עֲוֺנוֹתֵֽינוּ [בְּאַהֲבָה]
מִקְרָא קֹֽדֶשׁ, זֵֽכֶר לִיצִיאַת מִצְרָֽיִם.

*Some recite this traditional version; others continue on the next page with
A Prayer for Jewry in Distress.*

BECAUSE OF OUR SINS
מִפְּנֵי חֲטָאֵֽינוּ. The first
of the middle b'rakhot
of the Amidah is called
קְדֻשַּׁת הַיּוֹם (k'dushat
ha-yom), the expres-
sion of the holiness of
the day. The content
of this b'rakhah is
not prescribed in the
Talmud. During the first
millennium, the prayer
concerning the holiness
of the day came to be
centered on the Temple
and its offerings, as if
the utterance of the
words substituted for
the missing sacrifices.
Recently, some have
begun reciting alternate
prayers, which under-
stand the rebuilding
of the Temple as a
metaphor for the repair
of the world in which
we all need to engage.
(See the following page.)

וּמִפְּנֵי חֲטָאֵֽינוּ גָּלִֽינוּ מֵאַרְצֵֽנוּ וְנִתְרַחַֽקְנוּ מֵעַל אַדְמָתֵֽנוּ
וְאֵין אֲנַֽחְנוּ יְכוֹלִים לַעֲשׂוֹת חוֹבוֹתֵֽינוּ בְּבֵית בְּחִירָתֶֽךָ, בַּבַּֽיִת
הַגָּדוֹל וְהַקָּדוֹשׁ שֶׁנִּקְרָא שִׁמְךָ עָלָיו, מִפְּנֵי הַיָּד שֶׁנִּשְׁתַּלְּחָה
בְּמִקְדָּשֶֽׁךָ.

יְהִי רָצוֹן מִלְּפָנֶֽיךָ, יהוה אֱלֹהֵֽינוּ וֵאלֹהֵי אֲבוֹתֵֽינוּ [וְאִמּוֹתֵֽינוּ],
מֶֽלֶךְ רַחֲמָן הַמֵּשִׁיב בָּנִים לִגְבוּלָם, שֶׁתָּשׁוּב וּתְרַחֵם עָלֵֽינוּ
וְעַל מִקְדָּשְׁךָ בְּרַחֲמֶֽיךָ הָרַבִּים, וְתִבְנֵֽהוּ מְהֵרָה וּתְגַדֵּל
כְּבוֹדוֹ. אָבִֽינוּ מַלְכֵּֽנוּ, גַּלֵּה כְּבוֹד מַלְכוּתְךָ עָלֵֽינוּ מְהֵרָה,
וְהוֹפַע וְהִנָּשֵׂא עָלֵֽינוּ לְעֵינֵי כָּל־חָי, **וְקָרֵב פְּזוּרֵֽינוּ מִבֵּין
הַגּוֹיִם וּנְפוּצוֹתֵֽינוּ כַּנֵּס מִיַּרְכְּתֵי־אָֽרֶץ.**

וַהֲבִיאֵֽנוּ לְצִיּוֹן עִירְךָ בְּרִנָּה, וְלִירוּשָׁלַֽיִם בֵּית מִקְדָּשְׁךָ
בְּשִׂמְחַת עוֹלָם, שֶׁשָּׁם עָשׂוּ אֲבוֹתֵֽינוּ [וְאִמּוֹתֵֽינוּ] לְפָנֶֽיךָ אֶת־
קָרְבְּנוֹת חוֹבוֹתֵיהֶם, תְּמִידִים כְּסִדְרָם וּמוּסָפִים כְּהִלְכָתָם,

ON SHABBAT: וְאֶת־מוּסְפֵי יוֹם הַשַּׁבָּת הַזֶּה וְיוֹם הַכִּפּוּרִים הַזֶּה

On other days: וְאֶת־מוּסַף יוֹם הַכִּפּוּרִים הַזֶּה

On all days: עָשׂוּ וְהִקְרִֽיבוּ לְפָנֶֽיךָ בְּאַהֲבָה כְּמִצְוַת רְצוֹנֶֽךָ
כַּכָּתוּב בְּתוֹרָתֶֽךָ, עַל יְדֵי מֹשֶׁה עַבְדֶּֽךָ מִפִּי כְבוֹדֶֽךָ כָּאָמוּר:

You Alone, Adonai,
Will Rule

To long for the kingship
of God is to hope that the
image of God inscribed
in each person will be
recognized by each of us.
Recognizing that we are
all connected, that we are
dependent on one anoth-
er, and that we are called
to appreciate the special
qualities each of us brings
into the world is to gain
insight into the infinity
of God. We acknowledge
God as the only ultimate
authority, as our only
sovereign, when we help
the weak and the poor,
when we pursue justice,
when we come to love all
of creation. The servants
of God are those who
join in this process of
redemption.

You are holy, and Your name is revered, for there is no God but You. As Your prophet Isaiah wrote: "*Adonai Tz'va·ot* will be exalted through justice, the holy God sanctified through righteousness." *Barukh atah* ADONAI, the Holy Sovereign.

Fourth B'rakhah: The Holiness of Yom Kippur

You have chosen us among all peoples,
loving us, wanting us.
You have distinguished us among all nations,
making us holy through Your commandments,
drawing us close to Your service,
and calling us by Your great and holy name.

With love, You have bestowed on us, ADONAI our God, this [Shabbat, for sanctity and rest, and this] Yom Kippur for pardon, forgiveness, and atonement, that all our sins be forgiven [through Your love], a sacred time, recalling the Exodus from Egypt.

Some recite this traditional version; others continue on the next page with A Prayer for Jewry in Distress.

Because of our sins we have been exiled from our land and removed from our soil. And so, because of the hand which was set against Your sanctuary, we are unable to fulfill our obligations in that great and holy place which You chose to carry Your name.

May it be Your will, ADONAI our God and God of our ancestors, compassionate Sovereign who restores their descendants to their promised land, that You may once again have compassion on us and return in Your great mercy to Your sanctuary. May You speedily rebuild it and renew its glory. *Avinu Malkeinu*, speedily manifest the glory of Your dominion, reveal to all humanity that You are our sovereign. Gather our dispersed people from among the nations, and bring back those scattered to the ends of the earth.
v'kareiv p'zureinu mi-bein ha-goyim u-n'futzoteinu kanneis mi-yark'tei aretz.

Welcome back our dispersed from among the nations, and gather those scattered to the ends of the earth. Bring us exultantly to Zion, Your city, and with everlasting joy to Jerusalem Your sanctuary, where our ancestors once offered to You their obligatory daily and holy day sacrifices, each as prescribed. The [Shabbat and] Day of Atonement sacrifices were offered there in love, as You commanded, as it is written in Your Torah by Moses, Your servant, by Your instruction:

On Shabbat, those reciting the traditional sacrificial list add this paragraph:

וּבְיוֹם הַשַּׁבָּת שְׁנֵי כְבָשִׂים בְּנֵי שָׁנָה תְּמִימִם, וּשְׁנֵי
עֶשְׂרוֹנִים סֹלֶת מִנְחָה בְּלוּלָה בַשֶּׁמֶן וְנִסְכּוֹ: עֹלַת שַׁבַּת
בְּשַׁבַּתּוֹ, עַל עֹלַת הַתָּמִיד וְנִסְכָּהּ: במדבר כח ט-י

וּבֶעָשׂוֹר לַחֹדֶשׁ הַשְּׁבִיעִי הַזֶּה מִקְרָא־קֹדֶשׁ יִהְיֶה
לָכֶם וְעִנִּיתֶם אֶת־נַפְשֹׁתֵיכֶם כָּל־מְלָאכָה לֹא
תַעֲשׂוּ: וְהִקְרַבְתֶּם עֹלָה לַיהוה רֵיחַ נִיחֹחַ פַּר בֶּן־בָּקָר
אֶחָד אַיִל אֶחָד כְּבָשִׂים בְּנֵי־שָׁנָה שִׁבְעָה תְּמִימִם יִהְיוּ
לָכֶם: במדבר כט ז-ח

וּמִנְחָתָם וְנִסְכֵּיהֶם כִּמְדֻבָּר, שְׁלֹשָׁה עֶשְׂרֹנִים לַפָּר וּשְׁנֵי
עֶשְׂרֹנִים לָאַיִל וְעִשָּׂרוֹן לַכֶּבֶשׂ, וְיַיִן כְּנִסְכּוֹ, וּשְׁנֵי שְׂעִירִים
לְכַפֵּר, וּשְׁנֵי תְמִידִים כְּהִלְכָתָם.

A PRAYER FOR JEWRY IN DISTRESS

אֱלֹהֵינוּ וֵאלֹהֵי אֲבוֹתֵינוּ [וְאִמּוֹתֵינוּ], רַחֵם עַל אַחֵינוּ
בֵּית יִשְׂרָאֵל הַנְּתוּנִים בְּצָרָה וְהוֹצִיאֵם מֵאֲפֵלָה לְאוֹרָה.
וְקַבֵּל בְּרַחֲמִים אֶת־תְּפִלַּת עַמְּךָ בְּנֵי יִשְׂרָאֵל, בְּכָל־
מְקוֹמוֹת מוֹשְׁבוֹתֵיהֶם, הַשּׁוֹפְכִים אֶת־לִבָּם לְפָנֶיךָ בְּיוֹם
[הַשַּׁבָּת הַזֶּה וּבְיוֹם] הַכִּפּוּרִים הַזֶּה.

Those who recited the traditional sacrificial list now continue on the next page.

יְהִי רָצוֹן מִלְּפָנֶיךָ, יהוה אֱלֹהֵינוּ וֵאלֹהֵי אֲבוֹתֵינוּ
[וְאִמּוֹתֵינוּ], שֶׁיִּבָּנֶה בֵּית הַמִּקְדָּשׁ בִּמְהֵרָה בְיָמֵינוּ,
כְּפִי שֶׁהִבְטַחְתָּנוּ עַל יְדֵי נְבִיאֶךָ, כַּכָּתוּב:
וְהָיָה בְּאַחֲרִית הַיָּמִים,
נָכוֹן יִהְיֶה הַר בֵּית יהוה בְּרֹאשׁ הֶהָרִים וְנִשָּׂא מִגְּבָעוֹת,
וְנָהֲרוּ אֵלָיו כָּל־הַגּוֹיִם.
וְהָלְכוּ עַמִּים רַבִּים וְאָמְרוּ,
לְכוּ וְנַעֲלֶה אֶל הַר יהוה, אֶל בֵּית אֱלֹהֵי יַעֲקֹב,
וְיֹרֵנוּ מִדְּרָכָיו, וְנֵלְכָה בְּאֹרְחֹתָיו.
כִּי מִצִּיּוֹן תֵּצֵא תוֹרָה וּדְבַר יהוה מִירוּשָׁלָיִם.
וְשָׁפַט בֵּין הַגּוֹיִם וְהוֹכִיחַ לְעַמִּים רַבִּים,
וְכִתְּתוּ חַרְבוֹתָם לְאִתִּים וַחֲנִיתוֹתֵיהֶם לְמַזְמֵרוֹת,
לֹא יִשָּׂא גוֹי אֶל גּוֹי חֶרֶב וְלֹא יִלְמְדוּ עוֹד מִלְחָמָה.

MAY IT BE YOUR WILL יְהִי רָצוֹן. From *Siddur Va'ani Tefilati*, the prayerbook of the Masorti (Conservative) movement in Israel. This acknowledges the Jewish people's having returned to the Land of Israel. (The more traditional wording speaks of the exile, our inability to perform the Temple sacrifices, and the hope of return.)

AND IT SHALL COME TO PASS וְהָיָה בְּאַחֲרִית הַיָּמִים. Isaiah 2:2–4. Most contemporary biblical scholars think that this phrase points to the indefinite future. Classical exegetes thought of it as referring to a messianic end-time. This vision of universal peace is inscribed as the watchword of the United Nations.

LET US GO UP לְכוּ וְנַעֲלֶה. Isaiah's vision of universal religious unity.

INSTRUCTION SHALL GO FORTH תֵּצֵא תוֹרָה. The word *torah*, translated here as "instruction," can be understood in its widest sense: all that is right and true. Jewish mystics understood the verse as referring to a future divine revelation.

Our Sacrifice

Our worship is one of prayer and praise. But when we think of the piety of our ancestors, who from their meager store of cattle and grain, the yield of the shepherd's care and the farmer's toil, offered their best in the service of God, can we be content with a gift of mere words that costs us neither labor nor privation? Shall we not feel impelled to devote of our substance to the service of God? Shall we not give of our store to the relief of suffering, the healing of sickness, the dispelling of ignorance and error, the righting of wrongs and the strengthening of faith?

—MORDECAI KAPLAN
AND EUGENE KOHN
(adapted)

On Shabbat, those reciting the traditional sacrificial list add this paragraph:

On Shabbat: two yearling lambs without blemish, together with two-tenths of a measure of choice flour with oil mixed in as a grain offering, and with the proper libation. A burnt offering for every Shabbat, in addition to the regular burnt offering and its libation.   Numbers 28:9–10

On the tenth day of the seventh month, you shall observe a sacred occasion: you shall practice self-denial; you shall not work at your occupations. You shall prepare a burnt offering as a pleasing odor to ADONAI: one bull of the herd, one ram, seven yearling lambs, without blemish.   Numbers 29:7–8

As ordained, they shall be accompanied by grain offerings and by libations: three-tenths of a measure for the bull, two-tenths for the ram, one-tenth for each lamb, wine for its libation, two goats for expiation, and the two daily offerings as is their custom.

A PRAYER FOR JEWRY IN DISTRESS

Our God and God of our ancestors, show compassion to our brothers and sisters of the House of Israel, who suffer persecution; deliver them from darkness to light. Accept with compassion the prayers of Your people Israel who cry out to You on [this Shabbat and] this Day of Atonement, wherever they dwell.

Those who recited the traditional sacrificial list now continue on the next page.

May it be Your will, ADONAI our God and God of our ancestors, that the Holy Temple be rebuilt speedily in our time, as You promised, in the words of Your prophet Isaiah: "And it shall come to pass, in the end of days, that the House of ADONAI will be firmly established at the top of the mountain, raised high above all other hills. All peoples shall flow toward it, and nations shall say, 'Let us go up to the mountain of ADONAI to the house of the God of Jacob, and we shall learn from God's ways and walk in God's paths.' For instruction shall go forth from Zion and the word of ADONAI from Jerusalem. God will provide proper judgment among nations and admonish many peoples. They shall beat their swords into plowshares, and spears into pruning hooks. Nation shall not take up sword against nation, neither shall they learn war anymore."

יִשְׂמְחוּ בְמַלְכוּתְךָ שׁוֹמְרֵי שַׁבָּת וְקוֹרְאֵי עְנֶג, עַם מְקַדְּשֵׁי
שְׁבִיעִי, כֻּלָּם יִשְׂבְּעוּ וְיִתְעַנְּגוּ מִטּוּבֶךָ, וּבַשְּׁבִיעִי רָצִיתָ בּוֹ
וְקִדַּשְׁתּוֹ, חֶמְדַּת יָמִים אוֹתוֹ קָרָאתָ, זֵכֶר לְמַעֲשֵׂה בְרֵאשִׁית.

The ark is opened and we rise.

עָלֵינוּ לְשַׁבֵּחַ לַאֲדוֹן הַכֹּל, לָתֵת גְּדֻלָּה לְיוֹצֵר בְּרֵאשִׁית,
שֶׁלֹּא עָשָׂנוּ כְּגוֹיֵי הָאֲרָצוֹת, וְלֹא שָׂמָנוּ כְּמִשְׁפְּחוֹת
הָאֲדָמָה, שֶׁלֹּא שָׂם חֶלְקֵנוּ כָּהֶם, וְגֹרָלֵנוּ כְּכָל־הֲמוֹנָם.
וַאֲנַחְנוּ כּוֹרְעִים וּמִשְׁתַּחֲוִים וּמוֹדִים,
לִפְנֵי מֶלֶךְ, מַלְכֵי הַמְּלָכִים, הַקָּדוֹשׁ בָּרוּךְ הוּא.
שֶׁהוּא נוֹטֶה שָׁמַיִם וְיֹסֵד אָרֶץ, וּמוֹשַׁב יְקָרוֹ בַּשָּׁמַיִם מִמַּעַל,
וּשְׁכִינַת עֻזּוֹ בְּגָבְהֵי מְרוֹמִים, הוּא אֱלֹהֵינוּ אֵין עוֹד. אֱמֶת
מַלְכֵּנוּ אֶפֶס זוּלָתוֹ, כַּכָּתוּב בְּתוֹרָתוֹ: וְיָדַעְתָּ הַיּוֹם וַהֲשֵׁבֹתָ
אֶל־לְבָבֶךָ, כִּי יהוה הוּא הָאֱלֹהִים בַּשָּׁמַיִם מִמַּעַל וְעַל
הָאָרֶץ מִתָּחַת, אֵין עוֹד.

The ark is closed.

Congregation recites:

אֱלֹהֵינוּ וֵאלֹהֵי אֲבוֹתֵינוּ [וְאִמּוֹתֵינוּ], הֱיֵה עִם פִּיפִיּוֹת
שְׁלוּחֵי עַמְּךָ בֵּית יִשְׂרָאֵל, הָעוֹמְדִים לְבַקֵּשׁ תְּפִלָּה
וְתַחֲנוּנִים מִלְּפָנֶיךָ עַל עַמְּךָ בֵּית יִשְׂרָאֵל.

הוֹרֵם מַה שֶׁיֹּאמֵרוּ,   הֲבִינֵם מַה שֶׁיְּדַבֵּרוּ,
הֲשִׁיבֵם מַה שֶׁיִּשְׁאָלוּ,   יָדְעֵם אֵיךְ יְפָאֵרוּ.
בְּאוֹר פָּנֶיךָ יְהַלֵּכוּן,   בְּרֵךְ לְךָ יִכְרָעוּן,
עַמְּךָ בְּפִיהֶם יְבָרְכוּן,   וּמִבִּרְכוֹת פִּיךָ כֻּלָּם יִתְבָּרְכוּן.

Reader responds:

אוֹחִילָה לָאֵל, אֲחַלֶּה פָנָיו, אֶשְׁאֲלָה מִמֶּנּוּ מַעֲנֶה לָשׁוֹן.
אֲשֶׁר בִּקְהַל עָם אָשִׁירָה עֻזּוֹ, אַבִּיעָה רְנָנוֹת בְּעַד מִפְעָלָיו.
לְאָדָם מַעַרְכֵי לֵב, וּמֵיהוה מַעֲנֵה לָשׁוֹן.
יהוה שְׂפָתַי תִּפְתָּח, וּפִי יַגִּיד תְּהִלָּתֶךָ. יִהְיוּ לְרָצוֹן אִמְרֵי
פִי וְהֶגְיוֹן לִבִּי לְפָנֶיךָ, יהוה, צוּרִי וְגֹאֲלִי.

IT IS FOR US עָלֵינוּ. Aleinu is one of the best-known and oft-repeated prayers. Its central theme is a proclamation of God's sovereignty. It was originally written for the Rosh Hashanah service, where it introduces the Kingship (*Malkhuyot*) section of the Musaf service. When the prayer forms part of the daily and weekly liturgy, one bows formally from the waist down, but on the High Holy Days we ritually reenact Temple worship—the only time of year we do so—and many prostrate themselves on the floor of the synagogue in an act of humility and in full acknowledgment of God's sovereignty.

אוֹחִילָה לָאֵל. Although at the very beginning of the Musaf service the leader has asked God's help in leading the congregation in prayer, it was felt that another such prayer was needed before beginning the special sections of the Musaf Amidah: the *Avodah* (the service of the High Priest on the Day of Atonement) and the *Eilleh Ezk'rah* (the recounting of Jewish suffering). This *piyyut* was written in the first millennium and appears not only in the Ashkenazic tradition but in the Sephardic tradition as well, where it precedes the Amidah.

Aleinu

For the Rabbis who wrote the *Aleinu* prayer, God's sovereignty was contrasted with the rule of Rome, which they identified with the biblical Esau. Jacob/Israel is to seek God's sovereignty in this world; Rome/Esau seeks its own glory, wars against other peoples to subjugate them, revels in material existence, lives off the work of slave labor, allows many to die of poverty and starvation, and promotes entertaining circuses composed of gladiator fights in which humans are condemned to death. The Rabbis, picturing redemption, remark that the messianic age can be recognized when an end is brought to the rule of wickedness.

—SOLOMON SCHECHTER

ON SHABBAT, WE RECITE THIS PARAGRAPH:

Those who observe Shabbat and call it a delight rejoice in Your sovereignty. May the people who sanctify the seventh day be fulfilled and delighted with Your abundant goodness. You have loved the seventh day and sanctified it, calling it the treasured day, a sign of creation.

Yism'ḥu v'malkhut'kha shom'rei shabbat v'kor'ei oneg, am m'kad'shei sh'vi·i, kullam yisb'u v'yit·an'gu mi-tuvekha, u-va-sh'vi·i ratzita bo v'kiddashto, ḥemdat yamim oto karata, zeikher l'ma·aseih v'reishit.

The ark is opened and we rise.

Introduction to the Special Sections of Musaf

It is for us to praise the Ruler of all, to acclaim the Creator, who has not made us merely a nation, nor formed us as all earthly families, nor given us an ordinary destiny.

⨍ And so we bow, acknowledging the Supreme Sovereign, the Holy One, who is praised, the One who spreads out the heavens and establishes the earth, whose glorious abode is in the highest heaven, whose powerful presence is in the loftiest heights. This is our God, none else; ours is the true Sovereign, there is no other. As it is written in the Torah: "Know this day and take it to heart, that ADONAI is God in heaven above and on earth below, there is no other."

The ark is closed.

Congregation recites:

Our God and God of our ancestors, be with the messengers of Your people Israel as they stand praying for the ability to plead before You, on our behalf. Teach them what to say, inspire them in their speech, respond to their requests, instruct them how to properly glorify You. May they walk in the light of Your presence, and bend their knees to You. May Your people be blessed through the words of their mouths, and may all find blessing through the blessings of Your mouth.

Reader responds:

I pray to You, God, that I may come into Your presence. Grant me proper speech, for I would sing of Your strength amidst the congregation of Your people and utter praises describing Your deeds. A person may have the best of intentions, but it is God who grants the ability of expression. ADONAI, open my lips that my mouth may declare Your glory. And may the words of my mouth and the thoughts in my heart be acceptable to You, ADONAI, my stronghold and my redeemer.

At a certain hour, on a certain day of the year, all these four
　　holinesses met together.
This took place on the Day of Atonement, at the hour when
　　the High Priest entered the Holy of Holies and there revealed
　　the divine name.
And if he invoked God's name in purity, all of Israel was forgiven.

Wherever a person stands to lift up eyes to heaven, that place is
　　a Holy of Holies.
Every human being created by God in God's own image is a
　　High Priest.
Each day of a person's life is the Day of Atonement . . .

Each one of us can face God with the language of the heart.
Each one of us can be forgiven.
Each one of us can achieve atonement and be made pure
　　in the eyes of God.

The Yiddish playwright
and ethnographer Saul
Ansky (1863–1920)
combed the hinterlands
of Eastern Europe record-
ing aspects of Jewish life.
His dramatic play *The
Dybbuk*— first performed
in 1920—was based in
part on his studies, and
the *d'var torah* given by
a Ḥasidic master at the
beginning of the play was
one he actually recorded.
This Ḥasidic teaching is
presented here to offer
an understanding of the
Avodah service we are
about to read. Anksy's
ethnographic material
was held under lock and
key by the Soviet govern-
ment and it was only in
the 1990s that some of his
findings were finally made
available to the public.

THE TEMPLE SERVICE

The Service in the Temple on the Day of Atonement

INTRODUCTION:
The world of God is great and holy.

Of all the lands of the world, the Land of Israel was set aside
    to be holy for us;
and in the Land of Israel, the holiest city is Jerusalem.
In Jerusalem, the holiest place was the Holy Temple;
and the holiest site in the Temple was the Holy of Holies . . .

Our tradition is that in the world, there are seventy nations,
    and, of them, Israel was set aside to be holy unto God.
The holiest of the people Israel is the tribe of the Levites.
The holiest of the Levites are the priests;
and among the priests, the holiest was the High Priest.

The lunar year has 354 days.
Some days are set aside as holy days.
Holier than the festivals are the Shabbatot;
And the holiest of the Shabbatot is the Day of Atonement—
    the Shabbat of Shabbatot.

There are seventy languages in the world,
and of them, Hebrew was chosen as our holy tongue.
The holiest of all things written in the Hebrew language is
    the Holy Torah.
In the Torah, the holiest part is the Ten Commandments.
And the holiest of all the words in the Ten Commandments is
    the name of God.

אַזְכִּיר גְּבוּרוֹת אֱלוֹהַּ נֶאְדָּרִי,

יָחִיד וְאֵין עוֹד, אֶפֶס וְאֵין שֵׁנִי.

אַחֲרָיו אֵין בַּחֲלֹף, לְפָנָיו אֵין בַּשַּׁחַק,

אֵין בִּלְתּוֹ קֶדֶם, זוּלָתוֹ בְּעֵקֶב.

אָדוֹן לַחֲשֹׁב, אֱלֹהִים לַעֲשׂוֹת,

נִמְלַךְ וְאֵין נֶעְדָּר, שָׂח וְאֵין מְאַחֵר.

אוֹמֵר וְעוֹשֶׂה, יוֹעֵץ וּמֵקִים,

אַמִּיץ לָשֵׂאת וְגִבּוֹר לִסְבֹּל.

אֲשֶׁר לוֹ רְנָנוֹת מִפִּי יְצוּרָיו,

מִמַּעְלָה וּמִמַּטָּה יִשָּׂא תְהִלָּה.

אֵל אֶחָד בָּאָרֶץ קָדוֹשׁ בַּשָּׁמַיִם,

מִמַּיִם רַבִּים, אַדִּיר בַּמָּרוֹם

אֶדֶר מִתְּהוֹמוֹת, שֶׁבַח מִמְּאוֹרוֹת,

אֹמֶר מִיָּמִים, לֶמֶד מְלִילוֹת;

אֵשׁ תּוֹדִיעַ שְׁמוֹ, עֲצֵי־יַעַר יְרַנֵּנוּ,

בְּהֵמָה תְלַמֵּד עֱזוּז נוֹרְאוֹתָיו...

The description of the High Priest on Yom Kippur was the first major section to be added to the Musaf Amidah after the close of the Talmud. More than 100 poetic versions of this prayer have come down to us. They usually begin with words of praise of God, a description of creation, and then detail the service of Yom Kippur in the Temple. No rite preserves the same poem as another. The version here is an anthology of three of these poems: one by Yose ben Yose, who wrote in the 5th century and was probably the first of the post-talmudic poets in the Land of Israel; a second poem written by Yoḥanan Ha-Cohen ben Yehoshua (perhaps 10th century), which is recited in the Italian rite; and a third that is commonly found in the Ashkenazic rite, written by Meshullam ben Kalonymous in the 10th century.

YOSE BEN YOSE. Few of Yose's poems were known until the Cairo Genizah brought them to light in the 20th century, after a millennium of obscurity. Yose's importance was quickly recognized. He may be credited as the father of medieval *piyyut* and is certainly one of the originators of the Avodah service. All subsequent versions ultimately owe their form to his creativity and follow the pattern he developed: a description of creation, a rehearsal of some biblical narrative history, and then a poetic description of the service in the Temple on the Day of Atonement. The poem presented here is one of three he wrote for the Avodah; it was included by Saadiah Gaon (10th century) in his siddur. Yose wrote three such poems—perhaps so that each recitation of the Amidah (in the evening, in the morning, and the later Musaf service) would include an Avodah service.

THE AVODAH SERVICE. The Temple is no more, but evoking the service in the Temple through words had the power, in the minds of the ancient authors of the synagogue service, to reenact, and thus re-create, the experience. They taught, "Instead of bulls, we will give the offering of our lips" (Pesikta of Rav Kahana). For us, too, the visualization of the Avodah can evoke the fear and trembling of that moment when Israel came closest to the Divine, achieving forgiveness and atonement. For a moment we can try to experience how the Temple ritual inspired our people.

I WOULD SPEAK OF GOD'S GREATNESS אַזְכִּיר גְּבוּרוֹת אֱלוֹהַּ (literally, "I would recall"). Thus begins the Avodah. The next section of the service, the Martyrology, begins with the words אֵלֶּה אֶזְכְּרָה, "these I recall." The High Holy Days, which begin a new year and look to the future, do so by accounting for and remembering the past, beginning with Rosh Hashanah, which is known in the Bible as יוֹם הַזִּכְרוֹן, the Day of Remembrance. In looking to the past, we recall both the high and the low points.

FROM THE CREATION OF THE WORLD TO
THE SANCTUARY IN THE DESERT

I would speak of God's greatness,
the One who is my strength,
the single One, joined by no other.
None takes precedence on earth or in the heavens,
nor is there a past or future beyond God.

Master of thought, divine in deed,
God contemplates and nothing is left out.
God commands and nothing constrains:
thought is deed,
speech and act are one.

God supports the world in strength
and bears its suffering.

The song of all that is created rises up to God,
who receives the praise of those on high and below.

This is the one God, holy in heaven, present on earth,
to whom oceans sound praise,
the deep pays tribute,
galaxies extol,
each day speaks,
and night chants;

fire pronounces God's name,
as forests sing
and animals teach
the might of God's wonders . . .

יַחַד שְׁלִישִׁי לִרְאוֹת פְּנֵי־מֶלֶךְ, לְשׁוֹרֵר, לְשָׁרֵת, לָבוֹא חֲדָרָיו...

כְּגֶפֶן אַדֶּרֶת, יְפַת פֶּרִי וְעָנָף, הִצְמִיחַ עַמְרָם מִשֹּׁרֶשׁ לֵוִי, כִּי שָׁלַח שְׁלֹשֶׁת שָׂרִיגֵי חֶמֶד: מְכַהֵן וְרוֹעֶה וְאִשָּׁה נְבִיאָה.

כְּגֶשֶׁת עֵת דּוֹדִים, פִּרְחוֹ הוּקַם לְשַׁבֵּר מוֹסְרוֹת צֹעַן, וְלִפְרֹץ גֶּדֶר שׁוּעָל.

כֻּסָּה בֶּעָנָן וְנִתְקַדַּשׁ שָׁבוּעַ, נִצָּב בַּתּוֹךְ בְּעֵת מַתַּן אֹמֶר. כֹּחַ אַדִּירִים לְפָנָיו הִכְנַע, מִמּוֹרָאוֹ לֹא עָמַד אִישׁ. כִּלְכֵּל צֹאן קֹדֶשׁ שְׁאֵר בִּישִׁימוֹן, וּמַלְחֵם שְׁחָקִים עַד בּוֹאָם לָאָרֶץ.

כָּרְתָה בְּאֵר לְעָם עַלְמָה מְתוֹפֶפֶת, גָּוְעָה וְנֶאֶסְפָה וְלֹא הָיָה מָיִם.

◁ לְוֻיֵּי עַנְוֵי הוֹד יְדִידִים נֶחֱנֵנוּ, עַל יְדֵי מְכַהֵן בְּשָׁלוֹם וּמִישׁוֹר

לוֹ וּלְזַרְעוֹ בְּרִית אֱמֶת נֶחְקָקָה, בְּלִי תְשֻׁבוֹת מֶלַח בְּרִית הַנִּיחֹחַ.

לִמְּדָם מְחוֹקֵק סִדְרֵי עֲבוֹדוֹת, כִּי בְּשִׁבְתָּם פֶּתַח עֲלֵיהֶם הִפְקָד,

לִרְחוֹץ וְלָסוּךְ, לְקַדֵּשׁ יָד וָרֶגֶל, לִלְבּוֹשׁ בַּדִּים וְלַחְגּוֹר בַּמֶּזַח,

לְמַלֵּא יָדָם שִׁבְעָה יָמִים וַיְשִׂימֶהָ לְחוֹק לְדוֹרוֹת עוֹלָם.

THREE שְׁלֶשֶׁת. Yose ben Yose bases himself on Micah 6:4 where Moses, Aaron, and Miriam are mentioned together as the three classic personages who helped save Israel. Yose adds a metered phrase to describe them: Moses, the one who could enter the inner chambers; Aaron, the one who served in the Temple; and Miriam, the one who sang.

A PRIEST, A SHEPHERD, AND A PROPHETESS מְכַהֵן וְרוֹעֶה וְאִשָּׁה נְבִיאָה. Aaron, the High Priest; Moses, the people's shepherd; and Miriam, the prophetess. Interestingly, the poet views all three roles as equally critical to a well-ordered world.

TIME OF RIPENING עֵת דּוֹדִים. Literally, "the time of flowers" or "the time of lovers," a poetic allusion to the lovers in the Song of Songs. Passover, commemorating the Exodus, occurs in the spring and it is on Passover that the Song of Songs is read in the synagogue.

COVERED BY A CLOUD כֻּסָּה בֶּעָנָן. Moses.

STOOD BETWEEN נִצָּב בַּתּוֹךְ. According to the biblical account, Moses stood between God and Israel.

A WELL בְּאֵר. According to the midrash, a well accompanied the Israelites in the desert, but when Miriam died the well went dry (Babylonian Talmud, Taanit 9a).

THE PRIEST WHO SERVED RIGHTEOUSLY, MAKING PEACE מְכַהֵן בְּשָׁלוֹם וּבְמִישׁוֹר. The midrash gives this accolade (quoted from Malachi 2:6) to Aaron, because he did not question God after his sons Nadab and Abihu died in the sanctuary when they brought "a strange fire."

THE ETERNAL COVENANT בְּרִית מֶלַח. God promised an eternal covenant with the children of Aaron after Phineas, Aaron's son, slew the heretics in the desert. The phrase is literally translated as "a covenant of salt." In the ancient world, salt was chiefly used as a preservative, and therefore a "covenant of salt" is an eternal covenant. The poet also plays on another association of the word salt: all sacrifices in the Temple were salted.

THE LAWGIVER מְחוֹקֵק. Moses.

GOD'S ANOINTED IN THE DESERT

The third son of Jacob and Leah was chosen to see the face of
the Sovereign, to serve, to sing, to enter the inner chambers.
> Like the most beautiful vine,
> with attractive leaves and gorgeous fruit,
> Amram, rooted in the tribe of Levi,
> grew three beautiful branches:
> a priest, a shepherd, and a prophetess.
When the time of ripening came,
these flowered and were able to break the chains of Egypt
and breach the walls of the Sea.
> The first was covered by a cloud, purified for a week, and
> then stood between when the Word was delivered.
The mighty bent before him;
everyone had to yield in awe.
He nourished the holy flock in the desert
with bread from heaven, until they arrived in the land.
> The girl with the timbrel dug a well for the people,
> and when she died there was no water to drink.
The beloved people were favored with clouds of glory
because of the priest who served righteously, making peace.
A faithful promise was given to him and his descendants,
> that the eternal covenant of this sacred service never end.

PREPARATIONS FOR THE SERVICE

While they sat at the entrance to the Tent, the lawgiver taught
the priests the order of the service—for it was prescribed for
him to do so:
> how to wash, to anoint, to sanctify themselves, hand
> and foot:
> to wear white linen and to tie the sash.
He then ordained them after seven days,
legislating the same for future generations.

כַּכָּתוּב בְּתוֹרָתֶךְ: כַּאֲשֶׁר עָשָׂה בַּיּוֹם הַזֶּה
צִוָּה יהוה לַעֲשֹׂת לְכַפֵּר עֲלֵיכֶם;

נוֹעֲדוּ חֲצוֹת לַיְלָה, מַעֲבִירֵי דֶשֶׁן,
נִצְבּוּ תֵת פַּיִס, וְלֹא יֶהְדְּפוּ;
נִצְבְּעוּ שֵׁנִית, לְצוֹרֶךְ מִזְבֵּחַ חוּצָה,
נִקּוּי פְּנִימִי וְנֵר, וְלֹא יָמִירוּ;
שָׂח פָּקִיד, גּוֹשׁוּ חֲדָשִׁים לִקְטֹרֶת,
סוֹד מַצְבִּיעִים בַּפַּעַם, וְלֹא יִשְׁנוּ;
סִלּוּק נְתָחִים, בֵּין כֶּבֶשׁ לַמִּזְבֵּחַ,
סִדּוּרָם בַּפַּעַם כַּדָּת, וְלֹא יְאַחֵרוּ;
סֶגֶן יִשְׁאַל, אִם בָּרַק נֹגַהּ,
שָׂה לִקְרוֹץ בַּשַּׁחַר, וְלֹא בָאִישׁוֹן;
סְבָבוּהוּ חֲנִיכָיו, לְבֵית טְבִילַת חוּצָה,
סֵדֶר מְחִיצָה בַּתָּוֶךְ, וְלֹא יֵרָאֶה;
עֵירָם שְׁאֵרוֹ, וְטָבַל וְלָבַשׁ שְׁמֹנָה,
עוֹד יִתְקָרֵב כַּחֹק וְלֹא יָמוּשׁ;
עָרַף כֶּבֶשׂ, וְזָרַק וְהִקְטִיר וְהֵיטִיב,
עֶרְכּוֹ וְנִסְכּוֹ בְכֹשֶׁר, וְלֹא בִפְסוּל;
עוֹד בָּא לַפַּרְוָה, וְקִדֵּשׁ וְטָבַל,
עָטָה בְּהִתְקַדְּשׁוֹ בַדִּים, וְלֹא פָז;
עַל פָּרוֹ בְכוֹבֶד, יָדֵיהוּ סָמַךְ,
עֲוֹנוֹ וְנָוֵהוּ הוֹדָה, וְלֹא בוֹשׁ.

AS IT IS WRITTEN IN YOUR TORAH כַּכָּתוּב בְּתוֹרָתֶךְ. Leviticus 8:34, regarding the investiture of the High Priest. The Rabbis understood these verses also to apply to the High Priest's ritual on the Day of Atonement. Therefore, as in the investiture ceremony, the High Priest was separated for seven days before he was to enter the Holy of Holies on the Day of Atonement so that he entered in purity.

GATHERED AT MIDNIGHT נוֹעֲדוּ חֲצוֹת לַיְלָה. The elaborate ritual of the Day of Atonement demanded detailed preparation. Everything was to be made ready for the first crack of dawn, as the ceremony began with the very start of the day. This part of the Avodah service was written by Yoḥanan Ha-Cohen ben Yehoshua, who may have lived in the Land of Israel before the Muslim conquest. Many of his poems were found in the Genizah.

LINEN VESTMENTS בַּדִּים. The High Priest wore plain white linen when performing the special atonement ritual on this day—a sign of purity and humility. Thus it is the custom to dress the Torah in white for the High Holy Days and for the service leaders to wear white. Later custom had congregants do the same, thus symbolizing that on this day all were priests serving in the Temple. Note that at the end of the ceremony the High Priest once again dons the priestly clothing sewn with gold thread. The ancient Rabbis comment that the people sinned with gold at Sinai by worshipping the golden calf; were the High Priest to enter the Holy of Holies with gold, it would be a reminder of that sin. Once his sins and the sins of Israel were forgiven, the full magnificence of the office could be restored.

CONFESSED HIS SINS AND THOSE OF HIS HOUSEHOLD עֲוֹנוֹ וְנָוֵהוּ הוֹדָה. Although the biblical injunction is only that the High Priest pray for the atonement of the sins of Israel, the Rabbis insisted that the High Priest had to engage in personal expiation before he could atone for the community. "Better that someone who is innocent atone for one who is guilty; one who is guilty should not attempt to atone for another who is guilty" (Babylonian Talmud, Yoma 43b). Ḥasidic teaching similarly insists that no one upbraid a neighbor who has not first engaged in self-examination.

As it is written in Your Torah, "As was done on this day to atone for you, God has commanded to do henceforward."

When the priests gathered at midnight of Yom Kippur, they drew lots for the privilege of sweeping the altar, so that none might push ahead. Then they chose yet again to appoint those who would sweep clean the outer altar and wipe the inner sanctum's candelabrum; none could exchange places.

The priestly officer called out, "May the priests who were chosen through the secret lot for the privilege of lighting the incense and the removal of the innards before the sacrifice is brought to the altar come forward; and may none change places." Finally, the assistant would ask, "Has the dawn broken so that we may slaughter the morning sacrifice, not in the dark?"

Then the High Priest was surrounded by his acolytes who stood outside the pool with a curtain between so that they would not gaze upon him.

He bared his flesh, immersed himself, and then put on the eight priestly garments, for he had prepared himself in conformity with the unchanging law. Appropriately and unerringly, he slaughtered the sheep, spilled its blood, offered the incense, lit the lamp, arranged the sacrifice on the altar, and poured the libation.

THE FIRST CONFESSION

Then he once again came out to the porch to sanctify and immerse himself—this time putting on the white linen vestments, not the gold ones. He stretched his hands over the bull and confessed his sins and those of his household, withholding nothing in embarrassment.

וְכָךְ הָיָה אוֹמֵר:

אָנָּא הַשֵּׁם, חָטָאתִי, עָוִיתִי, פָּשַׁעְתִּי לְפָנֶיךָ אֲנִי וּבֵיתִי. אָנָּא בַשֵּׁם, כַּפֶּר־נָא לַחֲטָאִים, וְלָעֲוֹנוֹת וְלַפְּשָׁעִים, שֶׁחָטָאתִי וְשֶׁעָוִיתִי, וְשֶׁפָּשַׁעְתִּי לְפָנֶיךָ אֲנִי וּבֵיתִי, כַּכָּתוּב בְּתוֹרַת מֹשֶׁה עַבְדֶּךָ: כִּי בַיּוֹם הַזֶּה יְכַפֵּר עֲלֵיכֶם לְטַהֵר אֶתְכֶם, מִכֹּל חַטֹּאתֵיכֶם לִפְנֵי יהוה —

וְהַכֹּהֲנִים וְהָעָם הָעוֹמְדִים בָּעֲזָרָה, כְּשֶׁהָיוּ שׁוֹמְעִים אֶת־הַשֵּׁם הַנִּכְבָּד וְהַנּוֹרָא, מְפֹרָשׁ יוֹצֵא מִפִּי כֹהֵן גָּדוֹל בִּקְדֻשָּׁה וּבְטָהֳרָה, הָיוּ כּוֹרְעִים וּמִשְׁתַּחֲוִים וּמוֹדִים וְנוֹפְלִים עַל פְּנֵיהֶם, וְאוֹמְרִים: **בָּרוּךְ שֵׁם כְּבוֹד מַלְכוּתוֹ לְעוֹלָם וָעֶד.**

וְאַף הוּא הָיָה מִתְכַּוֵּן לִגְמֹר אֶת הַשֵּׁם כְּנֶגֶד הַמְבָרְכִים וְאוֹמֵר לָהֶם — תִּטְהָרוּ. וְאַתָּה בְטוּבְךָ מְעוֹרֵר רַחֲמֶיךָ וְסוֹלֵחַ לְאִישׁ חֲסִידֶיךָ.

צָעַד לֵילֵךְ לוֹ לְמִזְרַח עֲזָרָה,

צֶמֶד שְׂעִירִים שָׁם מֵהוֹן עֵדָה,

צְמוּדִים אֲחוּיִם שָׁוִים בְּתֹאַר וּבְקוֹמָה,

צָגִים לְכַפֵּר עֲוֹן בַּת הַשּׁוֹבֵבָה,

צָהוֹב חֲלָשִׁים טָרַף וְהֶעֱלָה מִקַּלְפִּי,

צָנַח וְהִגְרִיל לְשֵׁם גָּבוֹהַּ וְלַצּוּק,

צָעַק בְּקוֹל רָם לַיהוה חַטָּאת,

צוֹתְתָיו עָנוּ לוֹ וּבֵרְכוּ אֶת־הַשֵּׁם,

צֶבַע זְהוֹרִית קָשַׁר בְּרֹאשׁ הַמִּשְׁתַּלֵּחַ,

צִיּנָתוֹ אָמַן נֶגֶד בֵּית שִׁלּוּחַ,

צָלַח וּבָא אֵצֶל פָּרוֹ שֵׁנִית,

צָחַן מַטֵּהוּ פְּנֵי צוּר הַתּוֹדָה.

THE NAME EXPLICITLY ENUNCIATED הַשֵּׁם...מְפֹרָשׁ. In the Second Temple period, it was only on Yom Kippur that the personal name of God was pronounced, by the High Priest serving in the Holy of Holies. The Talmud reports that the proper pronunciation had been forgotten even before the destruction of the Temple. Certainly, today Jews view the name of God as ineffable and in this edition of the maḥzor the name of God is written without vowels to indicate that it is unpronounceable.

ON THIS DAY . . . YOU SHALL BE CLEANSED כִּי בַיּוֹם הַזֶּה...תִּטְהָרוּ. Leviticus 16:30.

WOULD BOW AND KNEEL AND FALL PROSTRATE TO THE GROUND הָיוּ כּוֹרְעִים וּמִשְׁתַּחֲוִים וּמוֹדִים וְנוֹפְלִים עַל פְּנֵיהֶם. Prostrations were integral to the service in the ancient synagogue, but later rabbis frowned upon its practice. However, on the High Holy Days it remains the custom of the leaders of the congregation—and even of some congregants—to prostrate themselves in imitation of Temple practice. The tradition is to touch one's head to the ground but not to lie completely flat on the ground.

PRAISED IS THE NAME OF THE ONE בָּרוּךְ שֵׁם כְּבוֹד. This is the same phrase that we recite following the first line of the Sh'ma.

It was a special feature of
the ritual of the Day of
Atonement that one goat
was sent to the desert, or
"to Azazel" (לַעֲזָאזֵל), in
the words of the Torah.
Whatever its meaning
was in biblical times, in
later Judaism these words
became paradigmatic
of the separating and
discarding of sin. The
desert is the area of no
life, where sin is sent
away from the realm of
the living. Abraham Ibn
Ezra (12th century, Spain
and Italy) recorded an
opinion that sending the
goat to the desert was
symbolic of sending it
back to Sinai—the place
of sin and forgiveness.
The Rabbis insisted that
the two goats—one of-
fered for sacrifice to God
and one sent off to the
desert—be as similar as
possible. This recalls the
teaching that the impulse
for sin and the impulse
for good reside next to
each other. It is not the
urges themselves that
are good or evil, but the
purposes to which we put
them.

And thus he would say:

Adonai, I have committed iniquity, I have transgressed, I
have sinned against You, *I and my household*. I beseech You,
Adonai, by Your holy name: forgive the iniquities and the
transgressions and the sins that I have committed against You,
I and my household, as is written in the Torah of Your servant
Moses: "On this day, atonement shall be made for you, to
cleanse you of all your sins before Adonai . . ."

When the priests and all the people standing in the Temple
Court would hear the glorious and awe-inspiring name explicitly enunciated, in holiness and purity, by the lips of the High
Priest, ʄthey would bow and kneel and fall prostrate to the
ground, saying, "Praised is the name of the One whose glorious
sovereignty will be forever and ever."
Barukh shem k'vod malkhuto l'olam va·ed.

The High Priest would intentionally prolong the utterance of
the name while the people recited their praise, whereupon he
would complete the verse, saying: ". . . you shall be cleansed."

And You, out of Your goodness, aroused Your love and forgave
the one who was faithful to You.

THE SECOND CONFESSION

He walked to the east of the courtyard, where two goats alike
in form and size stood ready, as the sacrificial offering for the
consequences of sin. He grabbed the gold lots, pulled them
from the urn, and cast them: "for heaven" and "for the wilderness." He called out for the one: "A purification offering unto
Adonai." Those who heard him responded by praising God's
name. On the head of the goat that was to be sent out, he tied
a crimson thread, directing the goat toward its destination. He
returned to the sacrificial bull, confessing the sin of his tribe
before the rock of Israel.

וְכָךְ הָיָה אוֹמֵר:

אָנָּא הַשֵּׁם, חָטָאתִי, עָוִיתִי, פָּשַׁעְתִּי לְפָנֶיךָ אֲנִי וּבֵיתִי
וּבְנֵי אַהֲרֹן עַם קְדוֹשֶׁךָ. אָנָּא בַשֵּׁם, כַּפֶּר־נָא לַחֲטָאִים,
וְלַעֲוֹנוֹת וְלַפְּשָׁעִים, שֶׁחָטָאתִי וְשֶׁעָוִיתִי, וְשֶׁפָּשַׁעְתִּי לְפָנֶיךָ
אֲנִי וּבֵיתִי וּבְנֵי אַהֲרֹן עַם קְדוֹשֶׁךָ, כַּכָּתוּב בְּתוֹרַת מֹשֶׁה
עַבְדֶּךָ: כִּי בַיּוֹם הַזֶּה יְכַפֵּר עֲלֵיכֶם לְטַהֵר אֶתְכֶם, מִכֹּל
חַטֹּאתֵיכֶם לִפְנֵי יהוה—

וְהַכֹּהֲנִים וְהָעָם הָעוֹמְדִים בָּעֲזָרָה, כְּשֶׁהָיוּ שׁוֹמְעִים
אֶת־הַשֵּׁם הַנִּכְבָּד וְהַנּוֹרָא, מְפֹרָשׁ יוֹצֵא מִפִּי כֹּהֵן גָּדוֹל
בִּקְדֻשָּׁה וּבְטָהֳרָה, הָיוּ כּוֹרְעִים וּמִשְׁתַּחֲוִים וּמוֹדִים
וְנוֹפְלִים עַל פְּנֵיהֶם, וְאוֹמְרִים: **בָּרוּךְ שֵׁם כְּבוֹד מַלְכוּתוֹ
לְעוֹלָם וָעֶד.**

וְאַף הוּא הָיָה מִתְכַּוֵּן לִגְמוֹר אֶת־הַשֵּׁם כְּנֶגֶד הַמְבָרְכִים
וְאוֹמֵר לָהֶם—תִּטְהָרוּ. וְאַתָּה בְּטוּבְךָ מְעוֹרֵר רַחֲמֶיךָ
וְסוֹלֵחַ לְשֵׁבֶט מְשָׁרְתֶיךָ.

קַח מַאֲכֶלֶת חַדָּה וּשְׁחָטוֹ כְּסֵדֶר,
קִבֵּל דָּם בְּמִזְרָק וּנְתָנוֹ לַמְמָרֵס...
קִישׁ צְעָדָיו לַפָּרֹכֶת וְקָרֵב לַבַּדִּים,
קְטֹרֶת שָׁם בֵּינֵימוֹ וְעָשָׁן וְיָצָא.
רוֹבֶה מְמָרֵס מֶנּוּ נָטַל דָּם, רָץ וְנִכְנַס וְקָם בֵּין שָׁדַיִם,
רְצוּי הַזָּיוֹת טָבַל וְהִצְלִיף בְּמִנְיָן, רוֹם מַעְלָה אַחַת
וּמַטָּה שֶׁבַע.

We repeat each number (aḥat . . .) following the reader's count:

וְכָךְ הָיָה מוֹנֶה: **אַחַת, אַחַת וְאַחַת, אַחַת וּשְׁתַּיִם, אַחַת
וְשָׁלֹשׁ, אַחַת וְאַרְבַּע, אַחַת וְחָמֵשׁ, אַחַת וָשֵׁשׁ, אַחַת וָשֶׁבַע.**

רָץ וְהִנִּיחוֹ בַּכֵּן וְשָׁחַט שָׂעִיר, רָצָה וְקִבֵּל דָּמוֹ בָּאַגָּן קֹדֶשׁ,
רֶגֶל וְעָמַד מָקוֹם וְעוֹד אָרוֹן, רָצָה הַזָּיוֹת
כְּמַעֲשֵׂה דַם פָּר.

וְכָךְ הָיָה מוֹנֶה: **אַחַת, אַחַת וְאַחַת, אַחַת וּשְׁתַּיִם, אַחַת
וְשָׁלֹשׁ, אַחַת וְאַרְבַּע, אַחַת וְחָמֵשׁ, אַחַת וָשֵׁשׁ, אַחַת וָשֶׁבַע.**

**THE SPRINKLING OF THE
BLOOD.** Blood was seen
as the source of life in the
ancient world. It is hard
to penetrate the mean-
ings of the biblical rituals
connected with sacrifice,
but perhaps the sprinkling
of blood on the cover of
the ark was meant to recall
that it is God who grants
life.

ONE, ONE AND ONE, אַחַת,
אַחַת וְאַחַת. Each time, the
High Priest would sprinkle
one drop of blood on the
top of the curtain and then
an increasing number on
the bottom.

And thus he would say:

ADONAI, I have committed iniquity, I have transgressed, I have sinned against You, *I and my household and the descendants of Aaron, Your consecrated people.* I beseech You, ADONAI, by Your holy name: forgive the iniquities and the transgressions and the sins that I have committed against You, I and my household, and the descendants of Aaron, Your consecrated people, as is written in the Torah of Your servant Moses: "On this day atonement shall be made for you, to cleanse you of all Your sins before ADONAI . . ."

When the priests and all the people standing in the Temple Court would hear the glorious and awe-inspiring name explicitly enunciated, in holiness and purity, by the lips of the High Priest, † they would bow and kneel and fall prostrate to the ground, saying, "Praised is the name of the One whose glorious sovereignty will be forever and ever."

Barukh shem k'vod malkhuto l'olam va·ed.

The High Priest would intentionally prolong the utterance of the name while the people recited their praise, whereupon he would complete the verse, saying: ". . . you shall be cleansed."

And You, out of Your goodness, aroused Your love and forgave the tribe who serve You.

THE SPRINKLING OF THE BLOOD

He then took a sharp knife, ritually slaughtered the sacrifice, receiving the blood in its bowl which he handed to his assistant . . . The sound of his footsteps was heard from between the curtains as he placed the incense within, allowing the smoke to rise, and then he exited. He took the swirled blood from his young assistant, returned to the hall, and stood between the two curtain rods; dipping in his finger, he sprinkled the designated number of times, upward one and downward seven.

We repeat each number (Aḥat . . .) following the reader's count:
And thus would he count: one, one and one, one and two, one and three, one and four, one and five, one and six, one and seven.
Aḥat, aḥat v'aḥat, aḥat u-sh'tayim, aḥat v'shalosh,
aḥat v'arba, aḥat v'hameish, aḥat va-sheish, aḥat v'sheva.
He quickly returned, placed the bowl on its pedestal, and slaughtered the goat. He offered it up and received its blood in a holy vessel; he then walked back again and stood in the presence of the Ark, and sprinkled the blood as before.

And thus would he count: one, one and one, one and two, one and three, one and four, one and five, one and six, one and seven.
Aḥat, aḥat v'aḥat, aḥat u-sh'tayim, aḥat v'shalosh,
aḥat v'arba, aḥat v'hameish, aḥat va-sheish, aḥat v'sheva.

רָהַט וְהִנִּיחוּ וְדַם פַּר נָטַל,
רַגְלָיו הֵרִיץ וְצָג חוּץ לַבַּדֶּלֶת,
רִקְמֵי פָרְכֶת יַז כְּמִשְׁפָּט כַּפְּרֶת,
רֶגֶשׁ וְשִׁנָּה וְהִזָּה מִדַּם שָׂעִיר.

שָׁב וּבְלָלָם וְחִטֵּא מִזְבֵּחַ סָגוּר,
שֶׁבַע עַל טָהֳרוֹ וּבְקַרְנָיו אַרְבַּע,
שָׁקַד וּבָא אֵצֶל שָׂעִיר הֶחָי,
שִׁגְיוֹן עָם וּזְדוֹנוֹ יוֹדֶה לָאֵל.

וְכָךְ הָיָה אוֹמֵר:
אָנָּא הַשֵּׁם, חָטָאוּ, עָווּ, פָּשְׁעוּ לְפָנֶיךָ עַמְּךָ בֵּית יִשְׂרָאֵל.
אָנָּא בַשֵּׁם, כַּפֶּר־נָא לַחֲטָאִים, וְלַעֲוֹנוֹת וְלַפְּשָׁעִים,
שֶׁחָטְאוּ וְשֶׁעָווּ, וְשֶׁפָּשְׁעוּ לְפָנֶיךָ עַמְּךָ בֵּית יִשְׂרָאֵל,
כַּכָּתוּב בְּתוֹרַת מֹשֶׁה עַבְדֶּךָ: כִּי בַיּוֹם הַזֶּה יְכַפֵּר עֲלֵיכֶם
לְטַהֵר אֶתְכֶם, מִכֹּל חַטֹּאתֵיכֶם לִפְנֵי יהוה —

וְהַכֹּהֲנִים וְהָעָם הָעוֹמְדִים בָּעֲזָרָה, כְּשֶׁהָיוּ שׁוֹמְעִים
אֶת־הַשֵּׁם הַנִּכְבָּד וְהַנּוֹרָא, מְפֹרָשׁ יוֹצֵא מִפִּי כֹּהֵן גָּדוֹל
בִּקְדֻשָּׁה וּבְטָהֳרָה, ֽ הָיוּ כּוֹרְעִים וּמִשְׁתַּחֲוִים וּמוֹדִים
וְנוֹפְלִים עַל פְּנֵיהֶם, וְאוֹמְרִים: **בָּרוּךְ שֵׁם כְּבוֹד מַלְכוּתוֹ
לְעוֹלָם וָעֶד.**

וְאַף הוּא הָיָה מִתְכַּוֵּן לִגְמוֹר אֶת־הַשֵּׁם כְּנֶגֶד הַמְבָרְכִים
וְאוֹמֵר לָהֶם — תִּטְהָרוּ. וְאַתָּה בְּטוּבְךָ מְעוֹרֵר רַחֲמֶיךָ
וְסוֹלֵחַ לַעֲדַת יְשֻׁרוּן.

JESHURUN יְשֻׁרוּן. A name
for Israel used promi-
nently in the Song of Moses
(Deuteronomy 32). Isaiah
comforts Israel and says:
"Fear not my servant Jacob,
Jeshurun, whom I have
chosen" (44:2). "Jeshurun"
is derived from the Hebrew
root meaning "straight."
The root meaning of the
name "Jacob" may be the
opposite: bent or dissem-
bling. Thus the use of the
name "Jeshurun" can be
symbolic of a final redemption when, in the words of
the prophet, "the crooked
(*akov*) shall be made
straight (*mishor*)" (Isaiah
40:4).

He bestirred himself and placed the bowl aside, now picking up the blood of the bull. He rushed and went out, standing in front of the embroidered curtain and sprinkled the blood as he had done on the Ark-cover. He hurried to repeat the procedure, sprinkling the blood of the goat.

THE THIRD CONFESSION

Mixing the two together, he purified the altar of gold: seven times to purify it, then four on each corner. He hurried to the live goat, confessing before God the mistakes and transgressions of the people.

And thus he would say:
ADONAI, Your people, the House of Israel, have committed iniquity, have transgressed, have sinned against You. I beseech You, ADONAI, by Your holy name: forgive the iniquities and the transgressions and the sins that Your people, the House of Israel, have committed against You, as is written in the Torah of Your servant Moses: "On this day atonement shall be made for you, to cleanse you of all Your sins before ADONAI . . ."

When the priests and all the people standing in the Temple Court would hear the glorious and awe-inspiring name explicitly enunciated, in holiness and purity, by the lips of the High Priest, ʄ they would bow and kneel and fall prostrate to the ground, saying, "Praised is the name of the One whose glorious sovereignty will be forever and ever."
Barukh shem k'vod malkhuto l'olam va·ed.
The High Priest would intentionally prolong the utterance of the name while the people recited their praise, whereupon he would complete the verse, saying: "...you shall be cleansed."

And You, out of Your goodness, aroused Your love and forgave the congregation of Jeshurun.

שִׁגְּרוּ בְּיַד אִישׁ עִתִּי לְמִדְבָּר עָז,

שָׁאַג סִדְרֵי יוֹם, קָדֵשׁ, וּפָשַׁט,

שִׁלֵּשׁ וְטָבַל, פְּזִים עָט וְקָדֵשׁ.

תֵּכֶף וְעָשׂ אֵילוֹ וְאֵיל עָם,

תֵּרֶב חַטָּאוֹת וּמוּסָפִין הִקְרִיב כַּחֹק,

תָּר וְקָדֵשׁ פָּשַׁט טָבַל וְקָדֵשׁ,

תַּכְרִיךְ בַּדִּים עָט וְנִכְנַס לַדְּבִיר,

תְּכוּנַת כְּלֵי קְטֹרֶת הוֹצִיא וְקָדֵשׁ,

תִּלְבֹּשֶׁת מַדָּיו הִפְשִׁיט וְגָנַז נֶצַח,

תֵּרַגֵּל וְטָבַל חֲרוּצִים עָט וְקָדֵשׁ,

תָּמִיד הִסְדִּיר וְתִמֵּר וְנֵרוֹת הֶעֱלָה,

תְּכֵל עֲבוֹדוֹת יָד וְרֶגֶל קָדֵשׁ,

תִּמֵּם טְבִילוֹת חָמֵשׁ וְקִדּוּשִׁים עֲשָׂרָה,

תֹּאַר מְגַמָּתוֹ כְּצֵאת הַשֶּׁמֶשׁ בִּגְבוּרָה,

תַּקֹּף וְדָץ וְעָטָה בִּגְדֵי הוֹנוֹ,

תַּמָּה תְלוּיָה צִיר נֶאֱמָן לַבַּיִת,

תָּגֵל בְּהִתְבַּשֵּׂר הַשֶּׁלַג אָדֵם תּוֹלַע,

תּוֹדָה נָתְנוּ אוֹסְפֵי זֶרַע שָׁלוֹם,

תְּהִלָּה בִּשְׂרוּ נוֹשְׂאֵי אֲלֻמּוֹת בְּרַנֵּן.

וְכָךְ הָיְתָה תְּפִלָּתוֹ שֶׁל כֹּהֵן גָּדוֹל בְּיוֹם הַכִּפּוּרִים בְּצֵאתוֹ מִבֵּית קֹדֶשׁ הַקֳּדָשִׁים בְּשָׁלוֹם:

יְהִי רָצוֹן מִלְּפָנֶיךָ, יהוה אֱלֹהֵינוּ וֵאלֹהֵי אֲבוֹתֵינוּ, שֶׁתְּהֵא הַשָּׁנָה הַזֹּאת הַבָּאָה עָלֵינוּ, וְעַל כָּל־עַמְּךָ בֵּית יִשְׂרָאֵל, שְׁנַת אָסָם,

שְׁנַת בְּרָכָה,

שְׁנַת גְּזֵרוֹת טוֹבוֹת מִלְּפָנֶיךָ,

שְׁנַת דָּגָן תִּירוֹשׁ וְיִצְהָר,

שְׁנַת הַרְוָחָה וְהַצְלָחָה,

שְׁנַת וְעוֹד בֵּית מִקְדָּשֶׁךָ,

HE REMOVED THE INSTRU-MENTS תְּכוּנַת כְּלֵי קְטֹרֶת הוֹצִיא. Yom Kippur was not only a Day of Atonement for the people but also a day of resanctifying the Temple and all its instruments.

DRESSED IN GOLD חֲרוּצִים עָט. Having atoned for the sins of Israel and purified the Temple, the High Priest now engages in the daily service dressed in the gold robes he usually wears. The white garments worn by the High Priest were buried, never to be worn again.

OFFERED UP THE DAILY SACRIFICE תָּמִיד הִסְדִּיר. Having completed the special rites connected with the Day of Atonement, the High Priest now turns to officiating over the daily tasks. On other days the daily offering would have been performed by regular members of the priest-hood.

RED THREAD HAD TURNED TO PURE WHITE הַשֶּׁלַג אָדֵם תּוֹלַע. According to rabbinic tradition, a red thread was hung in the Temple. After the goat was sent to the desert, if the thread turned white it was a sign from heaven that the sins of the people Israel had been forgiven.

GATHERING THE FRUITS OF PEACE אוֹסְפֵי זֶרַע שָׁלוֹם. The prophet Zechariah (8:12) says that in the past the people Israel have attacked each other and so destruction had been their harvest, but in the future, peace will enable them to harvest the fruits that had been planted.

THE COMPLETION OF THE CEREMONY

He sent out the goat to the harsh desert, accompanied by the appointed priest.

He read aloud the Torah portions. He undressed, washed his hands and feet, bathed again, put on the gold garments, and then washed his hands and feet again.

He immediately offered up his ram and the ram of the people. He sacrificed the fat of the purification offering and the holy day offering, according to the law. He walked away, washed his hands and feet, undressed, bathed and washed his hands and feet again, dressed in linens, and entered the inner sanctuary.

He removed the instruments for burning the incense and purified them, then took off his linen clothes and buried them forever. He walked away, bathed and sanctified, dressed in gold, and in sanctity offered up the daily sacrifice, burnt the incense, and lit the candles. So the service ended. Through the course of the day, he had washed his hands and feet ten times and bathed five times, and upon completion of the service his face shone like the sun in its zenith. He joyously hurried and put on his personal attire, and the crowd accompanied their faithful leader home, exulting that the red thread had turned to pure white.

They gave thanks, gathering the fruits of peace; they sang praises, reaping fulfillment.

THE PRAYER OF THE HIGH PRIEST FOR THE NEW YEAR

And this was the prayer of the High Priest as he emerged on the Day of Atonement from the Holy of Holies:

May it be Your will, ADONAI our God, and God of our ancestors, to grant us, with all Your people Israel,

A year of abundance,
a year of blessing,
a year of good fortune,
a year of bountiful harvest.
a year of prosperity and success,
a year of assembly in Your holy place,

שְׁנַת זִמְרָה,

שְׁנַת חַיִּים טוֹבִים מִלְּפָנֶיךָ,

שָׁנָה טְלוּלָה וּגְשׁוּמָה אִם שְׁחוּנָה,

שְׁנַת יַמְתִּיקוּ מְגָדִים אֶת־תְּנוּבָתָם,

שְׁנַת כַּפָּרָה וּסְלִיחָה עַל כָּל־עֲוֹנוֹתֵינוּ,

שְׁנַת לַחְמֵנוּ וּמֵימֵינוּ תְּבָרֵךְ,

שְׁנַת מְנוּחָה,

שְׁנַת נֶחָמָה,

שְׁנַת שֶׂבַע שְׂמָחוֹת,

שְׁנַת עֹנֶג,

שְׁנַת פְּרִי בִטְנֵנוּ וּפְרִי אַדְמָתֵנוּ תְּבָרֵךְ,

שְׁנַת צֵאתֵנוּ וּבוֹאֵנוּ תְּבָרֵךְ,

שְׁנַת קְהָלֵנוּ תּוֹשִׁיעַ,

שְׁנַת רַחֲמֶיךָ יִכָּמְרוּ עָלֵינוּ,

שְׁנַת שָׁלוֹם וְשַׁלְוָה,

שָׁנָה שֶׁתַּעֲלֵנוּ שְׂמֵחִים לְאַרְצֵנוּ,

שָׁנָה שֶׁלֹּא יִצְטָרְכוּ עַמְּךָ בֵּית יִשְׂרָאֵל זֶה לָזֶה וְלֹא לְעַם אַחֵר בְּתִתְּךָ בְרָכָה בְּמַעֲשֵׂה יְדֵיהֶם.

וְעַל אַנְשֵׁי הַשָּׁרוֹן הָיָה אוֹמֵר: יְהִי רָצוֹן מִלְּפָנֶיךָ יהוה אֱלֹהֵינוּ וֵאלֹהֵי אֲבוֹתֵינוּ, שֶׁלֹּא יֵעָשׂוּ בָתֵּיהֶם קִבְרֵיהֶם.

אַשְׁרֵי עַיִן רָאֲתָה כָל־אֵלֶּה,
הֲלֹא לְמִשְׁמַע אֹזֶן דָּאֲבָה נַפְשֵׁנוּ.
אַשְׁרֵי עַיִן רָאֲתָה אָהֳלֵנוּ, בְּשִׂמְחַת קְהָלֵנוּ,
הֲלֹא לְמִשְׁמַע אֹזֶן דָּאֲבָה נַפְשֵׁנוּ.

אֱלֹהֵינוּ וֵאלֹהֵי אֲבוֹתֵינוּ [וְאִמּוֹתֵינוּ], גָּלוּי וְיָדוּעַ לְפָנֶיךָ וְלִפְנֵי כִסֵּא כְבוֹדֶךָ,
שֶׁאֵין לָנוּ לֹא מְנַהֵל כַּיָּמִים הָרִאשׁוֹנִים,
לֹא כֹהֵן גָּדוֹל לְהַקְרִיב נִיחוֹחִים,
וְלֹא נָבִיא לְצַהֵל עֲבוּר מַיִם חַיִּים וּטְהוֹרִים.
◁ אָכֵן הַזְכְּרֵנוּ מִמַּעֲלָלוֹת קַדְמִים.

אֲבָל זִכִּיתָנוּ בַּעֲבוֹדָה אַחֶרֶת.

THE PRAYER OF THE HIGH PRIEST. The Mishnah (Yoma 7:1) indicates that the High Priest prayed after he exited the Holy of Holies. The Jerusalem Talmud offers a version of this prayer (Yoma 42c). During the Middle Ages it was expanded into an alphabetical acrostic of blessings and several different versions have come down to us. Many of the items mentioned in these prayers reflect those mentioned in the prayer for the new month recited each month at the prior Shabbat service. Tishrei, the month in which the High Holy Days occur, is never blessed on the preceding Shabbat (as was done for all other new moons), since Tishrei is the very beginning of the year. The hopes for the new month—indeed, for the whole year—are expressed in this expansive prayer.

AND TO THE PEOPLE OF SHARON וְעַל אַנְשֵׁי הַשָּׁרוֹן. The people of the Sharon Valley built their houses from mud bricks that were in constant danger of collapse as a result of flooding from the winter rains. The Jerusalem Talmud (38a) reports that their houses needed constant rebuilding. Thus the High Priest singled out in his prayers those living in poor or dangerous circumstances.

a year of song,
a year of a fulfilling life,
a year of dew and rain and sun,
a year of sweet fruit at the harvest,
a year of atonement and forgiveness for all our sins,
a year in which our bread and water are blessed,
a year of rest,
a year of consolation,
a year of abundant joy,
a year of delight,
a year in which the fruit of our womb and of our earth are blessed,
a year in which our going and coming are blessed,
a year in which our community achieves salvation,
a year in which Your mercy descends upon us,
a year of peace and tranquility,
a year in which we go up in joy to Your land,
a year in which Your people Israel will not require support from one another or from other people, the work of their hands being fully blessed.

And to the people of Sharon, he would say: May it be Your will, Adonai our God and God of our ancestors, that their homes not become their graves.

ATONEMENT FOR SIN IN A WORLD WITHOUT THE TEMPLE

Blessed were those who saw these things; sadly, we can only hear about them.
Ashrei ayin ra·atah khol eilleh, halo l'mishma ozen da·avah nafsheinu.
Blessed were those who saw the Temple filled with a joyous congregation; sadly, we can only hear about it.

Our God and God of our ancestors, it is known to You and revealed before Your throne of glory that we have no leader as we did in the days of old,
no High Priest to offer a sweet savor,
and no prophetess to sing over living and purifying waters.
And so we have recalled what the ancients did.

Fortunately, You have provided us with other forms of service.

פַּעַם אַחַת הָיָה רַבָּן יוֹחָנָן בֶּן־זַכַּאי יוֹצֵא מִירוּשָׁלַיִם
וְהָיָה רַבִּי יְהוֹשֻׁעַ הוֹלֵךְ אַחֲרָיו וְרָאָה אֶת־בֵּית הַמִּקְדָּשׁ
חָרֵב. אָמַר רַבִּי יְהוֹשֻׁעַ: אוֹי לָנוּ עַל זֶה שֶׁהוּא חָרֵב,
מָקוֹם שֶׁמְּכַפְּרִים בּוֹ עֲוֹנוֹתֵיהֶם שֶׁל יִשְׂרָאֵל! אָמַר לוֹ
רַבָּן יוֹחָנָן: בְּנִי, אַל יֵרַע לְךָ. יֵשׁ לָנוּ כַּפָּרָה אַחֶרֶת שֶׁהִיא
כְּמוֹתָהּ. וְאֵיזוֹ? גְּמִילוּת חֲסָדִים, שֶׁנֶּאֱמַר: כִּי חֶסֶד
חָפַצְתִּי וְלֹא זָבַח.

מַה־הוּא רַחוּם וְחַנּוּן, אַף אַתָּה.
מַה־הוּא מְתַקֵּן אֶת־הַכַּלָּה וּמְבַקֵּר חוֹלִים, אַף אַתָּה.
מַה־הוּא מְנַחֵם אֲבֵלִים וּמְלַוֶּה אֶת־הַמֵּת, אַף אַתָּה.
פְּרֹס לָרָעֵב לַחְמֶךָ וַעֲנִיִּים מְרוּדִים תָּבִיא בָיִת,
כִּי תִרְאֶה עָרֹם וְכִסִּיתוֹ וּמִבְּשָׂרְךָ לֹא תִתְעַלָּם.
לְמִי שֶׁעֶזְרָה אֵין לוֹ, תַּעֲזֹר,
וְעֵינַיִם לָעִוֵּר תִּהְיֶה וְרַגְלַיִם לַפִּסֵּחַ.
דַּעֲלָךְ סְנִי לְחַבְרָךְ לֹא תַעֲבֵיד,
וְאָהַבְתָּ לְרֵעֲךָ כָּמוֹךָ.
הֱוֵי מִתַּלְמִידָיו שֶׁל אַהֲרֹן הַכֹּהֵן, אוֹהֵב שָׁלוֹם וְרוֹדֵף
שָׁלוֹם, אוֹהֵב אֶת־הַבְּרִיּוֹת וּמְקָרְבָן לַתּוֹרָה.
מַה־הוּא רַחוּם וְחַנּוּן, אַף אַתָּה.
אָז יִבָּקַע כַּשַּׁחַר אוֹרֶךָ, וַאֲרֻכָתְךָ מְהֵרָה תִצְמָח,
וְהָלַךְ לְפָנֶיךָ צִדְקֶךָ, כְּבוֹד יהוה יַאַסְפֶךָ.
יִתֶּן־לָנוּ חָכְמַת לֵב וִיהִי שָׁלוֹם בֵּינֵנוּ.

זְכֹר רַחֲמֶיךָ יהוה וַחֲסָדֶיךָ, כִּי מֵעוֹלָם הֵמָּה. אַל תִּזְכָּר־
לָנוּ עֲוֹנוֹת רִאשֹׁנִים, מַהֵר יְקַדְּמוּנוּ רַחֲמֶיךָ כִּי דַלּוֹנוּ
מְאֹד. זָכְרֵנוּ יהוה בִּרְצוֹן עַמֶּךָ, פָּקְדֵנוּ בִּישׁוּעָתֶךָ.
זְכֹר עֲדָתְךָ קָנִיתָ קֶּדֶם, גָּאַלְתָּ שֵׁבֶט נַחֲלָתֶךָ, הַר צִיּוֹן
זֶה שָׁכַנְתָּ בּוֹ. זְכֹר יהוה חִבַּת יְרוּשָׁלַיִם.

ONCE AS פַּעַם אַחַת. The three passages on this page were arranged and translated by Jules Harlow.

RABBAN YOḤANAN BEN ZAKKAI. This story is found in the 3rd-century Avot of Rabbi Natan (Version A, chapter 4).

I DESIRE DEEDS כִּי חֶסֶד חָפַצְתִּי. Hosea 6:6.

AS GOD IS GRACIOUS מַה־הוּא רַחוּם. Mekhilta of Rabbi Ishmael, Shirata 3.

SHARE YOUR BREAD פְּרֹס לָרָעֵב לַחְמֶךָ. Isaiah 58:7.

EYES TO THE BLIND וְעֵינַיִם לָעִוֵּר. After Job 29:15.

WHAT IS HATEFUL TO YOU דַּעֲלָךְ סְנִי. Babylonian Talmud, Shabbat 31a.

LOVE YOUR NEIGHBOR וְאָהַבְתָּ לְרֵעֲךָ כָּמוֹךָ. Leviticus 19:18.

YOUR LIGHT SHALL BREAK FORTH AS DAWN אָז יִבָּקַע כַּשַּׁחַר אוֹרֶךָ. Isaiah 58:8, from the Haftarah for Yom Kippur, Isaiah defines the true fast as one in which the weak are freed from society's oppression.

CALL TO MIND זְכֹר רַחֲמֶיךָ. The recollection of the Temple service ends with a series of verses (Psalms 25:6, 79:8, 106:4, and 74:2), each containing plays on the Hebrew word for memory, זכר (zakhor). They were chosen for their mention of redemption and their connection to Zion and Jerusalem. The last sentence is not a biblical verse.

Once as Rabban Yoḥanan ben Zakkai was leaving Jerusalem, Rabbi Yehoshua, who was following him, looked back, saw the Temple in ruins, and remarked in despair, "How terrible for us! The place that atoned for the sins of all the people Israel lies in ruins!" Then Rabban Yoḥanan ben Zakkai said: "My son, do not grieve. There is another way of gaining atonement, equal to it. What is that? Performing deeds of kindness and love, as the prophet Hosea declared: 'I desire deeds of kindness and love, not burnt offerings.'"

As God is gracious and compassionate,
you be gracious and compassionate.
   Help the needy bride, visit the sick,
   comfort the mourners, attend to the dead,
share your bread with the hungry,
take the homeless into your home.
   Clothe the naked when you see them;
   do not turn away from people in need.
Help those who have no help;
be eyes to the blind, be feet to the lame.
   What is hateful to you, do not do to your fellow human beings,
   but love your neighbor as yourself.
Be a disciple of Aaron the priest.
Love peace and pursue peace,
love your fellow creatures and draw them to the Torah.
   As God is gracious and compassionate,
   you be gracious and compassionate.
Then your light shall break forth as dawn,
and your healing spread quickly.
Our righteousness will go before us,
and God's presence will gather us up.
   May God grant us wisdom of the heart.
   And may there be peace among us.

Call to mind Your acts of kindness, ADONAI, for they exist eternally. Do not hold the sins of our ancestors against us. May Your kindness soon greet us, for we are in great despair. Be mindful of us and take note of us as You favor Your people with salvation. Remember the congregation that long ago that You made Your very own when You redeemed the tribe You made Your inheritance. Remember Mount Zion, on which You once dwelled, and Your love of Jerusalem.

THE THIRTEEN ATTRIBUTES.
The explanation of the Thirteen Attributes that appears here is based on sources in the Babylonian Talmud (Rosh Hashanah 17b) and the Tosafists (France and Germany, 12th and 13th centuries) and by Abudarham (Spain, 13th century). The form found here was first published in *Sefer HaBakashah* by Moshe HaCohen Niral, Metz, 1788.

אֵל, אֶרֶךְ אַפַּיִם אַתָּה, וּבַעַל הָרַחֲמִים נִקְרֵאתָ, וְדֶרֶךְ תְּשׁוּבָה הוֹרֵיתָ. גְּדֻלַּת רַחֲמֶיךָ וַחֲסָדֶיךָ תִּזְכֹּר הַיּוֹם וּבְכָל־יוֹם לְזֶרַע יְדִידֶיךָ. תֵּפֶן אֵלֵינוּ בְּרַחֲמֶיךָ, כִּי אַתָּה הוּא בַּעַל הָרַחֲמִים.

בְּתַחֲנוּן וּבִתְפִלָּה פָּנֶיךָ נְקַדֵּם, כְּהוֹדַעְתָּ לֶעָנָו מִקֶּדֶם. מֵחֲרוֹן אַפְּךָ שׁוּב, כְּמוֹ בְּתוֹרָתְךָ כָּתוּב, וּבְצֵל כְּנָפֶיךָ נֶחֱסֶה וְנִתְלוֹנָן, כְּיוֹם וַיֵּרֶד יהוה בֶּעָנָן.

◁ תַּעֲבֹר עַל פֶּשַׁע וְתִמְחֶה אָשָׁם, כְּיוֹם וַיִּתְיַצֵּב עִמּוֹ שָׁם. תַּאֲזִין שַׁוְעָתֵנוּ וְתַקְשִׁיב מֶנּוּ מַאֲמָר כְּיוֹם וַיִּקְרָא בְשֵׁם יהוה.

וַיַּעֲבֹר יהוה עַל פָּנָיו וַיִּקְרָא:

יהוה יהוה, אֵל רַחוּם וְחַנּוּן, אֶרֶךְ אַפַּיִם, וְרַב־חֶסֶד וֶאֱמֶת. נֹצֵר חֶסֶד לָאֲלָפִים, נֹשֵׂא עָוֹן וָפֶשַׁע וְחַטָּאָה, וְנַקֵּה.

אֲנִי הוּא קֹדֶם שֶׁיֶּחֱטָא הָאָדָם	יהוה
אֲנִי הוּא לְאַחַר שֶׁיֶּחֱטָא הָאָדָם	יהוה
מִדַּת הָרַחֲמִים גַּם לָעַמִּים	אֵל
לְמִי שֶׁיֵּשׁ לוֹ זְכוּת	רַחוּם
לְמִי שֶׁאֵין לוֹ זְכוּת	וְחַנּוּן
לְמִי שֶׁאֵין לוֹ זְכוּת	אֶרֶךְ אַפַּיִם
לְנִצְרְכֵי־חֶסֶד	וְרַב־חֶסֶד
לְשַׁלֵּם שָׂכָר לְעוֹשֵׂי רְצוֹנוֹ	וֶאֱמֶת
נֹצֵר חֶסֶד לָאֲלָפִים כְּשֶׁאָדָם עוֹשֶׂה טוֹב	
לְעוֹשֶׂה בְזָדוֹן	נֹשֵׂא עָוֹן
הַמּוֹרְדִים לְהַכְעִיס	וָפֶשַׁע
הָעוֹשֶׂה בִשְׁגָגָה	וְחַטָּאָה
לַשָּׁבִים	וְנַקֵּה

וְסָלַחְתָּ לַעֲוֹנֵנוּ וּלְחַטָּאתֵנוּ וּנְחַלְתָּנוּ.

Some strike their heart when asking God to forgive and pardon:

סְלַח לָנוּ אָבִינוּ כִּי חָטָאנוּ, מְחַל לָנוּ מַלְכֵּנוּ כִּי פָשָׁעְנוּ, כִּי אַתָּה, אֲדֹנָי, טוֹב וְסַלָּח וְרַב חֶסֶד לְכָל־קוֹרְאֶיךָ.

THE THIRTEEN ATTRIBUTES

God, You are patient. You are known as the source of mercy. You taught the way of repentance. Today, and every day, call to mind the wonder of Your compassion and mercy toward the children of those You loved. Turn toward us in mercy, for You are the source of mercy.

We approach Your presence with supplication and prayer, and with the words You revealed to Moses, the humble one, long ago. Turn away from wrath, as it is written in Your Torah, and let us nestle under Your wings, *as on the day* "God descended in a cloud." Overlook sin, blot out guilt, *as on the day* "God stood beside him." Hear our cry, attend to our plea, *as on the day* "he called on the name ADONAI."

And God passed before him and called:
ADONAI, ADONAI, God, merciful and compassionate, patient, abounding in love and faithfulness, assuring love for thousands of generations, forgiving iniquity, transgression, and sin, and granting pardon.
Adonai, Adonai, El raḥum v'ḥannun, erekh appayim v'rav ḥesed ve-emet.
Notzer ḥesed la-alafim, nosei avon va-fesha v'ḥatta·ah v'nakkeih.

ADONAI . . . I am who I am before you sin
ADONAI . . . I am who I am after you sin
God . . . merciful to all, Gentile and Jew
merciful . . . to those with merit
and compassionate . . . to those without merit
patient . . . with the wicked, who may repent
abounding in love . . . with those in need of kindness
and faithfulness . . . rewarding those who do My will
assuring love for thousands of generations . . . when you do good deeds
forgiving iniquity . . . when you sin deliberately
transgression . . . when you rebel maliciously
and sin . . . when you sin unintentionally
and granting pardon . . . when you repent.

Forgive our transgressions and our sins; claim us for Your own.

Some strike their heart when asking God to forgive and pardon:
Forgive us, our creator, for we have sinned; pardon us, our sovereign, for we have transgressed—for You, ADONAI, are kind and forgiving;
You act generously to all who call on You.
S'laḥ lanu avinu ki ḥatanu, m'ḥal lanu malkeinu ki fashanu,
ki atah, Adonai, tov v'sallaḥ v'rav ḥesed l'khol kor'ekha.

אלה אזכרה

אֵלֶּה אֶזְכְּרָה וְנַפְשִׁי עָלַי אֶשְׁפְּכָה,
עַל קוֹרוֹתֵינוּ הַמָּרוֹת עֵינַי זוֹלְגוֹת דִּמְעָה.

א

כִּי בִימֵי הַשַּׂר לֹא עָלְתָה אֲרוּכָה לַעֲשָׂרָה הֲרוּגֵי מְלוּכָה.
וְשָׁנַיִם מֵהֶם הוֹצִיאוּ תְחִלָּה שֶׁהֵם גְּדוֹלֵי יִשְׂרָאֵל, רַבִּי
יִשְׁמָעֵאל כֹּהֵן גָּדוֹל וְרַבָּן שִׁמְעוֹן בֶּן־גַּמְלִיאֵל נְשִׂיא
יִשְׂרָאֵל. כְּרֹת רֹאשׁוֹ תְחִלָּה הִרְבָּה לִבְעוֹן וְנָם: הַרְגֵנִי
תְחִלָּה וְאַל אֶרְאֶה בְּמִיתַת מְשָׁרֵת לְדָר בְּמָעוֹן. וּלְהַפִּיל
גּוֹרָלוֹת צִוָּה צִפְעוֹן וְנָפַל הַגּוֹרָל עַל רַבָּן שִׁמְעוֹן.
לִשְׁפֹּךְ דָּמוֹ מִהֵר כְּשׁוֹר פָּר וּכְשֶׁנֶּחְתַּךְ רֹאשׁוֹ נְטָלוֹ וְצָרַח
עָלָיו בְּקוֹל מַר כַּשּׁוֹפָר: אֵי הַלָּשׁוֹן הַמְמַהֶרֶת לְהוֹרוֹת
בְּאִמְרֵי שֶׁפֶר, בַּעֲוֹנוֹת אֵיךְ עַתָּה לוֹחֶכֶת אֶת־הֶעָפָר.

אֵלֶּה אֶזְכְּרָה . . .

גְּזֵרָה מַלְכוּת הָרְשָׁעָה שֶׁלֹּא יַעַסְקוּ יִשְׂרָאֵל בַּתּוֹרָה.
וְרַבִּי עֲקִיבָא הָיָה מַקְהִיל קְהִלּוֹת בָּרַבִּים וְעוֹסֵק בַּתּוֹרָה.
תְּפָסוּהוּ וַחֲבָשׁוּהוּ בְּבֵית הָאֲסוּרִים. בְּשָׁעָה שֶׁהוֹצִיאוּ
אֶת־רַבִּי עֲקִיבָא לַהֲרֵגָה זְמַן קְרִיאַת שְׁמַע הָיָה וְהָיוּ
סוֹרְקִים אֶת־בְּשָׂרוֹ בְּמַסְרְקוֹת שֶׁל בַּרְזֶל וְהָיָה מְקַבֵּל
עָלָיו עוֹל מַלְכוּת שָׁמָיִם. אָמְרוּ לוֹ תַּלְמִידָיו: רַבֵּנוּ! עַד
כָּאן? אָמַר לָהֶם: כָּל־יָמַי הָיִיתִי מִצְטַעֵר עַל פָּסוּק זֶה —
"וּבְכָל־נַפְשְׁךָ", אֲפִלּוּ נוֹטֵל אֶת־נִשְׁמָתֶךָ. אָמַרְתִּי: מָתַי
יָבוֹא לְיָדִי וַאֲקַיְּמֶנּוּ? וְעַכְשָׁו שֶׁבָּא לְיָדִי, לֹא אֲקַיְּמֶנּוּ?!
הָיָה מַאֲרִיךְ בְּ"אֶחָד" עַד שֶׁיָּצְתָה נִשְׁמָתוֹ בְּ"אֶחָד."

אֵלֶּה אֶזְכְּרָה

THESE I RECALL אֵלֶּה
אֶזְכְּרָה. After the liturgical high point of the recollected Temple ritual, the service turns to recounting low points: scenes of martyrdom and destruction. The Avodah just recited offers a sense of our rapturous relationship with God; now we turn to prayers of sorrow, expressing a sense of abandonment by God.

Eilleh Ezk'rah, a late first-millennium rendering of the legend of martyrdom of ten rabbis killed by the Roman authorities following the Bar Kokhba revolt (132–135 C.E.), appears to have entered the Yom Kippur liturgy during the Crusades. Even earlier, mention of Jewish martyrdom and suffering had become a critical component of *s'liḥah* and *viddui* (forgiveness and confession). Indeed, each such service contained an *akeidah*, a martyrdom poem frequently drawing upon the image of the sacrifice of Isaac.

The Talmud records stories of the Bar Kokhba Revolt martyrs, which became the paradigms for later Jewish martyrdom. Rabbi Akiva, for instance, is reported to have died while reciting the Sh'ma,
saying that martyrdom expressed the extreme love of God. Subsequent generations of Jewish martyrs followed his example, going to their deaths reciting the Sh'ma. Strikingly, the Talmud (Babylonian Talmud, Menaḥot 29b) relates that Moses, seeing the fate of Rabbi Akiva, asks God, "Is this the Torah and its reward?" The question remains hanging. One can view this part of the service similarly, as a question to God that yet remains unanswered. Placing this question at the height of the day of Yom Kippur suggests a further question: "God, we have performed Your service in purity. We have fasted on this day, prayed to You, and pleaded our cause. But the reality we confront does not reflect our pious hopes. Why is that? If we are to give an accounting of ourselves on this day, are not You also to do so?"

The first line, as well as the story of the martyrdom of Rabbi Yishmael, is taken from the traditional *piyyut*. The story of the martyrdom of Rabbi Akiva is from Avot of Rabbi Natan, Version A, 38:3, and that of the other rabbis from the Talmud. The second line of the poetic rhyme, written for this maḥzor, introduces the historical series that follows.

EILLEH EZK'RAH: THESE I RECALL

These I recall, and my soul melts with sorrow;
for the bitter course of our history, tears pour from my eyes.
Eilleh ezk'rah v'nafshi alai eshp'khah,
al koroteinu ha-marot einai zol'got dim·ah.

א

The Rabbinic Martyrs Murdered by Rome

THE MARTYRDOM OF RABBAN SHIMON

In the time of the Roman Empire, God suffered ten rabbis to be martyred. Two of the most distinguished were taken out first: Rabbi Yishmael, the High Priest, and Rabban Shimon ben Gamliel, head of the Sanhedrin. Rabban Shimon pleaded to be executed first in order not to gaze upon the death of the one who had served God in the Temple. The tyrant commanded that lots be cast and it fell to Rabban Shimon to be martyred first and have his blood flow like a slaughtered bull. Rabbi Yishmael picked up his severed head and cried bitterly, like the shofar, "How the tongue that rushed to teach such beautiful words, now licks the earth because of our sins!"

  These I recall . . . Eilleh ezk'rah . . .

THE MARTYRDOM OF RABBI AKIVA

The Romans decreed that the people Israel no longer be allowed to study Torah. Rabbi Akiva publicly convened assemblies and continued to teach Torah. He was captured and imprisoned. The hour of execution was the time for the recitation of the morning Sh'ma, so as they scraped his skin with iron combs, he recited the Sh'ma, accepting the yoke of the sovereignty of heaven. His pupils cried out, "Even now?!" He said to them, "All my life, I was troubled that I could not fulfill the verse to love God 'with all your soul'—that is, even should God take your life. I asked myself, 'When will the time come that I can fulfill the verse?' Now that I have that possiblity, shouldn't I fulfill it?!" He prolonged the word "One" so that his soul left him as he uttered the word "One."

  These I recall . . . Eilleh ezk'rah . . .

אָמְרוּ עָלָיו עַל רַבִּי יְהוּדָה בֶּן־בָּבָא שֶׁלֹּא טָעַם חֵטְא
מִיָּמָיו וְיָשַׁב בְּתַעֲנִית עֶשְׂרִים וָשֵׁשׁ שָׁנָה. גָּזְרָה הַמַּלְכוּת
הָרְשָׁעָה עַל יִשְׂרָאֵל שֶׁכָּל־הַסּוֹמֵךְ יֵהָרֵג וְכָל־הַנִּסְמָךְ
יֵהָרֵג וְעִיר שֶׁסּוֹמְכִין בָּהּ תֵּחָרֵב וּתְחוּמֶיהָ תֵּחָרֵב. מֶה עָשָׂה רַבִּי
יְהוּדָה בֶּן־בָּבָא? הָלַךְ וְיָשַׁב לוֹ בֵּין שְׁנֵי הָרִים גְּדוֹלִים
וּבֵין שְׁתֵּי עֲיָרוֹת גְּדוֹלוֹת בֵּין אוּשָׁא לִשְׁפַרְעָם, וְסָמַךְ
שָׁם חֲמִשָּׁה זְקֵנִים. כֵּיוָן שֶׁהִכִּירוּ אוֹיְבֵיהֶן בָּהֶן, אָמַר לָהֶן:
בָּנַי, רוּצוּ! אָמְרוּ לוֹ: רַבִּי, מַה תְּהֵא עָלֶיךָ? אָמַר לָהֶן:
הֲרֵינִי מוּטָל לִפְנֵיהֶם כְּאֶבֶן שֶׁאֵין לוֹ הוֹפְכִים.
אָמְרוּ, לֹא זָזוּ מִשָּׁם עַד שֶׁנָּעֲצוּ בּוֹ שְׁלֹשׁ מֵאוֹת
לוֹנְכִיּוֹת שֶׁל בַּרְזֶל וַעֲשָׂאוּהוּ כְּכְבָרָה.

אֵלֶּה אֶזְכְּרָה . . .

מְצָאוּהוּ לְרַבִּי חֲנִינָא הָיָה מַקְהִיל קְהִלּוֹת בָּרַבִּים וְסֵפֶר
תּוֹרָה מֻנָּח לוֹ בְּחֵיקוֹ. כְּרָכוּהוּ בְּסֵפֶר תּוֹרָה וְהֶקִּיפוּהוּ
בַּחֲבִילֵי זְמוֹרוֹת וְהִצִּיתוּ בָהֶן אֶת־הָאוּר וְהֵבִיא סְפוֹגִין
שֶׁל צֶמֶר וּשְׂרָאוּם בְּמַיִם וְהִנִּיחוּם עַל לִבּוֹ כְּדֵי שֶׁלֹּא
תֵצֵא נִשְׁמָתוֹ מְהֵרָה. אָמְרוּ לוֹ תַּלְמִידָיו: רַבִּי, מָה אַתָּה
רוֹאֶה? אָמַר לָהֶן: גְּוִילִין נִשְׂרָפִין וְאוֹתִיּוֹת פּוֹרְחוֹת.

אֵלֶּה אֶזְכְּרָה . . .

ב

וַיְהִי כַּאֲשֶׁר שָׁמְעוּ אַנְשֵׁי קֹדֶשׁ חֲסִידֵי עֶלְיוֹן, קְהִלַּת
הַקֹּדֶשׁ אֲשֶׁר בְּמַעֲגְנְצָא, מָגֵן וְצִנָּה לְכָל־הַקְּהִילוֹת, אֲשֶׁר
נֶהֶרְגוּ קְצָת הַקָּהָל בִּשְׁפֵּיְרָא וְקָהָל וּוְרְמַיְישָׁא בְּפַעַם
שֵׁנִית וְנָגְעָה חֶרֶב עֲדֵיהֶם, אָז רָפְתָה יָדָם וְנָמֵס לָהֶם
וַיְהִי לְמַיִם. וַיִּצְעֲקוּ אֶל יהוה בְּכָל־לִבָּם וַיֹּאמְרוּ: יהוה
אֱלֹהֵי יִשְׂרָאֵל, הַאַתָּה עוֹשֶׂה אֶת־שְׁאֵרִית יִשְׂרָאֵל כָּלָה?
וְאַיֵּה כָּל־נִפְלְאוֹתֶיךָ הַנּוֹרָאוֹת אֲשֶׁר סִפְּרוּ לָנוּ
אֲבוֹתֵינוּ לֵאמֹר, הֲלֹא מִמִּצְרַיִם וּמִבָּבֶל הֶעֱלִיתָנוּ וְכַמָּה
פְעָמִים הִצַּלְתָּנוּ, וְאֵיךְ עַתָּה עֲזַבְתָּנוּ וּנְטַשְׁתָּנוּ יהוה,
לָתֵת אוֹתָנוּ בְּיַד אֱדוֹם הָרְשָׁעָה לְהַשְׁמִידֵנוּ. אַל תִּרְחַק
מִמֶּנּוּ, כִּי צָרָה קְרוֹבָה וְאֵין עוֹזֵר לָנוּ.

RABBI YEHUDAH BEN BAVA. The story is reported in the Babylonian Talmud, Avodah Zarah 8b and Sanhedrin 14a.

RABBI ḤANINA. The story is told in the Babylonian Talmud, Avodah Zarah 18a and Sanhedrin 14a.

THE CRUSADES. As the First Crusade passed through Europe, masses of Christian soldiers and commoners decided that they would murder "infidels" along the route to the Holy Land. Many Jewish communities were slaughtered, and nobles and even church authorities who tried to oppose the violence were ignored. At the time of the First Crusade there were three centers of Jewish learning in Germany: Mainz, Speyer, and Worms. In Mainz, more than 1,000 Jews were killed in 1096 and the synagogue was burnt to the ground. Many of the *piyyutim* we recite today were written by members of the Kalonymous family of Mainz. The account here was taken from the chronicle of Solomon bar Samson.

ARE YOU WIPING OUT THE REMNANT OF ISRAEL? הַאַתָּה עוֹשֶׂה אֶת שְׁאֵרִית יִשְׂרָאֵל כָּלָה. Ezekiel 11:13.

ESAU אֱדוֹם. Jews commonly used the generic name "Esau" or "Edom" for their enemies. The substitution served two purposes. Theologically, the enemies of Israel were identified with their biblical prototypes, and, practically, these allusions frequently escaped the censors.

THE MARTYRDOM OF RABBI YEHUDAH BEN BAVA

It is said of Rabbi Yehudah ben Bava that he never tasted sin in his life, but sat and fasted for twenty-six years. The Romans had decreed that anyone who ordained rabbis or anyone who was ordained would be killed, and that any city in which the ordinaton took place would be destroyed, as well as its suburbs. What did Rabbi Yehudah ben Bava do? He sat in a valley between two cities, Usha and Shefaram, and ordained five rabbis. When word got out, he told them to flee. They asked him, "But what will become of you?" He replied, "I will remain as an immovable rock." It is reported that the Romans did not leave until they had pierced him with 300 lances so that his body was like a sieve.

These I recall . . . Eilleh ezk'rah . . .

THE MARTYRDOM OF RABBI ḤANINA BEN TERADION

They also found Rabbi Ḥanina ben Teradion sitting and teaching Torah in public with a Sefer Torah in his lap. They wrapped the Sefer Torah around him, piled branches roundabout, lit them, and placed wet wool over his heart so that he would not die quickly. His disciples asked, "Master, what do you see?" He replied, "The parchment is burning, but the letters are flying free."

These I recall . . . Eilleh ezk'rah . . .

ב

The First Crusade

When the members of the pious and holy community in Mainz—whose reputation had spread throughout all the provinces as "a shield and protector" for all the Jewish communities—heard that the communities of Speyer and Worms had been attacked a second time and some had been killed, their hearts melted and they despaired. They cried out to the God of Israel with all their might, saying: "ADONAI, God of Israel, are You wiping out the remnant of Israel? Where are all Your awe-inspiring wonders, about which our ancestors told us, saying: 'Truly ADONAI brought us up from Egypt and Babylonia'? How many times have You saved us? Have You now abandoned and forsaken us, ADONAI, leaving us in the hands of wicked Esau, that they might destroy us? Do not distance Yourself from us, for tragedy is near and there is none to aid us."

וְהָיָה בַיּוֹם שְׁלוֹשָׁה בְּסִינַן אֲשֶׁר הָיָה יוֹם קָדוֹשׁ יוֹם קְדוֹשׁ וּפְרִישָׁה
לְיִשְׂרָאֵל בְּמַתַּן תּוֹרָה, בְּאוֹתוֹ יוֹם שֶׁאָמַר מֹשֶׁה רַבֵּנוּ
עָלָיו הַשָּׁלוֹם: "הֱיוּ נְכוֹנִים לִשְׁלוֹשֶׁת יָמִים", אוֹתוֹ הַיּוֹם
הוּפְרְשׁוּ קְהַל מַעֶגְנְצָא, חֲסִידֵי עֶלְיוֹן, בִּקְדֻשָּׁה
וּבְטָהֳרָה וְהוּקְדְּשׁוּ לַעֲלוֹת אֶל הָאֱלֹהִים כֻּלָּם יַחַד, כִּי
הָיוּ נְעִימִים בְּחַיֵּיהֶם וּבְמוֹתָם לֹא נִפְרָדוּ, כִּי כֻּלָּם בַּחֲצַר
הַהֶגְמוֹן. וַיִּחַר אַף בְּעַמּוֹ וְקִיֵּם עֲצַת הַתּוֹעִים וְעָלָה
בְיָדָם וְכָל־הוֹן לֹא הוֹעִיל, וְלֹא צוֹם וְעִנּוּי וְצַעֲקָה
וּצְדָקָה, וַאֲפִילוּ הַתּוֹרָה הַקְּדוֹשָׁה לֹא הֵגִינָה עַל לוֹמְדֶיהָ.
וַיֵּצֵא מִבַּת צִיּוֹן כָּל־הֲדָרָהּ, הִיא מַעֶגְנְצָא. עִיר תְּהִלָּתִי
קִרְיַת מְשׂוֹשִׂי, אֲשֶׁר כַּמָּה מֵאוֹת פִּזְּרָה לָאֶבְיוֹנִים, וְאֵין
לִכְתּוֹב בְּעֵט בַּרְזֶל בְּגִלְיוֹן סֵפֶר רוֹב מַעֲשִׂים אֲשֶׁר הָיָה
בָהּ מִימוֹת עוֹלָם, בְּמָקוֹם אֶחָד תּוֹרָה וּגְדֻלָּה וְעֹשֶׁר
וְכָבוֹד וְחָכְמָה וַעֲנָוָה וּמַעֲשִׂים טוֹבִים לַעֲשׂוֹת גָּדֵר עַל
גָּדֵר סְיָג לְדִבְרֵיהֶם, וְעַתָּה נִבְלְעוּ חֲכָמִים וְנִהְיוּ לִכְלָיָה
כִּבְנֵי יְרוּשָׁלַיִם בְּחֻרְבָּנָם.

אֵלֶּה אֶזְכְּרָה . . .

ג

יְהוּדָה וְיִשְׂרָאֵל דְּעוּ מַר לִי מְאֹד
לָכֵן בְּחָטֹאתִי אֲנִי אֶרְעַד רְעַד.

חָסְרָה נְגִינָתִי וְשִׂמְחָתִי בוֹד
אֶזְכּוֹר: שְׁבִילְיָא כִּי אֲבַדְנוּהָ אָבַד.

חָסְרָה עֲטֶרֶת כֹּל קְהִלּוֹת אַרְגּוֹן
גַּם קַאטִילוֹנְיָיא וּבָם שָׁלַט אוֹיֵב בְּשֹׁד.

חָסְרָה צְפִירַת הוֹד בְּקַשְׁטִילְיָיא לִיאוֹן
אֶבְכֶּה לְצָרָתָם מְלֹא דִמְעָה כְנֹאד.

חָסְרָה נְוַת תַּלְמוּד וְהַמִּשְׁנָה, וְהִיא
נִבְזֵית בְּעֵין אוֹיְבִים וּבוֹגְדִים בּוֹ בָגָד.

BE READY FOR THE THIRD DAY הֱיוּ נְכוֹנִים לִשְׁלוֹשֶׁת יָמִים. Exodus 19:15. Moses' exhortation to the people Israel before the revelation on Mount Sinai. The chronicler ironically argues that at this time, too, Israel was ready for a revelation; instead, its people were destroyed.

GONE FROM ZION וַיֵּצֵא מִבַּת צִיּוֹן. Lamentations 1:6. The destruction of the community of Mainz is thus identified with the destruction of the Temple. The chronicler makes this connection explicit in the last line of the text.

JUDAH AND ISRAEL יְהוּדָה וְיִשְׂרָאֵל. This *piyyut* was written in response to the destruction of the Jewish communities in Spain. It is recited to this day by the Sephardic community of Venice. It is a remarkable text in that it speaks openly of Jewish apostasy, while lamenting the loss of the learned communities in Spain (which the poet enumerates by region). It is equally surprising in the way the author stresses the loss of a sense of God's presence. For the poet, all is lost because both Jewish faithfulness and God's faithfulness are nowhere in evidence.

This piyyut by David ben Meshullam (12th century, Germany) bears poetic witness to the slaughter of the Jewish community of Mainz in the First Crusade. It is traditionally recited at this point of the Yom Kippur Musaf service.

God, do not be silent over my
   spilt blood,
do not be quiet, but avenge
   me.
Seek retribution from those
   who would destroy me
lest the whole earth be covered
   with my blood.

Innocent children, our holy
   seed, do not lie:
"This is my God whom I
   would glorify," they loudly
   sang.
These were to be our inheritors—of whom we were so
   proud—
they have now been wrapped
   in the bond of eternal life.

Women and children together
   covenanted to die;
these sheep were gathered in
   the slaughterhouse yard,
"O Holy One, bound and
   slaughtered we go up to You,"
refusing to be tied to another
   faith.

As year-old whole burnt offerings,
were these sacrifices made,
while instructing their mothers, "Do not be overcome,
for we are wanted as holocaust
   offerings by God on High."

Tears poured forth every-
   where,
the slaughtered and the slaugh-
   terers moaning to one other,
the blood of fathers mixing
   with their children,

(continued on next page)

But it came to pass on the third day of Sivan, which had been a day of sanctity and separation for ancient Israel in preparation of the giving of the Torah—on that day when Moses our teacher, may his memory be blessed, said: "Be ready for the third day . . ."—on that day the holy community of Mainz was designated for martyrdom; these pious people sanctified themselves by ascending to God as one. In life kindly toward each other, in death they were not parted, for they were all gathered together in the courtyard of the archbishop. The wrath of God was kindled against God's people and so the counsel of the Crusaders was fulfilled. Neither wealth nor fasting availed, nor self-affliction nor wailing nor charity. Even the holy Torah did not protect those who studied it. "Gone from Zion were all that were her glory"—namely Mainz. It was my glorious city, my citadel of joy, about which an iron stylus could not sufficiently inscribe in a ledger the number of righteous deeds performed there, including the untold sums distributed to the poor since antiquity. In this one place were found power and wealth, honor and wisdom, humility and good deeds, and Torah teachings which took innumerable precautions against transgression. But now their wisdom has been swallowed up and destroyed, as happened to the citizens of Jerusalem in their destruction.

These I recall . . . Eilleh ezk'rah . . .

ג

The Destruction of Spanish Jewry

Judah and Israel, know how bitter I am;
as I tremble, for my sins, shuddering and shaken.

For gone is my song, or any possible joy,
replaced by memories of Seville, now lost and forsaken.

Gone as well are the crown of Catalonia and Aragon;
ruled are you now by a pillaging crew.

Gone the splendid chant of Castile and Leon;
my tears could fill vessels, while weeping anew.

Gone the splendor of the Mishnah and Talmud,
reviled by foes and by traitors negating You!

חָסְרָה קְהִלַּת אֵל וְלוֹמְדֵי דָת וְדִין
עַל זֹאת יְהוּדָה קוּם וְיִשְׂרָאֵל סְפֹד.

חָסְרָה זְכוּת אָבוֹת וְלֹא תָלִין בְּעַד
זַרְעָם וְסַף גִּזְעָם וְנִכְחֲדוּ כְחַד.

חָסְרָה אֱמוּנַת אֵל בְּבוֹא עַמִּי בְּיַד
אוֹנֵס וְאוֹמֵר לוֹ: עֲבוֹדָתִי עֲבֹד!

חָסְרָה מְתִיקוּת מִבְּנֵי עַמּוֹ וְלֹא
חָסְרָה מְרִירוּתָם וְתִשְׁקֹד בָּם שְׁקֹד.

חָסְרָה עֲרֵבוּתָם וְטוֹבָתָם וְכָל־חָכְמַת
חֲכָמֵיהֶם וְנֶחְלָדָה חֲלֹד.

חָסְרָה יָדַעְתִּי בְּקוֹרוֹת הַזְּמָן
אֶמְאַס לְקוֹל שִׁירִים וּמָחוֹל גַּם רְקֹד.

חָסְרָה תְשׁוּבַת אֵל לְצַעֲקָתָם
אֵין עוֹנֶה וְאֵין חוֹמֵל וְנִלְאָה מִפְקֹד.

חָסְרָה חֲנִינַת אֵל וְרַחֲמָיו נִשְׁכְּחוּ
הוּא לִי כְּמוֹ אַכְזָר וְגַם אוֹיֵב וְעוֹד.

חָסְרָה נְבוּאָה בִּי וְנֶחְתַּם כָּל־חֲזוֹן
אוּרִים וְגַם תֻּמִּים וְצֵרוּף שֵׁם בְּסוֹד.

חָסְרָה בְּשׂוֹרַת אִישׁ אֵלִיָּהוּ נָבִיא
הָאֵל וְנֶעְכַּב שָׁם וְאָמְרוּ לוֹ: עֲמֹד!

חָסְרָה יְשׁוּעַת מֵעֲדַת עִבְרִים וּבָם
צָרוֹת מְחֻדָּשׁוֹת כְּאֵשׁ יֵקַד יְקֹד.

חָסְרָה שְׁכִינָה מִשְׁכַּן מַטָּה בְּתוֹךְ
מִקְדָּשׁ וּבְיִשְׂרָאֵל וְחָדְלָה מִן כְּבוֹד.

אֵלֶּה אֶזְכְּרָה . . .

(continued from previous page)
and all declaiming the
   blessing of the sacrifice,
   "Sh'ma yisrael..."

Has such ever been
   heard? A sight like
   this seen?
How can one believe
   such awful deeds:
leading children to
   slaughter as if to the
   marriage canopy?
Can the One on High
   hold back after this?

Gone God's congregations and students of the Law.
Rise then, Judah; for Israel, it is time to mourn.

Gone the patriarchs' merit, no longer able to defend their
     descendants,
their stock, oppressed and completely forlorn.

Gone faith in God as my people succumbed to the ravager
who declared, "Worship as I!"

Gone is sweetness from the people of God,
they are left only with this bitterness coming nigh.

Gone beauty, gone goodness; gone the teaching of the wise;
all have taken leave or have rotted away.

Gone awareness of everyday affairs.
I have come to despise singing and the dancer's sway.

Gone God's reply to the people's cry,
no one to answer or comfort or care.

Gone is God's pity, mercy forgotten,
now become cruel, my enemy's pair.

Gone prophetic dreams, and visions of hope,
priestly charm, or help from the Holy Name are past.

We will not hear the call of Elijah, God's prophet;
for Heaven has restrained him and he is told, "Stand fast!"

Salvation is gone from the Hebrew folk;
new troubles spring up as a fiery blaze.

For gone is God's Presence, no longer found on earth;
not in temple or folk, or amidst glorious praise.

   These I recall ... Eilleh ezk'rah ...

I SHALL REMEMBER. Jacob Glatstein's poem was published in 1966. Born Yankev Glatshteyn in Lublin, Poland, in 1896, Glatstein lived most of his life in the United States, having migrated as a teenager. He died in New York, in 1971. The poem evokes the Eastern European life of his youth and of his memory. In mourning his own family and in sharing his own remembrances, he creates a eulogy for all that was lost in the destruction of European Jewry in the Holocaust: a loss of a way of life, a loss of a language, a loss of so many individual people. The translation is by Benjamin and Barbara Harshav.

ד

נאָר די זאַכן וויל איך דערמאָנען,
די באַזונדערע קלענערע חורבנות,
וואָס זענען צייטיק געוואָרן אין מיר . . .
נאָר די זאַכן טו איך דערמאָנען.
די באַרוועסע חלום-סטעזשקע,
וואָס האָט ווי אַ פרידיקער שניט
דורכגעבליצט דורך דער מאַפע
פון מיין פאַרבענקטן שלאָף
דעם שטילן וועג וואָס האָט צוזאַמענגעקרייצט
אַלע לענדער, אַלע גאַסן, אַלע הייזער,
אויף איין אויפגעשראָקענער, אויפגעוואָאכטער יידנגאַס,
וואָס האָט מיט אירע ווארעמע שטיינער,
טוכלען געהילץ און מצבהדיקן ציגל
אויפגענומען מיינע אָנלויפנדיקע טריט.
די בשמים-געשעפטן,
די קאָשע- און מעל-קראָמען,
די הערינג-געוועלבלעך,
די נאַפט- קלייטן און די געזייפטע ראָזורעס,
די שייטל- און פּאַרוק-מאַכערס,
די מאַנדלען, טייטלען און פייגן,
דאָס פריש-געבאַקענע זויער-ברויט,
די מאַן-און-געציבלטע-פלעצלעך,
די חושכדיקע טשייניעס,
מיט די דרימלענדיקע, שווארצע ווערעם
אויפן וואָרעמן פּיעקעליק,
די מאָגערע לאָנקעס,
די פאַרדרימלטע און האַלב-לעבעדיקע בית-עלמינס,
וואָס האָבן שטענדיק באָוואַכט
דאָס אַנגעשראָקענע לעבן.

אַלץ האָט געווארט אויף דעם ברען און ברי
פון דעם יינגלס סאָפענדיקע,
אָנלויפנדיקע טריט
און איז זיך צוזאַמענגעקומען אויף דעם איינציקן,
שאַרפן און פרידיקן שניט,

ד

The Holocaust

I SHALL REMEMBER

And these too I want to remember,
The separate, smaller destructions,
That ripened in me . . .
And these too I shall remember.
The barefoot dream-path,
Like lightening,
A joyful flash through the map
Of my nostalgic sleep,
The quiet road that brought together
All the countries, streets, houses
Into one scared-awake Jewstreet,
With its warm stones,
Its moldy wood and somber bricks,
Accepting my light feet.
The spice shops,
The kasha-and-flour stores,
The herring stands,
The kerosene vendors, the soapy barbershops,
The toupee and wig-makers,
The almonds, dates and figs,
The freshly-baked sour-bread
The poppy-seed and onion rolls,
The dark tearooms
With drowsing, black worms
On their warm fireplace,
The meager pastures,
The sleepy, half-alive graveyards,
Forever watching over
The frightened life.

All this was waiting
For the fiery breath
Of the boy's panting, light feet,
All this came together on the single,
Sharp and joyful flash

Smoke

Through crematorium
  chimneys
a Jew curls toward the
  Eternal.
As soon as the smoke is
  gone,
upward cluster his wife
  and son.

And above, in the high
  heavens,
sacred smoke prays and
  weeps.
God—where You are—
we all disappear.

—JACOB GLATSTEIN
(trans. Richard J. Fein, adapted)

פֿון דער חלום-סטעזשקע,
וואָס האָט געהייסן היים . . .

נאָר דאָס דאַרף איך דערמאָנען:
די אויפֿגעציליעטע לידער
פֿון מײַן מאַמען,
די לאַכנדיקע, קלוגע און קוים-געגראַמטע ווערטער.
די מחיהדיקע, מוסר-השׂכלדיקע,
איר שטיל מויל, וואָס האָט זיך אַלעמאָל
פֿריִער קלוג באַדאַכט,
איידער ס'האָט זיך שײן געעפֿנט
און אַרומגעקײַלעכדיקט אַ באַטעמטן זאָג,
וואָס די גאַנצע משפּחה האָט געוואַרט דערויף.
ווי אויך אַן עצה-טובה.
מײַן מאַמע, די שטאָלצע דינסט פֿון איר הויזגעזינד,
האָט צווישן שײַערן, קאָכן,
און וואַשן גרעט,
מיר פֿאַרטרויט דאָס וואונדער
פֿון דעם פֿויעריש-ייִדישן גלײַכווערטל,
פֿויעריש-אײַנגעזעסן אויף אײגענער ערד,
מיט אײגענע קי, אײגענע סעדער,
אײגענער סמעטענע און רויטע יאַגדעס
און געפֿעפֿערטע, האַרטע, געטרוקנטע קעזלעך.
זי, די מאַמע מײַנע, האָב איך געקרוינט
פֿאַר דער מאַמע פֿון מײַן גאַנצן ייִדישן פֿאָלק.
און צו איר און נאָר איר
האָב איך מײַן גאַנץ לעבן געבענקט,
ווען ס'האָט אויפֿגעלויכט און אויפֿגעטונקלט
דאָס קלײנע פֿינטעלע אויף מײַן חלום-מאַמע . . .

און אַז מײַן צדקותדיקער טאַטע,
וואָס איז געווען מײַן פֿענצטערל צו דער גרויסער וועלט,
מײַן טאַטע, מיט די זיכערע, נחתדיקע טריט,
מיט די גלייביקע, בטחונדיקע טריט,
אַז ער האָט מיטגענומען מײַן ברודער בנימין,
מיט די גלײַיקע אויגן,

In responding to the Holocaust, Charles Reznikoff, an American poet, sees the Jewish people as aspiring to transform the evil of the world into the work of redemption.

¶ Out of the strong, sweetness;
and out of the dead body of the
    lion of Judah,
the prophecies and the psalms;
out of the slaves in Egypt,
out of the wandering tribesmen
    of the deserts
and the peasants of Palestine,
out of the slaves of Babylon and
    Rome,
out of the ghettos of Spain
    and Portugal, Germany and
    Poland,
the Torah and the prophecies,
the Talmud and the sacred
    studies, the hymns and
    songs of the Jews;
and out of the Jewish dead
of Belgium and Holland, of
    Rumania, Hungary, and
    Bulgaria,
of France and Italy and
    Yugoslavia,
of Lithuania and Latvia, White
    Russia and Ukrainia,
of Czechoslovakia and Austria,
Poland and Germany,
out of the greatly wronged
a people teaching and doing
    justice;
out of the plundered
a generous people;
out of the wounded a people of
    physicians;
and out of those who met only
    with hate,
a people of love, a compassion-
    ate people.

—CHARLES REZNIKOFF

Of the dream-path
Called home
. . .
And this too I should remember:
My mother's songs
Strung like beads,
The laughing, wise and barely-rhymed words,
The refreshing, moral tale,
That her quiet mouth, always
First pondered wisely
Before it opened beautifully
And rounded out a tasteful saying;
The whole family was waiting for it
As for good advice.
My mother, the proud servant of her household,
In between scrubbing, cooking,
And washing laundry,
Confided to me the wonder
Of the peasant-wise Jewish proverb,
Rooted like Gentile peasants on their own soil,
With their own cows, their own arbors,
Their own sweet cream and red strawberries
And peppered, hard, dried cheeses.
Her, my mother, I crowned
As the mother of my whole Jewish people.
For her I have longed my whole life,
When the little dot on my dream-map
Lit up and fell dark.
. . .

And when my saintly father,
Who was my small window on the great world,
My father with his sure, measured steps,
His believing, trusting steps,
When he took my brother Benjamin
With his glowing eyes

און מיט בנימין'ס ווײַב און קינד

זענען זיי אלע געגאנגען מיטן גאַנצן פאָלק,
האָבן זיי באַזונדערע, קלײַנע, געמאָסטענע, שנײַדיקע טריט
געמאַכט פאַר מיר.

זיי זענען באַזונדער געגאַנגען אויף מײַן שמאָלער אַלייע.
דאָרט, מיטן פאָלק זענען זיי געגאַנגען מיט טריט,
וואָס האָבן זיך געציילט, ווי זאַמד בײַם ים,
אָבער פאַר מיר זענען זיי געווען
באַזונדערדיקע טריט,
ווי אייגענע האַרץ-קלעפ.
מײַן אייגן פאָלק, וואָס מיט אים האָב איך אָנגעהויבן
מײַן באַשאַפענע וועלט –
שפּאַנט איצט צום סוף,
מײַן באַשאַפענע וועלט, וואָס האָט געהאַט אן אָנהייב,
ברענט איצט אין די לעצטע שעהן פון אונטערגאַנג.
דער גאַנצער הימל לעשט זיך,
אַ גאַנץ תּנכל ווערט פינצטער און שטום,
אַ גאַנץ לאַנד ווערט חרוב.
ס'גייען מיליאָנען און מיט זיי
מײַן טאַטע, מיט די ווײַצלדיקע אויגן,
מײַן ברודער בנימין,
מיט צוטרוילעכער ליבשאַפט, נאָכן טאַטן,
מיט ווײַב און קינד.
און באַזונדער שפּאַנען זיי
דורך מײַן חלום-סטעזשקע,
גייען פאַרבײַ, גייען אונטער,
און צערײַסן מײַן גאַנצן חלום,
ווי שפּינוועב.

נאָך די באַזונדערע קלענערע חורבנות,
וואָס זענען צײַטיק געוואָרן אין מיר,
האָב איך געמוזט טאָן דערמאָנען.

אֵלֶה אֶזְכְּרָה . . .

From "The Song of the Murdered People"

And it continued. Ten a day, ten thousand Jews a day.

That did not last very long. Soon they took fifteen thousand.

Warsaw! The city of Jews—the fenced-in, walled-in city,

Dwindled, expired, melted, like snow before my eyes.

The first to perish were the children, abandoned orphans,

The world's best, the bleak earth's brightest.

These children from the orphanages might have been our comfort.

From these sad, mute, bleak faces our new dawn might have risen.

They, the Jewish children, were the first to perish, all of them,

Almost all without father or mother, eaten by cold, hunger and vermin,

Saintly messiahs, sanctified by pain . . . O why such punishment?

Why were they first to pay so high a price to evil in the days of slaughter?

This is how it began, from the start . . . O heavens, tell me why,

Why must we be so shamed on this great earth?

The deaf-mute earth's eyes seem shut. But you, heavens, you saw,

You watched from above and yet did not collapse!

And Benjamin's wife and children,

When they went with the whole people,

They took separate small, measured, cutting steps for me.

They went separately through my narrow alley.

There, with the people, they walked with steps

Numerous as the sand of the sea,

But for me they were

Separate footsteps,

My own heartbeats.

My own people, with whom I began

My own created world—

Draws now to its end.

My created world—that had a beginning,

Now burns in the last hours of its doom.

The light of the sky goes out.

A whole Bible grows dark and mute.

A whole land is laid waste.

Millions walk and with them

My father with his witty eyes,

My brother Benjamin

Behind my father, with trustful love,

With wife and child.

And separately they stride

Through my dream-path,

Pass by, pass away,

And rip up my whole dream

Like a spider web.

These separate, smaller destructions too,

That grew ripe in me,

I had to remember.

These I recall . . .   *Eilleh ezk'rah* . . .

They are no more! Don't ask overseas about Kasrilevke, Yhupetz. Don't.

Don't look for Menachem Mendels, Tevye the dairymen, Nogids, Motke thieves.

Don't look—

They will, like the prophets, Isaiah, Jeremiah, Ezekiel, Hosea, and Amos from the Bible,

Cry to you from Bialik, speak to you from Sholem Aleichem and Sholem Asch's books.

—YITZHAK KATZNELSON
(trans. Noah H. Rosenbloom)

ALL MY WARS. History has not ended: to the losses of the past, we add our own contemporary losses. Early poems by the Israeli poet Yehuda Amichai talk of his participation in the Israeli wars of 1947–1948 and the loss of comrades in combat. Subsequently, among other themes, he has written of the tragedy of the Arab-Israeli conflict and of Jerusalem. In this poem, he reflects on his father's experience as a German soldier in World War I, his hopes for peace and an end to destruction and mayhem. Amichai concludes the poem with his own experience of continuing war and violence. The translation is by T. Carmi.

אָבִי הָיָה אַרְבַּע שָׁנִים בְּמִלְחַמְתָּם,
וְלֹא שָׂנֵא אוֹיְבָיו וְלֹא אָהַב.
אֲבָל אֲנִי יוֹדֵעַ, כִּי כְּבָר שָׁם
בָּנָה אוֹתִי יוֹם־יוֹם מִשַּׁלְוֹותָיו

הַמְּעַטוֹת כָּל־כָּךְ, אֲשֶׁר לָקַט
אוֹתָן בֵּין פְּצָצוֹת וּבֵין עָשָׁן,
וְשָׂם אוֹתָן בְּתַרְמִילוֹ הַמְמֻרְטָט
עִם שְׁאֵרִית עוּגַת־אִמּוֹ הַמִּתְקַשָּׁה.

וּבְעֵינָיו אָסַף מֵתִים בְּלִי שֵׁם,
מֵתִים רַבִּים אָסַף לְמַעֲנִי,
שֶׁאַכִּירֵם בְּמַבָּטָיו וְאֹהֲבֵם

וְלֹא אָמוּת כְּמוֹהֶם בַּזְּוָעָה . . .
הוּא מִלֵּא עֵינָיו בָּהֶם וְהוּא טָעָה:
אֶל כָּל־מִלְחֲמוֹתַי יוֹצֵא אֲנִי.

MY FATHER

My father took part in their war for four years, and he didn't hate his enemies or love them. But I know that already there, day after day, he was forming me out of his few—so very few—

tranquilities, which he scraped up between bombs and smoke, then put them in his tattered pack, together with the scraps of his mother's hardening cake.

And in his eyes he gathered the nameless dead, a great many dead he gathered for my sake, that I might recognize them in his look and love them

and not die, as they did, in such horror . . . He filled his eyes with them, and he was mistaken: I must go out to all my wars.

יִתְגַּדַּל
Kishinev

וְיִתְקַדַּשׁ
Warsaw

שְׁמֵהּ רַבָּא
Auschwitz

בְּעָלְמָא דִּי בְרָא, כִּרְעוּתֵיהּ,
Dachau

וְיַמְלִיךְ מַלְכוּתֵיהּ
Buchenwald

בְּחַיֵּיכוֹן וּבְיוֹמֵיכוֹן
Babi Yar

וּבְחַיֵּי דְכָל בֵּית יִשְׂרָאֵל,
Baghdad

בַּעֲגָלָא וּבִזְמַן קָרִיב,
Hebron

וְאִמְרוּ אָמֵן.

יְהֵא שְׁמֵהּ רַבָּא מְבָרַךְ
לְעָלַם וּלְעָלְמֵי עָלְמַיָּא.

יִתְבָּרַךְ וְיִשְׁתַּבַּח
Kfar Etzion

וְיִתְפָּאַר וְיִתְרוֹמַם
Mayence

וְיִתְנַשֵּׂא וְיִתְהַדָּר
Terezin

וְיִתְעַלֶּה וְיִתְהַלָּל שְׁמֵהּ דְּקֻדְשָׁא בְּרִיךְ הוּא לְעֵלָּא לְעֵלָּא
Vilna   Bergen-Belsen   Treblinka

מִכָּל־בִּרְכָתָא וְשִׁירָתָא תֻּשְׁבְּחָתָא וְנֶחָמָתָא דַּאֲמִירָן בְּעָלְמָא
Jerusalem   Massada   Usha

וְאִמְרוּ אָמֵן.

יְהֵא שְׁלָמָא רַבָּא מִן שְׁמַיָּא וְחַיִּים עָלֵינוּ
וְעַל כָּל־יִשְׂרָאֵל, וְאִמְרוּ אָמֵן.

עֹשֶׂה שָׁלוֹם בִּמְרוֹמָיו הוּא יַעֲשֶׂה שָׁלוֹם עָלֵינוּ
וְעַל כָּל־יִשְׂרָאֵל [וְעַל כָּל־יוֹשְׁבֵי תֵבֵל], וְאִמְרוּ אָמֵן.

מִמַּעֲמַקִּים קְרָאתִֽיךָ יהוה.

אַל־תַּסְתֵּר פָּנֶֽיךָ מִמֶּֽנִּי בְּיוֹם צַר לִי הַטֵּה־אֵלַי אָזְנֶֽךָ בְּיוֹם אֶקְרָא מַהֵר עֲנֵֽנִי. כִּי־כָלוּ בְעָשָׁן יָמָי וְעַצְמוֹתַי כְּמוֹקֵד נִחָֽרוּ.

דָּמִֽיתִי לִקְאַת מִדְבָּר הָיִֽיתִי כְּכוֹס חֳרָבוֹת.

אַל־תְּבוֹאֵֽנִי רֶֽגֶל גַּאֲוָה וְיַד־רְשָׁעִים אַל־תְּנִדֵֽנִי.

שָׁם נָפְלוּ פֹּֽעֲלֵי אָֽוֶן דֹּחוּ וְלֹא־יָֽכְלוּ קוּם.

נְפוּגֹֽתִי וְנִדְכֵּֽיתִי עַד־מְאֹד שָׁאַֽגְתִּי מִנַּהֲמַת לִבִּי.

אֲדֹנָי נֶגְדְּךָ כָל־תַּאֲוָתִי וְאַנְחָתִי מִמְּךָ לֹא־נִסְתָּֽרָה.

אַל־תַּֽעַזְבֵֽנִי יהוה אֱלֹהַי אַל־תִּרְחַק מִמֶּֽנִּי.

אֲדֹנָי שִׁמְעָה בְקוֹלִי תִּהְיֶֽינָה אָזְנֶֽיךָ קַשֻּׁבוֹת לְקוֹל תַּחֲנוּנָי.

הַמְצֵא לָֽנוּ בְּבַקָּשָׁתֵֽנוּ כְּמָה שֶׁכָּתוּב וּבִקַּשְׁתֶּם מִשָּׁם אֶת־יהוה אֱלֹהֶֽיךָ וּמָצָֽאתָ כִּי תִדְרְשֶֽׁנּוּ בְּכָל־לְבָבְךָ וּבְכָל־נַפְשֶֽׁךָ:

הֲבִיאֵֽנוּ אֶל הַר קָדְשֶֽׁךָ, וְשַׂמְּחֵֽנוּ בְּבֵית תְּפִלָּתֶֽךָ, כְּמָה שֶׁכָּתוּב: וַהֲבִיאוֹתִים אֶל הַר קָדְשִׁי, וְשִׂמַּחְתִּים בְּבֵית תְּפִלָּתִי, כִּי בֵיתִי בֵּית תְּפִלָּה יִקָּרֵא לְכָל־הָעַמִּים.

FROM THE DEPTHS
מִמַּעֲמַקִּים. The Eilleh Ezk'rah, recalling the history of Jewish martyrdom, is part of the S'liḥot section, the prayers that precede the confession and that focus on the theme of forgiveness. We now move to the culmination of the S'liḥot section, which is traditionally announced with a series of biblical verses. These are chosen from a variety of traditions. The verses recited here are Psalms 130:1; 102:3–4, 7; 36:12–13; 38:9–10, 22; 130:2.

I SHALL BRING YOU TO MY HOLY MOUNTAIN
וַהֲבִיאוֹתִים אֶל הַר קָדְשִׁי. The series of verses ends with a prayer for peace, including the universal message of Isaiah 56:7 that in the end of days all of humanity will worship as one.

Biblical Verses of Prayer

From the depths I call to You, God.

Do not hide Your face from me in the day of my affliction.

Turn Your ear to me.

On the day I call to You, answer me.

My days end like smoke; my bones are black as if charred in a conflagration.

I am like an owl in the desert,

like an owl among the ruins.

Do not let the foot of the arrogant tread on me,

nor the hand of the wicked push me away.

Lord, You know all my desires and needs,

my sighs are not hidden from You.

Do not abandon me, ADONAI;

do not distance Yourself from me.

Lord, hear my voice,

may your ear be attentive to the sound of my plea.

Respond to our supplications as You promised, "Wherever you are, when you seek ADONAI your God with all your heart and all your might, you will surely find Me."

Bring us to Your holy mountain; make us joyful in Your house of prayer, as Your prophet Isaiah wrote, "I shall bring you to My holy mountain and make you joyous in My house of prayer, for My house shall be called a house of prayer for all people."

שְׁמַע קוֹלֵנוּ, יהוה אֱלֹהֵינוּ, חוּס וְרַחֵם עָלֵינוּ,
וְקַבֵּל בְּרַחֲמִים וּבְרָצוֹן אֶת־תְּפִלָּתֵנוּ.

הֲשִׁיבֵנוּ יהוה אֵלֶיךָ וְנָשׁוּבָה, חַדֵּשׁ יָמֵינוּ כְּקֶדֶם.

אַל־תַּשְׁלִיכֵנוּ מִלְּפָנֶיךָ, וְרוּחַ קָדְשְׁךָ אַל־תִּקַּח מִמֶּנּוּ.

אַל־תַּשְׁלִיכֵנוּ לְעֵת זִקְנָה, כִּכְלוֹת כֹּחֵנוּ אַל־תַּעַזְבֵנוּ.

Said quietly:

אַל תַּעַזְבֵנוּ, יהוה אֱלֹהֵינוּ, אַל תִּרְחַק מִמֶּנּוּ.
עֲשֵׂה עִמָּנוּ אוֹת לְטוֹבָה, וְיִרְאוּ שׂוֹנְאֵינוּ וְיֵבֹשׁוּ,
כִּי אַתָּה יהוה עֲזַרְתָּנוּ וְנִחַמְתָּנוּ.
אֲמָרֵינוּ הַאֲזִינָה יהוה, בִּינָה הֲגִיגֵנוּ. יִהְיוּ לְרָצוֹן אִמְרֵי־פִינוּ
וְהֶגְיוֹן לִבֵּנוּ לְפָנֶיךָ, יהוה צוּרֵנוּ וְגוֹאֲלֵנוּ. כִּי לְךָ יהוה
הוֹחָלְנוּ, אַתָּה תַעֲנֶה, אֲדֹנָי אֱלֹהֵינוּ.

The ark is closed.

אֱלֹהֵינוּ וֵאלֹהֵי אֲבוֹתֵינוּ [וְאִמּוֹתֵינוּ],
אַל תַּעַזְבֵנוּ וְאַל תִּטְּשֵׁנוּ,
וְאַל תַּכְלִימֵנוּ וְאַל תָּפֵר בְּרִיתְךָ אִתָּנוּ.
קָרְבֵנוּ לְתוֹרָתֶךָ, לַמְּדֵנוּ מִצְוֹתֶיךָ, הוֹרֵנוּ דְּרָכֶיךָ,
הַט לִבֵּנוּ לְיִרְאָה אֶת־שְׁמֶךָ, וּמוֹל אֶת־לְבָבֵנוּ לְאַהֲבָתֶךָ,
וְנָשׁוּב אֵלֶיךָ בֶּאֱמֶת וּבְלֵב שָׁלֵם. וּלְמַעַן שִׁמְךָ הַגָּדוֹל תִּמְחַל
וְתִסְלַח לַעֲוֹנֵנוּ, כַּכָּתוּב בְּדִבְרֵי קָדְשֶׁךָ:
לְמַעַן־שִׁמְךָ יהוה, וְסָלַחְתָּ לַעֲוֹנִי כִּי רַב־הוּא.

שְׁמַע קוֹלֵנוּ **HEAR OUR VOICE**. The first sentence in this set of verses is a quotation from the concluding prayer of personal petition in the daily Amidah. It is typical of Jewish liturgy that before or after the main body of requests, there is a generalized plea that God hear our prayer. Sh'ma Koleinu ("Hear our voice") is a supplication that seeks to penetrate the silence surrounding us, to evoke a response from God, and to draw God into our prayer. "Hear our voice" may be among the most poignant words spoken in prayer.

The verses quoted here are Lamentations 5:21; Psalms 51:13; 71:9; 38:22. A millennium ago, the maḥzor's editors adapted the biblical text by changing singular wording to plural.

אַל תַּעַזְבֵנוּ **DO NOT ABANDON US**. Psalm 38:22. These sentences are recited quietly so as not to assert aloud that God might abandon us. The verses that follow represent personal pleas that God might heed our prayer: Psalms 86:17, 5:2, 19:15, 38:16.

עֲוֹנִי **MY SIN**. Though this entire prayer speaks in the plural, the verse from Psalm 25:11 is in the singular, as if to say that we each must eventually confront our own sinfulness. Some editions of the maḥzor change even this verse to the plural.

CULMINATION OF S'LIḤOT: HEAR OUR VOICE

The ark is opened. After the leader recites each verse, we repeat it.

Hear our voice, ADONAI our God, be kind, and have compassion
for us. Willingly and lovingly accept our prayer.

Turn us toward You, ADONAI, and we will return to You;
Make our days seem fresh, as they once were.

Do not cast us away from You;
Take not Your holy presence from us.

Do not cast us away as we grow old;
Do not desert us as our energy wanes.

Sh'ma koleinu, Adonai eloheinu, ḥus v'raḥeim aleinu, v'kabbeil b'raḥamim
u-v'ratzon et t'fillateinu.
Hashiveinu Adonai eilekha v'nashuvah ḥaddeish yameinu k'kedem.
Al tashlikheinu mi-l'fanekha, v'ru·aḥ kodsh'kha al tikkaḥ mimmenu.
Al tashlikheinu l'eit ziknah, ki-kh'lot koḥeinu al ta·azveinu.

Said quietly:

Do not abandon us, ADONAI our God, do not distance Yourself
    from us.
Give us a signal of hope, so that our enemies will understand
    and hesitate, knowing that You have been our help and comfort.
Hear our words, ADONAI, and consider our innermost thoughts.
May the words of our mouths and the meditations of our
    hearts be acceptable to You, ADONAI, our rock and redeemer.
It is for You we wait; surely You will respond, ADONAI our God.

The ark is closed.

Our God and God of our ancestors, do not abandon us, do not
forsake us, do not shame us, do not annul Your covenant with us.
Draw us close to Your Torah, teach us Your mitzvot, show us Your
ways. Open our hearts to revere Your name, circumcise our hearts
to love You; then, we will turn to You, faithfully, with a perfect
heart. And as befits Your own great name, pardon and forgive our
sins, as the psalmist wrote: "For the sake of Your own name, forgive
my sin, though it be great."

V'salaḥta la-avoni ki rav hu.

אֱלֹהֵינוּ וֵאלֹהֵי אֲבוֹתֵינוּ [וְאִמּוֹתֵינוּ],
סְלַח לָנוּ מְחַל לָנוּ, כַּפֶּר־לָנוּ.

כִּי

אָנוּ עַמֶּךָ,	וְאַתָּה אֱלֹהֵינוּ,
אָנוּ בָנֶיךָ,	וְאַתָּה אָבִינוּ.
אָנוּ עֲבָדֶיךָ,	וְאַתָּה אֲדוֹנֵנוּ,
אָנוּ קְהָלֶךָ,	וְאַתָּה חֶלְקֵנוּ.
אָנוּ נַחֲלָתֶךָ,	וְאַתָּה גוֹרָלֵנוּ,
אָנוּ צֹאנֶךָ,	וְאַתָּה רוֹעֵנוּ.
אָנוּ כַרְמֶךָ,	וְאַתָּה נוֹטְרֵנוּ,
אָנוּ פְעֻלָּתֶךָ,	וְאַתָּה יוֹצְרֵנוּ.
אָנוּ רַעְיָתֶךָ,	וְאַתָּה דוֹדֵנוּ,
אָנוּ סְגֻלָּתֶךָ,	וְאַתָּה קְרוֹבֵנוּ.
אָנוּ עַמֶּךָ,	וְאַתָּה מַלְכֵּנוּ,
אָנוּ מַאֲמִירֶךָ,	וְאַתָּה מַאֲמִירֵנוּ.

וידוי

אָנוּ עַזֵּי פָנִים,	וְאַתָּה רַחוּם וְחַנּוּן;
אָנוּ קְשֵׁי עֹרֶף,	וְאַתָּה אֶרֶךְ אַפַּיִם;
אָנוּ מְלֵאֵי עָוֹן,	וְאַתָּה מָלֵא רַחֲמִים;
אָנוּ יָמֵינוּ כְּצֵל עוֹבֵר,	וְאַתָּה הוּא וּשְׁנוֹתֶיךָ לֹא יִתָּמּוּ.

WE ARE YOUR PEOPLE
כִּי אָנוּ עַמֶּךָ. An early medieval poem, which expands on the verse from Song of Songs: "I am for my beloved and my beloved is mine" (2:16). It completes the S'liḥot/ Forgiveness section and forms the transition to the confession. Here we end in joyous song, then move to a meditative melody, as we begin the Viddui/ Confession. In this poem we emphasize our related-ness to God, whereas in the next we emphasize the stark difference between the human and the Divine.

VIDDUI—PRAYERS OF CON-FESSION וִדּוּי. In addition to fasting and otherwise afflicting oneself, the central mitzvah that must be performed on Yom Kip-pur is *viddui* (confession). The rabbinic requirement to confess is based on the biblical passage that describes the confession of the High Priest when performing the Temple ceremony. Following the destruction of the Temple, greater emphasis was placed on synagogue ritual and individual prayer, and it fell upon each person to make confession on Yom Kippur.

A PASSING SHADOW כְּצֵל עוֹבֵר. Psalm 144:4.

FOR TIME WITHOUT END וּשְׁנוֹתֶיךָ לֹא יִתָּמּוּ. "Of old You established the earth; / the heavens are the work of Your hands. / They shall perish, but You shall endure; / they shall all wear out like a garment; / You change them like clothing and they pass away. / But You are the same, and Your years never end" (Psalm 102:26–28).

Our God and God of our ancestors, forgive us, pardon us, grant us atonement.
For—

We are Your people,	and You are our God;
we are Your children	and You are our parent.
We are Your servants,	and You are our master;
we are Your congregation,	and You are our portion.
We are Your heritage,	and You are our destiny;
we are Your flock,	and You are our shepherd.
We are Your vineyard,	and You are our guardian;
we are Your creatures,	and You are our creator.
We are Your spouse,	and You are our beloved;
we are Your cherished ones,	and You are near to us.
We are Your people,	and You are our sovereign;
We are the ones You address,	and You are the One to whom we speak.

Ki

Anu ammekha,	*v'atah eloheinu,*
anu vanekha	*v'atah avinu.*
Anu avadekha	*v'atah adoneinu,*
anu k'halekha	*v'atah ḥelkeinu.*
Anu naḥalatekha	*v'atah goraleinu,*
anu tzonekha	*v'atah ro·einu.*
Anu kharmekha	*v'atah not'reinu,*
anu f'ullatekha,	*v'atah yotz'reinu.*
Anu ra·ayatekha	*v'atah dodeinu,*
anu s'gullatekha	*v'atah k'roveinu.*
Anu ammekha	*v'atah malkeinu,*
anu ma·amirekha	*v'atah ma·amireinu.*

VIDDUI—PRAYERS OF CONFESSION

We are insolent,
    You are gracious and compassionate.
We are obstinate,
    You are patient.
We are sinful,
    You are merciful.
Our days are a passing shadow,
    but You are the One who truly is, for time without end.

אֱלֹהֵינוּ וֵאלֹהֵי אֲבוֹתֵינוּ [וְאִמּוֹתֵינוּ],

תָּבֹא לְפָנֶיךָ תְּפִלָּתֵנוּ,

וְאַל תִּתְעַלַּם מִתְּחִנָּתֵנוּ,

שֶׁאֵין אֲנַחְנוּ עַזֵּי פָנִים וּקְשֵׁי עֹרֶף,

לוֹמַר לְפָנֶיךָ יהוה אֱלֹהֵינוּ וֵאלֹהֵי אֲבוֹתֵינוּ [וְאִמּוֹתֵינוּ],

צַדִּיקִים אֲנַחְנוּ וְלֹא חָטָאנוּ,

אֲבָל אֲנַחְנוּ וַאֲבוֹתֵינוּ [וְאִמּוֹתֵינוּ] חָטָאנוּ.

It is customary to strike one's heart as we recite each word of the confession.

אָשַׁמְנוּ, בָּגַדְנוּ, גָּזַלְנוּ, דִּבַּרְנוּ דֹפִי.

הֶעֱוִינוּ, וְהִרְשַׁעְנוּ, זַדְנוּ, חָמַסְנוּ, טָפַלְנוּ שֶׁקֶר.

יָעַצְנוּ רָע, כִּזַּבְנוּ, לַצְנוּ, מָרַדְנוּ, נִאַצְנוּ, סָרַרְנוּ,

עָוִינוּ, פָּשַׁעְנוּ, צָרַרְנוּ, קִשִּׁינוּ עֹרֶף.

רָשַׁעְנוּ, שִׁחַתְנוּ, תִּעַבְנוּ, תָּעִינוּ, תִּעְתָּעְנוּ.

סַרְנוּ מִמִּצְוֹתֶיךָ וּמִמִּשְׁפָּטֶיךָ הַטּוֹבִים, וְלֹא שָׁוָה לָנוּ.

וְאַתָּה צַדִּיק עַל כָּל־הַבָּא עָלֵינוּ, כִּי אֱמֶת עָשִׂיתָ וַאֲנַחְנוּ הִרְשָׁעְנוּ.

STRIKE OUR HEART. The custom of striking our heart while confessing our sins is first mentioned in a midrash on Ecclesiastes 7:2 ("the living will lay it to heart"): "Rabbi Meir said: 'Why do people strike their hearts [in remorse for their sins]? Because the heart is the seat and source of sin'" (Ecclesiastes Rabbah).

FOR WE AND OUR ANCES-TORS אֲנַחְנוּ וַאֲבוֹתֵינוּ. No one has walked the earth and not sinned. In ascribing sin to our ancestors, the liturgist is quoting Psalm 106:6. Similarly, Nehemiah reports that in rededicating themselves, the people gathered in the Temple courtyard and "confessed their own sins and the sins of their ancestors" (Nehemiah 9:2). Medieval authors argued that knowledge that previous generations sinned, just as we do, empowers us to ask for forgiveness—for is not our own failing part of the very nature of the human condition?

WE ABUSE אָשַׁמְנוּ. The liturgical list is alphabetical, with the hope that it will help us find our own words to name our transgressions. We might concentrate on one particular failing in our lives.

WE DESTROY שִׁחַתְנוּ. In this bilingual alphabetical list, the English word that represents the letter D means roughly the same as the Hebrew word that represents the letter שׁ (shin). The sin of בַּל תַּשְׁחִית (bal tash·ḥit), "not destroying anything needlessly," was enumerated by the Rabbis among the 613 commandments of the Torah. To destroy any part of creation is to undo God's work, to reject God's gift.

YOU HAVE ACTED FAITHFULLY וְאַתָּה צַדִּיק. Nehemiah 9:33. The prayer of the Levites at the rededication of the Temple, upon the return from the Babylonian Exile.

Before One Dies

Rabbi Eliezer said: "Repent one day before your death." His disciples asked: "Does anyone know on what day he or she will die?"

"All the more reason to repent today," answered Rabbi Eliezer, "in case you die tomorrow, and thus a person's whole life should be spent in repentance."

—BABYLONIAN TALMUD, SHABBAT
(*trans. Francine Klagsbrun*)

Repentance

Rabbi Abahu said: "In the place where penitents stand, even the wholly righteous cannot stand."

—BABYLONIAN TALMUD, BERAKHOT

Ashamnu

Jewish tradition requires a verbal confession—a confession in words—as part of the process

Our God and God of our ancestors, hear our prayer; do not ignore our plea. Our God and God of our ancestors, we are neither so insolent nor so obstinate as to claim in Your presence that we are righteous, without sin; for we, like our ancestors who came before us, have sinned.

The Shorter Confession—Ashamnu

It is customary to strike one's heart as we recite each word of the confession.

We **a**buse, we **b**etray, we are **c**ruel, we **d**estroy, we **e**mbitter, we **f**alsify, we **g**ossip, we **h**ate, we **i**nsult, we **j**eer, we **k**ill, we **l**ie, we **m**ock, we **n**eglect, we **o**ppress, we **p**ervert, we **q**uarrel, we **r**ebel, we **s**teal, we **t**ransgress, we are **u**nkind, we are **v**iolent, we are **w**icked, we are e**x**tremists, we **y**earn to do evil, we are **z**ealous for bad causes.

Ashamnu, bagadnu, gazalnu, dibbarnu dofi,
He·evinu, hirshanu, zadnu, ḥamasnu, tafalnu sheker,
Ya·atznu ra, kizzavnu, latznu, maradnu, ni·atznu,
Sararnu, avinu, pashanu, tzararnu, kishinu oref,
Rashanu, shiḥatnu, ti·avnu, ta·inu, titanu.

We have turned from Your goodly laws and commandments, but it has not profited us. Surely, You are in the right with respect to all that comes upon us, for You have acted faithfully, but we have been in the wrong.

of repentance. It is not enough simply to feel repentant or contrite, or to think thoughts of repentance.... But you can't confess in words without language, and there is no language without some kind of form, even if it's as rudimentary as a grammar or an alphabet. In this sense, the Ashamnu is language in its most pared-down, astringent form, the naked alphabet, as it were, the barest, most elemental expression of language. It is a list of sins whittled down to single words, and those single words go from *alef* to *tav*, relentlessly and inexorably.... the Viddui is alphabetical because it is about the confession of the totality of one's sins from aleph to tav, from alpha to omega.... [You cannot] hide any sins or forget them or inadvertently skip one sin or another, just as in reciting the alphabet you cannot leave out a letter. —DAVID STERN

Our Ancestors and Us

Throughout the long hours of prayer, we speak of all the reasons why God should care for us and forgive us: our remorse, our atonement, our acknowledgment of wrongdoing, God's own promise of mercy, God's wish to be known in the world as loving. In this prayer, we call on our association with our ancestors who were cared for by God. We subtly imply that since we are their children, we have inherited their spiritual legacy. In placing our own prayer in the context of theirs, perhaps what is implied as well is that we seek to live our lives in accordance with that which gave them honor. —NINA BETH CARDIN

א

הִרְשַׁעְנוּ וּפָשַׁעְנוּ, לָכֵן לֹא נוֹשַׁעְנוּ. וְתֵן בְּלִבֵּנוּ לַעֲזוֹב
דֶּרֶךְ רֶשַׁע וְחִישׁ לָנוּ יֶשַׁע, כַּכָּתוּב עַל יַד נְבִיאֶךָ: יַעֲזֹב
רָשָׁע דַּרְכּוֹ, וְאִישׁ אָוֶן מַחְשְׁבֹתָיו, וְיָשֹׁב אֶל יהוה
וִירַחֲמֵהוּ, וְאֶל אֱלֹהֵינוּ כִּי יַרְבֶּה לִסְלוֹחַ.

ב

אֱלֹהֵינוּ וֵאלֹהֵי אֲבוֹתֵינוּ [וְאִמּוֹתֵינוּ], סְלַח וּמְחַל
לַעֲוֹנוֹתֵינוּ בְּיוֹם [הַשַּׁבָּת הַזֶּה וּבְיוֹם] הַכִּפּוּרִים הַזֶּה.
מְחֵה וְהַעֲבֵר פְּשָׁעֵינוּ וְחַטֹּאתֵינוּ מִנֶּגֶד עֵינֶיךָ,
וְכֹף אֶת־יִצְרֵנוּ לְהִשְׁתַּעְבֶּד־לָךְ,
וְהַכְנַע עָרְפֵּנוּ לָשׁוּב אֵלֶיךָ,
וְחַדֵּשׁ כִּלְיוֹתֵינוּ לִשְׁמוֹר פִּקֻּדֶיךָ;
וּמוֹל אֶת־לְבָבֵנוּ לְאַהֲבָה וּלְיִרְאָה אֶת־שְׁמֶךָ,
כַּכָּתוּב בְּתוֹרָתֶךָ: וּמָל יהוה אֱלֹהֶיךָ אֶת־לְבָבְךָ,
וְאֶת־לְבַב זַרְעֶךָ, לְאַהֲבָה אֶת־יהוה אֱלֹהֶיךָ בְּכָל־לְבָבְךָ
וּבְכָל־נַפְשְׁךָ לְמַעַן חַיֶּיךָ.

ג

הַזְּדוֹנוֹת וְהַשְּׁגָגוֹת אַתָּה מַכִּיר, הָרָצוֹן וְהָאֹנֶס,
הַגְּלוּיִים וְהַנִּסְתָּרִים, לְפָנֶיךָ הֵם גְּלוּיִם וִידוּעִים.
מָה אָנוּ, מֶה חַיֵּינוּ, מֶה חַסְדֵּנוּ, מַה צִּדְקֵנוּ,
מַה יְשׁוּעֵנוּ, מַה כֹּחֵנוּ, מַה גְּבוּרָתֵנוּ.
מַה נֹּאמַר לְפָנֶיךָ, יהוה אֱלֹהֵינוּ וֵאלֹהֵי אֲבוֹתֵינוּ
[וְאִמּוֹתֵינוּ].
הֲלֹא כָּל־הַגִּבּוֹרִים כְּאַיִן לְפָנֶיךָ,
וְאַנְשֵׁי הַשֵּׁם כְּלֹא הָיוּ,
וַחֲכָמִים כִּבְלִי מַדָּע,
וּנְבוֹנִים כִּבְלִי הַשְׂכֵּל,

BLOT OUT AND DISREGARD
מְחֵה וְהַעֲבֵר. Both inner and outer parts of the body are mentioned in this prayer. Body and soul are intimately bound, as we seek to behave differently. It is as if we simultaneously ask the Creator to fashion for us a new, less sinful body as home to a purified soul.

CIRCUMCISE וּמָל. Deuteronomy 30:6. Circumcision is an act of completion and perfection. Removing the flesh—our sins, which mask our essential nature— reveals the true function of the heart: to lead us to a life of love, righteousness, and peace.

Merely to have survived is
  not an index of excellence,
Nor, given the way things go,
Even of low cunning.
Yet I have seen the wicked in
  great power,
. . .
And the good as if they had
  never been;
Their voices are blown away
  on the winter wind.
And again we wander the
  wilderness
For our transgressions
Which are confessed in the
  daily papers.

Except the Lord of hosts had
  left unto us
A very small remnant,
We should have been as
  Sodom,
We should have been like
  unto Gomorrah.
And to what purpose, as the
  darkness closes about,
. . .
Here, in this wilderness of
  comfort
In which we dwell.

        Shall we now consider
The suspicious posture of our
  virtue,
The deformed consequences
  of our love,
The painful issues of our
  mildest acts?
Shall we ask,
Where is there one
Mad, poor and betrayed
  enough to find
Forgiveness for us, saying,
"None does offend,
None, I say,
None"?
. . .

—ANTHONY HECHT

PENITENTIAL PRAYERS BEFORE
THE GREAT CONFESSION

One or more of the following penitential prayers may be included.

א

We have done wrong and transgressed, and so we have
not triumphed. Inspire our hearts to abandon the path
of evil, and hasten our redemption. And so Your prophet
Isaiah declared: "Let the wicked forsake their path, and
the sinful their design. Let them return to ADONAI, who
will show them compassion. Let them return to our God,
who will surely forgive them."

ב

Our God and God of our ancestors, forgive and pardon
our sins [on this Shabbat and] on this Day of Atonement.
Blot out and disregard our sins and errors;
subdue our instincts so that they may serve You.
Bend our stiffness so that we turn to You;
renew our passion for observing Your ordinances.
Circumcise our hearts to love and revere Your name, as it
is written in Your Torah: "Then ADONAI your God will
circumcise your heart and the hearts of your offspring to
love ADONAI your God with all your heart and all your
soul, that you may live."

ג

You recognize both our sins and our mistakes, acts of will
and those committed under compulsion; public acts and
private ones are equally revealed and known to You.
What are we?
What is our life?
Our goodness?
Our righteousness?
Our achievement?
Our power?
Our victories?
What shall we say in Your presence, ADONAI our God
and God of our ancestors?
Heroes count as nothing in Your presence,
famous people are as if they never existed,
the wise seem ignorant,
clever ones as if they lacked reason.

כִּי רֹב מַעֲשֵׂיהֶם תֹּהוּ,
וִימֵי חַיֵּיהֶם הֶבֶל לְפָנֶיךָ.
וּמוֹתַר הָאָדָם מִן הַבְּהֵמָה אָיִן,
כִּי הַכֹּל הָבֶל.

מַה־נֹּאמַר לְפָנֶיךָ יוֹשֵׁב מָרוֹם,
וּמַה־נְּסַפֵּר לְפָנֶיךָ שׁוֹכֵן שְׁחָקִים.
הֲלֹא כָּל־הַנִּסְתָּרוֹת וְהַנִּגְלוֹת אַתָּה יוֹדֵעַ.

ד

שִׁמְךָ מֵעוֹלָם עוֹבֵר עַל פֶּשַׁע,
שַׁוְעָתֵנוּ תַאֲזִין בְּעָמְדֵנוּ לְפָנֶיךָ בִּתְפִלָּה.
תַּעֲבוֹר עַל פֶּשַׁע לְעַם שָׁבֵי פֶשַׁע,
תִּמְחֶה פְּשָׁעֵינוּ מִנֶּגֶד עֵינֶיךָ.

ה

אַתָּה יוֹדֵעַ רָזֵי עוֹלָם, וְתַעֲלוּמוֹת סִתְרֵי כָל־חָי.
אַתָּה חוֹפֵשׂ כָּל־חַדְרֵי בָטֶן, וּבוֹחֵן כְּלָיוֹת וָלֵב.
אֵין דָּבָר נֶעְלָם מִמֶּךָּ, וְאֵין נִסְתָּר מִנֶּגֶד עֵינֶיךָ.
וּבְכֵן יְהִי רָצוֹן מִלְּפָנֶיךָ,
יהוה אֱלֹהֵינוּ וֵאלֹהֵי אֲבוֹתֵינוּ [וְאִמּוֹתֵינוּ],
שֶׁתִּסְלַח לָנוּ עַל כָּל־חַטֹּאתֵינוּ,
וְתִמְחַל לָנוּ עַל כָּל־עֲוֹנוֹתֵינוּ,
וּתְכַפֶּר־לָנוּ עַל כָּל־פְּשָׁעֵינוּ.

 שׁ בְּאוֹתוֹ עֶרֶב מוּזָר
מִישֶׁהוּ שָׁאַל:
הַאִם אֶפְשָׁר לְשַׁנּוֹת אֶת
הֶעָבָר?
וְהָאִשָּׁה הַחוֹלָנִית עָנְתָה בְּזַעַף:
הֶעָבָר אֵינֶנּוּ תַּכְשִׁיט
חָתוּם בְּתוֹךְ קֻפְסָה שֶׁל בְּדֹלַח
גַּם אֵינֶנּוּ
נָחָשׁ בְּתוֹךְ צִנְצֶנֶת שֶׁל כֹּהַל -
הֶעָבָר מִתְנוֹעֵעַ
בְּתוֹךְ הַהֹוֶה
וְכַאֲשֶׁר הַהֹוֶה נוֹפֵל לְתוֹךְ בּוֹר
נוֹפֵל אִתּוֹ הֶעָבָר -
כַּאֲשֶׁר הֶעָבָר מַבִּיט הַשָּׁמַיְמָה
זוֹ הֲרָמַת הַחַיִּים כֻּלָּם,
גַּם חַיֵּי עָבָר רָחוֹק עַד מְאֹד.

אַךְ הָאִישׁ הַגַּלְמוּד מִלְמֵל:
וַהֲלֹא הָיָה פַּעַם אַבְרָהָם בַּתֵּבֵל
זֶה שֶׁלֹּא לָקַח אֲפִלּוּ חוּט
מִנֶּפֶשׁ מוֹלִידוֹ.

In that strange night
someone asked:
Can you change the past?
And the sick woman
angrily responded:
The past is not a piece of
jewelry sealed in a crystal
box nor is it a snake
preserved in a bottle of
formaldehyde—
The past trembles within
the present
when the present falls
into a pit the past goes
with it—
when the past looks
toward heaven all of life
is upraised, even the
distant past.

But the lonely man
muttered:
Did not Abraham once
stride the earth,
he who did not seem
attached to even the cord
of the one who gave him
birth?   —ZELDA
          (trans. Edward Feld)

The sum of their acts is chaos;
in Your presence the days of their lives are futile.
Human beings have no superiority over beasts; all life is vanity.

What can we say before You, You who live in the transcendent?
And what can we tell about ourselves to You who dwell
    on high?
You surely know both the secret and the revealed.

ד

You have always been known as the one who overlooks
    transgression.
Hear our cry, as we stand before You, in prayer.
Overlook the transgressions of a people turning from
    transgression.
Wipe away our transgressions from Your sight.

ה

You know the mysteries of the universe,
the deepest secrets of everyone alive.
You probe our innermost depths;
You examine our thoughts and feelings.
Nothing escapes You;
nothing is secret from You.
Therefore, may it be Your will, our God and God of our
    ancestors,
to forgive us for all our sins,
to pardon us for all our iniquities,
to grant us atonement for all our transgressions.

עַל חֵטְא שֶׁחָטָאנוּ לְפָנֶיךָ בְּאֹנֶס וּבְרָצוֹן,

וְעַל חֵטְא שֶׁחָטָאנוּ לְפָנֶיךָ בְּאִמּוּץ הַלֵּב.

עַל חֵטְא שֶׁחָטָאנוּ לְפָנֶיךָ בִּבְלִי דָעַת,

וְעַל חֵטְא שֶׁחָטָאנוּ לְפָנֶיךָ בְּבִטּוּי שְׂפָתָיִם.

עַל חֵטְא שֶׁחָטָאנוּ לְפָנֶיךָ בְּגִלּוּי עֲרָיוֹת,

וְעַל חֵטְא שֶׁחָטָאנוּ לְפָנֶיךָ בַּגָּלוּי וּבַסָּתֶר.

עַל חֵטְא שֶׁחָטָאנוּ לְפָנֶיךָ בְּדַעַת וּבְמִרְמָה,

וְעַל חֵטְא שֶׁחָטָאנוּ לְפָנֶיךָ בְּדִבּוּר פֶּה.

עַל חֵטְא שֶׁחָטָאנוּ לְפָנֶיךָ בְּהוֹנָאַת רֵעַ,

וְעַל חֵטְא שֶׁחָטָאנוּ לְפָנֶיךָ בְּהִרְהוֹר הַלֵּב.

עַל חֵטְא שֶׁחָטָאנוּ לְפָנֶיךָ בִּוְעִידַת זְנוּת,

וְעַל חֵטְא שֶׁחָטָאנוּ לְפָנֶיךָ בְּוִדּוּי פֶּה.

עַל חֵטְא שֶׁחָטָאנוּ לְפָנֶיךָ בְּזִלְזוּל הוֹרִים וּמוֹרִים,

וְעַל חֵטְא שֶׁחָטָאנוּ לְפָנֶיךָ בְּזָדוֹן וּבִשְׁגָגָה.

עַל חֵטְא שֶׁחָטָאנוּ לְפָנֶיךָ בְּחִזֶּק יָד,

וְעַל חֵטְא שֶׁחָטָאנוּ לְפָנֶיךָ בְּחִלּוּל הַשֵּׁם.

עַל חֵטְא שֶׁחָטָאנוּ לְפָנֶיךָ בְּטֻמְאַת שְׂפָתָיִם,

וְעַל חֵטְא שֶׁחָטָאנוּ לְפָנֶיךָ בְּטִפְּשׁוּת פֶּה.

◁ עַל חֵטְא שֶׁחָטָאנוּ לְפָנֶיךָ בְּיֵצֶר הָרָע,

וְעַל חֵטְא שֶׁחָטָאנוּ לְפָנֶיךָ בְּיוֹדְעִים וּבְלֹא יוֹדְעִים.

וְעַל כֻּלָּם, אֱלוֹהַּ סְלִיחוֹת, סְלַח לָנוּ, מְחַל לָנוּ, כַּפֶּר־לָנוּ.

עַל חֵטְא שֶׁחָטָאנוּ לְפָנֶיךָ בְּכַחַשׁ וּבְכָזָב,

וְעַל חֵטְא שֶׁחָטָאנוּ לְפָנֶיךָ בְּכַפַּת שֹׁחַד.

עַל חֵטְא שֶׁחָטָאנוּ לְפָנֶיךָ בְּלָצוֹן,

וְעַל חֵטְא שֶׁחָטָאנוּ לְפָנֶיךָ בְּלָשׁוֹן הָרָע.

THE LONGER CONFESSION. Despite the double alphabetical acrostic in which the sins are enumerated, the Al Ḥet is not simply a formal list. The sins it enumerates are the stuff of daily life, and they point to our repeated moral failures. The Al Ḥet makes almost no specific reference to violations of the rituals of Judaism. Such infractions as the desecration of Shabbat and festivals, and the failure to abide by the disciplines that invest our daily life with sacred significance, are categorized by the Talmud as "sins between people and God." It is taken for granted that only sins "between one person and another" need to be detailed (Babylonian Talmud, Yoma 86b).

Amidst a community of imperfect humans, we gain the courage to confess our sins to God. Knowing that it is God whom we are facing, we are called to a level of honesty and truthfulness that is greater than any intermediary would demand.

The forty-four lines included in the Al Ḥet are an expansion of the six lines that appear in Saadiah Gaon's prayerbook (10th century), the twelve in Amram Gaon's (9th century), and the twenty-two in Maimonides' (12th century).

DEFRAUDING OTHERS הוֹנָאַת רֵעַ. Or, "oppressing others" (materially or spiritually), for so the Rabbis understood the related verb in Leviticus 19:33.

SPEAKING BADLY OF OTHERS בְּלָשׁוֹן הָרָע. The tradition distinguished between לְשׁוֹן הָרַע (l'shon ha-ra) and רְכִילוּת (r'khilut), both enumerated here. The first is the spreading of truthful yet damaging statements, even without intending any harm. The latter is the telling of outright falsehoods about another.

Embarrassment not
only precedes religious
commitment; it is the
touchstone of religious
existence. . . . What the
world needs is a sense
of embarrassment.
. . . We are guilty of
misunderstanding the
meaning of existence;
we are guilty of
distorting our goals and
misrepresenting our
souls. We are better than
our assertions, more
intricate, more profound
than our theories
maintain. . . .

What is the truth
of being human? The
lack of pretension,
the acknowledgment
of opaqueness,
shortsightedness,
inadequacy. But truth
also demands rising,
striving, for the goal is
both within and beyond
us. The truth of being
human is gratitude; its
secret is appreciation.
—ABRAHAM JOSHUA
HESCHEL

The Longer Confession—Al Ḥet

It is customary to strike one's heart when we say the words "We have sinned."

We have sinned against You unwillingly and willingly,
And we have sinned against You through hardening our hearts.
We have sinned against You thoughtlessly,
And we have sinned against You in idle chatter.
We have sinned against You through sexual immorality,
And we have sinned against You openly and in private
We have sinned against You knowingly and deceitfully,
And we have sinned against You by the way we talk.
We have sinned against You by defrauding others,
And we have sinned against You in our innermost thoughts.
We have sinned against You through forbidden trysts,
And we have sinned against You through empty confession.
We have sinned against You by scorning parents and teachers,
And we have sinned against You purposely and by mistake.
We have sinned against You by resorting to violence,
*And we have sinned against You by public desecration of
Your name.*
We have sinned against You through foul speech,
And we have sinned against You through foolish talk.
We have sinned against You through pursuing the impulse
to evil,
And we have sinned against You wittingly and unwittingly.

*For all these sins, forgiving God, forgive us, pardon us,
grant us atonement.*

V'al kullam elo·ah s'liḥot s'laḥ lanu, m'ḥal lanu, kapper lanu.

We have sinned against You through denial and deceit,
And we have sinned against You by taking bribes.
We have sinned against You by clever cynicism,
And we have sinned against You by speaking badly of others.

עַל חֵטְא שֶׁחָטָאנוּ לְפָנֶיךָ בְּמַשָּׂא וּבְמַתָּן,
וְעַל חֵטְא שֶׁחָטָאנוּ לְפָנֶיךָ בְּמַאֲכָל וּבְמִשְׁתֶּה.
עַל חֵטְא שֶׁחָטָאנוּ לְפָנֶיךָ בְּנֶשֶׁךְ וּבְמַרְבִּית,
וְעַל חֵטְא שֶׁחָטָאנוּ לְפָנֶיךָ בִּנְטִיַּת גָּרוֹן.
עַל חֵטְא שֶׁחָטָאנוּ לְפָנֶיךָ בְּשִׂיחַ שִׂפְתוֹתֵינוּ,
וְעַל חֵטְא שֶׁחָטָאנוּ לְפָנֶיךָ בְּשִׁקּוּר עָיִן.
◁ עַל חֵטְא שֶׁחָטָאנוּ לְפָנֶיךָ בְּעֵינַיִם רָמוֹת,
וְעַל חֵטְא שֶׁחָטָאנוּ לְפָנֶיךָ בְּעַזּוּת מֶצַח.

וְעַל כֻּלָּם, אֱלוֹהַּ סְלִיחוֹת, סְלַח לָנוּ, מְחַל לָנוּ, כַּפֶּר־לָנוּ.

עַל חֵטְא שֶׁחָטָאנוּ לְפָנֶיךָ בִּפְרִיקַת עֹל,
וְעַל חֵטְא שֶׁחָטָאנוּ לְפָנֶיךָ בִּפְלִילוּת.
עַל חֵטְא שֶׁחָטָאנוּ לְפָנֶיךָ בִּצְדִיַּת רֵעַ,
וְעַל חֵטְא שֶׁחָטָאנוּ לְפָנֶיךָ בְּצָרוּת עָיִן.
עַל חֵטְא שֶׁחָטָאנוּ לְפָנֶיךָ בְּקַלּוּת רֹאשׁ,
וְעַל חֵטְא שֶׁחָטָאנוּ לְפָנֶיךָ בְּקַשְׁיוּת עֹרֶף.
עַל חֵטְא שֶׁחָטָאנוּ לְפָנֶיךָ בְּרִיצַת רַגְלַיִם לְהָרַע,
וְעַל חֵטְא שֶׁחָטָאנוּ לְפָנֶיךָ בִּרְכִילוּת.
עַל חֵטְא שֶׁחָטָאנוּ לְפָנֶיךָ בִּשְׁבוּעַת שָׁוְא,
וְעַל חֵטְא שֶׁחָטָאנוּ לְפָנֶיךָ בְּשִׂנְאַת חִנָּם.
◁ עַל חֵטְא שֶׁחָטָאנוּ לְפָנֶיךָ בִּתְשׂוּמֶת־יָד,
וְעַל חֵטְא שֶׁחָטָאנוּ לְפָנֶיךָ בְּתִמְהוֹן לֵבָב.

וְעַל כֻּלָּם, אֱלוֹהַּ סְלִיחוֹת, סְלַח לָנוּ, מְחַל לָנוּ, כַּפֶּר־לָנוּ.

עַל מִצְוֹת עֲשֵׂה וְעַל מִצְוֹת לֹא תַעֲשֶׂה, בֵּין שֶׁיֵּשׁ בָּהּ קוּם עֲשֵׂה,
וּבֵין שֶׁאֵין בָּהּ קוּם עֲשֵׂה, אֶת־הַגְּלוּיִים לָנוּ וְאֶת־שֶׁאֵינָם
גְּלוּיִים לָנוּ. אֶת־הַגְּלוּיִים לָנוּ כְּבָר אֲמַרְנוּם לְפָנֶיךָ,
וְהוֹדִינוּ לְךָ עֲלֵיהֶם; וְאֶת־שֶׁאֵינָם גְּלוּיִים לָנוּ, לְפָנֶיךָ
הֵם גְּלוּיִים וִידוּעִים, כַּדָּבָר שֶׁנֶּאֱמַר: הַנִּסְתָּרֹת לַיהוה
אֱלֹהֵינוּ, וְהַנִּגְלֹת לָנוּ וּלְבָנֵינוּ עַד עוֹלָם, לַעֲשׂוֹת
אֶת־כָּל־דִּבְרֵי הַתּוֹרָה הַזֹּאת.

CONSPIRATORIAL GLANCES
בְּשִׁקּוּר עָיִן. Many sins in
this section and the next
refer to attitudes we hold in
relationships. The Hebrew
speaks of the way we "see"
the world. We confess to
שִׁקּוּר עָיִן (sikkur ayin),
"conspiratorial glances";
עֵינַיִם רָמוֹת (einayim
ramot), literally "eyes raised
high," which we translate as
"condescension"; צָרוּת עָיִן
(tzarut ayin), "selfishness,"
literally, "narrow vision."

SUPERFICIALITY בְּקַלּוּת
רֹאשׁ. Literally, "lightheadedness." The Rabbis used
this term to refer to a state
of mind in which we are
unable to exercise sound
judgment. Many Jewish
legal authorities oppose the
use of mind-altering drugs
if they deny us the ability to
make reasoned judgments.

CONFUSION בְּתִמְהוֹן לֵבָב.
Literally "with a doubting
heart." So many of the sins
enumerated here reference
body parts. The Hebrew
for arrogance translates as
"stiff-necked." The Hebrew
for selfishness translates as
"hard-headed." It is instruc-
tive that the last body part
mentioned is the heart.

SECRET MATTERS הַנִּסְתָּרֹת.
Deuteronomy 29:28.

No list of sins can
ever be complete. By
beginning with *alef* and
ending with *tav*, we
express our intention to
include in our confession
everything of which we
are guilty, from A to Z.
However, this form of the
Al Het does not relieve
us of our individual
obligation to confess the
particular sins for which
we are each personally
responsible. And we
are also called upon to
contemplate those sins
which are especially
prevalent in our world
today.

We have sinned against You by the way we do business,
And we have sinned against You in our eating and drinking.
We have sinned against You by greed and oppressive interest,
And we have sinned against You through arrogance.
We have sinned against You in everyday conversation,
And we have sinned against You through conspiratorial glances.
We have sinned against You through condescension,
And we have sinned against You through ego.

*For all these sins, forgiving God, forgive us, pardon us,
grant us atonement.*

V'al kullam elo·ah s'liḥot s'laḥ lanu, m'ḥal lanu, kapper lanu.

We have sinned against You by throwing off all restraint,
And we have sinned against You by rashly judging others.
We have sinned against You by plotting against others,
And we have sinned against You through selfishness.
We have sinned against You through superficiality,
And we have sinned against You through stubbornness.
We have sinned against You by rushing to do evil,
And we have sinned against You through gossip.
We have sinned against You through empty promises,
And we have sinned against You through baseless hatred.
We have sinned against You by betraying a trust,
And we have sinned against You by succumbing to confusion.

*For all these sins, forgiving God, forgive us, pardon us,
grant us atonement.*

V'al kullam elo·ah s'liḥot s'laḥ lanu, m'ḥal lanu, kapper lanu.

And forgive us the breach of all commandments and prohibitions, whether involving deeds or not, whether known to us or not. The sins known to us we have acknowledged, and those unknown to us are surely known to You, as the Torah states: "Secret matters are the concern of ADONAI our God; but in matters that are revealed, it is for us and our children to apply all teachings of the Torah till the end of time."

עַל חֵטְא שֶׁחָטָאנוּ לְפָנֶיךָ וְלִפְנֵיהֶם בַּאֲטִימַת אֹזֶן,

וְעַל חֵטְא שֶׁחָטָאנוּ לְפָנֶיךָ וְלִפְנֵיהֶם בִּבְגִידַת רֵעִים.

עַל חֵטְא שֶׁחָטָאנוּ לְפָנֶיךָ וְלִפְנֵיהֶם בְּהֶסּוֹס וּבְהִרְהוּר,

וְעַל חֵטְא שֶׁחָטָאנוּ לְפָנֶיךָ וְלִפְנֵיהֶם בִּוְעִידוֹת שָׁוְא.

עַל חֵטְא שֶׁחָטָאנוּ לְפָנֶיךָ וְלִפְנֵיהֶם בִּזְהִירוּת יֶתֶר,

וְעַל חֵטְא שֶׁחָטָאנוּ לְפָנֶיךָ וְלִפְנֵיהֶם בְּחִבּוּק יָדָיִם.

עַל חֵטְא שֶׁחָטָאנוּ לְפָנֶיךָ וְלִפְנֵיהֶם בַּטִּמְטוּם הַמֹּחַ,

וְעַל חֵטְא שֶׁחָטָאנוּ לְפָנֶיךָ וְלִפְנֵיהֶם בְּיֵאוּשׁ מִדַּעַת.

עַל חֵטְא שֶׁחָטָאנוּ לְפָנֶיךָ וְלִפְנֵיהֶם בְּסַבְלָנוּת,

וְעַל חֵטְא שֶׁחָטָאנוּ לְפָנֶיךָ וְלִפְנֵיהֶם בַּעֲלִיזוּת חַיֵּינוּ.

עַל חֵטְא שֶׁחָטָאנוּ לְפָנֶיךָ וְלִפְנֵיהֶם בְּפִצוּי וּבְפִיּוּס,

וְעַל חֵטְא שֶׁחָטָאנוּ לְפָנֶיךָ וְלִפְנֵיהֶם בְּצִדּוּק הַדִּין.

עַל חֵטְא שֶׁחָטָאנוּ לְפָנֶיךָ וְלִפְנֵיהֶם בְּשַׁאֲנַנּוּת רוּחַ,

וְעַל חֵטְא שֶׁחָטָאנוּ לְפָנֶיךָ וְלִפְנֵיהֶם בְּשִׂנְאַת חִנָּם.

וְעַל כֻּלָּם אֱלוֹהַּ סְלִיחוֹת, סְלַח לָנוּ, מְחַל לָנוּ, כַּפֶּר־לָנוּ.

עַל חֵטְא שֶׁחָטָאנוּ לְפָנֶיךָ בְּאֹנֶס,

וְעַל חֵטְא שֶׁחָטָאנוּ לְפָנֶיךָ בְּרָצוֹן.

עַל חֵטְא שֶׁחָטָאנוּ לְפָנֶיךָ בַּסֵּתֶר,

וְעַל חֵטְא שֶׁחָטָאנוּ לְפָנֶיךָ בַּגָּלוּי.

עַל חֵטְא שֶׁחָטָאנוּ לְפָנֶיךָ בְּשׁוֹגֵג,

וְעַל חֵטְא שֶׁחָטָאנוּ לְפָנֶיךָ בְּמֵזִיד.

וְעַל כֻּלָּם אֱלוֹהַּ סְלִיחוֹת, סְלַח לָנוּ, מְחַל לָנוּ, כַּפֶּר־לָנוּ.

עַל חֵטְא. Rabbi Avraham Holtz has written a contemporary Al Ḥet focused on the sins of the Jewish community in not focusing and reacting with zeal to contemporary crises. Though Rabbi Holtz had the Holocaust in mind when he wrote this alphabetical acrostic, the words can be applied to many situations in our time.

Sin and Repentance

No sin is so light that it may be overlooked; no sin is so heavy that it may not be repented of.

—MOSES IBN EZRA

Facing Ourselves

There is a law which states, "You should not deceive your fellow" (Leviticus 19:11), but to be faithful to God is to go beyond the law—not even to deceive one's self.

—JULES HARLOW

AN ALTERNATE CONFESSIONAL

We have sinned against You, and them, by refusing to hear,
and we have sinned against You, and them, by betraying friends.
We have sinned against You, and them, by hesitating,
and we have sinned against You, and them, by useless conferences.
We have sinned against You, and them, by being overcautious,
and we have sinned against You, and them, by not using our power.
We have sinned against You, and them, by senselessness,
and we have sinned against You, and them, by despairing.
We have sinned against You, and them, by being patient,
and we have sinned against You, and them, by frivolity at dreadful times.
We have sinned against You, and them, by appeasement,
and we have sinned against You, and them, by theological rationalizations.
We have sinned against You, and them, by complacency,
and we have sinned against You, and them, by communal strife.

For all these sins, forgiving God, forgive us pardon us, grant us atonement.
V'al kullam elo·ah s'liḥot s'laḥ lanu, m'ḥal lanu, kapper lanu.

We have sinned against You unwillingly,
and we have sinned against You willingly.
We have sinned against You in secret,
and we have sinned against You openly.
We have sinned against You by mistake,
and we have sinned against You purposely.

For all these sins, forgiving God, forgive us pardon us, grant us atonement.
V'al kullam elo·ah s'liḥot s'laḥ lanu, m'ḥal lanu, kapper lanu.

וְאַתָּה רַחוּם מְקַבֵּל שָׁבִים; וְעַל הַתְּשׁוּבָה מֵרֹאשׁ הִבְטַחְתָּנוּ, וְעַל הַתְּשׁוּבָה עֵינֵינוּ מְיַחֲלוֹת לָךְ.

אֱלֹהֵינוּ וֵאלֹהֵי אֲבוֹתֵינוּ [וְאִמּוֹתֵינוּ], מְחַל לַעֲוֹנוֹתֵינוּ בְּיוֹם [הַשַּׁבָּת הַזֶּה וּבְיוֹם] הַכִּפֻּרִים הַזֶּה. מְחֵה וְהַעֲבֵר פְּשָׁעֵינוּ וְחַטֹּאתֵינוּ מִנֶּגֶד עֵינֶיךָ, כָּאָמוּר: אָנֹכִי אָנֹכִי הוּא מֹחֶה פְשָׁעֶיךָ לְמַעֲנִי, וְחַטֹּאתֶיךָ לֹא אֶזְכֹּר. וְנֶאֱמַר: מָחִיתִי כָעָב פְּשָׁעֶיךָ וְכֶעָנָן חַטֹּאתֶיךָ, שׁוּבָה אֵלַי כִּי גְאַלְתִּיךָ. וְנֶאֱמַר: כִּי בַיּוֹם הַזֶּה יְכַפֵּר עֲלֵיכֶם לְטַהֵר אֶתְכֶם, מִכֹּל חַטֹּאתֵיכֶם לִפְנֵי יְהֹוָה תִּטְהָרוּ.

אֱלֹהֵינוּ וֵאלֹהֵי אֲבוֹתֵינוּ [וְאִמּוֹתֵינוּ], [רְצֵה בִמְנוּחָתֵנוּ] קַדְּשֵׁנוּ בְּמִצְוֹתֶיךָ וְתֵן חֶלְקֵנוּ בְּתוֹרָתֶךָ, שַׂבְּעֵנוּ מִטּוּבֶךָ וְשַׂמְּחֵנוּ בִּישׁוּעָתֶךָ [וְהַנְחִילֵנוּ, יְהֹוָה אֱלֹהֵינוּ, בְּאַהֲבָה וּבְרָצוֹן שַׁבַּת קָדְשֶׁךָ, וְיָנוּחוּ בָהּ יִשְׂרָאֵל מְקַדְּשֵׁי שְׁמֶךָ] וְטַהֵר לִבֵּנוּ לְעָבְדְּךָ בֶּאֱמֶת, כִּי אַתָּה סָלְחָן לְיִשְׂרָאֵל וּמָחֳלָן לְשִׁבְטֵי יְשֻׁרוּן בְּכָל-דּוֹר וָדוֹר, וּמִבַּלְעָדֶיךָ אֵין לָנוּ מֶלֶךְ מוֹחֵל וְסוֹלֵחַ אֶלָּא אָתָּה. בָּרוּךְ אַתָּה יְהֹוָה, מֶלֶךְ מוֹחֵל וְסוֹלֵחַ לַעֲוֹנוֹתֵינוּ וְלַעֲוֹנוֹת עַמּוֹ בֵּית יִשְׂרָאֵל, וּמַעֲבִיר אַשְׁמוֹתֵינוּ בְּכָל-שָׁנָה וְשָׁנָה, מֶלֶךְ עַל כָּל-הָאָרֶץ, מְקַדֵּשׁ [הַשַּׁבָּת וְ] יִשְׂרָאֵל וְיוֹם הַכִּפֻּרִים.

SINCE THE DAWN OF CRE-ATION מֵרֹאשׁ. The Midrash proposes that t'shuvah was one of the seven things that preceded the crea-tion of heaven and earth (Pesaḥim 54a). Another midrash maintains that the world could not be created and continue in existence until t'shuvah was created (Pirke d'Rabbi Eliezer, ch. 3).

I, SURELY I . . . אָנֹכִי אָנֹכִי. Isaiah 43:25.

I SWEEP ASIDE YOUR SINS LIKE A MIST מָחִיתִי כָעָב פְּשָׁעֶיךָ. Isaiah 44:22. Isaiah announces Israel's redemp-tion and says that even the heavens and hills will rejoice at Israel's return.

FOR ON THIS DAY כִּי-בַיּוֹם הַזֶּה. Leviticus 16:30.

FILL OUR LIVES WITH YOUR GOODNESS שַׂבְּעֵנוּ מִטּוּבֶךָ. Literally, "satiate us," as if our sustenance were no longer food but God's spiritual succor.

EACH YEAR SWEEPING AWAY OUR GUILT וּמַעֲבִיר אַשְׁמוֹתֵינוּ בְּכָל-שָׁנָה. We know that we are human and will sin, but the possi-bility of renewal is an equal part of our humanity.

We are afraid of things that cannot harm us, and we know it; and we crave things that cannot help us, and we know it. But actually, it is something within us that we are afraid of, and it is something within us that we crave.

—MARTIN BUBER

You are compassionate, welcoming those who turn back to You. You have promised, since the dawn of creation, that repentance would be received. Now, our eyes look toward You, to accept our repentance.

Conclusion of the Sanctification of the Day

Our God and God of our ancestors, forgive our sins on [this Shabbat and] this Yom Kippur. Blot out and disregard them, as the prophet Isaiah says in Your name: "I, surely I, am the One who wipes away sin, for this is My nature; I will not recall your errors," and the prophet adds: "I sweep aside your sins like a mist, and disperse your transgressions like a cloud. Turn back to Me, for I will redeem you." And in Your Torah it is written: "For on this day, atonement shall be made for you to purify you from all your transgressions. In the presence of ADONAI you shall be pure."

Our God and God of our ancestors: [embrace our rest,] make us holy through Your mitzvot and let the Torah be our portion. Fill our lives with Your goodness and gladden us with Your triumph. [ADONAI our God, grant that we inherit Your holy Shabbat, lovingly and willingly, so that the people Israel, who sanctify Your name, may find rest on this day.] Purify our hearts to serve You faithfully, for You forgive the people Israel and pardon the tribes of Jeshurun in every generation. Beside You, we have no sovereign who pardons and forgives. *Barukh atah ADONAI*, sovereign who pardons and forgives our sins and those of the people, the House of Israel, each year sweeping away our guilt—ruler of all the earth, who makes [Shabbat,] the people Israel and the Day of Atonement holy.

melekh al kol ha-aretz, m'kaddeish [ha-shabbat v'] yisra·el

רְצֵה יהוה אֱלֹהֵינוּ, בְּעַמְּךָ יִשְׂרָאֵל, וּבִתְפִלָּתָם, וּבִתְפִלָּתָם, וְהָשֵׁב אֶת־הָעֲבוֹדָה לִדְבִיר בֵּיתֶךָ. [וְאִשֵּׁי יִשְׂרָאֵל] וּתְפִלָּתָם בְּאַהֲבָה תְקַבֵּל בְּרָצוֹן, וּתְהִי לְרָצוֹן תָּמִיד עֲבוֹדַת יִשְׂרָאֵל עַמֶּךָ.

If the kohanim will be reciting the Priestly Blessing, this b'rakhah continues:

וְתֶעֱרַב עָלֶיךָ עֲתִירָתֵנוּ. וְתֶחֱזֶינָה עֵינֵינוּ בְּשׁוּבְךָ לְצִיּוֹן בְּרַחֲמִים, וְשָׁם נַעֲבָדְךָ בְּיִרְאָה כִּימֵי עוֹלָם וּכְשָׁנִים קַדְמוֹנִיּוֹת. בָּרוּךְ אַתָּה יהוה, שֶׁאוֹתְךָ לְבַדְּךָ בְּיִרְאָה נַעֲבוֹד.

If the kohanim will not be blessing the congregation, we proceed here:

וְתֶחֱזֶינָה עֵינֵינוּ בְּשׁוּבְךָ לְצִיּוֹן בְּרַחֲמִים. בָּרוּךְ אַתָּה יהוה, הַמַּחֲזִיר שְׁכִינָתוֹ לְצִיּוֹן.

While reciting the first words, by custom we remain seated while bowing our head.

Congregation recites:

מוֹדִים אֲנַחְנוּ לָךְ
שָׁאַתָּה הוּא יהוה אֱלֹהֵינוּ
וֵאלֹהֵי אֲבוֹתֵינוּ [וְאִמּוֹתֵינוּ]
אֱלֹהֵי כָל־בָּשָׂר, יוֹצְרֵנוּ,
יוֹצֵר בְּרֵאשִׁית. בְּרָכוֹת
וְהוֹדָאוֹת לְשִׁמְךָ הַגָּדוֹל
וְהַקָּדוֹשׁ, עַל שֶׁהֶחֱיִיתָנוּ
וְקִיַּמְתָּנוּ. כֵּן תְּחַיֵּנוּ
וּתְקַיְּמֵנוּ, וְתֶאֱסוֹף
גָּלֻיּוֹתֵינוּ לְחַצְרוֹת קָדְשֶׁךָ,
לִשְׁמוֹר חֻקֶּיךָ וְלַעֲשׂוֹת
רְצוֹנֶךָ, וּלְעָבְדְּךָ בְּלֵבָב
שָׁלֵם, עַל שֶׁאֲנַחְנוּ מוֹדִים
לָךְ. בָּרוּךְ אֵל הַהוֹדָאוֹת.

Leader recites:

מוֹדִים אֲנַחְנוּ לָךְ
שָׁאַתָּה הוּא יהוה אֱלֹהֵינוּ
וֵאלֹהֵי אֲבוֹתֵינוּ [וְאִמּוֹתֵינוּ]
לְעוֹלָם וָעֶד, צוּר חַיֵּינוּ
מָגֵן יִשְׁעֵנוּ אַתָּה הוּא.
לְדוֹר וָדוֹר נוֹדֶה לָּךְ
וּנְסַפֵּר תְּהִלָּתֶךָ, עַל חַיֵּינוּ
הַמְּסוּרִים בְּיָדֶךָ וְעַל
נִשְׁמוֹתֵינוּ הַפְּקוּדוֹת לָךְ,
וְעַל נִסֶּיךָ שֶׁבְּכָל־יוֹם עִמָּנוּ
וְעַל נִפְלְאוֹתֶיךָ וְטוֹבוֹתֶיךָ
שֶׁבְּכָל־עֵת, עֶרֶב וָבֹקֶר
וְצָהֳרָיִם. ◁ הַטּוֹב, כִּי לֹא
כָלוּ רַחֲמֶיךָ, וְהַמְרַחֵם כִּי
לֹא תַמּוּ חֲסָדֶיךָ מֵעוֹלָם
קִוִּינוּ לָךְ.

RESTORE WORSHIP TO YOUR SANCTUARY וְהָשֵׁב אֶת־הָעֲבוֹדָה לִדְבִיר בֵּיתֶךָ. A motif of Jewish theology is that we are in exile and that our collective relationship with God cannot be fulfilled. Yearning for the restoration of the Temple expresses the wish to have a direct relationship with God.

THE FIERY OFFERINGS וְאִשֵּׁי יִשְׂרָאֵל. The reference to the "fiery offerings," originally referring to the sacrifices that took place in the Temple, was understood by many Ḥasidic commentators as referring to the intensity of religious fervor in true prayer.

YOUR DIVINE PRESENCE שְׁכִינָתוֹ. The Hebrew word *shekhinah* has been used for centuries to refer to God's immanence, the presence of God that is felt in the world. The word *shekhinah* is grammatically feminine. Accordingly, the Jewish mystical tradition generally describes the Divine Presence—known as the Shekhinah—in feminine imagery.

A CONGREGATIONAL RESPONSE מוֹדִים. A second version of Modim, the b'rakhah of thanksgiving, was created by the Rabbis of the talmudic period to be recited by the congregation while the leader chants the official prayer (Babylonian

Talmud, Sotah 40a). In this way, both the leader and the congregation personally fulfill the imperative of acknowledging God. The central idea in this version is *modim anaḥnu lakh. . . . al she-anaḥnu modim lakh*, "we thank You for the ability to thank You." The prayer may be understood as an expression of appreciation for being part of a religious tradition that values reflection and gratitude. More radically, this prayer may be understood as expressing the thought that our prayers may be addressed to God, but God is the source of all—even the words of holiness we speak. The very ability to thank is thus a manifestation of the presence of God within us.

Fifth B'rakhah: The Restoration of Zion

ADONAI our God, embrace Your people Israel and their prayer. Restore worship to Your sanctuary. May [the fiery offerings and] the prayers of the people Israel be lovingly accepted by You, and may our service always be pleasing.

If the kohanim will be reciting the Priestly Blessing, this b'rakhah continues:

May our prayers be pleasing to You and may our eyes behold Your merciful return to Zion so that we may worship there as in days of old. *Barukh atah* ADONAI, for You alone shall we worship in awe.

If the kohanim will not be blessing the congregation, we proceed here:

Let our eyes behold Your merciful return to Zion. *Barukh atah* ADONAI, who restores Your Divine Presence to Zion.

Sixth B'rakhah: Gratitude for Life and Its Blessings

While reciting the first words, by custom we remain seated while bowing our head.

Gratitude

Gratitude is a fundamental religious stance. In reciting a blessing, we become conscious of our lives as a gift, and, in that moment, we experience the world around us as loving and good. Rabbi Meir asks us to recite a hundred *b'rakhot* each day in recognition of life and its many blessings (Babylonian Talmud, Menaḥot 43b). We then come to understand ourselves as guardians of the gifts we have received and thus feel called on to express our love and care in return.

Leader recites:

We thank You, You who are our God and the God of our ancestors through all time, protector of our lives, shield of our salvation. From one generation to the next we thank You and sing Your praises—
for our lives that are in Your hands,
for our souls that are under Your care,
for Your miracles that accompany us each day,
and for Your wonders and Your gifts that are with us each moment—
evening, morning, and noon. You are the One who is good, whose mercy is never-ending; the One who is compassionate, whose love is unceasing. We have always placed our hope in You.

Congregation recites:

ſ We thank You for the ability to acknowledge You. You are our God and the God of our ancestors, the God of all flesh, our creator, and the creator of all. We offer praise and blessing to Your holy and great name, for granting us life and for sustaining us. May You continue to grant us life and sustenance. Gather our dispersed to Your holy courtyards, that we may fulfill Your mitzvot and serve You wholeheartedly, carrying out Your will. May God, the source of gratitude, be praised.

וְעַל כֻּלָּם יִתְבָּרַךְ וְיִתְרוֹמַם שִׁמְךָ מַלְכֵּנוּ תָּמִיד לְעוֹלָם וָעֶד.

אָבִינוּ מַלְכֵּנוּ, זְכוֹר רַחֲמֶיךָ וּכְבוֹשׁ כַּעַסְךָ, וְכַלֵּה דֶּבֶר
וְחֶרֶב, וְרָעָב וּשְׁבִי, וּמַשְׁחִית וְעָוֹן, וּשְׁמַד וּמַגֵּפָה,
וּפֶגַע רַע וְכָל־מַחֲלָה, וְכָל־תַּקָּלָה וְכָל־קְטָטָה, וְכָל־מִינֵי
פֻרְעָנִיּוֹת, וְכָל־גְּזֵרָה רָעָה וְשִׂנְאַת חִנָּם, מֵעָלֵינוּ וּמֵעַל
כָּל־בְּנֵי בְרִיתֶךָ.

וּכְתוֹב לְחַיִּים טוֹבִים כָּל־בְּנֵי בְרִיתֶךָ.

וְכֹל הַחַיִּים יוֹדוּךָ סֶּלָה, וִיהַלְלוּ אֶת־שִׁמְךָ בֶּאֱמֶת
הָאֵל יְשׁוּעָתֵנוּ וְעֶזְרָתֵנוּ סֶלָה.
בָּרוּךְ אַתָּה יהוה, הַטּוֹב שִׁמְךָ וּלְךָ נָאֶה לְהוֹדוֹת.

If the kohanim do not bless the congregation, we continue on page 357.
We rise.

בִּרְכַּת כֹּהֲנִים

The kohanim recite quietly:
יְהִי רָצוֹן מִלְּפָנֶיךָ יהוה אֱלֹהֵינוּ וֵאלֹהֵי אֲבוֹתֵינוּ [וְאִמּוֹתֵינוּ],
שֶׁתְּהֵא הַבְּרָכָה הַזֹּאת שֶׁצִּוִּיתָנוּ לְבָרֵךְ אֶת־עַמְּךָ יִשְׂרָאֵל בְּרָכָה
שְׁלֵמָה, וְלֹא יִהְיֶה בָּהּ שׁוּם מִכְשׁוֹל וְעָוֹן מֵעַתָּה וְעַד עוֹלָם.

Leader:
אֱלֹהֵינוּ וֵאלֹהֵי אֲבוֹתֵינוּ [וְאִמּוֹתֵינוּ],
בָּרְכֵנוּ בַּבְּרָכָה הַמְשֻׁלֶּשֶׁת
בַּתּוֹרָה הַכְּתוּבָה עַל יְדֵי מֹשֶׁה עַבְדֶּךָ,
הָאֲמוּרָה מִפִּי אַהֲרֹן וּבָנָיו
כֹּהֲנִים עַם קְדוֹשֶׁךָ—כָּאָמוּר:

The kohanim recite:
בָּרוּךְ אַתָּה יהוה, אֱלֹהֵינוּ מֶלֶךְ הָעוֹלָם, אֲשֶׁר קִדְּשָׁנוּ
בִּקְדֻשָּׁתוֹ שֶׁל אַהֲרֹן, וְצִוָּנוּ לְבָרֵךְ אֶת־עַמּוֹ יִשְׂרָאֵל
בְּאַהֲבָה.

אָמֵן.

אָמֵן.   יְבָרֶכְךָ יהוה וְיִשְׁמְרֶךָ.

אָמֵן.   יָאֵר יהוה פָּנָיו אֵלֶיךָ וִיחֻנֶּךָּ.

אָמֵן.   יִשָּׂא יהוה פָּנָיו אֵלֶיךָ וְיָשֵׂם לְךָ שָׁלוֹם.

שָׁלוֹם שָׁלוֹם לָרָחוֹק וְלַקָּרוֹב, אָמַר יהוה, וּרְפָאתִיו.

We are seated.

FOR ALL THESE וְעַל כֻּלָּם. In the language of the Bible and the prayerbook, "God's name is exalted" when we acknowledge God, recognize God's goodness in creation, and act to enable God's justice and compassion to be visible in the world.

AND INSCRIBE וּכְתוֹב. This is the third of the four special insertions in the Amidah for the Ten Days of Repentance.

BIRKAT KOHANIM. This blessing (Numbers 6:24–26) is known as the Birkat Kohanim, the Priestly Blessing, as the Torah prescribes that it is to be recited by Aaron and his descendants, the *kohanim* (priests), to bring God's blessing upon the people Israel. Its words are the only biblical verses that have been found in archaeological digs of biblical times. In most synagogues in Israel, this blessing is recited every day by the *kohanim* in each community, who come to the front of the synagogue after preparing themselves ritually and extend their hands toward the community in a traditional gesture that serves as a conduit of blessing. In many synagogues in the Diaspora, the *kohanim* reenact this ancient blessing only during the Musaf service on High Holy Days and festivals. At other times, and at all times in many congregations, the blessing is recited by the service leader.

For all these blessings may Your name be praised and exalted, our sovereign, always and forever.

Avinu Malkeinu, remember Your compassion and subdue Your anger. Bring an end to pestilence, sword, and hunger; captivity and destruction, sin and oppression, plague and calamity; every illness, misfortune, and quarrel; all kinds of danger, every evil decree, and causeless hatred. Bring an end to these for us and for all the people of Your covenant.

And inscribe all the people of Your covenant for a good life.
U-kh'tov l'ḥayyim tovim kol b'nei v'ritekha.

May all that lives thank You always, and praise Your name faithfully forever, God of our deliverance and help.
Barukh atah ADONAI, whose name is goodness and to whom praise is fitting.

If the kohanim do not bless the congregation, we continue on page 357.
We rise.

The Priestly Blessing
The kohanim recite quietly:

May it be Your will, ADONAI our God and God of our ancestors, that this blessing with which You have instructed us to bless Your people Israel be perfect and complete, and that it not be diminished by any error or sin, now or ever.

Leader (quietly):

Our God and God of our ancestors: Bless us with the threefold blessing written in the Torah by the hand of Moses Your servant, recited by Aaron and his descendants, the *kohanim*, the consecrated priests of Your people:
am k'doshekha ka-amur.

The kohanim recite:

Barukh atah ADONAI, our God, ruler of time and space, who has made us holy with the sanctity of Aaron and has instructed us to bless the people Israel with love.   Amen.

May ADONAI bless and protect you.   Amen.

May ADONAI's countenance shine upon you and grant you kindness.
                                                              Amen.

May ADONAI's countenance be lifted toward you and grant you peace.
                                                              Amen.

Shalom, shalom—shalom to those who are far off, shalom to those who are near, says ADONAI, and I shall heal them.
We are seated.

If the kohanim do not bless the congregation, we continue here:

אֱלֹהֵינוּ וֵאלֹהֵי אֲבוֹתֵינוּ [וְאִמּוֹתֵינוּ], בָּרְכֵנוּ בַּבְּרָכָה
הַמְשֻׁלֶּשֶׁת בַּתּוֹרָה הַכְּתוּבָה עַל יְדֵי מֹשֶׁה עַבְדֶּךָ,
הָאֲמוּרָה מִפִּי אַהֲרֹן וּבָנָיו, כֹּהֲנִים, עַם קְדוֹשֶׁךָ, כָּאָמוּר:

כֵּן יְהִי רָצוֹן.   יְבָרֶכְךָ יהוה וְיִשְׁמְרֶךָ.

כֵּן יְהִי רָצוֹן.   יָאֵר יהוה פָּנָיו אֵלֶיךָ וִיחֻנֶּךָּ.

כֵּן יְהִי רָצוֹן.   יִשָּׂא יהוה פָּנָיו אֵלֶיךָ וְיָשֵׂם לְךָ שָׁלוֹם.

All services continue here:

שִׂים שָׁלוֹם בָּעוֹלָם, טוֹבָה וּבְרָכָה, חֵן וָחֶסֶד וְרַחֲמִים
עָלֵינוּ וְעַל כָּל־יִשְׂרָאֵל עַמֶּךָ. בָּרְכֵנוּ אָבִינוּ כֻּלָּנוּ כְּאֶחָד
בְּאוֹר פָּנֶיךָ, כִּי בְאוֹר פָּנֶיךָ נָתַתָּ לָּנוּ, יהוה אֱלֹהֵינוּ, תּוֹרַת
חַיִּים וְאַהֲבַת חֶסֶד, וּצְדָקָה וּבְרָכָה וְרַחֲמִים וְחַיִּים,
וְשָׁלוֹם. וְטוֹב בְּעֵינֶיךָ לְבָרֵךְ אֶת־עַמְּךָ יִשְׂרָאֵל, בְּכָל־עֵת
וּבְכָל־שָׁעָה בִּשְׁלוֹמֶךָ.

**בְּסֵפֶר חַיִּים, בְּרָכָה וְשָׁלוֹם וּפַרְנָסָה טוֹבָה, נִזָּכֵר וְנִכָּתֵב
לְפָנֶיךָ, אֲנַחְנוּ וְכָל־עַמְּךָ בֵּית יִשְׂרָאֵל, לְחַיִּים טוֹבִים
וּלְשָׁלוֹם.**

וְנֶאֱמַר: כִּי בִי יִרְבּוּ יָמֶיךָ, וְיוֹסִיפוּ לְךָ שְׁנוֹת חַיִּים.
לְחַיִּים טוֹבִים תִּכְתְּבֵנוּ, אֱלֹהִים חַיִּים.
כָּתְבֵנוּ בְּסֵפֶר הַחַיִּים,
כַּכָּתוּב: וְאַתֶּם הַדְּבֵקִים בַּיהוה אֱלֹהֵיכֶם, חַיִּים
כֻּלְּכֶם הַיּוֹם.

GRANT PEACE שִׂים שָׁלוֹם.
Every Jewish prayer service
ends with a prayer for
peace. The midrash says
that peace is one of the
names of God. The words
of Sim Shalom, "grant
peace," are related directly
to the conclusion of Birkat
Kohanim, the priestly
blessing: "May God grant
You peace." Additionally,
the paragraph uses the
metaphor of the light
of God's face as bestow-
ing blessing. Thus, this
b'rakhah is traditionally
recited at all services at
which Birkat Kohanim is
recited. On fast days such
as Yom Kippur, Birkat
Kohanim is recited at all
services throughout the
day.

**INSCRIBE US FOR A
GOOD LIFE** לְחַיִּים טוֹבִים
תִּכְתְּבֵנוּ (*l'ḥayyim tovim
tikht'veinu*). A final plea for
a year of life, a good life.

Peace

Peace is a great thing and quarrelsomeness is hateful. Peace is a great thing, for even during war peace is necessary, as it says: "When you approach a town to attack it you shall offer it terms of peace" (Deuteronomy 20:10). Great is peace, for God is called Peace, as it says: "And [Gideon] called the altar, 'ADONAI is peace'" (Judges 6:24).
—NUMBERS RABBAH, CHAPTER 11, SECTION 7

Three days before the Messiah arrives, Elijah will come and stand upon the mountains.... Elijah's voice will be heard from world's end to world's end. And then he will say: "Peace has come to the world."
—PESIKTA RABBATI, PISKA 35
(trans. Francine Klagsbrun)

Seventh B'rakhah: Prayer for Peace

If the kohanim do not bless the congregation, we continue here:
Our God and God of our ancestors,
bless us with the threefold blessing of the Torah
written by Moses Your servant,
recited by Aaron and his descendants, the *kohanim*,
the consecrated priests of Your people:

May ADONAI bless and protect you.
So may it be God's will. Kein y'hi ratzon.
May ADONAI's countenance shine upon you
and grant you kindness.
So may it be God's will. Kein y'hi ratzon.
May ADONAI's countenance be lifted toward you
and grant you peace.
So may it be God's will. Kein y'hi ratzon.

All services continue here:
Grant peace to the world: goodness and blessing, grace, love, and compassion to us and all the people Israel. Bless us, our creator, united as one in the light of Your countenance; by that light, ADONAI our God, You gave us a guide to life: the love of kindness, righteousness, blessing, compassion, life, and peace. May it please You to bless Your people Israel at every season and at all times with Your gift of peace.

May we and the entire House of Israel be called to mind and inscribed for life, blessing, sustenance, and peace in the Book of Life.
*B'seifer ḥayyim b'rakhah v'shalom u-farnasah tovah,
nizzakheir v'nikkateiv l'fanekha, anaḥnu v'khol am'kha beit yisra·el,
l'ḥayyim tovim u-l'shalom.*

As it is written: "Through Me shall your days be increased,
and years be added to your life."
Inscribe us for a good life,
You who are the God of life;
write us in the Book of Life,
as is written in Your Torah: "And those of you who cling to God
on this day are truly alive today."

The ark is opened.

הַיּוֹם תְּאַמְּצֵנוּ, אָמֵן.

הַיּוֹם תְּבָרְכֵנוּ, אָמֵן.

הַיּוֹם תְּגַדְּלֵנוּ, אָמֵן.

הַיּוֹם תִּדְרְשֵׁנוּ לְטוֹבָה, אָמֵן.

הַיּוֹם תִּכְתְּבֵנוּ לְחַיִּים טוֹבִים, אָמֵן.

הַיּוֹם תְּקַבֵּל בְּרַחֲמִים וּבְרָצוֹן אֶת־תְּפִלָּתֵנוּ, אָמֵן.

הַיּוֹם תִּשְׁמַע שַׁוְעָתֵנוּ, אָמֵן.

הַיּוֹם תִּתְמְכֵנוּ בִּימִין צִדְקֶךָ, אָמֵן.

The ark is closed.

כְּהַיּוֹם הַזֶּה תְּבִיאֵנוּ שָׂשִׂים וּשְׂמֵחִים בְּבִנְיַן שָׁלֵם,
כַּכָּתוּב עַל יַד נְבִיאֶךָ: וַהֲבִיאוֹתִים אֶל הַר קָדְשִׁי,
וְשִׂמַּחְתִּים בְּבֵית תְּפִלָּתִי, כִּי בֵיתִי בֵּית תְּפִלָּה יִקָּרֵא
לְכָל־הָעַמִּים. וּצְדָקָה וּבְרָכָה וְרַחֲמִים וְחַיִּים וְשָׁלוֹם
יִהְיֶה לָּנוּ לְכָל־יִשְׂרָאֵל וּלְכָל־יוֹשְׁבֵי תֵבֵל עַד הָעוֹלָם.
בָּרוּךְ אַתָּה יהוה, עוֹשֶׂה הַשָּׁלוֹם.

TODAY הַיּוֹם. The *piyyut* is an alphabetical acrostic, though it has become common to recite only the first four verses, a verse in the middle, and three concluding ones.

ON A DAY LIKE THIS כְּהַיּוֹם. Presumably at a moment like this, when our sins have been forgiven, we face God, the congregation, and the world in purity.

I SHALL BRING YOU וַהֲבִיאוֹתִים. Isaiah 56:7.

HA-YOM—THIS DAY: A PIYYUT

The ark is opened.

Strengthen us—today. *Amen.*

Bless us—today. *Amen.*

Exalt us—today. *Amen.*

Seek our well-being—today. *Amen.*

Inscribe us for a good life—today. *Amen.*

Lovingly accept our prayers—today. *Amen.*

Hear our plea—today. *Amen.*

Sustain us with the power of Your righteousness—today. *Amen.*

Ha-yom t'am'tzeinu. Amen.
Ha-yom t'var'kheinu. Amen.
Ha-yom t'gad'leinu. Amen.
Ha-yom tidr'sheinu l'tovah. Amen.
Ha-yom tikht'veinu l'ḥayyim tovim. Amen.
Ha-yom t'kabbel b'raḥamim u-v'ratzon et t'fillateinu. Amen.
Ha-yom tishma shavateinu. Amen.
Ha-yom titm'kheinu bimin tzidkekha. Amen.

The ark is closed.

On a day like this, bring us joyfully to the fullness of redemption. As Your prophet Isaiah said, "I shall bring you to My holy mountain and make you joyous in My house of prayer, for My house shall be called a house of prayer for all people." May we, the entire people Israel and all humanity, be granted justice, blessing, compassion, life, and peace forever. *Barukh atah ADONAI*, who brings peace.

קַדִּישׁ שָׁלֵם

יִתְגַּדַּל וְיִתְקַדַּשׁ שְׁמֵהּ רַבָּא, בְּעָלְמָא דִּי בְרָא, כִּרְעוּתֵהּ,
וְיַמְלִיךְ מַלְכוּתֵהּ בְּחַיֵּיכוֹן וּבְיוֹמֵיכוֹן וּבְחַיֵּי דְכָל־בֵּית
יִשְׂרָאֵל, בַּעֲגָלָא וּבִזְמַן קָרִיב, וְאִמְרוּ אָמֵן.

יְהֵא שְׁמֵהּ רַבָּא מְבָרַךְ לְעָלַם וּלְעָלְמֵי עָלְמַיָּא.

יִתְבָּרַךְ וְיִשְׁתַּבַּח וְיִתְפָּאַר וְיִתְרוֹמַם וְיִתְנַשֵּׂא וְיִתְהַדָּר
וְיִתְעַלֶּה וְיִתְהַלָּל שְׁמֵהּ דְּקֻדְשָׁא, בְּרִיךְ **הוּא** לְעֵלָּא לְעֵלָּא
מִכָּל־בִּרְכָתָא וְשִׁירָתָא תֻּשְׁבְּחָתָא וְנֶחָמָתָא דַּאֲמִירָן
בְּעָלְמָא, וְאִמְרוּ אָמֵן.

תִּתְקַבַּל צְלוֹתְהוֹן וּבָעוּתְהוֹן דְּכָל־יִשְׂרָאֵל קֳדָם אֲבוּהוֹן
דִּי בִשְׁמַיָּא, וְאִמְרוּ אָמֵן.

יְהֵא שְׁלָמָא רַבָּא מִן שְׁמַיָּא וְחַיִּים עָלֵינוּ וְעַל כָּל־
יִשְׂרָאֵל, וְאִמְרוּ אָמֵן.

עֹשֶׂה שָׁלוֹם בִּמְרוֹמָיו הוּא יַעֲשֶׂה שָׁלוֹם עָלֵינוּ וְעַל כָּל־
יִשְׂרָאֵל [וְעַל כָּל־יוֹשְׁבֵי תֵבֵל], וְאִמְרוּ אָמֵן.

KADDISH SHALEM. The Kaddish Shalem (literally "Full Kaddish") ends the Musaf service. It is called the "Full Kaddish" because it includes a plea that the prayers we have offered be acceptable.

Kaddish Shalem

May God's great name be exalted and hallowed throughout the created world, as is God's wish. May God's sovereignty soon be established, in your lifetime and in your days, and in the days of all the House of Israel. And respond with: *Amen.*

May God's great name be acknowledged forever and ever!
Y'hei sh'meih rabba m'varakh l'alam u-l'almei almayya.

May the name of the Holy One be acknowledged and celebrated, lauded and worshipped, exalted and honored, extolled and acclaimed—though God, who is blessed, *b'rikh hu*, is truly far beyond all acknowledgment and praise, or any expressions of gratitude or consolation ever spoken in the House of Israel. And respond with: *Amen.*

May the prayers and pleas of all Israel be accepted by their Creator in heaven. And respond with: *Amen.*

May abundant peace from heaven, and life, come to us and to all Israel. And respond with: *Amen.*

May the One who brings harmony on high, bring harmony to us and to all Israel [and to all who dwell on earth]. And respond with: *Amen.*

Oseh shalom bi-m'romav hu ya·aseh shalom aleinu v'al kol yisra·el [v'al kol yosh'vei teiveil], v'imru amen.

מנחה ליום כיפור   AFTERNOON SERVICE OF YOM KIPPUR

הוֹצָאַת הַתּוֹרָה

THE AFTERNOON SERVICE.
Today's Minḥah service
begins immediately with
a Torah reading, followed
by a Haftarah (the Book of
Jonah), before it continues
with the Amidah. The two
prayers that normally open
Minḥah—Ashrei (Psalm
145) and U-va L'tziyyon
Go·el—are deferred until
the Ne·ilah service. This is
done to ensure that Ne·ilah
will begin before sundown.

We rise as the ark is opened.

וַיְהִי בִּנְסֹעַ הָאָרֹן וַיֹּאמֶר מֹשֶׁה:
קוּמָה יהוה וְיָפֻצוּ אֹיְבֶיךָ, וְיָנֻסוּ מְשַׂנְאֶיךָ מִפָּנֶיךָ.

כִּי מִצִּיּוֹן תֵּצֵא תוֹרָה, וּדְבַר יהוה מִירוּשָׁלָיִם.
בָּרוּךְ שֶׁנָּתַן תּוֹרָה לְעַמּוֹ יִשְׂרָאֵל בִּקְדֻשָּׁתוֹ.

Leader:

AS THE ARK וַיְהִי בִּנְסֹעַ.
Numbers 10:35.

ℸ גַּדְּלוּ לַיהוה אִתִּי, וּנְרוֹמְמָה שְׁמוֹ יַחְדָּו.

Congregation and leader:

THEN TORAH SHALL GO
FORTH כִּי מִצִּיּוֹן. Isaiah 2:3.

ACCLAIM גַּדְּלוּ. Psalm 34:4.

YOURS גַּדְּלוּ. 1 Chronicles
29:11; Psalm 99:5, 9.

לְךָ יהוה הַגְּדֻלָּה וְהַגְּבוּרָה וְהַתִּפְאֶרֶת וְהַנֵּצַח וְהַהוֹד,
כִּי־כֹל בַּשָּׁמַיִם וּבָאָרֶץ,
לְךָ יהוה הַמַּמְלָכָה וְהַמִּתְנַשֵּׂא לְכֹל לְרֹאשׁ.
רוֹמְמוּ יהוה אֱלֹהֵינוּ וְהִשְׁתַּחֲווּ לַהֲדֹם רַגְלָיו,
קָדוֹשׁ הוּא.
רוֹמְמוּ יהוה אֱלֹהֵינוּ וְהִשְׁתַּחֲווּ לְהַר קָדְשׁוֹ,
כִּי־קָדוֹשׁ יהוה אֱלֹהֵינוּ.

אַב הָרַחֲמִים הוּא יְרַחֵם עַם עֲמוּסִים, וְיִזְכֹּר בְּרִית
אֵיתָנִים, וְיַצִּיל נַפְשׁוֹתֵינוּ מִן הַשָּׁעוֹת הָרָעוֹת, וְיִגְעַר
בְּיֵצֶר הָרָע מִן הַנְּשׂוּאִים, וְיָחֹן אוֹתָנוּ לִפְלֵיטַת עוֹלָמִים,
וִימַלֵּא מִשְׁאֲלוֹתֵינוּ בְּמִדָּה טוֹבָה יְשׁוּעָה וְרַחֲמִים.

TORAH SERVICE

Taking Out the Torah

We rise as the ark is opened.

As the Ark was carried forward, Moses would say:
ADONAI! Scatter Your foes, so that Your enemies flee Your
Presence.

Torah shall go forth from Zion,
and the word of ADONAI from Jerusalem.
Praised is the One who gave Torah to the people Israel
in holiness.

Ki mi-tziyyon teitzei torah, u-d'var Adonai mi-rushalayim.
Barukh she-natan torah l'ammo yisra·el bi-k'dushato.

Leader:

ℓ Acclaim ADONAI with me; let us exalt God's name together.

Congregation and leader:

Yours, ADONAI, is the greatness, the power, the splendor, the
triumph, and the majesty—for all in heaven and on earth is
Yours. Yours is the sovereignty, above all else. Exalt ADONAI
our God, and bow down at God's throne, for our God is holy.
Exalt ADONAI our God, bow toward God's holy mountain, for
ADONAI our God is holy.

L'kha Adonai ha-g'dullah v'ha-g'vurah
v'ha-tiferet v'ha-neitzaḥ v'ha-hod,
ki khol ba-shamayim u-va-aretz.
L'kha Adonai ha-mamlakhah v'ha-mitnassei l'khol l'rosh.
Rom'mu Adonai eloheinu v'hishtaḥavu la-hadom raglav,
kadosh hu.
Rom'mu Adonai eloheinu v'hishtaḥavu l'har kodsho,
ki kadosh Adonai eloheinu.

May the One who is the source of compassion, who has always
sustained us, have mercy on us, and remember the covenant
with our ancestors. May God save us in difficult times, restrain
the impulse to evil within us, and grace our lives with enduring deliverance. May our pleas be answered with a measure of
kindness, salvation, and compassion.

Torah Reader (or Gabbai):

וְתִגָּלֶה וְתֵרָאֶה מַלְכוּתוֹ עָלֵינוּ בִּזְמַן קָרוֹב, וְיָחֹן פְּלֵטָתֵנוּ
וּפְלֵטַת עַמּוֹ בֵּית יִשְׂרָאֵל לְחֵן וּלְחֶסֶד לְרַחֲמִים וּלְרָצוֹן,
וְנֹאמַר **אָמֵן.** הַכֹּל הָבוּ גֹדֶל לֵאלֹהֵינוּ, וּתְנוּ כָבוֹד לַתּוֹרָה.
(כֹּהֵן, קְרַב: יַעֲמֹד _____ בֶּן _____ הַכֹּהֵן.)
(בַּת כֹּהֵן, קִרְבִי: תַּעֲמֹד _____ בַּת _____ הַכֹּהֵן.)
(יַעֲמֹד _____ בֶּן _____ רִאשׁוֹן.)
(תַּעֲמֹד _____ בַּת _____ רִאשׁוֹנָה.)
בָּרוּךְ שֶׁנָּתַן תּוֹרָה לְעַמּוֹ יִשְׂרָאֵל בִּקְדֻשָּׁתוֹ.

Congregation and Torah Reader:

וְאַתֶּם הַדְּבֵקִים בַּיהוה אֱלֹהֵיכֶם, חַיִּים כֻּלְּכֶם הַיּוֹם.

בִּרְכוֹת הַתּוֹרָה

The person who is honored with an aliyah recites the following
before the Torah is read:

בָּרְכוּ אֶת־יהוה הַמְבֹרָךְ.

The congregation responds:

בָּרוּךְ יהוה הַמְבֹרָךְ לְעוֹלָם וָעֶד.

The person repeats the above response, then continues:

בָּרוּךְ אַתָּה יהוה אֱלֹהֵינוּ מֶלֶךְ הָעוֹלָם,
אֲשֶׁר בָּחַר בָּנוּ מִכָּל־הָעַמִּים וְנָתַן לָנוּ אֶת־תּוֹרָתוֹ.
בָּרוּךְ אַתָּה יהוה, נוֹתֵן הַתּוֹרָה.

The person who is honored recites the following after the Torah is read:

בָּרוּךְ אַתָּה יהוה אֱלֹהֵינוּ מֶלֶךְ הָעוֹלָם,
אֲשֶׁר נָתַן לָנוּ תּוֹרַת אֱמֶת, וְחַיֵּי עוֹלָם נָטַע בְּתוֹכֵנוּ.
בָּרוּךְ אַתָּה יהוה, נוֹתֵן הַתּוֹרָה.

For the traditional Torah reading, turn to the next page.
For an alternate Torah reading, turn to page 365.

THE TORAH READING.
As Yom Kippur moves toward its conclusion and we prepare to return to daily life in a new year, the traditional afternoon Torah reading invites us to assess the state of our most intimate relationships, Leviticus 18. While we refrain from normal activities on Yom Kippur, we reflect on how to make our future behavior match the sense of purity that we have achieved today. As a symbol of the transition already underway, this Torah reading is recited with ordinary Shabbat trope (cantillation) rather than High Holy Day trope. In the modern period, some prefer that the focus of the reading be on broader issues of holiness. To that end, some congregations substitute the very next passage in the Torah, Leviticus 19.

The Public Reading
of Torah

When I read Torah, I
am a link in a very long
chain that shapes my
identity; it is a ritual of
personal and communal
self-definition, as well
as a reenactment of the
first public reading of the
Torah by Ezra and the
scribes rededicating the
Temple. I enunciate the
words, and add my own
meaning to the centuries
of interpretation that
preceded me; thus they
serve both as a key to my
own inner life and as a
form of historical identification.

—RAYMOND SCHEINDLIN

Torah Reader (or Gabbai):

May God's sovereignty be revealed to us soon. May God favor
the remnant of the people Israel with grace and kindness, with
compassion and love.
And let us say: *Amen.*
Let us all declare the greatness of God and give honor to the
Torah as (*the first to be called to the Torah*) comes forward. Praised is
God who gave the Torah to Israel in holiness.

Congregation and Torah Reader:

You who cling to ADONAI your God have been sustained to
this day.
V'attem ha-d'veikim badonai eloheikhem ḥayyim kull'khem ha-yom.

B'RAKHOT RECITED BY ONE CALLED UP TO THE TORAH
The person who is honored with an aliyah recites the following
before the Torah is read:

Praise ADONAI, to whom all prayer is directed.

The congregation responds:

Praise ADONAI, to whom all prayer is directed forever and ever.
Barukh Adonai ha-m'vorakh l'olam va·ed.

The person repeats the above response, then continues:

Barukh atah ADONAI, our God, ruler of time and space, who
has chosen us from among all peoples, giving us the Torah.
Barukh atah ADONAI, who gives the Torah.

The person who is honored recites the following after the Torah is read:

Barukh atah ADONAI, our God, ruler of time and space, who
has given us a teaching of truth, planting eternal life in our
midst. *Barukh atah ADONAI,* who gives the Torah.

For the traditional Torah reading, turn to the next page.
For an alternate Torah reading, turn to page 365.

קְרִיאַת הַתּוֹרָה – מְקַבֶּלֶת

וַיִּקְרָא יח

רִאשׁוֹן א וַיְדַבֵּ֥ר יְהֹוָ֖ה אֶל־מֹשֶׁ֥ה לֵּאמֹֽר: ב דַּבֵּר֙ אֶל־בְּנֵ֣י יִשְׂרָאֵ֔ל וְאָמַרְתָּ֖ אֲלֵהֶ֑ם אֲנִ֖י יְהֹוָ֥ה אֱלֹֽהֵיכֶֽם: ג כְּמַעֲשֵׂ֧ה אֶֽרֶץ־מִצְרַ֛יִם אֲשֶׁ֥ר יְשַׁבְתֶּם־בָּ֖הּ לֹ֣א תַעֲשׂ֑וּ וּכְמַעֲשֵׂ֣ה אֶֽרֶץ־כְּנַ֡עַן אֲשֶׁ֣ר אֲנִי֩ מֵבִ֨יא אֶתְכֶ֥ם שָׁ֙מָּה֙ לֹ֣א תַעֲשׂ֔וּ וּבְחֻקֹּֽתֵיהֶ֖ם לֹ֥א תֵלֵֽכוּ: ד אֶת־מִשְׁפָּטַ֤י תַּֽעֲשׂוּ֙ וְאֶת־חֻקֹּתַ֣י תִּשְׁמְר֔וּ לָלֶ֖כֶת בָּהֶ֑ם אֲנִ֖י יְהֹוָ֥ה אֱלֹֽהֵיכֶֽם: ה וּשְׁמַרְתֶּ֤ם אֶת־חֻקֹּתַי֙ וְאֶת־מִשְׁפָּטַ֔י אֲשֶׁ֨ר יַעֲשֶׂ֥ה אֹתָ֛ם הָאָדָ֖ם וָחַ֣י בָּהֶ֑ם אֲנִ֖י יְהֹוָֽה:

שֵׁנִי ו אִ֥ישׁ אִישׁ֙ אֶל־כׇּל־שְׁאֵ֣ר בְּשָׂר֔וֹ לֹ֥א תִקְרְב֖וּ לְגַלּ֣וֹת עֶרְוָ֑ה אֲנִ֖י יְהֹוָֽה: ז עֶרְוַ֥ת אָבִ֛יךָ וְעֶרְוַ֥ת אִמְּךָ֖ לֹ֣א תְגַלֵּ֑ה אִמְּךָ֣ הִ֔וא לֹ֥א תְגַלֶּ֖ה עֶרְוָתָֽהּ: ח עֶרְוַ֥ת אֵֽשֶׁת־אָבִ֖יךָ לֹ֣א תְגַלֵּ֑ה עֶרְוַ֥ת אָבִ֖יךָ הִֽוא: ט עֶרְוַ֨ת אֲחֽוֹתְךָ֤ בַת־אָבִ֙יךָ֙ א֣וֹ בַת־אִמֶּ֔ךָ מוֹלֶ֣דֶת בַּ֔יִת א֖וֹ מוֹלֶ֣דֶת ח֑וּץ לֹ֥א תְגַלֶּ֖ה עֶרְוָתָֽן: י עֶרְוַ֤ת בַּת־בִּנְךָ֙ א֣וֹ בַֽת־בִּתְּךָ֔ לֹ֥א תְגַלֶּ֖ה עֶרְוָתָ֑ן כִּ֥י עֶרְוָתְךָ֖ הֵֽנָּה: יא עֶרְוַ֨ת בַּת־אֵ֤שֶׁת אָבִ֙יךָ֙ מוֹלֶ֣דֶת אָבִ֔יךָ אֲחֽוֹתְךָ֖ הִ֑וא לֹ֥א תְגַלֶּ֖ה עֶרְוָתָֽהּ: יב עֶרְוַ֥ת אֲחֽוֹת־אָבִ֖יךָ לֹ֣א תְגַלֵּ֑ה שְׁאֵ֥ר אָבִ֖יךָ הִֽוא: יג עֶרְוַ֥ת אֲחֽוֹת־אִמְּךָ֖ לֹ֣א תְגַלֵּ֑ה כִּֽי־שְׁאֵ֥ר אִמְּךָ֖ הִֽוא: יד עֶרְוַ֥ת אֲחִֽי־אָבִ֖יךָ לֹ֣א תְגַלֵּ֑ה אֶל־אִשְׁתּוֹ֙ לֹ֣א תִקְרָ֔ב דֹּדָֽתְךָ֖ הִֽוא: טו עֶרְוַ֥ת כַּלָּֽתְךָ֖ לֹ֣א תְגַלֵּ֑ה

LEVITICUS 18. This passage focuses on permitted and prohibited sexual unions, including the definition of incest. In pre-modern societies, privacy in the family rarely existed. A public recitation of the rules that define and protect the family was deemed important on this day—when the entire community gathered for prayer and reflection. For our generation, this recitation takes on additional meaning as an opportunity to think about the rules that should govern our sexual lives. The Babylonian Talmud muses that while the Temple still stood, on each Day of Atonement after the High Priest had completed the annual purification ritual in the sanctuary, the nation's young men and women would go out to the fields; there, marriage proposals were tendered. The reading aloud of Leviticus 18 represented a warning that this coupling not become licentious (Taanit 26b).

VERSE 3. YOU SHALL NOT COPY THE PRACTICES OF THE LAND OF EGYPT ... WHERE YOU DWELT כְּמַעֲשֵׂה אֶרֶץ־מִצְרַיִם אֲשֶׁר יְשַׁבְתֶּם־בָּהּ לֹא תַעֲשׂוּ. At certain periods in the history of ancient Egypt, it was the custom among the royal class to encourage brother-sister marriages. Some of the other prohibited acts found in this chapter may have been practiced in Canaanite culture.

VERSE 5. HUMAN BEINGS SHALL LIVE הָאָדָם וָחַי בָּהֶם. The Rabbis interpreted this wording as a positive command to preserve human life—one that overrides almost all other precepts. Except for the prohibitions against murder, sexual immorality, and idolatry, any commandment must be set aside for *pikku·aḥ nefesh*, to save a person's life (Babylonian Talmud, Yoma 44a). Accordingly, one may violate Shabbat to take someone to the hospital in an emergency; likewise, physicians must not hesitate to violate the laws of Shabbat to save the life of a human being.

VERSE 6. TO UNCOVER NAKEDNESS לְגַלּוֹת עֶרְוָה. "To uncover nakedness" is a euphemism for sexual intercourse. It may also serve to imply that, in a society where people dressed modestly, seeing a person undressed might lead to sexual contact. Nakedness, and the uncovering of nakedness, is a category that is particularly human. Judaism traditionally calls for modesty in dress, not only to avoid temptation but as a statement about the holiness of the body. According to the Book of Genesis, as Adam and Eve were leaving the Garden of Eden, God made clothes for them.

All of our acts, including our sexual ones, have social consequences. Therefore, while our sexual activities should reflect our own values and not simply peer-pressure, in shaping our individual sexual values we must consider the effects of what we do on others—not only those with whom we engage in sexual relations, but also the moral character of our people. In this, as in other areas of life, our actions should be a *kiddush hashem*, a sanctification of God's name, by reflecting well on the Jewish tradition, the Jewish people, and the God Jews worship. —ELLIOT DORFF

Sexual Morality: In the Bible and Today

The passage contains important insights that contemporary Jews can affirm: we need some boundaries in our sexual relationships; sexual behavior is not simply a private matter; individual behavior is connected with the ethical character of our social world. Leviticus 18 seeks to implement these ideas in its own time and place. But we need to find ways to express those insights in the context of an ethic of sexual holiness appropriate for the 21st century.
—JUDITH PLASKOW
(*adapted*)

Traditional Torah Reading

LEVITICUS 18

First aliyah

1 ADONAI spoke to Moses, saying: 2 Speak to the Israelite people and say to them:

I ADONAI am your God. 3 You shall not copy the practices of the land of Egypt where you dwelt, or of the land of Canaan to which I am taking you; nor shall you follow their laws. 4 My rules alone shall you observe, and faithfully follow My laws: I ADONAI am your God.

5 You shall keep My laws and My rules, by the pursuit of which human beings shall live: I am ADONAI.

Second aliyah

6 None of you men shall come near anyone of his own flesh to uncover nakedness: I am ADONAI.

7 Your father's nakedness, that is, the nakedness of your mother, you shall not uncover; she is your mother—you shall not uncover her nakedness.

8 Do not uncover the nakedness of your father's wife; it is the nakedness of your father.

9 The nakedness of your sister—your father's daughter or your mother's, whether born into the household or outside—do not uncover their nakedness.

10 The nakedness of your son's daughter, or of your daughter's daughter—do not uncover their nakedness; for their nakedness is yours.

11 The nakedness of your father's wife's daughter, who was born into your father's household—she is your sister; do not uncover her nakedness.

12 Do not uncover the nakedness of your father's sister; she is your father's flesh.

13 Do not uncover the nakedness of your mother's sister; for she is your mother's flesh.

14 Do not uncover the nakedness of your father's brother: do not approach his wife; she is your aunt.

15 Do not uncover the nakedness of your daughter-in-law:

אֵשֶׁת בִּנְךָ֙ הִ֔וא לֹ֥א תְגַלֶּ֖ה עֶרְוָתָֽהּ: יז עֶרְוַ֨ת אִשָּׁ֤ה וּבִתָּהּ֙ לֹ֣א תְגַלֵּ֔ה אֶֽת־בַּת־בְּנָ֞הּ וְאֶת־בַּת־בִּתָּ֗הּ לֹ֤א תִקַּח֙ לְגַלּ֣וֹת עֶרְוָתָ֔הּ שַׁאֲרָ֥ה הֵ֖נָּה זִמָּ֥ה הִֽוא: יח וְאִשָּׁ֥ה אֶל־אֲחֹתָ֖הּ לֹ֣א תִקָּ֑ח לִצְרֹ֗ר לְגַלּ֧וֹת עֶרְוָתָ֛הּ עָלֶ֖יהָ בְּחַיֶּֽיהָ: יט וְאֶל־אִשָּׁ֖ה בְּנִדַּ֣ת טֻמְאָתָ֑הּ לֹ֣א תִקְרַ֔ב לְגַלּ֖וֹת עֶרְוָתָֽהּ: כ וְאֶל־אֵ֨שֶׁת עֲמִֽיתְךָ֔ לֹא־תִתֵּ֥ן שְׁכָבְתְּךָ֖ לְזָ֑רַע לְטָמְאָה־בָֽהּ: כא וּמִֽזַּרְעֲךָ֥ לֹא־תִתֵּ֖ן לְהַעֲבִ֣יר לַמֹּ֑לֶךְ וְלֹ֧א תְחַלֵּ֛ל אֶת־שֵׁ֥ם אֱלֹהֶ֖יךָ אֲנִ֥י יְהוָֽה:

מפטיר כב וְאֶ֨ת־זָכָ֔ר לֹ֥א תִשְׁכַּ֖ב מִשְׁכְּבֵ֣י אִשָּׁ֑ה תּוֹעֵבָ֖ה הִֽוא: כג וּבְכָל־בְּהֵמָ֛ה לֹא־תִתֵּ֥ן שְׁכָבְתְּךָ֖ לְטָמְאָה־בָ֑הּ וְאִשָּׁ֗ה לֹֽא־תַעֲמֹ֞ד לִפְנֵ֧י בְהֵמָ֛ה לְרִבְעָ֖הּ תֶּ֥בֶל הֽוּא: כד אַל־תִּֽטַּמְּא֖וּ בְּכָל־אֵ֑לֶּה כִּ֤י בְכָל־אֵ֨לֶּה֙ נִטְמְא֣וּ הַגּוֹיִ֔ם אֲשֶׁר־אֲנִ֥י מְשַׁלֵּ֖חַ מִפְּנֵיכֶֽם: כה וַתִּטְמָ֣א הָאָ֔רֶץ וָאֶפְקֹ֥ד עֲוֺנָ֖הּ עָלֶ֑יהָ וַתָּקִ֥א הָאָ֖רֶץ אֶת־יֹשְׁבֶֽיהָ: כו וּשְׁמַרְתֶּ֣ם אַתֶּ֗ם אֶת־חֻקֹּתַי֙ וְאֶת־מִשְׁפָּטַ֔י וְלֹ֣א תַעֲשׂ֔וּ מִכֹּ֥ל הַתּוֹעֵבֹ֖ת הָאֵ֑לֶּה הָֽאֶזְרָ֔ח וְהַגֵּ֖ר הַגָּ֥ר בְּתֽוֹכְכֶֽם: כז כִּ֚י אֶת־כָּל־הַתּוֹעֵבֹ֣ת הָאֵ֔ל עָשׂ֥וּ אַנְשֵֽׁי־הָאָ֖רֶץ אֲשֶׁ֣ר לִפְנֵיכֶ֑ם וַתִּטְמָ֖א הָאָֽרֶץ: כח וְלֹֽא־תָקִ֤יא הָאָ֨רֶץ֙ אֶתְכֶ֔ם בְּטַמַּֽאֲכֶ֖ם אֹתָ֑הּ כַּאֲשֶׁ֥ר קָאָ֛ה אֶת־הַגּ֖וֹי אֲשֶׁ֥ר לִפְנֵיכֶֽם: כט כִּ֚י כָּל־אֲשֶׁ֣ר יַעֲשֶׂ֔ה מִכֹּ֥ל הַתּוֹעֵבֹ֖ת הָאֵ֑לֶּה וְנִכְרְת֛וּ הַנְּפָשׁ֥וֹת הָעֹשֹׂ֖ת מִקֶּ֥רֶב עַמָּֽם: ל וּשְׁמַרְתֶּ֣ם אֶת־מִשְׁמַרְתִּ֗י לְבִלְתִּ֞י עֲשׂ֤וֹת מֵחֻקּ֣וֹת הַתּוֹעֵבֹ֗ת אֲשֶׁ֤ר נַעֲשׂוּ֙ לִפְנֵיכֶ֔ם וְלֹ֥א תִטַּמְּא֖וּ בָּהֶ֑ם אֲנִ֥י יְהוָ֖ה אֱלֹהֵיכֶֽם:

VERSE 18. DO NOT TAKE [INTO YOUR HOUSEHOLD AS A WIFE] A WOMAN AS A RIVAL TO HER SISTER וְאִשָּׁה אֶל־אֲחֹתָהּ לֹא תִקַּח לִצְרֹר. Marrying two sisters would create a damaging rivalry. (The Rabbis saw Jacob's marriage to both Rachel and Leah as a negative model.) The prohibition continues as long as the first sister remains alive, regardless of divorce.

VERSE 21. TO MOLECH לַמֹּלֶךְ. We have archaeological evidence that some of the societies of the ancient Mediterranean world did indeed sacrifice children.

VERSE 22. DO NOT LIE WITH A MALE וְאֶת־זָכָר לֹא תִשְׁכַּב. Scholars debate this verse's original meaning and how Jewish law in our time should treat same-sex relations. One view is that the biblical text does not refer to homosexuality as we think of it today. Indeed, the notion of homosexuality as an identity is certainly modern. Aside from this verse and its parallel in Leviticus 20:13, the Bible mentions same-sex relations only in the context of rape (Genesis 19:5, Judges 19:22), and with regard to what seems to be male prostitution (Deuteronomy 23:18–19). In that vein, some commentators, noting that this verse's prohibition follows the verse excoriating the worship of Molech, speculate that the only homosexual acts prohibited here are those connected to sacred worship. (The Book of Kings mentions King Hezekiah's removal of male Temple prostitutes.) Sex with animals, mentioned in the next verse, likewise might have been part of ancient fertility rites, though obviously it is prohibited for other reasons as well.

VERSE 25. THE LAND BECAME DEFILED וַתִּטְמָא הָאָרֶץ. The gift of the Land of Israel is conditioned on moral behavior.

VERSE 26. NEITHER THE CITIZEN NOR THE STRANGER WHO RESIDES AMONG YOU הָאֶזְרָח וְהַגֵּר הַגָּר בְּתוֹכְכֶם. The same moral standard is required not only of the people Israel themselves, but also of those who dwell in the land with them.

We believe that we honor the image of God by honoring the body. Through our bodies we can connect with each other, the world, and the sacred. . . . All sexual activity between people must be consensual. . . . No person shall abuse, exploit, control, humiliate, do violence to, or harm another human being physically, emotionally, or in any other way in the course of sexual expression. . . . Each person must take responsibility for the consequences of sexual activity, including pregnancy and children. Sexuality shall not be used as an expression of status or power, and no person shall use status or power to gain consent for sexual activity. . . . It is the responsibility of the Jewish community to raise and discuss issues of sexuality and to help give parents the tools to discuss sexual issues with their children.

—FROM THE ETHIC OF THE SU KASHA HAVURAH
(as quoted by Judith Plaskow)

she is your son's wife; you shall not uncover her nakedness.

16 Do not uncover the nakedness of your brother's wife; it is the nakedness of your brother.

17 Do not uncover the nakedness of a woman and her daughter; nor shall you take [into your household as a wife] her son's daughter or her daughter's daughter and uncover her nakedness: they are kindred; it is depravity.

18 Do not take [into your household as a wife] a woman as a rival to her sister and uncover her nakedness in the other's lifetime.

19 Do not come near a woman during her menstrual period of impurity to uncover her nakedness.

20 Do not have carnal relations with your neighbor's wife and defile yourself with her.

21 Do not allow any of your offspring to be offered up to Molech, and do not profane the name of your God: I am ADONAI.

Maftir

22 Do not lie with a male as one lies with a woman; it is an abhorrence.

23 Do not have carnal relations with any beast and defile yourself thereby. Likewise for a woman: she shall not lend herself to a beast to mate with it; it is perversion.

24 Do not defile yourselves in any of those ways, for it is by such that the nations that I am casting out before you defiled themselves. 25 Thus the land became defiled; and I called it to account for its iniquity, and the land spewed out its inhabitants. 26 But you must keep My laws and My rules, and you must not do any of those abhorrent things, neither the citizen nor the stranger who resides among you; 27 for all those abhorrent things were done by the people who were in the land before you, and the land became defiled. 28 So let not the land spew you out for defiling it, as it spewed out the nation that came before you. 29 All who do any of those abhorrent things—such persons shall be cut off from their people.

30 You shall keep My charge not to engage in any of the abhorrent practices that were carried on before you, and you shall not defile yourselves through them: I ADONAI am your God.

קְרִיאַת הַתּוֹרָה – חֲלוּפָה

וַיִּקְרָא יט

ראשון א וַיְדַבֵּר יְהֹוָה אֶל־מֹשֶׁה לֵּאמֹר: ב דַּבֵּר אֶל־
כָּל־עֲדַת בְּנֵי־יִשְׂרָאֵל וְאָמַרְתָּ אֲלֵהֶם קְדֹשִׁים תִּהְיוּ
כִּי קָדוֹשׁ אֲנִי יְהֹוָה אֱלֹהֵיכֶם: ג אִישׁ אִמּוֹ וְאָבִיו תִּירָאוּ
וְאֶת־שַׁבְּתֹתַי תִּשְׁמֹרוּ אֲנִי יְהֹוָה אֱלֹהֵיכֶם: ד אַל־תִּפְנוּ
אֶל־הָאֱלִילִם וֵאלֹהֵי מַסֵּכָה לֹא תַעֲשׂוּ לָכֶם אֲנִי יְהֹוָה
אֱלֹהֵיכֶם:

שני ה וְכִי תִזְבְּחוּ זֶבַח שְׁלָמִים לַיהֹוָה לִרְצֹנְכֶם תִּזְבָּחֻהוּ:
ו בְּיוֹם זִבְחֲכֶם יֵאָכֵל וּמִמָּחֳרָת וְהַנּוֹתָר עַד־יוֹם הַשְּׁלִישִׁי
בָּאֵשׁ יִשָּׂרֵף: ז וְאִם הֵאָכֹל יֵאָכֵל בַּיּוֹם הַשְּׁלִישִׁי פִּגּוּל הוּא
לֹא יֵרָצֶה: ח וְאֹכְלָיו עֲוֺנוֹ יִשָּׂא כִּי־אֶת־קֹדֶשׁ יְהֹוָה חִלֵּל
וְנִכְרְתָה הַנֶּפֶשׁ הַהִוא מֵעַמֶּיהָ: ט וּבְקֻצְרְכֶם אֶת־קְצִיר
אַרְצְכֶם לֹא תְכַלֶּה פְּאַת שָׂדְךָ לִקְצֹר וְלֶקֶט קְצִירְךָ לֹא
תְלַקֵּט: י וְכַרְמְךָ לֹא תְעוֹלֵל וּפֶרֶט כַּרְמְךָ לֹא תְלַקֵּט לֶעָנִי
וְלַגֵּר תַּעֲזֹב אֹתָם אֲנִי יְהֹוָה אֱלֹהֵיכֶם:

LEVITICUS 19. This passage has been called the "holy of holies" of the Book of Leviticus. It contains some of the most central ethical teachings of Judaism. Hillel famously taught that the entire Torah rested on the principle enunciated in verse 18: "Love your fellow [Israelite] as yourself" (Sifra K'doshim).

VERSE 3. YOU SHALL EACH REVERE YOUR MOTHER AND YOUR FATHER אִישׁ אִמּוֹ וְאָבִיו תִּירָאוּ. In contrast, in the Decalogue (Exodus 20) the observance of Shabbat is mentioned first, before respect for parents. The reversed order here typifies this passage's emphasis on the mutual dependence of ritual practice and ethical awareness; neither one is given priority. (The two concerns are inseparable in much of Jewish thought. For example, the Book of Deuteronomy maintains that a function of Shabbat is to allow slaves—and even animals—to rest.) Gender priority is also reversed here: unlike in the Decalogue, mother is mentioned before father.

VERSE 5. AN OFFERING OF WELL-BEING זֶבַח שְׁלָמִים. This term—the focus of the only cultic provision in this afternoon's Torah reading—refers to a voluntary offering that worshippers ate at home, unsupervised by a priest. Its mention here implies that the holiness associated with the sanctuary can be cultivated at home, and in each individual's life.

VERSE 10. YOUR VINEYARD וְכַרְמְךָ. Underdeveloped clusters of grapes must be left unpicked until they mature. At that time, only the poor and the stranger may pick them. Similarly, fruit that falls to the ground during the harvest is to be left ungathered, so that the poor may pick it up.

You Shall Be Holy

"Holiness" is the language of invitation—that is, that you shall be vessels prepared and willing to receive. "For I . . . ADONAI am holy," that is: I am always ready and willing to be with you if only you would be ready and willing with holy thoughts.

—MENAḤEM MENDEL OF KOTZK

In what way can God demand that a human being attain the level of holiness? This does not mean that you must attain the level of angels—something that is impossible. Rather, what God demands is that you attain the level of which you are capable. Be holy: in whatever circumstances you find yourself, advance a little at a time in your holiness.

—MENAḤEM MENDEL OF WORKA

I . . . Am Holy

The Ḥasidic master Menaḥem Mendel of Kotzk said: At times, we think we have fulfilled our obligation and do not need to go any further. Regarding this the Midrash teaches: "Lest we infer that 'you shall be holy' means '. . . holy like Me,' the Torah adds, 'For I . . . am holy'—My holiness is higher than yours." No matter how much we sanctify ourselves, we must realize that God's holiness is even greater, and so we have not yet truly fulfilled our obligation.

—S. Y. AGNON
(adapted)

Alternate Torah Reading

LEVITICUS 19
First aliyah

1 ADONAI spoke to Moses, saying: 2 Speak to the whole Israelite community and say to them:

You shall be holy, for I, ADONAI your God, am holy.

3 You shall each revere your mother and your father, and keep My sabbaths: I ADONAI am your God.

4 Do not turn to idols or make molten gods for yourselves: I ADONAI am your God.

Second aliyah

5 When you sacrifice an offering of well-being to ADONAI, sacrifice it so that it may be accepted on your behalf. 6 It shall be eaten on the day you sacrifice it, or on the day following; but what is left by the third day must be consumed in fire. 7 If it should be eaten on the third day, it is an offensive thing, it will not be acceptable. 8 And one who eats of it shall bear the guilt for having profaned what is sacred to ADONAI; that person shall be cut off from kin.

9 When you reap the harvest of your land, you shall not reap all the way to the edges of your field, or gather the gleanings of your harvest. 10 You shall not pick your vineyard bare, or gather the fallen fruit of your vineyard; you shall leave them for the poor and the stranger: I ADONAI am your God.

מַפְטִיר יא לֹא תִּגְנֹבוּ וְלֹא־תְכַחֲשׁוּ וְלֹא־תְשַׁקְּרוּ אִישׁ
בַּעֲמִיתוֹ: יב וְלֹא־תִשָּׁבְעוּ בִשְׁמִי לַשָּׁקֶר וְחִלַּלְתָּ אֶת־
שֵׁם אֱלֹהֶיךָ אֲנִי יהוה: יג לֹא־תַעֲשֹׁק אֶת־רֵעֲךָ וְלֹא תִגְזֹל
לֹא־תָלִין פְּעֻלַּת שָׂכִיר אִתְּךָ עַד־בֹּקֶר: יד לֹא־תְקַלֵּל
חֵרֵשׁ וְלִפְנֵי עִוֵּר לֹא תִתֵּן מִכְשֹׁל וְיָרֵאתָ מֵּאֱלֹהֶיךָ אֲנִי
יהוה: טו לֹא־תַעֲשׂוּ עָוֶל בַּמִּשְׁפָּט לֹא־תִשָּׂא פְנֵי־דָל וְלֹא
תֶהְדַּר פְּנֵי גָדוֹל בְּצֶדֶק תִּשְׁפֹּט עֲמִיתֶךָ: טז לֹא־תֵלֵךְ רָכִיל
בְּעַמֶּיךָ לֹא תַעֲמֹד עַל־דַּם רֵעֶךָ אֲנִי יהוה: יז לֹא־תִשְׂנָא
אֶת־אָחִיךָ בִּלְבָבֶךָ הוֹכֵחַ תּוֹכִיחַ אֶת־עֲמִיתֶךָ וְלֹא־תִשָּׂא
עָלָיו חֵטְא: יח לֹא־תִקֹּם וְלֹא־תִטֹּר אֶת־בְּנֵי עַמֶּךָ
וְאָהַבְתָּ לְרֵעֲךָ כָּמוֹךָ אֲנִי יהוה:

VERSE 11. YOU SHALL NOT STEAL לֹא תִּגְנֹבוּ. This law follows directly after the laws of leaving part of the harvest for the poor. The juxtaposition may teach that keeping everything for ourselves is a form of stealing (Abraham Ibn Ezra). Alternatively, we are commanded to help the poor find enough to eat so that they will not be driven to steal (Joseph Kara).

VERSE 14. YOU SHALL NOT INSULT THE DEAF לֹא־תְקַלֵּל חֵרֵשׁ. You shall not insult anyone, even a deaf person whose feelings will not be hurt by your words (Babylonian Talmud, Shevuot 36a). Though no actual harm was caused, the image of God has been diminished through this act.

YOU SHALL NOT . . . PLACE A STUMBLING BLOCK BEFORE THE BLIND וְלִפְנֵי עִוֵּר לֹא תִתֵּן מִכְשֹׁל. The Rabbis expanded the meaning of the term "blind" to include someone who lacks necessary information, or who is morally blinded by emotion. One violates this law by deliberately giving bad advice (Sifra), or by providing someone who cannot resist temptation the means to do wrong (Babylonian Talmud, Pesaḥim 22b), or by provoking a short-tempered person to lash out in anger (Kiddushin 32a). This verse was also understood to prohibit our creating conditions that might tempt someone to transgress a mitzvah.

VERSE 16. DO NOT PROFIT BY THE BLOOD OF YOUR FELLOW לֹא תַעֲמֹד עַל־דַּם רֵעֶךָ. Or "do not stand by the blood of your fellow." The Babylonian Talmud understands this precept as obliging us to help someone in distress, even if we have to spend our own time and money to do so (Sanhedrin 73a).

VERSE 17. REPROVE YOUR KIN הוֹכֵחַ תּוֹכִיחַ אֶת־עֲמִיתֶךָ. The Sages forbid carrying reproach to the point of embarrassing someone (Sifra). The obligation to reprove is limited to cases in which one has reason to believe that the reproof will bring about a change in behavior.

VERSE 18. TAKE VENGEANCE . . . BEAR A GRUDGE לֹא־תִקֹּם וְלֹא־תִטֹּר. What's the difference between these misdeeds? If you say to someone, "I will not lend you my hammer, because you broke my saw," that is taking vengeance; whereas if you say, "I will lend you my hammer even though you wouldn't lend me your saw," that is bearing a grudge (Babylonian Talmud, Yoma 23a). It is said of the Eastern European sage Saul Katzenellenbogen that he had such a prodigious memory he never forgot anything he read or heard. Invariably, however, he would forget when someone offended him.

LOVE YOUR FELLOW [ISRAELITE] AS YOURSELF וְאָהַבְתָּ לְרֵעֲךָ כָּמוֹךָ. Much like Hillel before him, Rabbi Akiva said that this was the most basic principle of the Torah. Abraham Joshua Heschel added that this was the hardest mitzvah to observe.

A Second Ten Commandments

Rabbi Ḥiyya taught: This section [Leviticus 19] was spoken in the presence of a gathering of the whole assembly, because most of the essential principles of the Torah are attached to it. Rabbi Levi said: Because the Ten Commandments are included in them:

"I ADONAI am your God" (Exodus 20:2) and here it is written, "I ADONAI am your God" (Leviticus 19:3);

"You shall have no other gods" (Exodus 20:3) and here it is written, "Do not . . . make molten gods for yourselves" (Leviticus 19:4);

11 You shall not steal; you shall not deal deceitfully or falsely with one another. 12 You shall not swear falsely by My name, profaning the name of your God: I am ADONAI.

13 You shall not defraud your fellow [Israelite]. You shall not commit robbery. The wages of a laborer shall not remain with you until morning.

14 You shall not insult the deaf, or place a stumbling block before the blind. You shall fear your God: I am ADONAI.

15 You shall not render an unfair decision: do not favor the poor or show deference to the rich; judge your kin fairly. 16 Do not deal basely with members of your people. Do not profit by the blood of your fellow [Israelite]: I am ADONAI.

17 You shall not hate your kinsfolk in your heart. Reprove your kin but incur no guilt on their account. 18 You shall not take vengeance or bear a grudge against members of your people. Love your fellow [Israelite] as yourself: I am ADONAI.

"You shall not swear falsely by the name of your God ADONAI" (Exodus. 20:7) and here it is written, "You shall not swear falsely by My name" (Leviticus 19:12);

"Remember Shabbat" (Exodus 20:8) and here it is written, "You shall each . . . keep My Shabbatot" (Leviticus 19:3);

"Honor your father and your mother" (Exodus 20:12) and here it is written, "You shall each revere your mother and your father" (Leviticus 19:3);

"You shall not murder" (Exodus 20:13) and here it is written, "Do not profit by the blood of your fellow [Israelite]" (Leviticus 19:16);

"You shall not commit adultery" (Exodus 20:13) and here it is written, "The adulterer and the adulteress shall be put to death" (Leviticus 20:10);

"You shall not steal" (Exodus 20:13) and here it is written, "You shall not steal" (Leviticus 19:11);

"You shall not bear false witness" (Exodus 20:13) and here it is written, "Do not deal basely with members of your people" (Leviticus 19:16);

"You shall not covet . . . anything that is your neighbor's" (Exodus 20:14) and here it is written, "Love your fellow [Israelite] as yourself" (Leviticus 19:18). —LEVITICUS RABBAH 24:5

From the Most Distant To the Closest

The ethical commands in this chapter move from the corner of the field to your heart, from the stranger to your neighbor, from that which is distant to that which is most intimate. Jewish ethical training asks us to begin with simple acts but ultimately demands the most fundamental transformation in character and behavior: to be a truly loving and compassionate human being. The Torah commands us to love God and to love our neighbor. Each is a reflection of the other.

הַגְבָּהַת הַתּוֹרָה

*A Magbiah and Golel are called to raise and tie the Sefer Torah.
As the Torah is lifted, we rise and recite:*

וְזֹאת הַתּוֹרָה אֲשֶׁר־שָׂם מֹשֶׁה לִפְנֵי בְּנֵי יִשְׂרָאֵל,
עַל־פִּי יהוה בְּיַד־מֹשֶׁה.

בְּרָכָה שֶׁלִּפְנֵי הַהַפְטָרָה

בָּרוּךְ אַתָּה יהוה אֱלֹהֵינוּ מֶֽלֶךְ הָעוֹלָם, אֲשֶׁר בָּחַר
בִּנְבִיאִים טוֹבִים, וְרָצָה בְדִבְרֵיהֶם הַנֶּאֱמָרִים בֶּאֱמֶת.
בָּרוּךְ אַתָּה יהוה, הַבּוֹחֵר בַּתּוֹרָה וּבְמֹשֶׁה עַבְדּוֹ
וּבְיִשְׂרָאֵל עַמּוֹ וּבִנְבִיאֵי הָאֱמֶת וָצֶֽדֶק.

הַפְטָרָה

יוֹנָה א

א וַיְהִי דְּבַר־יהוה אֶל־יוֹנָה בֶן־אֲמִתַּי לֵאמֹר: ב קוּם לֵךְ
אֶל־נִינְוֵה הָעִיר הַגְּדוֹלָה וּקְרָא עָלֶֽיהָ כִּי־עָלְתָה רָעָתָם
לְפָנָי: ג וַיָּֽקָם יוֹנָה לִבְרֹֽחַ תַּרְשִׁישָׁה מִלִּפְנֵי יהוה וַיֵּֽרֶד
יָפוֹ וַיִּמְצָא אֳנִיָּה ׀ בָּאָה תַרְשִׁישׁ וַיִּתֵּן שְׂכָרָהּ וַיֵּֽרֶד בָּהּ
לָבוֹא עִמָּהֶם תַּרְשִׁישָׁה מִלִּפְנֵי יהוה: ד וַיהוה הֵטִיל
רֽוּחַ־גְּדוֹלָה אֶל־הַיָּם וַיְהִי סַֽעַר־גָּדוֹל בַּיָּם וְהָֽאֳנִיָּה
חִשְּׁבָה לְהִשָּׁבֵר: ה וַיִּֽירְאוּ הַמַּלָּחִים וַיִּזְעֲקוּ אִישׁ אֶל־
אֱלֹהָיו וַיָּטִֽלוּ אֶת־הַכֵּלִים אֲשֶׁר בָּֽאֳנִיָּה אֶל־הַיָּם לְהָקֵל
מֵֽעֲלֵיהֶם וְיוֹנָה יָרַד אֶל־יַרְכְּתֵי הַסְּפִינָה וַיִּשְׁכַּב וַיֵּרָדַם:

THE BOOK OF JONAH. Unlike other prophetic books, this one does not contain an extensive record of the prophet's words. Nor is it a historical book, for it nowhere indicates a specific era or date. Most biblical scholars think of it as a fable carrying an important religious message—though they differ on what that message is. For various interpretations, see the left-most column.

VERSE 1. JONAH SON OF AMITTAI יוֹנָה בֶן־אֲמִתַּי. A prophet with this name appears briefly elsewhere (2 Kings 14:25). "Amittai" may be a play on the root אמת (*emet*), meaning "truth."

VERSE 3. TARSHISH תַּרְשִׁישׁ. In the ancient Near East, ships hugged the coastline as they sailed. Tarshish (Tarsus) is located up the Mediterranean coast from Joppa (Jaffa or *Yafo*). Nineveh, where God was sending Jonah, is located east of the Land of Israel (in modern-day Iraq). Jonah, instead of traveling east by land, flees north by sea.

Alternatively, some scholars identify "Tarshish" with Tartusa in Spain. If so, then

---

Jonah travels in exactly the opposite direction from Nineveh.

AWAY FROM מִלִּפְנֵי. This word (*mi-lif'nei*) can be distinguished from a nearly identical preposition, *mi-p'nei*. According to Abraham ibn Ezra, the latter connotes a backing away motivated by fear, whereas the present term implies a rupture of contact, a turning of one's back.

WENT DOWN . . . WENT ABOARD וַיֵּֽרֶד . . . וַיֵּֽרֶד. The verb ירד ("go down") describes Jonah's movements three times in a row; in verse 5, we will learn that he "had gone down" into the boat's hold. This progressive descent marks his increasing distance from God (in heaven) and his growing depression.

VERSE 4. A GREAT STORM רֽוּחַ־גְּדוֹלָה. When God wants the wind to blow, it blows. When God wants a giant fish to appear, the natural world responds and it appears. Everything and everyone—even the foreign sailors— is responsive to God; only God's prophet doesn't listen.

VERSE 5. The piety of the pagan sailors is in stark contrast to Jonah's. They pray to their deities while he flees from his. Eventually they will pray to Adonai and even offer a sacrifice (verse 16).

Jonah: Understanding the Book

The Babylonian Talmud states that the Haftarah reading for Yom Kippur afternoon is the Book of Jonah; it gives no explanation for this choice (Megillah 31a). This book is, of course, about sin and forgiveness, yet we are left with many questions. Why on this day are we reading about a prophet who tries to run away from God's service and who seems angered by God's forgiving nature? Why does Jonah flee? And why is he so dejected after the people of Nineveh repent? Medieval Jewish commentators as well as contemporary biblical scholars have wrestled with these questions.

Jonah can be seen as demanding a standard of strict justice. Yet God opts for mercy. Jonah watches an entire city of evildoers escape punishment when they choose to repent—an unsettling outcome. (How can God not punish people for their wrongs? If they are not held to account, might not the world descend into chaos?) According to this view, the Rabbis chose this Haftarah in order to assure us that God's primary relationship with humanity is one of mercy, kindness, and love.

Others argue that Jonah flees because he is asked to reach out to the world beyond Israel. The story

(continued)

Lifting the Torah

A Magbiah and Golel are called to raise and tie the Sefer Torah. As the Torah is lifted, we rise and recite:

This is the Torah, God's word by Moses' hand, which Moses set before the people Israel.

V'zot ha-torah asher sam Mosheh lifnei b'nei yisra·el al pi Adonai b'yad Mosheh.

B'rakhah before the Haftarah

Barukh atah ADONAI, our God, ruler of time and space, who chose worthy prophets; and who was pleased by their words, spoken in truth. *Barukh atah* ADONAI, who has chosen the Torah, Moses Your servant, Your people Israel, and the prophets of truth and justice.

Haftarah

THE BOOK OF JONAH

Chapter 1

1 The word of ADONAI came to Jonah son of Amittai: 2 Go at once to Nineveh, that great city, and proclaim judgment upon it; for their wickedness has come before Me.

3 Jonah, however, started out to flee to Tarshish from ADONAI's service. He went down to Joppa and found a ship going to Tarshish. He paid the fare and went aboard to sail with the others to Tarshish, away from the service of ADONAI.

4 But ADONAI cast a mighty wind upon the sea, and such a great tempest came upon the sea that the ship was in danger of breaking up. 5 In their fright, the sailors cried out, each to his own god; and they flung the ship's cargo overboard to make it lighter for them. Jonah, meanwhile, had gone down into the hold of the vessel where he lay down and fell asleep.

ו וַיִּקְרַב אֵלָיו רַב הַחֹבֵל וַיֹּאמֶר לוֹ מַה־לְּךָ נִרְדָּם קוּם
קְרָא אֶל־אֱלֹהֶיךָ אוּלַי יִתְעַשֵּׁת הָאֱלֹהִים לָנוּ וְלֹא נֹאבֵד:
ז וַיֹּאמְרוּ אִישׁ אֶל־רֵעֵהוּ לְכוּ וְנַפִּילָה גוֹרָלוֹת וְנֵדְעָה
בְּשֶׁלְּמִי הָרָעָה הַזֹּאת לָנוּ וַיַּפִּלוּ גּוֹרָלוֹת וַיִּפֹּל הַגּוֹרָל עַל־
יוֹנָה: ח וַיֹּאמְרוּ אֵלָיו הַגִּידָה־נָּא לָנוּ בַּאֲשֶׁר לְמִי־הָרָעָה
הַזֹּאת לָנוּ מַה־מְּלַאכְתְּךָ וּמֵאַיִן תָּבוֹא מָה אַרְצֶךָ וְאֵי־
מִזֶּה עַם אָתָּה: ט וַיֹּאמֶר אֲלֵיהֶם עִבְרִי אָנֹכִי וְאֶת־יְהוָה
אֱלֹהֵי הַשָּׁמַיִם אֲנִי יָרֵא אֲשֶׁר־עָשָׂה אֶת־הַיָּם וְאֶת־
הַיַּבָּשָׁה: י וַיִּירְאוּ הָאֲנָשִׁים יִרְאָה גְדוֹלָה וַיֹּאמְרוּ אֵלָיו
מַה־זֹּאת עָשִׂיתָ כִּי־יָדְעוּ הָאֲנָשִׁים כִּי־מִלִּפְנֵי יְהוָה הוּא
בֹרֵחַ כִּי הִגִּיד לָהֶם: יא וַיֹּאמְרוּ אֵלָיו מַה־נַּעֲשֶׂה לָּךְ
וְיִשְׁתֹּק הַיָּם מֵעָלֵינוּ כִּי הַיָּם הוֹלֵךְ וְסֹעֵר: יב וַיֹּאמֶר
אֲלֵיהֶם שָׂאוּנִי וַהֲטִילֻנִי אֶל־הַיָּם וְיִשְׁתֹּק הַיָּם מֵעֲלֵיכֶם כִּי
יוֹדֵעַ אָנִי כִּי בְשֶׁלִּי הַסַּעַר הַגָּדוֹל הַזֶּה עֲלֵיכֶם: יג וַיַּחְתְּרוּ
הָאֲנָשִׁים לְהָשִׁיב אֶל־הַיַּבָּשָׁה וְלֹא יָכֹלוּ כִּי הַיָּם הוֹלֵךְ
וְסֹעֵר עֲלֵיהֶם: יד וַיִּקְרְאוּ אֶל־יְהוָה וַיֹּאמְרוּ אָנָּה יְהוָה
אַל־נָא נֹאבְדָה בְּנֶפֶשׁ הָאִישׁ הַזֶּה וְאַל־תִּתֵּן עָלֵינוּ דָּם
נָקִיא כִּי־אַתָּה יְהוָה כַּאֲשֶׁר חָפַצְתָּ עָשִׂיתָ: טו וַיִּשְׂאוּ
אֶת־יוֹנָה וַיְטִלֻהוּ אֶל־הַיָּם וַיַּעֲמֹד הַיָּם מִזַּעְפּוֹ: טז וַיִּירְאוּ
הָאֲנָשִׁים יִרְאָה גְדוֹלָה אֶת־יְהוָה וַיִּזְבְּחוּ־זֶבַח לַיהוָה
וַיִּדְּרוּ נְדָרִים:

(continued from previous page)

is largely about non-Israelites. Indeed, Nineveh
is not only a foreign
city but also the capital
of the very empire that
destroyed the Northern
Kingdom of Israel. In
this reading, the Rabbis
chose this Haftarah in
order to teach that God
is the sovereign of all
humanity, and that God's
justice and mercy extend
to all human beings—
even to Israel's enemies.

Still others perceive Jo-
nah's fleeing as the result
of inner turmoil over the
difficulty of his position.
Perhaps he fears that if
he brings God's message
to the Ninevites, they
will reject him; he will
fail. (The prophetic task
can be disheartening
when people ignore the
message or attack the
messenger: Elijah hides
in the desert in fear for
his life; Amos must flee
the temple precinct at
Beth El; and Jeremiah
wishes that he'd never
been born.) Yet if he
succeeds and the people
repent, what then? If
his dire predictions do not come to pass, he might be
ridiculed as a false prophet. According to this interpretation, the Rabbis chose this Haftarah to charge us with
taking on the difficult task of serving as loving critics to
one another.

Perhaps all of these readings can inspire us: We are
called upon to believe in a merciful God and, in turn,
to manifest kindness and caring. We are asked to take
responsibility for a larger world beyond our family and
friends, and to overcome our fears of either failure or
success—fears that may inhibit us from standing up for
God's teaching to uphold truth, demand justice, and exemplify love and kindness in our lives. At times we want
to flee from responsibility, because the task is difficult.
Like Jonah, we can learn to trust enough to love—and
allow ourselves to be loved.

6 The captain went over to him and cried out, "How can you be
sleeping so soundly! Up, call upon your god! Perhaps the god
will be kind to us and we will not perish."

7 The crew said to one another, "Let us cast lots and find out
on whose account this misfortune has come upon us." They
cast lots and the lot fell on Jonah. 8 They said to him, "Tell us,
you who have brought this misfortune upon us, what is your
business? Where have you come from? What is your country,
and of what people are you?" 9 "I am a Hebrew," he replied.
"I worship ADONAI, the God of Heaven, who made both sea
and land." 10 The crew was greatly terrified, and they asked
him, "What have you done?" And when the crew learned that
he was fleeing from the service of ADONAI—for so he told
them— 11 they said to him, "What must we do to you to make
the sea calm around us?" For the sea was growing more and
more stormy. 12 He answered, "Heave me overboard, and the
sea will calm down for you; for I know that this terrible storm
came upon you on my account." 13 Nevertheless, the crew
rowed hard to regain the shore, but they could not, for the sea
was growing more and more stormy about them. 14 Then they
cried out to ADONAI: "Oh, please, ADONAI, do not let us perish
on account of this fellow's life. Do not hold us guilty of killing
an innocent person! For You, O ADONAI, by Your will, have
brought this about." 15 And they heaved Jonah overboard, and
the sea stopped raging.

16 The crew feared ADONAI greatly; they offered a sacrifice to
ADONAI and they made vows.

א וַיְמַן יהוה דָּג גָּדוֹל לִבְלֹעַ אֶת־יוֹנָה וַיְהִי יוֹנָה בִּמְעֵי הַדָּג שְׁלֹשָׁה יָמִים וּשְׁלֹשָׁה לֵילוֹת: ב וַיִּתְפַּלֵּל יוֹנָה אֶל־יהוה אֱלֹהָיו מִמְּעֵי הַדָּגָה: ג וַיֹּאמֶר

קָרָאתִי מִצָּרָה לִי אֶל־יהוה   וַיַּעֲנֵנִי

מִבֶּטֶן שְׁאוֹל שִׁוַּעְתִּי   שָׁמַעְתָּ קוֹלִי:

ד וַתַּשְׁלִיכֵנִי מְצוּלָה   בִּלְבַב יַמִּים

וְנָהָר יְסֹבְבֵנִי

כָּל־מִשְׁבָּרֶיךָ וְגַלֶּיךָ   עָלַי עָבָרוּ:

ה וַאֲנִי אָמַרְתִּי נִגְרַשְׁתִּי   מִנֶּגֶד עֵינֶיךָ

אַךְ אוֹסִיף לְהַבִּיט   אֶל־הֵיכַל קָדְשֶׁךָ:

ו אֲפָפוּנִי מַיִם עַד־נֶפֶשׁ   תְּהוֹם יְסֹבְבֵנִי

סוּף חָבוּשׁ לְרֹאשִׁי:

ז לְקִצְבֵי הָרִים יָרַדְתִּי   הָאָרֶץ בְּרִחֶיהָ בַעֲדִי לְעוֹלָם

וַתַּעַל מִשַּׁחַת חַיַּי   יהוה אֱלֹהָי:

ח בְּהִתְעַטֵּף עָלַי נַפְשִׁי   אֶת־יהוה זָכָרְתִּי

וַתָּבוֹא אֵלֶיךָ תְּפִלָּתִי   אֶל־הֵיכַל קָדְשֶׁךָ:

ט מְשַׁמְּרִים הַבְלֵי־שָׁוְא   חַסְדָּם יַעֲזֹבוּ:

י וַאֲנִי בְּקוֹל תּוֹדָה   אֶזְבְּחָה־לָּךְ

אֲשֶׁר נָדַרְתִּי אֲשַׁלֵּמָה   יְשׁוּעָתָה לַיהוה:

יא וַיֹּאמֶר יהוה לַדָּג וַיָּקֵא אֶת־יוֹנָה אֶל־הַיַּבָּשָׁה:

א וַיְהִי דְבַר־יהוה אֶל־יוֹנָה שֵׁנִית לֵאמֹר: ב קוּם לֵךְ אֶל־נִינְוֵה הָעִיר הַגְּדוֹלָה וּקְרָא אֵלֶיהָ אֶת־הַקְּרִיאָה אֲשֶׁר אָנֹכִי דֹּבֵר אֵלֶיךָ: ג וַיָּקָם יוֹנָה וַיֵּלֶךְ אֶל־נִינְוֵה כִּדְבַר יהוה וְנִינְוֵה הָיְתָה עִיר־גְּדוֹלָה לֵאלֹהִים מַהֲלַךְ שְׁלֹשֶׁת יָמִים: ד וַיָּחֶל יוֹנָה לָבוֹא בָעִיר מַהֲלַךְ יוֹם אֶחָד וַיִּקְרָא וַיֹּאמַר עוֹד אַרְבָּעִים יוֹם וְנִינְוֵה נֶהְפָּכֶת: ה וַיַּאֲמִינוּ אַנְשֵׁי נִינְוֵה

2:3–9. Jonah's prayer is made up of a pastiche of phrases from the psalms. Its borrowed nature is evident from the fact that all the verbs are in the past tense and the author speaks of having already been saved.

VERSE 3. SHEOL שְׁאוֹל. In biblical Israel, Sheol was thought of as a nether-world to which the dead were gathered.

3:4. SHALL BE OVERTHROWN נֶהְפָּכֶת. Literally, "over-turned." In Genesis, the same word describes the destruction of Sodom and Gomorrah. Here it may refer equally to the process of repentance, through which the Ninevites might change their behavior and their way of life. As the Babylonian Talmud remarks: "Jonah was told that Nineveh would be overturned, but he did not know whether for good or for evil" (Sanhedrin 89b).

Chapter 2

1 ADONAI provided a huge fish to swallow Jonah; and Jonah remained in the fish's belly three days and three nights. 2 Jonah prayed to his God ADONAI from the belly of the fish. 3 He said:

In my trouble I called to ADONAI,   who answered me;
from the belly of Sheol I cried out,   and You heard my voice.
4 You cast me into the depths,   into the heart of the sea,
    the floods engulfed me;
all Your breakers and billows   swept over me.
5 I thought I was driven away   out of Your sight:
would I ever gaze again   upon Your holy Temple?
6 The waters closed in over me,   the deep engulfed me.
    Weeds twined around my head.
7 I sank to the base of the mountains;   the bars of the earth closed upon me forever.
Yet You brought my life up from the pit,   O my God ADONAI!
8 When my life was ebbing away,   I called ADONAI to mind;
and my prayer came before You,   into Your holy Temple.
9 They who cling to empty folly   forsake their own welfare,
10 But I, with loud thanksgiving,   will sacrifice to You;
what I have vowed I will perform.   Deliverance is ADONAI's!

11 ADONAI commanded the fish, and it spewed Jonah out upon dry land.

Chapter 3

1 The word of ADONAI came to Jonah a second time: 2 "Go at once to Nineveh, that great city, and proclaim to it what I tell you." 3 Jonah went at once to Nineveh in accordance with ADONAI's command.

Nineveh was an enormously large city a three days' walk across. 4 Jonah started out and made his way into the city the distance of one day's walk, and proclaimed: "Forty days more, and Nineveh shall be overthrown!"

בֵּאלֹהִים וַיִּקְרְאוּ־צוֹם וַיִּלְבְּשׁוּ שַׂקִּים מִגְּדוֹלָם וְעַד־קְטַנָּם: ו וַיִּגַּע הַדָּבָר אֶל־מֶלֶךְ נִינְוֵה וַיָּקָם מִכִּסְאוֹ וַיַּעֲבֵר אַדַּרְתּוֹ מֵעָלָיו וַיְכַס שַׂק וַיֵּשֶׁב עַל־הָאֵפֶר: ז וַיַּזְעֵק וַיֹּאמֶר בְּנִינְוֵה מִטַּעַם הַמֶּלֶךְ וּגְדֹלָיו לֵאמֹר הָאָדָם וְהַבְּהֵמָה הַבָּקָר וְהַצֹּאן אַל־יִטְעֲמוּ מְאוּמָה אַל־יִרְעוּ וּמַיִם אַל־יִשְׁתּוּ: ח וְיִתְכַּסּוּ שַׂקִּים הָאָדָם וְהַבְּהֵמָה וְיִקְרְאוּ אֶל־אֱלֹהִים בְּחָזְקָה וְיָשֻׁבוּ אִישׁ מִדַּרְכּוֹ הָרָעָה וּמִן־הֶחָמָס אֲשֶׁר בְּכַפֵּיהֶם: ט מִי־יוֹדֵעַ יָשׁוּב וְנִחַם הָאֱלֹהִים וְשָׁב מֵחֲרוֹן אַפּוֹ וְלֹא נֹאבֵד: י וַיַּרְא הָאֱלֹהִים אֶת־מַעֲשֵׂיהֶם כִּי־שָׁבוּ מִדַּרְכָּם הָרָעָה וַיִּנָּחֶם הָאֱלֹהִים עַל־הָרָעָה אֲשֶׁר־דִּבֶּר לַעֲשׂוֹת־לָהֶם וְלֹא עָשָׂה:

יונה ד

א וַיֵּרַע אֶל־יוֹנָה רָעָה גְדוֹלָה וַיִּחַר לוֹ: ב וַיִּתְפַּלֵּל אֶל־יְהֹוָה וַיֹּאמַר אָנָּה יְהֹוָה הֲלוֹא־זֶה דְבָרִי עַד־הֱיוֹתִי עַל־אַדְמָתִי עַל־כֵּן קִדַּמְתִּי לִבְרֹחַ תַּרְשִׁישָׁה כִּי יָדַעְתִּי כִּי אַתָּה אֵל־חַנּוּן וְרַחוּם אֶרֶךְ אַפַּיִם וְרַב־חֶסֶד וְנִחָם עַל־הָרָעָה: ג וְעַתָּה יְהֹוָה קַח־נָא אֶת־נַפְשִׁי מִמֶּנִּי כִּי טוֹב מוֹתִי מֵחַיָּי: ד וַיֹּאמֶר יְהֹוָה הַהֵיטֵב חָרָה לָךְ: ה וַיֵּצֵא יוֹנָה מִן־הָעִיר וַיֵּשֶׁב מִקֶּדֶם לָעִיר וַיַּעַשׂ לוֹ שָׁם סֻכָּה וַיֵּשֶׁב תַּחְתֶּיהָ בַּצֵּל עַד אֲשֶׁר יִרְאֶה מַה־יִּהְיֶה בָּעִיר: ו וַיְמַן יְהֹוָה־אֱלֹהִים קִיקָיוֹן וַיַּעַל | מֵעַל לְיוֹנָה לִהְיוֹת צֵל עַל־רֹאשׁוֹ לְהַצִּיל לוֹ מֵרָעָתוֹ וַיִּשְׂמַח יוֹנָה עַל־הַקִּיקָיוֹן שִׂמְחָה גְדוֹלָה: ז וַיְמַן הָאֱלֹהִים תּוֹלַעַת בַּעֲלוֹת הַשַּׁחַר לַמָּחֳרָת וַתַּךְ אֶת־הַקִּיקָיוֹן וַיִּיבָשׁ: ח וַיְהִי | כִּזְרֹחַ הַשֶּׁמֶשׁ וַיְמַן אֱלֹהִים רוּחַ קָדִים חֲרִישִׁית וַתַּךְ הַשֶּׁמֶשׁ עַל־רֹאשׁ יוֹנָה וַיִּתְעַלָּף וַיִּשְׁאַל אֶת־נַפְשׁוֹ לָמוּת וַיֹּאמֶר טוֹב מוֹתִי מֵחַיָּי:

VERSES 7–8. This may be an exaggerated—almost satirical—image, picturing even the animals as fasting and wearing sackcloth. It strengthens the contrast between the willingness of all creatures to do God's bidding, and Jonah's resistance to his assigned task. Scholars note that it was a Persian practice to drape animals in sackcloth as a way of appealing to their deity.

VERSE 9. WHO KNOWS מִי־יוֹדֵעַ. The people of Nineveh enter into fasting and repentance without knowing whether or not their acts will cause God to change the threatened outcome.

4:1. THIS DISPLEASED JONAH וַיִּחַר לוֹ. It seems that God's forgiving nature arouses Jonah's anger.

VERSE 2. Here Jonah quotes from the thirteen attributes of God that were revealed to Moses (Exodus 34:6–7). He omits that passage's reference to punishment—just as we do in the liturgy.

VERSE 6. RICINUS PLANT קִיקָיוֹן. This is the Bible's only occurrence of the term *kikkayon*. We cannot be sure which species is meant.

5 The people of Nineveh believed God. They proclaimed a fast, and great and small alike put on sackcloth. 6 When the news reached the king of Nineveh, he rose from his throne, took off his robe, put on sackcloth, and sat in ashes. 7 And he had the word cried through Nineveh: "By decree of the king and his nobles: No human or beast—of flock or herd—shall taste anything! They shall not graze, and they shall not drink water! 8 They shall be covered with sackcloth—human and beast—and shall cry mightily to God. Let everyone turn back from their evil ways and from the injustice of which they are guilty. 9 Who knows but that God may turn and relent? [God] may turn back from wrath, so that we do not perish."

10 God saw what they did, how they were turning back from their evil ways. And God renounced the punishment that had been planned for them, and did not carry it out.

Chapter 4

1 This displeased Jonah greatly, and he was grieved. 2 He prayed to ADONAI, saying, "O ADONAI! Isn't this just what I said when I was still in my own country? That is why I fled beforehand to Tarshish. For I know that You are a compassionate and gracious God, slow to anger, abounding in kindness, renouncing punishment. 3 Please, ADONAI, take my life, for I would rather die than live." 4 ADONAI replied, "Are you that deeply grieved?"

5 Now Jonah had left the city and found a place east of the city. He made a booth there and sat under it in the shade, until he should see what happened to the city. 6 God ADONAI provided a ricinus plant, which grew up over Jonah, to provide shade for his head and save him from discomfort. Jonah was very happy about the plant. 7 But the next day at dawn God provided a worm, which attacked the plant so that it withered. 8 And when the sun rose, God provided a sultry east wind; the sun beat down on Jonah's head, and he became faint. He begged for death, saying, "I would rather die than live."

ט וַיֹּאמֶר אֱלֹהִים אֶל־יוֹנָה הַהֵיטֵב חָרָה־לְךָ עַל־הַקִּיקָיוֹן
וַיֹּאמֶר הֵיטֵב חָרָה־לִי עַד־מָוֶת: י וַיֹּאמֶר יהוה אַתָּה
חַסְתָּ עַל־הַקִּיקָיוֹן אֲשֶׁר לֹא־עָמַלְתָּ בּוֹ וְלֹא גִדַּלְתּוֹ
שֶׁבִּן־לַיְלָה הָיָה וּבִן־לַיְלָה אָבָד: יא וַאֲנִי לֹא אָחוּס עַל־
נִינְוֵה הָעִיר הַגְּדוֹלָה אֲשֶׁר יֶשׁ־בָּהּ הַרְבֵּה מִשְׁתֵּים־עֶשְׂרֵה
רִבּוֹ אָדָם אֲשֶׁר לֹא־יָדַע בֵּין־יְמִינוֹ לִשְׂמֹאלוֹ וּבְהֵמָה רַבָּה:

מִיכָה ז

יח מִי־אֵל כָּמוֹךָ
נֹשֵׂא עָוֹן וְעֹבֵר עַל־פֶּשַׁע
לִשְׁאֵרִית נַחֲלָתוֹ
לֹא־הֶחֱזִיק לָעַד אַפּוֹ כִּי־חָפֵץ חֶסֶד הוּא:
יט יָשׁוּב יְרַחֲמֵנוּ
יִכְבֹּשׁ עֲוֹנֹתֵינוּ
וְתַשְׁלִיךְ בִּמְצֻלוֹת יָם כָּל־חַטֹּאתָם:
כ תִּתֵּן אֱמֶת לְיַעֲקֹב חֶסֶד לְאַבְרָהָם
אֲשֶׁר־נִשְׁבַּעְתָּ לַאֲבֹתֵינוּ מִימֵי קֶדֶם:

הַבְּרָכוֹת שֶׁלְּאַחַר הַהַפְטָרָה

בָּרוּךְ אַתָּה יהוה אֱלֹהֵינוּ מֶלֶךְ הָעוֹלָם, צוּר כָּל־
הָעוֹלָמִים, צַדִּיק בְּכָל־הַדּוֹרוֹת, הָאֵל הַנֶּאֱמָן הָאוֹמֵר
וְעֹשֶׂה, הַמְדַבֵּר וּמְקַיֵּם, שֶׁכָּל־דְּבָרָיו אֱמֶת וָצֶדֶק. נֶאֱמָן
אַתָּה הוּא יהוה אֱלֹהֵינוּ וְנֶאֱמָנִים דְּבָרֶיךָ, וְדָבָר אֶחָד
מִדְּבָרֶיךָ אָחוֹר לֹא יָשׁוּב רֵיקָם, כִּי אֵל מֶלֶךְ נֶאֱמָן וְרַחֲמָן
אָתָּה. בָּרוּךְ אַתָּה יהוה, הָאֵל הַנֶּאֱמָן בְּכָל־דְּבָרָיו.

רַחֵם עַל צִיּוֹן כִּי הִיא בֵּית חַיֵּינוּ. וְלַעֲלוּבַת נֶפֶשׁ תּוֹשִׁיעַ
בִּמְהֵרָה בְיָמֵינוּ. בָּרוּךְ אַתָּה יהוה, מְשַׂמֵּחַ צִיּוֹן בְּבָנֶיהָ.

שַׂמְּחֵנוּ, יהוה אֱלֹהֵינוּ בְּאֵלִיָּהוּ הַנָּבִיא עַבְדֶּךָ וּבְמַלְכוּת
בֵּית דָּוִד מְשִׁיחֶךָ. בִּמְהֵרָה יָבֹא וְיָגֵל לִבֵּנוּ, עַל כִּסְאוֹ לֹא
יֵשֵׁב זָר וְלֹא יִנְחֲלוּ עוֹד אֲחֵרִים אֶת־כְּבוֹדוֹ, כִּי בְשֵׁם
קָדְשְׁךָ נִשְׁבַּעְתָּ לּוֹ שֶׁלֹּא יִכְבֶּה נֵרוֹ לְעוֹלָם וָעֶד. בָּרוּךְ
אַתָּה יהוה, מָגֵן דָּוִד.

VERSE 10. YOU CARED
ABOUT THE PLANT אַתָּה
חַסְתָּ עַל־הַקִּיקָיוֹן. God
does not respond with an
intellectual argument. God
has to make Jonah realize
that he, too, requires God's
grace, undeserved though
that may be. God makes
Jonah feel the transitory
nature of all life and so
rouses his sense of pity for
all living creatures. (David
L. Lieber)

MICAH 7:18–19. The Micah
verses are added here
because of their theme
of forgiveness. Customar-
ily these verses are also
recited during the Tashlikh
ceremony on the afternoon
of the first day of Rosh
Hashanah. On that occa-
sion, the community enacts
the reference to God's
casting sins into the sea,
symbolizing faith in divine
forgiveness.

9 Then God said to Jonah, "Are you so deeply grieved about the plant?" "Yes," he replied, "so deeply that I want to die."

10 Then ADONAI said: "You cared about the plant, which you did not work for and which you did not grow, which appeared overnight and perished overnight. 11 And should not I care about Nineveh, that great city, in which there are more than a hundred and twenty thousand persons who do not yet know their right hand from their left, and many beasts as well!"

MICAH 7

18 Is there any divinity save You
who forgives the sins and pardons the transgressions
of the remnant, Your people?
You do not maintain anger forever, for You delight in love.
19 You will return to us compassionately—
overcoming the consequences of our sin,
hurling our sins into the depths of the sea.
20 You will keep faith with Jacob,
showing enduring love to Abraham,
as You promised our ancestors in days of old.

B'rakhot after the Haftarah

Barukh atah ADONAI, our God, ruler of time and space, eternal protector, righteous in all generations, the faithful God who fulfills what is promised, who accomplishes what is spoken, whose every word is true and just. Faithful are You, ADONAI, and Your words are trustworthy; not one of Your words will prove empty, for You are a faithful and compassionate sovereign. *Barukh atah* ADONAI, God who faithfully fulfills all Your words.

Show compassion to Zion, our true home, and speedily, in our time, bring redemption to those sad in spirit. *Barukh atah* ADONAI, who makes Zion happy with her children.

Make us joyful, ADONAI our God, with Elijah the prophet, Your servant, and with the kingdom of David, Your anointed—may he soon come and make our hearts rejoice. May no stranger sit on his throne and may no other inherit his glory, for You have promised him, by Your holy name, that his light shall never be extinguished. *Barukh atah* ADONAI, Shield of David.

We rise. Leader:

יְהַלְלוּ אֶת־שֵׁם יהוה, כִּי־נִשְׂגָּב שְׁמוֹ לְבַדּוֹ.

Congregation:

הוֹדוֹ עַל־אֶרֶץ וְשָׁמָיִם. וַיָּרֶם קֶרֶן לְעַמּוֹ,
תְּהִלָּה לְכָל־חֲסִידָיו, לִבְנֵי יִשְׂרָאֵל עַם קְרֹבוֹ, הַלְלוּ־יָהּ.

לְדָוִד מִזְמוֹר.
לַיהוה הָאָרֶץ וּמְלוֹאָהּ, תֵּבֵל וְיֹשְׁבֵי בָהּ.
כִּי־הוּא עַל־יַמִּים יְסָדָהּ, וְעַל־נְהָרוֹת יְכוֹנְנֶהָ.
מִי־יַעֲלֶה בְהַר־יהוה, וּמִי־יָקוּם בִּמְקוֹם קָדְשׁוֹ.
נְקִי כַפַּיִם וּבַר־לֵבָב, אֲשֶׁר לֹא־נָשָׂא לַשָּׁוְא נַפְשִׁי,
וְלֹא נִשְׁבַּע לְמִרְמָה.
יִשָּׂא בְרָכָה מֵאֵת יהוה, וּצְדָקָה מֵאֱלֹהֵי יִשְׁעוֹ.
זֶה דּוֹר דֹּרְשָׁו, מְבַקְשֵׁי פָנֶיךָ יַעֲקֹב, סֶלָה.
שְׂאוּ שְׁעָרִים רָאשֵׁיכֶם, וְהִנָּשְׂאוּ פִּתְחֵי עוֹלָם,
וְיָבוֹא מֶלֶךְ הַכָּבוֹד.
מִי זֶה מֶלֶךְ הַכָּבוֹד,
יהוה עִזּוּז וְגִבּוֹר, יהוה גִּבּוֹר מִלְחָמָה.
שְׂאוּ שְׁעָרִים רָאשֵׁיכֶם, וּשְׂאוּ פִּתְחֵי עוֹלָם,
וְיָבֹא מֶלֶךְ הַכָּבוֹד.
מִי הוּא זֶה מֶלֶךְ הַכָּבוֹד,
יהוה צְבָאוֹת הוּא מֶלֶךְ הַכָּבוֹד, סֶלָה. תהלים כד

PSALM 24. This psalm's dramatic imagery of gates that open for God's symbolic entrance to the Temple explains why it accompanies our Torah's return to the ark. Yet the psalm focuses first of all on the state of the worshipper: purity of action—especially verbal honesty—must characterize those who would enter this holy place and receive its blessing. This develops a theme of the b'rakhah recited just after each Torah reading, describing the Torah as "a teaching of truth": in order to live in accord with Torah, we must exemplify inner truthfulness while also pursuing truth in the world.

Returning the Torah

We rise. Leader:

Extol the name of ADONAI, for God's name alone is exalted.

Congregation:

God's glory encompasses heaven and earth; God extols the faithful—
raising up Israel, the people God keeps close. Halleluyah!

Hodo al eretz v'shamayim, va-yarem keren l'ammo;
t'hillah l'khol ḥasidav, liv'nei yisra·el am k'rovo. Hal'luyah!

PSALM 24

A SONG OF DAVID.

The earth is ADONAI's in all its fullness, the land and all who dwell on it.
For it was God who founded it upon the seas, and set it firm upon the
flowing streams. Who may ascend the mount of ADONAI? Who may
come forward in God's sanctuary? One who has clean hands and a pure
heart, who has not taken God's name in vain, nor sworn deceitfully. One
such as this will receive ADONAI's blessing, a just reward from God, the
deliverer. This generation searches for You; like Jacob, seeks Your presence, *selah.* Open up, arched gateways—open up, doors of the world;
may the sovereign who is exalted enter. Who is the sovereign who is
exalted? ADONAI, mighty and triumphant, triumphant in battle. Open up,
arched gateways—open up, doors of the world; may the sovereign who is
exalted enter. Who is the sovereign who is exalted? *Adonai Tz'va·ot* is the
sovereign who is exalted. *Selah.*

Ladonai ha-aretz u-m'lo·ah, teiveil v'yosh'vei vah.
  Ki hu al yammim y'sadah, v'al n'harot y'khon'neha.
Mi ya·aleh v'har Adonai, u-mi yakum bi-m'kom kodsho.
  N'ki khappayim u-var leivav, asher lo nasa la-shav nafshi,
  v'lo nishba l'mirmah.
Yissa v'rakhah mei-eit Adonai, u-tz'dakah mei-elohei yisho.
  Zeh dor dor'shav m'vakshei fanekha ya·akov, selah.
S'u sh'arim rasheikhem, v'hinnas'u pitḥei olam,
v'yavo melekh ha-kavod.
  Mi zeh melekh ha-kavod, Adonai izzuz v'gibbor,
  Adonai gibbor milḥamah.
S'u sh'arim rasheikhem, v'hinnas'u pitḥei olam,
v'yavo melekh ha-kavod.
  Mi hu zeh melekh ha-kavod,
  Adonai Tz'va·ot hu melekh ha-kavod, selah.

The Sefer Torah is placed in the ark.

וּבְנֻחֹה יֹאמַר: שׁוּבָה יהוה רִבְבוֹת אַלְפֵי יִשְׂרָאֵל.
קוּמָה יהוה לִמְנוּחָתֶךָ, אַתָּה וַאֲרוֹן עֻזֶּךָ.
כֹּהֲנֶיךָ יִלְבְּשׁוּ־צֶדֶק, וַחֲסִידֶיךָ יְרַנֵּנוּ.
בַּעֲבוּר דָּוִד עַבְדֶּךָ, אַל־תָּשֵׁב פְּנֵי מְשִׁיחֶךָ.
◁ כִּי לֶקַח טוֹב נָתַתִּי לָכֶם, תּוֹרָתִי אַל־תַּעֲזֹבוּ.
עֵץ־חַיִּים הִיא לַמַּחֲזִיקִים בָּהּ, וְתֹמְכֶיהָ מְאֻשָּׁר.
דְּרָכֶיהָ דַרְכֵי־נֹעַם, וְכָל־נְתִיבוֹתֶיהָ שָׁלוֹם.
הֲשִׁיבֵנוּ יהוה אֵלֶיךָ וְנָשׁוּבָה, חַדֵּשׁ יָמֵינוּ כְּקֶדֶם.

חֲצִי קַדִּישׁ

יִתְגַּדַּל וְיִתְקַדַּשׁ שְׁמֵהּ רַבָּא, בְּעָלְמָא דִּי בְרָא, כִרְעוּתֵהּ,
וְיַמְלִיךְ מַלְכוּתֵהּ בְּחַיֵּיכוֹן וּבְיוֹמֵיכוֹן וּבְחַיֵּי דְכָל־בֵּית
יִשְׂרָאֵל, בַּעֲגָלָא וּבִזְמַן קָרִיב, וְאִמְרוּ אָמֵן.

יְהֵא שְׁמֵהּ רַבָּא מְבָרַךְ לְעָלַם וּלְעָלְמֵי עָלְמַיָּא.

יִתְבָּרַךְ וְיִשְׁתַּבַּח וְיִתְפָּאַר וְיִתְרוֹמַם וְיִתְנַשֵּׂא וְיִתְהַדָּר
וְיִתְעַלֶּה וְיִתְהַלָּל שְׁמֵהּ דְּקֻדְשָׁא, בְּרִיךְ הוּא, לְעֵלָּא לְעֵלָּא
מִכָּל־בִּרְכָתָא וְשִׁירָתָא תֻּשְׁבְּחָתָא וְנֶחֱמָתָא דַּאֲמִירָן
בְּעָלְמָא, וְאִמְרוּ אָמֵן.

The Silent Amidah can be found on page 213.

The Silent Amidah can be found on page 213.

WHENEVER THE ARK WAS SET DOWN וּבְנֻחֹה יֹאמַר. Numbers 10:36. As the Torah completes its circuit through the synagogue, we recall Moses' words when the people finished a stage in their journey through the wilderness and came to rest in a new camp. This verse and the ones that follow (Psalm 132:8–10; Proverbs 4:2; 3:18, 3:17; Lamentations 5:21) can also serve to refer to our own inner journey—accompanied by Torah.

IT IS A TREE OF LIFE FOR THOSE WHO GRASP IT עֵץ חַיִּים הִיא לַמַּחֲזִיקִים בָּהּ This verse (Proverbs 3:18) is the source of the custom of holding onto the *atzei ḥayyim*, the Torah handles, while reciting the *b'rakhot* over the Torah— thus grasping the "tree of life" both physically and figuratively.

ITS WAYS ARE PLEASANT WAYS, AND ALL ITS PATHS ARE PEACE דְּרָכֶיהָ דַרְכֵי־נֹעַם, וְכָל־נְתִיבוֹתֶיהָ שָׁלוֹם. Proverbs 3:17. As we put away the Torah, we pray that our study should promote actions that lead to pleasantness and peace.

MAY GOD'S GREAT NAME יְהֵא שְׁמֵהּ. Whenever the people Israel enter the synagogue and house of study and proclaim: יְהֵא שְׁמֵהּ רַבָּא מְבָרַךְ לְעָלַם וּלְעָלְמֵי עָלְמַיָּא (Y'hei sh'meih rabba m'varakh l'alam u-l'almei almayya), "May God's great name be acknowledged forever and ever," the Holy One nods and says: "Happy is the sovereign in whose house such praise is spoken" (Babylonian Talmud, Berakhot 3a).

The Sefer Torah is placed in the ark.

Whenever the Ark was set down, Moses would say:
ADONAI, may You dwell among the myriad families of the
people Israel.

> Return, ADONAI, to Your sanctuary,
> You and Your glorious Ark.

Let Your priests be robed in righteousness,
and Your faithful sing for joy.

> For the sake of David, Your servant,
> do not turn away from Your anointed.

I have given you a precious inheritance:
Do not forsake My teaching.

> It is a tree of life for those who grasp it,
> and all who hold onto it are blessed.

Its ways are pleasant ways, and all its paths are peace.

> Turn us toward You, ADONAI, and we will return to You;
> make our days seem fresh, as they once were.

Eitz ḥayyim hi la-maḥazikim bah, v'tom'kheha m'ushar.
D'rakheha darkhei no·am, v'khol n'tivoteha shalom.
Hashiveinu Adonai eilekha v'nashuvah, ḥaddeish yameinu k'kedem.

Ḥatzi Kaddish

May God's great name be exalted and hallowed throughout the
created world, as is God's wish. May God's sovereignty soon be
established, in your lifetime and in your days, and in the days of
all the House of Israel. And respond with: *Amen.*

May God's great name be acknowledged forever and ever!
Y'hei sh'meih rabba m'varakh l'alam u-l'almei almayya.

May the name of the Holy One be acknowledged and celebrated, lauded and worshipped, exalted and honored, extolled
and acclaimed—though God, who is blessed, *b'rikh hu*, is truly
far beyond all acknowledgment and praise, or any expressions
of gratitude or consolation ever spoken in the world. And
respond with: *Amen.*

The Silent Amidah can be found on page 213.

We rise as the ark is opened.

כִּי שֵׁם יהוה אֶקְרָא, הָבוּ גֹדֶל לֵאלֹהֵינוּ.
אֲדֹנָי שְׂפָתַי תִּפְתָּח, וּפִי יַגִּיד תְּהִלָּתֶךָ.

Version with Patriarchs and Matriarchs:	*Version with Patriarchs:*

בָּרוּךְ אַתָּה יהוה,
אֱלֹהֵינוּ וֵאלֹהֵי אֲבוֹתֵינוּ
[וְאִמּוֹתֵינוּ], אֱלֹהֵי אַבְרָהָם,
אֱלֹהֵי יִצְחָק, וֵאלֹהֵי יַעֲקֹב,
אֱלֹהֵי שָׂרָה, אֱלֹהֵי רִבְקָה,
אֱלֹהֵי רָחֵל, וֵאלֹהֵי לֵאָה,
הָאֵל הַגָּדוֹל הַגִּבּוֹר וְהַנּוֹרָא,
אֵל עֶלְיוֹן, גּוֹמֵל חֲסָדִים
טוֹבִים, וְקוֹנֵה הַכֹּל, וְזוֹכֵר
חַסְדֵי אָבוֹת [וְאִמָּהוֹת],
וּמֵבִיא גוֹאֵל לִבְנֵי בְנֵיהֶם
לְמַעַן שְׁמוֹ בְּאַהֲבָה.

בָּרוּךְ אַתָּה יהוה,
אֱלֹהֵינוּ וֵאלֹהֵי אֲבוֹתֵינוּ,
אֱלֹהֵי אַבְרָהָם, אֱלֹהֵי
יִצְחָק, וֵאלֹהֵי יַעֲקֹב, הָאֵל
הַגָּדוֹל הַגִּבּוֹר וְהַנּוֹרָא,
אֵל עֶלְיוֹן, גּוֹמֵל חֲסָדִים
טוֹבִים, וְקוֹנֵה הַכֹּל, וְזוֹכֵר
חַסְדֵי אָבוֹת, וּמֵבִיא גוֹאֵל
לִבְנֵי בְנֵיהֶם לְמַעַן שְׁמוֹ
בְּאַהֲבָה.

מְסוֹד חֲכָמִים וּנְבוֹנִים,
וּמִלֶּמֶד דַּעַת מְבִינִים,
אֶפְתְּחָה פִי בִּתְפִלָּה וּבְתַחֲנוּנִים,
לְחַלּוֹת וּלְחַנֵּן פְּנֵי מֶלֶךְ מָלֵא רַחֲמִים
מוֹחֵל וְסוֹלֵחַ לַעֲוֹנִים.

The ark is closed.

AMIDAH. In every Amidah, the first three *b'rakhot* and the last three *b'rakhot* consistently address the same themes. On Yom Kippur, a single intermediate *b'rakhah* recounts the day's holiness. Our public confession is inserted into that *b'rakhah* whenever the leader repeats the Amidah.

ADONAI, OPEN MY LIPS אֲדֹנָי שְׂפָתַי תִּפְתָּח. Psalm 51:17. Every Amidah begins with this request asking God to afford us the appropriate attitude and words for prayer. Perhaps the phrase conveys a mystical sense that prayer originates in our soul, the part of God within us all.

GOD OF SARAH אֱלֹהֵי שָׂרָה. Many congregations add the names of the four matriarchs at the beginning of this *b'rakhah* because of their significance as founders of our people and as part of our effort to reclaim women's voices and to honor women's experiences.

GREAT, MIGHTY, AWE-INSPIRING הַגָּדוֹל הַגִּבּוֹר וְהַנּוֹרָא. This phrase is a quotation from Deuteronomy 10:17–18, where God's might is characterized by the befriending of the stranger, the widow, and the orphan.

REDEEMER גוֹאֵל. Judaism's messianic impulse reminds us that the world, as broken as it sometimes appears, is ultimately perfectible; God's teachings, carried out by us, will help the world achieve such perfection.

INSPIRED BY THE INSIGHT מְסוֹד חֲכָמִים. These lines serve to introduce *piyyutim*, poetic additions to the Amidah, that address the holy day's themes. The reference to "sages" and "those who acquired wisdom" is a relic of the era when adding *piyyutim* was a matter of controversy, which prompted this appeal to the authority of those sages who permitted them. This introduction proclaimed that the Amidah's *piyyutim* are faithful to tradition, in that they are saturated with biblical and midrashic quotations.

REPETITION OF THE AMIDAH

Meditation on Prayer

In the Bible, God speaks to us, and we listen. At the moment of prayer, we speak to God and God listens. —ISAAC ARAMA

Bending the Knees and Bowing

The Talmud encourages us to pay attention to the movement of each of our vertebrae as we bow, enabling us to focus on the miracle of our bodies' construction. We stand up straight when we reach God's name, for we speak to God face to face.

God of Abraham, God of Isaac, and God of Jacob

Why is the word "God" repeated each time? We might more easily have said it once. The repeated use of the word "God" highlights that each patriarch—and matriarch—knew God personally and sought a distinct relationship with God.

We rise as the ark is opened.

As I proclaim God's name, ADONAI, exalt our God.
ADONAI, open my lips that my mouth may speak Your praise.

First B'rakhah: Our Ancestors

Version with Patriarchs:

Barukh atah ADONAI,
our God and God of our
   ancestors,
God of Abraham, God of
   Isaac, and God of Jacob,
great, mighty, awe-inspiring,
   transcendent God,
who acts with lovingkindness
   and creates all things,
who remembers the loving
   deeds of our ancestors,
and who will send a redeemer
   to their children's children
   with love
   for the sake of divine honor.

Version with Patriarchs and Matriarchs:

Barukh atah ADONAI,
our God and God of our
   ancestors,
God of Abraham, God of
   Isaac, and God of Jacob,
God of Sarah, God of
   Rebecca, God of Rachel,
   and God of Leah,
great, mighty, awe-inspiring,
   transcendent God,
who acts with lovingkindness
   and creates all things,
who remembers the loving
   deeds of our ancestors,
and who will send a redeemer
   to their children's children
   with love
   for the sake of divine honor.

Inspired by the insight of sages
and the teachings of those who acquired wisdom,
I open my lips in prayer and supplication
to entreat the Merciful Sovereign,
who forgives and pardons sin.

The ark is closed.

זָכְרֵנוּ לְחַיִּים, מֶלֶךְ חָפֵץ בַּחַיִּים, וְכָתְבֵנוּ בְּסֵפֶר הַחַיִּים, לְמַעַנְךָ אֱלֹהִים חַיִּים.

Version with Patriarchs and Matriarchs:

Version with Patriarchs and Matriarchs:

מֶלֶךְ עוֹזֵר וּפוֹקֵד
וּמוֹשִׁיעַ וּמָגֵן.
בָּרוּךְ אַתָּה יהוה, מָגֵן
אַבְרָהָם וּפוֹקֵד שָׂרָה.

Version with Patriarchs:

מֶלֶךְ עוֹזֵר וּמוֹשִׁיעַ וּמָגֵן.
בָּרוּךְ אַתָּה יהוה, מָגֵן
אַבְרָהָם.

אַתָּה גִּבּוֹר לְעוֹלָם אֲדֹנָי, מְחַיֵּה מֵתִים אַתָּה, רַב לְהוֹשִׁיעַ.

מְכַלְכֵּל חַיִּים בְּחֶסֶד, מְחַיֵּה מֵתִים בְּרַחֲמִים רַבִּים, סוֹמֵךְ נוֹפְלִים, וְרוֹפֵא חוֹלִים, וּמַתִּיר אֲסוּרִים, וּמְקַיֵּם אֱמוּנָתוֹ לִישֵׁנֵי עָפָר. מִי כָמְוֹךָ בַּעַל גְּבוּרוֹת וּמִי דְוֹמֶה לָּךְ, מֶלֶךְ מֵמִית וּמְחַיֶּה וּמַצְמִיחַ יְשׁוּעָה.

מִי כָמְוֹךָ אַב הָרַחֲמִים, זוֹכֵר יְצוּרָיו לְחַיִּים בְּרַחֲמִים.

וְנֶאֱמָן אַתָּה לְהַחֲיוֹת מֵתִים. בָּרוּךְ אַתָּה יהוה, מְחַיֵּה הַמֵּתִים.

REMEMBER US זָכְרֵנוּ. This brief prayer is the first of four that are added on the ten days of the High Holy Day season. Each of the four phrases of this short addition ends with the word חַיִּים (ḥayyim), "life."

SHIELD OF ABRAHAM מָגֵן אַבְרָהָם. After Genesis 15:1.

GUARDIAN OF SARAH פוֹקֵד שָׂרָה. Or: "the One who remembered Sarah" (after Genesis 21:1). We, who stand here today, are the fruit of God's promise to Abraham and Sarah.

SUPPORT THE FALLING סוֹמֵךְ נוֹפְלִים. After Psalm 145:14.

HEAL THE SICK רוֹפֵא חוֹלִים. After Exodus 15:26.

LOOSEN THE CHAINS OF THE BOUND מַתִּיר אֲסוּרִים. Psalm 146:7.

BRINGS DEATH AND LIFE מֵמִית וּמְחַיֶּה. 1 Samuel 2:6.

WHO IS LIKE YOU, SOURCE OF COMPASSION מִי כָמְוֹךָ אַב הָרַחֲמִים. Jewish mystical tradition highlights the theological tension between God's qualities of power and strict judgment, גְּבוּרָה (g'vurah), and God's qualities of mercy and lovingkindness, חֶסֶד (ḥesed). Throughout the year, this b'rakhah reminds us that God is unsurpassed in power. At this season of judgment, we add this line to remind us—and God—that God is also unsurpassed in mercy.

GIVES LIFE TO THE DEAD מְחַיֵּה הַמֵּתִים. Over the millennia, many Jewish perspectives on the afterlife have been proposed. Many sages (including Saadiah Gaon, 10th century, and Maimonides, 12th century) caution against speculation about the specific implications of the doctrine of bodily resurrection of the dead. They understand it to be an articulation of God's supreme power: God cares for even the dead.

Each morning You
restore consciousness
to my sleep-filled body,
and I awake.
Each spring You restore
vitality to trees, plants,
and animals that have
hibernated through the
winter, and they grow
once more.
Each day I remember
those who have died;
they live on beyond the
grave.
Each moment I contem-
plate the rebirth of our
people; I recall that You
put the breath of life
into dry bones.
Praised are You, Adonai,
for planting immortal-
ity in my soul, in my
people, and in our
world.

—ROBERT SCHEINBERG

Remember us for life, Sovereign who delights in life,
and inscribe us in the Book of Life, for Your sake, God of life.
*Zokhreinu l'ḥayyim, melekh ḥafeitz ba-ḥayyim,
v'khotveinu b'seifer ha-ḥayyim, l'ma·ankha Elohim ḥayyim.*

Version with Patriarchs:
You are the Sovereign
who helps and saves and
shields.

Barukh atah ADONAI,
Shield of Abraham.

Version with Patriarchs and Matriarchs:
You are the Sovereign who
helps and guards, saves and
shields.

Barukh atah ADONAI,
Shield of Abraham and
Guardian of Sarah.

Second B'rakhah: God's Saving Care

You are mighty forever, ADONAI—
You give life to the dead;
great is Your saving power.

You sustain the living through love,
　　and with great mercy give life to the dead.
You support the falling, heal the sick,
　　loosen the chains of the bound,
　　and keep faith with those who sleep in the dust.
Who is like You, Almighty,
　　and who can be compared to You?—
　　Sovereign, who brings death and life,
　　and causes salvation to flourish.

*M'khalkeil ḥayyim b'ḥesed, m'ḥayyeih meitim b'raḥamim rabbim,
someikh nof'lim, v'rofei ḥolim, u-mattir asurim, u-m'kayyeim emunato
li-sheinei afar. Mi khamokha ba·al g'vurot u-mi domeh lakh, melekh
meimit u-m'ḥayyeh u-matzmi·aḥ y'shu·ah.*

Who is like You, source of compassion,
who remembers with compassion Your creatures for life?
Mi khamokha av ha-raḥamim, zokheir y'tzurav l'ḥayyim b'raḥamim.

You are faithful in bringing life to the dead.
Barukh atah ADONAI, who gives life to the dead.

יִמְלֹךְ יהוה לְעוֹלָם אֱלֹהַיִךְ צִיּוֹן לְדֹר וָדֹר, הַלְלוּ־יָהּ.
וְאַתָּה קָדוֹשׁ, יוֹשֵׁב תְּהִלּוֹת יִשְׂרָאֵל, אֵל נָא.

קְדֻשָּׁה

כַּכָּתוּב עַל יַד נְבִיאֶךָ, וְקָרָא זֶה אֶל זֶה וְאָמַר:
**קָדוֹשׁ, קָדוֹשׁ, קָדוֹשׁ יהוה צְבָאוֹת,
מְלֹא כָל־הָאָרֶץ כְּבוֹדוֹ.**

כְּבוֹדוֹ מָלֵא עוֹלָם, מְשָׁרְתָיו שׁוֹאֲלִים זֶה לָזֶה אַיֵּה מְקוֹם
כְּבוֹדוֹ. לְעֻמָּתָם בָּרוּךְ יֹאמֵרוּ:
בָּרוּךְ כְּבוֹד־יהוה מִמְּקוֹמוֹ.

מִמְּקוֹמוֹ הוּא יִפֶן בְּרַחֲמִים, וְיָחוֹן עַם הַמְיַחֲדִים שְׁמוֹ
עֶרֶב וָבֹקֶר בְּכָל־יוֹם תָּמִיד, פַּעֲמַיִם בְּאַהֲבָה שְׁמַע
אוֹמְרִים:
שְׁמַע יִשְׂרָאֵל יהוה אֱלֹהֵינוּ יהוה אֶחָד.

הוּא אֱלֹהֵינוּ, הוּא אָבִינוּ, הוּא מַלְכֵּנוּ, הוּא מוֹשִׁיעֵנוּ,
וְהוּא יַשְׁמִיעֵנוּ בְּרַחֲמָיו שֵׁנִית לְעֵינֵי כָּל־חַי, לִהְיוֹת לָכֶם
לֵאלֹהִים:
אֲנִי יהוה אֱלֹהֵיכֶם.

אַדִּיר אַדִּירֵנוּ יהוה אֲדֹנֵנוּ, מָה אַדִּיר שִׁמְךָ בְּכָל־הָאָרֶץ.
וְהָיָה יהוה לְמֶלֶךְ עַל כָּל־הָאָרֶץ, בַּיּוֹם הַהוּא יִהְיֶה יהוה
אֶחָד וּשְׁמוֹ אֶחָד. וּבְדִבְרֵי קָדְשְׁךָ כָּתוּב לֵאמֹר:
יִמְלֹךְ יהוה לְעוֹלָם, אֱלֹהַיִךְ צִיּוֹן לְדֹר וָדֹר, הַלְלוּ־יָהּ.

לְדוֹר וָדוֹר נַגִּיד גָּדְלֶךָ, וּלְנֵצַח נְצָחִים קְדֻשָּׁתְךָ נַקְדִּישׁ,
וְשִׁבְחֲךָ אֱלֹהֵינוּ מִפִּינוּ לֹא יָמוּשׁ לְעוֹלָם וָעֶד, כִּי אֵל מֶלֶךְ
גָּדוֹל וְקָדוֹשׁ אָתָּה.

We are seated.

KEDUSHAH. The Kedushah is a poetic elaboration of the third b'rakhah of the Amidah, in which the congregation and the leader proclaim God's holiness responsively. Antiphonal proclamations of God's holiness such as this are referred to as *d'varim she-bik'dushah*, "sections of holiness," and are recited only in the presence of a minyan. In this ancient mystic prayer, we pattern our praise after the angelic glorification of God. The Kedushah of the Amidah occurs in many different versions, but always contains three biblical quotations: "Holy, holy, holy" (Isaiah 6:3), "Praised is Adonai's glory wherever God dwells" (Ezekiel 3:12), and "Adonai will reign forever" (Psalm 146:10). The prayers surrounding these verses vary. On weekdays, they are brief. On Shabbat and holy days, they are more elaborate. On Yom Kippur, the Kedushah at all services is recited in its most elaborate version, which during the year is reserved for the Musaf service on Shabbat and festivals.
(adapted from Reuven Hammer)

HOLY קָדוֹשׁ. These are the words uttered by the angels, which Isaiah recorded when he had an overwhelming experience of being in the very presence of God. Holiness is God's essential quality, of which we can partake when we dedicate ourselves to God and undertake to imitate the divine qualities of mercy and love.

Third B'rakhah: God's Holiness

ADONAI will reign forever; your God, O Zion, from generation to generation, Halleluyah! And You, O Holy One, are enthroned through the praises of the people Israel. God, please hear us.

KEDUSHAH

Each cried out to the other:
"Holy, holy, holy is *Adonai Tz'va·ot*, the whole world is filled with God's glory!"
Kadosh, kadosh, kadosh Adonai Tz'va·ot, m'lo khol ha-aretz k'vodo.

God's glory fills the universe. As one angelic chorus asks, "Where is the place of God's glory?" another responds:
"Praised is ADONAI's glory wherever God dwells."
Barukh k'vod Adonai mi-m'komo.

From where God dwells, may God turn with compassion toward the people who twice each day, evening and morning, lovingly proclaim God's oneness, reciting the Sh'ma: "Hear, O Israel, ADONAI is our God, ADONAI alone."
Sh'ma yisra·el, Adonai eloheinu, Adonai eḥad.

The Holy One is our God, our creator, our sovereign, our redeemer. Yet again, God will in mercy proclaim to us before all that lives:
Hu eloheinu, hu avinu, hu malkeinu, hu moshi·einu, v'hu yashmi·einu b'raḥamav sheinit l'einei kol ḥai, lihyot lakhem leilohim.
"I, ADONAI, am your God."
Ani Adonai eloheikhem.

Majesty, our majesty, "ADONAI, our master, how majestic is Your name throughout the world!"

ADONAI shall be acknowledged sovereign of all the earth. On that day ADONAI shall be one, and the name of God, one.

As the psalmist sang:
ADONAI will reign forever; your God, O Zion, from generation to generation. Halleluyah!
Yimlokh Adonai l'olam, elohayikh tziyyon l'dor va-dor, hal'luyah.

From one generation to another we will declare Your greatness, and forever sanctify You with words of holiness. Your praise will never leave our lips, for You are God and Sovereign, great and holy.
We are seated.

חֲמֹל עַל מַעֲשֶׂיךָ
וְתִשְׂמַח בְּמַעֲשֶׂיךָ,
וְיֹאמְרוּ לְךָ חוֹסֶיךָ
בְּצַדֶּקְךָ עֲמוּסֶיךָ,
תִּקְדַּשׁ אָדוֹן עַל כָּל־מַעֲשֶׂיךָ.

וּבְכֵן תֵּן פַּחְדְּךָ יהוה אֱלֹהֵינוּ עַל כָּל־מַעֲשֶׂיךָ
וְאֵימָתְךָ עַל כָּל־מַה־שֶּׁבָּרָאתָ,
וְיִירָאוּךָ כָּל־הַמַּעֲשִׂים
וְיִשְׁתַּחֲווּ לְפָנֶיךָ כָּל־הַבְּרוּאִים,
וְיֵעָשׂוּ כֻלָּם אֲגֻדָּה אַחַת לַעֲשׂוֹת רְצוֹנְךָ בְּלֵבָב שָׁלֵם,
כְּמוֹ שֶׁיָּדַעְנוּ יהוה אֱלֹהֵינוּ,
שֶׁהַשִּׁלְטוֹן לְפָנֶיךָ, עֹז בְּיָדְךָ וּגְבוּרָה בִּימִינֶךָ,
וְשִׁמְךָ נוֹרָא עַל כָּל־מַה־שֶּׁבָּרָאתָ.

וּבְכֵן תֵּן כָּבוֹד יהוה לְעַמֶּךָ,
תְּהִלָּה לִירֵאֶיךָ וְתִקְוָה לְדוֹרְשֶׁיךָ,
וּפִתְחוֹן פֶּה לַמְיַחֲלִים לָךְ,
שִׂמְחָה לְאַרְצֶךָ וְשָׂשׂוֹן לְעִירֶךָ,
וּצְמִיחַת קֶרֶן לְדָוִד עַבְדֶּךָ,
וַעֲרִיכַת נֵר לְבֶן־יִשַׁי מְשִׁיחֶךָ, בִּמְהֵרָה בְיָמֵינוּ.

וּבְכֵן צַדִּיקִים יִרְאוּ וְיִשְׂמָחוּ,
וִישָׁרִים יַעֲלֹזוּ,
וַחֲסִידִים בְּרִנָּה יָגִילוּ,
וְעוֹלָתָה תִּקְפָּץ־פִּיהָ,
וְכָל־הָרִשְׁעָה כֻּלָּהּ כְּעָשָׁן תִּכְלֶה,
כִּי תַעֲבִיר מֶמְשֶׁלֶת זָדוֹן מִן הָאָרֶץ.

וְתִמְלֹךְ אַתָּה יהוה לְבַדֶּךָ, עַל כָּל־מַעֲשֶׂיךָ,
בְּהַר צִיּוֹן מִשְׁכַּן כְּבוֹדֶךָ,
וּבִירוּשָׁלַיִם עִיר קָדְשֶׁךָ,
כַּכָּתוּב בְּדִבְרֵי קָדְשֶׁךָ:
יִמְלֹךְ יהוה לְעוֹלָם, אֱלֹהַיִךְ צִיּוֹן לְדֹר וָדֹר, הַלְלוּ־יָהּ.

U-V'KHEIN וּבְכֵן. These three paragraphs, which are all introduced by the same word, וּבְכֵן (u-v'khein), are ascribed by many scholars to the 2nd or 3rd century, and may constitute the earliest poetic additions to the Amidah.

Stages of redemption are described in this series of prayers. The first paragraph implores God to cause the entire world to live with reverence for God.

The second paragraph discusses not the universal, but the particular: the return of the people Israel to its land (and specifically to Jerusalem), and the kingship of David.

The third paragraph describes the rejoicing that will come to the righteous "when You remove the tyranny of arrogance from the earth" and God will rule alone over the entire world from Zion and Jerusalem.
(adapted from Reuven Hammer)

AWE . . . FEAR . . . פַּחְדְּךָ . . . וְאֵימָתְךָ. These emotions are meant to describe obedience to God's will and inspire us to bring sanctity to the world.

THE LIGHT OF DAVID קֶרֶן לְדָוִד. See Psalm 132:17.

YOU ALONE . . . WILL RULE וְתִמְלֹךְ אַתָּה לְבַדֶּךָ. God's sovereignty is always envisioned as the rule of justice, and therefore a time of peace. It is the ultimate conclusion of history.

ADONAI WILL REIGN FOREVER יִמְלֹךְ יהוה לְעוֹלָם. Psalm 146:10.

The purpose of creation is not division, nor separation. The purpose of the human race is not a struggle to the death between classes, between nations. Humanity is meant to become a single body.... Our purpose is the great upbuilding of unity and peace. And when all nations are bound together in one association living in justice and righteousness, they atone for each other.   —MARTIN BUBER

Have compassion on Your creation,
and rejoice in Your handiwork.
As You vindicate Your people,
all who trust in You will declare:
"Be sanctified, Lord, throughout Your creation."

U-v'khein—Adonai our God,
instill Your awe in all You have made,
and fear of You in all You have created,
so that all You have fashioned revere You,
all You have created bow in recognition,
and all be bound together, carrying out Your will wholeheartedly.
For we know that true sovereignty is Yours,
power and strength are in Your hands,
and Your name is to be revered beyond any of Your creations.

U-v'khein—Bestow honor to Your people, Adonai,
praise to those who revere You,
hope to those who seek You,
recognition to those who await You,
joy to Your land, and gladness to Your city.
Simḥah l'artzekha v'sason l'irekha
May the light of David, Your servant, dawn,
and the lamp of the son of Jesse, Your anointed,
be kindled speedily in our day.

U-v'khein—The righteous, beholding this, will rejoice,
the upright will be glad,
the pious will celebrate with song,
evil will be silenced,
and all wickedness will disappear like smoke,
when You remove the tyranny of arrogance from the earth.

You alone, Adonai, will rule all Your creation,
from Mount Zion, the dwelling-place of Your glory,
and from Jerusalem, Your holy city.
As it is written in the Book of Psalms:
"Adonai will reign forever;
your God, O Zion, from generation to generation. Halleluyah!"

קָדוֹשׁ אַתָּה וְנוֹרָא שְׁמֶךָ, וְאֵין אֱלוֹהַּ מִבַּלְעָדֶיךָ, כַּכָּתוּב: וַיִּגְבַּה יהוה צְבָאוֹת בַּמִּשְׁפָּט, וְהָאֵל הַקָּדוֹשׁ נִקְדַּשׁ בִּצְדָקָה. בָּרוּךְ אַתָּה יהוה, הַמֶּלֶךְ הַקָּדוֹשׁ.

אַתָּה בְחַרְתָּנוּ מִכָּל־הָעַמִּים,
אָהַבְתָּ אוֹתָנוּ וְרָצִיתָ בָּנוּ,
וְרוֹמַמְתָּנוּ מִכָּל־הַלְּשׁוֹנוֹת,
וְקִדַּשְׁתָּנוּ בְּמִצְוֺתֶיךָ,
וְקֵרַבְתָּנוּ מַלְכֵּנוּ לַעֲבוֹדָתֶךָ,
וְשִׁמְךָ הַגָּדוֹל וְהַקָּדוֹשׁ עָלֵינוּ קָרָאתָ.

וַתִּתֶּן־לָנוּ יהוה אֱלֹהֵינוּ בְּאַהֲבָה אֶת־יוֹם [הַשַּׁבָּת הַזֶּה לִקְדֻשָּׁה וְלִמְנוּחָה וְאֶת־יוֹם] הַכִּפּוּרִים הַזֶּה לִמְחִילָה וְלִסְלִיחָה וּלְכַפָּרָה וְלִמְחָל־בּוֹ אֶת־כָּל־עֲוֺנוֹתֵינוּ [בְּאַהֲבָה] מִקְרָא קֹדֶשׁ, זֵכֶר לִיצִיאַת מִצְרָיִם.

אֱלֹהֵינוּ וֵאלֹהֵי אֲבוֹתֵינוּ [וְאִמּוֹתֵינוּ], יַעֲלֶה וְיָבֹא, וְיַגִּיעַ וְיֵרָאֶה, וְיֵרָצֶה וְיִשָּׁמַע, וְיִפָּקֵד וְיִזָּכֵר זִכְרוֹנֵנוּ וּפִקְדוֹנֵנוּ, וְזִכְרוֹן אֲבוֹתֵינוּ [וְאִמּוֹתֵינוּ], וְזִכְרוֹן מָשִׁיחַ בֶּן־דָּוִד עַבְדֶּךָ, וְזִכְרוֹן יְרוּשָׁלַיִם עִיר קָדְשֶׁךָ, וְזִכְרוֹן כָּל־עַמְּךָ בֵּית יִשְׂרָאֵל לְפָנֶיךָ לִפְלֵיטָה לְטוֹבָה, לְחֵן וּלְחֶסֶד וּלְרַחֲמִים, לְחַיִּים וּלְשָׁלוֹם, בְּיוֹם הַכִּפּוּרִים הַזֶּה.
זָכְרֵנוּ יהוה אֱלֹהֵינוּ בּוֹ לְטוֹבָה,   אָמֵן.
וּפָקְדֵנוּ בוֹ לִבְרָכָה,   אָמֵן.
וְהוֹשִׁיעֵנוּ בוֹ לְחַיִּים,   אָמֵן.
וּבִדְבַר יְשׁוּעָה וְרַחֲמִים, חוּס וְחָנֵּנוּ, וְרַחֵם עָלֵינוּ וְהוֹשִׁיעֵנוּ, כִּי אֵלֶיךָ עֵינֵינוּ, כִּי אֵל מֶלֶךְ חַנּוּן וְרַחוּם אָתָּה.

ADONAI TZ'VA·OT WILL BE EXALTED וַיִּגְבַּה יהוה צְבָאוֹת. Isaiah 5:16. In concluding the b'rakhah, this verse highlights its themes as expanded on the High Holy Days: We await the day when earthly powers become subservient to the divine ideals of justice and righteousness.

THE HOLY SOVEREIGN הַמֶּלֶךְ הַקָּדוֹשׁ. The rest of the year, this b'rakhah concludes with the words הָאֵל הַקָּדוֹשׁ "the Holy God." The High Holy Days, though, emphasize God's sovereignty.

CALLING US BY YOUR GREAT AND HOLY NAME וְשִׁמְךָ הַגָּדוֹל וְהַקָּדוֹשׁ עָלֵינוּ קָרָאתָ. The name "Israel" means "wrestling with God" (Genesis 32:28). Our relationship with God is part of our self-definition as Jews.

In Maimonides' view chosenness does not imply superiority or inherent sanctity, since the correct reading of the Bible in fact implies conditional chosenness. The election is one of duty, not of rights or attributes. Superiority and sanctity do not belong to historical Israel, to concrete individuals, but to a mythical Israel, held up as a model and ideal, defined by submission to God's commandments and respect for the covenant. . . . Judaism avoided being drawn into a universalistic, proselytizing monotheism through its interpretation of election as a duty, the particular relation between a people and its God in its social and historical reality.

—HENRI ATLAN

You are holy, and Your name is revered, for there is no God but You. As Your prophet Isaiah wrote: "*Adonai Tz'va·ot* will be exalted through justice, the holy God sanctified through righteousness."
Barukh atah ADONAI, the Holy Sovereign.

Fourth B'rakhah: The Holiness of Yom Kippur

You have chosen us among all peoples, loving us, wanting us. You have distinguished us among all nations, making us holy through Your commandments, drawing us close to Your service, and calling us by Your great and holy name.

With love, You have bestowed on us, ADONAI our God, this [Shabbat, for sanctity and rest, and this] Yom Kippur for pardon, forgiveness, and atonement, that all our sins be forgiven [through Your love], a sacred time, recalling the Exodus from Egypt.

Our God and God of our ancestors,
may the thought of us rise up and reach You.
Attend to us and accept us;
hear us and respond to us.
Keep us in mind,
and keep in mind the thought of our ancestors,
as well as the Messiah, the descendant of David;
Jerusalem, Your holy city;
and all Your people, the House of Israel.
On this Yom Kippur respond to us
with deliverance, goodness, compassion, love, life, and peace.

Remember us for good;   *Amen.*

respond to us with blessing;   *Amen.*

redeem us with life.   *Amen.*

Show us compassion and care with words of salvation and kindness; have mercy on us and redeem us. Our eyes are turned to You, for You are a compassionate and loving sovereign.

אֵל, מֶלֶךְ יוֹשֵׁב עַל כִּסֵּא רַחֲמִים, מִתְנַהֵג בַּחֲסִידוּת, מוֹחֵל עֲוֹנוֹת עַמּוֹ, מַעֲבִיר רִאשׁוֹן רִאשׁוֹן, מַרְבֶּה מְחִילָה לַחַטָּאִים, וּסְלִיחָה לַפּוֹשְׁעִים, עוֹשֶׂה צְדָקוֹת עִם כָּל־בָּשָׂר וָרוּחַ, לֹא כְרָעָתָם תִּגְמוֹל.

◁ אֵל, הוֹרֵיתָ לָנוּ לוֹמַר שְׁלֹשׁ עֶשְׂרֵה, זְכָר־לָנוּ הַיּוֹם בְּרִית שְׁלֹשׁ עֶשְׂרֵה, כְּמוֹ שֶׁהוֹדַעְתָּ לֶעָנָו מִקֶּדֶם, כְּמוֹ שֶׁכָּתוּב: וַיֵּרֶד יהוה בֶּעָנָן, וַיִּתְיַצֵּב עִמּוֹ שָׁם, וַיִּקְרָא בְשֵׁם יהוה.

וַיַּעֲבֹר יהוה עַל־פָּנָיו וַיִּקְרָא:

יהוה יהוה, אֵל רַחוּם וְחַנּוּן, אֶרֶךְ אַפַּיִם, וְרַב־חֶסֶד וֶאֱמֶת. נֹצֵר חֶסֶד לָאֲלָפִים, נֹשֵׂא עָוֹן וָפֶשַׁע וְחַטָּאָה, וְנַקֵּה.

וְסָלַחְתָּ לַעֲוֹנֵנוּ וּלְחַטָּאתֵנוּ וּנְחַלְתָּנוּ.

Some customarily strike their heart when asking God to forgive and pardon:

סְלַח לָנוּ אָבִינוּ כִּי חָטָאנוּ, מְחַל לָנוּ מַלְכֵּנוּ כִּי פָשָׁעְנוּ, כִּי אַתָּה, אֲדֹנָי, טוֹב וְסַלָּח וְרַב־חֶסֶד לְכָל־קֹרְאֶיךָ.

זְכָר־לָנוּ בְּרִית רִאשׁוֹנִים כַּאֲשֶׁר אָמַרְתָּ: וְזָכַרְתִּי לָהֶם בְּרִית רִאשׁוֹנִים, אֲשֶׁר הוֹצֵאתִי־אֹתָם מֵאֶרֶץ מִצְרַיִם לְעֵינֵי הַגּוֹיִם לִהְיוֹת לָהֶם לֵאלֹהִים, אֲנִי יהוה. מְחֵה פְשָׁעֵינוּ כָּעָב וְכֶעָנָן, כַּאֲשֶׁר אָמַרְתָּ: מָחִיתִי כָעָב פְּשָׁעֶיךָ וְכֶעָנָן חַטֹּאותֶיךָ, שׁוּבָה אֵלַי כִּי גְאַלְתִּיךָ. זְרֹק עָלֵינוּ מַיִם טְהוֹרִים וְטַהֲרֵנוּ כְּמָה שֶׁכָּתוּב: וְזָרַקְתִּי עֲלֵיכֶם מַיִם טְהוֹרִים וּטְהַרְתֶּם, מִכֹּל טֻמְאוֹתֵיכֶם וּמִכָּל־גִּלּוּלֵיכֶם אֲטַהֵר אֶתְכֶם.

THRONE OF MERCY כִּסֵּא רַחֲמִים. In rabbinic imagery, God is said to have two thrones: the seat of judgment and the seat of mercy. On Rosh Hashanah God sits in judgment; on Yom Kippur God moves to the throne of mercy.

GOD, YOU TAUGHT US אֵל הוֹרֵיתָ לָנוּ. The biblical verse is ambiguous as to whether it was Moses or God who recited the Thirteen Attributes of God. Rabbi Yoḥanan in the Babylonian Talmud (Rosh Hashanah 17b) describes God wearing a *tallit* like a leader of communal prayer and showing Moses how to pray. God said to Moses: "Whenever Israel sins, they should pray like this and I will forgive them." And then God recited the Thirteen Attributes.

FOR OUR SAKE, REMEMBER זְכָר־לָנוּ בְּרִית. Leviticus 26:45; Isaiah 44:22; Ezekiel 36:25; Leviticus 16:30; and Isaiah 56:7. These verses are taken from contexts in which God promises to show kindness to those who have been exiled. The quotations ask God to remember our relationship, forgive our sins, and see us as pure despite our failings. Taken together, their imagery progresses from the wiping away of sin to an ultimate scene of redemption, as all are gathered together in God's house.

S'LIḤOT: PRAYERS OF FORGIVENESS

❡ *From Ibn Gabirol's Keter Malkhut*

How can I repay You for
  having placed a soul in
  this body
and having granted me
  life,
to teach and direct me,
to save me from pitfalls?

You formed me from
  earth,
and breathed in me from
  birth.
You granted me wisdom,
fashioned me as more
  than animal,
instructed me to enter a
  higher realm. . . .

You placed in me a holy
  soul;
though I have sinned,
  and am not whole.
My instincts made me
  violate the gift of self.
Not against You have
  I sinned, but against
  myself. . . .

Terrible urges have
  pulled me apart.
I intend to act innocently,
then sow with guile and
  deceit;
I desire peace,
but cause contention and
  enmity. . . .

Do not repay me accord-
  ing to my deeds;
do not demean me;
do not desert me while
  my life is not yet over;
do not hide Your face
  from me.

Renew me with life,
raise me from the
  depths. . . .

THE THIRTEEN ATTRIBUTES

God, Sovereign who sits on a throne of mercy, acting with un-bounded grace, forgiving the sins of Your people, one by one, as each comes before You, generously forgiving sinners and pardon-ing transgressors, acting charitably with every living thing: do not repay them for their misdeeds.

God, You taught us how to recite the thirteen attributes of Your name; remember the promise implied in these thirteen attributes, which You first revealed to Moses, the humble one, as it is written: God descended in a cloud and stood beside him, and he called the name ADONAI.

And ADONAI passed before him and called:

ADONAI, ADONAI, God, merciful and compassionate, patient, abounding in love and faithfulness, assuring love for thou-sands of generations, forgiving iniquity, transgression, and sin, and granting pardon.

Adonai, Adonai, El raḥum v'ḥannun, erekh appayim v'rav ḥesed ve-emet. Notzeir ḥesed la-alafim, nosei avon va-fesha v'ḥatta·ah v'nakkeih.

Forgive our transgressions and our sins; claim us for Your own.

Some customarily strike their heart when asking God to forgive and pardon:

Forgive us, our creator, for we have sinned;
pardon us, our sovereign, for we have transgressed—
for You, ADONAI, are kind and forgiving;
You act generously to all who call on You.

S'laḥ lanu avinu ki ḥatanu, m'ḥal lanu malkeinu ki fashanu, ki atah Adonai tov v'sallaḥ, v'rav ḥesed l'khol kor'ekha.

For our sake, remember the covenant You made with our ances-tors, as You said in the Torah: "I will remember My covenant with their ancestors whom I took out of the land of Egypt in the sight of all nations, to be their God. I am ADONAI."

Sweep aside our transgressions like a mist, disperse them like a cloud, as You promised in the words of Isaiah: "I sweep aside your sins like a mist, and disperse your transgressions like a cloud. Turn back to Me, for I will redeem you."

Purify us, as Your prophet Ezekiel promised in Your name: "I will sprinkle purifying water upon you and you shall be cleansed; I will cleanse you of all your impurities and your idolatries."

כַּפֵּר חֲטָאֵינוּ בַּיּוֹם הַזֶּה וְטַהֲרֵנוּ, כְּמָה שֶׁכָּתוּב: כִּי־בַיּוֹם
הַזֶּה יְכַפֵּר עֲלֵיכֶם לְטַהֵר אֶתְכֶם, מִכֹּל חַטֹּאתֵיכֶם לִפְנֵי
יהוה תִּטְהָרוּ.
הֲבִיאֵנוּ אֶל הַר קָדְשֶׁךָ וְשַׂמְּחֵנוּ בְּבֵית תְּפִלָּתֶךָ, כְּמָה
שֶׁכָּתוּב: וַהֲבִיאוֹתִים אֶל־הַר קָדְשִׁי וְשִׂמַּחְתִּים בְּבֵית
תְּפִלָּתִי, כִּי בֵיתִי בֵּית־תְּפִלָּה יִקָּרֵא לְכָל־הָעַמִּים.

The ark is opened. After the leader recites each verse, we repeat it.

שְׁמַע קוֹלֵנוּ, יהוה אֱלֹהֵינוּ, חוּס וְרַחֵם עָלֵינוּ,
וְקַבֵּל בְּרַחֲמִים וּבְרָצוֹן אֶת־תְּפִלָּתֵנוּ.
הֲשִׁיבֵנוּ יהוה אֵלֶיךָ וְנָשׁוּבָה, חַדֵּשׁ יָמֵינוּ כְּקֶדֶם.
אַל־תַּשְׁלִיכֵנוּ מִלְּפָנֶיךָ, וְרוּחַ קָדְשְׁךָ אַל־תִּקַּח מִמֶּנּוּ.
אַל־תַּשְׁלִיכֵנוּ לְעֵת זִקְנָה, כִּכְלוֹת כֹּחֵנוּ אַל־תַּעַזְבֵנוּ.

Said quietly:

אַל־תַּעַזְבֵנוּ, יהוה אֱלֹהֵינוּ, אַל־תִּרְחַק מִמֶּנּוּ.
עֲשֵׂה־עִמָּנוּ אוֹת לְטוֹבָה, וְיִרְאוּ שׂוֹנְאֵינוּ וְיֵבֹשׁוּ,
כִּי־אַתָּה יהוה עֲזַרְתָּנוּ וְנִחַמְתָּנוּ.
אֲמָרֵינוּ הַאֲזִינָה יהוה, בִּינָה הֲגִיגֵנוּ. יִהְיוּ לְרָצוֹן אִמְרֵי־
פִינוּ וְהֶגְיוֹן לִבֵּנוּ לְפָנֶיךָ, יהוה צוּרֵנוּ וְגוֹאֲלֵנוּ.
כִּי־לְךָ יהוה הוֹחָלְנוּ, אַתָּה תַעֲנֶה, אֲדֹנָי אֱלֹהֵינוּ.

The ark is closed.

אֱלֹהֵינוּ וֵאלֹהֵי אֲבוֹתֵינוּ [וְאִמּוֹתֵינוּ],
אַל תַּעַזְבֵנוּ וְאַל תִּטְּשֵׁנוּ,
וְאַל תַּכְלִימֵנוּ וְאַל תָּפֵר בְּרִיתְךָ אִתָּנוּ.
קָרְבֵנוּ לְתוֹרָתֶךָ, לַמְּדֵנוּ מִצְוֹתֶיךָ, הוֹרֵנוּ דְּרָכֶיךָ,
הַט לִבֵּנוּ לְיִרְאָה אֶת־שְׁמֶךָ, וּמוֹל אֶת־לְבָבֵנוּ לְאַהֲבָתֶךָ,
וְנָשׁוּב אֵלֶיךָ בֶּאֱמֶת וּבְלֵב שָׁלֵם.
◁ וּלְמַעַן שִׁמְךָ הַגָּדוֹל תִּמְחַל וְתִסְלַח לַעֲוֹנֵנוּ,
כַּכָּתוּב בְּדִבְרֵי קָדְשֶׁךָ:
לְמַעַן־שִׁמְךָ יהוה, וְסָלַחְתָּ לַעֲוֹנִי כִּי רַב־הוּא.

Grant atonement and purify us this day, as it is written in the Torah, "For on this day, atonement shall be made for you to purify you from all your transgressions. In the presence of ADONAI you shall be pure."

Bring us to Your holy mountain and make us joyful in Your house of prayer, as Isaiah prophesied, "I shall bring you to My holy mountain and make you joyous in My house of prayer, for My house shall be called a house of prayer for all people."

CULMINATION OF S'LIḤOT: HEAR OUR VOICE

The ark is opened. After the leader recites each verse, we repeat it.

Hear our voice, ADONAI our God, be kind, and have compassion for us. Willingly and lovingly accept our prayer.

Turn us toward You, ADONAI, and we will return to You; make our days seem fresh, as they once were.

Do not cast us away from You; take not Your holy presence from us.

Do not cast us away as we grow old; do not desert us as our energy wanes.

Sh'ma koleinu, Adonai eloheinu, ḥus v'raḥeim aleinu, v'kabbeil b'raḥamim u-v'ratzon et t'fillateinu. Hashiveinu Adonai eilekha v'nashuvah, ḥaddeish yameinu k'kedem. Al tashlikheinu mi-l'fanekha, v'ru·aḥ kodsh'kha al tikkaḥ mimmennu. Al tashlikheinu l'eit ziknah, ki-kh'lot koḥeinu al ta·azveinu.

Said quietly:

Do not abandon us, ADONAI our God, do not distance Yourself from us.

Give us a signal of hope, so that our enemies will understand and hesitate, knowing that You have been our help and comfort.

Hear our words, ADONAI, and consider our innermost thoughts.

May the words of our mouths and the meditations of our hearts be acceptable to You, ADONAI, our rock and redeemer.

It is for You we wait; surely You will respond, ADONAI our God.

The ark is closed.

Our God and God of our ancestors, do not abandon us, do not forsake us, do not shame us, do not annul Your covenant with us. Draw us close to Your Torah, teach us Your mitzvot, show us Your ways. Open our hearts to revere Your name, circumcise our hearts to love You; then, we will turn to You, faithfully, with a perfect heart. And as befits Your own great name, pardon and forgive our sins, as the psalmist wrote: "For the sake of Your own name, forgive my sin, though it be great."

V'salaḥta la-avoni ki rav hu.

אֱלֹהֵֽינוּ וֵאלֹהֵי אֲבוֹתֵֽינוּ [וְאִמּוֹתֵֽינוּ],
סְלַח לָֽנוּ, מְחַל לָֽנוּ, כַּפֶּר־לָֽנוּ.

כִּי

אָֽנוּ עַמֶּֽךָ	וְאַתָּה אֱלֹהֵֽינוּ,
אָֽנוּ בָנֶֽיךָ	וְאַתָּה אָבִֽינוּ.
אָֽנוּ עֲבָדֶֽיךָ	וְאַתָּה אֲדוֹנֵֽנוּ,
אָֽנוּ קְהָלֶֽךָ	וְאַתָּה חֶלְקֵֽנוּ.
אָֽנוּ נַחֲלָתֶֽךָ	וְאַתָּה גוֹרָלֵֽנוּ,
אָֽנוּ צֹאנֶֽךָ	וְאַתָּה רוֹעֵֽנוּ.
אָֽנוּ כַרְמֶֽךָ	וְאַתָּה נוֹטְרֵֽנוּ,
אָֽנוּ פְעֻלָּתֶֽךָ	וְאַתָּה יוֹצְרֵֽנוּ.
אָֽנוּ רַעְיָתֶֽךָ	וְאַתָּה דוֹדֵֽנוּ,
אָֽנוּ סְגֻלָּתֶֽךָ	וְאַתָּה קְרוֹבֵֽנוּ.
אָֽנוּ עַמֶּֽךָ	וְאַתָּה מַלְכֵּֽנוּ,
אָֽנוּ מַאֲמִירֶֽךָ	וְאַתָּה מַאֲמִירֵֽנוּ.

וידוי

אָֽנוּ עַזֵּי פָנִים	וְאַתָּה רַחוּם וְחַנּוּן.
אָֽנוּ קְשֵׁי עֹֽרֶף	וְאַתָּה אֶֽרֶךְ אַפַּֽיִם.
אָֽנוּ מְלֵאֵי עָוֹן	וְאַתָּה מָלֵא רַחֲמִים.
אָֽנוּ יָמֵֽינוּ כְּצֵל עוֹבֵר	וְאַתָּה הוּא וּשְׁנוֹתֶֽיךָ לֹא יִתָּֽמּוּ.

אֱלֹהֵֽינוּ וֵאלֹהֵי אֲבוֹתֵֽינוּ [וְאִמּוֹתֵֽינוּ],
תָּבֹא לְפָנֶֽיךָ תְּפִלָּתֵֽנוּ, וְאַל תִּתְעַלַּם מִתְּחִנָּתֵֽנוּ,
שֶׁאֵין אֲנַֽחְנוּ עַזֵּי פָנִים וּקְשֵׁי עֹֽרֶף לוֹמַר לְפָנֶֽיךָ,
יהוה אֱלֹהֵֽינוּ וֵאלֹהֵי אֲבוֹתֵֽינוּ [וְאִמּוֹתֵֽינוּ],
צַדִּיקִים אֲנַֽחְנוּ וְלֹא חָטָֽאנוּ,
אֲבָל אֲנַֽחְנוּ וַאֲבוֹתֵֽינוּ [וְאִמּוֹתֵֽינוּ] חָטָֽאנוּ.

כִּי WE ARE YOUR PEOPLE אָנוּ עַמֶּךָ. An early medieval poem, which expands on the verse from Song of Songs: "I am for my beloved and my beloved is mine" (2:16). It completes the S'liḥot/Forgiveness section and forms the transition to the confession. Here we end in joyous song, then move to a meditative melody, as we begin the Viddui/Confession. In this poem we emphasize our relatedness to God, whereas in the next we emphasize the stark difference between the human and the Divine.

VIDDUI—PRAYERS OF CONFESSION וִידּוּי. In addition to fasting and otherwise afflicting oneself, the central mitzvah that must be performed on Yom Kippur is *viddui* (confession). The rabbinic requirement to confess is based on the biblical passage that describes the confession of the High Priest when performing the Temple ceremony. Following the destruction of the Temple, greater emphasis was placed on synagogue ritual and individual prayer, and it fell upon each person to make confession on Yom Kippur.

A PASSING SHADOW כְּצֵל עוֹבֵר. Psalm 144:4.

FOR TIME WITHOUT END וּשְׁנוֹתֶיךָ לֹא יִתָּמּוּ. "Of old You established the earth; / the heavens are the work of Your hands. / They shall perish, but You shall endure; / they shall all wear out like a garment; / You change them like clothing and they pass away. / But You are the same, and Your years never end" (Psalm 102:26–28).

WE, LIKE OUR ANCESTORS אֲנַחְנוּ וַאֲבוֹתֵינוּ. In the Babylonian Talmud, Mar Zutra remarked that anyone who says "we have sinned" has understood the meaning of confession (Yoma 87b). Every human being is imperfect. Even previous generations—whom we may idealize—contained sinners. As the Rabbis taught: no one has walked the earth and not sinned. In ascribing sin to our ancestors, the liturgist is quoting Psalm 106:6.

Our God and God of our ancestors, forgive us, pardon us, grant us atonement.

For—

We are Your people,	and You are our God;
we are Your children	and You are our parent.
We are Your servants,	and You are our master;
we are Your congregation,	and You are our portion.
We are Your heritage,	and You are our destiny;
we are Your flock,	and You are our shepherd.
We are Your vineyard,	and You are our guardian;
we are Your creatures,	and You are our creator.
We are Your spouse,	and You are our beloved;
we are Your cherished ones,	and You are near to us.
We are Your people,	and You are our sovereign;

we are the ones You address, and You are the One to whom we speak.

Ki

Anu ammekha,	*v'atah eloheinu,*
anu vanekha	*v'atah avinu.*
Anu avadekha	*v'atah adoneinu,*
anu k'halekha	*v'atah ḥelkeinu.*
Anu naḥalatekha	*v'atah goraleinu,*
anu tzonekha	*v'atah ro·einu.*
Anu kharmekha	*v'atah not'reinu,*
anu f'ullatekha,	*v'atah yotz'reinu.*
Anu ra·ayatekha	*v'atah dodeinu,*
anu s'gullatekha	*v'atah k'roveinu.*
Anu ammekha	*v'atah malkeinu,*
anu ma·amirekha	*v'atah ma·amireinu.*

VIDDUI — PRAYERS OF CONFESSION

We are insolent;	You are gracious and compassionate.
We are obstinate;	You are patient.
We are sinful;	You are merciful.
Our days are a passing shadow,	but You are the One who truly is,

for time without end.

Our God and God of our ancestors, hear our prayer; do not ignore our plea. Our God and God of our ancestors, we are neither so insolent nor so obstinate as to claim in Your presence that we are righteous, without sin; for we, like our ancestors who came before us, have sinned.

Sin and Repentance
No sin is so light that it may be overlooked; no sin is so heavy that it may not be repented of.

—MOSES IBN EZRA

Customarily, we each strike our heart as we recite every phrase of this confession.

אָשַׁמְנוּ, בָּגַדְנוּ, גָּזַלְנוּ, דִּבַּרְנוּ דֹּפִי.
הֶעֱוִינוּ, וְהִרְשַׁעְנוּ, זַדְנוּ, חָמַסְנוּ, טָפַלְנוּ שֶׁקֶר.
יָעַצְנוּ רָע, כִּזַּבְנוּ, לַצְנוּ, מָרַדְנוּ, נִאַצְנוּ.
סָרַרְנוּ, עָוִינוּ, פָּשַׁעְנוּ, צָרַרְנוּ, קִשִּׁינוּ עֹרֶף.
רָשַׁעְנוּ, שִׁחַתְנוּ, תִּעַבְנוּ, תָּעִינוּ, תִּעְתָּעְנוּ.

סַרְנוּ מִמִּצְוֹתֶיךָ וּמִמִּשְׁפָּטֶיךָ הַטּוֹבִים, וְלֹא שָׁוָה לָנוּ.
וְאַתָּה צַדִּיק עַל כָּל־הַבָּא עָלֵינוּ, כִּי אֱמֶת עָשִׂיתָ
וַאֲנַחְנוּ הִרְשָׁעְנוּ.

One or more of the following penitential prayers may be included.

א

הִרְשַׁעְנוּ וּפָשַׁעְנוּ, לָכֵן לֹא נוֹשָׁעְנוּ. וְתֵן בְּלִבֵּנוּ לַעֲזוֹב דֶּרֶךְ
רֶשַׁע וְחִישׁ לָנוּ יֶשַׁע, כַּכָּתוּב עַל יַד נְבִיאֶךָ: יַעֲזֹב רָשָׁע דַּרְכּוֹ,
וְאִישׁ אָוֶן מַחְשְׁבֹתָיו, וְיָשֹׁב אֶל־יהוה וִירַחֲמֵהוּ, וְאֶל־אֱלֹהֵינוּ
כִּי־יַרְבֶּה לִסְלוֹחַ.

ב

אֱלֹהֵינוּ וֵאלֹהֵי אֲבוֹתֵינוּ [וְאִמּוֹתֵינוּ],
סְלַח וּמְחַל לַעֲוֺנוֹתֵינוּ
בְּיוֹם [הַשַּׁבָּת הַזֶּה וּבְיוֹם] הַכִּפּוּרִים הַזֶּה.
מְחֵה וְהַעֲבֵר פְּשָׁעֵינוּ וְחַטֹּאתֵינוּ מִנֶּגֶד עֵינֶיךָ,
וְכֹף אֶת־יִצְרֵנוּ לְהִשְׁתַּעְבֶּד־לָךְ,
וְהַכְנַע עָרְפֵּנוּ לָשׁוּב אֵלֶיךָ,
וְחַדֵּשׁ כִּלְיוֹתֵינוּ לִשְׁמוֹר פִּקּוּדֶיךָ,
וּמוֹל אֶת־לְבָבֵנוּ לְאַהֲבָה וּלְיִרְאָה אֶת־שְׁמֶךָ,
כַּכָּתוּב בְּתוֹרָתֶךָ: וּמָל יהוה אֱלֹהֶיךָ אֶת־לְבָבְךָ,
וְאֶת־לְבַב זַרְעֶךָ, לְאַהֲבָה אֶת־יהוה אֱלֹהֶיךָ
בְּכָל־לְבָבְךָ וּבְכָל־נַפְשְׁךָ
לְמַעַן חַיֶּיךָ.

STRIKE OUR HEART. The custom of striking our heart while confessing our sins is first mentioned in a midrash on Ecclesiastes 7:2 ("the living will lay it to heart"): "Rabbi Meir said: 'Why do people strike their hearts [in remorse for their sins]? Because the heart is the seat and source of sin'" (Ecclesiastes Rabbah).

WE ABUSE אָשַׁמְנוּ. The liturgical list is alphabetical, with the hope that it will help us find our own words to name our transgressions. We might concentrate on one particular failing in our lives.

WE DESTROY שִׁחַתְנוּ. In this bilingual alphabetical list, the English word that represents the letter D means roughly the same as the Hebrew word that represents the letter שׁ (shin). The sin of בַּל תַּשְׁחִית (bal tash·ḥit), "not destroying anything needlessly," was enumerated by the Rabbis among the 613 commandments of the Torah. To destroy any part of creation is to undo God's work, to reject God's gift.

YOU HAVE ACTED FAITHFULLY וְאַתָּה צַדִּיק. Nehemiah 9:33. The prayer of the Levites at the rededication of the Temple, upon the return from the Babylonian Exile.

LET THE WICKED FORSAKE יַעֲזֹב רָשָׁע. Isaiah 55:7.

BLOT OUT AND DISREGARD מְחֵה וְהַעֲבֵר. Both inner and outer parts of the body are mentioned in this prayer. Body and soul are intimately bound, as we seek to behave differently. It is as if we simultaneously ask the Creator to fashion for us a less sinful body as the home for our newly purified self.

CIRCUMCISE וּמָל. Deuteronomy 30:6. Circumcision is an act of completion and perfection. Removing the flesh—our sins, which mask our essential nature—reveals the true function of the heart: to lead us to a life of love, righteousness, and peace.

We Betray

When we sin, we betray our true selves; when we repent, we rediscover the purity of our souls— and find, once again, that God dwells within us. As the 20th-century Jewish thinker and rabbi Joseph Ber Soloveitchik remarked, it is because we ourselves are God's temple that repentance and forgiveness are possible.

Repentance

Penitence can transform all our past sins into spiritual assets. From every error we can derive an important lesson, and from every lowly fall we can derive the inspiration to climb to spiritual heights.

Who Are We

Emotions ebb and flow throughout these holy days. Paradoxes swim in the stream of prayer. At one moment, we believe our deeds to be of such import that the world stands still so that we may take account of them. At another moment, we imagine ourselves so small, so insignificant that our lives are like a passing breath. We are great; we are small. We are the center of the universe; we are nothing at all. And yet, no matter how large we imagine our sins to be, and no matter how puny we imagine ourselves to be, God will never forsake us.

—NINA BETH CARDIN

The Shorter Confession—Ashamnu

Customarily, we each strike our heart as we recite every phrase of this confession.

We abuse, we betray, we are cruel, we destroy, we embitter, we falsify, we gossip, we hate, we insult, we jeer, we kill, we lie, we mock, we neglect, we oppress, we pervert, we quarrel, we rebel, we steal, we transgress, we are unkind, we are violent, we are wicked, we are extremists, we yearn to do evil, we are zealous for bad causes.

Ashamnu, bagadnu, gazalnu, dibbarnu dofi;
he·evinu, v'hirshanu, zadnu, ḥamasnu, tafalnu sheker;
ya·atznu ra, kizzavnu, latznu, maradnu, ni·atznu;
sararnu, avinu, pashanu, tzararnu, kishinu oref;
rashanu, shiḥatnu, ti·avnu, ta·inu, titanu.

We have turned from Your goodly laws and commandments, but it has not profited us. Surely, You are in the right with respect to all that comes upon us, for You have acted faithfully, but we have been in the wrong.

PENITENTIAL PRAYERS BEFORE THE GREAT CONFESSION
One or more of the following penitential prayers may be included.

א

We have done wrong and transgressed, and so we have not triumphed. Inspire our hearts to abandon the path of evil, and hasten our redemption. And so Your prophet Isaiah declared: "Let the wicked forsake their path, and the sinful their design. Let them return to ADONAI, who will show them compassion. Let them return to our God, who will surely forgive them."

ב

Our God and God of our ancestors,
forgive and pardon our sins
[on this Shabbat and] on this Day of Atonement.
Blot out and disregard our sins and errors;
subdue our instincts so that they may serve You.
Bend our stiffness so that we turn to You;
renew our passion for observing Your ordinances.
Circumcise our hearts to love and revere Your name,
as it is written in Your Torah: "Then ADONAI your God
will circumcise your heart and the hearts of your offspring
to love ADONAI your God with all your heart and all your soul,
that you may live."

הַזְּדוֹנוֹת וְהַשְּׁגָגוֹת אַתָּה מַכִּיר. הָרָצוֹן וְהָאֹנֶס,
הַגְּלוּיִים וְהַנִּסְתָּרִים, לְפָנֶיךָ הֵם גְּלוּיִים וִידוּעִים.
מָה אָנוּ, מֶה חַיֵּינוּ, מֶה חַסְדֵּנוּ, מַה צִּדְקֵנוּ,
מַה יִּשְׁעֵנוּ, מַה כֹּחֵנוּ, מַה גְּבוּרָתֵנוּ.
מַה נֹּאמַר לְפָנֶיךָ יהוה אֱלֹהֵינוּ
וֵאלֹהֵי אֲבוֹתֵינוּ [וְאִמּוֹתֵינוּ].
הֲלֹא כָּל־הַגִּבּוֹרִים כְּאַיִן לְפָנֶיךָ,
וְאַנְשֵׁי הַשֵּׁם כְּלֹא הָיוּ,
וַחֲכָמִים כִּבְלִי מַדָּע,
וּנְבוֹנִים כִּבְלִי הַשְׂכֵּל,
כִּי רֹב מַעֲשֵׂיהֶם תֹּהוּ,
וִימֵי חַיֵּיהֶם הֶבֶל לְפָנֶיךָ.
וּמוֹתַר הָאָדָם מִן הַבְּהֵמָה אָיִן,
כִּי הַכֹּל הָבֶל.
מַה־נֹּאמַר לְפָנֶיךָ יוֹשֵׁב מָרוֹם,
וּמַה־נְּסַפֵּר לְפָנֶיךָ שׁוֹכֵן שְׁחָקִים.
הֲלֹא כָּל־נִסְתָּרוֹת וְהַנִּגְלוֹת אַתָּה יוֹדֵעַ.

שִׁמְךָ מֵעוֹלָם עוֹבֵר עַל פֶּשַׁע,
שַׁוְעָתֵנוּ תַאֲזִין בְּעָמְדֵנוּ לְפָנֶיךָ בִּתְפִלָּה.
תַּעֲבוֹר עַל פֶּשַׁע לְעַם שָׁבֵי פֶשַׁע,
תִּמְחֶה פְּשָׁעֵינוּ מִנֶּגֶד עֵינֶיךָ.

אַתָּה יוֹדֵעַ רָזֵי עוֹלָם, וְתַעֲלוּמוֹת סִתְרֵי כָל־חָי.
אַתָּה חוֹפֵשׂ כָּל־חַדְרֵי בָטֶן, וּבוֹחֵן כְּלָיוֹת וָלֵב.
אֵין דָּבָר נֶעְלָם מִמֶּךָּ, וְאֵין נִסְתָּר מִנֶּגֶד עֵינֶיךָ.
וּבְכֵן יְהִי רָצוֹן מִלְּפָנֶיךָ,
יהוה אֱלֹהֵינוּ וֵאלֹהֵי אֲבוֹתֵינוּ [וְאִמּוֹתֵינוּ],
שֶׁתִּסְלַח לָנוּ עַל כָּל־חַטֹּאתֵינוּ,
וְתִמְחַל לָנוּ עַל כָּל־עֲוֹנוֹתֵינוּ,
וּתְכַפֵּר לָנוּ עַל כָּל־פְּשָׁעֵינוּ.

YOU RECOGNIZE אַתָּה מַכִּיר. Our confession is not to enlighten the High Court; God already knows all that we have done. Rather, we recite these words to proclaim in our own voice that we acknowledge and take responsibility for our deeds.

WHAT ARE WE מָה אָנוּ. This prayer, which originated here in the Yom Kippur liturgy, is now included in the daily prayerbook, as part of the introductory morning service throughout the year.

YOU HAVE ALWAYS BEEN KNOWN שִׁמְךָ מֵעוֹלָם. From a double alphabetical acrostic piyyut by Elijah the Elder (ca. 1040). It begins אַתָּה מֵבִין תַּעֲלוּמוֹת לֵב (atah meivin ta·alumot lev), "You understand the secrets of the heart." Almost all rites preserve only these final lines, corresponding to the Hebrew alphabet's last two letters.

YOU KNOW THE MYSTERIES OF THE UNIVERSE אַתָּה יוֹדֵעַ רָזֵי עוֹלָם. The Babylonian Talmud (Yoma 87b) offers various liturgies that fulfill the obligation of confession. This one is offered by Rav (3rd century, Babylonia).

בְּאוֹתוֹ עֶרֶב מוּזָר
מִישֶׁהוּ שָׁאַל:
הַאִם אֶפְשָׁר לְשַׁנּוֹת אֶת
הֶעָבָר?
וְהָאִשָּׁה הַחוֹלָנִית עָנְתָה בְּזַעַף:
הֶעָבָר אֵינֶנּוּ תַּכְשִׁיט
חָתוּם בְּתוֹךְ קֻפְסָה שֶׁל בְּדֹלַח
גַּם אֵינֶנּוּ
נָחָשׁ בְּתוֹךְ צִנְצֶנֶת שֶׁל כֹּהַל -
הֶעָבָר מִתְנוֹעֵעַ
בְּתוֹךְ הַהֹוֶה
וְכַאֲשֶׁר הַהֹוֶה נוֹפֵל לְתוֹךְ בּוֹר
נוֹפֵל אִתּוֹ הֶעָבָר -
כַּאֲשֶׁר הֶעָבָר מַבִּיט הַשָּׁמַיְמָה
זוֹ הֲרָמַת הַחַיִּים כֻּלָּם,
גַּם חַיֵּי עָבָר רָחוֹק עַד מְאֹד.

אַךְ הָאִישׁ הַגַּלְמוּד מִלְמֵל:
וַהֲלֹא הָיָה פַּעַם אַבְרָהָם בַּתֵּבֵל
זֶה שֶׁלֹּא לָקַח לָקַח אֲפִלוּ חוּט
מִנֶּפֶשׁ מוֹלִידוֹ.

In that strange night
someone asked:
Can you change the past?
And the sick woman
angrily responded:
The past is not a piece of
jewelry sealed in a crystal
box nor is it a snake
preserved in a bottle of
formaldehyde—
The past trembles within
the present
when the present falls
into a pit the past goes
with it—
when the past looks
toward heaven all of life
is upraised, even the
distant past.

But the lonely man
muttered:
Did not Abraham once
stride the earth,
he who did not seem
attached to even the cord
of the one who gave him
birth?   —ZELDA
(trans. Edward Feld)

ג

You recognize both our sins and our mistakes, acts of will and
those committed under compulsion; public acts and private
ones are equally revealed and known to You.
What are we? What is our life? Our goodness? Our righteousness? Our achievement? Our power? Our victories?
What shall we say in Your presence,
ADONAI our God and God of our ancestors?
Heroes count as nothing in Your presence,
famous people are as if they never existed,
the wise seem ignorant,
and clever ones as if they lack reason.
The sum of their acts is chaos;
in Your presence the days of their lives are futile.
Human beings have no superiority over beasts;
all life is vanity.

What can we say before You, You who live in the transcendent?
And what can we tell about ourselves to You who dwell on high?
You surely know both the secret and the revealed.

ד

You have always been known as the one who overlooks
transgression.
Hear our cry, as we stand before You, in prayer.
Overlook the transgressions of a people turning from
transgression.
Wipe away our transgressions from Your sight.

ה

You know the mysteries of the universe,
the deepest secrets of everyone alive.
You probe our innermost depths;
You examine our thoughts and feelings.
Nothing escapes You;
nothing is secret from You.
Therefore, may it be Your will, our God and God of our ancestors,
to forgive us for all our sins,
to pardon us for all our iniquities,
and to grant us atonement for all our transgressions.

Customarily, we each strike our heart as we recite the words עַל חֵטְא שֶׁחָטָאנוּ.

עַל חֵטְא שֶׁחָטָאנוּ לְפָנֶיךָ בְּאֹנֶס וּבְרָצוֹן,

וְעַל חֵטְא שֶׁחָטָאנוּ לְפָנֶיךָ בְּאִמּוּץ הַלֵּב.

עַל חֵטְא שֶׁחָטָאנוּ לְפָנֶיךָ בִּבְלִי דָעַת,

וְעַל חֵטְא שֶׁחָטָאנוּ לְפָנֶיךָ בְּבִטּוּי שְׂפָתָיִם.

עַל חֵטְא שֶׁחָטָאנוּ לְפָנֶיךָ בְּגִלּוּי עֲרָיוֹת,

וְעַל חֵטְא שֶׁחָטָאנוּ לְפָנֶיךָ בַּגָּלוּי וּבַסָּתֶר.

עַל חֵטְא שֶׁחָטָאנוּ לְפָנֶיךָ בְּדַעַת וּבְמִרְמָה,

וְעַל חֵטְא שֶׁחָטָאנוּ לְפָנֶיךָ בְּדִבּוּר פֶּה.

עַל חֵטְא שֶׁחָטָאנוּ לְפָנֶיךָ בְּהוֹנָאַת רֵעַ,

וְעַל חֵטְא שֶׁחָטָאנוּ לְפָנֶיךָ בְּהִרְהוֹר הַלֵּב.

עַל חֵטְא שֶׁחָטָאנוּ לְפָנֶיךָ בִּוְעִידַת זְנוּת,

וְעַל חֵטְא שֶׁחָטָאנוּ לְפָנֶיךָ בְּוִדּוּי פֶּה.

עַל חֵטְא שֶׁחָטָאנוּ לְפָנֶיךָ בְּזִלְזוּל הוֹרִים וּמוֹרִים,

וְעַל חֵטְא שֶׁחָטָאנוּ לְפָנֶיךָ בְּזָדוֹן וּבִשְׁגָגָה.

עַל חֵטְא שֶׁחָטָאנוּ לְפָנֶיךָ בְּחֹזֶק יָד,

וְעַל חֵטְא שֶׁחָטָאנוּ לְפָנֶיךָ בְּחִלּוּל הַשֵּׁם.

עַל חֵטְא שֶׁחָטָאנוּ לְפָנֶיךָ בְּטֻמְאַת שְׂפָתָיִם,

וְעַל חֵטְא שֶׁחָטָאנוּ לְפָנֶיךָ בְּטִפְּשׁוּת פֶּה.

◁ עַל חֵטְא שֶׁחָטָאנוּ לְפָנֶיךָ בְּיֵצֶר הָרָע,

וְעַל חֵטְא שֶׁחָטָאנוּ לְפָנֶיךָ בְּיוֹדְעִים וּבְלֹא יוֹדְעִים.

וְעַל כֻּלָּם, אֱלוֹהַּ סְלִיחוֹת, סְלַח לָנוּ, מְחַל לָנוּ, כַּפֶּר־לָנוּ.

עַל חֵטְא שֶׁחָטָאנוּ לְפָנֶיךָ בְּכַחַשׁ וּבְכָזָב,

וְעַל חֵטְא שֶׁחָטָאנוּ לְפָנֶיךָ בְּכַפַּת שֹׁחַד.

עַל חֵטְא שֶׁחָטָאנוּ לְפָנֶיךָ בְּלָצוֹן,

וְעַל חֵטְא שֶׁחָטָאנוּ לְפָנֶיךָ בְּלָשׁוֹן הָרָע.

THE LONGER CONFESSION. Despite the double alphabetical acrostic in which the sins are enumerated, the Al Het is not simply a formal list. The sins it enumerates are the stuff of daily life, and they point to our repeated moral failures. It makes almost no specific reference to violations of the rituals of Judaism. Such infractions as the desecration of Shabbat and festivals, and the failure to abide by the disciplines that invest our daily life with sacred significance, are categorized by the Talmud as "sins between people and God." It is taken for granted that only sins "between one person and another" need to be detailed (Babylonian Talmud, Yoma 86b).

Amidst a community of imperfect humans, we gain the courage to confess our sins to God. Knowing that it is God whom we are facing, we are called to a level of honesty and truthfulness that is greater than any intermediary would demand.

The forty-four lines included in the Al Het are an expansion of the six lines that appear in Saadiah Gaon's prayerbook (10th century), the twelve in Amram Gaon's (9th century), and the twenty-two in Maimonides' (12th century).

DEFRAUDING OTHERS הוֹנָאַת רֵעַ. Or, "oppressing others" (materially or spiritually), for so the Rabbis understood the related verb in Leviticus 19:33.

SPEAKING BADLY OF OTHERS בְּלָשׁוֹן הָרָע. The tradition distinguished between לָשׁוֹן הָרָע (l'shon ha-ra) and רְכִילוּת (r'khilut), both enumerated here. The first is the spreading of truthful yet damaging statements, even without intending any harm. The latter is the telling of outright falsehoods about another.

Embarrassment not only precedes religious commitment; it is the touchstone of religious experience.... What the world needs is a sense of embarrassment. ... We are guilty of misunderstanding the meaning of existence; we are guilty of distorting our goals and misrepresenting our souls. We are better than our assertions, more intricate, more profound than our theories maintain....

What is the truth of being human? The lack of pretension, the acknowledgment of opaqueness, shortsightedness, inadequacy. But truth also demands rising, striving, for the goal is both within and beyond us. The truth of being human is gratitude; its secret is appreciation.

—ABRAHAM JOSHUA HESCHEL

¶ All our secrets are known to You, Adonai, we cannot even fool ourselves. Lying is a vain exercise; help us not even to try.

How could we deceive You, within us, at once forming and knowing our most secret thoughts?

We live in a world of illusion. We each think we are separate, alone, cut off, misunderstood, unwanted. We forget we are part of Your glory, each of us a unique ray of Your light.

As we live our lives, rent asunder, each in our own small world, help us to remember what we often forget: We need one another; we each are part of the other; and in some place, so well known, yet so secret, we may find our true solace in You.

—JULES HARLOW *(adapted)*

The Longer Confession—Al Ḥet

Customarily, we each strike our heart as we recite the words "We have sinned."

We have sinned against You unwillingly and willingly,
And we have sinned against You through hardening our hearts.
We have sinned against You thoughtlessly,
And we have sinned against You in idle chatter.
We have sinned against You through sexual immorality,
And we have sinned against You openly and in private.
We have sinned against You knowingly and deceitfully,
And we have sinned against You by the way we talk.
We have sinned against You by defrauding others,
And we have sinned against You in our innermost thoughts.
We have sinned against You through forbidden trysts,
And we have sinned against You through empty confession.
We have sinned against You by scorning parents and teachers,
And we have sinned against You purposely and by mistake.
We have sinned against You by resorting to violence,
And we have sinned against You by public desecration of Your name.
We have sinned against You through foul speech,
And we have sinned against You through foolish talk.
We have sinned against You through pursuing the impulse to evil,
And we have sinned against You wittingly and unwittingly.

For all these sins, forgiving God, forgive us, pardon us, grant us atonement.
V'al kullam, elo·ah s'liḥot, s'laḥ lanu, m'ḥal lanu, kapper lanu.

We have sinned against You through denial and deceit,
And we have sinned against You by taking bribes.
We have sinned against You by clever cynicism,
And we have sinned against You by speaking badly of others.

עַל חֵטְא שֶׁחָטָאנוּ לְפָנֶיךָ בְּמַשָּׂא וּבְמַתָּן,

וְעַל חֵטְא שֶׁחָטָאנוּ לְפָנֶיךָ בְּמַאֲכָל וּבְמִשְׁתֶּה.

עַל חֵטְא שֶׁחָטָאנוּ לְפָנֶיךָ בְּנֶשֶׁךְ וּבְמַרְבִּית,

וְעַל חֵטְא שֶׁחָטָאנוּ לְפָנֶיךָ בִּנְטִיַּת גָּרוֹן.

עַל חֵטְא שֶׁחָטָאנוּ לְפָנֶיךָ בְּשִׂיחַ שִׂפְתוֹתֵינוּ,

וְעַל חֵטְא שֶׁחָטָאנוּ לְפָנֶיךָ בְּשִׁקּוּר עָיִן.

◁ עַל חֵטְא שֶׁחָטָאנוּ לְפָנֶיךָ בְּעֵינַיִם רָמוֹת,

וְעַל חֵטְא שֶׁחָטָאנוּ לְפָנֶיךָ בְּעַזּוּת מֵצַח.

וְעַל כֻּלָּם, אֱלוֹהַּ סְלִיחוֹת, סְלַח לָנוּ, מְחַל לָנוּ, כַּפֶּר־לָנוּ.

עַל חֵטְא שֶׁחָטָאנוּ לְפָנֶיךָ בִּפְרִיקַת עֹל,

וְעַל חֵטְא שֶׁחָטָאנוּ לְפָנֶיךָ בִּפְלִילוּת.

עַל חֵטְא שֶׁחָטָאנוּ לְפָנֶיךָ בִּצְדִיַּת רֵעַ,

וְעַל חֵטְא שֶׁחָטָאנוּ לְפָנֶיךָ בְּצָרוּת עָיִן.

עַל חֵטְא שֶׁחָטָאנוּ לְפָנֶיךָ בְּקַלּוּת רֹאשׁ,

וְעַל חֵטְא שֶׁחָטָאנוּ לְפָנֶיךָ בְּקַשְׁיוּת עֹרֶף.

עַל חֵטְא שֶׁחָטָאנוּ לְפָנֶיךָ בְּרִיצַת רַגְלַיִם לְהָרַע,

וְעַל חֵטְא שֶׁחָטָאנוּ לְפָנֶיךָ בִּרְכִילוּת.

עַל חֵטְא שֶׁחָטָאנוּ לְפָנֶיךָ בִּשְׁבוּעַת שָׁוְא,

וְעַל חֵטְא שֶׁחָטָאנוּ לְפָנֶיךָ בְּשִׂנְאַת חִנָּם.

◁ עַל חֵטְא שֶׁחָטָאנוּ לְפָנֶיךָ בִּתְשׂוּמֶת־יָד,

וְעַל חֵטְא שֶׁחָטָאנוּ לְפָנֶיךָ בְּתִמְהוֹן לֵבָב.

וְעַל כֻּלָּם, אֱלוֹהַּ סְלִיחוֹת, סְלַח לָנוּ, מְחַל לָנוּ, כַּפֶּר־לָנוּ.

וְעַל מִצְוַת עֲשֵׂה וְעַל מִצְוַת לֹא תַעֲשֶׂה, בֵּין שֶׁיֵּשׁ בָּה קוּם
עֲשֵׂה, וּבֵין שֶׁאֵין בָּה קוּם עֲשֵׂה, אֶת הַגְּלוּיִים לָנוּ וְאֶת־
שֶׁאֵינָם גְּלוּיִים לָנוּ. אֶת־הַגְּלוּיִים לָנוּ כְּבָר אֲמַרְנוּם לְפָנֶיךָ,
וְהוֹדִינוּ לְךָ עֲלֵיהֶם; וְאֶת־שֶׁאֵינָם גְּלוּיִים לָנוּ, לְפָנֶיךָ הֵם
גְּלוּיִים וִידוּעִים, כַּדָּבָר שֶׁנֶּאֱמַר: הַנִּסְתָּרֹת לַיהוה אֱלֹהֵינוּ,
וְהַנִּגְלֹת לָנוּ וּלְבָנֵינוּ עַד עוֹלָם, לַעֲשׂוֹת אֶת־כָּל־דִּבְרֵי
הַתּוֹרָה הַזֹּאת.

CONSPIRATORIAL GLANCES
בְּשִׁקּוּר עָיִן. Many sins in
this section and the next
refer to attitudes we hold in
relationships. The Hebrew
speaks of the way we "see"
the world. We confess to
שִׁקּוּר עָיִן (sikkur ayin),
"conspiratorial glances";
עֵינַיִם רָמוֹת (einayim
ramot), literally "eyes raised
high," which we translate as
"condescension"; צָרוּת עָיִן
(tzarut ayin), "selfishness,"
literally, "narrow vision."

SUPERFICIALITY בְּקַלּוּת
רֹאשׁ. Literally, "lightheadedness." The Rabbis used
this term to refer to a state
of mind in which we are
unable to exercise sound
judgment. Many Jewish
legal authorities oppose the
use of mind-altering drugs
if they deny us the ability to
make reasoned judgments.

SECRET MATTERS הַנִּסְתָּרֹת.
Deuteronomy 29:28.

Enumerating Sins
No list of sins can
ever be complete. By
beginning with *alef* and
ending with *tav*, we
express our intention to
include in our confession
everything of which we
are guilty, from A to Z.
However, this form of the
Al Ḥet does not relieve
us of our individual
obligation to confess the
particular sins of which
we are each personally
responsible. And we
are also called upon to
contemplate those sins
which are especially
prevalent in our world
today.

We have sinned against You by the way we do business,
And we have sinned against You in our eating and drinking.
We have sinned against You by greed and oppressive interest,
And we have sinned against You through arrogance.
We have sinned against You in everyday conversation,
And we have sinned against You through conspiratorial glances.
We have sinned against You through condescension,
And we have sinned against You through ego.

For all these sins, forgiving God, forgive us, pardon us,
grant us atonement.
V'al kullam, elo·ah s'liḥot, s'laḥ lanu, m'ḥal lanu, kapper lanu.

We have sinned against You by throwing off all restraint,
And we have sinned against You by rashly judging others.
We have sinned against You by plotting against others,
And we have sinned against You through selfishness.
We have sinned against You through superficiality,
And we have sinned against You through stubbornness.
We have sinned against You by rushing to do evil,
And we have sinned against You through gossip.
We have sinned against You through empty promises,
And we have sinned against You through baseless hatred.
We have sinned against You by betraying a trust,
And we have sinned against You by succumbing to confusion.

For all these sins, forgiving God, forgive us, pardon us,
grant us atonement.
V'al kullam, elo·ah s'liḥot, s'laḥ lanu, m'ḥal lanu, kapper lanu.

And forgive us the breach of all commandments and prohibitions, whether involving deeds or not, whether known to us or
not. The sins known to us we have acknowledged, and those
unknown to us are surely known to You, as the Torah states:
"Secret matters are the concern of Adonai our God; but in
matters that are revealed, it is for us and our children to apply
all teachings of the Torah till the end of time."

חַנָּה, מָרַת רוּחַ הִתְפַּלְלָה לְפָנֶיךָ, וַיִּמָּלֵא לִבָּהּ בֶּכִי, וְקוֹלָהּ
לֹא יִשָּׁמַע, אַךְ בָּחַנְתָּ אֶת־לִבָּהּ וַתִּפֶן אֵלֶיהָ. עֲנֵה לָנוּ בְּעֵת
בַּקָּשָׁתֵנוּ כְּשֶׁעָנִיתָ לְתַחֲנַת הָאִשָּׁה בְּשִׁילֹה וְנִזְכֶּה לָשִׁיר
כְּמוֹתָהּ: יהוה מַשְׁפִּיל אַף־מְרוֹמֵם, מֵקִים מֵעָפָר דָּל.

וְדָוִד עַבְדְּךָ אָמַר לְפָנֶיךָ: שְׁגִיאוֹת מִי־יָבִין, מִנִּסְתָּרוֹת נַקֵּנִי.
נַקֵּנוּ יהוה אֱלֹהֵינוּ מִכָּל־פְּשָׁעֵינוּ, וְטַהֲרֵנוּ מִכָּל־טֻמְאוֹתֵינוּ,
וּזְרוֹק עָלֵינוּ מַיִם טְהוֹרִים וְטַהֲרֵנוּ, כַּכָּתוּב עַל יַד נְבִיאֶךָ:
וְזָרַקְתִּי עֲלֵיכֶם מַיִם טְהוֹרִים וּטְהַרְתֶּם, מִכֹּל טֻמְאוֹתֵיכֶם
וּמִכָּל־גִּלּוּלֵיכֶם אֲטַהֵר אֶתְכֶם.

וְאַתָּה רַחוּם מְקַבֵּל שָׁבִים, וְעַל הַתְּשׁוּבָה מֵרֹאשׁ
הִבְטַחְתָּנוּ וְעַל הַתְּשׁוּבָה עֵינֵינוּ מְיַחֲלוֹת לָךְ.

אֱלֹהֵינוּ וֵאלֹהֵי אֲבוֹתֵינוּ [וְאִמּוֹתֵינוּ], מְחַל לַעֲוֹנוֹתֵינוּ
בְּיוֹם [הַשַּׁבָּת הַזֶּה וּבְיוֹם] הַכִּפּוּרִים הַזֶּה. מְחֵה וְהַעֲבֵר
פְּשָׁעֵינוּ וְחַטֹּאתֵינוּ מִנֶּגֶד עֵינֶיךָ, כָּאָמוּר: אָנֹכִי אָנֹכִי
הוּא מֹחֶה פְשָׁעֶיךָ לְמַעֲנִי, וְחַטֹּאתֶיךָ לֹא אֶזְכֹּר. וְנֶאֱמַר:
מָחִיתִי כָעָב פְּשָׁעֶיךָ וְכֶעָנָן חַטֹּאתֶיךָ, שׁוּבָה אֵלַי כִּי
גְאַלְתִּיךָ. וְנֶאֱמַר: כִּי־בַיּוֹם הַזֶּה יְכַפֵּר עֲלֵיכֶם לְטַהֵר
אֶתְכֶם מִכֹּל חַטֹּאתֵיכֶם, לִפְנֵי יהוה תִּטְהָרוּ.

אֱלֹהֵינוּ וֵאלֹהֵי אֲבוֹתֵינוּ [וְאִמּוֹתֵינוּ], [רְצֵה בִמְנוּחָתֵנוּ]
קַדְּשֵׁנוּ בְּמִצְוֹתֶיךָ וְתֵן חֶלְקֵנוּ בְּתוֹרָתֶךָ, שַׂבְּעֵנוּ מִטּוּבֶךָ
וְשַׂמְּחֵנוּ בִּישׁוּעָתֶךָ, [וְהַנְחִילֵנוּ יהוה אֱלֹהֵינוּ, בְּאַהֲבָה
וּבְרָצוֹן שַׁבַּת קָדְשֶׁךָ, וְיָנוּחוּ בָהּ יִשְׂרָאֵל, מְקַדְּשֵׁי שְׁמֶךָ]
וְטַהֵר לִבֵּנוּ לְעָבְדְּךָ בֶּאֱמֶת, כִּי אַתָּה סָלְחָן לְיִשְׂרָאֵל
וּמָחֳלָן לְשִׁבְטֵי יְשֻׁרוּן בְּכָל־דּוֹר וָדוֹר, וּמִבַּלְעָדֶיךָ אֵין
לָנוּ מֶלֶךְ מוֹחֵל וְסוֹלֵחַ אֶלָּא אָתָּה. בָּרוּךְ אַתָּה יהוה,
מֶלֶךְ מוֹחֵל וְסוֹלֵחַ לַעֲוֹנוֹתֵינוּ וְלַעֲוֹנוֹת עַמּוֹ בֵּית יִשְׂרָאֵל,
וּמַעֲבִיר אַשְׁמוֹתֵינוּ בְּכָל־שָׁנָה וְשָׁנָה, מֶלֶךְ עַל כָּל־הָאָרֶץ
מְקַדֵּשׁ [הַשַּׁבָּת וְ] יִשְׂרָאֵל וְיוֹם הַכִּפּוּרִים.

HANNAH חַנָּה. Hannah became, for the Rabbis, the model of proper prayer; David, the psalmist, was seen as the master of prayer.

I, SURELY I אָנֹכִי אָנֹכִי. Isaiah 43:25.

I SWEEP ASIDE YOUR SINS LIKE A MIST מָחִיתִי כָעָב פְּשָׁעֶיךָ. Isaiah 44:22.

FOR ON THIS DAY כִּי־בַיּוֹם הַזֶּה. Leviticus 16:30.

YOU FORGIVE אַתָּה סָלְחָן. The grammatical form of the nouns סָלְחָן (solhan) and מָחֳלָן (moholan) indicate an essential personal quality. For example, when one לוֹמֵד (lomed), "studies," until becoming a scholar, one is then called a לַמְדָּן (lamdan). The use of this form reflects the poet's belief that God's forgiving nature is, in fact, God's essence.

Throughout the long
hours of prayer, we speak
of all the reasons why
God should care for
us and forgive us: our
remorse, our atonement,
our acknowledgment
of wrongdoing, God's
own promise of mercy,
God's wish to be known
in the world as loving.
In this prayer, we call on
our association with our
ancestors who were cared
for by God. We subtly
imply that since we are
their children, we have
inherited their spiritual
legacy. In placing our
own prayer in the context
of theirs, perhaps what
is implied as well is that
we seek to live our lives
in accordance with that
which gave them honor.
—NINA BETH CARDIN

What Do I Want?

You know what is for
my good. If I recite my
wants, it is not to remind
You of them, but so that
I may better understand
how great is my depen-
dence on You. If, then,
I ask You for the things
that may not be for my
well-being, it is because I
am ignorant; Your choice
is better than mine and
I submit myself to Your
unalterable decree and
Your supreme direction.
—BAHYA IBN PAKUDA

Hannah, sad and depressed, prayed to You, her heart overflowing with tears, her voice inaudible. But You understood her
heartfelt cry and turned to her. Answer us in our time of need,
as You responded to the plea of the woman in Shiloh, that like
her we may sing: ADONAI "brings down and lifts up, raises up
the poor from the dust of the earth."

Your servant David pleaded before You: "Who can be aware of
error? Cleanse me of my most secret sins." Cleanse us, ADONAI
our God, of all our transgressions; purify us of all our foulness;
pour over us purifying water that we may be cleansed, as the
prophet Ezekiel wrote: "I will sprinkle purifying water upon
you and you shall be cleansed; I will cleanse you of all your
impurities and your idolatries."

You are compassionate, welcoming those who turn back to
You. You have promised, since the dawn of creation, that
repentance would be received. Now our eyes look toward
You, to accept our repentance.

Our God and God of our ancestors, forgive our sins on this
[Shabbat and this] Yom Kippur. Blot out and disregard them,
as the prophet Isaiah says in Your name: "I, surely I, am the
One who wipes away sin, for this is My nature; I will not recall
your errors," and the prophet adds: "I sweep aside your sins like
a mist, and disperse your transgressions like a cloud. Turn back
to Me, for I will redeem you." And in Your Torah it is written:
"For on this day, atonement shall be made for you to purify you
from all your transgressions. In the presence of ADONAI you
shall be pure."

Our God and God of our ancestors: [embrace our rest,] make
us holy through Your mitzvot and let the Torah be our portion. Fill our lives with Your goodness and gladden us with
Your triumph. [ADONAI our God, grant that we inherit Your
holy Shabbat, lovingly and willingly, so that the people Israel,
who sanctify Your name, may find rest on this day.] Purify our
hearts to serve You faithfully, for You forgive the people Israel
and pardon the tribes of Jeshurun in every generation. Beside
You, we have no sovereign who pardons and forgives. *Barukh
atah ADONAI*, sovereign who pardons and forgives our sins and
those of the people, the House of Israel, each year sweeping
away our guilt—ruler of all the earth, who makes [Shabbat,]
the people Israel and the Day of Atonement holy.

melekh al kol ha-aretz, m'kaddeish [ha-shabbat v'] yisra-el

רְצֵה, יהוה אֱלֹהֵינוּ, בְּעַמְּךָ יִשְׂרָאֵל וּבִתְפִלָּתָם, וְהָשֵׁב אֶת־הָעֲבוֹדָה לִדְבִיר בֵּיתֶךָ, [וְאִשֵּׁי יִשְׂרָאֵל] וּתְפִלָּתָם בְּאַהֲבָה תְקַבֵּל בְּרָצוֹן, וּתְהִי לְרָצוֹן תָּמִיד עֲבוֹדַת יִשְׂרָאֵל עַמֶּךָ.

וְתֶחֱזֶינָה עֵינֵינוּ בְּשׁוּבְךָ לְצִיּוֹן בְּרַחֲמִים. בָּרוּךְ אַתָּה יהוה, הַמַּחֲזִיר שְׁכִינָתוֹ לְצִיּוֹן.

While reciting the first words, by custom we remain seated while bowing our head.

Congregation recites:

◊ **מוֹדִים אֲנַחְנוּ לָךְ** שָׁאַתָּה הוּא יהוה אֱלֹהֵינוּ וֵאלֹהֵי אֲבוֹתֵינוּ [וְאִמּוֹתֵינוּ] אֱלֹהֵי כָל־בָּשָׂר, יוֹצְרֵנוּ, יוֹצֵר בְּרֵאשִׁית. בְּרָכוֹת וְהוֹדָאוֹת לְשִׁמְךָ הַגָּדוֹל וְהַקָּדוֹשׁ, עַל שֶׁהֶחֱיִיתָנוּ וְקִיַּמְתָּנוּ. כֵּן תְּחַיֵּנוּ וּתְקַיְּמֵנוּ, וְתֶאֱסוֹף גָּלֻיּוֹתֵינוּ לְחַצְרוֹת קָדְשֶׁךָ, לִשְׁמוֹר חֻקֶּיךָ וְלַעֲשׂוֹת רְצוֹנֶךָ, וּלְעָבְדְּךָ בְּלֵבָב שָׁלֵם, עַל שֶׁאֲנַחְנוּ מוֹדִים לָךְ. בָּרוּךְ אֵל הַהוֹדָאוֹת.

Leader recites:

מוֹדִים אֲנַחְנוּ לָךְ שָׁאַתָּה הוּא יהוה אֱלֹהֵינוּ וֵאלֹהֵי אֲבוֹתֵינוּ [וְאִמּוֹתֵינוּ] לְעוֹלָם וָעֶד, צוּר חַיֵּינוּ מָגֵן יִשְׁעֵנוּ אַתָּה הוּא. לְדוֹר וָדוֹר נוֹדֶה לְּךָ וּנְסַפֵּר תְּהִלָּתֶךָ, עַל חַיֵּינוּ הַמְּסוּרִים בְּיָדֶךָ וְעַל נִשְׁמוֹתֵינוּ הַפְּקוּדוֹת לָךְ, וְעַל נִסֶּיךָ שֶׁבְּכָל־יוֹם עִמָּנוּ וְעַל נִפְלְאוֹתֶיךָ וְטוֹבוֹתֶיךָ שֶׁבְּכָל־עֵת, עֶרֶב וָבֹקֶר וְצָהֳרָיִם. ◁ הַטּוֹב, כִּי לֹא כָלוּ רַחֲמֶיךָ, וְהַמְרַחֵם, כִּי לֹא תַמּוּ חֲסָדֶיךָ, מֵעוֹלָם קִוִּינוּ לָךְ.

וְעַל כֻּלָּם יִתְבָּרַךְ וְיִתְרוֹמַם שִׁמְךָ מַלְכֵּנוּ תָּמִיד לְעוֹלָם וָעֶד.

RESTORE WORSHIP TO YOUR SANCTUARY וְהָשֵׁב אֶת־הָעֲבוֹדָה לִדְבִיר בֵּיתֶךָ. According to the Babylonian Talmud, "Ever since the day when the Temple was destroyed, there has been an iron barrier separating Israel from God" (Berakhot 32b). Each destruction of the Temple in Jerusalem (first by the Babylonians in 586 B.C.E., then by the Romans in 70 C.E.) was a cataclysmic event in early Jewish history. In praying for the restoration of the Temple, we express our wish both for the sense of immediate connection with God that is believed to have characterized the Temple service, and for the common sense of purpose and religious community that was experienced there.

YOUR DIVINE PRESENCE שְׁכִינָתוֹ. The Hebrew word *shekhinah* has been used for centuries to refer to God's immanence, the presence of God that is felt in the world. The word *shekhinah* is grammatically feminine. Accordingly, Jewish mystical tradition has tended to personify as female the Divine Presence, who is known as the Shekhinah.

PROTECTOR OF OUR LIVES צוּר חַיֵּינוּ. God is our source of support and stability.

FROM ONE GENERATION TO THE NEXT לְדוֹר וָדוֹר. After Psalm 79:13. In a world where nations, values, and ideals rise and fall, our relationship with God is a constant truth.

Fifth B'rakhah: The Restoration of Zion

ADONAI our God, embrace Your people Israel and their prayer. Restore worship to Your sanctuary. May the [fiery offerings and] prayers of the people Israel be lovingly accepted by You, and may our service always be pleasing.

Let our eyes behold Your merciful return to Zion. *Barukh atah ADONAI*, who restores Your Divine Presence to Zion.

Sixth B'rakhah: Gratitude for Life and Its Blessings

While reciting the first words, by custom we remain seated while bowing our head.

Leader recites:

We thank You, You who are our God and the God of our ancestors through all time, protector of our lives, shield of our salvation. From one generation to the next we thank You and sing Your praises—

for our lives that are in Your hands,

for our souls that are under Your care,

for Your miracles that accompany us each day,

and for Your wonders and Your gifts that are with us each moment—

evening, morning, and noon. You are the One who is good, whose mercy is never-ending; the One who is compassionate, whose love is unceasing. We have always placed our hope in You.

Congregation recites:

ʃ We thank You for the ability to acknowledge You. You are our God and the God of our ancestors, the God of all flesh, our creator, and the creator of all. We offer praise and blessing to Your holy and great name, for granting us life and for sustaining us. May You continue to grant us life and sustenance. Gather our dispersed to Your holy court-yards, that we may fulfill Your mitzvot and serve You whole-heartedly, carrying out Your will. May God, the source of gratitude, be praised.

For all these blessings may Your name be praised and exalted, our sovereign, always and forever.

אָבִינוּ מַלְכֵּנוּ, זְכֹר רַחֲמֶיךָ וּכְבֹשׁ כַּעַסְךָ, וְכַלֵּה דֶּבֶר וְחֶרֶב וְרָעָב וּשְׁבִי וּמַשְׁחִית וְעָוֹן וְשַׁמָּד וּמַגֵּפָה וּפֶגַע רַע וְכָל־מַחֲלָה, וְכָל־תַּקָּלָה וְכָל־קְטָטָה, וְכָל־מִינֵי פֻרְעָנִיּוֹת וְכָל־גְּזֵרָה רָעָה וְשִׂנְאַת חִנָּם, מֵעָלֵינוּ וּמֵעַל כָּל־בְּנֵי בְרִיתֶךָ.

וּכְתֹב לְחַיִּים טוֹבִים כָּל־בְּנֵי בְרִיתֶךָ.

וְכֹל הַחַיִּים יוֹדוּךָ סֶּלָה, וִיהַלְלוּ אֶת־שִׁמְךָ בֶּאֱמֶת, הָאֵל יְשׁוּעָתֵנוּ וְעֶזְרָתֵנוּ סֶלָה. בָּרוּךְ אַתָּה יהוה, הַטּוֹב שִׁמְךָ וּלְךָ נָאֶה לְהוֹדוֹת.

אֱלֹהֵינוּ וֵאלֹהֵי אֲבוֹתֵינוּ [וְאִמּוֹתֵינוּ], בָּרְכֵנוּ בַּבְּרָכָה הַמְשֻׁלֶּשֶׁת בַּתּוֹרָה הַכְּתוּבָה עַל יְדֵי מֹשֶׁה עַבְדֶּךָ, הָאֲמוּרָה מִפִּי אַהֲרֹן וּבָנָיו, כֹּהֲנִים, עַם קְדוֹשֶׁךָ, כָּאָמוּר:

יְבָרֶכְךָ יהוה וְיִשְׁמְרֶךָ.   **כֵּן יְהִי רָצוֹן.**

יָאֵר יהוה פָּנָיו אֵלֶיךָ וִיחֻנֶּךָּ.   **כֵּן יְהִי רָצוֹן.**

יִשָּׂא יהוה פָּנָיו אֵלֶיךָ וְיָשֵׂם לְךָ שָׁלוֹם.   **כֵּן יְהִי רָצוֹן.**

שִׂים שָׁלוֹם בָּעוֹלָם, טוֹבָה וּבְרָכָה, חֵן וָחֶסֶד וְרַחֲמִים עָלֵינוּ וְעַל כָּל־יִשְׂרָאֵל עַמֶּךָ. בָּרְכֵנוּ אָבִינוּ כֻּלָּנוּ כְּאֶחָד בְּאוֹר פָּנֶיךָ, כִּי בְאוֹר פָּנֶיךָ נָתַתָּ לָּנוּ, יהוה אֱלֹהֵינוּ, תּוֹרַת חַיִּים וְאַהֲבַת חֶסֶד, וּצְדָקָה וּבְרָכָה וְרַחֲמִים וְחַיִּים, וְשָׁלוֹם. וְטוֹב בְּעֵינֶיךָ לְבָרֵךְ אֶת־עַמְּךָ יִשְׂרָאֵל, בְּכָל־עֵת וּבְכָל־שָׁעָה בִּשְׁלוֹמֶךָ.

בְּסֵפֶר חַיִּים, בְּרָכָה וְשָׁלוֹם וּפַרְנָסָה טוֹבָה, נִזָּכֵר וְנִכָּתֵב לְפָנֶיךָ, אֲנַחְנוּ וְכָל־עַמְּךָ בֵּית יִשְׂרָאֵל, לְחַיִּים טוֹבִים וּלְשָׁלוֹם.

בָּרוּךְ אַתָּה יהוה, עוֹשֶׂה הַשָּׁלוֹם.

ON SHABBAT, WE CONTINUE WITH KADDISH SHALEM ON PAGE 390.

AND INSCRIBE וּכְתֹב. This is the third of the four special insertions in the Amidah for the Ten Days of Repentance.

MAY ADONAI BLESS YOU AND PROTECT YOU יְבָרֶכְךָ יהוה וְיִשְׁמְרֶךָ. This blessing (Numbers 6:24–26) is known as Birkat Kohanim, the "Priestly Blessing," as the Torah prescribes that it is to be recited by Aaron and his descendants, the kohanim (priests), to bring God's blessing upon the people Israel. In most synagogues in Israel, this blessing is recited every day. The kohanim, who come to the front of the synagogue after preparing themselves ritually, extend their hands toward the community in a traditional gesture, thus serving as a conduit of blessing. In many synagogues in the Diaspora, the kohanim re-enact this ancient blessing during the Musaf service on High Holy Days and festivals.

GRANT PEACE שִׂים שָׁלוֹם. Generally in the Ashkenazic liturgy, the b'rakhah Sim Shalom is recited only during the morning (Shaharit and Musaf) services, whereas a similar b'rakhah, Shalom Rav ("Grant abundant peace"), is recited instead at afternoon and evening services. However, on fast days such as Yom Kippur, Sim Shalom is said at every service.

The Blessing of Shalom

When the blessing of *shalom* is lacking, however much we have of other blessings—wealth or power, fame or family, even health—these all appear as nothing. But when *shalom* is present, however little else we have somehow seems sufficient.

Shalom means "peace," of course, but it means so much more as well:
wholeness, fullness, and completion;
integrity and perfection;
healing, health, and harmony;
utter tranquility;
loving and being loved;
consummation;
forgiveness and reconciliation;
totality of well-being.

And even all of these together do not spell out sufficiently the meaning of *shalom*. But though we cannot accurately translate or adequately define *shalom*, we can experience it.

—HERSHEL J. MATT

Avinu Malkeinu, remember Your compassion and subdue Your anger. Bring an end to pestilence, sword, and hunger; captivity and destruction, sin and oppression, plague and calamity; every illness, misfortune, and quarrel; all kinds of danger, every evil decree, and causeless hatred. Bring an end to these for us and for all the people of Your covenant.

And inscribe all the people of Your covenant for a good life.
U-kh'tov l'ḥayyim tovim kol b'nei v'ritekha.

May all that lives thank You always, and praise Your name faithfully forever, God of our deliverance and help.
Barukh atah ADONAI, whose name is goodness
and to whom praise is fitting.

Seventh B'rakhah: Prayer for Peace

Our God and God of our ancestors, bless us with the threefold blessing of the Torah written by Moses Your servant, recited by Aaron and his descendants, the *kohanim*, the consecrated priests of Your people:

May ADONAI bless and protect you.
So may it be God's will. Kein y'hi ratzon.
May ADONAI's countenance shine upon you and
grant you kindness. *So may it be God's will. Kein y'hi ratzon.*
May ADONAI's countenance be lifted toward you and
grant you peace. *So may it be God's will. Kein y'hi ratzon.*

Grant peace to the world: goodness and blessing, grace, love, and compassion to us and all the people Israel. Bless us, our creator, united as one in the light of Your countenance; by that light, ADONAI our God, You gave us a guide to life: the love of kindness, righteousness, blessing, compassion, life, and peace. May it please You to bless Your people Israel at every season and at all times with Your gift of peace.

May we and the entire House of Israel be called to mind and inscribed for life, blessing, sustenance, and peace in the Book of Life.
B'seifer ḥayyim b'rakhah v'shalom u-farnasah tovah,
nizzakheir v'nikkateiv l'fanekha, anaḥnu v'khol am'kha beit yisra·el,
l'ḥayyim tovim u-l'shalom.

Barukh atah ADONAI, who brings peace.

ON SHABBAT, WE CONTINUE WITH KADDISH SHALEM ON PAGE 390.

Many congregations omit Avinu Malkeinu at Minḥah, reserving it for Ne·ilah.
We rise as the ark is opened. An alternate version begins on page 244.
Avinu Malkeinu is not recited on Shabbat.

אָבִינוּ מַלְכֵּנוּ! חָטָאנוּ לְפָנֶיךָ.

אָבִינוּ מַלְכֵּנוּ! אֵין לָנוּ מֶלֶךְ אֶלָּא אָתָּה.

אָבִינוּ מַלְכֵּנוּ! עֲשֵׂה עִמָּנוּ לְמַעַן שְׁמֶךָ.

אָבִינוּ מַלְכֵּנוּ! חַדֵּשׁ עָלֵינוּ שָׁנָה טוֹבָה.

אָבִינוּ מַלְכֵּנוּ! בַּטֵּל מֵעָלֵינוּ כָּל־גְּזֵרוֹת קָשׁוֹת.

אָבִינוּ מַלְכֵּנוּ! בַּטֵּל מַחְשְׁבוֹת שׂוֹנְאֵינוּ.

אָבִינוּ מַלְכֵּנוּ! הָפֵר עֲצַת אוֹיְבֵינוּ.

אָבִינוּ מַלְכֵּנוּ! כַּלֵּה כָּל־צַר וּמַשְׂטִין מֵעָלֵינוּ.

אָבִינוּ מַלְכֵּנוּ! כַּלֵּה דֶּבֶר וְחֶרֶב וְרָעָב וּשְׁבִי וּמַשְׁחִית וְעָוֹן
וּשְׁמַד מִבְּנֵי בְרִיתֶךָ.

אָבִינוּ מַלְכֵּנוּ! סְלַח וּמְחַל לְכָל־עֲוֹנוֹתֵינוּ.

אָבִינוּ מַלְכֵּנוּ! מְחֵה וְהַעֲבֵר פְּשָׁעֵינוּ וְחַטֹּאתֵינוּ מִנֶּגֶד עֵינֶיךָ.

After the leader has recited each of these lines, we repeat it:

◁ אָבִינוּ מַלְכֵּנוּ! הַחֲזִירֵנוּ בִּתְשׁוּבָה שְׁלֵמָה לְפָנֶיךָ.

אָבִינוּ מַלְכֵּנוּ! שְׁלַח רְפוּאָה שְׁלֵמָה לְחוֹלֵי עַמֶּךָ.

אָבִינוּ מַלְכֵּנוּ! זָכְרֵנוּ בְּזִכָּרוֹן טוֹב לְפָנֶיךָ.

אָבִינוּ מַלְכֵּנוּ! כָּתְבֵנוּ בְּסֵפֶר חַיִּים טוֹבִים.

אָבִינוּ מַלְכֵּנוּ! כָּתְבֵנוּ בְּסֵפֶר גְּאֻלָּה וִישׁוּעָה.

אָבִינוּ מַלְכֵּנוּ! כָּתְבֵנוּ בְּסֵפֶר פַּרְנָסָה וְכַלְכָּלָה.

אָבִינוּ מַלְכֵּנוּ! כָּתְבֵנוּ בְּסֵפֶר זְכֻיּוֹת.

אָבִינוּ מַלְכֵּנוּ! כָּתְבֵנוּ בְּסֵפֶר סְלִיחָה וּמְחִילָה.

אָבִינוּ מַלְכֵּנוּ! הַצְמַח לָנוּ יְשׁוּעָה בְּקָרוֹב.

אָבִינוּ מַלְכֵּנוּ! הָרֵם קֶרֶן יִשְׂרָאֵל עַמֶּךָ.

אָבִינוּ מַלְכֵּנוּ! הָרֵם קֶרֶן מְשִׁיחֶךָ.

אָבִינוּ מַלְכֵּנוּ! שְׁמַע קוֹלֵנוּ, חוּס וְרַחֵם עָלֵינוּ.

אָבִינוּ מַלְכֵּנוּ! קַבֵּל בְּרַחֲמִים וּבְרָצוֹן אֶת־תְּפִלָּתֵנוּ.

אָבִינוּ מַלְכֵּנוּ! נָא אַל תְּשִׁיבֵנוּ רֵיקָם מִלְּפָנֶיךָ.

אָבִינוּ מַלְכֵּנוּ! זְכוֹר כִּי עָפָר אֲנָחְנוּ.

אָבִינוּ מַלְכֵּנוּ! חֲמוֹל עָלֵינוּ וְעַל עוֹלָלֵינוּ וְטַפֵּנוּ.

אָבִינוּ מַלְכֵּנוּ! עֲשֵׂה לְמַעַן הֲרוּגִים עַל שֵׁם קָדְשֶׁךָ.

אָבִינוּ מַלְכֵּנוּ! עֲשֵׂה לְמַעַן טְבוּחִים עַל יָחוּדֶךָ.

AVINU MALKEINU אָבִינוּ
מַלְכֵּנוּ. The Babylonian Talmud reports: "It once happened that Rabbi Eliezer
led the congregation
and recited twenty-four
b'rakhot, but his prayers
were not answered. Then
Rabbi Akiva followed him
and led the congregation
in prayer, saying, 'Our
father, our sovereign, You
are truly our father. Our
father, our sovereign, we
have no ruler but You. Our
father, our sovereign, we
have sinned before You.
Our father, our sovereign,
have mercy on us. Our
father, our sovereign, do it
for Your name's sake,' and
his prayers were answered"
(Taanit 25b). Generations
have added many more
verses to this prayer. The
verses mentioning the
martyrs were added after
the Crusades.

Avinu Malkeinu was
first introduced as a prayer
for material blessing. It
then took on an added
layer of pleas against
devastation by human
enemies, and finally, special prayers for the High
Holy Days (for instance,
"inscribe us in the Book
of Life").

The image of God as
"father" represents relatedness and closeness; that
of God as Ruler conveys
authority and greater distance. Jewish theology has
always talked of transcendence and immanence,
God as ineffable and God
as close at hand. The ap-
peal here brings together
both aspects of God.

Avinu Malkeinu

Many congregations omit Avinu Malkeinu at Minḥah, reserving it for Ne·ilah. We rise as the ark is opened. An alternate version begins on page 244. Avinu Malkeinu is not recited on Shabbat.

Avinu Malkeinu, we have sinned in Your presence.

Avinu Malkeinu, we have no sovereign but You.

Avinu Malkeinu, act toward us kindly in accord with Your name.

Avinu Malkeinu, make this a good new year for us.

Avinu Malkeinu, annul every harsh decree against us.

Avinu Malkeinu, nullify the designs of our foes.

Avinu Malkeinu, frustrate the plots of our enemies.

Avinu Malkeinu, rid us of every oppressor and adversary.

Avinu Malkeinu, rid Your covenanted people of disease, war, hunger, captivity, and destruction.

Avinu Malkeinu, forgive and pardon all our sins.

Avinu Malkeinu, do not look toward our sins and transgressions; blot them out.

Avinu Malkeinu, return us to Your presence, fully penitent.

Avinu Malkeinu, send complete healing to the sick among Your people.

Avinu Malkeinu, remember us favorably.

Avinu Malkeinu, inscribe us for good in the Book of Life.

Avinu Malkeinu, inscribe us in the Book of Redemption.

Avinu Malkeinu, inscribe us in the Book of Sustenance.

Avinu Malkeinu, inscribe us in the Book of Merit.

Avinu Malkeinu, inscribe us in the Book of Forgiveness.

Avinu malkeinu, haḥazireinu bi-t'shuvah sh'leimah l'fanekha.
Avinu malkeinu, sh'laḥ r'fu·ah sh'leimah l'ḥolei ammekha.
Avinu malkeinu, zokhreinu b'zikkaron tov l'fanekha.
Avinu malkeinu, kotveinu b'seifer ḥayyim tovim.
Avinu malkeinu, kotveinu b'seifer g'ullah vi-shu·ah.
Avinu malkeinu, kotveinu b'seifer parnasah v'khalkalah.
Avinu malkeinu, kotveinu b'seifer z'khuyyot.
Avinu malkeinu, kotveinu b'seifer s'liḥah u-m'ḥilah.

Avinu Malkeinu, cause our salvation to flourish soon.

Avinu Malkeinu, cause Your people Israel to be exalted.

Avinu Malkeinu, raise up Your anointed with strength.

Avinu Malkeinu, hear our voice, be kind, sympathize with us.

Avinu Malkeinu, accept our prayer, willingly and lovingly.

Avinu Malkeinu, do not turn us away empty-handed.

Avinu Malkeinu, remember that we are but dust.

Avinu Malkeinu, have compassion for us, our infants, and our children.

Avinu Malkeinu, do this for the sake of those who were martyred for Your holy name.

Avinu Malkeinu, do this for the sake of those who were slaughtered for their exclusive devotion to You.

אָבִֽינוּ מַלְכֵּֽנוּ! עֲשֵׂה לְמַֽעַן בָּאֵי בָאֵשׁ וּבַמַּֽיִם עַל קִדּוּשׁ שְׁמֶֽךָ.

אָבִֽינוּ מַלְכֵּֽנוּ! עֲשֵׂה לְמַעַנְךָ אִם לֹא לְמַעֲנֵֽנוּ.

אָבִֽינוּ מַלְכֵּֽנוּ! חָנֵּֽנוּ וַעֲנֵֽנוּ, כִּי אֵין בָּֽנוּ מַעֲשִׂים, עֲשֵׂה עִמָּֽנוּ צְדָקָה וָחֶֽסֶד וְהוֹשִׁיעֵֽנוּ.

The ark is closed.

קַדִּישׁ שָׁלֵם

יִתְגַּדַּל וְיִתְקַדַּשׁ שְׁמֵהּ רַבָּא, בְּעָלְמָא דִּי בְרָא, כִרְעוּתֵהּ, וְיַמְלִיךְ מַלְכוּתֵהּ בְּחַיֵּיכוֹן וּבְיוֹמֵיכוֹן וּבְחַיֵּי דְכָל־בֵּית יִשְׂרָאֵל, בַּעֲגָלָא וּבִזְמַן קָרִיב, וְאִמְרוּ אָמֵן.

יְהֵא שְׁמֵהּ רַבָּא מְבָרַךְ לְעָלַם וּלְעָלְמֵי עָלְמַיָּא.

יִתְבָּרַךְ וְיִשְׁתַּבַּח וְיִתְפָּאַר וְיִתְרוֹמַם וְיִתְנַשֵּׂא וְיִתְהַדָּר וְיִתְעַלֶּה וְיִתְהַלָּל שְׁמֵהּ דְּקֻדְשָׁא, **בְּרִיךְ הוּא**, לְעֵֽלָּא לְעֵֽלָּא מִכָּל־בִּרְכָתָא וְשִׁירָתָא תֻּשְׁבְּחָתָא וְנֶחֱמָתָא דַּאֲמִירָן בְּעָלְמָא, וְאִמְרוּ אָמֵן.

תִּתְקַבַּל צְלוֹתְהוֹן וּבָעוּתְהוֹן דְּכָל־יִשְׂרָאֵל קֳדָם אֲבוּהוֹן דִּי בִשְׁמַיָּא, וְאִמְרוּ אָמֵן.

יְהֵא שְׁלָמָא רַבָּא מִן שְׁמַיָּא וְחַיִּים עָלֵֽינוּ וְעַל כָּל־ יִשְׂרָאֵל, וְאִמְרוּ אָמֵן.

עֹשֶׂה שָׁלוֹם בִּמְרוֹמָיו הוּא יַעֲשֶׂה שָׁלוֹם עָלֵֽינוּ וְעַל כָּל־ יִשְׂרָאֵל [וְעַל כָּל־יוֹשְׁבֵי תֵבֵל], וְאִמְרוּ אָמֵן.

KADDISH SHALEM קַדִּישׁ שָׁלֵם is recited at the end of every worship service that features an Amidah. Its distinguishing sentence is the line תִּתְקַבַּל צְלוֹתְהוֹן, "May the prayers . . . of all Israel be accepted."

PEACE . . . HARMONY שְׁלָמָא שָׁלוֹם. Like many traditional Jewish prayers, this one ends with thoughts of peace.

Avinu Malkeinu, do this for the sake of those who went through fire and water to sanctify Your holy name.

Avinu Malkeinu, do this for Your sake if not for ours.
Avinu Malkeinu, have mercy on us, answer us, for our deeds are insufficient, deal with us charitably and lovingly, and redeem us.

Avinu malkeinu, ḥonneinu va-aneinu, ki ein banu ma·asim, aseih immanu tz'dakah va-ḥesed v'hoshi·einu.

The ark is closed.

Kaddish Shalem

May God's great name be exalted and hallowed throughout the created world, as is God's wish. May God's sovereignty soon be established, in your lifetime and in your days, and in the days of all the House of Israel. And respond with: *Amen.*

May God's great name be acknowledged forever and ever!
Y'hei sh'meih rabba m'varakh l'alam u-l'almei almayya.

May the name of the Holy One be acknowledged and celebrated, lauded and worshipped, exalted and honored, extolled and acclaimed—though God, who is blessed, *b'rikh hu*, is truly far beyond all acknowledgment and praise, or any expressions of gratitude or consolation ever spoken in the world. And respond with: *Amen.*

May the prayers and pleas of all Israel be accepted by their creator in heaven. And respond with: *Amen.*

May abundant peace from heaven, and life, come to us and to all Israel. And respond with: *Amen.*

May the One who brings harmony on high, bring harmony to us and to all Israel [and to all who dwell on earth].
And respond with: *Amen.*

Oseh shalom bi-m'romav hu ya·aseh shalom aleinu v'al kol yisra·el [v'al kol yosh'vei teiveil], v'imru amen.

נעילה ליום כיפור   CONCLUDING SERVICE OF YOM KIPPUR

א

מִי יַעֲמֹד חֵטְא אִם תִּשְׁמֹר
וּמִי יָקוּם דִּין אִם תִּגְמֹר
הַסְּלִיחָה עִמְּךָ הִיא סָלַחְתִּי לֵאמֹר
הָרַחֲמִים גַּם לְךָ מִדָּתְךָ לִכְמוֹר.

הֲקִימֵנוּ בְּאוֹר פָּנֶיךָ וְחֶשְׁבּוֹן יִתְמַצֶּה
קִיּוּם מֶרֶדֶת שַׁחַת כֹּפֶר יִמָּצֵא
טֶרֶם נִקְרָא עוֹד דִּגּוּר יֵצֵא
נִדְבוֹת פִּינוּ יהוה נָא רְצֵה.

ב

אֱלֹהַי,
כִּמְהַת נַפְשִׁי
וּמְקוֹרָהּ,
הֲתוּכַל לִסְפֹּג
כָּל-פְּגָמַי?
הֲתוּכַל לְהָכִיל?
כִּי לֹא אוּכַל
עוֹד, בִּלְעָדֶיךָ
לְסָבְכִי.

ג

לֵילוֹת כִּי יַלְבִּינוּ
בְּאֵלֶּה לֵילֵי הַחֲלוֹם הַלְּבָנִים
שֶׁיַּחֲלֹם עוֹלָם עָיֵף,
יָדֹם יַקְשִׁיב הַזְּמַן אֶל-דָּפְקוֹ,
בְּהַרְנִין מַעֲיָנוֹת
רִנַּת עַצְמוּתָם.

וְעָבָר וְעָתִיד יִשְׁתַּלְּמוּ
שַׁלְוַת נְצָחִים בַּהֹוֶה –
בִּדְמוּמִיַּת חַיֶּיךָ
יִשְׁקְטוּ כּוֹכָבִים,
וְרוּחַ מִנְּצָחִים תְּפַכֶּה –
עֵינֶיךָ תִּרְחַבְנָה.

WHO CAN SURVIVE? מִי יַעֲמֹד. This *piyyut*, ascribed to Shlomo ben Yehudah the Babylonian (10th century), is traditionally recited at Ne·ilah. It emphasizes God's quality of compassion and the hope that something new will bear fruit in this coming year. The Hebrew word דִּגּוּר (*diggur*), which we have translated as "a new way of being born," is used to describe the warming of the egg by the mother bird and the hatching of the newborn.

MY GOD אֱלֹהַי. The author, Menachem Lorberbaum, is a contemporary Israeli philosopher and poet.

WHEN NIGHTS GROW WHITE לֵילוֹת כִּי יַלְבִּינוּ. The poet, Avraham Sonne (1883–1950), was born in the Galician city of Przemysl, Poland/Austria. Escaping the Nazi storming of Vienna in 1938, he emigrated to Israel and took the name Avraham ben Yitzḥak.

After a day of fasting and praying, Ne·ilah can be a moment of peaceful listening. What we may arrive at finally, by the end of the day, is a sufficient diminution of self so that we are open to hearing not the buzz of our busy minds but the pulse of the universe. As we become attuned to the natural rhythms of the world, we may emerge from the day with a rediscovered childlike sense of wonder.

The Day's End

The journey through Yom Kippur was a real journey—one to be measured not by what we feel when it is over, but by how we lead our lives in the days and weeks and years afterwards, when the final shofar blast has pierced not only the highest reach of the heavens, but also the deepest reach of our souls.

—JONATHAN MAGONET

Meditations Before Ne·ilah

א

If You were to keep an account of our sins, who could survive?
Who would be vindicated at the end of the day?
Forgiveness is Yours: for You to say, "I have forgiven";
for You to spread out Your quality of compassion.

Raise us up by the light of Your face, find a way
to give us life; do not send us down to the grave.
Before we pray to You once more, may a new way of
being be born.
May these words we utter of own free will be acceptable to You.

—SHLOMO BEN YEHUDAH

ב

My God,
my soul's desire
and its source,
can You absorb
all my faults?
Can You take them in?
For I cannot,
without You,
become untangled.

—MENACHEM LORBERBAUM

ג

WHEN NIGHTS GROW WHITE
In those dreams of white nights
that a tired world will dream,
silently, time will listen for its own pulse
as wellsprings sing
the song of their selves.

Past and future will be fulfilled
in an eternally present peace—
and in the silence of your life
stars will be quiet,
a wind of eternity will blow—
—and your eyes will grow wide.

—AVRAHAM BEN YITZHAK

עַד יוֹם מוֹתוֹ תְּחַכֶּה לּוֹ לִתְשׁוּבָה, לְהַנְטוֹתוֹ לִתְחִיָּה.

אֱנוֹשׁ מַה־יִּזְכֶּה, וּצְבָא דַק לֹא זַכּוּ בְעֵינֶיךָ?

בַּלָּחִים אִם תִּבְעַר הָאֵשׁ, מַה בֶּחָצִיר יָבֵשׁ?

גָּלוּי לְךָ חְשֶׁךְ כְּמוֹ אוֹר, מְשׁוֹטֵט כֹּל בְּעֵין.

דִּירָתְךָ בַּסֵּתֶר, וּגְלוּיוֹת לְךָ כָּל־נִסְתָּרוֹת.

הַדָּן יְחִידִי, וְהוּא בְאֶחָד וּמִי יְשִׁיבֶנּוּ.

וְעַל גּוֹי וְעַל אָדָם יַחַד יִנְטֶה קַו, וְאֵין מִי יַרְשִׁיעַ.

זֹאת יָבִין כָּל־יְצִיר, וְלֹא יַתְעוּ יֵצֶר לַחֲטֹא לְיוֹצֵר.

חִתְּלַת בְּאֵרוֹ, חֲפִירַת בּוֹרוֹ, חֶשְׁבּוֹן בּוֹרְאוֹ.

טָמֵא מִשְּׁאֵרוֹ, וּמְטַמֵּא בְעוֹדוֹ, וּמְטַמֵּא בְמוֹתוֹ.

יְמֵי חַיָּיו תֹּהוּ, וְלֵילוֹתָיו בֹּהוּ, וְעִנְיָנָיו הֶבֶל.

כַּחֲלוֹם מֵהָקִיץ נִדְמָה, בֶּהָלוֹת יְבַעֲתֻהוּ תָמִיד.

לַיְלָה לֹא יִשְׁכַּב, יוֹמָם לֹא יָנוּחַ, עַד יֵרָדַם בַּקֶּבֶר.

מַה־יִּתְאוֹנֵן אָדָם חַי, דַּיּוֹ אֲשֶׁר הוּא חָי.

נוֹלַד לְעָמָל וִיגִיעָה, אַשְׁרָיו אִם יַגִּיעוֹ יְהִי יִגִּיעוֹ בְּדַת אֱמֶת.

סוֹפוֹ עַל רֹאשׁוֹ מוֹכִיחַ, וְלָמָּה יַחֲנִיף?

עוֹד חוֹתָמוֹ מְעִידוּ עַל פָּעֳלוֹ, וּמַה־יִּגְנֹב דָּעַת?

פּוֹעֵל צְדָקוֹת אִם יְהִי, יְלַוְּוּהוּ לְבֵית עוֹלָמוֹ.

צוֹפֶה בְחָכְמָה אִם יְהִי, עִמּוֹ תִתְלוֹנֵן בְּכֵלְחוֹ.

קָצוּף בְּדָמִים וּמִרְמָה אִם יְהִי, חֲרוּצִים יָמָיו.

רְצוֹנוֹ וְחֶפְצוֹ בִּהְיוֹת בְּמוּסָר, יָנוּב בְּשֵׂיבָה טוֹבָה.

◁ שֵׁם טוֹב אִם יִקְנֶה, מִשְּׂמוֹת נְעִימִים אֲשֶׁר יִקְרָא.

תַּחַת כֵּן יוֹם הַמִּיתָה מִיּוֹם לֵידָה הוּטָב.

עַד יוֹם מוֹתוֹ תְּחַכֶּה לּוֹ לִתְשׁוּבָה, לְהַנְטוֹתוֹ לִתְחִיָּה.

UNTIL THE DAY OF DEATH עַד יוֹם מוֹתוֹ. This alphabetical *piyyut* is a meditation on human imperfection and finitude. Ascribed (some believe erroneously) to Meshullam ben Kalonymous (Italy and Germany, 10th–11th centuries), the poem reminds us that Yom Kippur has long been a day for confronting our own mortality—a notion heightened by the wearing of the *kittel* (the white garment that is analogous to burial shrouds).

WHAT MERIT CAN THERE BE TO A HUMAN BEING אֱנוֹשׁ מַה־יִּזְכֶּה. One of the greatest paradoxes of Jewish theology is that God continues to care for us despite our imperfections. This *piyyut* details at length the shortcomings of humanity, remarking that God holds us accountable to a high standard of behavior, but also that God is willing to forgive us when we fail to attain that standard.

YOU ALONE ARE ENTITLED TO JUDGE ALONE הַדָּן יְחִידִי. God may judge alone, but human courts are subject to imperfection. According to the Mishnah (Sanhedrin 1:1) we must have at least three judges, for human beings are influenced by subjective judgments.

OUR SIGNATURE ATTESTS TO OUR HANDIWORK עוֹד חוֹתָמוֹ מְעִידוּ עַל פָּעֳלוֹ. In the classic metaphor of the Book of Life, we ourselves have signed the list of our deeds and misdeeds.

SO THE DAY OF DEATH IS MORE TELLING THAN THE DAY OF BIRTH תַּחַת כֵּן יוֹם הַמִּיתָה מִיּוֹם לֵידָה הוּטָב. It is only the time of our death that allows for a summing up of our lives.

YOU AWAIT OUR REPENTANCE תְּחַכֶּה לּוֹ לִתְשׁוּבָה. One of the major themes of the High Holy Days is that it is never too late to seek repentance. In Ezekiel's words, God declares: "It is not My desire that the wicked shall die, but that the wicked turn from their evil ways and live. Turn back, turn back from your evil ways, House of Israel; why should you die?" (33:11).

ד

UNTIL THE DAY OF DEATH YOU AWAIT OUR REPENTANCE: A PIYYUT
Until the day of death You await our repentance, to turn us toward
true life.
What merit can there be to a human being, when even angels lack
merit in Your sight?
> *If fire ravages even the trees filled with sap, what chance is there
> for dry grass?*
Darkness is bright as light to You who, with Your vision, perceive all.
> *Your own abode is secret, but all our secrets are revealed to You.*
You alone are entitled to judge alone. Who could contradict You?
> *Over individuals and nations alike You render Your decree; who
> can challenge You?*
May impulse not drive us to sin against our creator. May all creatures
understand this:
> *Our origin is the womb; our destiny is the grave; our fate is to give
> a reckoning to our maker.*
We are corrupted by our flesh, are tarnished in our lives, and are
impure in our deaths.
> *Our days are chaotic, our nights are void, our pursuits are fleeting.*
Like startled dreamers, terrors frighten us constantly;
> *never at rest, day or night—until we finally slumber in the grave.*
But why complain? To be living at all is gift enough—
> *Born to labor and toil, happy are we if we labor in the teaching
> of truth.*
Our end proves our nature; why might we flatter ourselves?
> *At life's end, our signature attests to our handiwork; what use
> is deceit?*
Righteous deeds, when we perform them, escort us to the end
of time.
> *Wisdom, when we delve into it, accompanies us even in advanced
> years.*
And wrath, when it leads to bloodshed or deceit, defines our days.
> *If our will and desire is to be ethical, then even in old age we will
> flourish.*
If we acquire good names for ourselves, they are far better than
the sweetest names we are called by others.
> *So the day of death is more telling than the day of birth.*
And until the day of death You await our repentance, to turn us
toward true life.

אַשְׁרֵי יוֹשְׁבֵי בֵיתֶךָ, עוֹד יְהַלְלוּךָ סֶּלָה.
אַשְׁרֵי הָעָם שֶׁכָּכָה לּוֹ, אַשְׁרֵי הָעָם שֶׁיהוה אֱלֹהָיו.

תְּהִלָּה לְדָוִד.

אֲרוֹמִמְךָ אֱלוֹהַי הַמֶּלֶךְ, וַאֲבָרְכָה שִׁמְךָ לְעוֹלָם וָעֶד.
בְּכָל־יוֹם אֲבָרְכֶךָּ, וַאֲהַלְלָה שִׁמְךָ לְעוֹלָם וָעֶד.
גָּדוֹל יהוה וּמְהֻלָּל מְאֹד, וְלִגְדֻלָּתוֹ אֵין חֵקֶר.
דּוֹר לְדוֹר יְשַׁבַּח מַעֲשֶׂיךָ, וּגְבוּרֹתֶיךָ יַגִּידוּ.
הֲדַר כְּבוֹד הוֹדֶךָ, וְדִבְרֵי נִפְלְאֹתֶיךָ אָשִׂיחָה.
וֶעֱזוּז נוֹרְאוֹתֶיךָ יֹאמֵרוּ, וּגְדֻלָּתְךָ אֲסַפְּרֶנָּה.
זֵכֶר רַב־טוּבְךָ יַבִּיעוּ, וְצִדְקָתְךָ יְרַנֵּנוּ.
חַנּוּן וְרַחוּם יהוה, אֶרֶךְ אַפַּיִם וּגְדָל־חָסֶד.
טוֹב־יהוה לַכֹּל, וְרַחֲמָיו עַל־כָּל־מַעֲשָׂיו.
יוֹדוּךָ יהוה כָּל־מַעֲשֶׂיךָ, וַחֲסִידֶיךָ יְבָרְכוּכָה.

NE·ILAH נְעִילָה means "closing," and referred originally to the closing of the gates of the ancient Temple in Jerusalem. It then took on a more spiritual meaning, and was understood to refer to the symbolic closing of the gates of heaven.

On ordinary weekdays there are three services at which we recite the Amidah (Arvit, evening; Shaharit, morning, and Minhah, afternoon). On Shabbat and Festivals we add a fourth (Musaf, literally "addition"). In the Talmud, a fifth service, called Ne·ilah, was added on all fast days. Today, we recite a Ne·ilah service only on Yom Kippur.

Ne·ilah is one of the most moving of all services, bringing this sacred day to a close with poetic additions to the liturgy and unique melodies. It is a worthy parallel to Kol Nidrei, with which the Yom Kippur journey began. (adapted from Reuven Hammer)

JOYOUS ARE THEY אַשְׁרֵי. The afternoon service (Minhah) begins with this psalm every other day of the year, but on Yom Kippur, in the Ashkenazic rite, it is delayed until Ne·ilah.

Psalm 145, which is an alphabetic acrostic, forms the main body of the Ashrei prayer, but it is preceded by two verses beginning with the word ashrei (Psalms 84:5 and 144:15). The first verse notes that we are sitting in God's house, while the second acknowledges the community with whom we pray.

The use of the alphabet is not only a poetic device but also an aid to memory, making the psalm particularly well-suited to public recitation in an era when written texts were rare. It is also a psalm that is obviously designed to be recited by two groups, or perhaps by a leader with the congregation responding. The leader speaks the praise of God and calls upon others to bless God's name as well. The group then responds with statements in which God's qualities are enumerated. (adapted from Reuven Hammer)

Ne·ilah

The sun has begun to set and the holiest day of the year is about to come to a close; we are weak from fasting and tired from a long day of praying. On the one hand, we may be looking forward to resuming our normal lives, confident in our having cleansed ourselves and grateful for the chance to begin again. On the other hand, we are especially conscious of the passing of sacred time, of the spiritual work that remains undone, and of the extent to which we squander opportunities today and throughout the year. The service of Ne·ilah reflects these complicated emotions, containing both joyful expressions of confidence and urgent pleas for just a little more time before the gates close.

Ashrei

The first half of the psalm, through the line beginning with the letter *mem*, praises God's greatness, goodness, and sovereignty in general, abstract terms. There is then a break in the acrostic, with no verse beginning with the letter *nun*. With the very next verse (beginning with the *samekh*) the tone of the psalm shifts markedly, and we recount the very specific, particular ways in which God takes care of God's creatures: supporting those who

(continued)

ASHREI

Joyous are they who dwell in Your house;
they shall praise You forever.

> *Joyous the people who are so favored;*
> *joyous the people whose God is ADONAI.*

PSALM 145
A PSALM OF DAVID.

I exalt You, my God, my sovereign;
I praise Your name, always.

> *Every day I praise You, glorifying Your name, always.*

Great is ADONAI, greatly to be praised,
though God's greatness is unfathomable.

> *One generation praises Your works to another,*
> *telling of Your mighty deeds.*

I would speak of Your majestic glory
and of Your wondrous acts.

> *People speak of Your awe-inspiring deeds;*
> *I, too, shall recount Your greatness.*

They recount Your great goodness,
and sing of Your righteousness.

> *ADONAI is merciful and compassionate,*
> *patient, and abounding in love.*

ADONAI is good to all,
and God's mercy embraces all of creation.

> *All of creation acknowledges You,*
> *and the faithful bless You.*

Ashrei yosh'vei veitekha, od y'hal'lukha selah.
Ashrei ha-am she-kakhah lo, ashrei ha-am she-Adonai elohav.
T'hillah l'david.
Aromim'kha elohai ha-melekh, va-avar'kha shimkha l'olam va-ed.
B'khol yom avar'kheka, va-ahal'lah shimkha l'olam va-ed.
Gadol Adonai u-m'hullal m'od, v'li-g'dullato ein ḥeiker.
Dor l'dor y'shabbaḥ ma-asekha, u-g'vurotekha yaggidu.
Hadar k'vod hodekha, v'divrei nifl'otekha asiḥah.
Ve-ezuz nor'otekha yomeiru, u-g'dullat'kha asap'rennah.
Zeikher rav tuv'kha yabbi·u, v'tzidkat'kha y'ranneinu.
Ḥannun v'raḥum Adonai, erekh appayim u-g'dol ḥased.
Tov Adonai la-kol, v'raḥamav al kol ma·asav.
Yodukha Adonai kol ma·asekha, va-ḥasidekha y'var'khukha.

כְּבוֹד מַלְכוּתְךָ יֹאמֵרוּ, וּגְבוּרָתְךָ יְדַבֵּרוּ.
לְהוֹדִיעַ לִבְנֵי הָאָדָם גְּבוּרֹתָיו, וּכְבוֹד הֲדַר מַלְכוּתוֹ.
מַלְכוּתְךָ מַלְכוּת כָּל־עוֹלָמִים, וּמֶמְשַׁלְתְּךָ בְּכָל־דּוֹר וָדֹר.
סוֹמֵךְ יהוה לְכָל־הַנֹּפְלִים, וְזוֹקֵף לְכָל־הַכְּפוּפִים.
עֵינֵי־כֹל אֵלֶיךָ יְשַׂבֵּרוּ, וְאַתָּה נוֹתֵן לָהֶם אֶת־אָכְלָם בְּעִתּוֹ.
פּוֹתֵחַ אֶת־יָדֶךָ, וּמַשְׂבִּיעַ לְכָל־חַי רָצוֹן.
צַדִּיק יהוה בְּכָל־דְּרָכָיו, וְחָסִיד בְּכָל־מַעֲשָׂיו.
קָרוֹב יהוה לְכָל־קֹרְאָיו, לְכֹל אֲשֶׁר יִקְרָאֻהוּ בֶאֱמֶת.
רְצוֹן־יְרֵאָיו יַעֲשֶׂה, וְאֶת־שַׁוְעָתָם יִשְׁמַע וְיוֹשִׁיעֵם.
שׁוֹמֵר יהוה אֶת־כָּל־אֹהֲבָיו, וְאֵת כָּל־הָרְשָׁעִים יַשְׁמִיד.
◁ תְּהִלַּת יהוה יְדַבֶּר־פִּי,
וִיבָרֵךְ כָּל־בָּשָׂר שֵׁם קָדְשׁוֹ לְעוֹלָם וָעֶד. תהלים קמה

וַאֲנַחְנוּ נְבָרֵךְ יָהּ, מֵעַתָּה וְעַד־עוֹלָם. הַלְלוּ־יָהּ. **WE SHALL PRAISE** וַאֲנַחְנוּ
נְבָרֵךְ יָהּ. Psalm 115:18.

(continued from previous page)
stumble, raising the bowed, giving food to the hungry, and responding to our cries. As the High Holy Day period draws to a close, we too are called to particularize our generalized spiritual longings and to express the contents of our prayers in deeds. The *mem* verse recalls that we have crowned God as Sovereign on Rosh Ha-shanah; now it is up to us to be the agents through whom God's love extends to all created beings in concrete ways. The letter *nun*—missing from the psalm's acrostic—carries the numerical value of fifty. Our tradition associates the number fifty with completeness, but also with the unattainable. The midrash imagines fifty levels of purity and impurity, but we pass through only forty-nine. Similarly, there are fifty gates of wisdom, but even Moses reached only the forty-ninth; the fiftieth gate remained closed even to the greatest of prophets. Perhaps, then, the *nun* verse is not missing but concealed, a reminder of the limits of human understanding and capacity. Even at this moment, after all of our prayers and repentance, we humbly acknowledge the mystery that is ever unknowable, a level of holiness to which we can only aspire.

They speak of the glory of Your sovereignty;
and tell of Your might,
proclaiming to humanity Your mighty deeds,
and the glory of Your majestic sovereignty.
Your sovereignty is eternal,
Your dominion endures through each generation.
ADONAI supports all who falter,
and lifts up all who are bent down.
The eyes of all look hopefully to You,
and You provide them nourishment in due time.
You open Your hand,
satisfying all the living with contentment.
ADONAI is righteous in all that is done, faithful to all creation.
ADONAI is near to all who call, to all who sincerely call.
God fulfills the desire of those who are faithful,
listening to their cries, rescuing them.
ADONAI watches over all those who love the Holy One,
but will destroy all the wicked.
My mouth shall utter praise of ADONAI.
May all that is mortal praise God's name forever and ever.

We shall praise ADONAI now and always. Halleluyah!

K'vod malkhut'kha yomeiru, u-g'vurat'kha y'dabbeiru.
L'hodi·a li-v'nei ha-adam g'vurotav, u-kh'vod hadar malkhuto.
Malkhut'kha malkhut kol olamim, u-memshalt'kha b'khol dor va-dor.
Someikh Adonai l'khol ha-nof'lim, v'zokeif l'khol ha-k'fufim.
Einei khol eilekha y'sabbeiru, v'atah notein lahem et okhlam b'itto.
Potei·ah et yadekha, u-masbi·a l'khol hai ratzon.
Tzaddik Adonai b'khol d'rakhav, v'hasid b'khol ma·asav.
Karov Adonai l'khol kor'av, l'khol asher yikra·uhu ve-emet.
R'tzon y'rei·av ya·aseh, v'et shavatam yishma v'yoshi·eim.
Shomeir Adonai et kol ohavav, v'eit kol ha-r'sha·im yashmid.
T'hillat Adonai y'dabber pi, vi-vareikh kol basar shem kodsho l'olam va·ed.
Va-anahnu n'vareikh Yah, mei-atah v'ad olam. Hal'luyah.

ADONAI HAS ASSURED A REDEEMER וּבָא לְצִיּוֹן. This collection of biblical verses is known as the Kedushah D'sidra, most likely because it was recited after Torah study (sidra, the weekly Torah portion). It is part of the concluding section of the weekday morning service, but is recited at the afternoon service on Shabbat and festivals. In the Ashkenazic rite, it is delayed until Ne·ilah on Yom Kippur, to be certain that Minhah is not prolonged and Ne·ilah can start before sunset.

Kedushah D'sidra consists of four sections: verses of comfort from the prophet Isaiah (59:20–21); a statement of God's holiness (Psalm 22:40), followed by verses of holiness that are included in all versions of the Kedushah of the Amidah (Isaiah 6:3, Ezekiel 3:12, and Exodus 15:18), together with their Aramaic translation (shown here in gray type); verses about God's forgiving nature (1 Chronicles 29:18; Psalms 78:38, 86:5, 119:142; Micah 7:20; Psalms 68:20, 46:8, 84:13, 20:10); and a passage about the truth of Torah (found on the following page), which concludes with additional verses.

Unlike other versions of the Kedushah, this version includes quotations from Ezekiel's description of his personal experience of God. The prayer may be expressing the hope that we too may partake of that profound experience.

(adapted from Reuven Hammer)

וּבָא לְצִיּוֹן גּוֹאֵל וּלְשָׁבֵי פֶשַׁע בְּיַעֲקֹב, נְאֻם יהוה.

וַאֲנִי זֹאת בְּרִיתִי אוֹתָם, אָמַר יהוה, רוּחִי אֲשֶׁר עָלֶיךָ, וּדְבָרַי אֲשֶׁר־שַׂמְתִּי בְּפִיךָ, לֹא־יָמוּשׁוּ מִפִּיךָ וּמִפִּי זַרְעֲךָ וּמִפִּי זֶרַע זַרְעֲךָ, אָמַר יהוה, מֵעַתָּה וְעַד־עוֹלָם.

◁ וְאַתָּה קָדוֹשׁ, יוֹשֵׁב תְּהִלּוֹת יִשְׂרָאֵל.

וְקָרָא זֶה אֶל־זֶה וְאָמַר: קָדוֹשׁ קָדוֹשׁ קָדוֹשׁ יהוה צְבָאוֹת, מְלֹא כָל־הָאָרֶץ כְּבוֹדוֹ. וּמְקַבְּלִין דֵּין מִן דֵּין וְאָמְרִין: קַדִּישׁ בִּשְׁמֵי מְרוֹמָא עִלָּאָה בֵּית שְׁכִינְתֵּהּ, קַדִּישׁ עַל אַרְעָא עוֹבַד גְּבוּרְתֵּהּ, קַדִּישׁ לְעָלַם וּלְעָלְמֵי עָלְמַיָּא, יהוה צְבָאוֹת, מַלְיָא כָל־אַרְעָא זִיו יְקָרֵהּ.

◁ וַתִּשָּׂאֵנִי רוּחַ, וָאֶשְׁמַע אַחֲרַי קוֹל רַעַשׁ גָּדוֹל: בָּרוּךְ כְּבוֹד יהוה מִמְּקוֹמוֹ. וּנְטָלַתְנִי רוּחָא, וְשִׁמְעֵת בַּתְרַי קָל זִיעַ סַגִּיא, דִּמְשַׁבְּחִין וְאָמְרִין: בְּרִיךְ יְקָרָא דַיהוה מֵאֲתַר בֵּית שְׁכִינְתֵּהּ.

◁ יהוה יִמְלֹךְ לְעֹלָם וָעֶד. יהוה מַלְכוּתֵהּ קָאֵם לְעָלַם וּלְעָלְמֵי עָלְמַיָּא.

יהוה אֱלֹהֵי אַבְרָהָם יִצְחָק וְיִשְׂרָאֵל אֲבֹתֵינוּ, שָׁמְרָה־זֹּאת לְעוֹלָם לְיֵצֶר מַחְשְׁבוֹת לְבַב עַמֶּךָ, וְהָכֵן לְבָבָם אֵלֶיךָ.

וְהוּא רַחוּם יְכַפֵּר עָוֹן וְלֹא יַשְׁחִית, וְהִרְבָּה לְהָשִׁיב אַפּוֹ, וְלֹא־יָעִיר כָּל־חֲמָתוֹ.

כִּי אַתָּה אֲדֹנָי טוֹב וְסַלָּח, וְרַב חֶסֶד לְכָל־קֹרְאֶיךָ.

צִדְקָתְךָ צֶדֶק לְעוֹלָם, וְתוֹרָתְךָ אֱמֶת.

תִּתֵּן אֱמֶת לְיַעֲקֹב, חֶסֶד לְאַבְרָהָם, אֲשֶׁר נִשְׁבַּעְתָּ לַאֲבֹתֵינוּ מִימֵי קֶדֶם.

בָּרוּךְ אֲדֹנָי, יוֹם יוֹם יַעֲמָס־לָנוּ, הָאֵל יְשׁוּעָתֵנוּ סֶלָה.

יהוה צְבָאוֹת עִמָּנוּ, מִשְׂגָּב־לָנוּ אֱלֹהֵי יַעֲקֹב סֶלָה.

יהוה צְבָאוֹת, אַשְׁרֵי אָדָם בֹּטֵחַ בָּךְ.

יהוה הוֹשִׁיעָה, הַמֶּלֶךְ יַעֲנֵנוּ בְיוֹם־קָרְאֵנוּ.

ADONAI has assured a redeemer for Zion, for those of the House of
Jacob who turn from sin. ADONAI has said: "This is My covenant
with them: My spirit shall remain with you and with your descen-
dants. My words shall be upon your lips and upon the lips of your
children and your children's children, now and forever."
And You, O Holy One, are enthroned through the praises of the
people Israel.
The angels on high called out one to another: "Holy, holy, holy is
Adonai Tz'va·ot, the whole world is filled with God's glory."
Kadosh, kadosh, kadosh Adonai Tz'va·ot, m'lo khol ha-aretz k'vodo.

They receive sanction from one another, saying: "*Adonai Tz'va·ot* is
holy in the highest heavens, holy on the earth, and holy forever,
throughout all time; the radiance of God's glory fills the whole
world."
Then a wind lifted me up and I heard the sound of a great rushing
behind me, saying: "Praised is ADONAI's glory wherever God
dwells."
Barukh k'vod Adonai mi-m'komo.
ADONAI will reign forever and ever.
Adonai yimlokh l'olam va·ed.

ADONAI, God of our ancestors Abraham, Isaac, and Israel, impress
this always upon Your people, and direct our hearts toward You.
God, being merciful, grants atonement for sin and does not destroy.
Time and again God restrains wrath, refusing to let rage be all-
consuming.
You, ADONAI, are kind and forgiving, loving to all who call upon You.
Your righteousness is everlasting; Your Torah is truth.
You will be faithful to Jacob and merciful to Abraham, fulfilling the
promise You made to our ancestors.
Praised is ADONAI, the God of our deliverance, who sustains us day
after day.
Adonai Tz'va·ot is with us; the God of Jacob is our refuge.
Adonai Tz'va·ot, blessed is the one who trusts in You.
ADONAI, help us; answer us, Sovereign, when we call.

בָּרוּךְ הוּא אֱלֹהֵינוּ, שֶׁבְּרָאָנוּ לִכְבוֹדוֹ, וְהִבְדִּילָנוּ מִן הַתּוֹעִים, וְנָתַן לָנוּ תּוֹרַת אֱמֶת, וְחַיֵּי עוֹלָם נָטַע בְּתוֹכֵנוּ.

הוּא יִפְתַּח לִבֵּנוּ בְּתוֹרָתוֹ וְיָשֵׂם בְּלִבֵּנוּ אַהֲבָתוֹ וְיִרְאָתוֹ, וְלַעֲשׂוֹת רְצוֹנוֹ וּלְעָבְדוֹ בְּלֵבָב שָׁלֵם, לְמַעַן לֹא נִיגַע לָרִיק, וְלֹא נֵלֵד לַבֶּהָלָה.

יְהִי רָצוֹן מִלְּפָנֶיךָ, יהוה אֱלֹהֵינוּ וֵאלֹהֵי אֲבוֹתֵינוּ [וְאִמּוֹתֵינוּ], שֶׁנִּשְׁמֹר חֻקֶּיךָ בָּעוֹלָם הַזֶּה, וְנִזְכֶּה וְנִחְיֶה וְנִרְאֶה, וְנִירַשׁ טוֹבָה וּבְרָכָה, לִשְׁנֵי יְמוֹת הַמָּשִׁיחַ, וּלְחַיֵּי הָעוֹלָם הַבָּא.

לְמַעַן יְזַמֶּרְךָ כָבוֹד וְלֹא יִדֹּם, יהוה אֱלֹהַי לְעוֹלָם אוֹדֶךָּ. בָּרוּךְ הַגֶּבֶר אֲשֶׁר יִבְטַח בַּיהוה, וְהָיָה יהוה מִבְטַחוֹ. בִּטְחוּ בַיהוה עֲדֵי־עַד, כִּי בְּיָהּ יהוה צוּר עוֹלָמִים. ◁ וְיִבְטְחוּ בְךָ יוֹדְעֵי שְׁמֶךָ, כִּי לֹא־עָזַבְתָּ דֹרְשֶׁיךָ יהוה. יהוה חָפֵץ לְמַעַן צִדְקוֹ, יַגְדִּיל תּוֹרָה וְיַאְדִּיר.

חֲצִי קַדִּישׁ

יִתְגַּדַּל וְיִתְקַדַּשׁ שְׁמֵהּ רַבָּא, בְּעָלְמָא דִי בְרָא, כִּרְעוּתֵהּ, וְיַמְלִיךְ מַלְכוּתֵהּ בְּחַיֵּיכוֹן וּבְיוֹמֵיכוֹן וּבְחַיֵּי דְכָל־בֵּית יִשְׂרָאֵל, בַּעֲגָלָא וּבִזְמַן קָרִיב, וְאִמְרוּ אָמֵן.

יְהֵא שְׁמֵהּ רַבָּא מְבָרַךְ לְעָלַם וּלְעָלְמֵי עָלְמַיָּא.

יִתְבָּרַךְ וְיִשְׁתַּבַּח וְיִתְפָּאַר וְיִתְרוֹמַם וְיִתְנַשֵּׂא וְיִתְהַדָּר וְיִתְעַלֶּה וְיִתְהַלָּל שְׁמֵהּ דְּקֻדְשָׁא, בְּרִיךְ הוּא, לְעֵלָּא לְעֵלָּא מִכָּל־בִּרְכָתָא וְשִׁירָתָא תֻּשְׁבְּחָתָא וְנֶחֱמָתָא דַּאֲמִירָן בְּעָלְמָא, וְאִמְרוּ אָמֵן.

PRAISED IS OUR GOD בָּרוּךְ הוּא אֱלֹהֵינוּ. This sentence begins the prayerful ending of this passage. The phrase "not labor in vain, nor shall our children suffer confusion" is taken from Isaiah 65:23, but in its context here it may also be understood as "that we may not act meaninglessly or sow confusion."

THUS I WILL SING לְמַעַן יְזַמֶּרְךָ. Psalm 30:13.

BLESSED IS THE ONE בָּרוּךְ הַגֶּבֶר. Jeremiah 17:7.

TRUST IN ADONAI בִּטְחוּ בַיהוה. Isaiah 26:4.

THOSE WHO LOVE YOU וְיִבְטְחוּ בְךָ. Psalm 9:11.

ADONAI . . . EXALTS יהוה חָפֵץ. Isaiah 42:21.

MAY GOD'S GREAT NAME יְהֵא שְׁמֵהּ. Whenever the people Israel enter the synagogue and house of study and proclaim: יְהֵא שְׁמֵהּ רַבָּא מְבָרַךְ לְעָלַם וּלְעָלְמֵי עָלְמַיָּא (Y'hei sh'meih rabba m'varakh l'alam u-l'almei almayya), "May God's great name be acknowledged forever and ever," the Holy One nods and says: "Happy is the sovereign in whose house such praise is spoken" (Babylonian Talmud, Berakhot 3a).

Praised is our God who created us for the divine glory,
setting us apart from those who go astray, giving us the
Torah, which is truth, and planting within us eternal life.
May God open our hearts to the Torah—inspiring us to
love, revere, and wholeheartedly serve God. Thus shall we
not labor in vain, nor shall our children suffer confusion.
ADONAI, our God and God of our ancestors, may we fulfill
Your precepts in this world, to be worthy of happiness and
blessing in the messianic era and in the world to come.
Thus I will sing Your praise unceasingly; thus I will exalt
You, ADONAI my God, forever.
Blessed is the one who trusts in ADONAI.
Trust in ADONAI forever and ever; ADONAI is an unfailing
stronghold.
Those who love You trust in You; You never forsake those
who seek You, ADONAI.
ADONAI, through divine righteousness, exalts the Torah
with greatness and glory.

Ḥatzi Kaddish

May God's great name be exalted and hallowed throughout
the created world, as is God's wish. May God's sovereignty
soon be established, in your lifetime and in your days, and
in the days of all the House of Israel. And respond with:
Amen.

May God's great name be acknowledged forever and ever!
Y'hei sh'meih rabba m'varakh l'alam u-l'almei almayya.

May the name of the Holy One be acknowledged and
celebrated, lauded and worshipped, exalted and honored,
extolled and acclaimed—though God, who is blessed,
b'rikh hu, is truly far beyond all acknowledgment and
praise, or any expressions of gratitude or consolation ever
spoken in the world. And respond with: *Amen.*

Before the Amidah begins, it is customary to take three steps backward, as if we are leaving our familiar surroundings, and then three steps forward, as we approach God's presence.

When reciting the words בָּרוּךְ אַתָּה on this page, we customarily bend the knees and bow, standing up straight by the time we reach the word יהוה. We repeat these motions at the end of the first b'rakhah when we come to the words "barukh atah Adonai." The sign ֻ indicates the places to bow.

אֲדֹנָי שְׂפָתַי תִּפְתָּח, וּפִי יַגִּיד תְּהִלָּתֶךָ.

GOD OF ABRAHAM, GOD OF ISAAC, AND GOD OF JACOB אֱלֹהֵי אַבְרָהָם, אֱלֹהֵי יִצְחָק, וֵאלֹהֵי יַעֲקֹב. God begins the conversation with Moses at the burning bush with this self-description. We understand the world of prayer, first of all, through the experience of those who came before us—both in our immediate and our ancient past. Perhaps the quotation of these words expresses the hope that we too might feel the presence of God. Moses saw only a burning bush, but his inner ear heard so much more.

SEAL US וְחָתְמֵנוּ. Since Rosh Hashanah, we have included this and three other insertions in every Amidah every day. Until Ne·ilah, we have asked God to inscribe us in the Book of Life (וְכָתְבֵנוּ בְּסֵפֶר הַחַיִּים); now, we ask God to seal us in it (וְחָתְמֵנוּ).

Version with Patriarchs and Matriarchs:

ֻ בָּרוּךְ אַתָּה יהוה,
אֱלֹהֵינוּ וֵאלֹהֵי אֲבוֹתֵינוּ
[וְאִמּוֹתֵינוּ], אֱלֹהֵי אַבְרָהָם,
אֱלֹהֵי יִצְחָק, וֵאלֹהֵי יַעֲקֹב,
אֱלֹהֵי שָׂרָה, אֱלֹהֵי רִבְקָה,
אֱלֹהֵי רָחֵל, וֵאלֹהֵי לֵאָה,
הָאֵל הַגָּדוֹל הַגִּבּוֹר וְהַנּוֹרָא,
אֵל עֶלְיוֹן, גּוֹמֵל חֲסָדִים
טוֹבִים, וְקוֹנֵה הַכֹּל, וְזוֹכֵר
חַסְדֵי אָבוֹת [וְאִמָּהוֹת],
וּמֵבִיא גוֹאֵל לִבְנֵי בְנֵיהֶם
לְמַעַן שְׁמוֹ בְּאַהֲבָה.

Version with Patriarchs:

ֻ בָּרוּךְ אַתָּה יהוה,
אֱלֹהֵינוּ וֵאלֹהֵי אֲבוֹתֵינוּ,
אֱלֹהֵי אַבְרָהָם, אֱלֹהֵי
יִצְחָק, וֵאלֹהֵי יַעֲקֹב, הָאֵל
הַגָּדוֹל הַגִּבּוֹר וְהַנּוֹרָא,
אֵל עֶלְיוֹן, גּוֹמֵל חֲסָדִים
טוֹבִים, וְקוֹנֵה הַכֹּל, וְזוֹכֵר
חַסְדֵי אָבוֹת, וּמֵבִיא גוֹאֵל
לִבְנֵי בְנֵיהֶם לְמַעַן שְׁמוֹ
בְּאַהֲבָה.

זָכְרֵנוּ לְחַיִּים,
מֶלֶךְ חָפֵץ בַּחַיִּים,
וְחָתְמֵנוּ בְּסֵפֶר הַחַיִּים,
לְמַעַנְךָ אֱלֹהִים חַיִּים.

THE SILENT AMIDAH

An Alternate
Rendering

*Some may want to engage
in silent prayer by read-
ing through the prayers
and meditations in this
column through page 406.
Renderings of the opening
and closing b'rakhot are
by André Ungar. Medita-
tions on the themes of the
day are by other authors.*

Help me, O God,
to pray. Our ances-
tors worshipped You.
Abraham and Sarah,
Rebecca and Isaac,
Jacob, Rachel, and Leah
stood in awe before You.
We, too, reach for You,
infinite, awe-inspiring,
transcendent God,
source of all being,
whose truth shines
through our ancestors'
lives. We, their distant
descendants, draw
strength from their lives
and from Your redeem-
ing love. Be our help
and our shield, as You
were theirs. We praise
You, God, Guardian of
Abraham.

O sovereign God who
    delights in life,
make our lives worthy to
    be remembered.
Out of Your love for us,
    O living God,
Seal our names in the
    Ledger of Life.

*Before the Amidah begins, it is customary to take three steps backward, as if we
are leaving our familiar surroundings, and then three steps forward, as we approach God's presence.*

   *When reciting the words "barukh atah" on this page, we customarily bend the
knees and bow, standing up straight by the time we reach the word "Adonai." We
repeat these motions at the end of the first b'rakhah when we come to the words
"barukh atah Adonai." The sign ʄ indicates the places to bow.*

ADONAI, open my lips that my mouth may speak Your praise.

First B'rakhah: Our Ancestors

Version with Patriarchs:

ʄ *Barukh atah* ADONAI,
our God and God of our
    ancestors,
God of Abraham, God of
    Isaac, and God of Jacob,
great, mighty, awe-inspiring,
    transcendent God,
who acts with lovingkindness
and creates all things,
who remembers the loving
    deeds of our ancestors,
and who will send a redeemer
    to their children's children
    with love
for the sake of divine honor.

Version with Patriarchs and Matriarchs:

ʄ *Barukh atah* ADONAI,
our God and God of our
    ancestors,
God of Abraham, God of
    Isaac, and God of Jacob,
God of Sarah, God of
    Rebecca, God of Rachel,
    and God of Leah,
great, mighty, awe-inspiring,
    transcendent God,
who acts with lovingkindness
and creates all things,
who remembers the loving
    deeds of our ancestors,
and who will send a redeemer
    to their children's children
    with love
for the sake of divine honor.

Remember us for life,
Sovereign who delights in life,
and seal us in the Book of Life,
for Your sake, God of life.

Version with Patriarchs and Matriarchs: *Version with Patriarchs:*

מֶֽלֶךְ עוֹזֵר וּפוֹקֵד
וּמוֹשִֽׁיעַ וּמָגֵן.
♦ בָּרוּךְ אַתָּה יהוה, מָגֵן
אַבְרָהָם וּפוֹקֵד שָׂרָה.

מֶֽלֶךְ עוֹזֵר וּמוֹשִֽׁיעַ וּמָגֵן.
♦ בָּרוּךְ אַתָּה יהוה, מָגֵן
אַבְרָהָם.

אַתָּה גִבּוֹר לְעוֹלָם אֲדֹנָי, מְחַיֵּה מֵתִים אַתָּה,
רַב לְהוֹשִֽׁיעַ.

מְכַלְכֵּל חַיִּים בְּחֶֽסֶד, מְחַיֵּה מֵתִים בְּרַחֲמִים רַבִּים,
סוֹמֵךְ נוֹפְלִים, וְרוֹפֵא חוֹלִים, וּמַתִּיר אֲסוּרִים, וּמְקַיֵּם
אֱמוּנָתוֹ לִישֵׁנֵי עָפָר. מִי כָמֽוֹךָ בַּֽעַל גְּבוּרוֹת וּמִי דּֽוֹמֶה
לָּךְ, מֶֽלֶךְ מֵמִית וּמְחַיֶּה וּמַצְמִֽיחַ יְשׁוּעָה.

מִי כָמֽוֹךָ אַב הָרַחֲמִים, זוֹכֵר יְצוּרָיו לְחַיִּים בְּרַחֲמִים.

וְנֶאֱמָן אַתָּה לְהַחֲיוֹת מֵתִים. בָּרוּךְ אַתָּה יהוה,
מְחַיֵּה הַמֵּתִים.

אַתָּה קָדוֹשׁ וְשִׁמְךָ קָדוֹשׁ, וּקְדוֹשִׁים בְּכָל־יוֹם
יְהַלְלֽוּךָ, סֶּֽלָה.

MIGHTY FOREVER אַתָּה גִבּוֹר. This *b'rakhah*, which describes God's presence and activity in the world, centers on the kindness and care of God for the incapacitated—even the dead are in God's care.

GIVE LIFE TO THE DEAD מְחַיֵּה מֵתִים. To be sure, the primary meaning of this phrase was understood to refer to the afterlife, but the Rabbis also understood that the phrase could refer to a spiritual revival in this world as well. Fasting is a "taste of death," and as we end Yom Kippur, it is hoped that we will feel "revived."

WHO IS LIKE YOU, SOURCE OF COMPASSION מִי כָמֽוֹךָ אַב הָרַחֲמִים. A second insertion at each of the services in the High Holy Day season. The gift of life is an expression of God's kindness.

Your power sustains the universe. You breathe life into dead matter. With compassion You care for all who live. Your limitless love lets life triumph over death, heals the sick, upholds the exhausted, frees the enslaved, keeps faith even with the dead. Who is like You, God of splendor and power incomparable?

As a tender parent, You nurture our souls that we may grow into a life of compassion.

You govern both life and death; Your presence brings our souls to blossom. We praise You, God, who wrests life from death.

Sacred are You, sacred Your mystery. Seekers of holiness worship You all their lives.

Let all creation stand in awe of You;
let all humankind sense Your mystery.
May all people be united in doing Your will whole-heartedly.
We know that You judge those who govern,
that ultimate power is Yours alone,
that Your care embraces all Your creatures.

Make us all people of honor.
Smile on all who serve You.
Give hope to those who seek You,
courage to those who await the fulfillment of the messianic dream,
soon in our lifetime.

Version with Patriarchs:

You are the sovereign who helps and saves and shields.

ℓ *Barukh atah* ADONAI, God of our ancestors, Shield of Abraham.

Version with Patriarchs and Matriarchs:

You are the sovereign who helps and guards, saves and shields.

ℓ *Barukh atah* ADONAI, God of our ancestors, Shield of Abraham and Guardian of Sarah.

Second B'rakhah: God's Saving Care

You are mighty forever, ADONAI—
You give life to the dead;
great is Your saving power.

You sustain the living through love,
    and with great mercy give life to the dead.
You support the falling,
    heal the sick,
    loosen the chains of the bound,
    and keep faith with those who sleep in the dust.
Who is like You, Almighty,
    and who can be compared to You?—
Sovereign, who brings death and life,
    and causes salvation to flourish.

Who is like You, source of compassion,
    who remembers with compassion Your creatures for life?

You are faithful in bringing life to the dead.
Barukh atah ADONAI, who gives life to the dead.

Third B'rakhah: God's Holiness

Holy are You and holy is Your name;
    holy ones praise You each day.

וּבְכֵן תֵּן פַּחְדְּךָ יהוה אֱלֹהֵינוּ עַל כָּל־מַעֲשֶׂיךָ
וְאֵימָתְךָ עַל כָּל־מַה־שֶּׁבָּרָאתָ,
וְיִירָאוּךָ כָּל־הַמַּעֲשִׂים
וְיִשְׁתַּחֲווּ לְפָנֶיךָ כָּל־הַבְּרוּאִים,
וְיֵעָשׂוּ כֻלָּם אֲגֻדָּה אֶחָת לַעֲשׂוֹת רְצוֹנְךָ בְּלֵבָב שָׁלֵם,
כְּמוֹ שֶׁיָּדַעְנוּ יהוה אֱלֹהֵינוּ שֶׁהַשִּׁלְטוֹן לְפָנֶיךָ,
עֹז בְּיָדְךָ וּגְבוּרָה בִּימִינֶךָ,
וְשִׁמְךָ נוֹרָא עַל כָּל־מַה־שֶּׁבָּרָאתָ.

וּבְכֵן תֵּן כָּבוֹד יהוה לְעַמֶּךָ,
תְּהִלָּה לִירֵאֶיךָ וְתִקְוָה לְדוֹרְשֶׁיךָ,
וּפִתְחוֹן פֶּה לַמְיַחֲלִים לָךְ,
שִׂמְחָה לְאַרְצֶךָ וְשָׂשׂוֹן לְעִירֶךָ
וּצְמִיחַת קֶרֶן לְדָוִד עַבְדֶּךָ,
וַעֲרִיכַת נֵר לְבֶן־יִשַׁי מְשִׁיחֶךָ, בִּמְהֵרָה בְיָמֵינוּ.

וּבְכֵן צַדִּיקִים יִרְאוּ וְיִשְׂמָחוּ
וִישָׁרִים יַעֲלֹזוּ,
וַחֲסִידִים בְּרִנָּה יָגִילוּ,
וְעוֹלָתָה תִּקְפָּץ־פִּיהָ
וְכָל־הָרִשְׁעָה כֻּלָּהּ כְּעָשָׁן תִּכְלֶה,
כִּי תַעֲבִיר מֶמְשֶׁלֶת זָדוֹן מִן הָאָרֶץ.

וְתִמְלֹךְ אַתָּה יהוה לְבַדֶּךָ עַל כָּל־מַעֲשֶׂיךָ,
בְּהַר צִיּוֹן מִשְׁכַּן כְּבוֹדֶךָ
וּבִירוּשָׁלַיִם עִיר קָדְשֶׁךָ,
כַּכָּתוּב בְּדִבְרֵי קָדְשֶׁךָ:
יִמְלֹךְ יהוה לְעוֹלָם, אֱלֹהַיִךְ צִיּוֹן לְדֹר וָדֹר, הַלְלוּ־יָהּ.

קָדוֹשׁ אַתָּה וְנוֹרָא שְׁמֶךָ, וְאֵין אֱלוֹהַּ מִבַּלְעָדֶיךָ,
כַּכָּתוּב: וַיִּגְבַּהּ יהוה צְבָאוֹת בַּמִּשְׁפָּט, וְהָאֵל הַקָּדוֹשׁ
נִקְדַּשׁ בִּצְדָקָה. בָּרוּךְ אַתָּה יהוה, הַמֶּלֶךְ הַקָּדוֹשׁ.

U-V'KHEIN וּבְכֵן. These three paragraphs, which are introduced by the same word, וּבְכֵן (u-v'khein), are ascribed by many scholars to the 2nd or 3rd century, and may constitute the earliest poetic additions to the Amidah.

Stages of redemption are described in this series of prayers. The first paragraph implores God to cause the entire world to live with reverence for God. The next paragraph discusses not the universal, but the particular: the return of the people Israel to its land (and specifically to Jerusalem) and the kingship of David. The third paragraph describes the rejoicing that will come to the righteous "when You remove the tyranny of arrogance from the earth" and God will rule alone over the entire world from Zion and Jerusalem. *(adapted from Reuven Hammer)*

ADONAI WILL REIGN יִמְלֹךְ. In the context of this prayer, the words from Psalm 146:10 express a messianic hope.

ADONAI TZ'VA·OT WILL BE EXALTED וַיִּגְבַּהּ יהוה צְבָאוֹת. Isaiah 5:16. This verse, with which the b'rakhah concludes, highlights the themes of this b'rakhah, as it has been expanded on the High Holy Days: We await the day when earthly powers become subservient to the divine ideals of justice and righteousness.

May the righteous witness it and be happy,
may good people be filled with joy—
when at last all jeering stops and evil evaporates,
when the reign of violence vanishes from Earth.

And You, You alone, will rule over all Your creation
from Mount Zion, Your glorious dwelling place,
from Jerusalem, Your holy city,
as sacred Scripture proclaims:
"God will reign throughout the world,
Your God, O Zion, forever and ever.
Halleluyah!"

Sacred are You, sacred Your mystery. Seekers of holiness worship You all their lives.
We praise You, God, ultimate sacred mystery.

U-v'khein—ADONAI our God,
instill Your awe in all You have made,
and fear of You in all You have created,
so that all You have fashioned revere You,
all You have created bow in recognition,
and all be bound together, carrying out Your will wholeheartedly.
For we know that true sovereignty is Yours,
power and strength are in Your hands,
and Your name is to be revered beyond any of Your creations.

U-v'khein—Bestow honor to Your people, ADONAI,
praise to those who revere You,
hope to those who seek You,
recognition to those who await You,
joy to Your land, and gladness to Your city.
May the light of David, Your servant, dawn,
and the lamp of the son of Jesse, Your anointed, be kindled speedily in our day.

U-v'khein—The righteous, beholding this, will rejoice,
the upright will be glad,
the pious will celebrate with song,
evil will be silenced,
all wickedness will disappear like smoke,
when You remove the tyranny of arrogance from the earth.

You alone, ADONAI, will rule all Your creation,
from Mount Zion, the dwelling-place of Your glory,
and from Jerusalem, Your holy city.
As it is written in the Book of Psalms:
"ADONAI will reign forever;
your God, O Zion, from generation to generation. Halleluyah!"

You are holy, and Your name is revered,
    for there is no God but You.
As Your prophet Isaiah wrote: "*Adonai Tz'va·ot* will be exalted through justice, the holy God sanctified through righteousness."
Barukh atah ADONAI, the Holy Sovereign.

אַתָּה בְחַרְתָּנוּ מִכָּל־הָעַמִּים,
אָהַבְתָּ אוֹתָנוּ וְרָצִיתָ בָּנוּ,
וְרוֹמַמְתָּנוּ מִכָּל־הַלְּשׁוֹנוֹת,
וְקִדַּשְׁתָּנוּ בְּמִצְוֹתֶיךָ,
וְקֵרַבְתָּנוּ מַלְכֵּנוּ לַעֲבוֹדָתֶךָ,
וְשִׁמְךָ הַגָּדוֹל וְהַקָּדוֹשׁ עָלֵינוּ קָרָאתָ.

וַתִּתֶּן־לָנוּ, יְהֹוָה אֱלֹהֵינוּ, בְּאַהֲבָה אֶת־יוֹם [הַשַּׁבָּת הַזֶּה
לִקְדֻשָּׁה וְלִמְנוּחָה וְאֶת־יוֹם] הַכִּפֻּרִים הַזֶּה, לִמְחִילָה
וְלִסְלִיחָה וּלְכַפָּרָה, וְלִמְחָל־בּוֹ אֶת־כָּל־עֲוֹנוֹתֵינוּ
[בְּאַהֲבָה] מִקְרָא קֹדֶשׁ, זֵכֶר לִיצִיאַת מִצְרָיִם.

אֱלֹהֵינוּ וֵאלֹהֵי אֲבוֹתֵינוּ [וְאִמּוֹתֵינוּ], יַעֲלֶה וְיָבֹא, וְיַגִּיעַ
וְיֵרָאֶה, וְיֵרָצֶה וְיִשָּׁמַע, וְיִפָּקֵד וְיִזָּכֵר זִכְרוֹנֵנוּ וּפִקְדוֹנֵנוּ,
וְזִכְרוֹן אֲבוֹתֵינוּ [וְאִמּוֹתֵינוּ], וְזִכְרוֹן מָשִׁיחַ בֶּן־דָּוִד
עַבְדֶּךָ, וְזִכְרוֹן יְרוּשָׁלַיִם עִיר קָדְשֶׁךָ, וְזִכְרוֹן כָּל־עַמְּךָ בֵּית
יִשְׂרָאֵל לְפָנֶיךָ לִפְלֵיטָה לְטוֹבָה, לְחֵן וּלְחֶסֶד וּלְרַחֲמִים,
לְחַיִּים וּלְשָׁלוֹם, בְּיוֹם הַכִּפֻּרִים הַזֶּה.
זָכְרֵנוּ יְהֹוָה אֱלֹהֵינוּ בּוֹ לְטוֹבָה,
וּפָקְדֵנוּ בוֹ לִבְרָכָה,
וְהוֹשִׁיעֵנוּ בוֹ לְחַיִּים,
וּבִדְבַר יְשׁוּעָה וְרַחֲמִים חוּס וְחָנֵּנוּ, וְרַחֵם עָלֵינוּ
וְהוֹשִׁיעֵנוּ, כִּי אֵלֶיךָ עֵינֵינוּ,
כִּי אֵל מֶלֶךְ חַנּוּן וְרַחוּם אָתָּה.

אֱלֹהֵינוּ וֵאלֹהֵי אֲבוֹתֵינוּ [וְאִמּוֹתֵינוּ], מְחַל לַעֲוֹנוֹתֵינוּ
בְּיוֹם [הַשַּׁבָּת הַזֶּה וּבְיוֹם] הַכִּפֻּרִים הַזֶּה. מְחֵה וְהַעֲבֵר
פְּשָׁעֵינוּ וְחַטֹּאתֵינוּ מִנֶּגֶד עֵינֶיךָ, כָּאָמוּר: אָנֹכִי אָנֹכִי הוּא
מֹחֶה פְשָׁעֶיךָ לְמַעֲנִי, וְחַטֹּאתֶיךָ לֹא אֶזְכֹּר. וְנֶאֱמַר:
מָחִיתִי כָעָב פְּשָׁעֶיךָ וְכֶעָנָן חַטֹּאתֶיךָ, שׁוּבָה אֵלַי כִּי
גְאַלְתִּיךָ. וְנֶאֱמַר: כִּי־בַיּוֹם הַזֶּה יְכַפֵּר עֲלֵיכֶם לְטַהֵר
אֶתְכֶם, מִכֹּל חַטֹּאתֵיכֶם לִפְנֵי יְהֹוָה תִּטְהָרוּ.

CALLING US BY YOUR GREAT AND HOLY NAME וְשִׁמְךָ הַגָּדוֹל וְהַקָּדוֹשׁ עָלֵינוּ קָרָאתָ. The name "Israel" means "wrestling with God" (Genesis 32:28). Our relationship with God is part of our self-definition as a people.

FORGIVE OUR SINS יַעֲלֶה וְיָבֹא. In this prayer we mention all that we wish God to keep in mind at this hour. It is filled with synonyms and repetitions of the word "remember." We cannot imagine a different future, unless we keep in mind our past.

I, SURELY I אָנֹכִי אָנֹכִי. Isaiah 43:25.

I SWEEP ASIDE YOUR SINS LIKE A MIST מָחִיתִי כָעָב פְּשָׁעֶיךָ. Isaiah 44:22.

FOR ON THIS DAY כִּי־בַיּוֹם הַזֶּה. Leviticus 16:30.

You know what is for my good. If I recite my wants, it is not to remind You of them, but so that I may better understand how great is my dependence on You. If, then, I ask You for the things that may not be for my well-being, it is because I am ignorant; Your choice is better than mine and I submit myself to Your unalterable decree and Your supreme direction.

—BAHYA IBN PAKUDA

Fourth B'rakhah: The Holiness of Yom Kippur

You have chosen us among all peoples, loving us, wanting us. You have distinguished us among all nations, making us holy through Your commandments, drawing us close to Your service, and calling us by Your great and holy name.

With love, You have bestowed on us, ADONAI our God, this [Shabbat, for sanctity and rest, and this] Yom Kippur for pardon, forgiveness, and atonement, that all our sins be forgiven [through Your love], a sacred time, recalling the Exodus from Egypt.

Our God and God of our ancestors, may the thought of us rise up and reach You.
Attend to us and accept us;
hear us and respond to us.
Keep us in mind,
and keep in mind the thought of our ancestors, as well as the Messiah the descendant of David; Jerusalem, Your holy city; and all Your people, the House of Israel.
On this Yom Kippur respond to us with deliverance, goodness, compassion, love, life, and peace.
Remember us for good;
respond to us with blessing;
redeem us with life.
Show us compassion and care with words of salvation and kindness; have mercy on us and redeem us. Our eyes are turned to You, for You are a compassionate and loving sovereign.

Our God and God of our ancestors, forgive our sins on this [Shabbat and this] Yom Kippur. Blot out and disregard them, as the prophet Isaiah says in Your name: "I, surely I, am the One who wipes away sin, for this is My nature; I will not recall your errors," and the prophet adds: "I sweep aside your sins like a mist, and disperse your transgressions like a cloud. Turn back to Me, for I will redeem you." And in Your Torah it is written: "For on this day, atonement shall be made for you to purify you from all your transgressions. In the presence of ADONAI you shall be pure."

אֱלֹהֵינוּ וֵאלֹהֵי אֲבוֹתֵינוּ [וְאִמּוֹתֵינוּ], [רְצֵה בִמְנוּחָתֵנוּ]
קַדְּשֵׁנוּ בְּמִצְוֹתֶיךָ וְתֵן חֶלְקֵנוּ בְּתוֹרָתֶךָ, שַׂבְּעֵנוּ מִטּוּבֶךָ
וְשַׂמְּחֵנוּ בִּישׁוּעָתֶךָ, [וְהַנְחִילֵנוּ יהוה אֱלֹהֵינוּ, בְּאַהֲבָה
וּבְרָצוֹן שַׁבַּת קָדְשֶׁךָ, וְיָנוּחוּ בָהּ יִשְׂרָאֵל, מְקַדְּשֵׁי שְׁמֶךָ]
וְטַהֵר לִבֵּנוּ לְעָבְדְּךָ בֶּאֱמֶת, כִּי אַתָּה סָלְחָן לְיִשְׂרָאֵל
וּמָחֳלָן לְשִׁבְטֵי יְשֻׁרוּן בְּכָל־דּוֹר וָדוֹר, וּמִבַּלְעָדֶיךָ אֵין
לָנוּ מֶלֶךְ מוֹחֵל וְסוֹלֵחַ אֶלָּא אָתָּה. בָּרוּךְ אַתָּה יהוה,
מֶלֶךְ מוֹחֵל וְסוֹלֵחַ לַעֲוֹנוֹתֵינוּ וְלַעֲוֹנוֹת עַמּוֹ בֵּית יִשְׂרָאֵל,
וּמַעֲבִיר אַשְׁמוֹתֵינוּ בְּכָל־שָׁנָה וְשָׁנָה, מֶלֶךְ עַל כָּל־הָאָרֶץ
מְקַדֵּשׁ [הַשַּׁבָּת וְ] יִשְׂרָאֵל וְיוֹם הַכִּפּוּרִים.

רְצֵה, יהוה אֱלֹהֵינוּ, בְּעַמְּךָ יִשְׂרָאֵל וּבִתְפִלָּתָם, וְהָשֵׁב
אֶת־הָעֲבוֹדָה לִדְבִיר בֵּיתֶךָ, [וְאִשֵּׁי יִשְׂרָאֵל]
וּתְפִלָּתָם בְּאַהֲבָה תְקַבֵּל בְּרָצוֹן, וּתְהִי לְרָצוֹן תָּמִיד
עֲבוֹדַת יִשְׂרָאֵל עַמֶּךָ.

וְתֶחֱזֶינָה עֵינֵינוּ בְּשׁוּבְךָ לְצִיּוֹן בְּרַחֲמִים.
בָּרוּךְ אַתָּה יהוה, הַמַּחֲזִיר שְׁכִינָתוֹ לְצִיּוֹן.

מוֹדִים אֲנַחְנוּ לָךְ, שָׁאַתָּה הוּא, יהוה אֱלֹהֵינוּ וֵאלֹהֵי
אֲבוֹתֵינוּ [וְאִמּוֹתֵינוּ] לְעוֹלָם וָעֶד. צוּר חַיֵּינוּ, מָגֵן יִשְׁעֵנוּ,
אַתָּה הוּא. לְדוֹר וָדוֹר נוֹדֶה לְּךָ וּנְסַפֵּר תְּהִלָּתֶךָ
עַל חַיֵּינוּ הַמְּסוּרִים בְּיָדֶךָ,
וְעַל נִשְׁמוֹתֵינוּ הַפְּקוּדוֹת לָךְ,
וְעַל נִסֶּיךָ שֶׁבְּכָל־יוֹם עִמָּנוּ,
וְעַל נִפְלְאוֹתֶיךָ וְטוֹבוֹתֶיךָ שֶׁבְּכָל־עֵת,
עֶרֶב וָבֹקֶר וְצָהֳרָיִם.
הַטּוֹב, כִּי לֹא כָלוּ רַחֲמֶיךָ,
וְהַמְרַחֵם כִּי לֹא תַמּוּ חֲסָדֶיךָ,
מֵעוֹלָם קִוִּינוּ לָךְ.

402 נעילה ליום כיפור · תפילת העמידה בלחש

YOU FORGIVE אַתָּה סָלְחָן. The grammatical form of the nouns סָלְחָן (solhan) and מָחֳלָן (moholan) indicate an essential personal quality. For example, when one לוֹמֵד (lomed), "studies," until becoming a scholar, one is then called a לַמְדָן (lamdan). The use of this form reflects the poet's belief that God's forgiving nature is, in fact, God's essence.

RESTORE WORSHIP TO YOUR SANCTUARY וְהָשֵׁב אֶת־הָעֲבוֹדָה לִדְבִיר בֵּיתֶךָ. According to the Babylonian Talmud, "Ever since the day when the Temple was destroyed, there has been an iron barrier separating Israel from God" (Berakhot 32b). Each destruction of the Temple in Jerusalem (first by the Babylonians in 586 B.C.E. and then by the Romans in 70 C.E.) was a cataclysmic event in early Jewish history. In the exile, amidst the brokenness that surrounds us, we can never know whether our service to God is appropriate or not. The prayer for the restoration of the Temple carries with it the hope that we might someday be assured that our service to God is proper.

YOUR DIVINE PRESENCE שְׁכִינָתוֹ. The Hebrew word shekhinah has been used for centuries to refer to God's immanence, the presence of God that is felt in the world. The word shekhinah is grammatically feminine. Accordingly, the Jewish mystical tradition generally describes the Divine Presence—known as the Shekhinah—in feminine imagery.

PROTECTOR OF OUR LIVES צוּר חַיֵּינוּ. God is our source of support and stability.

FROM ONE GENERATION TO THE NEXT לְדוֹר וָדוֹר. After Psalm 79:13. In a world where nations, values, and ideals rise and fall, the relationship with God is a constant truth.

Would that Your people at prayer gained delight in You. Would that we were aflame with the passionate piety of our ancestors' worship. Would that You found our worship acceptable, and forever cherished Your people. If only our eyes could see Your glory perennially renewed in Jerusalem. We praise You, God whose presence forever radiates from Zion.

You are our God today as You were our ancestors' God throughout the ages; firm foundation of our lives, we are Yours in gratitude and love. Our lives are safe in Your hand, our souls entrusted to Your care. Our sense of wonder and our praise of Your miracles and kindnesses greet You daily at dawn, dusk, and noon. O Gentle One, Your caring is endless; O Compassionate One, Your love is eternal. You are forever our hope. Let all the living confront You with thankfulness, delight, and truth. Help us, O God; sustain us. We praise You, God whose touchstone is goodness.

May a life of goodness await all of us, children of Your covenant.

To pray to You is joy.

(continued)

Our God and God of our ancestors: [embrace our rest,] make us holy through Your mitzvot and let the Torah be our portion. Fill our lives with Your goodness and gladden us with Your triumph. [ADONAI our God, grant that we inherit Your holy Shabbat, lovingly and willingly, so that the people Israel, who sanctify Your name, may find rest on this day.] Purify our hearts to serve You faithfully, for You forgive the people Israel and pardon the tribes of Jeshurun in every generation. Beside You, we have no sovereign who pardons and forgives. *Barukh atah ADONAI*, sovereign who pardons and forgives our sins and those of the people, the House of Israel, each year sweeping away our guilt—ruler of all the earth, who makes [Shabbat,] the people Israel and the Day of Atonement holy.

Fifth B'rakhah: The Restoration of Zion

ADONAI our God, embrace Your people Israel and their prayer. Restore worship to Your sanctuary. May the [fiery offerings and] prayers of Israel be lovingly accepted by You, and may our service always be pleasing.

Let our eyes behold Your merciful return to Zion. *Barukh atah ADONAI*, who restores Your Divine Presence to Zion.

Sixth B'rakhah: Gratitude for Life and Its Blessings

ſ We thank You,
You who are our God and the God of our ancestors
    through all time,
    protector of our lives,
    shield of our salvation.
From one generation to the next we thank You
    and sing Your praises—
    for our lives that are in Your hands,
    for our souls that are under Your care,
    for Your miracles that accompany us each day,
    and for Your wonders and Your gifts that are
    with us each moment—
    evening, morning, and noon.
You are the One who is good, whose mercy is never-ending,
    the One who is compassionate,
    whose love is unceasing.
    We have always placed our hope in You.

וְעַל כֻּלָּם יִתְבָּרַךְ וְיִתְרוֹמַם שִׁמְךָ מַלְכֵּנוּ תָּמִיד
לְעוֹלָם וָעֶד.

וַחֲתוֹם לְחַיִּים טוֹבִים כָּל־בְּנֵי בְרִיתֶךָ.

וְכֹל הַחַיִּים יוֹדוּךָ סֶּלָה,
וִיהַלְלוּ אֶת שִׁמְךָ בֶּאֱמֶת,
הָאֵל יְשׁוּעָתֵנוּ וְעֶזְרָתֵנוּ סֶלָה.
בָּרוּךְ אַתָּה יהוה, הַטּוֹב שִׁמְךָ וּלְךָ נָאֶה לְהוֹדוֹת.

שִׂים שָׁלוֹם בָּעוֹלָם, טוֹבָה וּבְרָכָה, חֵן וָחֶסֶד וְרַחֲמִים
עָלֵינוּ וְעַל כָּל־יִשְׂרָאֵל עַמֶּךָ. בָּרְכֵנוּ אָבִינוּ כֻּלָּנוּ כְּאֶחָד
בְּאוֹר פָּנֶיךָ, כִּי בְאוֹר פָּנֶיךָ נָתַתָּ לָנוּ, יהוה אֱלֹהֵינוּ,
תּוֹרַת חַיִּים וְאַהֲבַת חֶסֶד, וּצְדָקָה וּבְרָכָה וְרַחֲמִים
וְחַיִּים, וְשָׁלוֹם. וְטוֹב בְּעֵינֶיךָ לְבָרֵךְ אֶת־עַמְּךָ יִשְׂרָאֵל,
בְּכָל־עֵת וּבְכָל־שָׁעָה בִּשְׁלוֹמֶךָ.

בְּסֵפֶר חַיִּים, בְּרָכָה וְשָׁלוֹם וּפַרְנָסָה טוֹבָה, נִזָּכֵר וְנֵחָתֵם
לְפָנֶיךָ, אֲנַחְנוּ וְכָל־עַמְּךָ בֵּית יִשְׂרָאֵל, לְחַיִּים טוֹבִים
וּלְשָׁלוֹם.

בָּרוּךְ אַתָּה יהוה, עוֹשֵׂה הַשָּׁלוֹם.

וידוי

אֱלֹהֵינוּ וֵאלֹהֵי אֲבוֹתֵינוּ [וְאִמּוֹתֵינוּ],
תָּבֹא לְפָנֶיךָ תְּפִלָּתֵנוּ, וְאַל תִּתְעַלַּם מִתְּחִנָּתֵנוּ,
שֶׁאֵין אֲנַחְנוּ עַזֵּי פָנִים וּקְשֵׁי עֹרֶף לוֹמַר לְפָנֶיךָ,
יהוה אֱלֹהֵינוּ וֵאלֹהֵי אֲבוֹתֵינוּ [וְאִמּוֹתֵינוּ],
צַדִּיקִים אֲנַחְנוּ וְלֹא חָטָאנוּ,
אֲבָל אֲנַחְנוּ וַאֲבוֹתֵינוּ [וְאִמּוֹתֵינוּ] חָטָאנוּ.

SEAL וַחֲתוֹם. The third insertion for the High Holy Day period. Again, instead of asking to be "inscribed in the Book of Life," we ask now to be "sealed."

MAY WE בְּסֵפֶר חַיִּים. The fourth insertion for the High Holy Day period. This culminating prayer asks not only for life but for peace and sustenance as well.

(continued from previous page)
O God, from whom all peace flows, grant serenity to Your Jewish people, with love and mercy, life and goodness for all. Shelter us with kindness, bless us with tranquility at all times and all seasons.

May we, and all Your people, the House of Israel, be deserving of a year of life, blessing, peace, and an honorable livelihood.

We praise You, God whose blessing is peace.

For all these blessings may Your name be praised and exalted, our sovereign, always and forever.

And seal all the people of Your covenant for a good life.

May all that lives thank You always, and praise Your name faithfully forever, God of our deliverance and help.
ſ *Barukh atah* ADONAI, whose name is goodness and to whom praise is fitting.

Seventh B'rakhah: Prayer for Peace

Grant peace to the world: goodness and blessing, grace, love, and compassion, for us and for all the people Israel. Bless us, our creator, united as one with the light of Your presence; by that light, ADONAI our God, You gave us a guide to life, the love of kindness, generosity, blessing, compassion, life, and peace. May it please You to bless Your people Israel at all times with Your peace.

May we and the entire House of Israel be called to mind and sealed for life, blessing, sustenance, and peace in the Book of Life.

Barukh atah ADONAI, who brings peace.

VIDDUI — PRAYERS OF CONFESSION

Because confession is an essential aspect of Yom Kippur, we add this liturgical confession each time that we recite the Amidah.

INTRODUCTION TO THE CONFESSION

Our God and God of our ancestors,
hear our prayer; do not ignore our plea.
Our God and God of our ancestors,
we are neither so insolent nor so obstinate
as to claim in Your presence
that we are righteous, without sin;
for we, like our ancestors who came before us, have sinned.

It is customary to strike one's heart with one's fist as each phrase is recited.

אָשַׁמְנוּ, בָּגַדְנוּ, גָּזַלְנוּ, דִּבַּרְנוּ דְּפִי. הֶעֱוִינוּ, וְהִרְשַׁעְנוּ, זַדְנוּ, חָמַסְנוּ, טָפַלְנוּ שֶׁקֶר. יָעַצְנוּ רָע, כִּזַּבְנוּ, לַצְנוּ, מָרַדְנוּ, נִאַצְנוּ, סָרַרְנוּ, עָוִינוּ, פָּשַׁעְנוּ, צָרַרְנוּ, קִשִּׁינוּ עֹרֶף. רָשַׁעְנוּ, שִׁחַתְנוּ, תִּעַבְנוּ, תָּעִינוּ, תִּעְתָּעְנוּ.

סַרְנוּ מִמִּצְוֹתֶיךָ וּמִמִּשְׁפָּטֶיךָ הַטּוֹבִים, וְלֹא שָׁוָה לָנוּ. וְאַתָּה צַדִּיק עַל כָּל־הַבָּא עָלֵינוּ, כִּי אֱמֶת עָשִׂיתָ וַאֲנַחְנוּ הִרְשַׁעְנוּ. מַה נֹּאמַר לְפָנֶיךָ יוֹשֵׁב מָרוֹם, וּמַה נְּסַפֵּר לְפָנֶיךָ שׁוֹכֵן שְׁחָקִים, הֲלֹא כָּל־הַנִּסְתָּרוֹת וְהַנִּגְלוֹת אַתָּה יוֹדֵעַ.

אַתָּה נוֹתֵן יָד לְפוֹשְׁעִים, וִימִינְךָ פְּשׁוּטָה לְקַבֵּל שָׁבִים. וַתְּלַמְּדֵנוּ יהוה אֱלֹהֵינוּ לְהִתְוַדּוֹת לְפָנֶיךָ עַל כָּל־עֲוֹנוֹתֵינוּ, לְמַעַן נֶחְדַּל מֵעֹשֶׁק יָדֵינוּ, וּתְקַבְּלֵנוּ בִּתְשׁוּבָה שְׁלֵמָה לְפָנֶיךָ כְּאִשִּׁים וּכְנִיחוֹחִים, לְמַעַן דְּבָרֶיךָ אֲשֶׁר אָמָרְתָּ. אֵין קֵץ לְאִשֵּׁי חוֹבוֹתֵינוּ, וְאֵין מִסְפָּר לְנִיחוֹחֵי אַשְׁמוֹתֵינוּ; וְאַתָּה יוֹדֵעַ שֶׁאַחֲרִיתֵנוּ רִמָּה וְתוֹלֵעָה, לְפִיכָךְ הִרְבֵּיתָ סְלִיחָתֵנוּ.

מָה אָנוּ, מֶה חַיֵּינוּ, מֶה חַסְדֵּנוּ, מַה צִּדְקֵנוּ, מַה יְּשׁוּעֵנוּ, מַה כֹּחֵנוּ, מַה גְּבוּרָתֵנוּ. מַה נֹּאמַר לְפָנֶיךָ, יהוה אֱלֹהֵינוּ וֵאלֹהֵי אֲבוֹתֵינוּ [וְאִמּוֹתֵינוּ]. הֲלֹא כָּל־הַגִּבּוֹרִים כְּאַיִן לְפָנֶיךָ, וְאַנְשֵׁי הַשֵּׁם כְּלֹא הָיוּ, וַחֲכָמִים כִּבְלִי מַדָּע, וּנְבוֹנִים כִּבְלִי הַשְׂכֵּל, כִּי רֹב מַעֲשֵׂיהֶם תֹּהוּ, וִימֵי חַיֵּיהֶם הֶבֶל לְפָנֶיךָ. וּמוֹתַר הָאָדָם מִן הַבְּהֵמָה אָיִן, כִּי הַכֹּל הָבֶל.

The Shorter Confession—Ashamnu

It is customary to strike one's heart with one's fist as each phrase is recited.

We abuse, we betray, we are cruel, we destroy, we embitter, we falsify, we gossip, we hate, we insult, we jeer, we kill, we lie, we mock, we neglect, we oppress, we pervert, we quarrel, we rebel, we steal, we transgress, we are unkind, we are violent, we are wicked, we are extremists, we yearn to do evil, we are zealous for bad causes.

Ashamnu, bagadnu, gazalnu, dibbarnu dofi, he·evinu, v'hirshanu, zadnu, hamasnu, tafalnu sheker, ya·atznu ra, kizzavnu, latznu, maradnu, ni·atznu, sararnu, avinu, pashanu, tzararnu, kishinu oref, rashanu, shihatnu, ti·avnu, ta·inu, titanu.

PRAYER ACCOMPANYING THE CONFESSION

We have turned from Your goodly laws and commandments, but it has not profited us. Surely, You are in the right with respect to all that comes upon us, for You have acted faithfully, but we have been in the wrong. What can we say to You who sit on high, and what can we tell You who dwell in heaven, for You know all that is hidden as well as all that is revealed.

You extend Your hand to those who sin, Your right hand to receive those who return. You have taught us, ADONAI our God, to confess each of our transgressions to You, so that we cease using our hands for oppression. Accept us fully when we turn to You, as You promised to accept the sweet-smelling sacrifices. Endless are the guilt-offerings that would have been required of us even in ancient Temple times, and You know that we will ultimately atone for our sins with our death. Accordingly, You have forgiven us many times over.

What are we? What is our life? Our goodness? Our
   righteousness? Our achievement? Our power? Our victories?
What shall we say in Your presence,
   ADONAI our God and God of our ancestors?
Heroes count as nothing in Your presence,
   famous people are as if they never existed,
   the wise seem ignorant,
   and clever ones as if they lack reason.
The sum of their acts is chaos;
   in Your presence the days of their lives are futile.
Human beings have no superiority over beasts;
   all life is vanity.

אַתָּה הִבְדַּֽלְתָּ אֱנוֹשׁ מֵרֹאשׁ, וַתַּכִּירֵהוּ לַעֲמוֹד לְפָנֶֽיךָ. כִּי מִי יֹאמַר לְךָ מַה תִּפְעָל, וְאִם יִצְדַּק מַה יִּתֶּן־לָךְ. וַתִּתֶּן־ לָֽנוּ יהוה אֱלֹהֵֽינוּ בְּאַהֲבָה אֶת־יוֹם הַכִּפֻּרִים הַזֶּה, קֵץ וּמְחִילָה וּסְלִיחָה עַל כָּל־עֲוֺנוֹתֵֽינוּ, לְמַֽעַן נֶחְדַּל מֵעֹֽשֶׁק יָדֵֽנוּ, וְנָשׁוּב אֵלֶֽיךָ לַעֲשׂוֹת חֻקֵּי רְצוֹנְךָ בְּלֵבָב שָׁלֵם.

וְאַתָּה בְּרַחֲמֶֽיךָ הָרַבִּים רַחֵם עָלֵֽינוּ, כִּי לֹא תַחְפֹּץ בְּהַשְׁחָתַת עוֹלָם, שֶׁנֶּאֱמַר: דִּרְשׁוּ יהוה בְּהִמָּצְאוֹ, קְרָאֻֽהוּ בִּהְיוֹתוֹ קָרוֹב. וְנֶאֱמַר: יַעֲזֹב רָשָׁע דַּרְכּוֹ, וְאִישׁ אָֽוֶן מַחְשְׁבֹתָיו, וְיָשֹׁב אֶל־יהוה וִירַחֲמֵֽהוּ, וְאֶל־אֱלֹהֵֽינוּ כִּי יַרְבֶּה לִסְלֽוֹחַ. וְאַתָּה אֱלֽוֹהַּ סְלִיחוֹת, חַנּוּן וְרַחוּם, אֶֽרֶךְ אַפַּֽיִם, וְרַב חֶֽסֶד וֶאֱמֶת, וּמַרְבֶּה לְהֵיטִיב; וְרוֹצֶה אַתָּה בִּתְשׁוּבַת רְשָׁעִים, וְאֵין אַתָּה חָפֵץ בְּמִיתָתָם, שֶׁנֶּאֱמַר: אֱמֹר אֲלֵיהֶם, חַי אָֽנִי, נְאֻם אֲדֹנָי יֱהֹוִה, אִם אֶחְפֹּץ בְּמוֹת הָרָשָׁע, כִּי אִם בְּשׁוּב רָשָׁע מִדַּרְכּוֹ וְחָיָה; שֽׁוּבוּ שֽׁוּבוּ מִדַּרְכֵיכֶם הָרָעִים, וְלָֽמָּה תָמֽוּתוּ בֵּית יִשְׂרָאֵל. וְנֶאֱמַר: הֶחָפֹץ אֶחְפֹּץ מוֹת רָשָׁע, נְאֻם אֲדֹנָי יֱהֹוִה, הֲלֹא בְּשׁוּבוֹ מִדְּרָכָיו וְחָיָה. וְנֶאֱמַר: כִּי לֹא אֶחְפֹּץ בְּמוֹת הַמֵּת, נְאֻם אֲדֹנָי יֱהֹוִה, וְהָשִֽׁיבוּ וִחְיוּ. כִּי אַתָּה סָלְחָן לְיִשְׂרָאֵל וּמָחֳלָן לְשִׁבְטֵי יְשֻׁרוּן בְּכָל־דּוֹר וָדוֹר, וּמִבַּלְעָדֶֽיךָ אֵין לָֽנוּ מֶֽלֶךְ מוֹחֵל וְסוֹלֵֽחַ אֶלָּא אָֽתָּה.

AND EVEN IF A PERSON WERE INNOCENT וְאִם יִצְדַּק. After Job 35:7.

SEEK דִּרְשׁוּ. Isaiah 55:6-7, emphasizing that God is always present, for those who seek God.

YOU, FORGIVING GOD וְאַתָּה אֱלֽוֹהַּ סְלִיחוֹת. Nehemiah, speaking to the remnants of the people Israel returning to the Land of Israel, emphasizes Moses' teaching of God's forgiving nature (9:17).

SAY TO THEM אֱמֹר אֲלֵיהֶם. Ezekiel speaks words of consolation to the exiles in Babylonia (33:11, 18:23, 32).

Yet from the beginning You distinguished human beings, acknowledging them that they might stand before You. For who can tell You how to behave? And even if a person were innocent, what difference would it make to You? ADONAI our God, You have lovingly given us this Day of Atonement, bringing an end to our sins with pardon and forgiveness, that we cease using our hands for oppression, and turn back to You, wholeheartedly acting in accord with the laws You deem desirable.

May You, with Your abundant mercy, have compassion for us; for You do not desire the destruction of the world, as Your servant Nehemiah declares: "Seek ADONAI, who can be found everywhere; call to God, who is close. Let evildoers abandon their path and the wicked their schemes, and return to ADONAI, who will have mercy on them; for our God will forgive, again and again."

You, forgiving God, are compassionate and merciful, patient, abounding in love and goodness, and desire the return of the evildoers—not their death. For You instructed Your prophet Ezekiel: "Say to them, 'As I live,' declares our Lord, ADONAI, 'I do not desire the death of the evildoers, but that they turn from their paths, and live. Turn back, turn back from your evil paths that you may not die, House of Israel!'... 'Is it My desire that the evildoer die,' declares the Lord, ADONAI, 'Is it not that they turn from their ways and live?'... 'It is not My desire that the wicked shall die, but that the wicked turn from their evil ways and live.'"... For You forgive Israel and pardon the tribes of Jeshurun in every generation. Beside You, we have no sovereign who pardons and forgives.

אֱלֹהַי, עַד שֶׁלֹּא נוֹצַרְתִּי אֵינִי כְדַאי, וְעַכְשָׁו שֶׁנּוֹצַרְתִּי כְּאִלּוּ
לֹא נוֹצַרְתִּי. עָפָר אֲנִי בְּחַיַּי, קַל וָחֹמֶר בְּמִיתָתִי. הֲרֵי אֲנִי
לְפָנֶיךָ כִּכְלִי מָלֵא בוּשָׁה וּכְלִמָּה. יְהִי רָצוֹן מִלְּפָנֶיךָ, יהוה
אֱלֹהַי וֵאלֹהֵי אֲבֹתַי [וְאִמּוֹתַי], שֶׁלֹּא אֶחֱטָא עוֹד. וּמַה
שֶּׁחָטָאתִי לְפָנֶיךָ מָרֵק בְּרַחֲמֶיךָ הָרַבִּים, אֲבָל לֹא עַל יְדֵי
יִסּוּרִים וָחֳלָיִים רָעִים.

אֱלֹהַי, נְצֹר לְשׁוֹנִי מֵרָע, וּשְׂפָתַי מִדַּבֵּר מִרְמָה, וְלִמְקַלְלַי
נַפְשִׁי תִדֹּם, וְנַפְשִׁי כֶּעָפָר לַכֹּל תִּהְיֶה. פְּתַח לִבִּי בְּתוֹרָתֶךָ,
וּבְמִצְוֹתֶיךָ תִּרְדּוֹף נַפְשִׁי. וְכָל־הַחוֹשְׁבִים עָלַי רָעָה, מְהֵרָה
הָפֵר עֲצָתָם וְקַלְקֵל מַחֲשַׁבְתָּם. עֲשֵׂה לְמַעַן שְׁמֶךָ, עֲשֵׂה
לְמַעַן יְמִינֶךָ, עֲשֵׂה לְמַעַן קְדֻשָּׁתֶךָ, עֲשֵׂה לְמַעַן תּוֹרָתֶךָ.
לְמַעַן יֵחָלְצוּן יְדִידֶיךָ, הוֹשִׁיעָה יְמִינְךָ וַעֲנֵנִי. יִהְיוּ לְרָצוֹן
אִמְרֵי פִי וְהֶגְיוֹן לִבִּי לְפָנֶיךָ, יהוה צוּרִי וְגוֹאֲלִי. עֹשֶׂה שָׁלוֹם
בִּמְרוֹמָיו, הוּא יַעֲשֶׂה שָׁלוֹם עָלֵינוּ, וְעַל כָּל־יִשְׂרָאֵל
[וְעַל כָּל־יוֹשְׁבֵי תֵבֵל] וְאִמְרוּ: אָמֵן.

MY GOD אֱלֹהַי. The Baby-
lonian Talmud says that
every Amidah must be
accompanied by a personal
prayer. These two private
prayers, the first attributed
to Rava and the second
to Mar son of Ravina, are
among the Talmud's exem-
plars (Berakhot 17a). They
were so admired that they
entered the formal liturgy.
Both prayers distinctively
use the first-person singular
("I"), whereas almost all
other prayers—including
the confessions—are in the
first-person plural ("we").

MAY THE WORDS יִהְיוּ לְרָצוֹן.
Psalm 19:15.

Concluding Meditation
May my tongue be innocent of malice and my lips free from lies. When confronted by enemies may my soul stay calm, truly humble to all. Open my heart with Your teachings, that I may be guided by You. May all who plan evil against me abandon their schemes. Hear my words and help me, God, because You are loving, because You reveal Your Torah. May You find delight in the words of my mouth and in the emotions of my heart, God, my strength and my salvation. As You maintain harmony in the heavens, give peace to us, the whole Jewish people, and to all who dwell on earth. Amen.

Personal Prayers Concluding the Amidah

My God, before I was created I was entirely lacking in substance; and now that I have been created, it is as if I never was. Dust and ashes am I in life, all the more so in death. I stand before You as a vessel full of embarrassment and shame. May it be Your will, Adonai my God and God of my ancestors, that I sin no more, and that in Your great mercy You erase the sins I have sinned before You, but not through great pain and suffering.

My God, keep my tongue from evil, my lips from lies. Help me ignore those who would slander me. Let me be humble before all. Open my heart to Your Torah, that I may pursue Your mitzvot. Frustrate the designs of those who plot evil against me; make nothing of their schemes. Act for the sake of Your name, Your power, Your holiness, and Your Torah. Answer my prayer for the deliverance of Your people. May the words of my mouth and the meditations of my heart be acceptable to You, Adonai, my rock and my redeemer. May the One who brings peace to the universe bring peace to us and to all the people Israel [and to all who dwell on earth]. Amen.

אֵל נוֹרָא עֲלִילָה

אֵל נוֹרָא עֲלִילָה   אֵל נוֹרָא עֲלִילָה
בִּשְׁעַת הַנְּעִילָה.   הַמְצֵא לָנוּ מְחִילָה

לְךָ עַיִן נוֹשְׂאִים   מְתֵי מִסְפָּר קְרוּאִים
בִּשְׁעַת הַנְּעִילָה.   וּמְסַלְּדִים בְּחִילָה

מְחֵה פְשָׁעָם וְכַחֲשָׁם   שׁוֹפְכִים לְךָ נַפְשָׁם
בִּשְׁעַת הַנְּעִילָה.   הַמְצִיאֵם מְחִילָה

וְחַלְּצֵם מִמְּאֵרָה   הֱיֵה לָהֶם לְסִתְרָה
בִּשְׁעַת הַנְּעִילָה.   וְחָתְמֵם לְהוֹד וּלְגִילָה

וְכָל־לוֹחֵץ וְלוֹחֵם   חֹן אוֹתָם וְרַחֵם
בִּשְׁעַת הַנְּעִילָה.   עֲשֵׂה בָהֶם פְּלִילָה

וְחַדֵּשׁ אֶת יְמֵיהֶם   זְכֹר צִדְקַת אֲבִיהֶם
בִּשְׁעַת הַנְּעִילָה.   כְּקֶדֶם וּתְחִלָּה

וְהָשֵׁב שְׁאֵרִית הַצֹּאן   קְרָא נָא שְׁנַת רָצוֹן
בִּשְׁעַת הַנְּעִילָה.   לְאָהֳלִיבָה וְאָהֳלָה

הַבָּנִים וְהַבָּנוֹת   תִּזְכּוּ לְשָׁנִים רַבּוֹת
בִּשְׁעַת הַנְּעִילָה.   בְּדִיצָה וּבְצָהֳלָה

אֵלִיָּהוּ וְגַבְרִיאֵל   מִיכָאֵל שַׂר יִשְׂרָאֵל
בִּשְׁעַת הַנְּעִילָה.   בַּשְּׂרוּ נָא הַגְּאֻלָּה

EL NORA ALILAH אֵל נוֹרָא עֲלִילָה. Attributed to Moshe Ibn Ezra (c. 1055–1135, Spain), this *piyyut* introduces Ne·ilah in the Sephardic rite. Note that the name משה (*Moshe*) and the word חזק (*ḥazak*, "be strong") are spelled out in the first letters of each verse. The poem is a plea for forgiveness. This *piyyut* entered the Ashkenazic maḥzor in the 20th century, marking the opening of the ark for Ne·ilah. The last two stanzas are not part of the original poem but have been attached to it in many editions.

L'OHOLIVAH V'OHOLAH לְאָהֳלִיבָה וְאָהֳלָה. Translated here as "former glory." The prophet Ezekiel uses these names to refer to Samaria and Jerusalem, the capitals of the two ancient kingdoms of Israel and Judah (Ezekiel 23:4). As the day ends, we pray for the unity of all Israel.

INTRODUCTION TO NE·ILAH: A PIYYUT

Awe-inspiring Creator, God,
 find forgiveness for us
We who are called "few in number"
 and tremblingly beseech You,
As we pour out our souls,
 craft forgiveness for us,
Be our protector.
 seal our fate for joy and glory
Be compassionate and loving toward us;
 who would oppress or war against us,
Remember our ancestors' righteousness
 as of old and as at the beginning,
May this year be one which is pleasing to You.
 to their former glory
May we, Your children,
 length of days merited
May Michael protector of Israel
 bring tidings of redemption

awe-inspiring Creator, God,
in this closing hour.
raise our eyes toward You,
in this closing hour.
wipe away our sins and denials,
in this closing hour.
Shield us from terror;
in this closing hour.
bring judgment on all
in this closing hour.
and renew our days,
in this closing hour.
Restore Your remaining flock
in this closing hour.
celebrate with joy and gladness,
in this closing hour.
along with Elijah and Gabriel
in this closing hour.

El nora alilah
hamtzei lanu m'ḥilah

M'tei mispar k'ru·im
u-m'sal'dim b'ḥilah

Shof'khim l'kha nafsham
hamtzi·eim m'ḥilah

Heyeih lahem l'sitrah
v'ḥotmeim l'hod u-l'gilah

Ḥon otam v'raḥeim
aseih vahem p'lilah

Z'khor tzidkat avihem
k'kedem u-t'ḥillah

K'ra na sh'nat ratzon
l'oholivah v'oholah

Tizku l'shanim rabbot
b'ditzah u-v'tzoholah

Mikha·el sar yisra·el
basru na ha-g'ulah

El nora alilah
bi-sh'at ha-n'ilah.

l'kha ayin nos'im
bi-sh'at ha-n'ilah.

m'ḥeih fisham v'khaḥasham
bi-sh'at ha-n'ilah.

v'ḥal'tzeim mi-m'eirah
bi-sh'at ha-n'ilah.

v'khol loḥeitz v'loḥeim
bi-sh'at ha-n'ilah.

v'ḥaddeish et y'meihem
bi-sh'at ha-n'ilah.

v'hasheiv sh'eirit ha-tzon
bi-sh'at ha-n'ilah.

ha-banim v'ha-banot
bi-sh'at ha-n'ilah.

eliyahu v'gavri·el
bi-sh'at ha-n'ilah.

*We rise as the ark is opened. The ark remains open throughout the leader's
repetition of the Amidah, during which it is customary for those who are able
to stand. In some congregations, while the ark remains open, congregants can
approach the ark for a final silent prayer.*

כִּי שֵׁם יהוה אֶקְרָא, הָבוּ גֹדֶל לֵאלֹהֵינוּ.
אֲדֹנָי שְׂפָתַי תִּפְתָּח, וּפִי יַגִּיד תְּהִלָּתֶךָ.

Version with Patriarchs and Matriarchs:

בָּרוּךְ אַתָּה יהוה,
אֱלֹהֵינוּ וֵאלֹהֵי אֲבוֹתֵינוּ
[וְאִמּוֹתֵינוּ], אֱלֹהֵי אַבְרָהָם,
אֱלֹהֵי יִצְחָק, וֵאלֹהֵי יַעֲקֹב,
אֱלֹהֵי שָׂרָה, אֱלֹהֵי רִבְקָה,
אֱלֹהֵי רָחֵל, וֵאלֹהֵי לֵאָה,
הָאֵל הַגָּדוֹל הַגִּבּוֹר וְהַנּוֹרָא,
אֵל עֶלְיוֹן, גּוֹמֵל חֲסָדִים
טוֹבִים, וְקוֹנֵה הַכֹּל, וְזוֹכֵר
חַסְדֵי אָבוֹת [וְאִמָּהוֹת],
וּמֵבִיא גוֹאֵל לִבְנֵי בְנֵיהֶם
לְמַעַן שְׁמוֹ בְּאַהֲבָה.

Version with Patriarchs:

בָּרוּךְ אַתָּה יהוה,
אֱלֹהֵינוּ וֵאלֹהֵי אֲבוֹתֵינוּ,
אֱלֹהֵי אַבְרָהָם, אֱלֹהֵי
יִצְחָק, וֵאלֹהֵי יַעֲקֹב, הָאֵל
הַגָּדוֹל הַגִּבּוֹר וְהַנּוֹרָא,
אֵל עֶלְיוֹן, גּוֹמֵל חֲסָדִים
טוֹבִים, וְקוֹנֵה הַכֹּל, וְזוֹכֵר
חַסְדֵי אָבוֹת, וּמֵבִיא גוֹאֵל
לִבְנֵי בְנֵיהֶם לְמַעַן שְׁמוֹ
בְּאַהֲבָה.

מְסוֹד חֲכָמִים וּנְבוֹנִים,
וּמִלֶּמֶד דַּעַת מְבִינִים,
אֶפְתְּחָה פִּי בִּתְפִלָּה וּבְתַחֲנוּנִים,
לְחַלּוֹת וּלְחַנֵּן פְּנֵי מֶלֶךְ מָלֵא רַחֲמִים
מוֹחֵל וְסוֹלֵחַ לַעֲוֹנִים.

זָכְרֵנוּ לְחַיִּים, מֶלֶךְ חָפֵץ בַּחַיִּים, וְחָתְמֵנוּ בְּסֵפֶר הַחַיִּים,
לְמַעַנְךָ אֱלֹהִים חַיִּים.

**GOD OF ABRAHAM, GOD OF
ISAAC, AND GOD OF JACOB**
אֱלֹהֵי אַבְרָהָם, אֱלֹהֵי יִצְחָק,
וֵאלֹהֵי יַעֲקֹב. God begins the
conversation with Moses
at the burning bush with
this self-description. We
understand the world of
prayer, first of all, through
the experience of those
who came before us—both
in our immediate and our
ancient past. Perhaps the
quotation of these words
expresses the hope that we
too might feel the presence
of God. Moses saw only a
burning bush, but his inner
ear heard so much more.

INSPIRED BY THE INSIGHT
מְסוֹד חֲכָמִים. A personal
plea of the prayer leader
that the prayers about to
be offered will be acceptable.

SEAL US וְחָתְמֵנוּ. Since
Rosh Hashanah, we have
included this and three
other insertions in every
Amidah every day. Until
Ne·ilah, we have asked
God to inscribe us in the
Book of Life (וְכָתְבֵנוּ בְּסֵפֶר
הַחַיִּים); now, we ask God to
seal us (וְחָתְמֵנוּ) in it.

REPETITION OF THE AMIDAH

We rise as the ark is opened. The ark remains open throughout the leader's repetition of the Amidah, during which it is customary for those who are able to stand. In some congregations, while the ark remains open, congregants can approach the ark for a final silent prayer.

Meditation

There is little we may claim to know about God, but this much is certain: one cannot come before God save in integrity of heart and mind. It would not do to try to feign or fib for the greater glory of God. It cannot be required of human beings, and surely it can never be made a duty, to plead falsely to the God of truth. . . . The fearless seeker of truth, even the honest blasphemer, is nearer to God than the liars for the benefit of religion.

—SHALOM SPIEGEL

As I proclaim God's name, ADONAI, exalt our God.
ADONAI, open my lips that my mouth may speak Your praise.

First B'rakhah: Our Ancestors

Version with Patriarchs:

Barukh atah ADONAI,
our God and God of our
  ancestors,
God of Abraham, God of
  Isaac, and God of Jacob,
great, mighty, awe-inspiring,
  transcendent God,
who acts with lovingkindness,
and creates all things,
who remembers the loving
  deeds of our ancestors,
and who will send a redeemer
  to their children's children
  with love
for the sake of divine honor.

Version with Patriarchs and Matriarchs:

Barukh atah ADONAI,
our God and God of our
  ancestors,
God of Abraham, God of
  Isaac, and God of Jacob,
God of Sarah, God of
  Rebecca, God of Rachel,
  and God of Leah,
great, mighty, awe-inspiring,
  transcendent God,
who acts with lovingkindness,
and creates all things,
who remembers the loving
  deeds of our ancestors,
and who will send a redeemer
  to their children's children
  with love
for the sake of divine honor.

Inspired by the insight of sages
and the teachings of those who acquired wisdom,
I open my lips in prayer and supplication
to entreat the Merciful Sovereign,
who forgives and pardons sin.

Remember us for life, Sovereign who delights in life,
and seal us in the Book of Life, for Your sake, God of life.
Zokhreinu l'ḥayyim, melekh ḥafeitz ba-ḥayyim,
v'ḥotmeinu b'seifer ha-ḥayyim, l'ma·ankha Elohim ḥayyim.

מֶֽלֶךְ עוֹזֵר וּפוֹקֵד
וּמוֹשִֽׁיעַ וּמָגֵן.
בָּרוּךְ אַתָּה יהוה, מָגֵן
אַבְרָהָם וּפוֹקֵד שָׂרָה.

מֶֽלֶךְ עוֹזֵר וּמוֹשִֽׁיעַ וּמָגֵן.
בָּרוּךְ אַתָּה יהוה, מָגֵן
אַבְרָהָם.

MIGHTY FOREVER אַתָּה
גִּבּוֹר. This b'rakhah, which
describes God's presence
and activity in the world,
centers on the kindness
and care of God for the
incapacitated—even the
dead are in God's care.

אַתָּה גִּבּוֹר לְעוֹלָם אֲדֹנָי, מְחַיֵּה מֵתִים אַתָּה,
רַב לְהוֹשִֽׁיעַ.

מְכַלְכֵּל חַיִּים בְּחֶֽסֶד, מְחַיֵּה מֵתִים בְּרַחֲמִים רַבִּים,
סוֹמֵךְ נוֹפְלִים, וְרוֹפֵא חוֹלִים, וּמַתִּיר אֲסוּרִים, וּמְקַיֵּם
אֱמוּנָתוֹ לִישֵׁנֵי עָפָר. מִי כָמֽוֹךָ בַּֽעַל גְּבוּרוֹת וּמִי דֽוֹמֶה
לָּךְ, מֶֽלֶךְ מֵמִית וּמְחַיֶּה וּמַצְמִֽיחַ יְשׁוּעָה.

מִי כָמֽוֹךָ אַב הָרַחֲמִים, זוֹכֵר יְצוּרָיו לְחַיִּים בְּרַחֲמִים.

וְנֶאֱמָן אַתָּה לְהַחֲיוֹת מֵתִים. בָּרוּךְ אַתָּה יהוה,
מְחַיֵּה הַמֵּתִים.

GIVE LIFE TO THE DEAD
מְחַיֵּה מֵתִים. To be sure, the
primary meaning of this
phrase was understood to
refer to the afterlife, but
the Rabbis also understood
that it could refer to a spiritual revival in this world as
well. Fasting is a "taste of
death," and as we end Yom
Kippur, it is hoped that we
will feel "revived."

**WHO IS LIKE YOU, SOURCE
OF COMPASSION** מִי כָמֽוֹךָ
אַב הָרַחֲמִים. A second
insertion at each of the
services in the High Holy
Day season. The gift of life
is an expression of God's
kindness.

יִמְלֹךְ יהוה לְעוֹלָם, אֱלֹהַֽיִךְ צִיּוֹן לְדֹר וָדֹר, הַלְלוּ־יָהּ.
וְאַתָּה קָדוֹשׁ, יוֹשֵׁב תְּהִלּוֹת יִשְׂרָאֵל, אֵל נָא.

I wanted a perfect
ending,
So I sat down to write the
book with the ending in
place before there even
was an ending.
Now I've learned the
hard way, that some
poems don't rhyme
and some stories don't
have a clear beginning,
middle, and end.
Like my life, this book
has ambiguity. Like my
life, this book is about
not knowing, having to
change, taking the mo-
ment and making the
best of it, not knowing.
—GILDA RADNER

Version with Patriarchs:

You are the Sovereign
who helps and saves and
shields.

Barukh atah ADONAI,
Shield of Abraham.

Version with Patriarchs and Matriarchs:

You are the Sovereign who
helps and guards, saves and
shields.

Barukh atah ADONAI,
Shield of Abraham and
Guardian of Sarah.

Second B'rakhah: God's Saving Care

You are mighty forever, ADONAI—
You give life to the dead;
great is Your saving power.

You sustain the living through love,
 and with great mercy give life to the dead.
You support the falling,
 heal the sick,
 loosen the chains of the bound,
 and keep faith with those who sleep in the dust.
Who is like You, Almighty,
 and who can be compared to You?—
 Sovereign, who brings death and life,
 and causes salvation to flourish.

*M'khalkeil ḥayyim b'ḥesed, m'ḥayyeih meitim b'raḥamim rabbim,
someikh nof'lim, v'rofei ḥolim, u-mattir asurim, u-m'kayyeim emunato
li-sheinei afar. Mi khamokha ba·al g'vurot u-mi domeh lakh, melekh
meimit u-m'ḥayyeih u-matzmi·aḥ y'shu·ah.*

Who is like You, source of compassion,
who remembers with compassion Your creatures for life?
Mi khamokha av ha-raḥamim, zokheir y'tzurav l'ḥayyim b'raḥamim.

You are faithful in bringing life to the dead.
Barukh atah ADONAI, who gives life to the dead.

Third B'rakhah: God's Holiness

ADONAI will reign forever; your God, O Zion, from generation to generation. Halleluyah! And You, O Holy One, are
enthroned through the praises of the people Israel. God, please
hear us.

שְׁמַע נָא, סְלַח נָא הַיּוֹם, עֲבוּר כִּי פָנָה יוֹם,
וּנְהַלֶּלְךָ נוֹרָא וְאָיוֹם, קָדוֹשׁ.

וּבְכֵן וּלְךָ תַעֲלֶה קְדֻשָּׁה,
כִּי אַתָּה אֱלֹהֵינוּ מֶלֶךְ מוֹחֵל וְסוֹלֵחַ.

פִּתְחוּ לָנוּ שַׁעֲרֵי צֶדֶק, נָבֹא בָם נוֹדֶה יָהּ.
דְּלָתֶיךָ דָּפַקְנוּ רַחוּם וְחַנּוּן.
נָא אַל תְּשִׁיבֵנוּ רֵיקָם מִלְּפָנֶיךָ.

פְּתַח לָנוּ וּלְכָל־יִשְׂרָאֵל אַחֵינוּ [וַאֲחֶיוֹתֵינוּ] בְּכָל־מָקוֹם.

שַׁעֲרֵי אוֹרָה, שַׁעֲרֵי בְרָכָה, שַׁעֲרֵי גִילָה,
שַׁעֲרֵי דִיצָה, שַׁעֲרֵי הוֹד וְהָדָר, שַׁעֲרֵי וַעַד טוֹב,
שַׁעֲרֵי זְכִיּוֹת, שַׁעֲרֵי חֶדְוָה, שַׁעֲרֵי טָהֳרָה,
שַׁעֲרֵי יְשׁוּעָה, שַׁעֲרֵי כַפָּרָה, שַׁעֲרֵי לֵב טוֹב,
שַׁעֲרֵי מְחִילָה, שַׁעֲרֵי נֶחָמָה, שַׁעֲרֵי סְלִיחָה,
שַׁעֲרֵי עֶזְרָה, שַׁעֲרֵי פַרְנָסָה טוֹבָה, שַׁעֲרֵי צְדָקָה,
שַׁעֲרֵי קוֹמְמִיּוּת, שַׁעֲרֵי רְפוּאָה שְׁלֵמָה,
שַׁעֲרֵי שָׁלוֹם, שַׁעֲרֵי תְשׁוּבָה.

וְחָתְמֵנוּ בְּסֵפֶר הַחַיִּים לִבְרָכָה וְלִקְדֻשָּׁה,
כִּי אַתָּה קָדוֹשׁ וְשִׁמְךָ קָדוֹשׁ
וּשְׁעָרֶיךָ בִּקְדֻשָּׁה נִכְנָס.

HEAR US שְׁמַע נָא. The rhythm of this fragment is staccato, expressing desperation at the end of the day. The author weaves in his name, Shimon (שִׁמְעוֹן), in the word *sh'ma* and the beginning of *u-n'hallekha*.

GATES. Appropriate to the theme of this service, Ne·ilah contains a series of *piyyutim* that speak of gates. They stress the many gates through which we may walk.

OPEN פְּתַח. This *piyyut* is found in the Sephardic rite for Yom Kippur.

בְּטֶרֶם

בְּטֶרֶם הַשַּׁעַר יִסָּגֵר,
בְּטֶרֶם כָּל־הָאָמוּר יֵאָמֵר,
בְּטֶרֶם אֶהְיֶה אַחֵר.
בְּטֶרֶם יַקְרִישׁ דָּם נָבוֹן,
בְּטֶרֶם יִסָּגְרוּ הַדְּבָרִים בָּאָרוֹן,
בְּטֶרֶם יִתְקַשֶּׁה הַבֶּטוֹן.
בְּטֶרֶם יִסָּתְמוּ כָּל־נִקְבֵי
הַחֲלִילִים,
בְּטֶרֶם יֻסְבְּרוּ כָּל־הַכְּלָלִים,
בְּטֶרֶם יִשָּׁבְרוּ אֶת הַכֵּלִים.
בְּטֶרֶם הַחֹק יִכָּנֵס לְתָקְפּוֹ,
בְּטֶרֶם אֱלֹהִים יִסְגּוֹר אֶת־כַּפּוֹ,
בְּטֶרֶם נֵלֵךְ מִפֹּה.

Before the gate closes,
before everything is said,
before I become
  estranged.
Before the discerning
  blood dries up,
before things are boxed
  in,
before the concrete
  hardens.
Before all the flute holes
  are blocked,
before all principles are
  explained,
before everything is
  broken,
before the law goes into
  effect,
before God's hand closes,
before we go away from
  here.

—YEHUDA AMICHAI
(trans. Alan Lettofsky)

We repeat the following verse after the leader:

Hear us, forgive us today, for the day is ending,
and we shall praise You, awe-inspiring Holy One.

Now, may our sanctification rise up to You,
for You, our God, are a forgiving and merciful sovereign.

THE GATES: A PIYYUT

Open the gates of righteousness for us,
that we may enter them and praise God.
We have knocked on Your doors, Merciful One;
do not turn us away empty-handed.

Open for us and for all Israel,
our people, wherever they are:
Gates of light, blessing, and joy,
  gates of gladness, splendor, and good counsel,
  gates of merit, love, and purity,
  gates of salvation, atonement, and kindness,
  gates of pardon, consolation, and forgiveness,
  gates of help, prosperity, and righteousness,
  gates of uprightness and complete healing,
  gates of peace and repentance.

Sha·arei orah, sha·arei v'rakhah, sha·arei gilah,
sha·arei ditzah, sha·arei hod v'hadar, sha·arei va·ad tov,
sha·arei z'khuyyot, sha·arei ḥedvah, sha·arei tohorah,
sha·arei y'shu·ah, sha·arei khapparah, sha·arei lev tov,
sha·arei m'ḥilah, sha·arei neḥamah, sha·arei s'liḥah,
sha·arei ezrah, sha·arei farnasah tovah, sha·arei tz'dakah,
sha·arei kom'miyyut, sha·arei r'fu·ah sh'leimah,
sha·arei shalom, sha·arei t'shuvah.

And seal us in the Book of Life for blessing and holiness,
for You are holy and Your name is holy;
allow us to enter Your gates in holiness.

קְדֻשָּׁה

וּבְכֵן תַּעֲרַץ וְתִקְדַּשׁ, כְּסוֹד שִׂיחַ שַׂרְפֵי קֹדֶשׁ,
הַמַּקְדִּישִׁים שִׁמְךָ בַּקֹּדֶשׁ, כַּכָּתוּב עַל יַד נְבִיאֶךָ,
וְקָרָא זֶה אֶל זֶה וְאָמַר:

**קָדוֹשׁ, קָדוֹשׁ, קָדוֹשׁ יהוה צְבָאוֹת,
מְלֹא כָל־הָאָרֶץ כְּבוֹדוֹ.**

כְּבוֹדוֹ מָלֵא עוֹלָם, מְשָׁרְתָיו שׁוֹאֲלִים זֶה לָזֶה אַיֵּה מְקוֹם
כְּבוֹדוֹ. לְעֻמָּתָם בָּרוּךְ יֹאמֵרוּ:

בָּרוּךְ כְּבוֹד־יהוה מִמְּקוֹמוֹ.

מִמְּקוֹמוֹ הוּא יִפֶן בְּרַחֲמִים, וְיָחוֹן עַם הַמְיַחֲדִים שְׁמוֹ
עֶרֶב וָבֹקֶר בְּכָל־יוֹם תָּמִיד, פַּעֲמַיִם בְּאַהֲבָה שְׁמַע
אוֹמְרִים:

שְׁמַע יִשְׂרָאֵל יהוה אֱלֹהֵינוּ יהוה אֶחָד.

הוּא אֱלֹהֵינוּ, הוּא אָבִינוּ, הוּא מַלְכֵּנוּ, הוּא מוֹשִׁיעֵנוּ,
וְהוּא יַשְׁמִיעֵנוּ בְּרַחֲמָיו שֵׁנִית לְעֵינֵי כָּל־חָי, לִהְיוֹת לָכֶם
לֵאלֹהִים:

אֲנִי יהוה אֱלֹהֵיכֶם.

אַדִּיר אַדִּירֵנוּ יהוה אֲדֹנֵנוּ, מָה אַדִּיר שִׁמְךָ בְּכָל־הָאָרֶץ.
וְהָיָה יהוה לְמֶלֶךְ עַל כָּל־הָאָרֶץ, בַּיּוֹם הַהוּא יִהְיֶה יהוה
אֶחָד וּשְׁמוֹ אֶחָד. וּבְדִבְרֵי קָדְשְׁךָ כָּתוּב לֵאמֹר:

יִמְלֹךְ יהוה לְעוֹלָם, אֱלֹהַיִךְ צִיּוֹן לְדֹר וָדֹר, הַלְלוּ־יָהּ.

The Kedushah is composed of an interweaving of two prophetic visions: Isaiah's vision of angels singing "holy, holy, holy…" and Ezekiel's vision of heavenly forces descending to earth, concluding with the phrase, "praised is Adonai's glory." Unlike the Kedushah D'sidra, which was recited at the beginning of Ne·ilah (page 396), this form of the Kedushah has an antiphonal quality: in heaven one chorus of angels responds to another, and on earth, leader and congregation respond to each other. Our recitation of the Sh'ma, evening and morning, is offered as a counterpoint to the angelic praise.

FROM WHERE GOD DWELLS מִמְּקוֹמוֹ. The Rabbis said that the word מָקוֹם (makom), "place," is one of the names of God. "God is the place of the world, but the world is not God's place" (Genesis Rabbah 68:10). The fact that God is everywhere allows us to recite the Kedushah outside of heaven and outside the Temple. Every synagogue filled with prayer can become God's place.

YET AGAIN שֵׁנִית. The first time was at the time of the Exodus. The second time will be the ultimate redemption of the world in messianic times.

Whether or not one accepts the imagery of angels and heavenly choirs found in the Kedushah literally, when we view it as poetry it is remarkably successful in invoking a sense of the mystery and awe of the incomprehensible world in which we live. As science expands the horizons of our knowledge and extends our view of the vastness of the universe, as space probes provide us with ever more spectacular and inspiring vistas of the magnificence of creation, the Kedushah fills our imagination with awe-inspiring glimpses of the mysterious realities beyond that which we can see and comprehend. It lifts our spirits into new realms of existence no less wondrous than the s'firot (spheres of existence) described in the Kabbalah (Jewish mysticism).

—REUVEN HAMMER

The Kedushah

Congregants who are sitting may rise for the Kedushah. The tradition recommends standing like angels, with feet together. Some have the custom of rising each time the word "holy" is recited.

Through the people Israel, may You be revered and hallowed, with the mystic language of the heavenly chorus, who sanctify Your name in Your holy realm, as recorded in Isaiah's vision:

Each cried out to the other:
"Holy, holy, holy is *Adonai Tz'va·ot*, the whole world is filled with God's glory!"
Kadosh, kadosh, kadosh Adonai Tz'va·ot, m'lo khol ha-aretz k'vodo.

God's glory fills the universe. As one angelic chorus asks, "Where is the place of God's glory?" another responds: "Praised is Adonai's glory wherever God dwells."
Barukh k'vod Adonai mi-m'komo.

From where God dwells, may God turn with compassion toward the people who twice each day, evening and morning, lovingly proclaim God's oneness, reciting the Sh'ma: "Hear, O Israel, Adonai is our God, Adonai alone."
Sh'ma yisra·el, Adonai eloheinu, Adonai ehad.

The Holy One is our God, our creator, our sovereign, our redeemer. Yet again, God will in mercy proclaim to us before all that lives:
Hu eloheinu, hu avinu, hu malkeinu, hu moshi·einu, v'hu yashmi·einu b'rahamav sheinit l'einei kol hai, lihyot lakhem leilohim.
"I, Adonai, am your God."
Ani Adonai eloheikhem.

Majesty, our majesty, Adonai, our master, how majestic is Your name throughout the world!

Adonai shall be acknowledged sovereign of all the earth. On that day Adonai shall be one, and the name of God, one.

As the psalmist sang:
Adonai will reign forever; your God, O Zion, from generation to generation. Halleluyah!
Yimlokh Adonai l'olam, elohayikh tziyyon l'dor va-dor, hal'luyah.

לְדוֹר וָדוֹר נַגִּיד גָּדְלֶךָ, וּלְנֵצַח נְצָחִים קְדֻשָּׁתְךָ נַקְדִּישׁ,
וְשִׁבְחֲךָ אֱלֹהֵינוּ מִפִּינוּ לֹא יָמוּשׁ לְעוֹלָם וָעֶד, כִּי אֵל מֶלֶךְ
גָּדוֹל וְקָדוֹשׁ אָתָּה.

חֲמוֹל עַל מַעֲשֶׂיךָ
וְתִשְׂמַח בְּמַעֲשֶׂיךָ,
וְיֹאמְרוּ לְךָ חוֹסֶיךָ
בְּצַדֶּקְךָ עֲמוּסֶיךָ,
תֻּקְדַּשׁ אָדוֹן עַל כָּל־מַעֲשֶׂיךָ.

בְּאֵין מֵלִיץ יֹשֶׁר
מוּל מַגִּיד פֶּשַׁע,
תַּגִּיד לְיַעֲקֹב דְּבַר חֹק וּמִשְׁפָּט,
וְצַדְּקֵנוּ בַּמִּשְׁפָּט, הַמֶּלֶךְ הַמִּשְׁפָּט.

וּבְכֵן תֵּן פַּחְדְּךָ יהוה אֱלֹהֵינוּ עַל כָּל־מַעֲשֶׂיךָ,
וְאֵימָתְךָ עַל כָּל־מַה־שֶּׁבָּרָאתָ,
וְיִירָאוּךָ כָּל־הַמַּעֲשִׂים
וְיִשְׁתַּחֲווּ לְפָנֶיךָ כָּל־הַבְּרוּאִים,
וְיֵעָשׂוּ כֻלָּם אֲגֻדָּה אַחַת לַעֲשׂוֹת רְצוֹנְךָ בְּלֵבָב שָׁלֵם,
כְּמוֹ שֶׁיָּדַעְנוּ יהוה אֱלֹהֵינוּ,
שֶׁהַשִּׁלְטוֹן לְפָנֶיךָ, עֹז בְּיָדְךָ וּגְבוּרָה בִּימִינֶךָ,
וְשִׁמְךָ נוֹרָא עַל כָּל־מַה־שֶּׁבָּרָאתָ.

וּבְכֵן תֵּן כָּבוֹד יהוה לְעַמֶּךָ,
תְּהִלָּה לִירֵאֶיךָ וְתִקְוָה לְדוֹרְשֶׁיךָ,
וּפִתְחוֹן פֶּה לַמְיַחֲלִים לָךְ,
שִׂמְחָה לְאַרְצֶךָ וְשָׂשׂוֹן לְעִירֶךָ,
וּצְמִיחַת קֶרֶן לְדָוִד עַבְדֶּךָ,
וַעֲרִיכַת נֵר לְבֶן־יִשַׁי מְשִׁיחֶךָ, בִּמְהֵרָה בְיָמֵינוּ.

U-V'KHEIN וּבְכֵן. These three paragraphs, which are all introduced by the same word, וּבְכֵן (u-v'khein), are ascribed by many scholars to the 2nd or 3rd century, and may constitute the earliest poetic additions to the Amidah.

Stages of redemption are described in this series of prayers. The first paragraph implores God to cause the entire world to live with reverence for God. The second paragraph discusses not the universal, but the particular: the return of Israel to its land (and specifically to Jerusalem) and the kingship of David. The third paragraph describes the rejoicing that will come to the righteous "when You remove the tyranny of arrogance from the earth" and God will rule alone over the entire world from Zion and Jerusalem. (*adapted from Reuven Hammer*)

Meditation on God and Prayer

Prayer is meaningless unless it is subversive, unless it seeks to overthrow and to ruin the pyramids of callousness, hatred, opportunism, falsehoods.
— ABRAHAM JOSHUA HESCHEL

From one generation to another we will declare Your greatness, and forever sanctify You with words of holiness. Your praise will never leave our lips, for You are God and Sovereign, great and holy.

REMEMBER US FOR GOOD: FRAGMENTS OF TWO PIYYUTIM

Have compassion on Your creation
and rejoice in Your handiwork.
As You vindicate Your people,
all who trust in You will declare:
"Be sanctified, Lord, throughout Your creation."

Though we have no one fully righteous to plead our cause
against the one who talks of our guilt,
speak to Jacob of Your judgment
finding us innocent, Sovereign of justice.

U-v'khein—ADONAI our God,
instill Your awe in all You have made,
and fear of You in all You have created,
so that all You have fashioned revere You,
all You have created bow in recognition,
and all be bound together, carrying out Your will wholeheartedly.
For we know that true sovereignty is Yours,
power and strength are in Your hands,
and Your name is to be revered beyond any of Your creations.

U-v'khein—Bestow honor to Your people, ADONAI,
praise to those who revere You,
hope to those who seek You,
recognition to those who await You,
joy to Your land, and gladness to Your city.
Simḥah l'artzekha v'sason l'irekha
May the light of David, Your servant, dawn,
and the lamp of the son of Jesse, Your anointed,
be kindled speedily in our day.

וּבְכֵן צַדִּיקִים יִרְאוּ וְיִשְׂמָחוּ, וִישָׁרִים יַעֲלֹזוּ, וַחֲסִידִים
בְּרִנָּה יָגִילוּ, וְעוֹלָתָה תִּקְפָּץ־פִּיהָ, וְכָל־הָרִשְׁעָה כֻּלָּהּ
כְּעָשָׁן תִּכְלֶה, כִּי תַעֲבִיר מֶמְשֶׁלֶת זָדוֹן מִן הָאָרֶץ.

וְתִמְלֹךְ אַתָּה יהוה לְבַדֶּךָ, עַל כָּל־מַעֲשֶׂיךָ,
בְּהַר צִיּוֹן מִשְׁכַּן כְּבוֹדֶךָ, וּבִירוּשָׁלַיִם עִיר קָדְשֶׁךָ,
כַּכָּתוּב בְּדִבְרֵי קָדְשֶׁךָ:
יִמְלֹךְ יהוה לְעוֹלָם, אֱלֹהַיִךְ צִיּוֹן לְדֹר וָדֹר, הַלְלוּ־יָהּ.

קָדוֹשׁ אַתָּה וְנוֹרָא שְׁמֶךָ, וְאֵין אֱלוֹהַּ מִבַּלְעָדֶיךָ,
כַּכָּתוּב: וַיִּגְבַּהּ יהוה צְבָאוֹת בַּמִּשְׁפָּט, וְהָאֵל הַקָּדוֹשׁ
נִקְדַּשׁ בִּצְדָקָה. בָּרוּךְ אַתָּה יהוה, הַמֶּלֶךְ הַקָּדוֹשׁ.

אַתָּה בְחַרְתָּנוּ מִכָּל־הָעַמִּים, אָהַבְתָּ אוֹתָנוּ וְרָצִיתָ בָּנוּ,
וְרוֹמַמְתָּנוּ מִכָּל־הַלְּשׁוֹנוֹת, וְקִדַּשְׁתָּנוּ בְּמִצְוֹתֶיךָ, וְקֵרַבְתָּנוּ
מַלְכֵּנוּ לַעֲבוֹדָתֶךָ, וְשִׁמְךָ הַגָּדוֹל וְהַקָּדוֹשׁ עָלֵינוּ קָרָאתָ.

וַתִּתֶּן־לָנוּ, יהוה אֱלֹהֵינוּ, בְּאַהֲבָה אֶת־יוֹם [הַשַּׁבָּת הַזֶּה
לִקְדֻשָּׁה וְלִמְנוּחָה וְאֶת־יוֹם] הַכִּפּוּרִים הַזֶּה לִמְחִילָה
וְלִסְלִיחָה וּלְכַפָּרָה, וְלִמְחָל־בּוֹ אֶת־כָּל־עֲוֹנוֹתֵינוּ
[בְּאַהֲבָה] מִקְרָא קֹדֶשׁ, זֵכֶר לִיצִיאַת מִצְרָיִם.

אֱלֹהֵינוּ וֵאלֹהֵי אֲבוֹתֵינוּ [וְאִמּוֹתֵינוּ], יַעֲלֶה וְיָבֹא, וְיַגִּיעַ
וְיֵרָאֶה, וְיֵרָצֶה וְיִשָּׁמַע, וְיִפָּקֵד וְיִזָּכֵר זִכְרוֹנֵנוּ וּפִקְדּוֹנֵנוּ,
וְזִכְרוֹן אֲבוֹתֵינוּ [וְאִמּוֹתֵינוּ], וְזִכְרוֹן מָשִׁיחַ בֶּן־דָּוִד עַבְדֶּךָ,
וְזִכְרוֹן יְרוּשָׁלַיִם עִיר קָדְשֶׁךָ, וְזִכְרוֹן כָּל־עַמְּךָ בֵּית יִשְׂרָאֵל
לְפָנֶיךָ לִפְלֵיטָה לְטוֹבָה, לְחֵן וּלְחֶסֶד וּלְרַחֲמִים, לְחַיִּים
וּלְשָׁלוֹם, בְּיוֹם הַכִּפּוּרִים הַזֶּה.

זָכְרֵנוּ יהוה אֱלֹהֵינוּ בּוֹ לְטוֹבָה,   אָמֵן.
וּפָקְדֵנוּ בוֹ לִבְרָכָה,   אָמֵן.
וְהוֹשִׁיעֵנוּ בוֹ לְחַיִּים,   אָמֵן.

וּבִדְבַר יְשׁוּעָה וְרַחֲמִים, חוּס וְחָנֵּנוּ, וְרַחֵם עָלֵינוּ
וְהוֹשִׁיעֵנוּ, כִּי אֵלֶיךָ עֵינֵינוּ,
כִּי אֵל מֶלֶךְ חַנּוּן וְרַחוּם אָתָּה.

ADONAI WILL REIGN יִמְלֹךְ
יהוה. In the context of this
prayer, the words from
Psalm 146:10 express a messianic hope.

**ADONAI TZ'VA·OT WILL BE
EXALTED** וַיִּגְבַּהּ יהוה צְבָאוֹת.
Isaiah 5:16. The liturgist
transforms Isaiah's call to
the people to repent into a
messianic wish.

יַעֲלֶה וְיָבֹא. In this prayer
we mention all that we
wish God to keep in mind
at this hour. It is filled with
synonyms and repetitions
of the word "remember."
We cannot imagine a different future, unless we keep
in mind our past.

The Holiness of the
Day and the Holiness
of the Hour
The contemporary
Jewish thinker Eliezer
Schweid remarks that at
the end of the day of fasting and prayer, we may
be left with feelings more
than with thoughts; with
a sense of how fragile life
is and how much we want
to live. It may be a time
when we feel most in-
tensely the pleas that the
day's prayers enunciate.

U-v'khein—The righteous, beholding this, will rejoice, the upright will be glad, the pious will celebrate with song, evil will be
silenced, all wickedness will disappear like smoke, when You
remove the tyranny of arrogance from the earth.

You alone, ADONAI, will rule all Your creation, from Mount
Zion, the dwelling-place of Your glory, Jerusalem, Your holy
city. As it is written in the Book of Psalms: "ADONAI will reign
forever, your God, O Zion, from generation to generation.
Halleluyah."

You are holy, and Your name is revered, for there is no God but
You. As Your prophet Isaiah wrote: "*Adonai Tz'va·ot* will be
exalted through justice, the holy God sanctified through righteousness." *Barukh atah* ADONAI, the Holy Sovereign.

Fourth B'rakhah: The Holiness of Yom Kippur

You have chosen us among all peoples, loving us, wanting us.
You have distinguished us among all nations, making us holy
through Your commandments, drawing us close to Your service, and calling us by Your great and holy name.

With love, You have bestowed on us, ADONAI our God, this
[Shabbat, for sanctity and rest, and this] Yom Kippur for pardon, forgiveness, and atonement, that all our sins be forgiven
[through Your love], a sacred time, recalling the Exodus from
Egypt.

Our God and God of our ancestors, may the thought of us
rise up and reach You. Attend to us and accept us; hear us
and respond to us. Keep us in mind, and keep in mind the
thought of our ancestors, as well as the Messiah the descendant of David; Jerusalem, Your holy city; and all Your people,
the House of Israel. On this Yom Kippur respond to us with
deliverance, goodness, compassion, love, life, and peace.

Remember us for good;	*Amen.*
respond to us with blessing;	*Amen.*
redeem us with life.	*Amen.*

Show us compassion and care with words of salvation and
kindness; have mercy on us and redeem us. Our eyes are
turned to You, for You are a compassionate and loving
sovereign.

The following three paragraphs are recited aloud, first by the leader and then by the congregation.

פְּתַח לָנוּ שַׁעַר,
בְּעֵת נְעִילַת שַׁעַר,
כִּי פָנָה יוֹם.

הַיּוֹם יִפְנֶה,
הַשֶּׁמֶשׁ יָבֹא וְיִפְנֶה,
נָבוֹאָה שְׁעָרֶיךָ.

אָנָּא אֵל נָא,
שָׂא נָא, סְלַח נָא, מְחַל נָא,
חֲמָל־נָא, רַחֶם־נָא, כַּפֶּר־נָא,
כְּבוֹשׁ חֵטְא וְעָוֹן.

אֵל, אֶרֶךְ אַפַּיִם אַתָּה,
וּבַעַל הָרַחֲמִים נִקְרֵאתָ,
וְדֶרֶךְ תְּשׁוּבָה הוֹרֵיתָ.
גְּדֻלַּת רַחֲמֶיךָ וַחֲסָדֶיךָ תִּזְכֹּר הַיּוֹם
וּבְכָל־יוֹם לְזֶרַע יְדִידֶיךָ.
תֵּפֶן אֵלֵינוּ בְּרַחֲמֶיךָ,
כִּי אַתָּה הוּא בַּעַל הָרַחֲמִים.

בְּתַחֲנוּן וּבִתְפִלָּה פָּנֶיךָ נְקַדֵּם,
כְּהוֹדַעְתָּ לֶעָנָו מִקֶּדֶם.
מֵחֲרוֹן אַפְּךָ שׁוּב,
כְּמוֹ בְּתוֹרָתְךָ כָּתוּב,
וּבְצֵל כְּנָפֶיךָ נֶחֱסֶה וְנִתְלוֹנָן,
כְּיוֹם וַיֵּרֶד יהוה בֶּעָנָן.
◁ תַּעֲבֹר עַל פֶּשַׁע וְתִמְחֶה אָשָׁם,
כְּיוֹם וַיִּתְיַצֵּב עִמּוֹ שָׁם.
תַּאֲזִין שַׁוְעָתֵנוּ וְתַקְשִׁיב מֶנּוּ מַאֲמָר
כְּיוֹם וַיִּקְרָא בְשֵׁם יהוה.

As in the Kol Nidrei service, we turn now to the two most important themes of Yom Kippur: *s'liḥah* (forgiveness) and *viddui* (confession). God is merciful and forgiving, and so confession brings forgiveness and atonement. Just as in the Kol Nidrei service, the Thirteen Attributes of God—which emphasize God's forgiving nature—are repeated three times. Each time, they are introduced with *piyyutim*.

Each of the lines here is actually the refrain from a separate *piyyut*, traditionally attributed to Elazar Kallir (6th century, Land of Israel). The staccato quality of these *piyyutim* emphasizes the urgency of the moment.

Following the very moment when Israel was closest to God—standing at Sinai, having heard God utter the Ten Commandments—the Torah sees the people as sinking from the greatest heights to terrible depths. It was then that Israel committed the greatest breach against God, making a golden calf and worshipping it. But Moses prayed and God forgave even this terrible sin. It is this quintessential moment of sin and forgiveness that is the model for Yom Kippur. God does not want to punish us for our sins, but rather wants us to return to the path that leads toward the Holy One. If the sin of the golden calf could be forgiven, so can any sin.

AS ON THE DAY כְּיוֹם. The phrases that follow are from Exodus 34:5, the scene of Moses on Mount Sinai following the shattering of the tablets. When Moses was on the mountain, he did not eat or drink. Just as Israel at Sinai was forgiven, so too may our sins be forgiven; just as Moses, after fasting and praying, was afforded God's comforting and loving presence, so too may we merit God's loving presence.

S'LIḤOT

My room
has many doors

Each leads to
another room
with many doors

Without a word I go
from door to door
from room to room

I hear my silence

hear strange voices
an echo of words
behind a door
that is shut

Where is the key
the key word
— ROSE AUSLANDER

*The following three paragraphs are recited aloud,
first by the leader and then repeated by the congregation.*

THE GATES ARE CLOSING: THREE POETIC FRAGMENTS

Keep open the gate for us,
at the time of the closing of the gate,
for the day is coming to an end.

The day will come to an end,
soon, the sun will set,
let us come into Your gates.

God, we pray:
turn to us, forgive us, pardon us,
have mercy upon us, have compassion on us,
grant us atonement,
conquer sin and transgression.

*P'taḥ lanu sha·ar,
b'eit n'ilat sha·ar,
ki fanah yom.*

*Ha-yom yifneh,
ha-shemesh yavo v'yifneh,
navo·ah sh'arekha.*

*Ana El na,
sa na, s'laḥ na, m'ḥal na,
ḥamol na, raḥem na, kapper na,
k'vosh ḥeit v'avon.*

God, You are patient. You are known as the source of mercy.
You have taught the way of repentance. Today, and every day,
call to mind the wonder of Your compassion and mercy toward
the children of those You loved. Turn toward us in mercy, for
You are the source of mercy.

We approach Your presence with supplication and prayer, and
with the words You revealed to Moses, the humble one, long
ago. Turn away from wrath, as it is written in Your Torah,
and let us nestle under Your wings,
     as on the day "God descended in a cloud."
Overlook sin, blot out guilt,
     as on the day "God stood beside him."
Hear our cry, attend to our plea,
     as on the day "he called on the name ADONAI."

וַיַּעֲבֹר יהוה עַל פָּנָיו וַיִּקְרָא:

יהוה יהוה, אֵל רַחוּם וְחַנּוּן, אֶרֶךְ אַפַּיִם, וְרַב־חֶסֶד
וֶאֱמֶת. נֹצֵר חֶסֶד לָאֲלָפִים, נֹשֵׂא עָוֹן וָפֶשַׁע וְחַטָּאָה,
וְנַקֵּה.

וְסָלַחְתָּ לַעֲוֹנֵנוּ וּלְחַטָּאתֵנוּ וּנְחַלְתָּנוּ.

Some customarily strike their heart when asking God to forgive and pardon:

סְלַח לָנוּ אָבִינוּ כִּי חָטָאנוּ, מְחַל לָנוּ מַלְכֵּנוּ כִּי פָשָׁעְנוּ,
כִּי־אַתָּה, אֲדֹנָי, טוֹב וְסַלָּח וְרַב־חֶסֶד לְכָל־קוֹרְאֶיךָ.

כְּרַחֵם אָב עַל בָּנִים, כֵּן תְּרַחֵם יהוה עָלֵינוּ. לַיהוה
הַיְשׁוּעָה, עַל עַמְּךָ בִרְכָתֶךָ סֶּלָה. יהוה צְבָאוֹת עִמָּנוּ,
מִשְׂגָּב לָנוּ אֱלֹהֵי יַעֲקֹב, סֶלָה. יהוה צְבָאוֹת, אַשְׁרֵי אָדָם
בֹּטֵחַ בָּךְ. יהוה הוֹשִׁיעָה, הַמֶּלֶךְ יַעֲנֵנוּ בְיוֹם קָרְאֵנוּ.

◁ סְלַח נָא לַעֲוֹן הָעָם הַזֶּה כְּגֹדֶל חַסְדֶּךָ, וְכַאֲשֶׁר נָשָׂאתָה
לָעָם הַזֶּה מִמִּצְרַיִם וְעַד הֵנָּה. וְשָׁם נֶאֱמַר:
וַיֹּאמֶר יהוה סָלַחְתִּי כִּדְבָרֶךָ.

THIRTEEN ATTRIBUTES.
After praying for Israel,
Moses asked to see God's
face. God replied that no
one can see God directly,
but human beings can
experience God indirectly.
God passed before Moses,
who then heard the words
of the Thirteen Attributes
(Exodus 34:6–7), which
speak of God's love. The
message of the liturgy is
that God is experienced
in moments of forgiveness
and love. Repeatedly, the
liturgy emphasizes God's
graciousness, mercy, and
love.

FORGIVE סְלַח Numbers
14:19–20. When the people
Israel proved faithless after
hearing the report of the
spies who had returned
from scouting the land,
Moses uttered this prayer.
God responded, "I forgive,
as you asked."

THE THIRTEEN ATTRIBUTES

And ADONAI passed before him and called:
ADONAI, ADONAI, God, merciful and compassionate, patient,
abounding in love and faithfulness, assuring love for thousands
of generations, forgiving iniquity, transgression, and sin, and
granting pardon.

Adonai, Adonai, El rahum v'hannun, erekh appayim v'rav hesed ve-emet.
Notzeir hesed la-alafim, nosei avon va-fesha v'hatta·ah v'nakkeih.

Forgive our transgressions and our sins; claim us for Your own.

Some customarily strike their heart when asking God to forgive and pardon:
Forgive us, our creator, for we have sinned;
pardon us, our sovereign, for we have transgressed—
for You, ADONAI, are kind and forgiving;
You act generously to all who call on You.

S'lah lanu avinu ki hatanu, m'hal lanu malkeinu ki fashanu,
ki atah, Adonai, tov v'sallah v'rav hesed l'khol kor'ekha.

As a parent looks kindly on a child, may You, God, look kindly on
us. Salvation is ADONAI's alone; pour blessings on Your people
forever. *Adonai Tz'va·ot* is with us, our support, the God of Jacob,
forever. Blessed is the one who trusts in You, *Adonai Tz'va·ot*.
ADONAI, save us. Surely the Sovereign will respond to us on the
day that we call out.

"As befits Your abundant love, please forgive this people's sin,
just as You have always forgiven this people from the time of the
Exodus from Egypt until now." When Moses recited this prayer it is
recorded:
ADONAI said, "I forgive, as you asked."

Va-yomer Adonai salahti ki-d'varekha.

אֶנְקַת מְסַלְּדֶיךָ,
תַּעַל לְפְנֵי כִסֵּא כְבוֹדֶךָ.
מַלֵּא מִשְׁאֲלוֹת עַם מְיַחֲדֶךָ,
שׁוֹמֵעַ תְּפִלַּת בָּאֵי עָדֶיךָ.

יִשְׂרָאֵל נוֹשַׁע בַּיהוה תְּשׁוּעַת עוֹלָמִים,
גַּם הַיּוֹם יִוָּשְׁעוּ מִפִּיךָ שׁוֹכֵן מְרוֹמִים,
כִּי אַתָּה רַב סְלִיחוֹת וּבַעַל הָרַחֲמִים.

יַחְבִּיאֵנוּ צֵל יָדוֹ תַּחַת כַּנְפֵי הַשְּׁכִינָה,
חֹן יָחֹן כִּי יִבְחֹן לֵב עָקֹב לְהָכִינָה,
קוּמָה נָא אֱלֹהֵינוּ עֻזָּה עֻזִּי נָא,
יהוה לְשַׁוְעָתֵנוּ הַאֲזִינָה.

יַשְׁמִיעֵנוּ סָלַחְתִּי יוֹשֵׁב בְּסֵתֶר עֶלְיוֹן,
בִּימִין יֶשַׁע לְהוֹשִׁיעַ עַם עָנִי וְאֶבְיוֹן,
בְּשַׁוְּעֵנוּ אֵלֶיךָ נוֹרָאוֹת בְּצֶדֶק תַּעֲנֵנוּ,
יהוה הֱיֵה עוֹזֵר לָנוּ.

These fragments of four *piyyutim* traditionally included in the Ashkenazic rite, were written by poets from Italy and France, who lived during the 9th to 13th centuries.

MAY ISRAEL, WHOM YOU PROMISED WOULD BE SAVED יִשְׂרָאֵל נוֹשַׁע. Isaiah declares that ultimately his work will be validated, and we too pray that our lives will be judged worthwhile. The poet has adapted Isaiah 49:2, Jeremiah 17:9, and Psalm 68:29.

THIS POOR AND DESTITUTE PEOPLE עַם עָנִי וְאֶבְיוֹן. God is the protector of the poor and the orphan, and in prayer, we come before God impoverished and bereft.

PLEAS TO GOD: FRAGMENTS OF FOUR PIYYUTIM

May the cry of those who pray to You rise up before the
    throne of Your glory.
Fulfill the requests of those who worship You alone,
You who hear the prayers of those who approach You.

May Israel, whom You promised would be saved in the end of days,
be saved today, as You, who dwell on high, utter words of forgiveness,
for You are abundantly forgiving and the source of compassion.

May the shadow of Your hand
shelter us beneath the wings of the Shekhinah.
Have compassion on us as You probe and set straight our deceitful hearts.
Our God, rise up and give us strength, and hear our plea.

Unfathomable God, let us hear the words "I forgive."
May this poor and destitute people
be delivered by Your right hand.
As we appeal to You,
respond to us with righteous and awe-inspiring deeds.
ADONAI, help us.

אֵל, מֶלֶךְ יוֹשֵׁב עַל כִּסֵּא רַחֲמִים,

מִתְנַהֵג בַּחֲסִידוּת, מוֹחֵל עֲוֹנוֹת עַמּוֹ,

מַעֲבִיר רִאשׁוֹן רִאשׁוֹן,

מַרְבֶּה מְחִילָה לַחַטָּאִים, וּסְלִיחָה לַפּוֹשְׁעִים,

עוֹשֶׂה צְדָקוֹת עִם כָּל־בָּשָׂר וָרְוּחַ, לֹא כְרָעָתָם תִּגְמוֹל.

◁ אֵל, הוֹרֵיתָ לָּנוּ לוֹמַר שְׁלֹשׁ עֶשְׂרֵה,

זְכָר־לָנוּ הַיּוֹם בְּרִית שְׁלֹשׁ עֶשְׂרֵה,

כְּמוֹ שֶׁהוֹדַעְתָּ לֶעָנָו מִקֶּדֶם,

כְּמוֹ שֶׁכָּתוּב: וַיֵּרֶד יהוה בֶּעָנָן, וַיִּתְיַצֵּב עִמּוֹ שָׁם,

וַיִּקְרָא בְשֵׁם יהוה.

וַיַּעֲבֹר יהוה עַל פָּנָיו וַיִּקְרָא:

יהוה יהוה, אֵל רַחוּם וְחַנּוּן, אֶרֶךְ אַפַּיִם, וְרַב־חֶסֶד
וֶאֱמֶת. נֹצֵר חֶסֶד לָאֲלָפִים, נֹשֵׂא עָוֹן וָפֶשַׁע וְחַטָּאָה,
וְנַקֵּה.

וְסָלַחְתָּ לַעֲוֹנֵנוּ וּלְחַטָּאתֵנוּ וּנְחַלְתָּנוּ.

Some customarily strike their heart when asking God to forgive and pardon:

סְלַח לָנוּ אָבִינוּ כִּי חָטָאנוּ, מְחַל לָנוּ מַלְכֵּנוּ כִּי פָשָׁעְנוּ,
כִּי־אַתָּה, אֲדֹנָי, טוֹב וְסַלָּח וְרַב־חֶסֶד לְכָל־קוֹרְאֶיךָ.

THE THIRTEEN ATTRIBUTES

God, Sovereign who sits on a throne of mercy,
acting with unbounded grace,
forgiving the sins of Your people, one by one,
as each comes before You,
generously forgiving sinners and pardoning transgressors,
acting charitably with every living thing:
do not repay them for their misdeeds.

God, You taught us how to recite the thirteen attributes of Your name;
remember the promise implied in these thirteen attributes,
which You first revealed to Moses, the humble one,
as it is written: God descended in a cloud and stood beside him, and he
called the name ADONAI:

And ADONAI passed before him and called:
ADONAI, ADONAI, God, merciful and compassionate, patient, abounding in
love and faithfulness, assuring love for thousands of generations, forgiving
iniquity, transgression, and sin, and granting pardon.
Adonai, Adonai, El raḥum v'ḥannun, erekh appayim v'rav ḥesed ve-emet.
Notzeir ḥesed la-alafim, nosei avon va-fesha v'ḥatta·ah v'nakkeih.

Forgive our transgressions and our sins; claim us for Your own.

Some customarily strike their heart when asking God to forgive and pardon:
Forgive us, our creator, for we have sinned; pardon us, our sovereign, for
we have transgressed—for You, ADONAI, are kind and forgiving; You act
generously to all who call on You.
S'laḥ lanu avinu ki ḥatanu, m'ḥal lanu malkeinu ki fashanu,
ki atah, Adonai, tov v'sallaḥ v'rav ḥesed l'khol kor'ekha.

לֵךְ בְּשִׂמְחָה אֱכֹל לַחְמֶךָ וּשְׁתֵה בְלֶב טוֹב יֵינֶךָ.

אֱלֹהִים הַדָּר בִּמְרוֹמְךָ שְׁמַע אַנְקַת אֱמוּנֶיךָ,
וּבַשֵּׂר אֶת־עַמְּךָ סָלַחְתִּי אֶת־זְדוֹנֶיךָ,
לֵךְ בְּשִׂמְחָה אֱכֹל לַחְמֶךָ וּשְׁתֵה בְלֶב טוֹב יֵינֶךָ.

מִטֶּרֶם עֲלוֹת שֶׁמֶשׁ לִמְעוֹנוֹ בַּמְּרוֹמִים,
וְעַד לֹא יָבוֹא אֱמֶשׁ הַקְשֵׁב שִׂיחַ תְּמִימִים,
וְכָל־פִּשְׁעֵיהֶם הַמֵּשׁ וְתַשְׁקִיעֵם בִּתְהוֹמִים,
וְצוֹרְרֵמוֹ צוּר הַכְמֵשׁ בַּחֲרוֹן אַף וּזְעָמִים,
וּלְעַם כָּפוּף בְּחֶרְמֵשׁ תַּשְׁמִיעַ בְּקוֹל רַחֲמִים,
קוּם לָמָּה זֶה בְּאֵימִים אַתָּה נוֹפֵל עַל פָּנֶיךָ,
לֵךְ בְּשִׂמְחָה אֱכֹל לַחְמֶךָ וּשְׁתֵה בְלֶב טוֹב יֵינֶךָ.

שַׁעֲרֵי רָצוֹן פְּתָחָה לְעַם קְנוּי לְגוֹרָלָךְ
וּלְכָל־חַטֹּאתָם סְלָחָה אֱלֹהִים חַי בְּרוֹב גָּדְלָךְ,
וְהָנֵס מֵהֶם אֲנָחָה וְשׁוּר כִּי הֵם פָּעֳלָךְ,
וּמַלְאָךְ, בְּרִית שְׁלָחָה לְגוֹי בָּחַרְתָּ לְחֶבְלָךְ,
וְחִישׁ לְהַשְׁמִיעוֹ בְּשִׂמְחָה בְּהוֹד נֹעַם מְלוּלָךְ,
עַמִּי מַה חָרָה לָךְ וְלָמָּה נָפְלוּ פָנֶיךָ,
לֵךְ בְּשִׂמְחָה אֱכֹל לַחְמֶךָ וּשְׁתֵה בְלֶב טוֹב יֵינֶךָ.

הָעֵת נְעִילַת שְׁעָרִים וְעֵת הַשֶּׁמֶשׁ לָבוֹא,
יַשְׁמִיעַ לַבְּחִירִים הַצּוּר לְמַעַן טוּבוֹ,
שְׂאוּ רָאשֵׁיכֶם שְׁעָרִים עַמִּי יָבוֹאוּ בוֹ,
וְיִזֶּה מֵי כִפּוּרִים עַל עַם בָּחַר לְחַבְּבוֹ,
וְיִגְאַל זֶרַע יְשָׁרִים וְיַעֲנֶה לְגוֹי אֲשֶׁר אֲהֵבוֹ,
זֶה הַדֶּרֶךְ לְכוּ בוֹ הִנְנִי עוֹמֵד לְפָנֶיךָ,
לֵךְ בְּשִׂמְחָה אֱכֹל לַחְמֶךָ וּשְׁתֵה בְלֶב טוֹב יֵינֶךָ.

GO FORTH JOYFULLY לֵךְ בְּשִׂמְחָה. Written by Moshe Ibn Ezra (12th century Spain) for Ne·ilah, this *piyyut* (based on Ecclesiastes 9:7) is included in the Italian rite for this day. The poem expresses the anticipated joy at the successful completion of the day.

THIS IS THE PATH זֶה הַדֶּרֶךְ. Isaiah 30:21.

Go forth joyfully, and with a full heart, partake of your meal and drink your wine.

Leikh b'simḥah ekhol laḥmekha u-sh'teih b'leiv tov yeinekha.

God, who dwells on high, hear the plea of Your faithful, and respond to Your people by saying: "I have forgiven your sins.
Go forth joyfully, and with a full heart, partake of your meal and drink your wine."

Leikh b'simḥah ekhol laḥmekha u-sh'teih b'leiv tov yeinekha.

Before the sun sets in the sky, and before the morrow comes, hear the words of Your simple people. Wipe away sins—tie them in a bundle and drown them in the deep—with divine anger reduce them to nothing. And to the people beaten down by the sickle, announce in a voice of compassion: "Stand up! Why are you falling on your face in fear?
Go forth joyfully, and with a full heart, partake of your meal and drink your wine."

Leikh b'simḥah ekhol laḥmekha u-sh'teih b'leiv tov yeinekha.

Open up the gates of favor to the people whose fate is so tied to You. Living God, in Your great mercy, forgive all their errors. Remove from them suffering and shackles, for this people is the work of Your hands. Send the herald of the covenant to the people with whom You have chosen to join; hasten joyfully and with glorious pleasure to tell them Your word: "My people, why do you trouble yourself, and why has your face fallen?
Go forth joyfully, and with a full heart, partake of your meal and drink your wine."

Leikh b'simḥah ekhol laḥmekha u-sh'teih b'leiv tov yeinekha.

At this hour of the closing of the gates and the setting of the sun, may the Stronghold of Israel, with kindness, announce to the chosen people, "Raise up high, O you gates, so that My people may enter." Pour the waters of atonement on the people whom You have chosen to adore You. Redeem the children of the upright and respond to the people who love You: "This is the path on which you shall walk. See, I stand before you."
Go forth joyfully, and with a full heart, partake of your meal and drink your wine."

Leikh b'simḥah ekhol laḥmekha u-sh'teih b'leiv tov yeinekha.

The following two verses are recited aloud, first by the leader
and then by the congregation.

רַחֶם־נָא קְהַל עֲדַת יְשֻׁרוּן.
סְלַח וּמְחַל עֲוֺנָם וְהוֹשִׁיעֵנוּ אֱלֹהֵי יִשְׁעֵנוּ.

שַׁעֲרֵי שָׁמַיִם פְּתַח, וְאוֹצָרְךָ הַטּוֹב לָנוּ תִפְתַּח,
תּוֹשִׁיעַ וְרִיב אַל תִּמְתַּח, וְהוֹשִׁיעֵנוּ אֱלֹהֵי יִשְׁעֵנוּ.

אֵל, מֶלֶךְ יוֹשֵׁב עַל כִּסֵּא רַחֲמִים,
מִתְנַהֵג בַּחֲסִידוּת, מוֹחֵל עֲוֺנוֹת עַמּוֹ,
מַעֲבִיר רִאשׁוֹן רִאשׁוֹן,
מַרְבֶּה מְחִילָה לַחַטָּאִים, וּסְלִיחָה לַפּוֹשְׁעִים,
עוֹשֶׂה צְדָקוֹת עִם כָּל־בָּשָׂר וָרוּחַ, לֹא כְרָעָתָם תִּגְמוֹל.
◁ אֵל, הוֹרֵיתָ לָּנוּ לוֹמַר שְׁלֹשׁ עֶשְׂרֵה,
זְכֹר־לָנוּ הַיּוֹם בְּרִית שְׁלֹשׁ עֶשְׂרֵה,
כְּמוֹ שֶׁהוֹדַעְתָּ לֶעָנָו מִקֶּדֶם,
כְּמוֹ שֶׁכָּתוּב: וַיֵּרֶד יהוה בֶּעָנָן, וַיִּתְיַצֵּב עִמּוֹ שָׁם,
וַיִּקְרָא בְשֵׁם יהוה.

וַיַּעֲבֹר יהוה עַל פָּנָיו וַיִּקְרָא:

יהוה יהוה, אֵל רַחוּם וְחַנּוּן, אֶרֶךְ אַפַּיִם, וְרַב־חֶסֶד
וֶאֱמֶת. נֹצֵר חֶסֶד לָאֲלָפִים, נֹשֵׂא עָוֺן וָפֶשַׁע וְחַטָּאָה,
וְנַקֵּה.

וְסָלַחְתָּ לַעֲוֺנֵנוּ וּלְחַטָּאתֵנוּ וּנְחַלְתָּנוּ.

Some customarily strike their heart when asking God to forgive and pardon:

סְלַח לָנוּ אָבִינוּ כִּי חָטָאנוּ, מְחַל לָנוּ מַלְכֵּנוּ כִּי פָשָׁעְנוּ,
כִּי־אַתָּה, אֲדֹנָי, טוֹב וְסַלָּח וְרַב־חֶסֶד לְכָל־קֹרְאֶיךָ.

THE THRONE OF MERCY
כִּסֵּא רַחֲמִים. Symbolically, God is said to have
two thrones: the seat of
judgment and the seat of
mercy. On Rosh Hashanah
God sits in judgment; on
Yom Kippur God moves to
the throne of mercy.

ONE BY ONE מַעֲבִיר רִאשׁוֹן
רִאשׁוֹן. According to the
Talmud, God counts only
one sin at a time. If the
totality of our sins were
counted altogether, we
might be judged negatively;
so God forgives each sin,
one by one. (Babylonian
Talmud, Rosh Hashanah
17a)

GOD, YOU TAUGHT US אֵל
הוֹרֵיתָ לָּנוּ. The biblical
verse is ambiguous as to
whether it was Moses
or God who recited the
thirteen attributes of God.
Rabbi Yoḥanan in the
Babylonian Talmud (Rosh
Hashanah 17b) describes
God wearing a *tallit* like a
cantor and showing Moses
how to pray. God said to
Moses: "Whenever Israel
sins, they should pray like
this and I will forgive them."
And then God recited the
thirteen attributes.

Meditation

God means: No one is ever alone; the essence of the temporal is the eternal; the moment is an image of eternity in an infinite mosaic.

—ABRAHAM JOSHUA
HESCHEL

The following two verses are recited aloud, first by the leader and then by the congregation.

Have mercy on the community of Jeshurun.
Forgive and pardon their sin and save us, God of our salvation.

Open the gates of heaven, and open for us Your goodly treasure.
Save us and do not press your quarrel with us; save us, God of our salvation.

Raḥem na k'hal adat y'shurun.
S'laḥ u-m'ḥal avonam v'hoshi·einu elohei yisheinu.
Sha·arei shamayim p'taḥ, v'otzar'kha ha-tov lanu tiftaḥ,
toshi·a v'riv al timtaḥ, v'hoshi·einu elohei yisheinu.

THE THIRTEEN ATTRIBUTES

God, Sovereign who sits on a throne of mercy,
acting with unbounded grace,
forgiving the sins of Your people, one by one,
as each comes before You,
generously forgiving sinners and pardoning transgressors,
acting charitably with every living thing:
do not repay them for their misdeeds.

God, You taught us how to recite the thirteen attributes of
Your name;
remember the promise implied in these thirteen attributes,
which You first revealed to Moses, the humble one,
as it is written: God descended in a cloud and stood beside him,
and he called the name Adonai:

And Adonai passed before him and called:
Adonai, Adonai, God, merciful and compassionate, patient,
abounding in love and faithfulness, assuring love for thousands
of generations, forgiving iniquity, transgression, and sin, and
granting pardon.

Adonai, Adonai, El raḥum v'ḥannun, erekh appayim v'rav ḥesed ve-emet.
Notzeir ḥesed la-alafim, nosei avon va-fesha v'ḥatta·ah v'nakkeih.

Forgive our transgressions and our sins; claim us for Your own.

Some customarily strike their heart when asking God to forgive and pardon:

Forgive us, our creator, for we have sinned; pardon us, our sovereign, for we have transgressed—for You, Adonai, are kind and forgiving; You act generously to all who call on You.

S'laḥ lanu avinu ki ḥatanu, m'ḥal lanu malkeinu ki fashanu,
ki atah, Adonai, tov v'sallaḥ v'rav ḥesed l'khol kor'ekha.

אֱלֹהֵינוּ וֵאלֹהֵי אֲבוֹתֵינוּ [וְאִמּוֹתֵינוּ],
סְלַח לָנוּ מְחַל לָנוּ, כַּפֶּר־לָנוּ.

כִּי

וְאַתָּה אֱלֹהֵינוּ,   אָנוּ עַמֶּךְ
וְאַתָּה אָבִינוּ.   אָנוּ בָנֶיךָ
וְאַתָּה אֲדוֹנֵנוּ,   אָנוּ עֲבָדֶיךָ
וְאַתָּה חֶלְקֵנוּ.   אָנוּ קְהָלֶךָ
וְאַתָּה נַחֲלָתֵךְ,   אָנוּ גוֹרָלֶךָ
וְאַתָּה רוֹעֵנוּ.   אָנוּ צֹאנֶךָ
וְאַתָּה נוֹטְרֵנוּ,   אָנוּ כַרְמֶךָ
וְאַתָּה יוֹצְרֵנוּ.   אָנוּ פְעֻלָּתֶךָ
וְאַתָּה דוֹדֵנוּ,   אָנוּ רַעְיָתֶךָ
וְאַתָּה קְרוֹבֵנוּ.   אָנוּ סְגֻלָּתֶךָ
וְאַתָּה מַלְכֵּנוּ,   אָנוּ עַמֶּךְ
וְאַתָּה מַאֲמִירֵנוּ.   אָנוּ מַאֲמִירֶךָ

WE ARE YOUR PEOPLE כִּי אָנוּ עַמֶּךְ. An early medieval poem, which expands on the well-known verse from Song of Songs: "I am for my beloved and my beloved is mine" (2:16). It completes the S'liḥot/Forgiveness section and forms the transition to the confession. Here we end in joyous song, then move to a meditative melody, as we begin the Viddui/Confession. In this poem we emphasize our relatedness to God, whereas in the next we emphasize the stark difference between the human and the Divine.

וידוי

וְאַתָּה רַחוּם וְחַנּוּן.   אָנוּ עַזֵּי פָנִים
וְאַתָּה אֶרֶךְ אַפַּיִם.   אָנוּ קְשֵׁי עֹרֶף
וְאַתָּה מָלֵא רַחֲמִים.   אָנוּ מְלֵאֵי עָוֹן
אָנוּ יָמֵינוּ כְּצֵל עוֹבֵר   וְאַתָּה הוּא וּשְׁנוֹתֶיךָ לֹא יִתָּמּוּ.

אֱלֹהֵינוּ וֵאלֹהֵי אֲבוֹתֵינוּ [וְאִמּוֹתֵינוּ],
תָּבֹא לְפָנֶיךָ תְּפִלָּתֵנוּ, וְאַל תִּתְעַלַּם מִתְּחִנָּתֵנוּ,
שֶׁאֵין אֲנַחְנוּ עַזֵּי פָנִים וּקְשֵׁי עֹרֶף לוֹמַר לְפָנֶיךָ,
יהוה אֱלֹהֵינוּ וֵאלֹהֵי אֲבוֹתֵינוּ [וְאִמּוֹתֵינוּ],
צַדִּיקִים אֲנַחְנוּ וְלֹא חָטָאנוּ,
אֲבָל אֲנַחְנוּ וַאֲבוֹתֵינוּ [וְאִמּוֹתֵינוּ] חָטָאנוּ.

WE, LIKE OUR ANCESTORS אֲנַחְנוּ וַאֲבוֹתֵינוּ. In the Babylonian Talmud, Mar Zutra remarked that anyone who says "we have sinned" has understood the meaning of confession (Yoma 87b). Every human being is imperfect. Even previous generations—whom we may idealize—contained sinners. As the Rabbis taught: no one has walked the earth and not sinned. In ascribing sin to our ancestors, the liturgist is quoting Psalm 106:6.

Our God and God of our ancestors, forgive us, pardon us, grant us atonement.

For—

We are Your people,	and You are our God;
we are Your children	and You are our parent.
We are Your servants,	and You are our master;
we are Your congregation,	and You are our portion.
We are Your heritage,	and You are our destiny;
we are Your flock,	and You are our shepherd.
We are Your vineyard,	and You are our guardian;
we are Your creatures,	and You are our creator.
We are Your spouse,	and You are our beloved;
we are Your cherished ones,	and You are near to us.
We are Your people,	and You are our sovereign;

We are the ones You address, and You are the One to whom we speak.

Ki

Anu ammekha,	*v'atah eloheinu,*
anu vanekha	*v'atah avinu.*
Anu avadekha	*v'atah adoneinu,*
anu k'halekha	*v'atah ḥelkeinu.*
Anu naḥalatekha	*v'atah goraleinu,*
anu tzonekha	*v'atah ro·einu.*
Anu kharmekha	*v'atah not'reinu,*
anu f'ullatekha,	*v'atah yotz'reinu.*
Anu ra·ayatekha	*v'atah dodeinu,*
anu s'gullatekha	*v'atah k'roveinu.*
Anu ammekha	*v'atah malkeinu,*
anu ma·amirekha	*v'atah ma·amireinu.*

VIDDUI — PRAYERS OF CONFESSION

We are insolent;	You are gracious and compassionate.
We are obstinate;	You are patient.
We are sinful;	You are merciful.
Our days are a passing shadow,	but You are the One who truly is, for time without end.

Our God and God of our ancestors, hear our prayer; do not ignore our plea. Our God and God of our ancestors, we are neither so insolent nor so obstinate as to claim in Your presence that we are righteous, without sin; for we, like our ancestors who came before us, have sinned.

It is customary to strike one's heart with one's fist as each phrase is recited.

אָשַׁמְנוּ, בָּגַדְנוּ, גָּזַלְנוּ, דִּבַּרְנוּ דְפִי.

הֶעֱוִינוּ, וְהִרְשַׁעְנוּ, זַדְנוּ, חָמַסְנוּ, טָפַלְנוּ שָׁקֶר.

יָעַצְנוּ רָע, כִּזַּבְנוּ, לַצְנוּ, מָרַדְנוּ, נִאַצְנוּ.

סָרַרְנוּ, עָוִינוּ, פָּשַׁעְנוּ, צָרַרְנוּ, קִשִּׁינוּ עֹרֶף.

רָשַׁעְנוּ, שִׁחַתְנוּ, תִּעַבְנוּ, תָּעִינוּ, תִּעְתָּעְנוּ.

סַרְנוּ מִמִּצְוֹתֶיךָ וּמִמִּשְׁפָּטֶיךָ הַטּוֹבִים, וְלֹא שָׁוָה לָנוּ. וְאַתָּה צַדִּיק עַל כָּל־הַבָּא עָלֵינוּ, כִּי אֱמֶת עָשִׂיתָ וַאֲנַחְנוּ הִרְשָׁעְנוּ. מַה נֹּאמַר לְפָנֶיךָ יוֹשֵׁב מָרוֹם, וּמַה נְּסַפֵּר לְפָנֶיךָ שׁוֹכֵן שְׁחָקִים, הֲלֹא כָּל הַנִּסְתָּרוֹת וְהַנִּגְלוֹת אַתָּה יוֹדֵעַ.

אַתָּה נוֹתֵן יָד לְפוֹשְׁעִים, וִימִינְךָ פְשׁוּטָה לְקַבֵּל שָׁבִים. וַתְּלַמְּדֵנוּ יהוה אֱלֹהֵינוּ לְהִתְוַדּוֹת לְפָנֶיךָ עַל כָּל־עֲוֹנוֹתֵינוּ, לְמַעַן נֶחְדַּל מֵעֹשֶׁק יָדֵינוּ, וּתְקַבְּלֵנוּ בִּתְשׁוּבָה שְׁלֵמָה לְפָנֶיךָ כְּאִשִּׁים וּכְנִיחוֹחִים, לְמַעַן דְּבָרֶיךָ אֲשֶׁר אָמַרְתָּ. אֵין קֵץ לְאִשֵּׁי חוֹבוֹתֵינוּ, וְאֵין מִסְפָּר לְנִיחוֹחֵי אַשְׁמוֹתֵינוּ. וְאַתָּה יוֹדֵעַ שֶׁאַחֲרִיתֵנוּ רִמָּה וְתוֹלֵעָה, לְפִיכָךְ הִרְבֵּיתָ סְלִיחָתֵנוּ.

מָה אָנוּ, מֶה חַיֵּינוּ, מֶה חַסְדֵּנוּ, מַה צִּדְקֵנוּ, מַה יִּשְׁעֵנוּ, מַה כֹּחֵנוּ, מַה גְּבוּרָתֵנוּ. מַה נֹּאמַר לְפָנֶיךָ, יהוה אֱלֹהֵינוּ וֵאלֹהֵי אֲבוֹתֵינוּ [וְאִמּוֹתֵינוּ]. הֲלֹא כָּל־הַגִּבּוֹרִים כְּאַיִן לְפָנֶיךָ, וְאַנְשֵׁי הַשֵּׁם כְּלֹא הָיוּ, וַחֲכָמִים כִּבְלִי מַדָּע, וּנְבוֹנִים כִּבְלִי הַשְׂכֵּל, כִּי רֹב מַעֲשֵׂיהֶם תֹּהוּ, וִימֵי חַיֵּיהֶם הֶבֶל לְפָנֶיךָ, וּמוֹתַר הָאָדָם מִן הַבְּהֵמָה אָיִן, כִּי הַכֹּל הָבֶל.

WE ABUSE אָשַׁמְנוּ. In Ne·ilah, we recite only this short confessional, the Ashamnu. It functions as a summary of the day, reminding us of the thoughts that have passed through our minds in these last twenty-four hours.

YOU EXTEND YOUR HAND אַתָּה נוֹתֵן יָד. These paragraphs replace the long confessional עַל חֵטְא (Al Het), which is recited in all other services on Yom Kippur.

WHAT ARE WE מָה אָנוּ. This paragraph is included in the daily morning service. This prayer expounds on the unimportance of our deeds and the meager nature of our goodness in comparison with God, concluding with the pessimistic words from Ecclesiastes 3:19: "Humans have no superiority over beasts; all life is vanity."
(Reuven Hammer)

ALL IS VANITY כִּי הַכֹּל הֶבֶל Ecclesiastes 3:19. *Hevel* (הֶבֶל) can also be translated as "breath" or "wind"; that is, our deeds are carried away like a passing wind.

To attain a degree of
spiritual security one
cannot rely upon one's
own resources. One
needs an atmosphere,
where the concern for the
spirit is shared by a community. We are in need
of students and scholars,
masters and specialists.
But we need also the
company of witnesses, of
human beings who are
engaged in worship, who
for a moment sense the
truth that life is meaningless without attachment
to God.

—ABRAHAM JOSHUA
HESCHEL

Concluding Confession—Ashamnu

It is customary to strike one's heart with each word of the confession.

We abuse, we betray, we are cruel, we destroy, we embitter,
we falsify, we gossip, we hate, we insult, we jeer, we kill, we lie,
we mock, we neglect, we oppress, we pervert, we quarrel, we
rebel, we steal, we transgress, we are unkind, we are violent, we
are wicked, we are extremists, we yearn to do evil, we are
zealous for bad causes.

Ashamnu, bagadnu, gazalnu, dibbarnu dofi,
he·evinu, v'hirshanu, zadnu, ḥamasnu, tafalnu sheker,
ya·atznu ra, kizzavnu, latznu, maradnu, ni·atznu,
sararnu, avinu, pashanu, tzararnu, kishinu oref,
rashanu, shiḥatnu, ti·avnu, ta·inu, titanu.

We have turned from Your goodly laws and commandments,
but it has not profited us. Surely, You are in the right with
respect to all that comes upon us, for You have acted faithfully,
but we have been in the wrong.

You extend Your hand to those who sin; Your right hand to
receive those who turn. You have taught us, ADONAI our God,
to confess each of our transgressions to You, so that we cease
using our hands for oppression. Accept us fully when we turn
to You, as You promised to accept the sweet smelling sacrifices.
Endless are the guilt-offerings that would have been required of
us in ancient Temple times.
You know that death is our end. Accordingly, You have afforded
us abundant opportunities to seek forgiveness.

What are we? What is our life? Our goodness? Our
righteousness? Our achievement? Our power?
Our victories?
What shall we say in Your presence,
ADONAI our God and God of our ancestors?
Heroes count as nothing in Your presence,
famous people are as if they never existed,
the wise seem ignorant,
and clever ones as if they lack reason.
The sum of their acts is chaos;
in Your presence the days of their lives are futile.
Human beings have no superiority over beasts;
all life is vanity.

אַתָּה הִבְדַּלְתָּ אֱנוֹשׁ מֵרֹאשׁ, וַתַּכִּירֵהוּ לַעֲמֹד לְפָנֶיךָ. כִּי מִי יֹאמַר לְךָ מַה תִּפְעָל, וְאִם יִצְדַּק מַה יִּתֶּן־לָךְ. וַתִּתֶּן־לָנוּ יהוה אֱלֹהֵינוּ בְּאַהֲבָה אֶת־יוֹם [הַשַּׁבָּת הַזֶּה וְאֶת־יוֹם] הַכִּפֻּרִים הַזֶּה, קֵץ וּמְחִילָה וּסְלִיחָה עַל כָּל־עֲוֹנוֹתֵינוּ, לְמַעַן נֶחְדַּל מֵעֹשֶׁק יָדֵנוּ, וְנָשׁוּב אֵלֶיךָ לַעֲשׂוֹת חֻקֵּי רְצוֹנְךָ בְּלֵבָב שָׁלֵם.

וְאַתָּה בְּרַחֲמֶיךָ הָרַבִּים רַחֵם עָלֵינוּ, כִּי לֹא תַחְפֹּץ בְּהַשְׁחָתַת עוֹלָם, שֶׁנֶּאֱמַר: דִּרְשׁוּ יהוה בְּהִמָּצְאוֹ, קְרָאֻהוּ בִּהְיוֹתוֹ קָרוֹב. וְנֶאֱמַר יַעֲזֹב רָשָׁע דַּרְכּוֹ, וְאִישׁ אָוֶן מַחְשְׁבֹתָיו, וְיָשֹׁב אֶל־יהוה וִירַחֲמֵהוּ, וְאֶל־אֱלֹהֵינוּ כִּי יַרְבֶּה לִסְלוֹחַ.

וְאַתָּה אֱלוֹהַּ סְלִיחוֹת, חַנּוּן וְרַחוּם, אֶרֶךְ אַפַּיִם, וְרַב חֶסֶד וֶאֱמֶת, וּמַרְבֶּה לְהֵיטִיב; וְרוֹצֶה אַתָּה בִּתְשׁוּבַת רְשָׁעִים, וְאֵין אַתָּה חָפֵץ בְּמִיתָתָם, שֶׁנֶּאֱמַר: אֱמֹר אֲלֵיהֶם, חַי אָנִי, נְאֻם אֲדֹנָי יֱהֹוִה, אִם אֶחְפֹּץ בְּמוֹת הָרָשָׁע, כִּי אִם בְּשׁוּב רָשָׁע מִדַּרְכּוֹ וְחָיָה; שׁוּבוּ שׁוּבוּ מִדַּרְכֵיכֶם הָרָעִים, וְלָמָּה תָמוּתוּ בֵּית יִשְׂרָאֵל. וְנֶאֱמַר: הֶחָפֹץ אֶחְפֹּץ מוֹת רָשָׁע, נְאֻם אֲדֹנָי יֱהֹוִה, הֲלֹא בְּשׁוּבוֹ מִדְּרָכָיו וְחָיָה. וְנֶאֱמַר: כִּי לֹא אֶחְפֹּץ בְּמוֹת הַמֵּת, נְאֻם אֲדֹנָי יהוה, וְהָשִׁיבוּ וִחְיוּ. כִּי אַתָּה סָלְחָן לְיִשְׂרָאֵל וּמָחֳלָן לְשִׁבְטֵי יְשֻׁרוּן בְּכָל־דּוֹר וָדוֹר, וּמִבַּלְעָדֶיךָ אֵין לָנוּ מֶלֶךְ מוֹחֵל וְסוֹלֵחַ אֶלָּא אָתָּה.

אֱלֹהֵינוּ וֵאלֹהֵי אֲבוֹתֵינוּ [וְאִמּוֹתֵינוּ], מְחַל לַעֲוֹנוֹתֵינוּ בְּיוֹם [הַשַּׁבָּת הַזֶּה וּבְיוֹם] הַכִּפּוּרִים הַזֶּה. מְחֵה וְהַעֲבֵר פְּשָׁעֵינוּ וְחַטֹּאתֵינוּ מִנֶּגֶד עֵינֶיךָ, כָּאָמוּר: אָנֹכִי אָנֹכִי הוּא מֹחֶה פְשָׁעֶיךָ לְמַעֲנִי, וְחַטֹּאתֶיךָ לֹא אֶזְכֹּר. וְנֶאֱמַר: מָחִיתִי כָעָב פְּשָׁעֶיךָ וְכֶעָנָן חַטֹּאתֶיךָ, שׁוּבָה אֵלַי כִּי גְאַלְתִּיךָ. וְנֶאֱמַר: כִּי־בַיּוֹם הַזֶּה יְכַפֵּר עֲלֵיכֶם לְטַהֵר אֶתְכֶם, מִכֹּל חַטֹּאתֵיכֶם לִפְנֵי יהוה תִּטְהָרוּ.

אֱלֹהֵינוּ וֵאלֹהֵי אֲבוֹתֵינוּ [וְאִמּוֹתֵינוּ], [רְצֵה בִמְנוּחָתֵנוּ] קַדְּשֵׁנוּ בְּמִצְוֹתֶיךָ וְתֵן חֶלְקֵנוּ בְּתוֹרָתֶךָ, שַׂבְּעֵנוּ מִטּוּבֶךָ וְשַׂמְּחֵנוּ בִּישׁוּעָתֶךָ, [וְהַנְחִילֵנוּ יהוה אֱלֹהֵינוּ, בְּאַהֲבָה

AND EVEN IF A PERSON WERE INNOCENT וְאִם יִצְדַּק. After Job 35:7.

YOU HAVE DISTINGUISHED אַתָּה הִבְדַּלְתָּ. This prayer contrasts with the one above, affirming the value of our lives, asserting that in the act of creation humans were separated from the rest of existence and given a special status.

(Reuven Hammer)

SEEK דִּרְשׁוּ. Isaiah 55:6–7, emphasizing that God is always present, for those who seek God.

SAY אֱמֹר. Ezekiel speaks words of consolation to the exiles in Babylonia (33:11, 18:23, 32).

I, SURELY I אָנֹכִי אָנֹכִי. Isaiah 43:25, 44:22.

JESHURUN יְשֻׁרוּן. Another biblical name for Israel.

FOR ON THIS DAY כִּי בַיּוֹם הַזֶּה. Leviticus 16:30. This verse summarizes the biblical description of Yom Kippur.

Yet from the beginning You distinguished human beings, acknowledging them that they might stand before You. For who can tell You how to behave? And even if a person were innocent, what difference would it make to You? ADONAI our God, You have lovingly given us this [Shabbat and this] Day of Atonement, bringing an end to our sins with pardon and forgiveness, that we cease using our hands for oppression, and turn back to You, wholeheartedly acting in accord with the laws You deem desirable.

May You, with Your abundant mercy, have compassion for us; for You do not desire the destruction of the world, as Your prophet declares: "Seek ADONAI, who can be found everywhere; call to God, who is close. Let evildoers abandon their path and the wicked their schemes, and return to ADONAI, who will have mercy on them; for our God will forgive, again and again." "You, forgiving God, are compassionate and merciful, patient, abounding in love" and goodness, and desire the return of the evildoers—not their death.

For You instructed Your prophet Ezekiel: "Say to them, 'As I live,' declares our Lord, ADONAI, 'I do not desire the death of the evildoers, but that they turn from their paths, and live. Turn back, turn back from your evil paths that you may not die, House of Israel!'... 'Is it My desire that the evildoer die,' declares the Lord, ADONAI, 'Is it not that they turn from their ways and live?'... 'It is not My desire that the wicked shall die, but that the wicked turn from their evil ways and live.".... For You forgive Israel and pardon the tribes of Jeshurun in every generation. Beside You, we have no sovereign who pardons and forgives.

CONCLUSION OF THE FOURTH B'RAKHAH
Our God and God of our ancestors, forgive our sins on this [Shabbat and this] Yom Kippur. Blot out and disregard them, as the prophet Isaiah says in Your name: "I, surely I, am the One who wipes away sin, for this is My nature; I will not recall your errors," and the prophet adds: "I sweep aside your sins like a mist, and disperse your transgressions like a cloud. Turn back to Me, for I will redeem you." And in Your Torah it is written: "For on this day, atonement shall be made for you to purify you from all your transgressions. In the presence of ADONAI you shall be pure."

Our God and God of our ancestors: [embrace our rest,] make us holy through Your mitzvot and let the Torah be our portion. Fill our lives with Your goodness and gladden us with Your triumph.

וּבִרְצוֹן שַׁבַּת קׇדְשֶׁךָ, וְיָנוּחוּ בָהּ יִשְׂרָאֵל, מְקַדְּשֵׁי שְׁמֶךָ]
וְטַהֵר לִבֵּנוּ לְעׇבְדְּךָ בֶּאֱמֶת, כִּי אַתָּה סׇלְחָן לְיִשְׂרָאֵל
וּמׇחֳלָן לְשִׁבְטֵי יְשֻׁרוּן בְּכׇל־דּוֹר וָדוֹר, וּמִבַּלְעָדֶיךָ אֵין
לָנוּ מֶלֶךְ מוֹחֵל וְסוֹלֵחַ אֶלָּא אָתָּה. בָּרוּךְ אַתָּה יהוה,
מֶלֶךְ מוֹחֵל וְסוֹלֵחַ לַעֲוֹנוֹתֵינוּ וְלַעֲוֹנוֹת עַמּוֹ בֵּית יִשְׂרָאֵל,
וּמַעֲבִיר אַשְׁמוֹתֵינוּ בְּכׇל־שָׁנָה וְשָׁנָה, מֶלֶךְ עַל כׇּל־הָאָרֶץ
מְקַדֵּשׁ [הַשַּׁבָּת וְ] יִשְׂרָאֵל וְיוֹם הַכִּפּוּרִים.

רְצֵה, יהוה אֱלֹהֵינוּ, בְּעַמְּךָ יִשְׂרָאֵל וּבִתְפִלָּתָם, וְהָשֵׁב
אֶת־הָעֲבוֹדָה לִדְבִיר בֵּיתֶךָ, [וְאִשֵּׁי יִשְׂרָאֵל]
וּתְפִלָּתָם בְּאַהֲבָה תְקַבֵּל בְּרָצוֹן, וּתְהִי לְרָצוֹן תָּמִיד
עֲבוֹדַת יִשְׂרָאֵל עַמֶּךָ.

וְתֶחֱזֶינָה עֵינֵינוּ בְּשׁוּבְךָ לְצִיּוֹן בְּרַחֲמִים. בָּרוּךְ אַתָּה
יהוה, הַמַּחֲזִיר שְׁכִינָתוֹ לְצִיּוֹן.

RESTORE WORSHIP TO YOUR SANCTUARY וְהָשֵׁב אֶת־הָעֲבוֹדָה לִדְבִיר בֵּיתֶךָ. According to the Babylonian Talmud, "Ever since the day when the Temple was destroyed, there has been an iron barrier separating Israel from God" (Berakhot 32b). Each destruction of the Temple in Jerusalem (first by the Babylonians in 586 B.C.E., then by the Romans in 70 C.E.) was a cataclysmic event in early Jewish history. In praying for the restoration of the Temple, we express our wish both for the sense of immediate connection with God that is believed to have characterized the Temple service, and for the common sense of purpose and religious community that was experienced there.

Congregation recites:

↑ מוֹדִים אֲנַחְנוּ לָךְ
שָׁאַתָּה הוּא יהוה אֱלֹהֵינוּ
וֵאלֹהֵי אֲבוֹתֵינוּ [וְאִמּוֹתֵינוּ]
אֱלֹהֵי כׇל־בָּשָׂר, יוֹצְרֵנוּ,
יוֹצֵר בְּרֵאשִׁית. בְּרָכוֹת
וְהוֹדָאוֹת לְשִׁמְךָ הַגָּדוֹל
וְהַקָּדוֹשׁ, עַל שֶׁהֶחֱיִיתָנוּ
וְקִיַּמְתָּנוּ. כֵּן תְּחַיֵּנוּ
וּתְקַיְּמֵנוּ, וְתֶאֱסוֹף
גָּלֻיּוֹתֵינוּ לְחַצְרוֹת קׇדְשֶׁךָ,
לִשְׁמוֹר חֻקֶּיךָ וְלַעֲשׂוֹת
רְצוֹנֶךָ, וּלְעׇבְדְּךָ בְּלֵבָב
שָׁלֵם, עַל שֶׁאֲנַחְנוּ מוֹדִים
לָךְ. בָּרוּךְ אֵל הַהוֹדָאוֹת.

Leader recites:

מוֹדִים אֲנַחְנוּ לָךְ
שָׁאַתָּה הוּא יהוה אֱלֹהֵינוּ
וֵאלֹהֵי אֲבוֹתֵינוּ [וְאִמּוֹתֵינוּ]
לְעוֹלָם וָעֶד, צוּר חַיֵּינוּ
מָגֵן יִשְׁעֵנוּ אַתָּה הוּא.
לְדוֹר וָדוֹר נוֹדֶה לְּךָ
וּנְסַפֵּר תְּהִלָּתֶךָ, עַל חַיֵּינוּ
הַמְּסוּרִים בְּיָדֶךָ וְעַל
נִשְׁמוֹתֵינוּ הַפְּקוּדוֹת לָךְ,
וְעַל נִסֶּיךָ שֶׁבְּכׇל־יוֹם עִמָּנוּ
וְעַל נִפְלְאוֹתֶיךָ וְטוֹבוֹתֶיךָ
שֶׁבְּכׇל־עֵת, עֶרֶב וָבֹקֶר
וְצׇהֳרָיִם. ◁ הַטּוֹב, כִּי לֹא
כָלוּ רַחֲמֶיךָ, וְהַמְרַחֵם, כִּי
לֹא תַמּוּ חֲסָדֶיךָ, מֵעוֹלָם
קִוִּינוּ לָךְ.

WE THANK YOU מוֹדִים אֲנַחְנוּ לָךְ. At this moment, after a day of fasting, we are particularly conscious of the gift of life.

וְעַל כֻּלָּם יִתְבָּרַךְ וְיִתְרוֹמַם שִׁמְךָ מַלְכֵּנוּ תָּמִיד לְעוֹלָם וָעֶד.

[ADONAI our God, grant that we inherit Your holy Shabbat, lovingly and willingly, so that the people Israel, who sanctify Your name, may find rest on this day.] Purify our hearts to serve You faithfully, for You forgive the people Israel and pardon the tribes of Jeshurun in every generation. Beside You, we have no sovereign who pardons and forgives. *Barukh atah ADONAI,* sovereign who pardons and forgives our sins and those of the people, the House of Israel, each year sweeping away our guilt—ruler of all the earth, who makes [Shabbat,] the people Israel and the Day of Atonement holy.

melekh al kol ha-aretz, m'kaddeish [ha-shabbat v'] yisra·el

Fifth B'rakhah: The Restoration of Zion

ADONAI our God, embrace Your people Israel and their prayer. Restore worship to Your sanctuary. May the [fiery offerings and] prayers of the people Israel be lovingly accepted by You, and may our service always be pleasing.

Let our eyes behold Your merciful return to Zion. *Barukh atah ADONAI,* who restores Your Divine Presence to Zion.

Sixth B'rakhah: Gratitude for Life and Its Blessings

Leader recites:

We thank You, You who are our God and the God of our ancestors through all time, protector of our lives, shield of our salvation. From one generation to the next we thank You and sing Your praises—
for our lives that are in Your hands,
for our souls that are under Your care,
for Your miracles that accompany us
  each day,
and for Your wonders and Your gifts
  that are with us each moment—
evening, morning, and noon.
You are the One who is good, whose mercy is never-ending; the One who is compassionate, whose love is unceasing. We have always placed our hope in You.

Congregation recites:

ⓕ We thank You for the ability to acknowledge You. You are our God and the God of our ancestors, the God of all flesh, our creator, and the creator of all. We offer praise and blessing to Your holy and great name, for granting us life and for sustaining us. May You continue to grant us life and sustenance. Gather our dispersed to Your holy courtyards, that we may fulfill Your mitzvot and serve You wholeheartedly, carrying out Your will. May God, the source of gratitude, be praised.

For all these blessings may Your name be praised and exalted, our sovereign, always and forever.

אָבִֽינוּ מַלְכֵּֽנוּ, זְכוֹר רַחֲמֶֽיךָ וּכְבוֹשׁ כַּעַסְךָ, וְכַלֵּה דֶּֽבֶר וְחֶֽרֶב, וְרָעָב וּשְׁבִי, וּמַשְׁחִית וְעָוֹן, וּשְׁמַד וּמַגֵּפָה, וּפֶֽגַע רָע וְכָל־מַחֲלָה, וְכָל־תַּקָלָה וְכָל־קְטָטָה, וְכָל־מִינֵי פֻרְעָנִיּוֹת, וְכָל־גְּזֵרָה רָעָה וְשִׂנְאַת חִנָּם, מֵעָלֵֽינוּ וּמֵעַל כָּל־בְּנֵי בְרִיתֶֽךָ.

וַחֲתוֹם לְחַיִּים טוֹבִים כָּל־בְּנֵי בְרִיתֶֽךָ.

וְכֹל הַחַיִּים יוֹדֽוּךָ סֶּֽלָה, וִיהַלְלוּ אֶת־שִׁמְךָ בֶּאֱמֶת, הָאֵל יְשׁוּעָתֵֽנוּ וְעֶזְרָתֵֽנוּ סֶֽלָה. בָּרוּךְ אַתָּה יהוה, הַטּוֹב שִׁמְךָ וּלְךָ נָאֶה לְהוֹדוֹת.

אֱלֹהֵֽינוּ וֵאלֹהֵי אֲבוֹתֵֽינוּ [וְאִמּוֹתֵֽינוּ], בָּרְכֵֽנוּ בַּבְּרָכָה הַמְשֻׁלֶּֽשֶׁת בַּתּוֹרָה הַכְּתוּבָה עַל יְדֵי מֹשֶׁה עַבְדֶּֽךָ, הָאֲמוּרָה מִפִּי אַהֲרֹן וּבָנָיו כֹּהֲנִים עַם קְדוֹשֶֽׁךָ, כָּאָמוּר.

כֵּן יְהִי רָצוֹן.	יְבָרֶכְךָ יהוה וְיִשְׁמְרֶֽךָ.
כֵּן יְהִי רָצוֹן.	יָאֵר יהוה פָּנָיו אֵלֶֽיךָ וִיחֻנֶּֽךָּ.
כֵּן יְהִי רָצוֹן.	יִשָּׂא יהוה פָּנָיו אֵלֶֽיךָ וְיָשֵׂם לְךָ שָׁלוֹם.

שִׂים שָׁלוֹם בָּעוֹלָם טוֹבָה וּבְרָכָה, חֵן וָחֶֽסֶד וְרַחֲמִים, עָלֵֽינוּ וְעַל כָּל־יִשְׂרָאֵל עַמֶּֽךָ. בָּרְכֵֽנוּ אָבִֽינוּ כֻּלָּֽנוּ כְּאֶחָד בְּאוֹר פָּנֶֽיךָ, כִּי בְאוֹר פָּנֶֽיךָ נָתַֽתָּ לָּֽנוּ, יהוה אֱלֹהֵֽינוּ, תּוֹרַת חַיִּים וְאַהֲבַת חֶֽסֶד, וּצְדָקָה וּבְרָכָה וְרַחֲמִים וְחַיִּים וְשָׁלוֹם. וְטוֹב בְּעֵינֶֽיךָ לְבָרֵךְ אֶת־עַמְּךָ יִשְׂרָאֵל בְּכָל־עֵת וּבְכָל־שָׁעָה בִּשְׁלוֹמֶֽךָ.

בְּסֵֽפֶר חַיִּים, בְּרָכָה וְשָׁלוֹם וּפַרְנָסָה טוֹבָה, נִזָּכֵר וְנֵחָתֵם לְפָנֶֽיךָ, אֲנַֽחְנוּ וְכָל־עַמְּךָ בֵּית יִשְׂרָאֵל, לְחַיִּים טוֹבִים וּלְשָׁלוֹם.

בָּרוּךְ אַתָּה יהוה, עוֹשֵׂה הַשָּׁלוֹם.

ALL THE PEOPLE OF YOUR COVENANT כָּל־בְּנֵי בְרִיתֶֽךָ. Having been together for a whole day of prayer, we may have a greater sense of community and a greater awareness of, and connection with, Jews throughout time and the Jewish people everywhere.

SEAL וַחֲתוֹם. The third insertion for the High Holy Day period. Once again, instead of asking to be "inscribed in the Book of Life," we ask now to be "sealed."

MAY ADONAI BLESS YOU יְבָרֶכְךָ. Numbers 6:24–26.

MAY WE בְּסֵֽפֶר חַיִּים. The fourth insertion for the High Holy Day period. At the end of the Amidah, we ask not only for life but for peace and prosperity as well.

The contemporary scholar Avi Ravitzky remarks that, in Jewish thought, the word שָׁלוֹם (shalom), "peace," refers to much more than the cessation of war or reconciliation after a quarrel, it also means wholeness or completeness and refers both to a physical and spiritual state. The greeting, hashalom lakh or l'kha?, inquires after both the physical and spiritual health of the person. The prayer for peace, then, is a prayer for fullness, for wholeness, for physical health and spiritual fulfillment. In one reading of the tradition, the striving for peace is turned into the goal of our being, "All that is written in the Torah was written for the sake of peace" (Midrash Tanḥuma, Shoftim).

Avinu malkeinu, remember Your compassion and subdue Your anger. Bring an end to pestilence, sword, and hunger; captivity and destruction, sin and oppression, plague and calamity; every illness, misfortune, and quarrel; all kinds of danger, every evil decree, and causeless hatred. Bring an end to these for us and for all the people of Your covenant.

And seal all the people of Your covenant for a good life.
Va-ḥatom l'ḥayyim tovim kol b'nei v'ritekha.

May all that lives thank You always, and praise Your name faithfully forever, God of our deliverance and help.
Barukh atah ADONAI, whose name is goodness and to whom praise is fitting.

Seventh B'rakhah: Prayer for Peace

Our God and God of our ancestors, bless us with the threefold blessing of the Torah written by Moses Your servant, recited by Aaron and his descendants, the kohanim, the consecrated priests of Your people:

May ADONAI bless and protect you.
          So may it be God's will. *Kein y'hi ratzon.*
May ADONAI's countenance shine upon you and
   grant you kindness. *So may it be God's will. Kein y'hi ratzon.*
May ADONAI's countenance be lifted toward you and
   grant you peace. *So may it be God's will. Kein y'hi ratzon.*

Grant peace to the world: goodness and blessing, grace, love, and compassion to us and all the people Israel. Bless us, our creator, united as one in the light of Your countenance; by that light, ADONAI our God, You gave us a guide to life: the love of kindness, righteousness, blessing, compassion, life, and peace. May it please You to bless Your people Israel at every season and at all times with Your gift of peace.

May we and the entire House of Israel be called to mind and inscribed for life, blessing, sustenance, and peace in the Book of Life.
B'seifer ḥayyim b'rakhah v'shalom u-farnasah tovah,
nizzakheir v'neiḥateim l'fanekha, anaḥnu v'khol am'kha beit yisrael,
l'ḥayyim tovim u-l'shalom.
Barukh atah ADONAI, who brings peace.

An alternate version of Avinu Malkeinu appears on the next page.

אָבִינוּ מַלְכֵּנוּ! חָטָאנוּ לְפָנֶיךָ.

אָבִינוּ מַלְכֵּנוּ! אֵין לָנוּ מֶלֶךְ אֶלָּא אָתָּה.

אָבִינוּ מַלְכֵּנוּ! עֲשֵׂה עִמָּנוּ לְמַעַן שְׁמֶךָ.

אָבִינוּ מַלְכֵּנוּ! חַדֵּשׁ עָלֵינוּ שָׁנָה טוֹבָה.

אָבִינוּ מַלְכֵּנוּ! בַּטֵּל מֵעָלֵינוּ כָּל־גְּזֵרוֹת קָשׁוֹת.

אָבִינוּ מַלְכֵּנוּ! בַּטֵּל מַחְשְׁבוֹת שׂוֹנְאֵינוּ.

אָבִינוּ מַלְכֵּנוּ! הָפֵר עֲצַת אוֹיְבֵינוּ.

אָבִינוּ מַלְכֵּנוּ! כַּלֵּה כָּל־צַר וּמַשְׂטִין מֵעָלֵינוּ.

אָבִינוּ מַלְכֵּנוּ! כַּלֵּה דֶּבֶר וְחֶרֶב וְרָעָב וּשְׁבִי וּמַשְׁחִית וְעָוֹן וּשְׁמַד מִבְּנֵי בְרִיתֶךָ.

אָבִינוּ מַלְכֵּנוּ! סְלַח וּמְחַל לְכָל־עֲוֹנוֹתֵינוּ.

אָבִינוּ מַלְכֵּנוּ! מְחֵה וְהַעֲבֵר פְּשָׁעֵינוּ וְחַטֹּאתֵינוּ מִנֶּגֶד עֵינֶיךָ.

We repeat the following lines after the leader:

◁ אָבִינוּ מַלְכֵּנוּ! הַחֲזִירֵנוּ בִּתְשׁוּבָה שְׁלֵמָה לְפָנֶיךָ.

אָבִינוּ מַלְכֵּנוּ! שְׁלַח רְפוּאָה שְׁלֵמָה לְחוֹלֵי עַמֶּךָ.

אָבִינוּ מַלְכֵּנוּ! זָכְרֵנוּ בְּזִכָּרוֹן טוֹב לְפָנֶיךָ.

אָבִינוּ מַלְכֵּנוּ! חָתְמֵנוּ בְּסֵפֶר חַיִּים טוֹבִים.

אָבִינוּ מַלְכֵּנוּ! חָתְמֵנוּ בְּסֵפֶר גְּאֻלָּה וִישׁוּעָה.

אָבִינוּ מַלְכֵּנוּ! חָתְמֵנוּ בְּסֵפֶר פַּרְנָסָה וְכַלְכָּלָה.

אָבִינוּ מַלְכֵּנוּ! חָתְמֵנוּ בְּסֵפֶר זְכֻיּוֹת.

אָבִינוּ מַלְכֵּנוּ! חָתְמֵנוּ בְּסֵפֶר סְלִיחָה וּמְחִילָה.

אָבִינוּ מַלְכֵּנוּ! הַצְמַח לָנוּ יְשׁוּעָה בְּקָרוֹב.

אָבִינוּ מַלְכֵּנוּ! הָרֵם קֶרֶן יִשְׂרָאֵל עַמֶּךָ.

אָבִינוּ מַלְכֵּנוּ! הָרֵם קֶרֶן מְשִׁיחֶךָ.

אָבִינוּ מַלְכֵּנוּ! שְׁמַע קוֹלֵנוּ, חוּס וְרַחֵם עָלֵינוּ.

אָבִינוּ מַלְכֵּנוּ! קַבֵּל בְּרַחֲמִים וּבְרָצוֹן אֶת־תְּפִלָּתֵנוּ.

אָבִינוּ מַלְכֵּנוּ! נָא אַל תְּשִׁיבֵנוּ רֵיקָם מִלְּפָנֶיךָ.

אָבִינוּ מַלְכֵּנוּ! זְכוֹר כִּי עָפָר אֲנָחְנוּ.

אָבִינוּ מַלְכֵּנוּ! חֲמוֹל עָלֵינוּ וְעַל עוֹלָלֵינוּ וְטַפֵּנוּ.

אָבִינוּ מַלְכֵּנוּ! עֲשֵׂה לְמַעַן הֲרוּגִים עַל שֵׁם קָדְשֶׁךָ.

אָבִינוּ מַלְכֵּנוּ! עֲשֵׂה לְמַעַן טְבוּחִים עַל יְחוּדֶךָ.

AVINU MALKEINU אָבִינוּ מַלְכֵּנוּ. The Babylonian Talmud reports: "It once happened that Rabbi Eliezer led the congregation and recited twenty-four *b'rakhot*, but his prayers were not answered. Then Rabbi Akiva followed him and led the congregation in prayer, saying, 'Our father, our sovereign, You are truly our father. Our father, our sovereign, we have no ruler but You. Our father, our sovereign, we have sinned before You. Our father, our sovereign, have mercy on us. Our father, our sovereign, do it for Your name's sake,' and his prayers were answered" (Taanit 25b). Generations have added many more verses to this prayer. The verses mentioning the martyrs were added after the Crusades.

Avinu Malkeinu was first introduced as a prayer for material blessing. It then took on an added layer of pleas against devastation by human enemies, and finally, special prayers for the High Holy Days (for instance, "inscribe us in the Book of Life").

The image of God as "father" represents relatedness and closeness; that of God as Ruler conveys authority and greater distance. Jewish theology has always talked of transcendence and immanence, God as ineffable and God as close at hand. The appeal here brings together both aspects of God.

Avinu Malkeinu

An alternate version of Avinu Malkeinu appears on the next page.

Avinu Malkeinu, we have sinned in Your presence.

Avinu Malkeinu, we have no sovereign but You.

Avinu Malkeinu, act toward us kindly in accord with Your name.

Avinu Malkeinu, make this a good new year for us.

Avinu Malkeinu, annul every harsh decree against us.

Avinu Malkeinu, nullify the designs of our foes.

Avinu Malkeinu, frustrate the plots of our enemies.

Avinu Malkeinu, rid us of every oppressor and adversary.

Avinu Malkeinu, rid Your covenanted people of disease, war, hunger, captivity, and destruction.

Avinu Malkeinu, forgive and pardon all our sins.

Avinu Malkeinu, do not look toward our sins and transgressions; blot them out.

Avinu Malkeinu, return us to Your presence, fully penitent.

Avinu Malkeinu, send complete healing to the sick among Your people.

Avinu Malkeinu, remember us favorably.

Avinu Malkeinu, seal us with goodness in the Book of Life.

Avinu Malkeinu, seal us in the Book of Redemption.

Avinu Malkeinu, seal us in the Book of Sustenance.

Avinu Malkeinu, seal us in the Book of Merit.

Avinu Malkeinu, seal us in the book of forgiveness.

Avinu malkeinu, haḥazireinu bi-t'shuvah sh'leimah l'fanekha.
Avinu malkeinu, sh'laḥ r'fu·ah sh'leimah l'ḥolei ammekha.
Avinu malkeinu, zokhreinu b'zikkaron tov l'fanekha.
Avinu malkeinu, ḥotmeinu b'seifer ḥayyim tovim.
Avinu malkeinu, ḥotmeinu b'seifer g'ullah vi-shu·ah.
Avinu malkeinu, ḥotmeinu b'seifer parnasah v'khalkalah.
Avinu malkeinu, ḥotmeinu b'seifer z'khuyyot.
Avinu malkeinu, ḥotmeinu b'seifer s'liḥah u-m'ḥilah.

Avinu Malkeinu, cause our salvation to flourish soon.

Avinu Malkeinu, cause Your people Israel to be exalted.

Avinu Malkeinu, raise up Your anointed with strength.

Avinu Malkeinu, hear our voice, be kind, sympathize with us.

Avinu Malkeinu, accept our prayer, willingly and lovingly.

Avinu Malkeinu, do not turn us away empty-handed.

Avinu Malkeinu, remember that we are but dust.

Avinu Malkeinu, have compassion for us, our infants, and our children.

Avinu Malkeinu, do this for the sake of those who were martyred for Your holy name.

Avinu Malkeinu, do this for the sake of those who were slaughtered for their exclusive devotion to You.

אָבִינוּ מַלְכֵּנוּ! עֲשֵׂה לְמַעַן בָּאֵי בָאֵשׁ וּבַמַּיִם עַל
קִדּוּשׁ שְׁמֶךָ.
אָבִינוּ מַלְכֵּנוּ! עֲשֵׂה לְמַעַנְךָ אִם לֹא לְמַעֲנֵנוּ.
אָבִינוּ מַלְכֵּנוּ! חָנֵּנוּ וַעֲנֵנוּ, כִּי אֵין בָּנוּ מַעֲשִׂים, עֲשֵׂה
עִמָּנוּ צְדָקָה וָחֶסֶד וְהוֹשִׁיעֵנוּ.

אָבִינוּ מַלְכֵּנוּ! חָטָאנוּ לְפָנֶיךָ.
בּוֹרְאֵנוּ מְבָרְכֵנוּ, אֵין לָנוּ מֶלֶךְ אֶלָּא אָתָּה.
גּוֹאֲלֵנוּ מִשְׁמְרֵנוּ, עֲשֵׂה עִמָּנוּ לְמַעַן שְׁמֶךָ.
דּוֹרְשֵׁנוּ מְפַרְנְסֵנוּ, חַדֵּשׁ עָלֵינוּ שָׁנָה טוֹבָה.
הוֹדֵינוּ מוֹשִׁיעֵנוּ, בַּטֵּל מֵעָלֵינוּ כָּל־גְּזֵרוֹת קָשׁוֹת.
וָתִיקֵנוּ מִפַּלְטֵנוּ, בַּטֵּל מַחְשְׁבוֹת שׂוֹנְאֵינוּ.
זָנֵנוּ מְנוּסֵנוּ, כַּלֵּה דֶּבֶר וְחֶרֶב וְרָעָב וּשְׁבִי וּמַשְׁחִית וְעָוֹן
וּשְׁמַד מִבְּנֵי בְרִיתֶךָ.
חוֹסֵנוּ מְחַיֵּינוּ, הָפֵר עֲצַת אוֹיְבֵינוּ.
טְהוֹרֵנוּ מְרַחֲמֵנוּ, סְלַח וּמְחַל לְכָל־עֲוֹנוֹתֵינוּ.
יוֹצְרֵנוּ מְלַמְּדֵנוּ, הַחֲזִירֵנוּ בִּתְשׁוּבָה שְׁלֵמָה לְפָנֶיךָ.
כּוֹנֵן מְכַלְכְּלֵנוּ, שְׁלַח רְפוּאָה שְׁלֵמָה לְחוֹלֵי עַמֶּךָ.
לְבוּבֵנוּ מְגַדְּלֵנוּ, זָכְרֵנוּ בְּזִכָּרוֹן טוֹב לְפָנֶיךָ.
אָבִינוּ מַלְכֵּנוּ, חָתְמֵנוּ בְּסֵפֶר חַיִּים טוֹבִים.
אָבִינוּ מַלְכֵּנוּ, חָתְמֵנוּ בְּסֵפֶר גְּאֻלָּה וִישׁוּעָה.
אָבִינוּ מַלְכֵּנוּ, חָתְמֵנוּ בְּסֵפֶר פַּרְנָסָה וְכַלְכָּלָה.
אָבִינוּ מַלְכֵּנוּ, חָתְמֵנוּ בְּסֵפֶר זְכֻיּוֹת.
אָבִינוּ מַלְכֵּנוּ, חָתְמֵנוּ בְּסֵפֶר סְלִיחָה וּמְחִילָה.

AVINU MALKEINU אָבִינוּ
מַלְכֵּנוּ. The images of God
as "our father" (avinu) and
"our sovereign" (malkeinu)
are central to much of the
High Holy Day liturgy. Yet
these images may not have
the same resonance for us
as they once did for our ancestors. At the same time,
the tradition is filled with
many different metaphors
for God. Therefore we offer
this alternative version, featuring a variety of imagery.
Its synonyms and meta-
phors for God are mostly
taken from usages in other
parts of the liturgy. Its
alphabetical listing conveys
the idea that we grasp the
ineffable God through an
infinite number of images.

Avinu Malkeinu, do this for the sake of those who went through fire and water to sanctify Your holy name.

Avinu Malkeinu, do this for Your sake if not for ours.

Avinu Malkeinu, have mercy on us, answer us, for our deeds are insufficient, deal with us charitably and lovingly, and redeem us.

Avinu malkeinu ḥonneinu va-aneinu ki ein banu ma·asim,
aseih immanu tz'dakah va-ḥesed v'hoshi·einu.

AVINU MALKEINU: ALTERNATE VERSION

Avinu Malkeinu, we have sinned in Your presence.

Our creator, who blesses us, we have no sovereign but You.

Our redeemer, who guards us, act kindly, in keeping with Your name.

You who seek us out and sustain us, make this new year a
good one for us.

You who are our glory, our savior, annul every harsh decree against us.

Ancient One, our rescuer, nullify the designs of our foes.

Provider, our refuge, rid Your covenanted people of disease, war, hunger, captivity, and destruction.

You who are our strength, who gives us life, rid us of every
oppressor and adversary.

You, who purify us, and have mercy on us, forgive and pardon all our sins.

You who form us and instruct us, return us to Your presence,
fully penitent.

You, who establish us, and provide for us, send complete healing to the sick among Your people.

You, our beloved, who raised us, remember us favorably.

Avinu Malkeinu, seal us with goodness in the Book of Life.

Avinu Malkeinu, seal us in the Book of Redemption.

Avinu Malkeinu, seal us in the Book of Sustenance.

Avinu Malkeinu, seal us in the Book of Merit.

Avinu Malkeinu, seal us in the Book of Forgiveness.

Avinu malkeinu, ḥotmeinu b'seifer ḥayyim tovim.
Avinu malkeinu, ḥotmeinu b'seifer g'ullah vishu·ah.
Avinu malkeinu, ḥotmeinu b'seifer parnasah v'khalkalah.
Avinu malkeinu, ḥotmeinu b'seifer z'khuyyot.
Avinu malkeinu, ḥotmeinu b'seifer s'liḥah u-m'ḥilah.

נוֹטְרֵנוּ מִפְלָטֵנוּ, הַצְמַח לָנוּ יְשׁוּעָה בְּקָרוֹב.

סוֹמְכֵנוּ מַצִּילֵנוּ, הָרֵם קֶרֶן יִשְׂרָאֵל עַמֶּךָ.

עָזְרֵנוּ מַקְשִׁיבֵנוּ שְׁמַע קוֹלֵנוּ, חוּס וְרַחֵם עָלֵינוּ.

פּוֹדֵנוּ מְשַׁמְּרֵנוּ, קַבֵּל בְּרַחֲמִים וּבְרָצוֹן אֶת־תְּפִלָּתֵנוּ.

צוּרֵנוּ מְנוּסֵנוּ, נָא אַל תְּשִׁיבֵנוּ רֵיקָם מִלְּפָנֶיךָ.

קְדוֹשֵׁנוּ מַצְדִּיקֵנוּ, זְכוֹר כִּי עָפָר אֲנָחְנוּ.

רַחֲמֵנוּ מְחַיֵּנוּ, חֲמוֹל עָלֵינוּ וְעַל עוֹלָלֵינוּ וְטַפֵּינוּ.

שׁוֹמְרֵנוּ מוֹשִׁיעֵנוּ, עֲשֵׂה לְמַעַן הֲרוּגִים עַל שֵׁם קָדְשֶׁךָ.

תּוֹמְכֵנוּ מִסְעָדֵנוּ, עֲשֵׂה לְמַעַנְךָ אִם לֹא לְמַעֲנֵנוּ.

אָבִינוּ מַלְכֵּנוּ, חָנֵּנוּ וַעֲנֵנוּ, כִּי אֵין בָּנוּ מַעֲשִׂים,
עֲשֵׂה עִמָּנוּ צְדָקָה וָחֶסֶד וְהוֹשִׁיעֵנוּ.

Our protector and savior, cause our salvation to flourish soon.

Our support and rescuer, cause Your people Israel to be exalted.

Our helper, who listens to us, hear our voice, be kind, sympathize with us.

Our redeemer, who watches over us, accept our prayer, willingly and lovingly.

Our fortress, who is our refuge, do not send us away empty-handed.

Holy One, who justifies us, remember that we are but dust.

Merciful One, who gives us life, have compassion for us, our infants, and our children.

Guardian, who grants us victory, do this for the sake of those who were martyred for Your holy name.

Benefactor, who provides for our welfare, do this for Your sake if not for ours.

Avinu Malkeinu, have mercy on us, answer us, for our deeds are insufficient; deal with us charitably and lovingly, and redeem us.

Avinu malkeinu ḥonnenu va-aneinu ki ein banu ma·asim,
aseih immanu tz'dakah va-ḥesed v'hoshi·enu.

קַדִּישׁ שָׁלֵם

יִתְגַּדַּל וְיִתְקַדַּשׁ שְׁמֵהּ רַבָּא, בְּעָלְמָא דִּי בְרָא, כִּרְעוּתֵהּ, וְיַמְלִיךְ מַלְכוּתֵהּ בְּחַיֵּיכוֹן וּבְיוֹמֵיכוֹן וּבְחַיֵּי דְכָל־בֵּית יִשְׂרָאֵל, בַּעֲגָלָא וּבִזְמַן קָרִיב, וְאִמְרוּ אָמֵן.

יְהֵא שְׁמֵהּ רַבָּא מְבָרַךְ לְעָלַם וּלְעָלְמֵי עָלְמַיָּא.

יִתְבָּרַךְ וְיִשְׁתַּבַּח וְיִתְפָּאַר וְיִתְרוֹמַם וְיִתְנַשֵּׂא וְיִתְהַדָּר וְיִתְעַלֶּה וְיִתְהַלָּל שְׁמֵהּ דְּקֻדְשָׁא, **בְּרִיךְ הוּא,** לְעֵלָּא לְעֵלָּא מִכָּל־בִּרְכָתָא וְשִׁירָתָא תֻּשְׁבְּחָתָא וְנֶחָמָתָא דַּאֲמִירָן בְּעָלְמָא, וְאִמְרוּ אָמֵן.

תִּתְקַבֵּל צְלוֹתְהוֹן וּבָעוּתְהוֹן דְּכָל־יִשְׂרָאֵל קֳדָם אֲבוּהוֹן דִּי בִשְׁמַיָּא, וְאִמְרוּ אָמֵן.

יְהֵא שְׁלָמָא רַבָּא מִן שְׁמַיָּא וְחַיִּים עָלֵינוּ וְעַל כָּל־יִשְׂרָאֵל, וְאִמְרוּ אָמֵן.

עֹשֶׂה שָׁלוֹם בִּמְרוֹמָיו הוּא יַעֲשֶׂה שָׁלוֹם עָלֵינוּ וְעַל כָּל־יִשְׂרָאֵל [וְעַל כָּל־יוֹשְׁבֵי תֵבֵל], וְאִמְרוּ אָמֵן.

Kaddish Shalem

May God's great name be exalted and hallowed throughout the created world, as is God's wish. May God's sovereignty soon be established, in your lifetime and in your days, and in the days of all the House of Israel. And respond with: *Amen.*

May God's great name be acknowledged forever and ever!
Y'hei sh'meih rabba m'varakh l'alam u-l'almei almayya.

May the name of the Holy One be acknowledged and celebrated, lauded and worshipped, exalted and honored, extolled and acclaimed—though God, who is blessed, *b'rikh hu,* is truly far beyond all acknowledgment and praise, or any expressions of gratitude or consolation ever spoken in the world. And respond with: *Amen.*

May the prayers and pleas of all Israel be accepted by their creator in heaven. And respond with: *Amen.*

May abundant peace from heaven, and life, come to us and to all Israel. And respond with: *Amen.*

May the One who brings harmony on high, bring harmony to us and to all Israel [and to all who dwell on earth]. And respond with: *Amen.*
Oseh shalom bi-m'romav hu ya·aseh shalom aleinu v'al kol yisra·el [v'al kol yosh'vei teiveil], v'imru amen.

Leader, then Congregation (once):

שְׁמַע יִשְׂרָאֵל יהוה אֱלֹהֵינוּ יהוה אֶחָד.

Recited three times:

בָּרוּךְ שֵׁם כְּבוֹד מַלְכוּתוֹ לְעוֹלָם וָעֶד.

Recited seven times:

יהוה הוּא הָאֱלֹהִים.

תקיעה גדולה

לַשָּׁנָה הַבָּאָה בִּירוּשָׁלָיִם!

Two different customs were developed by European Jewry: one tradition recites these verses before the final Kaddish (found on the previous page), and the other after the Kaddish.

HEAR שְׁמַע. How can this day be brought to an appropriate conclusion? Originally, the five services constituted the whole of the Yom Kippur experience. But just as Kol Nidrei emerged to raise the curtain on the day in the most powerful way possible, the recitation of the Sh'ma developed to bring down the curtain in a rousing finale. The final gesture of Yom Kippur consists of a confession of faith and the sounding of the shofar. (*adapted from Reuven Hammer*)

ADONAI יהוה. This affirmation comes from the story of Elijah's confrontation with the prophets of Ba'al at Mount Carmel. When the people are convinced that Adonai is indeed the only God, they shout, "Adonai is God!" (1 Kings 18:39). The sacredness of the number seven is well known.

SHOFAR. Some congregations recite Arvit (beginning on page 444) before the Sh'ma and the blowing of the shofar. According to Abudarham (Spain, 14th century), the blowing of the shofar at the end of the Yom Kippur services echoes the ancient practice of blowing the shofar to proclaim the beginning of the fiftieth year—the Jubilee— the time of freedom (Leviticus 25:9–10). Since we no longer know the cycle of the Jubilee year, *this* year may be the year in which we are to proclaim freedom to all. After the long blast of the shofar we proclaim, "Next year in Jerusalem"—signifying the hope for a return to a city that has symbolized hope and freedom for generations of Jews. (*adapted from Reuven Hammer*)

CONCLUSION

Meditation

For 25 hours we have prayed from our hearts and minds on this Day of Atonement. Now that evening approaches and the long fast draws to a close, tens of thousands of words must have been spoken and sung. And yet somehow we still feel that we have not penetrated to the heart of the matter; there are further unspoken feelings buried in us and interior courts in God's palace which we have not yet entered.

Therefore, we must muster the remaining physical and spiritual forces left under our command, and make one last desperate effort to descend into the human depths and to climb to the divine heights. But words have earlier proved futile. We cry out the Sh'ma—we repeat "Praised be the name of the One whose glorious sovereignty is forever and ever" three times—and we stammer, each time at a higher, and, as it were, more urgent pitch seven times the Hebrew words: "Adonai is God." No longer is it the meaning of the words but rather their rhythm, the scream of the soul that squeezes through them, the hammering of their insistent repetition, in which we place our hope. And, as if even this last resort had failed, finally we abandon the human voice and verbal expression altogether. We reach for the shofar and blow one long, piercing shriek: *t'kiah g'dolah*. This surely must rend the heavens!   —STE-VEN S. SCHWARZSCHILD *(adapted)*

Leader and then Congregation:

Hear, O Israel, Adonai is our God, Adonai alone.

Sh'ma yisra·el Adonai eloheinu Adonai eḥad.

Recited three times:

Praised be the name of the One whose glorious sovereignty is forever and ever.

Barukh shem k'vod malkhuto l'olam va·ed.

Recited seven times:

Adonai is God.

Adonai hu ha-Elohim.

T'ki·ah g'dolah

Next year in Jerusalem!

La-shanah ha-ba·ah bi-rushalayim!

מנחה לערב יום טוב   AFTERNOON SERVICE BEFORE THE HOLY DAY

אַשְׁרֵי יוֹשְׁבֵי בֵיתֶךָ, עוֹד יְהַלְלוּךָ סֶּלָה.
אַשְׁרֵי הָעָם שֶׁכָּכָה לּוֹ, אַשְׁרֵי הָעָם שֶׁיהוה אֱלֹהָיו.

תְּהִלָּה לְדָוִד.
אֲרוֹמִמְךָ אֱלוֹהַי הַמֶּלֶךְ,
וַאֲבָרְכָה שִׁמְךָ לְעוֹלָם וָעֶד.
בְּכָל־יוֹם אֲבָרְכֶךָּ,
וַאֲהַלְלָה שִׁמְךָ לְעוֹלָם וָעֶד.
גָּדוֹל יהוה וּמְהֻלָּל מְאֹד,
וְלִגְדֻלָּתוֹ אֵין חֵקֶר.
דּוֹר לְדוֹר יְשַׁבַּח מַעֲשֶׂיךָ,
וּגְבוּרֹתֶיךָ יַגִּידוּ.
הֲדַר כְּבוֹד הוֹדֶךָ,
וְדִבְרֵי נִפְלְאֹתֶיךָ אָשִׂיחָה.
וֶעֱזוּז נוֹרְאֹתֶיךָ יֹאמֵרוּ,
וּגְדֻלָּתְךָ אֲסַפְּרֶנָּה.
זֵכֶר רַב־טוּבְךָ יַבִּיעוּ,
וְצִדְקָתְךָ יְרַנֵּנוּ.
חַנּוּן וְרַחוּם יהוה,
אֶרֶךְ אַפַּיִם וּגְדָל־חָסֶד.
טוֹב יהוה לַכֹּל,
וְרַחֲמָיו עַל־כָּל־מַעֲשָׂיו.
יוֹדוּךָ יהוה כָּל־מַעֲשֶׂיךָ,
וַחֲסִידֶיךָ יְבָרְכוּכָה.
כְּבוֹד מַלְכוּתְךָ יֹאמֵרוּ,
וּגְבוּרָתְךָ יְדַבֵּרוּ.
לְהוֹדִיעַ לִבְנֵי הָאָדָם גְּבוּרֹתָיו,
וּכְבוֹד הֲדַר מַלְכוּתוֹ.
מַלְכוּתְךָ מַלְכוּת כָּל־עוֹלָמִים,
וּמֶמְשַׁלְתְּךָ בְּכָל־דּוֹר וָדֹר.
סוֹמֵךְ יהוה לְכָל־הַנֹּפְלִים,
וְזוֹקֵף לְכָל־הַכְּפוּפִים.

Joyous are they who dwell in Your house;
they shall praise You forever.

Joyous the people who are so favored;
joyous the people whose God is ADONAI.

PSALM 145
A PSALM OF DAVID

I exalt You, my God, my sovereign;
I praise Your name, always.

Every day I praise You, glorifying Your name, always.

Great is ADONAI, greatly to be praised,
though God's greatness is unfathomable.

One generation praises Your works to another,
telling of Your mighty deeds.

I would speak of Your majestic glory
and of your wondrous acts.

People speak of Your awe-inspiring deeds;
I, too, shall recount Your greatness.

They recount Your great goodness,
and sing of Your righteousness.

ADONAI is merciful and compassionate,
patient, and abounding in love.

ADONAI is good to all,
and God's mercy embraces all of creation.

All of creation acknowledges You,
and the faithful bless You.

They speak of the glory of Your sovereignty;
and tell of Your might,

proclaiming to humanity Your mighty deeds,
and the glory of Your majestic sovereignty.

Your sovereignty is eternal,
Your dominion endures through each generation.

ADONAI supports all who falter,
and lifts up all who are bent down.

עֵינֵי־כֹל אֵלֶיךָ יְשַׂבֵּרוּ,

וְאַתָּה נוֹתֵן־לָהֶם אֶת־אָכְלָם בְּעִתּוֹ.

פּוֹתֵחַ אֶת־יָדֶךָ,

וּמַשְׂבִּיעַ לְכָל־חַי רָצוֹן.

צַדִּיק יהוה בְּכָל־דְּרָכָיו,

וְחָסִיד בְּכָל־מַעֲשָׂיו.

קָרוֹב יהוה לְכָל־קֹרְאָיו,

לְכֹל אֲשֶׁר יִקְרָאֻהוּ בֶאֱמֶת.

רְצוֹן־יְרֵאָיו יַעֲשֶׂה,

וְאֶת־שַׁוְעָתָם יִשְׁמַע וְיוֹשִׁיעֵם.

שׁוֹמֵר יהוה אֶת־כָּל־אֹהֲבָיו,

וְאֵת כָּל־הָרְשָׁעִים יַשְׁמִיד.

◁ תְּהִלַּת יהוה יְדַבֶּר־פִּי,

וִיבָרֵךְ כָּל־בָּשָׂר שֵׁם קָדְשׁוֹ לְעוֹלָם וָעֶד.   תהלים קמה

וַאֲנַחְנוּ נְבָרֵךְ יָהּ, מֵעַתָּה וְעַד עוֹלָם. הַלְלוּ־יָהּ.

חֲצִי קַדִּישׁ

יִתְגַּדַּל וְיִתְקַדַּשׁ שְׁמֵהּ רַבָּא, בְּעָלְמָא דִּי בְרָא,

כִרְעוּתֵהּ, וְיַמְלִיךְ מַלְכוּתֵהּ בְּחַיֵּיכוֹן וּבְיוֹמֵיכוֹן וּבְחַיֵּי

דְכָל־בֵּית יִשְׂרָאֵל, בַּעֲגָלָא וּבִזְמַן קָרִיב, וְאִמְרוּ אָמֵן.

יְהֵא שְׁמֵהּ רַבָּא מְבָרַךְ לְעָלַם וּלְעָלְמֵי עָלְמַיָּא.

יִתְבָּרַךְ וְיִשְׁתַּבַּח וְיִתְפָּאַר וְיִתְרוֹמַם וְיִתְנַשֵּׂא וְיִתְהַדָּר

וְיִתְעַלֶּה וְיִתְהַלָּל שְׁמֵהּ דְּקֻדְשָׁא, **בְּרִיךְ הוּא,**

Before Rosh Hashanah:

לְעֵלָּא מִן כָּל־בִּרְכָתָא

Before Yom Kippur:

לְעֵלָּא לְעֵלָּא מִכָּל־בִּרְכָתָא

וְשִׁירָתָא תֻּשְׁבְּחָתָא וְנֶחֱמָתָא דַּאֲמִירָן בְּעָלְמָא,

וְאִמְרוּ אָמֵן.

The eyes of all look hopefully to You,
and You provide them nourishment in due time.
You open Your hand,
satisfying all the living with contentment.
ADONAI is righteous in all that is done,
faithful to all creation.
ADONAI is near to all who call,
to all who sincerely call.
God fulfills the desire of those who are faithful,
listening to their cries, rescuing them.
ADONAI watches over all those who love the Holy One,
but will destroy all the wicked.
My mouth shall utter praise of ADONAI.
May all that is mortal praise God's name forever and ever.
We shall praise ADONAI now and always. Halleluyah!

Psalm 145; 115:18

Ḥatzi Kaddish

May God's great name be exalted and hallowed throughout the
created world, as is God's wish. May God's sovereignty soon be
established, in your lifetime and in your days, and in the days of
all the House of Israel. And respond with: *Amen.*

May God's great name be acknowledged forever and ever!
Y'hei sh'meih rabba m'varakh l'alam u-l'almei almayya.

May the name of the Holy One be acknowledged and celebrated, lauded and worshipped, exalted and honored, extolled and
acclaimed—though God, who is blessed, *b'rikh hu,* is truly
[*before Yom Kippur add:* far] beyond all acknowledgment and
praise, or any expressions of gratitude or consolation ever spoken in the world. And respond with: *Amen.*

עֲמִידָה

כִּי שֵׁם יהוה אֶקְרָא, הָבוּ גֹדֶל לֵאלֹהֵינוּ.
אֲדֹנָי שְׂפָתַי תִּפְתָּח, וּפִי יַגִּיד תְּהִלָּתֶךָ.

Version with Patriarchs and Matriarchs:	*Version with Patriarchs:*

‏] **בָּרוּךְ** אַתָּה יהוה,
אֱלֹהֵינוּ וֵאלֹהֵי אֲבוֹתֵינוּ
[וְאִמּוֹתֵינוּ], אֱלֹהֵי אַבְרָהָם,
אֱלֹהֵי יִצְחָק, וֵאלֹהֵי יַעֲקֹב,
אֱלֹהֵי שָׂרָה, אֱלֹהֵי רִבְקָה,
אֱלֹהֵי רָחֵל, וֵאלֹהֵי לֵאָה,
הָאֵל הַגָּדוֹל הַגִּבּוֹר וְהַנּוֹרָא,
אֵל עֶלְיוֹן, גּוֹמֵל חֲסָדִים
טוֹבִים, וְקוֹנֵה הַכֹּל, וְזוֹכֵר
חַסְדֵי אָבוֹת [וְאִמָּהוֹת],
וּמֵבִיא גוֹאֵל לִבְנֵי בְנֵיהֶם
לְמַעַן שְׁמוֹ בְּאַהֲבָה.

בָּרוּךְ אַתָּה יהוה, ‏[
אֱלֹהֵינוּ וֵאלֹהֵי אֲבוֹתֵינוּ,
אֱלֹהֵי אַבְרָהָם, אֱלֹהֵי
יִצְחָק, וֵאלֹהֵי יַעֲקֹב, הָאֵל
הַגָּדוֹל הַגִּבּוֹר וְהַנּוֹרָא,
אֵל עֶלְיוֹן, גּוֹמֵל חֲסָדִים
טוֹבִים, וְקוֹנֵה הַכֹּל, וְזוֹכֵר
חַסְדֵי אָבוֹת, וּמֵבִיא גוֹאֵל
לִבְנֵי בְנֵיהֶם לְמַעַן שְׁמוֹ
בְּאַהֲבָה.

Before Yom Kippur add:

זָכְרֵנוּ לְחַיִּים, מֶלֶךְ חָפֵץ בַּחַיִּים,
וְכָתְבֵנוּ בְּסֵפֶר הַחַיִּים, לְמַעַנְךָ אֱלֹהִים חַיִּים.

Version with Patriarchs and Matriarchs:	*Version with Patriarchs:*

מֶלֶךְ עוֹזֵר וּפוֹקֵד
וּמוֹשִׁיעַ וּמָגֵן.
בָּרוּךְ אַתָּה יהוה, מָגֵן ‏[
אַבְרָהָם וּפוֹקֵד שָׂרָה.

מֶלֶךְ עוֹזֵר וּמוֹשִׁיעַ וּמָגֵן.
בָּרוּךְ אַתָּה יהוה, מָגֵן ‏[
אַבְרָהָם.

THE AMIDAH

When I call upon ADONAI, proclaim glory to our God!
ADONAI, open my lips that my mouth may speak Your praise.

Version with Patriarchs:

ℸ *Barukh atah ADONAI,*
our God and God of our
  ancestors,
God of Abraham, God of
  Isaac, and God of Jacob,
great, mighty, awe-inspiring,
  transcendent God,
who acts with lovingkindness
  and creates all things,
who remembers the loving
  deeds of our ancestors,
and who will send a redeemer
  to their children's children
  with love
  for the sake of divine honor.

Version with Patriarchs and Matriarchs:

ℸ *Barukh atah ADONAI,*
our God and God of our
  ancestors,
God of Abraham, God of
  Isaac, and God of Jacob,
God of Sarah, God of
  Rebecca, God of Rachel,
  and God of Leah,
great, mighty, awe-inspiring,
  transcendent God,
who acts with lovingkindness
  and creates all things,
who remembers the loving
  deeds of our ancestors,
and who will send a redeemer
  to their children's children
  with love
  for the sake of divine honor.

Before Yom Kippur add:

Remember us for life, Sovereign who delights in life,
and inscribe us in the Book of Life, for Your sake, God of life.

Version with Patriarchs:

You are the sovereign
who helps and saves and
shields.

ℸ *Barukh atah ADONAI,*
Shield of Abraham.

Version with Patriarchs and Matriarchs:

You are the sovereign who
helps and guards, saves and
shields.

ℸ *Barukh atah ADONAI,*
Shield of Abraham and
Guardian of Sarah.

אַתָּה גִבּוֹר לְעוֹלָם אֲדֹנָי, מְחַיֵּה מֵתִים אַתָּה,
רַב לְהוֹשִׁיעַ.

מְכַלְכֵּל חַיִּים בְּחֶסֶד, מְחַיֵּה מֵתִים בְּרַחֲמִים רַבִּים,
סוֹמֵךְ נוֹפְלִים, וְרוֹפֵא חוֹלִים, וּמַתִּיר אֲסוּרִים, וּמְקַיֵּם
אֱמוּנָתוֹ לִישֵׁנֵי עָפָר. מִי כָמוֹךְ בַּעַל גְּבוּרוֹת וּמִי דוֹמֶה לָךְ,
מֶלֶךְ מֵמִית וּמְחַיֶּה וּמַצְמִיחַ יְשׁוּעָה.

Before Yom Kippur add:

מִי כָמוֹךְ, אַב הָרַחֲמִים, זוֹכֵר יְצוּרָיו לְחַיִּים בְּרַחֲמִים.

וְנֶאֱמָן אַתָּה לְהַחֲיוֹת מֵתִים. בָּרוּךְ אַתָּה יהוה, מְחַיֵּה
הַמֵּתִים.

Read only when the Silent Amidah is recited:

אַתָּה קָדוֹשׁ וְשִׁמְךָ קָדוֹשׁ, וּקְדוֹשִׁים בְּכָל־יוֹם יְהַלְלוּךָ, סֶּלָה.

When the Amidah is said privately, continue on page 435.

Recited only when the Amidah is read aloud:

נְקַדֵּשׁ אֶת־שִׁמְךָ בָּעוֹלָם, כְּשֵׁם שֶׁמַּקְדִּישִׁים אוֹתוֹ בִּשְׁמֵי
מָרוֹם, כַּכָּתוּב עַל יַד נְבִיאֶךָ, וְקָרָא זֶה אֶל זֶה וְאָמַר:

קָדוֹשׁ, קָדוֹשׁ, קָדוֹשׁ יהוה צְבָאוֹת,
מְלֹא כָל־הָאָרֶץ כְּבוֹדוֹ.

לְעֻמָּתָם בָּרוּךְ יֹאמֵרוּ:
בָּרוּךְ כְּבוֹד יהוה מִמְּקוֹמוֹ.

וּבְדִבְרֵי קָדְשְׁךָ כָּתוּב לֵאמֹר:

יִמְלֹךְ יהוה לְעוֹלָם, אֱלֹהַיִךְ צִיּוֹן לְדֹר וָדֹר, הַלְלוּ־יָהּ.

לְדוֹר וָדוֹר נַגִּיד גָּדְלֶךָ, וּלְנֵצַח נְצָחִים קְדֻשָּׁתְךָ נַקְדִּישׁ,
וְשִׁבְחֲךָ אֱלֹהֵינוּ מִפִּינוּ לֹא יָמוּשׁ לְעוֹלָם וָעֶד,
כִּי אֵל מֶלֶךְ גָּדוֹל וְקָדוֹשׁ אָתָּה.

You are mighty forever, ADONAI—You give life to the dead;
great is Your saving power.

You sustain the living through love,
  and with great mercy give life to the dead.
You support the falling, heal the sick, loosen the chains of the bound,
  and keep faith with those who sleep in the dust.
Who is like You, Almighty, and who can be compared to You?—
Sovereign, who brings death and life, and causes salvation to flourish.

Before Yom Kippur add:
Who is like You, source of compassion,
  who remembers with compassion Your creatures for life?

You are faithful in bringing life to the dead.
Barukh atah ADONAI, who gives life to the dead.

Read only when the Silent Amidah is recited:
Holy are You and holy is Your name;
  holy ones praise You each day.
When the Amidah is said privately, continue on page 435.

The Kedushah
Recited only when the Amidah is read aloud:
Let us hallow Your name in this world as it is hallowed in the high
heavens, as Isaiah wrote of his vision, "Each cried out to the other:

'Holy, holy, holy is *Adonai Tz'va·ot*, the whole world is filled with
God's glory!'"
Kadosh, kadosh, kadosh Adonai Tz'va·ot, m'lo khol ha-aretz k'vodo.

Others respond with praise:
"Praised is ADONAI's glory wherever God dwells."
Barukh k'vod Adonai mim'komo.

And in Your holy scripture it is further declared:
"ADONAI will reign forever; your God, O Zion, from generation to
generation. Halleluyah!"
Yimlokh Adonai l'olam elohayikh tziyyon l'dor va-dor hal'luyah.

From one generation to another we will declare Your greatness, and
forever sanctify You with words of holiness. Your praise will never
leave our lips, for You are God and Sovereign, great and holy.

All services continue here:

Before Rosh Hashanah:

בָּרוּךְ אַתָּה יהוה, הָאֵל הַקָּדוֹשׁ.

Before Yom Kippur:

בָּרוּךְ אַתָּה יהוה, הַמֶּלֶךְ הַקָּדוֹשׁ.

אַתָּה חוֹנֵן לְאָדָם דַּעַת, וּמְלַמֵּד לֶאֱנוֹשׁ בִּינָה. חָנֵּנוּ מֵאִתְּךָ דֵּעָה בִּינָה וְהַשְׂכֵּל. בָּרוּךְ אַתָּה יהוה, חוֹנֵן הַדָּעַת.

הֲשִׁיבֵנוּ אָבִינוּ לְתוֹרָתֶךָ, וְקָרְבֵנוּ מַלְכֵּנוּ לַעֲבוֹדָתֶךָ, וְהַחֲזִירֵנוּ בִּתְשׁוּבָה שְׁלֵמָה לְפָנֶיךָ. בָּרוּךְ אַתָּה יהוה, הָרוֹצֶה בִּתְשׁוּבָה.

סְלַח לָנוּ אָבִינוּ כִּי חָטָאנוּ, מְחַל לָנוּ מַלְכֵּנוּ כִּי פָשָׁעְנוּ, כִּי מוֹחֵל וְסוֹלֵחַ אָתָּה. בָּרוּךְ אַתָּה יהוה, חַנּוּן הַמַּרְבֶּה לִסְלוֹחַ.

רְאֵה נָא בְעָנְיֵנוּ, וְרִיבָה רִיבֵנוּ, וּגְאָלֵנוּ מְהֵרָה לְמַעַן שְׁמֶךָ, כִּי גּוֹאֵל חָזָק אָתָּה. בָּרוּךְ אַתָּה יהוה, גּוֹאֵל יִשְׂרָאֵל.

רְפָאֵנוּ יהוה וְנֵרָפֵא, הוֹשִׁיעֵנוּ וְנִוָּשֵׁעָה, כִּי תְהִלָּתֵנוּ אָתָּה, וְהַעֲלֵה רְפוּאָה שְׁלֵמָה לְכָל־מַכּוֹתֵינוּ,

On behalf of one who is ill:

וִיהִי רָצוֹן מִלְּפָנֶיךָ יהוה אֱלֹהֵינוּ וֵאלֹהֵי אֲבוֹתֵינוּ וְאִמּוֹתֵינוּ, שֶׁתִּשְׁלַח מְהֵרָה רְפוּאָה שְׁלֵמָה מִן הַשָּׁמַיִם, רְפוּאַת הַנֶּפֶשׁ וּרְפוּאַת הַגּוּף, לְ _____ בֶּן / בַּת _____ בְּתוֹךְ שְׁאָר חוֹלֵי יִשְׂרָאֵל, וְחַזֵּק אֶת־יְדֵי הָעוֹסְקִים בְּצָרְכֵיהֶם, כִּי אֵל מֶלֶךְ רוֹפֵא נֶאֱמָן וְרַחֲמָן אָתָּה. בָּרוּךְ אַתָּה יהוה, רוֹפֵא חוֹלֵי עַמּוֹ יִשְׂרָאֵל.

בָּרֵךְ עָלֵינוּ יהוה אֱלֹהֵינוּ אֶת־הַשָּׁנָה הַזֹּאת וְאֶת־כָּל־מִינֵי תְבוּאָתָהּ לְטוֹבָה, וְתֵן בְּרָכָה עַל פְּנֵי הָאֲדָמָה, וְשַׂבְּעֵנוּ מִטּוּבָהּ, וּבָרֵךְ שְׁנָתֵנוּ כַּשָּׁנִים הַטּוֹבוֹת. בָּרוּךְ אַתָּה יהוה, מְבָרֵךְ הַשָּׁנִים.

תְּקַע בְּשׁוֹפָר גָּדוֹל לְחֵרוּתֵנוּ, וְשָׂא נֵס לְקַבֵּץ גָּלֻיּוֹתֵינוּ, וְקַבְּצֵנוּ יַחַד מֵאַרְבַּע כַּנְפוֹת הָאָרֶץ. בָּרוּךְ אַתָּה יהוה, מְקַבֵּץ נִדְחֵי עַמּוֹ יִשְׂרָאֵל.

All services continue here:

Before Rosh Hashanah:
Barukh atah ADONAI, Holy God.

Between Rosh Hashanah and Yom Kippur:
Barukh atah ADONAI, the Holy Sovereign.

You graciously endow human beings with knowledge and teach understanding to humanity. May You grace us with knowledge, understanding, and wisdom.
Barukh atah ADONAI, who bestows knowledge.

Return us, *avinu*, to Your teaching, and bring us closer,
malkeinu, to Your service—that we may truly turn and face You.
Barukh atah ADONAI, who desires our return.

Forgive us, *avinu*, for we have sinned: pardon us, *malkeinu*, for we have transgressed—for Your nature is to forgive and pardon.
Barukh atah ADONAI, gracious and forgiving.

Look upon our suffering and take up our cause; redeem us soon for the sake of Your name—for surely You are a mighty redeemer.
Barukh atah ADONAI, Redeemer of Israel.

Heal us, ADONAI, so that we may be truly healed; save us that we may be truly saved; You are the one deserving of praise. Bring complete healing to all our suffering.

> *On behalf of one who is ill:*
> Our God and God of our ancestors may it be Your will to send speedy and complete healing of body and soul to _____, along with all the others of Your people Israel who are ill; strengthen as well the hands of those concerned with their care—

for You are God and sovereign, a faithful and compassionate healer.
Barukh atah ADONAI, Healer of the afflicted among the people Israel.

ADONAI our God, make this a year of blessing for us: may its varied harvest yield prosperity. May the earth be blessed and satisfy us with its abundance. Bless this year that it be like the best of years.
Barukh atah ADONAI, who bestows blessing upon the years.

Sound the great shofar announcing our freedom, raise the banner signaling the ingathering of our exiles, and bring us together from the four corners of the earth.
Barukh atah ADONAI, who gathers the dispersed of the people Israel.

הָשִׁיבָה שׁוֹפְטֵינוּ כְּבָרִאשׁוֹנָה וְיוֹעֲצֵינוּ כְּבַתְּחִלָּה, וְהָסֵר מִמֶּנּוּ יָגוֹן וַאֲנָחָה, וּמְלוֹךְ עָלֵינוּ אַתָּה יהוה לְבַדְּךָ בְּחֶסֶד וּבְרַחֲמִים, וְצַדְּקֵנוּ בַּמִּשְׁפָּט.

Before Rosh Hashanah:

בָּרוּךְ אַתָּה יהוה, מֶלֶךְ אוֹהֵב צְדָקָה וּמִשְׁפָּט.

Before Yom Kippur:

בָּרוּךְ אַתָּה יהוה, הַמֶּלֶךְ הַמִּשְׁפָּט.

וְלַמַּלְשִׁינִים אַל תְּהִי תִקְוָה, וְכָל־הָרִשְׁעָה כְּרֶגַע תֹּאבֵד, וְכָל־אוֹיְבֶיךָ מְהֵרָה יִכָּרֵתוּ, וְהַזֵּדִים מְהֵרָה תְעַקֵּר וּתְשַׁבֵּר וּתְמַגֵּר וְתַכְנִיעַ בִּמְהֵרָה בְיָמֵינוּ. בָּרוּךְ אַתָּה יהוה, שֹׁבֵר אֹיְבִים וּמַכְנִיעַ זֵדִים.

עַל הַצַּדִּיקִים וְעַל הַחֲסִידִים וְעַל זִקְנֵי עַמְּךָ בֵּית יִשְׂרָאֵל, וְעַל פְּלֵיטַת סוֹפְרֵיהֶם, וְעַל גֵּרֵי הַצֶּדֶק וְעָלֵינוּ, יֶהֱמוּ נָא רַחֲמֶיךָ, יהוה אֱלֹהֵינוּ, וְתֵן שָׂכָר טוֹב לְכָל־הַבּוֹטְחִים בְּשִׁמְךָ בֶּאֱמֶת, וְשִׂים חֶלְקֵנוּ עִמָּהֶם, וּלְעוֹלָם לֹא נֵבוֹשׁ כִּי בְךָ בָּטָחְנוּ. בָּרוּךְ אַתָּה יהוה, מִשְׁעָן וּמִבְטָח לַצַּדִּיקִים.

וְלִירוּשָׁלַיִם עִירְךָ בְּרַחֲמִים תָּשׁוּב, וְתִשְׁכּוֹן בְּתוֹכָהּ כַּאֲשֶׁר דִּבַּרְתָּ, וּבְנֵה אוֹתָהּ בְּקָרוֹב בְּיָמֵינוּ בִּנְיַן עוֹלָם, וְכִסֵּא דָוִד מְהֵרָה לְתוֹכָהּ תָּכִין. בָּרוּךְ אַתָּה יהוה, בּוֹנֵה יְרוּשָׁלָיִם.

אֶת־צֶמַח דָּוִד עַבְדְּךָ מְהֵרָה תַצְמִיחַ, וְקַרְנוֹ תָּרוּם בִּישׁוּעָתֶךָ, כִּי לִישׁוּעָתְךָ קִוִּינוּ כָּל־הַיּוֹם. בָּרוּךְ אַתָּה יהוה, מַצְמִיחַ קֶרֶן יְשׁוּעָה.

שְׁמַע קוֹלֵנוּ יהוה אֱלֹהֵינוּ, חוּס וְרַחֵם עָלֵינוּ, וְקַבֵּל בְּרַחֲמִים וּבְרָצוֹן אֶת־תְּפִלָּתֵנוּ, כִּי אֵל שׁוֹמֵעַ תְּפִלּוֹת וְתַחֲנוּנִים אָתָּה, וּמִלְּפָנֶיךָ, מַלְכֵּנוּ, רֵיקָם אַל תְּשִׁיבֵנוּ. כִּי אַתָּה שׁוֹמֵעַ תְּפִלַּת עַמְּךָ יִשְׂרָאֵל בְּרַחֲמִים. בָּרוּךְ אַתָּה יהוה, שׁוֹמֵעַ תְּפִלָּה.

רְצֵה, יהוה אֱלֹהֵינוּ, בְּעַמְּךָ יִשְׂרָאֵל וּבִתְפִלָּתָם, וְהָשֵׁב אֶת־הָעֲבוֹדָה לִדְבִיר בֵּיתֶךָ, [וְאִשֵּׁי יִשְׂרָאֵל] וּתְפִלָּתָם בְּאַהֲבָה תְקַבֵּל בְּרָצוֹן, וּתְהִי לְרָצוֹן תָּמִיד עֲבוֹדַת יִשְׂרָאֵל עַמֶּךָ.

וְתֶחֱזֶינָה עֵינֵינוּ בְּשׁוּבְךָ לְצִיּוֹן בְּרַחֲמִים. בָּרוּךְ אַתָּה יהוה, הַמַּחֲזִיר שְׁכִינָתוֹ לְצִיּוֹן.

Restore our judges as once they ruled, and restore our counselors as of old. Remove sorrow and anguish. May You alone, ADONAI, rule over us with kindness and compassion. May You find our cause righteous.

Before Rosh Hashanah:
Barukh atah ADONAI, Sovereign who loves justice and compassion.

Before Yom Kippur:
Barukh atah ADONAI, Sovereign of judgment.

May the hopes of those who would defame us be dashed, may wickedness be instantly frustrated; may all Your enemies be quickly cut off. And speedily in our time may You root out, subdue, break, and humble the arrogant. *Barukh atah ADONAI*, who defeats enemies and humbles the arrogant.

Arouse Your compassion, ADONAI our God, toward the righteous, the pious, the leaders of the people Israel, the remnant of the wise, the righteous converts, and upon us all. May all those who trust in You be truly rewarded, and may our share be among them so that we never be ashamed—for we trust in You.
Barukh atah ADONAI, promise and support of the righteous.

In Your mercy, return to Your city, Jerusalem. Dwell there as You have promised; rebuild it permanently, speedily, in our day. May You soon establish the throne of David in its midst.
Barukh atah ADONAI, who rebuilds Jerusalem.

Cause the offspring of Your servant David to flourish; may his head be raised high with the coming of Your deliverance—for we await Your salvation each day.
Barukh atah ADONAI, who causes salvation to flourish.

Hear our voice, ADONAI our God, be kind and have compassion for us. Willingly and lovingly accept our prayers—for You, God, hear prayers and listen to pleas. Do not send us away empty-handed—for in Your kindness You listen to the prayers of Your people Israel.
Barukh atah ADONAI, who listens to prayer.

ADONAI our God, embrace Your people Israel and their prayer. Restore worship to Your sanctuary. May the [fiery offerings and] prayers of the people Israel be lovingly accepted by You, and may our service always be pleasing.

Let our eyes behold Your merciful return to Zion. *Barukh atah ADONAI*, who restores Your Divine Presence to Zion.

SILENT AMIDAH: We recite the paragraph on the right; while reciting its first words, we bow.

REPETITION OF THE AMIDAH: While reciting the first words, by custom we remain seated while bowing our head.

Congregation recites: *Leader recites:*

‡ מוֹדִים אֲנַחְנוּ לָךְ, שָׁאַתָּה
הוּא יהוה אֱלֹהֵינוּ וֵאלֹהֵי
אֲבוֹתֵינוּ [וְאִמּוֹתֵינוּ]
אֱלֹהֵי כָל־בָּשָׂר, יוֹצְרֵנוּ,
יוֹצֵר בְּרֵאשִׁית. בְּרָכוֹת
וְהוֹדָאוֹת לְשִׁמְךָ הַגָּדוֹל
וְהַקָּדוֹשׁ, עַל שֶׁהֶחֱיִיתָנוּ
וְקִיַּמְתָּנוּ. כֵּן תְּחַיֵּנוּ
וּתְקַיְּמֵנוּ, וְתֶאֱסוֹף
גָּלֻיּוֹתֵינוּ לְחַצְרוֹת קָדְשֶׁךָ,
לִשְׁמוֹר חֻקֶּיךָ וְלַעֲשׂוֹת
רְצוֹנֶךָ, וּלְעָבְדְּךָ בְּלֵבָב
שָׁלֵם, עַל שֶׁאֲנַחְנוּ מוֹדִים
לָךְ. בָּרוּךְ אֵל הַהוֹדָאוֹת.

מוֹדִים אֲנַחְנוּ לָךְ, שָׁאַתָּה
הוּא יהוה אֱלֹהֵינוּ וֵאלֹהֵי
אֲבוֹתֵינוּ [וְאִמּוֹתֵינוּ]
לְעוֹלָם וָעֶד, צוּר חַיֵּינוּ
מָגֵן יִשְׁעֵנוּ אַתָּה הוּא.
לְדוֹר וָדוֹר נוֹדֶה לְךָ
וּנְסַפֵּר תְּהִלָּתֶךָ עַל חַיֵּינוּ
הַמְּסוּרִים בְּיָדֶךָ, וְעַל
נִשְׁמוֹתֵינוּ הַפְּקוּדוֹת לָךְ,
וְעַל נִסֶּיךָ שֶׁבְּכָל־יוֹם עִמָּנוּ,
וְעַל נִפְלְאוֹתֶיךָ וְטוֹבוֹתֶיךָ
שֶׁבְּכָל־עֵת, עֶרֶב וָבֹקֶר
וְצָהֳרָיִם. ◁ הַטּוֹב, כִּי לֹא
כָלוּ רַחֲמֶיךָ, וְהַמְּרַחֵם, כִּי
לֹא תַמּוּ חֲסָדֶיךָ מֵעוֹלָם
קִוִּינוּ לָךְ.

וְעַל כֻּלָּם יִתְבָּרַךְ וְיִתְרוֹמַם שִׁמְךָ מַלְכֵּנוּ תָּמִיד לְעוֹלָם
וָעֶד.

Before Yom Kippur:

וּכְתוֹב לְחַיִּים טוֹבִים כָּל־בְּנֵי בְרִיתֶךָ.

וְכֹל הַחַיִּים יוֹדוּךָ סֶּלָה, וִיהַלְלוּ אֶת־שִׁמְךָ בֶּאֱמֶת, הָאֵל
יְשׁוּעָתֵנוּ וְעֶזְרָתֵנוּ סֶלָה.
‡ בָּרוּךְ אַתָּה יהוה, הַטּוֹב שִׁמְךָ וּלְךָ נָאֶה לְהוֹדוֹת.

Leader recites:

We thank You, You who are our God and the God of our ancestors through all time, protector of our lives, shield of our salvation. From one generation to the next we thank You and sing Your praises—

for our lives that are in Your hands,

for our souls that are under Your care,

for Your miracles that accompany us each day,

and for Your wonders and Your gifts that are with us each moment—evening, morning, and noon.

You are the One who is good, whose mercy is never-ending; the One who is compassionate, whose love is unceasing. We have always placed our hope in You.

Congregation recites:

ﬦ We thank You for the ability to acknowledge You. You are our God and the God of our ancestors, the God of all flesh, our creator, and the creator of all. We offer praise and blessing to Your holy and great name, for granting us life and for sustaining us. May You continue to grant us life and sustenance. Gather our dispersed to Your holy courtyards, that we may fulfill Your mitzvot and serve You wholeheartedly, carrying out Your will. May God, the source of gratitude, be praised.

For all these blessings may Your name be praised and exalted, our sovereign, always and forever.

Before Yom Kippur:

And inscribe all the people of Your covenant for a good life.
U-kh'tov l'ḥayyim tovim kol b'nei v'ritekha.

May all that lives thank You always, and praise Your name faithfully forever, God of our deliverance and help.
ﬦ *Barukh atah* ADONAI, whose name is goodness and to whom praise is fitting.

שָׁלוֹם רָב עַל יִשְׂרָאֵל עַמְּךָ וְעַל כָּל־יוֹשְׁבֵי תֵבֵל תָּשִׂים לְעוֹלָם,
כִּי אַתָּה הוּא מֶלֶךְ אָדוֹן לְכָל־הַשָּׁלוֹם. וְטוֹב בְּעֵינֶיךָ לְבָרֵךְ אֶת־
עַמְּךָ יִשְׂרָאֵל בְּכָל־עֵת וּבְכָל־שָׁעָה בִּשְׁלוֹמֶךָ.

Before Yom Kippur:

בְּסֵפֶר חַיִּים, בְּרָכָה וְשָׁלוֹם וּפַרְנָסָה טוֹבָה, נִזָּכֵר וְנִכָּתֵב לְפָנֶיךָ,
אֲנַחְנוּ וְכָל־עַמְּךָ בֵּית יִשְׂרָאֵל, לְחַיִּים טוֹבִים וּלְשָׁלוֹם.

Before Rosh Hashanah end with:

בָּרוּךְ אַתָּה יהוה, הַמְבָרֵךְ אֶת־עַמּוֹ יִשְׂרָאֵל בַּשָּׁלוֹם.

Before Rosh Hashanah, conclude with the final paragraph on page 441.

Before Yom Kippur end with:

בָּרוּךְ אַתָּה יהוה, עֹשֵׂה הַשָּׁלוֹם.

*The Confession, which begins here and continues through the top of page 441,
is recited in the Silent Amidah before Yom Kippur.*

וִדּוּי

אֱלֹהֵינוּ וֵאלֹהֵי אֲבוֹתֵינוּ [וְאִמּוֹתֵינוּ], תָּבֹא לְפָנֶיךָ
תְּפִלָּתֵנוּ, וְאַל תִּתְעַלַּם מִתְּחִנָּתֵנוּ, שֶׁאֵין אֲנַחְנוּ עַזֵּי פָנִים
וּקְשֵׁי עֹרֶף, לוֹמַר לְפָנֶיךָ יהוה אֱלֹהֵינוּ וֵאלֹהֵי אֲבוֹתֵינוּ
[וְאִמּוֹתֵינוּ], צַדִּיקִים אֲנַחְנוּ וְלֹא חָטָאנוּ, אֲבָל אֲנַחְנוּ
וַאֲבוֹתֵינוּ [וְאִמּוֹתֵינוּ] חָטָאנוּ.

Customarily, we each strike our heart as we recite every phrase of this confession.

אָשַׁמְנוּ, בָּגַדְנוּ, גָּזַלְנוּ, דִּבַּרְנוּ דֹפִי. הֶעֱוִינוּ, וְהִרְשַׁעְנוּ,
זַדְנוּ, חָמַסְנוּ, טָפַלְנוּ שֶׁקֶר. יָעַצְנוּ רָע, כִּזַּבְנוּ, לַצְנוּ,
מָרַדְנוּ, נִאַצְנוּ, סָרַרְנוּ, עָוִינוּ, פָּשַׁעְנוּ, צָרַרְנוּ, קִשִּׁינוּ עֹרֶף.
רָשַׁעְנוּ, שִׁחַתְנוּ, תִּעַבְנוּ, תָּעִינוּ, תִּעְתָּעְנוּ.

Grant abundant and lasting peace to Your people Israel and all who dwell on earth, for You are the sovereign master of all the ways of peace. May it please You to bless Your people Israel at all times with Your gift of peace.

Before Yom Kippur:

May we and the entire House of Israel be called to mind and inscribed for life, blessing, sustenance, and peace in the Book of Life.

Before Rosh Hashanah end with:

Barukh atah ADONAI, who blesses the people Israel with peace.

Before Rosh Hashanah, conclude with the final paragraph on page 441.

Before Yom Kippur: end with:

Barukh atah ADONAI, who brings peace.

The Confession, which begins here and continues through the top of page 441, is recited in the Silent Amidah before Yom Kippur.

Prayers of Confession

INTRODUCTION TO THE CONFESSION

Our God and God of our ancestors, hear our prayer; do not ignore our plea. Our God and God of our ancestors, we are neither so insolent nor so obstinate as to claim in Your presence that we are righteous, without sin; for we, like ancestors who came before us, have sinned.

The Shorter Confession—Ashamnu

Customarily, we each strike our heart as we recite every phrase of this confession.

We **a**buse, we **b**etray, we are **c**ruel, we **d**estroy, we **e**mbitter, we **f**alsify, we **g**ossip, we **h**ate, we **i**nsult, we **j**eer, we **k**ill, we **l**ie, we **m**ock, we **n**eglect, we **o**ppress, we **p**ervert, we **q**uarrel, we **r**ebel, we **s**teal, we **t**ransgress, we are **u**nkind, we are **v**iolent, we are **w**icked, we are **e**xtremists, we **y**earn to do evil, we are **z**ealous for bad causes.

Ashamnu, bagadnu, gazalnu, dibbarnu dofi,
he·evinu, v'hirshanu, zadnu, ḥamasnu, tafalnu sheker,
ya·atznu ra, kizzavnu, latznu, maradnu, ni·atznu,
sararnu, avinu, pashanu, tzararnu, kishinu oref,
rashanu, shiḥatnu, ti·avnu, ta·inu, titanu.

סָרְנוּ מִמִּצְוֹתֶיךָ וּמִמִּשְׁפָּטֶיךָ הַטּוֹבִים, וְלֹא שָׁוָה לָנוּ. וְאַתָּה
צַדִּיק עַל כָּל־הַבָּא עָלֵינוּ, כִּי אֱמֶת עָשִׂיתָ וַאֲנַחְנוּ
הִרְשָׁעְנוּ. מַה נֹּאמַר לְפָנֶיךָ יוֹשֵׁב מָרוֹם, וּמַה נְּסַפֵּר לְפָנֶיךָ
שׁוֹכֵן שְׁחָקִים, הֲלֹא כָּל־הַנִּסְתָּרוֹת וְהַנִּגְלוֹת אַתָּה יוֹדֵעַ.

אַתָּה יוֹדֵעַ רָזֵי עוֹלָם, וְתַעֲלוּמוֹת סִתְרֵי כָּל־חָי. אַתָּה
חוֹפֵשׂ כָּל־חַדְרֵי בָטֶן, וּבוֹחֵן כְּלָיוֹת וָלֵב. אֵין דָּבָר נֶעְלָם מִמֶּךָּ,
וְאֵין נִסְתָּר מִנֶּגֶד עֵינֶיךָ. וּבְכֵן יְהִי רָצוֹן מִלְּפָנֶיךָ, יהוה אֱלֹהֵינוּ
וֵאלֹהֵי אֲבוֹתֵינוּ [וְאִמּוֹתֵינוּ], שֶׁתִּסְלַח לָנוּ
עַל כָּל־חַטֹּאתֵינוּ, וְתִמְחַל לָנוּ עַל כָּל־עֲוֹנוֹתֵינוּ, וּתְכַפֶּר לָנוּ
עַל כָּל־פְּשָׁעֵינוּ.

Customarily, we each strike our heart as we recite the words עַל חֵטְא שֶׁחָטָאנוּ.

עַל חֵטְא שֶׁחָטָאנוּ לְפָנֶיךָ בְּאֹנֶס וּבְרָצוֹן,
וְעַל חֵטְא שֶׁחָטָאנוּ לְפָנֶיךָ בְּאִמּוּץ הַלֵּב.
עַל חֵטְא שֶׁחָטָאנוּ לְפָנֶיךָ בִּבְלִי דָעַת,
וְעַל חֵטְא שֶׁחָטָאנוּ לְפָנֶיךָ בְּבִטּוּי שְׂפָתָיִם.
עַל חֵטְא שֶׁחָטָאנוּ לְפָנֶיךָ בְּגִלּוּי עֲרָיוֹת,
וְעַל חֵטְא שֶׁחָטָאנוּ לְפָנֶיךָ בַּגָּלוּי וּבַסָּתֶר.
עַל חֵטְא שֶׁחָטָאנוּ לְפָנֶיךָ בְּדַעַת וּבְמִרְמָה,
וְעַל חֵטְא שֶׁחָטָאנוּ לְפָנֶיךָ בְּדִבּוּר פֶּה.
עַל חֵטְא שֶׁחָטָאנוּ לְפָנֶיךָ בְּהוֹנָאַת רֵעַ,
וְעַל חֵטְא שֶׁחָטָאנוּ לְפָנֶיךָ בְּהַרְהוֹר הַלֵּב.
עַל חֵטְא שֶׁחָטָאנוּ לְפָנֶיךָ בִּוְעִידַת זְנוּת,
וְעַל חֵטְא שֶׁחָטָאנוּ לְפָנֶיךָ בְּוִדּוּי פֶּה.
עַל חֵטְא שֶׁחָטָאנוּ לְפָנֶיךָ בְּזִלְזוּל הוֹרִים וּמוֹרִים,
וְעַל חֵטְא שֶׁחָטָאנוּ לְפָנֶיךָ בְּזָדוֹן וּבִשְׁגָגָה.

We have turned from Your goodly laws and commandments, but it has not profited us. Surely, You are in the right with respect to all that has come upon us, for You have acted faithfully, but we have been in the wrong. What can we say to You who sit on high, and what can we tell You who dwell in heaven, for You know all that is hidden as well as all that is revealed.

You know the mysteries of the universe, the deepest secrets of everyone alive. You probe our innermost depths; You examine our thoughts and feelings. Nothing escapes You; nothing is secret from You. Therefore, may it be Your will, our God and God of our ancestors, to forgive us for all our sins, to pardon us for all our iniquities, and to grant us atonement for all our transgressions.

The Longer Confession—Al Het

Customarily, we each strike our heart as we recite the words "We have sinned."

We have sinned against You unwillingly and willingly,
  and we have sinned against You through hardening our hearts.
We have sinned against You thoughtlessly,
  and we have sinned against You in idle chatter.
We have sinned against You through sexual immorality,
  and we have sinned against You openly and in private.
We have sinned against You knowingly and deceitfully,
  and we have sinned against You by the way we talk.
We have sinned against You by defrauding others,
  and we have sinned against You in our innermost thoughts.
We have sinned against You through forbidden trysts,
  and we have sinned against You through empty confession.
We have sinned against You by scorning parents and teachers,
  and we have sinned against You purposely and by mistake.

עַל חֵטְא שֶׁחָטָאנוּ לְפָנֶיךָ בְּחֹזֶק יָד,

וְעַל חֵטְא שֶׁחָטָאנוּ לְפָנֶיךָ בְּחִלּוּל הַשֵּׁם.

עַל חֵטְא שֶׁחָטָאנוּ לְפָנֶיךָ בְּטֻמְאַת שְׂפָתָיִם,

וְעַל חֵטְא שֶׁחָטָאנוּ לְפָנֶיךָ בְּטִפְשׁוּת פֶּה.

עַל חֵטְא שֶׁחָטָאנוּ לְפָנֶיךָ בְּיֵצֶר הָרָע,

וְעַל חֵטְא שֶׁחָטָאנוּ לְפָנֶיךָ בְּיוֹדְעִים וּבְלֹא יוֹדְעִים.

וְעַל כֻּלָּם, אֱלוֹהַּ סְלִיחוֹת, סְלַח לָנוּ, מְחַל לָנוּ, כַּפֶּר-לָנוּ.

עַל חֵטְא שֶׁחָטָאנוּ לְפָנֶיךָ בְּכַחַשׁ וּבְכָזָב,

וְעַל חֵטְא שֶׁחָטָאנוּ לְפָנֶיךָ בְּכַפַּת שֹׁחַד.

עַל חֵטְא שֶׁחָטָאנוּ לְפָנֶיךָ בְּלָצוֹן,

וְעַל חֵטְא שֶׁחָטָאנוּ לְפָנֶיךָ בְּלָשׁוֹן הָרָע.

עַל חֵטְא שֶׁחָטָאנוּ לְפָנֶיךָ בְּמַשָּׂא וּבְמַתָּן,

וְעַל חֵטְא שֶׁחָטָאנוּ לְפָנֶיךָ בְּמַאֲכָל וּבְמִשְׁתֶּה.

עַל חֵטְא שֶׁחָטָאנוּ לְפָנֶיךָ בְּנֶשֶׁךְ וּבְמַרְבִּית,

וְעַל חֵטְא שֶׁחָטָאנוּ לְפָנֶיךָ בִּנְטִיַּת גָּרוֹן.

עַל חֵטְא שֶׁחָטָאנוּ לְפָנֶיךָ בְּשִׂיחַ שִׂפְתוֹתֵינוּ,

וְעַל חֵטְא שֶׁחָטָאנוּ לְפָנֶיךָ בְּשִׁקּוּר עָיִן.

עַל חֵטְא שֶׁחָטָאנוּ לְפָנֶיךָ בְּעֵינַיִם רָמוֹת,

וְעַל חֵטְא שֶׁחָטָאנוּ לְפָנֶיךָ בְּעַזּוּת מֶצַח.

וְעַל כֻּלָּם, אֱלוֹהַּ סְלִיחוֹת, סְלַח לָנוּ, מְחַל לָנוּ, כַּפֶּר-לָנוּ.

עַל חֵטְא שֶׁחָטָאנוּ לְפָנֶיךָ בִּפְרִיקַת עֹל,

וְעַל חֵטְא שֶׁחָטָאנוּ לְפָנֶיךָ בִּפְלִילוּת.

עַל חֵטְא שֶׁחָטָאנוּ לְפָנֶיךָ בִּצְדִיַּת רֵעַ,

וְעַל חֵטְא שֶׁחָטָאנוּ לְפָנֶיךָ בְּצָרוּת עָיִן.

עַל חֵטְא שֶׁחָטָאנוּ לְפָנֶיךָ בְּקַלּוּת רֹאשׁ,

וְעַל חֵטְא שֶׁחָטָאנוּ לְפָנֶיךָ בְּקַשְׁיוּת עֹרֶף.

עַל חֵטְא שֶׁחָטָאנוּ לְפָנֶיךָ בְּרִיצַת רַגְלַיִם לְהָרַע,

וְעַל חֵטְא שֶׁחָטָאנוּ לְפָנֶיךָ בִּרְכִילוּת.

עַל חֵטְא שֶׁחָטָאנוּ לְפָנֶיךָ בִּשְׁבוּעַת שָׁוְא,

וְעַל חֵטְא שֶׁחָטָאנוּ לְפָנֶיךָ בְּשִׂנְאַת חִנָּם.

עַל חֵטְא שֶׁחָטָאנוּ לְפָנֶיךָ בִּתְשׂוּמֶת-יָד,

וְעַל חֵטְא שֶׁחָטָאנוּ לְפָנֶיךָ בְּתִמְהוֹן לֵבָב.

וְעַל כֻּלָּם, אֱלוֹהַּ סְלִיחוֹת, סְלַח לָנוּ, מְחַל לָנוּ, כַּפֶּר-לָנוּ.

We have sinned against You by resorting to violence,
 and we have sinned against You by public desecration of Your name.
We have sinned against You through foul speech,
 and we have sinned against You through foolish talk.
We have sinned against You through pursuing the impulse to evil,
 and we have sinned against You wittingly and unwittingly.

For all these sins, forgiving God, forgive us, pardon us, grant us atonement.

We have sinned against You through denial and deceit,
 and we have sinned against You by taking bribes.
We have sinned against You by clever cynicism,
 and we have sinned against You by speaking ill of others.
We have sinned against You by the way we do business,
 and we have sinned against You in our eating and drinking.
We have sinned against You by greed and oppressive interest,
 and we have sinned against You through arrogance.
We have sinned against You in everyday conversation,
 and we have sinned against You through conspiratorial glances.
We have sinned against You through condescension,
 and we have sinned against You through stubbornness.

For all these sins, forgiving God, forgive us, pardon us, grant us atonement.

We have sinned against You by throwing off all restraint,
 and we have sinned against You by rashly judging others.
We have sinned against You by plotting against others,
 and we have sinned against You through selfishness.
We have sinned against You through superficiality,
 and we have sinned against You through stubbornness.
We have sinned against You by rushing to do evil,
 and we have sinned against You through gossip.
We have sinned against You through empty promises,
 and we have sinned against You through baseless hatred.
We have sinned against You by betraying trust,
 and we have sinned against You by succumbing to confusion.

For all these sins, forgiving God, forgive us, pardon us, grant us atonement.

וְעַל מִצְוֹת עֲשֵׂה וְעַל מִצְוֹת לֹא תַעֲשֶׂה. בֵּין שֶׁיֵּשׁ בָּהּ קוּם עֲשֵׂה, וּבֵין שֶׁאֵין בָּהּ קוּם עֲשֵׂה, אֶת הַגְּלוּיִים לָנוּ וְאֶת־שֶׁאֵינָם גְּלוּיִים לָנוּ. אֶת־הַגְּלוּיִים לָנוּ כְּבָר אֲמַרְנוּם לְפָנֶיךָ וְהוֹדִינוּ לְךָ עֲלֵיהֶם, וְאֶת־שֶׁאֵינָם גְּלוּיִים לָנוּ, לְפָנֶיךָ הֵם גְּלוּיִים וִידוּעִים, כַּדָּבָר שֶׁנֶּאֱמַר: הַנִּסְתָּרֹת לַיהוה אֱלֹהֵינוּ, וְהַנִּגְלֹת לָנוּ וּלְבָנֵינוּ עַד עוֹלָם, לַעֲשׂוֹת אֶת־כָּל־דִּבְרֵי הַתּוֹרָה הַזֹּאת.

In all services the silent Amidah concludes here:

אֱלֹהַי, נְצֹר לְשׁוֹנִי מֵרָע, וּשְׂפָתַי מִדַּבֵּר מִרְמָה, וְלִמְקַלְלַי נַפְשִׁי תִדֹּם, וְנַפְשִׁי כֶּעָפָר לַכֹּל תִּהְיֶה. פְּתַח לִבִּי בְּתוֹרָתֶךָ, וּבְמִצְוֹתֶיךָ תִּרְדּוֹף נַפְשִׁי. וְכָל־הַחוֹשְׁבִים עָלַי רָעָה, מְהֵרָה הָפֵר עֲצָתָם וְקַלְקֵל מַחֲשַׁבְתָּם. עֲשֵׂה לְמַעַן שְׁמֶךָ, עֲשֵׂה לְמַעַן יְמִינֶךָ, עֲשֵׂה לְמַעַן קְדֻשָּׁתֶךָ, עֲשֵׂה לְמַעַן תּוֹרָתֶךָ. לְמַעַן יֵחָלְצוּן יְדִידֶיךָ, הוֹשִׁיעָה יְמִינְךָ וַעֲנֵנִי. יִהְיוּ לְרָצוֹן אִמְרֵי פִי וְהֶגְיוֹן לִבִּי לְפָנֶיךָ, יהוה צוּרִי וְגוֹאֲלִי. עֹשֶׂה שָׁלוֹם בִּמְרוֹמָיו, הוּא יַעֲשֶׂה שָׁלוֹם עָלֵינוּ, וְעַל כָּל־יִשְׂרָאֵל [וְעַל כָּל־יוֹשְׁבֵי תֵבֵל] וְאִמְרוּ: אָמֵן.

קַדִּישׁ שָׁלֵם

יִתְגַּדַּל וְיִתְקַדַּשׁ שְׁמֵהּ רַבָּא, בְּעָלְמָא דִּי בְרָא, כִּרְעוּתֵהּ,
וְיַמְלִיךְ מַלְכוּתֵהּ בְּחַיֵּיכוֹן וּבְיוֹמֵיכוֹן וּבְחַיֵּי דְכָל־בֵּית יִשְׂרָאֵל,
בַּעֲגָלָא וּבִזְמַן קָרִיב, וְאִמְרוּ אָמֵן.

יְהֵא שְׁמֵהּ רַבָּא מְבָרַךְ לְעָלַם וּלְעָלְמֵי עָלְמַיָּא.

יִתְבָּרַךְ וְיִשְׁתַּבַּח וְיִתְפָּאַר וְיִתְרוֹמַם וְיִתְנַשֵּׂא וְיִתְהַדָּר
וְיִתְעַלֶּה וְיִתְהַלָּל שְׁמֵהּ דְּקֻדְשָׁא, **בְּרִיךְ הוּא,**

Before Rosh Hashanah:

לְעֵלָּא מִן כָּל־בִּרְכָתָא

Before Yom Kippur:

לְעֵלָּא לְעֵלָּא מִכָּל־בִּרְכָתָא
וְשִׁירָתָא תֻּשְׁבְּחָתָא וְנֶחָמָתָא דַּאֲמִירָן בְּעָלְמָא, וְאִמְרוּ אָמֵן.

תִּתְקַבֵּל צְלוֹתְהוֹן וּבָעוּתְהוֹן דְּכָל־יִשְׂרָאֵל קֳדָם אֲבוּהוֹן
דִּי בִשְׁמַיָּא, וְאִמְרוּ אָמֵן.

יְהֵא שְׁלָמָא רַבָּא מִן שְׁמַיָּא וְחַיִּים עָלֵינוּ וְעַל כָּל־יִשְׂרָאֵל, וְאִמְרוּ אָמֵן.

עֹשֶׂה שָׁלוֹם בִּמְרוֹמָיו הוּא יַעֲשֶׂה שָׁלוֹם עָלֵינוּ וְעַל כָּל־יִשְׂרָאֵל
[וְעַל כָּל־יוֹשְׁבֵי תֵבֵל], וְאִמְרוּ אָמֵן.

And forgive us the breach of all commandments and prohibitions, whether involving deeds or not, whether known to us or not. The sins known to us we have acknowledged, and those unknown to us are surely known to You, as the Torah states: "Secret matters are the concern of ADONAI our God; but in matters that are revealed, it is for us and our children to apply all the teachings of the Torah till the end of time."

In all services the silent Amidah concludes here:

Personal Prayers Concluding the Amidah

My God, keep my tongue from evil, my lips from lies. Help me ignore those who would slander me. Let me be humble before all. Open my heart to Your Torah, that I may pursue Your mitzvot. Frustrate the designs of those who plot evil against me; make nothing of their schemes. Act for the sake of Your name, Your power, Your holiness, and Your Torah. Answer my prayer for the deliverance of Your people. May the words of my mouth and the meditations of my heart be acceptable to You, ADONAI, my rock and my redeemer. May the One who brings peace to the universe bring peace to us and to all the people Israel [and to all who dwell on earth]. Amen.

Kaddish Shalem

May God's great name be exalted and hallowed throughout the created world, as is God's wish. May God's sovereignty soon be established, in your lifetime and in your days, and in the days of all the House of Israel. And respond with: *Amen.*

May God's great name be acknowledged forever and ever!
Y'hei sh'meih rabba m'varakh l'alam u-l'almei almayya.

May the name of the Holy One be acknowledged and celebrated, lauded and worshipped, exalted and honored, extolled and acclaimed—though God, who is blessed, *b'rikh hu*, is truly [*before Yom Kippur add:* far] beyond all acknowledgment and praise, or any expressions of gratitude or consolation ever spoken in the world. And respond with: *Amen.*

May the prayers and pleas of all Israel be accepted by their creator in heaven. And respond with: *Amen.*

May abundant peace from heaven, and life, come to us and to all Israel. And respond with: *Amen.*

May the One who brings harmony on high, bring harmony to us and to all Israel [and to all who dwell on earth]. And respond with: *Amen.*

Oseh shalom bi-m'romav hu ya·aseh shalom aleinu v'al kol yisra·el [v'al kol yosh'vei teiveil], v'imru amen.

סִיּוּם הַתְּפִלָּה

עָלֵינוּ לְשַׁבֵּחַ לַאֲדוֹן הַכֹּל, לָתֵת גְּדֻלָּה לְיוֹצֵר בְּרֵאשִׁית,
שֶׁלֹּא עָשָׂנוּ כְּגוֹיֵי הָאֲרָצוֹת, וְלֹא שָׂמָנוּ כְּמִשְׁפְּחוֹת הָאֲדָמָה,
שֶׁלֹּא שָׂם חֶלְקֵנוּ כָּהֶם, וְגֹרָלֵנוּ כְּכָל־הֲמוֹנָם.
וַאֲנַחְנוּ כּוֹרְעִים וּמִשְׁתַּחֲוִים וּמוֹדִים,
לִפְנֵי מֶלֶךְ, מַלְכֵי הַמְּלָכִים, הַקָּדוֹשׁ בָּרוּךְ הוּא.
שֶׁהוּא נוֹטֶה שָׁמַיִם וְיֹסֵד אָרֶץ, וּמוֹשַׁב יְקָרוֹ בַּשָּׁמַיִם מִמַּעַל,
וּשְׁכִינַת עֻזּוֹ בְּגָבְהֵי מְרוֹמִים, הוּא אֱלֹהֵינוּ אֵין
עוֹד. אֱמֶת מַלְכֵּנוּ אֶפֶס זוּלָתוֹ, כַּכָּתוּב בְּתוֹרָתוֹ:
וְיָדַעְתָּ הַיּוֹם וַהֲשֵׁבֹתָ אֶל־לְבָבֶךָ, כִּי יהוה הוּא
הָאֱלֹהִים בַּשָּׁמַיִם מִמַּעַל, וְעַל הָאָרֶץ מִתָּחַת, אֵין עוֹד.

עַל כֵּן נְקַוֶּה לְךָ יהוה אֱלֹהֵינוּ, לִרְאוֹת מְהֵרָה בְּתִפְאֶרֶת עֻזֶּךָ,
לְהַעֲבִיר גִּלּוּלִים מִן הָאָרֶץ וְהָאֱלִילִים כָּרוֹת יִכָּרֵתוּן, לְתַקֵּן עוֹלָם
בְּמַלְכוּת שַׁדַּי, וְכָל־בְּנֵי בָשָׂר יִקְרְאוּ בִשְׁמֶךָ, לְהַפְנוֹת אֵלֶיךָ כָּל־
רִשְׁעֵי אָרֶץ. יַכִּירוּ וְיֵדְעוּ כָּל־יוֹשְׁבֵי תֵבֵל, כִּי לְךָ תִּכְרַע כָּל־בֶּרֶךְ,
תִּשָּׁבַע כָּל־לָשׁוֹן. לְפָנֶיךָ יהוה אֱלֹהֵינוּ יִכְרְעוּ וְיִפֹּלוּ, וְלִכְבוֹד שִׁמְךָ
יְקָר יִתֵּנוּ. וִיקַבְּלוּ כֻלָּם אֶת־עֹל מַלְכוּתֶךָ, וְתִמְלֹךְ עֲלֵיהֶם מְהֵרָה
לְעוֹלָם וָעֶד. כִּי הַמַּלְכוּת שֶׁלְּךָ הִיא, וּלְעוֹלְמֵי עַד תִּמְלוֹךְ בְּכָבוֹד.
כַּכָּתוּב בְּתוֹרָתֶךָ: יהוה יִמְלֹךְ לְעוֹלָם וָעֶד.
וְנֶאֱמַר: וְהָיָה יהוה לְמֶלֶךְ עַל כָּל־הָאָרֶץ,
בַּיּוֹם הַהוּא יִהְיֶה יהוה אֶחָד, וּשְׁמוֹ אֶחָד.

CONCLUDING PRAYERS

Aleinu

It is for us to praise the ruler of all, to acclaim the Creator, who has not made us merely a nation, nor formed us as all earthly families, nor given us an ordinary destiny.

ʄ And so we bow, acknowledging the supreme sovereign, the Holy One, who is praised—the One who spreads out the heavens and establishes the earth, whose glorious abode is in the highest heaven, whose powerful presence is in the loftiest heights. This is our God, none else; ours is the true sovereign, there is no other. As it is written in the Torah: "Know this day and take it to heart, that ADONAI is God in heaven above and on earth below; there is no other."

Aleinu l'shabbe·aḥ la-adon ha-kol, la-tet g'dullah l'yotzer b'reishit, she-lo asanu k'goyei ha-aratzot v'lo samanu k'mishp'ḥot ha-adamah, she-lo sam ḥelkeinu ka-hem, v'goraleinu k'khol hamonam.
ʄ *Va-anaḥnu kor'im u-mishtaḥavim u-modim lifnei melekh malkhei ha-m'lakhim ha-kadosh barukh hu.*

And so, ADONAI our God, we await You, that soon we may behold Your strength revealed in full glory, sweeping away the abominations of the earth, obliterating idols, establishing in the world the sovereignty of the Almighty. All flesh will call out Your name—even the wicked will turn toward You. Then all who live on earth will recognize and understand that to You alone knees must bend and allegiance be sworn. All will bow down and prostrate themselves before You, ADONAI our God, honor Your glorious name, and accept the obligation of Your sovereignty. May You soon rule over them forever and ever, for true dominion is Yours; You will rule in glory until the end of time.

As is written in Your Torah: "ADONAI will reign forever and ever." And as the prophet said: "ADONAI shall be acknowledged sovereign of all the earth. On that day ADONAI shall be one, and the name of God, one."

V'ne·emar v'hayah Adonai l'melekh al kol ha-aretz,
ba-yom ha-hu yihyeh Adonai eḥad u-sh'mo eḥad.

קַדִּישׁ יָתוֹם

Mourners and those observing Yahrzeit:

יִתְגַּדַּל וְיִתְקַדַּשׁ שְׁמֵהּ רַבָּא, בְּעָלְמָא דִּי בְרָא, כִּרְעוּתֵהּ, וְיַמְלִיךְ מַלְכוּתֵהּ בְּחַיֵּיכוֹן וּבְיוֹמֵיכוֹן וּבְחַיֵּי דְכָל־בֵּית יִשְׂרָאֵל, בַּעֲגָלָא וּבִזְמַן קָרִיב, וְאִמְרוּ אָמֵן.

Congregation and mourners:

יְהֵא שְׁמֵהּ רַבָּא מְבָרַךְ לְעָלַם וּלְעָלְמֵי עָלְמַיָּא.

Mourners:

יִתְבָּרַךְ וְיִשְׁתַּבַּח וְיִתְפָּאַר וְיִתְרוֹמַם וְיִתְנַשֵּׂא וְיִתְהַדָּר וְיִתְעַלֶּה וְיִתְהַלָּל שְׁמֵהּ דְּקֻדְשָׁא, בְּרִיךְ הוּא,

Before Rosh Hashanah:

לְעֵלָּא מִן כָּל־בִּרְכָתָא

Before Yom Kippur:

לְעֵלָּא לְעֵלָּא מִכָּל־בִּרְכָתָא

וְשִׁירָתָא תֻּשְׁבְּחָתָא וְנֶחָמָתָא דַּאֲמִירָן בְּעָלְמָא, וְאִמְרוּ אָמֵן.

יְהֵא שְׁלָמָא רַבָּא מִן שְׁמַיָּא וְחַיִּים עָלֵינוּ וְעַל כָּל־יִשְׂרָאֵל, וְאִמְרוּ אָמֵן.

עֹשֶׂה שָׁלוֹם בִּמְרוֹמָיו הוּא יַעֲשֶׂה שָׁלוֹם עָלֵינוּ וְעַל כָּל־יִשְׂרָאֵל [וְעַל כָּל־יוֹשְׁבֵי תֵבֵל], וְאִמְרוּ אָמֵן.

Mourner's Kaddish

May God's great name be exalted and hallowed throughout the created world, as is God's wish. May God's sovereignty soon be established, in your lifetime and in your days, and in the days of all the House of Israel. And respond with: *Amen.*

May God's great name be acknowledged forever and ever!

May the name of the Holy One be acknowledged and celebrated, lauded and worshipped, exalted and honored, extolled and acclaimed, though God is truly [*before Yom Kippur add:* far] beyond all acknowledgment and praise, or any expressions of gratitude or consolation ever spoken in the world. And respond with: *Amen.*

May abundant peace from heaven, and life, come to us and to all Israel. And respond with: *Amen.*

May the One who brings harmony on high, bring harmony to us and to all Israel [and to all who dwell on earth]. And respond with: *Amen.*

Mourners and those observing Yahrzeit:
Yitgaddal v'yitkaddash sh'meih rabba b'alma di v'ra ki-r'uteih v'yamlikh
malkhuteih b'hayyeikhon u-v'yomeikhon u-v'hayyei d'khol beit yisra·el
ba-agala u-viz'man kariv v'imru amen.

Congregation and mourners:
Y'hei sh'meih rabba m'varakh l'alam u-l'almei almayya.

Mourners:
Yitbarakh v'yishtabbah v'yitpa·ar v'yitromam v'yitnassei v'yit·haddar
v'yit·alleh v'yit·hallal sh'meih d'kudsha b'rikh hu l'ella [before Yom Kippur add: l'ella] mi-kol
birkhata v'shirata tushb'hata v'nehamata da-amiran b'alma v'imru amen.

Y'hei sh'lama rabba min sh'mayya v'hayyim aleinu v'al kol yisra·el v'imru amen.

Oseh shalom bi-m'romav hu ya·aseh shalom aleinu v'al kol yisra·el [v'al kol
yosh'vei teiveil] v'imru amen.

עֲרְבִית לְמוֹצָאֵי יוֹם טוֹב   EVENING SERVICE AFTER THE HOLY DAY

וְהוּא רַחוּם יְכַפֵּר עָוֹן וְלֹא יַשְׁחִית, וְהִרְבָּה לְהָשִׁיב אַפּוֹ וְלֹא יָעִיר כָּל־חֲמָתוֹ. יהוה הוֹשִׁיעָה, הַמֶּלֶךְ יַעֲנֵנוּ בְיוֹם קָרְאֵנוּ.

We rise. Leader:

בָּרְכוּ אֶת־יהוה הַמְבֹרָךְ.

Congregation, then the leader repeats:

⟩ בָּרוּךְ יהוה הַמְבֹרָךְ לְעוֹלָם וָעֶד.

We are seated.

בָּרוּךְ אַתָּה יהוה אֱלֹהֵינוּ מֶלֶךְ הָעוֹלָם,
אֲשֶׁר בִּדְבָרוֹ מַעֲרִיב עֲרָבִים,
בְּחָכְמָה פּוֹתֵחַ שְׁעָרִים,
וּבִתְבוּנָה מְשַׁנֶּה עִתִּים,
וּמַחֲלִיף אֶת־הַזְּמַנִּים,
וּמְסַדֵּר אֶת הַכּוֹכָבִים בְּמִשְׁמְרוֹתֵיהֶם בָּרָקִיעַ כִּרְצוֹנוֹ.
בּוֹרֵא יוֹם וָלָיְלָה,
גּוֹלֵל אוֹר מִפְּנֵי חֹשֶׁךְ, וְחֹשֶׁךְ מִפְּנֵי אוֹר.
◁ וּמַעֲבִיר יוֹם וּמֵבִיא לָיְלָה,
וּמַבְדִּיל בֵּין יוֹם וּבֵין לָיְלָה,
יהוה צְבָאוֹת שְׁמוֹ.
אֵל חַי וְקַיָּם, תָּמִיד יִמְלוֹךְ עָלֵינוּ לְעוֹלָם וָעֶד.
בָּרוּךְ אַתָּה יהוה, הַמַּעֲרִיב עֲרָבִים.

Bar'khu: The Call to Worship Together

God, being merciful, grants atonement for sin and does not destroy. Time and again God restrains wrath, refuses to let rage be all-consuming. Save us, ADONAI. Answer us, O Sovereign, when we call.

We rise. Leader:
Praise ADONAI, to whom all prayer is directed.

Congregation, then the leader repeats:
ſ Praise ADONAI, to whom all prayer is directed
forever and ever.
Barukh Adonai ha-m'vorakh l'olam va·ed.

We are seated.

First B'rakhah before the Sh'ma: The Evening Light

Barukh atah ADONAI, our God, ruler of time and space,
whose word brings the evening dusk,
whose wisdom opens the gates of dawn,
whose understanding changes the day's division,
whose will sets the succession of seasons and arranges the
    stars in their places in the sky,
who creates day and night,
who rolls light before darkness and darkness from light,
who makes day pass into night,
who distinguishes day from night;
Adonai Tz'va·ot is Your name.
Living and ever-present God,
May Your rule be with us, forever and ever.
Barukh atah ADONAI, who brings each evening's dusk.

אַהֲבַת עוֹלָם בֵּית יִשְׂרָאֵל עַמְּךָ אָהָבְתָּ, תּוֹרָה וּמִצְוֹת, חֻקִּים וּמִשְׁפָּטִים אוֹתָנוּ לִמַּדְתָּ. עַל כֵּן יהוה אֱלֹהֵינוּ, בְּשָׁכְבֵנוּ וּבְקוּמֵנוּ נָשִׂיחַ בְּחֻקֶּיךָ, וְנִשְׂמַח בְּדִבְרֵי תוֹרָתֶךָ וּבְמִצְוֹתֶיךָ לְעוֹלָם וָעֶד. ◁כִּי הֵם חַיֵּינוּ וְאֹרֶךְ יָמֵינוּ, וּבָהֶם נֶהְגֶּה יוֹמָם וָלָיְלָה, וְאַהֲבָתְךָ אַל תָּסִיר מִמֶּנּוּ לְעוֹלָמִים. בָּרוּךְ אַתָּה יהוה, אוֹהֵב עַמּוֹ יִשְׂרָאֵל.

קְרִיאַת שְׁמַע

Some people may wish to pause here for a moment. Some may close their eyes; others place a hand over their eyes. The intention is to concentrate on the one-ness of God. These words are added in the absence of a minyan: אֵל מֶלֶךְ נֶאֱמָן

שְׁמַע יִשְׂרָאֵל יהוה אֱלֹהֵינוּ יהוה אֶחָד.
בָּרוּךְ שֵׁם כְּבוֹד מַלְכוּתוֹ לְעוֹלָם וָעֶד.

וְאָהַבְתָּ אֵת יהוה אֱלֹהֶיךָ בְּכָל־לְבָבְךָ וּבְכָל־נַפְשְׁךָ וּבְכָל־מְאֹדֶךָ: וְהָיוּ הַדְּבָרִים הָאֵלֶּה אֲשֶׁר אָנֹכִי מְצַוְּךָ הַיּוֹם עַל־לְבָבֶךָ: וְשִׁנַּנְתָּם לְבָנֶיךָ וְדִבַּרְתָּ בָּם בְּשִׁבְתְּךָ בְּבֵיתֶךָ וּבְלֶכְתְּךָ בַדֶּרֶךְ וּבְשָׁכְבְּךָ וּבְקוּמֶךָ: וּקְשַׁרְתָּם לְאוֹת עַל־יָדֶךָ וְהָיוּ לְטֹטָפֹת בֵּין עֵינֶיךָ: וּכְתַבְתָּם עַל־מְזֻזוֹת בֵּיתֶךָ וּבִשְׁעָרֶיךָ: דברים ו ד-ט

Second B'rakhah before the Sh'ma: Torah and God's Love

You have loved Your people, the House of Israel, with infinite love; You taught us Torah and mitzvot, statutes and laws. Therefore, ADONAI our God, as we lie down or rise up, we shall think of Your laws and speak of them, rejoicing in Your words of Torah and Your mitzvot forever and ever. For they are our life and the fullness of our days, and on them we will meditate day and night. May You never withdraw Your love from us. *Barukh atah* ADONAI, who loves the people Israel.

Recitation of the Sh'ma

These words are added in the absence of a minyan: **God is a faithful Sovereign.**

Hear, O Israel, ADONAI is our God, ADONAI alone.
Praised be the name of the One whose glorious
sovereignty is forever and ever.

Sh'ma yisra·el Adonai eloheinu Adonai eḥad.
Barukh shem k'vod malkhuto l'olam va·ed.

You shall love ADONAI your God with all your heart, with all your soul, and with all that is yours. These words that I command you this day shall be taken to heart. Teach them again and again to your children, and speak of them when you sit in your home, when you walk on your way, when you lie down, and when you rise up. Bind them as a sign upon your hand and as a symbol above your eyes. Inscribe them upon the doorposts of your home and on your gates.   Deuteronomy 6:4–9

V'ahavta eit Adonai elohekha b'khol l'vav'kha u-v'khol nafsh'kha
u-v'khol m'odekha. V'hayu ha-d'varim ha-eilleh asher anokhi
m'tzav'kha ha-yom al l'vavekha. V'shinnantam l'vanekha v'dibbarta bam,
b'shivt'kha b'veitekha u-v'lekht'kha va-derekh u-v'shokhb'kha
u-v'kumekha. U-k'shartam l'ot al yadekha v'hayu l'totafot bein
einekha. U-kh'tavtam al m'zuzot beitekha u-vi-sh'arekha.

וְהָיָה אִם־שָׁמֹעַ תִּשְׁמְעוּ אֶל־מִצְוֹתַי אֲשֶׁר אָנֹכִי מְצַוֶּה
אֶתְכֶם הַיּוֹם לְאַהֲבָה אֶת־יְהוָה אֱלֹהֵיכֶם וּלְעָבְדוֹ בְּכָל־
לְבַבְכֶם וּבְכָל־נַפְשְׁכֶם: וְנָתַתִּי מְטַר־אַרְצְכֶם בְּעִתּוֹ
יוֹרֶה וּמַלְקוֹשׁ וְאָסַפְתָּ דְגָנֶךָ וְתִירֹשְׁךָ וְיִצְהָרֶךָ: וְנָתַתִּי
עֵשֶׂב בְּשָׂדְךָ לִבְהֶמְתֶּךָ וְאָכַלְתָּ וְשָׂבָעְתָּ: הִשָּׁמְרוּ לָכֶם
פֶּן־יִפְתֶּה לְבַבְכֶם וְסַרְתֶּם וַעֲבַדְתֶּם אֱלֹהִים אֲחֵרִים
וְהִשְׁתַּחֲוִיתֶם לָהֶם: וְחָרָה אַף־יְהוָה בָּכֶם וְעָצַר אֶת־
הַשָּׁמַיִם וְלֹא־יִהְיֶה מָטָר וְהָאֲדָמָה לֹא תִתֵּן אֶת־יְבוּלָהּ
וַאֲבַדְתֶּם מְהֵרָה מֵעַל הָאָרֶץ הַטֹּבָה אֲשֶׁר יְהוָה נֹתֵן
לָכֶם: וְשַׂמְתֶּם אֶת־דְּבָרַי אֵלֶּה עַל־לְבַבְכֶם וְעַל־נַפְשְׁכֶם
וּקְשַׁרְתֶּם אֹתָם לְאוֹת עַל־יֶדְכֶם וְהָיוּ לְטוֹטָפֹת בֵּין
עֵינֵיכֶם: וְלִמַּדְתֶּם אֹתָם אֶת־בְּנֵיכֶם לְדַבֵּר בָּם בְּשִׁבְתְּךָ
בְּבֵיתֶךָ וּבְלֶכְתְּךָ בַדֶּרֶךְ וּבְשָׁכְבְּךָ וּבְקוּמֶךָ: וּכְתַבְתָּם עַל־
מְזוּזוֹת בֵּיתֶךָ וּבִשְׁעָרֶיךָ: לְמַעַן יִרְבּוּ יְמֵיכֶם וִימֵי בְנֵיכֶם
עַל הָאֲדָמָה אֲשֶׁר נִשְׁבַּע יְהוָה לַאֲבֹתֵיכֶם לָתֵת לָהֶם
כִּימֵי הַשָּׁמַיִם עַל־הָאָרֶץ:

דברים יא יג-כא

וַיֹּאמֶר יְהוָה אֶל־מֹשֶׁה לֵּאמֹר: דַּבֵּר אֶל־בְּנֵי יִשְׂרָאֵל
וְאָמַרְתָּ אֲלֵהֶם וְעָשׂוּ לָהֶם צִיצִת עַל־כַּנְפֵי בִגְדֵיהֶם
לְדֹרֹתָם וְנָתְנוּ עַל־צִיצִת הַכָּנָף פְּתִיל תְּכֵלֶת: וְהָיָה לָכֶם
לְצִיצִת וּרְאִיתֶם אֹתוֹ וּזְכַרְתֶּם אֶת־כָּל־מִצְוֹת יְהוָה
וַעֲשִׂיתֶם אֹתָם וְלֹא־תָתוּרוּ אַחֲרֵי לְבַבְכֶם וְאַחֲרֵי עֵינֵיכֶם
אֲשֶׁר־אַתֶּם זֹנִים אַחֲרֵיהֶם: לְמַעַן תִּזְכְּרוּ וַעֲשִׂיתֶם
אֶת־כָּל־מִצְוֹתָי וִהְיִיתֶם קְדֹשִׁים לֵאלֹהֵיכֶם: אֲנִי יְהוָה
אֱלֹהֵיכֶם אֲשֶׁר הוֹצֵאתִי אֶתְכֶם מֵאֶרֶץ מִצְרַיִם לִהְיוֹת
לָכֶם לֵאלֹהִים אֲנִי ◄ יְהוָה אֱלֹהֵיכֶם:

במדבר טו לז-מא

אֱמֶת
וֶאֱמוּנָה כָּל־
זֹאת, וְקַיָּם עָלֵינוּ, כִּי הוּא יְהוָה אֱלֹהֵינוּ וְאֵין זוּלָתוֹ,
וַאֲנַחְנוּ יִשְׂרָאֵל עַמּוֹ.

הַפּוֹדֵנוּ מִיַּד מְלָכִים, מַלְכֵּנוּ הַגּוֹאֲלֵנוּ מִכַּף כָּל־הֶעָרִיצִים.
הָאֵל הַנִּפְרָע לָנוּ מִצָּרֵינוּ, וְהַמְשַׁלֵּם גְּמוּל לְכָל־אֹיְבֵי נַפְשֵׁנוּ,

If you will hear and obey the mitzvot that I command you this day, to love and serve ADONAI your God with all your heart and all your soul, then I will grant the rain for your land in season, rain in autumn and rain in spring. You shall gather in your grain and wine and oil—I will also provide grass in your fields for cattle—and you shall eat and be satisfied. Take care lest your heart be tempted, and you stray to serve other gods and bow to them. Then ADONAI's anger will flare up against you, and God will close up the sky so that there will be no rain and the earth will not yield its produce. You will quickly disappear from the good land that ADONAI is giving you.

Therefore, impress these words of mine upon your heart and upon your soul. Bind them as a sign upon your hand and as a symbol above your eyes; teach them to your children, speaking of them when you sit in your home, when you walk on your way, when you lie down and when you rise up; inscribe them upon the doorposts of your home and on your gates.

Then the length of your days and the days of your children, on the land that ADONAI swore to give to your ancestors, will be as the days of the heavens over the earth.

Deuteronomy 11:13–21

ADONAI said to Moses: Speak to the people Israel, and instruct them that in every generation they shall put *tzitzit* on the corners of their garments, placing a thread of blue on the *tzitzit*, the fringe of each corner. That shall be your *tzitzit* and you shall look at it, and remember all the mitzvot of ADONAI, and fulfill them, and not be seduced by your heart and eyes as they lead you astray. Then you will remember and fulfill all My mitzvot, and be holy before your God. I am ADONAI your God, who brought you out of the land of Egypt to be your God. I am ADONAI your God—

Numbers 15:37–41

Truly–

This is our faithful affirmation, binding on us: that ADONAI is our God and there is none other, and we, Israel, are God's people. God redeems us from earthly rulers, our sovereign delivers us from the hand of all tyrants,

God brings judgment upon our oppressors, retribution upon all our mortal enemies,

הָעֹשֶׂה גְדוֹלוֹת עַד אֵין חֵקֶר, וְנִפְלָאוֹת עַד אֵין מִסְפָּר.
הַשָּׂם נַפְשֵׁנוּ בַּחַיִּים, וְלֹא נָתַן לַמּוֹט רַגְלֵנוּ,
הַמַּדְרִיכֵנוּ עַל בָּמוֹת אוֹיְבֵינוּ, וַיָּרֶם קַרְנֵנוּ עַל כָּל־
שׂוֹנְאֵינוּ. הָעֹשֶׂה לָּנוּ נִסִּים וּנְקָמָה בְּפַרְעֹה, אוֹתוֹת
וּמוֹפְתִים בְּאַדְמַת בְּנֵי חָם. הַמַּכֶּה בְעֶבְרָתוֹ כָּל־בְּכוֹרֵי
מִצְרָיִם, וַיּוֹצֵא אֶת־עַמּוֹ יִשְׂרָאֵל מִתּוֹכָם לְחֵרוּת עוֹלָם.
הַמַּעֲבִיר בָּנָיו בֵּין גִּזְרֵי יַם סוּף, אֶת־רוֹדְפֵיהֶם וְאֶת־
שׂוֹנְאֵיהֶם בִּתְהוֹמוֹת טִבַּע, וְרָאוּ בָנָיו גְּבוּרָתוֹ, שִׁבְּחוּ
וְהוֹדוּ לִשְׁמוֹ.
◁ וּמַלְכוּתוֹ בְּרָצוֹן קִבְּלוּ עֲלֵיהֶם, מֹשֶׁה וּמִרְיָם וּבְנֵי
יִשְׂרָאֵל לְךָ עָנוּ שִׁירָה בְּשִׂמְחָה רַבָּה, וְאָמְרוּ כֻלָּם:

**מִי־כָמֹכָה בָּאֵלִם יהוה, מִי כָּמֹכָה נֶאְדָּר בַּקֹּדֶשׁ,
נוֹרָא תְהִלֹּת, עֹשֵׂה פֶלֶא.**

מַלְכוּתְךָ רָאוּ בָנֶיךָ, בּוֹקֵעַ יָם לִפְנֵי מֹשֶׁה, זֶה אֵלִי עָנוּ
וְאָמְרוּ:

יהוה יִמְלֹךְ לְעוֹלָם וָעֶד.

וְנֶאֱמַר: כִּי־פָדָה יהוה אֶת־יַעֲקֹב, וּגְאָלוֹ מִיַּד חָזָק מִמֶּנּוּ.
בָּרוּךְ אַתָּה יהוה, גָּאַל יִשְׂרָאֵל.

God performs wonders beyond understanding,
marvels beyond all reckoning.

> *God places us among the living,*
> *not allowing our steps to falter,*
> *and leads us past the false altars of our enemies.*

God exalted us above all those who hated us,
avenged us with miracles before Pharaoh,
offered signs and wonders in the land of Egypt.

> *God smote, in anger, all of Egypt's firstborn,*
> *brought Israel from its midst to lasting freedom,*
> *led them through the divided water of the Sea of Reeds.*

As their pursuing enemies drowned in the depths,
God's children beheld the power of the Divine;

> *they praised and acknowledged God's name,*
> *willingly accepting God's rule.*

Then Moses, Miriam, and the people Israel joyfully sang this
song to You:

> *"Who is like You, ADONAI, among the mighty! Who is like You,*
> *adorned in holiness, revered in praise, working wonders!"*
>
> Mi khamokha ba-eilim Adonai, mi kamokha ne·dar ba-kodesh,
> nora t'hillot, oseih fele.

Your children recognized Your sovereignty, as You split the sea
before Moses. "This is my God," they responded, and they said:

> *"ADONAI will reign forever and ever."*
>
> Adonai yimlokh l'olam va·ed.

And so it is written: "ADONAI has rescued Jacob and redeemed
him from the hand of those more powerful than he."
Barukh atah ADONAI, who redeemed the people Israel.

הַשְׁכִּיבֵנוּ יהוה אֱלֹהֵינוּ לְשָׁלוֹם,

וְהַעֲמִידֵנוּ מַלְכֵּנוּ לְחַיִּים,

וּפְרוֹשׂ עָלֵינוּ סֻכַּת שְׁלוֹמֶךָ,

וְתַקְּנֵנוּ בְּעֵצָה טוֹבָה מִלְּפָנֶיךָ,

וְהוֹשִׁיעֵנוּ לְמַעַן שְׁמֶךָ,

וְהָגֵן בַּעֲדֵנוּ,

וְהָסֵר מֵעָלֵינוּ אוֹיֵב, דֶּבֶר, וְחֶרֶב, וְרָעָב וְיָגוֹן,

וְהָסֵר שָׂטָן מִלְּפָנֵינוּ וּמֵאַחֲרֵינוּ,

וּבְצֵל כְּנָפֶיךָ תַּסְתִּירֵנוּ.

כִּי אֵל שׁוֹמְרֵנוּ וּמַצִּילֵנוּ אָתָּה,

כִּי אֵל מֶלֶךְ חַנּוּן וְרַחוּם אָתָּה,

◁ וּשְׁמֹר צֵאתֵנוּ וּבוֹאֵנוּ, לְחַיִּים וּלְשָׁלוֹם, מֵעַתָּה וְעַד עוֹלָם.

בָּרוּךְ אַתָּה יהוה, שׁוֹמֵר עַמּוֹ יִשְׂרָאֵל לָעַד.

חֲצִי קַדִּישׁ

יִתְגַּדַּל וְיִתְקַדַּשׁ שְׁמֵהּ רַבָּא, בְּעָלְמָא דִּי בְרָא, כִּרְעוּתֵהּ,
וְיַמְלִיךְ מַלְכוּתֵהּ בְּחַיֵּיכוֹן וּבְיוֹמֵיכוֹן וּבְחַיֵּי דְכָל־בֵּית
יִשְׂרָאֵל, בַּעֲגָלָא וּבִזְמַן קָרִיב, וְאִמְרוּ אָמֵן.

יְהֵא שְׁמֵהּ רַבָּא מְבָרַךְ לְעָלַם וּלְעָלְמֵי עָלְמַיָּא.

יִתְבָּרַךְ וְיִשְׁתַּבַּח וְיִתְפָּאַר וְיִתְרוֹמַם וְיִתְנַשֵּׂא וְיִתְהַדָּר
וְיִתְעַלֶּה וְיִתְהַלָּל שְׁמֵהּ דְּקֻדְשָׁא, **בְּרִיךְ הוּא,**

After Rosh Hashanah:

לְעֵלָּא לְעֵלָּא מִכָּל־בִּרְכָתָא

After Yom Kippur:

לְעֵלָּא מִן כָּל־בִּרְכָתָא
וְשִׁירָתָא תֻּשְׁבְּחָתָא וְנֶחֱמָתָא דַּאֲמִירָן בְּעָלְמָא,
וְאִמְרוּ אָמֵן.

Second B'rakhah after the Sh'ma: Peace in the Night

Allow us, ADONAI our God, to sleep peacefully
and to awaken again to life, our sovereign.
Spread over us Your canopy of peace,
restore us with Your good counsel,
and save us for the sake of Your name.
Shield us: Remove from us enemies and pestilence, sword,
starvation, and sorrow, and remove the evil forces that surround us.
Shelter us in the shadow of Your wings,
for You, God, watch over and deliver us,
and You are the Sovereign, merciful and compassionate.
Ensure our going and coming for life and peace, now and forever.
Barukh atah ADONAI, who eternally watches over Your people Israel.

Ḥatzi Kaddish

May God's great name be exalted and hallowed throughout the
created world, as is God's wish. May God's sovereignty soon be
established, in your lifetime and in your days, and in the days of
all the House of Israel. And respond with: *Amen.*

May God's great name be acknowledged forever and ever!
Y'hei sh'meih rabba m'varakh l'alam u-l'almei almayya.

May the name of the Holy One be acknowledged and celebrated,
lauded and worshipped, exalted and honored, extolled and
acclaimed— though God, who is blessed, *b'rikh hu*, is truly
[*after Rosh Hashanah add:* far] beyond all acknowledgment and praise,
or any expressions of gratitude or consolation ever spoken in the
world. And respond with: *Amen.*

תְּפִלַּת הָעֲמִידָה בַּלַּחַשׁ

Before the Amidah begins, it is customary to take three steps backward, as if we are leaving our familiar surroundings, and then three steps forward, as we approach God's presence.

אֲדֹנָי שְׂפָתַי תִּפְתָּח, וּפִי יַגִּיד תְּהִלָּתֶךָ.

Version with Patriarchs and Matriarchs:	*Version with Patriarchs:*

Version with Patriarchs:

בָּרוּךְ אַתָּה יהוה
אֱלֹהֵינוּ וֵאלֹהֵי אֲבוֹתֵינוּ,
אֱלֹהֵי אַבְרָהָם, אֱלֹהֵי
יִצְחָק, וֵאלֹהֵי יַעֲקֹב, הָאֵל
הַגָּדוֹל הַגִּבּוֹר וְהַנּוֹרָא,
אֵל עֶלְיוֹן, גּוֹמֵל חֲסָדִים
טוֹבִים, וְקוֹנֵה הַכֹּל, וְזוֹכֵר
חַסְדֵי אָבוֹת, וּמֵבִיא גוֹאֵל
לִבְנֵי בְנֵיהֶם לְמַעַן שְׁמוֹ
בְּאַהֲבָה.

Version with Patriarchs and Matriarchs:

בָּרוּךְ אַתָּה יהוה,
אֱלֹהֵינוּ וֵאלֹהֵי אֲבוֹתֵינוּ
[וְאִמּוֹתֵינוּ], אֱלֹהֵי אַבְרָהָם,
אֱלֹהֵי יִצְחָק, וֵאלֹהֵי יַעֲקֹב,
אֱלֹהֵי שָׂרָה, אֱלֹהֵי רִבְקָה,
אֱלֹהֵי רָחֵל, וֵאלֹהֵי לֵאָה,
הָאֵל הַגָּדוֹל הַגִּבּוֹר וְהַנּוֹרָא,
אֵל עֶלְיוֹן, גּוֹמֵל חֲסָדִים
טוֹבִים, וְקוֹנֵה הַכֹּל, וְזוֹכֵר
חַסְדֵי אָבוֹת [וְאִמָּהוֹת],
וּמֵבִיא גוֹאֵל לִבְנֵי בְנֵיהֶם
לְמַעַן שְׁמוֹ בְּאַהֲבָה.

After Rosh Hashanah add:

זָכְרֵנוּ לְחַיִּים, מֶלֶךְ חָפֵץ בַּחַיִּים, וְכָתְבֵנוּ
בְּסֵפֶר הַחַיִּים, לְמַעַנְךָ אֱלֹהִים חַיִּים.

THE SILENT AMIDAH

Before the Amidah begins, it is customary to take three steps backward, as if we are leaving our familiar surroundings, and then three steps forward, as we approach God's presence.

ADONAI, open my lips that my mouth may speak Your praise.

Version with Patriarchs:

ʄ *Barukh atah* ADONAI,
our God and God of our
  ancestors,
God of Abraham, God of
  Isaac, God of Jacob,
great, mighty, awe-inspiring,
  transcendent God,
who acts with lovingkindness
and creates all things,
who remembers the loving
  deeds of our ancestors,
and who will send a redeemer
  to their children's children
  with love
for the sake of divine honor.

Version with Patriarchs and Matriarchs:

ʄ *Barukh atah* ADONAI,
our God and God of our
  ancestors,
God of Abraham, God of
  Isaac, God of Jacob,
God of Sarah, God of
  Rebecca, God of Rachel,
  and God of Leah,
great, mighty, awe-inspiring,
  transcendent God,
who acts with lovingkindness
and creates all things,
who remembers the loving
  deeds of our ancestors,
and who will send a redeemer
  to their children's children
  with love
for the sake of divine honor.

After Rosh Hashanah add:

Remember us for life,
Sovereign who delights in life,
and inscribe us in the Book of Life,
for Your sake, God of life.

מֶלֶךְ עוֹזֵר וּמוֹשִׁיעַ וּמָגֵן.
בָּרוּךְ אַתָּה יהוה, מָגֵן
אַבְרָהָם.

מֶלֶךְ עוֹזֵר וּפוֹקֵד
וּמוֹשִׁיעַ וּמָגֵן.
בָּרוּךְ אַתָּה יהוה, מָגֵן
אַבְרָהָם וּפוֹקֵד שָׂרָה.

אַתָּה גִבּוֹר לְעוֹלָם אֲדֹנָי, מְחַיֵּה מֵתִים אַתָּה,
רַב לְהוֹשִׁיעַ.

מְכַלְכֵּל חַיִּים בְּחֶסֶד, מְחַיֵּה מֵתִים בְּרַחֲמִים רַבִּים,
סוֹמֵךְ נוֹפְלִים, וְרוֹפֵא חוֹלִים, וּמַתִּיר אֲסוּרִים, וּמְקַיֵּם
אֱמוּנָתוֹ לִישֵׁנֵי עָפָר. מִי כָמוֹךָ בַּעַל גְּבוּרוֹת וּמִי דּוֹמֶה
לָּךְ, מֶלֶךְ מֵמִית וּמְחַיֶּה וּמַצְמִיחַ יְשׁוּעָה.

After Rosh Hashanah add:

מִי כָמוֹךָ אַב הָרַחֲמִים, זוֹכֵר יְצוּרָיו לְחַיִּים בְּרַחֲמִים.

וְנֶאֱמָן אַתָּה לְהַחֲיוֹת מֵתִים. בָּרוּךְ אַתָּה יהוה,
מְחַיֵּה הַמֵּתִים.

אַתָּה קָדוֹשׁ וְשִׁמְךָ קָדוֹשׁ, וּקְדוֹשִׁים בְּכָל־יוֹם
יְהַלְלוּךָ, סֶּלָה.

After Rosh Hashanah add:

בָּרוּךְ אַתָּה יהוה, הַמֶּלֶךְ הַקָּדוֹשׁ.

After Yom Kippur add:

בָּרוּךְ אַתָּה יהוה, הָאֵל הַקָּדוֹשׁ.

You are the sovereign
who helps and saves and
shields.

ſ *Barukh atah ADONAI,*
Shield of Abraham.

You are the sovereign who
helps and guards, saves and
shields.

ſ *Barukh atah ADONAI,*
Shield of Abraham and
Guardian of Sarah.

You are mighty forever, ADONAI—
You give life to the dead;
great is Your saving power.

You sustain the living through love,
    and with great mercy give life to the dead.
You support the falling,
    heal the sick,
    loosen the chains of the bound,
    and keep faith with those who sleep in the dust.
Who is like You, Almighty,
    and who can be compared to You?—
Sovereign, who brings death and life,
    and causes salvation to flourish.

After Rosh Hashanah add:
Who is like You, source of compassion,
    who remembers with compassion Your creatures for life?

You are faithful in bringing life to the dead.
Barukh atah ADONAI, who gives life to the dead.

Holy are You and holy is Your name;
    holy ones praise You each day.

After Rosh Hashanah add:
Barukh atah ADONAI, the Holy Sovereign.

After Yom Kippur add:
Barukh atah ADONAI, Holy God.

אַתָּה חוֹנֵן לְאָדָם דַּעַת, וּמְלַמֵּד לֶאֱנוֹשׁ בִּינָה. אַתָּה חוֹנַנְתָּנוּ לְמַדַּע תּוֹרָתֶךָ, וַתְּלַמְּדֵנוּ לַעֲשׂוֹת חֻקֵּי רְצוֹנֶךָ, וַתַּבְדֵּל יהוה אֱלֹהֵינוּ בֵּין קֹדֶשׁ לְחוֹל, בֵּין אוֹר לְחשֶׁךְ, בֵּין יִשְׂרָאֵל לָעַמִּים, בֵּין יוֹם הַשְּׁבִיעִי לְשֵׁשֶׁת יְמֵי הַמַּעֲשֶׂה. אָבִינוּ מַלְכֵּנוּ, הָחֵל עָלֵינוּ הַיָּמִים הַבָּאִים לִקְרָאתֵנוּ לְשָׁלוֹם, חֲשׂוּכִים מִכָּל־חֵטְא, וּמְנֻקִּים מִכָּל־עָוֹן, וּמְדֻבָּקִים בְּיִרְאָתֶךָ. וְחָנֵּנוּ מֵאִתְּךָ דֵּעָה בִּינָה וְהַשְׂכֵּל. בָּרוּךְ אַתָּה יהוה, חוֹנֵן הַדָּעַת.

הֲשִׁיבֵנוּ אָבִינוּ לְתוֹרָתֶךָ, וְקָרְבֵנוּ מַלְכֵּנוּ לַעֲבוֹדָתֶךָ, וְהַחֲזִירֵנוּ בִּתְשׁוּבָה שְׁלֵמָה לְפָנֶיךָ. בָּרוּךְ אַתָּה יהוה, הָרוֹצֶה בִּתְשׁוּבָה.

סְלַח לָנוּ אָבִינוּ כִּי חָטָאנוּ, מְחַל לָנוּ מַלְכֵּנוּ כִּי פָשָׁעְנוּ, כִּי מוֹחֵל וְסוֹלֵחַ אָתָּה. בָּרוּךְ אַתָּה יהוה, חַנּוּן הַמַּרְבֶּה לִסְלֹחַ.

רְאֵה נָא בְעָנְיֵנוּ, וְרִיבָה רִיבֵנוּ, וּגְאָלֵנוּ מְהֵרָה לְמַעַן שְׁמֶךָ, כִּי גוֹאֵל חָזָק אָתָּה. בָּרוּךְ אַתָּה יהוה, גּוֹאֵל יִשְׂרָאֵל.

רְפָאֵנוּ יהוה וְנֵרָפֵא, הוֹשִׁיעֵנוּ וְנִוָּשֵׁעָה, כִּי תְהִלָּתֵנוּ אָתָּה, וְהַעֲלֵה רְפוּאָה שְׁלֵמָה לְכָל־מַכּוֹתֵינוּ,

On behalf of one who is ill:

וִיהִי רָצוֹן מִלְּפָנֶיךָ יהוה אֱלֹהֵינוּ וֵאלֹהֵי אֲבוֹתֵינוּ וְאִמּוֹתֵינוּ, שֶׁתִּשְׁלַח מְהֵרָה רְפוּאָה שְׁלֵמָה מִן הַשָּׁמַיִם, רְפוּאַת הַנֶּפֶשׁ וּרְפוּאַת הַגּוּף, לְ _____ בֶּן / בַּת _____ בְּתוֹךְ שְׁאָר חוֹלֵי יִשְׂרָאֵל, וְחַזֵּק אֶת־יְדֵי הָעוֹסְקִים בְּצָרְכֵיהֶם, כִּי אֵל מֶלֶךְ רוֹפֵא נֶאֱמָן וְרַחֲמָן אָתָּה. בָּרוּךְ אַתָּה יהוה, רוֹפֵא חוֹלֵי עַמּוֹ יִשְׂרָאֵל.

בָּרֵךְ עָלֵינוּ יהוה אֱלֹהֵינוּ אֶת־הַשָּׁנָה הַזֹּאת וְאֶת־כָּל־מִינֵי תְבוּאָתָהּ לְטוֹבָה, וְתֵן בְּרָכָה עַל פְּנֵי הָאֲדָמָה, וְשַׂבְּעֵנוּ מִטּוּבָהּ, וּבָרֵךְ שְׁנָתֵנוּ כַּשָּׁנִים הַטּוֹבוֹת. בָּרוּךְ אַתָּה יהוה, מְבָרֵךְ הַשָּׁנִים.

You graciously endow human beings with knowledge and teach understanding to humanity. You have graced us with the ability to know Your teaching, and taught us to observe the precepts that accord with Your will. ADONAI, our God, You have distinguished between the holy and the weekday, light and darkness, Israel and the peoples of the world, the seventh day and the six days of creation. *Avinu Malkenu*, bestow peace on the days ahead, free them of all sin, cleanse them of all wrongdoing, and fill them with awe-inspired attachment to You. May You grace us with knowledge, understanding, and wisdom. *Barukh atah* ADONAI, who bestows knowledge.

Return us, *Avinu*, to Your teaching, and bring us closer, *Malkeinu*, to Your service—that we may truly turn and face You. *Barukh atah* ADONAI, who desires our return.

Forgive us, *Avinu*, for we have sinned; pardon us, *Malkeinu*, for we have transgressed—for Your nature is to forgive and pardon. *Barukh atah* ADONAI, gracious and forgiving.

Look upon our suffering and take up our cause; redeem us soon for the sake of Your name—for surely You are a mighty redeemer. *Barukh atah* ADONAI, Redeemer of Israel.

Heal us, ADONAI, so that we may be truly healed; save us that we may be truly saved. You are the one deserving of praise. Bring complete healing to all our suffering.

> *On behalf of one who is ill:*
> Our God and God of our ancestors may it be Your will to send speedy and complete healing of body and soul to _____, along with all the others of Your people Israel who are ill; strengthen as well the hands of those concerned with their care—

for You are God and sovereign, a faithful and compassionate healer. *Barukh atah* ADONAI, Healer of the afflicted among the people Israel.

ADONAI our God, make this a year of blessing for us; may its varied harvest yield prosperity. May the earth be blessed and satisfy us with its abundance. Bless this year that it be like the best of years. *Barukh atah* ADONAI, who bestows blessing upon the years.

תְּקַע בְּשׁוֹפָר גָּדוֹל לְחֵרוּתֵנוּ, וְשָׂא נֵס לְקַבֵּץ גָּלֻיּוֹתֵינוּ, וְקַבְּצֵנוּ יַחַד מֵאַרְבַּע כַּנְפוֹת הָאָרֶץ. בָּרוּךְ אַתָּה יהוה, מְקַבֵּץ נִדְחֵי עַמּוֹ יִשְׂרָאֵל.

הָשִׁיבָה שׁוֹפְטֵינוּ כְּבָרִאשׁוֹנָה וְיוֹעֲצֵינוּ כְּבַתְּחִלָּה, וְהָסֵר מִמֶּנּוּ יָגוֹן וַאֲנָחָה, וּמְלוֹךְ עָלֵינוּ אַתָּה יהוה לְבַדְּךָ בְּחֶסֶד וּבְרַחֲמִים, וְצַדְּקֵנוּ בַּמִּשְׁפָּט.

After Rosh Hashanah:

בָּרוּךְ אַתָּה יהוה, הַמֶּלֶךְ הַמִּשְׁפָּט.

After Yom Kippur:

בָּרוּךְ אַתָּה יהוה, מֶלֶךְ אוֹהֵב צְדָקָה וּמִשְׁפָּט.

וְלַמַּלְשִׁינִים אַל תְּהִי תִקְוָה, וְכָל־הָרִשְׁעָה כְּרֶגַע תֹּאבֵד, וְכָל־אוֹיְבֶיךָ מְהֵרָה יִכָּרֵתוּ, וְהַזֵּדִים מְהֵרָה תְעַקֵּר וּתְשַׁבֵּר וּתְמַגֵּר וְתַכְנִיעַ בִּמְהֵרָה בְיָמֵינוּ. בָּרוּךְ אַתָּה יהוה, שֹׁבֵר אֹיְבִים וּמַכְנִיעַ זֵדִים.

עַל הַצַּדִּיקִים וְעַל הַחֲסִידִים וְעַל זִקְנֵי עַמְּךָ בֵּית יִשְׂרָאֵל, וְעַל פְּלֵיטַת סוֹפְרֵיהֶם, וְעַל גֵּרֵי הַצֶּדֶק וְעָלֵינוּ, יֶהֱמוּ נָא רַחֲמֶיךָ, יהוה אֱלֹהֵינוּ, וְתֵן שָׂכָר טוֹב לְכָל־הַבּוֹטְחִים בְּשִׁמְךָ בֶּאֱמֶת, וְשִׂים חֶלְקֵנוּ עִמָּהֶם, וּלְעוֹלָם לֹא נֵבוֹשׁ כִּי בְךָ בָּטָחְנוּ. בָּרוּךְ אַתָּה יהוה, מִשְׁעָן וּמִבְטָח לַצַּדִּיקִים.

וְלִירוּשָׁלַיִם עִירְךָ בְּרַחֲמִים תָּשׁוּב, וְתִשְׁכּוֹן בְּתוֹכָהּ כַּאֲשֶׁר דִּבַּרְתָּ, וּבְנֵה אוֹתָהּ בְּקָרוֹב בְּיָמֵינוּ בִּנְיַן עוֹלָם, וְכִסֵּא דָוִד מְהֵרָה לְתוֹכָהּ תָּכִין. בָּרוּךְ אַתָּה יהוה, בּוֹנֵה יְרוּשָׁלָיִם.

אֶת־צֶמַח דָּוִד עַבְדְּךָ מְהֵרָה תַצְמִיחַ, וְקַרְנוֹ תָּרוּם בִּישׁוּעָתֶךָ, כִּי לִישׁוּעָתְךָ קִוִּינוּ כָּל־הַיּוֹם. בָּרוּךְ אַתָּה יהוה, מַצְמִיחַ קֶרֶן יְשׁוּעָה.

שְׁמַע קוֹלֵנוּ יהוה אֱלֹהֵינוּ, חוּס וְרַחֵם עָלֵינוּ, וְקַבֵּל בְּרַחֲמִים וּבְרָצוֹן אֶת־תְּפִלָּתֵנוּ, כִּי אֵל שׁוֹמֵעַ תְּפִלּוֹת וְתַחֲנוּנִים אָתָּה, וּמִלְּפָנֶיךָ, מַלְכֵּנוּ, רֵיקָם אַל תְּשִׁיבֵנוּ. כִּי אַתָּה שׁוֹמֵעַ תְּפִלַּת עַמְּךָ יִשְׂרָאֵל בְּרַחֲמִים. בָּרוּךְ אַתָּה יהוה, שׁוֹמֵעַ תְּפִלָּה.

רְצֵה, יהוה אֱלֹהֵינוּ, בְּעַמְּךָ יִשְׂרָאֵל וּבִתְפִלָּתָם, וְהָשֵׁב אֶת־הָעֲבוֹדָה לִדְבִיר בֵּיתֶךָ, [וְאִשֵּׁי יִשְׂרָאֵל] וּתְפִלָּתָם בְּאַהֲבָה תְקַבֵּל בְּרָצוֹן, וּתְהִי לְרָצוֹן תָּמִיד עֲבוֹדַת יִשְׂרָאֵל עַמֶּךָ.

וְתֶחֱזֶינָה עֵינֵינוּ בְּשׁוּבְךָ לְצִיּוֹן בְּרַחֲמִים. בָּרוּךְ אַתָּה יהוה, הַמַּחֲזִיר שְׁכִינָתוֹ לְצִיּוֹן.

Sound the great shofar announcing our freedom, raise the banner signaling the ingathering of our exiles, and bring us together from the four corners of the earth. *Barukh atah* ADONAI, who gathers the dispersed of the people Israel.

Restore our judges as once they ruled, and restore our counselors as of old. Remove sorrow and anguish. May You alone, ADONAI, rule over us with kindness and compassion. May You find our cause righteous.

After Rosh Hashanah:
Barukh atah ADONAI, Sovereign of judgment.

After Yom Kippur:
Barukh atah ADONAI, Sovereign who loves justice and compassion.

May the hopes of those who would defame us be dashed, may wickedness be instantly frustrated; may all Your enemies be quickly cut off. And speedily in our time may You root out, subdue, break, and humble the arrogant.
Barukh atah ADONAI, who defeats enemies and humbles the arrogant.

Arouse Your compassion, ADONAI our God, toward the righteous, the pious, the leaders of the people Israel, the remnant of the wise, the righteous converts, and upon us all. May all those who trust in You be truly rewarded, and may our share be among them so that we never be ashamed —for we trust in You.
Barukh atah ADONAI, promise and support of the righteous.

In Your mercy, return to Your city, Jerusalem. Dwell there as You have promised; rebuild it permanently, speedily, in our day. May You soon establish the throne of David in its midst.
Barukh atah ADONAI, who rebuilds Jerusalem.

Cause the offspring of Your servant David to flourish; may his head be raised high with the coming of Your deliverance—for we await Your salvation each day.
Barukh atah ADONAI, who causes salvation to flourish.

Hear our voice, ADONAI our God, be kind, and have compassion for us. Willingly and lovingly accept our prayer—for You, God, hear prayers and listen to pleas. Do not send us away empty-handed—for in Your kindness You listen to the prayers of Your people Israel.
Barukh atah ADONAI, who listens to prayer.

ADONAI our God, embrace Your people Israel and their prayer. Restore worship to Your sanctuary. May the [fiery offerings and] prayers of the people Israel be lovingly accepted by You, and may our service always be pleasing.

Let our eyes behold Your merciful return to Zion.
Barukh atah ADONAI, who restores Your Divine Presence to Zion.

מוֹדִים אֲנַחְנוּ לָךְ, שָׁאַתָּה הוּא יהוה אֱלֹהֵינוּ וֵאלֹהֵי
אֲבוֹתֵינוּ [וְאִמּוֹתֵינוּ] לְעוֹלָם וָעֶד, צוּר חַיֵּינוּ מָגֵן יִשְׁעֵנוּ
אַתָּה הוּא. לְדוֹר וָדוֹר נוֹדֶה לְךָ וּנְסַפֵּר תְּהִלָּתֶךָ
עַל חַיֵּינוּ הַמְּסוּרִים בְּיָדֶךָ,
וְעַל נִשְׁמוֹתֵינוּ הַפְּקוּדוֹת לָךְ,
וְעַל נִסֶּיךָ שֶׁבְּכָל־יוֹם עִמָּנוּ,
וְעַל נִפְלְאוֹתֶיךָ וְטוֹבוֹתֶיךָ שֶׁבְּכָל־עֵת,
עֶרֶב וָבֹקֶר וְצָהֳרָיִם.
הַטּוֹב, כִּי לֹא כָלוּ רַחֲמֶיךָ,
וְהַמְרַחֵם, כִּי לֹא תַמּוּ חֲסָדֶיךָ,
מֵעוֹלָם קִוִּינוּ לָךְ.

וְעַל כֻּלָּם יִתְבָּרַךְ וְיִתְרוֹמַם שִׁמְךָ מַלְכֵּנוּ תָּמִיד לְעוֹלָם וָעֶד.

After Rosh Hashanah:

וּכְתוֹב לְחַיִּים טוֹבִים כָּל־בְּנֵי בְרִיתֶךָ.

וְכֹל הַחַיִּים יוֹדוּךָ סֶּלָה, וִיהַלְלוּ אֶת־שִׁמְךָ בֶּאֱמֶת, הָאֵל
יְשׁוּעָתֵנוּ וְעֶזְרָתֵנוּ סֶלָה.
בָּרוּךְ אַתָּה יהוה, הַטּוֹב שִׁמְךָ וּלְךָ נָאֶה לְהוֹדוֹת.

שָׁלוֹם רָב עַל יִשְׂרָאֵל עַמְּךָ וְעַל כָּל־יוֹשְׁבֵי תֵבֵל תָּשִׂים
לְעוֹלָם, כִּי אַתָּה הוּא מֶלֶךְ אָדוֹן לְכָל־הַשָּׁלוֹם. וְטוֹב
בְּעֵינֶיךָ לְבָרֵךְ אֶת־עַמְּךָ יִשְׂרָאֵל בְּכָל־עֵת וּבְכָל־שָׁעָה
בִּשְׁלוֹמֶךָ.

After Rosh Hashanah:

בְּסֵפֶר חַיִּים, בְּרָכָה וְשָׁלוֹם וּפַרְנָסָה טוֹבָה, נִזָּכֵר וְנִכָּתֵב
לְפָנֶיךָ, אֲנַחְנוּ וְכָל־עַמְּךָ בֵּית יִשְׂרָאֵל, לְחַיִּים טוֹבִים
וּלְשָׁלוֹם.

After Rosh Hashanah end the b'rakhah with:

בָּרוּךְ אַתָּה יהוה, עֹשֵׂה הַשָּׁלוֹם.

After Yom Kippur end the b'rakhah with:

בָּרוּךְ אַתָּה יהוה, הַמְבָרֵךְ אֶת־עַמּוֹ יִשְׂרָאֵל בַּשָּׁלוֹם.

ꜰ We thank You, You who are our God and the God of our ancestors through all time, protector of our lives, shield of our salvation.
From one generation to the next we thank You
   and sing Your praises:
   for our lives that are in Your hands,
   for our souls that are under Your care,
   for Your miracles that accompany us each day,
   and for Your wonders and Your gifts that are
   with us each moment,
   evening, morning, and noon.
You are the One who is good, whose mercy is never-ending;
   the One who is compassionate,
   whose love is unceasing.
   We have always placed our hope in You.

For all these blessings may Your name be praised and
exalted, our sovereign, always and forever.

After Rosh Hashanah:
And inscribe all the people of Your covenant for a good life.

May all that lives thank You always, and praise Your name
faithfully forever, God of our deliverance and help.
ꜰ *Barukh atah* ADONAI whose name is goodness and to whom
praise is fitting.

Grant abundant and lasting peace to Your people Israel and
all who dwell on earth, for You are the sovereign master of all the
ways of peace. May it please You to bless Your people Israel at all
times with Your peace.

After Rosh Hashanah:
May we and the entire House of Israel be called to mind and
inscribed for life, blessing, sustenance, and peace in the Book
of Life.

After Rosh Hashanah end the b'rakhah with:
Barukh atah ADONAI, who brings peace.

After Yom Kippur end the b'rakhah with:
Barukh atah ADONAI, who blesses the people Israel with peace.

אֱלֹהַי, נְצוֹר לְשׁוֹנִי מֵרָע, וּשְׂפָתַי מִדַּבֵּר מִרְמָה, וְלִמְקַלְלַי נַפְשִׁי תִדֹּם, וְנַפְשִׁי כֶּעָפָר לַכֹּל תִּהְיֶה. פְּתַח לִבִּי בְּתוֹרָתֶךָ, וּבְמִצְוֹתֶיךָ תִּרְדּוֹף נַפְשִׁי. וְכָל־הַחוֹשְׁבִים עָלַי רָעָה, מְהֵרָה הָפֵר עֲצָתָם וְקַלְקֵל מַחֲשַׁבְתָּם. עֲשֵׂה לְמַעַן שְׁמֶךָ, עֲשֵׂה לְמַעַן יְמִינֶךָ, עֲשֵׂה לְמַעַן קְדֻשָּׁתֶךָ, עֲשֵׂה לְמַעַן תּוֹרָתֶךָ. לְמַעַן יֵחָלְצוּן יְדִידֶיךָ, הוֹשִׁיעָה יְמִינְךָ וַעֲנֵנִי. יִהְיוּ לְרָצוֹן אִמְרֵי פִי וְהֶגְיוֹן לִבִּי לְפָנֶיךָ, יהוה צוּרִי וְגוֹאֲלִי. עֹשֶׂה שָׁלוֹם בִּמְרוֹמָיו, הוּא יַעֲשֶׂה שָׁלוֹם עָלֵינוּ, וְעַל כָּל־יִשְׂרָאֵל [וְעַל כָּל־יוֹשְׁבֵי תֵבֵל] וְאִמְרוּ: אָמֵן.

קַדִּישׁ שָׁלֵם

יִתְגַּדַּל וְיִתְקַדַּשׁ שְׁמֵהּ רַבָּא, בְּעָלְמָא דִּי בְרָא, כִּרְעוּתֵהּ, וְיַמְלִיךְ מַלְכוּתֵהּ בְּחַיֵּיכוֹן וּבְיוֹמֵיכוֹן וּבְחַיֵּי דְכָל־בֵּית יִשְׂרָאֵל, בַּעֲגָלָא וּבִזְמַן קָרִיב, וְאִמְרוּ אָמֵן.

יְהֵא שְׁמֵהּ רַבָּא מְבָרַךְ לְעָלַם וּלְעָלְמֵי עָלְמַיָּא.

יִתְבָּרַךְ וְיִשְׁתַּבַּח וְיִתְפָּאַר וְיִתְרוֹמַם וְיִתְנַשֵּׂא וְיִתְהַדָּר וְיִתְעַלֶּה וְיִתְהַלָּל שְׁמֵהּ דְּקֻדְשָׁא, בְּרִיךְ הוּא,

After Rosh Hashanah:

לְעֵלָּא לְעֵלָּא מִכָּל־בִּרְכָתָא

After Yom Kippur:

לְעֵלָּא מִן כָּל־בִּרְכָתָא

וְשִׁירָתָא תֻּשְׁבְּחָתָא וְנֶחָמָתָא דַּאֲמִירָן בְּעָלְמָא, וְאִמְרוּ אָמֵן. תִּתְקַבֵּל צְלוֹתְהוֹן וּבָעוּתְהוֹן דְּכָל־יִשְׂרָאֵל קֳדָם אֲבוּהוֹן דִּי בִשְׁמַיָּא, וְאִמְרוּ אָמֵן.

יְהֵא שְׁלָמָא רַבָּא מִן שְׁמַיָּא וְחַיִּים עָלֵינוּ וְעַל כָּל־יִשְׂרָאֵל, וְאִמְרוּ אָמֵן.

עֹשֶׂה שָׁלוֹם בִּמְרוֹמָיו הוּא יַעֲשֶׂה שָׁלוֹם עָלֵינוּ וְעַל כָּל־יִשְׂרָאֵל [וְעַל כָּל־יוֹשְׁבֵי תֵבֵל], וְאִמְרוּ אָמֵן.

My God, keep my tongue from evil, my lips from lies. Help me ignore those who would slander me. Let me be humble before all. Open my heart to Your Torah, that I may pursue Your mitzvot. Frustrate the designs of those who plot evil against me; make nothing of their schemes. Act for the sake of Your power, Your holiness, and Your Torah. Answer my prayer for the deliverance of Your people. May the words of my mouth and the meditations of my heart be acceptable to You, ADONAI, my rock and my redeemer. May the One who brings peace to the universe bring peace to us and to all the people Israel [and to all who dwell on earth]. Amen.

Kaddish Shalem

May God's great name be exalted and hallowed throughout the created world, as is God's wish. May God's sovereignty soon be established, in your lifetime and in your days, and in the days of all the House of Israel. And respond with: *Amen.*

May God's great name be acknowledged forever and ever!
Y'hei sh'meih rabba m'varakh l'alam u-l'almei almayya.

May the name of the Holy One be acknowledged and celebrated, lauded and worshipped, exalted and honored, extolled and acclaimed—though God, who is blessed, *b'rikh hu,* is truly [*after Rosh Hashanah add:* far] beyond all acknowledgment and praise, or any expressions of gratitude or consolation ever spoken in the world. And respond with: *Amen.*

May the prayers and pleas of all Israel be accepted by their creator in heaven. And respond with: *Amen.*

May abundant peace from heaven, and life, come to us and to all Israel. And respond with: *Amen.*

May the One who brings harmony on high, bring harmony to us and to all Israel [and to all who dwell on earth]. And respond with: *Amen.*

Oseh shalom bi-m'romav hu ya·aseh shalom aleinu v'al kol yisra·el [v'al kol yosh'vei teiveil], v'imru amen.

סיום התפילה

עָלֵינוּ לְשַׁבֵּחַ לַאֲדוֹן הַכֹּל,
לָתֵת גְּדֻלָּה לְיוֹצֵר בְּרֵאשִׁית,
שֶׁלֹּא עָשָׂנוּ כְּגוֹיֵי הָאֲרָצוֹת,
וְלֹא שָׂמָנוּ כְּמִשְׁפְּחוֹת הָאֲדָמָה,
שֶׁלֹּא שָׂם חֶלְקֵנוּ כָּהֶם,
וְגֹרָלֵנוּ כְּכָל־הֲמוֹנָם.
וַאֲנַחְנוּ כּוֹרְעִים וּמִשְׁתַּחֲוִים וּמוֹדִים,
לִפְנֵי מֶלֶךְ, מַלְכֵי הַמְּלָכִים, הַקָּדוֹשׁ בָּרוּךְ הוּא.
שֶׁהוּא נוֹטֶה שָׁמַיִם וְיוֹסֵד אָרֶץ, וּמוֹשַׁב יְקָרוֹ בַּשָּׁמַיִם מִמַּעַל,
וּשְׁכִינַת עֻזּוֹ בְּגָבְהֵי מְרוֹמִים, הוּא אֱלֹהֵינוּ אֵין
עוֹד. אֱמֶת מַלְכֵּנוּ אֶפֶס זוּלָתוֹ, כַּכָּתוּב בְּתוֹרָתוֹ:
וְיָדַעְתָּ הַיּוֹם וַהֲשֵׁבֹתָ אֶל־לְבָבֶךָ, כִּי יהוה הוּא
הָאֱלֹהִים בַּשָּׁמַיִם מִמַּעַל, וְעַל הָאָרֶץ מִתָּחַת, אֵין עוֹד.

עַל כֵּן נְקַוֶּה לְךָ יהוה אֱלֹהֵינוּ, לִרְאוֹת מְהֵרָה בְּתִפְאֶרֶת עֻזֶּךָ,
לְהַעֲבִיר גִּלּוּלִים מִן הָאָרֶץ וְהָאֱלִילִים כָּרוֹת יִכָּרֵתוּן, לְתַקֵּן עוֹלָם
בְּמַלְכוּת שַׁדַּי, וְכָל־בְּנֵי בָשָׂר יִקְרְאוּ בִשְׁמֶךָ, לְהַפְנוֹת אֵלֶיךָ כָּל־
רִשְׁעֵי אָרֶץ. יַכִּירוּ וְיֵדְעוּ כָּל־יוֹשְׁבֵי תֵבֵל, כִּי לְךָ תִּכְרַע כָּל־בֶּרֶךְ,
תִּשָּׁבַע כָּל־לָשׁוֹן. לְפָנֶיךָ יהוה אֱלֹהֵינוּ יִכְרְעוּ וְיִפֹּלוּ, וְלִכְבוֹד שִׁמְךָ
יְקָר יִתֵּנוּ. וִיקַבְּלוּ כֻלָּם אֶת־עוֹל מַלְכוּתֶךָ. וְתִמְלֹךְ עֲלֵיהֶם מְהֵרָה
לְעוֹלָם וָעֶד. כִּי הַמַּלְכוּת שֶׁלְּךָ הִיא, וּלְעוֹלְמֵי עַד תִּמְלֹךְ בְּכָבוֹד.
כַּכָּתוּב בְּתוֹרָתֶךָ: יהוה יִמְלֹךְ לְעוֹלָם וָעֶד.
וְנֶאֱמַר: וְהָיָה יהוה לְמֶלֶךְ עַל כָּל־הָאָרֶץ,
בַּיּוֹם הַהוּא יִהְיֶה יהוה אֶחָד, וּשְׁמוֹ אֶחָד.

CONCLUDING PRAYERS

Aleinu

It is for us to praise the ruler of all, to acclaim the Creator, who has not made us merely a nation, nor formed us as all earthly families, nor given us an ordinary destiny.

ſ And so we bow, acknowledging the supreme sovereign, the Holy One, who is praised—the One who spreads out the heavens and establishes the earth, whose glorious abode is in the highest heaven, whose powerful presence is in the loftiest heights. This is our God, none else; ours is the true sovereign, there is no other. As it is written in the Torah: "Know this day and take it to heart, that ADONAI is God in heaven above and on earth below, there is no other."

Aleinu l'shabbe·aḥ la-adon ha-kol, la-tet g'dullah l'yotzer b'reishit, she-lo asanu k'goyei ha-aratzot v'lo samanu k'mishp'hot ha-adamah, she-lo sam ḥelkeinu ka-hem, v'goraleinu k'khol hamonam.

ſ *Va-anaḥnu kor'im u-mishtaḥavim u-modim lifnei melekh malkhei ha-m'lakhim ha-kadosh barukh hu.*

She-hu noteh shamayim v'yosed aretz, u-moshav y'karo ba-shamayim mi-ma·al, u-sh'khinat uzzo b'govhei m'romim, hu eloheinu ein od. Emet malkeinu efes zulato, ka-katuv b'torato: v'yadata ha-yom va-hashevota el l'va-vekha, ki Adonai hu ha-Elohim ba-shamayim mi-ma·al, v'al ha-aretz mi-taḥat ein od.

And so ADONAI our God, we await You, that soon we may behold Your strength revealed in full glory, sweeping away the abominations of the earth, obliterating idols, establishing in the world the sovereignty of the Almighty. All flesh will call out Your name—even the wicked will turn toward You. Then all who live on earth will recognize and understand that to You alone knees must bend allegiance be sworn. All will bow down and prostrate themselves before You, ADONAI our God, honor Your glorious name, and accept the obligation of Your sovereignty. May You soon rule over them forever and ever, for true dominion is Yours; You will rule in glory until the end of time.

As is written in Your Torah: "ADONAI will reign forever and ever." And as the prophet said: "ADONAI shall be acknowledged Ruler of all the earth. On that day ADONAI shall be one, and the name of God, one."

V'ne·emar v'hayah Adonai l'melekh al kol ha-aretz,
ba-yom ha-hu yihyeh Adonai eḥad u-sh'mo eḥad.

Some congregations recite Mourner's Kaddish after Aleinu;
some, after the recitation of Psalm 27 (next page).

קַדִּישׁ יָתוֹם

Mourners and those observing Yahrzeit:

יִתְגַּדַּל וְיִתְקַדַּשׁ שְׁמֵהּ רַבָּא,
בְּעָלְמָא דִּי בְרָא, כִרְעוּתֵהּ,
וְיַמְלִיךְ מַלְכוּתֵהּ בְּחַיֵּיכוֹן וּבְיוֹמֵיכוֹן
וּבְחַיֵּי דְכָל־בֵּית יִשְׂרָאֵל,
בַּעֲגָלָא וּבִזְמַן קָרִיב,
וְאִמְרוּ אָמֵן.

Congregation and mourners:

יְהֵא שְׁמֵהּ רַבָּא מְבָרַךְ לְעָלַם וּלְעָלְמֵי עָלְמַיָּא.

Mourners:

יִתְבָּרַךְ וְיִשְׁתַּבַּח
וְיִתְפָּאַר וְיִתְרוֹמַם
וְיִתְנַשֵּׂא וְיִתְהַדָּר
וְיִתְעַלֶּה וְיִתְהַלָּל
שְׁמֵהּ דְּקֻדְשָׁא, בְּרִיךְ הוּא,

After Rosh Hashanah:

לְעֵלָּא לְעֵלָּא מִכָּל־בִּרְכָתָא

After Yom Kippur:

לְעֵלָּא מִן כָּל־בִּרְכָתָא
וְשִׁירָתָא תֻּשְׁבְּחָתָא וְנֶחֱמָתָא
דַּאֲמִירָן בְּעָלְמָא,
וְאִמְרוּ אָמֵן.

יְהֵא שְׁלָמָא רַבָּא מִן שְׁמַיָּא וְחַיִּים
עָלֵינוּ וְעַל כָּל־יִשְׂרָאֵל,
וְאִמְרוּ אָמֵן.

עֹשֶׂה שָׁלוֹם בִּמְרוֹמָיו
הוּא יַעֲשֶׂה שָׁלוֹם
עָלֵינוּ וְעַל כָּל־יִשְׂרָאֵל
[וְעַל כָּל־יוֹשְׁבֵי תֵבֵל],
וְאִמְרוּ אָמֵן.

Some congregations recite Mourner's Kaddish after Aleinu;
some, after the recitation of Psalm 27 (next page).

Mourner's Kaddish

May God's great name be exalted and hallowed throughout the created world, as is God's wish. May God's sovereignty soon be established, in your lifetime and in your days, and in the days of all the House of Israel. And respond with: *Amen.*

May God's great name be acknowledged forever and ever!

May the name of the Holy One be acknowledged and celebrated, lauded and worshipped, exalted and honored, extolled and acclaimed—though God, who is blessed, *b'rikh hu*, is truly [*after Rosh Hashanah add:* far] beyond all acknowledgment and praise, or any expressions of gratitude or consolation ever spoken in the world. And respond with: *Amen.*

May abundant peace from heaven, and life, come to us and to all Israel. And respond with: *Amen.*

May the One who brings harmony on high, bring harmony to us and to all Israel [and to all who dwell on earth]. And respond with: *Amen.*

Mourners and those observing Yahrzeit:
Yitgaddal v'yitkaddash sh'meih rabba, b'alma di v'ra, ki-r'uteih, v'yamlikh malkhuteih b'hayyeikhon u-v'yomeikhon u-v'hayyei d'khol beit yisra·el, ba-agala u-viz'man kariv, v'imru amen.

Congregation and mourners:
Y'hei sh'meih rabba m'varakh l'alam u-l'almei almayya.

Mourners:
Yitbarakh v'yishtabbah v'yitpa·ar v'yitromam v'yitnassei v'yit·haddar v'yit·alleh v'yit·hallal sh'meih d'kudsha, b'rikh hu, l'eilla l'eilla mi-kol birkhata v'shirata tushb'hata v'nehamata da-amiran b'alma, v'imru amen.

Y'hei sh'lama rabba min sh'mayya v'hayyim aleinu v'al kol yisra·el, v'imru amen.

Oseh shalom bi-m'romav hu ya·aseh shalom aleinu v'al kol yisra·el [v'al kol yosh'vei teiveil], v'imru amen.

לְדָוִד.

יהוה אוֹרִי וְיִשְׁעִי מִמִּי אִירָא,

יהוה מָעוֹז־חַיַּי מִמִּי אֶפְחָד.

בִּקְרֹב עָלַי מְרֵעִים לֶאֱכֹל אֶת־בְּשָׂרִי,

צָרַי וְאֹיְבַי לִי הֵמָּה כָשְׁלוּ וְנָפָלוּ.

אִם־תַּחֲנֶה עָלַי מַחֲנֶה לֹא־יִירָא לִבִּי,

אִם־תָּקוּם עָלַי מִלְחָמָה בְּזֹאת אֲנִי בוֹטֵחַ.

אַחַת שָׁאַלְתִּי מֵאֵת־יהוה, אוֹתָהּ אֲבַקֵּשׁ,

שִׁבְתִּי בְּבֵית־יהוה, כָּל־יְמֵי חַיַּי

לַחֲזוֹת בְּנֹעַם־יהוה וּלְבַקֵּר בְּהֵיכָלוֹ.

כִּי יִצְפְּנֵנִי בְּסֻכֹּה בְּיוֹם רָעָה,

יַסְתִּרֵנִי בְּסֵתֶר אָהֳלוֹ, בְּצוּר יְרוֹמְמֵנִי.

וְעַתָּה יָרוּם רֹאשִׁי עַל אֹיְבַי סְבִיבוֹתַי

וְאֶזְבְּחָה בְּאָהֳלוֹ זִבְחֵי תְרוּעָה,

אָשִׁירָה וַאֲזַמְּרָה לַיהוה.

שְׁמַע־יהוה קוֹלִי אֶקְרָא, וְחָנֵּנִי וַעֲנֵנִי.

לְךָ אָמַר לִבִּי בַּקְּשׁוּ פָנָי, אֶת־פָּנֶיךָ יהוה אֲבַקֵּשׁ.

אַל־תַּסְתֵּר פָּנֶיךָ מִמֶּנִּי,

אַל תַּט־בְּאַף עַבְדֶּךָ, עֶזְרָתִי הָיִיתָ,

אַל־תִּטְּשֵׁנִי וְאַל־תַּעַזְבֵנִי אֱלֹהֵי יִשְׁעִי.

כִּי־אָבִי וְאִמִּי עֲזָבוּנִי, וַיהוה יַאַסְפֵנִי.

הוֹרֵנִי יהוה דַּרְכֶּךָ, וּנְחֵנִי בְּאֹרַח מִישׁוֹר, לְמַעַן שׁוֹרְרָי.

אַל־תִּתְּנֵנִי בְּנֶפֶשׁ צָרָי,

כִּי קָמוּ־בִי עֵדֵי־שֶׁקֶר וִיפֵחַ חָמָס.

◁ לוּלֵא הֶאֱמַנְתִּי, לִרְאוֹת בְּטוּב־יהוה בְּאֶרֶץ חַיִּים.

קַוֵּה אֶל־יהוה, חֲזַק וְיַאֲמֵץ לִבֶּךָ וְקַוֵּה אֶל־יהוה. תהלים כז

Some congregations recite Mourner's Kaddish after the recitation of this psalm;
see previous page.

A Psalm for the Season of Repentance—Psalm 27

A PSALM OF DAVID.

ADONAI is my light and my help. Whom shall I fear?
ADONAI is the stronghold of my life. Whom shall I dread?
When evil people assail me to devour my flesh
it is they, my enemies and those who besiege me,
who stumble and fall.
Should an armed camp be arrayed against me,
my heart would show no fear;
should they war against me, of this I would be sure.

One thing I ask of ADONAI—this I seek:
to dwell in the House of God all the days of my life,
to behold God's beauty and visit in God's sanctuary.

Aḥat sha·alti mei·eit Adonai, otah avakkeish
shivti b'veit Adonai, kol y'mei ḥayyai
la-ḥazot b'no·am Adonai u-l'vakkeir b'heikhalo.

Were God to hide me in God's *sukkah* on the calamitous day,
were God to enfold me in the secret recesses of God's tent,
I would be raised up in a protecting fort.
Now, I raise my head above the enemies that surround me,
and come with offerings, amidst trumpet blasts, to God's tent,
chanting and singing praise to ADONAI.
ADONAI, hear my voice as I cry out;
be gracious to me, and answer me.
It is You of whom my heart said, "Seek my face!"
It is Your presence that I seek, ADONAI.
Do not hide Your face from me; do not act angrily toward me.
You have always been my help; do not forsake me;
do not abandon me, my God, my deliverer.
Though my father and mother abandon me,
ADONAI will gather me in.
Show me Your way, ADONAI, and lead me on a straight path
despite those arrayed against me.
Do not hand me over to the grasp of those who besiege me;
for false witnesses and those who seek ill have risen against me.

If only I could trust that I would see God's goodness
in the land of the living . . .
Place your hope in ADONAI.
Be strong, take courage, and place your hope in ADONAI.

Some congregations recite Mourner's Kaddish after the recitation of this psalm;
see previous page.

The first three paragraphs are omitted in the synagogue.

הִנֵּה אֵל יְשׁוּעָתִי, אֶבְטַח וְלֹא אֶפְחָד. כִּי עָזִּי וְזִמְרָת יָהּ יהוה, וַיְהִי לִי לִישׁוּעָה. וּשְׁאַבְתֶּם מַיִם בְּשָׂשׂוֹן מִמַּעַיְנֵי הַיְשׁוּעָה. לַיהוה הַיְשׁוּעָה עַל עַמְּךָ בִרְכָתֶךָ סֶּלָה. יהוה צְבָאוֹת עִמָּנוּ, מִשְׂגָּב לָנוּ אֱלֹהֵי יַעֲקֹב, סֶלָה. יהוה צְבָאוֹת, אַשְׁרֵי אָדָם בֹּטֵחַ בָּךְ. יהוה הוֹשִׁיעָה, הַמֶּלֶךְ יַעֲנֵנוּ בְיוֹם קָרְאֵנוּ.

לַיְהוּדִים הָיְתָה אוֹרָה וְשִׂמְחָה וְשָׂשׂוֹן וִיקָר. כֵּן תִּהְיֶה לָּנוּ.

כּוֹס יְשׁוּעוֹת אֶשָּׂא וּבְשֵׁם יהוה אֶקְרָא.

When Havdalah is recited in the synagogue, we begin here:

בָּרוּךְ אַתָּה יהוה, אֱלֹהֵינוּ מֶלֶךְ הָעוֹלָם, בּוֹרֵא פְּרִי הַגָּפֶן.

On Saturday night, we add this b'rakhah over spices.

בָּרוּךְ אַתָּה יהוה, אֱלֹהֵינוּ מֶלֶךְ הָעוֹלָם, בּוֹרֵא מִינֵי בְשָׂמִים.

After Yom Kippur:

בָּרוּךְ אַתָּה יהוה, אֱלֹהֵינוּ מֶלֶךְ הָעוֹלָם, בּוֹרֵא מְאוֹרֵי הָאֵשׁ.

בָּרוּךְ אַתָּה יהוה אֱלֹהֵינוּ מֶלֶךְ הָעוֹלָם, הַמַּבְדִּיל בֵּין קֹדֶשׁ לְחוֹל, בֵּין אוֹר לְחֹשֶׁךְ, בֵּין יִשְׂרָאֵל לָעַמִּים, בֵּין יוֹם הַשְּׁבִיעִי לְשֵׁשֶׁת יְמֵי הַמַּעֲשֶׂה. בָּרוּךְ אַתָּה יהוה, הַמַּבְדִּיל בֵּין קֹדֶשׁ לְחוֹל.

HAVDALAH. Just as a *b'rakhah* over wine begins each Shabbat and holy day—except Yom Kippur for obvious reasons—so too a *b'rakhah* over wine concludes them. Additionally, since the use of fire is not permitted on Shabbat and on Yom Kippur, on these occasions, the concluding ritual includes that which is now permissible. Shabbat has brought its own sweetness and, with its departure, something else is needed to arouse our senses and draw us into the world and so on the conclusion of Shabbat, the havdalah ceremony includes the smelling of the fragrance of spices or flowers. And so the weekday begins with a *b'rakhah*.

HAVDALAH AT HOME. When reciting Kiddush or Havdalah at home, biblical verses precede the blessing over wine. On Shabbat and Festivals, Kiddush is introduced with the Torah verses mandating the observance of the day; Havdalah is introduced with a series of verses on the theme of redemption: Isaiah 12:2–3; Psalm 3:9, 46:12 84:13, 20:10; Esther 8:16 (to which the wish expressed by the words "Grant us [what was]… brought to our ancestors" is added); and Psalm 116:13. These verses were probably not incorporated in the synagogue service so as not to delay the congregation from being able to go home and enjoy their dinner.

HAVDALAH

The first three paragraphs are omitted in the synagogue.

God is indeed my deliverance; I am confident and unafraid. ADONAI is my strength, my might, my deliverance. With joy shall you draw water from the wells of deliverance. Deliverance is ADONAI's; may You bless Your people. *Adonai Tz'va·ot* is with us; the God of Jacob is our Refuge. *Adonai Tz'va·ot*, blessed is the one who trusts in You. Help us, ADONAI; answer us, O Sovereign, when we call.

Grant us the blessings of light, gladness, joy, and honor that the miracle of deliverance brought to our ancestors.
La-y'hudim hay'tah orah v'simḥah v'sason vikar; ken tihyeh lanu.

As I lift up the cup of deliverance, I call upon ADONAI.

When Havdalah is recited in the synagogue, we begin here:
Barukh atah ADONAI, our God, ruler of time and space, who creates fruit of the vine.
Barukh atah Adonai eloheinu melekh ha-olam, borei p'ri ha-gafen.

On Saturday night, we add this b'rakhah over spices.
Barukh atah ADONAI, our God, ruler of time and space, who creates fragrant spices.
Barukh atah Adonai eloheinu melekh ha-olam, borei minei v'samim.

After Yom Kippur:
Barukh atah ADONAI, our God, ruler of time and space, who creates lights of fire.
Barukh atah Adonai eloheinu melekh ha-olam, borei m'orei ha-esh.

Barukh atah ADONAI, our God, ruler of time and space, who has distinguished between the sacred and the everyday, light and darkness, Israel and the peoples of the world, and the seventh day from the other days of creation. *Barukh atah* ADONAI, who distinguishes between the sacred and the ordinary.
Barukh atah Adonai eloheinu melekh ha-olam, ha-madvil bein kodesh l'ḥol,
bein or l'ḥoshekh,
bein yisra·el la'ammim,
bein yom ha-sh'vi·i l'sheshet y'mei ha-ma·aseh.
Barukh atah Adonai, ha-mavdil bein kodesh l'ḥol.

God's four-wheeled throne described in the first chapters of Ezekiel.

Midrash (plural: *Midrashim*). The interpretation of biblical verses. Ancient rabbinic biblical midrashim are collected in several books edited between the 3rd and 9th centuries in the Land of Israel.

Mitzvah (plural: *mitzvot*). Sometimes translated as "command." The 613 positive and negative precepts of the Torah. They represent the pathways for holy living.

Minḥah. The daily afternoon service comprising primarily the recitation of the AMIDAH. On the Sabbath and fast days (including Yom Kippur), a Torah reading is included in the service.

Minyan. A congregation is formed when ten people are gathered for a service or a ritual act. Certain prayers, such as the KADDISH, may be recited only when a minyan is present.

Musaf. Additional service following the Torah service on Shabbat and Festivals.

Nisan. The 7th month in the Jewish calendar but the first month in the biblical count.

P'sukei D'zimra. Literally, "Verses of Song." Psalmic and other biblical texts praising God and setting the mood for the formal beginning of the morning prayer service.

Piyyut (plural: *piyyutim*). A liturgical poem.

Rosh Hashanah. The beginning of the new year in the Hebrew calendar, the first day of the month of Tishrei and the beginning of ASERET Y'MEI T'SHUVAH.

Sephardic. Sepharad is the Hebrew name for Spain. After the exile from Spain in 1492 (and from Portugal in 1497), Jews from Iberia spread throughout the Mediterranean, parts of Europe, and as far as India and the New World. The term "Sephardic" is applied to Jews of Iberian descent.

Shekhinah. Literally, "Presence." Rabbinically, it is a term referring to God's presence in the world. Its feminine form gave rise to the mystical expression of God's feminine attributes.

Sh'ma. Literally, "Listen!" It refers to Deuteronomy 6:4–9, which, along with Deuteronomy 11:13–21 and Numbers 15:37–41, is recited in the morning and evening prayer service.

Shabbat. The seventh day of the week, on which God rested and on which Jews are commanded to rest. Yom Kippur is referred to in the Bible as Shabbat Shabbaton, the Sabbath of Sabbaths.

Shaddai. A biblical name of God, thought to express God's multiple powers. The ancient rabbis interpreted it to mean the One who placed a limit on creation.

Shaḥarit. The morning service.

Sh'varim. Literally, "fragments." The set of three broken blasts sounded by the SHOFAR.

Sh'vat. The 5th month of the Jewish calendar. In the Land of Israel, the first growth of spring appear during this month.

Shofar. The ram's horn blown on Rosh Hashanah and at the conclusion of Yom Kippur. It recalls the ram that was substituted for Isaac on the altar.

Sukkah (plural: *Sukkot*). The temporary booth, or hut, built in celebration of the holiday of Sukkot. In biblical times, farmers used booths for rest at harvest time. Sukkot refers to the autumn harvest festival that begins five days after Yom Kippur.

T'fillah. Hebrew for "prayer"; often used to refer to the AMIDAH.

T'ki·ah. Literally "blow," a single unbroken blast. The blowing of the shofar is called T'ki'at Shofar. The final blast of the shofar service is sustained and is called a *t'ki·ah g'dolah* (a long *t'ki·ah*).

T'ru·ah. Literally, "fanfare" or "blast." The nine staccato blasts of the shofar.

T'shuvah. Repentance, literally, "return."

Tallit. Prayer shawl, each corner of which contains TZITZIT, fringes.

Tishrei. The first month of the Jewish calendar (September or October); the month in which the High Holy Days occur.

Tz'dakah. Literally, "righteousness" or "justice," often translated as "charity," referring to money and works donated or volunteered toward good causes.

Tzitzit. The four fringes of the TALLIT commanded to be worn (Numbers 15:37–41). The Bible instructs that they contain a string of blue, *t'khelet*. That practice, lost for almost two millennia, has been revived in some communities in recent years.

Viddui. "Confession." The liturgical list of sins, appearing in the High Holy Day liturgy in both long and short forms, AL HET and ASHAMNU.

Yahrzeit. The anniversary of a death.

Yizkor. Literally, "may God remember." Memorial prayer for the dead, recited by ASHKENAZIC Jews on Yom Kippur and on each of the three pilgrimage festivals.

Yom Kippur. The Day of Atonement. The 10th day of TISHREI, devoted to T'SHUVAH and prayer, and marked by fasting and abstinence. By tradition, it is the day when Moses descended from Mt. Sinai, announcing that God had forgiven the people for the sin of the golden calf.

GLOSSARIES

Glossary of Hebrew Terms and Phrases

Adar. The sixth month of the Jewish calendar (March or April).

Akedah. Literally, the "binding," referring to Abraham's binding of Isaac on the altar as a sacrifice (as told in Genesis 22, the Torah reading for the second day of Rosh Hashanah).

Aliyah (plural: *Aliyot*). Literally, "going up," referring to ascending to the reader's desk for the honor of reciting the blessings before and after the reading (see K'RI·AH) of the Torah.

Amidah. Literally "standing." The central prayer of every service, recited standing in heightened reverence.

Arvit. Also known as MA'ARIV; the evening service recited each day, comprising the Sh'ma and its attendant blessings as well as the Amidah.

Ashkenazic. Originally, the term referred to German Jews but later came to include all the Jews in lands that were influenced by German religious practice: Central and Eastern European Jewry.

Av. The eleventh month of the Jewish calendar (July or August).

Avodah. Literally, "work," "service," or "worship." In the Maḥzor, the term "Avodah" refers to the sacrificial rites of performed by the High Priest, as retold in the MUSAF liturgy on Yom Kippur.

Avodah she-ba-lev. Avodah ("worship") was understood to refer to sacrificial rituals. Rabbinic literature frequently refers to prayer as *Avodah she-ba-lev* ("service of the heart").

B'rakhah (plural: *B'rakhot*). A prayer of gratitude or praise of God, either starting or ending with the *Barukh atah Adonai* formula; popularly called a "blessing."

Bimah. "Stage" or "platform." Located toward the front or placed in the center of a congregation. The Torah is read from the Bimah.

Birkat Kohanim. The Priestly Benediction (Numbers 6:24) recited by the *kohanim* ("priests") of the congregation—or by the service leader.

Birkhot Ha-shaḥar. Literally, "Morning Blessings," originally recited daily on waking up. In most modern Jewish practice, it is recited at the beginning of the morning synagogue service.

D'var Torah. Literally, "a word of Torah"; a lesson based on Torah.

Elul. The final month of the Jewish calendar (August/September). It is a month of preparation for the High Holy Days, which begin on the first day of the next month, TISHREI.

Haftarah. A reading from the Prophets following the reading of the Torah.

Ḥevra Kaddisha. Literally, the "Holy Community," the burial society trained to prepare the deceased for a proper Jewish burial and to assist the bereaved in traditional Jewish mourning rituals.

K'ri·ah. Literally, "reading." The term refers to a liturgical reading of a biblical text. K'ri·at Sh'ma refers to the required daily recitation of the Sh'ma. K'ri·at Ha-Torah refers to the public reading of the Torah.

Kaddish. A prayer in Aramaic praising and sanctifying God, recited in several forms, marking the end of sections of the service.

Kaddish Shalem. "Complete" Kaddish found at the end of a service, including a verse asking that our prayers be accepted.

Ḥatzi Kaddish. A partial Kaddish, dividing sections within a service. It does not contain either the final sentences asking that prayers be accepted or the prayer for peace.

Kaddish D'Rabbanan. An extended Kaddish recited after study, with a paragraph inserted asking for blessings on those who teach and study Torah.

Mourner's Kaddish. Kaddish recited by mourners during the period of mourning and on Yahrzeits.

Kavvanah. Literally, "intention" or "direction." The term can refer either to one's intention while praying or a particular meditation intended to spiritually direct one's consciousness while performing a ritual.

Kedushah. Literally, "holiness." The term refers to the recitation of the passages ascribed to the angels in Isaiah's and Ezekiel's visions of the heavenly court.

Kiddush. A blessing sanctifying the day accompanied by the blessing over wine.

Kohen (plural: *kohanim*). A descendant of Aaron. A priest, who would serve in the ancient Temple.

Ma·ariv. See ARVIT.

Maḥzor. A written compilation of the order of the prayer service usually for a specific occasion or festival.

Merkavah. Literally, "chariot." Merkavah mysticism is an early (first millennium) form of Jewish mysticism focused on imagery derived from the vision of the four-winged, four-faced creatures carrying

Hanover, Nathan Neta (died 1683). Ukrainian rabbi. Chronicler of the Chmielnicki Massacre of 1648 and 1649.

Ḥayim of Tzanz (1793–1876). Ḥayim Halberstam, founder of the Tzanz Ḥasidic dynasty.

Ḥazon Ish (1878–1953). Modern halakhist, known by the name of his most famous work. Born Avraham Isaiah Karelitz in Poland. Emigrated to Israel in 1933.

Ibn Ezra, Moses (ca. 1060–ca. 1138). Spanish poet, philosopher, and grammarian.

Ibn Gabirol, Solomon (ca. 1021–ca. 1058). Andalusian Hebrew poet and grammarian. Respected philosopher in Muslim and Christian circles.

Ibn Pakuda, Baḥya (11th century). Spanish rabbi, philosopher, and author.

Isserles, Moses (died 1572). One of the great halakhic authorities.

Kallir, Elazar (6th century). Resident of Tiberias in the Land of Israel and prolific author of many classical piyyutim. Italian and German rites preserve part of his work.

Katznelson, Yitzhak (1886–1944). Yiddish poet and dramatist, murdered in Auschwitz.

Kook, Abraham Isaac (1865–1935). Modern mystic who served as the first Ashkenazic Chief Rabbi of the Jewish community in the Land of Israel.

Luria, Isaac (1534–1572). Safed mystic. Innovator of the most influential system of Kabbalah in the late Middle Ages.

Maimonides, or **Rambam** (1135–1204). Moses ben Maimon. Born in Spain, died in Egypt. An innovative philosopher and halakhist, author of *The Guide for the Perplexed* and the *Mishneh Torah*. Many consider him the greatest medieval philosopher.

Mecklenburg, Jacob Tzvi (1785–1865). German rabbi. Author of an important siddur commentary, *Siddur Iyyun Tefillah*.

Menaḥem Mendel of Kotzk (1787–1859). A revolutionary Ḥasidic master who emphasized the devoted search for truth and inner purity.

Menaḥem Mendel of Worka (Vorki) (1819–1868). Ḥasidic master, son and successor of Yitzhak of Vorki.

Menaḥem Mendel of Rymanov (1745–1815). An influential leader of Ḥasidism.

Menaḥem Naḥum of Chernobyl (1730-1797). Ḥasidic master, storyteller, and author.

Meshullam ben Kalonymus (10th century). Scholar and poet credited for bringing Talmudic learning from Italy to Germany.

Molodowsky, Kadya (1894–1975). Polish-born Yiddish poet, playwright, fiction writer, and essayist who lived in the United States and Israel.

Naḥman of Bratzlav (1772–1810). Ḥasidic master and the great-grandson of the Baal Shem Tov, the founder of Ḥasidism.

The Nazir. See David HaCohen.

Rabbi of Ger (1798–1866). Isaac Meir Alter, founder of the Ger Ḥasidic dynasty in Poland.

Rabbi of Lublin (1745–1815). Jacob Isaac Horowitz, Polish Ḥasidic Master.

Rashi (1040–1105). Rabbi Solomon ben Isaac. French scholar and commentator on the Bible and Talmud.

Reznikoff, Charles (1894–1976). Jewish American poet.

Rosenzweig, Franz (1886–1929). Noted German-Jewish philosopher and theologian.

Schechter, Solomon (1850–1915). Anglo-German Jewish scholar and a founder of the Conservative movement in America.

Shmelke of Nikolsberg (1726–1778). Rabbi Shmuel Shmelke, early Ḥasidic master.

Simḥah Bunam (1765–1827). Rabbi Simḥah Bunam Bonhart of Przysucha, a Ḥasidic master.

Solomon bar Samson (11th–12th century). European Jew who witnessed and, in Hebrew verse, chronicled the Crusades.

Sternharz, Nathan (1780–1845). NAḤMAN OF BRATZLAV's closest disciple, who transcribed, published, edited and embellished many of his instructor's teachings.

Szalet, Leon (1892–1958). Polish-born memoirist who survived Sachsenhausen concentration camp.

Tussman, Malka Heifetz (1893–1987). Yiddish poet who wrote mainly in the United States.

Zangwill, Israel (1864–1926). English novelist and essayist. One of the first Jewish writers in England to gain prominence.

Ze'ev Wolf of Zhitomir (died 1800). Ḥasidic preacher.

Glossary of Books

Avot of Rabbi Natan. One of the so-called Minor Tractates of the Talmud. A commentary on an early version of the Mishnah tractate Avot, probably compiled in the 3rd century.

Babylonian Talmud. See TALMUD.

Ecclesiastes Rabbah. Midrash on the Book of Ecclesiastes, compiled between the 8th century and the 10th century.

Genesis Rabbah. Midrash on Genesis, edited in the land of Israel probably around the beginning of the 5th century.

Heikhalot Rabbati. A Jewish mystical text from the early first millennium C.E.

Leviticus Rabbah. Midrash on the Book of Leviticus, probably composed in the 5th century in the Land of Israel.

Mekhilta Pisḥa. A section of the 2nd-century midrashic work Mekhilta d'Rabbi Ishmael, dealing with the Passover, Exodus 12:1–13:16.

Mekhilta Shirata. A section of the 2nd-century midrashic work Mekhilta d'Rabbi Ishmael, commenting on the Song of Moses, Exodus 15.

Midrash Hagadol. An anonymous 14th-century collection of midrashim on the Torah.

Mishnah. The collection of rabbinic teachings edited in the Land of Israel about 225 C.E. by Judah the Prince. Organized by subject matter and dealing with both ritual and civil law, it became the basis for all subsequent developments within Jewish law.

Mishneh Torah. Code of Jewish law written by Moses Maimonides in the late 12th century.

Numbers Rabbah. Midrash on Numbers compiled in the late Middle Ages.

Pesikta of Rav Kahana. A collection of sermonic material for Festivals and special Sabbaths, perhaps compiled in the 8th century.

Pesikta Rabbati. Similar in form and content to PESIKTA OF RAV KAHANA but compiled at least a century later.

Pirkei Avot. A tractate of the Mishnah, distinctively formatted as a series of sayings attributed to various rabbis.

Pirkei D'rabbi Eliezer. A 9th-century work of Midrash attributed to Rabbi Eliezer ben Hyrcanus.

Sifra. Early Midrash on Leviticus, probably compiled in the 2nd or 3rd century.

Sifre Deuteronomy. Midrash on Deuteronomy, probably compiled in the 2nd or 3rd century.

Sifre Numbers. Midrash on Numbers, probably compiled in the 2nd or 3rd century.

Sof'rim. Post-talmudic minor tractate related to the laws of Soferut (the occupation of a ritual scribe), including laws relating to prayer. Perhaps written in the 8th century.

Talmud. The central work of rabbinic literature, comprising two parts: the MISHNAH, and the discussions based on it (known in Aramaic as Gemara). Of the Talmud's two versions, the earliest—called variously the Jerusalem Talmud, Talmud Yerushalmi, or Palestinian Talmud—was compiled in the Land of Israel in the 5th century. The later version—the Babylonian Talmud, or Talmud Bavli—is much larger and has been considered more authoritative. It reflects discussions that took place in the Babylonian academies and was compiled in the 6th and 7th centuries.

Tanna D'vei Eliyyahu. A mystical work of Midrash composed by the 10th century.

Yalkut Shimoni. A 13th-century European compilation of midrashim on the entire Bible.

Zohar. The central text of Jewish mysticism, ascribed to Shimon bar Yohai and compiled by a circle of Spanish Kabbalists headed by Moses de Leon in the late 13th century.

Glossary of Historical Figures Whose Work We Quote

Abraham of Slonim (1804–1884). Abraham ben Isaac Weinberg. Founder of the Hasidic dynasty of Slonim.

Abudarham, David (14th century). Author of a siddur commentary published in 1340 in Seville.

Arama, Isaac (ca. 1420–1494). Spanish rabbi and philosopher.

Baeck, Leo (1874–1956). German-born rabbi, scholar, and theologian. Leader of German Reform Jewry. Survivor of Theresienstadt concentration camp.

Benjamin son of Abraham min Ha-anavim (13th century). Jewish Italian writer who composed many *piyyutim*.

Bialik, Hayim Naḥman (1873–1934). Pioneer of modern Hebrew poetry.

Buber, Martin (1878–1975). Religious philosopher and popularizer of Hasidic life.

Danziger, Abraham (1748–1820). Rabbi. Author of *Hayyei Adam*, a popular compendium of Jewish law.

David HaCohen (1887–1972, the Land of Israel). Known as the Nazir, he was a student of ABRAHAM ISAAC KOOK and one of the chief propagators of his teacher's work.

Pages 90, 269: *Thankfulness*. Abraham Joshua Heschel, *Moral Grandeur and Spiritual Audacity*.

Pages 91, 270: *The Blessings of Peace*. From Midrash Sifrei Numbers, in Reuven Hammer, *Or Hadash (Shabbat)*.

Pages 96, 274: *What Torah Means*. Jacob Petuchowski, *Ever Since Sinai: A Modern View of Torah*.

Pages 97, 275: *Avinu Malkeinu*. Nathan Sternharz (trans. Jules Harlow), in Maḥzor for Rosh Hashanah and Yom Kippur, ed. Jules Harlow. | *As Soon As the Torah Scroll*. The Zohar, part 2, 206a (trans. David Goldstein), in *The Wisdom of the Zohar: An Anthology of Texts*, ed. Isaiah Tishby.

Pages 98, 276: *A Personal Meditation*. Navah Harlow, "Private Meditation," in Maḥzor for Rosh Hashanah and Yom Kippur, ed. Jules Harlow.

Pages 99, 183, 277, 362: *The Public Reading of Torah*. Raymond Scheindlin, "Judaism Is My Art Form," in *The Unfolding Tradition: Jewish Law After Sinai*, ed. Elliot Dorff.

Pages 100, 278: *Liturgical Practice*. Abraham Zvi Idelsohn, *Jewish Music In Its Historical Development*.

Page 103: *Here I Am*. Adele Berlin and Marc Zvi Brettler, eds., *The Jewish Study Bible*.

Page 104: *Verse 5. Then Abraham Said to His Servants*. Adele Berlin and Marc Zvi Brettler, eds., *The Jewish Study Bible*. | *Do Not Raise Your Hand Against the Boy*. Abraham Joshua Heschel, *Moral Grandeur and Spiritual Audacity*.

Page 105: *Where is Sarah?* Ellen Frankel, *Five Books of Miriam*. | *Heritage*. Ḥayim Gouri, "Heritage," in *The Penguin Book of Hebrew Verse*, ed. T. Carmi.

Pages 106, 282: *The Holy Day Sacrifice*. Babylonian Talmud Megillah, (trans. Jules Harlow), in Maḥzor for Rosh Hashanah and Yom Kippur, ed. Jules Harlow.

Page 109: *Sarah's Laughter and Hannah's Prayer*. Francine Klagsbrun, "Sarah and Hannah: The Laughter and the Prayer," in *Beginning Anew*, ed. Gail Twersky Reimer and Judith A. Kates.

Page 110: *What Do We Pray For?* Zvi Freeman, "Chana's Prayer," www.chabad.org.

Page 115: *Mi She-beirakh*. Lyrics by Debbie Friedman.

Pages 117, 288: *An Alternative Prayer for Our Country*. Adapted from Louis Ginzberg, "A Prayer for Our Country," in *Siddur Sim Shalom*, Jules Harlow, ed.

Page 118: *Soundless*. Everett Gendler, "The Consciousness of Time." | *Meditation Before Shofar Blowing*. Hershel J. Matt, Mahzor Hadash. | *In Your Great Mercy*. From Maḥzor for Rosh Hashanah and Yom Kippur, ed. Jules Harlow. | *Listening*. The Nazir HaRav David Cohen (adapted and trans. Aubrey L. Glazer), from *Ha-n'vu'ah: Ha-higgayon Ha-ivri Ha-sh'mi'i*. | *The Shofar*. Esther Ettinger, "Ha-shofar," in *Hayyei Burganiyyim L'hafli*.

Pages 123, 298: *God Gave Adam a Secret*. Elie Wiesel, *Messengers of God: Biblical Portraits and Legends*.

Pages 125, 300, 398: *Help Me, O God, to Pray*. André Ungar, in *Siddur Sim Shalom*, ed. Jules Harlow.

Pages 128, 152, 324: *Our Sacrifice*. Mordecai Kaplan and Eugene Kohn, *Sabbath Prayer Book with a Supplement Containing Prayers, Readings and Hymns and with a New Translation*.

Pages 129, 152, 324: *May It Be Your Will*. From *Siddur Va'ani Tefilati*, ed. Simchah Roth, trans. Edward Feld et al.

Page 129: *Israel and the World*. Martin Buber, *The Origin and Meaning of Hasidism*.

Page 130: *God's Sovereignty*. Abraham Joshua Heschel, *God in Search of Man*. | *How to Serve God*. Rabbi Baer of Radoshitz, in Martin Buber, *Hasidism and Modern Man*.

Pages 131, 156: *Establishing in the World*. Arthur Green, *These Are the Words: A Vocabulary of the Jewish Spiritual Life*.

Pages 132, 305: *Our God, Our Ancestor's God*. André Ungar, in *Siddur Sim Shalom*, ed. Jules Harlow.

Pages 133, 160: *Remember*. David Kraemer, in *Sh'ma: A Journal of Jewish Responsibility*, April 26, 1996.

Page 135: *Meditations on Redemption*. Leo Baeck (trans. Irving Howe and Victor Grubwieser), *The Essence of Judaism*.

Page 136: *Revelation Is of the Past*. Will Herberg, *Judaism and Modern Man*.

Page 137: *The Shofar Has Revelatory Power*. Jan Uhrbach.

Pages 138, 306, 402: *Would That Your People*. André Ungar, in *Siddur Sim Shalom*, ed. Jules Harlow.

Pages 139, 311, 406: *May My Tongue Be Innocent*. André Ungar, in *Siddur Sim Shalom*, ed. Jules Harlow.

Pages 139, 307: *O God, from whom*. André Ungar, in *Siddur Sim Shalom*, ed. Jules Harlow.

Page 141: *The Individual Worshipper and Public Prayer*. Adin Steinsaltz, *A Guide to Jewish Prayer*.

Page 144: *Piyyut for Musaf of Rosh Hashanah*. Admiel Kosman (trans. Aubrey L. Glazer), from *Alternative Prayerbook for 71 Poems*.

Pages 148, 319: *I Believe*. Yehuda Amichai (trans. Edward Feld), "Elim Miṭhal'fim, Ha-t'fillot Nish'arot La-ad," from *Patu-aḥ Sagur Patu-aḥ*. | *Belief*. Martin Buber.

Pages 152, 304: *The Sacrifices of God*. Piska 24:5 by R. Kahana (trans. William G. Braude and Israel J. Kapstein), in *Pesikta De-rab Kahana*, ed. William G. Braude.

Page 154: *Tikkun Olam—The Repair of the World*. Menachem Mendel Schneerson.

Pages 155: *The Thread*. Denise Levertov, *Poems 1960–1967*.

Pages 159: *The Broken Tablets*. Rodger Kamenetz, *The Lowercase Jew*.

Page 160: *On Linking the Generations*. Abraham Joshua Heschel, *Who Is Man?* and *Moral Grandeur and Spiritual Audacity*.

Pages 161: *God Does Not Forget Those*. Rachel Kahn-Troster.

Pages 163-4: *Will Forgiving and Graceful Days Yet Come*. Leah Goldberg (trans. Edward Feld et al.), from *Al Hapriha*. | *Night Visitors*. Kadya Molodowsky (trans. Kathryn Hellerstein), *Paper Bridges: Selected Poems of Kadya Molodowsky*.

Pages 169, 357: *Three Days Before*. Pesikta Rabbati, Piska 35, from Francine Klagsbrun, *Voices of Wisdom: Jewish ideals and ethics for everyday living*.

Pages 175, 249: *Adon Olam*. Adapted from Reuven Hammer, *Or Hadash (Shabbat)*.

Pages 180, 396: *Adonai Has Assured a Redeemer*. Reuven Hammer, "Kedusha D'Sidra" in *Or Hadash (Shabbat)*.

Pages 190, 378: *Chosenness*. Henri Atlan, "Chosen People," in *Contemporary Jewish Religious Thought*, ed. Arthur A. Cohen and Paul Mendes-Flohr.

Page 199: *Lighting the Yahrzeit Candle*. Merle Feld.

Page 200: *Meditation Before Yom Kippur for One Who Cannot Fast*. Simkha Y. Weintraub, in Paul Steinberg, *Celebrating the Jewish Year: Rosh Hashanah, Yom Kippur, Sukkot*, ed. Janet Greenstein Potter.

Page 202: *Wearing a Tallit*. Reuven Hammer, *Entering Jewish Prayer: A Guide to Personal Devotion and the Worship Service* | *The Meaning of the Day*. Jonathan Magonet, "Meditation," in *Forms of Prayer for Jewish Worship III: Prayers for the High Holy Days*, eds. Jonathan Magonet and Lionel Blue. | *Entering Community*. Reuven Hammer, *Entering Jewish Prayer: A Guide to Personal Devotion and the Worship Service*.

Page 203: *A Prayer for Purity*. Abraham Danziger (adapted Edward Feld). | *Forgiveness Is Not Forgetting*. Charles Klein, "How to Forgive When You Can't Forget," in *Women's League Outlook*, Fall 1996.

Page 204: *A Meditation on Kol Nidrei*. Ze'ev Falk (trans. Stanley Schachter), in Maḥzor for Rosh Hashanah and Yom Kippur, ed. Jules Harlow. | *Kol Nidrei*. Merle Feld, *Finding Words*.

Page 205: *A Deathless Prayer*. Leon Szalet (trans. Catherine Bland Williams), *Experiment "E"*.

Page 206: *Yom Kippur and Shabbat*. Or HaMeir, retold by S. Y. Agnon, *Days of Awe*.

Page 210: *Redemption: Interpretive Reading*. Chaim Stern, *Gates of Repentance: The New Union Prayerbook for the Days of Awe*.

Page 211: *God's Presence*. Merle Feld.

Pages 224, 383: *B'oto Erev Muzar / In That Strange Night*. Zelda Schneerson Mishkovsky (trans. Edward Feld), *Shirei Zeldah*.

Page 225: *Body and Soul*. Abraham Joshua Heschel, *Man Is Not Alone: A Philosophy of Religion*.

Page 233: *On Your Wings*. Edward Feld.

Page 235, 382: *We Betray*. Joseph Ber Soloveitchik and Hayyim Volozhin, *Yom Kippur Mahzor*, ed. Arnold Lustiger and Michael Taubes. | *Who Are We*. Nina Beth Cardin.

Page 236: *All Our Secrets*. in Maḥzor for Rosh Hashanah and Yom Kippur, ed. Jules Harlow.

SOURCES AND CREDITS

Sources for Rabbinic and liturgical texts are not listed.
Full citations for works requiring permission begin on page 467.

Page 2: *To Seek Renewal*. Hershel J. Matt, *Mahzor Hadash*. | *This Rosh Hashanah*. Chaim Stern, *Gates of Repentance: The New Union Prayerbook for the Days of Awe*.

Page 3: *Now Is the Time for Turning*. Jack Riemer, *New Prayers for the High Holy Days*.

Pages 4, 206: *Psalm 93—An Interpretive Translation*. Edward Feld.

Page 5: *Beginning to Pray*. Harold Schulweis, *Shalom Aleichem! Aleichem Shalom!*

Pages 5, 207: *God and Nature: An Interpretive Translation*. André Ungar, in *Siddur Sim Shalom*, ed. Jules Harlow.

Pages 6, 208: *Faith*. Abraham Joshua Heschel, *Man's Quest for God*. | *Sh'ma: Declaration of Faith*. Marcia Falk, *The Book of Blessings: New Jewish Prayers for Daily Life, the Sabbath, and the New Moon Festival*.

Pages 7, 209: *Faithfulness: An Interpretive Translation*. André Ungar, in *Siddur Sim Shalom*, ed. Jules Harlow.

Page 8: *A Prayer for Redemption*. Richard N. Levy, *On Wings of Awe*.

Pages 9, 212: *And Rested*. Reuven Hammer, *Or Hadash (Shabbat)*. | *Shabbat*. Lawrence Kushner, *The Book of Words: Talking Spiritual Life, Living Spiritual Talk*.

Page 9: *Peace*. Edward Feld.

Pages 11, 187, 213, 374: *Meditation on Prayer*. Isaac Arama, trans. Robert Scheinberg.

Pages 12, 188, 214, 375: *A Meditation on Immortality*. Robert Scheinberg.

Pages 13, 87, 126, 149, 189, 215, 258, 301, 321, 377, 400, 412: *U-v'khein*. Reuven Hammer, *Entering the High Holy Days*.

Pages 13, 189, 215, 377: *May All Be Bound Together*. Martin Buber, *Israel and the World: Essays in a Time of Crisis*.

Pages 14: *You Have Chosen Us*. David Wolpe, *Why Be Jewish?*

Pages 16, 193, 218, 388: *The Blessing of Shalom*. Hershel J. Matt, by arrangement with Media Judaica.

Pages 17, 139: *Yehi Ratzon/Creator of Beginnings*. From *Sha'arei Tziyon* (Prague, 1662), adapted and trans. Jules Harlow, in *Mahzor for Rosh Hashanah and Yom Kippur*, ed. Jules Harlow.

Pages 20–1: *B'reishit*. Merle Feld, *Finding Words*.

Page 21: *Khavatselet ha-Sharon/The Rose of Sharon*. Zelda Schneerson Mishkovsky (trans. Edward Feld), *Shirey Zelda*.

Page 22: *In Your Image*. Myriam Kubovy (trans. Alan Lettofsky, Hebrew; trans. Amy Gottlieb, English), "Si tu ne nous avais pas crées, mon Dieu," from *Monologues Avec Dieu*.

Page 23: *Y'hi Ratzon Mil'fanekha / May It Be Your Will*. Chaim Stern, *Gates of Repentance: The New Union Prayerbook for the Days of Awe*.

Pages 26, 247: *The Blessing of Memory*. Chaim Stern, *Gates of Prayer*.

Pages 27, 248: *Do Not Hide Your Face From Me*. Robert Alter, *The Book of Psalms: A Translation With Commentary*.

Page 27: *To Hold on to Life*. Simḥah Bunam, "To Clutch at Life," in Martin Buber and Olga Marx, *Tales of the Hasidim*, vol. 2. | *Psalm 27*. Benjamin Segal, "Where Liturgy and Bible Meet: Psalm 27, for the Time of Repentance," in *Conservative Judaism* 54:4.

Pages 28, 250: *Yigdal*. Macy Nulman, *The Encyclopedia of Jewish Prayer*.

Page 30: *With These Lights*. Mitchell Silver, *Respecting the Wicked Child: A Philosophy of Secular Jewish Identity and Education*. | *T'hinnah for Today*. Merle Feld. | *La Orasion De La Mujer/The Woman's Prayer*. Lyrics by Flory Jagoda.

Page 31: *Two Personal Prayers for the New Year*. Bernard Raskas.

Page 34: *The Effect of Prayer*. Reuven Hammer, *Or Hadash (Shabbat)*.

Page 44: *Love Me*. Malka Heifetz Tussman (trans. Marcia Falk), in *With Teeth in the Earth*.

Page 45: *Psalms*. Nahum M. Sarna, *On the Book of Psalms: Exploring the Prayers of Ancient Israel*.

Page 48: *Spiritual Living*. Abraham Joshua Heschel, *Who Is Man?*

Page 51: *Psalm 19—A Personal Prayer*. Stephen Mitchell, in *The Enlightened Heart: An Anthology of Sacred Poetry*, ed. Stephen Mitchell.

Page 52: *Taste and See How Good Adonai Is*. Joseph Ber Soloveitchik, *Out of the Whirlwind*, vol. 3, and *Worship of the Heart*, vol. 2.

Page 53: *Psalm 90—A Poetic Rendering*. Stephen Mitchell, *A Book of Psalms: Selected and Adapted from the Hebrew*.

Page 54: *I Know Not Your Ways*. Malka Heifetz Tussman (trans. Marcia Falk), *With Teeth in the Earth*.

Page 55: *Idols*. Abraham Joshua Heschel, *God in Search of Man*.

Page 56: *Exodus*. Michael Walzer, *Exodus and Revolution*.

Page 58: *Psalm 92—An Interpretive Translation*. Stephen Mitchell, *A Book of Psalms: Selected and Adapted from the Hebrew*. | Lines "but every secret . . . wrong is redressed," Ralph Waldo Emerson, "Compensation," in *Essays: First Series*. | Line "in the depths all becomes law," Rainer Maria Rilke (trans. Stephen Mitchell), *Letters to a Young Poet*.

Page 59: *Psalm 93—An Interpretive Translation*. Stephen Mitchell, *A Book of Psalms: Selected and Adapted from the Hebrew*.

Pages 60, 179: *Day In, Day Out*. "Challonot," Miriam Baruch Halfi (trans. Edward Feld et al.), *Kimmahon*.

Page 62: *The Sun Lit a Wet Branch*. Zelda Schneerson Mishkovsky (trans. Marcia Falk), *The Spectacular Difference: Selected Poems*.

Page 63: *Psalm 150—A Rendering*. Stephen Mitchell, *A Book of Psalms: Selected and Adapted from the Hebrew*.

Page 66: *Miracles*. Martin Buber, *Moses: The Revelation and the Covenant*.

Page 69: *The Life of the Soul*. Reuven Hammer, *Or Hadash (Shabbat)*.

Page 70: *Out of the Depths: Mimma'amakim*. Herman Kieval, *The High Holy Days: Book One: Rosh Hashanah*. | *The Words We Speak*, Abraham Joshua Heschel, *Man's Quest for God*.

Page 71: *Prayer*. Abraham Joshua Heschel, *Moral Grandeur and Spiritual Audacity*.

Page 72: *Almighty, Blessed*. Joel L. Hoffman, *My People's Prayer Book: Traditional Prayers, Modern Commentaries, Vol. 1: The Sh'ma and Its Blessings* ed. Lawrence A. Hoffman | *Renewing Creation*, Daniel C. Matt, *God and The Big Bang: Discovering Harmony Between Science and Spirituality*. | *The Sense of Wonder*, Abraham Joshua Heschel, *Man Is Not Alone: A Philosophy of Religion*. | *From the Zohar*, Daniel C. Matt, *The Essential Kabbalah*.

Page 75: *Angels*. Adin Steinsaltz, trans. Yehuda Hanegbi, *The Thirteen Petalled Rose*.

Page 76: *God's Love*. Richard N. Levy, *On Wings of Awe*. | *Unify Our Hearts*. Ze'ev Wolf of Zhitomir, from "Chasidism," commentary by Lawrence Kushner and Nehemia Polen, in *My People's Prayer Book: Traditional Prayers, Modern Commentaries Vol. 1: The Sh'ma and Its Blessings*, ed. Lawrence A. Hoffman.

Page 77: *Monotheism*. Judith Plaskow, in *My People's Prayer Book: Traditional Prayers, Modern Commentaries, Vol. 1: The Sh'ma and Its Blessings*, ed. Lawrence A. Hoffman.

Page 78: *Redemption*. Michael Walzer, *Exodus and Revolution*.

Page 79: *Renewing the Miracle of Redemption*. Hershel J. Matt, by arrangement with Media Judaica. | *Redemption*. Martin Buber and Olga Marx, *Ten Rungs, Hasidic Sayings*, The Schocken Library, vol. 8.

Page 80: *What the Exodus Taught*. Michael Walzer, *Exodus and Revolution*.

Page 81: *Prayer*. Abraham Joshua Heschel, *Man's Quest for God*.

Page 83: *Images of God*. Elliot Dorff, *Knowing God: Jewish Journeys to the Unknown*. | *The Crown of Glory*, adapted from Solomon Ibn Gabirol (trans. Peter Cole), *Selected Poems of Solomon Ibn Gabirol*.

Pages 86, 257: *Kedushah*. Reuven Hammer, *Or Hadash (Shabbat)*.

Page 87: *Many Faiths. One God*. Abraham Joshua Heschel, *Moral Grandeur and Spiritual Audacity*.

Pages 88, 216: *You Have Chosen Us*. Leo Baeck (trans. Albert H. Friedlance), *This People Israel: The Meaning of the Jewish Experience*.

The Rabbinical Assembly gratefully acknowledges the publishers and authors of the following works for granting permission to reprint them here. Any omissions or errors are inadvertent and will be corrected in future editions.

AGNON. Quote adapted from *Or Ha-Meir*, retold in *Days of Awe*, by S.Y. Agnon, published by Schocken Books © 1965, 1975; Quotation from Menaḥem Mendel of Kotzk, as quoted in *Present at Sinai*, published by The Jewish Publication Society © 1994, trans. from *Atem Re'item*, published by Schocken Publishing House © 1959. Reprinted with permission of the publishers.

ALTER. Adapted from *The Book of Psalms: A Translation With Commentary*, by Robert Alter, published by W. W. Norton and Company © 2007.

AMICHAI. "Elim Miṭhal'fim, Ha-t'fillot Nish'arot La-ad" by Yehuda Amichai, *Patu-aḥ Sagur Patu-aḥ*, published by Schocken Publishing House © 1998; "My Father," by Yehuda Amichai, in *The Penguin Book of Hebrew Verse*, ed. by T. Carmi, published by Penguin Books © 1981 T. Carmi, trans. from "Ahaveinu Kan—Soneta A."; "Before" and "Ahaveinu Kan—Soneta A" by Yehuda Amichai, from *Shirim 1948–1962*, published by Schocken Publishing House © 1963; Reprinted with permission of the publishers.

ATLAN. "Chosen People," by Henri Atlan, in *Contemporary Jewish Religious Thought*, ed. by Arthur A. Cohen and Paul Mendes-Flohr, published by Charles Scribner's Sons © 1987. Reprinted with permission of the author.

AUSLANDER. "The Key," by Rose Auslander, in *Forms of Prayer for Jewish Worship III: Prayers for the High Holy Days*, ed. by Jonathan Magonet and Lionel Blue, published by The Reform Synagogues of Great Britain, London © 1985; trans. from "Der Schlüssel," from *Hügel aus Äther unwiderbringlich, Gedichte und Prosa 1966–1975*, published by S. Fischer Verlag GmbH, Frankfurt am Main © 1984. Reprinted with permission of the editor and S. Fischer Verlag.

BAECK. *This People Israel: The Meaning of the Jewish Experience*, by Leo Baeck, trans. by Albert H. Friedlander, published by Holt, Rinehart and Winston © 1964 Union of American Hebrew Congregations; *The Essence of Judaism* by Leo Baeck, trans. by Irving Howe and Victor Grubwieser, published by Schocken Books © 1948.

BEN YITZḤAK. *Collected Poems* by Avraham Ben Yitzḥak, published by Hakibbutz Hameuchad Publishers © 1992. Reprinted with permission of the publisher.

BERLIN AND BRETTLER. *The Jewish Study Bible*, edited by Adele Berlin and Marc Zvi Brettler, published by Oxford University Press © 2004.

BITON AND KOSMAN. "The Hazon Ish," trans. by Aubrey L. Glazer from *Shira Hadasha*, *Apiryon* 44–45, Fall/Winter 1996–1997, ed. by Erez Biton and Admiel Kosman. Reprinted with permission of the author and translator.

BRAUDE AND KAPSTEIN. *Pesikta De-rab Kahana*, trans. by William G. Braude and Israel J. Kapstein, published by The Jewish Publication Society of America © 1975.

BUBER. Adapted from *Hasidism and Modern Man*, by Martin Buber, published by Horizon Press © 1958; *Israel and the World: Essays in a Time of Crisis*, by Martin Buber, published by Schocken Books © 1948; *Moses: The Revelation and the Covenant*, by Martin Buber, published by Harper and Row © 1946; *The Origin and Meaning of Hasidism*, by Martin Buber, published by Horizon Press © 1960; *Tales of the Hasidim*, Volume 2, by Martin Buber and Olga Marx, published by Schocken Books © 1948; *Ten Rungs, Hasidic Sayings*, by Martin Buber and Olga Marx, published by Schocken Books © 1947. Reprinted with permission of the Estate of Martin Buber.

COHEN. Adapted from The Nazir, HaRav David Cohen, adapted and trans. by Aubrey L. Glazer from *Ha-n'vu'ah: Ha-higgayon Ha-ivri Ha-sh'mi'i*, published by Mossad Harav Kook, 5730, no. 75. Reprinted with permission of the publisher and the translator.

COLE. Adapted from *Selected Poems of Solomon Ibn Gabirol*, trans. Peter Cole, published by Princeton University Press © 2001. Reprinted with permission of the publisher.

DORFF. *Love Your Neighbor and Yourself*, by Elliot N. Dorff, published by The Jewish Publication Society © 2003; *Knowing God: Jewish Journeys to the Unknown*, by Elliot N. Dorff, published by Jason Aronson © 1992.

ETTINGER. "Ha-shofar," by Esther Ettinger in *Hayyei Burganiyyim L'hafli (Poems)*, published by Am Oved Publishers Ltd. © 1998. Reprinted with permission of the author.

FALK, MARCIA. *The Book of Blessings: New Jewish Prayers for Daily Life, the Sabbath, and the New Moon Festival*, by Marcia Lee Falk, published by Harper San Francisco © 1996 Marcia Lee Falk. Reprinted with permission of the author.

FALK, ZE'EV. "A Meditation on Kol Nidrei," by Ze'ev Falk, trans. by Stanley Schachter, in *Mahzor for Rosh Hashanah and Yom Kippur*, edited by Jules Harlow, published by The Rabbinical Assembly © 1972. Reprinted with permission of the publisher.

FELD. "B'reishit" and "Kol Nidrei," by Merle Feld, in *Finding Words*, published by Union for Reform Judaism Press © 2010. Reprinted with permission of the author. "Lighting the yahrzeit candle," "God's Presence," and "T'hinnah for Today" by Merle Feld © 2010. Printed with permission of the author. "Though I stared earnestly at my fingernail," from *A Spiritual Life: Exploring the Heart and Jewish Tradition*, published by State University of New York Press, revised edition © 2007. Reprinted with permission of the publisher.

FINE. Adapted from "Birth is a beginning…" by Alvin Fine, in Chaim Stern, *Gates of Repentance: The New Union Prayerbook for the Days of Awe*, published by Central Conference of American Rabbis © 1999. Reprinted with permission of the publisher.

FRANKEL. *Five Books of Miriam* by Ellen Frankel, published by G.P Putnam's Sons, a division of Penguin Group (USA) Inc. © 1996 Ellen Frankel. Reprinted with permission of the publisher.

FREEMAN. Adapted from "Chana's Prayer," by Zvi Freeman, from www.chabad.org. Reprinted with permission from Chabad.

FRIEDMAN. "Mi She-beirakh," lyrics by Debbie Friedman © 1990. Reprinted with permission of the author.

GENDLER. "The Consciousness of Time," by Everett Gendler. Reprinted with permission of the author.

GLATSHTEYN. "I Shall Remember" by Yankev Glatshteyn, from *American Yiddish Poetry: A Bilingual Anthology*, ed. and trans. by Benjamin and Barbara Harshav, published by Stanford University Press © 1986, 2007 Benjamin and Barbara Harshav; "Nach Di…" by Yankev Glatshteyn, in *A Yid fun Lublin*, published by CYCO © 1966; "Smoke" by Yankev Glatshteyn, from *Selected Poems of Yankev Glatshteyn*, trans. by Richard Fein, published by the Jewish Publication Society © 1987. Reprinted with permission from the publishers.

GOLDBERG. Leah Goldberg, from *Al Hapriha* by Leah Goldberg, published by Sifriyat Poalim/Hakibbutz Hameuchad Publishing © 1948. Reprinted with permission of the publisher.

GOURI. "Heritage," by Ḥayim Gouri, *The Penguin Book of Hebrew Verse*, ed. by T. Carmi (Allen Lane, 1981). © Ḥayim Gouri and ACUM, English translation © T. Carmi, 1981. Used with permission from Penguin Books Ltd. and ACUM.

GREEN. Adapted from *These Are the Words: A Vocabulary of the Jewish Spiritual Life* by Arthur Green, published by Jewish Lights Publishing © 2000 Arthur Green. Reprinted with permission of the publisher.

HALFI. "Challonot," by Miriam Baruch Halfi, from *Kimmahon*, published by Hakibbutz Hameuchad Publishing © 1999. Reprinted with permission of the publisher.

HAMMER. Selections from *Or Hadash: A Commentary on Siddur Sim Shalom for Shabbat and Festivals*, published by The Rabbinical Assembly © 2003. Reprinted with permission of the publisher; *Entering the High Holy Days*, published by The Jewish Publication Society © 1998. Reprinted with permission of the publishers and author; *Entering Jewish Prayer: A Guide to Personal Devotion and the Worship Service*, published by Schocken Books © 1994.

HARLOW. Selections and adaptations from *Mahzor for Rosh Hashanah and Yom Kippur*, ed. by Jules Harlow, published by The Rabbinical Assembly © 1972; *Siddur Sim Shalom*, ed. by Jules Harlow, published by The Rabbinical Assembly © 1985. Reprinted with permission of the publisher.

HECHT. "Rites and Ceremonies" from *Collected Earlier Poems* by Anthony Hecht, published by Alfred A. Knopf, a division of Random House, Inc., © 1990 Anthony Hecht. Reprinted with permission of the publisher and the Estate of Anthony Hecht.

Pages 237, 266, 351, 384: *Kavvanah for Al Ḥet.* Abraham Joshua Heschel, *Who Is Man?*

Pages 239, 352, 386: *Our Ancestors and Us.* Nina Beth Cardin.

Pages 240–1: *Each of Us Has a Name.* Zelda Schneerson Mishkovsky (adapted and trans. Marcia Falk), in Marcia Falk, *The Book of Blessings: New Jewish Prayers for Daily Life, the Sabbath, and the New Moon Festival.*

Pages 241–2: *Birth Is a Beginning.* Alvin Fine (Hebrew trans. Alan Lettofsky), in Chaim Stern, *Gates of Repentance: The New Union Prayerbook for the Days of Awe.*

Page 244: *God's Names.* Jonathan Magonet, in *Forms of Prayer for Jewish Worship III: Prayers for the High Holy Days*, eds. Jonathan Magonet and Lionel Blue.

Page 253: *Life and Death.* Elisabeth Kübler-Ross, *Death: The Final Stage of Growth.*

Page 260: *S'liḥah.* The Ḥazon Ish (trans. Aubrey L. Glazer), from *Shira Hadasha*, in *Apiryon* 44–45, Fall/Winter 1996-1997, eds. Erez Biton and Admiel Kosman.

Pages 263, 353: *Facing Ourselves. Maḥzor for Rosh Hashanah and Yom Kippur*, ed. Jules Harlow. | *Ashamnu.* David Stern, "The ABC's of Confession," in *Kerem*, vol. 11, 2007–08.

Page 265: *Our Sins.* Max J. Routtenberg, *Seedtime and Harvest: Essays and Commentaries.*

Page 267: *For the Sin of Destroying God's Creation.* Daniel Nevins.

Page 286: *Here I Am.* Jan Uhrbach.

Page 289: *A Prayer for Peace.* From *Siddur Sim Shalom*, ed. Jules Harlow.

Page 290: *When I Stray from You.* From *Siddur Sim Shalom*, ed. Jules Harlow. | *Backwards and Forwards.* Harold Schulweis. | *We Recall.* Mordecai Kaplan, Eugene Kohn, and Ira Eisenstein, *Mahzor Hadash.*

Page 291: *Though I Stared Earnestly at My Fingernail.* Merle Feld, *A Spiritual Life: A Jewish Feminist Journey.*

Page 292: *A Yizkor Meditation in Memory of a Parent Who Was Hurtful.* Robert Saks.

Page 293: *My Peace.* Zelda Schneerson Mishkovsky (trans. Marcia Falk), *The Spectacular Difference: Selected Poems.*

Page 303: *Our agony.* From *Maḥzor for Rosh Hashanah and Yom Kippur*, ed. Jules Harlow.

Page 304: *May It Be Your Will.* Conservative Liturgical Committee, Israel. | *The Pathology of the Self.* Abraham Joshua Heschel, *Who Is Man?* | Judah the Patriarch, Piska 24:12 by R. Kahana, trans. William G. Braude and Israel J. Kapstein, in *Pesikta De-rab Kahana*, ed. William G. Braude.

Page 315: *Most of Us Prefer.* Leonard Gordon.

Page 320: *Doubt.* Edward Feld.

Page 341: *I Shall Remember.* Yankev Glatshteyn (trans. Benjamin and Barbara Harshav), in *American Yiddish Poetry: A Bilingual Anthology*, ed. Benjamin and Barbara Harshav; *Nach Di...* Yankev Glatshteyn, *A Yid fun Lublin.* | *Smoke.* Yankev Glatshteyn (trans. Richard J. Fein), *Selected Poems of Yankev Glatshteyn.*

Page 342: *Out of the Strong Sweetness.* Charles Reznikoff, *The Poems of Charles Reznikoff: 1918–1975*, ed. Seamus Cooney.

Page 343: *From the Song of the Murdered People.* Yitzhak Katznelson (trans. Noah H. Rosenbloom), *The Song of the Murdered Jewish People.*

Page 344: *My Father.* Yehuda Amichai, in *The Penguin Book of Hebrew Verse*, ed. T. Carmi. Translated from "Ahaveinu Kan – Soneta A," by Yehuda Amichai, *Shirim 1948–1962.*

Page 348: *Before One Dies.* Babylonian Talmud Shabbat 153a, trans. by Francine Klagsbrun, *Voices of Wisdom: Jewish ideals and ethics for everyday living.*

Page 349: *Rites and Ceremonies.* Anthony Hecht, *Collected Earlier Poems.*

Page 353: *Al Chet She'chatanu Lefanecha/ We Have Sinned Against You.* Avraham Holtz, in *Mahzor for Rosh Hashanah and Yom Kippur*, ed. Jules Harlow.

Page 354: *What We Seek.* Martin Buber and Olga Marx, *Ten Rungs, Hasidic Sayings*, The Schocken Library, vol. 8.

Page 363: *All of Our Acts.* Elliot N. Dorff, *Love Your Neighbor and Yourself.* | *Sexual Morality: In the Bible and Today.* Adapted from Judith Plaskow.

Page 364: *A One Contemporary Code.* Su Kasha, in Judith Plaskow, *The Coming of Lilith.*

Page 365: *I... Am Holy.* Menaḥem Mendel of Kotzk, in S. Y. Agnon, *Present at Sinai.*

Page 371: *You Cared About the Plant.* From *Etz Hayim: Torah and Commentary*, ed. David L. Lieber.

Page 392: *Leilot Ki Yalbinu / When Nights Grow White.* Avraham Ben Yitzḥak (trans. Edward Feld et al.), from *Collected Poems | Day's End.* Jonathan Magonet, "The journey through Yom Kippur...," in *Forms of Prayer for Jewish Worship III: Prayers for the High Holy Days*, eds. Jonathan Magonet and Lionel Blue. | *Elohai, Kmihat Nafshi / My God, My Soul's Desire.* Menachem Lorberbaum (trans. Edward Feld), *Magaim Mar'ot: Shirim.*

Page 394: *Ne-ilah.* Reuven Hammer, *Entering the High Holy Days.* | *Joyous are they.* Reuven Hammer, *Or Hadash (Shabbat).*

Pages 394–5: *Ashrei.* Jan Uhrbach.

Page 396: *Adonai Has Assured a Redeemer.* Edward Feld.

Pages 404, 421: *We Abuse.* Reuven Hammer, *Entering the High Holy Days.*

Pages 405, 422: *This Prayer Contrasts.* Reuven Hammer, *Entering the High Holy Days.*

Page 408: *Meditation.* Shalom Spiegel, in *Siddur Sim Shalom*, ed. Jules Harlow.

Page 409: *The Book of Life Uncertainty.* Gilda Radner, *It's Always Something.*

Page 410: "*Before*," Yehuda Amichai (trans. Alan Lettofsky) "*Before the Gate Closes...*," from *Shirim 1948–1962.*

Page 411: *The Kedushah.* Reuven Hammer, *Or Hadash (Shabbat).*

Page 412: *Meditation on God and Prayer.* Abraham Joshua Heschel, *Moral Grandeur and Spiritual Audacity.*

Page 414: *My Room.* Rose Auslander, "The Key," trans. from "Der Schlüssel," *Hügel aus Äther unwiderbringlich, Gedichte und Prosa 1966–1975*, in *Forms of Prayer for Jewish Worship III: Prayers for the High Holy Days*, eds. Jonathan Magonet and Lionel Blue.

Page 419: *Meditation.* Abraham Joshua Heschel, *Man Is Not Alone: A Philosophy of Religion.*

Page 421: *Spiritual Security.* Abraham Joshua Heschel, *The Insecurity of Freedom.*

Page 429: *Hear* and *Shofar.* Reuven Hammer, *Entering the High Holy Days.* | *Meditation.* Steven S. Schwarzschild, "Speech and Silence Before God," in *Judaism*, 10:3 (1961).

Hashanah and Yom Kippur, ed. Jules Harlow, published by The Rabbinical Assembly © 1972. Reprinted with permission of the publisher.

RADNER. It's Always Something, by Gilda Radner, published by Simon & Schuster © 1989 Gilda Radner.

REZNIKOFF. From The Poems of Charles Reznikoff: 1918–1975 by Charles Reznikoff, ed. by Seamus Cooney, published by Black Sparrow Books, an imprint of David R. Godine, Publisher, Inc. © 2005 Charles Reznikoff. Reprinted with permission of the publisher.

RIEMER. Jack Riemer, New Prayers for the High Holy Days, ed. by Jack Riemer and Harold Kushner © 1987 and 1970 by Media Judaica, New York and Bridgeport, CT. Reprinted with permission of the publisher.

RILKE. Letters to a Young Poet, by Rainer Maria Rilke, trans. by Stephen Mitchell, published by Vintage © 1986.

ROTH. Siddur Va'ani Tefilati, ed. Simchah Roth, published by Israeli Masorti Movement and The Rabbinical Assembly of Israel © 1998. Reprinted with permission of the publisher.

ROUTTENBERG. Seedtime and Harvest: Essays and Commentaries, by Max J. Routtenberg, published by Bloch Publishing Company © 1969. Reprinted with permission of the publisher.

SAKS. "A Yizkor Meditation in Memory of a Parent Who Was Hurtful," by Robert Saks. Reprinted with permission of the author.

SARNA. On the Book of Psalms: Exploring the Prayers of Ancient Israel, by Nahum M. Sarna, published by Schocken Books © 1993 Nahum M. Sarna.

SCHEINDLIN. Adapted from "Judaism is My Art Form," by Raymond Scheindlin in The Unfolding Tradition: Jewish Law After Sinai, ed. Elliot Dorff, published by Aviv Press © 2005. Reprinted with permission of the publisher and author.

SCHNEERSON. "Tikkun Olam—The Repair of the World," by Menachem Mendel Schneerson. Reprinted with permission from Chabad.

SCHULWEIS. Adapted from Shalom Aleichem! Aleichem Shalom!, by Harold Schulweis, published by Valley Beth Shalom, n.d.; "Backwards and Forwards," by Harold Schulweis. Reprinted with permission of the author.

SCHWARZSCHILD. Adapted from "Speech and Silence Before God," by Steven S. Schwarzschild, in Judaism, vol. 10, no. 3, 1961. Reprinted with permission of Maimon Schwarzschild.

SEGAL. Adapted from "Where Liturgy and Bible Meet: Psalm 27, for the Time of Repentance," by Benjamin Segal, in Conservative Judaism, vol. 54, no. 4 (Summer 2002). Reprinted with permission of the publisher.

SILVER. Adapted from "With These Lights," by Mitchell Silver, from Respecting the Wicked Child: A Philosophy of Secular Jewish Identity and Education, published by University of Massachusetts Press © 1998. Reprinted with permission of the publisher.

SOLOVEITCHIK. Adapted from Out of the Whirlwind, volume 3, by Joseph Ber Soloveitchik, published by KTAV © 2003, and from Worship of the Heart, volume 2, published by KTAV © 2003.

SOLOVEITCHIK AND VOLOZHIN. After Joseph Ber Soloveitchik and Hayyim Volozhin; from Yom Kippur Maḥzor, ed. and adapted by Arnold Lustiger and Michael Taubes, published by K'Hal Publishing © 2006, trans. © 1986–2006 Mesorah Publications, Ltd.

SPIEGEL. "Meditation," by Shalom Spiegel, in Siddur Sim Shalom, ed. Jules Harlow, published by The Rabbinical Assembly © 1985. Reprinted with permission of the publisher.

STEINSALTZ. Adapted from The Thirteen Petalled Rose, by Adin Steinsaltz, trans. by Yehuda Hanegbi, published by Basic Books, a member of the Perseus Book Group, © 2006 Adin Steinsaltz; A Guide to Jewish Prayer, by Adin Steinsaltz, published by Schocken Books, © 2002.

STERN, CHAIM. Adapted from Gates of Repentance: The New Union Prayerbook for the Days of Awe, by Chaim Stern, published by Central Conference of American Rabbis © 1999; Gates of Prayer, by Chaim Stern, published by Central Conference of American Rabbis © 1975. Reprinted with permission of the publisher.

STERN, DAVID. "The ABC's of Confession," by David Stern, in Kerem, vol. 11, 5768/2007–2008. Reprinted with permission of the author.

STERNHARZ. Nathan Sternharz, adapted and trans. by Jules Harlow, in Mahzor for Rosh Hashanah and Yom Kippur. published by The Rabbinical Assembly © 1972. Reprinted with permission of the publisher.

SZALET. "A Deathless Prayer," by Leon Szalet, trans. by Catherine Bland Williams, from Experiment "E," published by Didier Press © 1945. Reprinted with permission of the Estate of Leon Szalet and Madeleine Lejwa.

TISHBY. Selections from The Wisdom of the Zohar: An Anthology of Texts, arranged with extensive introductions and explanations by Isaiah Tishby and trans. from the Hebrew by David Goldstein, published by the Littman Library of Jewish Civilization, Oxford and Portland, Oregon, © 1989. Reprinted with permission of the publisher.

TUSSMAN. "Love Me" and "I Know Not Your Ways," by Malka Heifetz Tussman, trans. by Marcia Falk, in With Teeth in the Earth, published by Wayne State University Press © 1992 by Marcia Lee Falk. Reprinted with permission of the translator.

UNGAR. Selections by André Ungar from Siddur Sim Shalom, ed. Jules Harlow, published by The Rabbinical Assembly © 1985. Reprinted with permission of the publisher.

WALZER. Adapted from Exodus and Revolution, by Michael Walzer, published by Basic Books, a member of the Perseus Books Group, © 1986 Michael Walzer. Reprinted with permission of the publisher.

WEINTRAUB. "Meditation before Yom Kippur for One Who Cannot Fast" by Simkha Y. Weintraub, reprinted from Celebrating the Jewish Year: Rosh Hashanah, Yom Kippur, Sukkot, by Paul Steinberg, ed. Janet Greenstein Potter, published by the Jewish Publication Society © 2007. Reprinted with permission of the publisher.

WIESEL. Messengers of God: Biblical Portraits and Legends, by Elie Wiesel, published by Simon and Schuster 2005, © 1976 by Elirion Associates, Inc.

WOLPE. Adapted from Why Be Jewish? by David Wolpe, published by Henry Holt © 1995 David Wolpe. Reprinted with permission of the author.

ZELDA. Adapted from "B'oto erev muzar" and "Khavatselet ha-Sharon," by Zelda Schneerson Mishkovsky, from Shirey Zelda, published by Hakibbutz Hameuchad Publishing © 1985. Reprinted with permission of the publisher; "Each of Us Has a Name," by Zelda Schneerson Mishkovsky, adapted from the Hebrew by Marcia Falk, in The Book of Blessings: New Jewish Prayers for Daily Life, the Sabbath, and the New Moon Festival, published by Harper San Francisco © 1996 Marcia Lee Falk; "My Peace" and "The Sun Lit a Wet Branch," by Zelda Schneerson Mishkovsky, trans. by Marcia Falk, in The Spectacular Difference: Selected Poems, published by Hebrew Union College Press © 2004 Marcia Lee Falk. Reprinted with permission of Marcia Lee Falk.

HERBERG. *Judaism and Modern Man* by Will Herberg, published by the Jewish Publication Society of America © 1951.

HESCHEL. Excerpts from *Man's Quest for God* by Abraham Joshua Heschel. Copyright © 1954 Abraham Joshua Heschel. Copyright renewed 1982 by Susannah Heschel and Sylvia Heschel. Reprinted by permission of Farrar, Straus and Giroux, LLC on behalf of the Estate of Abraham Joshua Heschel; Excerpts from *God in Search of Man* by Abraham Joshua Heschel. Copyright © 1955 by Abraham Joshua Heschel. Copyright renewed 1983 by Sylvia Heschel. Excerpts from *The Insecurity of Freedom* by Abraham Joshua Heschel. Copyright © 1966 by Abraham J. Heschel. Copyright renewed 1994 by Sylvia Heschel. Excerpts from *Man Is Not Alone: A Philosophy of Religion* by Abraham Joshua Heschel. Copyright © 1951 by Abraham Joshua Heschel. Copyright renewed 1979 by Sylvia Heschel. Excerpts from *Moral Grandeur and Spiritual Audacity* by Abraham Joshua Heschel. Copyright © 1996 Sylvia Heschel. Excerpts from *Who Is Man?* by Abraham Joshua Heschel. Copyright © 1965 by Abraham Joshua Heschel. Reprinted by permission of Farrar, Straus and Giroux, LLC.

HOFFMAN. Excerpt by Joel L. Hoffman from *My People's Prayer Book: Traditional Prayers, Modern Commentaries Vol. 1: The Sh'ma and Its Blessings* published by Jewish Lights Publishing © 1997 Lawrence A. Hoffman. Reprinted with permission of the publisher.

HOLTZ. Excerpt from Avraham Holtz in *Maḥzor for Rosh Hashanah and Yom Kippur*, ed. Jules Harlow, published by The Rabbinical Assembly © 1972. Reprinted with permission of the publisher.

IDELSOHN. *Jewish Music In Its Historical Development* by Abraham Zvi Idelsohn, published by Henry Holt and Company © 1929.

JAGODA. "La Orasion De La Mujer"/"The Woman's Prayer," lyrics by Flory Jagoda, composer and lyricist © April 16, 2005. Reprinted with permission of the author.

KAMENETZ. "The Broken Tablets," from *The Lowercase Jew* by Rodger Kamenetz, published by Triquarterly Books/Northwestern University Press © 2003 Rodger Kamenetz, first published in *Louisiana Cultural Vistas* © 1999 Rodger Kamenetz. Reprinted with permission.

KAPLAN, KOHN, AND EISENSTEIN. Mordecai Kaplan, Eugene Kohn, and Ira Eisenstein (adapted), *Mahzor Hadash*, ed. by Rabbi Sidney Greenberg and Rabbi Jonathan D. Levine © 2009 and 1977 by The Prayer Book Press of Media Judaica, Bridgeport, CT. Adapted from *High Holiday Prayer Book: With Supplementary Prayers and Readings and with a New English Translation, Volume II, Prayers for Yom Kippur*, by Mordecai Kaplan, Eugene Kohn, and Ira Eisenstein, published by The Jewish Reconstructionist Federation © 1948. Reprinted with permission of the publishers.

KAPLAN AND KOHN. Adapted from *Sabbath Prayer Book with a Supplement Containing Prayers, Readings and Hymns and with a New Translation* by Mordecai M. Kaplan and Eugene Kohn, published by the Jewish Reconstructionist Federation © 1945. Reprinted with permission of the publisher.

KATZNELSON. *The Song of the Murdered Jewish People* by Yitzhak Katznelson, trans. by Noah H. Rosenbloom, published by Beit Lohamei Haghetaot/Ghetto Fighters' House Ltd./Hakibbutz Hameuchad Publishing House © 1980. Reprinted with permission of the publisher.

KIEVAL. Adapted from *The High Holy Days: Book One: Rosh Hashanah*, by Herman Kieval, published by The Burning Bush Press © 1959.

KLAGSBRUN. *Voices of Wisdom: Jewish ideals and ethics for everyday living*, ed. by Francine Klagsbrun, published by Pantheon Books, 1980; "Sarah and Hannah: The Laughter and the Prayer," by Francine Klagsbrun, in *Beginning Anew*, ed. by Gail Twersky Reimer and Judith A. Kates, published by Simon and Schuster © 1997. Reprinted with permission of the author.

KLEIN. "How to Forgive When You Can't Forget," by Charles Klein, in *Women's League Outlook*, Fall 1996. Reprinted with permission of the publisher.

KOSMAN. *Alternative Prayerbook for 71 Poems*, by Admiel Kosman; trans. by Aubrey L. Glazer. Reprinted with permission of the author and translator.

KRAEMER. "Remember," by David Kraemer, from *Sh'ma: A Journal of Jewish Responsibility*, April 26, 1996. Reprinted with permission of the publisher.

KÜBLER-ROSS. *Death: The Final Stage of Growth* by Elisabeth Kübler-Ross, published by Prentice Hall © 1975.

KUBOVY. "Si Tu Ne Nous Avais pas Créés, Mon Dieu," by Myriam Kubovy, from *Monologues Avec Dieu*, published by Editorial Losada, S.A., © 1957 Myriam Kubovy. Reprinted with permission of Michael Kubovy.

KUSHNER. Ze'ev Wolf of Zhitomir, adapted from "Chasidism," commentary by Lawrence Kushner and Nehemia Polen from *My People's Prayer Book: Traditional Prayers, Modern Commentaries Vol. 1: The Sh'ma and Its Blessings*, ed. by Lawrence A. Hoffman, published by Jewish Lights Publishing © 1997 Lawrence A. Hoffman; *The Book of Words: Talking Spiritual Life, Living Spiritual Talk* by Lawrence Kushner, published by Jewish Lights Publishing © 1993 Lawrence Kushner. Reprinted by permission of the publisher.

LEVERTOV. "The Thread" by Denise Levertov, from *Poems 1960–1967*, published by New Directions Publishing Corp. © 1966 Denise Levertov. Reprinted with permission of the publisher.

LEVY. Adapted from *On Wings of Awe*, by Richard N. Levy, published by B'nai B'irth Hillel Foundation © 1985. Reprinted with permission of the author.

LIEBER. Excerpt from *Etz Hayim: Torah and Commentary*, ed. David L. Lieber, published by The Rabbinical Assembly, The United Synagogue of Conservative Judaism, The Jewish Publication Society © 2001 David L. Lieber.

LORBERBAUM. *Magaim Mar'ot: Shirim*, by Menachem Lorberbaum, published by Carmel Publishing, Jerusalem. Reprinted with permission of the author.

MAGONET. *Forms of Prayer for Jewish Worship III: Prayers for the High Holy Days*, ed. by Jonathan Magonet and Lionel Blue, published by The Reform Synagogues of Great Britain © 1985. Reprinted with permission of the editor.

MATT, DANIEL C. *The Essential Kabbalah* by Daniel C. Matt, published by HarperCollins © 1995 Daniel C. Matt; *God and The Big Bang: Discovering Harmony Between Science and Spirituality*, published by Jewish Lights Publishing © 1996 Daniel C. Matt. Reprinted with permission of the publishers.

MATT, HERSHEL. Hershel J. Matt, *Mahzor Hadash*, ed. by Rabbi Sidney Greenberg and Rabbi Jonathan D. Levine © 2009 and 1977 by The Prayer Book Press of Media Judaica, Bridgeport, CT; Hershel J. Matt, *Walking Humbly with God*, ed. by Daniel Matt, published by KTAV, 1993, by arrangement with The Prayer Book Press of Media Judaica. Reprinted with permission.

MITCHELL. Psalm 19 from *The Enlightened Heart: An Anthology of Sacred Poetry*, ed. by Stephen Mitchell, copyright © 1989 by Stephen Mitchell. Psalm 90, Psalm 92, Psalm 93, and Psalm 150 from *A Book of Psalms: Selected and Adapted from the Hebrew* by Stephen Mitchell, copyright © 1993 by Stephen Mitchell. Reprinted by permission of HarperCollins Publishers.

MOLODOWSKY. "Night Visitors," by Kadya Molodowsky, trans. by Kathryn Hellerstein, in *Paper Bridges: Selected Poems of Kadya Molodowsky*, ed. Kathryn Hellerstein, published by Wayne State University Press © 1999. Reprinted with permission of the translator.

NEVINS. "For the Sins of Destroying God's Creation," by Daniel Nevins. Reprinted with permission of the author.

NULMAN. "Yigdal," from *The Encyclopedia of Jewish Prayer*, by Macy Nulman, published by Jason Aronson © 1993. Reprinted with permission of the publisher.

PETUCHOWSKI. *Ever Since Sinai: A Modern View of Torah* by Jacob Petuchowski, published by Scribe Publications © 1961.

PLASKOW. "Monotheism," by Judith Plaskow, excerpted from *My People's Prayer Book: Traditional Prayers, Modern Commentaries Vol. 1: The Sh'ma and Its Blessings*, by Lawrence A. Hoffman, published by Jewish Lights Publishing © 1997 Lawrence A. Hoffman; *The Coming of Lilith: Essays on Feminism, Judaism, and Sexual Ethics 1972–2003*, published by Beacon Press, Boston, © 2005 Judith Plaskow. Reprinted with permission of the publishers.

RABINOWITZ. "When We Really Begin" by Stanley Rabinowitz, adapted by Shamai Kanter and Jack Riemer, in *Maḥzor for Rosh*